CRITICAL SURVEY OF

Long Fiction

Fourth Edition

CRITICAL SURVEY OF

Long Fiction

Fourth Edition

Volume 7
Walter Pater—Anna Seghers

Editor
Carl Rollyson
Baruch College, City University of New York

SALEM PRESS
Pasadena, California   Hackensack, New Jersey

Editor in Chief: Dawn P. Dawson

Editorial Director: Christina J. Moose	*Research Supervisor:* Jeffry Jensen
Development Editor: Tracy Irons-Georges	*Research Assistant:* Keli Trousdale
Project Editor: Judy Selhorst	*Production Editor:* Joyce I. Buchea
Manuscript Editor: Desiree Dreeuws	*Design and Graphics:* James Hutson
Acquisitions Editor: Mark Rehn	*Layout:* William Zimmerman
Editorial Assistant: Brett S. Weisberg	*Photo Editor:* Cynthia Breslin Beres

Cover photo: Sir Walter Scott (The Granger Collection, New York)

Library of Congress Cataloging-in-Publication Data

Critical survey of long fiction / editor, Carl Rollyson. — 4th ed.
    p. cm.
Includes bibliographical references and index.
  ISBN 978-1-58765-535-7 (set : alk. paper) — ISBN 978-1-58765-536-4 (vol. 1 : alk. paper) —
ISBN 978-1-58765-537-1 (vol. 2 : alk. paper) — ISBN 978-1-58765-538-8 (vol. 3 : alk. paper) —
ISBN 978-1-58765-539-5 (vol. 4 : alk. paper) — ISBN 978-1-58765-540-1 (vol. 5 : alk. paper) —
ISBN 978-1-58765-541-8 (vol. 6 : alk. paper) — ISBN 978-1-58765-542-5 (vol. 7 : alk. paper) —
ISBN 978-1-58765-543-2 (vol. 8 : alk. paper) — ISBN 978-1-58765-544-9 (vol. 9 : alk. paper) —
ISBN 978-1-58765-545-6 (vol. 10 : alk. paper)
1. Fiction—History and criticism. 2. Fiction—Bio-bibliography—Dictionaries. 3. Authors—Biography—
Dictionaries. I. Rollyson, Carl E. (Carl Edmund)
  PN3451.C75 2010
  809.3—dc22

      2009044410

First Printing

PRINTED IN CANADA

CONTENTS

COMPLETE LIST OF CONTENTS

VOLUME 1

VOLUME 2

VOLUME 3

VOLUME 4

VOLUME 5

VOLUME 6

Volume 7

Contents

VOLUME 8

VOLUME 9

LONG FICTION IN HISTORY

WORLD LONG FICTION

VOLUME 10

PRONUNCIATION KEY

Foreign and unusual or ambiguous English-language names of profiled authors may be unfamiliar to some users of the *Critical Survey of Long Fiction*. To help readers pronounce such names correctly, phonetic spellings using the character symbols listed below appear in parentheses immediately after the first mention of the author's name in the narrative text. Stressed syllables are indicated in capital letters, and syllables are separated by hyphens.

VOWEL SOUNDS

Symbol	Spelled (Pronounced)
a	answer (AN-suhr), laugh (laf), sample (SAM-puhl), that (that)
ah	father (FAH-thur), hospital (HAHS-pih-tuhl)
aw	awful (AW-fuhl), caught (kawt)
ay	blaze (blayz), fade (fayd), waiter (WAYT-ur), weigh (way)
eh	bed (behd), head (hehd), said (sehd)
ee	believe (bee-LEEV), cedar (SEE-dur), leader (LEED-ur), liter (LEE-tur)
ew	boot (bewt), lose (lewz)
i	buy (bi), height (hit), lie (li), surprise (sur-PRIZ)
ih	bitter (BIH-tur), pill (pihl)
o	cotton (KO-tuhn), hot (hot)
oh	below (bee-LOH), coat (koht), note (noht), wholesome (HOHL-suhm)
oo	good (good), look (look)
ow	couch (kowch), how (how)
oy	boy (boy), coin (koyn)
uh	about (uh-BOWT), butter (BUH-tuhr), enough (ee-NUHF), other (UH-thur)

CONSONANT SOUNDS

Symbol	Spelled (Pronounced)
ch	beach (beech), chimp (chihmp)
g	beg (behg), disguise (dihs-GIZ), get (geht)
j	digit (DIH-juht), edge (ehj), jet (jeht)
k	cat (kat), kitten (KIH-tuhn), hex (hehks)
s	cellar (SEHL-ur), save (sayv), scent (sehnt)
sh	champagne (sham-PAYN), issue (IH-shew), shop (shop)
ur	birth (burth), disturb (dihs-TURB), earth (urth), letter (LEH-tur)
y	useful (YEWS-fuhl), young (yuhng)
z	business (BIHZ-nehs), zest (zehst)
zh	vision (VIH-zhuhn)

WALTER PATER

Born: London, England; August 4, 1839
Died: Oxford, England; July 30, 1894
Also known as: Walter Horatio Pater

PRINCIPAL LONG FICTION

Marius the Epicurean: His Sensations and Ideas, 1885 (2 volumes)
Gaston de Latour: An Unfinished Romance, 1896

OTHER LITERARY FORMS

Walter Pater (PAYT-ur) is principally remembered as a critic. His most influential work, *Studies in the History of the Renaissance* (1873; revised as *The Renaissance: Studies in Art and Poetry*, 1877, 1888, 1893), decisively changed the Victorian conception of art as a vehicle for the expression of uplifting sentiments or edifying ideals. Pater, whose unnamed antagonist was John Ruskin, argued that art is preeminently concerned with the dextrous elaboration of its own sensuous ingredients. Form, color, balance, and tone: These are the elements of which art is constituted. Hence, the imposition of a moral upon a painting, a poem, or a musical composition subverts the integrity of the work and distorts the function of criticism. The genuine critic begins with an analysis of the impression that a painting or a poem communicates and then endeavors to trace that impression to the structural elements of which the work is composed. Ultimately, as the notorious conclusion to *The Renaissance* makes clear, art is chiefly to be cherished as a means of enhancing, expanding, and enlarging the faculties of sensuous apprehension and as a catalyst in the pursuit of more varied, exquisite, and complex sensations. In the last analysis, Pater was inclined to evaluate and judge life itself as an aesthetic phenomenon.

Pater qualified this position in his later works, however, and since *Marius the Epicurean*—his one completed novel—was expressly written to revise and reevaluate the conclusion of *The Renaissance*, it is necessary to acquire some preliminary understanding of Pater's earlier and less complex point of view.

By way of preparation for *Marius the Epicurean*, Pater composed a series of stories that foreshadow the mature techniques of his novel. The best of these stories, "The Child in the House," traces the influence of a child's environment upon the formation of his sensibility and character. Here, in a statement that may be regarded as a keynote to the author's subsequent utterances, Pater expresses through the character of Florian Deleal the distinguishing quality that informs not only his own sensibility but also the sensibility of Marius and, indeed, of all his protagonists: "For with the desire of physical beauty," observes Pater of Florian, "mingled itself early the fear of death—the fear of death intensified by the desire of beauty."

Before examining the implications of this sentiment in the context of *Marius the Epicurean*, it is interesting to note that virtually all of Pater's other works—in both criticism and fiction—are meditations on the propinquity of beauty and death and on the desire that this meditation engenders in Pater to conceive of an absolute that defines itself in and gives broader significance to the sensuous flux of existence. As Pater observes in his study of Plato, "to realize unity in variety, to discover *cosmos*—an order that shall satisfy one's reasonable soul—below and within apparent chaos: is from first to last the continuous purpose of what we call philosophy."

In addition to *The Renaissance*, then, Pater's other works include *Imaginary Portraits* (1887), a collection of stories that prefigure *Marius the Epicurean* in their emphasis on the aesthetic quality and philosophical repercussions of experience upon a sensitive and circumspect temperament rather than with the dramatization of experience itself; *Appreciations: With an Essay on Style* (1889), a heterogeneous collection of literary criticisms that apply the principles adduced in *The Renaissance* to the examination of English and French literary figures; *Plato and Platonism: A Series of Lectures* (1893), the philosophical and theoretical counterpart to *Marius the Epicurean*, which examines the respective relations between the temporal and the eternal, the relative and the absolute, the ideal and the real in the works of Plato; *Greek Studies: A Series of Essays* (1895), an examination of the myths of Dionysus and Persephone and their symbolic relation to the spirit of art; and *Miscellaneous*

Studies (1895), a grouping of Pater's most important writings on figures of literary, religious, and artistic significance. Of special interest in the latter is the short essay "Diaphaneite," wherein Pater delineates those attributes that go into the making of an ideal and yet realizable humanity. Finally, *Essays from the "Guardian"* (1896) is a collection of Pater's reviews on the writers of his day.

ACHIEVEMENTS

Walter Pater's achievement as a novelist and a critic is central to the modern vision of art. Though he was not always edified by the scandalous manner in which his disciples interpreted his message, nor gratified by the distortion of his ideas by an entire generation of aesthetes and decadents, Pater, when he is fully understood, emerges as a figure of incalculable importance in the evolution of twentieth century literature. In the first place, he did away with much of the fustian approach that obscured the appreciation of art in his own day, and he left a critical legacy, which extended into the twentieth century in the works of Bernard Berenson and Roger Fry. Moreover, as Harold Bloom observes of Pater's most memorable character, "Marius, more than any fictional character of our age, is the representative modern poet as well as the representative man of literary culture who remains the only audience for that poet."

As a stylist, too, Pater was wonderfully suggestive and original. Adapting the rich and ornate cadences of Ruskin to his more subtle purpose, Pater evolved a style that is the last word in delicacy, refinement, and understated eloquence. His sentences are characterized by elaborate parentheses, delicately wrought rhythms, and mannered circumlocutions—annoying to some readers—and his malleable prose matches with minute accuracy the uncertainties, doubts, and deliberations of a mind in debate with itself, a mind fastidiously alive to the full complexity of human experience and scrupulously intent upon a verbal music that, in its hesitant rhythms, remains faithful to that experience. In this regard, he clearly anticipates Marcel Proust.

It is not, however, on the level of style alone that Pater's influence has been indelible. *Marius the Epicurean*, in the role that it assigns to memory, its tone of melancholy retrospect, its analysis of a highly developed sensi-

bility enamored of perfection yet resigned to uncertainty, anticipates, to a remarkable degree, the structural, tonal, and thematic underpinnings of Proust's novels. When one adds to this Pater's lasting influence on Oscar Wilde, James Joyce, André Gide, and William Butler Yeats—the last of whom claimed that *Marius the Epicurean* is "the only great prose in modern English"—one is compelled to admit that Pater was one of the first major sensibilities of the modern age.

BIOGRAPHY

For a writer who was to become the subject of numerous debates and controversies regarding the tendency of his works, the quality of his influence, and the dubiety of his doctrines, Walter Horatio Pater's life seems, at first glance, a singularly colorless affair. The youngest son of a dedicated physician who died prematurely, Pater, born in London on August 4, 1839, was reared in a household dominated by his sisters, his mother, and his godmother. He remained, throughout childhood, indifferent to the activities or sports of his peers, preferring to imagine a world of ceremonious gallantry and hieratic ritual. He manifested a deep attachment to the solemn devotions and sumptuous worship of the Anglican Church. A need to remain true to the irrepressible skepticism and intellectual scrupulousness of his own nature prevented him, at the last, from acting upon his early impulses and taking orders. With a temperament more than commonly inclined to self-analysis and introspection, Pater, following his matriculation at Queens College, Oxford, chose to pursue an academic career. He was elected a junior fellow at Brasenose College in 1864.

From the first, the young don was regarded with certain suspicions, "having acquired," as Humphry Ward observed, "a new and daring philosophy of his own, and a wonderful gift of style." Benjamin Jowett, the famous translator of Plato, was acutely displeased with the seemingly subversive conclusion to *The Renaissance* and successfully hindered Pater's advancement at Oxford. In defiance, however, of Jowett's reprobations, Pater continued to enjoy a steady advance in influence and reputation. Ultimately, his increased fame warranted the taking of additional rooms in London, and there, in the company of sisters and friends, Pater enjoyed the sympathy and civility that were sometimes denied him at Oxford.

Modest, retiring, elusive, and enigmatic: These are the epithets that most frequently occur in contemporary portraits of Pater. It was doubtless these qualities that won for him the admiration of his most famous pupil: Gerard Manley Hopkins. It is interesting to note (and much to Pater's credit) that, in the surcharged evangelical atmosphere of Oxford, where professors more often strove to win converts than to foster independence of mind, Pater was the single instructor who continued to be loyal to Hopkins after his embrace of Catholicism. Indeed, Pater's elasticity and insouciance, his careful cultivation of what John Keats called "negative capability," were as characteristic of the man as they were of the artist. Pater died as a result of a heart attack in 1894.

ANALYSIS

Walter Pater's *Marius the Epicurean* is the culminating expression of a fictional genre that began in the 1830's and continued until the turn of the century. This genre, a peculiar mixture of religious speculation and personal confession, developed almost synchronously with the assault of science against traditional Christianity, beginning with the publication, in 1832, of Sir Charles Lyell's *Principles of Geology*. Lyell's book, which exploded the biblical account of creation, was the first of several books—the most famous being Charles Darwin's—that shook Western culture to its foundations. The passage of the Reform Bill, the theories of Darwin and Karl Marx, the development of the so-called higher criticism in the exegesis of biblical texts, the rise in population, and the spread of revolution, were but a few events that challenged the inherited certainties of Victorian England. People were forced to reevaluate old beliefs, to doubt discredited traditions, to revise social policies, to change moral valuations. It is not surprising that the confessional novel, the novel of doubt and faith, should acquire an unprecedented significance during such a period. The absence of reliable guideposts threw people back upon themselves and obliged them to search for unity, purpose, and direction in the kaleidoscopic sequence of their own lives.

MARIUS THE EPICUREAN

Marius the Epicurean is one of the finest offshoots of a literary tradition inaugurated by Thomas Carlyle's *Sartor Resartus* (1835) and sustained in such works as

John Henry Newman's *Loss and Gain* (1848), William Hale White's *The Autobiography of Mark Rutherford* (1885), and Mary Ward's *Robert Elsmere* (1888; written as Mrs. Humphry Ward). Pater chose to set his search for meaning and purpose amid the disintegrating spectacle of Antonine Rome, but its bearing on the condition of late Victorian England is emphatically underlined: "Let the reader pardon me if here and there I seem to be passing from Marius to his modern representatives—from Rome, to Paris or London," Pater interpolates at one point. Marius is clearly meant to be prototypical: He dramatizes a quest for religious values that satisfies the demands of modern consciousness and reflects the ambiguity of a shattered world.

This is not to say that his growth is haphazard or random; on the contrary, Pater implies an underlying teleology in Marius's development: However dim and faint the sense of a superintending providence, his life is oriented toward the climactic moment of self-sacrifice with which the novel ends. Marius does not, however, fully

Walter Pater. (Library of Congress)

resolve the conflicting calls of conscience and sensation, beauty and duty, engagement and withdrawal, in the fulfillment of that end. Though Pater evidently sees Marius's entire existence as an elaborate preparation for the revelatory moment in which his moral and spiritual being are ultimately defined, critics have generally judged that this is accomplished, if at all, without dramatic conviction.

Marius's youth is characterized, as was Pater's, by a more than common susceptibility to sensuous impressions. His home, White Nights, a villa with adjacent farm, contributes to these susceptibilities. The note of grave beauty, of life lived under the conditions of animal sacrifice and seasonal change, develops in the boy a wistful reverence and wonder, which deepen with the passage of years. The Wordsworthian element in all this is not fortuitous, for Marius is destined to enact precisely that pattern of spiritual growth enunciated in "Lines Composed a Few Miles Above Tintern Abbey" and "Ode: Intimations of Immortality"—a pattern that involves a gradual conversion from the sensory to the spiritual planes of existence, a slow but steady ascension from the "aching joys" and "dizzy raptures" of his first impulsive response to beauty to the sober steadfastness of a mind that recognizes "a sense sublime of something far more deeply interfused." This conversion, if such it may be called, does not, for Marius, issue in the renunciation of his former pleasures, but rather a deepening awareness of their ultimate origin and tendency.

In brief, Marius comes to dwell consciously in the presence of a spirit that is implied in his first naïve responses to nature and beauty. Hence, the pagan ceremonies, which solicit Marius's devotion and awe, already foreshadow "certain heavy demands" that will not become apparent to the lad until he acquires the mature self-consciousness of adulthood. It is then, on the level of discursive thought, that he will begin to recognize "some ampler vision, which should take up into itself and explain this world's delightful shows." White Nights is, therefore, as Pater suggests, not only a domestic dwelling place but also a state of mind peculiar to youth and prior to the self-dedication that maturity exacts.

In any event, it is not long before Marius is obliged to abandon the "world's delightful shows" in the pursuit of a more bracing conception of beauty. To cure a childhood illness, Marius is sent to the Temple of Aesculapius. The process of healing is complemented by meditations on Platonic texts. While these constitute a cherishable legacy for Marius, the boy reacts against a world of abstract essences. The impalpable ideas of Plato attract him only insofar as they fuse with the world of spatiotemporal objects, "green fields, for instance, or children's faces." Here, Pater is clearly attempting to revise the "impressionism" of his youth, itself a recrudescence of the Heraclitean theory of perpetual flux, with a Symbolist theory of correspondences. Beauty will no longer be an end in itself but "an outward imagery identifying itself with unseen moralities." While Marius does not achieve such an identification at once or without great difficulty, Pater clearly intends that the boy's unthinking empiricism should be shaken and unsettled. In a word, the exhortation "to burn with a hard gem-like flame," which Pater formerly enunciated in *The Renaissance*, is now being duly qualified by an obligation "to discriminate, ever more and more fastidiously, select form and colour in things from what was less select."

Pater is avid to demonstrate, through his hero Marius, the correct application of the aesthetic theory to life, an application that requires a transvaluation of the concept "beauty" to include "not pleasure, but fulness of life, and insight as conducting to that fulness . . . whatever form of human life, in short, might be heroic, impassioned, ideal." Marius's stay at the temple initiates an intellectual or moral awakening, a search for a hieratic order of conduct and beauty that is truly serviceable to that ideal. Dissatisfied with the abstractness of the Platonic method, Marius rejects the world of ideal forms in the pursuit of its equivalent in a living community, a veritable body of fellow aspirants. His search for this community determines the subsequent shape of the novel.

Immediately prior to his departure from the temple, Marius is vouchsafed a distant view of a city that appears to be an earthly incarnation of the Platonic archetype he is seeking. This first glimpse of Rome kindles in Marius the illusion that it, perhaps, is that "new city coming down 'like a bride out of heaven,'" of which Plato discoursed so eloquently. Accordingly, Marius takes practical steps to bring him closer to "the most religious city in the world." He moves next to Pisa, preparing for his future obligations as secretary to the emperor Aurelius. He is soon befriended by an aspiring youth of literary ambitions by the name of Flavian—a character who clearly represents one aspect of Marius's own divided consciousness.

Flavian's function in the novel is to bear involuntary witness to the limitations of aesthetic hedonism. Pater clearly intends through this subordinate character to disabuse his devotees of the notion that burning with a hard, gemlike flame is equivalent to self-indulgent dissipation. Beneath "the perfection of form" that Flavian achieves in his bearing and his poetry, Marius recognizes "a depth of corruption," which compels him to follow his friend only so far. Pater anticipates, here, to a remarkable degree the theme of Thomas Mann's *Death in Venice* (1912): the awareness that an exclusive preoccupation with artistic form may have the effect of neutralizing both good and evil by reducing them to complementary colors, lights, and shades in a composition. Nevertheless, Flavian performs a vital role in the drama of Marius's development, for it is he who introduces Marius to the "golden book" of Apuleius.

At this point, Pater reproduces in full Apuleius's tale of Cupid and Psyche. Through subtle and strategic modifications of the original, Pater conceives of the tale as a presentiment of Marius's spiritual development. Evoking the solemn harmonies of the King James version of the Bible and softening the racy idiom of Apuleius, Pater endows the story of Cupid and Psyche with a "gentle idealism" and facilitates its interpretation as an allegory. Just as Psyche, symbol of the human soul, is redeemed from death by the intervention of Cupid, so Marius—bewildered, distracted, and divided by the contradictory sects and philosophical schools of decadent Rome—is presumably redeemed from despair by the appearance of a community that claims to satisfy the deepest needs of the human spirit. The road to that community is, however, difficult, uncertain, and devious.

Flavian's life is prematurely ended by an outbreak of plague. Marius, who remains, as ever, faithful to the evidence of his senses, is convinced of "nothing less than the soul's extinction." It may be parenthetically observed that despite his later sympathy with the Christian response to suffering, Marius never fully abandons those scruples "which can make no sincere claim to have ap-

prehended anything beyond the veil of immediate experience." With his departure for Rome, he remains in a state of suspended judgment with regard to the ultimate destiny appointed for the human soul.

The actual journey to the capital of the ancient world includes a number of incidents that undermine the philosophical detachment of the young Marius. Notwithstanding the glory of the Roman *campagna*, the many idyllic details of which Marius, with his habitual eye for the concrete, discerns with "a fresh, primeval poetry," he is plunged, following a scarcely averted accident, into further uncomfortable wrestling with the eternal questions. This accident—a loosened boulder falls from a wall beside the path Marius is following—has the effect of shaking him into a recognition that "his elaborate philosophy had not put beneath his feet the terror of mere bodily evil." The force, however, that is destined to correct the deficiencies in Marius's scheme of existence is not far away. Stopping at an inn to revive his spirits, Marius orders a glass of wine and muses vacantly over the "ring of delicate foam" that sparkles in his cup. Presently, his attention is arrested by a voice—"a youthful voice, with a reassuring clearness of note, which completes his cure." As he will soon learn, it is the voice of Cornelius, a young Roman soldier whose influence is destined to supersede that of Flavian. It is not, however, until much later in his pilgrimage that Marius discovers that the origin of Cornelius's gracious alacrity of spirit is traceable to "some new knighthood or chivalry, just then coming into the world."

Marius, however, is not yet in a position to be irresistibly won over to that knighthood. He must first extend his philosophical hypotheses beyond the immediate circle of his own sensations; the role of Marcus Aurelius in the novel is to facilitate this extension. Unlike Flavian and Cornelius, the philosophical emperor of Rome is more than merely a shadowy personification of Marius's fractured ego: Aurelius is a figure of vital warmth and sympathy who encourages Marius to enlarge his spiritual perspective and to discover that an exclusive preoccupation with the passing moment may actually narrow the range of experience, curtail the development of character, and inhibit the acquisition of wisdom. The upshot of Aurelius's teachings is to reinforce Marius's search for a "comely order . . . to which, as to all other beautiful phenomena in life, he must, for his own peace, adjust himself."

While his influence is certainly salutary, Aurelius remains, in the final analysis, incapable of reconciling his devotion to that "comely order" with the debased reality of Antonine Rome. It is not long before Marius discovers a number of serious shortcomings in Aurelius's view of existence. To be sure, Marius accepts the merits of a philosophical scheme that posits a universal reason, or *logos*, a point of rest and a center of calm from which to withstand the vertiginous whirl of feelings and events, the traumatic blows of fate and destiny. Such a scheme, as Marius equally recognizes, may easily devolve into a pretext for neglecting one's peers in the present, for averting one's eyes from the plenitude and plurality of the living world. While freely granting the efficacy of believing in a "universal commonwealth of mind"—the sense of expanded horizons, the freedom from petty vexations, the glimpse of imperishable ideals that it allows—Marius rejects the concomitant calm and serenity that Aurelius, for example, maintains in the middle of human misery.

Two episodes in particular underline the deficiencies of the Stoical system. The first of these occurs during a performance at the Colosseum over which Aurelius, notwithstanding his own aversion to the gladiatorial games, presides with an air of tolerance. This indifference to the unspeakable butchery of men and animals, a consequence of the Stoic divorce of reason from reality, provokes Marius "to mark Aurelius as his inferior, now and for ever, on the question of righteousness." When it comes, however, to the suffering and death of his son, Lucius Verus, Aurelius is presented in a more sympathetic light. This episode, too, leaves an indelible mark in Marius's consciousness. The disparity between the imperturbable calm of the professed Stoic and the irrepressible grief of the stricken parent is poignantly dramatized when the boy, after an operation of surpassing agony, lapses into a coma from which he never recovers.

The chapter that immediately follows this episode signals the direction that Marius henceforth will take. An epigraph from the Psalms—"My heart is ready, O God, a ready heart is mine"—clearly enunciates the imminence of that spiritual crisis toward which his whole life has been moving. It would be a mistake, however, to construe this crisis as a sudden shattering encounter with the divine. On the contrary, nothing in the sense of a clear dramatic conversion may be said to happen.

The epiphany that Marius is vouchsafed has all the character of a Wordsworthian "spot of time." In one of his vagrant wanderings on the outskirts of Rome, Marius pauses at an outdoor inn to gaze at the extensive Roman *campagna*. His attention is divided among a number of apparently trivial and unrelated details—"a bird came and sang among the wattled hedge-roses: an animal feeding crept nearer: the child who kept it was gazing quietly"—when, suddenly, the entire scene presents itself as the outward and tangible emblem of "that . . . Ideal, to which the Old Testament gives the name of Creator, which for the philosophers of Greece is the Eternal Reason, and in the New Testament the Father of Men." The mundane world is transfigured and transvalued in a moment of privileged perception: no less and no more. The departure of this mood is as quiet and unobtrusive as its inception, but it leaves Marius with the firm conviction that the remainder of his life must be "a search for the equivalent of that Ideal . . . a gathering together of every trace and token of it, which his actual experience might present." The event is clearly something of a watershed.

At this juncture, Marius is given the opportunity to visit a pair of houses that represent two opposing visions of reality. The first house represents the finest flowering of classical antiquity. It is here that Marius meets his former idol, the poet Apuleius; enjoys the refined pleasures and urbane conversation of the Roman intelligentsia; and delights in the delectations of a banquet replete with music, dance, and fine condiments. The whole proceedings, however, are tainted by a certain foppish connoisseurship, a pampered elegance, a "facility" and "self-complacency" in the exchange of ideas. Marius departs with a nagging sense of weariness and disillusion.

The second house, to which he is introduced by Cornelius, is that of the Christian saint, Cecilia. It is characteristic that Pater should choose the canonized patron of music as the agent of Marius's contact with Christianity. Presumably, if art can obscure the moral being of humans, as in the case of Flavian, it can also reveal that moral being. The grave, refined, and simple dignity of the Christian community—its air of domestic and filial piety, its comely rectitude of spirit, its solicitude for the departed, care for the living, and faith in things to come—stands in favorable contrast to the enervating amusements and facile wit of the Roman upper crust. Yet it is important to note that the early Church, as Pater presents it, has nothing of that apocalyptic fervor that looks forward to the end of the world and the last things. On the contrary, "the contrast between the church and the world" Pater tells us, "was becoming less pronounced." By far the largest part of Marius's attraction to this community derives from his contemplation of "the beautiful house of Cecilia, its lights and flowers, of Cecilia herself, moving among the lilies, with an enchanted grace."

The fact is that Marius remains ultimately indifferent to the dogmatic foundations of Christianity. To be sure, he returns to his childhood home and supervises the reburial of his ancestors according to the usages of the early Church. Furthermore, he willingly intercedes on Cornelius's behalf following an officially sanctioned purge of the growing Christian community. There is, however, a considerable degree of ambiguity involved in Marius's position vis-à-vis the Christian faith.

Marius is arrested along with Cornelius for being present at a community act of worship. An outbreak of plague shatters the fragile tolerance extended to the Church and initiates widespread persecution of the Christians. On the strength of his relations with Aurelius, Marius contrives to have Cornelius released. He is compelled, however, to give a deposition on his friend's behalf and to join the other prisoners in the long and arduous journey to Rome. This generosity of spirit on the part of Marius is prompted by a mistaken notion that Cornelius is Cecilia's intended: The latter's vows of chastity entirely elude Marius's understanding. Traveling to Rome in company with the other captives, Marius is stricken with plague and abandoned at a neighboring farm that, as it turns out, is the dwelling of some recent converts. Lying in a state of partial delirium for several days, he finds consolation, during the lucid intervals allowed him, in "the scent of newmown hay . . . and the sounds of cattle . . . from the green places around." The occupants, erroneously assuming that he is a Christian, administer to the dying Marius the last rites of their faith.

Is Marius, then, a Christian? This question has been the subject of critical debate since the novel's appearance. For Paul Elmer More, *Marius the Epicurean* is "only another manifestation of that aestheticism which Pater sucked from the Romantic school of his century and disguised in the phraseology of ancient faith." He further adds, "to write thus was to betray Christianity with a kiss." T. S. Eliot has no hesitation in asserting that "of the essence of the Christian Faith . . . Pater knew almost nothing." Arthur Benson is equally forthright in claiming that "the very peace which Marius discerns in Christianity is the old philosophical peace over again." The point is that Marius fails to grasp and remains largely indifferent to the theoretical foundations of Christianity. "Our creeds," as Pater observes, "are but the brief abstract of our prayer and song." Inasmuch as Christianity invests that song with a deeper pathos, frees the mind from its empirical trammels, and endows existence with a warmer hope, it is clearly a serviceable hypothesis for the questing human spirit. Its dogmatic underpinnings, however, are of secondary importance.

Some might claim that Pater's enterprise in *Marius the Epicurean* is fundamentally affiliated with the Christian existentialism of Søren Kierkegaard. There is, however, one signal and important difference. Unlike Kierkegaard, who posits a leap of faith in which reason is virtually annihilated, Pater viewed all such leaps as a source of potential fanaticism. Christianity, for Pater, is clearly a stage in the development of human potential, but he would jealously protect that potential from any claim that might threaten its autonomy. The Church of Cecilia is, at bottom, a fictive structure in which there is "no forced opposition between soul and body, the world and the spirit." It is even identified, at one point, with that "half-humorous placidity of soul, of a kind illustrated later very effectively by Montaigne."

Just as modern-day theologians who attempt to gerrymander Christianity into the camps of Marx, Sigmund Freud, Friedrich Nietzsche, or Ludwig Feuerbach, Pater has created a church of his own making—distinctly unrecognizable to the average believer. From the perspective of Christ's statement, "He who is not with me is against me," Marius is most certainly not a Christian; on the other hand, if one considers the earlier phrasing of this statement in the gospel of Mark, "He who is not against us is for us," then the question of Marius's death as "a kind of sacrament with plenary grace" remains open.

GASTON DE LATOUR

Moreover, as Pater was to recognize in *Gaston de Latour*, institutional Christianity, insofar as it defines itself in what a person professes rather than in what he or she is, is as prodigal of sectarian bigotry and bloodshed as the worst excesses of pagan Rome. Like *Marius the Epicurean*, *Gaston de Latour* examines the situation of faith in an "age of transition . . . when the problem of man's destiny and his relations to the unseen was undergoing a new solution." Though Pater never lived to complete the novel—it remains, at best, a series of discontinuous meditations on the religious and political ferment of the Reformation—its essential outlines are as follows.

Born in the middle of growing strife between Huguenots and Catholics, Gaston comes of age in "the cornlands of France," in close proximity to the cathedral of Chartres and amid the luxuries of his rustic manor house. He becomes acquainted with King Charles IX, joins the "episcopal household of Chartres as a page," and falls under the influence of the poetry of Pierre de Ronsard. Like Marius, in a different context, he becomes the votary of a great philosopher—in this instance, Michel de Montaigne. He eventually travels to Paris and takes up with a spirited Huguenot girl; under the pressure of her brothers, he marries her in a Protestant ceremony that exerts no real claim upon him: "The transaction seemed to have but that transitoriness as also the guilt of a vagrant love." Miscalculating the forces of destruction gathered on the eve of St. Bartholomew, Gaston returns to his homestead at Deux-manoirs, "his wife left behind there in Paris." He later learns of the death of his wife "while the stairways of the Louvre, the streets, the trap-doors of Paris, run blood." Following the banishment of King Charles, Gaston returns to Paris and falls under the influence of the heterodox monk Giordano Bruno. Here the novel abruptly ends.

What is clearly significant about this work is its relation to *Marius the Epicurean*. Just as Marius qualifies the hedonism of *The Renaissance*, so *Gaston de Latour* qualifies the Christianity of *Marius the Epicurean*. Indeed, of Gaston himself the reader is told that "the very genius of qualification followed him through his keen, constant, changeful consideration of men and things."

Pater's attitude is obvious. He clearly distrusts the external machinery of a church that absorbs the individual conscience and resolves all doubts in cozy conformity, irresponsible anonymity, and superstitious fear. Pater rejects dogmatic formulations and ideologies of any kind, especially insofar as these inhibit the cultivation of human sympathy or the development of individual character. "The man who never alters his opinion is like standing water, and breeds reptiles of the mind," wrote William Blake, and Pater would have most certainly agreed. Indeed, the true saint of the Reformation, for Pater, is Montaigne, and the legitimate attitude in all matters speculative and religious is not the intransigence of the doctrinaire but the suspended judgment of a humanist. "It was something to have been," writes Pater of Montaigne, "in the matter of religious tolerance, as in so many other matters of justice and gentleness, the solitary conscience of the age."

In the final analysis, the question of whether Pater's protagonists are ultimately Christian pales before the question of whether they are comprehensively human. Thoughtful, but without energy; sensitive, but without resolve; scrupulous, but without conviction; both Marius and Gaston remain imprisoned, each in his own consciousness and incapable of genuine community with others. The essentially selfish conviction that informs these novels and that may be taken as a motto for Pater's life and work is perhaps stated most succinctly in one of the Pythian Odes of the Latin poet Pindar: "O my soul, do not aspire to immortal life, but exhaust the limits of the possible." Pater once remarked of Marius that his was a philosophy that at least guaranteed its possessor of living a life without harm to others. The question remains, however, whether such a philosophy is adequate to the full range of human experience. In the absence of more solid and substantial convictions than those that Pater demonstrates in his writings, this question remains a point of legitimate concern in any final estimate of his achievement.

Stephen I. Gurney

OTHER MAJOR WORKS

SHORT FICTION: *Imaginary Portraits*, 1887.

NONFICTION: *Studies in the History of the Renaissance*, 1873, 1877, 1888, 1893 (revised as *The Renais-*

sance: Studies in Art and Poetry); *Appreciations: With an Essay on Style,* 1889; *Plato and Platonism: A Series of Lectures,* 1893; *Greek Studies: A Series of Essays,* 1895; *Miscellaneous Studies: A Series of Essays* (1895); *Essays from the "Guardian,"* 1896.

BIBLIOGRAPHY

Bann, Stephen, ed. *The Reception of Walter Pater in Europe.* New York: Thoemmes Continuum, 2004. Essays examine how Pater's novels and other works were received, translated, and published in Italy, France, Germany, Hungary, the former Czechoslovakia, Poland, and Spain.

Bloom, Harold, ed. *Walter Pater.* New York: Chelsea House, 1985. Bloom has compiled some of the best criticism available on Pater, creating a valuable and well-rounded study. Includes a bibliography and an index.

Brake, Laurel, Lesley Higgins, and Carolyn Williams, eds. *Walter Pater: Transparencies of Desire.* Greensboro, N.C.: ELT Press, 2002. Essays explore Pater's entire body of work. Includes discussion of *Marius the Epicurean,* Pater and modernism, and Pater's reception outside England. Includes a bibliography and an index.

Brake, Laurel, and Ian Small, eds. *Pater in the 1990's.* Greensboro, N.C.: ELT Press, 1991. While half of these essays reflect the older New Criticism approach to literature, the other half demonstrate the shift in Pater criticism toward consideration of his works in historical and biographical contexts. Topics range from editing the novel *Gaston de Latour* to Pater's friends and literary influences.

Buckler, William E. *Walter Pater: The Critic as Artist of Ideas.* New York: New York University Press, 1987. This scholarly study examines the breadth and depth of Pater's prose and poetry, as well as his role as a critic, acknowledging him as a major but underrated writer.

Daley, Kenneth. *The Rescue of Romanticism: Walter Pater and John Ruskin.* Athens: Ohio University Press, 2001. Daley examines the relationship of the two prominent Victorian art critics, focusing on their different theories of Romanticism. He demonstrates how Pater's theory was a response to Ruskin, whom Pater considered a conservative thinker.

Donoghue, Denis. *Walter Pater: Lover of Strange Souls.* New York: Alfred A. Knopf, 1995. An exceptional biographical and critical source. Donoghue defines Pater as a precursor of modernism who influenced the later works of James Joyce, T. S. Eliot, Virginia Woolf, and other authors.

Moliterno, Frank. *The Dialectics of Sense and Spirit in Pater and Joyce.* Greensboro, N.C.: ELT Press, 1998. A comparison of the themes and aesthetic theories of the two authors, demonstrating how Pater exerted a major influence on the work of James Joyce. Includes bibliographical references and an index.

Monsman, Gerald. *Walter Pater.* Boston: Twayne, 1977. A chronological look at Pater's work and life. Examines the heroes in his works, in particular the hero in *Marius the Epicurean.* A useful study for the beginning reader of Pater. Includes a selected bibliography.

Shuter, William. *Rereading Walter Pater.* New York: Cambridge University Press, 1997. A reevaluation of Pater's writings. Shuter initially provides a conventional account of the texts in the order in which they were written; he then returns to the earlier books, demonstrating how the later work, paradoxically, offers an introduction to the earlier.

ALAN PATON

Born: Pietermaritzburg, Natal, South Africa;
  January 11, 1903
Died: Botha's Hill, Natal, South Africa; April 12,
  1988
Also known as: Alan Stewart Paton

PRINCIPAL LONG FICTION

Cry, the Beloved Country, 1948
Too Late the Phalarope, 1953
Ah, but Your Land Is Beautiful, 1981

OTHER LITERARY FORMS

Before his first two novels, Alan Paton (PAYT-uhn) wrote only juvenile poems and a play, while at college. A collection of his short stories, *Tales from a Troubled Land*, published in 1961, was republished that same year as *Debbie Go Home*. In 1964, he produced a play, *Sponono*, with Krishna Shah. His major work of biography is *Hofmeyr* (1964), better known in its abridged American version, *South African Tragedy: The Life and Times of Jan Hofmeyr* (1965). Paton's autobiographies are titled *Towards the Mountain* (1980) and *Journey Continued* (1988).

ACHIEVEMENTS

Alan Paton burst upon the international literary scene with his novel *Cry, the Beloved Country*. Seldom has a first work had such immediate and yet such long-lasting impact. This first novel, published when its author was already forty-five years of age, sold fifteen million copies by the time of Paton's death in 1988, forty years later. The persistence of the book's popularity can also be seen in its having been made into films in 1951 and 1995. In addition to popular acclaim, Paton has been awarded considerable critical respect, receiving both British and American awards within a year of the publication of *Cry, the Beloved Country*.

His accomplishments as an author are impressively paradoxical. Paton's novels are set concretely in the landscape of South Africa, based specifically on the social conditions of that country, incorporating actual political events into their plots; however, from those localized elements emerges not the narrow regionalism that might be expected but rather cosmic concern with shared humanity. Deeply concerned with issues of political justice, Paton seldom degenerates into preaching or sentimentality. Carefully crafted as his lyrical style is, it is mostly admired not for its aesthetic competence but rather for its simplicity and naturalness.

BIOGRAPHY

Much that matters in his writing stems from the fact that Alan Stewart Paton was born in 1903 in Pietermaritzburg in Natal, South Africa. He loved that local land as much as he loved books. He learned both passions, which figure prominently in his writings, from his father, James Paton, an immigrant from Scotland, and his mother, Eunice Warder James Paton, the daughter of English immigrants. His father was a deeply religious Christian and a strict authoritarian, so strict that his disciplinary practices provoked Paton to resist authoritarianism in any form.

Paton married Doris "Dorrie" Olive Francis in 1928, and they had two sons, David and Jonathan. Following Dorrie's death in 1967, he married Anne Hopkins. After teaching chemistry and mathematics in high school and college, Paton worked as principal of the Diepkloof reformatory from 1935 until the publication of *Cry, the Beloved Country*, his first novel, written from the homesick perspective gained during a three-month tour of prisons in England and the United States.

Among the earliest voices for racial equality in South Africa, Paton helped create and vigorously promoted the Liberal Party during the 1950's, actively opposing his country's policy of apartheid. That opposition resulted in confiscation of his passport, eventual dissolution of the party, and the South African government's banning of his beloved Defence and Aid Fund, which had provided legal fees for oppressed blacks. By the time of his death at age eighty-five, Paton had been honored throughout the world with international awards for his humanitarian work and honorary degrees in recognition of his writing from such prestigious universities as Harvard, Yale, and Edinburgh.

ANALYSIS

Paton's novels are much admired for their lyrical language, their closeness to the land, and their heartfelt moral purpose. Although some readers feel that Paton falters in his attempt to integrate native and English elements into an archaic prose, most readers enjoy the lyrical quality of his style. His ear for the rhythms and nuances of spoken South African English is as sensitive as writer Mark Twain's ear for Americanisms. As a result of that linguistic giftedness, readers hear in his writing an impressive chorus of voices: the clamoring voices of South Africa, the sonorous voice of the Old Testament, the still, sad voice of humanity, and, integrating all of these, the earnestly reforming voice of Alan Paton.

Paton's second literary virtue is the realism of his fiction. Precise awareness of his South African home pervades every page, and the narrative is illuminated by Paton's honesty of perspective. Paton sees with a clear eye the complex urban degeneracies of Johannesburg and the tragedies of modern life. He is perhaps at his best viewing the simple natural glories of the Natal countryside. The plot of *Too Late the Phalarope*, for instance, hinges on his hero's awareness of the phalarope, a little-known bird of his homeland, a creature Pieter and his father understand better than the outland expert who writes the definitive book on Natal birds. Critic Edward Callan compares Paton's sensitivity to the natural life of South Africa to poet Robert Frost's keen awareness of the landscape of New England.

For most readers the most profound power of Alan Paton's fiction is generated by his moral earnestness. Some have worried that the directness of his moral purpose verges on melodrama, even propaganda. Consensus assessment of Paton's fiction, however, is that his insistence on the value of individual human dignity and worth "plumbs deep into human suffering and punishment" without "moralizing or . . . maudlin sentimentality." Fierce passion for reform without the downside of preaching is a rare literary achievement. Paton wrote *Cry, the Beloved Country* after reading American author John Steinbeck's classic novel of social protest, *The Grapes of Wrath* (1939). It may be, as critic F. Charles Rooney has suggested, that Paton captures in his writing "all Steinbeck's heart, plus *soul*."

CRY, THE BELOVED COUNTRY

Paton's first novel is also his best. Written from his personal experience with issues of freedom in his native South Africa, it is a lament for conditions that imprison the human spirit, a cry for freedom. Old Stephen Kumalo, pastor of the church in his Zulu village, ventures into sophisticated Johannesburg in search of his sister Gertrude, his brother John, and his son Absalom. He finds there a parable of the erosion of tribal society under the storm of white culture. He discovers Absalom in jail, the confessed murderer of a gentle and generous white man. In ironic confirmation of the relatedness of all humanity, the murdered man turns out to be the son of the plantation owner in Kumalo's home valley. Kumalo's sister, unable to find the husband who has deserted her, has become a prostitute. Kumalo's brother John has sold out totally to urban temptations of materialistic politics.

Alan Paton. (Library of Congress)

Kumalo also finds amid the corruptions of Johannesburg, however, the generosity of fellow priest Msimangu, whose Christian compassion reaches so far as to cause him to worry even about whites, "that one day when they turn to loving, they will find we are turned to hating." Kumalo finds along with the sin in this modern Sodom the determined social restructurings of the reformatory teacher, a man strikingly reminiscent of Paton himself. The weary old Zulu returns home to the father of the man his son has killed to tell him he is sorry, and they share across the abyss of race their mutual grief.

Kumalo's quest for his family ends in the worst of disasters. Fictional Johannesburg swallows the villagers who venture there as destructively as Western culture sapped the tribal values in mid-twentieth century South Africa. Paton's humanitarian ideals somehow prevail, however. When "that dawn will come, of our emancipation, from the fear of bondage and the bondage of fear" we cannot know, yet we can see even through the "clouded eyes" of those two bereaved fathers, looking toward a dawn that signals the end to the wasted life of Absalom Kumalo, the hope of that "faint steady lightening in the east."

The magnificent simplicity of the sad but hopeful plot is reflected in Paton's expression. The author has a gift for capturing in naturally lyrical prose the rhythms of Zulu, of Afrikaans, and of his King James Bible-steeped central characters. "Quietly, my child, there is a lovely valley where you were born. The water sings over the stones, and the wind cools you. The cattle come down to the river, they stand there under the trees. Quietly my child." The style, at its best, is reminiscent of the lean profundity of the book of Genesis and functions to much the same purpose—Paton's heartfelt expression makes *Cry, the Beloved Country* a psalm, a cry to repentance, and a prophecy.

TOO LATE THE PHALAROPE

Paton's first novel documents the destructiveness of racist attitudes on the world of black South Africans. His second book shifts focus to look at the havoc wrought by racism among whites. The fall of Pieter van Vlaanderen is tragic. Pieter is a white man drawn to black women, trapped in a society that views racial mixing as the ultimate sin. This good man is crushed by the racism of such Afrikaaners as his rigid father, Jakob, a man who under-

stands justice better than he comprehends mercy, so convinced of his racist perspective he can write his son out of the family Bible when he learns of his adultery with a black woman. Those fierce social attitudes are as realistic as the economic evils of Johannesburg painted in *Cry, the Beloved Country*. Harsh as it may seem, Paton wrote, in *Toward the Mountain*, as late as twenty years after the publication of *Too Late the Phalarope*, "Three white men have committed suicide in the last few weeks rather than face trial."

As in *Cry, the Beloved Country*, redemptive forces temper the destructiveness of the racist attitudes. Pieter's Jewish friend Kappie talks him out of suicide. His wife Nella, steeped as strictly in South African racism as Pieter, stands by him at the trial. Thoughtful Captain Massingham decides that the worst human offense may not be racial mixing but what is being done to Pieter, "to punish and not to restore, that is the greatest of all offences . . . the sin against the Holy Ghost."

Too Late the Phalarope is a fine novel, a haunting examination of a man's conscience. At its best the narrative is reminiscent of the soul-searching novels of religious inner torment of English writer Graham Greene. The book suffers from the usual problem of sequels, however: diminution from the power of the original. Perhaps because of the European rather than native viewpoint, *Too Late the Phalarope* does not reach for most readers the profound levels of compassion tapped by *Cry, the Beloved Country*.

AH, BUT YOUR LAND IS BEAUTIFUL

The title of Paton's final novel is based on comments from foreign visitors, who wonder how such a lovely landscape can tolerate, let alone produce, such intense racial hatreds as those that scar South African attitudes. The land is so beautiful that outsiders are surprised such ugly attitudes can inhabit the souls of its inhabitants. Prem Bodasingh, heroine of the novel, is an eighteen-year-old South African equivalent of Rosa Parks, the African American who sparked the Montgomery, Alabama, bus boycott in 1955 by refusing to give up her seat on a bus to a white passenger. This graceful Native African teenager, a model student, quietly rebels against apartheid by sitting down in the Durban Library to read, a position forbidden to her as a nonwhite by South African laws against racial intermixing in places such as libraries (and, as we discover later, at funerals).

In counterpoint to Prem's personal resistance to the evil political system of her country, the novel traces the public resistance to apartheid, mainly through the genesis of the Liberal Party, which Paton presided over from 1958 to 1968. It is a tribute to Paton's competence as a writer that he focuses always on the immediate human dilemma rather than on larger political forces. His conviction of the moral significance of every person's experience, however, makes the action of the novel take on cosmic significance—Paton believes deeply, and from our perspective it appears almost prophetically, that things can be better in South Africa.

Ah, but Your Land Is Beautiful is not only competent as a novel but also heartfelt. However, this work continues the diminishment of Paton's writing from the high-water mark of *Cry, the Beloved Country.* Perhaps that evaporation of the author's literary force was inevitable. His first novel looks at the brutalities of racism from the perspective of blacks, for whom it is a matter of life and death. *Too Late the Phalarope* approaches racist issues from the viewpoint of whites, for whom racism is personal tragedy. *Ah, but Your Land Is Beautiful* broaches Paton's inevitable subject from a less involved viewpoint, that of relative South African outsiders, such as Indians and Jews, for whom racist political policy is more a matter of economics than the issue of moral urgency it is for whites, let alone the matter of life and death it is for blacks. Whatever the reason for its neglect, *Ah, but Your Land Is Beautiful* is the least read of Paton's novels and the least discussed by critics.

Steven C. Walker

OTHER MAJOR WORKS

SHORT FICTION: *Tales from a Troubled Land*, 1961 (also known as *Debbie Go Home*).

PLAY: *Sponono*, pr. 1964 (with Krishna Shah).

NONFICTION: *The Land and People of South Africa*, 1955; *South Africa in Transition*, 1956 (with Dan Weiner); *Hope for South Africa*, 1958; *Hofmeyr*, 1964 (abridged as *South African Tragedy: The Life and Times of Jan Hofmeyr*, 1965); *Instrument of Thy Peace*, 1968; *For You Departed*, 1969 (also known as *Kontakion for You Departed*, 1969); *Apartheid and the Archbishop:*

The Life and Times of Geoffrey Clayton, Archbishop of Cape Town, 1973; *Towards the Mountain*, 1980 (autobiography); *Journey Continued*, 1988 (autobiography).

BIBLIOGRAPHY

Alexander, Peter F. *Alan Paton: A Biography*. New York: Oxford University Press, 1994. Thorough, vast study of Paton's life is as engagingly written as it is well documented. Provides informative background on Paton's novels.

Baker, Sheridan, ed. *Paton's "Cry, the Beloved Country": The Novel, the Critics, the Setting*. New York: Charles Scribner's Sons, 1968. Collection of critical essays examines the novel from many points of view. Includes Baker's own classic analysis, "Paton's Beloved Country and the Morality of Geography."

Bloom, Harold, ed. *Alan Paton's "Cry, the Beloved Country."* Philadelphia: Chelsea House, 2004. Helpful resource is designed to help students understand the novel. Includes a biographical sketch of Paton, list of characters, summary and analysis of the novel, and essays examining the book from a variety of perspectives.

Callan, Edward. *Alan Paton*. Rev. ed. Boston: Twayne, 1982. Offers a critical assessment of Paton's writings along with background on the events of the author's life and on South African history. Includes bibliography and index.

_____. *"Cry, the Beloved Country": A Novel of South Africa—A Study*. Boston: Twayne, 1991. Discusses the themes and critical reception of the novel and places it within the context of apartheid and South African culture. Includes bibliography and index.

Chiwengo, Ngwarsungu. *Understanding "Cry, the Beloved Country": A Student Casebook to Issues, Sources, and Historical Documents*. Westport, Conn.: Greenwood Press, 2007. Presents a literary analysis of the novel along with supplemental primary documents and other materials providing background on apartheid and on the social and economic conditions of segregated South Africa. Places the novel clearly within its historical context. Includes a chronology of South African history.

Coetzee, J. M. "South African Liberals: Alan Paton, Helen Suzman" In *Stranger Shores: Literary Essays,*

1986-1999. New York: Viking Press, 2001. Brief discussion of Paton places him within the tradition of South African liberalism. Part of a collection of literary essays by a South African novelist who has won the Nobel Prize in Literature and two Booker Prizes.

Paton, Jonathan. "Comfort in Desolation." In *International Literature in English: Essays on the Major Writers*, edited by Robert L. Ross. New York: Garland, 1991. Paton's youngest son describes the Christian call for comfort that underlies his father's first novel, *Cry, the Beloved Country*.

Peck, Richard. "The Liberal Tradition in South African Writings: Alan Paton and Laurens van der Post." In *A Morbid Fascination: White Prose and Politics in Apartheid South Africa*. Westport, Conn.: Greenwood Press, 1997. Discussion of Paton's work is part of a larger examination of the English-language literature of white South Africa that asserts that this literature demonstrates both a "morbid fascination" with political issues and a distrust of politics.

Van der Vlies, Andrew Edward. "Whose Beloved Country? Alan Paton and the Hypercanonical." In *South African Textual Cultures: White, Black, Read All Over*. New York: Manchester University Press, 2007. Essay on Paton is part of a volume devoted to an exploration of the publication, promotion, and reception of a series of South African writers and their works between 1883 and 2005.

GARY PAULSEN

Born: Minneapolis, Minnesota; May 17, 1939

PRINCIPAL LONG FICTION

The Implosion Effect, 1976
The Foxman, 1977
Tracker, 1984
Dogsong, 1985
Hatchet, 1987
Murphy, 1987
Murphy's Gold, 1988
Murphy's Herd, 1989
The Voyage of the Frog, 1989
The Winter Room, 1989
Canyons, 1990
Murphy's War, 1991
The River, 1991
Murphy's Stand, 1993
Murphy's Ambush, 1995
Brian's Winter, 1996
Murphy's Trail, 1996
Soldier's Heart, 1998
Brian's Return, 1999
Brian's Hunt, 2003
Molly McGinty Has a Really Good Day, 2004

OTHER LITERARY FORMS

Gary Paulsen has written more than two hundred books as well as hundreds of articles and short stories for children and adults. He is best known for his young adult novels, but his first published writings were nonfiction works aimed at adults. *The Special War* (1966), his first book, shares some of his own experiences along with those of other soldiers as they returned from the Vietnam War. Paulsen has stated that he considers *Some Birds Don't Fly* (1968), a satirical piece about problems in the American missile program, to be his first real book. He has also written how-to books on construction topics for adults as well as nonfiction for both young adults and children. In addition, he has written a few children's books, including *The Tortilla Factory* (1995).

ACHIEVEMENTS

Gary Paulsen's works for young adults in particular have received numerous awards and honors. In 1997, Paulsen received the Margaret A. Edwards Award for lifetime achievement in writing young adult fiction. He also won the Western Writers of America Golden Spurs Award for *The Haymeadow* (1992). In 1991, *The Boy Who Owned the School* (1990) won the ALAN Award

Gary Paulsen. (AP/Wide World Photos)

His higher education includes several years at Bemidji College (now Bemidji State University) in Minnesota, where he worked as a trapper to pay tuition, and later he was a student at the University of Colorado. His widely varied work career has included jobs as a carnival worker, a farm laborer, an engineer, a construction worker, a ranch hand, a trucker, a sailor, a satellite technician, and a magazine proofreader/editor.

Paulsen found childhood comfort in books, so his final choice of career is not surprising. While he was working on the magazine, he decided to start writing on his own. He published *The Special War* in 1966, and over the next eleven years he produced almost forty books in addition to a number of magazine articles and short stories. In 1977, he was involved in a lawsuit over his novel *Winterkill* (1976), and although he won, he stopped writing for a short period of time.

Paulsen's personal interests include extreme sports, so his raising and training of sled dogs for the annual Iditarod Trail Sled Dog Race fits him perfectly. He participated in two Iditarods, but an angina attack forced him to slow down in 1985. A heart attack in 1990 slowed him further. He has attempted the Iditarod on more than one occasion, withdrawing at the last minute in 2005 and after only a few days in 2006. He and his wife, Ruth Wright Paulsen, an artist, have established homes in Minnesota, New Mexico, and Alaska. The couple have one grown son.

ANALYSIS

Gary Paulsen has written a series of Western novels for adult readers, but he is best known for his action-adventure stories for young adults. He writes many stories of survival in which the main conflict is that of character versus nature, and many of his characters experience rites of passage into adulthood. Some of his best adventure works, such as the Brian books, are parts of series that center on particular characters. Paulsen's writing style is most often visual, with a stress on realistic settings. Additionally, his novels frequently revolve around imperfect families; often the main character must seek a person other than his or her parents to provide a support system, and many times this person is a part of the character's extended family. Paulsen has also ventured into humorous novels for a younger audience.

(presented by the Assembly on Literature for Adolescents) and received a Parents' Choice Citation. *Dogsong*, *Hatchet*, and *The Winter Room* are all Newbery Honor Books, and in 1985, *Tracker* won the Society of Midland Authors Award. *Dancing Carl* (1983) won the American Library Association's Best Young Adult Books Citation.

BIOGRAPHY

Gary Paulsen was born in May, 1939, in Minneapolis, Minnesota, to an unhappy family life. His father, a soldier, served in World War II during Paulsen's early years, and his mother worked in a factory. His parents were alcoholics who were unable to care for him adequately, so after living in the Philippines, where his father was stationed from 1946 to 1949, Paulsen lived with a variety of relatives, mainly his grandmother and a series of aunts, until he set out on his own at age fourteen.

HATCHET

One active character dominates *Hatchet*, which is ultimately about survival, maturity, and coming to terms with the divorce of one's parents. One of the main literary tools Paulsen uses in the book is foreshadowing. This is seen in the first chapter as thirteen-year-old Brian Robeson, who is setting off to spend the summer with his father, learns how to fly the small plane in which he is traveling while the pilot is still healthy and as he reveals that Brian's mother has a secret. On the way, the pilot has a heart attack and dies. Brian is quickly thrust into the role of an adult as he must decide how he will survive not only the plane crash but also being lost in the wilderness.

As Brian faces the next days alone, lost and desperate, he learns to depend on his own common sense to survive. He draws on his limited knowledge of what to do if lost in the wilderness and begins to be proactive, learning along the way. As he faces many character-versus-nature conflicts, Brian also deals with conflicts within himself as he tries to understand the reasons behind his parents' divorce and his mother's secret affair. He matures physically and psychologically during the long period he is forced to fend for himself. He learns to protect himself from dangerous animals, to provide food for himself, and to forgive others for what he perceives as their leaving him.

The novel ends with a number of ironic twists: Brian has learned to survive on his own, and yet he has finally recovered the survival kit from the plane; he has learned to accept that he may not be rescued for a long time, and yet he is finally rescued; he has learned that sharing his mother's secret may not be the best thing for anyone, but that is okay. This novel, the first in Paulsen's Brian saga, has been followed by others with Brian as the central character, including *The River*, *Brian's Winter*, *Brian's Return*, and *Brian's Hunt*.

THE VOYAGE OF THE FROG

Another survival story, *The Voyage of the Frog* places the story of fourteen-year-old David Alspeth on the Pacific Ocean rather than in the woodlands of the Brian books. David's uncle Owen has died, leaving the boy his twenty-two-foot sailboat along with the request that his ashes be scattered in the ocean. David sets sail to fulfill this request but does not take the time to think the trip through carefully. He does not file a trip plan, he

does not check the weather reports, and he does not let his parents know where he is going. During the first night, just as David has scattered his uncle's ashes, the boat is hit by a storm. While David is attempting to fight the storm and get the sails safely tied down, he is so badly injured that he loses time. When he wakes, he finds that the boat is damaged and he is some three hundred miles out to sea.

The novel follows David as he fights against nature to get the boat in sailing condition, as the boat is almost capsized by a large steamer in a shipping channel, and as he struggles against sharks that attack the boat, among other problems. As he works through these conflicts, David also deals with his grief over his uncle's death; ultimately, he arrives home much more mature than when he left. The survival conflict is the main focus of the story, with the setting being central to the conflict. Characterization comes in second as David's growth from childhood to adulthood takes place during the journey.

THE WINTER ROOM

In *The Winter Room*, eleven-year-old Eldon tells the story of his family's farm and how it runs from season to season. He explains the daily workings of the farm in great detail, sharing the thaw of spring, the work of summer, the killing of fall, and the peace of winter. Setting is the central focus of this novel until the end, when winter arrives. In the winter, Eldon, his older brother Wayne, his parents, his great uncle David, and David's brother Nels sit in the winter room of their home, watching the fire and listening to Uncle David, the family storyteller.

One winter, Wayne comes to believe that the stories Uncle David has been telling are not true; he believes his uncle has just been bragging about himself. When Uncle David overhears Wayne tell Eldon that the stories are lies, he crumbles. However, one day Eldon and Wayne are wrestling in the hayloft and they see Uncle David behind the barn. While they watch, he becomes young again for a moment and accomplishes a feat that Wayne had doubted that he could do. Things get better after Uncle David proves to himself, and inadvertently to the boys, that he still has worth. As life passes on the farm and Uncle David tells stories in the winter room, Eldon shares the ebb and flow of life, love, and death on a farm. These themes are intertwined in the novel with messages about forgiveness and self-worth. Although characterization is not the central focus of the novel, Uncle David particularly stands out as unforgettable.

MOLLY MCGINTY HAS A REALLY GOOD DAY

In one of Paulsen's few ventures into stories with female protagonists, *Molly McGinty Has a Really Good Day* provides a humorous view of one day in the life of a sixth-grade girl. The novel starts with Molly obsessing over the loss of her notebook, a three-ring binder in which she has meticulously organized not only her school life, her grandmother's business, their household affairs, and their varied appointments but also her friends' and schoolmates' likes and dislikes as well as multiple family details. The loss of her beloved notebook becomes secondary, however, to the embarrassment Molly struggles with all day at school as Irene, her guardian grandmother, attends school for the annual Senior Citizens Day. Carefree and flamboyant, Irene gains the admiration of all the other kids as she interacts with even the strictest teachers. As Molly watches, she begins to learn the value of sometimes just letting fun, friendship, and impulsive behavior rule.

By the end of the novel, Molly is starting to appreciate Irene in new ways. She also begins to understand that too much regimentation in life limits a person in unexpected ways, sometimes even keeping that person from having a really good day. The role reversal between Molly and Irene in this novel reflects one of Paulsen's common themes—that of a child having to take on adult responsibilities too early in life. The characterization of the grandmother, however, is more lighthearted than Paulsen's depictions of many of his irresponsible adult characters. Like *Winterkill* and a number of his other novels, *Molly McGinty Has a Really Good Day* is episodic in nature; the only real conflict is the one within Molly as she learns to accept her grandmother as others do. Paulsen's focus on a flawed adult provides readers with an endearing character whose main fault is that she loves her granddaughter.

Theresa L. Stowell

OTHER MAJOR WORKS

SHORT FICTION: *The Madonna Stories*, 1989.

NONFICTION: *The Special War*, 1966; *Some Birds Don't Fly*, 1968; *Eastern Sun, Western Moon: An Autobiographical Odyssey*, 1993; *Father Water, Mother Woods: Essays on Fishing and Hunting in the North Woods*, 1994; *Winterdance: The Fine Madness of Running the Iditarod*, 1994; *Puppies, Dogs, and Blue Northers: Reflections on Being Raised by a Pack of Sled Dogs*, 1996; *Pilgrimage on a Steel Ride: A Memoir About Men and Motorcycles*, 1997; *Caught by the Sea: My Life on Boats*, 2001; *Guts*, 2001.

CHILDREN'S/YOUNG ADULT LITERATURE: *Winterkill*, 1976; *The Foxman*, 1977; *The Night the White Deer Died*, 1978; *The Spitball Gang*, 1980; *Dancing Carl*, 1983; *Popcorn Days*, 1983; *Sentries*, 1986; *The Crossing*, 1987; *The Island*, 1988; *The Boy Who Owned the School*, 1990; *Woodsong*, 1990; *The Cookcamp*, 1991; *The Monument*, 1991; *A Christmas Sonata*, 1992; *The Haymeadow*, 1992; *Harris and Me*, 1993; *Nightjohn*, 1993; *Mr. Tucket*, 1994; *Call Me Francis Tucket*, 1995; *Escape from Fire Mountain*, 1995; *The Rifle*, 1995; *The Tent*, 1995; *The Tortilla Factory*, 1995; *Amos Binder, Secret Agent*, 1997; *Sarny*, 1997; *The Schernoff Discoveries*, 1997; *The Transall Saga*, 1998; *Alida's Song*, 1999; *Tucket's Gold*, 1999; *The Beet Fields: Memories of a Sixteenth Summer*, 2000; *Tucket's Home*, 2000; *The White Fox Chronicles*, 2000; *The Glass Café*, 2003; *How Angel Peterson Got His Name*, 2003; *The Quilt*, 2004; *The Time Hackers*, 2005; *The Amazing Life of Birds: (The Twenty-Day Puberty Journal of Duane Homer Leech)*, 2006; *The Legend of Bass Reeves*, 2006; *Lawn Boy*, 2007.

EDITED TEXT: *Shelf Life: Stories by the Book*, 2003.

BIBLIOGRAPHY

Golden, Bernice. *Critical Reading Activities for the Works of Gary Paulsen*. Portland, Maine: J. Weston Walch, 1999. Provides study and teaching guides, as well as reproducible activities, for secondary students reading the works of Gary Paulsen.

Gutner, Howard. *Teaching the Novels of Gary Paulsen*. New York: Scholastic Professional Books, 2000. Teaching guide for *Hatchet*, *Dogsong*, *Brian's Winter*, *The River*, and *Woodsong* includes lessons, activities, discussion questions, and writing prompts based on the novels.

Macken, JoAnn Early. *Gary Paulsen: Voice of Adventure and Survival*. Berkeley Heights, N.J.: Enslow, 2006. Provides intelligent critical commentary on

Paulsen's fiction for the young adult audience most interested in his books.

Salvner, Gary M. *Presenting Gary Paulsen*. New York: Twayne, 1996. One of the first book-length works to offer critical analysis and interpretation of some of Paulsen's works. Includes bibliography and index.

Thomson, Sarah L. *Gary Paulsen*. New York: Rosen Central, 2003. Provides an examination of Paulsen's works and writing habits. Includes both serious and humorous biographical information through interview with the author.

CESARE PAVESE

Born: Santo Stefano Belbo, Italy; September 9, 1908
Died: Turin, Italy; August 27, 1950

PRINCIPAL LONG FICTION

Paesi tuoi, 1941 (*The Harvesters*, 1961)
La spiaggia, 1942 (*The Beach*, 1963)
Il compagno, 1947 (*The Comrade*, 1959)
Il carcere, 1949 (*The Political Prisoner*, 1959)
Il diavolo sulle colline, 1949 (*The Devil in the Hills*, 1954)
La bella estate, 1949 (includes *Il diavolo sulle colline* and *Tra donne sole*; *The Beautiful Summer*, 1959)
La casa in collina, 1949 (*The House on the Hill*, 1956)
Prima che il gallo canti, 1949 (includes *Il carcere* and *La casa in collina*)
Tra donne sole, 1949 (*Among Women Only*, 1953)
La luna e i falò, 1950 (*The Moon and the Bonfire*, 1952)
Fuoco grande, 1959 (with Bianca Garufi; *A Great Fire*, 1963)
The Selected Works of Cesare Pavese, 1968

OTHER LITERARY FORMS

Although Cesare Pavese (pah-VAY-zay) is best known as a novelist, his oeuvre includes work in a number of other literary forms. Like many novelists, he began as a poet and continued to return to that genre throughout his career. His poems are collected in *Lavorare stanca* (1936, 1943; *Hard Labor*, 1976) and in *Verrà la morte e avrà i tuoi occhi* (1951), among other volumes. Pavese's poetry is also available in a comprehensive edition, *Poesie edite e inedite* (1962), which includes previously uncollected work, and English translations of many poems were published in 1969 in *A Mania for Solitude: Selected Poems, 1930-1950*. Pavese also published a number of short stories, some of which are collected in *Feria d'agosto* (1946; *Summer Storm, and Other Stories*, 1966) and *Notte di festa* (1953; *Festival Night, and Other Stories*, 1964); these stories, as well as previously uncollected ones, are also available in *Racconti* (1960; *Told in Confidence, and Other Stories*, 1971). Pavese also wrote works of nonfiction—*Dialoghi con Leucò* (1947; *Dialogues with Leucò*, 1966) and *La letteratura americana e altri saggi* (1951; *American Literature: Essays and Opinions*, 1970)—and his diaries and letters have been collected in several volumes.

ACHIEVEMENTS

Cesare Pavese's fiction, which contributed significantly to the development of the modern Italian novel, reflects his intense, lifelong interest in American literature, in which he found the elements of local color, psychological and social realism, and cultural symbolism that he strove to incorporate into his own works. He employed these elements to construct an alternative to the convention-bound Hermetic tradition of his Italian predecessors, whose excessive, abstract formalism isolated art from life. Pavese became for many readers the greatest of all the Italian neorealists—that group of writers and filmmakers including such major figures as Ignazio Silone, Alberto Moravia, and Vittorio De Sica.

Pavese's personal contribution to modern Italian literature is not limited to the aesthetic formulated in his own work, however, for he also conveyed the shift in literary values that neorealism represented through his translations of, and critical essays on, major American novelists and poets from whom—in Pavese's case at least—these aesthetic values and precedents were in part derived. Pavese's first translation, and undoubtedly his most important contribution in terms of its effect on his contemporaries, was of Herman Melville's *Moby Dick* (1851), appearing in 1932. The intense and monumental effort Pavese devoted to this work is apparent in the numerous letters he exchanged with an Italian American friend, Antonio Chiuminatto, during the period in which he was working on this project. The translation of *Moby Dick* was followed by translations of other works by Melville, as well as of novels by such important modern authors as Sinclair Lewis, Sherwood Anderson, John Dos Passos, Gertrude Stein, and John Steinbeck, and critical essays not only on these authors but also on Edgar Lee Masters, O. Henry, Theodore Dreiser, Walt Whitman, and Richard Wright.

Pavese's second important contribution to neorealism was his abandonment of the detached, omniscient perspective of the refined narrator speaking in the standard *lingua pura* dialect of literary Italian—as was conventional in novels—for the first-person narrator speaking a region vernacular. The vernacular of Pavese's unlettered narrators was Piedmontese, which he was accustomed to hearing in the vicinity of Turin, where he lived.

Pavese was not the only neorealist to eschew the worn-out diction of literary Italian; his contemporary Moravia frequently employed working-class narrators speaking the modern Roman vernacular. These two writers occupy a position of importance in the history of Italian literature somewhat analogous to that of William Wordsworth and Samuel Taylor Coleridge in England and Mark Twain and the southwestern humorists in the United States: They revolutionized the literary language of their time.

Finally, Pavese's novels are important as a response to fascism and, in a larger sense, to totalitarianism, the disease of the twentieth century. Pavese himself was only fourteen when ruler Benito Mussolini came to power, and he lived under the shadow of fascist repression for more than twenty years. In fact, one might claim, as some critics have done, that Pavese's sense of social and national commitment as a writer, as well as his hesitant engagement with the Communist Party, was largely a defensive reaction to the destructive effects of totalitarianism on the modern Italian consciousness.

It is on these elements that Pavese's reputation as an important modern novelist rests. Taken singly, each element is a great accomplishment; taken together, they place Pavese with Silone and Moravia as one of the greatest twentieth century Italian novelists.

BIOGRAPHY

Cesare Pavese was born on September 9, 1908, in Santo Stefano Belbo, a small rural community in the hilly Langhe district of Piedmont, a province in northwestern Italy. His father, who was a minor official in the municipal court of Turin, died in 1914, when Pavese was six. His mother, whom Pavese described as strict and authoritarian in bearing, rarely showed either himself or his sister, Maria, who was six years older, any parental affection or support. Despite this fact, Pavese seems to have been strongly attached to her, and he continued living with her in the family home, remaining unmarried. Following her death in 1930, he moved to his sister's home, where he lived for the remainder of his life, entertaining friends and callers in the single room that served him as bedroom, study, and parlor.

Though Pavese's family belonged to the middle class, after the death of his father, the family had to sell the few assets it had to maintain this position. Nevertheless, Pavese received an excellent education. During his early years, he attended school in Turin, spending every summer in the country at the family's farm in Santo Stefano Belbo, where he had been born. By 1918, however, only four years after the death of his father, the family could no longer afford the privilege of a second home, and the farm was sold, ending what Pavese saw as a vital part of his childhood experience. With the loss of the farm, his direct, personal contact with the simple peasants of the region and the renewing forces of the natural environment, which were so entwined with their agricultural lifestyle, was severed.

Cesare Pavese. (The Granger Collection, New York)

In 1923, Pavese entered a Turin *liceo*, or secondary school, where he received the classical education that was to form him into that special type of scholar, the humanistic intellectual. In 1927, he entered the University of Turin, from which he took his degree in letters in 1930 with a dissertation on Walt Whitman. The interest Pavese developed in American literature during this period had an important effect on his later development as a writer. This interest in American literature, which was not well known in Italy at the time, seems to have been stimulated in part by his friendship with Antonio Chiuminatto, a young Italian American who came to study at the University of Turin in the summer of 1929. In any event, Pavese's interest in American literature and culture is clearly evident in his choice of Walt Whitman for his dissertation topic—against the counsel of his advisers.

Following his graduation, Pavese remained in Turin, making his living by teaching and tutoring. Because of the increasing power of the Fascist Party—which, by the time he graduated, was in complete control of all

levels of government bureaucracy—Pavese joined in 1932, as did everyone who wished to secure or maintain any position controlled by the government. That this action was a matter of convenience, not conviction, is attested by the fact that Pavese was one of the first contributors to the leftist journal *La cultura*, which was produced by the newly formed Einaudi publishing house, founded in 1933 by one of Pavese's university friends. During the next two years, Pavese became increasingly involved with *La cultura* and its publisher, Einaudi, as well as with those who shared its leftist, and therefore anti-Fascist, sympathies.

In 1934, Pavese took charge of *La cultura* after its previous editor, Leone Ginzburg, was arrested by the Fascist authorities. Pavese must have realized the danger in which he was placing himself, for the authorities were becoming more and more openly intolerant of dissent. Moreover, by 1935, Pavese had become romantically involved with a young woman named Tina, who was an active member of the clandestine Communist resistance and who used his address to receive communications from other Party members.

In May of 1935, the Fascist authorities entered and searched Pavese's room, finding in Tina's letters what they believed was incriminating evidence. Besides, they reasoned, was not Pavese himself the editor of *La cultura*—a magazine that openly sympathized with such views? Pavese was arrested and sentenced to three years of political confinement, though this sentence was later reduced to ten months. He served the first two months of his sentence in jails at Turin and Rome and then was sent to serve the remainder of his confinement in the small village of Brancaleone, in remote southern Calabria, where he was isolated under police supervision.

It was there, in the later months of his confinement, that Pavese began the journal he kept from 1935 until his death. This work, posthumously published in 1952 as *Il mestiere di vivere: Diario, 1935-1950 (The Burning Brand: Diaries, 1935-1950*, 1961) has brought Pavese nearly as much fame as his novels and has led critics to see in his work a strong autobiographical element as well as a resigned philosophical orientation that links him to the existentialists Albert Camus and Jean-Paul Sartre.

When Pavese returned from his Calabrian exile early in 1936, he arrived in Turin to discover that Tina, the woman for whom he had been imprisoned, had married someone else the day before. This was the first, and undoubtedly the most intense, of the many disappointments in love he suffered from this time on. In 1936, Pavese's first collection of poetry, *Hard Labor*, appeared, and he resumed his association with Einaudi. In 1941, he published his novel *The Harvesters*, a work that revealed Pavese's renewed interest in the nonintellectual, primal world of the rural poor who live in direct contact with the creative and destructive forces of nature. Late in 1943, Pavese again left Turin to escape the German occupation of the city, moving to Serralunga di Crea in Monferrato, where he lived with his sister's family for nearly two years. Following the Allied liberation of northern Italy from German occupation in April, 1945, Pavese returned to Turin, and in the same year he was named editor in chief at Einaudi and became an official member of the Italian Communist Party.

The period that followed World War II was the final and most productive phase of Pavese's career as a writer. Seven of his ten novels were published between 1946 and 1950, as well as a collection of short stories, *Summer Storm, and Other Stories*, and *Dialogues with Leucò*. In 1950, Pavese was awarded the prestigious Strega Prize for his novel *Among Women Only*. No matter how much Pavese the author was successful, however, the man himself was plagued by a strong sense of frustration—particularly in his inability to commit himself effectively to political and social action. Moreover, his sense of failure in romantic endeavors still continued to torment him. One of Pavese's closest friends, Natalia Ginzburg, described Pavese's dilemma at this time in a moving tribute to the novelist published after his death: "He devised for himself over the years a system of ideas and principles, so entangled and severe as to bar him from the simplest decisions of everyday life." As Pavese himself implies in the revealing foreword to *Dialogues with Leucò*, the imaginary philosophical debates he constructs in that volume treat, in projected and universalized form, the personal dilemmas of existence with which he struggled in his own life: "Had it been possible, I would have gladly done without all this mythology. . . . When we retell an old myth . . . we are expressing . . . a general and comprehensive fact, a core of reality . . . an entire conceptual complex."

In 1950, Pavese formed another of the hopeless, unrequited romantic attachments that he had suffered repeatedly since his first tragic experience in 1935. This time, the woman was an American actor, Constance Dowling, and when she lost interest in Pavese upon her return home, he experienced again the deep depression and bitter resignation to his fate that played a significant part in his despairing assessment of man's absurd existence in a world stripped of meaning.

On the evening of August 26, 1950, Pavese left his sister's home, presumably to wander through the city, as he often did at night, visiting little bars and cafés. This time, however, he had in mind a more permanent remedy to his lifelong feelings of frustration and loneliness. He checked in at a hotel near the main railroad station, where he was not known, and made a few calls to friends. On the morning of August 27, 1950, at the age of forty-one, he was found dead from an overdose of sleeping pills.

ANALYSIS

Of the many elements that characterize Cesare Pavese's novels, those that have received most attention from critics are his preference for local color and the vernacular speaker, his affinity for unusual narrative perspectives, his use of lyric elements in discursive prose, his method of developing (or not developing) characters and plot conflicts, and his treatment of recurring symbols and themes. Each of these elements contributes in its own way to the artistic complexity of Pavese's work; taken together, they form his particular version of the neorealist aesthetic.

THE POLITICAL PRISONER

Although it was not published until shortly before his death, *The Political Prisoner* was the first novel Pavese wrote. It was written very quickly, between November, 1938, and April, 1939. Chronologically, it falls between his return from Calabria in 1936 and the publication of *The Harvesters*, which was the first of Pavese's novels to be published.

The Political Prisoner, as the title suggests, draws on Pavese's own political confinement, from which he had been only recently released, and thus seems autobiographical to a degree. Whatever his reasons for not publishing it at the time of its composition—whether because of its painful autobiographical disclosure, its technical immaturity, or the threat of Fascist censorship—the subject it treated was obviously an important one to Pavese. This novel, like the story from which the plot is partly derived—"Terra d'esilio" ("Land of Exile"), Pavese's first attempt at fiction—treats the isolating, alienating effects of totalitarian politics on human relations.

The technical shortcomings of *The Political Prisoner* are readily apparent: the melodramatic shallowness of every character except the protagonist, the inadequate exposition of the protagonist's past and the way this flaw impinges on his present motivation, the inadequate distancing of the protagonist as character from the author's own experience, and the mistaken choice of a limited omniscient point of view, which serves not to disguise but rather to compound the author's lack of narrative objectivity in the novel. Despite these technical defects, the novel is not the miserable failure some have claimed. Seen in the light of Pavese's mature novels, it constitutes the most powerful thematic expression of his fundamental alienation from the world, even if that expression is not always accomplished in an elegant, aesthetically pleasing way.

The Political Prisoner tells the story of a young northerner named Stefano who is sentenced to a period of isolation in a remote southern village because of his political activities. In this respect, the protagonist is like Pavese. There the resemblances end, however, for Stefano is an engineer, not a writer, and his experiences in the novel are based on his developing awareness of the contrast between the urban life led by the working classes in the north—where the economy is based on factory labor, capital investment, and wages—and the agrarian routine and grinding poverty of the rural inhabitants of the undeveloped, economically primitive south. For Stefano, this awareness of the influence of economic factors on social conduct is the beginning of his feeling of alienation from the simple people around him. He receives with indifference small gifts and food from Concia and Elena, the two women with whom he becomes acquainted in the village although he is unable to establish any authentic relationship with either of them—or with Giannino, another political prisoner, who tries to communicate with him from a nearby village. For

Stefano, these people remain wholly other, having no relationship to himself. His political isolation has become an ontological exile: Confronted with the primary facts of totalitarian repression and the loss of his own freedom, he comes to see the situation of the individual in the modern world as a sort of absurd, metaphysical imprisonment into which man is thrust by accident and from which the isolated, reflecting self cannot escape. In this respect, Pavese's novel closely resembles such works as Camus's *The Stranger* (1942) and Sartre's play *No Exit* (1944).

THE HARVESTERS

In *The Harvesters*, one finds Pavese's first attempt to use the vernacular narrator that was to become such an important element of his mature work. Naturally, Berto, the unemployed mechanic who narrates the story, employs the Piedmontese dialect with which Pavese himself was so familiar, yet the language of this novel is not entirely vernacular, but rather a careful mixture of Piedmontese with the *lingua pura* (the standard literary language), which Pavese called "naturalistic impressionism." No doubt he learned this technique from his studies of American literature, in which this impressionistic use of the vernacular has been popular since the time of Mark Twain, though Pavese was probably familiar with it through his translation of works by Anderson and Steinbeck. *The Harvesters* marked an important turning point in Pavese's development as a neorealist, for the narrative strategy he worked out in this novel came to maturity in *Among Women Only* and *The Moon and the Bonfire*, which were based on his experiences among the peasants of Serralunga.

The Harvesters was composed even more rapidly than Pavese's first novel, being completed in about ten weeks between June and August of 1939. When published, in 1941, the novel was criticized on two counts: for the use of an uneducated narrator and for the sensational nature of the subject matter. The first of these objections can be summarily dismissed; the second objection, however, is a much more serious one and does point to a shortcoming of the novel. The plot of *The Harvesters* focuses on the actions of the narrator, Berto, and his friend Talino. When the story begins, they have just been released from prison and have decided to escape the life of frustration and poverty they have known in the city by returning to Talino's home, the little Piedmontese hamlet of Monticello. When they arrive, however, they find not a carefree life of pastoral bliss but a round of ceaseless, backbreaking agrarian labor, which Berto gradually learns to accept with satisfaction. Talino, however, seems incorrigible, and the hostile impulses that led him to commit arson in the city are soon revealed to be part of a long history of senseless aggression that is aggravated and intensified both by his return home and by Berto's growing romantic involvement with Talino's sister, Gisella. As the tension builds between the two men, additional facts are revealed that make a tragic and violent outcome seem inevitable: Talino's incestuous desire for his sister, which culminates in her rape and subsequent abortion, and her betrayal of his arson to the authorities to exact revenge. Talino murders Gisella during the harvest in a moment of blind rage, and the villagers avenge her death. *The Harvesters* is strongly reminiscent of William Faulkner's novels of violence and revenge, such as *The Sound and the Fury* (1929), *Sanctuary* (1931), *Light in August* (1932), and *Absalom, Absalom!* (1936). Perhaps it is no accident that *Il borgo*, Pavese's translation of Faulkner's *The Hamlet* (1940)—which tells the story of the Snopes family, whose violent, perverse history resembles that of Talino and Gisella's family in striking ways—came out in 1942, the year following publication of *The Harvesters*.

This impression of borrowing from Faulkner is not limited to the plot. The quality for which Pavese most admired Faulkner was the latter's skillful blending of mythic and symbolic elements with psychological and historical realism. The attempt to achieve this blending is apparent in *The Harvesters*—which, as critics such as Sergio Pacifici have pointed out, is heavily laden with suggestive imagery and symbolism. This new style of figurative associations mixed with narrative objectivity, however inconsistently and clumsily it is used in *The Harvesters*, came to fruition in *Among Women Only* and *The Moon and the Bonfire*, in which Pavese mastered this powerful stylistic technique.

THE BEACH

Pavese's shortest novel, *The Beach*, was written between November of 1940 and January of the following year. It was the only one of Pavese's novels to be serialized, appearing in the journal *Lettere d'oggi* in 1941 and,

the following year, in a limited edition issued by the same journal. Though Pavese himself was dissatisfied with the novel and the conditions under which it was produced, *The Beach* illuminates an important portion of his work. Like his later novel *The Devil in the Hills* and like many of his mature short stories, *The Beach* neither employs a vernacular speaker nor focuses on portraying agrarian life; rather, it portrays the life of leisure led by the affluent middle class and employs a cultured, intellectual narrator.

The unnamed speaker of *The Beach* is a thirty-five-year-old *liceo* professor who, like Pavese himself, proudly asserts that he has managed to retain his youthful freedom from responsibility by remaining a bachelor. The story he tells recounts the summer vacation he spent at the beach with his boyhood friend Doro and Doro's wife, Clelia, who describes herself as "a spoiled child who doesn't know how to do anything." The main part of the action is set at Doro's villa on the Italian Riviera, and the narrator's intense, lyric evocation of summer life on the Ligurian coast illustrates the imagistic, poetic quality of Pavese's prose at its best.

The lyric prose style of *The Beach*, along with the novel's portrayal of the idle activities of the affluent, reminds one of the novels of F. Scott Fitzgerald, for which Pavese had such great admiration that he refused to translate them, fearing Fitzgerald's influence on his own work would become too strong. The reader's impression of Fitzgerald's influence on *The Beach* is reinforced by the unusual narrative strategy Pavese chose to employ in this novel. The unnamed narrator, much like Nick in Fitzgerald's *The Great Gatsby* (1925), is a detached observer of other people's actions—a character to whom little or nothing happens during the course of the novel. That, at least, is the way the narrator of *The Beach* sees himself as he tells the story of his summer with Doro and Clelia. Unlike Fitzgerald, however, Pavese makes the narrator himself—in his egotistical, Olympian detachment from the lives and concerns of those around him—the butt of the novel's irony. Fitzgerald's Nick calmly but compassionately reports the tragic downfall of his friend Jay Gatsby, while the tragedy of *The Beach* lies in the failure of the isolated, selfish narrator to establish any meaningful contact with those around him.

The irony implicit in the contrast between the reality

of the characters' situation and the narrator's uncomprehending report of it is linked to Pavese's concept of characterization in the modern novel, which he explains in his diary: "The art of the nineteenth century was centered on the development of situations . . . the art of the twentieth, on static essentials. In the first, the hero was not the same at the beginning of the story as he was at the end; now he remains the same." Though uncomprehending critics have sometimes accused Pavese of creating nothing but static characters, this is not really true, for it is only the heroes of his novels who are static. The dynamism of Pavese's novels resides not within the hero himself but in the conflict that arises from his intransigence in the face of a world that demands growth, adaptation, and change. In this type of plot, the recognition takes place within the reader, not within the characters of the fiction. It is the failure to realize this intention that has prevented many readers from seeing the degree to which *The Beach* is an outstanding example of Pavese's methods of novelistic construction.

THE HOUSE ON THE HILL

The House on the Hill is perhaps the most balanced representative of Pavese's later novels, because it successfully combines all the important themes and qualities of his work as a novelist: the competing claims of self and society; the contrast between agrarian and urban life; the use of first-person narrative; the conflict between static and dynamic characters; and the mingling of the material, objective nature of reality with a mythic, symbolic dimension.

Corrado, the unmarried professor at a Turin *liceo* from whose perspective the story is told, is another one of those detached, egotistical narrators one so often finds in Pavese's fiction. Corrado is more aware of his disengagement from others than is the anonymous narrator of *The Beach*, however, as the former's reflections often make clear. Of the effects of war on human relations, at least, he has a clear understanding: "The war had made it legitimate to turn in on oneself and live from day to day without regretting lost opportunities."

This novel, which was written between September, 1947, and February, 1948, clearly draws on Pavese's experiences during the long period from 1943 to 1945 he spent at Serralunga. After the war, he frequently commented on his sense of guilt in retreating to the safety of

the hills while many of his friends remained in Turin, joining the armed resistance to German occupation and braving the frequent Allied bombing attacks on the city. Indeed, some critics have suggested that Pavese's espousal of allegiance to the Communist Party following the war was an attempt to assuage this sense of guilt. *Prima che il gallo canti* (before the cock crows), the title of the volume in which *The House on the Hill* was first published together with *The Political Prisoner*, makes apparent, in its clear allusion to the biblical story of Saint Peter's cowardly denial of Christ, the central theme of commitment and betrayal that the novels share.

When the novel opens, Corrado describes his situation simply and directly, without any sense of guilt about his actions: "A whole class of people, the lucky, the top drawer, were going, or had gone, to their villas in the mountains or by the sea. There they lived pretty much as usual. . . . The war raged away, methodical and futile." Into the secure, complacent life of this static protagonist comes a disturbing catalyst named Cate—an old lover who is now actively engaged in the anti-Fascist Resistance in Turin, returning to the countryside only to avoid capture. In reflecting on the differences between himself and Cate, Corrado reveals many of the egotistical weaknesses of Pavese's other static heroes. He says, for example, "I was happy not to have in my days any real affection or encumbrance, to be alone, not tied to anyone." This is especially true of his thoughts about love, as when he reflects on his affair with Cate eight years before, and the possibility that her son, Dino, might well be his own unacknowledged offspring: "Once in a while I bought her a lipstick that filled her with joy, and then I began to see that you could maintain a woman, educate her, bring her to life, but if you know what her elegance is made out of, it loses its savor."

The outcome of this novel establishes a new, more satisfying pattern of development that is entirely absent from *The Beach*. In *The House on the Hill*, the hero overcomes his alienation from life, developing some measure of compassion for humankind by the end of the novel. When Cate is eventually captured by the Fascists, Corrado, fearful that he will meet the same fate, takes refuge in a seminary where—in posing as a teacher—he encounters Dino, who soon afterward runs away to join the beleaguered partisans. Corrado, becoming fearful that the Fascists have discovered his priestly masquerade, flees even farther from the city. He returns to the hills where he was born and joins his family in hiding, but even there Corrado cannot hide from the reality of the war; on his journey home, he witnesses the murder of a Fascist patrol by partisans lying in ambush. Of the dead soldiers, whose physical reality he cannot escape, he says: "It is they who have awakened me. . . . They are no longer somebody else's business, you don't feel that you have stumbled upon them by accident." He is now prepared for a recognition, and he remembers what Cate told him earlier: "Whoever lets things go and is satisfied is already a fascist." Corrado, unwilling to accept the consequences of his secure isolation, ends his experience by sitting down to tell his tale, which—he is now finally able to admit—is the "story of a long illusion."

Cesare Pavese was more than another literary suicide, for—whatever the failures of his personal life—in the nine novels he published before his death, he succeeded in creating a body of fiction that has won international acclaim. He is one of the leading figures of Italian neorealism, equaled only by Silone and Moravia. In his short life, he made wide-ranging contributions to the development of the modern Italian novel: the vernacular narrator he first developed in *The Harvesters*, the existential perspective on modern life portrayed in *The Political Prisoner*, the alienation of the static character trapped in a dynamic world in *The Beach*, and the complex mingling of realism with symbolism in *The House on the Hill*. It is for these reasons that Pavese is, and will continue to be, considered one of the greatest Italian novelists of the twentieth century.

Steven E. Colburn

OTHER MAJOR WORKS

SHORT FICTION: *Feria d'agosto*, 1946 (*Summer Storm, and Other Stories*, 1966); *Notte di festa*, 1953 (*Festival Night, and Other Stories*, 1964); *Racconti*, 1960 (*Told in Confidence, and Other Stories*, 1971); *The Leather Jacket: Stories*, 1980; *Stories*, 1987.

POETRY: *Lavorare stanca*, 1936 (expanded 1943; *Hard Labor*, 1976); *La terra e la morte*, 1947; *Verrà la morte e avrà i tuoi occhi*, 1951; *Poesie edite e inedite*, 1962; *A Mania for Solitude: Selected Poems, 1930-1950*, 1969.

NONFICTION: *Dialoghi con Leucò*, 1947 (*Dialogues with Leucò*, 1966); *La letteratura americana e altri saggi*, 1951 (*American Literature: Essays and Opinions*, 1970); *Il mestiere di vivere: Diario, 1935-1950*, 1952 (*The Burning Brand: Diaries, 1935-1950*, 1961; also known as *The Business of Living*); *Lettere*, 1966 (partial translation *Selected Letters, 1924-1950*, 1969).

TRANSLATIONS: *Il nostro signor Wrenn*, 1931 (of Sinclair Lewis's *Our Mr. Wrenn*); *Moby-Dick*, 1932 (of Herman Melville's novel); *Riso nero*, 1932 (of Sherwood Anderson's *Dark Laughter*); *Il 42 parallelo*, 1935 (of John Dos Passos's *Forty-second Parallel*); *U omini e topi*, 1938 (of John Steinbeck's *Of Mice and Men*); *Tre esistenze*, 1940 (of Gertrude Stein's *Three Lives*); *Il borgo*, 1942 (of William Faulkner's *The Hamlet*).

BIBLIOGRAPHY

Biasin, Gian-Paolo. *The Smile of the Gods: A Thematic Study of Cesare Pavese's Works*. Translated by Yvonne Freccero. Ithaca, N.Y.: Cornell University Press, 1968. Excellent study focuses on the importance of mythology in Pavese's thinking and provides a guide to the major themes in the author's work.

Binetti, Vincenzo. "Contextualizing Marginality: Urban Landscape and Female Communities in Cesare Pavese's *Among Women Only*." In *Italian Women and the City: Essays*, edited by Janet Levarie Smarr and Daria Valentini. Madison, N.J.: Fairleigh Dickinson University Press, 2003. Binetti's discussion of female communities in Pavese's novel is included in a collection of essays that examine the meanings of the city for Italian women as depicted in works of Italian literature and art.

Bondanella, Peter, and Andrea Ciccarelli, eds. *The Cambridge Companion to the Italian Novel*. New York: Cambridge University Press, 2003. Historical overview of the Italian novel contains many references to Pavese, but the majority of information about his novels can be found in chapter 7, "Neorealist Narrative: Experience and Experiment."

Fiedler, Leslie A. "Introducing Cesare Pavese." *Kenyon Review* 16 (Autumn, 1954): 536-553. Stresses Pavese's importance to the Italian and European literary worlds and places him in his worldwide literary context. Fiedler is credited with introducing Pavese to the American reading public.

Lajolo, Davide. *An Absurd Vice: A Biography of Cesare Pavese*. New York: New Directions, 1983. Lajolo was a friend of Pavese and his first biographer. His friendship with Pavese gave him special insights, but later scholars distrusted some of his psychological and political speculations about his subject.

O'Healy, Áine. *Cesare Pavese*. Boston: Twayne, 1988. Short, excellent biography clears away many of the myths about Pavese. Recommended as a good place for students to begin learning about Pavese and his work.

Simborowski, Nicoletta. *Secrets and Puzzles: Silence and the Unsaid in Contemporary Italian Writing*. Oxford, England: Legenda and European Humanities Research Centre, 2003. Examines post-World War II works by Pavese and three other Italian writers, focusing on the issue of self-censorship. These writers were alive during the Fascist era, and although that era's censorship no longer existed after the war, Simborowski describes how the writers chose to omit parts of their texts.

Thompson, Doug. *Cesare Pavese: A Study of the Major Novels and Poems*. New York: Cambridge University Press, 1982. Clearly written, insightful study avoids many of the biographical myths that have marred many examinations of Pavese. Locates the major themes that run through all of Pavese's work.

Ward, David. *Antifascisms: Cultural Politics in Italy, 1943-46: Benedetto Croce and the Liberals, Carlo Levi and the "Actionists."* Madison, N.J.: Fairleigh Dickinson University Press, 1996. Pavese's novels *The Political Prisoner* and *The House on the Hill* are among the books, films, and other media discussed in this study of the significant political changes that occurred in Italy during the mid-1940's.

THOMAS LOVE PEACOCK

Born: Weymouth, England; October 18, 1785
Died: Halliford, England; January 23, 1866
Also known as: T. L. Peacock

PRINCIPAL LONG FICTION

Headlong Hall, 1816
Melincourt, 1817
Nightmare Abbey, 1818
Maid Marian, 1822
The Misfortunes of Elphin, 1829
Crotchet Castle, 1831
Gryll Grange, 1860

OTHER LITERARY FORMS

Before turning his talents to the satiric novel, Thomas Love Peacock wrote poetry. His early works include *Palmyra, and Other Poems* (1806), *The Genius of the Thames* (1810), *The Philosophy of Melancholy* (1812), and *Sir Proteus: A Satirical Ballad* (1814). When his principal efforts turned to prose, Peacock continued to produce the occasional elegant lyric or rousing song, many of them incorporated into his novels. His long narrative poem *Rhododaphne* (1818), "a nympholeptic tale," attracted considerable contemporary attention and has retained a measure of continued critical esteem; his satiric *Paper Money Lyrics* (1837), topical and crochety, is largely ignored.

Early in his literary career Peacock also wrote two farces, "The Dilettanti" and "The Three Doctors," both of which were unpublished. Throughout his life, and particularly during the periods when his responsibilities at the East India Company precluded sustained literary projects, Peacock wrote essays and reviews, the most famous being his unfinished but incisive "Essay on Fashionable Literature," in *The Four Ages of Poetry* (1820), the satiric critique of contemporary poetry's debasement that provoked Percy Bysshe Shelley's *A Defense of Poetry* (1840) and Peacock's four-part *Memoirs of Percy Bysshe Shelley* (1858-1862), which the reserved and fastidious Peacock, who deplored the publication of private matters, wrote grudgingly, as a corrective to the muddled enthusiasms and posthumous scandal-retailing that admirers and acquaintances of Shelley were offering as literary biography.

ACHIEVEMENTS

From the beginning of his career as a satiric novelist, Thomas Love Peacock always had an attentive audience but never a wide one. His career in several ways has invited comparison with that of his contemporary Jane Austen. Both writers set out to please themselves, uninfluenced by desire for fame or gold. Both swam against the Romantic mainstream. Each produced a slim shelf of novels distinguished by elegance, irony, and—detractors might add—limited scope. Whereas Austen limited herself to matters suitable to the notice of a lady, Peacock restricted himself yet more narrowly. Except for *Maid Marian* and *The Misfortunes of Elphin*, respectively set in the picturesque past of "Merrie England" and Arthurian Wales, Peacock's novels take place in an idyllic country-house world where conversation—varied by singing, dining, drinking, flirtation, and sightseeing—is the chief activity. Even so, in this Pavonian realm, the reader who is able to read the signs aright can find, as critic Marilyn Butler reveals, serious and well-grounded discussion of moral, political, aesthetic, economic, and scientific concerns.

The dense if oblique topicality of these conversations is something of an obstacle for the twentieth century reader. Another hurdle for the general public in any age is Peacock's learning: Only those who share Peacock's passion for the past, especially classical antiquity, can enjoy the novels' esoterica and allusions, and only readers nurtured in Greek and Latin (or possessing editions whose annotations compensate for such deficiency) can smile at the puns and scholarly jokes Peacock presents in the names and adventures of his characters. Writing for a few congenial spirits, Peacock attained in his own time the respect of Shelley, Lord Byron, and John Cam Hobhouse. He has retained the appreciative but limited audience Shelley's lines from *Letter to Maria Gisbourne* (1820) seem to prophesy: "his fine wit/ Makes such a wound, the knife is lost in it;/ A strain too learned for a shallow age,/ Too wise for selfish bigots."

BIOGRAPHY

Thomas Love Peacock was born at Weymouth in Dorset, England, in 1785. His father, Samuel, was a London merchant, and his mother, Sarah, was a woman of Devonshire. The young Peacock attended a private school at Englefield Green until he was thirteen years old. After leaving school, he served for some time as a clerk at a mercantile house and as a private secretary. In his youth, Peacock found employment uncongenial, however, and his private resources, although insufficient to send him to a university, did preclude his having to work. Peacock used his leisure well.

An apt and diligent student, Peacock became a sound classicist through his independent reading. In 1812, he met Shelley through the agency of a mutual friend, Thomas Hookham. For the next few years he was often a part of the Shelley circle. Closely involved in Shelley's tangled domestic affairs, Peacock attempted to be true to his friend, fair to the poet's wife, Harriet, and civil to Shelley's new love, Mary Godwin. When Shelley went abroad, Peacock corresponded with him and transacted business for him. When Shelley died, Peacock, along with Byron, was named executor of the estate.

In 1819, Peacock was appointed assistant to the examiner in the East India Office. The salary he derived from his position enabled him to marry Jane Gryffydh, a rector's daughter whom he had last seen in 1811, when he had been on a walking tour of Wales. The marriage was not a particularly happy one; the professional appointment proved rather more auspicious. In 1837, on the retirement of James Mill, Peacock became examiner at East India House. He capably held this important administrative post until his retirement in 1856.

The pleasures of Peacock's maturity were those he ascribes to various characters (most of them urbane clergymen) in his novels: good wine, good dinners, hours in the garden or in his study with the classics, rural walks from his house at Halliford in the Thames valley. One of the few new friends Peacock made during the latter half of his life was Hobhouse, Lord Broughton. Peacock's peaceful old age was saddened by the unhappiness of his favorite daughter, the talented Mary Ellen, who had imprudently married novelist George Meredith, and by her death in 1861. Peacock died at Halliford in 1866.

ANALYSIS

A writer with strong intelligence but weak invention is not likely to become a novelist. His or her talents would seem to be most serviceable elsewhere in the literary realm. Even so, the example of Thomas Love Peacock suggests that such a deficiency need not be fatal to a writer of fiction. True, his plots are often insignificant or implausible, and his characters tend to be sketches rather than rounded likenesses or, if three-dimensional, to have more opinions than emotions. His novels are nevertheless readable and rereadable, for he excels in anatomizing the follies, philosophies, and fashions that the age presents to his satiric eye. It is not enough for Peacock to make clear the inconsistencies and absurdities of pre-Reform Toryism, Byronic misanthropy, or the modern educational system: His talent for phrase-making ensures that even the bores and halfwits he creates spout golden epigrams.

Clear thinking and stylish writing are not the rarest of

Thomas Love Peacock. (Getty Images)

Peacock's gifts, though. Perhaps his distinctive excellence is his ability to embrace limitation without accepting diminution. He revels in ideas and delights in the good things of the world. A thoroughgoing classicist in his own views, he accurately understands most of the contemporary opinions and ideas he attacks (Samuel Taylor Coleridge's transcendentalism is a notable exception). He is opinionated without being ill humored. His erudition does not preclude strong practicality. The narrow range of emotions he articulates is the result of a positive rather than a negative quality, of brave stoicism rather than heartlessness. Although Peacock's novels are for the most part slender, they never seem the productions of a small mind.

HEADLONG HALL

Headlong Hall, Peacock's first novel, is far from being his finest piece, but it is a mature work in which the characteristic devices of Peacock's career are effectively, if not perfectly, deployed. One finds charming description of picturesque countryside, in this case Wales, where Peacock had happily traveled in 1809. One finds a rich rural lover of good conversation, Squire Headlong of the Hall, who, to gratify his taste, assembles a diverse set of wise and foolish talkers. Most important, one finds the talkers themselves.

In this novel, as in several of the later ones, Peacock's satire is general; his own perspective is not to be precisely identified with that of any one character. The principal way of grouping the speakers at Squire Headlong's symposium is to distinguish the philosophers, who genuinely seek to discover truth via Socratic dialogue, from the cranks, who find in conversation a chance to ride forth on their particular intellectual hobbyhorses, and who would rather lecture than learn. When Peacock wrote *Headlong Hall* in 1815, he was in daily contact with the Shelley circle, and the novel's three philosophers reason from stances that Shelley, Peacock, and their friend Thomas Jefferson Hogg adopted in their intellectual discussions. Peacock's naming of the three characters indicates their respective positions. Foster the perfectabilian articulates a position that Shelley sometimes took, that the human race is improving largely through technological advances. At the other pole is Escot the deteriorationist, who takes the Jean-Jacques Rousseau-derived view that humankind has fallen from pristine excellence largely because, as Shelley's friend J. F. Newton argued, humans eat meat. Balancing these opposites is Jenkinson, the embracer of the status quo, who gives voice to Hogg's skepticism.

To fan the flames of intellectual discourse, Peacock provides an assortment of windy enthusiasts and eccentrics, none so finely drawn as later incarnations were to be, but none failing to amuse. The Reverend Mr. Gaster begins Peacock's series of gormandizing clergymen; Panscope is his first and thinnest burlesque of Coleridge's transcendentalism. Marmaduke Milestone speaks for the Reptonian school of picturesque gardening, a taste Peacock deplored. The phrenologist Mr. Cranium leads off the series of freakish scientists that continues down through *Gryll Grange*. Representing literary enterprises, if not strictly speaking literature, are the poets Nightshade and Maclaurel, the reviewers Gall and Treacle, and Miss Philomela Poppyseed, a writer of feminine novels and one of the few stupid women in Peacock's gallery. Lest the fine arts be neglected, Peacock supplies Sir Patrick O'Prism, a painting dilettante, and Cornelius Chromatic, an amateur violinist.

The characters feast, drink, talk, sing. Having served their host's (and their author's) purposes, they are paired in the ordering dance of marriage, an inevitable conclusion according to the systems of both Foster and Escot, and an empirical state in which one suspects the two philosophers' theories will prove of precisely equal value.

MELINCOURT

Peacock's second and longest novel, *Melincourt*, is generally considered his weakest. At the time of its composition, Peacock's principal association was with Shelley, and in this novel Peacock drops the objectivity of the "laughing philosopher" and presents political views he shared with the poet, who was even then giving them poetic form in what was to be Shelley's *The Revolt of Islam* (1818). Melincourt sincerely satirizes the Tory government and, as Lord Byron's *The Vision of Judgment* (1822) would later do, former liberals such as the Lake Poets—Robert Southey, William Wordsworth, and Coleridge (Feathernest, Paperstamp, and Mystic in the novel)—who had grown less critical of the establishment as their places in that order grew more comfortable.

Certain episodes in *Melincourt* are memorable. The election at Onevote presents a marvelous empirical case

for parliamentary reform, and the Anti-Saccharine Fête celebrates Peacock's belief that sugar, because its production permitted the West Indian slave trade to prosper, was a morally and politically abominable commodity to be abjured by all true philanthropists "till it were sent them by freemen." For the most part, though, this sort of candor makes *Melincourt* shrill rather than forceful.

The romantic thread on which the beads of satiric incident are strung is likewise not among Peacock's strongest. The heroine of the piece and owner of its principal location is Anthelia Melincourt, "at the age of 21, mistress of herself and of ten thousand a year, and of a very ancient and venerable castle in one of the wildest valleys of Westmoreland." More than one critic has noticed that the assets mentioned and the rhetoric employed in this, *Melincourt*'s opening passage, call to mind the famous first sentence of Austen's *Emma* (1816). Unlike Austen's charming and self-deluded Miss Woodhouse, Miss Melincourt is an earnest and judicious lady, a fit match for Mr. Sylvan Forester, the second Peacock hero to embody Shelley's intellectual idealism.

These two young people, so obviously suited for each other, lose no time in discovering their mutual regard. The novel's complications and the lovers' tribulations must come from without: Anthelia is abducted to Alga Castle by the enamored Lord Anophel Achthar. Having lost his bride-to-be, Forester, ostensibly seeking her, wanders about England's Lake District and calls on poets and reviewers at Mainchance Villa and Cimmerian Lodge. His dilatory pursuit gives Lord Anophel time to tire of waiting for Anthelia to yield to his repeated proposals. He threatens to compromise her, and, even though the lady is too strong minded to think that his wickedness will be her disgrace, she is nevertheless grateful enough to be rescued from a test of her theory by Forester and his companion Sir Oran Hautton, who is barely prevented from administering "natural justice" by throwing Lord Anophel out the window.

The fierce, faithful, mute Sir Oran is, most readers agree, the book's chief delight, curious though it might seem for a speechless character to be the chief excellence in a book by a writer noted largely for his characters' conversations. In Sir Oran, who plays the flute, goes out in society, and gains a parliamentary seat, Peacock presents with only slight exaggerations a theory of the Scottish jurist Lord Monboddo that the orangutan is a "noble savage" distinguished from the rest of the human race only by its inability to speak. In the world of literature at least, Monboddo's argument may have more validity than readers might expect: A literary Charles Darwin examining popular fiction might well be tempted to see in the still thriving breed of strong, silent, active heroes Sir Oran's not-too-distant descendants.

NIGHTMARE ABBEY

Peacock began writing his third novel, *Nightmare Abbey*, after Shelley and Godwin departed England for Italy in March of 1818. The book is arguably his finest, certainly his best-focused and plotted, and easily his most controversial. In this novel, Peacock, one of the great English admirers of Aristophanes, lays himself open to the same sort of unfair criticisms that have been heaped on the Greek dramatist for his comedy *The Clouds* (423 B.C.E.). Just as Aristophanes was censured by various critics, from Plato on, for inaccurately and irresponsibly portraying Socrates, so Peacock has been condemned for faithlessness and poor taste by readers who consider *Nightmare Abbey* an unseemly depiction of one of the less commendable interludes in Shelley's life—his period of wanting to have Godwin without giving up his wife, Harriet.

There are indeed resemblances between Shelley and the novelist's protagonist Scythrop—part romantic idealist, part misanthrope, part would-be reformer. Marionetta O'Carroll, the sprightly coquettish cousin Scythrop professes to love, is like Harriet Shelley in spirit and appearance. Scythrop's other love, the heiress Celinda Toobad (known to him as Stella) is tall and raven-haired, the physical opposite of Godwin, but very like Peacock's impression of that grave lady in her passion for philosophical speculation, political discussion, and transcendental romantic literature. Invention of detail was at no time Peacock's strong suit; he was obliged to borrow from real life.

Yet, despite having drawn certain details of his novel from Shelley's situation in 1814, Peacock was neither so tasteless nor so unkind as to write a book centering on his friend's romantic and domestic difficulties. The surest sign of Peacock's goodwill is Shelley's own admiration of the novel: "I am delighted with *Nightmare Abbey*," he wrote from Italy. "I think Scythrop a character admira-

bly conceived and executed; and I know not how to praise sufficiently the lightness, chastity, and strength of the language of the whole." Rather than personalities, Peacock's targets were the dark gloom of modern literature, Byron's *Childe Harold's Pilgrimage* (1812-1818), and such other determinedly dismal works, and the black bile and blue devils introduced by this literature into the lives of its readers.

Nightmare Abbey is the only Peacock novel to take place at one scene only, namely, the dreary and dilapidated seat of Christopher Glowry, a gentleman "naturally of an atrabilarious temperament, and much troubled with those phantoms of indigestion which are commonly called *blue devils*." Disappointed in love and marriage, the gloomy squire of the Abbey surrounds himself with owls, ivy, water weeds, and servants with the most dismal names: Raven, Crow, Graves, Deathshead. His son, Scythrop, a reader of gothic novels and transcendental philosophies, stalks the Abbey like a grand inquisitor. The young man is ruled by two passions: reforming the world by repairing the "crazy fabric of human nature" and drinking Madeira. These preoccupations alter materially when Mr. Glowry's sister and brother-in-law, their niece and ward Marionetta, and a host of other guests arrive for an extended taste of what hospitality the Abbey can afford.

Among the house guests are a particularly fine array of representative embodiments of morbid romanticism. The Honorable Mr. Listless, who spends whole days on a sofa, has perfected ennui. Mr. Flosky, who "plunged into the central opacity of Kantian metaphysics, and lay *perdu* several years in transcendental darkness, till the common daylight of common sense became intolerable to his eyes," is one of Peacock's more successful sketches of Coleridge. Mr. Toobad is a Manichaean Millenarian, the Byronic Mr. Cypress, a poet who, having quarreled with his wife, feels absolved from all duty and is about to set off on his travels.

Finely drawn though the gentlemen may be, as Marilyn Butler has noted in her treatment of *Nightmare Abbey*, Scythrop's two ladies divide the book between themselves. Scythrop's attraction to the volatile Marionetta, who playfully spurns him when he seems devoted and charms him when he seems distant, dominates the first half of the book, while his fascination for the mysterious and brilliant Stella, a creature of veils and conspiracies, overshadows lesser matters in the second half of the story. Scythrop can bring himself to dispense with neither lady: "I am doomed to be the victim of eternal disappointment," he laments in the tone of German high tragedy, "and I have no resource but a pistol." The two unrenounceable ladies, however, find it possible to renounce their suitor. Wishing Scythrop joy of Miss O'Carroll, Celinda/Stella turns to the metaphysical Mr. Flosky. Wishing him all happiness with Miss Toobad, Marionetta engages herself to Mr. Listless. His disappointment validated, his misanthropy doubly confirmed, Scythrop thinks himself unlikely to make a figure in the world. His story ends not with a gunshot but with a sound more familiar in the Peacock world: "Bring some Madeira."

Peacock's next two novels, *Maid Marian* and *The Misfortunes of Elphin*, depart from the prevailing "country-house conversation" pattern. Both works are generally labeled "satiric romances," being set in the picturesque past but laying out oblique observations on present-day situations.

MAID MARIAN

The first of these romances is perhaps Peacock's most widely known story, primarily because it forms the basis for a popular operetta by J. R. Planché (*Maid Marian: Or, The Huntress of Arlingford*, 1822). Peacock was sometimes considered to have borrowed portions of his novel from Sir Walter Scott's *Ivanhoe* (1819), but actually Scott and Peacock, who wrote most of his novel in 1818, shared their primary source: Joseph Ritson's *Robin Hood*, a collection of ancient poems, songs, and ballads about that hero.

Like Scott's work, Peacock's novel is no plausible portrait of medieval life. Robin Hood is not a responsible steward of the wealth he commandeers; his superiority lies in being less hypocritical than his adversaries, the sheriff and Prince John. Friar Tuck is one in Peacock's long gallery of wine-loving clergymen; Maid Marian, whose swordsmanship and archery are commendable, and who decides in liberated fashion at the novel's end to retain her virginal title "though the appellation was then as much a misnomer as that of Little John," is one of Peacock's admirably independent heroines. The satiric object of the forest idyll? To mock the repressive and reac-

tionary Holy Alliance, on which Byron, too, was then turning his sights in his *Don Juan* (1819-1824).

THE MISFORTUNES OF ELPHIN

As a perennial wandering woodsman, particularly in Windsor Forest, which had recently been enclosed, Peacock might have grown up with an interest in the Robin Hood material. His interest in the legendary past presented in *The Misfortunes of Elphin* dates to a more specific series of events. In 1820, Peacock married Jane Gryffydh, the young woman he had met on his travels in Wales ten years before, and her fluency in Welsh reawakened his interest in the Celtic legends of Elphin, Taliesin, and Arthur on which his story is based. Peacock's pastiche of Welsh myths is notable for its rousing songs and its depiction of the splendidly amoral inebriate Seithenyn. Its political satire is particularly effective. The crumbling of the ruinous seawall and castle administered by the drunken Seithenyn could be an apt allegory for any self-indulgent, backward-looking ruling class blind to imminent revolution and indifferent to public responsibility. The situation and the speeches of Seithenyn, however, superbly transmuted from those of the nineteenth century politician George Canning, are particularly relevant to an England on the brink of parliamentary reform.

CROTCHET CASTLE

Crotchet Castle, written two years after *The Misfortunes of Elphin*, returns to the Pavonian mainstream. Here the mansion is a glorified villa; the owner, a rich and recently retired Scottish stockbroker; the target, progressive hypocrisy, represented in real life by Henry Brougham and in the novel by the "March of Mind." The novel divides into three parts. A house party at Crotchet Castle, carefully designed by its host to pit "the sentimental against the rational, the intuitive against the inductive, the ornamental against the useful, the intense against the tranquil, the romantic against the classical," is followed by a floating caravan proceeding up the Thames to the rural depths of Wales. The novel concludes with a Christmas gathering, more than a little Pickwickian, at the quasi-medieval residence of Mr. Chainmail, a sturdy but sensitive anachronist patterned, as critic David Garnett has observed, on Sir Edward Strachey.

This tale of past and present—that is, the past as it

should have been and the future that the present shows all too much promise of becoming—sets Mr. Chainmail and the Reverend Dr. Folliot, one of Peacock's fiercer Tory clergymen, against the liberal utilitarians of the March of Mind school, preeminent among them one Mr. MacQuedy ("*Mac Q.E.D.*, son of a demonstration," as Peacock annotates his own pun). Two pairs of lovers require proper pairing as well. Mr. Chainmail, by story's end, overcomes his excessive regard for old names and blood and marries Susannah Touchandgo, a financier's daughter once engaged to the prospering speculator Crochet, Jr. Having lost her fiancé when her father lost his fortune and decamped for America, Miss Touchandgo has withdrawn to a salubrious Welsh seclusion of music, country cream, fresh air, and exercise, in which charming situation Mr. Chainmail comes upon her.

If old names must be foresworn, so must new money; in the romance dovetailed with the Chainmail-Touchandgo one, Lady Clarinda Bossnowl, generally acclaimed as the most delectable of Peacock's exceptionally pleasing heroines, breaks her engagement to young Crotchet and commits herself to the poor, pedigreed, and talented Captain Fitzchrome. Perhaps the best philosopher in the Crotchet Castle party, Lady Clarinda begins by playing at utilitarianism, intent on not giving her heart away when she can sell it. The journey from the stockbroker's villa to romantic Wales, however, gives her judgment time to concur with what her feelings long have suggested: that love in a cottage—and not even a *cottage ornée*—with the Captain is better than comfort at the Castle. Lady Clarinda's raillery, Folliot's prejudices, and Chainmail's enthusiasms make the novel's conversation particularly fine, and the climax, a spirited defense of Chainmail Hall against "Captain Swing" and that "coming race," the mob, is perhaps Peacock's most active.

GRYLL GRANGE

Peacock, preoccupied with official duties and family concerns, did not write another novel for thirty years, but *Gryll Grange*, his last one, is of a vintage worth waiting for. Few readers would suspect that the author of this suave and mellow production was well acquainted with sorrow and disappointment. The satire here is less incisive and the development of character richer than in the earlier books—in part because the people portrayed

have feelings as well as opinions, in part because Peacock's wit plays not on the characters but on the world outside Gryll Grange, the modern England of scientific advance, technological development, competitive examinations, and spiritualism—a society mocked by the Gryll Grange house party in their own satiric comedy "Aristophanes in London."

For the plot of *Gryll Grange*, Peacock harks back to the situation of *Melincourt*. Morgana, the niece and heiress of Gregory Gryll (the family, we learn, is descended from that Gryllus who alone among Ulysses' crewmen declined being released from the spell by which Circe has turned him into a pig), needs a fit husband who will take her name. Squire Gryll's friend the Reverend Dr. Opimian, a hearty man much like Peacock in his relish for "a good library, a good dinner, a pleasant garden, and rural walks," finds just such a suitor in Mr. Falconer, the new resident of a nearby tower significantly called the "Duke's Folly" by the neighborhood. Falconer, the last of Peacock's fictional projections of the young Shelley, is an idealistic recluse who lives a comfortable, scholarly life with seven beautiful sisters who manage his household and make his music. Once juxtaposed by the well-tried divine machine of a thunderstorm, Miss Gryll and Falconer are mutually attracted: The subsequent story in large measure centers on the hero's vacillations. Should he renounce his monastic retreat and the seven maidens who have been his companions since childhood, or should he forswear the social world so fetchingly represented by Gryll Grange and the one lady he loves?

Also staying at the Grange are Lord Curryfin, a lively, inventive, and engagingly ridiculous fellow, and the serenely beautiful Miss Niphet. Their presence further complicates the romantic dilemma. Lord Curryfin, at first drawn to Miss Gryll, finds himself increasingly enamored of the other charmer and knows not where to offer his heart and title. Miss Niphet, a good friend to Morgana, loves the young lord but hesitates to bag a bird on whom she believes her friend's sights to be trained. Miss Gryll, who knows she loves Falconer but doubts whether she can get him, believes she can get Lord Curryfin but wonders whether she could truly love him. This tangled web of love, honor, and jealousy, so mild that it never becomes a vice, is straightened out by an event yet more providential than the convenient thunderstorm: the appearance and acceptance of seven stalwart rustics who want to marry the maidens of the tower and who thereby free Falconer from his reservations. The novel ends with all the lovers properly betrothed, a multiple wedding, and, as is fitting in the Peacock world, a salute. Addressing the wedding party, Dr. Opimian concludes,

> Let all the corks, when I give the signal, be discharged simultaneously; and we will receive it as a peal of Bacchic ordnance, in honor of the Power of the Joyful Event, whom we may assume to be presiding on this auspicious occasion.

Peter W. Graham

OTHER MAJOR WORKS

POETRY: *The Monks of St. Mark*, 1804; *Palmyra, and Other Poems*, 1806; *The Genius of the Thames*, 1810; *The Philosophy of Melancholy*, 1812; *Sir Proteus: A Satirical Ballad*, 1814; *Rhododaphne*, 1818; *Paper Money Lyrics*, 1837.

NONFICTION: *The Four Ages of Poetry*, 1820; *Memoirs of Percy Bysshe Shelley*, 1858-1862; *The Letters of Thomas Love Peacock*, 2001 (2 volumes; Nicholas A. Joukovsky, editor).

BIBLIOGRAPHY

Butler, Marilyn. *Peacock Displayed: A Satirist in His Context*. Boston: Routledge & Kegan Paul, 1979. A first-rate study of Peacock. Focuses not only on his life but also on the society in which he lived and worked and on his satiric abilities.

Cavaliero, Glen. "Feasts of Reason: Thomas Love Peacock." In *The Alchemy of Laughter: Comedy in English Fiction*. New York: St. Martin's Press, 2000. Peacock's novels are included in this examination of comedy in English fiction. Cavaliero discusses how parody, irony, satire, and other types of humor are evident in Peacock's works.

Kiernan, Robert F. *Frivolity Unbound: Six Masters of the Camp Novel*. New York: Continuum, 1990. Examines Peacock in the company of Max Beerbohm, Ronald Firbank, E. F. Benson, P. G. Wodehouse, and Ivy Compton-Burnett, including analysis of Peacock's novels *Headlong Hall* and *Nightmare Abbey*.

McKay, Margaret. *Peacock's Progress: Aspects of Artistic Development in the Novels of Thomas Love Peacock*. Stockholm: Almqvist and Wiksell, 1992. Contains chapters on Peacock's poems and plays as well as on his novels. Good background on the literary figures and movements satirized by Peacock.

Mulvihill, James. *Thomas Love Peacock*. Boston: Twayne, 1987. An excellent short sourcebook on Peacock, providing biographical background and sound context for each of his major works, as well as his essays and reviews.

Prance, Claude A. *The Characters in the Novels of Thomas Love Peacock, 1785-1866*. Lewiston, N.Y.: Edwin Mellen Press, 1992. Includes a chronology of Peacock's life, descriptions of the characters in his novels and other works, an appendix listing the contemporaries upon whom he may have based his characters, and bibliographies of work by and about him.

Sage, Lorna, ed. *Peacock—The Satirical Novels: A Casebook*. London: Macmillan, 1976. Collection of essays by and about Peacock, including pieces by nineteenth century writers Percy Bysshe Shelley and William Makepeace Thackeray and twentieth century critics Virginia Woolf and Northrop Frye.

Schmid, Thomas H. *Humor and Transgression in Peacock, Shelley, and Byron: A Cold Carnival*. Lewiston, N.Y.: Edwin Mellen Press, 1992. A study that focuses on the shared themes in Peacock and the works of his Romantic friends Lord Byron and Percy Bysshe Shelley, rather than on their more usually emphasized differences.

Tomkinson, Neil. *The Christian Faith and Practice of Samuel Johnson, Thomas De Quincey, and Thomas Love Peacock*. Lewiston, N.Y.: Edwin Mellen Press, 1992. Examines the religious views of Peacock as demonstrated in his works and conversations, including his ideas about the clergy, worship, faith, sin, and death. Includes a bibliography and an index.

Vidal, Gore. "Thomas Love Peacock: The Novel of Ideas." In *The Essential Gore Vidal*, edited by Fred Kaplan. New York: Random House, 1999. This collection of fiction, essays, and reviews includes Vidal's appraisals of the work of several writers, including Peacock and his novels. Includes a chronology and a bibliography.

WALKER PERCY

Born: Birmingham, Alabama; May 28, 1916
Died: Covington, Louisiana; May 10, 1990

PRINCIPAL LONG FICTION

The Moviegoer, 1961
The Last Gentleman, 1966
*Love in the Ruins: The Adventures of a Bad
    Catholic at a Time Near the End of the World*,
    1971
Lancelot, 1977
The Second Coming, 1980
The Thanatos Syndrome, 1987

OTHER LITERARY FORMS

As a writer of imaginative literature, Walker Percy devoted himself exclusively to the novel. However, he also wrote more than fifty reviews and essays on many of the same topics that inform his novels: existential philosophy, language theory, modern scientific method, contemporary American culture, the South, and literature. With one or two exceptions, the most important of these essays are collected in *The Message in the Bottle* (1975), which has as its peculiarly Percyean subtitle *How Queer Man Is, How Queer Language Is, and What One Has to Do with the Other*. An indispensable book, *The Message in the Bottle* not only clarifies the author's major concerns as well as his commitment to that most basic philosophical question, "What is man?" but also details the formidable intellectual foundation on which his fiction so unpretentiously rests. That unpretentiousness is especially evident in *Lost in the Cosmos* (1983), ironically subtitled *The Last Self-Help Book*, in which Percy employs satire and semiotics in an effort to clarify the human being's social and more especially spiritual predicament as a uniquely "lost" creature needing the good news of the gospels but all too often willing to settle for the insights of scientists and talk-show hosts.

ACHIEVEMENTS

Walker Percy is perhaps most easily described as a Catholic-existentialist-American-southern novelist, a baggy phrase that at least has the virtue of identifying the various currents that are blended together in his distinctive works. In Percy's fiction, Mark Twain's Huck Finn from the novel *Adventures of Huckleberry Finn* (1884) and Jean-Paul Sartre's Antoine Roquentin from the play *Nausea* (1938) meet in a single character adrift in a world where, despite the formless sprawl of mass society, the possibility of grace still exists. Percy's fiction is readily identifiable by its distinctive narrative voice. That voice—laconic yet disarmingly honest and filled with wonder—gained for Percy both critical respect and a dedicated readership. Percy received the National Book Award for *The Moviegoer*, the Los Angeles Times Book Prize for *The Second Coming*, and the St. Louis Literary Award for *Lost in the Cosmos*. Among his other literary honors were memberships in the National Institute of Arts and Letters and the American Academy of Arts and Sciences.

BIOGRAPHY

Walker Percy was born in Birmingham, Alabama, on May 28, 1916. When his father, lawyer Leroy Percy, committed suicide in 1929, the young Percy, his two brothers, and their mother moved to Greenville, Mississippi, where they lived with Leroy's bachelor cousin, William Alexander Percy. William adopted the boys in 1931, following their mother's death in an automobile accident. The Greenville home served as something of a local cultural center; the uncle, the author of several works, including an autobiographical memoir of the South titled *Lanterns on the Levee* (1941), entertained such house guests as William Faulkner, Carl Sandburg, Langston Hughes, David Cohn, and Harry Stack Sullivan.

In the early 1930's, Percy attended Greenville High School, where he wrote a gossip column and became the close friend of Shelby Foote, who was by then already committed to a literary career. At the University of North Carolina, which was noted for its school of behaviorism, Percy majored in chemistry and received a bachelor of science degree in 1937. He then enrolled in Columbia's College of Physicians and Surgeons and received his medical degree in 1941. In addition to his studies, Percy underwent psychoanalysis and became a frequent filmgoer. The turning point in his life came in early 1942 when, as a medical resident at Bellevue Hospital in New York, Percy contracted tuberculosis. During his two-year convalescence at Saranac Lake, he began reading extensively in philosophy and literature (Sartre, Albert Camus, Søren Kierkegaard, Gabriel Marcel, Fyodor Dostoevski, Nikolai Gogol, Leo Tolstoy, Franz Kafka). What he discovered was that as a medical doctor he knew much about people but had no idea how to define a human.

Following a relapse and further convalescence in 1944, Percy seemed sure of only two things: He was a doctor who did not wish to practice medicine; he was literally as well as existentially homeless (his uncle having died in 1942). In 1945, he traveled with Foote to New Mexico and then stayed on alone for a time. On November 7, 1946, he married Mary Bernice Townsend, and less than a year later they both converted to Catholicism. (The decision to convert was, Percy said, in large measure the result of their reading of Kierkegaard's essay, "The Difference Between a Genius and an Apostle.") Soon after, the Percys moved from Sewanee, Tennessee, to New Orleans, Louisiana, where Percy continued his contemplative life. Financially secure—thanks to his uncle's estate—and intellectually rich, his landlord, Julius Friend, a professor of philosophy, introduced him to the writings of Charles Saunders Peirce, whose triadic theory of language formed the basis of Percy's own linguistic speculations. (Percy's interest in language had another and more personal source: The younger of his two daughters was born deaf.) In 1950, the Percys moved to Covington, Louisiana, "a pleasant non-place," Percy said, where it is possible to live as a stranger in one's own land; it is neither the "anyplace" that characterizes mass society nor the "someplace" of New Orleans or a Richmond, where the past haunts the present.

In the 1950's, Percy began publishing essays in such journals as *Thought, Commonweal,* and *Philosophy and Phenomenological Research.* After discarding two early novels, he began writing *The Moviegoer* in 1959, revising it four times before its publication two years later. Until his death on May 10, 1990, Percy lived quietly in Covington, a serious and meditative novelist pondering the world in thought, fiction, and an occasional essay.

ANALYSIS

Walker Percy acknowledged that Kierkegaard's writings provided him with "a theoretical frame of reference," and one of the most important ideas that he adapted from this frame is Kierkegaard's rejection of Hegelian rationalism in favor of a subjective and intensely passionate commitment on the part of the individual. In Percy's view, modern science in general and the social sciences in particular have mistakenly and indiscriminately adopted the behaviorist, or biological, method and have consequently defined the human being reductively and abstractly.

Existentialism, including the existential novel, on the other hand, presents an alternative to behaviorism: a concrete phenomenological approach whose aim is the recovery of humankind's uniqueness. Percy admits that the behaviorist method is valid to a point; ultimately, however, it must fail because, in classifying the human

Walker Percy. (© Nancy Crampton)

as a biological organism acting in accordance with rules applicable to all biological organisms, it fails to deal with what is distinctly human, the nonbiological goals. Concerned solely with sameness, the scientific method cannot account for Dostoevski's "underground man" except as a deviation from the norm. Existentialism, Percy believes, does account for this, as does Christianity, which acknowledges the Fall of Man and his distance from God, and defines existence as "the journey of a wayfarer along life's way." Denying the Fall, modern science makes the Gnostic mistake; it attempts to build Eden, the secular city, where human guilt and anxiety are conditioned away, where all biological needs are met, and where existence is certified by experts.

Percy rejects this "brave new world" and calls instead for a radical anthropology that can account for the ontological as well as the biological aspects of human existence. Guilt and anxiety, he points out, are not symptoms of maladjustment to be gotten rid of so that the individual (as human organism) can live the life of the satisfied consumer; rather, these signs of estrangement serve to summon a person not to self-fulfillment but to authentic existence. Humanity is on earth not to have needs met, Percy says, not to surrender sovereignty to the theories of experts (a view raised again by Christopher Lasch in his controversial book *The Culture of Narcissism*, 1979), but to be saved, and that necessitates consciousness of the human situation.

It is important to realize that Percy's sovereign wayfarer, or castaway, is not entirely identifiable with Kierkegaard's knight of faith. In place of Kierkegaard's extreme subjectivity, Percy posits the intersubjectivity of Gabriel Marcel, a Christian existentialist whose *we are* stands in stark contrast with both Kierkegaard's *I choose* and René Descartes's *I think*. We know we exist, Marcel says, by participating in the world. He does not think of being as experience, however, but as a presence within experience that is to be understood as simultaneously transcendent and immanent. To separate the two components of being is to pervert them and to transmogrify the individual as sovereign wayfarer into either angel—the abstract knower, the objective consciousness—or beast—a culture organism satisfying its needs. (The terms are Percy's, borrowed from Blaise Pascal.)

Marcel's quest for being, which is the quest for salvation as well, manifests itself in Percy's theory of language as intersubjective communication, where *we name* implies the same religious affirmation as Marcel's *we are* and Martin Buber's *I-Thou*. Percy originally turned to language theory to answer the question "What is man?" because the answer provided by the behaviorist method was reductive and because the old theological view, along with the words in which it was couched, has been rendered ineffective by the general acceptance of the scientific method, which predisposed modern humanity to view itself as the behaviorists had defined it. Percy then set himself the task of finding "the delta factor": that which makes the human what it is and not something else.

According to the old theological view, humankind's singularity is its "soul," a meaningless word in a scientific age that demands empirical proof. For soul, Percy substitutes language, which he defines not as a sign system (the behaviorist position) but as the uniquely human process of symbolization. At the heart of language (and therefore at the heart of humanity as well) is something mysterious (compare Marcel's "mystery of being"). The mystery is explained by what Percy calls the "coupling process," the intersubjective human context by which people name, or symbolize, the world and in this way come both to know it and to share it. Language is, therefore, an attempt to bridge the gap between self and other, or, considered in the religious context of the Fall of Man, between self and God. What complicates the situation is the fact that in the late twentieth century, Percy believed, language became as meaningless, as clichéd, as the old theology. Before there can be intersubjective communication, humankind must again learn how to speak.

To learn to name and therefore to know and share that knowledge with another is the basic plot of a Percy novel. As Robert Coles has pointed out, Percy's novels trace the protagonist's movement from lofty observation to active participation in the openness of life—its possibilities and the necessity of making choices. Each of his major characters feels estranged

> from being, from his own being, from the being of other creatures in the world, from the transcendent being. He has lost something, but what he does not know; he only knows that he is sick to death with the loss of it.

Since this quest for being is a quest for God, it involves the hero's progress through Kierkegaard's three stages: the aesthetic (the pursuit of pleasure; the self becomes an uncommitted ironic spectator detached from him- or herself and from others); the ethical (living within a general human code, such as marriage); the religious (requiring an entirely personal and—Kierkegaard would say—absurd leap of faith). The hero's search for being begins only when he or she becomes conscious of his or her despair and tries either to understand it or to alleviate it in one of two ways: rotation or repetition.

Rotation—the quest for new experiences to offset everydayness—makes up the comic substance of Percy's novels. Repetition—the return to the past—may be rendered comically, but more often it serves a darker purpose, for Percy's heroes are, like those of William Faulkner, haunted by the past; as a result, they do not live fully in the present. Only when they confront the past directly and become conscious of it can they break its spell and become sovereign wayfarers.

Frequently, Percy equates the past with the southern stoicism his uncle espoused, which, in Percy's judgment, leads only to pessimism, obsession with death, and "the wintry kingdom of self"; in short, it is the very antithesis of Percy's Christian existentialism. Rotation and repetition provide only temporary relief from the malaise that prevails within the aesthetic stage. The only escape from "aesthetic damnation" is through ordeal, especially the death of a loved one. Ordeal brings heroes face-to-face with mortality and enables them to see their world and themselves as if for the first time. The search they then begin is in effect a rejection of the absurdist position of aesthetic existentialists such as Camus and Sartre. The world is not absurd; it is a world to be named, known, and shared by the authentic self and the other in a mode of existence that is not so much religious *or* ethical as a synthesis of the two.

There are analogues for Walker Percy's religious-phenomenological conception of the human search for being in his method of composition and in his prose style. The author's search for narrative form parallels the hero's search for being. Beginning with a situation rather than a plot or set of characters, Percy wrote with no fixed purpose or end in mind. As he explained, the writing, while not "haphazard," involved "many false starts,

many blind detours, many blind passages, many goings ahead and backing up." Stylistically, his elegantly and precisely written novels suggest wonder, humor, and forbearance rather than the ponderous solemnity of other existential novelists such as Sartre. Moreover, his prose is richly and sensuously detailed; like two other converts to Catholicism, Marcel and even more particularly Gerard Manley Hopkins, he took pleasure in a natural and human world that is, although marred by evil, essentially sacramental.

THE MOVIEGOER

John Bickerson Bolling—Binx—is the narrator and main character of *The Moviegoer* and the first of Percy's spiritually "sick" protagonists. At age twenty-nine, he is a successful broker in a modern world where the church has been replaced by the brokerage house. Although financially secure, Binx feels uneasy; although adept at planning his client's futures, he has trouble living his own life from day to day, fearful that he may at any moment succumb to that worst of all plagues, the malaise of everydayness. To counter its effects, Binx becomes a moviegoer, partly because films project a "heightened . . . resplendent reality," albeit temporarily, and partly because films provide Binx with accepted role models: thus his impersonations of such canonized figures as Gregory Peck, Clark Gable, Dana Andrews, and Rory Calhoun (who also serves as his confidant). The impersonation can never fully satisfy the moviegoer, however, who must eventually face the fact that the reality of his own life can never attain the heightened illusion of the star's gestural perfection. Moviegoing serves Binx in two additional ways: It enables him to view his world through the perspective of the films he has seen and, more important, to observe the world as if it were itself a film and he the passive audience.

Binx's detachment is both a virtue and a vice. As the detached spectator, he observes those around him closely and accurately, thus exposing the roles they have unknowingly adopted. Appropriately, the novel's temporal setting is the week before Mardi Gras, the period of rehearsals for New Orleans' citywide impersonation. Instead of recognizing their situation as castaways, these others feel serenely at home in the world, whereas in fact they are, as Binx understands, dead. Neither virtuous nor sinful, they are merely "nice"; they speak, but in clichés;

they ask questions, but neither expect nor desire answers. Binx, who fears becoming invisible—losing his identity—is right to keep his distance from these shadowy others. At the same time, however, he longs to be like them, to have his identity certified for him by such spurious means as films, identity cards, *Consumer Reports*, newspaper advice columns, and radio shows such as "This I Believe," which broadcasts the meaningless affirmations of abstracted religionists to a half-believing, half-skeptical Binx.

If it is his ironic detachment that saves Binx from the unreflective life of mass humanity, then it is his search that most clearly characterizes his longing for authenticity and being. "To become aware of the possibility of the search is to be onto something," Binx says. "Not to be onto something is to be in despair." Binx distinguishes two kinds of search. The "vertical" leads to abstraction: theories that explain the world but fail to explain what humankind is. (One alternative to such abstraction is the romanticism that killed Binx's father and that the son wisely rejects.) The other is the "horizontal" or phenomenological search that Percy himself counsels in *The Message in the Bottle*. While Binx is indeed "onto something," his search is different from Percy's; it constitutes a "debased" form of the religious search because, as Percy explained, Binx, like Sartre, "has already ruled God out." His search takes a purely aesthetic form. To ease "the pain of loss," he pursues money and women, but the pursuit leads only to boredom and depression because the novelty of his possessions quickly wears off and everydayness inevitably returns to remind him of his inauthenticity and his position as a castaway.

Fortunately, Binx's yearning has a deeper current. As a college student, he found himself "lost in the mystery of being alive at such a time and place"; upon his return from the Korean War, he began his eight-year "exile" in the New Orleans suburb of Gentilly, which, like Covington, is a nonplace; as a broker he has taken to reading *Arabia Deserta*, by the self-styled "God's pilgrim," Charles Montagu Doughty, concealed inside a Standard & Poor's binder.

Binx's search begins with the fact of his own "invincible apathy" and eventually leads, after many wrong turns, to authenticity and intersubjective relationships with his fourteen-year-old half brother, Lonnie Smith,

and his twenty-five-year-old cousin, Kate Cutrer. There exists a complicity between Binx and the dying Lonnie, who faces life with true serenity because he understands it religiously. Like the other dying children in Percy's novels, Lonnie represents the paradox of unmerited suffering in a world ruled by a supposedly benevolent God, a paradox Percy resolves by depicting their spiritual victory in a "world full of God's grace where sorrow and death do not have the final word." Binx attends to the "good news" that Lonnie embodies because, in part, Lonnie's monotonous way of talking makes his words fresh and therefore meaningful, "like a code tapped through a wall."

Kate, unlike Lonnie, lives in pure anxiety, swinging wildly between various extremes, especially the longing to be free and the desire "to be an anyone who is anywhere." Although she lacks Binx's degree of awareness as well as his ironic detachment and is more prone to impersonation than he, Kate, like Binx, is aware of her disease, which others can only understand in psychological terms. (Thus, the novel's epigraph, taken from Kierkegaard: "the specific character of despair is precisely this: it is unaware of being despair.") Binx and Kate neatly complement each other: His childlike "simplemindedness" allows her to feel secure enough to speak honestly, while she correctly points out that in his search Binx may be overlooking something "obvious." Her request that Binx be her God—by which she means he is to tell her what to do—is not at all absurd given Marcel's brand of Christian existentialism. Significantly, her other suitors play the part of intersubjective God rather badly: One wants to send her to a high-priced psychoanalyst; the other promises an interminable vista of "niceness" and everydayness.

Binx's leap from nominal Catholic existing in despair to sovereign wayfarer and authentic being occurs very late in the novel and is effected by what, in a parallel context, Percy calls "some dim dazzling trick of grace." In fact, only a few pages from the end Binx laments that, having but one gift, "a good nose for merde," the only course for him to follow is "to fall prey to desire." There is even some justice to his Aunt Emily's judgment of him: In crucial situations, Binx invariably chooses to "default," to exit. Yet, in the final pages, it is clear that Binx will do so no longer. Neither, however, will he play the part his aunt has chosen for him—southern stoic. He will go to medical school, not because she wants him to but because now he knows what to do: to observe *and* to serve others.

Binx's leap is reflected in the very texture of Percy's prose. Until the epilogue, which takes place one year later, Binx has narrated his tale chiefly in what may be termed his detached, matter-of-fact, moviegoer style, against which the very few lyrical passages, used to underscore Binx's wonder and the gracefulness of his world, stand in vivid contrast. In the epilogue, Binx drops the moviegoer style (and the references to films) entirely; instead, he speaks easily, authentically, authoritatively. The man who earlier had been cousin, half brother, and ironic impersonator, now is husband, brother, and sovereign wayfarer.

THE LAST GENTLEMAN

Williston Bibb Barrett, or Billy Barrett, the protagonist of Percy's second novel, *The Last Gentleman*, is a modern-day version of Dostoevski's Prince Myshkin in *The Idiot* (1868). Although far less ironic than Binx Bolling, Barrett is far more disturbed, as his periodic fugue states and bouts of amnesia and déjà vu attest. Existing in a state of pure possibility, he is incapable of making any one decisive act or choice. He has tried and failed both to live the therapeutic life and to engineer his own destiny. Knowing something is missing in his life, Barrett seeks to recover reality and find his being in the "gap" between self and other. Specifically, these others are the members of the Vaught family, and his search is a spiritual odyssey, modeled on Twain's *Adventures of Huckleberry Finn*, which takes him from New York to his native Ithaca, then on to Mississippi, and finally to Santa Fe (Holy Faith), New Mexico, and the Sangre de Cristo (Blood of Christ) mountains.

The search begins when Barrett accidentally discovers Kitty Vaught and her sister-in-law, Rita, in Central Park. Rita, a secular humanist and advocate of self-fulfillment, quickly realizes she will not be able either to control or to convert Barrett and tries unsuccessfully to get rid of him. Barrett, however, has already fallen in love with Kitty, a rather pale version of Kate Cutrer—less anxiety-ridden, more successful in her impersonations. Barrett's love affair is both furthered and complicated by Kitty's younger brother, Jamie, whose traveling

companion he becomes. The fact that Jamie is dying establishes definite limits to the pure possibility of his and Barrett's lives and causes Barrett to consider his search more profoundly when he meets another sister, Val, and brother, Sutter, the two "absentee experts" (as Barrett calls them) who force him to make his existential choice. Val, a convert to Catholicism and a nun, has dedicated herself to teaching mute children to speak and to believe the Catholic religion. (All people are like her children, she claims; they are waiting to be told what to do.) Whereas she is hopeful and apostolic, Sutter, a diagnostician and pathologist, is suicidal and ironically quixotic. He rejects her belief in the human as wayfarer, claiming "We are doomed to the transcendence of abstraction and I choose the only reentry into the world which remains to us": cynicism, lewdness, and detachment.

Sutter's mistake, as Barrett well understands, is the positing of extreme alternatives such as God or no God, transcendence or immanence. Moreover, Sutter's concern for Jamie betrays his basically religious nature, and it is this, more than his medical expertise, that has led Barrett to look to him for answers. At Jamie's baptism, it is Sutter who comprehends what is happening. Barrett, although he acts as interpreter between Jamie and the priest, misses the religious significance. He does understand that something has happened, however, and to discover what that something is he tracks down Sutter, who has decided to commit suicide. Barrett's search for an answer is, as Percy noted, a search for a father, ultimately for the Father, God; his own father, Barrett finally realizes, had looked for his answer in all the wrong places—solitude, "old sad poetry," and the music of Johannes Brahms. The son's "wait" did not keep the father from killing himself, but it does save Sutter, who appears in the final tableau less as an oracle than as Barrett's self-chosen—and therefore sovereign—responsibility.

LOVE IN THE RUINS

Subtitled *The Adventures of a Bad Catholic at a Time Near the End of the World*, Percy's *Love in the Ruins* is a broad satire on the state of the modern world—in particular, its behaviorist assumptions and political absurdities. The novel may be flawed, as some reviewers have contended, by the author's insistent and at times rather heavy-handed social criticism; there is, however, a comic vitality in this novel that seems to offset such reservations about it as literary art. This comic vitality, quite unlike the irony and understatement that characterize Percy's earlier novels, is appropriate to a work that has the topics of community and reconciliation as two of its major concerns. As Percy explained in his essay "Notes for a Novel about the End of the World," the apocalyptic novelist serves two purposes: As prophet, or canary in the coal mine, he cries out in order to avert disaster; and as coupling agent, he connects humankind with reality. It is by means of the coupling process that disaster is averted, as Percy quietly suggests in the novel's closing image of a couple "twined about each other as the ivy twineth," in which what has been a sign of ruin (the ivy) is transformed into a symbol of intersubjective love.

The story, which is spoken into a pocket tape recorder by the hero, Tom More, as he keeps watch for snipers, follows a five-part structure (July Fourth, First, Second, Third, Fourth) that progressively becomes more chaotic until, in the epilogue ("Five Years Later"), peace and order are restored. The time of the novel is a not too distant future that bears a clear, if comically exaggerated, resemblance to the American 1960's: The fifteen-year war in Ecuador continues, racial tensions and Bantu uprisings are increasing, and the Catholic Church has split into three factions. In short, "the center did not hold." The physical setting is just as perverse as the social-political: Paradise Estates, home of the well-to-do and the spiritually impoverished; Fedville, a sprawling compound that includes a Masters and Johnson Love Clinic, where former priest Kev Kevin reads *Commonweal* and presides over the vaginal console; Honey Island Swamp, a counterculture retreat; and the golf course, where a banner proclaims "Jesus Christ, the Greatest Pro of Them All."

Percy's hero is as troubled as his society but in a different way. Forty-five years old and a collateral descendant of Sir/Saint Thomas, he is at once a doctor and a mental patient, a diagnostician but also a metaphysician in a world of behaviorists ready and willing to condition away any remaining feelings of guilt he may have. He is of the type that Kierkegaard termed aesthetic damnation, as he loves, in descending order of importance, women, music, science, God, and, "hardly at all," his fellow human. He has lost that thread in the world labyrinth that,

until the death of his daughter, Samantha, made the world seem sensible and holy. His faith gone, Tom More has his own messianic ambition, a plan to "save" America with More's Qualitative Quantitative Ontological Lapsometer. His invention—"the stethoscope of the spirit . . . the first caliper of the soul"—is designed to measure the gap between the outer, social self and true, inner being; he hopes to modify the lapsometer so that it can cure as well as diagnose humankind's fall from being, to put together what Descartes tore apart. Like Percy and, to a degree, like Sutter Vaught, More is troubled by the modern world's indifference to being and people's willingness to define themselves in half measures: the angel that, falling prey to abstraction, is unable to "reenter the lovely ordinary world," or the beast that adapts to its environment and so becomes the organism behaviorists say the human is.

Art Immelmann (Mephistopheles to More's Faust) tempts him with spurious "good news": a multimillion dollar development grant and the Nobel Prize. The price is, of course, More's soul—his being, his sense of personal responsibility. More resists the devil and so escapes aesthetic damnation; by not committing the unpardonable sin (refusing God's grace), he puts an end to the "feasting on death" that has preoccupied him since the onset of his daughter's illness and begins to live in the "lovely ordinary world" once again. Instead of an apocalypse, the novel ends with a new beginning, a Christmas morning. Reborn, Tom More no longer loves abstractly or bestially; he has married his former nurse, Ellen Oglethorpe, a Georgia Presbyterian, whose belief takes the form of charity. Equally important, More now knows what it is he wants: not prizes or women, but

> just to figure out what I've hit on. Some day a man will walk into my office as ghost or beast or ghost-beast and walk out as a man, which is to say sovereign wayfarer, lordly exile, worker and waiter and watcher.

LANCELOT

Percy's fourth novel, *Lancelot*, is by far his most troubling. Structurally, it follows the odd dialogue form of Camus's *The Fall* (1956); until the last two pages, only the voice of the protagonist is heard, addressing a "you" whose responses are not given. More disturbing is that, as Joyce Carol Oates has pointed out, the views of the main character, a self-righteous and unrepentant murderer, are strikingly similar to those of the author. Readers must recognize, as Percy surely does, the nature of the protagonist's grotesque mistake—the sources from which it derives and the ends to which it leads.

Lancelot Andrewes Lamar speaks his Poe-like tale from the Center for Aberrant Behavior in New Orleans, where he has been confined for one year. Although in the course of his apologia/confession Lance identifies his wife Margot's infidelity as the immediate cause of his murdering her and the members of the film company with whom she was involved, the actual causes go much further back and have less to do with Margot than with his own wasted life and his position as the last in a fallen line of southern aristocrats. As a Lamar, Lance has inherited not only the family homestead, Belle Isle, but also a way of judging humankind in absolute terms. His first wife, Lucy, was (or so Lance remembers her) an angel, whereas Margot, who for a time he turned into a goddess, became beast or devil.

Dividing his life into two parts—before he discovered his wife's adultery and after—he proclaims that the past is "absolutely dead" and the future will be "absolutely new." This penchant for absolutes suggests Lance's inability or unwillingness to confront the ambiguity and mystery of human existence and is related to the way the Lamars view human life in terms of individual, historically significant events. Thus, Lance's life is reduced to his 110-yard touchdown run against Alabama and his destruction of Belle Isle and everyone in it. Lance does understand that performing such feats is actually less difficult than living an ordinary life, but when he turns Margot's infidelity into a quest for the "unholy grail," he in effect sidesteps the ordinary life that is far "more complicated and ambiguous" than either the historical events venerated by the Lamars or the clichéd films of Margot and her friends.

Like their film, Lance's quest is superficial and derivative (it is cast in the mold of the Raymond Chandler detective novels he has been reading). Moreover, it leads Lance, as Cleanth Brooks has demonstrated, to commit a modern version of the Gnostic heresy. Claiming that the original sin was something God did to humans and judging Christianity as much a failure as southern stoicism, Lance determines to destroy the present age, which he

cannot tolerate, and start over in a new Eden with his new Eve, a fellow patient named Anna who, he believes, as the victim of a brutal gang rape, has been restored to innocence. Lance is wrong about Anna, however; she never lost her innocence. He also is wrong about Christianity, if one distinguishes, as Kierkegaard did, between Christianity (as embodied in Percival, Lance's listener to whom the novel is spoken) and Christendom, which Lance is right to reject as a viable alternative to his intolerable age.

Lance's confession, as well as his predicament, brings his friend Percival's spiritual ambivalence into sharp focus; Percival, the Prince Hal of their early manhood who has since been ordained Father John, is torn between two roles—priest and psychiatrist—and two approaches to human existence—the religious and the behavioral. It is Percival's fellow psychiatrists who certify Lance as sane, even though both Lance and Percival know there is still something wrong, something missing. As a psychiatrist, Percival cannot help Lance, whose problem is ontological and spiritual rather than psychological, and whose self-righteous ranting masks his deeper uncertainty and longing. When, at the very end of the novel, Lance asks, "Is there anything I can do for you before I leave?" Percival's "Yes" identifies him as the apostolic Father John, the bearer of the good news for which Lance has been waiting. Against such grand gestures as blowing up Belle Isle, Percy offers the power of a small, ordinary word freshly heard.

THE SECOND COMING

The Second Coming was, as Percy noted, his "first unalienated novel." Instead of the ambiguity that characterizes the endings of his earlier novels, here the author celebrates the unequivocal victory of love over death. While such a conclusion did not please all reviewers, many of whom found it unconvincing or even sentimental, it is consistent with Percy's religious vision and his flexible aesthetic with its various tones and broad range of narrative structures: the novelist's version of God's plenty.

The novel picks up the life of Will Barrett some twenty years after *The Last Gentleman*. At the age of forty-three, Will is a retired lawyer, a wealthy widower living in Linwood, North Carolina, and a recent recipient of the Rotary's man-of-the-year award; yet, he is still a sick man, subject to dizzy spells and tricks of memory. What troubles Will is not the loss of his wife, Marion, but the sudden realization that he has wasted his life and been "only technically alive." At the brink of the abyss, he sees himself as a total stranger; only two percent of himself, he sets out to find the missing ninety-eight percent. His search takes him in a number of directions. One is back to his father, or more specifically to the only "event" in his life. This is a hunting accident that he comes to realize was no accident at all but instead the father's attempt to kill his son and then himself and so free them both from lives not worth living.

Like his father, Will rejects the "death in life" that characterizes modern believers as well as unbelievers; Will also rejects his father's solution, suicide, because it proves nothing. Instead, he devises the "ultimate scientific experiment" that will, he believes, provide conclusive proof of either God's existence or His nonexistence/ noninvolvement. As the narrator points out, Will is mad; moreover, his plan (to starve himself and so force God either to save or abandon him) is badly flawed in two important ways. The language Will uses to define his experiment (actually more a "covenant") betrays his egotism as well as his legalistic frame of reference; to his "huge" bequest (his life), he attaches a "huge" condition (God's appearing to him). Not until much later in the novel does he learn "the economy of giving and getting" and the superiority of ordinary existence to his own ultimate experiments or his father's extraordinary "events."

In addition, Will is looking for God in the wrong place. While waiting in the cave for "a clear yes [or] no," he misses the unambiguous beauty of Indian summer; and while he assails God's "unavailability," his own "fade outs," such as the cave experiment, preclude the very intersubjective relationships through which God manifests Himself to humankind. The sign he does receive, a toothache, is "a muddy maybe" that cuts short the experiment and sends Will howling in pain out of the wilderness of self and into a world that, while not physically new, can be seen in an original way.

The person who changes Will's angle of vision is Allison Huger (Kitty Vaught's daughter), who has just escaped her own cave, a mental hospital, and begun a new life in an abandoned greenhouse. She resembles Will in that she feels uncomfortable around other people,

as well she should, for the Allison they see is the mentally disturbed organism for whom they can imagine nothing better than "the best-structured environment money can buy." Although she wants to live an entirely self-reliant life, each afternoon about four o'clock she experiences a sense of loss or emptiness. What she feels is identical to one of the symptoms of Will's disease (Hausmann's syndrome), which the doctors call "inappropriate longing." There is a pill to control Will's disease, but there is only one way to satisfy the longing, and that is by loving Allison, by finding his being in her just as she finds hers in him. As Allison explains in her characteristically melodic way, "Our lapses are not due to synapses." Percy's love story is not, therefore, simply romantic; rather, it is religious in the Christian existential sense. Their love is, to quote Allison again, "be-all" but not "end-all." When, in the novel's concluding scene, Will confronts Father Weatherbee, an old priest, Will's

> heart leapt with joy. What is it I want from her and him, he wondered, not only want but must have? Is she a gift and therefore a sign of the giver? Could it be that the Lord is here, masquerading behind this simple holy face? Am I crazy to want both, her and Him? No, not want, must have. And will have.

Here, as in the four earlier novels, one finds what Sartre called humanity's useless passion, but for Percy this passionate longing is not useless at all because the world is not absurd. Percy's search is not one of Sartre's purely arbitrary projects; rather it is a thoroughly modern and, for many readers, an entirely convincing rendition of John Bunyan's *The Pilgrim's Progress* (1678, 1684) in an age mired in the slough of behaviorism and unbelief.

THE THANATOS SYNDROME

The Thanatos Syndrome, Percy's sixth and last novel, ends a bit differently, which is to say less insistently. Narrator-protagonist Dr. Tom More's "well well well" befits the smaller scale of his latter-day desires, yet this fit proves ironic, given the novel's overgrand, at times messianic ambitions (of the kind More himself had in *Love in the Ruins*). Similarities between the two novels are obvious (they share a number of the same characters and the same futurist-fantasy approach), but both the strengths and the weaknesses of *The Thanatos Syndrome* owe far more to *Lost in the Cosmos* than to *Love in the Ruins*: the satirizing of contemporary absurdities (inauthenticity in some of its craziest manifestations) and, unfortunately, the hardening of that spiritual need, which characterizes Will Barrett and Binx Bolling, into religious dogma. What was a translation of Christian belief into psychological, cultural, and semiotic terms inthe earlier novels has begun to sound here like a propounding of conservative Catholic teachings, which undermines a novel that otherwise effectively mixes Sir Thomas More's 1516 *Utopia*, medieval romance, Dostoevski, and Robin Cook.

The novel picks up the life and times of Tom More in the mid-1990's, a short while after his release from federal prison, where he has served a two-year term for illegally selling drugs. A brilliant diagnostician, More describes himself as "a psyche-iatrist, an old-fashioned physician of the soul" who believes that it is better, psychologically and spiritually speaking, to be sick (anxious, even terrified) than well, for disease is the natural state of the prelapsarian human being. Many of the people around him are, he realizes, anything but anxious. They are, instead, content: without inhibitions, without anxiety, without anything more than rudimentary language skills, and, most important, without a sense of self. With the help of his epidemiologist cousin Lucy Lipscomb, More discovers Blue Boy, a clandestinely funded pilot project that involves introducing heavy sodium into the local water supply in order to stem the tide of social deterioration (crime, teenage pregnancy, even acquired immunodeficiency syndrome).

The ironically "graceful" Bob Comeaux (née Robert D'Angelo Como), who calls Blue Boy "our Manhattan Project," is the director of Blue Boy and indeed of the entire "Fedville" complex (including an Equalitarian Center with facilities for "pedeuthanasia" and "gereuthanasia" and a propensity for obfuscating acronyms). He tries to cajole, seduce, bribe, and threaten More into complicity, all to no avail. Although he remains a lapsed Catholic throughout, the doctor nevertheless sides with the enigmatic, certainly depressed, previously alcoholic, perhaps mad Father Simon (as in Simeon Stylites and Simon Peter) Smith. Father Simon spends all of his time in a fire tower silently triangulating the positions of forest fires, atoning for his sins, and, on one notable occasion, claiming that all tenderness inevitably leads to the gas

chamber (or to the Equalitarian Center, which may be the same thing in a different, more socially acceptable, guise). Comeaux would make everyone happy, at the cost of his or her freedom as well as awareness of him- or herself as a distinctly human being: a creature caught in the malaise, lost in the cosmos, in need of something other than heavy sodium or self-help.

As in Saul Bellow's *The Dean's December* (1982), *The Thanatos Syndrome* expresses More's faith (in there being "more" than Comeaux allows) in the form of a doubt concerning the modern belief that the causes and cures of humankind's problems are invariably physical. To the extent that *The Thanatos Syndrome* articulates this doubt, it, like Percy's other novels, succeeds extraordinarily well. To the extent that it propounds Catholic dogma in response to a host of topical issues (abortion, quality of life, sexual freedom, child abuse, bio- and behavioral engineering, among others), it fails according to the very terms that Percy himself adopted at the time of his conversion, turning the triadic mystery of Kierkegaard's apostle into dyadic pronouncement, sign into signal, and spiritual predicament into position paper.

Robert A. Morace

OTHER MAJOR WORKS

NONFICTION: *The Message in the Bottle*, 1975; *Lost in the Cosmos: The Last Self-Help Book*, 1983; *Conversations with Walker Percy*, 1985 (Lewis A. Lawson and Victor A. Kramer, editors); *The State of the Novel: Dying Art or New Science?*, 1987; *Signposts in a Strange Land*, 1991 (Patrick Samway, editor); *More Conversations with Walker Percy*, 1993 (Lawson and Kramer, editors); *A Thief of Peirce: The Letters of Kenneth Laine Ketner and Walker Percy*, 1995 (Samway, editor); *The Correspondence of Shelby Foote and Walker Percy*, 1997 (Jay Tolson, editor).

BIBLIOGRAPHY

Allen, William Rodney. *Walker Percy: A Southern Wayfarer*. Jackson: University Press of Mississippi, 1986. Allen reads Percy as a distinctly American, particularly Southern writer, claiming that the formative event in Percy's life was his father's suicide, not his reading of existentialist writers or conversion to Roman Catholicism.

Coles, Robert. *Walker Percy: An American Search*. Boston: Little, Brown, 1978. An early but always intelligent and certainly sensitive reading of Percy's novels and essays by a leading psychiatrist whose main contention is that Percy's work speaks directly to modern humanity.

Desmond, John F. *Walker Percy's Search for Community*. Athens: University of Georgia Press, 2004. Desmond examines Percy's six published novels to analyze his concerns about community. Discusses how Percy formed his own ideas about community from the ideas of philosophers and from his Catholic beliefs.

Dupuy, Edward J. *Autobiography in Walker Percy: Repetition, Recovery, and Redemption*. Baton Rouge: Louisiana State University Press, 1996. Discusses Percy's autobiographical novels as psychological fiction. Includes bibliographical references and an index.

Hardy, John Edward. *The Fiction of Walker Percy*. Urbana: University of Illinois Press, 1987. The originality of this book derives from Hardy's choosing to read the novels in terms of internal formal matters rather than, as is usually the case, in terms of Percy's essays, existentialism, Catholicism, or Southern background.

Kobre, Michael. *Walker Percy's Voices*. Athens: University of Georgia Press, 2000. Analyzes Percy's novels from the theoretical perspective of Russian theorist Mikhail Bakhtin. Kobre is especially interested in Percy's characters, who must sort out the conflicting inner voices of friends, therapists, family, and others until they eventually determine their own identities.

Lawson, Lewis A. *Following Percy: Essays on Walker Percy's Work*. Troy, N.Y.: Whitston, 1988. A collection of essays originally published between 1969 and 1984 by one of Percy's most dedicated, prolific, and knowledgeable commentators. Discussions of *The Moviegoer* and *Lancelot* predominate.

Pridgen, Allen. *Walker Percy's Sacramental Landscapes: The Search in the Desert*. Selingsgrove, Pa.: Susquehanna University Press, 2000. An examination of the imagery, themes, and other elements of literary technique in four of Percy's novels—*The Last Gentleman, Love in the Ruins, The Second Coming*, and *The Thanatos Syndrome*.

Quinlan, Kieran. *Walker Percy: The Last Catholic Novelist*. Baton Rouge: Louisiana State University Press, 1996. Features chapters on Percy as novelist and philosopher, existentialist, and explorer of modern science. Recommended for the advanced student who already has some knowledge of the religious themes in Percy's writing. Includes notes and a bibliography.

Samway, Patrick H. *Walker Percy: A Life*. New York: Farrar, Straus and Giroux, 1997. The authorized biography, written with Percy's approval and assistance. Samway portrays Percy, whom he met in a writing program, as a writer of great intellect and passion.

Tolson, Jay. *Pilgrim in the Ruins: A Life of Walker Percy*. New York: Simon & Schuster, 1992. A comprehensive account of Percy's life and work, written with Percy's assistance. Tolson describes how Percy was guided by his religious faith; he maintains that Percy's life was a heroic contrast to that of his ancestors, including his father and grandfather, who committed suicide.

Wyatt-Brown, Bertram. *The Literary Percys: Family History, Gender, and the Southern Imagination*. Athens: University of Georgia Press, 1994. Wyatt-Brown explores Percy within the context of his nineteenth century ancestors, including women, who were writers, and analyzes the melancholy that pervades the family.

RAMÓN PÉREZ DE AYALA

Born: Oviedo, Spain; August 9, 1880
Died: Madrid, Spain; August 5, 1962
Also known as: Ramón Pérez de Ayala y Fernández del Portal

PRINCIPAL LONG FICTION

Tinieblas en las cumbres, 1907
A.M.D.G., 1910
La pata de la raposa, 1912 (*The Fox's Paw*, 1924)
Troteras y danzaderas, 1913
"Prometeo," "Luz de domingo," "La caída de los Limones": Tres novelas poemáticas de la vida española, 1916 (*"Prometheus," "Sunday Sunlight," "The Fall of the House of Limón": Three Poematic Novels of Spanish Life*, 1920)
Belarmino y Apolonio, 1921 (*Belarmino and Apolonio*, 1931)
Luna de miel, luna de hiel and *Los trabajos de Urbano y Simona*, 1923 (combined in *Honeymoon, Bittermoon*, 1972)
Tigre Juan and *El curandero de su honra*, 1926 (combined in *Tiger Juan*, 1933)
Justicia, 1928

OTHER LITERARY FORMS

With the exception of the novel *A.M.D.G.*, the major writings of Ramón Pérez de Ayala (PAY-rayz day ah-YAH-lah) are compiled in the four volumes of his *Obras completas* (1964), edited by J. García Mercadel. Pérez de Ayala's canon shows that he was an author of varied talents and interests. Although he is best known for his novels, Pérez de Ayala began his career with the publication of a volume of poems, *La paz del sendero* (1904; the peace of the path). This was followed by two more poetry collections, *El sendero innumerable* (1916; the path of infinite variations) and *El sendero andante* (1921; the flowing path).

Pérez de Ayala was also a prolific essayist, contributing about one thousand articles to newspapers on topics ranging from literary criticism to politics and travel. Most of these essays were subsequently compiled and published.

ACHIEVEMENTS

Ramón Pérez de Ayala's accomplishments can best be summarized in terms of the attributes of the famed *generación del 1898*, or Generation of '98, of which he is generally considered a member. Like most of the leading writers of this generation, he was active in the political as well as the literary arenas of his time, seeking radical changes in both and hoping to effect a cultural and literary renaissance in Spain. Accordingly, he excelled in writing essays on current political and cultural topics together with novels that had no less a goal than the improvement of the world. In these novels, he was able both to express and to transcend the circumstances of his time and place. Combining an intensely regional viewpoint with universal human concerns, Pérez de Ayala fused invention and philosophy in an artful rendering of reality. His greatest achievements in the novel derive from the classical vision that informs his work, transforming individuals into archetypes, local politics into universal motifs.

It is undoubtedly as a result of this vision that Pérez de Ayala's novels have been translated into English, German, Japanese, Italian, French, Portuguese, and Swedish. Many of them have received a great deal of international critical attention and acclaim, particularly *Belarmino and Apolonio*, widely regarded as his best. Critics of Pérez de Ayala may note that he exposes the fictionality of his characters with the aplomb of Miguel de Unamuno y Jugo, ironically invites the reader to skip "superfluous" sections with no less technical dexterity than Julio Cortázar, and explores the boundary between dream and reality with the eloquence of Jorge Luis Borges. Pérez de Ayala received considerable recognition during his lifetime. He was awarded the Spanish National Prize for Literature for *Tiger Juan* in 1926, was elected to the Royal Spanish Academy in 1928, and was spoken of in that same year as a candidate for the Nobel Prize.

BIOGRAPHY

Ramón Pérez de Ayala y Fernández del Portal was born on August 9, 1880, in Oviedo, a major city of the mountainous Asturian region in the northwest of Spain—a region whose natural beauty would later find lyric expression in his novels. At the age of eight, he was sent to the Jesuit school of San Zoilo in nearby Carrión de los Condes. After studying there for two years, he went on to finish his baccalaureate at the Jesuit Colegio de la Inmaculada in Gijón, where he remained until the age of fourteen. His studies under the Jesuits, particularly in Greek, Latin, and the classics, gave him the basis of a sound humanistic education.

On the other hand, Pérez de Ayala would always consider the rigors of the Jesuit system of education to have done permanent damage to his sensitive nature. His second novel, *A.M.D.G.*, whose title is taken from the Jesuit motto, "ad majorem dei gloriam" (to the greater glory of God), is bitterly critical of that early educational experience. The author later described himself as having possessed an inquisitive and discontented nature—thus earning the nickname the Anarchist.

After four years at the Jesuit school in Gijón, Pérez de Ayala returned to Oviedo to study law at the university under what was at that time a highly distinguished faculty. After finishing his courses in law, he traveled to England, where he wrote, read, and dabbled in painting. His sojourn was interrupted by the suicide of his father following the collapse of the bank in which his money was invested. It may have been as a result of this family tragedy that Pérez de Ayala decided to become a professional writer. At any rate, he moved to Madrid intending to study for a doctorate in law at the university, and there he became acquainted with the major literary figures of his time. In 1903, he helped found the journal *Helios* and went on to collaborate in many of the leading periodicals of the epoch. He published his first book of poetry, *La paz del sendero*, in 1904 and his first novel, *Tinieblas en las cumbres* (darkness on the heights), shortly thereafter. In 1911, he obtained a grant to study art in Germany and Italy. It was in Italy that he met the American Mabel Rick; in 1913, they were married in the United States. By this time, he had written his four autobiographical novels and was about to enter what he himself later called a "transitional phase" in his life and narrative.

During this transitional period, Pérez de Ayala replaced personal themes with political ones, prompted by the outbreak of World War I as well as by his increasing involvement in Spanish politics. He visited the Italian front as a war correspondent and in 1917 published a collection of essays, *Hermann, encadenado* (Hermann, enchained), based on those experiences. In general, the many essays Pérez de Ayala wrote between 1913 and 1919 represent an attempt to gain a philosophical perspective on human history. His novels *Prometheus, Sunday Sunlight*, and *The Fall of the House of Limón* belong to this phase of his career. Between 1919 and 1920, Pérez de Ayala again traveled in the United States, sending articles to newspapers in Madrid.

The third period of Pérez de Ayala's career as a novelist stretched from 1921 until 1926, and it was during those years that he wrote his three major novels. His last full-length novel, *Tiger Juan*, received the National Prize for Literature in 1926. In 1928, Pérez de Ayala published his last known work of fiction, the short novel *Justicia*; in the remaining thirty-four years of his life, he published no more fiction. This prolonged silence continues to puzzle critics and biographers, who attribute it in part to Pérez de Ayala's disillusionment over the Spanish Civil War and the fall of the Second Spanish Republic, an ideal for which he and many of his literary colleagues had worked. Pérez de Ayala served the Republic as ambassador to London from 1931 until his resignation in 1936, upon the outbreak of the civil war.

Pérez de Ayala then spent the war years, 1936 to 1939, abroad, and during the next fifteen years, he would return to Madrid only for brief visits, taking up residence in France, Lima, and Buenos Aires and continuing to publish newspaper articles on a variety of topics. After his final return to Madrid in 1954, he lived a quiet and private life, receiving a few friends, reading classical literature, and publishing occasional articles on cultural topics in a Madrid paper. By the time of his death on August 5, 1962, he had been virtually forgotten by the literary world.

ANALYSIS

Ramón Pérez de Ayala's novels can be divided into three categories: the four interrelated autobiographical novels (*Tinieblas en las cumbres, A.M.D.G., The Fox's*

Paw, and *Troteras y danzaderas*), the transitional novels of Spanish life (*Prometheus*, *Sunday Sunlight*, and *The Fall of the House of Limón*), and the mature works that focus on major themes (*Belarmino and Apolonio*, *Honeymoon*, *Bittermoon*, and *Tiger Juan*). Despite the author's development between the composition of his early novels and that of his later ones, several features remain constant: the tragic sense of life and the humanistic spirit that inform his work, the classical vision that conceives of the universe as an ultimately harmonious confluence of antitheses, and the narrative techniques that are necessary for expressing the complexity of such a worldview.

Pérez de Ayala's novels reflect the various influences that were brought to bear on them. At the basis of his vision is the excellent foundation he had in the classics of Greek and Latin literature. His novels abound in allusions to classical heroes and mythological figures, and he often gives their names ironically to rural characters singularly devoid of grace. More important, however, is his classical conception of the universe as an assemblage of warring elements. Individuals, from their limited perspectives, can discern only the discontinuity of the parts rather than the harmony of the whole. Because the perception of cosmic unity is beyond the grasp of the rational mind, the happy coexistence of contradictory truths may approach expression only in aesthetic orders. Thus, the task of the novelist is to challenge constantly the partial truths that constitute the individual perspective and open them up to new vistas.

Pérez de Ayala's technique is, on the whole, Jamesian. It serves his belief in a multifaceted reality and his advocacy for the virtue of tolerance. By providing multiple points of reference and juxtaposing conflicting opinions, Pérez de Ayala reminds readers of the inadequacy of the individual perspective and of the necessity to expand the mind to encompass alternative realities. In *Troteras y danzaderas* (mummers and dancers), a spokesman for the author insists that all so-called golden ages have been social states brought about by a few conspicuous thinkers who believed in the compatibility of intelligence and strength, art and money, science and religion, philosophy and arms. By way of encouraging such marriages, Pérez de Ayala constantly reminds his readers that what they perceive as truth is merely one side of a coin. For example, in the prologue to the stories of *El ombligo del mundo* (1924; the umbilical center of the world), the narrator explains that everything that happens in the world is equally a cause for laughter and tears. The comic and the dramatic, he asserts, depend on one's perspective. Pérez de Ayala's own worldview as presented in the novels is tragicomic.

Pérez de Ayala's literary friends and associates, among them many prominent members of the Generation of '98, had a hand in shaping his views on art and life. Among his acquaintances were Antonio Machado, Ramón María del Valle-Inclán, Miguel de Unamuno y Jugo, José Ortega y Gasset, and the Nicaraguan poet Rubén Darío. An outspoken admirer of Darío's poetry, Pérez de Ayala appears to have been affected by his sense of the burden of consciousness. Pérez de Ayala's early novels bring to mind lines from Darío's well-known poem "Lo fatal" ("Fatality"): "For there is no greater grief than the grief of being alive/ No greater affliction than conscious life."

Unamuno's basically existentialist philosophy and his "tragic sense of life" also exerted an undeniable influence on Pérez de Ayala, whose humanism, like Unamuno's, arose from his knowledge of pain and his sympathy for the suffering that is the lot of all people. These feelings were no doubt intensified by the historical events of the period: the two world wars, the Spanish Civil War, and the Spanish-American War. Particularly in his later works, Pérez de Ayala deplores the shortsightedness that makes adversaries of people. His response to the events of his time took the form of a comprehensive humanism and desire for social reform—much the same spirit expressed in Ortega y Gasset's famous statement in *Meditaciones del Quixote* (1942; *Meditations on Quixote*, 1961): "I am I and my circumstance, and if I do not save it, I do not save myself."

TINIEBLAS EN LAS CUMBRES

Pérez de Ayala's first novel, *Tinieblas en las cumbres*, is a fitting introduction to his canon. It is the story of a young artist, Alberto Díaz de Guzmán, resembling Pérez de Ayala himself, who makes a trip to a mountain summit with a group of friends and prostitutes to witness a solar eclipse. Nearing the summit, they are enveloped in a dense fog; this fog becomes a symbol for the crisis in consciousness that Alberto is about to experience and is thus a precursor of the mist of Unamuno's novel *Niebla*

(1914; *Mist*, 1929). As Alberto approaches the peak, he engages in a colloquy with an intellectual friend, a discussion that leaves him questioning the meaning of existence. His friend, Yiddy, demolishes his romantic illusions concerning the transcendent value of the natural world and the immortality of art, and also informs him that consciousness is a nervous phenomenon.

This conversation is typical of Pérez de Ayala in its presentation of radically opposing viewpoints and metaphysical speculations that digress from the action of the novel. Also typical is the author's statement at the beginning of the "digression" that the reader may skip this "superfluous colloquy" if he or she desires. This section, rather than being expendable, contains the key to the novel. A person's unique ability to contemplate his or her own death forms the basis of the "tragic sense of life," as defined by Unamuno. A corresponding alienation from nature is a logical consequence of this awareness of impending death. Alberto's question at the end of *Tinieblas en las cumbres* is how one should live in the face of such understanding. He seems to decide in favor of hedonism, a decision that is followed by intimations of the Apocalypse. It has been suggested throughout the expedition that this solar phenomenon might signal the end of the world. Certainly, for Alberto it means the end of innocence as he feels a permanent darkness engulfing his soul. Deciding to embrace momentary pleasures, he proceeds to drink his way home and falls unconscious in his room as the novel closes.

Tinieblas en las cumbres is interesting as a first novel in that Pérez de Ayala begins his narrative career by exploring the existential void of a man overwhelmed by the reality of death. Unlike certain bildungsromans, such as D. H. Lawrence's *Sons and Lovers* (1913), in which the character is formed by his experiences of life and becomes the author of his own existence, this novel sees the character-artist stripped of his certainties and left half-dead. It was, for Pérez de Ayala, a fit beginning. In fact, his art—his humanism and his search for meaning—grew out of such an existential necessity, but before he was able to develop completely the comprehensive philosophy that shaped his later novels, he pursued the causes and effects of Alberto's mental state in the three autobiographical works that followed *Tinieblas en las cumbres*.

A.M.D.G.

Pérez de Ayala's second novel, *A.M.D.G.*, continues the story of Alberto Díaz de Guzmán by flashing back to his education (based on the author's own) in a Jesuit school, which is presumably at the root of his spiritual dilemma. The novel itself created a scandal upon its publication because of its shocking, and perhaps overstated, portrayal of the cruelty and hypocrisy of the Jesuits' methods of educating the young. Artistically, it is a failure, but it reveals both the best and the worst aspects of Pérez de Ayala's work.

Pérez de Ayala's novels being typically novels of ideas, the essayist is never far from the surface. Occasionally, the proper balance is not observed and the message becomes obtrusive. *A.M.D.G.* is an impassioned criticism somewhat lacking in the aesthetic detachment and spirit of tolerance that characterize Pérez de Ayala's best novels, yet the motivation behind it, to expose and thereby correct injustice, is also characteristic of his best work. Ortega y Gasset praised the novel for that very reason. Having had similar experiences with the Jesuits, he claimed that the novel transcended literature and was a valuable document for pedagogical reform. Pérez de Ayala never forgot his case against the Jesuits, but he did gain greater artistic control over it. Representatives of the order appear in unflattering contexts in his later fiction, and many of their basic principles, such as the separation of body and spirit, are severely criticized.

THE FOX'S PAW

The Fox's Paw resumes the story of Alberto Díaz de Guzmán at the point where *Tinieblas en las cumbres* concluded. The title is a reference to the fox's strategy of biting off its own paw when caught in a trap. Alberto wakes the morning after the eclipse feeling trapped by the conditions of life. Existence, he feels, is a flame between two shadows. Thus begins his search for meaning. Throughout the novel, Alberto vacillates between the desires of the flesh and the possibility of artistic commitment. Whenever he finds himself lured into demeaning emotional or physical involvements, he longs for the detachment from life that art affords. Life, he finds, enslaves the man, but the artist controls life. There is one possibility available to him for incorporating the real and the ideal, the flesh and the spirit. This is in the love offered him by his fiancé Fina—a love he has not the wisdom to accept nor the will to pursue.

Alberto, it is clear, has not made much progress since his setback on the mountaintop in *Tinieblas en las cumbres*. In fact, he seems to be moving in reverse. In the course of the novel, and in the process of trying to find himself, he joins a circus, travels to England, lives in Madrid writing books, and goes bankrupt. At his best moments, he is able to feel himself part of a cosmos that is harmonious and all-encompassing. He is never able to sustain that feeling; hence, he wanders. At the conclusion of the novel, he decides to return once again to Fina, but as a punishment for his moral failure, he is told by her furious old aunt that she is dead and that his desertion killed her. Pérez de Ayala's later novels show the main characters achieving the wholeness that eludes Alberto here. This novel, however, like *Tinieblas en las cumbres*, ends in a void. The last novel in the series, *Troteras y danzaderas*, fittingly descends with Alberto into the underworld of the Madrid literati and accounts for a gap in the chronology of *The Fox's Paw*.

TROTERAS Y DANZADERAS

Something of a departure from the other autobiographical novels, *Troteras y danzaderas* shifts its focus from Alberto in order to portray several of the literary figures with whom Pérez de Ayala associated in Madrid, among them Valle-Inclán and Ortega y Gasset. An involved, intelligent, ambitious, and finally an ungainly novel, it is interesting from the viewpoint of literary history and also for the insights into human nature and the lectures on art that the author delivers through Alberto, who in this work has become more of a mouthpiece than a character.

Nevertheless, the novel does not lack for characters; it contains innumerable starving artists, politicians, prostitutes, and related entertainers. Ultimately, it is a novel about people of mainly mediocre talents living a bohemian existence that has been divested of the innocence of Bohemia. The nadir of this Madrid underworld is an expedition Alberto and some friends make to the brothels, with each successive visit more horrifying than the last. The novel ends with the death of one tubercular artist, a discussion of politics, and Alberto's ironic response when asked what Spain has produced: "Mummers and dancers, my friend, mummers and dancers."

If, on the whole, this work appears to be a collection of loosely related episodes, many of its parts are excellent. One particularly noteworthy feature is the author's experimentation with multiple narrative perspectives. In one instance, Pérez de Ayala calls particular attention to his perspectivism: He describes a comic situation in which a "kept woman" is surprised by her keeper in a tête-à-tête with a poet, providing in separate paragraphs an account of the incident from the perspectives of the three principals in addition to that of a baby who happens to be in the room. He then laments the fact that no one knows the viewpoint of the pet turtle. More seriously, he later describes the dying poet from the perspectives of both sympathetic and unsympathetic observers. His mature works show a mastery of this technique and of the philosophy of tolerance and the necessary coexistence of opposites that underlies it.

Alberto's statement at the conclusion of *Troteras y danzaderas* provides an appropriate introduction to the novels belonging to this transitional phase of Pérez de Ayala's career. It concludes the autobiographical series with a shift of focus from individual concerns to national ones and indicates the overwhelming pessimism of Pérez de Ayala's political sentiments at that time.

PROMETHEUS

Strikingly unlike any of his other novels, the three-poematic novels of Spanish life are tales of failure and utter despair, related in a highly lyric style. *Prometheus*, the first of these short novels, begins with a humorous adaptation of Homer's *Odyssey* (c. 800 B.C.E.). Juan Pérez Setignano, who prefers to think of himself as Marco de Setiñano, is a modern-day Odysseus and a professor of Greek. A man of thought, like the author himself, he dreams of begetting a son who will be a man of action. He will call the son Prometheus, and Prometheus will redeem humankind. Juan sets out seeking a mother for Prometheus. He finds and marries his Nausicaa, who is called Perpetua Meana. The son is born precocious but deformed and malicious, and at the end of the novel, he hangs himself from a fig tree. The story appears to be an allegory of Pérez de Ayala's own desires—to engender from his art a corresponding action in the world—and a measure of his feelings of failure. A comment made by Juan's uncle confirms this reading. He wisely tells Juan that Prometheus is born of men yearning to soar and vanquished by their aspirations.

The other two works are somewhat less allegorical, referring as they do to existing political and social conditions.

SUNDAY SUNLIGHT

Sunday Sunlight, despite its promising title, is a tale of injustice. It takes place in a town controlled by a large family of aristocratic bosses, the Becerriles, whose power comes from Madrid. The Chorizos, an opposing faction of workmen and merchants, are fighting for power in the town. The hero, Cástor, is caught in the middle. When he refuses to support the Becerriles, a group of them take turns raping his fiancé in what is probably the cruelest scene in any of Pérez de Ayala's novels. Cástor tells her she is still innocent and marries her, but the stigma remains. By this point, the fault is not only with the Becerriles but also with the society that punishes the victim rather than the perpetrator of the crime. Cástor, of course, represents the only humane attitude. Wherever the couple go, they are unable to escape the gossip that follows them. Even on a boat bound for the New World, they meet with people who know their story and tell them that the Chorizos, now in power, are even worse than the Becerriles. While in Pérez de Ayala's later fiction a merging of polarities will generally be cause for optimism, here it can only mean despair. Thus, when the ship sinks, Cástor and his wife are grateful to go to a land where there are neither Becerriles nor Chorizos.

THE FALL OF THE HOUSE OF LIMÓN

The third novel, *The Fall of the House of Limón*, combines the themes of defective offspring, political oppression, and human pettiness of the other two. It begins in a Spanish boardinghouse, a favorite setting and topic for Pérez de Ayala. Two sisters, Dominica and Fernanda Limón, arrive and arrange to have mourning garments made for the following day. The narration then flashes back to the history of the family, their father's establishment of a political empire and his gradual transfer of power to Fernanda. The other daughter, Dominica, and the future heir, Arias, grow up in the rear of the family residence. They are left to themselves in this childhood kingdom. The boy, while not physically deformed, matures in a fantasy world that leaves him morally blemished and unable to distinguish fact from fiction. Neither

Arias nor Dominica realizes that the town is beginning to rebel against the dominion of the Limóns. It is Arias who precipitates their downfall by raping and killing a young woman without quite grasping the reality of his act.

If justice is conspicuously absent in *Sunday Sunlight*, here the entire concept is called into question by Arias's execution, a punishment as cruel as the crime. Morever, the smug pronouncement of the boardinghouse residents that justice has been done is deeply disturbing. Prompted by their sense of moral superiority, they proceed to insist, within hearing of the sisters, that Fernanda should have been hanged as well. As with *Sunday Sunlight*, readers are initially convinced that the evil resides in the political bosses, but Pérez de Ayala's perspective is never that simple. Another framework reveals that the cruelty and pettiness so pervasive in these two stories are a function of human nature, a view that may have been the real reason the author felt the world was not ready for his Promethean redeemer.

In his three major novels, Pérez de Ayala uses the same themes and narrative techniques found in his previous fiction. Here, though, he puts aside disillusionment and existential anxiety to present a vision of wholeness at once optimistic and tenuous. In these works, he strikes what is for his purposes a perfect balance between fiction and essay. All three hinge upon a philosophical premise. At the same time, the author develops characters that are not mere vehicles of the novel's message but are uniquely believable and sympathetic. These novels, particularly *Belarmino and Apolonio*, show Pérez de Ayala to be in full control of his perspectivist technique and the accompanying philosophy of mutually beneficial oppositions. Even while urging his own humanistic position, he uses the novels as forums for antagonistic points of view, in keeping with his insistence that all beliefs are valid, although some are less informed than others.

HONEYMOON, BITTERMOON

Honeymoon, Bittermoon is primarily a novel about male-female relationships and human sexuality. It focuses on two characters, Urbano and Simona, who marry without any knowledge of sex, even the most basic. Urbano's mother, Doña Micaela, is a sterile, domineering, and rigidly spiritual woman; she recalls D. H. Lawrence's cerebral and castrating females who will not give themselves over to sensuality. In fact, Pérez de Ayala's novel, like those of Lawrence, his contemporary, has as its goal the exposure of the folly of the prevailing sexual attitudes of the time. Here, however, they are the unique product of Spanish Catholicism.

Doña Micaela has overseen her son's education, even in his law courses, to the point of making certain that questionable pages have been torn from his books. At the end of this education, he is totally ignorant of the world, and his mother engages him to a young lady who is equally innocent. Urbano's father does not agree with his wife's actions, and their dispute constitutes one of Pérez de Ayala's famous polemics. The ensuing events attest Doña Michaela's error. Urbano, not knowing what is expected of him, leaves his wife on their honeymoon without consummating the marriage. Yet, Simona believes she is pregnant. For either lack of information or extreme modesty, no one is able to acquaint the pair with the facts of life. They are left to weather a series of catastrophes and separations until they gain enough knowledge of the world to be reunited.

The novel also considers some peripheral sexual relationships and attitudes, all highly unusual. Urbano's tutor, for example, is redeemed from his sexual ignorance and lack of practical knowledge by a servant, one of the healthiest characters in the novel. Another character is not so lucky. He is in his fifties and has been engaged for thirty-five years because his mother thinks he is too young to marry. All in all, the novel is Pérez de Ayala's perceptive analysis of the sexual foibles of his society and an argument for a reasonable, and humane, sex education.

In *Honeymoon, Bittermoon*, harmony hinges on the successful reconciliation of female and male, mind and matter. Most of the novel's characters are grotesques, unable to fuse with their counterparts or join flesh to spirit.

TIGER JUAN

The union of male and female sensibilities also supplies the theme of *Tiger Juan*, which surveys the related topics of matrimonial honor and "Don Juanism" in the context of Spanish cultural history. Tiger Juan, the protagonist, is a misogynist. Females are altogether alien to his fiercely masculine, and egotistical, nature. Based on past experience, he links them with extramarital activities and the resulting dishonor to the unlucky hus-

band. His perspective is, of course, limited, and the novel chronicles its growth. Initially, Juan esteems one woman only: Doña Iluminada, in whose widowhood he perceives complete faithfulness to her dead husband. He is unaware that she had, inexplicably and unwillingly, remained a virgin throughout her marriage.

Doña Iluminada is one of those bountiful virgins so prevalent in Pérez de Ayala's novels who, denied happiness for themselves, contrive to unite others. At the opposite extreme, Tiger Juan's male friend, Don Vespasiano, represents the Don Juan figure who, despite his apparent sexual activity, is barren. Tiger Juan's inordinate affection for this man derives from his notion that the Don Juan type is the scourge of womankind and an avenger of Eve's curse. Tiger Juan regularly argues with his son, Colás (a "child of air," as Tiger Juan is "salt of the earth"), about Don Juanism and about a husband's right to kill an unfaithful wife. Colás's ample and humane perspective is counterposed to Tiger Juan's selfishly narrow one. Tiger Juan receives an opportunity to broaden his views when he falls reluctantly in love with a young woman, Herminia. Repulsed by his bestial demeanor, Herminia is assured by Doña Iluminada that what she feels is the irresistible attraction of her opposite. When Herminia and Juan become engaged, without her ever having the opportunity to refuse, Juan anticipates marital disgrace. To ward it off, he gives Herminia a bracelet engraved with the words "I belong to Tiger Juan." For the occasion of their wedding, he buys her shoes several sizes too small—in emulation, the narrator explains, of the estimable Asian practice of footbinding. Pérez de Ayala is at his tragicomic best in his portrayal of Tiger Juan; the reader wishes at once to cry for Juan's ignorance and laugh at his folly.

Tiger Juan's expectation of dishonor is nearly self-fulfilling. Rebelling against Juan and the society that demands her domination by him, Herminia escapes with Vespasiano; she loses the desire to be unfaithful, however, when she realizes that she is pregnant by Tiger Juan, her ideal counterpart. She returns home, and Tiger Juan has a corresponding change of heart. Instead of killing her for the blemish to his honor her desertion has caused, he opens a vein in his own arm. As proof that he has incorporated the feminine principle into his fierce male nature, when the baby comes, Juan howls in pain while Herminia preserves stoic silence. Later, he takes on the mother's role by bottle-feeding the baby. As is so often the case in Pérez de Ayala's fiction, while the individual perspective has been amplified, the society remains small-minded. The end of *Tiger Juan* finds Juan and Herminia leaving their home to escape the censure of their neighbors.

Tiger Juan, like *Honeymoon, Bittermoon*, concludes with the merging of the antithetical qualities necessary to human happiness: spirit and flesh, femininity and masculinity, self and other. In order to show the confluence of these polarities, Pérez de Ayala expands upon his usual perspectivist technique and juxtaposes the radically different forms of consciousness represented by Herminia and Juan. When Herminia deserts Juan, the author records their separate thoughts and experiences in adjacent vertical columns. Trapped by their subjectivity, the characters do not have the perceptual advantage of the reader, who recognizes the harmony between the opposing columns even before they flow together in reconciliation.

A related innovation that Pérez de Ayala had gradually developed throughout his fiction reached fullness of expression here: his open declaration of the fiction of his constructs. This exposure of artifice serves his perspectivism by opening the hermetically sealed work into a larger context: the world. He admits his fabrication in the "Parergon," or accessory document, attached to the story's conclusion. Noting that the careful reader will have detected a gap in the narrative, the author explains that his "characters" were at that time discussing their warring emotions. Not wanting to distract the normal reader from the plot, he decided to append those dialogues. As usual, these "superfluous" debates present the philosophical basis of the novel, affirming as they do that truth is the sum of individual perspectives.

BELARMINO AND APOLONIO

Pérez de Ayala's perspectivism and his "diaphenomenal vision" reach a brilliant culmination in *Belarmino and Apolonio*. The novel has a bipolar structure and theme, as announced in the title, that derives from the conflict between two shoemakers: the dramatist Apolonio and the philosopher Belarmino. Their rivalry begins quite simply when Apolonio establishes his business on the same street as Belarmino's and they become competitors. Apolonio, although he quickly helps put Belarmino out of business, recognizes in his rival certain qualities that he does not possess, and he feels an instant antipathy that he assumes is mutual. There are many points of contrast between them, but the main conflict is that between philosophy and drama. As a philosopher, Belarmino invents his own language and eventually, when tragedy befalls him, lapses into silence. The everloquacious Apolonio borrows his language from tradition and is unable to refrain from speaking in verse. He converts tragedy to words, exploiting experience in the creation of dramas. Desiring fame, Apolonio produces a play that is a failure; Belarmino, without desiring it, becomes a prominent community figure because of his philosophizing. In fact, the town divides into two factions, Belarmines and anti-Belarmines, arguing whether he actually speaks a comprehensible language.

The dispute between Apolonio and Belarmino leads to a secondary bifurcation when Apolonio prevents the marriage of his son and Belarmino's daughter. The son then develops into a gregarious, hypocritical priest, while the disgraced daughter becomes an innocent, introspective prostitute—in yet another of the novel's unusual dichotomies. The narrator intercedes to reunite priest and prostitute, and when news of this event comes to Apolonio and Belarmino, now in a rest home, they embrace and speak to each other for the first time, admitting their mutual need.

These are but a few of the many schisms and reconciliations that make up the world of the novel. The conceptual and structural frame of the work is provided by two opposing points of view on the relationship between Belarmino and Apolonio, or drama and philosophy. The prologue records the musings of Don Amaranto, a boardinghouse philosopher, who believes that the dramatist immerses himself in experience while the philosopher removes himself to attain a better vantage point. The epilogue quotes from the notes of Froilán Escobar, who reverses these poles. He maintains that the dramatist acts out his life in borrowed gestures while the philosopher conceals his emotions with a cool exterior. Both opinions are correct, but in the context of the story, the latter is more informed. More important, these thinkers, like the narrator, affirm that philosopher and dramatist need each other.

On this level, the novel's theme and technique coalesce. While Pérez de Ayala generally combines philosophy and drama in his fiction, in *Belarmino and Apolonio*, he engages both with the object of illustrating their interdependence. At the same time, he juxtaposes conflicting opinions and perspectives on events to demonstrate the relativity of knowledge. The second chapter of the novel, another of those essential digressions that Pérez de Ayala labels "superfluous," contains a discussion of perspective and artistic creation. It begins with Don Amaranto's ghost confronting the narrator with a disquisition on the limits of narration. The apparition insists that because the novel unfolds in time, it is unable to match the human visual apparatus, which sees in depth. The narrator responds with an exercise in point of view and narrative dexterity. He relates an anecdote about a poet, Lirio, and a positivist, Lario, viewing the street where Belarmino and Apolonio lived. In an involved dispute typical of Pérez de Ayala, Lirio insists on the absurd beauty of the street while Lario finds it ugly for its lack of symmetry. The debate concludes when Lirio shows Lario his painting of the street. Lario replies that the street is ugly but the painting is beautiful.

In *Belarmino and Apolonio*, Pérez de Ayala achieved an ideal balance between the fictional and empirical narrative modes that characterize his novels while making that balance the very subject of the work. As a measure of his success, when the narrator states in the epilogue that Belarmino and Apolonio have existed only as his creations but that he has loved them, the reader does not doubt it. Even as symbols of antithetical elements of artistic creation, they are uniquely real and lovable. Through their story, the author demonstrates once again that "there are as many irreducible truths as there are points of view."

Barbara L. Hussey

OTHER MAJOR WORKS

SHORT FICTION: *Bajo el signo de Artemisa*, 1924; *El ombligo del mundo*, 1924.

POETRY: *La paz del sendero*, 1904; *El sendero innumerable*, 1916; *El sendero andante*, 1921.

NONFICTION: *Hermann, encadenado*, 1917; *Las máscaras*, 1917-1919 (2 volumes); *Política y toros*, 1918; *Divagaciones literarias*, 1958; *El país del futuro: Mis viajes a los Estados Unidos*, 1959; *Más divagaciones literarias*, 1960; *Amistades y recuerdos*, 1961; *Pequeños ensayos*, 1963; *Tributo a Inglaterra*, 1963; *Escritos políticos*, 1967.

MISCELLANEOUS: *Obras completas*, 1964 (4 volumes; J. García Mercadel, editor).

BIBLIOGRAPHY

Best, Marigold. *Ramón Pérez de Ayala: An Annotated Bibliography of Criticism*. London: Grant & Cutler, 1980. A dated but useful resource for finding critical analyses of Pérez de Ayala's work. Includes indexes.

Johnson, Roberta. "From the Generation of 1898 to the Vanguard." In *The Cambridge Companion to the Spanish Novel: From 1600 to the Present*, edited by Harriet Turner and Adelaida López de Martínez. New York: Cambridge University Press, 2003. Johnson includes a discussion of several of Pérez de Ayala's novels in her analysis of Spanish literature in the early years of the twentieth century.

Longhurst, C. A. "Modernist Narrative in the 1920's." In *The Cambridge History of Spanish Literature*, edited by David T. Gies. New York: Cambridge University Press, 2004. The novels of Pérez de Ayala are among the works examined in Longhurst's discussion of modernist literature; this article places Pérez de Ayala within the broader context of Spanish literary history.

Macklin, John. "Constructing the '98: Peréz de Ayala's 1942 Prologue to *Troteras y danzaderas*." In *Spain's 1898 Crisis: Regenerationism, Modernism, Post-Colonialism*, edited by Joseph Harrison and Alan Hoyle. New York: Manchester University Press, 2000. In 1898, Spain was defeated in the Spanish American War, a loss that marked the end of the Spanish Empire and led to a national identity crisis. Macklin's essay discusses Peréz de Ayala's fictional response to that crisis.

_____. *The Window and the Garden: The Modernist Fictions of Ramón Pérez de Ayala*. Boulder, Colo.: Society of Spanish and Spanish-American Studies, 1988. A thorough study of Pérez de Ayala's work, relating it to both realistic and modernistic fiction. The text is primarily in English, but some of the quotations are in Spanish. Includes a bibliography.

Rand, Marguerite C. *Ramón Pérez de Ayala*. New York:

Twayne, 1971. One of the volumes in the Twayne World Authors series, this book provides a biography as well as analysis of Pérez de Ayala's fiction. Includes a bibliography.

Stock, Margaret Pol. *Dualism and Polarity in the Novels of Ramón Pérez de Ayala*. London: Tamesis Books, 1988. Stock focuses on the use of paired opposites in Pérez de Ayala's novels, such as spectator versus actor, ideal versus real, and male versus female, and discusses how his work seeks to unify these dualities.

Weber, Frances Wyers. *The Literary Perspectivism of Ramón Pérez de Ayala*. Chapel Hill: University of North Carolina Press, 1966. Weber provides an ideological portrait of Pérez de Ayala and a multifaceted analysis of his writings. Includes lists of his works and bibliographical footnotes.

BENITO PÉREZ GALDÓS

Born: Las Palmas, Canary Islands; May 10, 1843
Died: Madrid, Spain; January 4, 1920

PRINCIPAL LONG FICTION

La fontana de oro, 1868 (*The Golden Fountain Cafe*, 1989)

El audaz, 1871

La sombra, 1871 (*The Shadow*, 1980)

La corte de Carlos IV, 1873 (*The Court of Charles IV: A Romance of the Escorial*, 1888)

Trafalgar, 1873 (English translation, 1884)

Episodios nacionales, 1873-1912 (46 historical novellas written in 5 series, many of which were also published separately and are included in this list)

Gerona, 1874

Zaragoza, 1874 (*Saragossa: A Story of Spanish Valor*, 1899)

La batalla de los Arapiles, 1875 (*The Battle of Salamanca: A Tale of the Napoleonic War*, 1895)

Doña Perfecta, 1876 (English translation, 1880)

Gloria, 1876-1877 (English translation, 1879)

La familia de León Roch, 1878 (*The Family of León Roch*, 1888; also known as *León Roch: A Romance*, 1888)

Marianela, 1878 (English translation, 1883)

La desheredada, 1881 (*The Disinherited Lady*, 1957)

El amigo Manso, 1882 (*Our Friend Manso*, 1987)

El doctor Centeno, 1883

La de Bringas, 1884 (*The Spendthrifts*, 1951; also known as *That Bringas Woman*, 1996)

Tormento, 1884 (*Torment*, 1952)

Lo prohibido, 1884-1885 (*The Forbidden*, 2006)

Fortunata y Jacinta, 1886-1887 (*Fortunata and Jacinta: Two Stories of Married Women*, 1973)

Miau, 1888 (English translation, 1963)

La incógnita, 1889 (*The Unknown*, 1991)

Realidad, 1889 (*Reality*, 1992)

Torquemada en la hoguera, 1889 (*Torquemada in the Flames*, 1956; also known as *Torquemada at the Stake*, 1986)

Ángel Guerra, 1890-1891 (English translation, 1990)

La loca de la casa, 1892

Tristana, 1892 (English translation, 1961)

Torquemada en la cruz, 1893 (*Torquemada's Cross*, 1973; also known as *Torquemada on the Cross*, 1986)

Torquemada en el purgatorio, 1894 (*Torquemada in Purgatory*, 1986)

Halma, 1895

Nazarín, 1895 (English translation, 1993)

Torquemada y San Pedro, 1895 (*Torquemada and Saint Peter*, 1986)

El abuelo, 1897

Misericordia, 1897 (*Compassion*, 1962)

Casandra, 1905

Prim, 1906 (English translation, 1944)

El caballero encantado, 1909

La razón de la sinrazón, 1915

Torquemada, 1986 (collection contains
    Torquemada at the Stake, *Torquemada on the
    Cross*, *Torquemada in Purgatory*, and
    Torquemada and Saint Peter)

OTHER LITERARY FORMS

The work of Benito Pérez Galdós (PAY-rayz gahl-DOHS) in other literary forms can be divided into three groups: twenty-two plays, including six dramatizations of previous novels: *Realidad* (pr., pb. 1892), *La loca de la casa* (pr., pb. 1893), *Gerona* (pr. 1893), *Doña Perfecta* (pr., pb. 1896), *El abuelo* (pr., pb. 1904; *The Grandfather*, 1910), and *Casandra* (pr., pb. 1910); nonfiction works, such as *Discursos académicos* (1897), *Memoranda* (1906), *Fisonomías sociales* (1923), *Arte y crítica* (1923), *Política española* (1923), *Nuestro teatro* (1923), *Cronicón* (1924), *Toledo* (1924), *Viajes y fantasías* (1928), *Memorias* (1930), *Crónica de Madrid* (1933), *Cartas de Pérez Galdós a Mesonero Romanos* (1943), *Crónica de la Quincena* (1948), and *Madrid* (1956); and hundreds of newspaper articles, many unsigned.

ACHIEVEMENTS

The Spanish Romantics of the middle decades of the nineteenth century sought to re-create the local color of the past or the fantasy of exotic surroundings, while the *costumbristas* (regionalists) described the peculiar atmosphere of particular Spanish regions and customs. It remained for the realists of the last part of the century to transcend the picturesque sketches and emotional excesses of their predecessors. The realists directed their attention to the multiplicity and variety of observable reality in an attempt to enhance the verisimilitude of their productions. At first, they concentrated on the surface elements of this multiple panorama, while presenting psychological portraits that displayed only a few dominant and usually harmonious traits.

For more than half a century, the novel had viewed people as conforming to general social patterns, and individual character was seen as constant and without development. A descriptive delineation of a person's dominant motives or reactions to particular situations was the novelist's goal. The change from this strictly social viewpoint to a preoccupation with distinct individuals became possible when people were given the role of persistent striving, when personality itself was seen as subject to psychological and environmental influences. These new novelistic perspectives were partly the result of the rise of the theory of evolution.

Also contributing to the birth of the realistic novel was the development of new ideas concerning society (a rising middle class represented a new sector of reading public that looked for a literature depicting individual citizens amid a recognizable environment), history (seen now in relation to the ordinary person), and science (the growth of which stimulated the desire for more acute observation and documentation). Some critics view the rise of realism in the Spanish novel as a result of the intellectual ferment caused by the Revolution of 1868, which overthrew Queen Isabella II. During this period, writers began to place equal emphasis on plot and environment, with the two elements functioning within a unified, verisimilar whole.

Benito Pérez Galdós belonged to the mature stage of the realistic movement. He rejected the portrayal of static elements of human nature and turned instead to the description of the varying relationships between the individual personality and the environment. Next to Miguel de Cervantes, Pérez Galdós is perhaps the most important novelist that Spain has produced; he is the only Spaniard of his age who can be compared to Honoré de Balzac, Charles Dickens, Leo Tolstoy, or Fyodor Dostoevski. In the course of his long career, he alone succeeded in reconciling the traditional and the liberal ideological currents then prevalent in Spain, demonstrating the significance of both past events and recent developments. In spite of the fact that most of his works were set in Madrid, he alone was able to transcend the regionalism of the Spanish realistic novel. Although his works represent a historical, social, and literary synthesis of his era, he was able to penetrate and develop themes of truly universal significance—ideas concerning charity and spiritual values, problems of modern science and of materialism, the yearning for social justice, the necessity of tolerance and of personal liberty, and the notion of human equality achieved through love.

Pérez Galdós was clearly a realistic writer. His choice of verisimilar subject matter, his convincing psychological portraits, the minimization of overt didacticism (in later novels), his basically objective organizational techniques, and the naturalness, descriptive immediacy, and dialogic emphasis of his style all attest this fact. Yet there are other factors unique to Pérez Galdós that suggest a transcendence of mere nineteenth century realism: symbolic representations, the inclusion of seemingly fantastic elements, and impressionistic descriptions, among others.

This particular combination of realistic and "idealistic" elements was one of the traits that Pérez Galdós seems to have inherited from Cervantes. A basic goodness, a positive, conciliatory spirit, a special kind of ironic humor also came from the master. Like Cervantes, Pérez Galdós was able to penetrate beneath the psychological facades of his characters. He exposed the consistently contradictory nature of human reality, revealing wisdom in the insane, a sense of honor in the humble, charity among beggars, and the anguish for salvation in the person of a miserly moneylender.

Pérez Galdós was also one of the few Spanish writers of his time to recognize the importance and the greatness of contemporary literature of other countries. Indeed, the realistic movement can be said to have developed first and most completely in France with writers such as Balzac, Gustave Flaubert, and Émile Zola. It was Pérez Galdós who first incorporated these foreign elements into a truly Spanish creation.

Above all, Pérez Galdós's realism was a *social* one, centered not on the delineation of regionalistic characters and landscape, not on the psychological investigation of isolated personalities, but rather on the complicated interaction between individual perspectives and aspirations and the social, usually urban milieu within which these viewpoints and desires are expressed. In short, Pérez Galdós's realism was a *human* one, focusing on the physical, psychic, and emotional effects that people have on one another and showing how these elements function within, against, or in line with the pressures of society. With *The Disinherited Lady*, Pérez Galdós recognized that an individual's personal charac-

teristics are partly the result of social and cultural forces; conversely, societies and cultures gain a particular flavor from the individuals who constitute them. He was able to strengthen his picture of both levels (individual and social) by virtue of his perception of their interdependence and interplay.

Yet the individual-society conflict is not merely social or psychological. When the characters suffer from the extreme discrepancy between dream (illusions, romance) and reality, the conflict becomes a metaphysical one, reflecting the Hegelian dialectic implicit in the theories of realism proposed by such critics as Harry Levin, Arnold Hauser, José Ortega y Gasset, and György Lukács. In Pérez Galdós's mature novels, this dialectic operates in the individual's growth toward self-consciousness through his relationships with others, in the conflict between (and eventual integration of) social classes, and in the opposition and interplay of different elements within a character.

In part, the historical importance of Pérez Galdós's novels is that of having united and perfected the prevailing literary tendencies of the times: the interest in history and the past, initiated by the Romantics (whose sentimentality and imaginative excesses he avoided); the didactic or "thesis" approach, offered now without the sacrifice of psychological verisimilitude or artistic balance; and the emphasis on *costumbrismo*, extended from a local, regional level to a broader, national perspective in order to analyze and interpret the life and character of the entire Spanish community. For Pérez Galdós, these three aims were combined toward achieving a constant objective: to help his countryfolk become conscious of their reality as a people, searching in the recent past for the explanation of current conditions, for a sense of direction that would work toward a future ideal of *trabajo y educación* (work and education), an ideal that would encourage an atmosphere of tolerance instead of constant civil strife.

Biography

Benito Pérez Galdós was born in Las Palmas on May 10, 1843, the last of ten children. Some critics believe that his place of birth, geographically and socially separate from the mainstream of Spanish life, contributed to his subsequent ability to view national events with relative candor and objectivity. Benito's father, Sebastián Pérez, sixteen years older than his wife and more a grandfather than a father to his younger children, had inherited sufficient property to maintain his family in comfort and had ample leisure time to regale his youngest offspring with tales of his military exploits, events that were to become part of *Episodios nacionales* (national episodes). However, it was Benito's mother, Doña Dolores, who was to dominate the family. Her rigid, puritanical religiosity, intolerance, strength of will, and constant need for order were to be reflected in several of Pérez Galdós's characters, most particularly Doña Perfecta. From his mother, Pérez Galdós seems to have inherited a Basque physique, stubbornness, and the ability to adhere to an unswerving, ordered routine.

Although interested in painting and music, the young Pérez Galdós found little to enjoy in his childhood schooling, usually appearing bored and absentminded. In 1862, he was sent to Madrid by Doña Dolores to study law, a course that, despite poor grades, irregular class attendance, and extensive extracurricular writing, he finished in 1869. His real interest during these years was the Ateneo, a literary and artistic club in Madrid that housed a remarkably good library and sponsored lectures and discussion groups. Here, Pérez Galdós developed the progressive, liberal spirit that would dominate his first novels, became exposed to the Krausist perspective of tolerance toward opposing views, and discovered the works of such European writers as Balzac, whose eighty volumes he himself collected.

It was during these years that Pérez Galdós began to write for such newspapers as *La nación*, *Las cortes*, and *El debate*. Later, in 1872 and 1873, he himself was the general director of the prestigious *Revista de España*. He traveled widely and in 1866 witnessed the uprising of *los sargentos de San Gil*, a historical event that perhaps stimulated him to initiate the first series of *Episodios nacionales*. The composition of these works, which he undertook in 1873 and continued intermittently until his death, reflected a conception of history as a slow but inevitable development toward the establishment of a just and equitable society, one in which the growing

Benito Pérez Galdós. (Library of Congress)

bourgeoisie would absorb a decadent aristocracy and a well-meaning but ignorant lower class. The series was instantly popular, perhaps because of its stress on the importance of everyday events in the lives of common citizens. At first, the *Episodios nacionales* gave him the economic stability that he needed; later, however, even the resounding financial success of his play *Electra* (pr., pb. 1901; English translation, 1911) was not enough to liquidate the debts that were to plague him sporadically throughout his life.

In 1886, Pérez Galdós entered politics, and in 1889, he accepted the governmentally rigged election results that made him a deputy for Puerto Rico; he served in congress until 1890. While he did little to improve the well-being of his constituents across the ocean, he did subsequently devote considerable energy to liberal causes and eventually expended much of his meager financial resources on republican politics.

It was also in 1889 that Pérez Galdós traveled to the Rhine Valley, where he met and had a brief affair with the Galician novelist Emilia Pardo Bazán. Despite her wish to continue the relationship, however, Pérez Galdós soon broke it off when he became involved with Lorenza Cobián, the woman who was to be the mother of his daughter, María, born January 12, 1891. After Lorenza became insane and committed suicide in 1906, the novelist took charge of María's education and made her his legal beneficiary.

In 1889, Pérez Galdós was elected to the Royal Spanish Academy, but he did not take his seat until 1897. This, says Walter Pattison, was "owing in part to his timidity about making a public speech and perhaps partly to his resentment at having been passed over on the first vote."

In later years, Pérez Galdós served further republican terms in congress—in 1907 and 1910—but his health deteriorated rapidly. To the problem of arteriosclerosis was added a hemiplegic stroke in 1905. Several operations on his eyes were not enough to prevent blindness. These events, coupled with the disdain of the reactionaries and the indifference of the young *generación del 1898*, or Generation of '98, left him bitter and resentful. The failure of his proponents to gain for him the Nobel Prize and the continued financial insecurity that came from his mismanagement of money matters added to the aging novelist's despair. Pérez Galdós had outlived his literary career. When his statue in Madrid's Retiro Park was unveiled in 1919, few prominent figures were present. Death came from uremia on January 4, 1920.

In his prime, Pérez Galdós had been reported as

> tall and somewhat roughhewn in body and features, as if carved of stone. . . . His eyes were small and timid, his face not very expressive, his manner of speaking brief, fragmentary, and low-pitched; in short, he did not give . . . that impression of genius that we imagine in great men.

He was shy, withdrawn, given to stage fright (he refused once to come to a large banquet in his honor, until friends pursued him and brought him back from Toledo). He preferred to listen and observe, rather than talk. Yet on the printed page, he could fight stubbornly and valiantly for his ideals. His outward simplicity was so great, said one friend, "that at times it bordered on commonness." The *generación del 1898* called him *Don Benito el garbancero* (Mister Benito the grocer). Nevertheless, his remarkably exact and detailed descriptions attest his acute observational powers, and his fecundity and creativity amply demonstrate his remarkable imaginative capabilities.

Pérez Galdós was thought to have had few close personal relationships, even within his own family; but his letters have now revealed a profound involvement with his relatives and with a broad circle of intimate acquaintances, all of whom he treated with sensitivity and charity, and with whom he was an entertaining and witty conversationalist. The tender care he offered to Lorenza Cobián and their daughter—another reason for his later impoverishment—reveals that he was indeed a warm and loving person.

Also erroneous is the notion that Pérez Galdós was an obsessive womanizer. It is true that he had an affair with Pardo Bazán, produced an illegitimate daughter with Lorenza, and in his old age nurtured a close relationship with a refined lady named Teodosia Gandarias, but his interest in women was far from licentious or "pathological," as early critics have claimed. Perhaps a desire for individual freedom lay behind his reluctance to marry.

Despite his anticlerical activities and his hatred for the ritual and beliefs of the neo-Catholics, Pérez Galdós developed a deeply spiritual and religious orientation related to a profound love of nature and to a Krausist upbringing that stressed tolerance, everyday ethics, and the basic goodness and harmony of human faculties. This orientation was particularly pronounced during the third phase of his literary career.

ANALYSIS

Through more than fifty years of literary creation, Benito Pérez Galdós's work underwent an evolution, a process of growth that both reflected and harmonized with broader European novelistic movements. In general, these shifts suggest a change from didacticism to more thorough, realistic documentary and later to a kind of symbolic spiritualism.

Pérez Galdós's initial orientation, however, was mostly historical. The Romantics had turned to the study of history in a desire to embrace the phenomenon of human temporality, but they had focused primarily on an atmosphere of the past—poetic, distant, and vague. Pérez Galdós and the realists inherited this historical sense, but utilized it primarily in an effort to understand the present. Pérez Galdós's first two novels, *The Golden Fountain Café* and *El audaz*, reflect such a historical orientation.

It was also during these early years that Pérez Galdós began the *Episodios nacionales*. These works, forty-six in all, were written throughout his long literary career. They narrate the then-recent history of Spain, from the Battle of Trafalgar (1805) against Napoleon Bonaparte through the Restoration in 1874. Again, the author's aim was to guide his fellow Spaniards toward a greater understanding of contemporary psychological and social circumstances. His artistic formula was that of combining novelistic fiction—the continuing story of certain literary characters, which gives a loose unity to each series—with the graphic presentation of historical events. Aside from their literary merits, these works represent in their totality the most vivid and most complete documentary of nineteenth century history that has yet been compiled.

Aside from Pérez Galdós's almost unbroken historical preoccupations, his novelistic output can be divided into four general periods. Between the years 1876 and 1879, many of Pérez Galdós's so-called *novelas de la primera época* (novels of the first epoch) appeared. Three *novelas de tesis* (thesis novels) represented a pronounced didactic intention, promulgating a liberal and *progresista* (progressive) spirit, opposed to religious and clerical intolerance and traditional absolutism. These novels expressed a youthful rebelliousness, a distinctly iconoclastic fervor. Indeed, the abstract, often symbolic level on which the young writer constructed such an ideological rebellion was in many respects distant from the objective immediacy of the contemporary European realists. *Doña Perfecta* describes the struggle of liberalism against outdated moral codes and religious bigotry, *Gloria* the mutual intolerance between Catholics and Jews, and *The Family of León Roch* a marriage that is the product of Catholic dogmatism.

In his second period, between 1881 and 1888, Pérez Galdós initiated the *novelas españolas contemporáneas* (contemporary Spanish novels). In these years, the au-

thor clearly settled into conformity with accepted European realistic techniques and attempted to offer something positive to replace those codes that he had tried to destroy during his early rebelliousness. *The Disinherited Lady* marks the change. A wholehearted adaptation of the use of background detail, a more complete treatment of central characters, increasing firsthand studies of his novels' milieus, a "biographical" method for exploring the interrelationships between the individual and society, and a constant attention to the ordinary circumstances of daily life—these factors suggest a stricter adherence to nineteenth century realistic practices and the influence of French naturalism. During these years also, a significant anomaly developed in Pérez Galdós's use of authorial perspective: Whereas the author appeared frequently as a minor character to enhance the effects of realism and autonomy, he allowed himself, at the same time, abundant revelations of a character's hidden thoughts, thus betraying authorial control.

Many of these novels attempted to depict Madrid society as representing a synthesis of national life. Among these works were some of Pérez Galdós's most important productions: *Our Friend Manso*, *The Spendthrifts*, *Miau*, the first of the Torquemada novels, and the four-volume masterpiece *Fortunata and Jacinta*.

If the novels of Pérez Galdós's second period placed greater emphasis on the individual and his complicated relationships with the broad scope of society, those written between 1889 and 1897 presented the spiritual and philosophical aspects of that individual's predicament. An increasing tendency toward the theme of tolerance and compromise, along with a stronger emphasis on the values of love, compassion, self-discipline, and individual creativity characterized this phase. Pérez Galdós's realistic techniques were continued and refined, while a more profound sense of universality was added to an already deep patriotic sentiment. The author no longer attempted to define morality in absolute terms; his spiritualist hero struggles to purify himself rather than to find the ultimate meaning of existence. He accepts the reality of the life around him, a reality marked by pain but suggesting an abiding hope in the future. The priest in *Nazarín* and the beggar woman of *Compassion* practice Christian charity and come to ennoble the miserable surroundings in which they live. This last novel in particular seems to represent a synthesis of Galdosian techniques: Its theme, realistic—even naturalistic—documentation, and spiritualistic emphasis are united in a harmonious whole. Here, Pérez Galdós demonstrated that, while fiction is an illusion created by the imagination, life itself is also unreal—an illusion created by the senses as one encounters the external world.

In the works of his fourth and final period, beginning in 1898, Pérez Galdós revealed a profound change in artistic perspective. His seminaturalistic objectivism gave way to a kind of subjective impressionism. The third series of *Episodios nacionales* and novels such as *Casandra* and *El caballero encantado* marked the mellowness of old age, an increase in fantasy and symbolism, and, to a certain extent, a diminishing of artistic excellence. It was during this period that Pérez Galdós turned to the theater, adapting some previous "dialogue novels" to the stage (novels such as *Reality* and *El abuelo*) and presenting such thesis plays as *Electra*, based on a condemnation of clerical intolerance and malpractice. Pérez Galdós, however, lacked true dramatic ability. Many of his plays were weighed down by psychological abstraction and slow-moving plots.

The first three stages of Pérez Galdós's literary production, then, reflect variations of general European realistic techniques of the nineteenth century. His youthful rebelliousness and abstractionism were an expression of the controversial atmosphere and ideological emphasis of the 1870's. Novels such as *The Disinherited Lady* and *The Forbidden* reflect the moderate propagation of naturalistic ideas in Spain during the 1880's, as the author attempted a more detailed study of the individual and his environment. Pérez Galdós's interest in transcending spiritual values in turn suggests a similar reaction throughout Europe during the 1890's.

To summarize those factors relating to the author's choice of subject matter, one may say that Pérez Galdós's realism grew out of the careful exercise of his powers of observation; it was supported by verisimilitude; its guiding concern was with society, and, more specifically, the individual's complex relationships with that society; it dwelt, in proportion to their numbers, on authentic treatment of the various social classes, breaking new ground in its inclusion of the middle class, and possibly showing some preference, in later years, for the humbler members of the social order. Pérez Galdós's version of realism reflected the organic, evolutionary quality of society. It incorporated, at least superficially, some vestiges of the costumbristic tradition, from which the author attempted to liberate himself during the latter part of his career. Finally, it assimilated historical materials, to the degree that they could shed light on contemporary social circumstances.

With respect to authorial point of view, Pérez Galdós was a realist in the humoristic tradition. He recognized that irony is implicit in realism because it exposes the often odious comparison between actuality and what one desires of life. A fundamentally comic vision came most clearly into play when he ironically deflated pretentious aspirations, or when he exposed human extravagance and self-deception. Another target of his humor was the delusion that the merely relative is the absolute. His novels offer a vast comic panorama in which moments of tragedy seem to eclipse the fundamental spiritual truth. Consonant with Cervantes' notions of the interplay of fiction and reality and of the ambiguity of truth, then, Pérez Galdós came to accept the view that finite truth changes. Any particular instance of human experience is only partially "true"; the total interrelation of these momentary revelations constitutes ultimate truth. Just as the multiplicity of realities remained a mystery to Pérez Galdós, so his characters fail to grasp absolute truth because they are permitted only glimpses of relative "realities."

Pérez Galdós's narrative point of view is a multiple one, suggesting the Cervantine idea that any person's view of reality is relative. These varied viewpoints include strictly impartial, omniscient commentary; total immersion within one character (made most striking by the use of *estilo indirecto libre* (free indirect style) and the *monólogo interior* (interior monologue); slanted (as opposed to neutral) omniscient perspectives; appearances of Pérez Galdós as omniscient author, speaking directly to his readers; moments in which Pérez Galdós appears as one of the characters, himself ignorant of facts and circumstances because of his limited personal vision (striking examples of this can be found in *The Spendthrifts* and *Our Friend Manso*); and total lack of direct authorial presence or intrusion, as manifested in the *novelas dialogadas*.

Thus, Pérez Galdós's attempts to describe all facets of contemporary Spanish society: his frequently lengthy, often unemotional descriptions, his basically impartial selectivity and means of organization, his shifting points of view—all of these contribute to a relative objectivity. At the same time, his didacticism or irony, his occasional failures to maintain authorial autonomy, and a strong, sympathetic identification with some of his characters serve to limit that very objective approach. His creations have life. They demonstrate verisimilitude, balance, and an almost infinite variety; but they come from the heart, and not the sociologist's notebook.

Pérez Galdós's characters are usually realistic in the sense that they are distinct individuals. At the same time, they are symbols: They are combinations of abstract types and concrete, humanized personalities. Torquemada, for example, symbolizes the coarse materialism of the rising Spanish middle class, but takes on a personal dimension in the emotionalism that erupts when his son dies, in his criticism at the banquet of businessmen like himself, his helplessness before the implacable Cruz, his comic attempts at verbal refinement, and his "transactions" with the Almighty. All of these factors particularize his predicament and suggest some measure of potential "roundness." Pérez Galdós's protagonists move within a double reality, reflecting the Cervantine notion that the human condition exists divided between secret, inner personality and acted, overt experience. Indeed, the constructs of the mind often seem more real than ordinary physical reality.

Despite Pérez Galdós's double emphasis upon social and individual characteristics, he does not attempt to explore the complexities and incongruities of personality in the manner of Dostoevski or some modern novelists. Often his characters are, by comparison, somewhat less complicated creatures, dominated generally by a limited number of motives (such as ambition, guilty conscience, charity, greed, and, above all, love).

With respect to style, Pérez Galdós was committed to painting even the smallest, seemingly least significant elements of reality. He was firmly convinced that the least noticeable facets of human existence and the least conspicuous details of a historical milieu are as important as the items that blaze from newspaper headlines. (Miguel de Unamuno y Jugo would later term this sphere

of reality an *intra-historia*.) Quite often, these small details are worked into descriptions of surprising length, and the *generación del 1898* was quick to condemn the author's extraordinary descriptive elaboration. This trait is most noticeable in the novels of the 1880's, especially *Fortunata and Jacinta*. While it is true that this abundance occasionally tires the reader, one can still detect in it Pérez Galdós's larger motives: to picture the total sweep of contemporary Spanish life, to imply its actual magnitude and multiplicity.

The relative absence of natural settings is a well-known characteristic of Pérez Galdós's novels. The reason behind this is not hard to discern: Above all, Pérez Galdós was interested in people, and portraits of nature were subordinated to character treatment. Only rarely does one find lyric descriptions of landscape that are designed to capture the poetic nuances of the setting itself. As might be expected, such elaborations are important only for their symbolic or psychological enhancement of the people involved. Thus, the delightful description of an evening in the countryside in *Torquemada in Purgatory* is contrasted ironically with Torquemada's imperviousness to its beauty.

Other stylistic features of Pérez Galdós's novels are especially pertinent to a discussion of realistic technique. One such feature is the naturalness of his vocabulary and phrasing: Despite its remarkable richness and variety, Pérez Galdós's language is unaffected, often colloquial. His imagery, though based on ordinary, concrete, even prosaic elements, is remarkably rich and vivid. Similes appear frequently, since they are found so often in common speech. Frequent dialogue functions as a means of actualizing his material; in one way, it helps to typify characters (to identify them as representatives of a social or vocational class), and, on the other hand, it helps to individualize them (by the use of distinguishing speech "tags"). Finally, Pérez Galdós frequently employs interior monologues; although such passages differ from the arbitrary, "free-association" techniques of the twentieth century, the novelist certainly anticipated the formulation of the stream of consciousness method.

DOÑA PERFECTA

Doña Perfecta best exemplifies Pérez Galdós's thesis novels, the type of writing produced during the more militant, aggressive years of his youth. It illustrates graphically Pérez Galdós's reaction to the intolerance expressed in the Constitution of 1876, which was widely discussed during the weeks when the work was appearing in installments in the *Revista de España*. The plot centers on Pepe Rey, a progressive, modern young engineer whose visit to the home of his aunt results in his sudden, tragic death. The author's main purpose is to depict the young man's struggle against the enemies of contemporary, liberal thought: bigotry, hypocrisy, reactionism, provincialism, and the weight of dead tradition.

At the suggestion of his father, Pepe goes to the remote cathedral town of Orbajosa (city of garlic), in order to survey the region for mining and irrigation projects, with the idea of meeting and possibly marrying his cousin Rosario. As the novel progresses, the conflict slowly develops between reactionary traditionalism (his aunt, Doña Perfecta, the priest Inocencio, and the latter's niece, María Remedios, who wants to marry her son, Jacinto, to Rosario) and modern thought (Pepe Rey, with the help of an army officer whose company is sent to Orbajosa to quell any possible uprisings of guerrilla bands). Finally, as Pepe tries to elope with Rosario, Doña Perfecta orders his execution. Afterward, Rosario becomes insane and is confined to an asylum, and Doña Perfecta continues her religious activities.

Thematically, then, Pérez Galdós condemns hypocrisy, fanatical religiosity, intolerance, and provincialism. On a slightly deeper level, however, he is also expressing his disdain for extremism of any kind, that passion that allows reason to be clouded by emotion. Spaniards, he says, must cast off a blind local patriotism rooted in ignorance, as well as the intolerance of many modern progressives (for Pepe's dogmatism and tactless inflexibility are also criticized). When violence engenders violence, when an oversimplified polarization of "them" and "us," of *moros* (Moors) and *cristianos* (Christians), takes place, there is no significant difference between the progressive and the reactionary perspectives. On the other hand, honesty, clearness of vision, restraint, charitable tolerance, and, above all, love are held up as factors that may unite the country and offer hope for the future. The lesson of the novel is ultimately a moral one that transcends the immediate political message about Spain of the 1870's.

Doña Perfecta, then, aptly demonstrates the Krausist justification of literature as an instrument of reform and education, as well as exemplifying the movement's belief that the moral and intellectual regeneration of the individual is the only path to the moral and intellectual reform of society. The Krausists' quest for "racial harmony," their recognition of the relationships between the whole and the part, relate directly to the technique in which biography and history are blended—the framework for this novel as well as for all the novellas in *Episodios nacionales*. Hence, Pepe's clash with his aunt, for example, is mirrored by the arrival of the troops from Madrid.

The artistic weakness of the novel lies primarily in its blatant didacticism and in the relative superficiality of its characterizations. Doña Perfecta, Pepe, Inocencio, Rosario, and María Remedios are what Stephen Gilman calls "rounded archetypes," symbolic representations of ideological viewpoints or human characteristics or passions (mostly negative).

Pepe himself is a kind of modern Don Quixote. His inevitable death, furthermore, is foreshadowed repeatedly by dramatic parallels and references to the Passion of Christ. He is individualized only by his flaws (inflexibility, tactlessness) and by his development from a straightforward, friendly, rational human being to a very intemperate, precipitous, even unethical conspirator. Generally, however, he remains a symbol.

Doña Perfecta, while more a symbolic type (almost a caricature) than a unique personality, is nevertheless also individualized somewhat and made understandable by aspects of her family background, her sincerity, and her own measure of development in the course of the novel. Rosario, whose main role is as a catalyst to the action, is nevertheless the most interesting of the characters, and Pérez Galdós's study of her conflicts, her dreams, and her neuroses is a superb precursor of the more profound pathological portraits that were to appear in later novels.

The author's style also points to later techniques. It is natural, direct, and at times even colloquial. A tone of irony predominates throughout the novel, usually expressed through dramatic contrast (Orbajosa's glorious past versus modern banditry; the symbolic dawn with which the novel opens versus the subsequent ineffectiveness of Pepe's actions; and so on). Theatrical elements abound, from the frequent use of dialogue to the descriptions of gestures and the author's "stage directions." Particular to this novel are the stress on animal imagery, classical references (as a means of revealing the ironic discrepancy between name and reality), and the symbolic use of sounds (such as the opening train whistle, the cockcrow, bugles, and the creaking of the cathedral weathercock).

The compact structure of the novel has been analyzed by two leading critics. Sherman H. Eoff has demonstrated that the movement of the plot is based on three decisive, progressively more intense moments of peripeteia: Pepe's "vehement defense of science at the end of chapter 8," his announcement of his intention to marry Rosario, and Doña Perfecta's ordering of his assassination. Stephen Gilman has suggested a number of parallels between the structure of the novel and that of neoclassical tragedy, in which "perfection" passes to "imperfection" through Pepe's tragic flaw and by way of a series of theatrically presented "acts." Indeed, the overt nature of the conflict (far different from the aim of synthesis and reconciliation evident in later works) made it an easy task to adapt the novel to the stage.

Doña Perfecta is far from a great work, and its tremendous popularity is probably undeserved. It is too schematized and melodramatic and lacks the warmth and humor, the feeling of movement, the depth of characterization, and the panorama of realistic detail that were to typify Pérez Galdós's best creations. Yet the skillful use of irony, the suggestion of pathological analysis (Rosario), and the start of a relativistic perspective in which a situation is viewed from several perspectives point to the more mature works that followed.

THE DISINHERITED LADY

The Disinherited Lady heralded a new phase in Pérez Galdós's career. The author no longer concentrated on examining merely the social implications of certain ideologies; rather, *The Disinherited Lady* reveals Pérez Galdós's forceful attempt to incorporate into the novel the world of external appearances, to accumulate innumerable, detailed images of outward, as well as inward, reality. Here, one finds the faithful representation of environment, daily customs, psychological motivation, and the formation of the new middle class—in short, the creation of an "accurate mirror of the society in which

we live." This was now the author's central purpose, and the core of his subsequent realistic aspirations.

Pérez Galdós now went to work on a broader canvas, including naturalistic suggestions of hereditary and environmental influence; he introduced "collective" characters (*manicomio, fábrica, taller, asilo, barrio bajo*) and the theme that people must face reality; he initiated the idea that the real world and the world of fiction interact and are mutually dependent. Finally, *The Disinherited Lady* represents a closer joining of the two narrative paths expressed previously in a more separate form: the *episodio* of contemporary history (here the abdication of Amadeo, the floundering of the First Republic, and the advent of the Restoration) and the didactic representation of society seen in the early *novelas contemporáneas*.

The plot deals with the life of a woman, Isidora Rufete, who tries in vain to prove her claims of nobility. As Isidora clings to the illusion of noble birth, which is her major standard of personal worth, she comes to live with, first, a man of aristocratic family and, later, one whose money can satisfy her desire for luxury. Only two episodes suggest actual narrative "movement"—the heroine's visit to the Marquesa whose kinship she has claimed, and her eventual imprisonment for having supposedly falsified the documents that could prove her relation to the Marquesa's family. Isidora, says Eoff, thus

> subordinates her wholesome inclinations of friendliness, sympathy, and honesty as she tries to prove her nobility; . . . she is increasingly tyrannized by the love of wealth and luxury; and . . . her integrity dissolves completely after the final disillusionment following her imprisonment.

At the end, her illusions irreparably shattered, she descends to a life of prostitution.

Although Pérez Galdós's attitude and beliefs are less prominent here than in his earlier thesis novels, the tone of the work is far from objective. Most important is its pervasive air of indulgent, yet pointed, Cervantine irony; this is evident from the beginning, when Pérez Galdós draws a contrast between the beauty of nature and the frenzied self-occupation of the asylum inmates. It is seen also in the use of caricature (as in the descriptions of Isidora's friend Don José and of such minor characters as

Tomás Rufete, Botín, and Juan Bou), in euphemism and in self-deception (in the moments of *estilo indirecto libre*, when self-deception is most conspicuous), and in the way in which the reader himself is deceived into identifying with the heroine.

Thematically, Pérez Galdós is saying that one must face reality as it is and reject false values and the worship of appearances; he condemns the attitude of *"quiero pero no puedo* (I want to but cannot),"* supports the need for better educational facilities and opportunities (for the sake of children such as Pecado, Isidora's brother), and criticizes social parasites (such as her lover, Joaquín). There are specific commentaries about the Spanish propensity for civil war (symbolized in the children's battle), the Catholic Church ("Entreacto en la iglesia"), nepotism, *caciquismo*, politics, and mental institutions. Only in his more mature novels was Pérez Galdós able to incorporate his desire to teach into a more completely artistic framework.

Many critics who have dealt with *The Disinherited Lady* have been specifically interested in the novel's naturalistic content. Most of them have concluded that this is one of Pérez Galdós's most naturalistic novels (and one that probably demonstrates stronger naturalistic influence than any other Spanish novel of its time), but they agree that it still offers no evidence of Pérez Galdós's complete adherence to the philosophical and linguistic tenets of Zola. Elements that suggest naturalistic influence include the force of heredity, some measure of environmental determinism, the topic of the *bestia humana* (humans driven by their own mechanistic or animalistic impulses), and occasional frankness of language. Nowhere, however, does one find the morbidity of many of Zola's works. Despite Pérez Galdós's detail, he consciously avoided presenting the seamier aspects of Isidora's love affairs. There is no true fatalistic determinism. Above all, the novel is a moral work that acknowledges the power and possibilities open to the human will. Finally, Pérez Galdós avoided the cold, objective tone of the naturalists. Zola's rigor is neutralized here by *la risa cervantina* (Cervantine humor).

With respect to style, the growing force of realism in Pérez Galdós's new manner reveals itself most dramatically in the increased use of colloquial speech and in the descriptive atmosphere of the novel. The author "takes

possession" of Madrid as the broad stage that was to form the background for so many of his works, leading the reader into all corners of the city and illuminating the contradictory, often oppressive aspects of the modern nineteenth century metropolis. Costumbristic scenes abound. Other linguistic techniques include theatrical elements, the fuller use of the *estilo indirecto libre*, the adaptation of language to circumstances and characters, and descriptions with an occasional impressionistic flavor. The last characteristic is evident, for example, at those moments when the author blurs the boundary between waking reality and reverie: *"insomnio número cinquenta y tantos"* and so on. The chapters titled "Beethoven" and "Sigue Beethoven" are deliberate linguistic tours de force; here Pérez Galdós uses the modernistic techniques of triple and quadruple adjectival construction, *sinestesia*, and musical elements to produce two moods analogous to major and minor keys.

In *The Disinherited Lady*, Pérez Galdós thus subordinated moralistic militancy to a relative stress on character delineation for its own sake. He continued to base his personages on one or two central attitudes or passions, but this focal impulse now became more personal. The real interest of the work lies in the evolution of the heroine. Only this progression gives the novel's structure continuity. The psychological movement of the story shows how Isidora subordinates her instincts of honesty, friendliness, and sympathy to her tyrannical obsession with her noble beginnings and her hunger for wealth and luxury. Ultimately, her integrity dissolves completely, in the final disillusionment that follows her imprisonment.

Through Isidora, one sees Pérez Galdós's first real venture into a further extension of "environment," what may be termed the world of "fiction," as opposed to that of immediate, physical circumstance. The intangible realm of the heroine's thoughts and beliefs is as real as the visible reality around her, although contrasting with it. The reader is left uncertain about the reality of Isidora's situation until her climactic conversation with the Marquesa de Aransis at the end of the first part. Pérez Galdós makes full use of the idea that men and women depend on their dreams. Isidora "dies" when her illusions are smashed, having declared that *"mejor es soñar que ver"* (it is better to dream than to see). The author demonstrates how critically trauma or psychic shock can function in the sphere of nominal sanity. As in Pérez Galdós's later novels, dreams serve two basic functions in *The Disinherited Lady*: as a means of characterization (Isidora's obsession, Don José's feelings toward the heroine) and as foreshadowing (Isidora's premonitions in jail concerning her lawyer's failure). The fact that almost all the major characters are prone to dreams and illusions echoes the Cervantine ambiguity of reality, with its intimation that "real" existence is a complicated blend of exterior and interior perceptions.

Certainly, Isidora is in part symbolic, representing aspects of the Spanish people as a whole. Yet, more important, she is a unique case of semi-insanity, individualized both by her faults (her aristocratic obsession, her fear of vulgarity, egotistical pride, financial ineptness, extreme nervousness) and by her virtues (in particular, her generosity).

Don José, probably one of Pérez Galdós's finest and most poignant psychological creations, serves primarily to dramatize the heroine's downfall with his own incidental destruction. Like Isidora, he is both a type-character (a kind of pathetic Don Quixote whose Dulcinea is the protagonist) and a peculiar blend of self-sacrificing, Platonic generosity and senile sexual illusions. The minor characters in the novel contribute in an essentially static fashion to Isidora's negative development.

The work's structure is not a tight one. In a way, the plot starts and ends in medias res. At times, one feels that Pérez Galdós is improvising, guided only by a plan to study the process of Isidora's psychological degeneration. Nevertheless, there is considerable evidence in the novel of careful structural techniques: the framework of two parts, each with its *suicidio*, each with a criminal act by Pecado, and so on (the first part contains the confirmation of Isidora's illusions and the second the gradual destruction of those hopes when the world of reality gains mastery); the careful social progression of the heroine's lovers in part 2; and finally, a series of parallels and correspondences: the two key events (the meeting with the Marquesa, Isidora's imprisonment), Pecado's world versus Isidora's interior world, the parallel scenes involving both Isidora and Joaquín, the two "Beethoven" chapters, the crimes of Pecado, the *cordelería* versus Bou's shop, the manner in which Pecado and his playmate Majito are eventually united after separate, but related descriptions, and so on.

The Disinherited Lady, then, was an experiment, and as such a turning point for Pérez Galdós. The novel retains at least something of the argumentative quality and abstractness of his thesis novels, yet points ahead to the greater psychological depth of such later characters as Fortunata and Benina. The work, viewed as a whole, adds in two ways to Pérez Galdós's maturing realistic technique: His details now fill in the canvas of external reality, and his insights take the reader deeper into the labyrinth of human psychology.

FORTUNATA AND JACINTA

Fortunata and Jacinta is Pérez Galdós's most complex creation and can be considered his masterpiece, probably one of the three greatest novels in Spanish literature. The framework for the action is a broad, detailed social record of Madrid life in the 1870's, with a veritable encyclopedia of customs, national types, and topographical minutiae. Above all, the work is an extraordinary study of the mutual influence of individual personalities and an exhibition of how one person's freedom can vanquish the potentially lethal effects of an immensely materialistic and erotic collectivity. The naturalistic semideterminism of *The Disinherited Lady* has passed to a Cervantine open-ended quest for rehabilitating values.

In broadest outline, the story concerns the fortunes of two women, linked by Juanito Santa Cruz, an idle, pampered bourgeois. In the first half of the book, Juanito marries his cousin, Jacinta, a woman obsessed with the idea of bearing a child. Fortunata, a beautiful woman of the *pueblo* and Juanito's lover, marries the sickly Maximiliano Rubín. As the novel progresses, Juanito vacillates between the security and conformity of his upper-middle-class marriage to Jacinta and the spontaneous vitality of society's lower rank (Fortunata). Eventually, Fortunata, the real protagonist of the work, gravitates toward her refined rival, whom she comes to see as a victim of Juanito, as she is. In the end, Fortunata gives birth to Juanito's son and, in a final gesture of understanding and self-expression, gives the child over to Jacinta. Around these personalities, Pérez Galdós weaves a web of interrelating stories, events, and minor characters that is astounding in its richness and complexity.

Pérez Galdós's novelistic techniques had matured considerably since the publication of *The Disinherited Lady*, clearly visible in characterization, theme, and style. Although the two heroines are meant to symbolize the clash between natural and social law, they are above all extremely complex individuals. There are no exclusively malevolent or benevolent figures in the novel. Fortunata, purposely presented first without background description, makes a slow and intricate voyage through self-consciousness toward self-discovery. By the end, she has surpassed jealousy, emulation, and fear of inferiority. While maintaining her original straightforward sincerity, emotional temperament, compassion, and disregard for social convention, she undergoes the "civilizing" influence of Maxi's widowed aunt, Doña Lupe, the elderly bachelor, Evaristo Feijóo, the social conventionalism of the charity worker, Guillermina Pacheco, and, above all, the model of Jacinta. In comparison to the psychological penetration Pérez Galdós offered in *The Disinherited Lady* in his portrayal of the insomniac Isidora, whose consciousness is marked by the relentless ticking of the clock, the study of Fortunata allows for a kind of autonomous interior time in which development occurs more slowly, more hesitatingly, and more meaningfully. This psychological trajectory is the very essence of the novel and gives the work its structure.

Jacinta hides her feelings, at least most of the time, under a veneer of social propriety. She is dominated throughout the novel by her obsession with children. She is gentle and affectionate rather than passionate and volatile by nature. Her evolution is marked by a lessening of sentimentality, an increase in independence, and, later, by a deepening maturity as she clashes with and then is drawn to Fortunata. Juanito functions as a catalyst in the plot and is more a type-character: the idle, well-off, essentially superficial *señorito* (young master). The diminutive that is inevitably applied to his name suggests the apron strings to which he has been tied. While not a despicable Joaquín Pez (of *The Disinherited Lady*), he is frivolous, pedantic, selfishly unremorseful, and vain, calculating, and insatiable in his search for novelty. In general, his personality is too shallow to allow room for subtlety or surprise.

The character of Maximiliano is, in Geoffrey Rib-

bans's words, "second only to Don Quixote as a highly sympathetic study of madness in Spanish literature." One of Pérez Galdós's supreme examples of the dreamer given over to imagination, he conceives the romantic mission of redeeming Fortunata; Maxi's "madness" actually allows him to see her true worth. His development, marked by vacillations between outward anger and inward anguish, reveals the writer's most original techniques of characterization. The minor figures serve primarily as links between or foils for the major characters, but many of their own individualized personalities demonstrate a marked tendency to evolve.

Thematically, *Fortunata and Jacinta* is less a study of the evils of Madrileñan society (although ample evidence of injustice, immorality, and ignorance is presented) than a demonstration that good cannot be neatly separated from evil and that, within the shifting relationships between the individual and his community, one person's expression of freedom, one act of giving, can, in Gilman's words, "be considered a final, self-justifying epic deed, an autonomous affirmation of humanity in the very teeth of history." While not complacent or overly optimistic, the author is hopeful, calling on the untapped potential for human progress.

In *Fortunata and Jacinta*, Pérez Galdós achieves an almost obsessive probing of the limits of daily speech, staged within a specificity of setting and topographical detail never before seen in the Spanish novel. Nowhere, with the possible exception of Leopoldo Alas's *La regenta* (1884), could readers find such richness, such fullness of descriptive elaboration. Particularly original to this work is the consistent bird imagery (for the purposes of characterization and structural development of the plot), the remarkable proto-Freudian use of dreams, and the increasingly complicated manipulations of point of view: authorial narrative, dialogue, *estilo indirecto libre*, and direct interior monologue (the recording of unspoken dialogue). Pérez Galdós's more frequent use of the unreliable narrator and the omnipresence of situational and verbal irony add to the ambiguities of the major characterizations and of the theme.

Fortunata and Jacinta presents a world of profound, interacting psychological portraits amid an incredibly detailed material setting; in its denouement, it reveals the end of Pérez Galdós's naturalistic phase and the beginning of a spiritual emphasis that was to dominate many of his later works.

COMPASSION

Written during a time of great financial and legal difficulties for Pérez Galdós, *Compassion* nevertheless demonstrates a spirit of understanding, a philosophical serenity, and a proclamation of profound optimism for humankind. The novel represents the fullest and most artistic expression of Pérez Galdós's "spiritual" phase. The setting—the misery and poverty of the beggars' world in old Madrid—is portrayed with the same seminaturalistic verisimilitude seen in earlier works, but the unresolved struggle between good and evil seen in *Fortunata and Jacinta* gives way to a deeper humanization of outlook in which love, charity, and basic Christian values indicate the clear potential of final triumph for all human beings.

In contrast to *Fortunata and Jacinta*, *Compassion* presents a world of reduced dimensions. Although the technique of detailed examination is similar, the author has been more selective, more attuned to the proportion of microcosm, rather than macrocosm. Further, out of the process of increasing interiorization manifested in earlier works came a profound evolutionary step: the inclusion of fantasy and illusion as integral components in the creation of actual, physical, living entities.

Benina, the elderly protagonist, begs to provide the daily bread for her spendthrift mistress Doña Paca, telling her that this income is wages from work in the house of a fictitious priest, Don Romualdo. As the story develops, Benina's charity extends to Paca's daughter, Obdulia, the pretentious Frasquito Ponte, and an increasingly broad circle of dependents. When she and her blind companion Almudena are arrested for begging in a prohibited area, she is taken to the poorhouse of Misericordia (compassion). During her absence, Paca, Paca's children, and Ponte are redeemed from poverty by an inheritance delivered to them by a priest named Romualdo Cedrón, whom they take to be Benina's Don Romualdo. Paca's domineering daughter-in-law Juliana comes forward to manage the new wealth, and when Benina finally returns, she is turned away. Her devotion to Paca has spawned only ingratitude.

Ironically, the inheritance leads only to misery. The dismissal of Benina and the lack of energy needed to ful-

fill their own pretentious visions lead the family to a life of spiritual emptiness. Benina goes with Almudena to live in a hut near the outskirts of Madrid, where she is eventually visited by Juliana. Like Saint Paul, the latter has experienced a sudden conversion and begs Benina to bless her and assure her of her children's future well-being.

The novel is constructed on a series of thematic, structural, and psychological dualities. With respect to characterization, Benina (based perhaps on Pérez Galdós's family nurse in Las Palmas) is particularized by her *sisa* (pilfering from her "earnings"), her superstition, and occasional naïveté. Yet she stands as the personification of charity and is presented symbolically as a Christ figure who suffers and accepts sacrifice (parallels to the life and words of Jesus abound in the novel). In addition, she bears more than a little resemblance to traditional type figures of Spanish literature (Lazarillo, Don Quixote). Her development consists of an expansion and intensification of her charitable ways toward a point of increased confidence and adjustability, in which charity and self-sacrifice are actually essential to her being. Through contact with others, she evolves toward a conscious recognition of the morality inherent in what originally were purely spontaneous acts of compassion.

Ponte is likewise a "dual" character. Born of costumbristic satire, he is the *proto-cursi* who attempts to relive the past; yet, when a fall from a horse leads to madness, he (like Maxi Rubín) is able to perceive the more profound truths concerning others. Almudena, one of Pérez Galdós's unique and most memorable creations, symbolizes the Moors and Jews who have been rejected and expelled from Spain and represents also the mystic exaltation of fantasy. His vices (egotism, jealousy, and so on) and his particular mixture of emotions toward Benina serve to individualize him. Paca embodies selfishness and irresponsibility, and the minor characters act as foils, parallels, or contrasts to Benina.

With respect to theme, the need to face reality is demonstrated, but (as the other side of the coin) certain kinds of fantasy or illusion (those with proper motives) are exalted as powerful, creative factors. The apparently "supernatural" appearance of Don Romualdo—which Benina herself feels may be the result of her own imagination—is the single most striking point of the novel and is meant to demonstrate this concept. A second general theme (the primary message) concerns the nature and importance of true charity. As a very significant link between the two main thematic statements, charity is seen to be the motive behind Benina's creature of fantasy, Don Romualdo. An additional bridge between the two messages lies in the thought that true charity provides a way of facing the hardships of reality.

Many elements of technique, tone, and style have been refined in *Compassion* but relate closely to those of Pérez Galdós's earlier works: expressive force, colloquial naturalness, frequent dialogue, naturalistic precision, costumbristic description, Cervantine irony, humor, the use of dreams. The gently ironic force of free indirect style is gradually abandoned in the later chapters, as Pérez Galdós identifies more closely with Benina, while allowing the heroine and others to testify more on their own behalf. The dualities of appearance and reality, seen throughout the author's career, are omnipresent here: Hunger becomes beneficial, blindness means vision, madness is wisdom, the servant is the leader, defeat equals victory.

The structure, based generally on Benina's development, reveals a dual or two-part organization. The first section (a week long, suggesting the Passion of Christ) is seen through Benina's eyes and presents the physical and temporal details of the beggars' lives and the heroine's expanding role; the second is a more generalized narration while Benina is in the poorhouse, leading to Paca's climactic rejection and the protagonist's final victory. Despite the relative haste with which Pérez Galdós composed the novel, the plot line is constructed with extraordinary care, exemplified by the steps leading to the meeting of Benina and the miserly Don Carlos at the start and by the careful stages in preparation for Don Romualdo's astonishing appearance with the news of the inheritance.

Compassion, then, is representative of Pérez Galdós's most mature creations. Within a framework of "spiritual" intentions, the work stands as the most artistic rendering of nineteenth century Cervantine dualities, seen from the two "faces" of the San Sebastián church, on the first page, through the seemingly contradictory reconciliations of charity and *la sisa* (Benina), Judaism/ Mohammedanism and Christianity (Almudena), fantasy and truth (Don Romualdo), matter and spirit, naturalism and idealistic humanism. At the same time, one sees here the real culmination of Pérez Galdós's development as a novelist.

At this stage, Pérez Galdós was able to anticipate the twentieth century's expansion of the realistic approach; he recognized that one must go beyond the perceptible elements of physical surroundings to fill out a realistic perspective. The writer must also integrate into his or her picture qualities of transcendent, universal, or symbolic significance. The nineteenth century realistic novel did generally move in this direction; although it looked critically at the inclusion of imaginary events, it sometimes ended by absorbing the stuff of the imagination. A dose of "poetic substance" entered realistic transcription; myth was simultaneously destroyed and assimilated into the real. Influenced by the Cervantine interplay of diverse "fictions" and "realities," Pérez Galdós demonstrated that "fiction" and "reality" are not dichotomous; rather, they are interacting components of the substance of human existence.

Jeremy T. Medina

OTHER MAJOR WORKS

PLAYS: *Realidad*, pr., pb. 1892 (adaptation of his novel); *Gerona*, pr. 1893 (adaptation of his novel); *La loca de la casa*, pr., pb. 1893; *Los condenados*, pr. 1894; *La de San Quintín*, pr., pb. 1894 (*The Duchess of San Quintín*, 1917); *Voluntad*, pr. 1895; *Doña Perfecta*, pr., pb. 1896 (adaptation of his novel); *La fiera*, pr. 1896; *Electra*, pr., pb. 1901 (English translation, 1911); *Alma y vida*, pr., pb. 1902; *El hombre fuerte*, pb. 1902 (wr. 1864-1868); *Mariucha*, pr., pb. 1903; *El abuelo*, pr., pb. 1904 (adaptation of his novel; *The Grandfather*, 1910); *Amor y ciencia*, pr., pb. 1905; *Bárbara*, pr., pb. 1905; *Pedro Minio*, pr. 1908; *Zaragoza*, pr., pb. 1908 (music by Arturo Lapuerto; adaptation of his novel); *Casandra*, pr., pb. 1910 (adaptation of his novel); *Celia en los infiernos*, pr., pb. 1913; *Alceste*, pr., pb. 1914; *Sor Simona*, pr., pb. 1915; *El tacaño Salomón*, pr., pb. 1916; *Santa Juana de Castilla*, pr., pb. 1918; *Antón Caballero*, pr. 1921 (completed by Serafín and Joaquín Álvarez Quintero); *Un joven de provecho*, pb. 1935 (wr. 1867).

NONFICTION: *Discursos académicos*, 1897; *Memoranda*, 1906; *Arte y crítica*, 1923; *Fisonomías sociales*,

1923; *Nuestro teatro*, 1923; *Política española*, 1923; *Cronicón*, 1924; *Toledo*, 1924; *Viajes y fantasías*, 1928; *Memorias*, 1930; *Crónica de Madrid*, 1933; *Cartas de Pérez Galdós a Mesonero Romanos*, 1943; *Crónica de la Quincena*, 1948; *Madrid*, 1956.

BIBLIOGRAPHY

Anderson, Lara. *Allegories of Decadence in Fin-de-Siècle Spain: The Female Consumer in the Novels of Emila Pardo Bazán and Benito Pérez Galdós.* Lewiston, N.Y.: Edwin Mellen Press, 2006. Anderson examines seven novels by Pérez Galdós and Pardo Bazán, focusing on the connections between Spanish decadence and the character of the female spendthrift. Discusses how this character reflects late nineteenth century concerns about Spain's decline.

Fuentes Peris, Teresa. *Galdos's "Torquemada" Novels: Waste and Profit in Late Nineteenth-Century Spain.* Cardiff: University of Wales Press, 2007. A study of the character of Francisco Torquemada, a Madrid moneylender, analyzing how his ideas about waste and profit enhance an understanding of the novels in which he appears.

Gilman, Stephen. *Galdós and the Art of the European Novel, 1867-1887.* Princeton, N.J.: Princeton University Press, 1981. Divided into three sections, with one part on the historical novelist and the remainder on *Fortunata and Jacinta.* A perceptive work of scholarship that provides an important context for understanding the novels. Includes an appendix on classical references in *Doña Perfecta.*

Gold, Hazel. *The Reframing of Realism: Galdós and the Discourses of the Nineteenth-Century Spanish Novel.* Durham, N.C.: Duke University Press, 1993. Excellent discussions of individual novels as well as a concluding chapter on Pérez Galdós's place in his native tradition. Recommended for advanced students.

Larsen, Kevin. *Cervantes and Galdós in "Fortunata y Jacinta: Tales of Impertinent Curiosity."* Lewiston, N.Y.: Edwin Mellen Press, 1999. Examines the significance of Cervantes to Pérez Galdós's writing of the novel *Fortunata and Jacinta.*

McGovern, Timothy Michael. *Galdós Beyond Realism: Reading and the Creation of Magical Worlds.* Newark, Del.: Juan de la Cuesta, 2004. McGovern argues that Perez Galdós should not be defined solely as a realist writer, arguing that some of his works feature nonrational or magical events and other aspects of "nonrealism."

Pattison, Walter T. *Benito Pérez Galdós.* Boston: Twayne, 1975. A very helpful introduction, with a chapter on the novelist's life, his journalism and early novels, his first contemporary novels, his naturalistic style, and the end of his career. Includes a chronology, detailed notes, and a bibliography.

Percival, Anthony. *Galdós and His Critics.* Buffalo, N.Y.: University of Toronto Press, 1985. An analysis and interpretation of the works of Pérez Galdós, with emphasis on critical reaction to his work. Includes a bibliography and an index.

Turner, Harriet S. *Benito Pérez Galdós, "Fortunata and Jacinta."* New York: Cambridge University Press, 1992. A painstaking study of this masterpiece, with a chronology of the novel's main events; genealogical tables; a biographical introduction to the author; chapters on the social and historical contexts, the characters, and the novel's metaphors; and a guide to further reading.

Willem, Linda M. *Galdós's "Secunda Manera": Rhetorical Strategies and Affective Response.* Chapel Hill: University of North Carolina Press, 1999. Willem examines how Pérez Galdós's narrative style became more sophisticated and varied with the publication of *The Disinherited Lady*, his first contemporary novel.

_____, ed. *A Sesquicentennial Tribute to Galdós, 1843-1993.* Newark, Del.: Juan de la Cuesta, 1993. A collection of essays on various aspects of Pérez Galdós's life and works, including analyses of the novels *The Forbidden*, *Tristana*, and *Compassion*. Includes a bibliography.

JAYNE ANNE PHILLIPS

Born: Buckhannon, West Virginia; July 19, 1952

PRINCIPAL LONG FICTION

Machine Dreams, 1984
Shelter, 1994
MotherKind, 2000
Lark and Termite, 2009

OTHER LITERARY FORMS

In addition to her novels, Jayne Anne Phillips has published essays, book reviews, and short stories. In her essays she often focuses on writing and the publishing process. For example, in "The Widow Speaks" (1999; in *The Eleventh Draft*, edited by Frank Conroy) she discusses writing from the writer's point of view, and in "Why She Writes" (1999; in *Why I Write*, edited by Will Blythe) she addresses the need of writers to associate with other writers. Phillips's essay "Home After Dark: Letter from Paducah," which deals with a school shooting incident in Kentucky, appeared in *Harper's* in 1999. Her book reviews have appeared in such periodicals as *New York* magazine and *The New York Times*. Her collections of short stories include *Black Tickets* (1979) and *Fast Lanes* (1987).

ACHIEVEMENTS

Jayne Anne Phillips's fiction has been translated into twelve languages, and her stories have been widely anthologized, including in the *Norton Anthology of Contemporary Fiction*. Phillips has won the Pushcart Prize four times, for individual stories and for collections, and an O. Henry Award. She has also received the Fels Award in Fiction from the Coordinating Council of Literary Magazines (1978), the St. Lawrence Award for Fiction (1979), and the Sue Kaufman Prize for First Fiction (for *Black Tickets*).

Phillips has been the recipient of a Guggenheim Fellowship, two fellowships from the National Endowment for the Arts (1978, 1985), and a Bunting Institute Fellowship (1981). Her novels have won numerous honors, including a National Book Critics Circle Award nomination, an American Library Association Notable Book

citation, a *New York Times* Best Books citation (1984), an Academy Award in Literature from the American Academy of Arts and Letters (1997), a nomination for Britain's Orange Prize (2001), and a Massachusetts Book Award for *MotherKind* (2001).

BIOGRAPHY

Born July 19, 1952, in Buckhannon, West Virginia, Jayne Anne Phillips was the middle child of Russell B. Phillips and Martha Jane Thornhill Phillips. Like many of the women in Phillips's novels, her mother was a teacher; she introduced Phillips to reading and storytelling. After graduating magna cum laude from West Virginia University in 1974, Phillips moved to the West Coast to become a writer chronicling her generation, the 1970's generation, which she believed retained the rebelliousness but lacked the passion of the 1960's. Like several of her contemporaries, she chose to work as a food server rather than as a teacher until her writing gained recognition.

During this period, Phillips's focus shifted from poetry to fiction—initially the short story—and she enrolled in the Iowa Writers' Workshop, earning her master of fine arts degree in 1978. *Sweethearts*, her first volume of stories, was published in a limited edition in 1976. Three other limited-edition story collections followed: *Counting* in 1978, *How Mickey Made It* in 1981, and *The Secret Country* in 1982. Phillips quickly gained recognition for her work. *Sweethearts* won the Pushcart Prize and the Fels Award from the Coordinating Council of Literary Magazines. *Counting* received the St. Lawrence Award for Fiction. Phillips's first volume of short stories to be published in a trade edition, *Black Tickets*, earned the Sue Kaufman Award for First Fiction from the American Academy and Institute of Arts and Letters.

In 1985, Phillips married Mark Brian Stockman; the couple have three sons. Although Phillips prefers writing to teaching, she has taught creative writing at a number of universities and work centers, including Humboldt State University in California, Williams College, Harvard University, the Bunting Institute, Boston University, and Brandeis University. She lives with her husband and children in Waltham, Massachusetts, and holds the positions of professor of English and director of the Master of Fine Arts Program at Rutgers University-Newark.

ANALYSIS

In style and technique, Jayne Anne Phillips has been compared with earlier writers of the American South, such as William Faulkner and Eudora Welty. Recurring themes in her work include those of family, change, loss, and the difficulty of communication.

MACHINE DREAMS

Machine Dreams, Phillips's first novel, has been widely praised as the first nonpolemical treatment of the Vietnam War. Phillips uses World War II and the war in Vietnam as background and metaphor for the family conflicts of the Hampsons. Because the primary focus is on the families at home, both wars are described through letters: those of Mitch, fighting in the Pacific in World War II, and his son Billy, fighting in Vietnam. Just as Phillips parallels the combatants' letters home, she also contrasts the reactions to the wars of their families and of American society as a whole. The saga of the Hampson family is thus a microcosm of the conflicts in American society during the twentieth century.

Family is clearly the most important theme in *Machine Dreams* as Phillips, like earlier twentieth century southern novelists, employs multiple narrators to portray the Hampsons' family history and internal conflicts. Initially the focus is on the multigenerational story of the Danners and the Hampsons. The novel begins with Jean Danner Hampson's letter to her daughter, Danner, chronicling the Danner family history. When Mitch Hampson, Jean's husband, tells his story in the next section, it too begins with an account of his parents, insofar as Mitch knows their story. Soon, however, the focus shifts to the changes within the Hampson family and their society. In many ways the family member most responsive to the changes taking place, Danner narrates six sections, in contrast with her mother (three), her father (four), and her brother (four). Ultimately Danner also seems the most logical member of

the family; in contrast, Billy's fatalism is seen in his refusal even to try to avoid military service, though he is certain he will be sent to Vietnam.

Another significant theme of the novel is change, usually accompanied by a kind of loss. Mitch responds with anger to any change, but Jean gradually develops the self-confidence to initiate change. Jean describes the losses that have changed her life—specifically, the deaths of her mother and her fiancé Tom. For Mitch, the losses began even earlier; he has been told that his mother left immediately after his birth and his father died in the mines a few years later. Mitch has been raised by his father's sisters, especially Bess, whom he regards as a mother figure. When he believes his actions have put Katie, Bess's delicate daughter, in jeopardy, his nightmares about the Pacific are replaced by terrible dreams of Katie's funeral. Mitch's losses continue, however, when the death of his business partner leads to the company's bankruptcy. At the same time, Jean has earned

Jayne Anne Phillips. (© Jerry Bauer)

teacher certification and become the family's primary breadwinner. This change, even more than the loss of his business, fuels Mitch's anger, which is directed especially at Jean. The family's greatest loss occurs, however, when Billy is declared missing in action in Vietnam and neither Danner nor Mitch can discover the truth about his fate.

Throughout *Machine Dreams*, family members simply cannot communicate with one another. Jean's parents shout at each other through locked doors, and she repeats the pattern as she argues with Mitch, who seems to yell at his family much more often than he converses with them. Eventually Jean and Mitch realize that their failures of communication have damaged both of their children. Danner adopts the types of rebellion common among young people in the 1960's, and Billy drops out of college without telling either parent. In addition, neither Danner nor Billy seems able to establish a healthy romantic relationship.

Machine Dreams consists of a series of vignettes, perhaps reflecting Phillips's original preference for short stories. Most of these vignettes reflect the personalities of their narrators, but the language is consistently lyrical—from the beginning, when Danner dreams of horses and Billy dreams of airplanes, to the conclusion, when Danner must try to understand what has happened.

SHELTER

Set in July, 1963, Phillips's second novel, *Shelter*, takes place at a Girl Guides camp (logically and symbolically named Camp Shelter) in Shelter County, West Virginia. The camp director, Mrs. Thompson-Warner, believes the isolated location and the structured environment of the camp itself provide both political and sexual protection for the young girls at the camp. Caught up in the Cold War mentality, Mrs. Thompson-Warner regularly lectures the campers on dangers from the Soviet Union, insisting that the girls prepare themselves for the threatening world outside the camp. She sees no sexual threat for the campers, however, because she believes the Girl Guides are essentially innocent, and she fails to realize the potential for trouble when she employs Frank, a teenage boy, as the camp bugler.

The four young girls at the center of the novel seemingly regard the camp as "shelter" from difficult family lives. The counselors realize the need to protect Delia, whose father has apparently committed suicide. Delia's best friend, Alma, is especially protective because she knows the details of an affair between her mother, Audrey, and Delia's father, Nickel, including the stories Nickel told Audrey about Delia's mother, Mina. As a result, Alma (whose name also seems symbolically appropriate) tries to take responsibility for Delia, and she is pleased to escape the emotional turmoil in both households. Other families in the novel are equally dysfunctional. Alma's older sister, Lenny, is also avoiding the tension at home, where her parents frequently argue and some nights her drunken father enters her bedroom and touches her inappropriately. At camp, Lenny and her best friend, Catherine, known as Cap, can no longer reenact the verbal fights between Cap's parents.

The woods surrounding the camp provide a haven for two male characters. Buddy Carmody, the young son of Hilda, the camp cook, practices "slipping through" the woods to escape his physically and sexually abusive stepfather. Buddy likes to pretend that he and Hilda are the only people in the area. At the same time, he has a crush on Lenny and wishes he could give her presents. In contrast, Parson is an adult, probably schizophrenic. Also abused in his youth, he sees ghosts and embodied figures of evil, and when his prison cell mate, Carmody, was released, Parson simply followed him to Shelter County because he believes Carmody will be the instrument of grace that will redeem him.

Even though none of these characters is absolutely innocent, *Shelter* is an initiation novel in which the girls experience sexual awakening and confront evil. Fifteen-year-old Lenny realizes that she is no longer a child; she sleeps naked and agrees to skinny-dipping in Turtle Hole, even when Cap attracts the attention of Frank, who is fishing nearby. Her sexual encounter with Frank and Cap stops just short of intercourse, but she readily agrees when Cap suggests inviting Frank to meet them there again. After Alma intercepts Cap's note and goes to Turtle Hole with Delia instead, the four girls believe themselves alone until they encounter the drunken Carmody.

In this novel Phillips uses multiple narrators: The book's forty-three sections are told from the perspectives of four characters—Lenny, Alma, Buddy, and Parson. This technique facilitates Phillips's use of the recurring motif of secrets or hiding. Each girl knows secrets involving her parents, but she also has her own secrets. Some are minor, such as Alma's doing Delia's camp chores, but some are more significant, such as Lenny's midnight encounter with Frank. Likewise, Buddy has been forced to find a secret place to hide from Carmody, who has threatened to kidnap him. Finally, there is Parson, who works with the pipe-laying crew but hides at night in a deserted henhouse. Eventually, at the novel's climax, the most sinister secret of all links these characters, a secret all of them vow to keep.

MOTHERKIND

Phillips's third novel, *MotherKind*, draws its title from the name of the postpartum service employed by the protagonist-narrator, Kate, who gradually realizes that she is part of "motherkind," a web unifying all nurturers, female and male. Caring for her dying mother, Katherine, and her newborn son, Alexander, Kate finally intuits the meaning of *namaste*, the Hindu word for the "oneness" of all, as she sees the paradoxical interrelationships of birth, living, and dying. Repeatedly told that she cannot handle all of her caregiver tasks alone, Kate relies increasingly on her neighbor Camille, the babysitter Amy, and finally the women sent by a home-care service. Phillips presents vivid sensory details as, within descriptions of daily events, she interjects Kate's memories of a trip to Nepal and her most recent visit "home" to West Virginia to show how Kate learns to "bow to the divine" in everyone.

Until news of Katherine's cancer brought her back to the United States, Kate had traveled in Nepal, searching for a unifying philosophy she had not found in her West Virginia family's traditional Christianity. Although Kate recalls attending church services, her family's religion has neither satisfied her nor prevented the fragmentation of her family; her parents divorced when Kate was in her teens, and she describes her relationship with her father, Waylon, in language borrowed from the poet Sylvia Plath. Her parents' only daughter, Kate has long been her mother's confidant and the sensible child. Her brothers seem self-centered, but their southern society has not demanded "caregiving" of them. Kate eventually reconciles with Waylon, but he rejects the idea of moving to Boston, where Kate is caring for her dying mother, citing his nurturing role at home in West Virginia.

To achieve "oneness" in her immediate family, Kate

must recognize the nurturing role that Matt, Alexander's father, fills with all his sons and eliminate the emotional distinction she initially makes between Alexander and her two stepsons, Sam and Jonah. Until she leaves Alexander safely ensconced on the beach and swims out to save Jonah, who is floating out to sea, even Kate does not recognize the imperceptible change as she becomes a parent to her stepsons. The recurring symbol of water culminates in the unity of Kate's family: Eventually, in Kate's dreams, Katherine is the one adrift on the ocean, and, as Katherine dies, the two of them are traveling the "birth road" in Sri Lanka.

Charmaine Allmon Mosby

OTHER MAJOR WORKS

SHORT FICTION: *Sweethearts*, 1976; *Counting*, 1978; *Black Tickets*, 1979; *How Mickey Made It*, 1981; *The Secret Country*, 1982; *Fast Lanes*, 1987.

BIBLIOGRAPHY

Larson, Leslie. "A Window on the Underworld: Jayne Anne Phillips' Writing Style." *Women's Review of Books* 12, no. 7 (April, 1995): 5-12. Examines Phillips's voice, characterization, and themes, with particular focus on her novel *Shelter*.

Lassner, Phyllis. "Jayne Anne Phillips: Women's Narrative and the Recreation of History." In *American Women Writing Fiction: Memory, Identity, Family, Space*, edited by Mickey Pearlman. Lexington: University Press of Kentucky, 1989. Emphasizes the symbolism that Phillips employs in *Machine Dreams* as well as the dissolution of traditional gender roles in her fiction.

Phillips, Jayne Anne. "Interview with Jayne Anne Phillips." Interview by Thomas C. Douglass. *Appalachian Journal* 21, no. 2 (1994): 182-189. Phillips discusses her work, particularly her use of West Virginia settings.

_____. "The Mystery of Language." Interview by Bonnie Lyons and Bill Oliver. In *Passion and Craft: Conversations with Notable Writers*, edited by Bonnie Lyons and Bill Oliver. Urbana: University of Illinois Press, 1998. Phillips discusses the poetic quality of her novels and her use of the "secret" as motif.

_____. "Taking Cues from the Work Itself." Interview by Sarah Anne Johnson. In *Conversations with American Women Writers*. Lebanon, N.H.: University Press of New England, 2004. Phillips addresses the topic of the importance of sensory associations in developing fiction.

Robertson, Sarah. *The Secret Country: Decoding Jayne Anne Phillips' Cryptic Fiction*. New York: Rodopi, 2007. Examination of Phillips's work focuses on the characteristics that link the author to earlier southern writers.

ROBERT PINGET

Born: Geneva, Switzerland; July 19, 1919
Died: Tours, France; August 25, 1997

PRINCIPAL LONG FICTION

Mahu: Ou, Le Matériau, 1952 (*Mahu: Or, The Material*, 1966)
Le Renard et la boussole, 1953
Graal flibuste, 1956
Baga, 1958 (English translation, 1967)
Le Fiston, 1959 (*No Answer*, 1961; also known as *Mr. Levert*)
Clope au dossier, 1961
L'Inquisitoire, 1962 (*The Inquisitory*, 1966)
Quelqu'un, 1965 (*Someone*, 1984)
Le Libéra, 1968 (*The Libera Me Domine*, 1972)
Passacaille, 1969 (*Recurrent Melody*, 1975; also known as *Passacaglia*, 1978)
Fable, 1971 (English translation, 1980)
Cette voix, 1975 (*That Voice*, 1982)
L'Apocryphe, 1980 (*The Apocrypha*, 1980)
Monsieur Songe, 1982 (English translation, 1989)
Le Harnais, 1984
Charrue, 1985
L'Ennemi, 1987 (*The Enemy*, 1991)
Du nerf, 1990 (*Be Brave*, 1995)
Théo: Ou, Le Temps neuf, 1991 (*Theo: Or, The New Era*, 1995)
Taches d'encre, 1997 (*Traces of Ink*, 2000)

OTHER LITERARY FORMS

In addition to his novels, Robert Pinget (pihn-ZHAY) wrote short stories as well as a number of plays for the ra-

dio and the stage. His dramatic works include *Lettre morte* (pr., pb. 1959; *Dead Letter*, 1963), *Ici ou ailleurs* (pr., pb. 1961; *Clope*, 1963), *L'Hypothèse* (pr., pb. 1961; *The Hypothesis*, 1967), *Architruc* (pr., pb. 1961; English translation, 1967), *Abel et Bela* (pr., pb. 1971; *Abel and Bela*, 1987); and *Un Testament bizarre* (pb. 1986; *A Bizarre Will*, 1989).

ACHIEVEMENTS

Hailed by John Updike as "one of the noblest figures in world literature," winner of the Prix de la Critique (1962), the Prix Femina (1965) and the Grand Prix National des Lettres (1987), a writer whose works have been translated into at least nineteen languages and whose plays have been performed by the Comédie-Française, and recognized by his peers among the French New Novelists as a "writer's writer," Robert Pinget was one of the most innovative of modern French authors. His work serves as an informative bridge between the conventions of traditional fiction and the experimental forms of the post-World War II years, and it illuminates indirectly the theoretical explorations of late twentieth century French literary criticism.

BIOGRAPHY

Robert Pinget was born in Geneva, Switzerland, on July 19, 1919. He studied law and entered the legal profession. After practicing law for a relatively short period of time, he became disappointed with his career and in 1946 moved to Paris, where he studied painting with Jean Souverbie at the École des Beaux-Arts. By 1950, he had once again become dissatisfied in his profession and, after an exhibition of his works at Boulevard Saint

Germain, he redirected his creative talents, devoting himself to writing full time. He became involved with the new literary movement of the time, known as *le nouveau roman*, or the New Novel, and associated himself with writers such as Alain Robbe-Grillet.

In 1951, he published his first book, a collection of short stories titled *Entre Fantoine et Agapa* (*Between Fantoine and Agapa*, 1982). Both Robbe-Grillet and Albert Camus praised the work. In 1955, Pinget met the Irish author Samuel Beckett, with whom he developed a lasting friendship. Beckett played a significant role in Pinget's career, providing advice and encouragement and, even more important, introducing him in both Dublin and New York to individuals who were influential in the literary world. The two writers carried on an extensive correspondence through 1988 (Beckett died in 1989). Both novelists and playwrights, each translated one of the other's radio plays: Beckett translated Pinget's *La Manivelle* (1960; *The Old Tune*, 1963), and Pinget translated Beckett's *All That Fall* (1957).

In 1962, six of Pinget's poems were set to music by Germaine Taillefer in a song cycle titled *Pancarte pour une porte d'entrée* (handbill for an entrance). In 1987, five of his plays were performed at the prestigious theater festival held in Avignon, France. In the spring of 1997, he published his last novel, *Traces of Ink*, and shortly after its publication a colloquium honoring Pinget was held in Tours, France, where he was living. Pinget suffered a stroke and died on August 26, 1997.

ANALYSIS

Three major unifying threads run through Robert Pinget's absorbing and outlandish fictional world. Most obviously, in terms of its overall structure, Pinget's writings unfold as corollaries to his unstated underlying belief that all writing comes to life as a sort of parallel song, a *para odos*, reacting to what has been written before. The second aspect of Pinget's work that catches the reader's attention is a fascination with the paradox of the potential and limits of language. Finally, Pinget is one of the very few writers of modern avant-grade French prose who possesses and displays what English-speaking readers could recognize as a sense of humor.

The years immediately preceding and following the publication of Pinget's first book, *Between Fantoine and*

Agapa, constitute a literary watershed in the history of post-World War II French letters. Taking into account the discoveries of relativity in physics, inquiries into the irrational nature of human behavior in psychiatry, and the growing uneasiness about the relationship between words and things among linguists, and recalling the moral and political horrors of World War II, the existentialist writers in vogue in France in the late 1940's and early 1950's returned again and again to the common theme of the absurd. Put simply, the characters in their novels and plays struggle to find meaning in a world that has none.

The depiction and exploration of the absurdity of the human condition have continued to dominate French fiction, but the literary expression of the theme has changed. The existentialist writers (Jean-Paul Sartre, Albert Camus, and others) described and presented the absence of meaning and the alienation attending it in a style that was both limpid and precise. In short, they wrote as if the absurd were an abstract philosophical concept with little or no direct bearing on language itself.

In the early 1950's, Alain Robbe-Grillet called for the creation of a "new novel," one that would incorporate the joys and frustrations of humankind's search for meaning into the very fabric of its prose. Robbe-Grillet was an editor and a strong moving force at Les Éditions de Minuit, and although the forms and techniques the two authors used were very different, Robbe-Grillet sensed in Pinget's work a desire similar to his own to renew the novel by breaking out of outworn restrictions and concepts. This general goal was shared by Michel Butor, Samuel Beckett, Claude Simon, Nathalie Sarraute, and Claude Ollier—all of whom were published by Les Éditions de Minuit, with the exception of Butor. It is therefore no accident that from his fourth book on, Pinget published there. His subsequent novels were to bear out Robbe-Grillet's intuition about the subversively innovative direction that Pinget's work would take.

An overview of the novels of Pinget's second period would be incomplete without mention of his work for the theater. Beginning in 1963 and throughout his career, Pinget rewrote, restructured, and transposed the themes elaborated in his novels for theatrical presentation, creating more and more original work for the theater. As innovative and challenging as his narratives, Pinget's plays have had considerable success. As the preceding discussion of Pinget's fiction would suggest, transposing these spiraling, inconclusive narratives from page to stage would prove to be no easy task, but Pinget succeeded in doing so.

The Hypothesis sets forth a most harrowing dramatic development of a situation that Pinget first explored in the novel *Clope au dossier* and in the play *Clope:* the loss of a manuscript and the circumstances surrounding it. Circumvented communication runs throughout Pinget's work. The last word can never be written about anything; if it is written, the text containing it must be found wanting and rewritten, for there can be no one single hypothesis, only a proliferation of hypotheses. In *The Hypothesis*, the curtain rises on Alexander Mortin,

Robert Pinget. (Roger Viollet/Getty Images)

pacing about as he revises a paper he is planning to present to an audience. At first, Mortin seems confidently in control both of himself and of the words he strings out in long, somewhat boring sentences, but when he reaches the point in the talk where he brings up the lost manuscript, the play's tone and structure undergo progressive and disturbing changes. The linear account branches off into a paradigmatic series of variants meant to explain or reconstruct the disappearance. Those variants give rise to other variants concerning Mortin's family. When Mortin reaches the point at which his story becomes hopelessly lost in contradictions, he stops, goes back, and begins again from the beginning. As he does so, a filmed image of him is projected on a screen at the rear of the stage. As he drones on, it grows larger and more menacing. This filmed Mortin interrupts the actor Mortin with increasing frequency, contradicting, correcting, offering ever more complicated and elaborate hypotheses until the curtain falls on the shattered scrivener, muttering muddled, circular phrases that come to no conclusion.

Pinget's early work incorporates and acts out a kinetic, highly generative, irrationally poetic approach to

word association reminiscent of the Surrealists. His later, somewhat forbidding narratives are the tightly crafted texts of a writer who has found his distinctive voice and means of expression. The novels and plays of Pinget's second period use intertextual references to call attention to the narrative structures they are making fun of while striking out resolutely in new directions. In these works, Pinget provides plots that are comprehensible (up to a point), quests that develop in a linear fashion before branching out into a bewildering plethora of variants, and language that follows the syntactic patterns of narrational discourse before doubling back on itself in associative spirals. These novels and plays are therefore of particular interest to the general reader inasmuch as they bridge old forms and new. More accessible than Pinget's initial experiments, they provide useful keys to the vital, often puzzling world of Pinget's later novels and plays.

Pinget's later fiction turns even further away from linear narration. The anecdotal fragments are shorter, more frequently interrupted or broken off, and even less causally sequential. As Laurent Jenny has remarked of the New Novel generally, "The book becomes simply a system of variants upon which it is impossible to impose an 'authentic' version of the story being told." In the works of this period, Pinget brings his mastery of the techniques of repetition and alternation to bear on words themselves. Themes and images accumulate and come into focus only to be transformed through new associations. That Pinget's fiction should have evolved in this direction is hardly surprising in the light of his deep and continuing fascination with poetry. Indeed, his later texts come as close to becoming "poèmes en prose" as the New Novel is likely to go.

Although Pinget's work may appear inaccessible at first, it offers rewards of great interest and value to the patient reader. His novels and plays give a gripping, totally honest, unself-indulgent account of the writer at grips with his exacting craft, and the oscillation between old forms and new in Pinget's works makes them an invaluable resource for anyone interested in the theory and practice of French fiction since the 1950's.

The definitive study of the relationships between the practices and techniques of the New Novelists since the 1950's, on the one hand, and the numerous new critical approaches to literature that developed in France in the 1960's and 1970's, on the other hand, has yet to be attempted. Considerable light was shed on this fascinating subject in a 1984 National Endowment for the Humanities summer seminar at Princeton University, "Modern Criticism and Narration," directed by Professor François Rigolot. Suffice it to say, however, that to the reader intrigued by Pinget's narrative strategies, many of these critical approaches yield helpful insights. The converse is also true. Many of Pinget's texts may be considered as forming a fruitful field of study for such diverse approaches to fiction as structural analysis, textuality, audience-oriented criticism, and deconstruction.

Finally, Pinget's quest is worthwhile in its own right. To be sure, the theme of incompletion and the impossibility of communication are depressing, and the steadfast refusal to accept any fixed form is daunting, but humor never abandons Pinget even at his most despairing moments. Humor presupposes a belief in the Divine, which, in turn, presupposes the possibility of transcendence. The letter may never be sent, the manuscript may never be completed, but somehow in these texts that doubt themselves, in these words that question themselves and one another and in so doing generate more words, new words, there is faintly audible the "puny inexhaustible voice still talking" to which William Faulkner alluded in his Nobel Prize acceptance speech. As in Faulkner's work, although in a different register altogether, one finds in Pinget's fiction the profound hope and conviction, against all rational explanation or justification, that the speaking voice and the writing hand will not merely survive but will prevail.

Pinget's first fictional work, *Between Fantoine and Agapa*, was remarkably prescient. Many of its goals and narrative strategies would be taken up later by the New Novelists. Pinget describes this quietly subversive work in a preface written for Barbara Wright's English translation in 1982 as follows:

> This little book is the first I wrote in prose. I had written a number of poems in my youth and I was still very much under the influence of the surrealists, of attempts to approach the unconscious; in short, of experiments made on language in what might be called its nascent state, that's to say: independent of any rational order. A gratuitous game with the vocabulary—that was my passion. Logic seemed to me to be incapable of attaining the very special domain of literature, which in any case I still equate with that of poetry. And so it was a fascination with the possibilities, the absolute freedom of creation, an intense desire to abolish all the constraints of classical writing, that made me produce these exercises.

The collection of stories takes the reader haphazardly through some twenty flights of fancy and concludes with a voyage journal reminiscent of the most freely associative pages of Lewis Carroll or Edward Lear. Pinget delights in playing off literal and figurative expressions, levels of language, cliché, and neologism. Figures of speech become characters; inanimate objects come to life. The formation of sentences results from unexpected and revivifying substitutions and juxtapositions. Through all of this, Pinget taps the vital infralanguage of speech, which refuses to be limited or bound by the normative rules and syntax characteristic of the written. As a result, the prose of Pinget's first book seems at the same time commonplace and bizarre:

I spent my childhood in soap boxes. My father was a film-maker, my mother a glass blower at Murano. She had left me with my grandmother, who lived in a garret. This good old woman was a bit of a bat. I kept in a casket the membrane that joined her arms to her ribs: they're like parchment today. . . . Our everyday fare at the time consisted of bits of plaster and raw rabbits.

Looking back at his first book, Pinget saw in it "all the forms in embryo taken by my later work." In terms of the three common threads mentioned above, it is obvious that Pinget took up such Surrealistic verbal exercises as automatic writing and free association in order to liberate his style from what he terms "the prisons of rationalizing reason." It is equally obvious, however, that the resulting flow of words has been edited and ordered to some degree by the conscious mind. Characteristically, then, from the very beginning, Pinget appropriates a preexisting stylistic approach, modifies it, and makes it his own.

Like his favorite author, Miguel de Cervantes, who used the process of parody to give expression to his vision of life, Pinget pokes fun at the reader's expectations of what a narrative should be and do. As in Cervantes' *Don Quixote de la Mancha* (1605, 1615), the act of writing becomes the book's subject and object, and the reader is invited into a world whose contours are softened and blurred by a gentle, inventive whimsy.

THE INQUISITORY

In the novels of his second period, Pinget uses the presuppositions and formulaic repetitiveness of the mystery story as comic foils. His distortion of the detective story becomes a *reductio ad absurdum* of the narrative strategies and conventions underpinning the "old novel"—its reliance on predictable psychology, linear plot, an omniscient author, an inevitable denouement, and consequential development. In *The Inquisitory*, Pinget taps the intertextual energies of parody as a generative principle, not only in terms of literary genres in the broadest sense but also in his treatment of the informational building blocks that move the *récit* along from one point to the next. The reader of Pinget's previous works may have noted in passing the repetition of familiar names and occurrences. In *The Inquisitory*, the phenomenon of recurrence takes on truly epic proportions. In its four-hundred-odd pages, almost all of the persons, places, and events mentioned in previous works recur, as in the cyni-

cal novels of Honoré de Balzac and Émile Zola. In Pinget's hands, however, recurring material reappears with a difference. Instead of coming into sharper and sharper focus, as it does in the novels of the nineteenth century, Pinget's cross-references to his own work become more and more blurred each time they appear, challenging, disrupting, and sabotaging the novel's linear development by generating new, alternative interpretations.

The Inquisitory begins with the cautionary phrase "Yes or no answer" and is cast in the form of dialogue from the first page to the last. The interlocutors in this often-belligerent verbal exchange appear to be a half-deaf, retired manservant and an investigator or inquisitor of some kind. With dogged persistence, the questioner attempts to ferret out some scandal or other to which the servant may have been privy during his long years of service to the chatelains of the local château—hence the neologism of the title. The old man responds to the questions with apparent goodwill, but the reader soon senses a certain reticence on his part to let slip any potentially scandalous revelations.

Moreover, whenever the questions seem to be about to narrow in on unsavory and satisfactorily conclusive revelations, the old man's answers trail off into interminable lists, endless anecdotes, topographical descriptions, and truncated reminiscences. The linguistic presupposition on which the pursuer in this verbal game of hide-and-seek (or deafman's buff) relies heavily is that the Socratic dialogue will eventually arrive at a single, all-encompassing truth. If this simplistic formulation were true, the narrative would unfold like a Chinese box. The hermeneutic process would inexorably produce a kernel of irreducible truth. In fact, it does not. Instead, the process of question and answer wheels about in long arabesques and ellipses, ending inconsequentially with the old man's refusal to continue.

Beckett would hardly have praised *The Inquisitory* as "one of the most important novels since the War," however, if it were simply the account of a garbled investigation that goes nowhere. In fact, that cautionary initial phrase, "Yes or no answer," sets in motion a far more interesting subdialogue maintained throughout the book, the novelist's interior monologue as he sits down at the typewriter and tries to summon his imaginary world from the void. Considered from this perspective, the novel opens into a simultaneous dialogue on three levels. The interrogator questions the old man, the author cudgels his brain to provide material to fill in the outlines of his imaginary province, and Pinget tacitly invites the reader to be present at the creation of the text. The manuscript pages of *The Inquisitory* illustrate the ebb and flow of the process in visible terms as their margins are crammed with floor plans, maps, sketches of furniture, and doodles as well as the usual cross-outs and emendations.

Determining what actually "happened" at the castle becomes completely unimportant and irrelevant (as well as downright impossible). Instead, Pinget shows to what degree the elements that make up the novel function as paradigmatic, indeterminate series. What appear to be "factual" elements of the story can be related to one another and expressed only approximately or relatively. By programming the paradigmatic elements that undercut the validity of the narrative's linear progression along the syntagmatic axis that moves the text from one anecdotal fragment to another, Pinget causes the novel to produce the reversed, mirror image of a novel as it moves along. As Denis Diderot had done earlier, in *Jacques le fataliste et son maître* (1796; *Jacques the Fatalist and His Master*, 1797), another narrative in question-and-answer form, Pinget effectively defies the reader's expectation of what a novel "should" be by querying implicitly, How can you challenge the novel without writing a novel? It is not surprising, then, that in *The Inquisitory* a thing can be itself and the contrary of itself at the same time. Truly, the search for meaning has made its way into the text at all levels—and with a vengeance.

This systematic frustration of the desire for clarity and definition irritates and troubles the reader, yet few novels capture the agony of the writer facing the blank page as compellingly, and the book's spiral development generates a manic, comic energy. The approximate nature of everything else in *The Inquisitory* spills over into its language, often with extremely amusing results. Because the retired servant is quite deaf, his reception and retransmission of words and phrases (particularly those of foreign derivation) are frequently garbled, resulting in numerous barbarisms, spoonerisms, and malapropisms: "kleptomane" for "clergyman," "tripe-tease" for "striptease," "Ross Royce" for "Rolls-Royce." In this absorbing novel, language generates itself through a process of

translingual inversion, and the "incorrect" transcriptions of words and phrases are often more poetically expressive than the clichés that brought them into being.

THE LIBERA ME DOMINE

In *The Libera Me Domine*, Pinget once again delves into an aspect of the human voice that fascinates him, that of gossip. The novel is set in a small French village. Very little actually happens in the narrative; the intrigue is rather a recounting of the various accounts of events as they are retold by the narrator, who plays a double role—as a villager retelling tales and addressing the reader as a person who is an insider in the village's activity. He often refers to "you know who" and "you know where" rather than mentioning the names of people and places, and thus creates an ambiance of sharing secrets and of complicity with the reader. It is a false relationship, however, because the reader does not know the stories about which the villagers gossip.

The narrator is also the author, with all of the author's privileges and dilemmas. He constantly begins the various stories he is telling and then changes the facts, such that he is writing the novel as the reader is reading it. The reader, however, is denied any creative part in the writing of the novel, being limited to the role of an observer listening to the author's thoughts as he develops the work. Pinget further confuses and disorients the reader/observer by sliding from one past happening to another without any transition.

Pinget breaks the novel form as he denies his narrative any chronological form and any actual fictional plot. The narrative is a compilation of gossip. Pinget uses the ever-changing nature of gossip—which is embellished, deformed, and sensationalized as it is repeated—to create a continuous undercurrent of danger, decay, and death. There are allusions to a boy who was murdered in the woods, to a drunken truck driver who has run someone over, and to the dangers that lurk—especially for children—behind each bush and in every deserted place.

The novel is an excellent example of Pinget's preoccupation not only with voice but also with tone. The repetition of words, names, phrases, and stories, coupled with the rhythmic nature of the prose, re-creates the musical tone of religious chant, especially that of the requiem. Hence the title *The Libera Me Domine* (Deliver me O Lord), the phrase from the requiem or funeral mass that is repeated in the final scenes of the funeral.

THAT VOICE

In *That Voice*, one of Pinget's most resonant and structurally complex texts, a voice localizes itself as "that voice." That voice speaks about and mimics many things: women's gossip over groceries in a country store, words that appear and disappear on a slate, Mortin's last days, the passage of the seasons, the disposition of shops in a small town, a murder that might have been a suicide, the writing of wills, the disappearance of papers, the posthumous validation of a manuscript. In the original French text, there was no punctuation in this flow of prose from fragment to fragment save a period at the end of each paragraph, but Pinget consented to the placement of commas in Barbara Wright's English translation. In both versions, however, the narrative's guiding structural principle relies on fade-outs and cuts as one subject dovetails into another or is abruptly interrupted. Toward the middle of the book, Pinget returns to the subjects of his narrative fragments in reverse order, like someone trying to go further and further back in an effort to remember. Pinget's working title for this book was "Amnesis." The word's literal meaning is "the recalling to memory of things past"; in the context of psychoanalysis it refers to "a patient's remembrance of the early stages of his illness."

The "illness" at issue here is the quest in *Between Fantoine and Agapa*. Pinget attempts to use words to find meaning and transcendence in the confusion and contradictions of daily life and to share the joy and anguish of that attempt as closely as possible with the reader. Viewed from the perspective of linear development, the narrative fails, since by doubling back it "deconstructs" itself into the silence from which it originated. In the supralogical poetic context in which the text is written, however, Pinget succeeds in suggesting a transcendence (life-in-death, the cycle of the seasons, the birth of a new voice from old words) that validates his work.

> The new law.
>
> A window open onto the night.
>
> Crescent moon, July on the wane, the harvest will soon be at an end.

A different voice, but all of a sudden, like a dew, the love of what has been said. . . .

A new law requires a new fable, let's wait until it takes shape with the passing days. . . .

All regrets stifled, task accepted, to recompose as a defense against anguish, no matter where it may come from, that unforgotten dream, then finally leave it far behind . . . for fear of never dying.

TRACES OF INK

Traces of Ink, written shortly before Pinget's death, is the last of the notebooks of Monsieur Songe; it is also Pinget's last commentary on the act of writing and on himself as a writer. Monsieur Songe was Pinget's alter ego. Through this character, Pinget recorded his own autobiography or portrait imbued with a humorous tone. Presented as a collection of random thoughts, Monsieur Songe/Pinget's self-doubts, concerns about the importance of writing, and preoccupation with death are reiterated, as are Monsieur Songe/Pinget's never-ending fascination with words and his faith in writing that flows from a free play of the unconscious.

Robert Henkels
Updated by Shawncey Webb

OTHER MAJOR WORKS

SHORT FICTION: *Entre Fantoine et Agapa*, 1951 (*Between Fantoine and Agapa*, 1982).

PLAYS: *Lettre morte*, pr., pb. 1959 (*Dead Letter*, 1963); *Architruc*, pr., pb. 1961 (English translation, 1967); *L'Hypothèse*, pr., pb. 1961 (*The Hypothesis*, 1967); *Ici ou ailleurs*, pr., pb. 1961 (*Clope*, 1963); *Plays*, 1963 (revised 1967); *Abel et Bela*, pr., pb. 1971 (*Abel and Bela*, 1987); *Identité*, pr., pb. 1971; *Paralchimie*, pr., pb. 1973; *Un Testament bizarre, et autre pieces*, 1986 (*A Bizarre Will, and Other Plays*, 1989; includes *Un Testament bizarre* [*A Bizarre Will*], *Mortin pas mort* [*Mortin Not Dead*], *Dictée* [*Dictation*], *Sophisme et sadisme* [*Sophism and Sadism*], *Le Chrysanthème* [*The Chrysanthemum*], and *Lubie* [English translation]).

RADIO PLAYS: *La Manivelle*, 1960 (*The Old Tune*, 1963); *Autour de Mortin*, 1965 (*About Mortin*, 1967); *Lubie*, 1981.

NONFICTION: *Robert Pinget à la lettre*, 1993.

MISCELLANEOUS: *Trio*, 2005 (includes *Between Fantoine and Agapa*, *That Voice*, and *Passacaglia*).

BIBLIOGRAPHY

Henkels, Robert M., Jr. *Robert Pinget: The Novel as Quest*. Tuscaloosa: University of Alabama Press, 1979. Examines the overriding themes of search and journey in Pinget's works.

Livingston, Beverly. "From A to F and Back: Pinget's Fictive Arena." *Yale French Studies* 57 (1979): 72-85. Provides a close reading of Pinget's novel *Someone*.

Oppenheim, Lois, ed. *Three Decades of the French New Novel*. Urbana: University of Illinois Press, 1986. Collection of essays from a literature colloquium includes discussion of Pinget's work.

Prieto, Eric. *Listening In: Music, Mind, and the Modernist Narrative*. Lincoln: University of Nebraska Press, 2002. Discusses Pinget's interest in music, especially baroque, and his use of musical elements of composition in his works, in particular repetition and variation.

Review of Contemporary Fiction 3, no. 2 (Summer, 1983). Special issue is devoted to the fiction of Pinget and American author Jack Kerouac.

Rosmarin, Leonard A. *Robert Pinget*. New York: Twayne, 1995. Provides criticism and interpretation of Pinget's works as well as information about his life. Includes bibliography and index.

Updike, John. Introduction to *Trio*, by Robert Pinget. Translated by Barbara Wright. Normal, Ill.: Dalkey Archive Press, 2005. One of Pinget's greatest admirers discusses the works of fiction collected in the volume: the short-story collection *Between Fantoine and Agapa* and the novels *That Voice* and *Passacaglia*.

Wright, Barbara. Afterword to *Traces of Ink*, by Robert Pinget. Translated by Barbara Wright. New York: Red Dust, 2000. Insightful discussion of Pinget's work is offered by the translator who has so adeptly brought his fiction to the English-speaking world.

LUIGI PIRANDELLO

Born: Girgenti (now Agrigento), Sicily, Italy; June 28, 1867

Died: Rome, Italy; December 10, 1936

PRINCIPAL LONG FICTION

L'esclusa, 1901 (*The Outcast*, 1925)

Il turno, 1902 (*The Merry-Go-Round of Love*, 1964)

Il fu Mattia Pascal, 1904 (*The Late Mattia Pascal*, 1923)

Suo marito, 1911 (revised 1941; *Her Husband*, 2000)

I vecchi e i giovani, 1913 (*The Old and the Young*, 1928)

Si gira . . . , 1916 (*Shoot! The Notebooks of Serafino Gubbio, Cinematograph Operator*, 1926)

Uno, nessuno, centomila, 1925 (*One, None, and a Hundred Thousand*, 1933)

Tutti i romanzi, 1941 (collected novels)

OTHER LITERARY FORMS

Luigi Pirandello (pee-rahn-DEHL-loh) was an exceptionally prolific writer. In addition to seven novels, he produced numerous volumes of short stories, several collections of poetry, more than forty plays, and a considerable number of essays, reviews, and journalistic pieces. He produced most of his poetry between 1889 and 1912, in the earlier part of his career, and it is as a poet that Pirandello is least remembered. His lyrics are relatively traditional, although they do mirror the writer's inner restlessness. The first compositions recall the strong moral fiber and tones of Giosuè Carducci, the most influential late nineteenth century Italian poet, as well as some of the darkly pessimistic character of critic Arturo Graf's lyrics, whereas the later collections were somewhat influenced by the melancholy and distressed quality of the crepuscular poets.

The short stories are more interesting not only because they contain a number of Pirandellian motifs, narrative devices, and ideas but also because they continued to intrigue the author as a genre. Pirandello produced his first short story as an adolescent; the last appeared the day before his death, although the majority of his stories were penned at the same time as his longer fiction. Pirandello's early stories reflect the influence of Verism; like his literary mentors, Luigi Capuana and Giovanni Verga, Pirandello drew a pessimistic portrait of lives stifled by social conventions and imbued with a tragic fatalism. Unlike his fellow Sicilians, however, Pirandello added elements of irony and paradox, which were to become standard ingredients of his fiction. The irrational pervades these narratives; characters fall prey to chance as the unexpected intrudes on them, all attempts at controlling life being futile; the bizarre and the grotesque are also staples of the Pirandellian diet, distinguishing the author from other *veristi*.

This same universe houses the plays. Pirandello is unquestionably Italy's greatest modern playwright, yet his theater is closely allied in theme and thought to his prose fiction. The critic E. Allen McCormick has pointed out this artistic fraternity, suggesting that novel, short story, and drama "derive their peculiar Pirandellian shape through the interplay of plot and commentary on plot" or, in other terms, the fusion of "action and exposition of action." It is not incidental that more than twenty of Pirandello's plays were based on novellas or sections of novels. One example is *Liolà* (pr. 1916; English translation, 1952), a lighthearted version of an episode taken from the first part of *The Late Mattia Pascal*, which presents a similar plot with a darker sense of humor and a moralizing constituent.

Significantly, Pirandello's serious involvement in theater corresponded to his abandonment of the novel: Only *One, None, and a Hundred Thousand* was published after his first great dramatic success, and that book had been fifteen years in the making. While Pirandello did change genres, he did not radically alter his vision. The author's perceptions of the relativity of reality, the multiplicity of the individual, and the chaos of life recur throughout his fiction and his plays. It is the message of *Così è (se vi pare)* (pr. 1917; *Right You Are [If You Think So]*, 1922), in which an entire town persecutes an unusual family triangle—husband, wife, and mother-in-law—in order to discover the "facts" surrounding their relationship. Is Mrs. Ponza the first or second wife? Is

Mrs. Frola her mother or a sweet madwoman? Who is really crazy, the old woman or her son-in-law? Facts in Pirandello are not solutions: The documents that might answer these questions are unattainable. Thus the truth is irretrievable, as it often is for this writer. The holder of the key is Mrs. Ponza—first or second?—who enters the final scene veiled, only to declare to the assembled busybodies who are destroying her family's precarious emotional equilibrium: "As for myself, I am whoever you believe me to be." Lamberto Laudisi ends the play with his ironic laugh, a final statement on the impossibility of being known.

Laudisi is the playwright's spokesperson, a cerebral protagonist who challenges friends and family to define him or themselves, noting that each person sees others differently, thus creating a series of diverse selves, every one distinguishable from another. The individual himself (or herself) cannot totally know or control these different selves he contains, as symbolized by the utilization of the mirror—a common prop in both drama and fiction—which reflects the individual but also distorts reality: The image of ourselves is inevitably a perversion. This psychological lacuna is a source of pain as well as tragedy in the Pirandellian universe.

A number of the author's characters soothe their existential suffering by rationalizing or by evading their relative selves, or both, as in Henry IV's feigned madness, in Pirandello's *Enrico IV* (pr., pb. 1922; *Henry IV*, 1923), which allows him to live within the fixed confines of medieval history as an emperor—but at the expense of his original identity and of human fellowship. To be aware is to be alone in this fictional universe where communication is blocked because of people's inherent inability to express themselves to others. Pirandello suitably termed his plays *maschere nude* (naked masks), for on the stage his characters uncover their painful humanity to themselves and to the public.

The playwright's themes and technical innovations are illustrated in his best-known work, *Sei personaggi in cerca d'autore* (pr., pb. 1921; *Six Characters in Search of an Author*, 1922), in which the contrast between the fluidity of existence and the stability of form (in this case, art) is embodied in the protagonists. On one hand, there are the six who come to a theater proposing to "be" the subject for a writer; they are unfulfilled characters, conceived but never written down, seeking the eternal life of art. On the other hand, the actors and directors who encounter them offer the flux and change of life. The two groups inevitably clash; the actors who mimic the words and gestures to the characters can only deform them, to the pained realization of the six that they can never be copied but only approximated at best. Art and life, form and flux, remain separate. Within this principal action, the "melo-drama" of the characters' "story" reiterates other Pirandellian motifs: human misunderstanding; the lack of love; the impossibility of communicating one's vision of oneself to others; the multiple aspects of the human personality and the roles deriving from it, which are both social and private; the tragedy of the disintegration of ties; and the need to express rationally passion and suffering. It is the dilemma of the characters that they can neither change their past—for it is Form and thus fixed—nor find absolute realization at the hands of a new writer or within the imitation of themselves offered by the thespians.

Just as *Six Characters in Search of an Author* defied traditional notions of subject matter or content, so too it challenged expectations concerning dramatic form. Indeed, this play marked the end of the traditional stage. In it, the action overflows into the main floor and behind the scenes; acts are abolished in favor of "accidental" divisions, such as the sudden drop of a curtain; there are no sets or backdrops, the stage is bare; characters come and go naturally, utilizing the entire theater. The action unfolds spontaneously, similar to the creative process at work. A character, Madame Pace, is necessary for the continuation of the story; she appears from nowhere, ready to take on her role. The demarcation between art and life disappears: The six relive their story; the actors re-create them, becoming characters. Illusion is made concrete for the audience, causing considerable intellectual and psychological discomfort. The technique of the play within a play is repeated later in *Ciascuno a suo modo* (pr., pb. 1924; *Each in His Own Way*, 1923) and *Questa sera si recita a soggetto* (pr., pb. 1930; *Tonight We Improvise*, 1932), in which reality and illusion are intertwined so completely as to befuddle audience and protagonists alike.

In his later years, Pirandello produced a series of three theatrical myths that encompass his final thoughts

on people and art. *La nuova colonia* (pr., pb. 1928; *The New Colony*, 1958) proposes the social myth of creating a new world, or, at least, a new social order. A group of misfits and undesirables bands together on an island to start their own utopia, only to have their formal social behavior reassert itself, exploding into violence and destruction. *Lazzaro* (pr., pb. 1929; *Lazarus*, 1952) contrasts the inadequacy of dogmatic (and bigoted) religion and the instinctive faith of the natural woman Sara and her simple and sage mate. The last play of the trilogy is Pirandello's final, if incomplete, work.

I giganti della montagna (act 1 pb. 1931, act 2 pb. 1934, act 3 pr. 1937; *The Mountain Giants*, 1958) celebrates the mystery and magic of the imagination. Fantasies come to life, dreams materialize, and reality is suspended in this myth of art, but it is a delicate balance. The death of the main protagonist, an actor obsessed with her mission of bringing the masterpiece of a dead playwright to the world, is often interpreted as the allegory of the impossibility of art to survive in a materialistic world—the realm of the Giants. Unaware of the value of her gift, the brutish henchmen of the Giants kill the actress; they seek entertainment, not art. Crotone, the master of the realm of fantasy, warns that the creative imagination can only prosper in his small space, being doomed in the outside world. It is an appropriately ambiguous conclusion for a writer who states that a feeling for the incongruity of things is an apt basis for literature. *The Mountain Giants* is both an affirmation of the power of art and its mystery and a declaration of its fragility.

ACHIEVEMENTS

Luigi Pirandello was one of the first writers to give voice to the dilemma of modern people. From the outset of his literary career, he exhibited what literary critic Carlo Salinari justly termed "the awareness of crisis," a feeling for the inherent absurdity of life and a sense of the anguish people experience when faced with chaos and nothingness. Pirandello challenged the postulates of Western civilization by subverting their very existence. Denying the possibility of an objective reality, declaring people's fundamental unknowability and multiplicity, and stressing the inherent fluidity of truth and the power of chance, this writer created a tragic vision of the human

Luigi Pirandello. (© The Nobel Foundation)

condition that would influence future generations of thinkers and artists, from the existentialists to Bertolt Brecht, from Eugène Ionesco to Samuel Beckett to Edward Albee.

Signaling the end of a belief in a structured and well-ordered universe, Pirandello opened the doors to anarchy and angst; his works are a death knell for nineteenth century optimism, with its faith in the human ability to shape reality and mold life. His protagonists are caught in uncertainties, trapped in their social masks, unable to forge some measure of meaning in their existence. The Pirandellian character is often disoriented and anxious, struggling in his attempt to establish a fragile inner balance to counteract the chaos and limitations around him. These attempts are illusory but necessary for survival. Often the protagonist who is aware seeks to control this inner turmoil by rationalizing it, by using logic to signify

the irrational. For this reason, Pirandello has often been considered a cerebral writer, a philosopher of sorts, whose spokesmen are his heroes, eloquently arguing their points, in a continuous dialectic with themselves, society, their audience, and life itself.

Having declared the relativity of truth and the inconsistency of the human personality in his uniquely ironic manner, Pirandello poses some of the major themes of twentieth century literature in his own works: the individual's fractured sense of identity, the oppressive nature of society, the inability of words to communicate and reach others, the insufficiency of reason, the conflict between appearances and reality, the pain of living, the difficulty if not impossibility of finding authenticity, the categorizing of the individual into socially determined roles, the fruitless search for absolutes, the existence of unconscious motivations, the condemnation of traditional institutions as instruments of coercion. Pirandello's greatness may well derive from his ability to give these ideas human form and individual names—life—as the characters of dramatic fiction and stirring theater.

BIOGRAPHY

Luigi Pirandello was born a few years after the achievement of Italian unification, into a prosperous middle-class Sicilian family. Stefano Pirandello and Caterina Ricci-Gramitto had initially come together because of their shared patriotic zeal, an enthusiasm whose ashes their son was to depict in his historical novel *The Old and the Young*. Following an early interest in literature, Pirandello studied classics and humanities at the University of Palermo, then at Rome, and finally at Bonn. During these student years, the fledgling writer experienced his first sentimental attachments and briefly flirted with Socialist ideas.

Upon finishing his thesis in linguistics on the dialect of his native Agrigento, Pirandello began his teaching career as a professor of Italian, first in Germany as a university lecturer and later at a women's teaching college in Rome. It was in the Italian capital that the young intellectual developed his first enduring friendships with some of the nation's leading literary figures, notably his fellow Sicilian Luigi Capuana, the father of Verism. It was the beginning of a prolific writing career that was to include numerous articles and reviews, hundreds of short stories, and seven novels, as well as more than forty theatrical works.

In 1894, Pirandello agreed to an arranged marriage to the daughter of a business associate of his father. Maria Antonietta Portulano was a typical southern Italian of limited education, and Pirandello set out to mold her into his ideal woman. The naïve Pygmalion soon discovered that his wife did not share his intellectual interests; indeed, she resented his literary associations and chose to center her life on marital and maternal duties. The marriage was not unhappy, however, and the couple had three children and a comfortable life financed by the family mining business in Sicily.

By 1903, the dilettante author had to his name two novels, three poetry collections, a literary journal, and a play. The collapse of the family's sulfur mine in that year, however, permanently altered the lives of Pirandello and his wife; financial ruin was soon followed by Antonietta's nervous collapse. Pirandello was forced to publish, tutor, and teach to survive. His work for some of the established national periodicals and the appearance of *The Late Mattia Pascal*—critically regarded as his most successful novel—opened the doors to Treves, Italy's most prestigious publishing house. These were years of intense activity but also years of living with a depressed, morbidly jealous wife whose paranoia served to foster his ideas on the multiplicity of the human personality. Antonietta's health deteriorated, as did her mental state, until Pirandello was forced to have her institutionalized in 1919, adding to his distress over his children: Both sons had enlisted in World War I, the elder spending considerable time as a prisoner of war, while his daughter attempted suicide because of the stress of the family situation.

From narrative prose, Pirandello turned to the theater, his first successes coming with Angelo Musco's productions of two plays in Sicilian dialect. The stage became the center of the author's life. Play followed play, more than forty in all. The first typically Pirandellian drama was *Right You Are (If You Think So)*. Like the proverbial prophet, the playwright was not recognized in his own land; Pirandello's first major successes and international fame came from abroad, most notably with *Six Characters in Search of an Author*, the Roman premiere of which was a fiasco—the dramatist and his daughter were mobbed by the crowd and had to be rescued. Acclaim came in Paris, London, and New York. As early as 1923, Manhattan's Fulton Theater created a "Pirandello Season" with the author in attendance. Pirandello's plays gradually entered the standard repertory of European companies. With fame, the writer was able to give up teaching and dedicate himself to his work and to constant international travel. Hoping to create a national theater, Pirandello became the artistic director of the Teatro d'Arte di Roma (1925-1928). The company drew some of Italy's finest acting talent, including Marta Abba, the young first lady who was to become Pirandello's friend, confidant, and inspiration. The now famous dramatist also wrote his last novel in 1925: *One, None, and a Hundred Thousand*.

Pirandello's final years were no less intense: more plays, more travel, cinematic screenplays, constant acclaim. In 1929, he was named to the Italian Academy; the Nobel Prize in Literature followed in 1934. At the time of his death, in 1936, he was an institution, but he went to his final resting place as he desired: Naked, wrapped in a shroud, on a pauper's hearse, without ceremony or accompaniment, Luigi Pirandello was cremated.

ANALYSIS

Luigi Pirandello's first narratives were greatly influenced by the theories and stylistic attitudes of Verism: objective presentations, careful and detailed description, and an impersonal narrator, composing a "photograph" of a specific environment—generally that of the petite bourgeoisie or the proletariat in a regional setting. At first glance, *The Outcast*, composed in 1893, appears as an ideal companion to the novels of the major Sicilian naturalists: Verga's *I malavoglia* (1881; *The House by the Medlar Tree*, 1964) and *Mastro-don Gesualdo* (1889; English translation, 1893, 1923), Capuana's *Il marchese di Roccaverdina* (1901), and Federico De Roberto's *I vicere* (1894; *The Viceroys*, 1962). In point of fact, the plot of Pirandello's novel is very similar to the story line of his friend Capuana's *Ribrezzo* (1885; revulsion): An attractive wife is mistakenly accused of adultery by her husband, is spurned by her father, becomes a social outcast, only to find herself actually committing the act for which she was unjustly blamed, almost as justification for her social leprosy. In naturalistic terms, it seems a stock plot, intended to criticize the prejudices and tyranny of a closed provincial environment that smothers the individual with its notions of propriety, honor, and male supremacy. In *The Outcast*, however, such social commentary gives way to a Pirandellian twist: The punished but innocent wife demonstrates great self-awareness and independence, regaining a measure of her self-respect in her work, only to return to her contrite husband *after* having consummated the adulterous affair that caused so much pain and degradation to her and her entire family. It is a paradoxical, totally unexpected conclusion that clearly points to the novelist's fundamental sense of irony. The innocent victim is rejected while the guilty party is embraced.

THE MERRY-GO-ROUND OF LOVE

In a scholarly essay titled *L'umorismo* (1908; revised 1920; *On Humour*, 1974), Pirandello defines his own inherently ironic voice while proposing a general psychoartistic frame of mind based on a "feeling for the incongruous," which generates literary works that, in turn, create a similar feeling in their audience. His second novel captures just such humor, or irony, in a comic vein. The location is once again the Sicily of small towns and little minds in which *The Merry-Go-Round of Love* is initiated by a well-meaning father who decides to marry off his pretty daughter to an elderly four-time widower who should soon leave her well-to-do and free to follow her heart. In typically Pirandellian fashion, chance intervenes. Unwilling to wait, her lovesick young admirer calls on an influential relative to help him dissolve the girl's abhorrent union; the aggressive lawyer, in turn, falls in love with her, has the marriage annulled, whisks her off to a convent, convinces her of the inevitability of their meeting, and weds her himself in place of the young swain. Soon, however, the possessive and bilious groom dies suddenly; it can be assumed that it will finally be the turn of the patient youth. In this tale of succeeding husbands, unpredictable events accompany the plot to its unanticipated resolution, while the lively old widower contemplates a new bride.

THE OLD AND THE YOUNG

In a far different temper, *The Old and the Young* returns to the Sicily of the earlier novels to present a sweeping picture of the political and social events that dominated the island in the 1890's. In this historical novel, various factual occurrences are depicted—the rise of the middle class, the development of the Socialist Party, the atmosphere of social agitation leading to the proclamation of a state of siege and military repression, and the Banca Romana financial scandal that shook the peninsula—from the author's pessimistic viewpoint, painting a tableau of collective and personal failures, ranging from the betrayal of the Romantic ideals of the Italian struggle for unification to the fall of southern socialism, from moral and financial bankruptcy to madness and murder. Numerous characters weave in and out of a complex narrative of social and private ambitions, class conflict, personal corruption, doomed loves, and human loss. The old are responsible for the demise of patriotic and social ideals and for the state of current ills; the young are caught in the crystallized social structures that suffocate them. It is a bitter vision, without any moderating illusions. Individuals fall under forces greater than themselves in a world full of misfits and alienated souls. In this novel, individual turmoil flows uneasily into historical chaos. The failed illusions of Pirandello's only historical novel are basically social—liberty, justice, equality, patriotism—but they evoke a similar defeat at the personal level. The novelist's best-known and most appreciated works are told by narrators/protagonists who concurrently expose their inner selves and comment on the world about them: Mattia Pascal, Serafino Gubbio, and Vitangelo Moscarda.

THE LATE MATTIA PASCAL

In *The Late Mattia Pascal*, Pascal's life story is quintessential Pirandello. After a happy and reckless childhood, Mattia is thrust into adulthood by his marriage to the lovely and pregnant Romilda, who comes to resent their poverty and becomes quite the shrew. Unhappily married, losing both his gentle mother and beloved baby, the hero runs off to Monte Carlo for a temporary reprieve. There he has some unusual encounters and wins a tidy sum at the casino. On the way back to Romilda (and his difficulties), Mattia reads about his own death, having been mistakenly recognized in the deformed body of a drowned suicide. This unexpected turn of events offers him a great opportunity to be free, or so he believes. Taking on a new identity, a new presence, and a new lifestyle, Mattia becomes Adriano Meis, wanderer. After a lengthy period of travel, Adriano decides to settle in Rome awhile, becoming one of the pensioners in the Paleari family. Gradually, inevitably, Meis involves himself in society and in the lives of others, particularly interested in the delicate and sensitive Adriana Paleari. It is through these relationships and because of a series of casual events, such as the theft of some money, that the new man realizes he has no valid identity, lacking any documents and thus, any legal right to exist. Without social credentials, Adriano Meis cannot marry, own a dog, file a police report. Without a past, without human ties, his life and freedom become meaningless. Having sought authenticity, Mattia Pascal has become a shadow man instead. In order to exist once more, Adriano fakes a suicide and returns home as Mattia, only to find his wife contentedly remarried with a baby. The only solution is to remain dead, legally nonexistent but at least equipped with a social identity. The sign of this existential absurdity is the narrator's visits to the grave of the late Mattia Pascal.

Setting aside the naturalist emphasis on objective narration, Pirandello dives headlong into modernism. *The Late Mattia Pascal* is fictional autobiography and private confession, a work that is declaratively subjective. The novel is also a parable on people's relationship to the social environment; it is, in some ways, an ironic and modernized version of the Prodigal Son returning to a bitter homecoming. Caught in the prison of tradition and conventions, Pascal is a victim. He is not yet aware that his social roles define him and compose his connection to the world of others. Such awareness comes through his alter ego, Adriano Meis. Having believed in his escape into freedom, the dual hero, Adriano/Mattia, must come face-to-face with the price of such presumed liberty: rootlessness and solitude. More important, he comes to the realization that liberty from oneself is impossible. Having become free of his past, he has become the spectator of life but can no longer be a participant. He is truly an outlaw, outside the law's reach and also its security, excluded from all emotional fellowship and totally self-dependent and alone.

From an understandable impulse to escape, Mattia progresses to a meditative understanding of the absurdity of an anchorless existence, preferring subordination to the social ties and conventions that bind the individual

but also define him. Pascal is one of Pirandello's first self-conscious protagonists, a type defined within the text by Anselmo Paleari, Adriano's philosophical landlord who has developed an ontological system called "lanternosophy" that speaks to modern man's sad privilege of "seeing himself live," which Paleari compares to a marionette, Orestes. Intent on his passionate thoughts of revenge (that is, "living"), Orestes suddenly perceives a rip in the paper sky of his puppet stage; action becomes contemplation. Aware of himself, Orestes stops, unable to act. He has been transformed into Hamlet, the embodiment of existential incongruity and psychological impotence. Modern man is this absurdly aware puppet of life.

Notwithstanding these themes of alienation and inescapability, the tone of *The Late Mattia Pascal* is not tragic, but humorous, as befits a narrator who has developed "a taste for laughing at all my misfortunes and at my every torment" and is well aware of "our infinite smallness." Naturally, it is the ironic lightness proposed in Pirandello's essay *On Humour*, with its emphasis on the incongruous. Much of the comedy in the novel is offered by the minor characters, for it is peopled with amusing, funny, and grotesque *macchiette*—character studies—that moderate the book's serious elements. Even death is presented for its mystery, unpredictability, and absurdity in much of the plot: Mattia wins at Monte Carlo using his mother's funeral money; it is the unknown suicide that allows him to become Adriano Meis, and it is a second suicide, planned and false, that permits him to resurrect Mattia; there is even Max, an obliging ghost, in attendance at Anselmo Paleari's séances. The unknown and the unexpected rule this fictional universe, appropriately symbolized by the roulette game, godmother of Pascal's transformation, wheel of fortune, goddess of chance. In his "Notice on the Scruples of Imagination" that accompanies this novel, Pirandello justifies the use of fantasy in its plot and in art in general, stating that there is no need to defend such absurdities "that have no need to appear probable, for they are true."

SHOOT! THE NOTEBOOKS OF SERAFINO GUBBIO, CINEMATOGRAPH OPERATOR

Shoot! The Notebooks of Serafino Gubbio, Cinematograph Operator is a far less whimsical work. Set in the Roman world of silent filmmaking, its tale is unfolded in the pages of a diary or journal kept by Serafino

Gubbio, cameraman by accident, as he observes and comments on what he sees. "Seeing" is Gubbio's peculiar characteristic; his watching is really study, an attempt to glimpse in others what he lacks, namely, "the certainty that they understand what they're doing" in the midst of their frenetic lives. Seeing is also part of his job: He is the eyes of his camera. Gubbio's is the most modern of Pirandellian alienations: people at the service of machines, seeking to become machinelike themselves, that is, to acquire a similar imperturbability—having already determined they had no need of a soul. Gubbio allows himself to grow depersonalized as a protective measure against the pain of living, hoping to become as desensitized to his surroundings as the camera he holds. If Mattia Pascal tries for an impossible authenticity, Gubbio prefers to escape his humanity altogether, watching everything, including himself, from a distance.

One of the objects of his visual study is the actor Varia Nestoroff, a Russian femme fatale, whose shady past has also touched the cameraman's former life. A young and gifted painter had loved her purely and completely; unable to bear his devotion, the woman proceeded to seduce his sister's fiancé, Aldo Nuti. Gubbio had known the family of the painter well, and they had formed the one idyllic memory of his existence until it was destroyed by the foreign beauty. Nestoroff is tortured by her inner demons and the weight of her secret guilt. Gubbio soon notes that the woman's acting is an externalization of her inner being: violent, dramatic, sensual, and overpowering.

For a brief period, the protagonist allows himself to be sucked into life. He feels compassion for Nestoroff, his landlord, a caged tiger, a vagabond musician, and the tormented Aldo Nuti, who also joins the film company. He also falls hopelessly in love with sweet little Luisetta, who, in turn, is equally and hopelessly fond of Nuti, who still loves the memory of his former lost fiancé and hates the woman who seduced him. The past swarms into Gubbio's memory as well, filling him with nostalgic regret and pity for the tragic family he had loved. Nudged out of his impassiveness, Gubbio soon realizes the futility of his emotional expenditures. Thus, he returns behind the glass eye of his "black spider": It is a desire for oblivion. In front of him, the imitation of life with all of its frantic manifestations—the film scenes—plays on

as he mechanically turns the handle. Arcangelo Leone De Castris suggests that shooting pictures is a way of portraying one's own absence from life, and it is to the state of nonbeing that Gubbio moves, distraught by his recently renewed connections to society and existence. The camera functions as a barrier between him and others. In this identity as a passive, mechanical spectator, Serafino Gubbio becomes totally enclosed in his "thing's silence" in the final pages of his notebooks. Shooting the last scene of an important adventure film, the cameraman is caught in the tragedy of Aldo Nuti and Varia Nestoroff. Instead of killing the tiger, Nuti turns his gun on his former mistress and is then torn to pieces by the cat. The perfect machine, Gubbio obeys the call of the camera, automatically registering it all, glued to the handle, and shocked into muteness, forever a willing thing in its silence.

Somewhat experimental stylistically, *Shoot! The Notebooks of Serafino Gubbio, Cinematograph Operator* is, however, an inconsistent work, accused of actually being three novels in one by critic Umberto Bosco, who catalogs it as a story of the destructive mechanization of modern life, an idyll in the nostalgic recovery of Gubbio's past memories, and a book about the early years of the cinema and its odd denizens. The novel is held together by the coexistence of all three threads in the single consciousness of its protagonist narrator.

ONE, NONE, AND A HUNDRED THOUSAND

One, None, and a Hundred Thousand takes introspective narration one step further. The protagonist of *The Late Mattia Pascal* tells the story of his life factually and chronologically, interspersing it with personal commentaries and insights; Serafino Gubbio presents a diary, notebooks that recount the inner man as well as external episodes; Vitangelo Moscarda's tale is the story of a spiritual journey. Pirandello was absorbed by *One, None, and a Hundred Thousand*, working on it for more than a decade. Its themes are not new but evoke those contained in his earlier books. If Mattia Pascal attempts a new identity and Serafino Gubbio chooses "thing"-hood, Vitangelo Moscarda opts for madness.

Moscarda is thrown into self-awareness and self-analysis by his nose or, more exactly, by his wife Dida's banal remark on the tilt of his nose. Discovering that he is unfamiliar with his body, Moscarda quickly progresses to the realization that he is even more unfamiliar with his inner self. The next step in his road to insight is the perception that others do not know him as he knows himself but have their own images of him, which they firmly believe to be the true man. Like the Orestes/Hamlet puppet, Vitangelo Moscarda catches himself in the act of living, forcing him to contemplate his identity. At first it is the stranger reflected in a window or mirror that concerns him, but it soon becomes the stranger in himself that obsesses the young man. He analyzes his social roles, against which he quickly rebels, unwilling to be the idiotic "Gengè" his wife sees and loves, the "usurer" the town believes him to be, or any of a number of his other multiple selves. Moscarda makes a supreme effort to see himself from the outside, as others see him, as he cannot see himself, and soon intuits that the belief in a unified personality is a mirage. The novel's title is exegetical: People believe in their wholeness but are actually numerous persons, chameleons who adapt to their changing environments and audience; being the object of so many differing views, there are a hundred thousand "I"s and actually no *one* self.

Aware of being the daily construction of himself and others, Moscarda is driven by his discovery, feeling imprisoned in his body, his name(s), his house, his reputation, his town, his roles, and his very historical situation. Desperate to be for others what he wishes to be for himself, he challenges "normal" behavior. For example, to prove he is not a usurer, he first evicts a poor tenant and then gives him an attractive new home, thus obtaining the collective appellation of "madman." In a frenzy to take control of his own existence, Moscarda initially determines to stop the regular flow of his life by a series of abnormal acts that reflect his recognition of the relativity of all and challenge the world about him to reassess and redefine him as he himself has already done. Instead, the others react in disbelief, for they do not recognize "their" Vitangelo Moscarda(s). His wife leaves him, and his business managers view him as an idiot, particularly when he expresses a desire to give away all of his possessions because they do not come from "him" but rather are inherited. Lacking common (collective) sense, searching for self-determination free of all encumbrances, and frightfully aware of the innate solitude of every person— since no one can ever truly know another—Moscarda

chooses spiritual liberation in the only way open to him: apart, one with nature, poor, and mad. Pirandello's novel concludes on this paradoxical note also sounded by his first novel: to be someone, the (anti)hero must resolve to live as no one, dying and being reborn at every moment, "alive and whole, no longer in myself, but in every thing outside myself."

Fiora A. Bassanese

OTHER MAJOR WORKS

SHORT FICTION: *Amori senza amore*, 1894; *Quando'ero matto . . .*, 1902; *Beffe della morte e della vita*, 1902-1903 (2 volumes); *Bianche e nere*, 1904; *Erma bifronte*, 1906; *La vita nuda*, 1910; *Terzetti*, 1912; *Le due maschere*, 1914; *Erba del nostro orto*, 1915; *La trappola*, 1915; *E domani, lunedì*, 1917; *Un cavallo nella luna*, 1918; *Berecche e la guerra*, 1919; *Il carnevale dei morti*, 1919; *A Horse in the Moon, and Twelve Short Stories*, 1932; *Better Think Twice About It!, and Twelve Other Stories*, 1933; *The Naked Truth, and Eleven Other Stories*, 1934; *Four Tales*, 1939; *The Medals, and Other Stories*, 1939; *Short Stories*, 1959; *Selected Stories*, 1964; *Short Stories*, 1964; *The Merry-Go-Round of Love, and Selected Stories*, 1964.

PLAYS: *La morsa*, pb. 1898 (as *L'epilogo*, pr. 1910; *The Vise*, 1928); *Scamandro*, pb. 1909; *Lumìe di Sicilia*, pr. 1910 (*Sicilian Limes*, 1921); *Il dovere del medico*, pb. 1912 (*The Doctor's Duty*, 1928); *Se non così . . .*, pr. 1915; *All'uscita*, pr. 1916 (*At the Gate*, 1928); *Liolà*, pr. 1916 (English translation, 1952); *Pensaci, Giacomino!*, pr. 1916; *Il berretto a sonagli*, pr. 1917 (*Cap and Bells*, 1957); *Così è (se vi pare)*, pr. 1917 (*Right You Are [If You Think So]*, 1922); *La giara*, pr. 1917 (*The Jar*, 1928); *Il piacere dell'onestà*, pr. 1917 (*The Pleasure of Honesty*, 1923); *Il giuoco delle parti*, pr. 1918 (*The Rules of the Game*, 1959); *Ma non è una cosa seria*, pr. 1918; *La patente*, pb. 1918 (*The License*, 1964); *L'innesto*, pr. 1919; *L'uomo, la bestia, e la virtù*, pr., pb. 1919 (*Man, Beast, and Virtue*, 1989); *Come prima, meglio di prima*, pr. 1920; *La Signora Morli, una e due*, pr. 1920; *Tutto per bene*, pr., pb. 1920 (*All for the Best*, 1960); *Sei personaggi in cerca d'autore*, pr., pb. 1921 (*Six Characters in Search of an Author*, 1922); *Enrico IV*, pr., pb. 1922 (*Henry IV*, 1923); *L'imbecille*, pr. 1922 (*The Imbecile*, 1928); *Vestire gli ignudi*, pr. 1922 (*Na-*

ked, 1924); *L'altro figlio*, pr. 1923 (*The House with the Column*, 1928); *L'uomo dal fiore in bocca*, pr. 1923 (*The Man with the Flower in His Mouth*, 1928); *La vita che ti diedi*, pr. 1923 (*The Life I Gave You*, 1959); *Ciascuno a suo modo*, pr., pb. 1924 (*Each in His Own Way*, 1923); *Sagra del Signore della nave*, pb. 1924 (*Our Lord of the Ship*, 1928); *Diana e la Tuda*, pr. 1926 (in Switzerland; *Diana and Tudo*, 1950); *L'amica della mogli*, pr., pb. 1927 (*The Wives' Friend*, 1949); *Bellavita*, pr. 1927 (English translation, 1964); *La nuova colonia*, pr., pb. 1928 (*The New Colony*, 1958); *The One-Act Plays of Luigi Pirandello*, 1928; *Lazzaro*, pr., pb. 1929 (*Lazarus*, 1952); *O di uno o di nessuno*, pr., pb. 1929; *Sogno (ma forse no)*, pb. 1929 (*I'm Dreaming, but Am I?*, 1964); *Come tu mi vuoi*, pr., pb. 1930 (*As You Desire Me*, 1931); *Questa sera si recita a soggetto*, pr., pb. 1930 (*Tonight We Improvise*, 1932); *I giganti della montagna*, act 1 pb. 1931, act 2 pb. 1934, act 3 pr. 1937 (*The Mountain Giants*, 1958); *Trovarsi*, pr., pb. 1932 (*To Find Oneself*, 1943); *Quando si è qualcuno*, pr. 1933 (*When Someone Is Somebody*, 1958); *La favola del figlio cambiato*, pr., pb. 1934; *Non si sa come*, pr. 1934 (*No One Knows How*, 1960); *Naked Masks: Five Plays*, 1952.

POETRY: *Mal giocondo*, 1889; *Pasqua di Gea*, 1891; *Pier Gudrò*, 1894; *Elegie renane*, 1895; *Scamandro*, 1909 (dramatic poem); *Fuori de chiave*, 1912.

NONFICTION: *Arte e scienze*, 1908; *L'umorismo*, 1908 (revised 1920; *On Humour*, 1974); *Saggi*, 1939.

TRANSLATION: *Elegie romane*, 1896 (of Johann Wolfgang von Goethe's *Römische Elegien*).

MISCELLANEOUS: *Opere*, 1966.

BIBLIOGRAPHY

Bassanese, Fiora A. *Understanding Luigi Pirandello*. Columbia: University of South Carolina Press, 1997. Informative introduction to Pirandello's work focuses largely on his thought and the relationship of his life to his writings. Includes discussions of some of his novels as well as his plays.

Biasin, Gian-Paolo, and Manuela Gieri, eds. *Luigi Pirandello: Contemporary Perspectives*. Buffalo: University of Toronto Press, 1999. Collection of essays provides modern perspectives on the work of Pirandello, including analyses of his novel *The Late Mattia Pascal*. Includes bibliographical references.

Caesar, Ann. *Characters and Authors in Luigi Pirandello*. New York: Clarendon Press, 1998. Thorough study focuses on the importance of character in all of Pirandello's writings, including his novels. Examines how his fictional characters fight to maintain their own identities.

Cambon, Glauco, ed. *Pirandello*. Englewood Cliffs, N.J.: Prentice-Hall, 1967. Collection of twelve essays includes Adriano Tilgher's seminal Pirandello criticism and moves on through critical views of the 1960's, a period of intense interest in Pirandello's influence on world literature of the early twentieth century. Includes a detailed chronology and a select bibliography.

Caputi, Anthony. *Pirandello and the Crisis of Modern Consciousness*. Urbana: University of Illinois Press, 1988. Discusses Pirandello as the source of the twentieth century's literary recognition and explication of the crisis of self-awareness. Includes equal reference to all forms of Pirandello's work, not limiting itself to his plays. Supplemented by an extensive Italian and English bibliography and an index.

DiGaetani, John Louis, ed. *A Companion to Pirandello Studies*. Westport, Conn.: Greenwood Press, 1991. Comprehensive volume contains twenty-seven essays on Pirandello's biography and work as well as an excellent introduction and informative appendixes. Several essays focus on Pirandello as a novelist, although the majority discuss his plays.

O'Grady, Deidre. *Piave, Boito, Pirandello: From Romantic Realism to Modernism*. Lewiston, N.Y.: Edwin Mellen Press, 2000. Traces the development of Italian literature through analysis of the works of Pirandello, Arrigo Boito, and Francesco Maria Piave, among others. Helps to place Pirandello's work in a larger context. Includes bibliography and index.

O'Rawe, Catherine. *Authorial Echoes: Textuality and Self-Plagiarism in the Narrative of Luigi Pirandello*. London: Legenda, 2005. Focuses on Pirandello's novels and other narrative fiction, including the historical novel *The Old and the Young* and the autobiographical *Her Husband*. Argues that Pirandello was a "self-plagiarist" who constantly revised his work and reused his own material.

Radcliff-Umstead, Douglas. *The Mirror of Our An-*

guish: A Study of Luigi Pirandello's Narrative Writing. Rutherford, N.J.: Fairleigh Dickinson University Press, 1978. Provides an introduction to Pirandello's seven novels and other narrative fiction. Includes an excellent opening chapter on Pirandello's philosophy of literature and its role in literary history. Supplemented with an extensive bibliography and an index.

Starkie, Walter. *Luigi Pirandello*. 3d ed. Berkeley: University of California Press, 1965. Classic work by a widely recognized Pirandello scholar focuses on the author's position as inheritor of one literary tradition

and forerunner of another. Provides one of the few extended commentaries available on Pirandello's prose fiction, novels, and short stories, and does so in nontechnical style. Includes bibliography and index.

Stella, M. John. *Self and Self-Compromise in the Narratives of Pirandello and Moravia*. New York: Peter Lang, 2000. Analyzes works by Pirandello, including his novel *The Late Mattia Pascal*, and by Alberto Moravia to examine how the two authors treat issues of identity. Emphasizes how their concepts of individual identity were influenced by Buddhist doctrines.

DAVID PLANTE

Born: Providence, Rhode Island; March 4, 1940
Also known as: David Robert Plante

PRINCIPAL LONG FICTION

The Ghost of Henry James, 1970
Slides, 1971
Relatives, 1972
The Darkness of the Body, 1974
Figures in Bright Air, 1976
The Family, 1978
The Country, 1981
The Woods, 1982
The Francoeur Novels, 1983 (includes previous 3 novels)
The Foreigner, 1984
The Catholic, 1985
The Native, 1987
The Accident, 1991
Annunciation, 1994
The Age of Terror, 1999
ABC, 2007

OTHER LITERARY FORMS

In addition to his novels, David Plante has published short stories and essays as well as two memoirs. He has been a frequent contributor of short fiction to *The New Yorker* magazine, including stories such as "Mr. Bonito" (1980), "Work" (1981), "The Accident" (1982), and "A

House of Women" (1986). He has also served as a reviewer and features writer for *The New York Times Book Review* and has contributed essays and introductions to works such as *Wrestling with the Angel: Faith and Religion in the Lives of Gay Men* (1995), edited by Brian Bouldrey. Plante's *Difficult Women: A Memoir of Three* (1983) is an account of his relationships with Sonia Orwell, George Orwell's widow, and writers Jean Rhys and Germaine Greer. *American Ghosts* (2005) is a personal memoir in which Plante focuses on how writing has served to link his past to his present by helping him to come to grips with his lineage as a French Canadian in New England, his Catholic upbringing, and his sexual orientation.

ACHIEVEMENTS

Although David Plante has never enjoyed a large readership, he has achieved considerable recognition among his peers, winning the acclaim of Philip Roth and other prominent contemporaries. Plante began his career with several self-consciously artistic novels, but in his later works he fashioned a spare, radically simplified style with a deceptive look of artlessness. In contrast to the minimalist writers to whose works his fiction bears a superficial resemblance, Plante uses this pared-down style as a vehicle to explore the consciousness of his protagonists, which he presents in a manner that differs sharply from the involuted style of most novels of consciousness. This is Plante's distinctive achievement in contemporary American fiction.

Plante's sixth novel, *The Family*, was nominated for the National Book Award in 1979. In 1983, while teaching writing at the University of Tulsa in Tulsa, Oklahoma, Plante received a Guggenheim grant, and in the same year he won the Prize for Artistic Merit from the American Academy and Institute of Arts and Letters. He also received an award from the British Arts Council Bursary and was named a fellow of the Royal Society of Literature.

BIOGRAPHY

David Plante was born in Providence, Rhode Island, on March 4, 1940, the son of Anaclet Joseph Adolph Plante and Albina (Bison) Plante. In 1959-1960, he attended the University of Louvain in Belgium, and in 1961 he earned a B.A. from Boston College. After graduation, Plante taught at the English School in Rome, Italy, at the Boston School of Modern Languages, and at St. John's Preparatory School. He also worked for two years (1962-1964) as a researcher for *Hart's Guide to New York* in New York City. In 1966, inspired, in part, by the example of the Anglo-American novelist Henry James, Plante settled in England, where he met Nickos Stangos, who would become his life partner.

Although he became a British citizen, Plante continued to spend time on both sides of the Atlantic; he was a writer-in-residence at the University of Tulsa (1979-1983) and at King's College, Cambridge (1984-1985). The first Westerner allowed to teach at the Gorky Institute of Literature in Moscow, Plante also served as writer-in-residence at the University of East Anglia (1977-1978), Adelphi University (1980-1989), and L'Université du Quebec à Montreal (1990). In 1998, he was named professor of writing at Columbia University. He divides his residency between New York and London.

ANALYSIS

David Plante's work is significant primarily for its contribution to the genre of the modernist novel of consciousness. His early experimental novels, although static and highly derivative, adumbrate the techniques Plante would later refine in novels that artfully explore the self-consciousness of individuals as they strive to understand their relationship with the external world. Plante succeeds in creating, through an often masterful command of language, a powerful synesthesia, blending paintings of the mind with the art of storytelling.

The dominant themes in Plante's novels concern the nature of relationships and the efforts of the individual to break out of self-consciousness in order to participate in these relationships. He explores the forces that unite people, whether family members, friends, or lovers, and the ability of these forces to bind as well as alienate, create as well as destroy.

Plante's method of narration in his early works reveals unconventional techniques that he later incorporated into his more traditional novels. In his earliest works, such as *The Ghost of Henry James*, *Slides*, *Relatives*, *The Darkness of the Body*, and *Figures in Bright Air*, Plante experiments with an almost plotless structure with an emphasis on language and the expression of consciousness, echoing Henry James, Nathaniel Hawthorne, James Joyce, and Gertrude Stein. Instead of a narrative of progression and movement within a defined space and time, these novels present random associations from constantly changing perspectives. Plante often creates snapshots of consciousness in the form of numerous brief narrative sections that flash in front of the reader, revealing not concrete images but glimpses of various characters' impressions, perceptions, and emotions. Through this technique, Plante attempts to use a character's consciousness to define and describe meaning, leading many critics to observe that these early novels are not novels at all but rather collections of psychological fragments that, though often powerful, ultimately confuse and disappoint the reader.

THE FRANCOEUR NOVELS

With the publication of his largely autobiographical trilogy *The Francoeur Novels* (which includes *The Family*, *The Country*, and *The Woods*) in 1983, Plante continued to develop his theme of relationships between family members through the perspective of subjective consciousness and fragmented images, but he integrated these experimental techniques into a more traditionally defined narrative. The first book of the trilogy, *The Family*, introduces Daniel Francoeur, Plante's autobiographical counterpart in the trilogy, and his six brothers, born to a Catholic, working-class French Canadian couple,

Jim and Reena Francoeur. The novel is set primarily in Providence, Rhode Island, at the Francoeurs' newly acquired lake home. Plante traces the emotional struggle of the nine family members to remain unified, communicative, and productive in the face of internal tension and external threat. Because of their ethnic background and unsophisticated social orientation, the family members feel alienated from the Providence community, and when Jim loses his job through union pressure, the internal problems within the family are magnified at the same time the bonds of love and dependence between individual members are tested.

Although most of the narrative is seen and evaluated through Daniel's consciousness, the focus of the novel is not on him or on any one character; rather, it is on the Francoeur family as a single living organism trying to support and nurture all of its parts for the survival of the whole. The dependence of each family member on the well-being of the others is exemplified by the hysterical disintegration of the family unit when Reena experiences a recurrence of an emotional illness.

Plante develops Reena's character more fully than he does the others in *The Family*, and he examines her closely through Daniel's eyes, making her the touchstone for the novel's major theme: the fragility of the seemingly indestructible. Reena possesses the objectivity to see quite clearly the flaws in the character of each of her sons while simultaneously loving each totally; she is unable, however, to acknowledge her husband's inability to cope with his unemployment. Her failure to deal with her husband as a fallible human being forces her sons to take sides against their father and ultimately to question their familial duties.

Despite her strength and authority as the Francoeur matriarch, Reena remains a child-wife, puzzled and victimized by an uncommunicative, brooding husband. She confides frequently in Daniel, who comes to see his mother's position in the family as isolated and vulnerable. The only woman in a world full of men, an interloper in a fraternity house environment, Reena has tried to remain as unobtrusive as possible in her husband's and sons' world, from avoiding bringing into the house flowers and lacy decorations that might intrude on their male starkness to suppressing her fears and anger. She has created, literally, seven times over, a world that she can

never enter. When her emotional breakdown occurs and Jim resists getting medical help for her, afraid she might come back from the sanatorium as something other than his submissive wife, the family organism suffers a shock and responds with violence: sons against father, mother against sons, brothers against brothers. The novel concludes with a semblance of unity, but the organism has been damaged.

The damage is subtly revealed in the second (although last-written) book of the trilogy, *The Woods*. Peace has returned to the Francoeur home, but only because Jim and Reena have surrendered to a self-imposed isolation and stagnant existence. They appear only peripherally in the novel, and the focus remains on Daniel, who visits his parents' home during a vacation from college. An extremely self-conscious adolescent, Daniel finds himself facing terrifying indecision and overwhelming freedom. Though little action takes place in the novel's three brief chapters, Plante conveys in simple yet intense language Daniel's need to belong, to anchor himself somewhere, to overcome his apathy and lack of ambition. Daniel's first sexual experience brings him no closer to what he wants as he becomes increasingly obsessed with the maleness of his own body. His decision to file with the draft board as a conscientious objector, despite the influence of his older brother Albert, a lifelong military man, role model, and major source of financial support for the Francoeurs, does give Daniel a sense of definition, though it is mixed with shame. In *The Woods*, Plante creates in Daniel a representation of the time in adolescence when passivity is the safest action, when any other action seems too great a risk, and when even one's own body appears strange and threatening.

This period in Daniel's life has long passed when *The Country* opens. Once again, Daniel, now a writer living in London, returns to his parents' home in Providence, where he joins his six brothers, not for any holiday or family celebration but as a response to the final assault on the family unit: the slow, degrading physical and mental deterioration of Reena and Jim Francoeur. Now in their eighties, they are weakened to the point of partial immobility and senility. The sons, some with wives and children, gather to take care of their parents' basic needs as well as to attempt, in quiet desperation, to restore the bonds of familial understanding and love. Reena's mental problems have intensified with age, and Daniel listens, as always, to her frightened and often bitter ramblings about her sacrifices for her husband and family. In more tender moments, however, Reena shows her devotion to her dying husband, frequently enveloping his withered body in her arms, grasping his hands in silence, and kissing his cheek. Reena is also still able to express love toward her sons, sharing their secrets and laughing at the jokes whispered to her in French.

The Country does not, however, use Reena as a symbol for the state of the Francoeur family as the first novel did. Except for a brief flashback to twenty years earlier at a tense family gathering at the lake house, the last book of the Francoeur trilogy explores the character of Jim, who in the earlier works receives uneven and ambiguous treatment. Through a first-person narrative, Daniel attempts to understand the complexities of a man who once seemed so simple. In moments of lucidity, Jim expresses to Daniel his doubts about having been a good father, husband, and worker, and Daniel realizes that, despite his father's domination over his mother and the unrelenting sense of social and familial duties imposed on his sons, Jim loved his family in every way that his Old World cultural background permitted, limited greatly by an inability to express his emotions.

As Daniel witnesses the pathetic deterioration of his once hearty and active father, he frantically tries to re-establish communication and a sense of tradition. In response, his father awkwardly attempts to understand his son's life as a writer in a foreign country. Ultimately, the father, drifting in and out of the present in a cloudy mind, leaves his son the only wisdom he knows: "Work hard. . . . And be a good boy." When his father dies, Daniel is able to grieve honestly for a man who, he now realizes, "could not think of himself, but had to think of his duty to the outside world." Reena, after an initial feeling of emancipation from her husband's authority, reacts to his death by retreating into incessant speech and fearful imaginings, once again alone among the men she created.

In *The Country*, the strongest work in the trilogy, Plante achieved what he had been working toward since his first novels: the subordination of plot with an emphasis on emotion and perception. The only significant action in *The Country* is the observation of time and death, but the helplessness of every member of the Francoeur

family is a haunting and consistent echo throughout the novel. This echo gives *The Country* a power not realized in Plante's earlier works.

THE FOREIGNER

In the two novels succeeding the Francoeur trilogy, Plante's protagonist continues to narrate in the first person, though he is never mentioned by name in the earlier work, *The Foreigner*; only through allusions to the hero's family background does the author identify him as a member of the Francoeur family, probably Daniel once again. Adam Mars-Jones has suggested in a review of *The Foreigner* that the narrator may be Daniel's older brother Andre, noting that at the end of *The Family* the Francoeurs receive a postcard from Andre, who is in Europe, the same postcard that is mentioned in *The Foreigner*. This connection does exist, but the narrator of *The Foreigner* undeniably possesses the same history, voice, and sensibility as the protagonist of *The Francoeur Novels*, whatever name the reader gives him.

The Foreigner does not relate to the trilogy in any other way, nor does it follow the previous work chronologically. In this novel, the hero is twenty and leaving his Rhode Island home in 1959 to travel to Europe, hoping to shed his "Americanisms" and experience the expatriate lifestyle in the fashion of Ernest Hemingway, whose epigraph, "In Spain you could not tell anything," introduces the book. Instead of the romance and rebirth he expected, the narrator discovers loneliness and alienation from the environment and the people, even his American college friends who meet him in France. Wanting to get as far away as possible from what these friends represent, he is grateful to find a mysterious black woman he met previously on his crossing from America. From the moment he links himself with Angela Johnson and her emotionally disturbed lover Vincent, the strangeness and danger he craved are never far from him, though never fully defined.

Angela and Vincent demand all of their new friend's money, leaving him totally dependent on them by the time he realizes that they are possibly involved in illegal activities. The narrator's odd relationship with Angela and Vincent is revealed in the Hemingway style of terse dialogue and matter-of-fact description blended with Plante's characteristically fragmented narrative and vivid images of consciousness. *The Foreigner* is a unique work for Plante, however, in that it does make some attempt, though sporadic and uneven, to provide a climactic scene, the street-dance suicide of Vincent. No previous Plante novel uses this traditional narrative element. The circumstances that lead up to the story's climax, however, remain subordinate to Plante's interest in the objective correlatives of his protagonist's consciousness, the means of representing his thoughts and emotions as concrete objects or communicable expressions. Many of these thoughts reflect the narrator's voyeuristic, homosexual obsession with Vincent and the total sense of alienation brought about by this attraction.

THE CATHOLIC

Daniel's homosexuality, only implied in *The Francoeur Novels*, is made explicit in *The Foreigner* and becomes the major focus of *The Catholic*. Early in the Francoeur trilogy, Daniel becomes obsessed with the figure of the nude, crucified Christ, a ubiquitous presence in his Catholic home. As he grows older, Daniel develops strange correlations between the body of Christ and the power of male sexuality. In *The Catholic*, Daniel decides that the only way for him to overcome his intense self-consciousness and escape from his body's prison is to surrender himself physically and spiritually to another man. Women, in Daniel's perception, have no spirituality: They are fixed, concrete, earthbound objects and therefore can only give him back to himself as a mirror does, thus increasing his awareness of himself. Although Daniel turns to women as confidants and advisers, sexually they cannot provide the transcendental experience he seeks.

When Daniel falls in love with Henry, he mistakes sexual obsession for heightened consciousness. They spend only one night together, and Daniel immediately realizes that Henry wants to maintain his autonomy and selfhood as desperately as Daniel wants to lose his. The novel becomes little more than an explication of Daniel's frightening sexual compulsions and the aftermath of grief and guilt. *The Catholic* does not develop the narrative structures attempted in *The Francoeur Novels* and *The Foreigner*; it resembles more closely Plante's earlier novels in its extremely obscure language and disturbing images.

ANNUNCIATION

Plante's thirteenth novel, *Annunciation*, represents a culmination of many of the themes and images of the earlier novels as well as something of a departure from their terseness and almost plotless structure. Intertwining the tale of art historian Claire O'Connel and her teenage daughter Rachel with that of art editor Claude Ricard, Plante examines the darkness that envelops and threatens to overwhelm the characters. Attempting to shelter her daughter from the truth of her husband's suicide, Claire brings Rachel to England, where she is raped and becomes pregnant. The already tenuous relationship between the mother, sensual and with a survival instinct, and the daughter, ethereal and painfully like her father, is strained even more when Claire becomes engaged. Ironically, Claire's fascination with the subject of her thesis, Baroque artist Pietro Testa, and her quest to find a previously uncataloged painting titled, once again ironically, *Annunciation* eventually brings mother and daughter together.

Along the way other characters are able to touch the enigmatic Rachel in a way her mother has not been able to, including Belorussian Maurice Kurigan and Claude Ricard, a young art editor of Russian descent. Although he is still stinging from a physical but unfulfilling relationship with an Englishwoman and the suicide of a distant cousin, Claude finds that his depression and rage abate when he and Maurice throw themselves into helping Claire. To do so they travel to Moscow, where Maurice's contacts, the Poliakoffs, are unhelpful, Maurice dies, and Claude is stricken with fever before Claire's arrival. In a climactic scene, Rachel, even more determined than her mother to find the painting, walks away from her mother, who has finally told her of her father's suicide. Overwrought, Claire, led to the ailing Claude by Poliakoff, asks him to take her to the picture, which he had previously discovered. Stricken by the purity of the angel and the Virgin in the painting, Claire falls to her knees, overwhelmed with tears. In the final scene the Americans are together in the Poliakoff apartment as the Russians try to imagine the West. The novel ends with Claude's reverie on God—"No, I don't believe in God, but I can imagine him. . . . That vast dark space behind the image of a sunlit glass of water is the only way I can imagine God"—an ending that brings the novel a redemptive full circle from the eight-word opening chapter: "A glass of water in a dark room—."

THE AGE OF TERROR

More experimental in form than *Annunciation* and set almost exclusively in the Soviet Union during its final days, *The Age of Terror* traces a spiritual journey of sorts for twenty-three-year-old Joe, which begins the moment he sees an archival photograph of Russian partisan Zoya Kosmodemyanskaya, who had been hanged and mutilated by invading German troops during World War II. Impotent and without faith but hoping nonetheless to rekindle his dormant idealism, Joe quits college in New England and travels to Leningrad, where he encounters a modern Zoya, a former KGB operative now engaged in a joint venture with the American expatriate Gerald in selling people into prostitution under the guise of helping them flee the country. Interspersed with bleak, wintry scenes of life during the breakup of the Soviet Union are surreal vignettes inspired by the Russian past, all of which prophesy a "different world," one beyond imagination, that will replace this "terrible" world.

Joe is both beckoned and repulsed by the soulless landscape of Leningrad and Moscow in the last days of the Soviet Union and by the innate despair of the native population as they go about their daily struggle for existence. His ambivalence is counterpointed by Gerald's certainty: "The truth, which makes men of boys, is that no one will be saved, that we're all bad." No matter how much one wants to feel "something beyond the age of terror," there is nothing. Befuddled, in part, by a persistent low fever, Joe eventually succumbs to the strength of Gerald's cynical conviction, and, against Zoya's express wishes, he confirms to Gerald the existence of her beautiful son Yura, whose desire to be a ballet dancer is an ironic consequence of the many years that his mother secretly monitored the movements of the ballet company's artists and their contacts with foreigners.

This betrayal is the turning point of the book. Later, Zoya belatedly embraces the nationalism of her namesake, whose photograph attracted both Joe and Gerald to Russia as if it were a place that embodied all of their personal suffering and longing; she announces to Gerald that she has taken a job with the publications department at the Bolshoi Ballet and that their partnership is at an end. Zoya decides that she will no longer be Gerald's willing accomplice in the hope that he will get her out of the country; instead, she has thrown in her lot with her fellow citizens. In revenge and perhaps in an effort to bind Zoya solely to him, Gerald has both Yura and his dance partner Larissa kidnapped and sold into the sex trade.

The novel concludes as Joe, still hallucinating from a fever, accompanies the now-devastated Zoya into the midst of a snow-covered forest, the forest he had once worshiped in his dreams. As he follows her into a snowdrift, Joe glimpses over Zoya's shoulder the brown clapboard house that had been his childhood home. Thus, the final vision of *The Age of Terror* is of two individuals bound by and reconciled through their sorrow.

ABC

Plante's next novel, *ABC*, published eight years after *The Age of Terror*, provides yet another exploration of one of the author's favorite themes in both his fictional and his autobiographical works: how vividly the lingering presence of the dead informs the experience of the living. In this case, the principal character, Gerard Chauvin, is so traumatized by the accidental death of his six-year-old son, Henry, in a deserted house near the family's summer residence that he abandons his wife, Margaret, and his career and sets out on an international quest to make some sense of the senselessness of his loss. Gerard's search is triggered by the fact that he was distracted from keeping an eye on his son by his presumably accidental discovery of a scrap of paper on which was written the alphabet in Sanskrit; his subsequent struggle to contend with his guilt and grief becomes inextricably tied to his newfound obsession with patterns of arrangement, such as the disposition of objects on the shelf in his son's room or the ordering of the letters of the alphabet.

A college teacher of French Canadian extraction, much like Plante himself, Chauvin becomes incrementally drawn to other individuals who have experienced similar personal tragedies: a Chinese woman named Catherine, whose daughter Susan committed suicide with a drug overdose; a Sephardic Jew named David Sasson, whose wife, Dirouhi, an Armenian art historian, is murdered by Greek terrorists; and a Chechen woman named Aminat, whose daughter is raped and murdered by Russian troops during Chechnya's ongoing struggle for independence. The unbearable suffering felt by each of these characters is translated into an irrational but compelling desire to discover why the letters of the alphabet are arranged as they are. It is as if all four characters believe that by finding the answer to why "a" comes before "b" and "b" before "c," they will discover that there is some ordering principle to the apparent randomness of life.

The momentum of Gerard's philological inquiry, impelled both by the chronological nature of the subject matter and by the consecutive narratives of his compatriots, takes him from his hometown of Manchester, New Hampshire, across the Atlantic to England and eventually to the Eastern Mediterranean. His journey and eventually that of the whole group, like the study of the origins of written language, propels them farther and farther east toward the traditional geographic cradle of ancient civilization. In particular, after Gerard meets Catherine on the second floor of the central public library on Copley Square in Boston, the two travel, by her invitation, to her flat in London and then to Cambridge University, where Catherine's daughter Susan had studied philology with an eccentric don named Charles Craig. In the latter's rooms at King's College, they encounter David Sasson, himself in search of whether there might be some prototype of all Indo-European alphabets, some original system of written symbols from which all other languages evolved. David, in turn, invites Gerard and Catherine to his houses in Athens and on the island of Paros, where they all find on the beach the distracted Aminat, who has hitched her way illegally from Chechnya in an effort to reach the site of ancient Ugarit in present-day Syria. Grief is the tie that binds these "abecedarians" together.

Each stage of their progressive journey comes with commentary on the attempts by generations of scholars to trace the origin of the Roman alphabet. In fact, some critics have compared the novel, in this regard, to Dan Brown's immensely popular *The Da Vinci Code* (2003) in that both can be read as historical detective stories. This injection of academic research is applauded by some critics, who find that such didacticism adds texture to the narrative; at various points in their travels, for example, Gerard and the others find copies of James Février's seminal text *Histoire de l'écriture* (1948; history of writing), the primary source Plante uses for most of the linguistic discoveries of his characters. Every time the book resurfaces, someone reads a passage from the

text, which adds another piece to the philological puzzle. Other critics, however, find such instructional moments inexpertly handled, and they cite Plante's inclusion of Charles Craig in his cast of characters apparently only for the purpose of having someone deliver a lesson on how all letters most likely originated as pictograms, representing physical objects.

Beyond any knowledge of language formation, Gerard, Catherine, David, and Aminat are looking for the organizing principle behind all verbal communication and, thus, trying to find the answer to a question that no one has answered before. In so doing, they hope to end their feeling of helplessness by discovering some ultimate meaning. Perhaps, in this regard, their quest is essentially spiritual. In a trailer park near the site of Gerard's son's death, for example, a young Indian girl links the letters of the alphabet to humanity's sense of the divine when she recites a line from the ancient Hindu sacred text the Bhagavad Gita in which the god Krishna asserts: "Of sounds I am the first sound, A."

In the final analysis, it could be said that, like Plante himself in his memoir *American Ghosts*, Gerard is simply seeking some form of transcendence, some link to the universal as embodied, in this instance, in the concept of the alphabet. Perhaps by studying history the members of the group will find the answers that they seek; David, spokesman for this perspective, argues that "the history of humankind is the history of gods" and that historical study may ultimately prove the existence of God or the gods who revealed the first alphabet to humankind.

Several aspects of *ABC* have attracted the most critical comment. The novel's first chapter has been praised consistently for its emotional impact, particularly Plante's vivid evocation of a family's impromptu summer "adventure" gone terribly wrong. Disagreement has arisen, however, over the relative success of the rest of the book, with some critics annoyed by the plot's many improbable coincidences and what they see as the ending's formless mysticism; still others find the book a lyrical record of the mysteries of human life and applaud the dreamlike conclusion, which is reminiscent of the ghost-haunted walk in the forest at the end of *The Age of Terror*.

Penelope A. LeFew; Jaquelyn W. Walsh
Updated by S. Thomas Mack

OTHER MAJOR WORKS

NONFICTION: *Difficult Women: A Memoir of Three*, 1983; *American Ghosts: A Memoir*, 2005.

BIBLIOGRAPHY

Dukes, Thomas. "David Plante." In *Contemporary Gay American Novelists: A Bio-bibliographical Sourcebook*, edited by Emmanuel S. Nelson. Westport, Conn.: Greenwood Press, 1993. Provides a brief biography and then presents a discussion of Plante's major works and themes.

Plante, David. "Creating the Space for a Miracle." Interview by Suzi Gablik. In *Conversations Before the End of Time*. New York: Thames and Hudson, 1995. Interview with Plante is part of a collection of interviews with philosophers, writers, and other artists that aims to address the meaning of art in culture at the end of the twentieth century.

_____. "My Parents, My Religion, and My Writing." In *Catholic Lives, Contemporary America*, edited by Thomas J. Ferraro. Durham, N.C.: Duke University Press, 1997. Plante discusses the influence of Catholicism on his fiction.

_____. "Portrait of the Artist: Interview with David Plante." Interview by Aaron Hamburger. *Lambda Book Report* 13 (April/May, 2005): 6-8. Plante, an avowed atheist, argues for the existence of some collective consciousness that connects not only the living but also the dead.

_____. "Seeing Through a Glass, Darkly: David Plante." Interview by Paul Baumann. *Commonweal* 121 (August 19, 1994): 14, 21-22. Plante discusses the significance of religious themes in his work, the influence of Ernest Hemingway on his writing, the importance of his French Blackfoot Indian heritage to his style, his fears about the lack of redemption in masterpieces of American literature, and his belief that writing can lead one outside oneself.

Summer, Claude J, ed. *The Gay and Lesbian Literary Heritage*. Rev. ed. New York: Routledge, 2002. Includes a short article focusing on Plante's place in the tradition of gay literature and argues that in his fiction he covers a wide range of homosexual identity, from the overt to the underdeveloped and the ambiguous.

KATHERINE ANNE PORTER

Born: Indian Creek, Texas; May 15, 1890
Died: Silver Spring, Maryland; September 18, 1980
Also known as: Callie Russell Porter

PRINCIPAL LONG FICTION

Noon Wine, 1937 (novella)
Old Mortality, 1937 (novella)
Pale Horse, Pale Rider, 1938 (novella)
Pale Horse, Pale Rider: Three Short Novels,
    1939 (includes the 3 novellas above)
Ship of Fools, 1962

OTHER LITERARY FORMS

Katherine Anne Porter is best known for her short fiction. Her stories appear in *Flowering Judas, and Other Stories* (1930), *The Leaning Tower, and Other Stories* (1944), and *The Old Order* (1944) and were gathered in *The Collected Stories of Katherine Anne Porter* (1965). Criticism, essays, and poems were collected in *The Days Before* (1952) and *The Collected Essays and Occasional Writings* (1970).

ACHIEVEMENTS

Katherine Anne Porter's solid and lasting reputation as a writer is based on a very small output of published work: one novel, a handful of novellas, and fewer than two dozen stories. This slender output, however, represents only a small portion of the fiction she wrote during her lifetime. Exacting and self-critical, she discarded many more stories than she published. By the time her first story appeared in print, she had already developed her fictional techniques to near perfection, and the maturity and craft of her style in *Flowering Judas, and Other Stories*, her first published collection, never was surpassed by her later fiction.

Porter early established her reputation with literary critics and only later became widely known and read. In 1931, one year after the publication of her first volume, she was granted a Guggenheim Fellowship, an award she received again in 1938. The Society of Libraries of New York University awarded her its first annual gold medal for literature in 1940 upon the publication of *Pale Horse, Pale Rider*. A Modern Library edition of *Flowering Judas, and Other Stories* appeared that same year. In 1943, she was elected a member of the National Institute of Arts and Letters, and in 1949, she accepted her first appointment as writer-in-residence and guest lecturer at Stanford University. In later years, she held similar positions in many other colleges and universities, including the University of Chicago, the University of Michigan, Washington and Lee University, the University of Liège, and the University of Virginia.

By the time she published *Ship of Fools* in 1962, Porter had received three more honors: a Ford Foundation grant in 1959, the O. Henry Memorial Award in 1962 for her story "Holiday," and the Emerson-Thoreau bronze medal of the American Academy of Arts and Sciences. *Ship of Fools* became a Book-of-the-Month Club selection and an immediate best seller. In the face of its overwhelming popular success, some critics charged that Porter had forsaken her artistic standards in favor of writing a book that would appeal to a large audience. *Ship of Fools* also was criticized for its pessimism and for its failure to conform neatly to the structure of a novel, a supposed flaw especially irksome to those who had admired the formal perfection of Porter's earlier works. Porter herself was surprised by the book's popularity. She had abandoned the form of her earlier work—with its tight plots centered on the fate of a single character—but she had moved deliberately on to something else. She was still writing "honest," she said, a quality that characterized all her fiction. First and last, she was still an artist, a label she applied to herself unhesitatingly.

Though Porter published no new fiction after *Ship of Fools*, her critical and public acclaim grew. It reached its

Katherine Anne Porter. (Washington Star Collection, D.C. Public Library)

peak when she received both the Pulitzer Prize and the National Book Award in fiction in 1966.

BIOGRAPHY

Katherine Anne Porter was born Callie Russell Porter in Indian Creek, Texas, on May 15, 1890. She was the third of five children born to Harrison and Mary Alice Jones Porter. When her mother died in 1892, she and her brothers and sisters moved to Kyle, Texas, where they were cared for by their paternal grandmother, Catherine Anne Porter. When Grandmother Porter died in 1901, Harrison Porter sold the farm in Kyle and moved with his family to San Antonio.

Facts about Porter's early life and education have been difficult to substantiate, partly because Porter's own accounts were evasive or inconsistent. Although her family apparently was Methodist, Porter attended convent schools, possibly for a time in New Orleans, which may be why later researchers have reported that she was a Roman Catholic from birth. Porter denied this allegation when it appeared in a biographical sketch published by the University of Minnesota series on American writers. Precocious as a child and rebellious as a teenager, she ran away from school at age sixteen to marry. The name of her first husband is not known, although the marriage lasted three years.

After the divorce, Porter moved to Chicago, already cherishing the ambition of becoming a professional writer. She worked as a reporter on a Chicago newspaper for a time and signed on as an extra with a motion-picture company for a few months. Passing up the opportunity to travel to Hollywood with the film company, she returned to Texas, where she reported that she made a living as a traveling entertainer, singing Scottish ballads, dressed in a costume she made herself. Thereafter, she wrote drama criticism and society gossip for a Fort Worth weekly, *The Critic*. One year later, she moved to Denver, Colorado, and became a reporter for the *Rocky Mountain News*. In Denver, during the influenza epidemic of 1918, she became severely ill and almost died. This experience, which she fictionalized in *Pale Horse, Pale Rider*, affected her profoundly. "I really had participated in death," she said years later in an interview with Barbara Thompson of *The Paris Review*. She had had "what the Christians call the 'beatific vision'"; she was no longer "like other people."

In 1919, Porter moved to New York City, where for a brief time she worked as a hack and ghostwriter. The following year she went to study in Mexico. Again she stayed only a short time, but for the next ten years Mexico was to be the center of her intellectual and imaginative life. Returning to Fort Worth, she began to write the stories based on her experiences there. During the next decade she traveled extensively, reviewed books for leading national magazines and newspapers, and worked and reworked the stories that were published in 1930 in *Flowering Judas, and Other Stories*.

Supported by a Guggenheim Fellowship granted that year, Porter returned to Mexico. In 1931, she sailed aboard a German ship from Veracruz to Bremerhaven. This voyage gave her the setting for *Ship of Fools*, which was not to be published for another thirty years. She lived until the mid-1930's in Paris, marrying and later divorcing Eugene Pressly, a member of the American Foreign Service, and working on her fiction. After her divorce from Pressly, she married Albert Erskine, Jr., of the Louisiana State University faculty. Until her divorce from Erskine in 1942, she lived in Baton Rouge. During this time, she continued to work on her short fiction, but not until the late 1950's did she begin sustained effort on her only full-length novel, *Ship of Fools*. Although by that time many of her acquaintances believed she never would finish it, fragments of the novel appeared in magazines. In 1962, *Ship of Fools* was published. Porter wrote no more new fiction after that, although *The Collected Essays and Occasional Writings* appeared in 1970. On September 18, 1980, at the age of ninety, Porter died in Silver Spring, Maryland.

ANALYSIS

Katherine Anne Porter once suggested that when she sat down to write about her life as accurately as possible, it turned into fiction; indeed, she knew no other way to write fiction. Whether this anecdote is true, it is certain that capturing the past with great detail was an important ingredient in her writing. In a number of the short stories, and in two of the best short novels, Miranda, the central character, is very close to being Porter herself. These stories follow Miranda's life from infancy in her grandmother's house in South Texas to her scrape with death from influenza in Colorado at the age of twenty-four—her first major step toward maturity.

Concerning the time of her illness, Porter has said that it was as though a line were drawn through her life, separating everything that came before from everything that came after. She had been given up and then had survived, and in some ways all her time after that was borrowed. Perhaps that is why her overtly autobiographical stories deal with the time before that line, the time when she was "alive" and therefore had a life to record. The stories that take place after that incident present her, if at all, as an observer, as someone slightly distant and alienated from life. (It is a question of degree: Miranda is also, of course, an acute observer in the stories in which she takes part. Her name, in fact, means "observer" in Spanish.) Porter was in real life a passenger on the ship about which her novel *Ship of Fools* was written, but she speaks of herself as purely an observer, who scarcely spoke a word on the entire voyage. She does not appear directly as a character in the novel.

OLD MORTALITY

Miranda, the girl in the short novel *Old Mortality*, runs away from school to get married, in part to escape from her family, so suffocatingly steeped in its own past. At the conclusion of the novella, she is determined to free herself once and for all from that past, so that she can begin to consider her own future; but she determines this, the reader is told in the ironic concluding lines, "in her hopefulness, her ignorance." The irony is that Miranda (Porter) herself became so obsessed with that past that much of her best work is devoted to it. The explanation for Porter's obsession with the past can perhaps be guessed from the conclusion of *Pale Horse, Pale Rider*. Everything of importance to Miranda has died; only her ravaged body, her spark of a soul somehow survives. She finds that she has no future, only the slow progression to death once again. The past, then, is all she has, yet the past is finally intangible, as the girl in *Old Mortality* discovers as she sifts through all the evidence. At last no truth can be discovered, no objectivity, only the combined and contradictory subjectives: The only truth, once again, is the truth of fiction.

Porter said that in her fiction she is not interested in actions so much as she is interested in the various and subtle results of actions. Certainly, of all her works, *Old Mortality* deals directly with the ramifications of past actions. This short novel spans ten years in the life of the protagonist, Miranda, from the age of eight to the age of eighteen. In that time, the reader learns little of Miranda's life, except that she is bad tempered and that, unlike many of the young women in her widely extended family, she is not going to be a "beauty." She is, rather, the recording center of the novel: The events are brought to her and have their effect on the person she is becoming.

The crucial actions have occurred in the preceding generation. Miranda's family is obsessed by a past event. Miranda's aunt, Amy, was a great beauty, the measure, in fact, against which all the current crop of beauties are found wanting. She was glamorous, racy, even though tubercular, and for a long time spurned Gabriel's devoted courtship. Gabriel was himself wild, ran a string of racehorses, and was heir to the fortune. Only when he was disinherited and Amy found herself in the terminal stage of her illness did she consent to marry him. The couple went to New Orleans on their honeymoon, and almost immediately Amy died. Miranda tries to sift out the truth of the story. She looks at the photograph of Amy and does not find her so impossibly beautiful and indeed thinks she looks silly in her out-of-fashion dress. Later, she is introduced to Gabriel, and instead of the dashing young man who had once challenged a rival to a duel over Amy, she finds him fat and drunken, down on his luck; the woman whom he married after Amy is bitter and depressed from living with a ne'er-do-well who has spent their whole married life talking about Amy. Later still, Miranda meets Eva, a homely spinster cousin from Gabriel's generation, and Eva says the real truth is that Amy was a lewd woman, who married only because someone else got her pregnant, and took her own life with an overdose of drugs.

After a moment of shock, Miranda realizes that Eva's version, in its negative way, is just as romantic as the others. Miranda does not want to know where the truth lies. By this time, she has left school and has run off to get married. Her father is cool with her, thinking she has deserted the family; indeed she has, and deliberately. She refuses to be trapped in the past, represented by this unknowable woman whose brief life still haunts the family. She wants instead to discover who she—Miranda—is; she wants her own life to exist in the present and future. This is what she determines—in the novel's ironic final line—"in her hopefulness, her ignorance."

In her ignorance, Miranda learns that her past is what she is, the result of those past actions. She has been touched by Amy even more than the others, for she has become Amy, the Amy who refused to live by the others' rules, and at last ran off, married, and never returned— just as Miranda has done. In so doing, Amy and Miranda become separated from the rest of the family, freezing its members in their moment of history just as Porter herself became separated from her family so that she could re-create them forever in her stories.

NOON WINE

Noon Wine is set in the rural southern Texas of Porter's childhood but does not deal with her family. The characters in this short novel, set at the turn of the twentieth century, are poor and uneducated farmers, but this does not stop the story from being an intricate and subtle moral allegory. The lingering effect of past actions is not the central theme, as it was in *Old Mortality*, but a sense of the cumulative force of a man's actions gives the story a tragic inevitability.

Mr. Thompson is a proud man, and as a result he marries above himself. Instead of a strong woman to help him in the strenuous operation of his farm, he marries a delicate and genteel woman who quickly becomes a near invalid. Further, she insists that they have a dairy, a bit higher class than an ordinary row-crop farm. In the end, Thompson is left with a wife who cannot help him and a kind of farmwork that he does not feel is masculine and that he therefore shirks. The farm is deteriorating, and the couple is about to go under entirely, when a strange taciturn Swede from North Dakota arrives, asking for work. Instantly there is a revolution. The Swede fixes, paints, repairs everything, and shortly the failing farm becomes productive. As the years go by, the couple is able to buy such luxuries as an icebox, and Mr. Thompson is able to sit on the porch while the work is being done. One day Hatch arrives, a thoroughly evil man. He is a bounty hunter; the Swede, it is revealed, is an escaped homicidal maniac who in a berserk fury stabbed his own brother to death. Thompson refuses to give up the Swede. There is a scuffle; the Swede suddenly appears and steps between them; Thompson, believing he sees Hatch stabbing the Swede in the stomach, smashes Hatch's skull with an ax.

The confrontation is remarkably complex. Hatch, as he is presented in the story, seems a pure manifestation of evil, and so perhaps he should be killed, but ironically he has in fact done nothing. The Swede is a primal murderer, a brother-killer like Cain, and is a threat to murder again. Thompson believes Hatch has stabbed the Swede and acts to defend him, but after he has killed Hatch, the Swede does not have a mark on him, not even, perhaps, the mark of Cain, which has been transferred to Thompson.

Thompson is easily acquitted of the crime in court, but his fundamentalist neighbors in the close-knit community look on him as a murderer. Most important, he must examine his own motives. Was he defending the Swede, or was he defending the success of his farm, which, he must have guiltily realized, was not the result of his work, but of the work of another, a sinner, a primal murderer? With his mark of Cain, Thompson goes the rounds of his neighbors, trying to tell his side of the story, believing it less each time himself, until he kills himself, the final consequence of his original pride.

PALE HORSE, PALE RIDER

Porter has called sleep "that little truce of God between living and dying." If dreams, therefore, take place in a landscape somewhere between life and death, it is appropriate that *Pale Horse, Pale Rider* begins with one of Miranda's many dreams to be recorded. Although the story is set during World War I in a small town in Colorado where Miranda is working for a newspaper, symbolically the story takes place in the dreamlike zone between life and death. In that initial dream, Death rides alongside Miranda, but she tells him to ride on ahead; she is not quite ready to go with him. She wakes up only to be reminded of the war, which is poisoning the lives of many people, who are full of despair because of their inability to control their destinies. The streets are filled with funerals, as the influenza epidemic kills people like a medieval plague. Miranda's work on the paper is hateful, and her only release is when, after work, she meets Adam. Adam, as his name suggests, is the man who should be her companion, her mate in life. He is a soldier, however, on his way to war and committed wholly to death, and so Miranda struggles to withhold her love from him.

The war and the plague, as presented in the novel, are symbols of the struggle of life and its vulnerability. Miranda and Adam differ from others in being existentially aware; all that exists for them is the present tense of their lives. They dance together in a cheap café, knowing that it is all they will ever have. Because they have so little—a brief moment of troubled life, and then death—the integrity of their actions becomes their only value. Miranda tells Adam that he is stupid to fight in a war in which old men send young men to die. He agrees, saying, however, that if he does not go, he can no longer face himself. Miranda has her own costly sense of integrity: As a reporter for the paper, she witnesses a pathetic scandal, and when the victims beg her not to write the story, she does not. The rival papers do, however, and her editor is furious; her colleagues think she is senseless. She is demoted to writing entertainment reviews. Even there, when she writes an unfavorable review of a vaudeville act, she is confronted by the old, broken, has-been actor, and her subsequent compassion struggles against her dedication to her job. Her colleagues counsel her to fake the reviews and make everyone happy, but writing honest reviews is an important value to her.

Miranda gets the flu, and in a long delirious dream comes to the point of death and has a beatific vision. The doctor and nurse fighting to preserve her, working with their own existential integrity, bring her back, but it is so painful being taken away from her vision and back to life, that when life-giving drugs are injected into her, she feels them like "a current of agony."

Miranda had fought, with her tiny spark of consciousness, to survive, to survive for Adam. Then she learns that Adam, perhaps having caught flu from her, has himself died. Her dream of heaven had been so brilliant that the real world seems to her a monochrome, a bleak field in which, with Adam gone, she has nothing. The reader, however, can see beyond this point. Earlier, Miranda and Adam had sung an old spiritual together, of a pale horse with a pale rider, who takes a girl's lover away, leaving her behind to mourn. Miranda is the singer who is left behind to mourn and to record the story for the rest of the world.

SHIP OF FOOLS

Porter has described her fiction as an investigation of the "terrible failure of the life of man in the Western World." Her one full-length novel, *Ship of Fools*, is a bleak cross section of modern civilization. It follows the lives of literally dozens of characters, from all levels of the particular society it is observing. More than forty characters of various nationalities are presented in some detail: American, Spanish, Mexican, Cuban, German, Swiss, Swedish. The time is 1931, and chaos is spreading. Soon Adolf Hitler will be in power, the extermination camps will be in operation, and another world war will be under way. The title *Ship of Fools* is a translation of Sebastian Brant's medieval moral allegory, *Das Narrenschiff* (1494). The ship is the world; the time of the journey is the lifetime of the characters. They, of course, do not see it that way. They think of it as a temporary voyage. The lies they tell, the treacheries they enact, the hopeless relationships they form, are only temporary, have nothing to do with the course of their real lives, with the objectives they mean to obtain, the moral codes by which they mean to live.

The ship, the *Vera* (truth), leaves Veracruz, Mexico, for the nearly monthlong journey to Bremerhaven. It is a German ship, and the German passengers sit at the captain's table. From the pompous and second-rate captain on down, they are comic grotesques, guzzling their food swinishly and looking suspiciously at everyone who does not eat pork, or who has a slightly large nose, as potentially Jewish. The only seemingly human Germans are Wilhelm Freytag, concealing as long as he can his Jewish wife, and Dr. Schumann, the ship's doctor and the novel's most sympathetic character. He is urbane, gentle, and wise, and to his own horror, commits perhaps the basest act of anyone on board. The American characters are only slightly less grotesque. William Denny, the Texan, is pure caricature: To him everyone but a white Texan is a "nigger," "spick," "wop," or "damyankee." He devotes all his time to pursuing sexual pleasures but is fearful that he will be cheated into paying too much for it. The comic result is that he pays out everything and gets nothing in return but a severe drubbing.

Mrs. Treadwell, a forty-five-year-old divorcé, is utterly selfish, yet she wonders why she gets nothing from life. David Scott and Jenny Brown, who live together and fight constantly, are, with Dr. Schumann and Freytag, the novel's main characters. David Scott is tied up within himself and will give up nothing to another. Jenny Brown sporadically gives up everything to mere acquaintances yet seems to have nothing of her own within.

One character after another debates humanity's nature: Are all people basically good? Are all people naturally depraved? Are the pure races good and the mongrel races evil? The characters seem intent on acting out all these possibilities. The most disciplined of them regularly lapse into helpless sentimentality. Freytag thinks that each woman he meets is the beautiful love of his life. One of these women is a Jew, whom he married during a period of extreme romanticism, and now he is déclassé among his German compatriots and cannot admit to himself how regretful he is. David and Jenny, needing everything from each other, have only gone as far as learning each other's weaknesses, of which they take full advantage to lacerate each other. They continue to cling together, always saying they will separate at some later time. Most painful is the folly of the sympathetic Dr.

Schumann. He convinces himself that he is in love with a neurotic Spanish countess (he has a wife at home), and under pretense of caring for her as her doctor, he turns her into a hopeless and helpless drug addict in order to keep his power over her.

The most purely evil characters on the ship are the shoddy Spanish dance troupe. Through herculean efforts they almost take control of the ship and certainly take control of the lives of the characters, bringing out their deepest and worst traits, but at the end they sit listless and exhausted, as though the effort were immensely greater than any return they have had from it. This troupe of carnival performers cheats, steals, blackmails, and even kills right before the others, who remark on it, but do nothing to stop them, each character feeling it is not his place to do anything. At length, the troupe is sitting confidently at the captain's table, having rearranged everyone's position on the ship. In a kind of Walpurgis Night, they bring the many characters to some sort of climax in an eruption of drunken violence. It is Porter's vision of how World War II began: low thugs and gangsters taking power with the casual, half-intentional connivance of the world.

In the middle of this bleak and pessimistic picture of the Western world, there is one possibility of redemption. The rare positive moments in the novel are when the characters suddenly, often to their own surprise, come together in the act of sex—Porter emphasizing the sensuality of the contact rather than any spiritual qualities. Perhaps Porter is saying that in their fallen state human beings must start at the bottom, with earthly sensuality, in order to slowly acquire a knowledge of spiritual beauty.

Norman Lavers

OTHER MAJOR WORKS

SHORT FICTION: *Flowering Judas, and Other Stories*, 1930; *Hacienda*, 1934; *The Leaning Tower, and Other Stories*, 1944; *The Old Order*, 1944; *The Collected Stories of Katherine Anne Porter*, 1965.

POETRY: *Katherine Anne Porter's Poetry*, 1996 (Darlene Harbour Unrue, editor).

NONFICTION: *My Chinese Marriage*, 1921; *Outline of Mexican Popular Arts and Crafts*, 1922; *What Price Marriage*, 1927; *The Days Before*, 1952; *A Defence of*

Circe, 1954; *A Christmas Story*, 1967; *The Collected Essays and Occasional Writings*, 1970; *The Selected Letters of Katherine Anne Porter*, 1970; *The Never-Ending Wrong*, 1977; *Letters of Katherine Anne Porter*, 1990.

BIBLIOGRAPHY

Bloom, Harold, ed. *Katherine Anne Porter*. Bromall, Pa.: Chelsea House, 2001. A book of essays interpreting Porter's fiction, with a biography and chronology of her life. Includes a bibliography.

Brinkmeyer, Robert H., Jr. *Katherine Anne Porter's Artistic Development: Primitivism, Traditionalism, and Totalitarianism*. Baton Rouge: Louisiana State University Press, 1993. Brinkmeyer traces Porter's development as a writer, dividing her work into three stages: the early work written in Mexico, the rediscovery of her southern identity, and a period of cynicism and obsession that resulted in *Ship of Fools*. Argues that she achieved her height as an artist when she created a memory-based dialogue with her southern roots.

Givner, Joan. *Katherine Anne Porter: A Life*. Rev. ed. Athens: University of Georgia Press, 1991. Givner, Porter's chosen biographer, provides a well-balanced account of the author's life. This revision of the biography originally published in 1982 includes updated information, as well as previously embargoed material.

Hartley, Lodwick, and George Core, eds. *Katherine Anne Porter: A Critical Symposium*. Athens: University of Georgia Press, 1969. A collection of seminal essays, this book includes an interview with Porter conducted in 1963, as well as a personal assessment by Porter's friend, Glenway Wescott. A group of five essays provide general surveys of her writing. Includes a bibliography and an index.

Hendrick, George. *Katherine Anne Porter*. New York: Twayne, 1965. A biographical sketch precedes studies grouped according to settings from Porter's life: The first group from Mexico, the second from Texas, and the third from New York and Europe. After a chapter on *Ship of Fools*, this book surveys Porter's essays and summarizes major themes. Includes notes, an annotated bibliography, an index, and a chronology.

Liberman, Myron M. *Katherine Anne Porter's Fiction.* Detroit, Mich.: Wayne State University Press, 1971. In his study of the techniques and intentions of Porter's fiction, Liberman devotes seven chapters to an analysis of *Ship of Fools.* Includes notes and an index.

Stout, Janis. *Katherine Anne Porter: A Sense of the Times.* Charlottesville: University Press of Virginia, 1995. Contains chapters on Porter's background in Texas, her view of politics and art in the 1920's, her writing and life between the two world wars, and her relationship with the southern agrarians. Also addresses the issue of gender, the problem of genre in *Ship of Fools,* and the quality of Porter's "free, intransigent, dissenting mind." Includes notes and a bibliography.

Titus, Mary. *The Ambivalent Art of Katherine Anne Porter.* Athens: University of Georgia Press, 2005. A look at the ways in which Porter confronted issues of gender in her work and life. Includes a study of some of her unpublished papers.

Unrue, Darlene Harbour. *Katherine Anne Porter: The Life of an Artist.* Jackson: University Press of Mississippi, 2005. The first biography written since Givner's book. A comprehensive account that offers insight into Porter's turbulent personal life and her writing.

Walsh, Thomas F. *Katherine Anne Porter and Mexico: The Illusion of Eden.* Austin: University of Texas Press, 1992. Contains chapters on Porter and Mexican politics, her different periods of residence in Mexico, and *Ship of Fools.* Includes notes and a bibliography.

CHAIM POTOK

Born: Bronx, New York; February 17, 1929
Died: Merion, Pennsylvania; July 23, 2002
Also known as: Herman Harold Potok; Chaim Tzvi

PRINCIPAL LONG FICTION

The Chosen, 1967
The Promise, 1969
My Name Is Asher Lev, 1972
In the Beginning, 1975
The Book of Lights, 1981
Davita's Harp, 1985
The Gift of Asher Lev, 1990
I Am the Clay, 1992
Old Men at Midnight, 2001 (3 novellas)

OTHER LITERARY FORMS

The book *Wanderings: Chaim Potok's History of the Jews* (1978) is a personal reconstruction of four thousand years of Jewish history. Chaim Potok (POH-tawk) also wrote essays and book reviews for Jewish and secular periodicals and newspapers. In January, 1988, his stage adaptation of *The Chosen* opened as a short-lived Broadway musical, with music by Philip Springer and lyrics by Mitchell Bernard. Potok wrote two picture books for young children, *The Tree of Here* (1993) and *The Sky of Now* (1995), both illustrated by Tony Auth. Potok also published essays and stories in various magazines and a collection of short stories about troubled young people, *Zebra, and Other Stories* (1998). In addition, he wrote a few full-length works of nonfiction, including *The Gates of November: Chronicles of the Slepak Family* (1996), the epic story of the families of Solomon Slepak, a Bolshevik and one of the founders of the Soviet Union. Slepak managed to survive all of Joseph Stalin's purges without being imprisoned. The book also focuses on his son, Volodya Slepak, a refusenik and one of the Russian Jews who applied for and was for years refused permission by the Soviet government to immigrate to Israel.

ACHIEVEMENTS

Critical acceptance and public acclaim have greeted Chaim Potok's novelistic explorations of the conflict between Orthodox Judaism and secular American culture. Potok received the Edward Lewis Wallant Award and a National Book Award nomination for *The Chosen,* his first novel. He received the Athenaeum Award for its sequel, *The Promise*. He also received the National Jewish Book Award for Fiction for *The Gift of Asher Lev* and the National Foundation for Jewish Culture Achievement Award for Literature. His sympathetic (critics would say sentimental) portrayal of Jewish fundamentalism and those who choose to leave it highlights the poignancy of an individual's break with tradition. Indeed, Potok's novels test the ability of traditional communities to contribute to the modern world without themselves being assimilated. His evocation of Jewish life in New York in the latter two-thirds of the twentieth century has universal appeal and disturbing implications.

BIOGRAPHY

Born of Orthodox Jewish parents in the Bronx in 1929, Chaim Potok was reared in a fundamentalist culture. Potok's father, Benjamin Potok, was a Polish émigré and no stranger to the pogroms of Eastern Europe. The young Potok was taught that the profound suffering of the Jews would one day transform the world. Yet, as Potok suggests in *Wanderings*, his service as a Jewish chaplain with the U.S. Army in Korea (1956-1957) confronted him with a world of good and evil that had never heard of Judaism. His attempt to come to terms with this larger world led Potok to a critical investigation of his own Jewish heritage and the limitations of the fundamentalist perspective. Though he was ordained a Conservative rabbi in 1954, attracted by doctrines more liberal than those of strict Jewish Orthodoxy, Potok continued his struggle to reconcile fundamental Judaism with the findings of science (as historiography and textual criticism shed new light on ancient traditions). *The Chosen* inaugurated his public search for a voice with which to speak to his heritage as well as to the larger world.

In the early 1960's, Potok taught at the Jewish Theological Seminary in New York and edited *Conservative Judaism*. In 1965, he became editor in chief at the Jewish Publication Society of Philadelphia, and in 1975, he took the position of special projects editor. He was married to Adena Mosevitzky in 1958, and they took up residence in Merion, Pennsylvania. The Potoks had three children: Rena, Naama, and Akiva. Potok served as a visiting professor at the University of Pennsylvania, Bryn Mawr College, and Johns Hopkins University.

ANALYSIS

In his novels, Chaim Potok returns again and again to the story of a young protagonist coming of age in a culture (usually Jewish) at once mysterious, beautiful, sad, and somehow inadequate. Usually told in the first person, Potok's stories surround the reader with forebodings of the larger, evil world (news of pogroms in Europe, the Holocaust, the first atom bomb) into which his characters are plunged. Potok creates a microcosm of feeling and reaction to events that shake the world. His sentences are simple and reportorial, at times almost a parody of the staccato style of Ernest Hemingway. The stories develop chronologically, though they are frequently invaded by dreams, visions, or voices from the "Other Side."

In each of his stories, Potok sets for himself a question to be answered and reworks his own experiences until he is satisfied with at least a provisional resolution. Controlling metaphors help shape the questions. In *The Chosen*, the baseball game symbolizes the competition between two Jewish cultures, the very strict Hasidic and the more openly assimilationist. What happens to those caught in between those two traditions? The vision of pups being born in *The Book of Lights* represents the entrance of fertile Kabbala mysticism into a world of strict Jewish law. How can Jewish mysticism enrich Orthodoxy? Asher Lev's dreams of his mythical ancestor foreshadow the young artist's confrontation with his own culture. What happens when art brings great hurt? The sound of a little door harp symbolizes the transforming power of the imagination for Ilana Davita Chandal (Potok's first female protagonist) of *Davita's Harp*. What is the place of the imagination in Jewish Orthodoxy? What is the place of women?

THE CHOSEN

The Chosen recounts the story of Danny Saunders, brilliant son of a Hasidic rabbi, chosen by tradition to one day succeed his father as leader of the fundamentalist community in Brooklyn, New York. Yet Danny is less interested in studying the Talmud (Jewish law) than in probing the works of Sigmund Freud and other secular psychologists. The story closes with the inevitable confrontation between Danny and his father, which is mediated by Danny's friend Reuvan Malter. In the climactic scene in Reb Saunders's office, the old rabbi turns to his son and addresses him as a father for the first time. (For years, Danny had been reared in silence, except for times of Talmud study.) With fatherly tears, Reb Saunders explains that the years of silence created a soul of compassion within his brilliant son. Though he may well leave the Hasidic community for secular studies, Danny will always carry with him the legacy of Jewish suffering. That legacy will provide the moral force to change the world.

Reuvan, son of a Talmud scholar of the new school of textual criticism, chooses to become a rabbi. The choices, for Reuvan and for Danny, do not, however, come easily. Reuvan faces ostracism by the Hasidic community for suggesting that some Talmudic texts were of inferior quality and subject to misinterpretation. Danny must seemingly turn against his father if he is to pursue secular studies and abandon his leadership obligations.

The novel is structured almost as a diary, with pages of detailed descriptions of schoolwork in the Jewish high school, visits to the local synagogue, and the ebb and flow of Reuvan's life. Though at times tedious, the very innocence of the language contributes to a certain dramatic intensity. The conflict in the novel is mirrored in the frequent news reports of World War II and in the ensuing controversy over the creation of a Jewish state, Israel, in 1949. The Hasidic community is content to wait for the Messiah to create such a state; Reuvan's father calls for an immediate political settlement. Political questions are present in each of Potok's novels and are of central interest in *Davita's Harp*.

THE PROMISE

Silence is again present in Potok's second novel, *The Promise*, which continues the story of Danny Saunders and Reuvan Malter as they enter their professional lives. The novel begins with shouts of rage from young Michael Gordon, the son of Professor Abraham Gordon, a controversial Jewish philosopher. Michael has been cheated at a carnival booth by an old Jewish man, and both Reuvan and his date, Rachel Gordon, Michael's cousin, stare in horror as Michael angrily denounces Orthodoxy. Michael's father had questioned the supernatural accounts in the Hebrew Bible and, as a result, was excommunicated from the Orthodox community; now Michael is releasing his hate on those who persecuted

Professor Gordon. Subsequently, Michael is taken to Danny Saunders, now a psychologist at a residential treatment center. When the boy refuses to speak, Danny isolates him. The agonizing silence breaks Michael's will and he reveals the hate he feels for his father and his writings, writings that have brought condemnation to them both. Eventually, Michael is finally able to accept his own feelings and reconcile with his parents, and Danny and Rachel are married, the powerful coupling of the brilliant Hasid with the cosmopolitan daughter of a secularist philosopher.

The Promise continues the exploration of Reuvan's choice to receive his rabbinate from an Orthodox seminary and his refusal to become a secular Jew, as Professor Gordon has done. Yet Reuvan is uneasy with the traditional method of Talmud study advanced by Rav Kalman, one of his teachers. If the Talmud is the sacred oral tradition of the Jews in written form, contradictory commentaries from rabbis down through the centuries

Chaim Potok. (© Jerry Bauer)

must always be reconciled by newer interpretations, so as not to call God's Word into question. For Reuvan, there is another possibility; a corrupt text could be the source of confusion. Any correction, however, would mean violence to sacred scripture. Reuvan will become a rabbi so that he might debate Rav Kalman and the others from within a common tradition.

Reuvan's father, David Malter, is the voice of quiet wisdom throughout both books. Though a proponent of the new Talmud studies, he is sympathetic toward those whose tightly knit culture is being threatened. As he tells Reuvan in *The Promise*, "We cannot ignore the truth. At the same time, we cannot quite sing and dance as they do. . . . That is the dilemma of our time, Reuvan. I do not know what the answer is." Earlier, Reuvan's father had challenged his son to make his own meaning in the world. Those who had committed themselves to the Hasidic traditions had kept the faith alive through incomprehensible persecution. Now, Reuvan must also choose with the greatest seriousness and fervency, for he, too, must make a mark on the world and endure hardship of his own.

MY NAME IS ASHER LEV

Potok picks up this theme in his third novel, *My Name Is Asher Lev*. Covering the period of the late 1940's through the late 1960's, the book is an apologia for the artist. The Orthodox Jewish surroundings are familiar, but this time the controversy is not over textual criticism but rather representational art. Painting is not strictly forbidden to the Orthodox Jew, but it is regarded as useless, as foolishness, as a waste of time better devoted to the study of the Torah, the five books of Moses. Moreover, certain pictures could come close to violating the commandment forbidding graven images. Asher Lev is a born painter, however, and throughout the novel, as he develops his talent, he is increasingly isolated from his family and culture.

Asher is born in Crown Heights in Brooklyn in 1943. His father travels extensively for the local Rebbe in an effort to establish Ladover Hasid communities throughout Europe and to aid families immigrating to the United States. Asher's mother must stay with her son in New York because Asher refuses to leave his familiar streets to join his father in Europe. There are long nights of loneliness, waiting for Asher's father to return from some

mission or other. Asher's mother suffers a breakdown when her brother, also on a mission for the Rebbe, is killed. She begins to find herself again by plunging into her Russian studies, picking up the work her brother left unfinished. Metaphors of things unfinished and things completed permeate the novel. Asher's father is continually on the move because of the great unfinished work of the Ladover. Asher himself finds that he must bring some kind of completeness to the world by painting not only what he sees with his eyes but also what his inner vision reveals to him. Those visions are not always beautiful; his paintings can be like knives, plunging the reality of evil into the soul of the onlooker. The wise Rebbe, sensing Asher's vast talent, entrusts him to Jacob Kahn, himself an artistic genius and a nonobservant Jew. Kahn forces Asher to absorb the work of Pablo Picasso, especially *Guernica* (1937), a painting inspired by the German bombing of the Basque capital during the Spanish Civil War. In time, Asher begins to surpass his teacher.

Asher becomes virtually a stranger to his father. At the end of the novel, Asher's parents stare with mixed rage and amazement at the two crucifixions he has painted. Both are of his mother, looking in abstract fashion at Asher the stranger on one side and at the always-traveling husband on the other. The image of the cross for Asher has become the supreme symbol of suffering, devoid of any Christian preoccupation. The image is too much, however, for his parents, Orthodox Jews. As the Rebbe tells him, "You have crossed a boundary. I cannot help you. You are alone now. I give you my blessings."

There is a marked contrast between Asher's sensitive paintings (an effort to say what must be said about the evil in the world) and his selfish behavior toward his parents. He is one of the least sympathetic of Potok's protagonists because he struggles less with his own anguish than with his need to express his artistic gift at whatever cost. Jacob Kahn's advice, "Be a great painter, Asher Lev. . . . That will be the only justification for all the pain your art will cause," seems too facile. Asher is determined to remain an observant Jew, but he will do so on his own terms. The commandment about honoring one's parents must be radically reinterpreted. The book suffers from the technical difficulty that Asher Lev must be identified as a genius early in the story in order for Potok to create the kind of tension he needs to interest a reader. A mediocre artist who causes pain is merely self-indulgent.

Yet the book reveals something of Potok's larger purpose. Art must be true to itself even if that means surprise or hurt. The artist, painter, or writer must speak from the heart; anything else is mere propaganda. Potok sought to provide a rationale for his novelistic critiques of fundamentalist communities.

Potok introduces something else into Asher's story: Asher often dreams of his "mythic ancestor," a Jew who served a nobleman only to have the nobleman unleash evil upon the world. Just as Asher envisioned that ancient Jew traveling the world, seeking to redress the wrong he had a part in, so must the artist reshape evil into art and so bring a kind of balance to the world. Asher's visions are forerunners of Potok's use of mysticism or imaginative visions themselves as ways of coming to terms with a world gone crazy.

IN THE BEGINNING

In the Beginning is the story of young David Lurie and his childhood in an Orthodox family in the Bronx in the 1920's. The novel is patterned on the biblical book of Genesis: David falls from his mother's arms, develops a keen interest in the accounts of the Flood, and learns through the study of the Torah the power of words to shape a world. Potok's fourth novel was his most complex to date, departing from the forthright exposition found in *The Chosen* in favor of a more subtle panoply of impressions of growing up.

Like all Potok's protagonists, David is precocious, constantly questioning the world around him, trying to have it make sense. He is sickly, bullied by other boys, and plagued with recurring nightmares. David functions in the novel as an idealized figure to focus the reader's attention on how Orthodoxy confronts anti-Semitism and growing secularization. David imagines the Golem of Prague crushing those who would harm the Jews like some powerful living robot; as David grows, though, he learns that words can be more powerful than the Golem. Eventually, helped by those who practice textual critique of the Torah, David heads for graduate study at the University of Chicago. Yet, as in Potok's other works, there must also be some kind of reconciliation of the demands of Jewish Orthodoxy with those of secular learning. It is achieved through a vision David has years later as he

tours the site of the Bergen-Belsen death camp. David's vision of his dead father, and of his father's brother, David's namesake, is a moving conclusion to the book. David's father despairs that he has lost his son to the evil world, to the very world that took the lives of millions of Jews. He is reassured by David's uncle, however, that the son must journey into that world in order to bring something back to enrich Orthodoxy, which has become moribund. The son must venture out but must never forget his own roots. No anger of humanity can strike evil from the world. Only the patient use of words, with faith in their power to transform creation, can accomplish the task. That will be a new beginning for the world, and for Orthodoxy.

Potok's earlier novels tell the story of those in conflict with their Orthodox heritage. For the first time, *In the Beginning* pictures a reconciliation as a vision or story within the context of the novel. It is a kind of blessing from the beyond; here is the artist at work, crafting the resolution to the story.

THE BOOK OF LIGHTS

The Book of Lights, narrated in the third person, uses the technique of mystical reconciliation for a more universal purpose. If the Master of the Universe truly exists, how is a believer to accept the death light of the twentieth century, the atomic bomb? Potok's answer is that through the imaginative use of Jewish mysticism, the spark of God can be found in an evil world.

The story departs from Potok's previous novels, which traced the childhood of the protagonist. Only a few pages are devoted to Gershon Loran's early life before his seminary days and subsequent chaplaincy in Korea. Those first pages, however, are significant. Gershon witnesses the birth of some pups on a rooftop in the midst of his rundown neighborhood; he is awed by the presence of life even amid wreckage.

In seminary, Gershon is introduced to the study of the Kabbala and its *Zohar*, a Jewish mystical work from the thirteenth century. The *Zohar* is the book of lights of the novel's title, describing the creation of the world through the emanations of God. There are places where God has withdrawn His light; that has enabled humankind to come on the scene but it has also ushered in great evil. Now the mystic is called to ascend through those emanations to find God.

Such mystical tradition is complex and even contradictory. For Gershon, however, it is the pounding heart of a living faith. Gershon's quiet moments of reverie serve him well during his chaplaincy. Though Potok paints a detailed picture of Gershon's activities in Korea, the crucial story is elsewhere. Gershon's seminary friend, Arthur Leiden, travels with him to Kyōto and Hiroshima. At the Hiroshima monument, Arthur reads from the Psalms and pleads to God in vain for some kind of atonement. Arthur's father had worked with other scientists in developing the atom bomb, and Arthur is haunted by the memory. Later, Arthur is killed in a plane crash; Gershon, visiting Arthur's parents, hears a portion of one of Arthur's letters: "All the world, it seems, is a grayish sea of ambiguity, and we must learn to navigate in it or be drowned." That is Potok's message in the novel; "Loran" is itself a navigational acronym. If Judaism were merely the law, the faith would break on the shoals of the gritty world. Its mystical tradition infuses the faith with the ambiguity of real life. It does not explain but rather affirms the nature of God's creation. The *Zohar* is an imaginative understanding of the nature of God; in it, God enfolds both good and evil. It is a light by which to view a decaying civilization, a light that will survive the death light. In his final mystical vision of his old Kabbala teacher, Gershon learns that the mystical light will help mend the world so that it can be broken again in yet new acts of creation.

DAVITA'S HARP

It is the "mending power" of imagination that is at the heart of *Davita's Harp*. The harp referred to is a small instrument that fits on a door, with little balls that strike piano wires when the door is opened or closed. Here Potok returns to the first-person narrative, tracing the childhood of Ilana Davita Chandal, his first female lead character. She is the daughter of a nonbelieving Jewish mother and a nonbelieving Christian father. Spanning the years from the mid-1930's to 1942, the novel speaks with a new voice yet recapitulates some familiar themes.

Davita grows up in the New York area; she remembers frequent moves, strange people coming and going, and the constant singing of the door harp. Her parents are involved in the Communist Party, attempting to fight fascism in Spain and in the United States. Davita is precocious and inquisitive and her mother intelligent and cool, forever supplying Davita with the meaning of new words: proletariat, strike, idea, magic, war. Davita is spurred in her imaginative development by Aunt Sarah, a devout Episcopalian nurse, who tells her Bible stories, and by Jakob Daw, an Austrian writer, now suffering from having been gassed in World War I, who had loved Davita's mother when they were both in Vienna. Daw is sheltered for a time by Davita's parents and spins odd stories for her. There is the story of the little bird, flying to find the source of a beautiful music that soothes the world from the horrors of war. Only if the bird could stop the deceitful music would the world wake to its pain.

Davita's father, Michael Chandal, a journalist with *New Masses*, is killed during the bombing of Guernica during the Spanish Civil War. Soon after, both Jakob Daw and Davita's mother, Channah, become disillusioned with the Stalinists because the Communists, too, have committed atrocities. Davita has taken to attending a Jewish high school and becomes an outstanding student. Jakob Daw returns to Europe, where he dies, though his stories live in Davita's heart. Not long afterward, Ezra Dinn, an Orthodox Jew who had loved Davita's mother years before, marries Channah. Slowly, Davita's mother regains her sense of place.

Davita's time of innocence is over. Before Jakob Daw left for Europe, he finished his strange story of the bird. The bird, he said, gave up searching for the music of the world and became very small to fit inside the door harp. There, said Daw, the music was not deceitful but full of innocence. Now, however, Davita encounters something sinister in her adopted tradition. She is the most brilliant student at her yeshiva but she is passed over for the Akiva Award because, she is told, she is a woman. It is 1942. Another student is selected for the award but learns the truth and refuses it. He is Reuvan Malter, first introduced in *The Chosen*.

Ilana Davita had wanted the prize because it would have given her the opportunity to tell her Jewish community a few words of farewell. "I had made this community my home, and now I felt betrayed by it. . . . I felt suddenly alone. And for the first time I began to understand how a single event could change a person's life." Later, in a vision, Jakob Daw and Davita's father appear, as well as Aunt Sarah. They want to hear her words, and so Davita speaks. She does not understand a world that kills its very best. She had wanted to speak public words of good-bye to her father and Jakob Daw the storyteller. The harp appears in her vision as well, singing in memorial to all the Davitas who would never have an opportunity to "speak their few words to this century."

In the end, Davita will go on to public school, angry with "sacred discontent." In an interview, Potok explained that Davita's experience was based on that of his wife, who was passed over as valedictory speaker because of her gender. *Davita's Harp* is a new exploration for Potok, that of Orthodoxy and feminism. Yet the novel also draws from Gershon Loran, David Lurie, and Asher Lev in recognizing the power of the artist's imagination to transform pain and ambiguity into some kind of meaning. A writer is a kind of harp, playing new music that mends the world.

THE GIFT OF ASHER LEV

The Gift of Asher Lev is framed by death. It begins with the funeral of Yitzchok Lev, Asher's uncle, and the ending of Asher's exile in France to attend the services in Brooklyn. Asher Lev is forty-five; he is joined by his wife, Devorah; their daughter, Rocheleh, eleven; and five-year-old son, Avrumel. Though his family adapts well to the life of the Brooklyn Hasidim, Asher is haunted by the memory of a strange telephone call he received eighteen years earlier, the last time he had visited his parents in New York. It was a voice from the "Other Side," threatening death.

Asher is unable to paint (though he is given to sketching) and he seems to wander aimlessly through the local shops and galleries, as if waiting for a renewal of his gift. In the last year, critics had detected Asher's repetition of old themes, and he feels in danger of losing his gift should he become acclimated to his parents' community. Morose and determined to flee to France again, Asher is asked by the Rebbe to stay, at least for a while. Eventually it becomes clear to Asher that he and the aging Rebbe are woven inextricably together, as darkness and light. The Rebbe has no heir, and it is apparent that the leadership of the Ladover must pass soon to Asher's father; but there can be stability in the community only if there is assurance of the line of succession. If not Asher, then the next heir must be Avrumel, Asher's only son.

By the end of the novel, which takes Asher's story to the late 1980's, the artist has exiled himself again to France, but not without sacrifice. He has left his wife and children in New York, promising to return to them several months hence; yet in his isolation he has begun to paint again. "What kind of God creates such situations?" Asher asks himself as he walks with Devorah. "He gives me a gift and a son, and forces me to choose between them." Later, in France, Asher is visited by the image of the far-away Rebbe: "Slowly you begin to unravel the riddle," the vision says,

> Your answer may save us and return you to your work. . . . It is sometimes possible for a man to acquire all of the world to come by means of a single act in this world. . . . You will redeem all that you have done and all that you are yet to do.

Paradoxically, the sacrifice of Avrumel for the good of the community is a kind of death that redeems that artist himself; a gift on behalf of the world to come in exchange for the gift of the world as it is, in all its ambiguity and horror, and the ability to capture it on canvas.

I AM THE CLAY

Like *The Book of Lights*, *I Am the Clay* is a third-person narrative that grew in part from Potok's experiences in Korea. As they flee the North Korean and Chinese armies, a nameless old man and a woman named Gyu find a boy, Kim Sin, who is terribly wounded. The man wants to leave the boy, but the woman insists on taking him with them and heals him of his wounds. Eventually, they return to the village of the old couple to discover that it has not been destroyed. The boy then travels to his village, discovers that it has been razed, and returns to the village of the man and woman. Nearby is an American military installation where the boy gets a job, eventually working for a Jewish chaplain. After the boy reluctantly gets involved with a thief, the chaplain helps him escape by finding him a job in Seoul. By this time, the woman is dead, and the man has learned to love the boy.

The book treats the conflicts between the old, rural way of life and the new, technological way of life as well as between the old religious ideas and the reality of war. When the old man and woman return to their village, they think things will be the same because it has been spared, but they are wrong.

Like the biblical Job, to whom the novel's title alludes, the man, woman, and boy do not understand why they suffer. The woman has learned the words "I am the clay" from a missionary, from whom she has also learned to make the sign of the cross. Blending the sign of the cross into her own ideas about magic, she illustrates Potok's idea of the unity of all people. Although the novel has little to do with Jews, *I Am the Clay* treats one of Potok's central problems: testing one's beliefs in the face of an ambiguous, often harsh, and rapidly changing reality.

Dan Barnett
Updated by Richard Tuerk

OTHER MAJOR WORKS

NONFICTION: *Wanderings: Chaim Potok's History of the Jews*, 1978; *Tobiasse: Artist in Exile*, 1986; *The Gates of November: Chronicles of the Slepak Family*, 1996; *My First Seventy-nine Years*, 1999 (with Isaac Stern); *Conversations with Chaim Potok*, 2001 (Daniel Walden, editor).

CHILDREN'S LITERATURE: *The Tree of Here*, 1993; *The Sky of Now*, 1995.

BIBLIOGRAPHY

Abramson, Edward A. *Chaim Potok*. Boston: Twayne, 1986. The first book-length study of Potok, this volume is the fullest available introduction to his life and works. After a biographical sketch, Abramson discusses each of Potok's novels through *Davita's Harp*. Supplemented by a chronology, notes, an index, and a good selected bibliography, including a list of secondary sources with brief annotations.

Bloom, Harold, ed. *Chaim Potok's "The Chosen."* Philadelphia: Chelsea House, 2005. This student guide to the novel contains a biographical sketch of Potok, an account of the conditions under which the novel was written, a list of characters, a plot summary and analysis, and a critical opinion of the book. Also includes an annotated bibliography.

Daum, Robert A. "Crossing Cruci-Fictional Boundaries: Transgressive Tropes in Chaim Potok's *My Name Is Asher Lev*." In *Jesus in Twentieth-Century Literature, Art, and Movies*, edited by Paul C. Burns. New York: Continuum, 2007. This analysis of Potok's novel focuses on its treatment of a crucified Jesus. Part of a collection of essays that analyze the representation of Jesus in the work of twentieth century novelists, artists, and filmmakers.

Furman, Andrew. "Zionism in Chaim Potok's *The Chosen*, Messianic Complications and Current Crises." In *Israel Through the Jewish-American Imagination: A Survey of Jewish-American Literature on Israel, 1928-1995*. Albany: State University of New York Press, 1997. Furman analyzes *The Chosen* and works by seven other Jewish-American authors to chart the evolution of the relationship of American Jews with the state of Israel.

Shaked, Gershon. "Shadows of Identity: A Comparative Study of German Jewish and American Jewish Literature." In *What Is Jewish Literature?*, edited by Hana Wirth-Nesher. Philadelphia: Jewish Publication Society, 1994. Shaked briefly places *The Chosen* in the context of literature in which Jewish authors and their characters have a dual identity: Jewish as well as that of the country in which they live.

Sternlicht, Sanford. *Chaim Potok: A Critical Companion*. Westport, Conn.: Greenwood Press, 2000. A straightforward and useful guide to the novelist's works through *I Am the Clay*. Includes two biographical chapters and a bibliography of primary and secondary sources.

Studies in American Jewish Literature 4 (1985). This special issue devoted to Potok includes several valuable critical essays, an interview with Potok conducted in 1981 by S. Lillian Kremer, and an autobiographical essay by Potok, "The First Eighteen Years." An indispensable source.

University of Pennsylvania, Jewish Studies Program. *Chaim Potok and Jewish-American Culture: Three Essays*. Philadelphia: Author, 2002. These essays, delivered at a memorial symposium for Potok, reappraise *The Chosen*, discuss "Potok and the Question of Jewish Writing," and examine how the author was a *Zwischenmensch*, or a person who negotiated between two cultures.

Walden, Daniel, ed. *Conversations with Chaim Potok*. Jackson: University Press of Mississippi, 2001. Reprints numerous interviews with Potok, in which he discusses a range of topics, including his view on writing and other writers, his religious faith, and his novels.

ANTHONY POWELL

Born: London, England; December 21, 1905
Died: Frome, Somerset, England; March 28, 2000
Also known as: Anthony Dymoke Powell

PRINCIPAL LONG FICTION

Afternoon Men, 1931
Venusberg, 1932
From a View to a Death, 1933
Agents and Patients, 1936
What's Become of Waring, 1939
A Question of Upbringing, 1951
A Buyer's Market, 1952
The Acceptance World, 1955
At Lady Molly's, 1957
Casanova's Chinese Restaurant, 1960
The Kindly Ones, 1962
The Valley of Bones, 1964
The Soldier's Art, 1966
The Military Philosophers, 1968
Books Do Furnish a Room, 1971
Temporary Kings, 1973
Hearing Secret Harmonies, 1975
A Dance to the Music of Time, 1951-1975, 1976
    (collective title for previous 12 titles)
O, How the Wheel Becomes It!, 1983
The Fisher King, 1986

OTHER LITERARY FORMS

Although Anthony Powell (pohl) produced much writing other than his long fiction, he remained primarily a novelist. Powell was an editor, an author of prefaces, a prolific book reviewer, and a screenwriter. While his miscellaneous writing includes light verse and fictional sketches, the stories, such as the ironic sequels to Charles Dickens's *A Christmas Carol* (1843) and D. H. Lawrence's *Lady Chatterley's Lover* (1928), are facile parodies, amusing but of limited interest. His skill in characterization and the fine art of gossip, basic to his major work, *A Dance to the Music of Time*, helps explain Powell's empathy with a seventeenth century expert in these matters, John Aubrey, author of *Lives of Eminent Men* (1813; also known as *Brief Lives*, 1898). Powell ed-

ited Aubrey's works and wrote a biographical study, *John Aubrey and His Friends* (1948, 1963). Powell also wrote two plays, *The Garden God* and *The Rest I'll Whistle* (published together in 1971). These comedies of manners, while containing crisp dialogue and entertaining dramatic scenes, do not suggest that Powell was a dramatist manqué. Finally, wrote his memoirs, in four volumes under the general title *To Keep the Ball Rolling* (1976-1982). These books provide a valuable account of experiences that Powell transmuted into fiction; they also present vivid characterizations of many of Powell's contemporaries, including Constant Lambert, the Sitwells, Evelyn Waugh, Cyril Connolly, and George Orwell. In 1990, Powell published a substantial selection of his essays and reviews, *Miscellaneous Verdicts: Writings on Writers, 1946-1989*, followed in 1991 by a second collection, *Under Review: Further Writings on Writers, 1946-1989*. Three volumes of Powell's journals were also published between 1995 and 1997.

ACHIEVEMENTS

Powell's career as a novelist started with five novels published in the 1930's. These books had generally favorable reviews and reasonable sales; they established Powell's reputation as a skilled and successful, if perhaps minor, novelist. His reputation grew steadily with his twelve-volume sequence *A Dance to the Music of Time*, begun after World War II and completed in 1975, and by the 1980's he was generally recognized as one of the major English writers of the century. He is frequently compared to Marcel Proust, although, as Evelyn Waugh pointed out, Powell's *roman-fleuve* is more realistic and much funnier.

A Dance to the Music of Time is indeed funny. Becoming more somber in tone as it proceeds, incorporating numerous tragic events, never lacking a certain fundamental seriousness, the series nevertheless remains comic, a comedy in more aspects than Honoré de Balzac's meaning of a broad social portrait. The series does present a picture of various segments of English society—essentially the privileged segments—during the British Empire's decline since World War I. It has, thus, a certain limited value as sociological documentation—as what W. D. Quesenbery termed an "anatomy of decay"—but this is at best a secondary aspect. Primarily as excellent entertainment, the novels are appreciated by a wide range of readers. One may enjoy, in each of the individual novels, the wit, especially in dialogue, the characterization, and incident. In the series as a whole, there is the additional pleasure of observing the complex interactions of the characters as they appear, disappear, and reappear, forming unexpected patterns in the "dance," the whole bound together, if somewhat loosely, by theme.

From the first volume of the sequence, *A Question of Upbringing*, the work was well received, although it was, of course, only as subsequent volumes appeared that readers, in increasing numbers, came to appreciate the complex interconnections of the separate books. Powell's wit and style were commended, as was his characterization, especially the creation, in Kenneth Widmerpool, of one of the great comic villains in all of English literature. It was the narrative structure, however, that eventually produced the most critical interest.

Although the series moves chronologically forward, through the half century from 1921 to 1971, it is presented through the memory of the narrator, Nicholas Jenkins, who employs flashback and foreshadowing in a complex manner, recalling, for example, in the sixth book, his childhood in 1914. Such a structure suggests Proust's *À la recherche du temps perdu* (1913-1927; *Remembrance of Things Past*, 1922-1931). The comparison is relevant, and both Powell and his protagonist Nick Jenkins admire the French writer. Powell's narrator is not similar to Proust's however; Nick's mind operates differently. In addition, Henri Bergson's theory of time, so important to Proust, has limited relevance to Powell's work.

If Powell was not an English Proust, comparisons with other novel sequences make even clearer the unique quality of *A Dance to the Music of Time*. In its focus on the individuality of character, it is diametrically opposed, for example, to "unanimism," the ideology of collective experience that informs Jules Romains's *roman-fleuve Les Hommes de bonne volonté* (1932-1946; *Men of Good Will*, 1933-1946). One of the few English novel sequences of comparable length, C. P. Snow's *Strangers and Brothers* (1940-1970), employs a structure quite dif-

ferent from Powell's. The eleven volumes of Snow's work shift between those that focus on the life of the central figure, Lewis Eliot, and those that do not, whereas Nick Jenkins remains in each book simultaneously a participant in, and an observer of, the "dance" that the series chronicles.

Powell's achievement, springing from an interest in character, expressed through matchless style, and distinctly structured, has then, as does any great work of art, a sui generis excellence. It won Powell a devoted and varied audience; the British Broadcasting Corporation (BBC) has produced the series; *A Dance to the Music of Time*'s translations include a Bulgarian version. A share of worldly honors, such as an honorary fellowship in the Modern Language Association of America and an honorary D.Litt. from Oxford, came to Powell. Perhaps more significantly, he earned the respect of fellow writers, those his own age and those younger, those who share his conservative beliefs and those who do not. In sincere flattery, at least one other writer, the major Canadian novelist Hugh Hood, is writing his own series of novels in admiring emulation of Powell's work.

BIOGRAPHY

Anthony Dymoke Powell was born December 21, 1905, in London, England. His mother was the daughter of a barrister; his father, himself the son of a colonel, was a lieutenant in the army who was to win decoration in World War I and retire as a lieutenant colonel. Powell, his parents' only child, spent his early years in a military environment. He was to have a continuing respect for the service; General Conyers, in *A Dance to the Music of Time*, is only one of a number of sympathetically portrayed army officers in Powell's fiction.

As a member of a well-to-do family, Powell had an upper-class education and acquired the values of his class. He entered Eton in 1918, where he made friends, such as Hubert Duggan, a source for Stringham, who were to contribute to his subsequent characterizations. When, in 1923, Powell matriculated at Balliol College, Oxford, he continued to collect the friends and the personal impressions that were to serve him well when he later described Nick Jenkins's experiences. Powell's memoirs, *To Keep the Ball Rolling*, written after *A Dance to the Music of Time*, are invaluable for helping

Anthony Powell. (Express Newspapers/Archive Photos)

readers deal with the complex issue of the relation between fiction and "real life," but it may be said that Powell was not always entirely forthcoming and that many of his fictional characters are based, often rather closely, on particular prototypes.

While at Oxford, Powell made various vacation trips to the Continent; in 1924, he traveled to Finland, where his father was stationed. Later, he drew on this travel in his early novel *Venusberg*. Powell graduated from Oxford in 1926 and went to work for the publishing firm of Duckworth, in London. There, Powell lived the quasi-bohemian life that is described in *A Buyer's Market* and subsequent volumes in *A Dance to the Music of Time* and is also reflected in his five prewar novels. He spent much time in the company of painters and musicians, meeting, among them, the composer Constant Lambert, who was to become a lifelong friend and the prototype for Hugh Moreland in Powell's series.

On December 3, 1934, Powell married Lady Violet Packenham; they were to have two sons, Tristam and John. With his marriage, Powell acquired a large set of interesting in-laws; collectively, they were to contribute something to his fictional portrait of the Tollands; his brother-in-law Frank Pakenham, the seventh earl of Longford, was to serve as a major source for the character Kenneth Widmerpool.

After his wedding, Powell left Duckworth's. In 1936, he worked as a scriptwriter for Warner Bros. in London, where he met Thomas Phipps, the original of Chips Lovell. In 1937, he went with his wife, via the Panama Canal, to Hollywood, California, in search of a scriptwriting job. Although the job did not work out, before they returned to England the Powells enjoyed an interesting interlude that included a meeting with F. Scott Fitzgerald. Upon his return to London, Powell engaged in journalism and wrote his fifth novel, *What's Become of Waring*.

In 1939, as World War II began, Powell was commissioned a lieutenant in the Welsh Regiment. His war experiences are fairly accurately portrayed in the military trilogy, the third "movement" of the four in *A Dance to the Music of Time*. Powell, like Nick Jenkins, served first in a line regiment in Northern Ireland; he was transferred, in 1941, to Army Intelligence, worked as a liaison officer with Allied forces, served in France and Belgium, and gained the rank of major.

Just as Nick, after leaving the army at the end of the war, worked on a study of Robert Burton, so did Powell engage in historical research on John Aubrey, publishing his study in 1948, and an edited collection of Aubrey's work the next year. With Aubrey "finally out of the way," as Powell writes, he turned again to novel writing and began, with *A Question of Upbringing*, his *roman-fleuve*. The novels in the series appeared at fairly regular intervals, averaging one every two years from 1951 until 1975. During these years, Powell continued his career in journalism, contributing sketches, articles, and reviews to *Punch*, the London *Daily Telegraph*, and other periodicals. In 1956, he was made a Commander of the Order of the British Empire. In 1961, he lectured in the United States at Dartmouth College, Amherst College, and Cornell University, and he was appointed a trustee of the National Portrait Gallery in 1962. His plays, *The Garden God* and *The Rest I'll Whistle*, were published together in 1971, the same year in which the University of Sussex awarded him the D.Litt.

During his outwardly quiet postwar years, Powell continued to enjoy and expand his circle of friends, thereby finding some additional prototypes for the characters introduced in the later volumes of his series. The writer Julian Maclaren-Ross, the prototype of X. Trapnel, is a notable example.

Upon completing *A Dance to the Music of Time*, Powell began his memoirs, publishing *Infants of the Spring* in 1976, followed, at two-year intervals, by *Messengers of Day*, *Faces in My Time*, and *The Strangers All Are Gone*. In 1983, a year after the appearance of the final volume of his memoirs, Powell published the short novel *O, How the Wheel Becomes It!*, a satiric *jeu d'esprit*, his first work of fiction since the completion of *A Dance to the Music of Time*. This was followed in 1986 by *The Fisher King*, a full-length novel published to ex-

cellent reviews. During most of the period of his major work, Powell and his wife lived at Somerset. In the 1980's Powell continued to receive honors for writing, including a D.Litt. from Oxford in 1980.

Anthony Powell was one of the major figures of British letters since the 1920's and 1930's, and by the late 1990's he was the last surviving member of the so-called Brideshead generation, as described by Waugh. While he was a student at Eton, perhaps England's most prestigious public school, Powell's contemporaries included Harold Acton, Cyril Connolly, and George Orwell. At Oxford University he was a colleague of Waugh, Peter Quennell, and Maurice Bowra. Powell died in March, 2000, in Somerset.

ANALYSIS

Of the many pleasures and rewards offered by Anthony Powell's novels, none surpasses that to be found in coming to know, and continually being surprised by what happens to, a variety of fascinating characters. For Powell, an interest in character was primary. This can be seen in his absorption in the biographies sketched by John Aubrey, in the series of verbal portraits that dominate *To Keep the Ball Rolling*, and in his statement that a concern for character was central in his beginning *A Dance to the Music of Time*. Successful fiction, though, involves more than the presentation of a series of characters, however intriguing. When characterization is conveyed with wit, both in dialogue and description, when the style becomes a pleasure in itself, as it does in Powell's work, one has enough ingredients for writing worth reading, but not enough for a novel, certainly not for a novel of the scope and stature of *A Dance to the Music of Time*. Such a novel, like any successful work of art, must satisfy the aesthetic requirement of unity—it must convey a sense of structure and order.

A DANCE TO THE MUSIC OF TIME

Although not the sole ingredient on which the unified structure of *A Dance to the Music of Time* depends, character does help provide this sense of balance in the work. For example, Powell achieves a degree of unity by having a single narrator, Nicholas Jenkins, yet *A Dance to the Music of Time* is not really the story of Nick Jenkins, just as it is not essentially the story of Kenneth Widmerpool, important as both these characters are. Although himself a participant in the "dance," Nick basically observes and reports; he does not give structure to the events that he relates: No persona, only Powell himself, could do this.

Many writers, certainly, achieve structure through plot, which may be the soul of fiction as Aristotle thought it was of drama. For Powell, however, the demands normally implied by "plot" run counter to his fundamental sense of time's complex mutability; to give his work a definite beginning, middle, and end, with action rising to and falling from a specific climax, would be justified neither by his sense of reality nor his artistic intentions.

This is not to say that conscious arrangement of incident is not present in *A Dance to the Music of Time*. On the contrary, because the author has exercised intelligent concern for such arrangement, continual surprises are enjoyed in a first reading, and anticipation of the irony of coming events gives a special pleasure to rereading the series. It would be yielding too readily to the seductive appeal of paradox, however, to claim that it is a crafted sense of the random that gives basic structure to *A Dance to the Music of Time*—that its order lies in its apparent lack of order.

If not to be found primarily in character or plot, what is the key to the structure of the dance? Unwilling, with reason, to accept the idea that it *has* no clear structure, that it is, even if cut from a loaf made of remarkably milled flour, essentially "a slice of life," critics have proposed a variety of answers.

The title of the series, as Powell has explained, derives from an allegorical painting in the Wallace Collection in London, Nicolas Poussin's *A Dance to the Music of Time*. Comparisons between the painting and the novel may be ingeniously extended, but it seems improbable that they were extensively worked out by Powell as he began a series that, he writes in *Faces in My Time*, would consist of a number of volumes, "just how many could not be decided at the outset." It would appear more probable that the Poussin painting, expressing the French artist's sense of the permutations time produces in human life, while an important analogue to Powell's intention in the series, was only one of a number of sources of the work's pattern. Another source might have been Thomas Nashe's *Summer's Last Will and Testament*

(1592), a masque organized around the four seasons, contrasting the arts and the utilitarian spirit, and involving a sophisticated, semidetached "presenter"; it was the basis of a musical composition by Powell's close friend Constant Lambert.

Other structural keys have been proposed, including the importance of mysticism (the Dr. Trelawney, Mrs. Erdleigh aspect) and the signs of the zodiac. There would seem to be some validity in most of these interpretations, but the attempt to see any one as a single key to the series appears reductionist, in the sense that a strict Freudian or Marxist reading of William Shakespeare is too limiting. Insofar as the pattern of the dance can be extrapolated from the work itself, most critics have agreed that it must be seen as a reflection of theme.

Of the many thematic strands, that which is central appears to be the conflict between power and art, or imagination and will. Jenkins himself suggests this at more than one point in the series. From the perspective of this conflict, in which Widmerpool, the extreme example of the self-centered power seeker, is thematically contrasted to Hugh Moreland the musician, and later to X. Trapnel the writer, the characters and their actions fall into a meaningful, if somewhat shadowy, pattern. The pattern is hardly simple, though; few characters are purely villainous or heroic; some artists seek power; some professional soldiers and businessmen are artistic and imaginative; both victories and defeats tend to be temporary.

Furthermore, the sexual designs woven in the "dance" complicate a bipolar view of theme. Sexual attraction, or love, in the novel usually involves both an imaginative appreciation of a perceived beauty in the desired partner, and some attempt to impose one's will on another. Thus, with vagaries of desire, thematic antitheses and syntheses may fluctuate within individual characters. It is clear, however, that when Matilda Wilson goes from the artist Moreland to the industrialist Sir Magnus Donners, or Pamela Flitton leaves Widmerpool for the novelist X. Trapnel, a thematic point is made. (Indeed, the women in the series, generally less convincingly presented than the men, often seem to serve as scoring markers in the thematic game.)

That this thematic conflict, while it should not be simplistically defined, was essential to Powell's concept of the work's structure is shown additionally by the way prototypes were transmuted into fictional characters. Frank Pakenham, for example, unlike his fictional "counterpart" Widmerpool, not only would seem to have a number of virtues but also has enjoyed a long and happy marriage, blessed by eight children. Clearly, the structure of the series requires that such satisfaction be denied its thematic villain.

A suggestion, then, may be made as to the probable way Powell proceeded in constructing his series. He apparently started with a novelist's interest in certain people that he knew, those he felt would be worth portraying. Then, to create order in his work, he fitted these people's fictional representatives into thematic patterns, changing reality as needed to accomplish this patterning. Using the thematically identified characters, he then, at a lower order of priority, considered and manipulated the plot, using plot itself to demonstrate another major theme, that of "mutability." The result was a uniquely constructed work of art.

AFTERNOON MEN

Before beginning his major work, Powell wrote five novels; a case can be made for their being excellent works in their own right. Had Powell not gone on to write his *roman-fleuve*, they may have gained him a certain lasting recognition. As it is, inevitably they are regarded primarily as preparation for his masterpiece. The use of the "detached" narrator, coincidence in plot, ironic style, clipped dialogue, the theme of power, art, and love—all these attributes of *A Dance to the Music of Time* are anticipated in the early novels. *Afternoon Men*, picturing a London social scene the young Powell knew well, is the first of the five early novels. Powell described it as "something of an urban pastoral . . . depicting the theme of unavailing love," with not much plot in the conventional sense. He saw the design of this first novel to be "not without resemblance to the initial framework" of the sequence. Although the protagonist, William Atwater, is not the narrator—the story is told mainly from his point of view, with the author occasionally intruding in his own voice—he may be compared, in his wit and detached forbearance, to Nicholas Jenkins. It is essentially in its ironic style, however, especially in the dialogue, that *Afternoon Men* anticipates the later series.

VENUSBERG *and* FROM A VIEW TO A DEATH

Venusberg, Powell's second novel, also has a protagonist, Lushington, who is comparable to Nick Jenkins. Flashback, a technique later significant to the series, is employed in this novel's construction, and the theme of love is extended to include adultery, while power and clairvoyance, topics prominent in *A Dance to the Music of Time*, are introduced. Powell's next novel, *From a View to a Death*, dealing with the interrelated themes of art, love, and power, emphasizes the latter. Arthur Zouch, a painter and womanizer, uses art and love in his search for the power he believes is his by right of his being an *Übermensch*. Fittingly, for one who not only debases the gift of imagination but is also a would-be social climber, he is defeated by a member of the country gentry. Technically, the book is interesting in that Powell experiments with a shifting point of view.

AGENTS AND PATIENTS

Art, sex, and power—specifically power derived from money—are the subjects that provide structure in *Agents and Patients*. In this novel, each of two confidence men, Maltravers and Chipchase, attempts to fleece a naïve young man, Blore Smith, Maltravers by playing on Smith's sexual innocence, Chipchase by playing on his artistic innocence. As the title, drawn from John Wesley, suggests, the issue of free will and determinism, significant in a less direct way in *A Dance to the Music of Time*, is an underlying theme. Excellent as it is as satiric comedy, *Agents and Patients* puts such an emphasis on plot and theme that the characterization, usually Powell's strongest suit, tends somewhat toward caricature.

WHAT'S BECOME OF WARING

What's Become of Waring, Powell's last novel before the war, is perhaps a less impressive achievement than the four that preceded it. It is, however, close to *A Dance to the Music of Time* in more than chronology. Although it has a carefully worked out, conventional plot, Powell still manages, as James Tucker observes, to "slip out of it and pursue his concern for people." In this work, a first-person narrator is employed. He is a publisher's reader; the work draws on Powell's experience at Duckworth's. Never named, the narrator, in his overall attitude and as a partial alter ego for Powell, resembles Nicholas Jenkins. Again, the mystical element, later present in the series, is introduced through séances. Significantly, given the thematic center of *A Dance to the Music of Time*, *What's Become of Waring* ends with the narrator, as he drifts off to sleep, free-associating on the idea of power.

A QUESTION OF UPBRINGING

That Powell, after his lengthy hiatus from novel writing, returned to the idea of the quest for power is clear even from the first of the three volumes that constitute "Spring," the initial movement of his sequence. *A Question of Upbringing* introduces, at the very start, the series' most important character, Widmerpool, and it is clear that even as a schoolboy he is determined to dominate.

The early introduction of the major themes is an important aid to unity, for the start of a long series poses particular problems for its author. As Powell suggests in *Faces in My Time*, early volumes, in preparation for future ones, must introduce undeveloped characters and potential situations; additionally, some characters and situations, in view of their subsequent importance, must be overemphasized. These requirements may tend to confuse the reader, unless patterns are perceived.

A Question of Upbringing, which covers Nick's youth at public school and university, introduces an important pattern of repetition of related incidents by having Nick meet his Uncle Giles at both the beginning and the end of the volume. Another recurring structural device, the alternation of scenes described in dramatic detail with linking sections provided by Nick's subjective impressions, is present, as are the patterning devices of allusion and symbolism. The series begins with a scene of workmen gathered around a fire, repeated at the conclusion of the sequence, twelve volumes later, and mentions the Poussin painting that provides the title for the whole sequence. References to paintings are important throughout the series, including the Giovanni Battista Tiepolo ceiling in *Temporary Kings* and the oft-mentioned drawing by Amedeo Modigliani that is rescued in the final volume.

A BUYER'S MARKET

Although the themes of love and art (which, along with the interrelated theme of power, dominate the series) are present in the first volume, they are more prominent in the second, *A Buyer's Market*. In this book, dominated by the social life of parties and dances that Nick, down from the university, enjoys, not only do sexual activities become important to Nick (a late bloomer as compared to his friends Templer and Stringham), but also the theme of the quest for power is extended to include politics. The radical young woman Gypsy Jones (with whom Nick apparently loses his virginity) is utilized in one of Powell's recurring attacks on the political Left as well as to serve as an object of frustrated lust for Widmerpool, whose sex life is to be, throughout the series, eccentric and unsatisfactory.

THE ACCEPTANCE WORLD

The Acceptance World, the third volume in this movement, begins with another meeting between Nick and his Uncle Giles, who is now associated with Mrs. Erdleigh, a clairvoyant. She plays a major role in the dramatization of the subtheme of mysticism. Mysticism in the series, as seen later in Dr. Trelawney and finally in Scorpio Murtlock, is related to attempts to escape from what Mrs. Erdleigh calls the "puny fingers of Time" and to gain power. Power in *The Acceptance World*, however, is considered more in political terms; there is an extension of the political satire against the Left, especially through Quiggin (whose character owes something to Cyril Connolly's), a university friend of Jenkins who moves in left-wing intellectual circles.

The volume's love interest involves Nick in a serious affair with Jean Templer, a school friend's sister. Much later in the series, in *The Military Philosophers*, Nick realizes that Jean, who breaks off the affair, really is attracted to money and power; she ultimately marries a Colonel Flores, who becomes a Latin American dictator. As Nick reflects in the first volume, "being in love is a complicated matter"; staying in love is even more so. The balance of thematic opposites, necessary to love, is seldom maintained. Nick is to be virtually unique in the series by virtue of his lasting, successful marriage, but the reader is given little direct insight into the secret of his success.

AT LADY MOLLY'S

Nick's courtship and engagement are described in the first volume of the second movement, "Summer." This volume is titled *At Lady Molly's*; Lady Molly Jeavons is a fictional amalgam of actual people including Rosa Lewis, the famous proprietor of the Cavendish Hotel, and Lady Astor, celebrated mistress of the magnificent country mansion, Cliveden, the prototype of the novel's Dogdene. Lady Molly, whose easygoing hospitality attracts a variety of guests, is the aunt of Chips Lovell (a character based on Thomas Phipps), who works with Nick as a scriptwriter for films. Powell here, as throughout the series, introduces new characters, thereby continually revivifying his novel, personifying its themes with variety, and causing the reader to wonder who, as well as what, is coming next. The actions of the two most permanent characters, Nick and Widmerpool, form the core of the volume; Nick's developing and successful love for Isobel Tolland is contrasted with the debacle that occurs when Widmerpool attempts a premarital seduction of his fiancé, Mildred Haycock.

CASANOVA'S CHINESE RESTAURANT

Love and marriage are even more central to the next book, *Casanova's Chinese Restaurant*, which introduces and focuses on one of the series' most important and attractively realized characters, the composer Hugh Moreland, who becomes one of Nick's closest friends, just as Moreland's real-life prototype, Constant Lambert, became very important to Powell. Moreland is, thematically, *the* artist. As such, he is Widmerpool's antithesis, even though the two have too little in common to be antagonists other than thematically—the few occasions when they encounter each other are singularly, but not surprisingly, undramatic. One critic has suggested that even their names, Widmerpool's suggesting wetness, and Moreland's the opposite, indicate their antithesis. (Powell's names, as most readers will have noticed, are frequently suggestive and apt, as well as sometimes amusing—consider, for example, the name of the sexually experienced woman whom Widmerpool so decidedly fails to satisfy, Mrs. Haycock.)

A more significant difference between Moreland and Widmerpool is in their way of talking. Moreland produces very witty and pleasurable conversation; Widmerpool is given to pompous pronouncements that often entertain the reader by their unconscious self-satire. Like Widmerpool, however, although quite differently and for different reasons, Moreland has trouble with his love life; interconnections of art and love form much of the subject matter of the volumes in this movement.

THE KINDLY ONES

Other perspectives on love are introduced in *The Kindly Ones*, the last volume of "Summer," in which Widmerpool temporarily fades into the background, until the last chapter. The work begins with a flashback to Nick's childhood in 1914, thereby relating World War I to the approach of World War II in 1938, the time to which the book returns. The chronology is particularly complicated in this volume, and coincidence, always a feature of the series' plotting, is pushed to its limits when Nick, having gone to the seaside hotel where his Uncle Giles has died, meets, along with others from his past, Bob Duport, the former husband of Nick's past lover, Jean. The fact that for many readers, the complex structure of *The Kindly Ones* is unobtrusively successful, provides some measure of Powell's legerdemain.

At the end of *The Kindly Ones*, Nick has arranged for his commission in the army; the third movement, "Autumn," carries him though World War II. The reader learns from the autobiographical *Faces in My Time* that Nick's army experiences closely parallel Powell's own. Nick's service is distinguished, but the focus is more on the tedium of war than on its heroism.

In treating this often tedious but different world of the service, Powell faced technical problems. He had to maintain the structure of his series within an entirely new environment. New characters, some from social backgrounds that the novel had previously ignored, had to be used in a manner in accordance with the controlling themes. Furthermore, the style had to make some adaptation to the grim subject matter. Powell was not going to emphasize the comic elements of war, even though they are not ignored. The basic solution to these problems was to alternate the army scenes with those occurring when Nick is on leave. Thereby, the reader is able to experience the new, while still maintaining an interest in the old characters and themes.

THE VALLEY OF BONES

The first volume of the movement, *The Valley of Bones*, introduces, among many new characters, a particularly significant one, Captain Gwatkin. Gwatkin, while no artist—he had worked in a local Welsh bank—is a man of imagination, a sort of Miniver Cheevy actually in armor. He has romantic ambitions to be a perfect soldier, ambitions doomed to failure in his encounters with the men of power who are his superiors. Although he is eventually relieved of his command, Gwatkin finds some consolation in love, only to lose it when he learns of the infidelity of his beloved barmaid Maureen. Between these army scenes, Nick, while on leave, observes the continued amatory maneuvers of his friends and relations. The book ends with the dramatic appearance of Widmerpool as an influential major.

THE SOLDIER'S ART

In the next volume, *The Soldier's Art*, Nick is working as Widmerpool's junior assistant, in a position to observe his superior's continuing struggle for power, transferred from civilian to military life. Widmerpool hovers on the verge of disaster, but at the end of the book his career is saved. Previously, he had failed to assist an old school fellow of his and Nick's, Stringham, now reduced to being an enlisted man working in the officers' mess, subsequently to die in a Japanese prisoner-of-war camp. Meanwhile, personal entanglements continue to form new patterns, while some of the characters, including Chips Lovell and Lady Molly, are killed in a bombing raid.

THE MILITARY PHILOSOPHERS

The final volume of the movement, *The Military Philosophers*, finds Nick in the war office, working on liaison with Allied troops. This book, stylistically notable for its increased use of allusion, presents a number of the real personnel with whom Powell worked, little changed in their fictional guises. It is, however, an imagined character, or at least one for whom no prototype has been established, who reappears at this point, having been briefly introduced earlier as a young girl, subsequently to be a major figure. Pamela Flitton is, like Widmerpool, Stringham, Moreland, and Trapnel, one of the series' most memorable creations. She is a kind of ubiquitous nemesis, capable of bringing down the men of both art and power. Outstanding even in a cast of remarkably unusual and individual characters, she is made by Powell larger than life and yet believable, beautiful and yet repulsive, contemptible and yet capable of arousing the reader's sympathies. Although not all readers find her entirely convincing, she is certainly one of Powell's most fascinating characters. As the war ends, she is engaged to Widmerpool. No one could deserve her less, or more. With Pamela's entrance into the series, the tone, previously not essentially grim, even with the many deaths occurring during the war, changes.

BOOKS DO FURNISH A ROOM

In the final movement of the series, "Winter," the style also changes as Powell moves toward a concluding "wintery silence." While a sense of the comic is never abandoned, the mood becomes more somber, the action more direct. The first novel in this movement, *Books Do Furnish a Room*, is primarily the story of X. Trapnel, a novelist based on Powell's friend Julian Maclaren Ross. Trapnel, the artist, is juxtaposed with Widmerpool, the man of power, through the agency of Pamela Flitton, who leaves Widmerpool to live with Trapnel. The triumph of the artist is temporary, however, for not only is Pamela discovered to be both sexually insatiable and frigid, but she also destroys a manuscript of Trapnel's most recent novel by dumping it in the Maida Vale Canal, and returns to Widmerpool.

TEMPORARY KINGS

In the next volume, *Temporary Kings*, which begins at an international literary conference in Venice, where the first half of the novel is set, Pamela is a dominant character. Her sexual debauchery continues, unsettling Widmerpool, but she encounters a man on whom her charms fail, Professor Russell Gwinnett. Continuing his ability to rejuvenate the series by introducing new characters, Powell brings in this American scholar with necrophilic tastes, who is writing a book on Trapnel. Nick finds him "an altogether unfamiliar type," with "nothing simple" about his personality.

Thematically, Gwinnett, a curious variant of the deus ex machina, may embody a kind of resolution of the conflict between art and power. Having both an involvement with art and an exceptionally strong will, Gwinnett, whose superior psychic strength provokes Pamela's suicide, perhaps in a necrophilic ritual, may be thought to have avenged Trapnel, if not Widmerpool. Any resolution with Gwinnett is, however, a dark one, incorporating the cult rites with which he becomes involved before returning to America, and necessarily suggesting that to which he is most strongly related, death.

HEARING SECRET HARMONIES

The final volume of the sequence, *Hearing Secret Harmonies*, is focused on Widmerpool, who, with the exception of Nick himself, is the series' most enduring character. After becoming a kind of hero to rebellious youth, he joins a pagan religious cult and struggles with its leader, Scorpio Murtlock, for dominance. Finally, running at the end, just as he was in his first appearance in the sequence, he falls dead, exhausted by his effort to take the lead in a ritual run.

The ending of such a long work poses a particular problem. After twelve books, certainly some feeling of conclusion must be produced, yet the whole structure, the whole sense of the continually evolving dance of time, renders any strong sense of climax inappropriate. Powell, by having Nick learn at second hand of Widmerpool's death, and then returning to the initial image of the workmen's fire, quoting Robert Burton, and providing a carefully worded final image, skillfully solves this problem. The ending is a final reminder of the quality of literary skill and talent that is sustained through all the volumes of singularly satisfactory achievement.

THE FISHER KING

The Fisher King was Powell's second novel to be published after the completion of *A Dance to the Music of Time*. Most of the action involves a group of characters taking a summer cruise around the British Isles. Aboard the cruise ship *Alecto* is Saul Henchman, a famous photographer who received disabling and disfiguring injuries in World War II. He is traveling with his assistant and companion, a beautiful woman named Barberina Rookwood. Much of the story is narrated by another passenger, Valentine Beals, a writer of historical novels. As the cruise progresses, Henchman reveals himself as a thoroughly unpleasant individual, Beals is seen to be gossipy and pretentious, and Rookwood inspires the admiration of men and women alike. Three men on the cruise—Henchman, Gary Lamont, and Robin Jilson—vie for her attention.

The Fisher King provides numerous connections between its characters and mythological figures, generally commented on by Beals. Beals's interpretations and speculations are flawed in a number of ways, however, and Powell is perhaps suggesting that myth can still illuminate intriguing aspects of human behavior but cannot truly predict how humans will act. Throughout, Powell is less concerned with drawing precise mythological parallels than with providing an amusing and intellectually entertaining story of people and their foibles.

William B. Stone
Updated by Eugene Larson and McCrea Adams

OTHER MAJOR WORKS

PLAYS: *"The Garden God" and "The Rest I'll Whistle": The Text of Two Plays*, 1971.

POETRY: *Caledonia: A Fragment*, 1934.

NONFICTION: *John Aubrey and His Friends*, 1948, 1963; *To Keep the Ball Rolling*, 1976-1982 (includes *Infants of the Spring*, 1976; *Messengers of Day*, 1978; *Faces in My Time*, 1980; *The Strangers All Are Gone*, 1982); *Miscellaneous Verdicts: Writings on Writers, 1946-1989*, 1990; *Under Review: Further Writings on Writers, 1946-1989*, 1991; *Journals*, 1995-1997 (3 volumes); *A Writer's Notebook*, 2000.

BIBLIOGRAPHY

Barber, Michael. *Anthony Powell: A Life*. Woodstock, N.Y.: Overlook Press, 2004. Comprehensive biography chronicles Powell's career and places him within the context of literary life in twentieth century England. Although Barber was not Powell's official biographer, he was able to conduct several interviews with his subject. Includes photographs.

Berberich, Christine. "Dancing to the Music of Widmerpool: The Gentleman in Anthony Powell's *A Dance to the Music of Time*." In *The Image of the English Gentleman in Twentieth-Century Literature: Englishness and Nostalgia*. Burlington, Vt.: Ashgate, 2007. Discussion of Powell's character Kenneth Widmerpool is included in a study of how the English gentleman has been portrayed in twentieth century literature. Demonstrates how writers use the gentleman character as a means to critique society and to represent changing concepts of gender, class, and nationality.

Birns, Nicholas. *Understanding Anthony Powell*. Columbia: University of South Carolina Press, 2004. Examines all of Powell's work, including his novels *Afternoon Men*, *Venusberg*, and *The Fisher King*. Pays particular attention to *A Dance to the Music of Time*, placing the novel series within its social and historical context.

Brennan, Neil. *Anthony Powell*. Rev. ed. New York: Twayne, 1995. One-third of this study is devoted to *A Dance to the Music of Time*, Powell's tour de force; the rest provides analyses of the author's other works, including early novels such as *Afternoon Men* and

From a View to a Death. Contains a chronology of Powell that includes information on his ancestry.

Joyau, Isabelle. *Investigating Powell's "A Dance to the Music of Time."* New York: St. Martin's Press, 1994. Insightful and appreciative analysis of Powell's novel sequence discusses its structure and characters as well as the literary techniques Powell employs.

Morris, Robert K. *The Novels of Anthony Powell*. Pittsburgh, Pa.: University of Pittsburgh Press, 1968. First book-length study of Powell's writings discusses all of Powell's novels up to 1968. Focuses on Powell's central theme of the struggle between the power-hungry and the sensualists. Also provides analysis of the first eight volumes of *A Dance to the Music of Time*.

Selig, Robert L. *Time and Anthony Powell*. Cranbury, N.J.: Associated University Presses, 1991. Examines how Powell uses time within *A Dance to the Music of Time* and how the novel sequence affects the reader's sense of time.

Spurling, Hilary. *Invitation to the Dance: A Guide to Anthony Powell's "Dance to the Music of Time."* Boston: Little, Brown, 1977. Useful guide helps readers to navigate the complexities of Powell's novel series. Contains a synopsis of each volume, by chapter and time sequence, and an extensive character index.

Tucker, James. *The Novels of Anthony Powell*. New York: Columbia University Press, 1976. Extensive appraisal of the twelve volumes of *A Dance to the Music of Time* includes a "who's who" of characters as well as discussion of themes, style, narrative, and method. A scholarly work, but quite readable. Includes bibliography.

DAWN POWELL

Born: Mount Gilead, Ohio; November 28, 1897
Died: New York, New York; November 14, 1965

PRINCIPAL LONG FICTION

Whither, 1925
She Walks in Beauty, 1928
The Bride's House, 1929
Dance Night, 1930
The Tenth Moon, 1932
The Story of a Country Boy, 1934
Turn, Magic Wheel, 1936
The Happy Island, 1938
Angels on Toast, 1940, 1989 (revised as *A Man's Affair*, 1956)
A Time to Be Born, 1942, 1991
My Home Is Far Away, 1944, 1995
The Locusts Have No King, 1948, 1990
The Wicked Pavilion, 1954, 1990
A Cage for Lovers, 1957
The Golden Spur, 1962
Novels, 1930-1942, 2001 (Tim Page, editor)
Novels, 1944-1962, 2001 (Page, editor)

OTHER LITERARY FORMS

Though Dawn Powell is known primarily as a novelist, she had originally intended to write for the theater. Her play *Big Night* was produced by the Group Theatre in 1933, and *Jig Saw: A Comedy* had a short run in 1934. Powell also wrote a musical comedy and scripts for radio, television, and film and published essays, reviews, and short stories in distinguished national magazines. A number of her short stories were collected in *Sunday, Monday, and Always* (1952).

ACHIEVEMENTS

While such contemporaries as Ernest Hemingway and John Dos Passos considered Dawn Powell one of the finest writers of their time, she never attained their popularity. Shortly before her death in 1965, Powell was honored with an honorary doctorate and an award from the National Institute of Arts and Letters, but despite occasional attempts by her admirers, such as Edmund Wilson, to call attention to her achievements, she remained relatively obscure, and her sixteen novels, all out of print, were difficult to find. Fortunately, in the next two decades, there was a revolution in the American sensibility. One of the results of the feminist movement was that critics and publishers had to admit sins of omission; they had minimized the talent of many fine women writers simply because they were women. Powell, who has been called an American equivalent to English satiric novelists such as Evelyn Waugh and Anthony Powell, is an obvious example.

In 1987, author and critic Gore Vidal launched the campaign to obtain proper recognition for Powell. In a lengthy essay published in *The New York Review of Books*, he traced her life and her literary career and concluded by bemoaning the fact that the novels of the person he considered America's best comic novelist were all out of print. As a result of his article, several of her later books were reprinted, all with Vidal's essay as an introduction, and the reviews that followed suggest that Powell may at last receive the recognition denied her during her lifetime.

BIOGRAPHY

Dawn Powell was born in Mount Gilead, Ohio, on November 28, 1897, the daughter of Roy K. Powell, a traveling salesman, and Hattie B. Sherman Powell. For six years, after the death of her mother when Powell was six, she and her two sisters lived with various relatives on farms and in small towns. After her father's remarriage, the girls went to live with him and their stepmother on a farm. Powell already was a dedicated writer; indeed, after her stepmother punished her by burning her stories, Powell fled to the home of an aunt. After graduating from high school, Powell went to Lake Erie College, where she received her bachelor of arts degree in 1918. That year she moved to New York to serve in the U.S. Navy auxiliary, remaining there working in public relations and in advertising.

In 1920, Powell married Joseph Roebuck Gousha, an executive with an advertising agency, with whom she had one son, Joseph Roebuck Gousha, Jr. Failing in her attempts to break into the theatrical world as a playwright, Powell began writing novels, publishing the first, *Whither*, in 1925. Over the next four decades, she published fifteen more novels, the early ones set in her native Ohio, most of the later ones in New York City's Greenwich Village, in what became her world, the small

circle of writers, publishers, actors, producers, artists, and critics who were at the intellectual center of the United States. Still without wide recognition, Powell died of cancer at St. Luke's Hospital in New York City on November 14, 1965.

ANALYSIS

The primary purpose of a Dawn Powell novel is to describe a society. To do so, Powell brings a number of characters together, perhaps in an Ohio boardinghouse, perhaps at a New York party or a bar. Then the characters seem to take over, as if they are determined to dramatize their own world. They act and interact, they talk, they boast, they scheme, they lie, and they confess to one another. To this extent, Powell's novels could be called realistic. They also, however, include an element of satire. It is primarily noticeable in the characters' inner deliberations, which Powell reveals to her readers in illuminating detail. The characters' confusion about facts, their muddled reasoning, and above all their clearly selfish motivations, reported with such painstaking care, leave the reader no doubt as to Powell's satiric intentions, which are further stressed in her occasional wry and witty comments.

Although Powell's first book, *Whither*, was set in New York City, all but one of the six novels published during the next six years were placed in the rural Midwest. These works introduce the themes that would dominate Powell's later work: the alienation of an individual from society, the frustration of the failing artist, the random nature of love, the limits of friendship, and above all the rule of money. Beginning with *Turn, Magic Wheel*, Powell wrote a series of seven novels to which Vidal refers as her "New York cycle." Most critics consider these novels to represent Powell's highest artistic achievement and, indeed, a unique contribution to American literature.

ANGELS ON TOAST

The third of these novels, *Angels on Toast*, illustrates Powell's approach. The world that she both summarizes and satirizes is defined in the first chapter of the book. The story begins with two businessmen, Jay Oliver and Lou Donovan, on a train from Chicago to New York. The self-absorption that marks most of Powell's characters is evident from the first.

Their world is neither abstract nor cosmopolitan. At its simplest it is made up of their own bodies and their own clothes. Jay admires his own shoes, which he thinks reflect his polished personality, and his socks, which are so dazzling that he must mention how expensive they were. Lou contemplates and assesses his weight, his shoulders, then is delighted to tell Jay how much his shirt cost and to invite him to feel the material. For men so fascinated with the most trivial details about themselves, it is not surprising that both friendship and love are limited in depth. From the facile comment that Jay is his best friend, Lou soon has moved to the notion that Jay may know too much about him; indeed, it is Jay's company that is his best friend, not Jay himself, Lou muses. If Jay were replaced, the new man would become Lou's best friend. Lou's capacity for love is similarly limited by circumstances. For example, when he married above himself, he found it convenient to forget having been married before, and he is now worried because that former wife has turned up in Chicago. In a typical Powell passage, however, Lou congratulates himself because he has been faithful to his wife, except for casual encounters in places where she would never go. Jay, on the other hand, is shockingly unfaithful, picking up his regular mistress on the train and taking her to New York with him. It is not adultery, but taking such chances, that Lou considers immoral.

Thus, by re-creating conversations and by reporting her characters' thoughts, Powell reveals their attitudes and values. Her satiric intention is clear, when she lets Lou congratulate himself for what are in fact very low moral standards; it is obvious that for him and his society, love and friendship will never stand in the way of making money.

In Powell's later novels, New York itself might as well be listed as one of the characters. It is symbolic that the first chapter takes place on the way to New York, instead of on the way back to Chicago. In New York, the businessmen think they can get away with anything. It is, of course, ironic that the city proves to be much smaller than the out-of-town visitors think it is; unfortunately, paths do cross, and wives do find out what is occurring.

In *Angels on Toast*, the compelling attraction of New York is also dramatized in the attitude of an eccentric old lady who lives in a seedy hotel. When her daughter sug-

gests that they both move to Connecticut, the idea is greeted with horror. Obviously, even a dingy hotel in New York is better than a mansion anywhere else. Actually, the old lady's real home is the hotel bar; its inhabitants are the only people she needs or wishes to know.

Except for the fact that Ebie Vane is a commercial artist, the conflict between the creator and his crass, indifferent world is not as important in *Angels on Toast* as it is in Powell's last three novels, in which the alienation of the artist from society is a major theme. The cohesiveness of New York's literary and theatrical world is suggested by the title of the first of these books, *The Locusts Have No King*. The quotation, which comes from the biblical Proverbs, emphasizes the idea that although there is no single leader among locusts, they seem to have a mysterious single direction. They move in hordes and, it should be added, destructive hordes. It is such mindless human groups that can destroy the will and the

Dawn Powell. (Library of Congress)

hopes of an artist or, perhaps worse, turn an artist into a commercial success at the cost of creative integrity and personal relationships.

THE LOCUSTS HAVE NO KING

At the beginning of *The Locusts Have No King*, there seems to be no possibility that the protagonist, Frederick Olliver, a writer of scholarly books, will ever become successful enough to find his soul endangered. In contrast, his mistress, Lyle Gaynor, a successful playwright, is a celebrity who knows every other celebrity in the literary world. Lyle is completely devoted to Frederick. Indeed, she would marry him except that she feels a duty to remain with her ill-tempered husband because he is disabled. To help Frederick, Lyle includes him in every party she gives and arranges for him to be invited to every party she attends. Nevertheless, Frederick always feels that he is an alien in Lyle's world. In response, he voices his scorn of the successful, including his generous mistress. The fact that one lover is inside the magic circle and the other is outside clearly imperils their relationship.

Powell's theme of alienation appears in three different typical situations. The first involves characters such as Frederick, who, though they are not new to New York, have simply not had enough success to be accepted. The second involves a young person who, like Jonathan Jaimison in *The Golden Spur* and like the young Powell herself in 1918, has recently arrived in New York, usually from the Midwest, and must be initiated into its ways. Although the misunderstandings and mistakes of the innocent can be highly comic, they do not provide the occasions of satire that Powell sees in the third kind of alienation. Like all the great satirists, she delights in exposing the pretensions of characters who attempt to be accepted in a complex, cultivated society but who are too foolish to master its mannerisms or even its idiom.

An example of this kind of alienated character, who unlike the other types has no hope of being accepted as a result of eventual success or deliberate adaptation, is Dodo Brennan in *The Locusts Have No King*. Dodo has chosen to think of herself as a southern belle, and she has come from Baltimore to conquer New York with cuteness. Unfortunately, her poses and her baby talk make her ludicrous. Although Frederick becomes involved with Dodo and introduces her into Lyle's circle, Dodo's vulgarity, her stupidity, and her inability to realize that her idiotic speeches have no resemblance to wit ensure her status as a permanent alien in the literary world.

In *The Locusts Have No King*, however, the theme of alienation is most important as it relates to the central love story. When by chance Frederick and Lyle reverse their places in society, when Lyle's fortunes decline and Frederick becomes a commercial success, ironically the psychological barriers to their union disappear. Unlike most of Powell's lovers, whose short-term entanglements are motivated by chance, lust, and ambition, Frederick and Lyle prove to be capable of profound attachment, which only grows stronger in the face of change.

THE WICKED PAVILION

Even though sexual liaisons are important in Powell's novels, the real action takes place not in bedrooms but in the living rooms and bars where her characters gather. Although the title of her next novel, *The Wicked Pavilion*, is taken from a reference to the Brighton Pavilion in England, Powell's pavilion is simply a New York café, where many of the characters from her preceding books reappear, now older but hardly wiser. The book is carefully crafted, with two plots that are intertwined, both of which depend on frequent appearances in the Café Julien. One of them involves an incomplete love story. Haunted by the memory of his passion for a young woman whom he met at the café during the war, Rick Prescott has returned to search for her and for the happiness he believes that he somehow lost. In developing this plot, Powell again emphasizes the transitory nature of most human relationships, especially love, which, despite lovers' illusions, depends heavily on chance and on the imagination.

The second plot exposes the phoniness of the artistic world. When a painter dies, two of his unsuccessful fellow artists discover that they can make a large amount of money by forging works supposedly painted by him; their scheme is complicated, however, when they find that he is not dead but has pretended to die and is now profiting by the greatly increased value of his old paintings, as well as of the new ones he is producing, which he can market as lost masterpieces. It is evident that Powell is in sympathy with the artists, who on at least one occasion have thus triumphed over the commerciality of art dealers and the arrogant stupidity of art critics.

THE GOLDEN SPUR

In Powell's final novel, *The Golden Spur*, it is not the artist but the innocent who triumphs over the glittering and corrupt world that Powell knew, loved, and satirized. Again, the title refers to a bar, but in this case the reference is not oblique. The Golden Spur is indeed the name of a bar that has a special significance to a young man from the Midwest. In her youth, his mother, then Constance (Connie) Birch, had come to New York as a real innocent, had fallen in love with the city and with one of its residents, and then, pregnant, had returned to Ohio to marry an unsuspecting flour salesman named John Jaimison. Now another innocent, Connie's son, has come to New York.

In his response to the city, the son is like his mother. Within eighteen hours he is hopelessly in love with it. Unlike her, however, he is not destined to become a victim. As he seeks out the various men mentioned in his mother's diaries, any of whom might possibly be his father, he finds that instead of being horrified at the prospect of scandal, they are all pleased. Even those who cannot remember Connie would like to talk themselves into the memory of an affair with her, which could have produced this appealing son. Yet the prospective son is less than enthusiastic about the various candidates, who, though they may be rich and famous, do not live up to the dream father who has appeared in his imagination.

Certainly, Powell is pointing out that reality rarely equals illusion. In this final book, however, there is a special significance in Jonathan's disenchantment. Like Powell herself, in her sixties at the time *The Golden Spur* appeared, the people of the magic circle have aged, and the old New York is dead. At the end of *The Wicked Pavilion*, the Café Julien was torn down; at the end of *The Golden Spur*, an artist insists that the real money of the twenty-first century will be not in creation but in demolition. His ambition does not stop with seedy hotels and run-down cafés; he yearns to take the big ball to the Metropolitan Museum of Art. Thus, Powell's final book does not mark merely the end of a young man's dream; it commemorates the end of the world Powell knew.

In Robert van Gelder's book of interviews, *Writers and Writing* (1946), Powell answered the repeated criticism of her work—that she did not deal with significant people—by pointing out that most people have no real goals in life. The answer was that of a realist. Still, she might better have appealed to the standards of her genre. The satirist causes readers to laugh at people, not to revere them. In her last and best novels, Powell points out the follies and the vices of New Yorkers like those she knew: the vulnerable or vulgar innocence of newcomers, the desperate need of the alien to become accepted, the misuse of reason to justify lust and ambition, the betrayal of love and friendship, and above all, the enslavement to greed.

It is appropriate that Powell has had a revival. Certainly she immortalized a society forever gone, but more important, she created characters whose weaknesses are all too universally human.

Rosemary M. Canfield Reisman

OTHER MAJOR WORKS

SHORT FICTION: *Sunday, Monday, and Always*, 1952; *Dawn Powell at Her Best*, 1994 (Tim Page, editor).

PLAYS: *Big Night*, pr. 1933; *Jig Saw: A Comedy*, pr., pb. 1934; *The Lady Comes Across*, pr. 1941; *Four Plays*, 1999 (Michael Sexton and Tim Page, editors).

NONFICTION: *The Diaries of Dawn Powell, 1931-1965*, 1995 (Page, editor); *Selected Letters of Dawn Powell, 1913-1965*, 1999 (Tim Page, editor).

BIBLIOGRAPHY

Levy, Barbara. "Forerunners: Dorothy Parker, Dawn Powell, Betty MacDonald." In *Ladies Laughing: Wit as Control in Contemporary American Women Writers*. Amsterdam: Gordon and Breach, 1997. Levy analyzes the use of wit in the works of seven contemporary American writers. The study includes a biographical chapter about Powell.

Page, Tim. *Dawn Powell: A Biography*. New York: Holt, 1998. Page, one of Powell's finest critics and the major force behind her literary resurrection, provides the first comprehensive account of her life and work. Includes detailed notes and an extensive bibliography.

Rice, Marcelle Smith. *Dawn Powell*. New York: Twayne, 2000. More of an overview than a traditional biography, this book concentrates on Powell's novels, their creation, and their relation to the author's life experiences. Includes an index and bibliographical references.

Rovit, Earl. "A Memorable Reality." *Sewanee Review* 110, no. 2 (Spring, 2002). An overview of Powell's life and literary career, discussing the work that Powell herself described as her "Ohio novels" and her "New York stories." Rovit speculates on why Powell never attained significant success as a novelist.

Vidal, Gore. "Dawn Powell, the American Writer." *The New York Review of Books*, November 5, 1987. This essay, which also serves as the introduction to the Vintage Press editions of *Angels on Toast, The Golden Spur*, and *The Wicked Pavilion*, is an important work of Powell criticism. In it, Vidal summarizes Powell's life, suggests reasons for her obscurity, presents a chronological summary of her novels, and discusses her importance to American literature.

_____. "Dawn Powell: Queen of the Golden Age." In *The Last Empire: Essays, 1992-2000*. New York: Doubleday, 2001. Vidal admired Powell and called her America's "best mid-century novelist." This analysis of her work is included in his collection of essays

about literature, politics, and American society and culture.

Wetzsteon, Ross. *Republic of Dreams: Greenwich Village, the American Bohemia, 1910-1960*. New York: Simon & Schuster, 2002. Wetzsteon recounts the history of the New York City neighborhood in the chapter "Dawn Powell: The Village as an Idea of Itself." Recounts stories about some of Greenwich Village's most creative residents, including Powell, Eugene O'Neill, and Edna St. Vincent Millay.

Wilson, Edmund. "Greenwich Village in the 50's." *The New Yorker*, November 17, 1962. A review of *The Golden Spur* by one of the literary giants who shared Powell's world. Wilson compares her genius to that of Anthony Powell, Evelyn Waugh, and Muriel Spark.

Wilson, Edmund, and Leon Edel, eds. *The Thirties: From Notebooks and Diaries of the Period*. New York: Farrar, Straus and Giroux, 1980. An excellent source, not only because of the references to Powell but also because it provides a full picture of the period in which she lived. Edel's introduction is also illuminating. Includes illustrations.

J. F. POWERS

Born: Jacksonville, Illinois; July 8, 1917
Died: Collegeville, Minnesota; June 12, 1999
Also known as: James Farl Powers

PRINCIPAL LONG FICTION

Morte d'Urban, 1962
Wheat That Springeth Green, 1988

OTHER LITERARY FORMS

J. F. Powers was highly regarded for his prowess as a short-story writer. "Lions, Harts, Leaping Does" (1943), only his second story to be published, appeared in the O. Henry and Martha Foley anthologies in 1944. His first short-story collection, *Prince of Darkness, and Other Stories*, was published by Doubleday in 1947. (Random House reissued the collection in 1979.)

Doubleday published his second collection of stories, *The Presence of Grace*, in 1956. In 1963, Time published *Lions, Harts, Leaping Does, and Other Stories*, a collection culled from Powers's first two books. His next collection, *Look How the Fish Live*, was published by Knopf in 1975. Powers's stories appeared first in magazines such as *Accent, Colliers, Commonweal, The Nation, Kenyon Review, Partisan Review*, and *The New Yorker*. Powers also wrote reviews of poetry and fiction, autobiographical pieces, and articles dealing with social issues. His nonfiction, like most of his fiction, is often satiric in tone.

ACHIEVEMENTS

J. F. Powers is to be numbered among those American writers—others include Katherine Anne Porter and

J. D. Salinger—who produced a relatively small body of work distinguished by meticulous craftsmanship. Powers was praised by critics and fellow writers such as Alfred Kazin, William H. Gass, Thomas Merton, and Stanley Edgar Hyman. The Irish master of the short story, Frank O'Connor, judged Powers to be "among the greatest of living storytellers." When Powers drew negative critical response, it was often for what were deemed to be his overly parochial concerns and his narrow focus on the world of the Catholic Church in the United States, especially of the clergy. In fact, Powers's narrow focus can be seen as a source of strength; he wrote about what he knew best and, like excellent writers everywhere, discovered the universal in the particular. He has a permanent place in American literature as one of the most accomplished short-story writers of the twentieth century.

J. F. Powers. (Hugh Powers)

BIOGRAPHY

James Farl Powers was born in Jacksonville, Illinois, on July 8, 1917, to James Ansbury and Zella Routzong Powers. He is one of three children. His father was a manager for Swift and Company, and the family lived in comfortable circumstances. Jacksonville was a predominantly Protestant community, and that made the Catholic Powers family part of a minority.

In 1924, the Powers family moved to Rockford, Illinois, where they lived for seven years and where James attended public schools. After another move, in 1931 to Quincy, Illinois, Powers became a student at the Franciscan-run Quincy Academy, from which he graduated in 1935. He then moved to Chicago, where, over the next eight years, he held various jobs: insurance salesman, clerk at Marshall Field department store, chauffeur, editor with the Chicago Historical Records Survey, and clerk at Brentano's bookstore. From 1938 to 1940, he took night courses at Northwestern University. While working at Brentano's, in 1942, he wrote his first story, "He Don't Plant Cotton," published the following year in *Accent* magazine. He was fired from Brentano's for refusing to buy war bonds.

In 1943, Powers experienced what critic John V. Hagopian (in *J. F. Powers*, 1968) described as a religious crisis. Since moving to Chicago, he had become increasingly sensitive to social issues; the status of African Americans and war were two issues with which he was particularly concerned. His moral revulsion at the injustices to which African Americans were subjected was tellingly expressed in such stories as "He Don't Plant Cotton" and "The Trouble." Powers became a pacifist in 1943. Arrested two weeks after he failed to report for induction, he was, after pleading not guilty and waiving trial by jury, sentenced to serve three years in Sandstone Federal Prison in Minnesota. He was paroled in late 1944 after serving thirteen months of his sentence. He then went to St. Paul and worked as a hospital orderly. In 1945, he met Elizabeth Alice Wahl at St. Benedict's College in St. Joseph's, Minnesota, and the following year they were married. She, like Powers, pursued a writing career.

Powers was a resident at the Yaddo community in 1947, the year in which *Prince of Darkness, and Other Stories*, his first collection of stories, was published. The book met with favorable critical response. In 1948,

Powers received grants from the Guggenheim Foundation and the National Institute of Arts and Letters (NIAL), and taught at St. John's University of Collegeville, Minnesota. He continued teaching for several years, this time at Marquette University, and had another residency at Yaddo. Throughout the 1950's, Powers and his growing family (he and his wife had five children—Katherine, Mary, James, Hugh, and Jane) lived in either Minnesota or Ireland. In 1956, the year in which his second collection of stories, *The Presence of Grace*, was published, he taught at the University of Michigan. Powers once said that teaching was something he turned to out of need, when he ran out of money.

Powers's first novel, *Morte d'Urban*, was published by Doubleday in 1962. It won the 1963 National Book Award and the Thermod Monsen Award, given by the Chicago critics for the best book written by a midwesterner. Powers was writer-in-residence at Smith College between 1965 and 1966. The short-story collection *Look How the Fish Live* appeared in 1975. His second novel, *Wheat That Springeth Green*, was published in 1988. Besides receiving grants from the NIAL and the Guggenheim, Powers received a Rockefeller Fellowship on three occasions.

ANALYSIS

J. F. Powers was an idealist; he also was a moralist. The two attitudes need not necessarily be incorporated in a single person, but they naturally combine when, as is the case with Powers, the ideal is perceived to be something that is to not only be admired but also sought. The vision of the pure idealist tends to be illuminated chiefly by aesthetic considerations; a discrepancy between the ideal and the real is seen primarily as an artistic failure. For the idealist-moralist, on the other hand, the discrepancy between the ideal and the real, while it can profitably be seen in aesthetic terms, is essentially a matter of morality. To call Powers an idealist is not to say that he was a perfectionist. Falling short of the ideal is, for fallen human beings, to be expected; but to abandon the ideal, to give up the pursuit of perfection, is to fail morally. As a moralist, Powers had quite distinct notions of what constitutes good and evil, and the difference between them is sharp. His morality was based on Catholic theology.

Powers's "world," his equivalent of William Faulkner's Yoknapatawpha County, is the American Catholic Church, more particularly that Church as it manifests itself in the Midwest, more particularly still, the clergy of that Church. Unquestionably, Powers's best fiction is that written about Catholic priests. Choosing to write about priests was in itself an ingenious artistic ploy. The priest is by vocation, if not by disposition, an idealist, and therefore presents for an idealist-moralist an excellent focal point for examining the discrepancy between the ideal and the real. His characters are not drawn from the common people but from a kind of scaled-down aristocracy, people from whom readers would be justified in expecting more because more has been given them.

MORTE D'URBAN

Some of the critical reaction that followed immediately upon the publication of *Morte d'Urban* was adverse. Perhaps because of the fact that certain chapters had previously been published individually as short stories, the judgment was made that the work lacked the unity of structure necessary for a novel and was only a gathering of loosely associated tales. Only the most superficial reading of the work could sustain a judgment of this sort, for the novel is possessed of remarkable unity of theme and structure. The chief unifying element in the novel is its main character, Father Urban Roche. Father Urban is presented as a very attractive character, but a peculiar kind of deceptive satire, at which Powers excels, is at work in the novel. So attractive is Father Urban that the unwary reader might be led erroneously to conclude that the novel demonstrates the insensitivity of the powers-that-be within the Catholic Church, treating in shabby fashion a man of Father Urban's talent and charm.

Morte d'Urban is essentially a comic novel, not only in the sense that it is funny, which it certainly is, but also, and more important, in the sense that it is the obverse of tragic. It is the story of a priest who, though by no means a bad man, is not manifesting in his life the type of goodness of which he is capable and, more pointedly, to which he is dedicated by vows. Father Urban is a Roman Catholic priest, but on the basis of the attitudes that dominate his consciousness and the behavior in which he engages, he is more appropriately identifiable as the all-American boy. He is Sinclair Lewis's George F. Babbitt with a Roman collar, always on the lookout for the ecclesiastical main chance. He is intelligent, imaginative, witty, well spoken, and possessed of a seemingly inexhaustible fund of energy. He is doubtless sincere in his conviction that the various projects to which he dedicates his talents are eminently worthwhile—that is, for the good of the Church and, ultimately, for the greater glory of God. Father Urban is an activist, and there is something almost intrinsically admirable in the activist, but he is a person for whom activity has become altogether too much. His "can do" attitude toward his vocation, which puts a premium on tangible results, has been nurtured over the years at the expense of his interior life. While ostensibly oriented toward the spiritual, he is in fact a materialist.

Father Urban is a member of the Order of St. Clement, the Clementines, of whom it has been said that their uniqueness consists in their being noted for nothing at all. He concurs in this cruel judgment, but if he belongs to a third-rate order, he takes consolation in the fact that he is its star, the scintillating exception in an organization composed, for the most part, of bland mediocrities. He behaves toward his confreres with pro forma charitableness, a disguise for condescension. He is in fact an accomplished preacher, and in much demand as a conductor of parish missions. When he is assigned to the order's latest white elephant, a retreat house in rural Minnesota, his paranoid conviction that he is persecuted by his foolish superiors because they are jealous of his talents is only more firmly established.

After a depressing first few months in his new assignment, and thanks to the reinvigorating experiences associated with his filling in as pastor at a nearby parish, Father Urban regains his old gusto. His term as acting pastor of St. Monica's allows him to display with verve all his talents as a get-up-and-go priest, a cleric with zip who knows the right people to befriend and is always building for the future—a brisk optimist and a "bricks and mortar man" par excellence. When the priest for whom he is substituting dies suddenly (of a heart attack while vacationing in the Bahamas), Father Urban entertains the possibility that the bishop might appoint him as the permanent pastor of St. Monica's. He cleverly attempts to further his cause with the bishop, but to no avail. The appointment is given to another priest.

Father Urban, though disappointed, is not floored by this turn of events, for by this time, he has begun to see possibilities for the retreat house, St. Clement's Hill. With the financial backing of Billy Cosgrove, a wealthy Chicago layman and friend, he secures the permission of the Clementine provincial superior and the local bishop to build a nine-hole golf course at St. Clement's Hill. The idea behind the venture is to make the facility more attractive for the better sort of Catholic laypeople, those who will not only come there to make a retreat but also leave behind them a generous donation. It would seem that Father Urban's characteristic modus operandi has stood him in good stead even in the backlands of Minnesota, but his streak of successes is put in jeopardy by the rumor that the bishop may take the retreat house away from the Clementine Order and turn it into a seminary for his diocese.

The bishop visits St. Clement's Hill with a young priest of the diocese who is an expert golfer. They all take to the links together, and as the game progresses, it becomes evident to Father Urban that in his match with the young priest, the bishop's man, he has symbolically entered the lists and is involved in a trial of strength. Whatever might be the eventual fate of St. Clement's Hill, it becomes a point of honor for him that he win the golf match. Having made a nice approach shot to the final green, he is apparently on the verge of doing so when events are suddenly reversed: Father Urban is struck on the head and knocked unconscious by a golf ball hit by the bishop. This seemingly absurd incident marks the turning point of the novel.

After the accident on the golf course, as a result of which the bishop drops his plans to take over the retreat house, Father Urban's attitude toward life and toward his vocation slowly changes. His being felled by a golf ball, while not comparable to St. Paul's being knocked off his horse on the road to Damascus, precipitates a period of reassessment. During this period, Father Urban undergoes three trials, which is consonant with the Arthurian theme—one of the informing elements of the novel. In one trial, he tries and fails to persuade Mrs. Thwaites, an elderly benefactor, with whom he had previously attempted to ingratiate himself, to restore to an innocent employee money that she had effectively stolen from her. His eyes are thus opened to the unpretty realities of

Thwaites's hypocrisy and stark avariciousness, which in the past he was inclined to overlook as supportable eccentricities.

In the second trial, Urban goes on a fishing trip with his friend Billy Cosgrove, which results in the dissolution of the friendship. The experience proves to be painful but educational. He is made fully aware that Cosgrove is not a noble human being. He is rich, yes, but he is also egotistical, childish, and pathologically cruel. In the third trial, Urban is put upon by Mrs. Thwaites's daughter, Sally Hopwood, who is rich, sophisticated, bored, and bereft of principles and who attempts to seduce him. She fails, but out of the ordeal, Urban comes to a new, and disturbing, consciousness of himself; he realizes that had he chosen to follow a vocation other than the priesthood, his outlook on life would not have been appreciably different from the one he entertains as a priest. He is brought to see that there is something fundamentally lacking in the quality of his priestly life.

The novel is brought to an abrupt and significant close after Urban is elected as the provincial superior of the Chicago Province of the Clementines. It is a position for which, when he was possessed of the consciousness of the "old man," he had often longed, as it would provide him with the power base to implement the kind of progressive reforms about which he had always dreamed. Here would be his chance to get the Clementines off dead-center, to shake them up, to move them toward becoming a first-rate order that had a reputation for gumption. Those who elect Urban to the post have in mind the type of person who can make the right kind of friends for the order, people such as Cosgrove, people who have the money to make things happen. The Father Urban who moves back to Chicago from Minnesota to become Father Provincial, however, is a radically changed man. He has undergone a conversion.

Urban does not die physically, but as the title *Morte d'Urban* suggests, a death does take place. Urban dies to the kind of life, superficial and meretricious, to which he had devoted the better part of his days and turns to a life that, though less flamboyant, is decidedly more promising.

Wheat That Springeth Green

Powers's long-awaited second novel, *Wheat That Springeth Green*, was published in 1988. Although it

was nominated for a National Book Award shortly after its publication, that honor was to elude Powers this time around. Like its predecessor, *Morte d'Urban*, this second novel is primarily the story of a priest. In this case, the protagonist is Father Joe Hackett, who is a member of the presbyterate of an unnamed diocese in Minnesota. The novel might be described as a portrait of a modern priest that is set against the background of a church, as well as a larger society, that finds itself in a state of disorientation and turmoil.

The narrative covers the whole of Father Hackett's life, but equal time is not given to every stage. Most of the action of the novel takes place in the late 1960's, when the protagonist is in his forties. The reader is introduced to Joe Hackett when he is little more than a toddler, but even at so tender an age he comes across as someone with a penchant for easy egocentrism. One's next glimpse of him is as a boy of grade-school age, revealing two incongruous personality traits that seem to be permanent by the time he reaches adulthood—a scrappy competitiveness and a tendency to run and hide when the world is not going the way he wants it to go.

Next, Powers provides a brief look at Joe's adolescent years, the centerpiece of which is a set of rather fantastical sexual escapades with the girls next door. One suspects that this chapter is to be read as a parody of the adolescent imagination. In the following chapter, Joe is in his early twenties; he has put his sinful ways behind him and is now a seminary student, preparing for the Catholic priesthood. He is an earnest seminarian, possessed of a considerable capacity to take himself with the utmost seriousness. This displays itself in odd behavior at times. For one who is an advanced student in theology, and apparently doing quite well in his studies, he nurtures comically crude and naïve notions concerning the nature and requirements of the spiritual life.

The reader next encounters Joe as a young priest. One watches, and is not terribly surprised, as his tenuously founded idealism begins to give way to a spiritless pragmatism. Discovering that the daily life of a priest is often composed of prosaic and undramatic demands, he loses his initial fervor. He makes accommodations. Slowly and subtly, he becomes worldly, although his worldliness is not something of which he himself is fully aware. In fact, he tends to interpret this worldliness as something positive: his own peculiar, and canny, brand of antiestablishment fervor. An ominous accompaniment of this downward slide is a steady increase in his drinking. Joe is, indeed, in the incipient stages of alcoholism, which, typically, he does not admit to himself.

The latter two-thirds of the novel takes place in the present, relative to the narrative. The year is 1968; Father Joe, now forty-four years old, is the comfortably established pastor of a well-to-do suburban parish. He fulfills his rather tightly circumscribed duties in a conscientious fashion and shows a lively alertness to the particulars of his situation. Significantly, he is guided by what has now become a conviction that his is the right way of doing things. He has developed a strong, although low-key, propensity to regard himself as somewhat the ecclesiastical "genuine article." On occasion, he seems to view himself as a lonely warrior for the right, engaged in constant battle on several fronts with several varieties of benighted bumblers and pretenders, both inside and outside the Church, by whom he is surrounded. By this time, he has become a habitual drinker, dependent upon alcohol to see him through the day.

The novel ends abruptly, as if in medias res, after Father Joe seemingly undergoes a sort of conversion experience, which is as sudden as it is difficult to understand. In his final state, which is simply announced to the reader, Father Joe has given up drinking, as well as his suburban pastorate; he now ministers among the poor in the inner city. Somehow, the authenticity of this latest transformation is less than fully convincing. Has Father Joe finally found himself and his proper place in the Church and in the world, or is it but the stage to a further impetuous move?

It is possible to read *Wheat That Springeth Green* as an extended exercise in irony, the kind of thing one would expect from Powers. Clues to such a reading can be found, for example, in the parallels one can make between the objects of Father Joe's constant criticism and the patterns of his own behavior. He is an acute and relentless critic, in general, of the ways of the world and, in particular, of certain ways and personality types to be found within the Church. Specifically, he has what comes close to being an obsessive concern for what he regards as the Church's preoccupation with money.

Father Joe strives to present himself as the refreshing antithesis of the type of pastor who is absorbed with money, but whether his own way of handling the finances of his parish does not in the end succeed in giving more, or at least as much, attention to money matters is debatable. He appears to have convinced himself that he is virtuously antimaterialistic because he is not concerned with "big bucks," but what the reader witnesses is a man whose daily concerns are taken up primarily with things material. Materialism is no less materialism for being low-budget. The point is that the demands of a genuine poverty of spirit do not seem to be key factors in Father Joe's life. In addition, Father Joe has a low tolerance for those among his fellow clerics whom he sees as mindless and unimaginative—not to say cowardly—functionaries, people with little or no understanding of the Church's mission and how a priest should be leading his life.

This attitude of Father Joe is in many respects commendable. Yet it loses much of its moral force when one considers that he himself scarcely comes across as a paragon of priestly virtue. He is not what would be identified as "pastoral" in his inclinations; he is anything but outgoing, and any thought to the continuing spiritual needs of his parishioners that he may have fails to manifest itself in his day-to-day activities. Moreover, he has a habit of confining himself to the immediate precincts of the rectory.

Father Joe's idea of a good pastor is all too easily reducible to the role of the faithful middle manager, someone who keeps regular office hours, makes sure the parish books are kept in the black, and maintains an eccentrically rigid control over the population of the parish school. In sum, it is difficult to see how Father Joe's interpretation of the proper duties of the conscientious priest stands as a marked improvement over the behavior he vigorously criticizes. Hence the irony.

Father Joe Hackett, then, is an intensely ordinary priest, a priest who is running outside the track, and perhaps a bit behind the pack, but who has long since persuaded himself that all the while he has been sticking to the inside rail. He is certainly not a bad man. For that matter, neither is he mediocre. Nevertheless, he is possessed of a kind of ordinariness that can prove dangerous because of its penchant for mistaking moral limitations for real moral advantages. Be that as it may, Father Joe falls far short of qualifying as the great midwestern hope of a confused and blundering Church.

Dennis Q. McInerny
Updated by William Hoffman

OTHER MAJOR WORKS

SHORT FICTION: *Prince of Darkness, and Other Stories*, 1947; *The Presence of Grace*, 1956; *Lions, Harts, Leaping Does, and Other Stories*, 1963; *Look How the Fish Live*, 1975; *The Old Bird: A Love Story*, 1991 (originally published in *Prince of Darkness, and Other Stories*); *The Stories of J. F. Powers*, 2000.

BIBLIOGRAPHY

Evans, Fallon, ed. *J. F. Powers*. St. Louis, Mo.: Herder, 1968. A collection of essays and appreciations emphasizing the Catholic context of Powers's fiction. Among the contributors are Hayden Carruth, William H. Gass, Thomas Merton, and John Sisk. Also includes an interview with Powers and a bibliography.

Hagopian, John V. *J. F. Powers*. New York: Twayne, 1968. The first book-length study of Powers, this overview comprises a biographical sketch and a survey of Powers's work through *Morte d'Urban*. Includes a useful bibliography.

Labrie, Ross. "J. F. Powers (b. 1917)." In *The Catholic Imagination in American Literature*. Columbia: University of Missouri Press, 1997. Labrie analyzes representative works by Powers and other Catholic writers and poets to describe how these works express each writer's particular interpretation of Catholic teaching.

Long, J. V. "Clerical Character(s)." *Commonweal* 125, no. 9 (May 8, 1998): 11-16. Long offers a retrospective analysis of the leading characters in *Morte d'Urban* and *Wheat That Springeth Green* and the sacred-versus-secular issues confronting them. It is an interesting look back in the light of changes in American Catholicism since the 1950's.

Powers, Katherine A. "Reflections of J. F. Powers: Author, Father, Clear-Eyed Observer." *Boston Globe*, July 18, 1999. A reminiscence of Powers by his daughter; discusses the writers that most influenced Powers, particularly his admiration for Evelyn Waugh, and comments on his writing and reading habits.

Preston, Thomas R. "Christian Folly in the Fiction of J. F. Powers." *Critique* 16, no. 2 (1974): 91-107. The theme of the "fool for Christ," whose actions confound the wisdom of this world, has a long tradition. Focusing on the novel *Morte d'Urban* and the stories "Lions, Harts, Leaping Does" and "The Forks," Preston explores Powers's handling of this theme, showing how Powers uses priests as protagonists, not to dwell on concerns peculiar to the priesthood but rather to illumine the nature of the Christian life.

Wood, James. "Church Mice." *The New Yorker*, December 11, 2000. Wood, a prominent literary critic, evaluates Powers's novels and other works and assesses the characters in his fiction. He compares Powers's work to that of other Catholic writers.

RICHARD POWERS

Born: Evanston, Illinois; June 18, 1957
Also known as: Richard S. Powers

PRINCIPAL LONG FICTION

Three Farmers on Their Way to a Dance, 1985
Prisoner's Dilemma, 1988
The Gold Bug Variations, 1991
Operation Wandering Soul, 1993
Galatea 2.2, 1995
Gain, 1998
Plowing the Dark, 2000
The Time of Our Singing, 2003
The Echo Maker, 2006

OTHER LITERARY FORMS

Richard Powers first appeared in print nationally with "Computer-Assisted English Instruction," a chapter in *Education in the 80's: English* (1981). Powers has published book reviews and has frequently contributed opinion pieces to *The New York Times*, including "A Game We Couldn't Lose" (February 18, 1996) and "Losing Our Souls, Bit by Bit" (July 15, 1998). His contributions to *The New York Times Magazine* include "Life by Design: Too Many Breakthroughs" (November 19, 1998), "Eyes Wide Open" (April 18, 1999), "American Dreaming: The Limitless Absurdity of Our Belief in an Infinitely Transformable Future" (May 7, 2000), and "A Head for Music" (January 8, 2006). Shortly after the terrorist attack on New York City of September 11, 2001, he wrote about the disaster in "The Simile," which also appeared in *The New York Times Magazine* (September 23, 2001). Powers also contributed "An Artificial Being" to *Making Things Public: Atmospheres of Democracy*, a volume edited by Bruno Latour and Peter Weibel and published in 2005. In "My Music" (in *Gramophone*, October, 2005) Powers details the significance of music in his life.

ACHIEVEMENTS

In 1985, in recognition of *Three Farmers on Their Way to a Dance*, Richard Powers received the Rosenthal Award of the American Academy and Institute of Arts and Letters, a PEN/Hemingway Special Citation, and a nomination from the National Book Critics Circle. In 1989, he became the youngest recipient of a MacArthur Fellowship, a so-called genius award. In 1998, Powers was named Swanlund Professor of English at the University of Illinois at Urbana-Champaign, where, in 2000, he became a fellow at the Center for Advanced Study. *Gain* brought him an award as Best Business Book of 1990 as well as the James Fenimore Cooper Prize of the American Society of Historians. Many of Powers's novels have been named notable books by *The New York Times* (1991, 1995, 1998, 2000, 2003), and his works were finalists for the National Book Critics Circle Award in 1985, 1991, 1995, and 2003. *The Echo Maker* received the National Book Award for fiction in 2006 and was also a finalist for a Pulitzer Prize for fiction. Powers's novels have been translated into more than a dozen languages.

BIOGRAPHY

Richard Powers's roots in Illinois are deep and of long standing. Born in Evanston in 1957, he was the fourth of Donna and Richard Franklin Powers' five children. He attended elementary school in Lincolnwood, a heavily Jewish suburb of Chicago. On Jewish holidays, the Powers children were among a handful of non-Jewish children attending school.

When Powers was eleven years old, his father, a secondary school principal, accepted a position at the International School in Bangkok, Thailand. During his family's five-year stay in Thailand, Powers perfected his skill in playing the cello, heightened his understanding of Johann Sebastian Bach's complex compositions, and joined a chorus that traveled within Asia to perform. His vocal abilities were substantial, and his exposure to Asian culture had a considerable effect on him.

Upon returning to the United States, Powers's family settled in De Kalb, Illinois, where the father became a school administrator and Donna Powers worked as a secretary and administrative assistant for the Wurlitzer Corporation. Powers, who was six feet, seven inches tall, played high school basketball, but he also read voraciously, taking careful notes on his reading.

When he completed high school, Powers entered the University of Illinois at Urbana, an institution familiar to him because his family had lived near the campus in the mid-1960's. His father had completed a doctorate there in 1967. Uncertain of what studies he wanted to pursue, Powers considered becoming a physics major. During his freshman year, however, he took an honors seminar with Professor Robert Schneider of the university's English department. Schneider ignited in him a spark that eventuated in Powers's becoming an English and rhetoric major. In 1977, he completed his undergraduate degree, having maintained a perfect A average. He then pursued graduate studies in English and received a master's degree late in 1979.

Spurning the university's attempts to lure him into the doctoral program, Powers moved to Boston in 1980, where he became a computer programmer and data processor for a large corporation. When his employers tried to advance him into management, he quit his job, became a freelance computer specialist, and devoted himself to writing.

In Boston, Powers visited the Museum of Fine Arts every Saturday, when visitors were admitted free before noon. During one such excursion, he stumbled upon an August Sander photograph of three country bumpkins, bedecked in weekend finery, on their way to a dance. This photograph haunted Powers because its date was 1914 and the dance to which these three peasants were going was, metaphorically, World War I. Powers used the picture as a central reference point in his first novel, *Three Farmers on Their Way to a Dance*.

In 1987, Powers relocated to the Netherlands, where he polished the first draft of *Prisoner's Dilemma* and completed *The Gold Bug Variations*. In 1991, he became writer-in-residence at Cambridge University. During his tenure there, he completed *Operation Wandering Soul*, a disturbing book that reflects some of his personal upheavals and has elicited mixed responses.

Returning to the United States, Powers gravitated to the campus of the University of Illinois at Urbana-Champaign, where he had an ad hoc arrangement to be a writer-in-residence in return for room and board. Here he wrote *Galatea 2.2*. By 1996 he had reluctantly accepted a full professorship in the university's English department, and in 1998 he became the university's first Swanlund Professor of English. In 2001, he married Jane Kuntz, a doctoral candidate in Romance languages.

ANALYSIS

Richard Powers's novels are not designed for casual reading. Deeply intellectual novels of ideas, they tackle such daunting questions as the meaning and purpose of life. As his biographer Joseph Dewey has noted, Powers's novels involve a staggering breadth of knowledge: "game theory, genetic recombination, saponification, corporate economic theory, computer programming, photographic reproduction, polyphonic music, pediatric medicine, tropical botany, and oncology." To this list, one might add ornithology, neuropsychology, and ecology, central elements in *The Echo Makers*.

Every Powers novel demonstrates that the author has become an expert, generally self-taught, in the fields he treats. His encompassing curiosity leads him constantly

Richard Powers.

into fresh fields of study, but his approach is neither cursory nor superficial. Once he sets his intelligence loose on a subject, he masters it as any expert might. Powers's expertise in computers has made available to him worlds of knowledge of which he has availed himself fully. His knowledge of computers and of computer programming is most evident in *Galatea 2.2*, in which an English major joins forces with a computer expert to create a computer capable of passing the master's comprehensive examination in English. His close association with the Beckman Center at the University of Illinois provided a stimulus for this compelling postmodern novel.

THREE FARMERS ON THEIR WAY TO A DANCE

In his first novel, *Three Farmers on Their Way to a Dance*, Powers establishes the contrapuntal pattern of presentation that pervades most of his subsequent work. Two strands of this book are devoted to telling the stories of the three farmers—Hubert, Adolphe, and Peter—and of the people who come into contact with them or with Sander's picture of them. The unnamed narrator, whose name begins with the initial "P" (as in "Powers"), is a thirtyish stockbroker who stumbles upon Sander's photograph of the three farmers when he changes trains during a six-hour layover in Detroit en route from Chicago to Boston, to which he is moving.

Integral to the story is Mrs. Schreck, a cleaning woman who immigrates from Germany to Boston. She has lost the love of her life in World War I. She has a print of Sander's picture, which she bought before she left Germany—seemingly from Sander himself—because one of the peasants in it is her lost love, Peter Schreck.

Peter Mays, a technical editor for an electronics magazine, has also been affected by the Sander photograph, having found a print of it in his mother's attic, in which he has been rummaging in search of information about a picture of Henry Ford. He had seen the Ford photograph when it was projected on the stage of a theater during a mixed-media show about the life of social reformer Jane Addams. The person in the picture with Ford looks remarkably like Peter, although he clearly is someone else. Spurred by the possibility that someone in his family had a connection with Ford, Peter journeys to his mother's house in Illinois, where he finds a letter signed by Ford establishing a trust fund for one of Peter's forebears, a fund that turns out to be worthless. In his search for this document, he unearths a print of the Sander photograph and is haunted by it. He also finds an envelope with the name Schreck written on it.

In the Henry Ford interchapters that occur throughout the novel's twenty-seven chapters, Powers weaves the story of Ford's sailing to Europe with a boatload of well-known pacifists in December, 1915, in an attempt to end World War I. Other interchapters deal with the technology of war, the immediacy of events captured by photography, the actress Sarah Bernhardt, and the remarkable interconnectedness of seemingly disparate events.

THE GOLD BUG VARIATIONS

Still pursuing his curiosity about the interconnectedness of all things, Powers, in his third novel, *The Gold Bug Variations*, links Johann Sebastian Bach's musical work the *Goldberg Variations* (1741) and Edgar Allan Poe's mystery story "The Gold-Bug" (1843). Like Bach's counterpoint, Powers's novel is complicated and closely structured. The book has thirty chapters, mirroring the musical *Goldberg Variations*, of which there are thirty. In this novel, Powers focuses on four central characters, all of whom work with information: Jan O'Deigh, a reference librarian in Brooklyn, New York; Franklin Todd, a graduate student in art history who was once Jan's lover; Stuart Ressler, now dead, who at age twenty-five helped to uncover the mysteries of the DNA (deoxyribonucleic acid) molecule; and Jeanette Koss, a married woman who had an affair with Ressler.

Just as Bach's *Goldberg Variations* are based on four musical phrases, Powers shapes his novel around various elements that involve the number four. There are four central characters, two couples, and in each couple the members' ages are separated by four years: Jan is thirty-four and Franklin is thirty; Stuart was twenty-six when he was involved Jeanette, who was thirty. Powers also mentions the four seasons, the four corners of the earth, the four chambers of the heart, and the four winds. Stuart begins his work at the University of Illinois with the Cyfer team assembled to determine the genetic structure of the DNA molecule, joining the group four years after James Watson and Francis Crick articulated the double-helix theory of DNA, which involves linking strands of four chemical bases.

Jan first meets Franklin when he approaches her at

the reference desk of the Brooklyn branch of the New York Public Library, where he is searching for information about a man who was instrumental in unraveling the mystery of the double helix but who has now faded into the shadows. Franklin works with Ressler on the night shift at a computer billing operation. In time, Franklin takes Jan to New Hampshire for a weekend with Ressler, and by this time, Jan has fallen in love with Franklin.

Ressler lives a minimalist's existence in which he has no reason to compete as he had when he was part of the high-powered team pursuing the mystery of DNA at the University of Illinois. He has withdrawn from society, putting behind him the years that led to his being pictured in *Life* magazine at age twenty-five.

Jan receives a card from Franklin one day informing her of Ressler's death from lung cancer. Deciding to devote herself to unearthing more information about Ressler, she immediately quits her job and embarks on an investigation of him. The novel proceeds from this investigation and deals with life's largest questions and most elusive mysteries.

The Echo Maker

Twenty-seven-year-old Mark Schluter, a mechanic in a Kearney, Nebraska, slaughterhouse, skids off an icy road on his way home from a bar where he has been drinking with his buddies. Mark is pulled from the wreckage and rushed to a hospital, where he remains in a coma for some weeks. His sister, thirty-one-year-old Karin Schluter, rushes to Mark's bedside.

Eventually, Mark emerges from his coma, but his severe brain injuries have rendered him mute. When he was an infant, Karin taught him to speak. Now that he is reduced to a virtually infantile state, she quits her job in Sioux City and helps Mark to recover. The greatest problem she faces is that Mark's injuries have resulted in his developing a rare condition, Capgras syndrome, that makes it impossible for him to accept Karin as his sister. Although she looks familiar to him, he views her as an impostor and discourages her efforts to help him.

Karin, who is well read in psychology, is familiar with the writings on neuropsychology of Dr. Gerald Weber, who practices on Long Island. Lately, he has been discredited as exploitative in both *The New York Times* and *Harper's*, criticized for the anecdotal nature of his neuropsychological investigations. Even worse,

he has been parodied in *The New Yorker*. (The character of Weber strongly resembles the neurologist and popular author Oliver Sacks.)

Karin persuades Weber to come to Nebraska to work with her brother. His story runs contrapuntally to the Mark-Karin story, as does the story of the migrating sandhill cranes, the only witnesses to Mark's accident. The cranes add an ecological element to the novel. When they migrate, following instincts embedded in them for eons, bird-watchers flock to see them. Now a developer wants to create a bird-watching center that would drain the Platte River to the point, ironically, that the cranes might not land there.

Powers has written before about various illnesses— for example, cancer in *Gain* and *The Gold Bug Variations* and progeria in *Operation Wandering Soul*. In *The Echo Maker*, he uses Capgras syndrome to explore the human brain and to question the complex nature of identity and of relationships among people.

R. Baird Shuman

Other major works

NONFICTION: "Computer-Assisted English Instruction," 1981 (in *Education in the 80's: English*, R. Baird Shuman, editor); "A Game We Couldn't Lose," 1996; "Life by Design: Too Many Breakthroughs," 1998; "Losing Our Souls, Bit by Bit," 1998; "Eyes Wide Open," 1999; "All That Is Solid Melts into Air," 2000; "American Dreaming: The Limitless Absurdity of Our Belief in an Infinitely Transformable Future," 2000; "The Simile," 2001; "An Artificial Being," 2005 (in *Making Things Public: Atmospheres of Democracy*, Bruno Latour and Peter Weibel, editors); "My Music," 2005; "A Head for Music," 2006.

Bibliography

Atwood, Margaret. "In the Heart of the Heartland." Review of *The Echo Maker*, by Richard Powers. *The New York Review of Books*, December 21, 2006. Very favorable review discusses the complexity of Powers's fiction and provides an overview of the novel.

Birkerts, Sven. "Mystical Powers." Review of *Plowing the Dark*, by Richard Powers. *Esquire*, July, 2000. Offers a perceptive discussion of Powers's writing, with commentary on his earlier novels as well as on *Plowing the Dark*.

Burns, Stephen J., and Peter Dempsey, eds. *Intersections: Essays on Richard Powers*. Urbana, Ill.: Dalkey Archive Press, 2008. Comprehensive collection presents critical essays on Powers's fiction by leading critics and philosophers. Topics addressed include Powers's narrative innovations. Includes an essay by Powers in which he discusses his philosophy of the novel.

Dewey, Joseph. *Understanding Richard Powers*. Columbia: University of South Carolina Press, 2002. First book-length consideration of Powers's fiction offers in-depth discussion of his novels through *Plowing the Dark*.

Howard, Maureen. "Facing the Footage." Review of *Prisoner's Dilemma*, by Richard Powers. *The Nation*, May 14, 1988. Examination of Powers's most autobiographical novel is penetrating, sensitive, and compelling.

Hurt, James. "Narrative Powers: Richard Powers as Storyteller." *Review of Contemporary Fiction* 18, no. 3 (1998): 24-41. Presents detailed analyses of Powers' first four novels, with a focus on their narrative structure.

LeClair, Tom. "The Prodigious Fiction of Richard Powers, William Vollman, and David Foster Wallace." *Critique* 38, no. 1 (Fall, 1996): 12-37. Provides a comparative consideration of the works of three writers whom LeClair labels "post-postmodern."

Leonard, John. "Mind Painting." Review of *Plowing the Dark*, by Richard Powers. *The New York Review of Books*, January 11, 2001. Brilliant, extensive essay considers the full body of Powers's work and presents a shrewd assessment of the author's writing.

Mallon, Thomas. "Going to Extremes." Review of *The Time of Our Singing*, by Richard Powers. *The Atlantic Monthly*, January/February, 2003. Comments incisively on Powers's fiction in general and provides an overview of the novel.

ABBÉ PRÉVOST

Born: Hesdin, France; April 1, 1697
Died: Courteuil, France; November 25, 1763
Also known as: Antoine François Prévost; Prévost d'Exiles

PRINCIPAL LONG FICTION

Mémoires et avantures d'un homme de qualité, qui s'est retiré du monde, 1728-1731 (6 volumes; volumes 1-4 as *Memoirs of a Man of Quality: Written Originally in the French Tongue by Himself, After His Retirement from the World*, 1738; volumes 5-6 as *The Memoirs and Adventures of a Man of Quality*, 1770; known in its entirety as *Memoirs of a Man of Quality*)

Histoire du chevalier des Grieux et de Manon Lescaut, 1731, 1733, 1753 (*Manon Lescaut*, 1734, 1786)

Le Philosophe anglois: Ou, Histoire de Monsieur Cleveland, fils naturel de Cromwell, 1732-1739 (8 volumes; *The Life and Entertaining Adventures of Mr. Cleveland, Natural Son of Oliver Cromwell*, 1734, 1735; also known as *The English Philosopher: Or, History of Monsieur Cleveland*, 1742)

Le Doyen de Killerine, 1735-1740 (4 volumes; *The Dean of Killerine*, 1744)

Histoire d'une Grecque moderne, 1740 (*The History of a Fair Greek*, 1755)

Mémoires d'un honnête homme, 1745 (2 volumes; *Memoirs of a Man of Honor*, 1747)

Le Monde moral: Ou, Mémoires pour servir à l'histoire du cœur humain, 1760-1764 (4 volumes)

OTHER LITERARY FORMS

Abbé Prévost (pray-VOH) has been described as the first truly self-supporting man of letters in France. According to the Henry Harrisse edition, Prévost published more than 120 volumes during his career, including more than forty translations; histories of travel; moral and didactic tracts on various subjects of contemporary interest; and more than thirty volumes of prose fiction. He also founded the literary journal *Le Pour et contre*, which appeared from 1733 to 1740 and was designed as a forum for the discussion of European writers. Prévost's work was highly esteemed by some of the most acute literary commentators of his own time, but aside from *Manon Lescaut*, more recent French critics have regarded his work as a part of literary history rather than living literature. Among those books that are of interest to the modern reader are the novels *The Dean of Killerine*, *The History of a Fair Greek*, and *Le Monde moral*.

ACHIEVEMENTS

Although Abbé Prévost was a very versatile writer who did significant work in several areas of literary endeavor, the novel *Manon Lescaut* is undoubtedly his masterwork and the primary reason for his reputation as an author of note. The book was an immediate success in Europe, and in spite of its suppression in France in 1733, it has always been available there, with new editions, featuring comments by popular writers, issued regularly. *Manon Lescaut* was translated into English the year after its publication in Amsterdam in 1733, and a new English translation has appeared every thirty years or so since then.

During the nineteenth century, the novel was the inspiration for three operas, the light and airy *Manon Lecaut* of Daniel-François-Esprit Auber (1856), the well-known *Manon* of Jules Massenet (1884), and the darkly powerful *Manon Lescaut* of Giacomo Puccini (1893), which is the most faithful rendition of Prévost's work. As Alexandre Dumas, *fils*, remarked, "Manon is now exploited like steam or photography," and Manon and the young Chevalier inhabit the same mythic landscape that features Romeo and Juliet and Héloïse and Abélard, among others. Guy de Maupassant's assertion, referring to Manon Lescaut, that "no other woman was ever so completely evoked" is an example of the intensely emotional responses that the novel has drawn.

In addition to *Manon Lescaut*, Prévost's other novels are an important early part of the great tradition of the European novel. Like Samuel Richardson—whose work

Prévost translated so successfully that Richardson was, for a time, more popular in France than in England— Prévost developed a language and style that defined and expressed the sensibility of an age. Jules Janin, who calls Prévost's books "charming tales . . . which, we, ungrateful, no longer read," maintains that "in these forgotten books you find in their entirety the precious remnants of that exquisite and elegant society of Louis XIV which Prévost depicts for us and which the world is never to know again." More than two centuries later, Prévost's style still seems distinctive, capable of capturing in language the moral consciousness of an era and reflecting in its tone the temper and mood of an ancient culture.

While Prévost's novels are burdened with bizarre contrivances of plot, melodramatic excess, and much repetitious and superfluous detail, the originality of their conception demonstrated for many other authors how much the novel could do. Certainly Denis Diderot, François-René de Chateaubriand, and Jean-Jacques Rousseau were influenced by Prévost's writing, and one critic has speculated that Rousseau's *La Nouvelle Héloïse* (1761) might not have been written had Prévost remained in Holland. As a testament to Prévost's power, Alexander Vinet writes, "There are certain styles which occur only once: no one will again write like the Abbé Prévost, and *Manon Lescaut* is the last example of a lost style."

Prévost was also the founder of *Le Pour et contre*, a journal modeled on Joseph Addison and Richard Steele's *The Spectator*. Prévost presented to the French people their first really penetrating, impartial picture of England. His discussion of James Thomson's poetry encouraged the developing Romantic revival, and his ideas on English tragedy helped to shape Voltaire's essay on William Shakespeare. Prévost's depiction of England is partially responsible for a radical reversal of Franco-British relations, and his open attitude toward other nations contributed to a mutuality of insight and a cross-cultural stance that formed an important part of the Romantic movement. He was one of the first writers to preach the "cosmopolitanism of genius."

BIOGRAPHY

Antoine François (Abbé) Prévost in 1697 in the town of Hesdin (near Calais), the second son of a family that had achieved some distinction in government service

Abbé Prévost. (Getty Images)

and ecclesiastical affairs. His father was a *procureur du roi*, an important local magistrate with considerable influence in community matters. At the age of fourteen, Prévost enrolled in the local college administered by the Jesuits, but he left the school two years later to join the king's Musketeers. His military career was cut short by the Treaty of Utrecht. He reentered the Jesuit novitiate, only to drop out twice to pursue secular adventure before beginning his third novitiate at a Benedictine monastery near Rouen in 1720. He took his final vows in 1721, but according to his own account, he had considerable reservations about the religious life. "Forced by necessity," he wrote in a letter, "I only pronounced the formula of our vows with all the inward restrictions which could authorize me to break them."

Nevertheless, Prévost served the order admirably. He won respect as a brilliant student of theology at Saint Omer, as a teacher of the humanities at Saint Germer,

and as a popular preacher at Évreux during the Lenten season. In 1728, he was called to the abbey of Saint-Germain-des-Prés in Paris, where, he told a friend, the Church believed he would be "less dangerous than elsewhere." There he completed an entire volume of the enormous *Gallia Christiana*, but he felt severely restricted by the life of the order and had written, in secret, at least the first and second volumes of *Memoirs of a Man of Quality* (the first two volumes of which bear the suggestive subtitle *Written Originally in the French Tongue by Himself, After His Retirement from the World*). Prévost asked to be transferred to the less rigorous order at Amiens, and the authorities in Rome agreed, but the bishop of the Cluny order delayed the petition to make further inquiries.

Apparently, Prévost doubted that his request would be granted, and he left his post. To explain his actions, Prévost asserted that "My books were my faithful friends; but like myself, they were dead," and he threatened to expose the Benedictines as fools if he were harshly treated. His justification for his actions was his belief that he had taken nothing with him: "You have kept me for eight years, I have served you well; thus whatever was owed is paid." The Church appealed to the police for his arrest, calling him "a fugitive monk" and adding that he was the author of a "little novel" that slandered the duke of Tuscany. When a warrant was issued for Prévost's arrest in November, 1728, he fled to Holland.

Prévost's six-year exile in Holland and England was one of his most productive periods. The third and fourth volumes of *Memoirs of a Man of Quality* were published in 1728, with two more volumes appearing in 1731. The seventh volume, which is actually a separate book connected only by the device of the Man of Quality meeting a young couple in transit, is the story of Manon Lescaut and the Chevalier des Grieux. The October 3, 1733, edition of the *Journal de la cour et de Paris* notes the appearance of an *histoire* that is "the prose equivalent of Voltaire's verse."

In spite of the book's immediate acceptance by the reading public, Prévost had incurred so many debts in Holland that he had to leave the country, and although he was very active in English society, within a year (in December, 1733) he was convicted in England of fabricating a bill of exchange and was almost sent to the gallows. Aside from his continuing financial difficulties, Prévost seems to have thrived during the years of his banishment, but his resentment at being forced to leave France is expressed in his adopted name, Prévost d'Exiles.

Through the intercession of the princede Conti, a patron of many other men of letters, and Cardinal de Bissy, who acted as Prévost's ecclesiastical sponsor, Prévost was able to return to France in October, 1734, and in February, 1735, he was accepted into the abbey of La Grènetière in Vendée. His appointment as almoner to de Conti freed him from the confines of monastic residence, and for the remaining twenty-eight years of his life, he lived comfortably with his vocation. *Manon Lescaut* continued to appear in France after its suppression in 1733, but in pirated editions published abroad. Nevertheless, Prévost was famous, and one who, as one Parisian wrote, "would make his fortune just by appearing at the fair." To capitalize on this fame, Prévost wrote the eight-volume series called *The English Philosopher* between 1732 and 1739 and, as a kind of literary penance, compiled the fifteen-volume *Histoire générale des voyages* as an ongoing project assembled from English sources. The set was published from 1745 to 1759. During this period, Prévost also translated Dryden's *All for Love* (1735); founded the journal *Le Pour et contre*, which ran from 1733 to 1740 on a biweekly schedule; wrote a history of William the Conqueror (1742); and wrote several novels, including the triumph of his mature years, *Memoirs of a Man of Honor.*

Prévost's life as a celebrated author and prominent figure in the artistic and intellectual circles of Parisian society was generally uneventful compared to the adventures and escapades of his early years, but in 1741, he obligingly corrected the proofs of an underground broadsheet for a friend who had included some libelous statements about several people in power. The "friend" accused Prévost of complicity, perhaps hoping to hide behind Prévost's celebrity. The strategy failed, the pamphleteer was jailed, but Prévost had to endure another year in exile in Belgium and Frankfurt. By this time, his friends were men of sufficient influence to overcome the envy of various factions angered by Prévost's singularity, and Prévost was recalled to France. His publisher af-

ter 1745, Pierre Didot, assisted Prévost in the acquisition of a rural retreat at Saint Firmin, near Chantilly, and Prévost spent his last years "happy with my cows and two chickens." During this time, he revised the original manuscript of *Manon Lescaut* for a kind of "official" edition (1753), changing many direct statements into partial euphemisms. Referring to an old lecher, for instance, Manon says in the 1753 edition, "He will not be able to boast of any advantages I have given him over me," instead of her much more direct claim in the 1731 edition, "He will not have the satisfaction of having slept with me for even one night." The loss in directness is balanced, according to some critics, by an increased precision and a reduction of unnecessary epithets and nouns.

Prévost died suddenly in November, 1763, as he was returning through the forest of Chantilly to his house at Saint Firmin. He had been dining with his Benedictine colleagues of the Church of Saint Nicolas d'Acy.

ANALYSIS

Abbé Prévost began the composition of *Memoirs of a Man of Quality* shortly after he had arrived at Saint-Germain-des-Prés. Writing covertly in his chamber at night, Prévost had no real models to follow, and *Memoirs of a Man of Quality* is an example of a genre in development, retaining some aspects of the familiar picaresque genre while enlarging the boundaries of the new form that was the novel in its earliest conception. Because he was discovering this "form" through the process of composition, *Memoirs of a Man of Quality* is a string of digressions almost casually tied together by the vague and intermittent progress of the protagonist toward some nebulous destination. While these digressions often seem distracting, if not completely pointless, they are written with considerable energy and invention, and they are a necessary prelude to Prévost's final digression, the story of Manon Lescaut and the Chevalier des Grieux. *Memoirs of a Man of Quality* is essentially a preparation for *Manon Lescaut*, both in terms of Prévost's mastery of his craft and in terms of what Prévost had to express before he could reach that part of his mind and heart that are revealed in his masterpiece.

MEMOIRS OF A MAN OF QUALITY

Like other early examples of the novel, *Memoirs of a Man of Quality* is composed of a series of adventures related by a narrator from the perspective of his retirement into tranquillity. As in the first days of film, the new novel offered the French audience a fresh view of the world, and as motion pictures later enthralled audiences no matter what the subject, so the novel in its infancy provided descriptions of exotic locales and thrilling escapades of intrigue and suspense whose novelty alone provided sufficient reason for existence. Prévost supplied information enlivened by imagination; *Memoirs of a Man of Quality* was an immediate success upon the publication of its first volumes in 1728.

In addition to its value as entertainment, *Memoirs of a Man of Quality* has as its central theme an examination of the ways in which a man learns about himself and the world, and then how he transmits this wisdom or *quality* to his son. Ultimately, the novel explores the evolving relationship between a son and his father, concentrating on the son's determination to justify himself in his father's eyes by the correctness of his actions and on the father's attempt to guide his son toward proper action.

Significantly, the Man of Quality is of French ancestry, but reared in Spain by a family on the run. Prévost's own struggle between his genuine attraction toward the Church (solid, legitimate authority) and his desire for liberty (freedom to create) is reflected in his depiction of a man who is the scion of a disinherited couple condemned to a life of exile. Almost instinctively, the Man of Quality decides to cultivate those aspects of will and spirit that might make him feel at home anywhere—in other words, at ease with himself and his existence. His formal education is conducted by the Jesuits, but his true education results from his adventures. Nearly all of volume 2 is set in Turkey, and at the conclusion of the volume, the Man of Quality is prepared to transmit all that he has learned to his surrogate "son" (his daughter is consigned to a convent), as he becomes the guardian of and guide to a young marquis.

The second "book," which consists of the remaining four volumes, has as its vital center the Man of Quality's sojourn in England. This section has the feeling for political geography and the sense of place of an excellent travel journal. During the Jacobite uprising, the Man of Quality introduces the Marquis to the ways of the world. Actual historical figures appear throughout the narrative to authenticate the milieu and give the reader a feeling

that he or she is reading an insider's report. As the Man of Quality attempts to instruct the Marquis by gentle admonition and proper personal example, they are both exposed to all the temptations of life in a vibrant, growing metropolis. Prévost creates a vision of English life designed to shatter the smugness and expand the insularity of a Continental audience, and his praise of English democracy and English institutions is one of the first descriptions of the modern world emerging from the Middle Ages to be found in world literature. Prévost was strongly attracted to the democratic tendencies in English society, and his depiction of the rough equality of life in the street, the free press, and the chaotic debate among citizens in the coffeehouse has a vitality that stands in strong contrast to the patterns of life in old, monarchical European cities. At the same time, Prévost is skilled enough as a storyteller to avoid didacticism, intertwining his ideas with tales of love, sex, intrigue, and scandal based on accounts he had read in *The Spectator* and learned from William Hogarth's depictions of harlots, gamblers, base men, and sporting blades.

In each episode, the moral education of the young Marquis continues. The Man of Quality offers his carefully considered discourse on proper behavior in any sort of conflict or challenge, underscoring the lesson of each encounter in Prévost's felicitous prose. The style is so graceful and the Man of Quality so appealingly modest that his maxims, aphorisms, and principles are easy to accept. Still, compared to modern prose fiction, the book is severely limited. The action is rarely subtle, and each episode is separate, without resonance for the others; there is a sense of stasis in psychological development, as the Man of Quality is essentially fixed and the young Marquis mostly a prop or vehicle to offer his mentor an opportunity to present his reflections on an incident.

MANON LESCAUT

Upon the publication of *Memoirs of a Man of Quality* and the beginning of his own exile, Prévost returned to the world to become fully involved in several relationships, which formed the basis for the extraordinary relationship he describes in *Manon Lescaut*. In *Manon Lescaut*, Prévost wrote the only book in his oeuvre that concerns the one subject he could not regard with any sense of detachment. Generally, when he used his own experiences as the basis for a narrative, he filtered the actual events through a reflective apparatus that enabled him to cultivate the graceful style that has been described as "the taste of fresh water." In *Manon Lescaut*, his subject is romantic fervor in its most consuming form, approached with no reserve, no distancing devices, and no digressions to lessen the fierce tension. The book moved Voltaire to remark that Prévost's language is the "natural language of passion," and the book's effect derives in part from Prévost's ability to maintain the tension of the relationship it portrays without losing the natural grace of his best prose.

The book has become famous as the story of the extraordinarily beautiful Manon Lescaut. In the original title, however, the Chevalier des Grieux is placed first, and while it is Manon who is the focus of attention, the reader knows her only through his eyes; it is his soul and psyche that are explored in the course of the book. Manon is hardly a character at all; she is more like a spirit of sexual intoxication, an inspiration for absolute romantic devotion, and, finally, the motive and cause of a young man's madness. Her effect is like that of the mythical Sirens, and every man who sees her is beguiled and transformed by her incredible presence. The reader learns the power of Manon's beauty not through description but through reaction. Prévost's story of a man possessed by an uncontrollable passion is an expression of the primal male fear of a woman's powers; it is a tale of terror induced by a mysterious essence that is as irresistible as it is incomprehensible. The continuing popularity of the story and the three operas based on it stems from a public perception that it is an account of doomed, idyllic young lovers. In actuality, Prévost's novel is the story of lovesickness akin to madness, and because Manon is a fixed force that never changes or dims, the progress of the fatal passion must be measured by its awesome, almost horrifying effect on the Chevalier des Grieux.

The correspondence between Prévost's life during the early years of his exile and the adventures of the Chevalier des Grieux has been established by Prévost scholars, and while *Manon Lescaut* is not literally autobiographical, its matter is clearly derived from events that Prévost knew from firsthand experience. The most crucial aspect of this source is not the events themselves but Prévost's examination of the psychology of des Grieux as the events occur. The Chevalier knows what is hap-

pening to him, but he believes that any sacrifice is worthwhile if it helps him to maintain Manon's love. Watching des Grieux lose his honor, his reason, his wit, his health, and, finally, his love with an almost ghastly fascination, the reader is nevertheless likely to be convinced that the Chevalier has acted correctly—that his is "a world well lost." Prévost generates an unusual sense of sympathy for des Grieux, encouraging an identification that engenders, if not a sharing of his passion, at least a shared desire to see it gratified. The suspense that builds as the Chevalier tries everything to remain with Manon and keep her happy drives the narrative along with powerful surges of energy that illuminate his character.

The Chevalier is especially interesting in this situation because he seems such an unlikely person to be so obsessed. He would never have chosen to live a tragedy of love—it is almost as if, with cosmic irony, love has chosen him. When the story begins, he is only seventeen years old, finishing a philosophy course at Amiens, the beloved son of "one of the best families," a young man "leading such a docile and orderly life that my masters held me up as a model to the school." He describes his temperament as "naturally gentle and tranquil," with an inclination to study and a career of promise awaiting him in either the Church or the army. Then, as if by a stroke of destiny, he meets Manon, a woman younger than he, and is instantly, totally caught in an all-consuming love affair that completely alters his life. While professing his desire to be guided by rational principles and traditional religious precepts, the Chevalier becomes a man of instinctive, emotional responses whose only vital religion is a worship of the cult of love. What makes him so compelling as a character is his (and Prévost's) ability to make his behavior seem logical and his commitment almost holy. Thus, his actions are entirely consistent with his nature. The lesson is that none among us is safe.

Although Manon never wavers in her profession of ardor for des Grieux, she is also always ready to respond to the offers or advances of any wealthy admirer. Whenever des Grieux chastises her, she claims that her actions are motivated by a wish to provide the means for the couple to enjoy a comfortable, carefree life. Her sincerity is never in doubt, but her instinct seems always directed toward the protection of her position and her pleasure. Her self-possession and her selfishness begin to counteract her beauty in the eyes of des Grieux, but he neverthe-less remains completely in her power. He understands what is happening to him, but he cannot control his actions or feelings.

As the narrative continues, the Chevalier gradually is drawn into a narrowing cycle of action. Short episodes of satisfaction with Manon are interrupted again and again by other suitors and jealous rivals. He is always in combat against some adversary for her heart or his honor, and his life is reduced to a series of schemes and calculations to avenge himself, get more money, and find a hideout for himself and Manon. Never really a criminal (even when he gambles, steals, swindles or, finally, kills without compunction), he becomes an outlaw to the "honest" world, an outcast among his friends and family, and a figure of opprobrium in his own eyes. No longer capable of calm reflection, he has become a man of radical extremes whose rage is only partly against his fate because it is also against himself for what he knows he has become. Even then, he still believes in love, for not only Manon but as one position of certainty amid the chaos of existence.

When Manon dies in his arms in the American wilderness, to which they have been exiled, he is finally freed from his obsession, but his freedom is empty, for he has lost the energy that, as William Blake observes, is the source of eternal delight. Like Achilles, he has agreed with his fate, which was to blaze fiercely, if briefly, in the firmament of love. For most people, this life would be as destructive as it is for the Chevalier, but after reading Prévost's account, how many would not be tempted to take the same risks?

MEMOIRS OF A MAN OF HONOR

Near the end of his literary career, Prévost was able to summon the creative energy that illuminated *Manon Lescaut* one last time. In 1745, he completed *Memoirs of a Man of Honor*, the story of a young man from the country who tests his principles against the temptations of a wicked, fascinating city. *Memoirs of a Man of Honor* is similar to *Memoirs of a Man of Quality*, but in the later work, Prévost has removed the distancing device of the older narrator and has permitted the young man to tell his own story with no intervening devices to soften the impact. The young man is similar to des Grieux (and to Prévost), but his sacred honor is strong enough to resist the charms of the demi-Manons he meets. The social

world in which he moves is almost a character in itself—society as an endless pleasure party, with Paris a cross between Daniel Defoe's teeming London and John Cleland's world of sex in *Memoirs of a Woman of Pleasure* (1749; better known as *Fanny Hill*, 1938).

The Man of Honor is discovered by the author in a dungeon somewhere in Germany, where he relates the events of his life, beginning with the end. "I come from a deep and horrid dungeon," he begins, and then proceeds to explain how he got there. The narrative is essentially the development of a philosophy and a sensibility—the test of unpolished, rustic virtue by the allure of a decadent, too-knowing city. It is as if a walking embodiment of the philosophies of John Locke and Jean-Jacques Rousseau were set as a challenge to the old order, the ancien régime trying to convert the force that eventually will destroy it. At the conclusion, the force is temporarily confined but still fresh and unconverted.

As the narrative commences, the young man, well-born, wealthy, and educated by the conversation of "the most polite men of the province," travels to Paris to take part in the delights of Parisian society and to be instructed further by the most prominent men and women of the haut monde, or high society. There is, however, an interesting complication in the young man's life, as he is also leaving the country because he is being ardently pursued by the young woman his widowed father wishes to marry.

While attempting to extricate himself honorably from an alliance conceived in a confusion of motives, and trying to decide how to deal with his own passion for a married woman while having to keep those motives hidden, the Man of Honor escapes into the world of the soiree, where he is alternately appalled or charmed by wit, gossip, posture, and slander. In addition, he uses his fortune to extricate innocent young women from the grasp of rich, ruthless men and to rescue decent young men from ruin at the hands of the greedy.

Because his time is his own, the Man of Honor is involved in a continuing cycle of visits and parties. These visits form the structure of the book, and he seems always to be either en route to a social engagement or returning from one. Since there is little extended dialogue, the visits are occasions for reflection, and the young man concludes each sequence by evaluating what he has seen, thus providing Prévost with an opportunity to judge and evaluate everything. Throughout, the Man of Honor is informed by the idea that "wit is very enchanting, but it ought not to be exercised at the expense of truth and justice." He is particularly critical of the cynical citizens who are skilled in the practice of turning everything into a commodity with its own relative measure of value. Finally, he is the ultimate noble "square," but his sincerity—while sometimes a bit tiresome—never becomes the burden it is in Richardson, and while he is presented without much irony by Prévost, the humor is sometimes, gently, at his expense.

Although Prévost approves of the young man's character and style, he places him in a world in which the Man of Honor is overcome by circumstance. While attempting to act according to his principles without the loathsome habit of expecting everyone else to measure up to his exceptional standards, the Man of Honor is overwhelmed by what seems to be a series of bizarre occurrences. Actually, he is a man of a new time, a figure from the future born too early. Like the young Prévost, he is unable to reconcile his own true nature with the demands of the world, even with all of its advantages for him. He is living in Paris in a world about to collapse under the weight of its own rot, but the famous Revolution is still four decades away. Although this society is about to die, its perverse power is still so great that, to the Man of Honor, it is almost as if the zeitgeist is poisoned. The Man of Honor does not have a sufficient antidote, and because he is so pure, he is also very vulnerable.

His downfall is ultimately caused by his own glorious weakness, his capacity for total commitment to what he believes is right. Were he merely a moralizing prig, like some character of Tobias Smollett or John Henry MacKenzie, he would endure, but his traits would suffocate the book. His undoing through his devotion to his honor is also his saving grace, the mark of his true humanity among the charlatans, poseurs, manipulators, and malefactors of the intricately detailed Parisian milieu. He must, therefore, suffer a duel with the brother of the woman pursuing him, support serious wounds leading to gangrene, accept his father's injunction to marry the woman to preserve *her* reputation, and eventually wind up exiled and imprisoned in a foreign land. For Prévost, this is an analogue to the trials of his own free spirit and to the spirit of France, which he is trying to pre-serve amid the decay and sterility of a rigid, entrapping social order.

The complexity of Prévost's attitude is expressed in the Man of Honor's struggle to remain true to himself while exploring that realm of excitement that he finds simultaneously intriguing and repulsive. Prévost's exile and return to his country and his religious commitment are paralleled by the hardship the Man of Honor must endure. The book ends with the Man of Honor's marriage of necessity—with his imprisonment within the larger prison of an unjust world. Yet within his chains, he is truly free, because, like Prévost, he remains an *honnête homme*, or honest man.

Leon Lewis

OTHER MAJOR WORKS

NONFICTION: *Le Pour et contre*, 1733-1740; *Voyages du capitaine Robert Lade*, 1744; *Histoire générale des voyages*, 1745-1759 (15 volumes).

TRANSLATIONS: *Paméla*, 1742 (of Samuel Richardson's *Pamela*); *Histoire de Miss Clarisse Harlowe*, 1751 (of Richardson's *Clarissa*); *Grandisson*, 1755-1758 (of Richardson's *Sir Charles Grandison*).

BIBLIOGRAPHY

Bloom, Rori. *Man of Quality, Man of Letters: The Abbé Prévost Between Novel and Newspaper*. Lewisburg, Pa.: Bucknell University Press, 2009. A study of the concepts of authorship and readership in the context of Prévost's novels and journalistic writings.

Coleman, Patrick. *Reparative Realism: Mourning and Modernity in the French Novel, 1730-1830*. Geneva, Switzerland: Librairie Droz, 1998. Coleman examines *Manon Lescaut* and novels by Jean-Jacques Rousseau, Benjamin Constant, Madame de Staël, and Honoré de Balzac in this study of issues of grief and bereavement in eighteenth and nineteenth century French fiction.

Kory, Odile A. *Subjectivity and Sensitivity in the Novels of the Abbé Prévost*. Montreal: Didier, 1972. Kory explores the psychological and moral components in Prévost's fiction, including the novels *Manon Lescaut* and *The History of a Fair Greek*. Includes a bibliography.

Mander, Jenny. *Circles of Learning: Narratology and*

the Eighteenth Century French Novel. Oxford, England: Voltaire Foundation, 1999. Mander's study of narration and autobiography in the eighteenth century French novel focuses on works by Prévost and Marivaux. Includes bibliographical references and an index.

Miller, Nancy K. *The Heroine's Text: Readings in the French and English Novel, 1722-1782*. New York: Columbia University Press, 1980. A feminist interpretation of eighteenth century French novels, including *Manon Lescaut*, which Miller persuasively argues is the lodestone of Prévost's career. Includes a bibliography and an index.

Mylne, Vivienne. "Prévost: The New Realism." In *The Eighteenth Century French Novel: Techniques of Illusion*. 2d ed. New York: Cambridge University Press, 1981. Mylne's thirty-page essay adds considerable luster to Prévost's influential position as purveyor of the sentimental novel and places him within the broader context of eighteenth century French literature.

Segal, Naomi. *The Unintended Reader: Feminism and "Manon Lescaut."* New York: Cambridge University Press, 1986. Segal presents a feminist interpretation of *Manon Lescaut* and examines the novel's themes of money, woman, "the double," and fatality.

REYNOLDS PRICE

Born: Macon, North Carolina; February 1, 1933
Also known as: Edward Reynolds Price

PRINCIPAL LONG FICTION

A Long and Happy Life, 1962
A Generous Man, 1966
Love and Work, 1968
The Surface of Earth, 1975
The Source of Light, 1981
Mustian: Two Novels and a Story, Complete and Unabridged, 1983
Kate Vaiden, 1986
Good Hearts, 1988
The Tongues of Angels, 1990
Blue Calhoun, 1992
The Honest Account of a Memorable Life: An Apocryphal Gospel, 1994
The Promise of Rest, 1995
Roxanna Slade, 1998
A Great Circle: The Mayfield Trilogy, 2001 (includes *The Surface of Earth*, *The Source of Light*, and *The Promise of Rest*)
Noble Norfleet, 2002
The Good Priest's Son, 2005

OTHER LITERARY FORMS

Reynolds Price is best known as a novelist, but he has also produced sensitively written short fiction, poetry, and dramas, as well as retellings of biblical stories. Although these works are not consistently of the quality of his best novels, all are clearly the work of an author with a strong sense of his craft. His collections of essays include some extremely interesting insights into what Price is trying to accomplish philosophically and stylistically in his long fiction. His poetry has been collected in several volumes, including *Late Warning: Four Poems* (1968), *Vital Provisions* (1982), *The Laws of Ice* (1986), and *The Use of Fire* (1990). Since his early collection of short stories *The Names and Faces of Heroes* appeared in 1963, several other volumes of his stories have been published. *Things Themselves: Essays and Scenes* (1972) and *A Common Room: Essays, 1954-1987* (1987) contain his most salient essays on writing. Among Price's retellings of biblical stories are *Presence and Absence: Versions from the Bible* (1973), *Oracles: Six Versions from the Bible* (1977), and *A Palpable God: Thirty Stories Translated from the Bible with an Essay on the Origins and Life of Narrative* (1978). His dramas include *Early Dark* (pb. 1977), *Private Contentment* (pb.

1984), and the teleplay *House Snake* (1986). The plays in his trilogy *New Music* premiered in 1989 and have subsequently been produced throughout the United States. Price's autobiography *Clear Pictures: First Loves, First Guides* was published in 1989.

ACHIEVEMENTS

Early in his career, Reynolds Price won the literature award from the National Institute of Arts and Letters, and he has received the Sir Walter Raleigh Award for Fiction, presented by the North Carolina Literary and Historical Association, six times (in 1962, 1976, 1981, 1984, 1986, and 1999). In 1986, he received the National Book Critics Circle Award for *Kate Vaiden*, and in 1994 Price's *The Collected Stories* (1993) was a finalist for the Pulitzer Prize in fiction. In 1988, in recognition of his achievements, Price was elected to the American Academy of Arts and Letters. In 1993, early in his presidency, Bill Clinton, a devoted reader of Price's novels, entertained the author at a White House dinner.

BIOGRAPHY

Born on February 1, 1933, in the rural North Carolina town of Macon, the son of William Solomon Price and Elizabeth Rodwell Price, Edward Reynolds Price was a child of the Great Depression. Although, because of the closeness of his family structure, his welfare was not seriously threatened by the social dislocations around him, the boy was aware of them and developed what his biographer Constance Rooke calls Dickensian terrors of abandonment and destitution. His parents, hard-pressed economically, lost their house when they could not raise a fifty-dollar mortgage payment.

Upon graduation from Needham-Broughten High School in Raleigh, where his English teacher, Phyllis Peacock, appreciated his ability and took a particular interest in him, Price became an English major at Duke University in 1951. There he came under the influence of William Blackburn, a legendary teacher of creative writing who numbered among his former students such luminaries as William Styron, Anne Tyler, Max Hyman, and Fred Chappell. Through Blackburn, Price met Eudora Welty, who respected his work and ten years later was instrumental in helping to get Price's first book, *A Long and Happy Life*, published.

Upon receiving his bachelor's degree from Duke, Price attended Merton College, University of Oxford, as a Rhodes scholar. He received a bachelor of letters degree from Oxford in 1958 and returned to Duke University in that year as an assistant professor of English. Except for brief intervals, Price continued to teach there for the rest of his career. Since 1977, he has held the position of James B. Duke Professor of English at Duke, where he has regularly taught courses in creative writing and on the poetry of John Milton.

Price, who never married, burst on the literary scene auspiciously when *Harper's* magazine devoted the whole of its April, 1962, issue to printing *A Long and Happy Life*, which was being released in hardcover at about the same time. The critical reception of this first novel was enthusiastic and brought Price the prestigious Faulkner Foundation Award for a first novel.

In 1963, Price visited England, and in the same year a collection of his short stories, *The Names and Faces of Heroes*, was released. This collection includes "Michael Egerton," the short story that had first impressed Eudora Welty when she gave a reading at Duke in the early 1950's. The title story, told from the perspective of a young boy, is an especially sensitive study in point of view.

Price's second novel, *A Generous Man*, appeared in 1966; this work focuses on the Mustian family, as does his first book. The second book is a warm, rollicking story based on a hunt for a python named Death that has escaped from a snake show after being bitten by a dog diagnosed as rabid. The concept is openly allegorical, and Price drives home the allegory well while also presenting an extremely amusing story, with the hydrophobic python probably qualifying as the most outrageous phallic symbol in American literature. In 1977, Price published a play, *Early Dark*, based on the Mustian cycle, and, in 1983, *Mustian: Two Novels and a Story, Complete and Unabridged* was issued, consisting of the first two novels and "The Chain of Love," a short story.

Price's novel *Love and Work* and his loosely woven short-story collection *Permanent Errors* (1970) both explore matters of heredity and its effects on people. Neither received overwhelming praise, although they had support among some critics. Price, however, was busy with a much larger project, an ambitious saga of the

Kendal-Mayfield family through four generations. The first novel of this story, *The Surface of Earth*, was received with skepticism by some critics when it appeared in 1975, but few could deny the creative zeal it reflected. The second volume of the Kendal-Mayfield story was published in 1981 under the title *The Source of Light*, and it, too, received mixed reviews.

A turning point in Price's life came in 1984, when he was well into writing *Kate Vaiden*. He was stricken with spinal cancer, and the surgery that saved his life also left him a paraplegic. Pain drove Price to seek the help of a psychiatrist, who introduced him to hypnosis as a method of pain control. Little did Price suspect that through hypnosis he would be put in touch with a distant past that he had not realized existed. Suddenly details of his earliest childhood and of his family surfaced. When *Kate Vaiden* was published in 1986, it was, because of these unexpected insights, a quite different novel from the one Price had originally projected. Price's hypnosis unlocked the memories from which his autobiography, *Clear Pictures*, published in 1989, evolved. *The Tongues of Angels*, a novel published in 1990, is also a product of Price's hypnotic communication with his past.

A further literary product of Price's painful illness is his personal narrative *A Whole New Life* (1994), which not only offers a detailed account of his "mid-life collision with cancer and paralysis" but also celebrates his emergence from that trial into a new and, he affirms, better life. Price's own confrontation with mortality no doubt added resonance to all his subsequent writing, such as the poignant description of Wade's suffering and death in *The Promise of Rest*. Furthermore, as an affirmation of God's strange grace, *A Whole New Life* displays kinship with Price's numerous retellings of stories from the Bible.

ANALYSIS

Any reading of a number of Reynolds Price's novels quickly demonstrates that Price's work, throughout his career, has grappled with puzzling questions. Preeminent among these questions is the effect that families have on communities and on the broader societies outside the isolated communities that provide Price with his microcosms.

Focusing on a single region of North Carolina just

Reynolds Price. (Margaret Sartor)

south of the Virginia border, Price has moved beyond the limitations sometimes found in the works of regional writers. His work deals with universal themes, particularly with those that concern original sin and free choice; biological determinism, particularly as it is reflected in heredity; and the meanings of and relationships between life and death. In Price's novels, children inherit the burden of sin passed on by their parents, and, try as they will, they cannot escape this burden. They have free will, they can make choices, but the choices they make are almost identical to the choices their progenitors have made before them, so they grow up to be like those who have spawned them, no matter how much they struggle to avoid such a resemblance.

Price has always been attuned to current events, some of which have provided the impetus for elements in some of his later works. In 2001, the massacre in Texas of five young children by their clinically depressed mother, Andrea Yates, received sustained national attention. The following year, Price published *Noble Norfleet*, in which the mother, Edith Norfleet, murders her two younger children by stabbing them with an icepick. Additionally, in this novel, the seventeen-year-old protagonist, Noble Norfleet, loses his virginity to his high school Spanish teacher. In 1996, the affair of Mary Kay Letourneau, a middle school teacher, and her thirteen-year-old student Vili Fualaau made national headlines and resulted in the revelation of other sexual liaisons between female teachers and their male students. The public had been prepared for some of the events in *Noble Norfleet* by the publicity that accompanied these events.

Price's 2005 novel *The Good Priest's Son* also draws on a national event that transfixed the public, in this case the destruction by terrorists of the World Trade Center towers on September 11, 2001. As the novel opens, Mabry Kincaid, the novel's protagonist, is grounded in Nova Scotia on a return trip from Europe because of the ban on air travel imposed immediately following the events of September 11. Price depends on his readers' knowledge of such events to orient them to elements in his novels that refer to similar events.

KATE VAIDEN

Price harbored from his earliest memories questions about his mother and about his parents' relationship to each other. He seldom forgot that his mother almost died in bearing him and that she was left mutilated by his difficult birth. His later relationships with her were always colored by that recollection and by the feeling of guilt it aroused in him. The guilt of the child is reflected most clearly in *Kate Vaiden*, in which Kate blames herself for an act that was as much out of her control as Elizabeth Price's difficult confinement was out of her son's control.

Despite Kate's innocence of any fault in the matter, she continues to blame herself after her father murders her mother and then turns the gun on himself. Her entire adult life—indeed, her life from age eleven onward—is so profoundly affected by this single event, which brought an end to her childhood innocence, that it takes her forty-five years to begin to come to grips with her problems in any effective way. *Kate Vaiden* does not end on any realistic note of hope or promise. Rather, it ends with a large question mark. Through writing the novel,

however, Price presumably enhanced his understanding of his mother, who, like Kate, was orphaned at an early age.

LOVE AND WORK

Price was working toward the solution of problems like those that *Kate Vaiden* poses in his earlier *Love and Work*, in which Thomas Eborn, like Price himself a novelist and a professor, is forced to examine his relationship to his mother and his parents' relationship to each other and to society at large when his mother dies unexpectedly. Tom has been a dutiful son; he has helped provide for his mother financially. He is also, however, a compulsive writer who husbands his time and guards it jealously, organizing his life in such a way that he will always be able to write. Because of this dedication, he misses his mother's last telephone call; he is busy writing and will not talk with her. Shortly thereafter, she is dead.

Price creates in this novel a story that uses place most effectively. Tom Eborn teaches in a southern town not unlike Durham, North Carolina, where Price has spent his professional career. Tom has arranged his life to eliminate from it any unnecessary distractions, and in doing this he has excluded from it as well much human contact. Tom's turf—completely his own—is his study. It is his inviolable space where he can be alone, where he can create. No one dares intrude on it. His mother's unanticipated death, however, makes Tom realize the inhumanity of isolating himself as fully as he has from humankind.

It is clear that much of Reynolds Price can be seen in Tom Eborn, but to make a simple equation between the two would be misleading. *Love and Work* is a novel, and although Price once said that a writer's experience and background have as much to do with writing fiction as has imagination, he also warned that writers slip in and out of autobiography, so that their novels cannot be read as accurate autobiographical statements. One can profitably read *Love and Work* against Price's consciously constructed autobiography, *Clear Pictures*, and find both the correspondences and the differences between his life and Eborn's. The same can be said regarding *Kate Vaiden*, which strongly reflects Price's background but is far from an authentic autobiographical representation.

A LONG AND HAPPY LIFE

Price's consuming interest in the family as the fundamental unit of society is found in his first novel, *A Long and Happy Life*, and pervades his future writing. *A Long and Happy Life* and *A Generous Man*, along with several of Price's short stories and his novel *Good Hearts*, focus on the members of the Mustian family, who live in Macon, North Carolina, the small southern town on the North Carolina/Virginia border in which Price was born and reared. *A Long and Happy Life* revolves around the romance between twenty-year-old Rosacoke Mustian and her boyfriend of six years, Wesley Beavers, two years her senior.

Wesley rides his motorcycle to his native Macon to visit Rosacoke whenever he can take a weekend away from the naval base in Norfolk, 130 miles to the northeast. Wesley is sexually experienced, but Rosacoke is a virgin when the story opens in July. On a scorching day, Rosacoke rides on the back of Wesley's motorcycle to the black church from which her friend Mildred Sutton is to be buried. Mildred has died while giving birth to her child Sledge.

Wesley roars up to the church, deposits Rosacoke, and stays outside polishing his bike. Those in the church moan in ecstasies of religious transport. One woman cries, "Sweet Jesus," and Wesley, hearing her cry, is transported to a sweaty bed in Norfolk, where one of his many women uttered an identical cry at a crucial moment in their lovemaking. Reminded of this, Wesley zooms off on his motorcycle in a cloud of red dust so dry and thick that reading about it almost makes one want to wash it off. Wesley has to get ready for the afternoon, for the church picnic that he and Rosacoke will attend. Price's descriptions in this portion of the book are masterful and memorably comic, although the import of what is being communicated is deadly serious and universally significant.

At the church picnic, Wesley tries to seduce Rosacoke, but she resists him, as she always has in the past. The picnic itself is a jolly affair. As the picnickers are about to sit down to their meals, Uncle Simon discovers that his false teeth are missing. Those who have not already begun to consume their barbecued pork and Brunswick stew help Simon look for his teeth. Someone asks him when he last remembers having them. After due deliber-

ation, he proclaims that he took them out while he was stirring the large kettle of Brunswick stew. With this revelation, all eating comes to an abrupt halt. Simon eventually finds his teeth—they were in his back pocket all along. Still, the eating never quite gets back to normal, given the general uncertainty about where the lost dentures were. Vignettes like this help Price to convey an inherently philosophical message to readers without immersing them in specialized terminology or in abstruse and abstract thinking.

A GENEROUS MAN

In *A Generous Man*, published four years after *A Long and Happy Life*, Price goes back several years in time and writes about the Mustian family before Wesley Beavers was known to them. Rosacoke is only eleven years old during the action of this later novel. The basic concept of the book is so outrageous that it would have seemed completely ridiculous if not handled delicately and well. The novel is essentially about a young boy's coming-of-age. Milo, Rosacoke's fifteen-year-old brother, has just lost his virginity to Lois Provo, the girl who runs the snake show at the Warren County Fair. Years ago, Lois's mother was impregnated by a bounder, who proves to be Milo's cousin. Once the truth was known, he abandoned the woman, leaving her only her memories and his eighteen-foot python, Death, which still thrives.

On the morning after his maiden voyage with Lois, Milo wakens to find that his dog, Phillip, is ill. The family gathers for a trip to the alcoholic veterinarian, who promptly diagnoses the dog's illness as rabies. For reasons that are never disclosed, the vet neither confines the dog nor destroys it. Instead, he provides a muzzle, and the Mustians leave with their muzzled mutt to go to the fair. Rato, the family's retarded son, takes the dog's muzzle off. Despite his retardation, Rato has known all along that the dog does not have rabies but is merely suffering from worms, a bit of information he keeps to himself, not wanting to put his knowledge of dogs and their maladies up against that of the vet.

As it turns out, Phillip has a prejudice against snakes, and when he encounters Death, he attacks the python. By the time the dust has settled, the dog, the snake, and the retarded Rato have disappeared into the woods. Sheriff Rooster Pomeroy, citing the dangers of having a hydrophobic snake abroad among the loblolly and kudzu, collects a posse, a group of men keen for excitement and camaraderie, to hunt down the missing boy, the dog, and, most urgently, the snake. Spirits are high, and liquor flows freely.

In the course of the hunt, Milo, unaccustomed to alcohol, gets drunk enough to wander out of the woods, straight to Pomeroy's house, where Mrs. Pomeroy has been left alone. Because the sheriff is impotent, Mrs. Pomeroy finds her sexual satisfaction wherever she can, and Milo looks very good to her. They end up in her bed, where, during their pillow talk, Milo learns that Mrs. Pomeroy's first sexual encounter was with his cousin, the same bounder who sired Lois and gave Death to her mother.

Despite his prurient intentions, Milo cannot complete his act because the doorbell rings, prompting him to bolt through the open window, carrying his clothing with him. He rejoins the unlikely search, and it is he who ultimately finds Death. The snake wraps itself around Milo, almost choking the life out of him, but ironically Sheriff Pomeroy comes to the rescue and defeats Death with a well-placed shot from his gun.

Soon Milo wants to resume his lovemaking with Lois, but she is unwilling, because their first encounter left her quite unsatisfied. She classifies Milo among those men who are takers rather than givers in love encounters, and she lets him know it. He promises to reform. In his second encounter with her, his performance is indeed altered. Thus the book's title: Milo has become a man, but, having learned that he must give as well as take, he must mature further to become a generous man.

KENDAL-MAYFIELD SAGA

Price's difficulties with the critics when he produced the first volume of the Kendal-Mayfield saga, *The Surface of Earth*, stemmed largely from the inability of many northeastern critics to respond with understanding to this convoluted familial saga with heavy biblical overtones, having to do fundamentally with original sin, guilt, conflicted race relations, incestuous feelings, incredibly frequent suicides, and many elements that are more common to rural southern experience than to urban northern experience. Southern families like the two that Price writes about in the Kendal-Mayfield novels are smothering families. Their members sometimes try to

escape, but the magnetic pull back into the decaying bosom of the family is too strong for them to resist. In that respect, this saga is not unlike William Faulkner's *The Sound and the Fury* (1929), in which the Compsons can never escape their heredity and all that it has predestined for them.

It is significant that the family members in the Kendal-Mayfield saga (including those in *The Source of Light* and *The Promise of Rest*, sequels to *The Surface of Earth*) resemble one another closely. Not only do they sound alike but, more tellingly, they also think alike and act alike from generation to generation. Readers become particularly aware of this because of the compression of the novels: A large time span is telescoped into a few hundred pages.

On a literal level, the events of the saga might seem unlikely; taken symbolically, they assume a broader and deeper meaning and a greater artistic plausibility. Perhaps reflection on the outrageous unreality of parts of *A Generous Man* can help readers to understand some of the quintessential symbolic elements of the Kendal-Mayfield saga. Such comparable sagas as the five novels that make up John Galsworthy's *The Forsyte Saga* (1922) and the three novels of Sigrid Undset's *Kristin Lavransdatter* (1920-1922) suffer from a similar sense of unreality if they are read without conscious consideration of their symbolic contexts.

A considerable amount of the symbolic content of Price's Kendal-Mayfield novels can be found in the dream sequences that are integral to the books (more than twenty appear in the first novel). These sequences serve many purposes beyond suggesting the subconscious states of the characters who have the dreams.

The beginning of the Kendal family history as Price reveals it in *The Surface of Earth* is Bedford Kendal's rendition to his children of their grandparents' tragedy. Their grandmother died while giving birth to their mother. Their grandfather, considering himself responsible for his wife's death, killed himself, leaving his newborn daughter (like Price's own mother) an orphan. Bedford, having married this orphan when she grew to adulthood, soon realized that she was consumed by guilt and that she had a strong aversion to sex, all tied up with the guilt she suffered at the thought of having, through her birth, killed her own mother and driven her father to suicide.

Bedford's children, hearing this story, build up their own guilt feelings and their own aversions to sex. His daughter Eva, the strongest student of thirty-two-year-old Latin teacher Forrest Mayfield, elopes with him. Forrest is looking for family ties and thinks that he has found them among the Kendals, who, on the surface, seem to be an enviable family. His marrying Eva disrupts the family's delicate balance, however, so all that Forrest hopes for in the marriage is unavailable to him.

The title of book 1 in the novel, "Absolute Pleasures," seems to be both an irony and a warning. Eva has her absolute pleasure, her unremitting sexual release on her wedding night, but then guilt possesses her. She dreams an Electra dream of her father stretched out over her body, and she is never able to enjoy sex again. She passes her sexual aversion on to her children, suggesting to her son Rob that he masturbate rather than become ensnared in love relationships with women.

Forrest, meanwhile, has his own hereditary baggage to carry. Forrest and Eva, whose names, as Rooke notes, suggest something primal and essentially sexual, ironically are trapped by their pasts. Price emphasizes another theme on which he has dwelt before: Marriage disrupts the family balance, but guilt over that disruption—at least among the Kendals and the Mayfields—in turn disrupts the marriage. The family and heredity are exacting taskmasters, and they are inescapable.

Eva, like many of Price's women, barely survives the birth of her son Rob, and in this difficult birth, which also severely threatens the life of the infant, one sees an entire cycle recurring. The mother, with her cargo of guilt about sex and about her mother's death in childbirth, has a difficult delivery that will increase her aversion to sex and that will impose on her newborn child the same guilt with which she has lived. So has it always been with the Kendals; so presumably it will always be.

Eva and Forrest both settle for lives of frequent masturbation, and their masturbation fantasies are tied to their respective father and mother. Forrest, having abjured further sexual encounters with Eva, meditates on a poem by Gaius Valerius Catullus that has to do with ritual castration. He ultimately leaves Eva and makes a ritualized journey back to Bracey, his hometown, to live with his sister Hatt, a widow.

Book 2 of *The Surface of Earth*, the real heart of the novel, is the story of Eva and Forrest's son, Rob Mayfield, named for his paternal grandfather. Rob, now seventeen, is leaving the family nest, but an awareness of family surges within him. He has no more hope of leaving it than did any of the Kendals before him. There is no escape from either the biological heredity or the strong pull of memory and custom that families impose.

Rob, obsessed with Oedipal feelings since the onset of puberty, hopes that contact with other women will help him to overcome the shameful feelings that disturb his equilibrium. He tries to seduce his date for the senior prom, but she denies him, whereupon he sheds her. Like Milo in *A Generous Man*, his sexual thoughts are only of his own gratification, and his masturbation gives him an independence when he is rebuffed.

Rob contemplates suicide several times in his period of flight from the nest. He comes closest to it when he sees a clutch of boys shooting at a turtle, trying to kill it. The turtle comes to represent for Rob all the isolation and insensitivity that have plagued his recent life, that have brought him closer to suicide than ever in the past.

Rob seeks to overcome his problems by marrying Rachel, whose father manages a hotel, Panacea Springs, in Goshen. Not in love with Rachel, Rob wavers in his commitment to marry her, and he goes—as his father before him had gone to the first Rob—to his father for counsel. Forrest is now living in a heterodox arrangement with Polly, a woman with whom he makes love only ten times a year, fearing that more frequent contact would jeopardize what they have struggled to achieve. Having seen his father's relationship, Rob can now return to Rachel and marry her.

The dinner on the night before the wedding brings together all the elements of the family that Price needs to show to make his story work. In this evening of premarital celebration, the family history, and all that it implies, is made clear. That being done, the only task remaining to Price artistically is to kill Rachel off in childbirth, which he promptly does. Rachel dies giving birth to Hutch, whose story becomes the next portion of the saga.

The Source of Light is a more optimistic book than its predecessor. It focuses on Hutch and on the aging and death of his father. In this second novel of the trilogy, both Hutch and Rob seem to have reached an accord in their lives, to have matured into acceptance of what seems for them inevitable. The pull of the family and the inevitability of their heredity are both still operative, but they are less oppressive than they were in the earlier book.

The Promise of Rest, which completes the Mayfield trilogy, boldly confronts the twin furies of sexuality and race that have tormented the Mayfields for nine decades. After more than thirty years of marriage, Ann has left Hutch. Although Hutch has been faithful to her, she feels isolated because of his close friendship with Strawson Stewart, who was once Hutch's student and lover and is still the tenant on the Mayfield home place.

Hutch remains a successful poet and teacher at Duke University, but he is devastated by news that his only son, Wade, is suffering from acquired immunodeficiency syndrome (AIDS) in New York City. Wade was estranged from his family, not because of his homosexuality but because his black lover, Wyatt, condemned Hutch and Ann as racists. After Wyatt commits suicide, Hutch brings Wade home to die. At first Hutch tries to exclude Ann from the deathbed watch, but their mutual pain eventually pulls them back together. After Wade's death they learn that he loved not only Wyatt but also Wyatt's sister, Ivory, and with her he fathered a child. This child, Raven, bears the given name of both Hutch and Wade, and he is proof that the Mayfield clan will not soon become extinct.

Raven's link with his grandparents remains tenuous, but in the final scene of the novel he goes with Hutch to visit an aging black cousin and to spread Wade's ashes on the Mayfield farm. In this way, the book affirms racial unity and solace after the pain of death. With a long heritage of sexual confusion and miscegenation, the Mayfields may not readily achieve peaceful rest, but its potential promise is surely genuine.

The Tongues of Angels

Set primarily at a summer camp for boys in western North Carolina, *The Tongues of Angels* is the story of a young man's rite of passage and a commentary on his continuing source of inspiration as a mature artist. Bridge Boatner is now a successful painter, but when his sons ask about the inscription on the back of his first significant landscape, he recounts the circumstances under which he produced it. At the age of twenty-one, Bridge recoiled from the recent death of his father by becoming

a counselor at Camp Juniper. There he formed a brief but intense friendship with a troubled but immensely gifted camper, Raphael (Rafe) Noren, for whom the painting was intended as a gift.

Raphael's angelic name suggests the mysterious nature of his great talents (especially in Native American dancing), but he also exhibits a profound need for love. Having seen his own mother murdered, Rafe is drawn toward Bridge even though he confides little. Bridge enlists Rafe as a model for sketches of angels, and in so doing he, perhaps inadvertently, contributes to the camper's death. In recalling that traumatic event, however, Bridge observes that even now he creates as an artist not merely because of his past errors but by actually using those errors as instruments.

Noble Norfleet

The title character of *Noble Norfleet* is a handsome seventeen-year-old, a high school senior in northeastern North Carolina in a town much like Macon, where Price lived much of his early life. Noble, who runs track, comes of age quickly and violently within the span of a few hours. He has just lost his virginity to his high school Spanish teacher, Nita Acheson, a woman considerably his senior, who is married but whose husband is away in Vietnam with the military (the story takes place in the late 1960's, during the Vietnam War). Exhausted from the exertions of strenuous lovemaking, Noble wakens in his home the next morning to discover that his mother, Edith Norfleet, has killed his brother and sister by stabbing them with an icepick. Edith, who had for many years shown signs of a deep-seated psychosis, might have turned the icepick on Noble but for some unfathomable reason did not do so.

Edith's precipitous actions are not wholly surprising to those who know her. Deserted by her husband some years earlier, she has always been considered odd, but, for the most part, she has appeared to be harmless. Now it falls to Noble to take charge of his mother's legal problems and to arrange for her to be committed to a hospital for the criminally insane, where she will remain for many years. Meanwhile, her son, in many ways a model citizen, has no recourse other than to get on with his life. His only remaining close family member, an uncle, has little interest in helping the youth.

The one person Noble can depend on is Hesta James,

a stalwart black woman who has been Edith's cleaning lady for some years. Noble also seeks continued solace from Nita Acheson, who carries on her involvement with him for some months. Noble hopes to receive some helpful counseling from Tom Landingham, a local clergyman who is, like Nita, interested in Noble largely as a sexual object. Noble becomes the passive recipient of Landingham's advances as he struggles with his rapidly developing sexual identity. Consumed with guilt, Landingham commits suicide.

Noble than enlists in the Army and is sent to Vietnam as a medic. On his return home, he becomes a nurse and has a relationship with a young woman named Fare Langston, but he cannot sustain such a relationship and eventually the two go their separate ways. Noble settles for a life that involves his working hard and looking in occasionally on his mother, who has now been released from custody. The one constant in Noble's life is Hesta James, on whom he can always depend.

THE GOOD PRIEST'S SON

The Good Priest's Son is a novel of confessions, reconciliations, and strong emotions. The protagonist of the novel is Mabry Kincaid, a fifty-three-year-old art conservator with an encroaching case of multiple sclerosis. On his way home from a business trip to Europe, Mabry is grounded in Nova Scotia following the freeze on air travel immediately following the September 11, 2001, terrorist attacks on the World Trade Center towers and the Pentagon. His New York apartment was in the shadows of the World Trade Center, a site so devastated by the towers' destruction that he cannot return to it. Instead, he goes to North Carolina to stay temporarily with Tasker Kincaid, his aged father, an Episcopal priest.

In the course of his brief sojourn in North Carolina, Mabry learns of his father's checkered past when the old man confesses to him some of his sexual indiscretions. After a few traumatic days during which Mabry's own checkered past is also revealed in some detail, he returns to New York to confront the task of putting his life back together. There he reconnects with his daughter, Charlotte, an adult with whom he has had strained relations since he departed from his family when she was twelve. As he has in the past, Price deals here with matters of heredity and family, but he does so less successfully than in some of his other novels.

Throughout his writing, Price is concerned with showing that people cannot outrun their pasts. Price's characters are dots on a long, seemingly infinite continuum, and the continuum assumes a life of its own. It is like a steadily flowing river that moves unrelentingly toward the sea. Anything in it that tries to swim upstream is destined to be defeated. Even the strongest of swimmers, the ones who make a little progress against the inevitable flow, will be caught ultimately by the flow and swept along with it. Underlying Price's theme of the strength of the family and the inability of people to resist their heredity is a pervasive theme of guilt, all of it tied up with pleasure, as manifested by sex, versus death or mutilation, as represented by the childbirth catastrophes of many of Price's characters.

Price's intimate and sensitive knowledge of southern rural life enables him to write some of the most accurate and memorable descriptions ever published of the locale in which most of his stories are set. He portrays the speech rhythms, vocabulary, and syntax of northern North Carolina with an authenticity that remains consistent throughout his novels and stories, as do the unshakably consistent points of view of his characters.

R. Baird Shuman
Updated by Albert Wilhelm

OTHER MAJOR WORKS

SHORT FICTION: *The Names and Faces of Heroes*, 1963; *Permanent Errors*, 1970; *The Foreseeable Future: Three Long Stories*, 1991; *The Collected Stories*, 1993.

PLAYS: *Early Dark*, pb. 1977; *Private Contentment*, pb. 1984; *New Music: A Trilogy*, pr. 1989; *Full Moon, and Other Plays*, 1993.

POETRY: *Late Warning: Four Poems*, 1968; *Lessons Learned: Seven Poems*, 1977; *Nine Mysteries (Four Joyful, Four Sorrowful, One Glorious)*, 1979; *Vital Provisions*, 1982; *The Laws of Ice*, 1986; *The Use of Fire*, 1990; *The Collected Poems*, 1997.

TELEPLAY: *House Snake*, 1986.

NONFICTION: *Things Themselves: Essays and Scenes*, 1972; *A Common Room: Essays, 1954-1987*, 1987; *Clear Pictures: First Loves, First Guides*, 1989; *Conversations with Reynolds Price*, 1991 (Jefferson Humphries, editor); *A Whole New Life*, 1994; *Three Gospels*, 1996;

Learning a Trade: A Craftsman's Notebooks, 1955-1997, 1998; *Letter to a Man in the Fire: Does God Exist and Does He Care?*, 1999; *Feasting the Heart: Fifty-two Essays for the Air*, 2000; *A Serious Way of Wondering: The Ethics of Jesus Imagined*, 2003; *Letter to a Godchild: Concerning Faith*, 2006.

TRANSLATIONS: *Presence and Absence: Versions from the Bible*, 1973; *Oracles: Six Versions from the Bible*, 1977; *A Palpable God: Thirty Stories Translated from the Bible with an Essay on the Origins and Life of Narrative*, 1978.

CHILDREN'S LITERATURE: *A Perfect Friend*, 2000.

BIBLIOGRAPHY

Hovis, George. "Reynolds Price: Plain Folk in the Tobacco Belt." In *Vale of Humility: Plain Folk in Contemporary North Carolina Fiction*. Columbia: University of South Carolina Press, 2007. Places Prices's fiction within the context of the southern literary tradition. Part of a larger study of the ways in which modern southern writers approach their regional experiences.

Humphries, Jefferson, ed. *Conversations with Reynolds Price*. Jackson: University Press of Mississippi, 1991. Collection of interviews, originally published between 1966 and 1989 in literary journals, newspapers, and magazines, offers insight into Price's views and methods. Includes an informative introduction, chronology, and index.

Poteat, William Mark. *Gay Men in Modern Southern Literature: Ritual, Initiation, and the Construction of Masculinity*. New York: Peter Lang, 2006. Examines the creation of gay characters in the works of three writers: Price, Tennessee Williams, and Charles Nelson.

Powell, Tara. "The Fiction of Mercy: Suffering Delight in Reynolds Price's *The Promise of Rest*." *Mississippi Quarterly* 53 (Spring, 2000): 251-264. Looks at Price's depiction of suffering and salvation within a Christian context in his novel.

Price, Reynolds. Interview by Wendy Smith. *Publishers Weekly*, May 9, 1994. Price discusses his sense of malevolent fate, his troubled family history, his discovery of himself as a writer, his previous works, and the process of writing about his ordeal with cancer.

_____. "Outlaw Christian: An Interview with Reynolds Price." Interview by Sarah J. Fodor. *Christian Century* 112 (November 22-29, 1995): 1128-1131. Among other topics, Price discusses eroticism in literature, the role of children in his fiction, the women in his novels, the importance of solitude in his life, and his views on religion.

Rooke, Constance. *Reynolds Price*. Boston: Twayne, 1983. Good introduction to Price's fiction focuses on his consistency of vision. Includes a brief biography and discussion of Price's work within a literary and geographic context as well as detailed analyses of his first five novels. Supplemented with a chronology and a select bibliography.

Sadler, Lynn Veach. "Reynolds Price and Religion: The 'Almost Blindlingly Lucid' Palpable World." *Southern Quarterly* 26 (Winter, 1988): 1-11. Examines religious underpinnings, especially the influence of biblical narrative, in Price's fiction, and also investigates Price's perceptions of the deeper reality of life underlying what is commonly visible.

Schiff, James A., ed. *Critical Essays on Reynolds Price*. New York: G. K. Hall, 1998. Collection of essays serves as a good resource for the beginning student of Price's fiction. Includes bibliography and index.

_____. *Understanding Reynolds Price*. Columbia: University of South Carolina Press, 1996. Collection of essays provides a general introduction to Price's work, focusing primarily on the novels but also commenting on the relationship of Price's short stories to his longer fiction and memoirs.

J. B. PRIESTLEY

Born: Bradford, Yorkshire, England; September 13, 1894

Died: Stratford-upon-Avon, Warwickshire, England; August 14, 1984

Also known as: John Boynton Priestley; Peter Goldsmith

PRINCIPAL LONG FICTION

Adam in Moonshine, 1927

Benighted, 1927

Farthing Hall, 1929 (with Hugh Walpole)

The Good Companions, 1929

Angel Pavement, 1930

Faraway, 1932

I'll Tell You Everything, 1933 (with George Bullett)

Wonder Hero, 1933

They Walk in the City: The Lovers in the Stone Forest, 1936

The Doomsday Men: An Adventure, 1938

Let the People Sing, 1939

Blackout in Gretley: A Story of—and for— Wartime, 1942

Daylight on Saturday; A Novel About an Aircraft Factory, 1943

Three Men in New Suits, 1945

Bright Day, 1946

Jenny Villiers: A Story of the Theatre, 1947

Festival at Farbridge, 1951 (also known as *Festival*)

Low Notes on a High Level: A Frolic, 1954

The Magicians, 1954

Saturn over the Water: An Account of His Adventures in London, South America, and Australia by Tim Bedford, Painter, 1961

The Thirty-first of June: A Tale of True Love, Enterprise, and Progress in the Arthurian and Ad-Atomic Ages, 1961

The Shape of Sleep: A Topical Tale, 1962

Sir Michael and Sir George: A Tale of COMSA and DISCUS and the New Elizabethans, 1964

(also known as *Sir Michael and Sir George: A Comedy of New Elizabethans*)

Lost Empires: Being Richard Herncastle's Account of His Life on the Variety Stage from November, 1913, to August, 1914, Together with a Prologue and Epilogue, 1965

Salt Is Leaving, 1966

It's an Old Country, 1967

The Image Men: "Out of Town" and "London End," 1968

The Carfitt Crisis, 1975

Found, Lost, Found: Or, The English Way of Life, 1976

My Three Favorite Novels, 1978

OTHER LITERARY FORMS

In addition to the nearly thirty novels that he published after *Adam in Moonshine* in 1927, J. B. Priestley wrote approximately fifty plays, on which his future reputation will largely depend. These include such memorable works as *Dangerous Corner* (1932), *Eden End* (1934), *Time and the Conways* (1937), *An Inspector Calls* (1946), *The Linden Tree* (1947), and *The Scandalous Affair of Mr. Kettle and Mrs. Moon* (1955). He also collaborated with Iris Murdoch on the successful stage adaptation of her novel *A Severed Head* (1963).

In addition, a long list of impressive works characterize Priestley as the twentieth century equivalent of an eighteenth century man of letters, a term he professed to despise. This list includes accounts of his travels both in England and abroad, the best of these being *English Journey: Being a Rambling but Truthful Account of What One Man Saw and Heard and Felt and Thought During a Journey Through England During the Autumn of the Year 1933* (1934), *Russian Journey* (1946), and *Journey down a Rainbow* (1955), written in collaboration with Jacquetta Hawkes. Priestley produced several books of reminiscence and recollection, which include *Rain upon Godshill: A Further Chapter of Autobiography* (1939), *Margin Released: A Writer's Reminiscences and Reflections* (1962), and *Instead of the Trees* (1977). His literary criticism includes studies of George Meredith, Charles Dickens, and Anton Chekhov; and his familiar essays, thought by many to be among his finest works, are represented in the volume titled *Essays of Five Decades* (1968), and by *Postscripts* (1940), a collection of transcripts of his broadcasts in support of England at war. Priestley created several picture books of social criticism, such as *The Prince of Pleasure and His Regency, 1811-1820* (1969), *The Edwardians* (1970), and *Victoria's Heyday* (1972), and his far-reaching historical surveys detail an idiosyncratic view of people in time: *Literature and Western Man* (1960) and *Man and Time* (1964). Priestley's short-story collections include *Going Up: Stories and Sketches* (1950) and *The Other Place, and Other Stories of the Same Sort* (1953).

As this list indicates, no aspect of modern life escaped Priestley's scrutiny, and no genre was left untried. In a long and prestigious career, he earned for himself a secure place in the annals of literature.

ACHIEVEMENTS

Although J. B. Priestley's accomplishments in the theater may prove more significant than his work in the novel, perhaps because of his experimentation within the dramatic genre, his fiction has nevertheless secured for him a high place in contemporary literature; it has been read and cherished by a large and very appreciative audience. *The Good Companions*, a runaway best seller in 1929, allowed Priestley to turn his attention from journalism and the novel to the theater in the 1930's, but he kept returning to the novel form throughout his career.

Priestley produced no novel that equals James Joyce's *Ulysses* (1922) in scope or intellectual subtlety, no novel as prophetic as D. H. Lawrence's *The Rainbow* (1915), no novel illustrative of the intuitive faculty equal to Virginia Woolf's *To the Lighthouse* (1927), or of ethical concern equal to Joseph Conrad's *The Secret Agent* (1907) or William Faulkner's *Light in August* (1932). His place on the scale of literary achievement may be lower than theirs, but his audience has been, by and large, greater. Priestley aimed for and caught a popular audience that remained loyal to him through five decades of writing. His novels and plays have been widely translated and acted, most notably in the Soviet Union. His craft in the novel genre shows the influence of

Charles Dickens, of the English Romantics, especially of William Wordsworth and William Hazlitt, and of the English music hall and its traditions. Priestley himself made no great claims for his fiction, beyond good-naturedly protesting once or twice that there is more to it than meets the top-speed reviewer's eye. His finest novel, *Bright Day*, however, earned general critical approval when it was published in 1946, and merited the praise of Carl Jung, who found its theme consonant with his notion of the oneness of all people.

BIOGRAPHY

John Boynton Priestley was born in Bradford, Yorkshire, on September 13, 1894. His mother died soon after his birth, and he was reared by a kind and loving stepmother. His father, Jonathan, was a schoolmaster; in his autobiographical work *Margin Released*, Priestley characterizes his father as the man Socialists have in mind when they write about Socialists.

In Priestley's early years, Bradford offered much to feed a romantic boy's imagination: theater, the music halls, a playgoer's society, an arts club, the concert stage, a busy market street, and a grand-scale arcade called the Swan. A tram ride away were the Yorkshire Dales and moors. As a young man, Priestley worked in a wool office, writing poetry and short stories into handmade notebooks in his spare time. An important early influence was Richard Pendlebury, his English master. Priestley later observed that Bradford and its environs did more for his education than did Cambridge University, which he attended years later.

In 1915, Priestley enlisted in the army. He was sent to France, invalided back to England after being wounded, and then sent back to France. Significantly, his experience of war does not figure explicitly in any fictional piece, with the single exception of the haunting short story *The Town Major of Miraucourt*, which was published on its own in 1930. Priestley's entire creative output may, however, have been an attempt to put war and its ravages into a long-range context, a notion that pervades his *Postscripts* broadcasts for the British Broadcasting Corporation (BBC) during World War II. At the end of his army service, Priestley went to Cambridge, where he studied, between 1919 and 1922, literature, history, and political theory. His first book, *Brief Diver-*

sions: Being Tales, Travesties, and Epigrams (1922), received good reviews but did not sell.

Leaving Cambridge for London and the precarious life of a journalist, Priestley worked for J. C. Squire and the *London Mercury*, for the *Daily News*, and for the Bodley Head Press. Meanwhile, he published critical books on George Meredith, Thomas Love Peacock, and modern literature. His first novel, *Adam in Moonshine*, appeared in 1927. Shortly thereafter, Hugh Walpole offered to collaborate with Priestley on a novel called *Farthing Hall* in order to give the younger writer a much-needed publisher's advance so that he could continue his work. In 1929, *The Good Companions* appeared, and Priestley was fully embarked on a long and distinguished career.

Priestley was married three times; his first marriage, to Pat Tempest, came in 1919. A year after her death, in

J. B. Priestley. (Library of Congress)

1925, he married Mary Holland Wyndham Lewis, from whom he was divorced in 1952. The two marriages produced four daughters and a son. In 1953, he married the distinguished anthropologist Jacquetta Hawkes. During his adult life, Priestley resided in London, on the Isle of Wight, and in Alveston, just outside Stratford-upon-Avon. He traveled widely, frequently using his journeys as background for his novels and plays. During World War II, he and his wife ran a hostel for evacuated children; after the war he campaigned vigorously for nuclear disarmament. He served as a delegate to the United Nations Educational, Scientific, and Cultural Organization (UNESCO) and on the board of the National Theatre. He refused a knighthood and a life peerage but did, in 1977, accept membership in the Order of Merit. In 1973, he happily accepted conferment of the Freedom of the City from his native Bradford.

Priestley did not retire from his writing work until well after he turned eighty. He died in 1984, one month shy of his ninetieth birthday.

ANALYSIS

In his novels J. B. Priestley largely portrays a romantic view of life. His focus is primarily on England and the English national character, and on those aspects of people that ennoble and spiritualize them. His fiction also portrays a no-nonsense view of life, however; hard work, dedication to ideals, and willingness to risk all in a good cause are themes that figure prominently. At times, the darker aspects of humanity becloud this gruff but kindly Yorkshireman's generally sunny attitudes. Ultimately, life in Priestley's fictional universe is good, provided the individual is permitted to discover his or her potential. In politics, this attitude reduces to what Priestley has called "Liberal Socialism." For Priestley, too much government is not good for the individual.

Romanticism largely dictated characterization in Priestley's novels, and his most valid psychological portraits are of individuals who are aware of themselves as enchanted and enchanting. These characters are usually portrayed as questers. It is Priestley's symbolic characters, however, who are the most forcefully portrayed, occasionally as god figures, occasionally as devil figures, but mostly as organizers—as stage managers, impresarios, factory owners, butlers. Priestley's female characters fall generally into roles as ingenues or anima figures. There are, however, noteworthy exceptions, specifically, Freda Pinnel in *Daylight on Saturday*.

It is primarily through the presentation of his organizers that Priestley's chief plot device emerges: the common cause. A group of disparate characters is assembled and organized into a common endeavor; democratic action follows as a consequence. "Liberal democracy. Expensive and elaborate, but best in the end," says a choric figure in *Festival at Farbridge*, echoing one of his author's deepest convictions.

A romantic view of people in space and time also dictated the kind of novels that Priestley wrote. His fiction falls easily into three main categories. The first is the seriously conceived and carefully structured novel, in which symbolism and consistent imagery figure as aspects of craft. The best of this group are *Angel Pavement*, *Bright Day*, and *It's an Old Country*. The second category can be termed the frolic or escapade. This group includes *The Good Companions*, *Festival at Farbridge*, and the delightful *Sir Michael and Sir George*. The third category is the thriller or entertainment, which includes such science-fiction works as *The Doomsday Men* and *Saturn over the Water* as well as the detective story *Salt Is Leaving*. Priestley's favorite novel, and his longest, *The Image Men*, published in two volumes in 1968 and as one in 1969, incorporates these three categories within a controlled and incisive satiric mode.

In many of his works, but more so in his plays than in his fiction, Priestley dramatized a theory concerning the nature of time and experience that derived from his understanding of John William Dunne's *An Experiment with Time* (1927) and *The Serial Universe* (1934) and P. D. Ouspensky's *A New Model of the Universe* (1931). Briefly stated, this time theory, most explicit in *The Magicians*, a gothic tale that presents Priestley's characterizations of the Wandering Jew, and *Jenny Villiers*, originally written as a play for the Bristol Old Vic, proposes a means of transcendence. Priestley believed that Dunne's serialism—"we observe something, and we are conscious of our observation . . . and we are conscious of the observation of the observation, and so forth"—permitted him to deal with character "creatively." For the ordinary individual, to "Observer One," the fourth dimension appears as time. The self within dreams becomes

"Observer Two," to whom the fifth dimension appears as time. Unlike the three-dimensional outlook of Observer One, Observer Two's four-dimensional outlook enables him or her to receive images from coexisting past and future times. From Ouspensky, Priestley refined the notion that time, like space, has three dimensions; these three dimensions, however, can be regarded as a continuation of the dimensions of space. Wavelike and spiral, time provides for eternal recurrence, but a recurrence not to be confused with Friedrich Nietzsche's "eternal retour," with reincarnation, or with the Bergsonian *durée*. Ouspensky provided Priestley with the possibility of re-creation—that is, of intervention in space and time through an inner development of self. In other words, self-conscious awareness of self in past time can re-create the past in the present; sympathetic recreation of self and others in what Priestley terms "time alive" can give new meaning to the present and shape the future. For Priestley, the seer—whether he or she be a painter or a musician, or the organizer of a festival or of a traveling group of entertainers, or even a butler in a country house—by looking creatively into the past, ameliorates the present and shapes a brighter future. Consequently, the organizer is Priestley's most forceful and symbolic character, and the thematic purpose of his novels depends on an understanding of this character's motives.

THE GOOD COMPANIONS

Priestley's first successful novel, *The Good Companions*, presents a cozy fairy tale against an essentially realistic background, the English music halls of the 1920's. A determined spinster, Elizabeth Trant, organizes a down-and-out group of entertainers who have called themselves the Dinky Doos into a successful group renamed the Good Companions. The picaresque adventures of these troupers on the road and on the boards provide the novel with its zest and comedy.

ANGEL PAVEMENT

Angel Pavement is in some ways a departure from this earlier work inasmuch as its tone appears dark and ominous. In *Angel Pavement*, the organizer is not a cheerful woman of thirty-seven giving herself a holiday on the roads as an impresario but a balding, middle-aged adventurer named Golspie. "A thick figure of a man but now slow and heavy," Golspie enters the London firm of

Twigg and Dersingham, dealers in wood veneers, and breathes new life into the business in a period of economic depression. With his only commitment being his daughter Lena, Golspie seems at first the firm's savior, for he provides a supply of veneer from the Baltic at half the domestic price. Perhaps because he and his daughter are rejected by the more polite segments of London society, Golspie feels it unnecessary to play fair with his employers. Eventually, he ruins Twigg and Dersingham, putting the employees out of work. At the novel's end, he and Lena leave London for South America and new adventure.

What most distinguishes *Angel Pavement* is its portrayal of the city, London, in the midst of the Depression, and of those who people it. Lilian Matfield, the head secretary, is fascinated by Golspie but refuses to accept the life of adventure he offers her, and Henry Smeeth, the bookkeeper, accepts a raise in salary, only to discover that once Golspie has abandoned Twigg and Dersingham, the company is bankrupt and he is out of work. The streets, the offices, the pubs, the tobacco stands, the amusements, all combine to present a view of human enervation and despair. A confidence man but not exactly a charlatan, Golspie locks the novel to a seemingly pessimistic view. Despite the enervation and apathy portrayed, Golspie offers freedom. Through his sinister organizer, Priestley portrays the life of romance that lies beneath the ordinary. What *Angel Pavement* finally achieves is a startling view of the modern metropolis as a prison from which only the romantic can escape.

BRIGHT DAY

One of his own favorite works, Priestley's *Bright Day* has been justly admired by critics and readers alike. Its uniqueness lies not so much in its dexterous use of such novelistic techniques as the time shift and memory digression as in the way it looks behind and beyond its immediate focus into that sense of race and identity all people share. Although the novel deals with time, Priestley here shows a greater indebtedness to Henri Bergson and Marcel Proust than he does to Ouspensky and Dunne.

Music, specifically a Franz Schubert trio, returns a middle-aged screenwriter, Gregory Dawson, the narrator, who has taken refuge from his unhappy life in a genteel hotel in Cornwall, to a memory of youth and joy. An old couple reminds him of the boy of eighteen he was when he fell in love with a family called Alington in Bruddersford, a wool-producing northern town. The Alingtons, charming and gracious, had sentimentally attached the young Gregory to themselves and had introduced the would-be writer to their world, which he had seen as one of grace and beauty. Ironically, the old couple who trigger the middle-aged Dawson's memories are in fact the Eleanor and Malcolm Nixey who had opportunistically intruded on his youthful idyll and brought an end to the prosperous wool business on which the Alingtons and their gracious world depended, and to Gregory's idealism as well.

In *Bright Day*, Priestley, concerned with a rite of passage, presents Gregory's initiation into a world of greed and suspicion, of appearance and falsehood; his is in fact an initiation into the modern world, and the novel symbolically spans the period of the two world wars. In the course of reconstructing the past, Gregory comes to terms with himself in the present, and it is his recognition of self in time that makes a commitment to the future possible for him. This liberation is confirmed by the stunning revelation made to him by Laura Bradshaw, who had also known the Alingtons, that Joan Alington in a jealous rage had pushed her sister Eva to her death from a cliff. The cancer of destruction had been in the Alingtons themselves; the Nixeys had merely served as catalysts.

Although Gregory Dawson is a quester for truth through self-knowledge, he is much more than a symbolic character. His psychological validity makes his growth in the course of the novel persuasive and compelling. The rediscovery of his romantic self in the present time of the novel is the rediscovery of a moment of beauty that had lain dormant in the rich soil of his memory. Many of Priestley's novels largely describe romance; *Bright Day* re-creates its essence, as does Evelyn Waugh's *Brideshead Revisited* (1945, 1959), with which it has much in common.

LOST EMPIRES

Published in 1965 and representative of the novels Priestley produced in the later stages of his career, *Lost Empires* is in some ways a return to the world of *The Good Companions*, employing as it does the music hall as background. Unlike *The Good Companions*, however, the chief interest of which is the high jinks of the troupers on the road, the theater serves here as a metaphor for the theme of appearance and reality and allows Priestley to allegorize loosely the politics of a world destined for war.

The protagonist, Dick Herncastle, one of Priestley's romantic questers here presented as an artist, is contrasted to his uncle, Nick Ollanton, the organizer, who is portrayed as a magician or mesmerizer. Ollanton and his "turn" allegorize the political activist and his propaganda techniques as he bends people to his will, much as does Thomas Mann's Cipolla in "Mario and the Magician." A time perspective on Ollanton's influence on young Dick, who works as his assistant, is presented by means of a deftly presented prologue and epilogue, which encompass the action proper of the novel, set in the period of World War I. The main action ends with Dick succumbing to the illusion of a better world after the end of the war, and with Ollanton himself leaving the Old World for the United States, revealing his bag of tricks as a private escape from the "bloody mincing machine" of global war. There, he will manufacture machine-gun sights for warplanes. The novel proper, however, ends with the account in the prologue of Dick's return from the war and his successful career as a watercolorist, an illusionist of another sort.

The charm of *Lost Empires* goes well beyond its symbolic dimension; it lies chiefly in the presentations of the performers and the turns they perform on the boards. The juggler Ricardo, the comedian Beamish, the ballad singer Lily Farrish, and many others add to the plot and charm of the novel. That they are logically placed within the melodramatic and symbolic structure of the novel is simply another testimony to the skill of the author.

A. A. DeVitis

OTHER MAJOR WORKS

SHORT FICTION: *The Town Major of Miraucourt*, 1930; *Going Up: Stories and Sketches*, 1950; *The Other Place, and Other Stories of the Same Sort*, 1953; *The Carfitt Crisis, and Two Other Stories*, 1975.

PLAYS: *The Good Companions*, pr. 1931 (adaptation of his novel; with Edward Knoblock); *Dangerous Corner*, pr., pb. 1932; *The Roundabout*, pr. 1932; *Laburnum Grove*, pr. 1933; *Eden End*, pr., pb. 1934; *Cornelius*, pr., pb. 1935; *Duet in Floodlight*, pr., pb. 1935; *Bees on the Boat Deck*, pr., pb. 1936; *Spring Tide*, pr., pb. 1936 (with George Billam); *I Have Been Here Before*, pr., pb. 1937; *People at Sea*, pr., pb. 1937; *Time and the Conways*, pr., pb. 1937; *Music at Night*, pr. 1938; *Mystery at Greenfingers*, pr., pb. 1938; *When We Are Married*, pr., pb. 1938; *Johnson over Jordan*, pr., pb. 1939; *The Long Mirror*, pr., pb. 1940; *Goodnight, Children*, pr., pb. 1942; *They Came to a City*, pr. 1943; *Desert Highway*, pr., pb. 1944; *The Golden Fleece*, pr. 1944; *How Are They at Home?*, pr., pb. 1944; *Ever Since Paradise*, pr. 1946; *An Inspector Calls*, pr. 1946; *The Linden Tree*, pr. 1947; *The Rose and Crown*, pb. 1947 (one act); *The High Toby*, pb. 1948 (for puppet theater); *Home Is Tomorrow*, pr. 1948; *The Plays of J. B. Priestley*, 1948-1950 (3 volumes); *Summer Day's Dream*, pr. 1949; *Bright Shadow*, pr., pb. 1950; *Seven Plays of J. B. Priestley*, 1950; *Dragon's Mouth*, pr., pb. 1952 (with Jacquetta Hawkes); *Treasure on Pelican*, pr. 1952; *Mother's Day*, pb. 1953 (one act); *Private Rooms*, pb. 1953 (one act); *Try It Again*, pb. 1953 (one act); *A Glass of Bitter*, pb. 1954 (one act); *The White Countess*, pr. 1954 (with Hawkes); *The Scandalous Affair of Mr. Kettle and Mrs. Moon*, pr., pb. 1955; *These Our Actors*, pr. 1956; *The Glass Cage*, pr. 1957; *The Pavilion of Masks*, pr. 1963; *A Severed Head*, pr. 1963 (with Iris Murdoch; adaptation of Murdoch's novel); *An Inspector Calls, and Other Plays*, 2001.

POETRY: *The Chapman of Rhymes*, 1918.

SCREENPLAY: *Last Holiday*, 1950.

NONFICTION: *Brief Diversions: Being Tales, Travesties, and Epigrams*, 1922; *Papers from Lilliput*, 1922; *I for One*, 1923; *Figures in Modern Literature*, 1924; *Fools and Philosophers: A Gallery of Comic Figures from English Literature*, 1925 (also known as *The English Comic Characters*); *George Meredith*, 1926; *Talking: An Essay*, 1926; *The English Novel*, 1927, 1935, 1974; *Open House: A Book of Essays*, 1927; *Thomas Love Peacock*, 1927; *Apes and Angels: A Book of Essays*, 1928; *Too Many People, and Other Reflections*, 1928; *The Balconinny, and Other Essays*, 1929 (also known as *The Balconinny*, 1931); *English Hu-*

mour, 1929, 1976; *The Lost Generation: An Armistice Day Article*, 1932; *Self-Selected Essays*, 1932; *Albert Goes Through*, 1933; *English Journey: Being a Rambling but Truthful Account of What One Man Saw and Heard and Felt and Thought During a Journey Through England During the Autumn of the Year 1933*, 1934; *Four-in-Hand*, 1934; *Midnight on the Desert: A Chapter of Autobiography*, 1937 (also known as *Midnight on the Desert: Being an Excursion into Autobiography During a Winter in America, 1935-1936*); *Rain upon Godshill: A Further Chapter of Autobiography*, 1939; *Britain Speaks*, 1940; *Postscripts*, 1940 (radio talks); *Out of the People*, 1941; *Britain at War*, 1942; *British Women Go to War*, 1943; *The Man-Power Story*, 1943; *Here Are Your Answers*, 1944; *The New Citizen*, 1944; *Letter to a Returning Serviceman*, 1945; *Russian Journey*, 1946; *The Secret Dream: An Essay on Britain, America, and Russia*, 1946; *The Arts Under Socialism: Being a Lecture Given to the Fabian Society, with a Postscript on What Government Should Do for the Arts Here and Now*, 1947; *Theatre Outlook*, 1947; *Delight*, 1949; *Journey down a Rainbow*, 1955 (with Jacquetta Hawkes); *All About Ourselves, and Other Essays*, 1956; *The Writer in a Changing Society*, 1956; *The Art of the Dramatist: A Lecture Together with Appendices and Discursive Notes*, 1957; *Thoughts in the Wilderness*, 1957; *Topside: Or, The Future of England, a Dialogue*, 1958; *The Story of Theatre*, 1959; *Literature and Western Man*, 1960; *William Hazlitt*, 1960; *Charles Dickens: A Pictorial Biography*, 1962; *Margin Released: A Writer's Reminiscences and Reflections*, 1962; *The English Comic Characters*, 1963; *Man and Time*, 1964; *The Moments and Other Pieces*, 1966; *All England Listened: J. B. Priestley's Wartime Broadcasts*, 1968; *Essays of Five Decades*, 1968 (Susan Cooper, editor); *Trumpets over the Sea: Being a Rambling and Egotistical Account of the London Symphony Orchestra's Engagement at Daytona Beach, Florida, in July-August, 1967*, 1968; *The Prince of Pleasure and His Regency, 1811-1820*, 1969; *Anton Chekhov*, 1970; *The Edwardians*, 1970; *Over the Long High Wall: Some Reflections and Speculations on Life, Death, and Time*, 1972; *Victoria's Heyday*, 1972; *The English*, 1973; *Outcries and Asides*, 1974; *A Visit to New Zealand, Particular Pleasures: Being a Personal Record of Some Varied Arts and Many*

Different Artists, 1974; *The Happy Dream: An Essay*, 1976; *Instead of the Trees*, 1977 (autobiography).

CHILDREN'S LITERATURE: *Snoggle*, 1972.

EDITED TEXTS: *Essayists Past and Present: A Selection of English Essays*, 1925; *Tom Moore's Diary: A Selection*, 1925; *The Book of Bodley Head Verse*, 1926; *The Female Spectator: Selections from Mrs. Eliza Heywood's Periodical, 1744-1746*, 1929; *Our Nation's Heritage*, 1939; *Scenes of London Life, from "Sketches by Boz" by Charles Dickens*, 1947; *The Best of Leacock*, 1957; *Four English Novels*, 1960; *Four English Biographies*, 1961; *Adventures in English Literature*, 1963; *An Everyman Anthology*, 1966.

BIBLIOGRAPHY

Atkins, John. *J. B. Priestley: The Last of the Sages*. New York: Riverrun Press, 1981. Describes Priestley's development as novelist, essayist, critic, dramatist, autobiographer, social commentator, historian, and travel writer. Particularly informative concerning the political, social, and economic background of the late 1920's and 1930's, the period during which Priestley made his most significant contributions to literature.

Baxendale, John. *Priestley's England: J. B. Priestley and English Culture*. New York: Manchester University Press, 2007. Scholarly study recounts the events of Priestley's life and his literary career within the context of twentieth century English social history. Includes bibliography and index.

Brome, Vincent. *J. B. Priestley*. London: Hamish Hamilton, 1988. Offers an affectionate but candid portrait of Priestley in public and private life. Argues that the prolific Priestley has been denied his proper niche by overly harsh critics who do not deal fairly with those who write for a wide, general audience.

Cook, Judith. *Priestley*. London: Bloomsbury, 1997. Biography includes examination of Priestley's novels, nonfiction works, and dramatic works. Includes bibliography and index.

DeVitis, A. A., and Albert E. Kalson. *J. B. Priestley*. Boston: Twayne, 1980. Begins with a biographical chapter that includes a discussion of Priestley's time theories, then addresses the author's work in two sections, one devoted to his novels and the other to his plays. Discusses all of Priestley's works in the two genres, the more significant ones in some detail. Includes a chronology of the important events in Priestley's life and a useful bibliography.

Gray, Dulcie. *J. B. Priestley*. Stroud, England: Sutton, 2000. Provides a concise look at Priestley's life and many works. Includes a bibliography.

Klein, Holger. *J. B. Priestley's Fiction*. New York: Peter Lang, 2002. Examines Priestley's novels and short stories, with the discussion organized by themes, including escape, people and work, rebellion and commitment, and dimensions of crime. Also discusses Priestley's narrative technique.

V. S. PRITCHETT

Born: Ipswich, England; December 16, 1900
Died: London, England; March 20, 1997
Also known as: Victor Sawdon Pritchett

PRINCIPAL LONG FICTION

Claire Drummer, 1929
Shirley Sanz, 1932 (also known as *Elopement into Exile*)
Nothing Like Leather, 1935
Dead Man Leading, 1937
Mr. Beluncle, 1951

OTHER LITERARY FORMS

V. S. Pritchett (PRIHCH-iht) is recognized above all as a master of the short story. His stories rely less on plot than on character—character revealed principally through dialogue. Many of Pritchett's stories were first published in magazines; they have been collected, however, in more than a dozen volumes.

Pritchett is also widely known as a travel writer and a literary critic and biographer. As the former, he produced several works, among which *The Spanish Temper* (1954) was perhaps most highly praised. *The Offensive Traveller* (1964; also known as *Foreign Faces*) is a collection of numerous previously published travel essays. Pritchett's literary biographies include *Balzac: A Biography* (1973), *The Gentle Barbarian: The Life and Work of Turgenev* (1977), and *Chekhov: A Spirit Set Free* (1988). His criticism ranges across more than four decades, from *In My Good Books* (1942) to *A Man of Letters* (1985). Two autobiographical works by Pritchett, *A*

Cab at the Door (1968) and *Midnight Oil* (1972) are regarded as classics of the genre.

ACHIEVEMENTS

During the second half of the twentieth century, V. S. Pritchett's readership and influence in the United States grew considerably. After the 1950's, his stories appeared frequently in *The New Yorker*, and selections of his reviews appeared yearly in *The New York Review of Books*. He was the Christian Gauss Lecturer at Princeton University (1953), writer-in-residence at Smith College (1966), Beckman Professor at the University of California at Berkeley (1962), and visiting professor at Brandeis University (1968). His fiction and criticism alike were enjoyed and praised by American critics—his fiction for its social comedy, acute characterization, and subtle manner, his criticism for its focus, lucidity, and balance. As a "literary journalist," he has been compared to Edmund Wilson, and his sentences, whether in fiction or nonfiction, are thought to be among the best written in English in the twentieth century. In England, he was an elder statesman of letters, many times honored. He was the Clark Lecturer at Cambridge University (1969) and was awarded a D.Litt. by Leeds University (1972). He served as president of the British Association of Poets, Playwrights, Editors, Essayists, and Novelists (PEN) in 1970 and of the International PEN Club in 1974. He was the recipient of two awards for nonfiction, the Heinemann in 1969 and the International PEN Club in 1974. He was a fellow of the Royal Society of Literature and an honorary member of the American Academy of

Arts and Letters. In 1969, he was made a Commander of the British Empire, and in 1975, he was knighted.

BIOGRAPHY

In December of 1900, in lodgings over a toy shop in Ipswich, England, Victor Sawdon Pritchett was born, the first child of Beatrice Martin and Walter Pritchett, who had met in the milliner's shop where they both worked. The marriage apparently began passionately, three children following quickly after Victor, but because of Walter's many business misadventures and his conversion to Christian Science, the marriage was soon unsettled and its passion converted to quarrelsomeness. Although the Pritchetts were not shiftless, their household was often shifted about: By the time Pritchett was twelve, the family had moved around London at least fourteen times, usually so that Walter Pritchett could escape creditors, twice to hide his bankruptcy. Beatrice Pritchett lived in constant fear of creditors (once denying her identity on opening the door to an officer attempting to serve a writ) and in outspoken jealousy of the "other women" in her husband's life—his mother, his business partner ("Miss H"), and Mary Baker Eddy (founder of the Christian Science Church).

Because the family never stayed in one place for long, Pritchett felt that he belonged nowhere, that he was an outsider everywhere but in his own, rather strange, family. In addition to moving with his parents, he was sent at intervals to his grandparents in Yorkshire, an arrangement contrived, apparently, to ease the burden on Walter Pritchett's purse. New problems complicated their home life from 1910, when in Camberwell, Walter was converted to Christian Science. His conversion brought on quarrels with Beatrice about "that woman" that lasted well into the night, and later his business failed. After a year's separation, during which time Pritchett formed a vague idea that he would become a painter, Beatrice and the children rejoined Walter in Dulwich, where he had established an art needlework trade with his former bookkeeper, Miss H.

Until he moved to Dulwich, Pritchett had received only sporadic schooling, and then only in rough Methodist and penny-a-day schools, because his father did not trouble himself about the children's education. Finally, Beatrice grew impatient with Walter's ruminations over the prospectuses from Eton and Harrow, for which Pritchett would never have qualified because, among other things, he knew no Latin, and she enrolled him in Rosendale Road School. There he was awarded a copy of John Ruskin's *Modern Painters* (1843-1860) for one of his paintings, and there, too, under a man named Bartlett, he read his first literature. He promptly began to read whatever he could find, having decided to become a writer. He became known in the family as "Dirty Poet" and "Professor."

Two years later, to impress Miss H, his father allowed him to sit for an examination for a scholarship to the Strand School (Streatham), which he failed. Pritchett identifies this failure in *A Cab at the Door* as a turning point in his life, for he believed that had he won the scholarship, he surely would have continued at a university and died as a writer. Instead, at Miss H's expense, he entered Alleyn's School, a London grammar school founded to educate the lower middle classes. There he learned that he was good at languages, and he also enjoyed a few classroom successes with his writing. Around this time, he sprained his ankle, and this accident was the occasion of his first hearing the Christian Science argument from his father. Not long afterward, Pritchett professed his belief in it, probably out of a need to please his father, but his faith seems never to have been very strong. Church provided a social outlet for him, the children otherwise not being allowed to go out.

In 1916, at the instigation of his grandfather, Pritchett was taken from school and put to work as a clerk in a London firm that manufactured leather goods. After fighting with another clerk on the office floor, he was promoted out of the office to learn the other phases of the trade. For four years he commuted into London, so happy with the idea of thoroughly learning a trade that for a while he abandoned his literary ambitions. At the end of 1920, however, he fell ill, and when he recovered, he did not go back to the leather business but instead went to Paris, which he had dreamed of doing for several years.

With two hundred pounds saved from his earnings and a typewriter from his father, Pritchett arrived in Paris in the spring of 1921. He found a job as a photographer's assistant and settled joyfully into Parisian life. Christian Science had taught him that sex should be avoided as the chief avenue of Animal Magnetism, the force that created the illusion of Evil, but by this time, it is fair to say, he was tormented by his virginity. Finally, he managed a brief affair with a Danish girl, who soon after returned to Denmark and married another man. Pritchett had a few other friends, mostly from the church, but he knew no writers, least of all the American expatriates. He spent most of his time alone, continuing the autodidacticism that for the most part had been his education; it was in his room, remembering author Sir James Barrie's advice to write about small things, that he began his career as a writer. His first three sketches were taken almost immediately by *The Saturday Westminster*, *Time and Tide*, and *The Christian Science Monitor*. Soon he was emboldened to quit the photographer's shop for a job as a shellac salesman. He was happy to be part of the workaday city, to walk the streets with his samples, but he sold

nothing and was fired. Once again, he began to write and to place articles, but then his luck changed, he ran out of money, and *The Christian Science Monitor* did not pay him for a series of articles he had written. When he was on the verge of starvation, he was fed by his landlady and given money by friends. Storing his belongings in Paris, he returned to England, two years after leaving, to see the London editor of *The Christian Science Monitor*.

In Paris, Pritchett had proven to himself and to his father that he could lead an independent and manly life as a writer, so once back in London, he looked for regular work writing. At *The Christian Science Monitor*, the new editor was not immediately forthcoming, but eventually he paid Pritchett and gave him a trial assignment in Ireland, where Pritchett met Æ, James Stephens, Sean O'Casey, and William Butler Yeats himself, with whom he argued about George Bernard Shaw. In Ireland, too, he fell in love with another journalist and rashly married her after agreeing to go to Spain for *The Christian Science Monitor*. He did not much like his role as foreign correspondent because he disliked politics, preferring instead to write about places, people, customs, and manners. Tiring of journalism, he began to write short stories, none of which was published for several years. Over a period of three years of writing from Ireland, Spain, and the United States, his writing (by his own account) had grown self-conscious and contorted. At long last, *The Christian Science Monitor* tired of it and fired him.

In London again, Pritchett sustained himself by translating business letters for a foreign language school, serving as the librarian to the Bath Club for one pound a week, and selling a few stories and sketches. Unable to find a publisher for a collection of sketches, poor, and inspired by D. H. Lawrence's *Sea and Sardinia* (1921), he decided to walk across Spain and write a book about it upon his return to England. *Marching Spain* (1928) sold only six hundred copies before it was remaindered, but it won Pritchett two contracts, one for a book of stories and another for a novel. In the meantime, he was hired again by *The Christian Science Monitor*, this time as a reviewer, a job he kept until he published "The

V. S. Pritchett. (© Nancy Crampton)

Saint" in the 1930's and was fired for the last time. Also in 1928, he began what proved to be a long association with the *New Statesman* (he eventually became the director), published a few stories in *The Fortnightly Review*, and became the novel reviewer for *The Spectator*. In 1929, his first novel, *Claire Drummer*, was published, and his first book of stories, *The Spanish Virgin, and Other Stories*, followed in 1930. The book of stories surprised everyone by selling three thousand copies; the novel sold fewer than a thousand.

Throughout the 1920's, Pritchett and his wife had been separated much of the time, partly because she was pursuing an acting career. By the 1930's, Pritchett had earned some measure of peace and security from his writing, but it was not until 1934 that the transience and emotional tension that had characterized his entire life were relieved. In that year, he met Dorothy Rudge Roberts, who, after his divorce in 1936, became his second wife. It was not merely to fulfill a tedious convention that he dedicated all of his subsequent books to her, for—believing that love released the tension responsible for his bad writing—it was to her and their marriage that he attributed the great burst of creativity that overtook him. Through the 1930's he published three more novels, but, as portended by the response to *The Spanish Virgin*, it was in the short story that he excelled. During the war years, he gardened and reviewed books; in the 1950's, he published his only truly successful novel, *Mr. Beluncle*, and *The Spanish Temper*, which is generally thought to be one of the best books ever written on Spain; throughout the 1960's, 1970's, and 1980's he continued to write stories and reviews. He also completed two volumes of memoirs in 1968 and 1971.

Pritchett continued to live in London with his wife until his death there at the age of ninety-six. The critical praise he received for his 1988 biography, *Chekhov*, was testimony to the fact that even as he approached ninety he remained a masterful scholar and wordsmith.

ANALYSIS

Two central forces shaped V. S. Pritchett's artistry: his family and his urge to break away from it. The picture that Pritchett gives of his home life in *A Cab at the Door* is of a fantastic edifice of dreams, resounding with the words of Walter Pritchett—self-complacent, moraliz-

ing, and sometimes angry words. The family life Walter tried to create was a fantasy at which Beatrice chipped away. She wailed jealous complaints and remonstrated; she told stories about dead relatives, dead pets, and dead royalty; above all, she told jokes that ended with her bursting into hysterical laughter, rocking on her chair, and peering out at her audience from behind spread fingers, her skirts hoisted above her knees and her bloomers showing. If his father's words imprisoned the young Pritchett, his mother's opened a chink into the world where people voiced their feelings and cried, and where, most important, they laughed.

When Pritchett began to read widely, he discovered fictions other than his father's and was led to a consideration of the worlds that prompted them. (That he thought there was some literal place where life was better is demonstrated by his early desire to travel.) It is characteristic of his imagination that as a young man going to work in London he was reminded of Charles Dickens, rather than of London when reading Dickens, and that as a septuagenarian, in *Midnight Oil*, he described himself as two people—the writer, "the prosing man at the desk," and the other self, "the valet who dogs him and does the living." For Pritchett, in short, life followed art, and this order of things is important for understanding the writer.

Probably because Pritchett's interest in literature arose suddenly from his recognition that print is like paint, that it can create pictures that open onto other perspectives, his writing is predominantly descriptive, his narrative perhaps more lyric than dramatic. Added to his visual acuity is a good ear for dialect, developed from adjusting his own language to whatever new neighborhood he found himself in as a boy and from speaking French and Spanish as a young man. The mundane world, consequently, is richly evoked in his works. He is not primarily concerned with recording the details of the external world, however, for he is too much of an essentialist in purpose and too richly comic in manner to be preoccupied with strict representationalism. Like the Victorians, he studies characters in social settings; like Dickens and Thomas Hardy, his first-loved novelists, he concerns himself with the social environment as a condition of character. Place and class are important as limiters—of experience, language, and the stuff of fantasy. He evokes them with selected, exaggerated, and often symbolic images, usually visual, and through the words the characters speak. Perhaps no other twentieth century writer is as adept as Pritchett at representing society through these brilliant half-strokes. In the sense of upholding the value—whether mythical, political, or moral—of one class above another, however, he is ultimately one of the least class-conscious of English writers. His authorial position is class-free, his attitude independent.

His real divergence from social realism is most obvious in his characters, who ring true, but not because they are singly imitative of individuals with whom one might rub shoulders in the real world. The eccentrics who populate his books are instead caricatures through which are enacted certain emotional, intellectual, and aesthetic problems. The conflicting versions of the world created by the various characters produce a collision at the climax that is often understated and ironic, and perhaps it is the frequency of this "silent" climax that has led to the charge by critics that Pritchett's plotting is weak. Then, too, character and situation above all capture his attention. In a relatively static fashion, one resembling portraiture more than dramatic literature, he touches and retouches his central point.

The unifying theme of Pritchett's fiction concerns dreaming as an ambiguous mechanism of the imagination, for it can lead either to freedom or to imprisonment. According to their way of dreaming, his characters fall loosely into two categories. The first is the egotist. He has many faces, but essentially he is the one who, as is said of Mr. Beluncle, never dreams at all—except when he is awake. Usually he is treated humorously, under a Dickensian light, and when there is an objective narrator, in the Meredithian manner: incisively, ironically, and epigrammatically. The egotist, by placing himself at the center of things and acting out his dreams, tries to negate the three-dimensional world. His dreams are for the most part unrealizable and his version of the world untenable, and he appears comically two-dimensional as a result. The second character type, the artist, recognizes and belongs to the world where perspectives shift. Like the egotist, he dreams, but, unlike the egotist's desires, his longings and aspirations are curbed by an awareness of actual conditions. He is, moreover, capable of holding contradictory dreams, or accounts of the world, in his mind at the same time.

Dead Man Leading

Pritchett's first three novels draw on his experiences in Ireland, Spain, and London. They were not successful, and in *Midnight Oil* he writes that they were "machines for conveying [his] characters into a trap." In *Dead Man Leading*, he tried something new. Instead of looking for essences in the stuff of his own experience, he concocted a material world to convey the essence of masochism. His idea, that explorers are motivated by masochism, he inferred from reading biographies; his setting, Brazil, was known to him only through literature. To pick up mundane details he read missionaries' diaries and talked about Manaos with a drunken businessman on leave, and to fix the setting clearly in mind, he made a small model of the river in his garden. This method of writing the book is partly responsible for both its strengths and its weaknesses. It is overloaded with the pop-Freudianism that infects the literature of the 1930's and is too imitative in its symbolism, whether consciously or not, of Joseph Conrad. Still, it shows an uncommon force of imagination in other respects and a strong narrative power, and—being a symbolic tale approaching psychological allegory—it sheds light on his other works.

The story concerns an expedition by three men, each of whom is an egotist of sorts. The first is Charles Wright, a famous explorer, now middle-aged, who is making the expedition to complete a former, aborted one. The second is Harry Johnson, the chosen companion of Wright, a young Englishman who works in the Brazilian timber industry and uses his leaves to explore the far reaches of the world. He and Wright are "camp companions," initiates into the thoroughly masculine world where women are "bad luck." The third is Gilbert Phillips, who stands outside their circle, a stranger to their code. He envied Harry when they were boys together, and now, as a journalist, he is trying to acquire courage by following bold men. These characters—especially Wright and Johnson—are less persuasive as people than as Freudian symbols.

Despite Wright's nominal leadership, Johnson is at the head of the group. The expedition, which occurs in three stages (not counting the long expository flashback), is a primal regression into the interior of Johnson's being, a gradual peeling-back of his adult self. The flashback, in which we learn that Johnson has had an affair with Wright's stepdaughter, Lucy, and is now burdened with guilt and a desire for self-punishment, lays the foundation for the analysis of his puritanical, masochistic psychology, according to which Wright and Lucy (to whom Wright had been attracted before marrying her mother) serve as father and mother surrogates. Through the first stage of the expedition, the journey upriver with Phillips to meet Wright, Johnson grows feverish and, in an irrational effort to avoid Wright, tries to persuade Phillips to disembark and strike out over land. When they do rendezvous with Wright, Johnson is put to bed in the house of a whiskey-besotted Cockney named Calcott, who entertains him while Wright and Phillips are off hunting turtle eggs. He encourages Johnson in his misogyny ("all women are dagoes") and insists that Johnson is there to look for his father, a missionary who slept in the same room before disappearing into the jungle years earlier. Calcott's Portuguese confidant, Jose Silva, lends support to Calcott by pretending to be the voice of the dead man in a séance arranged for Johnson's benefit. When Phillips and Wright are detained for several days by a storm and Johnson grows impatient to try his luck, Silva, thinking there might be gold in it for him, encourages Johnson to set out and to take him along. When Phillips and Wright return, then, Johnson is gone—now leading the expedition.

The second stage consists of Johnson's trip with Silva. Johnson, making a conscious decision neither to flee his friends nor to follow his father, simply goes on without turning back. Loosened from the "net" the minds of others cast over him, he drifts into a world where the birds whistle "like boys" and Silva chatters and frolics in the sand. Silva is like a boy-genie (an "artist," the narrator calls him) released by Harry's subconscious to grant his deepest wishes. After several days, however, Johnson is overtaken and, in a strained reunion with Wright, breaks down, regressing to an angry child wishing for the death of his father. Wright, attempting to restore harmony, invites him to go out hunting. While they are spearing fish in a mud hole, a jaguar surprises them and, in the panic of the moment, Wright shoots himself. By the time Johnson is able to bring him in, Wright is dead. Characteristically, Johnson thinks this accident has been caused by his own weakness and that his weakness has been brought upon him by Lucy.

He now feels "that he had no longer a self, that he was scattered, disintegrated—nothing."

So begins the third and final stage of the expedition. Johnson's idea, if he has one, is to walk until he encounters the South American Indians who are presumed to have killed his father. Although Phillips has lost his interest in the expedition with the death of Wright, he has promised Lucy, with whom he also has had an affair, that he will take care of Johnson. Consequently, when Silva and the crew turn back, Phillips follows him overland, hoping to save him from the ultimate solitude of the grave. At first, Johnson tolerates his company, but after a few days, Phillips conceives the idea that he intends to leave him behind. When Phillips is nearly dead of thirst, Johnson decides to search for water, leaving a note and his gun behind. Roused from delirium before Johnson is out of sight, Phillips believes he is being abandoned and fires at him. Johnson is last seen looking back at Phillips before turning and automatically marking a trail he will not follow back. Without Phillips, representative perhaps of the social aspect of the ego, Johnson is finally alone, free to rejoin his father, death.

The setting, seemingly so important to the action, is largely created by images drawn from the characters' private states of mind. When England to Gilbert is a fresh memory, for example, the wake of the boat is "like an old mat," and the "slow clapping" of vultures' wings is "like dusty and ragged rugs being shaken." Later, when he is obsessed with keeping the fire low, the vultures wheeling overhead are "like two bits of charred paper tossed up by the draught of a fire." As it is imagined by the characters, the setting helps to describe and explain their motivations. As a stage for playing out a psychological drama, it is nowhere better adapted to the purpose than in the chapter presenting Wright's death. In the topography, the mud hole, and the appearance of the jaguar, the imagery binds character to setting, and the action expresses subconscious desires.

The role of language in shaping the world surfaces as an explicit theme in each stage of the expedition. In the first, Silva speaks in the "voice" of Johnson's father and in the second in the voice of the child within. By a Freudian model, Silva can be understood as the voice of Johnson's ego, at one time speaking out of the superego and at another out of the id. In the third stage of the expedition, when Johnson feels disintegrated, Silva is absent. In this last stage, Johnson and Phillips develop a special camaraderie, complete with its own vocabulary, which the narrator explains at some length. First they coin new words for the essentials of their life—"water" becoming "mud," for example—then they abbreviate them, and then they lapse into nearly total silence. This loss of society, of language, of the vocabulary necessary for cultivating the physical world, parallels Johnson's regression.

As analyzed in *Dead Man Leading*, the desire to explore is masochistic, and masochism arises from the sexual guilt produced by puritanism. Puritanism, Walter Allen has noted, is Pritchett's main study, and in no other book is his recurring theme more evident, yet Pritchett's attitude toward Johnson's puritanism and toward Johnson himself is not clear. Although Johnson behaves ridiculously, he is not treated as a comic character. Indeed, Pritchett creates a good deal of sympathy for him, portraying him as a troubled, possibly even tragic, hero. Certainly, by doing what others cannot do, he is great: He cuts through the world of social convention and conscious activity directly into the world of unadulterated egotism, into the dreamworld where accidents really do make wishes come true. In this sense, Johnson is like Beluncle, an artist of egotism. The general ambivalence of the authorial attitude toward Johnson, however, is probably caused by the thorny subject matter: the relationships among father, mother, and son, which Pritchett eventually mastered in late middle age.

MR. BELUNCLE

It was not until 1951, after a decade of book reviewing and short-story writing, that Pritchett published his next novel. *Mr. Beluncle* is concerned with what he calls in *Midnight Oil* his "obsessive subject": his father. *Dead Man Leading* is concerned with this obsessive subject, too, but the father in question is not drawn directly from Pritchett's own, and it is the son's, not the father's, story. *Mr. Beluncle*, in contrast, presents an unmistakable portrait of Walter Pritchett. Pritchett's manner in this book is not, as it is in *Dead Man Leading*, to approach his subject and character earnestly but to create an attitude, which can be termed "objective sympathy," out of a barbed, epigrammatic wit reminiscent of George Meredith. Both books concern the quality of the individual's imagination and the power of dreaming, but *Mr.*

Beluncle is far superior, its subject and manner being natural to Pritchett's genius and fully under control. Indeed, all of Pritchett's strengths are united in *Mr. Beluncle* to produce what is surely his finest novel.

Compared with *Dead Man Leading*, so like a boy's adventure story, *Mr. Beluncle* is a quiet book. Both books are, in a sense, character studies, but in *Dead Man Leading*, to the extent that it is psychological allegory, the primary means of characterization is action, whereas in *Mr. Beluncle*, it is portraiture. *Mr. Beluncle* works largely through long gazes at Beluncle penetrated by a quick narrative omniscience, through set presentations of monologues and incremental repetition of ritualized behavior, and through a panorama of supporting characters. Many of the minor characters are eccentrics in their own right, but in the narrative, they serve Mr. Beluncle in his fantastic egotism.

Mr. Beluncle occupies two domains, in each of which he possesses a helpmate and a family. At home, it is his wife, Ethel, and his sons, Henry, George, and Leslie. At work, it is his business partner, Mrs. Linda Truslove, his junior partner, Mr. Everard Chilly, and his typist. At home, he is a tyrant, self-complacently moralizing to his family, filling his drawers with expensive clothing while neglecting to give Ethel housekeeping money, and refusing to allow the family members to go out alone or to have friends. A fleshy man himself, he does not want them to leave him because he feels diminished; they are "like vultures pulling his flesh off him." At work, he is a fake, busying himself with writing aphorisms on slips of paper, daydreaming about a new house, issuing commands, and driving the company car over to the showroom. It is in fact Mrs. Truslove who runs the company, who has bought the car, and who has tried to save the business from Beluncle's extravagances.

Mrs. Truslove has been in love with Beluncle for years and subject to his persuasions, but it is not she who basically enables him to live in his house of delusion. That role is reserved for his other "mistress," the Church of the Last Purification. With its easy transcendentalism and its central doctrine that evil is illusion, the religion has enabled him to dismiss as illusory anything unpleasant and to achieve such a degree of self-importance that God, like his family and associates, serves him. "God is a radio station," he asserts in an expansive moment; "God is Supply," in a moment of financial need. His most immediate need, he thinks, is another new house; having heard that in the Father's house are many mansions, he is certain that "one has been prepared" for him. Especially congenial to his sensibility is the church's equating evil and sex. A very clean man married to a somewhat slovenly woman, Beluncle finds it "hard to realize that woman is a Divine Idea." Because his "sexual instinct interfered with the acquisitive," he is gratified by church doctrine, since, as Lady Roads, head of the local church, says, "it takes sex out of love." His way is thus clear to express it more naturally, by using his attractiveness to women (his sister, his mother, Lady Roads, Mrs. Truslove, and Mrs. Robinson, a tearoom manageress) to seduce them out of their money. He manages everything with charm and righteousness, always depending on God, who is (as Mrs. Truslove thinks of it) the "joker in his pack." The story is about the collapse of his house of cards.

Beluncle's huge capacity for dreaming has produced his success to date, but it is the very thing that destroys him in the end. Encouraged to daydream by the transcendental aspect of Purification theology, he ignores factual circumstances. Accountants, for example, amaze him because they actually believe the figures on paper. "You can add it up this way, you can add it up that way and every time you get a different answer," he opines and adds, "As Shakespeare says, it's all in your mind." Mrs. Truslove, though, is one who believes the figures on paper, and because she is finished loving him, signals her intention of withdrawing from the business. At home, he has disappointments too. Chief among them is his son Henry, who without Beluncle's knowledge has fallen in love with the stationmaster's daughter, Mary Phibbs. When Beluncle confronts Henry with the "idea" of Mary, the boy is unable to stand up to him, but, in defeat and humiliation, he flings the more cutting decision at him: He has no intention of entering the business. Thus Beluncle's dream for his son, who would have belonged to him forever and brought him a girl with money for the business, collapses. The more the world submits evidence that his dreams are ashes, however, the harder he clings to them. All that is needed, he thinks, is a miracle to vindicate and save him, so when Judy Dykes, the crippled sister of Mrs. Truslove, is brought to her feet by the verbal assault of a fanatical newspaper vendor, he

launches into a new round of expenditures. Instead of saving him, this miracle completes his ruin. It calls into question the soundness of the Purification, for Judy's recovery is the prelude to her death, and once she is gone, Mrs. Truslove is free to pursue a new life. When Mr. Beluncle receives word of Judy's death, he is prompted to make his first and last speech in his new boardroom, to an imaginary board of directors. He begins by denying the death. "It's a mistake, a dream and—by the way, I'll give you a thought there, where is the dream when you wake up?"

Everyone in *Mr. Beluncle* dreams: Judy Dykes that she will walk, Mrs. Truslove that someday something will come of her love for Beluncle, Henry that he will free himself from his father. Each character attempts to force reality to conform to the dream: Judy Dykes by accumulating fashionable shoes; Mrs. Truslove by using the business as a marriage; Henry by loading the slender figure of Mary Phibbs with his many nameless desires. Judy dies, however, and Mrs. Truslove parts with her desire for Beluncle, which has been "exhausted by the imagination." Henry, who has imitated his father in many respects, observes Mary's reaction to his declaration that he has lost his faith and realizes for the first time that she is "not an extension of himself, but another human being." Everyone wakes up to find the dream gone, except for Mr. Beluncle, who uses language to keep it alive.

If the quality of the individual's dream is the moral topic of the book, then the manner by which language serves the imagination is its aesthetic corollary. Mr. Beluncle's extraordinary force of personality expresses itself by his physical substance and demeanor but also, and more important, by his words. He is a man who likes to roll words in his mouth like fine chocolates and bestow his thoughts on those around him like a king. Never mind that what he says is absurd, his manner convinces. To Mr. Chilly, one of Beluncle's admirable traits is his ability to "make a statement and then appear to lean physically upon it." One thought uttered, he is hoisted to another, word by word exchanging fact for fancy, as if to speak were to make the world anew. To Beluncle, the narrator explains, talking is "a way of turning realities into unrealities," and placing written messages, such as "Eternity = Now," next to letters from creditors is typical of his way of doing business. In various other ways, too, the fundamental connection between dreaming and speaking, image and word, is emphasized. One major way is by the character of Henry, who imitates his father in his love of the creative power of language, especially when he is with Mary Phibbs. To her, he tells stories about his family, improved by an artistic juggling of detail, without noticing that she hates them because of "their importance to him and his pride in them"—because, basically, of their self-centeredness. Other characters, too, spin their wishful accounts of the world.

A second, more symbolic way in which the role of language in projecting the dreamworld surfaces is in two characters who exist primarily as "voices"—a technique Pritchett had practiced in *Dead Man Leading*. One is the youngest Beluncle boy, Leslie, who emerges in the middle of the book to utter the blunt, innermost thoughts of the family, which are ordinarily blurred by Beluncle's rich discourse; the other is Mary's sister. Leslie attaches himself to Henry in one key scene in the garden, and Mary's sister sleeps with her and teases her with the things that Mary is afraid to think directly. Henry and Mary do not, however, give in entirely to this dream voice, as does Harry Johnson. Rather, they hear it along with another one, that of the waking world, and out of the two they harmonize a public voice. Mr. Beluncle, unlike them, is afraid of hearing two voices. He is afraid of the inner voice, because it whispers to him of his own mortality, but he is also afraid of the outer voice, because it denies the complete gratification of his infantile desires. A puritan who has adopted a transcendental explanation of human nature in order to live with himself, he has succeeded, it would seem, in killing one of the voices—exactly which one is moot. It is enough to say that his inner voice has been made public, that his dream is his life. He is thus one-dimensional, hollow, his ego merely an expanding shell.

That Henry hears two voices makes possible a doubling of perspective that will eventually lead him out of egotistic confinement into artistic freedom. Henry is the foil to Beluncle's charlatanry, the nascent artist of the book, and clearly the autobiographical character; what is especially remarkable about the book is that he never nudges Beluncle out of the limelight. For being an autobiographical novel of sorts, and one incorporating elements of comedy, *Mr. Beluncle* is surprisingly unconcerned in any overt way with the triumph of son over father, youth over age. In this, his major study of egotism, Pritchett never forgets that the archetypal egotist in his private imagination is his father. If his earliest desire was to surmount him, then he succeeds in this novel, not by assuming center stage himself, not by painting himself large, but by reducing himself, by exercising the artist's negative capability to create one of the most memorable eccentrics in English literature.

Linda F. Tunick

OTHER MAJOR WORKS

SHORT FICTION: *The Spanish Virgin, and Other Stories*, 1930; *You Make Your Own Life, and Other Stories*, 1938; *It May Never Happen, and Other Stories*, 1945; *Collected Stories*, 1956; *The Sailor, The Sense of Humour, and Other Stories*, 1956 (also known as *The Saint, and Other Stories*, 1966); *When My Girl Comes Home*, 1961; *The Key to My Heart*, 1963; *Blind Love, and Other Stories*, 1969; *The Camberwell Beauty, and Other Stories*, 1974; *The Fly in the Ointment*, 1978; *Selected Stories*, 1978; *On the Edge of the Cliff*, 1979; *Collected Stories*, 1982; *More Collected Stories*, 1983; *A Careless Widow, and Other Stories*, 1989; *Complete Collected Stories*, 1990.

NONFICTION: *Marching Spain*, 1928; *In My Good Books*, 1942; *The Living Novel and Later Appreciations*, 1946; *Why Do I Write? An Exchange of Views Between Elizabeth Bowen, Graham Greene, and V. S. Pritchett*, 1948; *Books in General*, 1953; *The Spanish Temper*, 1954; *London Perceived*, 1962; *The Offensive Traveller*, 1964 (also known as *Foreign Faces*); *New York Proclaimed*, 1965; *Shakespeare: The Comprehensive Soul*, 1965; *The Working Novelist*, 1965; *Dublin: A Portrait*, 1967; *A Cab at the Door*, 1968; *George Meredith and English Comedy*, 1970; *Midnight Oil*, 1972; *Balzac: A Biography*, 1973; *The Gentle Barbarian: The Life and Work of Turgenev*, 1977; *The Myth Makers: Literary Essays*, 1979; *The Tale Bearers: Literary Essays*, 1980; *The Other Side of the Frontier: A V. S. Pritchett Reader*, 1984; *A Man of Letters*, 1985; *Chekhov: A Spirit Set Free*, 1988; *Lasting Impressions*, 1990; *The Complete Essays*, 1991.

MISCELLANEOUS: *The Pritchett Century*, 1997.

BIBLIOGRAPHY

Angell, Roger. "Marching Life." *The New Yorker* 73 (December 22-29, 1997): 126-134. Offers commentary on Pritchett along with a biographical sketch. Contends that although Pritchett was called First Man of Letters, the title never fit properly because he was neither literary nor a stylist, and he liked to say he was a hack long before he was a critic.

Baldwin, Dean. *V. S. Pritchett*. Boston: Twayne, 1987. Slim volume contains a superb short biography of Pritchett followed by a clear-cut analysis of his novels, short stories, and nonfiction. Includes bibliography and index.

Pritchett, V. S. "An Interview with V. S. Pritchett." Interview by Ben Forkner and Philippe Sejourne. *Journal of the Short Story in English* 6 (1986): 11-38. Interview in a question-and-answer format provides a straightforward record of Pritchett's views. The author reveals a number of salient details about his opinions on writing in general and the influences on his work of authors such as H. G. Wells and Arnold Bennett. He discusses at length the Irish predilection for storytelling and Irish ideas about morality and the art of concealment and also reveals his penchant for the ironic and pays homage to Anton Chekhov, one of his models. Pritchett notes that he believes that the comic is really a facet of the poetic.

Stinson, John J. *V. S. Pritchett: A Study of the Short Fiction*. New York: Twayne, 1992. Introduction to Pritchett's short fiction suggests that the author's stories have been largely ignored by critics because they do not have the symbolic image pattern favored by formalist critics. Provides interpretations of a number of Pritchett's stories as well as essays on his short fiction by Eudora Welty and William Trevor. Also includes Pritchett's own comments on writers who have influenced him.

Theroux, Paul. "V. S. Pritchett." *The New York Times Book Review*, May 25, 1997. Biographical tribute notes that Pritchett worked slowly and with confidence. Asserts that Pritchett was probably the last man who could be called a man of letters.

Treglown, Jeremy. *V. S. Pritchett: A Working Life*. New York: Random House, 2004. Admiring and engaging biography examines both the breadth of Pritchett's literary production and the highs and lows of his personal life.

FREDERIC PROKOSCH

Born: Madison, Wisconsin; May 17, 1908
Died: Plan de Grasse, France; June 2, 1989

PRINCIPAL LONG FICTION

The Asiatics, 1935
The Seven Who Fled, 1937
Night of the Poor, 1939
The Skies of Europe, 1941
The Conspirators, 1943
Age of Thunder, 1945
The Idols of the Cave, 1946
Storm and Echo, 1948
Nine Days to Mukalla, 1953
A Tale for Midnight, 1955
A Ballad of Love, 1960
The Seven Sisters, 1962
The Dark Dancer, 1964
The Wreck of the Cassandra, 1966
The Missolonghi Manuscript, 1968
America, My Wilderness, 1972

OTHER LITERARY FORMS

Frederic Prokosch (proh-KAWSH) published five books of poetry. Some of his poems enjoyed a transitory popularity and appeared in anthologies, notably those of Oscar Williams. In addition, he translated the love sonnets of Louise Labé in 1947, some of the poetry of Friedrich Hölderlin in 1943, and Euripides' *Medea* (431 B.C.E.) in 1947.

Many of the poems in Prokosch's first collection, *The*

Assassins (1936), celebrate places and journeys and aspire to create an exotic mood. The collection also contains one of his most anthologized poems, "The Dolls," where Prokosch writes at his musical best of the sweet, crescent-eyed shapes that, reaching into the poet's "secret night," become the "furies" of his sleep. Dylan Thomas later parodied this poem, giving to his own poem the title "The Molls."

Prokosch's second volume of poems, *The Carnival* (1938), depends less on the dazzling imagery of geography and more on the ordinary things of life and was an attempt, according to the author, to convey the darkness of the prewar decade, as in "Fable," where the "rippled snow is tracked with blood,/ And my love lies cold in the burning wood." The volume contains a long, autobiographical "Ode" that describes the phases of Prokosch's first thirty years of life and his various discoveries (of fairy tales, his body, the past, Asia). His "Nocturne," beginning "Close my darling both your eyes,/ Let your arm lie still at last," shares similarities with W. H. Auden's well-known poem "Lay your sleeping head, my love,/ Human on my faithless arm."

The poems contained in *Death at Sea* (1940) concern the plight of the individual in a chaotic world. In "The Festival," for example, a pair of lovers who are apparently homosexual note the "coming tempest" and follow "Silent the paths of longing and regret/ Which all our learning taught us to despise"; the poem is set against a backdrop of earrings trembling in the dark and fairies huddling by a bridge.

Reviewers were not kind to Prokosch the poet, and time itself has been still less kind. Although he assembled an anthology, *Chosen Poems*, in 1944, it was not until 1983 that he published his next volume of verse, *The Sea*, a collection of sonnets that once again reflects Prokosch's fascination with geography. Finally, in 1983, Prokosch published his memoirs, *Voices*, a series of vignettes in which many of the literary giants of the twentieth century appear in a decidedly unheroic light.

ACHIEVEMENTS

Frederic Prokosch is said to have created the novel of geography, a distillate of the reflective travelogue. More than half of his sixteen novels fall into this category, and even those that do not are dominated in some way by the theme of geography and involve cosmopolitan, travel-loving characters. With the publication of his first novel, *The Asiatics*, in 1935, a book highlighted by Asian scenes and attitudes when other American novelists were writing realistic novels set in their own country, Prokosch achieved instant fame and maintained a high reputation for approximately the next ten years. William Butler Yeats was deeply struck by Prokosch's poetic gifts, and André Gide, Thomas Mann, and Albert Camus all praised his works during his stellar decade. Even his later works were praised by W. Somerset Maugham, Thornton Wilder, and Marianne Moore.

The Asiatics, which was translated into seventeen foreign languages and was even more popular in Europe than in the United States, would remain in print for more than fifty years. *The Seven Who Fled* won the Harper Novel Prize, awarded by a panel of judges consisting of Wilder, Sinclair Lewis, and Louis Bromfield. In 1944, Warner Bros. released a film adaptation of *The Conspirators* starring Hedy Lamarr and Paul Henreid.

Radcliffe Squires observed that Prokosch's recurring theme—the death-defying search for truth in travel—began to seem irrelevant to a postwar generation looking for stability in suburbia. Subsequently, his novels were not so much condemned by the critics as they were ignored. Nevertheless, no complete discussion of twentieth century literature can afford to gloss over the fictional subgenre—the novel of geography—pioneered by the wunderkind Prokosch.

BIOGRAPHY

Frederic Prokosch was born in Madison, Wisconsin, on May 17, 1908, the middle child of three children born to Eduard and Mathilde Depprich Prokosch. His father, who had left Austria to escape a duel, was professor of Germanic philology at the University of Wisconsin, and his mother was an accomplished pianist. In 1913, Eduard Prokosch assumed a position at the University of Texas at Austin, which he lost six years later as a result of the anti-German hysteria that followed World War I.

Prokosch was sent in 1914 to spend a year in Europe, visiting his grandfather in Austria and attending private schools there and in Munich. His Austrian-Slavic-Germanic ancestry and his early acquaintance with European culture encouraged Prokosch's cosmopolitan spirit and love for geography. As a child, he developed an interest in fairy tales, and this he credits for his fascination as a novelist with picaresque and allegorical characters who strive inexorably for fulfillment.

In 1920, the family moved to Bryn Mawr, where Prokosch attended high school; in 1922, he entered Haverford College. In college, he became an athlete, particularly in tennis and squash, which he continued to play for years to come; he won the national squash championship of France in 1939 and that of Sweden in 1944. An avid lepidopterist, in later years he became as dexterous wielding his butterfly net as he had been with a racket.

After receiving his first master's degree from Haverford in 1928, Prokosch proceeded to earn a second one from King's College, Cambridge, in 1930. Two years later, he earned his doctorate at Yale. While a doctoral student, Prokosch taught English (from 1931 to 1933), continuing as a research fellow in 1934. The following year, *The Asiatics* appeared, and he returned to England, later visiting Africa and Asia. In 1936 and 1937, he was teaching at New York University, but when in 1937 he received both a Guggenheim Fellowship and the Harper Novel Prize of seventy-five hundred dollars, he abandoned teaching altogether. He was then at the apogee of his renown as a writer, and he could write from Prague in 1937 that one of his main interests was "trying to avoid the vulgarizations of money and publicity." Ironically, the vagaries of the reading public would facilitate this goal considerably in coming years.

After the fall of France, Prokosch spent two years in Lisbon, which served as the setting for *The Conspirators*. When the United States entered World War II, Prokosch returned home to enter government service in the Office of War Information and then spent two years (1943 to 1944) as an attache in the American Legation in Stockholm, Sweden. After the war, he went to Rome (1947 to 1953), where, on a Fulbright scholarship (1951 to 1952), he researched in the Vatican Library the material for his first attempt at a historical novel, *A Tale for Midnight*, about the Renaissance Cenci family.

The 1960's found Prokosch living in Paris; he finally settled in Grasse in the south of France. He continued his writing—now largely ignored by critics—and indulged his interest in rare books. Between 1968 and 1970, he

Frederic Prokosch. (Library of Congress)

printed and bound a series of elegant gift books, each containing a single poem by a well-known modern writer; these books' imprints dated the printing between 1933 and 1940, making them collectors' items. Eventually, Nicolas Barker exposed these "self-forgeries" and Prokosch admitted to the books' late date. Prokosch died in June, 1989, in Plan de Grasse, France.

ANALYSIS

Frederic Prokosch was a lover of travel and even of maps themselves. In *America, My Wilderness*, he defines the place-name as a "talisman that guides us through the terror of anonymity," and his novelist's fascination with place-names is, at its best, lyrical and evocative, at its worst, pedantic and tedious. It follows that such a lover of the places of this world would be a proponent of internationalism, and in most of his novels written after 1940, Prokosch urged his American readers to abandon their isolationism and to nurture links and bonds with the other peoples of the world.

All of Prokosch's fiction is an attempt in some way to probe the spiritual malaise characteristic of the twentieth century. In his novels of the 1930's, there is an abiding, non-Western fatalism. A sense of impending doom for the world saturates *The Asiatics* as the natives philosophize to the young American traveler about the resignation implicit in the Asian personality. This doom is counterbalanced by the lyrical nature of the writing and by the luxuriance of detail, however, and the beguiling, unutterable beauty of life strains to prevail even in these prewar novels. When the fear and foreboding of the 1930's was eventually replaced by worldwide optimism after the war, the tenor of Prokosch's novels changed in tune with the times. In *Storm and Echo*, the emphasis is on Africa as a new continent rather than on Asia as a dying one, and the hint of a positive note in the destiny of humankind is unmistakable.

THE ASIATICS

In the picaresque narrative of *The Asiatics*, the nameless young American hero crosses the entire Asian continent from Lebanon to China. The character of the hero is elusive and vague, and many of the secondary characters with whom he forms friendships—friendships that are sometimes intense but always temporary—seem to take on more life than he. The hero is jailed in Turkey and suffers a plane crash in Iran, but always keeps his mind open and unbiased in order to soak up all the aphorisms proffered him both by the Asians and by the Western travelers whom he encounters. There is a chillingly prophetic mood to the novel; Asia is old and tired and waiting for death. When the hero enters a snowy-domed *dagoba* in Kandy and begins to converse with an old monk, it is of the coming of the twenty-fifth Buddha and of the accompanying dissolution of the world into Nirvana that they speak. The novel never ceases to analyze and emphasize the decadence and resignation of the enigma that is Asia.

THE SEVEN WHO FLED

In *The Seven Who Fled*, Prokosch weaves an allegory around a group of seven travelers, each representing a country in Europe (England, France, Spain, Germany, Austria, Belgium, and Russia), set adrift in the hostile vastness of Chinese Turkestan. After their caravan reaches Aqsu from Kashgar, the two German-speaking geologists are put into prison by local authorities; two others are kept as hostages; the Frenchman de la Scaze

falls prey to a fever. Only the Englishman Layeville and de la Scaze's beautiful Spanish wife are free to proceed; the former joins a caravan to Tibet, and the latter continues eastward on a caravan in the company of Dr. Liu, a wealthy Chinese merchant. Much of the first half of the book details the disintegration and eventual death of Layeville in the icy summits of Tibet. In his relationship with the barbaric and tantalizing Tansang, his Turgot guide whose powerful face combines the strengths of "a young man, a woman and a child," Layeville feels the possibility of a renewal of his spirit, but he loses his last chance when Tansang dies.

Like Layeville and Tansang, the hostages back in Aqsu, the Russian Serafimov (an inarticulate bear of a man) and the Belgian thief Goupilliere, form an uneasy pair. When Serafimov is rejected by the Russian prostitute Madame Tastin while his companion Goupilliere is accepted, Serafimov consummates his hatred for the Belgian by murdering him. The two geologists, the German Wildenbruch (who worships heroism and ambition) and the blond, angelic Austrian Von Wald, escape from prison together and travel to Shanghai, where the tubercular Wildenbruch departs for home and Von Wald decides to remain. The last pair, the most mismatched of all, are Paul and Olivia de la Scaze. Olivia, who abandons her husband in Aqsu, comes under the complete control of Dr. Liu and ends up joining a house of prostitution in Shanghai. Paul recovers from his fever, eventually catches cholera from a dancing girl, and dies.

Although the seven characters do not correspond exactly to the seven cardinal sins of medieval theology, each sin is very much in evidence. Certainly sloth is implied in the flight of the seven from the responsibilities of their European lives to the distractions of adventure abroad. Lust is evident in Layeville's reminiscences of homosexuality, in Olivia's eventual choice of occupation, and in Serafimov's obsession with Madame Tastin. Wildenbruch feels envy for the innocence of Von Wald, and only Von Wald seems relatively immune to the ravages of the deadly sins.

NINE DAYS TO MUKALLA

Nine Days to Mukalla is the story of four plane-crash survivors who make their way from an island in the Indian Ocean to Mukalla in Arabia (now Saudi Arabia, Yemen, and the Persian Gulf states), where they will be able to get a boat for Aden and return to civilization. The novel employs the rich, evocative style that characterizes Prokosch's best work and allegorizes the contrasting sensibilities of the four victims lost in a mysterious Arabia, which, in its capacity to distill good and evil, "reveals the human skeleton."

The group is composed of two Englishwomen, Miss Todd and Sylvia Howard; and two Americans, an archaeologist, Dr. Moss, and David Gilbert, who is the only survivor by the end of the novel. David, described by Miss Todd as not quite a typical American, seems symbolic of a new, postwar, cosmopolitan America. Miss Todd, although she dies early in the narrative, possesses such great vitality that her spirit persists throughout the novel. It is the gift of her jewelry to David that enables him to reach Mukalla successfully. Dr. Moss is Miss Todd's foil, and just as the party's Bedouin guide thinks of Miss Todd as their good spirit, Moss is viewed by him as their bad spirit. He steals some of Miss Todd's jewels, abandons the party in his own interest, and is finally murdered in the desert. The primness of Sylvia Howard, the sketchiest of the four characters, is broken down in the Arabian desert, and before she dies of exhaustion when she actually reaches Mukalla, she asks David to make love to her.

THE SEVEN SISTERS

The Seven Sisters is Prokosch's first novel in which an American setting (Bishop's Neck, Maryland) is handled as powerfully as the foreign settings are in his earlier works. Each of the seven Nightingale sisters has a story, and the story of each sheds light on the character of Peter, an orphan who lives with the family. Peter is another of Prokosch's searching artists, but this time, untypically for Prokosch, his search ends in a kind of maturity. Five of the seven sisters, after frantic struggles, gradually achieve a kind of maturity as well.

The death of one of the sisters, young Elizabeth, who succumbs to a snakebite while still innocent, signals the real start of the action of the novel, suggesting a world divested of its innocence. The oldest sister, the repressed Augusta, marries a neighboring aristocrat, recognizes that the marriage is a mistake, and returns to her parents' home. Daphne leaves home dressed as a boy, falls in with a lesbian, meets a runaway New Yorker named Pancho, loses him to another man and to death, rejects

the lesbian, and returns home. The elfin and visionary Grace never leaves home, but follows the advice of a ouija board, becomes pregnant, and goes to a cave, where she dies in the act of childbirth.

Consuelo, Barbara, and Freya, in the company of Peter and their mother, go to Europe. Consuelo links up with a Hungarian refugee. Blond, beautiful Barbara marries a wealthy, aging Italian prince, falls in love with his handsome nephew, and ends up, after losing both, praying for forgiveness for her vanity and pride. Freya gives up her career as a painter and goes to Brazil as a social worker, where she perishes in the jungle. It is the character of Peter that acts as the cohesive force in the novel; it is with him that the novel begins and ends.

THE SKIES OF EUROPE

The Skies of Europe is Prokosch's first realistic novel and covers the events that led up to World War II. Philip, a young American journalist, loves Saskia, a failed artist who does not love him. The novel abounds in characters who are unsuccessful artists and neglected poets; one such unnamed character seems intended to represent Adolf Hitler. *The Skies of Europe* has affinities with a later novel, *A Ballad of Love,* Prokosch's most nearly autobiographical novel, his "portrait of the artist as a young man." It is, moreover, a portrait of a defeated artist. The hero, Henry, is a poet who grows up in Austria, Texas, and Wisconsin and becomes involved in a disastrous love affair similar to those in *The Skies of Europe* and *The Idols of the Cave.*

STORM AND ECHO

Storm and Echo follows the pattern of Prokosch's first two novels, and the landscape of Africa is even more brilliantly painted than that of Asia in his earlier novels. There is a Conradian power in this tale of an American's search for a mysterious friend who has gone off to Mount Nagala. Central Africa is typically fraught with dangers of all kinds, but the friend is found (albeit as a corpse impaled upon a rock), and the protagonist emerges victorious over his own death wish.

THE WRECK OF THE CASSANDRA

The Wreck of the Cassandra is similar to *Nine Days to Mukalla* but lacks the latter's allegorical sweep. Here, nine survivors of a shipwreck somewhere between Hong Kong and Australia reach a large island and settle down idyllically for a short time before the spirit of the island distills their personalities into various shades of good and evil. The presence of hostile natives adds to the tensions in the group, they confront one another violently, and some of their number are lost before their inevitable rescue.

WORLD WAR II NOVELS

Three of Prokosch's novels are set against the backdrop of World War II. *Night of the Poor*, the title of which was taken from a painting by Diego Rivera, is perhaps the author's weakest novel and amounts to little more than a conventional travelogue. It is the first of Prokosch's novels that has an American setting, and American place-names are savored and enumerated to such an extent that they tax the reader's patience. The plot chronicles the travels of Tom on his way to Texas after the death of an uncle in Wisconsin, and the gamut of depravity and inhumanity that he encounters on the way.

Thirty-three years later, Prokosch would rework the same idea in *America, My Wilderness*, dressing it up with generous amounts of Surrealism and modernistic bizarrerie. After the murder of his uncle in the Midwest, a half-black outcast named Pancho Krauss wanders from the Atlantic to the Pacific, savoring the "slow transition of one landscape into another."

Prokosch is destined to be remembered, if not as a great novelist, as a pioneer of the novel of geography and as an internationalist. He focused on the exotica of far-away lands but always called his fellow Americans to abandon their parochialism and recognize the underlying unity of humankind.

Jack Shreve

OTHER MAJOR WORKS

POETRY: *The Carnival: Poems*, 1938; *Death at Sea: Poems*, 1940; *Chosen Poems*, 1944; *The Sea*, 1983.

NONFICTION: *Voices: A Memoir*, 1983.

TRANSLATIONS: *Some Poems of Friedrich Hölderlin*, 1943; *Love Sonnets of Louise Labé*, 1947; *Medea*, 1947 (in *Greek Plays in Modern Translation*, Dudley Fitts, editor).

BIBLIOGRAPHY

Austen, Roger. *Playing the Game: The Homosexual Novel in America*. Indianapolis, Ind.: Bobbs-Merrill, 1977. Contains a useful discussion of Prokosch and his works, situating him in the context of twentieth century American literature about homosexuality. Includes a bibliography and an index.

Carpenter, Richard C. "The Novels of Frederic Prokosch." *College English* 18 (1957): 261-267. Provides much insight into the development of Prokosch's novelistic style. An appreciative essay by a sympathetic critic of Prokosch.

Iyer, Pico. "The Perfect Traveler." *The New York Review of Books*, November 18, 2004. This portrait of Prokosch focuses on *The Asiatics*, describing how Prokosch came to write the novel and examining its plot and its critical and popular reception. Iyer, a noted writer of place-related works, situates *The Asiatics* within the context of Prokosch's life and literary career.

Squires, Radcliffe. *Frederic Prokosch*. New York: Twayne, 1964. Presents Prokosch's works in a chronological format and is useful as a critical introduction. Squires focuses on the timeless qualities of "interplay of emotion and intellect" in Prokosch's work but acknowledges that his writing was a "casualty" of World War II, which changed the values of the reading public. A selected bibliography is provided.

FRANCINE PROSE

Born: Brooklyn, New York; April 1, 1947

PRINCIPAL LONG FICTION

Judah the Pious, 1973
The Glorious Ones, 1974
Marie Laveau, 1977
Animal Magnetism, 1978
Household Saints, 1981
Hungry Hearts, 1983
Bigfoot Dreams, 1986
Primitive People, 1992
Hunters and Gatherers, 1995
Guided Tours of Hell: Novellas, 1997 (includes
    Guided Tours of Hell and *Three Pigs in Five
    Days*)
Blue Angel, 2000
A Changed Man, 2005
Goldengrove, 2008

OTHER LITERARY FORMS

Francine Prose is a prolific writer who, in addition to her novels, has published critically acclaimed short stories, translations, children's books, collections of Jewish folktales, and essays that explore topics that range widely from art history and the power of writing to gluttony. Over the course of her career as a writer, Prose has published articles, stories, and book reviews in numerous magazines and journals as diverse as *Hudson Review*, *The Atlantic Monthly*, *The New Yorker*, *People*, *Redbook*, *The New York Times Book Review*, *The New Republic*, *Yale Review*, and *Art News*, among others. She has written several novels for young adults, including *After* (2003) and *Bullyville* (2007), which deal with the pervasiveness of violence in American society and explore themes of power, authority, and security.

Prose has contributed to Oxford University Press's series of books on the seven deadly sins with the satiric volume *Gluttony* (2003), and her books *Caravaggio: Painter of Miracles* (2005) and *The Lives of the Muses: Nine Women and the Artists They Inspired* (2002) not only offer powerful insights into artists and their worlds but also provide moving meditations on the nature of art and on the little-explored role of women in the history of art. In *Reading Like a Writer: A Guide for People Who Love Books and for Those Who Want to Write Them* (2006), Prose invites readers to explore with her the writings of Jane Austen, Marcel Proust, Charles Dickens, Gustave Flaubert, and others as a way of demonstrating that becoming a good writer requires being a close and observant reader. Prose's nonfiction is marked by the same close observation of the world that characterizes her novels.

ACHIEVEMENTS

From the beginning of her career, Francine Prose has been critically acclaimed as a splendid writer and often regarded by critics as a prophet for her wise and deep social observation. She has won four Pushcart Prizes for her short stories, and many of her books, novels and nonfiction, have been national best sellers. Her first novel, *Judah the Pious*, was awarded the Jewish Book Council Award for 1973. Two years later, in 1975, she was *Mademoiselle* magazine's Mademoiselle Award winner and was recognized as one of "Twelve Women Working to Make Things Better" in an article accompanying the announcement of the award.

Prose often gets her inspiration from her travels, and in 1989 she was awarded a Fulbright grant for travel to Yugoslavia. She won grants from the National Endowment for the Arts in 1979 and 1985, and she received a Guggenheim Fellowship in 1991. Her contribution to children's literature was recognized when she received the Sydney Taylor Award for books for younger children. Prose's novel *Blue Angel* was a finalist for the National Book Award in 2000, and her young adult novel *After* was nominated for the Los Angeles Times Book Prize in 2003. Prose was awarded the first Dayton Literary Peace Prize in fiction for her novel *A Changed Man* in 2006. The film adaptation of her novel *Household Saints*, starring Tracey Ullman and directed by Nancy Savoca, was released in 1993.

BIOGRAPHY

Francine Prose began reading when she was four years old and never stopped. She has told numerous interviewers that the only reason she wanted to become a writer was that she was such an avid reader and that she could not imagine any other career. Born on April 1, 1947, in Brooklyn, New York, to two physicians, Philip Prose and Jessie Rubin Prose, the young Francine grew up listening to her father discuss medical cases with his colleagues. She learned the knack of narrative storytelling from these sessions, and she also learned how to be closely observant of details from her parents. In addition, she developed her keen ear and eye by paying close attention to the lives of her family's neighbors and to the larger social world in which she grew up.

Prose graduated summa cum laude with a bachelor's degree in English in 1968 from Radcliffe College. In 1969, she entered an M.A. program at Harvard, but she soon grew tired of the claustrophobic atmosphere there. In 1971, she left the program to travel for almost a year in Bombay (now Mumbai), India, where she read the classic novels of authors from Fyodor Dostoevski to Marcel Proust. During that year, she scrapped the autobiographical novel on which she had been working and started writing what would become her first published novel, *Judah the Pious*. After that novel appeared, her career as a writer was launched, and she never looked back, producing a new book almost every three years and also writing articles and stories.

In 1976, Prose married Howard "Howie" Michaels, an artist and sculptor. The couple's first son, Bruno, was born in 1978, and their second, Leon, was born in 1982. After Leon's birth, Prose embarked on a teaching career, and, between 1982 and 1989, she taught at the University of Arizona, the Iowa Writers' Workshop, Sarah Lawrence College, the Bread Loaf Writers' Conference, and the Sewanee Writers' Conference. During these years she continued to write and publish novels, including *Household Saints*, *Hungry Hearts*, and *Bigfoot Dreams*. In 1999, Prose was a director's fellow at the New York Public Library's Center for Scholars and Writers, and she has been a fellow of the New York Institute of the Humanities. She continues to teach and has

Francine Prose. (© Miriam Berkley)

held the position of visiting professor of literature at Bard College. In 2007, she became president of the PEN/American Center in New York.

ANALYSIS

In her book *Reading Like a Writer*, Francine Prose provides some insights into her own life as a writer as she analyzes the writings of other writers she admires. Reading and rereading writers whom she loves—Dostoevski, Flaubert, Austen, Dickens, Philip Roth, Franz Kafka—Prose admits that writing, like reading, puts every word on trial for its life. Much as she reads her favorite writers closely for the ways they use words and language, in writing her own novels Prose weighs every word, every phrase, for the way it tells the story, the way it expresses emotions, the way it shocks or surprises a reader, the way it elicits a snicker or a belly laugh, the way it haunts the spirit, or the way it evokes the beauty of the world and the human soul.

In her early fiction, such as *Judah the Pious*, Prose

turned a folklorist's eye to the stories of rabbis and their families that she retold in her fiction. She preserved the traditions of these folktales by weaving colorful narratives of the modern world around them. While she has never abandoned the use of these tales in her fiction (she has published several books of them for children), her later novels have focused on the modern world. *Bigfoot Dreams*, for example, features Vera (whose name means "truth"), a writer for a supermarket tabloid who composes stories about UFO sightings, Elvis Presley's being alive and well on Mars, and a ninety-one-year-old woman bearing a child; the novel explores the challenges that writing such fictions presents to Vera's real life. In almost all of Prose's novels, the characters struggle to distinguish between the real world and imaginary worlds, worlds they have very often created for themselves as places of retreat from the real world. In both *Blue Angel* and *Goldengrove*, the main characters often delude themselves about their real lives and create for themselves, if only momentarily, alternate universes in which they feel safe and secure. Much like Kafka, Prose creates a universe in which life is often turned upside down with no reason and in which men and women must right themselves in order to move through life.

Prose's novels also often deal with the spiritual. *Judah the Pious* follows the adventures of the Polish Rabbi Eliezer and his attempts to help his people. *Marie Laveau* chronicles the life of the great New Orleans voodoo queen and her magic. In *Hunters and Gatherers*, Prose narrates the exploits of New Age priestess Isis Moonwagon and her followers, and *Household Saints* recounts the story of a Catholic family striving to understand the ways in which the spiritual impinges on the ordinary. Through the use of satire and comedy, Prose explores the spiritual longings of human beings and their attempts to reconcile those longings with everyday life. Prose's sharp and cunning long fiction provides incisive glimpses into various situations, reflecting the humor, the sorrow, and the pathos in human lives.

HOUSEHOLD SAINTS

Like many of Prose's early writings, *Household Saints* weaves elements of folklore and legend into a tale of revelation and hope. In this stunning novel, Prose captures the intensity of family life lived in close quarters as well as the details that shape the everyday lives of the mem-

bers of a close-knit social community. Her prose evokes the smells, sights, and sounds of Little Italy in New York in the 1950's so that the setting becomes as much of a character in the novel as the men and women who live on the neighborhood's streets. This splendid little morality tale, as many critics have observed, is reminiscent of the powerful stories of Isak Dinesen and Isaac Bashevis Singer. The novel offers readers a study in character and confronts readers with troublesome questions about the nature of evil, the character of the good, and the promise of hope. Above all, it asks readers to consider the ways in which human beings' mundane lives can be transformed by ancient ways and by something beyond themselves.

The novel opens with the startling and comic assertion that Joseph Santangelo has won his wife, by the grace of God, in a game of pinochle. As in most of the rest of his life, Joseph, a butcher in Little Italy, has had to depend on some power outside himself to help him navigate life's waters. Since he often discovers that little help is forthcoming from those quarters, he cheats his customers at his butcher shop and he cheats at cards. Joseph's mother sees evil in every aspect of the world around her and prays to her saints for good health and wealth from the sausages that her son sells in his store. Joseph's wife, Catherine, is caught between the old world and the new as she tries to teach her daughter, Theresa, the lessons of the saints of old and the lessons the girl will need to survive in the modern world. Theresa, much like her namesake, Theresa of Avila, does discover the ways in which the mundane is infused with the sacred. Although the novel ends in surprising ways, the events depicted confirm that the veneration of everyday objects can keep alive the memory of those household saints who have graced our lives.

Household Saints depicts one family's struggles to reconcile the ordinary and the extraordinary, in this case, the spiritual. Prose offers readers a beautiful little morality tale of despair and hope, loss and redemption, and family and society.

A CHANGED MAN

What happens when a former skinhead walks into a human rights organization and declares that he is a changed man? What happens when this young man declares that he wants to help prevent other young men from making the choices he made in the past? Should the organization be extremely wary and suspicious that the newly changed individual is lying, or should the organization and its founders embrace this person and allow him to work to bring about good in the world? In her typically satiric fashion, Prose raises these and other questions in her often hilarious, and always bitingly incisive, novel *A Changed Man*.

One spring afternoon, young Vincent walks into the offices of World Brotherhood Watch, a human rights organization run by Meyer Maslow, a Holocaust survivor. Vincent, a former neo-Nazi whose arms are covered with Nazi tattoos, claims to have been transformed and wants to change his life. Vincent tells Maslow that he would like to convince other young men not to choose the life of a neo-Nazi but instead to choose a life of moderation and charity. Can Maslow afford to believe him? Vincent appears at a time in Maslow's life when Maslow himself is beginning to question his own effectiveness at stopping intolerance and injustice. As the plot progresses, Vincent begins to transform everyone around him. Much like Albert Camus's Dr. Rieux in *La Peste* (1947; *The Plague*, 1948), Vincent transforms the world around him through his actions and his active commitment to social justice. He is no mere cheerleader for the right ways; rather, he leads others to perform those right actions. Maslow himself is eventually transformed and regains and renews his dedication to bringing an end to anti-Semitism and intolerance. Bonnie Kalen, the fundraiser for the organization, who has been devoted to Maslow over the years, warily eyes Vincent from the beginning but is won over by his commitment and honesty. Bonnie's son, Danny, also changes his life after an encounter with Vincent.

With her characteristic humor, Prose raises challenging questions about human nature and the nature of the world. Is it possible to overcome evil? Is it possible to change for the good and for that change to last and to influence the lives of others? What is the nature of morality? What does it mean to be human? How can one determine what it means to live a moral life? Prose couches these questions in a fast-paced, satiric narrative that asks readers to consider how they live their own lives.

BLUE ANGEL

From Kingsley Amis's *Lucky Jim* (1954) and Lionel Trilling's *The Middle of the Journey* (1947) to Randall

Jarrell's *Pictures from an Institution* (1954) and Richard Russo's *Straight Man* (1997), the academic novel has often comically portrayed the ways in which power relations between professors and students go awry. Most of the main characters in these novels are older males who take advantage of younger female students who have become enamored of them. These professors find themselves losing not only their sexual fire but also their desire for the subjects about which they were once passionate. Prose's *Blue Angel* joins the rank of these campus novels, but her novel is more than simply a story about the lust of an older professor for a younger student; it revolves around themes of loneliness and insecurity. In this work Prose also explores the banality of an educational system that at once encourages such relationships by the passions inherent in its very structure and condemns these dynamic relationships through static sets of rules that do not account for human passions.

Ted Swenson, a professor of creative writing at a small, rural New England college, is going through the motions of teaching and writing. It has been years since he has written a novel, and his fame has steadily declined as his name has disappeared from the bookstore shelves. His new class is more frustrating than exciting, and most of his students are writing stories about having sex with dead animals. Living with his wife in an isolated wooded area near the campus and estranged from his only child, Swenson exists in a bubble, striving vainly now and then to work on a new novel and to impart some wisdom to his students. His life is revived by one of those students, Angela Argo, a purple-haired waif whose own novel seduces Swenson with its mature prose and its depiction of a relationship between an older man and a younger woman. As Angela seeks his help with her novel, Swenson becomes more and more entangled in a web of lust and infatuation. Filled with stereotypical characters from a college campus—the haughty dean, the feminist English professor, the English professor who tried to live as if his real life were determined by the elements of literary theory—*Blue Angel* is a compelling satire of academic novels as well as an examination of loss and loneliness.

Prose ingeniously takes Josef von Sternberg's 1930 movie *The Blue Angel*, starring Marlene Dietrich, as the model for her campus novel. In the film, an older professor becomes so enamored of a burlesque dancer that he loses everything. In Prose's novel, Swenson watches this film over and over for some clue to his own demise and ponders how one man can so easily lose everything in the quest for the unreachable. Unlike other campus novels, Prose's novel astutely explores the challenges of life in an artificial environment such as a college campus and the foibles of the men and women who live there.

GOLDENGROVE

Coming of age in a small town where everyone knows your every move is hard enough to do, but coming of age in such an environment grows even harder when you must face that experience without your best friend, who has died unexpectedly. Such is the life that thirteen-year-old Nico must face in Prose's novel *Goldengrove*. One Sunday in early May, Nico and her older sister, Margaret, are spending the afternoon lazily drifting on Mirror Lake, as they have on many Sunday afternoons before. The novel's opening sentence almost warns of the ominous events to follow, for Nico reflects that for many years her and her sister's lives were as calm and transparent as the waters. On this Sunday afternoon, the waters open to swallow Margaret forever—she drowns while making the short swim back to the dock near their house. Suddenly, Nico must navigate life's rough waters alone, and she struggles to understand the mysteries of life and death that have left her alone and that have snatched her sister from her.

Nico's mother escapes into drugs and drink as she tries to blunt her feelings of loss, and Nico's father, who runs a bookstore called Goldengrove in their town, retreats into his attempts to write a novel about an apocalyptic religious sect. Both parents are so engrossed in their own grief that neither can help Nico with her own struggles. Seeking refuge from the tragedy that has changed her life, Nico starts to hang around with Margaret's boyfriend, Aaron, as both of them try to grow closer to her dead sister. In a summer full of halting attempts to recover from her monumental loss, Nico learns about the inadequacy of love, the disappointments of hope, the shortcomings of family and friends, and the insufficiency of both emotional and rational responses to loss.

Prose wrote *Goldengrove* as her own mother was dying (the novel is dedicated to her) and as she was struggling with her own losses. The novel takes its name from Gerard Manley Hopkins's poem "Spring and Fall: To a Young Child," which features a young woman whose mourning over the falling of leaves in Goldengrove is actually a mourning over the loss of her youth. Prose effectively uses this poem as a springboard into an extended meditation on a young girl's realization that she is alone in this world and must face its joys and sorrows without the consolation of her parents or her friends.

Henry L. Carrigan, Jr.

OTHER MAJOR WORKS

SHORT FICTION: *Women and Children First, and Other Stories*, 1988; *The Peaceable Kingdom*, 1993.

NONFICTION: *The Lives of the Muses: Nine Women and the Artists They Inspired*, 2002; *Gluttony: The Seven Deadly Sins*, 2003; *Sicilian Odyssey*, 2003; *Caravaggio: Painter of Miracles*, 2005; *Reading Like a Writer: A Guide for People Who Love Books and for Those Who Want to Write Them*, 2006.

TRANSLATIONS: *A Scrap of Time, and Other Stories*, 1987 (with Madeline Levine; of Ida Fink's novel); *The Journey*, 1992 (with Johanna Weschler; of Fink's novel).

CHILDREN'S/YOUNG ADULT LITERATURE: *Stories from Our Living Past*, 1974; *Dybbuk: A Story Made in Heaven*, 1996; *The Angel's Mistake: Stories of Chelm*, 1997; *You Never Know: A Legend of the Lamedvavniks*, 1998; *The Demon's Mistake: A Story from Chelm*, 2000; *After*, 2003; *Leopold, the Liar of Leipzig*, 2005; *Bullyville*, 2007; *Touch*, 2009.

EDITED TEXTS: *The "Mrs. Dalloway" Reader*, 2003; *Best New American Voices, 2005*, 2004.

BIBLIOGRAPHY

Aarons, Victoria. "Responding to an Old Story: Susan Fromberg, Leslea Newman, and Francine Prose." In *Daughters of Valor: Contemporary Jewish American Writers*, edited by Jay L. Halia and Ben Siegel. Newark: University of Delaware Press, 1997. Helpful essay explores the works of Prose and two other writers and discusses these authors' canny abilities to retell Jewish folktales for a new generation of children.

Hogan, Randolph. "The Butcher Won a Wife." Review of *Household Saints*, by Francine Prose. *The New York Times Book Review*, July 12, 1981. Positive review provides an overview of the novel and praises Prose as a splendid writer.

Hooper, Brad. Review of *Blue Angel*, by Francine Prose. *Booklist* 96, no. 16 (April 15, 2000). Positive review observes that Prose breathes new life into the standard story of academe.

Maslin, Janet. "An Aura of Grief Surrounds a Stunned Family." Review of *Goldengrove*, by Francine Prose. *The New York Times*, September 11, 2008. Thoughtful review describes *Goldengrove* as one of Prose's gentler books and praises Prose's "mostly effortless narrative verve."

Nebroso, Donna L. Review of *Household Saints*, by Francine Prose. *Library Journal* 106, no. 11 (June 1, 1981). Describes the novel as a simple but powerful tale that elevates the commonplace into the mythic.

Potok, Rena. "Francine Prose." In *Jewish-American Women Writers: A Bio-Bibliographical and Critical Sourcebook*, edited by Sara R. Horowitz. Westport, Conn.: Greenwood Press, 1994. Informative article provides a biographical sketch and offers an overview of Prose's early work.

Prose, Francine. "Francine Prose." Interview by Mickey Pearlman. In *Inter/View: Talks with America's Writing Women*, edited by Mickey Pearlman and Katherine Usher Henderson. Lexington: University of Kentucky Press, 1990. Prose discusses her early novels and stories and provides insights into her writing methods.

Publishers Weekly. Review of *Household Saints*, by Francine Prose. May 8, 1981. Positive review summarizes the novel and praises Prose for her insight into families and their shortcomings.

Tierney, William G. "Interpreting Academic Identities: Reality and Fiction on Campus." *Journal of Higher Education* 73, no. 1 (January, 2002): 161-173. Compares Prose's *Blue Angel* with two other campus novels, Philip Roth's *The Human Stain* (2000) and Saul Bellow's *Ravelstein* (2000), and describes Prose's novel as a masterpiece of comic despair.

E. ANNIE PROULX

Born: Norwich, Connecticut; August 22, 1935
Also known as: Edna Annie Proulx

PRINCIPAL LONG FICTION

Postcards, 1992
The Shipping News, 1993
Accordion Crimes, 1996
That Old Ace in the Hole, 2002

OTHER LITERARY FORMS

Before E. Annie Proulx (prew) began her career as a fiction writer in her mid-fifties, she had done considerable freelance writing in such disparate fields as cider making, driveway and fence repair, canoeing, cooking, and gardening. Having built her own house, she had experience with which to inform how-to books. She also wrote articles of interest to adolescent girls, publishing them regularly in *Seventeen*. Although she dismisses such work as writing for hire, it promoted her development as a writer of fiction because she researched her topics thoroughly and presented them in the clear and precise prose that would come to characterize her fiction. Her early nonfiction writing served as a valuable apprenticeship for the writing of the fiction that followed.

In 1984, Proulx founded a rural Vermont monthly newspaper, *The Vershire Behind the Times*, for which she wrote regularly during the years of its existence, 1984-1986. She has published several collections of short stories, including *Close Range: Wyoming Stories* (1999), *Bad Dirt: Wyoming Stories 2* (2004), and *Fine Just the Way It Is: Wyoming Stories 3* (2008).

ACHIEVEMENTS

Before she had gained a reputation for writing fiction, E. Annie Proulx received the 1986 Garden Writers of America Award following the publication of *The Gardener's Journal and Record Book* (1983) and *The Fine Art of Salad Gardening* (1985). After the publication of her first collection of short fiction, *Heart Songs, and Other Stories*, in 1988, Proulx received a Vermont Council of the Arts Fellowship, an award from the National Endowment for the Arts, and, in 1992, a Guggenheim Fellowship. Following the praise her short stories elicited, Proulx's publisher urged her to write a novel. The grants she received enabled her to produce her first novel, *Postcards*, which received the PEN/ Faulkner Award for Fiction in 1993 and was also nominated for a National Book Critics Circle Award for fiction. Proulx was the first female recipient of the PEN/ Faulkner Award for Fiction.

In 1998, Proulx's short story "The Half-Skinned Steer" was selected for inclusion in *The Best American Short Stories 1998*, and the story was also later included in *The Best American Short Stories of the Century*. Also in 1998, Proulx received the National Magazine Award for her short story "Brokeback Mountain," which was subsequently adapted for film by Larry McMurtry and Diana Ossana. This daring story tells of two Wyoming ranch hands who, spending a summer together on the range tending flocks of sheep, become lovers. Both ultimately marry women and return to heterosexual lifestyles, although they continue to have brief encounters together in the ensuing years.

Proulx's novel *The Shipping News*, which was also adapted as a motion picture (released in 2001), has been praised for its accuracy of dialect and for the authenticity of its descriptions of the harsh Newfoundland landscape where it is set. Proulx studied the language patterns of the people about whom she was writing and also became well versed in the folklore of their communities. This novel received the National Book Award for fiction as well as the *Chicago Tribune*'s Heartland Prize for Fiction and the Irish Times International Fiction Prize in 1993. In 1994, it was awarded the Pulitzer Prize for fiction. In that year, the University of Maine bestowed on Proulx an honorary doctor of humane letters degree. In 1997, Proulx received the John Dos Passos Prize for the full body of her work. In 2002, *That Old Ace in the Hole* won the Best American Novel Award.

BIOGRAPHY

Edna Annie Proulx is the oldest of the five daughters of George Napoleon Proulx and Lois "Nelly" Gill Proulx. Her father's ancestors immigrated to Quebec from France in 1637 and then, around the time of the American Civil War, to New England to work in the textile mills. Her mother's family had immigrated to America from England in 1635. George Proulx began working in the textile industry as a bobbin boy but quickly advanced to the vice presidency of a textile mill and served as an internationally recognized consultant in textiles. His work involved assignments in various venues, and the family moved with him.

The family had lived in North Carolina, Vermont, Rhode Island, and Maine by the time Proulx finished secondary school at Deering High School in Portland, Maine, in 1953. Her mother was an amateur artist and devoted naturalist. She passed these interests along to her daughters, including Annie, much of whose freelance writing would later explore naturalist topics.

Proulx enrolled in Colby College in Waterville, Maine, with the class of 1957, but she dropped out of college in 1955 to marry the first of her three husbands, all of whom she eventually divorced. She had a daughter by her first husband, two sons by her second, and another son by her third. The daughter, from whom Proulx was estranged, lived with her father, who raised her. Eventually her relationship with Proulx, who was always close to her sons, improved. Proulx helped to raise her sons and partially supported them with the income from her freelance writing.

Proulx enrolled in the University of Vermont at Burlington in 1963 and in 1969 was awarded a bachelor's degree cum laude in history. She was elected to Phi Beta Kappa. She then pursued graduate studies in history at Sir George Williams University, now Concordia University, in Montreal, earning a master's degree in 1973. She continued her graduate studies, pursuing a doctorate in Renaissance history. In 1975 she passed her doctoral oral examinations, but she failed to complete the doctoral dissertation she had contemplated producing on Renaissance economic history.

As early as 1964, Proulx published articles in *Seventeen*, which continued to publish her work through the next fifteen years, as did *Gray's Sporting Journal*. As early as 1979, *Gourmet* published a piece Proulx wrote. She has said in interviews that she made a decent living from freelance writing.

Proulx's writing soon attracted favorable attention. Her short stories were well received, so when her publisher urged her to write a novel, she obliged, producing *Postcards* in 1992. In the 1980's, looking for a good place to go canoeing, Proulx found a map of Newfoundland and was intrigued by such place-names in this stark land as Blow-Me-Down, Snake's Bight, Come-by-Chance, and Run-by-Guess. Newfoundland became the setting for her next novel, *The Shipping News*. She eventually bought a house in Newfoundland and began to visit there regularly, although in 1995 she moved to Wyoming and has contin-

E. Annie Proulx. (Getty Images)

ued to live there for part of every year. She first went to Wyoming for a six-week residency at the Ucross Foundation and found it such a compatible writing environment that she settled there.

ANALYSIS

Thematically most of E. Annie Proulx's writing is concerned with the gradual disappearance of the rural America that she cherishes, as urban sprawl overtakes the farmlands and forests that once constituted a major part of the United States. Proulx has always avoided cities, preferring to live in rural areas. As city dwellers have pushed farther and farther into rural America, family farms have virtually disappeared, as Proulx shows in *Postcards*.

Proulx is also concerned with the necessity for people to have roots, and in her novels she shows how, in an expanding society, it becomes difficult to maintain such roots. In *The Shipping News*, the protagonist, Quoyle, born in Brooklyn, is a deeply disturbed person who has cast about in New York State for most of his thirty-odd years, unhappy with the person he is. Only when he makes a break from his unsatisfactory life following the

death of his oversexed, unfaithful wife in an automobile wreck does he develop a self-image he can live with. He leaves his sorrow at his wife's death behind and moves with his two daughters to Newfoundland, to a dilapidated property that his family has owned for years. In returning to his ancestral roots, he begins to build a new life for himself, one based on self-acceptance.

Proulx usually employs third-person omniscient narrators in her writing. She uses her narrators to provide "flash-forwards," which, unlike flashbacks, inform readers of the fates of characters outside the immediate time frame of the narrative. By using this device, Proulx is able to add to the intensity of occurrences in her stories by giving readers clues to impending events.

Sentimentality seldom intrudes on Proulx's writing. An admirer of Icelandic author Halldór Laxness's novel *Sjálfstætt fólk* (1934-1935; *Independent People*, 1946), she, like Laxness, writes about harsh, unforgiving landscapes populated by people strong enough to survive them. She understands well the dialects of her characters, using them authentically to make her characters credible. Doing her research for *The Shipping News*, she spent a great deal of time in Newfoundland listening to how Newfoundlanders speak and doggedly studying the *Dictionary of Newfoundland English*.

Proulx does not mourn for a lost agrarian past; rather, she creates situations with which her characters must cope on a day-to-day basis. Her characters do not have easy lives. Those involved in farming or fishing live at the mercy of changing variables that are indifferent to their suffering. Much that she writes about is horrific, but she tempers the horror with humor, albeit often a black humor. She admits to avoiding scrupulously what she terms a "pastoral nostalgia."

POSTCARDS

Loyal Blood has lived most of his early life on the family farm, improving it through backbreaking work. He has a clear vision of the farm's potential. His roots are firmly entrenched in this farm, where he lives with his father and brother. The story Proulx relates in *Postcards* details events that occur in Loyal's life between 1944 and 1988. Critics have pointed out that John Dos Passos chronicled the first three decades of the twentieth century in his trilogy *U.S.A.* (1937) and suggest that Proulx has taken up where Dos Passos left off. She has undertaken the herculean task of chronicling, through Loyal Blood's adventures, more than four decades in mid-century America.

Loyal Blood has killed his girlfriend, Billy; she had rejected his advances, leading the aroused Loyal to rape her, and in the course of the rape, she died. This clearly is not a case of premeditated murder, but nevertheless it is an act that can destroy Loyal's life. Panicked by what he has done, Loyal hides Billy's body in an abandoned root cave. He then tells his father, Mink, that he and Billy have decided to run away and that they are leaving immediately, without even saying goodbye to Billy's family. Mink is furious.

Postcards unfolds over the next forty-four years, during which Loyal, whose fervent wish has been to stay on the family farm, is ironically forced to live life on the run. His presence is essential to the farm's survival, as Loyal alone understands how to make the most of its potential. Now Loyal's only contact with his family is through infrequent postcards—always the same card, with a picture of a bear on it—sent to them with no return address. One card informs the family that Loyal and Billy have separated, and nobody seems eager to pursue finding her.

Ever running, Loyal moves from one menial job to another. His emotional response to Billy's death is reflected in his having a violent asthma attack every time he tries to involve himself sexually with a woman. Meanwhile, part of the family farm has been sold to a Boston doctor who has found Billy's skeleton, but the doctor thinks the remains are those of someone the Indians killed earlier, so nothing comes of his discovery.

Proulx's careful research is evident in *Postcards*, as it is in all her writing. For example, at one point in Loyal's meandering, he decides to search for uranium. He scans maps for places with names like "Poison Spring" and "Badwater Canyon" because such names suggest the presence of arsenic or selenium in these places, and where these elements exist, uranium may be present.

THE SHIPPING NEWS

R. G. Quoyle, the protagonist of *The Shipping News*, is an unhappy, overweight widower who, born in Brooklyn, has drifted around New York State. He falls in love with Petal Bear, a promiscuous vamp, and marries her, but she is unfaithful to him. She is fleeing from him and their two daughters when she crashes her car into a tree and dies. Still in love with Petal, Quoyle suffers the pangs of a disabling grief, but his aunt, Agnis Hamm, an unsentimental, practical woman, urges him to leave his past behind and resettle on a dilapidated family property in Newfoundland.

Quoyle and his daughters, one of whom is emotionally disturbed, follow Agnis's advice and land in a stark world that is totally unfamiliar to them. There, Quoyle builds a new life. He finds work as a reporter for the local newspaper, *The Gammy Bird*, where his assignments are the shipping news and car wrecks. Quoyle thinks that he cannot endure reporting on the latter, but Agnis views his doing so as a necessary rite of passage.

Quoyle eventually fits in, making friends with the owner of *The Gammy Bird* and with other locals, including Wavey Prowse, a widow with a disabled son. The two find that they are kindred spirits and, for the first time in his life, Quoyle experiences something that approaches contentment and self-acceptance.

ACCORDION CRIMES

In *Accordion Crimes*, Proulx explores the melting-pot nature of the United States. Her cast of characters is large, making for a complex narrative of epic proportions. The story focuses on the successive owners of a green accordion that was made in Sicily and, over the century from around 1890 to the 1990's, is owned by people in the United States in places ranging from Louisiana and Texas to Minnesota and Illinois. Each of the eight chapters in the novel focuses on someone who has possession of the instrument.

The accordion is made a by Sicilian accordion maker who, with his son, Silvano, is about to set sail for the New World, and the instrument comes to America with them. Lured to New Orleans, probably by a pitchman employed to find greenhorns about to sail for the United States and divert them to that city, where they are needed as cheap laborers, the accordion maker is soon beaten to death by people who hate Italians. Silvano, blaming himself for his father's death, attempts to mask his Italian heritage and changes his name to Bob Joe. In time, the green accordion passes on to his black friend, Polio, who soon dies, as do most of the people involved with the instrument. The green accordion is ultimately found by two children in a Dumpster in the 1990's. They fish it out, place it on a highway, and watch an eighteen-wheeler run over and destroy it.

R. Baird Shuman

OTHER MAJOR WORKS

SHORT FICTION: *Heart Songs, and Other Stories*, 1988; *Close Range: Wyoming Stories*, 1999; *Bad Dirt: Wyoming Stories 2*, 2004; *Fine Just the Way It Is: Wyoming Stories 3*, 2008.

NONFICTION: *Great Grapes! Grow the Best Ever*, 1980; *Making the Best Apple Cider*, 1980; *Sweet and Hard Cider: Making It, Using It, and Enjoying It*, 1980 (also known as *Cider: Making, Using, and Enjoying Sweet and Hard Cider*, 1997; with Lew Nichols); *"What'll You Take for It?": Back to Barter*, 1981; *Make Your Own Insulated Window Shutters*, 1981; *The Complete Dairy Foods Cookbook: How to Make Everything from Cheese to Custard in Your Own Kitchen*, 1982 (with Lew Nichols); *Plan and Make Your Own Fences and Gates, Walkways, Walls, and Drives*, 1983; *The Gardener's Journal and Record Book*, 1983; *The Fine Art of Salad Gardening*, 1985; *The Gourmet Gardener: Growing Choice Fruits and Vegetables with Spectacular Results*, 1987.

EDITED TEXT: *The Best American Short Stories, 1997: Selected from U.S. and Canadian Magazines*, 1997 (with Katrina Kenison).

MISCELLANEOUS: *"Brokeback Mountain": Story to Screenplay*, 2006 (with Larry McMurtry and Diana Ossana).

BIBLIOGRAPHY

Hunt, Alex, ed. *The Geographical Imagination of Annie Proulx: Rethinking Regionalism*. Lanham, Md.: Lexington Books, 2009. Collection of essays focuses on the role of place and landscape in Proulx's fiction and addresses the significance of regionalism in contemporary fiction in general.

Proulx, E. Annie. "On Hemingway and His Influence: Conversations with Writers." Interview by Steve Paul. *Hemingway Review* 18 (Spring, 1999): 115-132. Proulx acknowledges her debt to Ernest Hemingway in this interesting interview.

Rood, Karen Lane. *Understanding Annie Proulx*. Columbia: University of South Carolina Press, 2001. Presents discussion of all of Proulx's novels through *Accordion Crimes* as well as analysis of her short fiction. Includes an informative biographical chapter.

Stacy, Jim, ed. *Reading "Brokeback Mountain": Essays on the Story and the Film*. Jefferson, N.C.: McFarland, 2007. Collection of fifteen essays focuses on the short story "Brokeback Mountain" and on the award-winning film based on it, but includes essays on Proulx's style and her use of locale that provide valuable insights into her longer fiction.

Varvogli, Aliki. *Annie Proulx's "The Shipping News": A Reader's Guide*. New York: Continuum, 2002. Comments on the importance of Proulx's use of locale and provides a valuable assessment of the novelist's method of developing of characters. Includes an exhaustive bibliography.

MARCEL PROUST

Born: Auteuil, France; July 10, 1871
Died: Paris, France; November 18, 1922
Also known as: Valentin Louis Georges Eugène
Marcel Proust

PRINCIPAL LONG FICTION

Du côté de chez Swann, 1913 (*Swann's Way*,
1922)
À l'ombre des jeunes filles en fleurs, 1919
(*Within a Budding Grove*, 1924)
Le Côté de Guermantes, 1920-1921 (*The
Guermantes Way*, 1925)
Sodome et Gomorrhe, 1922 (*Cities of the Plain*,
1927)
Albertine disparue, 1925 (*The Sweet Cheat Gone*,
1930)
La Prisonnière, 1925 (*The Captive*, 1929)
Le Temps retrouvé, 1927 (*Time Regained*, 1931)
À la recherche du temps perdu, 1913-1927
(collective title for all of the above;
Remembrance of Things Past, 1922-1931,
1981)
Jean Santeuil, 1952 (English translation, 1955)

OTHER LITERARY FORMS

In addition to his magnum opus, *Remembrance of Things Past*, Marcel Proust (prewst) wrote a number of less well-known works. His first book, *Les Plaisirs et les jours* (1896; *Pleasures and Regrets*, 1948), a collection of stories and some verse, was published in 1896. Its primary value lies in its preliminary statement of themes that are developed more fully in *Remembrance of Things Past*, as Edmund Wilson has pointed out.

Proust's fascination with John Ruskin led to prefaces for and translations of Ruskin's *The Bible of Amiens* (1880-1885) in 1904 and of his *Sesame and Lilies* (1865) in 1906. Before turning his full attention to the novel, Proust also wrote a series of parodies of his favorite French writers, which were published in *Le Figaro*. Of considerable interest to Proust scholars is *Contre Sainte-Beuve* (*By Way of Sainte-Beuve*, 1958), written in 1908 but not published until 1954. In it, Proust uses a variety

of essays, autobiographical pieces, and fiction to attack criticism that claims to be scientific and objective. Proust argues instead that only memory and the unconscious can break through the barriers of habit that impede art. Of somewhat less interest is *Pastiches et mélanges*, a volume of miscellaneous pieces published in 1919. Proust's brother, Robert, collected magazine and newspaper articles written by Proust as late as 1921 and published them in *Chroniques* (1927).

ACHIEVEMENTS

Marcel Proust's monumental achievement in writing *Remembrance of Things Past* consists not simply in the work's multivolume length or the complexity of the extended and intermingled lives of its characters, although these elements alone are impressive. It is above all the intense psychological realism with which the novel's characters—particularly the author's alter ego, Marcel—are rendered that has influenced other writers and has drawn critical acclaim. That "realism" is internal: Proust was fascinated by the interplay between external events and the mind, especially by the way human perception synthesizes and interprets events in time—by "the symbolic omnitemporality of an event fixed in a remembering consciousness," as Erich Auerbach put it. These concerns are reflected in much of twentieth century literature—notably in the works of James Joyce, Thomas Mann, and Virginia Woolf—and Proust may be said to have introduced their full exposition in his magnum opus.

Although, at the beginning of his writing career, Proust received little recognition outside his literary milieu, he was awarded the Prix Goncourt in 1919 for *Within a Budding Grove*. This recognition helped establish him as a serious and significant author, and since his death, his reputation and influence have continued to grow.

BIOGRAPHY

Marcel Proust was born in Auteuil, a suburb of Paris, on July 10, 1871. He was the son of the happily married Dr. Adrien Proust and Jeanne Weil. Adrien Proust had left the devoutly Catholic home of his candlemaker father in Illiers to go to Paris, where he ultimately found acclaim as a professor and hygienist. Adrien's family returned to Illiers, the "Combray" of *Remembrance of Things Past*, for frequent holidays. The home there of Adrien's sister, Elisabeth, became the model for the famous house and garden of Marcel's Aunt Léonie. Marcel's mother was the daughter of a wealthy Jewish family from Lorraine. Although Marcel was baptized a Catholic, he remained close to his mother's family throughout his life. His novels reveal little interest in religion other than aesthetic pleasure in church architecture, and Proust practiced no religion during his adult life.

From his birth, Proust was plagued by ill health; indeed, his parents feared he would die shortly after his birth. In spite of careful attention given to his well-being, he suffered a severe attack of asthma at the age of nine. Such frailty doubtless contributed to his acute sensitivity. While both his father and younger brother, Robert (later also a doctor), were committed to science, duty, and routine, Marcel and his mother were of a more emotional, artistic, and intellectual sensibility.

Poor health did not restrict Proust's movement entirely. He attended the Lycée Condorcet, and during his years there (1882-1889), he played in the gardens of the Champs-Elysées, where he fell in love with Marie de Banardaky. Although he had numerous friendships at school, even at that early age he found pleasure in the solitary task of writing. That did not, however, prevent him from attending the salons of his classmates' mothers. At the age of seventeen, Proust had already entered the world of Parisian society that he would depict so brilliantly in *Remembrance of Things Past*.

After receiving his *baccalauréat* in 1889, Proust volunteered for his one year of military duty. It was one of the happiest, most "normal" years of his life. He became friends with Gaston Arman de Caillavet, one of the models for Robert de Saint-Loup. On his return to Paris, he studied at the Sorbonne and at the École des Sciences Politiques, where he was deeply influenced by the lectures of the French philosopher Henri Bergson. In spite of his father's wish that he enter diplomatic service, Proust found himself more attracted to the worlds of society and literature. He became a favorite in the salons of

both the haute bourgeoisie and the nobility. At the salon of Madame Arman de Caillavet, he met Anatole France, a meeting that provided the model in part for Bergotte. Although women such as the Comtesse Greffulhe and Princess Mathilde provided invaluable opportunities for Proust to observe the mannerisms and style of the pinnacle of Parisian society, it was perhaps the salon of Madame Straus, widow of Georges Bizet and mother of Marcel's Condorcet friend, Jacques, that was most influential in Proust's development. Madame Straus was noted for her beauty and wit, and along with the Comtesse de Chevigné, she contributed significantly to the characterization of the chief denizen of Proust's fictional Parisian suburb Faubourg Saint-Germain, Madame de Guermantes.

In his mid-twenties, Proust gradually withdrew from the brilliant world he had both participated in and observed so carefully. From an early age he had felt that artistic endeavor and social life were largely incompatible; he may also have grown disillusioned with the vanities of high society.

During these early years of maturity, Proust developed intense platonic relationships with both men and women. His sexual interest was primarily in men. Among his earliest affairs was one with Reynaldo Hahn, a composer. It was Comte Robert de Montesquiou, however, who served as chief model for Proust's greatest gay character, the Baron de Charlus. Perhaps Proust's most compelling involvement was with Alfred Agostinelli, who served as his chauffeur and secretary. Agostinelli, who enrolled in aviation school under the name Marcel Swann, drowned as the result of an airplane crash off the French coast in 1914. It has been suggested frequently that Proust's tortured experience with Agostinelli was the inspiration for the characterization of Albertine.

Proust's father died in 1903, and his mother's death in 1905 left Proust utterly grief-stricken. Within a year after his mother's death, he began an early version of *Remembrance of Things Past*. In the remaining years of that decade, he wrote widely, penning parodies, some fiction, and essays in criticism. In January, 1909, Proust returned on a snowy evening to the warmth of his kitchen for a cup of tea and dry toast; while idly savoring the humble repast, he involuntarily recalled precious childhood memories. The significance of spontaneous memory as a condition for art struck Proust, providing the missing link in his theory of literature. This revelation was to shape his writing of *Remembrance of Things Past* as he labored in his cork-lined Paris apartment.

Proust was physically unfit to serve during World War I, although the suffering of France affected him deeply. During the war, his life was more solitary than ever before, although he dined so frequently at a famous Paris hotel that he became known as Marcel of the Ritz. Thus, the image of the dandy, the snob, the fop followed Proust throughout most of his life. Nevertheless, he had a huge coterie of loyal friends and servants and a reputation for courage (he once fought a duel with a libelous critic) and generosity. Before his death from asthma in 1922, he not only had been awarded the Prix Goncourt but also had received the recognition of his contemporaries as a genius.

Marcel Proust. (Getty Images)

ANALYSIS

Like Gustave Flaubert, Marcel Proust believed that of all literary forms, the novel most fully reveals the temperament of its writer. As George Painter's exhaustive biography of Proust demonstrates, there are innumerable, indeed seemingly endless, parallels between the lives of Marcel Proust and Marcel, the narrator of *Remembrance of Things Past*.

REMEMBRANCE OF THINGS PAST

While the novel reveals much of Proust's character and values, it is not an autobiography but a work of fiction in which the raw materials of personal experience and remembrance are transformed by the imagination into art of the highest order. Rather than yield to the temptation of a biographical reading of the novel, it is perhaps more profitable to concentrate on the development of the themes and to note the techniques that Proust employs to create his vision of humankind in their emotional, moral, and aesthetic worlds.

Like Dante and Honoré de Balzac before him, Proust creates a vast and teeming world, depicting the immense social changes that took place in French life between the end of the Franco-Prussian War in 1871 and the post-

World War I era. While *Remembrance of Things Past* focuses on the wealthy bourgeois and nobility of Paris, it by no means excludes other classes. The detailed and sympathetic characterizations of Jupien the tailor, Françoise, and Aimé, the headwaiter at the Grand Hotel, testify to the social range of the novel. Given the work's considerable time span and its scope of social inquiry, it is not surprising that Proust is able to develop a variety of themes: the Dreyfus affair, homosexuality, the difficulties of love, the growth of the artist, the vanity of society, and so on. By doing this, Proust invests the worlds of Paris, Combray, and Balbec with solidity and seriousness. Each thematic concern is ultimately registered on the growing consciousness of the protagonist, Marcel; all themes are subordinated to the dominant thematic concern of the novel: Marcel's attempt to overcome the disappointments of love, the false social expectations and the faulty imaginings and appearances that separate him from reality. With the aid of memory, prompted involuntarily by physical stimuli, Marcel ultimately defeats time, and through art, he finds the joy that has eluded him in love and social life. It is difficult, therefore, to understand Wilson's characterization of the novel as "the gloomiest book ever written"; while Proust's world is obviously complex and borders on the tragic, the existence in it of a sensuous and moral art belies the charge of pessimism.

The need to give structure and unity to a work as thematically ambitious as *Remembrance of Things Past* was a major challenge for Proust. While Wilson may have been off the mark thematically, his observation that the novel's structure is symphonic, a series of shifting images with "multiplied associations," is accurate. In so describing Proust, Wilson, like other critics, emphasized Proust's debt to Symbolism specifically and Romanticism generally. Proust's appreciation of introspection, his attentiveness to and enthusiasm for the natural world, his awareness of the power of the subjective and unconscious, and his use of image as symbol—all are variations on themes and techniques developed by nineteenth century French Romantics. Proust's affinity with the Symbolists was reinforced by his appreciation of the metaphysics of Henri Bergson, who was one of Proust's professors and a cousin by marriage. Although Proust denied any debt to Bergson, he, like Bergson, appreciated the role of intuition as a source of knowledge. Bergson also believed, as Wallace Fowlie has pointed out in his book *A Reading of Proust* (1964), that the capacity of an object to stimulate the memory lies in the individual himself, not in the object. By embracing the Symbolists and Bergson, Proust aligned himself clearly with those who resisted a purely scientific interpretation of reality.

Proust employs a variety of specific means to give shape to his world. Most important, perhaps, is the organization of *Remembrance of Things Past* into three major quests undertaken by the protagonist, Marcel. The first is the quest for love, a search that prompts much subjective analysis by the protagonist. In contrast, the second quest, Marcel's emergence into society, draws upon Proust's brilliant and often comic observations of both manners and morals. The quest for love begins with young Marcel's desperate desire for a goodnight kiss from his mother, a desire frustrated by Swann's call on his parents. Marcel's subsequent infatuations with Gilberte, the Duchess de Guermantes, and Albertine are paralleled by other, equally vain quests for love by

Swann for Odette, Robert de Saint-Loup for Rachel, and Baron de Charlus for Morel. The quest for love is symbolized in part by Swann's Way, one of the two paths that leads young Marcel and his family from their home in Combray to the outside world. The other road, the Guermantes Way, symbolizes the quest for society that leads Marcel from the secure world of family, servants, and neighbors in Combray to the drawing room of Odette Swann and, later, to a higher echelon of society symbolized by the salon of the slightly déclassé "bluestocking" Madame de Villeparisis. From there, Marcel finds his way into the much sought-after world of the Duke and Duchess de Guermantes and ultimately to the most socially exalted milieu of all, the soirees given by Prince and Princess de Guermantes.

In the same way that Swann's Way and Guermantes Way are finally united when Swann's daughter marries a Guermantes, these two quests, one private, one public, come together in mutual disillusionment. What saves the novel from utter despair is the persistence of those things that are not defeated by time and human vanity: Marcel's memories of his grandmother's selflessness and love, his involuntary recollection of sensations that produced great happiness, his realization of the eternity that lies within art. Thus, failure in the first two quests allows for success in the third: Marcel's pursuit of a career as an artist. The quest for art, initially overshadowed by love and society, is hinted at, however, by the presence in the novel of three artists who, in spite of their foibles and miseries, have created enduring works of art: the novelist Bergotte, the painter Elstir, and the composer Vinteuil. Indeed, although the emphasis shifts from book to book, all three quests figure in each of the seven novels that together make up *Remembrance of Things Past*.

SWANN'S WAY

Swann's Way, the chronicle of Marcel's childhood, begins and ends with memories of the protagonist, the mature Marcel. The first memory, recounted in a section called "Overture," is preceded by a description of the disorientation and pleasure that come from awakening in a darkened room at night. This sensation is one that Marcel has learned to relish, because it leads him to recall other rooms, particularly those of Combray, his childhood home. Marcel recalls the particular evening when Swann called on his family. Wealthy, Jewish, suave, and sophisticated, Swann visits Marcel's family frequently when he is home from Paris. Swann's visit upsets Marcel because it interrupts the ritual of his mother's nightly kiss. In his room, young Marcel grows so desperate that he sends Françoise, the cook, to deliver a note to his mother. His mother does not come until Swann leaves, but Marcel's stern father suggests unexpectedly that she sleep in Marcel's room to comfort him. The triumph of Marcel, touching yet disturbing in its power to manipulate, proves to be paradoxical. Even though he possesses his mother's attention, Marcel senses that such happiness, such a moment of unexpected success, is fleeting. "I knew that such a night could not be repeated." One function of this incident is clear: Marcel's quest for love has a most ambiguous beginning.

Immediately following the famous scene of the mother's kiss, Proust draws a crucial distinction between two types of memory. The first is voluntary, or recollection associated with intellect, "an exercise of the will." Voluntary memory is largely sterile and in vivid contrast to the sensations created by the second type, involuntary memory. Proust makes this distinction clear by recounting the episode of *la petite madeleine*, or little cake. The adult Marcel comes home on a winter day to tea and cakes. The crumbs in the spoon of tea give him exquisite pleasure, much to his surprise and delight. Initially puzzled by the sensation, Marcel suddenly recovers the memory: His Aunt Léonie had once given him tea and madeleines. An entire vision of forgotten elements of Combray surges over him. The incident is charming in itself, but it also anticipates a larger movement in the novel, Marcel's quest for the source of artistic inspiration.

Having resurrected memories of his youthful home in the madeleine incident, Proust logically moves to the next section, titled "Combray." Here emerges Marcel's childhood as it is shaped by family, an occasional school friend such as the pugnacious Bloch, and his reading of novels, particularly the works of Bergotte, an acquaintance of Swann. While Proust has been accused of being careless, casual, and prolix, the Combray section indicates quite the opposite. The characters and the quest motifs and themes are introduced without diverting the reader's attention away from the immediate concern, the characterization of Marcel's early years. Like Charles

Dickens, Proust creates characters that seem to have their own independent lives. The bedridden Aunt Léonie, for example, delights the reader with her quixotic pursuit of local gossip, yet her attachment to her sickroom clearly anticipates Marcel's own frequent retirements to his bed.

The Combray section also introduces the two "ways" that will influence Marcel's life, Swann's and Guermantes'. These two walks, the first represented by the lover Swann and the second by the socially prominent Duchess de Guermantes, will be the symbolic means by which Marcel will come to know the world outside Combray. While walking Swann's Way, Marcel first sees Swann's daughter, Gilberte, who will be the object of Marcel's first quest outside the confines of family. In an irony that is distinctly Proustian, Gilberte, standing under the pink hawthorns, makes an obscene gesture that to Marcel has the appearance of anger and rejection. The adult Marcel discovers that the reality was quite the opposite: Gilberte's youthful intentions were entirely sexual. This misreading of appearances emerges as one of the novel's central themes.

The Combray incidents are followed by what may seem an unlikely sequel, a novel within a novel titled "Swann in Love." Although audacious technically, its position within the larger work is logical and effective. Swann's affair with Odette contributes to the whole in terms of both style and theme. Proust reveals first of all his flexibility in use of point of view. The entire episode is told by an omniscient narrator; Proust recognizes that there is no way that either the youthful or the adult Marcel could be privy to the history of Swann's romance. Focusing on the sophisticated Swann also allows Proust to characterize the social world of Paris that Marcel will someday pursue. Of particular interest is Proust's use of the Verdurins and their "little nucleus" of friends. Not only do they enlarge one's knowledge of the teeming social life of Paris, but also they form a comic, ironic backdrop for Swann's tender love. Comically vulgar, the Verdurins are on the bottom rung of the social ladder— bohemians, as Marcel's grandfather calls them. Madame Verdurin will ultimately become much more than a backdrop, however; she will marry the Prince de Guermantes and prove herself to be the most vivid example of the immensity of the social change that occurs in the full novel's fifty-year time span. Another theme, similar in its social character, is also introduced in "Swann in Love." It occurs in a passing comment made by Oriane, the Princess des Laumes, about Swann's being a Jew. While apparently irrelevant in the early part of *Remembrance of Things Past*, the question of anti-Semitism, raised by the Dreyfus affair, later divided France profoundly.

This section's title indicates the primary focus of "Swann in Love." Swann's obsession with Odette, replete with ironies and contradictions, foreshadows Marcel's own loves; Swann is indeed the archetype of the Proustian lover. Whether heterosexual or "inverted" (Proust's term for homosexual), the lover chooses as his object someone who at best only obliquely shares his values. Swann—a member of the Jockey Club, a friend of the Prince of Wales, a man whose eye is so sensitive that he sees reflections of Giotto's *Charity* in a kitchen maid, the very spiritual and artistic father of Marcel—is also a man who seeks after prostitutes. He is continually vulnerable to "the sight of healthy, abundant, rosy human flesh." Similarly, the elegant, manly Robert de Saint-Loup is obsessed with the plain, whorish Rachel, and the Baron de Charlus freely spends his social, moral, and emotional capital on the unscrupulous grandson of a valet, Morel. While Odette de Crécy is no ordinary courtesan, she nevertheless has little of Swann's sophistication and sensibility. Once Swann has possessed Odette physically, their love is composed of lies, infidelities, perhaps lesbian sexuality on Odette's part, and jealousy and obsession on Swann's. Most significant, "this malady, which was Swann's love," will afflict Marcel as perniciously in his quest of Albertine.

A particularly brilliant scene, Swann attending a soiree at Madame de Sainte-Euverte's, illustrates both the function of Swann in the larger work and the tightly woven texture of Proust's art. Wishing to leave a drawing room—a room off-limits to Odette—Swann is irritated that he has been entrapped by the beginning of a musical piece. He soon recognizes a series of notes that proves to be a phrase from a sonata by the fictional composer Vinteuil, the same piece Swann had earlier called the national anthem of his love for Odette. Swann's experience as he listens to the piece foreshadows Marcel's most profound discoveries: involuntary memory as the source of

revelation and disappointment in love. As he listens, Swann "could see it all: the snowy, curled petals of the chrysanthemum . . . the address 'Maison Dorée' embossed on the note paper . . . the frowning contraction of her eyebrows." From the moment he hears the sonata, Swann knows he can never revive his love for Odette.

Not only does Swann's epiphany, rooted in involuntary memory, foreshadow Marcel's in the final volume of the novel, but also it indicates how Proust develops a number of themes simultaneously. The party at Madame de Sainte-Euverte's is also fine social satire, one of Proust's major concerns. The important theme of music, represented by Vinteuil, is present. The works of Vinteuil will eventually play as large a role in Marcel's life as in Swann's. Most important, Swann is, as Vladimir Nabokov, in his *Lectures on Literature* (1980), calls him, "a kind of fancy mirror of the narrator himself," one who "sets the pattern." Significant, too, is the pervading sense of paradox and irony that attends Swann's realization of love gone stale. The scene unobtrusively knits together elements of plot and theme that preceded it, renders them with clarity in a fully realized present, and anticipates further enrichments of plot and theme to come. The scene does not conclude Swann's concern for Odette; their love goes through death throes described in images of disease and decay. As "Swann in Love" ends, it appears that Swann and Odette have separated permanently; as it turns out, however, only Swann's love has been lost.

Swann's Way concludes with a section titled "Place-Names: The Name." The reader has reentered the world of Marcel's childhood, now set in Paris. Thematically, even in matters of plot, this last section is still clearly connected to "Swann in Love." Marcel wishes to travel; the names of Venice, Florence, and Balbec are magical to him. Because of his health, however, Marcel is forced to remain in Paris. While playing in the Champs-Elysées, he meets Gilberte, Odette, and Swann's daughter, the same girl he had seen in Combray. Initially, Gilberte is kind to Marcel; she gives him an agate marble and an essay by Bergotte on Jean Racine. Gilberte's enthusiasm is in contrast to Marcel's, however, much as her mother's feelings had been for Swann. Marcel is aware that he loves alone, but he still maintains his keen interest for her parents. He tries to imitate Swann's mannerisms, and when Gilberte chooses not to be available, he watches the resplendent Odette walk along the Allée des Acacias. In this same locale twenty years later, the adult Marcel makes the closing observations of *Swann's Way*. On a somber November day, Marcel finds that "vulgarity and fatuity" have replaced the standards of elegance that Odette had set years before. More important, Marcel is led to reflect on memory and its relationship to reality: "The reality that I had known no longer existed." The sadness of Marcel as he feels the onslaught of fugitive time is not yet assuaged by the knowledge that time can, in fact, be regained with all of its color and truth. All he knows is that physical space, in this instance the Bois de Boulogne, does not contain the reality of the past. Marcel can remember Odette, but he experiences none of the ecstasy associated with involuntary memory. Thus, the melancholy tone of these closing pages indicates clearly that Marcel's goals of love, society, and an artistic vocation have not yet been achieved.

WITHIN A BUDDING GROVE

Even though Marcel's exact age is not stated, *Swann's Way* concerns itself generally with the years of Marcel's childhood, while *Within a Budding Grove* develops his adolescence. A sign of Marcel's increasing independence is his frequent visits to the drawing room of Madame Swann, whom Marcel's parents will not receive, despite their warm feelings for her husband. Thus, the first long chapter of *Within a Budding Grove* is titled "Madame Swann at Home." The second, somewhat shorter section, "Place-Names: The Place," and the third and concluding chapter, "Seascape, with Frieze of Girls," depict Marcel's first venture away from his parents. Even though his grandmother accompanies him for reasons of health to the seaside hotel at Balbec, Marcel experiences considerable freedom. He mingles with the lower classes, young women, the members of the aristocratic Guermantes family, and the Impressionist painter Elstir (who, like the composer Vinteuil, is a composite of several real artists), all of whom contribute to his largely unconscious search for the real. Indeed, appearances still make their claim on Marcel, but new realities begin to make themselves felt.

In spite of *Within a Budding Grove*'s concentration on Marcel's life apart from parental influence, its first great scene occurs within the confines of the family;

furthermore, it is one of the few scenes in which Marcel's father emerges with much clarity. The occasion is a small dinner for the Marquis de Norpois, a distinguished member of the Foreign Office (Marcel's father is Permanent Secretary there). While Norpois reappears frequently in later novels, his primary function at the dinner is to introduce subtly the themes that will find elaboration in subsequent scenes. Marcel's career as a writer, the major concern of *Remembrance of Things Past*, is first discussed openly at the dinner. Norpois champions the vocation of writer, an important gesture, because Marcel's father has opposed it. In the hands of Dickens, Norpois would be the archetype of the good uncle who intervenes on behalf of a young boy beset by an incompetent or hostile father figure.

While Proust's method of characterization does seek out the type in the individual, as Swann sees the Botticellian possibilities in Odette, the type is always fully rounded, almost to the point of contradicting the type. Françoise is the good, faithful servant, but her limitations are never ignored. Similarly, Swann is the connoisseur, yet, as Norpois points out, since his marriage to Odette he has at times played the parvenu. In the case of Norpois, while he promotes Marcel's writing career, he nearly cuts it short by agreeing with Marcel's falsely modest assertion that his first writing exercise was "childish scribbling." Norpois goes on to attack Marcel's beloved Bergotte, judging him precious and an "evil influence." In a manner typical of him, Proust makes twofold use of Norpois's literary remarks. They obviously frustrate and antagonize the sensitive Marcel; they also contain many of the objections that Proust's own novels met critically. Norpois particularly dislikes "all those Chinese puzzles of form," saying that "all these deliquescent mandarin subtleties seem to me to be quite futile." Ironically, when Marcel soon thereafter meets Bergotte at Odette's, he is immensely disappointed and recalls Norpois's assessment. Marcel's lofty vision of the novelist, inferred from his work, is mocked by Bergotte's disappointing physical qualities and his snobbery and ambition.

In addition to its effect on Marcel's writing career, Norpois's conversation reminds the reader of other topics and themes. Norpois's personal political credentials are established by his recollections of service to France under reactionary and radical governments; later he appears as the most reasonable of the anti-Dreyfusards. While Swann's Jewishness is not mentioned by Norpois, he does provide the missing exposition on Swann's marriage, and the reader is once again reminded of the love theme, which is reinforced by Norpois's insistence that Marcel be allowed to see the famous actress Berma perform as Phèdre in Jean Racine's great play. Norpois also plays a minor but important role in Marcel's growing social awareness; his influence extends from Odette's drawing room to the court of kings, yet he will not honor Marcel's simple, enthusiastic request that he mention his, Marcel's, name to Odette.

Before his journey to Balbec, Marcel does find admittance to Odette's salon. Marcel himself describes his time spent at Swann's house as a stage in his movement upward in society. Ironically, it was Marcel's quest for love, not society, that originally attracted him to Swann's. His first visit comes after Gilberte invites him to tea following his attack of asthma. He continues to call, but Odette takes more pleasure in his presence than does Gilberte. Finally, while coyly refusing to see Gilberte, Marcel remains faithful to Odette, among her chrysanthemums and coterie of bourgeois acquaintances. Marcel discontinues his visits when he learns another fact of love: Absence breeds forgetfulness. He still visits the Bois de Boulogne, knowing the exact time when Odette walks there, the very personification of Woman as she strolls with her mauve parasol, followed by Swann and his friends from the Jockey Club. This particular vision of Odette leads the adult Marcel to conclude that one's memories of "poetical sensations" are much greater than one's memory of suffering.

Two years pass before Marcel takes the 1:22 train to Balbec with his grandmother. The summer and fall Marcel passes there greatly increase his knowledge of society and, to a lesser extent, his knowledge of love. Although he longs to die when he first sees the unfamiliar room in the Grand Hotel, habit and the presence of Françoise and his grandmother soon make this new world bearable, even pleasurably exciting.

The much-desired world of society appears at first to be closed off to Marcel. He must resign himself to the presence of chattering, vulgar provincials and disdainful members of the local aristocracy. Circumstances, however, prove kind, and an accidental meeting between his grandmother and the Marquise de Villeparisis, her old schoolmate, slowly opens up a new world to Marcel. The Marquise is a member of the distinguished Guermantes family, and she proves to be an indispensable step in Marcel's movement to the very top of the social hierarchy. To demonstrate her fondness for Marcel, she takes him on carriage rides about the countryside. Proust identifies her closely with the arts; her family owns paintings by Titian, and her father entertained Stendhal. She herself will write a highly regarded memoir. She is also, unbeknown to Marcel, the Marquis de Norpois's lover. Madame de Villeparisis illustrates one of the central principles of Proust's world: A character's identity cannot be known at once; time will unfold its secrets, and the reader comes to see, as Nabokov has put it, that Proust's characters wear a series of masks.

Madame de Villeparisis also introduces Marcel to her nephews, two characters who figure prominently in the evolution of a variety of themes, including love and the analysis of society. Marcel's first impression of the handsome, elegant Robert, Marquis de Saint-Loup, is negative. His apparent insolence, however, masks a generosity that conquers both Marcel and his unpretentious, socially indifferent grandmother. The other, older nephew, Palamède, Baron de Charlus, wears an even more impenetrable mask. To characterize the Baron for Marcel, Robert relates an incident that illustrates both the Baron's virility and his hostility to inversion; Robert clearly is unaware that the Baron, who has stared fixedly at Marcel, is, in fact decidedly homosexual. Robert also points out with some family pride that the Baron, who moves with ease in the Faubourg Saint-Germain, the pinnacle of Parisian society, has a list at the Jockey Club of two hundred members to whom he would not permit himself to be introduced.

The Baron will play one of the central roles in Marcel's drama. His two major functions, furthering Marcel's social awareness and explicating the homosexual theme, are joined by a third: His formal social demeanor provides a vivid contrast to the crude behavior of Bloch, Marcel's Jewish friend. Part of Marcel's social education is his exposure to the Bloch family as well as to the Guermanteses. Lest Proust's portrayal of the vulgarity of the Blochs be seen as anti-Semitic, however, one must recall that Proust's mother and her family, whom he loved and honored, were Jewish, as were many of his closest friends. As in his treatment of other minorities—ethnic, social, and sexual—Proust proves to be compassionate without indulging in apologies or sentimentality. No character would have been more offended by the Bloch family's lack of decorum than the Jewish Swann. Also, Robert's Jewish mistress, Rachel, while seen as manipulative, "had opened his mind to the invisible, had brought a serious element into his life, delicacy into his heart."

While Marcel finds pleasure in his new acquaintances at Balbec, his attention is most avidly focused on a band of young girls whom he sees about the town and countryside. He meets them through an unexpected source, the famous painter Elstir. Marcel's easy access to Elstir brings to mind one of the most frequent criticisms of the novel: The young, inexperienced Marcel makes a quick conquest of almost everyone he meets, from duchesses and novelists to lift boys. The reader's only direct clue to Marcel's charm is found in *The Guermantes Way*, when Marcel wittily entertains Robert's friends at the army town of Doncières. Marcel is usually passive both in tête-à-têtes and in society. Elstir nevertheless takes Marcel seriously enough to deliver a stirring monologue on aesthetic matters and the nature of wisdom. Marcel, however, seems more concerned with the failure to appear of a young girl who occasionally visits Elstir's studio. Marcel does eventually meet this young girl, Albertine. His immediate response to her is distinctly Proustian: The real Albertine is less than the imagined one. Following an innocent courtship that thrives on games played in the sand dunes with a band of girls, Marcel chooses Albertine to be his love interest. When Marcel makes advances toward her, however, she repulses them, and Marcel's initiation into the larger world of Balbec ends, as does *Swann's Way*, on a melancholy, cool note. The novel has, however, furthered Marcel's quest for love and prepared for his entry into the salons of Parisian society.

THE GUERMANTES WAY

The Guermantes Way begins with a mundane fact, but one crucial to the success of Marcel's dual quest for love and society. Marcel's family has moved to the Hôtel Guermantes, the Paris residence of the Duke and Duchess de Guermantes and Madame de Villeparisis; there,

too, is Jupien's tailor shop. While it is conceivable that Marcel might have made his way into the most distinguished drawing rooms of Paris without this change, it clearly makes Proust's plotting easier, even though plot is, perhaps, comparatively a lesser concern in such an expansive, comprehensive work as *Remembrance of Things Past*. Proust's keen psychological analyses, his brilliant use of metaphors to give depth and clarity to his themes, his elegance of style, and his sense of comedy are his chief virtues. Perhaps of all the novels of Proust's epic, *The Guermantes Way* best illustrates the truth of such a proposition.

The key organizing principle of *The Guermantes Way* is a series of social engagements: matinees, dinners at restaurants, and evening parties. Their only interruption, by what might appear to be an incongruity, is the death of Marcel's grandmother. There is, however, a unity of action provided by Marcel's growing consciousness, fostered by his exposure to the world of the Guermanteses. Once exposed, Marcel, relieved of his obsession with Oriane, the Duchess de Guermantes, states that "what troubled me now was the discovery that almost every house sheltered some unhappy person. . . . Quite half of the human race was in tears." He discovers the disparity between the romance that envelops a royal name and the reality of the royal person. Proust makes Marcel's disillusionment clearer by the use of metaphor. Marcel observes that

> each of my fellow guests at dinner, smothering the mysterious name under which I had only at a distance known and dreamed of them with a body and with a mind similar or inferior to those of all the people I knew, had given me the impression of flat vulgarity which the view on entering the Danish port of Elsinore would give to any passionate admirer of *Hamlet*.

Having met and conquered two of the members of the Guermantes family in Balbec, Madame de Villeparisis and Robert de Saint-Loup, Marcel, at the beginning of *The Guermantes Way*, sets his sights on Oriane, the beautiful Duchess de Guermantes. Marcel's own dreamlike state is reinforced by the magic of the great Berma's performance in Jean Racine's *Phèdre* (1677.) To Marcel's utter surprise, the Duchess acknowledges him with a wave of her hand. In comedy reminiscent of Dickens,

Marcel thereafter stalks the Duchess, loitering in the streets in the hope of seeing her. When word reaches Marcel that his infatuation irritates the Duchess, he employs a new tactic: He goes to the military camp at Doncières to visit Robert de Saint-Loup, hoping to gain access to the Duchess through Robert's influence.

Even though Robert is unable to help Marcel, the rekindling of their friendship allows Proust the novelist to develop themes previously introduced. Robert's obsession with his mistress Rachel reminds the reader of Swann's relationship with Odette and anticipates both the Baron de Charlus's mad pursuit of Morel and, most important, Marcel's tortured relationship with Albertine. Even an apparently insignificant incident in which Robert strikes a gay man is preparation for Robert's own sexual inversion later.

Robert's pursuit of his mistress brings him and Marcel back to Paris. Marcel is encouraged by his father to attend a matinee at the home of Madame de Villeparisis. While this occasion is of greater social significance than the gatherings Marcel had previously attended at Odette Swann's, it has limited status. Madame de Villeparisis, from the point of view of the Faubourg Saint-Germain, has been careless of her famous family name. She has married beneath her station, has had liaisons, and has associated herself closely with the academic and artistic worlds. Although the Duchess de Guermantes and the Baron de Charlus attend the matinee, they do so out of family loyalty. The matinee, essentially comic in tone, focuses in part on the foibles of guests such as Legrandin, a shameless flatterer, and Marcel's boyhood friend Bloch, who upsets a vase of apple blossoms. Few of Proust's scenes are as comic as that of Madame de Villeparisis pretending to be asleep when the humiliated Bloch comes to bid her farewell. The comic, however, is interwoven with themes of tragic potential, such as Norpois's discussion with Bloch about the Dreyfus affair and the pervasive evidence of vicious snobbery. Most important, Marcel and the reader gain a clearer picture of the complexity of the Guermanteses: Oriane, the Baron, and Madame de Marsantes, the mother of Robert. The Baron's comically indirect, elegant propositioning of Marcel as he leaves the matinee develops the homosexual theme and reveals Marcel's naïveté.

A hiatus of sorts follows Marcel's initiation into the world of the Guermanteses. First, Marcel's grandmother dies. Having been convinced by an eminent physician, Dr. de Boulbon, that her ill health is psychosomatic, Marcel's grandmother follows his advice and accompanies Marcel to the Champs-Élysées. She rather suddenly interrupts their stroll to go into a public toilet. During the interim, Marcel talks to "la marquise," who attends the toilet, to which she refers as her "salon." Her conversation, coming so soon after the de Villeparisis matinee, is brutally satiric, as is Marcel's experience with a doctor, Professor E——, to whom he turns when it is apparent that the grandmother has suffered a stroke. Although he does examine her, Professor E—— is clearly more concerned with the mending of a buttonhole, a repair that is necessary before he calls on the Minister of Commerce. The protracted suffering of the grandmother and the devotion of Marcel's mother to her are set in stark contrast to the vanity, insinuations, and archness of the drawing room. Marcel will continue his social ascent, but the vision of his grandmother's love will provide a vivid contrast to the falseness of the *beau monde*.

Deeply touched by his grandmother's death, Marcel's attention nevertheless turns again to women. Although he successfully pursues a Madame de Stermaria, he is consoled by the reappearance of Albertine, finding that she no longer repulses his physical advances. Albertine's return coincides with a number of discoveries by Marcel. In spite of the kind of attention that Robert de Saint-Loup gives him, Marcel concludes that friendship is basically incompatible with the vocation of writing. Most important, he discovers that he has grown indifferent to the Duchess de Guermantes, as he had to Gilberte. This realization occurs ironically when Marcel receives an invitation from the Duchess to dine with her. Marcel's observations during the dinner, more than one hundred pages in length, are an excellent example of what Nabokov calls "Marcel the eavesdropper." Marcel's personality and concerns intrude little, if at all, in the description of the Guermanteses at home. At the center is Oriane, the Duchess herself. One learns that as a young woman she was, by the Guermanteses' standards, poor. What distinguished her was her beauty, her style, and her spirit: "She had had the audacity to say to the Russian Grand Duke: 'Well, Sir, I hear you would like to have Tolstoy murdered?'" In spite of her liberal views, she was most careful to marry well. With the aid of her aunt, Madame de Villeparisis, she married the Prince des Laumes, the future Duke de Guermantes. Their marriage has scarcely been a happy one. The Duke is tight with money but profligate in his affection for other women. The Duke admires his wife, however, particularly her sharp "Guermantes wit," which in reality often consists of terrible puns, poor imitations, cruel characterizations of her friends and family, and fatuous literary judgments. Marcel nevertheless finds something of value in the Faubourg Saint-Germain world that she represents. Like the peasants, the great noblemen still have a concern for the land, for history, for custom. In this way, they are superior to the bourgeoisie, who are interested only in money.

Although Marcel's social education is not yet complete, his evening with the Duchess does much to strip away the appearances and the magic of the world of names. Before the evening is out, however, Marcel will receive one more lesson. Invited by the Baron de Charlus to call on him after dinner, Marcel encounters a hostile Baron, who accuses Marcel of ingratitude and talebearing. Marcel retaliates by trampling the Baron's new silk hat and begins his exit. The formerly imperious Baron seems sobered by Marcel's anger. A civilized conversation follows, one that reveals the Baron's quixotic intelligence and sensitivity, as well as his appreciation for his family. The scene, both comic and touching, reveals him in his fullness and has led Wilson to compare Proust's characterization of the Baron to William Shakespeare's characterization of Falstaff.

In the final scene of *The Guermantes Way*, Proust provides—as he had in the episode of the grandmother's death—a brilliant gloss on the artificiality and vacuity of the Guermanteses' world. Marcel has received an invitation from the Princess de Guermantes, and being unsure of its authenticity, he goes to visit the Duke and Duchess upon their return to Paris. While he is there, Swann arrives with a photograph for a book he is writing on the knights of the Order of Malta. Oriane claims a great interest in Swann's project, but the Duke hurries her off to a dinner at a relative's. As they leave, Swann announces that he is dying. Although Swann is one of her oldest friends, the Duchess yields to her husband's demands that they leave for the dinner. The Duke tells Swann that he will outlive them all. The detail that fully reveals the cruelty of the Guermanteses, however, is the Duke's concern for Oriane's forgotten red shoes. The Duke and his world chose to ignore whatever unpleasant reality discomforts them in favor of a dramatic appearance.

CITIES OF THE PLAIN

Cities of the Plain, a novel of brilliantly contrasted scenes, records the beginning of Marcel's descent into his own personal hell, fuller description of which occurs in *The Captive* and *The Sweet Cheat Gone*. In *Cities of the Plain*, Marcel moves from the pinnacle of Parisian society, symbolized by the soiree given by the Prince and Princess de Guermantes, downward to the ridiculously comic Wednesdays at the Verdurins' home at La Raspelière. More significantly, Marcel himself reluctantly changes from detached observer to subjective sufferer because of the emergence of the phenomenon that dominates the novel: homosexuality.

One of the lingering criticisms of *Remembrance of Things Past* is that it gives excessive attention to the homosexual theme, thus presenting a distorted picture of society as it was in Paris at the beginning of the twentieth century. Some consider Proust's fascination with the subject merely self-indulgent; others, seeking to justify the theme, have called it a symbol of Original Sin or a symbol of the corruption and coming destruction of the aristocracy. Both the critics and Proust's defenders miss the point. Within the self-contained world of the larger novel, homosexuality functions primarily as an aesthetic device. Without its presence, there would be no Baron de Charlus, Proust's most brilliantly drawn character. Homosexuality also contributes to other major concerns of the novel, such as the characterization of much of the aristocracy, the love theme, and the education of the narrator. Without homosexuality, the central plot would not advance; had Albertine not mentioned her friendship with the lesbian who was the companion of Vinteuil's daughter, Marcel would not have urged her to come to Paris. One may further assume that the heterosexual Marcel's inability to find human love is directly connected to his ultimate quest for salvation in art. To see the function of homosexuality in terms of plot, theme, and characterization does not, however, negate its intrinsic interest. Like the characterization of the aristocracy and the descriptions of life in a provincial French town or sea resort, homosexuality resonates with the tragicomic complexity of human experience.

Cities of the Plain begins as an apparent extension of Marcel's pursuit of the world of the Guermanteses. In a flashback, Marcel awaits the return of the Duke and Duchess de Guermantes to ask about the authenticity of an invitation he has received from the Princess de Guermantes. Marcel sees instead the Baron de Charlus meeting Jupien, the tailor. Although Marcel could scarcely be ignorant of the Baron's sexual proclivities, he is still surprised by the cooperation of Jupien in such matters. Marcel is, nevertheless, fascinated by the coquetry that takes place, and he uses an extended botanical metaphor, comparing Jupien to an orchid and the Baron to a bee. The effect of the metaphor is to suggest that, while the encounter is unusual, it is in the larger scheme of things natural, "a miracle."

Jupien is just another member of the "human herbary" that intrigues Marcel, a "moral botanist." Samuel Beckett has noted the importance of Proust's use of "vegetal" images, stating,

> This preoccupation accompanies very naturally his complete indifference to moral values and human justices. Flowers and plants have no conscious will. They are shameless exposing their genitals. And so in a sense are Proust's men and women.

Although Beckett perhaps overstates the case, there is indeed no moral censure on young Marcel's part; neither is there a defense of homosexuality. Marcel concludes that gays are essentially men-women and that in spite of the Baron's pretension of virility, he, in fact, has the sensibility of a woman. Marcel concludes that homosexuals are like "an Oriental colony, cultured, musical, malicious, which has certain charming qualities and intolerable defects." Proust's objective characterization of homosexuals is perfectly consistent with those of other minorities: Jews, aristocrats, artists, and so on. Thus, Marcel later says that, like his extremely moral grandmother, he also "enjoyed the diversity of other people without expecting anything of them or resenting anything that they did."

There is another Marcel in *Cities of the Plain* who does not take such a sanguine view of humankind or homosexuality. The Marcel who captures the comedy,

homosexual and otherwise, of the soiree at the Guermanteses' (where the Baron shamelessly pursues two vapid brothers in the presence of their unwittingly cooperative mother) is quite different from the Marcel who returns to Balbec and discovers that he is not immune to the sting of "vice."

Marcel's return to Balbec with his mother marks a general movement toward a more somber, reflective, subjective protagonist. Upon reaching his old room at the Grand Hotel, Marcel takes off his boots, and involuntarily his memory returns to his grandmother. For the first time, he feels the effect of her death and learns from Françoise of the courage and sacrifice his grandmother concealed from him during their earlier stay at Balbec. His suffering diminishes, however, with Albertine's return to town. His comfort proves to be short-lived. While visiting a casino with Cottard, the doctor, Marcel sees Albertine dancing with Andrée. Cottard casually remarks that the two women are aroused. Unlike his detached response to the Baron de Charlus and Jupien, Marcel is deeply distressed by the possibility of a lesbian liaison between Albertine and Andrée. From this point on, *Cities of the Plain* develops the torturous relationship of Marcel and Albertine, a relationship that reveals the sometimes sadistic, paranoiac, and self-indulgent aspects of Marcel's character.

In *Cities of the Plain*, Proust does not yet entirely extricate Marcel and Albertine from the larger social fabric. Their physical but loveless affair grows within the context of life at the Grand Hotel and, more important, the Wednesdays at the Verdurins' home. The "nucleus" that gathers around "The Mistress" has changed little since they first appeared in *Swann's Way*. If possible, they are even more ridiculously savage in their comedy. The evenings at La Raspelière are the supreme achievement of Proust's comedy. Whether it is the Faithful mistaking Meyerbeer for Claude Debussy, or Madame Cottard falling asleep, or the Baron de Charlus revealing his sexual proclivities by choosing strawberry juice rather than orangeade, the comedy is sublime. Madame Verdurin herself has become even more imperious and amoral. To her, the death of Deschampes the pianist is essentially a nuisance that threatens to spoil her first entertainment in her new country residence. Besides, she has a new protégé, the violinist Charles Morel.

Morel, the grandson of Marcel's Uncle Adolphe's valet, emerges as one of Proust's greatest achievements in characterization. A fit companion for the Verdurins, Morel is utterly amoral, available either to men or women, entirely free of any loyalty, and he almost proves to be the Baron's nemesis. The Baron is so in love with Morel that he suffers the vulgarities and ignorance of the Verdurins and their circle in order to promote the young man's career and simply be in his presence. Like Odette and Albertine, Morel is one of those faithless creatures that ironically have the power to enslave a sensibility finer than their own. Morel's affair with the Baron is one panel in Proust's triptych of the vanity of human love.

In time, Marcel's jealousy and paranoia concerning Albertine lead him to resemble the Baron in his pursuit of Morel. At Balbec, however, Marcel's feelings are at best ambivalent. He is indeed possessive of Albertine and even jealous of her attention to his old friend Robert de Saint-Loup. So corrosive is the effect of this attachment on his moral behavior that he refuses to leave her alone with Saint-Loup in order to speak even briefly to Bloch's father. Marcel still dreams of traveling, however, and he finally resolves that he will abandon her. Only when Marcel inadvertently discovers that Albertine is an old friend of the lover of Vinteuil's daughter does the specter of lesbian sexuality rise up to shatter his resolution. It is scarcely the same detached Marcel, the moral botanist who watched Jupien lure the Baron, who announces to his mother that he will return to Paris and marry Albertine. While *The Guermantes Way* reveals Marcel's disillusionment in his quest for society, *Cities of the Plain* does the same for his quest for love. Salvation, if it exists it all, has thus far eluded Marcel.

THE CAPTIVE

Coupled with *The Sweet Cheat Gone*, *The Captive* has as its central concern Marcel's destructive relationship with the elusive Albertine. Although the love theme appears earlier, in the histories of Swann and Odette, Robert and Rachel, and the Baron de Charlus and Morel, it is in the painstaking treatment of Marcel's paranoid obsession with Albertine that Proust most fully explores the paradoxes of love. Wilson describes their relationship as "trying" at best: "It is quite without tenderness, glamour, or romance." There is in it neither "idealism [nor] enjoyment." This extended episode is crucial to the

central concern of the novel, however: Marcel's discovery of his true vocation as an artist. Once love has proved itself impossible for Marcel, the only salvation is the world of art—as the final volume of *Remembrance of Things Past* will show.

Although *The Captive* includes one of Proust's most brilliant social scenes, the Verdurins' quarrel with the Baron de Charlus, it begins and ends with Marcel's life with Albertine. The novel opens with Marcel in his bedroom in Paris. As a number of critics have pointed out, the bedroom functions as one of the primary motifs in the work. Marcel's recurring bouts of ill health make his stays in bed, be it at Combray, Balbec, or Paris, credible; however, the emphasis in each instance is elsewhere. Consciously or not, Marcel's retirements represent a power struggle of sorts. His delicate health as a child guarantees the attention of his mother, and the famous scene at Combray where Marcel awaits and ultimately receives his mother's kiss represents an ambivalent victory for Marcel over his father. At his Balbec hotel room, the adolescent Marcel, although he is unaware of it, has a rival for his grandmother's attention: death itself. Again, Marcel temporarily wins the struggle. As an adult, Marcel once again retires to his bedroom and uses this withdrawal to imprison the third important woman in his life, Albertine. Her presence is in part a repetition of earlier experience. Marcel himself twice sees Albertine's kisses late at night as a reenactment of his mother's visit to his side after Swann had left that fateful night in *Swann's Way*. As was true with his mother and grandmother, Marcel has a rival for Albertine, her probable inclinations toward lesbian sexuality.

It has been suggested that Albertine's presence in the home of Marcel's parents violates credibility. Bourgeois values would not have allowed it. Proust does, however, cover his tracks. First, Marcel's father is away on diplomatic business, and his indulgent mother is conveniently in Combray, attending a sick relative. Only the disapproving Françoise is present. Moreover, Marcel conceals Albertine's residency from friends. Most important, Marcel has never particularly adhered to social strictures, as is indicated by his moral indifference to the male citizens of Sodom and Gomorrah.

While Marcel the social observer is admirably tolerant, Marcel the lover has little to recommend him other than his lucid candor; why Albertine accepts Marcel's paranoia and jealousy as long as she does is not clear. Marcel's motives and behavior, on the other hand, are scrutinized uncompromisingly. Marcel tells Albertine that the doctor has ordered him to stay in bed. In truth, Marcel is so jealous of Albertine that he cannot bear to see her responses to other people in public. Thus, the tyrant Marcel permits Albertine to go out only with Andrée or alone with the chauffeur, but he also asks both, in effect, to spy on her.

Marcel's desire for control over Albertine leads him to like her best when she is sleeping or just awakening. Marcel compares the waking Albertine to Eve come from the side of Adam—"astonished and submissive." So consuming is Marcel's jealousy that he finds he is less interested in Albertine's frequent intelligent comments than he is in some unguarded remark that will fuel his paranoia.

While his jealousy proves intensely painful to Marcel, he does find some pleasure in life with Albertine. He both admires and takes some credit for her intelligence. She does provide him physical titillation and satisfaction. His greatest pleasure seems to reside in his capacity simply to control her, to hold her captive. Whether he is choosing her clothing after consultation with the Duchess de Guermantes or begging her to return home from the Trocadéro, Marcel seeks to reduce Albertine to merely an instrument of his will. Marcel is fully conscious not only that his attachment to Albertine prevents him from traveling and working but also that he himself has become a captive to Albertine's lies and his own mania. Although unable to act on his knowledge, Marcel sees clearly that "I had clipped her wings, she had ceased to be a Victory, was a burdensome slave of whom I would fain have been rid."

The Captive does not develop Marcel's relationship with Albertine exclusively. Another love story, the Baron de Charlus's obsession with Morel, is also carried to a disastrous climax at the musical soiree held at the Verdurins'. The humiliation of the imperious Baron at the hands of the Verdurins is but one of the important events that this brilliant scene develops. Its objectively cruel satire, directed toward the aristocrats and the members of the Verdurins' circle, provides a necessary contrast in tone and texture to the Albertine-Marcel story.

The playing of Vinteuil's lost septet during the soiree also allows Marcel to consider questions crucial to his development as an artist.

In *The Captive*, the theme of the artist is like an underground stream that slowly makes its way to the surface. Marcel points out early in the novel that when he is not with the Duchess, he examines an album of Elstir's work, or one of Bergotte's books, or Vinteuil's sonata. Later, Marcel learns of Bergotte's death as he is viewing a Vermeer at an exhibition. Proust, anticipating *Time Regained*, suggests that the dead Bergotte's books, arranged three by three, are the symbol of his resurrection, his salvation. Marcel, while awaiting Albertine's return from the Trocadéro, plays Vinteuil's sonata. Fowlie points out that this scene is of primary importance in the transition of Marcel from lover to artist. After the sonata, Marcel plays a score of Richard Wagner's *Tristan und Isolde* (1859), and this arouses a number of questions in him. He admires the giants of the nineteenth century—Wagner, Honoré de Balzac, Victor Hugo—and their capacity to produce "Vulcan-like" massive works leaves Marcel unhappy and unsure whether a commitment to art is preferable to life as he leads it. At the Verdurins', Marcel hears Vinteuil's septet, and he realizes that Vinteuil's later work has been enriched by his love and suffering for his daughter. In this septet, Vinteuil, like Bergotte, has found a means of defeating time.

In contrast to the violet mist in which Vinteuil's immortal work is shrouded is the unheroic world of the Verdurins. The Baron's aristocratic guests ignore Madame Verdurin, and to get revenge, she poisons Morel's mind against the Baron. Even in this atmosphere of snobbery and viciousness, Proust avoids caricature. At evening's end, the Verdurins decide to provide anonymously for the financially broken Saniette, whom they have abused in the past. More dramatic, however, is the Queen of Naples, who returns to the Verdurins' for a misplaced fan and rather magnificently comes to the aid of the devastated Baron de Charlus. Thus, the major concerns that propel the previous novels—homosexuality, the development of the artist, the vanity of love, the emptiness of the aristocracy, the Janus-like nature of reality—are in this scene recapitulated seamlessly.

Marcel returns home to Albertine. They quarrel, and Marcel asks Albertine to leave. A reconciliation follows, but Marcel learns more disquieting facts about Albertine's past. Albertine herself grows restless, as symbolized by her violent opening of her window. When Marcel plans to end the relationship, Albertine ensures his continued bondage to jealousy by leaving him first. It would appear that Marcel's quest for love has reached its nadir. The descent, however, is not yet complete.

THE SWEET CHEAT GONE

The Sweet Cheat Gone, more than any of the novels that precede it, concerns itself with Marcel's loss of innocence. Proust emphasizes this theme by ending the novel with Marcel's return to the Combray of his childhood. There he finds the youthful object of his imagination and love, Gilberte, living in a fallen world. For Marcel, not only has Gilberte lost her appeal, but also her husband and his friend, Robert de Saint-Loup, seems stripped of nobility. Most poignant, the once beautiful Vivonne is now little more than "a meagre, ugly rivulet."

The novel begins with Marcel's desperate strategies to bring Albertine back to him. He recognizes the irony of seeking the return of one who afforded him mediocre pleasures while preventing him from realizing loftier goals. Alas, she had become a habit. No longer having Albertine about to lie to him, Marcel lies to himself. He persuades himself that her departure is an attempt to negotiate better terms. He therefore dispatches a letter telling Albertine that her departure is final, while Robert de Saint-Loup is sent to bribe Albertine's aunt. A second letter reveals an even baser Marcel; in it, he suggests that a Rolls-Royce and a yacht might be in the offing. The final communication, a telegram, asks Albertine to name her terms; all he wants is to hold her three times a week. So summarized, Marcel's actions are comic. The news of Albertine's death in a riding accident alters the tone, as does her last letter, in which she asks Marcel to take her back on any terms. Proust, however, makes no attempt to sentimentalize her death. There is a peculiar flatness in its description that undercuts any pronounced emotional response. The reader has known so little of Albertine that he is moved only by the irony of events.

The ironic tone is sustained in the treatment of Marcel's grief. The former captor is now enslaved by memory, and Marcel discovers that each season brings with it a new set of painful recollections. Temporarily affectionate memories of Albertine replace his former suspicions. Marcel feels guilt, as though he had murdered her. He deifies her, calls her "my sister, my child, my tender mistress." The exaggerated, unexpected sincerity of Marcel's grief once again approaches comedy. He begins to believe that Albertine is not dead and considers the possibility of immortality. At the same time, Marcel has commissioned Aimé, a former headwaiter at Balbec, to investigate Albertine's life at the resort; Aimé writes that Albertine had been an active lesbian. Aimé, on a second mission, discovers a laundress from whom Albertine had received profound pleasure, and Aimé believes the laundress's report because she has excited him sexually as well. Such revelations Marcel both believes and doubts. He continues his quest for the true Albertine, and while Andrée admits to having lesbian feelings, she denies any involvement with Albertine. Marcel is thus frustrated in his attempt to locate the one, the absolute Albertine. Instead, he discovers that memory crumbles, and the time will soon come when Albertine's room will be occupied by someone else.

Although Marcel's relationship with Albertine will surface again, the novel abandons it in favor of another and crueler kind of oblivion, which has taken place without Marcel's knowledge. Marcel is introduced in the drawing room of the Duchess de Guermantes to Mademoiselle de Forcheville, who is Gilberte Swann. While she had earlier recognized Marcel, Marcel had thought, indeed hoped, that she was a young woman of easy virtue whom Robert de Saint-Loup had once known. The return of Gilberte allows Proust to recall the aftermath of Swann's death. To everyone's surprise, Odette exhibited a long and sincere grief. She then married Forcheville, who in time adopted Gilberte. Gilberte has inherited an immense fortune from an uncle and has thus been received in aristocratic houses. Even the Duchess de Guermantes receives her, an event devoutly desired by Swann but denied to him during his life. Although Gilberte has inherited her father's tact and charm, she contributes to Swann's oblivion by addressing Forcheville as father, and soon no one mentions Swann's name in her presence. Her hypocrisy and snobbery are seen in her signature, "G. S. Forcheville." The Guermanteses, whom Marcel now describes as "people whose lives have no purpose," aid in the destruction of Swann's memory. When Gilberte notices some Elstir sketches in the Guermanteses' drawing room, the Duchess remarks that "some friends" recommended Elstir rather than embarrass Gilberte with the name of Swann.

While the scene serves the necessary function of reintroducing Gilberte to the plot, it also reveals the growth of Marcel, who no longer is enamored of names and rank. The concerted attempt to erase Swann's memory is particularly offensive to Marcel, because it was Swann who so unobtrusively provided a type of paternal authority for Marcel. In his affair with Albertine, Marcel constantly sees Swann's life with Odette as the prototype of love. Swann has also introduced Marcel to Bergotte and to an appreciation of Vinteuil. Had it not been for Swann's remarks about the Persian quality of the church at Balbec, Marcel believes, he might never have met Albertine or Elstir. Appropriately, the connoisseur of art, Swann, will himself be immortalized in the art of his aesthetic son, Marcel.

Albertine has not yet been forgotten either. Marcel speaks again with Andrée, from whom he receives "a terrible revelation." Andrée has lied previously about her lack of contact with Albertine; moreover, she tells Marcel that Albertine and Morel together enticed virginal girls into occasional orgiastic revels. Suggesting that while Albertine lived with Marcel she had reformed and looked to him to save her, Andrée further implies that Albertine's death was a suicide related to a lesbian scandal. The effect of Andrée's tales, however, is less than might be expected. Marcel no longer feels the need to believe in Albertine's innocence; so detached has he become that he now realizes that Albertine's lesbian orientation was perhaps a precondition for her frank and open manner, one that permitted their special camaraderie. Marcel realizes he will never know the truth about Albertine, and sorrow is finally replaced by exhaustion. Marcel knows that oblivion has made a conquest of him when, in Venice, he receives a telegram from Gilberte that at first appears to be from Albertine. Even the possibility that Albertine is alive does not interest him.

Once the Albertine theme has reached its inevitable conclusion, Proust uses the closing pages of the novel to foreshadow the major concerns of the final volume, *Time Regained*. Foremost among them is the theme of time. While visiting Venice with his mother and an old friend, Madame Sazerat, Marcel sees Madame de Villeparisis seated with her old lover, Monsieur de Norpois. Time has grievously altered the Marquise; Madame Sazerat, whose father was ruined by a youthful affair with the noblewoman, can scarcely believe that the woman once "beautiful as an angel, wicked as a demon" is now "hunch backed, red-faced . . . hideous." A second theme, the social change brought by time, is contained in the news of two marriages: Gilberte to Robert de Saint-Loup and Jupien's niece to the nephew of Legrandin. In the union of Gilberte and Robert, Swann's Way and Guermantes Way unexpectedly come together. More startling is the story of Jupien's niece. Adopted by the Baron de Charlus and given a name, she dies shortly after her marriage to an impoverished member of the provincial aristocracy. This young girl, enamored of and abused by Morel, through her death sends the royal houses of Europe into mourning. It is the same sense of irony and dramatic change that will permeate *Time Regained*.

The Sweet Cheat Gone concludes with a series of revelations that further strip away from Marcel any remaining romantic illusions. Gilberte's marriage to Robert is not a happy one; Robert appears to have inherited both his uncle's proclivities and his infatuation with Morel. Gilberte tries to make herself look like Rachel in a vain attempt to stop his infidelity, but she reaps only lies and melodramatic confessions of guilt. Marcel learns also that Gilberte's childhood gesture under the arch of hawthorns had been intentionally vulgar, a revelation that serves to reinforce one of Proust's central tenets. There is not a single Gilberte, but many Gilbertes: the little girl amid the hawthorns, the loving daughter of Swann, the snob, the suffering wife. What exists is not an absolute Gilberte but a series of Gilbertes relative to time and place. Even places fail to present an absolute image, as Marcel's disappointment in his walks in Combray reveals. Innocence has been stripped away. The only quest left is the one for art.

The final installment of an ambitious and lengthy chronicle has a considerable number of tasks to perform. The reader nurtured on the nineteenth century novel expects to see the numerous loose threads of the plot knotted and the conflicts resolved. Themes must evolve, ripen, and produce; the characters that reflect such truths must complete their move from ignorance to greater knowledge. Most of all, there must be a sense of the conclusion's inevitability. Proust brilliantly fulfills such expectations in the final volume of *Remembrance of Things Past*. The matinee at the new mansion of the Prince and Princess de Guermantes allows Marcel to arrive at a knowledge that has eluded him previously in his various quests for society and love. Marcel, no longer young, himself victim of the onslaughts of time, discovers that, indeed, he is capable of the literary vocation that he had previously considered beyond his grasp. *Time Regained* is nothing less than a gallery of transformations. The guests at the matinee have aged so that Marcel first thinks he has come to a masquerade. French society itself has undergone a massive upheaval. Most significant, however, is the transformation in Marcel after he fortuitously steps on the uneven paving stones outside the Guermantes mansion.

TIME REGAINED

Time Regained begins in Combray, where Marcel lives among the shattered images of his youth. His own first love, Gilberte, now suffers from the same-sex infidelities of Marcel's dearest friend, Robert de Saint-Loup. In addition to these disappointments, a book given to Marcel by Gilberte, an unpublished *Journal* of the Goncourt brothers, convinces Marcel that he has no vocation in literature. A passage from the *Journal* describes an evening at the Verdurins'. The description of Cottard and other members of the clan makes Marcel feel that he lacks the capacity to see and hear accurately. Also, if the Goncourts' work is genuine art, then art lies, for Marcel knows that the circle surrounding the Verdurins has little of the glamour that the Goncourts' account suggests. Although realistic in its detail, the passage has failed, because it has not penetrated the surface. Marcel recalls that Bergotte succeeded where the *Journal* fails, because he had the ability to become a mirror that reflected life accurately. His reading of the *Journal* leaves Marcel in a state of artistic depression, one that will not be relieved until he steps on the uneven stones.

The Goncourt *Journal* has a second function: Its description of society prepares the way for Marcel's return to the Paris of World War I. Although the war rages less than an hour away, Paris seems largely unaffected; the feud between Madame Verdurin and the Baron de Charlus continues. Although Madame Verdurin, with the aid of Morel's journalistic pieces, appears to have turned

society against the supposedly pro-German Baron, he has lost none of his intellectual or sexual fervor. What the Baron dislikes about wartime France is its love of the hypocritical chauvinistic cant written by men such as Norpois and Brichot. The Baron, however, does find the soldiers attractive; indeed, when Marcel encounters him, he is following two Zouaves. By chance, Marcel also learns of the Baron's preference for the sexually bizarre. Jupien has come to operate a male brothel for the sake of the Baron's pleasures, among which is a whipping administered to him while he is chained to an iron bed. Robert de Saint-Loup also frequents Jupien's establishment, but the war has restored his old nobility: Robert dies when he returns to the front in order to cover the retreat of his men. Gilberte, in the meantime, is in Tansonville, and Marcel learns from her that the Méséglise Way of his childhood has been the scene of an eight-month battle in which 600,000 Germans have died.

The final scene in the novel comes several years after the war has ended. Marcel has returned to Paris from a sanatorium. He continues to regret his lack of talent for literature; even his desire to produce a great work is apparently dying. Having thus no reason to avoid society, banal as it is, he accepts the invitation of the Prince and Princess de Guermantes to a matinee. The afternoon produces two major surprises. First, Marcel discovers that the past can be profoundly recaptured, although involuntarily; then, he witnesses the shocking effect time has wrought on the people he has known. His afternoon reaffirms his judgment that society has little to offer and that his one hope is to cheat death long enough to complete the work he now knows he must write.

Marcel's discoveries begin as he walks the last, short distance to the Guermanteses' new mansion. He encounters an aged Baron de Charlus supported by Jupien. The Baron brings to Marcel's mind the image of great tragic figures such as Lear and Oedipus. In this accidental meeting, the larger spectacle of aging apparent at the matinee is anticipated. Filled with gloom, Marcel approaches the mansion, but, in avoiding a passing car, he trips against the uneven paving stones. Immediately, a happiness like that evoked by the madeleine his Aunt Léonie had fed him, the trees at Balbec, and the music of Vinteuil dispels his melancholy. He then remembers the experience that lies at the source of this pleasure: The uneven stones have produced the same sensation he experienced when he stood on similar stones in the baptistery of Saint Mark's. Once inside the Guermanteses' mansion, Marcel continues to savor such memories: The sound of a spoon, the stiffness of a napkin invoke involuntary recollections. As Marcel relives the past, he is conscious of moving outside time.

Once cognizant of his ability to recapture past time, Marcel explores its relevance to creativity. In a profusion of brilliant, often aphoristic observations, Marcel indicates that the role of the artist is that of a translator of the impressions and sensations that lie within him into spiritual equivalencies. As Proust's own prose reveals, this transformation is accomplished primarily through the use of metaphor. Metaphor aids the artist in his search for the truths that lie obscured by conventional knowledge: "Through art alone are we able to emerge from ourselves, to know what another person sees of a universe which is not the same as our own." Unlike ordinary men, the artist understands that the images of daily life, the people one meets, are symbols waiting to be interpreted and read. As Wilson points out, Proust sees the role of the artist as prophetic and moral. Ideally, as Marcel states, "every reader is, while he is reading, the reader of his own self."

As Marcel savors his discoveries about the nature of art, he also perceives that Swann has indeed been his primary mentor and inspiration. Through Swann's influence, he has gone to Balbec and subsequently made the acquaintance of both the Guermanteses and Albertine. Marcel observes that even the Guermantes Way has emanated from Swann's Way, an idea reinforced when he meets Mademoiselle de Saint-Loup at the matinee. In this granddaughter of Swann, the two ways have literally become one. This recollection of Swann also provides a smooth transition back to Marcel's immediate concern, the matinee. With irony characteristic of the novel as a whole, Marcel discovers, with something akin to horror, the destructive effect of time precisely at the moment that he conceives of a work that depends on memories existing outside time. Gathered at the Guermanteses' home are most of the personages—the "interwoven threads," as Marcel calls them—that have populated the novel: Bloch, Legrandin, Gilberte, Odette, the Baron, the Duke and Duchess de Guermantes, Morel, even Rachel, Robert de Saint-Loup's old mistress. Marcel discovers curious reversals and startling revelations: The Duchess de Guermantes now patronizes Rachel, whom she once had snubbed; the Duke, described as a "magnificent ruin," loves Odette; most shocking of all, the new Princess de Guermantes is Madame Verdurin. Marcel is struck by the vast change that has taken place in a society that he once considered stable, monumental, and without flux.

The vivid display of decay and cruelty that Marcel sees at the matinee, coupled with the news of the tragic death of the great actress, Berma, produces the appropriate effect on Marcel and the reader. The physical world, awash in the tide of time, is rendered absurd by the inevitability of suffering and death. For Marcel, the visceral knowledge of such a fact is the necessary spur to action. Rather than sink into despair, he sees that life can be restored to its "pristine shape" only within the confines of a book; he repeatedly insists that his purpose in writing such a work is that others may examine their own lives.

The end of *Remembrance of Things Past* is also its beginning. Marcel removes himself from society, and, under the shadow of its own approaching death, he begins the work that will immortalize Swann, the Guermanteses, Albertine, and himself. While the quests for love and society fail or lead to disappointment, the greater quest for immortality in art succeeds.

John K. Saunders

OTHER MAJOR WORKS

SHORT FICTION: *Les Plaisirs et les jours*, 1896 (*Pleasures and Regrets*, 1948); *The Complete Short Stories of Marcel Proust*, 2001.

NONFICTION: *Pastiches et mélanges*, 1919; *Chroniques*, 1927; *Contre Sainte-Beuve*, 1954 (wr. 1908; *By Way of Sainte-Beuve*, 1958); *Marcel Proust: Selected Letters*, 1983-1992 (3 volumes; Philip Kolb, editor); *Letters of Marcel Proust*, 2006 (Mina Curtiss, editor).

TRANSLATIONS: *Le Bible d'Amiens*, 1904 (of John Ruskin's *The Bible of Amiens*); *Sésame et les lys*, 1906 (of Ruskin's *Sesame and Lilies*).

BIBLIOGRAPHY

Aciman, André, ed. *The Proust Project*. New York: Farrar, Straus and Giroux, 2004. Twenty-eight authors discuss their favorite passages in Proust's *Remembrance of Things Past*. Among the contributors are Judith Thurman, Edmund White, and J. D. McClatchy.

Bales, Richard, ed. *The Cambridge Companion to Proust*. New York: Cambridge University Press, 2001. Collection of essays about *Remembrance of Things Past* includes discussions of the novel's birth and development, the novel's structure, its narrator, and love, sex, and friendship in the novel. Also addressed are the changes seen in French society from the belle époque to World War I.

Bloom, Harold, ed. *Marcel Proust*. New York: Chelsea House, 1987. Collection features essays by Proust's most distinguished critics, including Germaine Brée, Samuel Beckett, and Walter Benjamin. Topics covered include Proust's reading and his handling of time, narrative, and metaphor. Begins with an informative editor's introduction and includes a chronology and a bibliography.

_____. *Marcel Proust's "Remembrance of Things Past."* New York: Chelsea House, 1987. Overlaps somewhat with Bloom's other edited volume of essays (above) but contains important essays by Georges Bataille ("Proust and Evil") and Georges Poulet ("Proustian Space"). Includes an introduction, chronology, and bibliography.

Brady, Patrick. *Marcel Proust*. Boston: Twayne, 1977. Good introductory study presents discussion of Proust's voice and tone as well as selves, relationships, things, symbols, patterns, memories, and art in his works. Includes chronology, notes, and annotated bibliography.

Brown, Stephen Gilbert. *The Gardens of Desire: Marcel Proust and the Fugitive Sublime*. Albany: State University of New York Press, 2004. Provides a psychological critique of *Remembrance of Things Past*, applying theories of Sigmund Freud, Jacques Derrida, and Otto Rank to analyze the origins of the novels' creative impulse.

Cano, Christine M. *Proust's Deadline*. Urbana: University of Illinois Press, 2006. Interesting history describes the publishing and reception of *Remembrance of Things Past*. Includes discussion of how the later discovery of unpublished drafts touched off a debate about the novel's authenticity.

Carter, William C. *Marcel Proust: A Life*. New Haven, Conn.: Yale University Press, 2000. Meticulous account of Proust's life and literary career traces his development as a writer. Demonstrates how his earlier writings, including the abandoned novel *Jean Santeuil*, led him to create *Remembrances of Things Past*.

Hodson, Leighton, ed. *Marcel Proust: The Critical Heritage*. New York: Routledge, 1989. Carefully tracks the reception of the author's work, from contemporary reviews to later critical essays. Includes a bibliography.

Murphy, Michael. *Proust and America*. Liverpool, England: Liverpool University Press, 2007. Interprets Proust's work within the context of American art, literature, and culture. Describes how the French writer was influenced by American authors Ralph Waldo Emerson and Edgar Allan Poe as well as by American neurologist George Beard's writings on neurasthenia and "American nervousness."

Painter, George. *Proust: The Early Years*. Boston: Little, Brown, 1959.

_____. *Proust: The Later Years*. Boston: Little, Brown, 1965. Two-volume work is renowned not only as a great biography of Proust but also as an exemplary work of biography in and of itself. Painter is noted for his extraordinary grasp of the autobiographical materials from which *Remembrance of Things Past* evolved.

White, Edmund. *Marcel Proust*. New York: Viking, 1999. Excellent concise biography of Proust. White, a gay literary critic and novelist, perceptively and honestly discusses Proust's homosexuality. Includes bibliographical references.

MANUEL PUIG

Born: General Villegas, Argentina; December 28, 1932
Died: Cuernavaca, Mexico; July 22, 1990
Also known as: Juan Manuel Puig

PRINCIPAL LONG FICTION

La traición de Rita Hayworth, 1968 (*Betrayed by Rita Hayworth*, 1971)
Boquitas pintadas, 1969 (*Heartbreak Tango: A Serial*, 1973)
The Buenos Aires Affair: Novela policial, 1973 (*The Buenos Aires Affair: A Detective Novel*, 1976)
El beso de la mujer araña, 1976 (*Kiss of the Spider Woman*, 1979)
Pubis angelical, 1979 (English translation, 1986)
Maldición eterna a quien lea estas páginas, 1980 (*Eternal Curse on the Reader of These Pages*, 1982)
Sangre de amor correspondido, 1982 (*Blood of Requited Love*, 1984)
Cae la noche tropical, 1988 (*Tropical Night Falling*, 1991)

OTHER LITERARY FORMS

Although he is best known for his novels, Manuel Puig (pweeg) was also an author of nonfiction, a playwright, and a screenwriter. His screenplays for his own *Boquitas pintadas* (1974) and for José Donoso's novel *El lugar sin límites* (1978) both won prizes at the San Sebastián Festival. His plays include *El beso de la mujer araña* (pb. 1983; *Kiss of the Spider Woman*, 1986), an adaptation of his novel, and *Misterio del ramo de rosas* (pb. 1987; *Mystery of the Rose Bouquet*, 1988).

ACHIEVEMENTS

Manuel Puig established himself both as a Latin American novelist and as a writer capable of providing insight into contemporary American society. For many years, Puig was a highly mobile exile from Argentina, spending considerable stretches of time in New York City and also favoring other cosmopolitan centers, such as Rio de Janeiro. In the process, he became a cross-cultural writer, exploring such phenomena as the effects of mass communications and culture, the issues of changing gender roles and variant sexualities, and the need to establish new types of bonds in an impermanent and rapidly changing social environment.

In addition to the university audience that is likely to gravitate toward Latin American authors, Puig's work appeals to various subcultures such as those found in New York. Film enthusiasts are understandably drawn to this novelist, who used a storehouse of cinematic knowledge in his fiction. Film critic Andrew Sarris, among others, has directed his readers toward Puig's novels and followed Puig's career with interest. The growth of the gay people's liberation movement and the general interest in alternative sexualities also increased Puig's readership, and he, in turn, was willing to learn from this movement, with its stress on the validation of nonstandard sexual expression. The author was receptive to the idea that some readers would come to his works, lectures, and public readings specifically attracted by this content, and he discussed his thoughts about sexuality in the magazine *Christopher Street* and other gay forums. Puig also became a figure admired by many members of another subculture, science-fiction readers and writers, who feel drawn not only to Puig's *Pubis angelical*, with its unmistakable borrowings from science fiction, but also to the author's overall production, for its critique of culture and society.

Puig's work thus reaches an audience more diverse than the literary sophisticates who are the only audience for many experimental writers. The excellent relationships the author established with cultural subgroups in the United States reveal his profound willingness to reach out to many types of readers, including the special enclaves that may be considered marginal or bizarre by the literary establishment.

BIOGRAPHY

Juan Manuel Puig was born on December 28, 1932, in General Villegas, Argentina. His early life, however confusing it may have been to him, provided him with excellent insight into the problems of mass-media saturation and contemporary uncertainties about sexuality and sex-role definition. As the author reported it, his almost daily filmgoing began before he had reached the age of four. The boy favored films with a strong element of glamour and fantasy, especially the extravagantly mounted musical comedies and dramas imported from the United States. His attention, he recalled, was directed almost exclusively to the female lead performers; male actors failed to provoke an empathetic response.

At the age of ten, Puig suffered a traumatic experience: an attempted rape by another male. Because Puig chose to make public this very troubling incident in his early life, one may assume that it is associated with his later literary interest in showing the effects of formative experiences in the shaping of one's identity, particularly in the emergence of a conflicted or uneasy sense of one's sexual self.

Puig's hometown was severely limited in its cultural and educational opportunities, but U.S. films provided continual reminders of the larger, cosmopolitan world. Puig's mother was an urban woman who had gone to the pampas to work in the provincial health services and ended up staying there and marrying a local man. This woman stood out from her surroundings in many ways; with her great passion for reading and filmgoing, she seems to have had a streak of Gustave Flaubert's Madame Bovary in her character. At any rate, the provincial's longing for a cosmopolitan environment became powerfully represented in Puig's first two novels.

A secondary factor in Puig's development was the disjunction between his Spanish-language environment and the English-language film world. The language used in Hollywood films, as conventionalized as it often is, cannot be considered representative of any spontaneously occurring form of expression, but Puig nevertheless identified the English language with Hollywood (indeed, as he later explained, it made him feel close to Hollywood), and he sought to bridge the gap between his world and the cinematic world by mastering English. The idea of English as the language of film persisted with Puig, to the extent that his first few writing efforts were film scripts in English. He was an active consultant in the translation of his novels into English, and he actually wrote the first version of *An Eternal Curse on the*

Reader of These Pages in English, later composing a Spanish equivalent; the published English version of the novel was based on both the unpublished English original and the Spanish "translation."

Puig's early career was marked by various unsuccessful attempts to find an outlet for his special love and knowledge of film and other popular forms. From 1955 to 1962, Puig sought to break into screenwriting and directing but was consistently unable to make progress in the film industry. A scholarship in 1957 to the Experimental Film Center permitted him to study filmmaking in Rome; later, he tried Spanish-language script work in Argentina, but he seemed to be insufficiently attuned to national realities. To become comfortable with an Argentine Spanish suitable for screenwriting, Puig worked at reproducing the voices he had heard around him in his hometown. The re-creation of these voices from a long-ago small-town world proved more absorbing than the task of screenwriting and allowed Puig to begin writing novels.

The sets of concerns referred to above are, essentially, the crucial issues of Puig's first two novels. In

Manuel Puig. (© Jerry Bauer)

1963, the restless Puig moved to New York, took a fairly undemanding job as an airline employee, and set about writing narrative, the literary form that would eventually prove his most successful medium. The author was soon able to obtain praise for his work, but it was 1968 before *Betrayed by Rita Hayworth* was published, and then without attaining a wide readership. *Heartbreak Tango* followed, as popular and readable as a soap opera, which it resembled. It drew readers to his earlier novel, and Puig became a celebrated feature of the Buenos Aires scene, which during those "boom" years tended to make celebrities of innovative writers.

In 1973, however, his third novel, *The Buenos Aires Affair*, was confiscated by authorities. After the impounding of the copies of this work, Puig published with the Barcelona firm of Seix Barral. Well established as a novelist with an international reputation, Puig traveled widely, spending considerable time in New York. He died in Cuernavaca, Mexico, on July 22, 1990.

Analysis

Although Manuel Puig took pains to introduce new variants on his favored thematic issues and to seek new solutions to the formal problems of organizing a novel, he has tended to remain identified in many minds with his first work. The highly memorable title of this novel would seem to make actor Rita Hayworth a character in the plot, and, indeed, this implication is in a sense accurate, though the action takes place far from Hollywood.

Betrayed by Rita Hayworth

In *Betrayed by Rita Hayworth*, Hayworth and other luminaries of the late 1930's and early 1940's figure as vivid presences in the decidedly unglamorous lives of a group of small-town Argentine children growing into a troubled adolescence, continually turning to the films to supply satisfactions that are missing in their existence.

Betrayed by Rita Hayworth also introduced a type of character common throughout Puig's writings: the young person confused about sex. Here, the protagonist Toto is particularly prominent in this role. Toto's early stream-of-consciousness narratives reveal his inability to make the standard distinction between male and female; he identifies himself with Shirley Temple and his unreliable father with the treacherous Rita Hayworth. As is evident from the beginning, his uncertain notions about

sexuality and sex roles are entwined with his popular-culture fantasy vision of life. The two themes come together in Toto's essay about the 1938 film *The Great Waltz*. Attempting to convey the film's ambience of a rapturous, waltz-mad Old Vienna, Toto inadvertently signals his conflict-filled view of sex. Among other things, he expresses the idea that heterosexual sex, even in the form of simple embracing and kissing, is physically harmful to women; he inserts his own element of voyeurism not found in the original film; and he dwells on the theme of insecurity about one's sexual attractiveness.

Betrayed by Rita Hayworth shows with extraordinary vividness the ability of a popular medium to bedazzle and distract consumers, particularly when audience members lack other sources of stimulation. The novel, however, does not constitute simply a lovingly nostalgic evocation of a filmgoer's paradise, for Puig also offers a critique of popular culture. It becomes clear that his characters are suffering the effects of the acritical and unquestioning consumption of a mass-culture product.

As well as including material on the sexual lives of very young characters (both real and imaginary), this first novel was unusual enough in its approach to appear risky to publishers. The small, daring Buenos Aires firm of Jorge Álvarez launched the work but then was forced to close. Later, a more prestigious house, Editorial Sudamericana, reprinted it, but only after the publication of Puig's second novel, the playfully nostalgic appeal of which convinced the public that Puig was readable. Although *Betrayed by Rita Hayworth* subsequently became a best seller, it remains a difficult work to assess and to characterize. Perhaps most difficult of all the issues involved is that of establishing the work's relation to the phenomenon of popular culture.

Sudamericana's publicity for *Betrayed by Rita Hayworth* characterized the text as a "pop novel," certainly an attractive and catchy phrase. Along with the merrily kitsch cover, which showed a tawdry Art Deco fantasy vision of Hollywood-style glamour, the publicity surrounding the work suggested that Puig had produced either an item of pop culture or a denunciatory satire of the Hollywood culture. As Puig noted, these two options seem to account for most of the readings of his works, although neither is especially accurate. *Betrayed by Rita Hayworth*, for example, cannot be critically restricted to a mere part of pop culture, for the simple reason that it evinces complex new structures characteristic of the twentieth century novel. The narration is not undertaken by a recognizable and reliable narrative voice, as it typically is in the easy-to-read formula best seller; rather, one must discover what is happening to the characters by extracting information from a variety of types of narration. These include a babble of neighborhood voices discussing the hero's birth and his mother's situation, extracts from a young girl's diary, diverse forms of stream-of-consciousness writing, a prizewinning school essay by the protagonist, letters, and other modes, all designed to look like transcriptions from the flow of thought and language. Because the novel is so strikingly anomalous, with its paradoxical joining of sophisticated novelistic form and popular culture, it conveys the impression of a somewhat uneasy synthesis.

HEARTBREAK TANGO

Heartbreak Tango is much easier to read than its predecessor. It was an immediate best seller when it appeared and, in effect, served to draw readers to Puig's more complex early novel. *Heartbreak Tango* takes the form of an old-fashioned installment novel, with each chapter revealing a new, tantalizing glimpse of a fairly intricate but banal plot. The reader is drawn along by two major lines of development: how a wondrously handsome young man of fairly good family came to an impoverished, tubercular end, and how the tense relations between a housemaid and her upwardly mobile seducer culminated in the latter's murder. Further interest comes from following the fates of three other young women: the handsome young rake's scheming sister; a local cattle baron's daughter, who rendezvouses with the rake while waiting to marry into the landed aristocracy; and another of the hero's conquests, an ambitious blond who can never manage to rise above the lower middle class.

The characters, however sympathetic they may be at moments, are satirized for their obsession with status and standing. Puig warned against placing too great an emphasis on the satiric element. While well-educated urban readers might see the book as turning the members of the provincial middle class into figures of fun, such a reading fails to take into account the great amount of material dedicated to the exploration of Puig's twin themes of popular culture and concepts of sexuality.

One of the most telling indicators of the extent to which the media have saturated the culture is the language used by the characters to speak of their own lives. So enthralled are they by the commercially standardized language of sentimental and romantic films, advertising copy charged with mass-appeal allure, and other popular subgenres (song lyrics, sportscasting, "tearjerker" novels, and so on) that this language becomes second nature to them. The problem is the lack of correlation between their own existence and the rapturous, adventurous, or "macho" language they employ. The incongruity is especially acute in the area of courtship mores. The reader sees a small society in which both marriage and informal liaisons are heavily governed by questions of prestige and economic power, while the characters see love and sexuality through a haze of dreamily romantic or aggressively Don Juanesque phrases.

The presentation of popular culture in *Heartbreak Tango* is much more diverse than it is in *Betrayed by Rita Hayworth*. The characters, no longer children growing into adolescence, are young adults moving toward an early, disaffected middle age. Their patterns of pop-culture consumption reflect this shift. They have lost the child's ability to be enraptured by a film, and they turn to the cinema house as a meeting place, a distraction in which they indulge by ingrained habit. Concerned with presenting themselves impressively, they rely on advertising and magazine materials in order to master style. The artifacts of mass culture—photo albums, commercial art, decorative product packaging, dance-hall decor, and household bric-a-brac—surround them. They are living in the "golden age" of radio, and the airwaves are full of gimmicky programs, including variety shows, serial dramas, and musicals.

On one hand, the young people present the classic picture of "junk-culture addicts"; they show many signs of a virtual dependence on their pop culture. (One young woman, for example, cannot forgo her daily radio soap opera, even when a long-absent friend shows up at her house.) Despite this constant consumption of media, however, their satisfaction with it lessens. The rakish hero reports attending the cinema without feeling any interest in the film shown, while an observant heroine notices that her town is being shipped films that are too out-of-date to screen elsewhere. These expressions of ennui with the homogeneous mass media do not, however, entail a critical questioning of mass culture. The young people are not moved by their boredom and dissatisfaction with certain pop-culture artifacts to ask whether the massive standardization of this culture might be unwarranted and intellectually unhealthy, nor do they attempt to find alternative forms of diversion. The young men and women remain fixed in their accustomed patterns.

The focus on sexuality is less concerned with individual cases than it is with the social codes that govern the expression of sexual feelings. The small-town young people try to satisfy various conflicting sets of standards. On the surface, the unmarried women are expected to remain chaste, while men are given more leeway, although they are required to satisfy conditions of respectability. Overlapping this Victorian standard, and at times in conflict with it, is the code of machismo, which demands of the young men a constant effort to conquer numbers of women, to cultivate a swaggering style, and to appear unconcerned with their own well-being. An additional set of factors has to do with the intense and widespread desire for upward mobility.

Apart from the inherent passion between the sexes, the desire for prestige is the most powerful force in determining the characters' involvements with one another. The Don Juanesque hero's sister continually schemes to link him with the cattleman's daughter and to steer him away from the blond social climber, while the stockbroker seeks to guide his daughter toward a landowning customer. Meanwhile, the blond attempts to minimize a loss of status incurred by an earlier seduction, hoping to charm her Casanova-lover into marriage. In a subplot, the hero masterminds the amorous life of a lower-class friend. Under this tutelage, the aspiring policeman seduces a servant, avoiding any lasting commitment that might impede his rise in society.

Of the various liaisons contracted during the novel, all are somehow colored by the dream of acquiring an advantageous match in marriage. The schemes uniformly come to nothing, for the hero dies without marrying any of his lovers; the wealthy landowner rejects the stockbroker's daughter, along with a shipment of diseased cattle; the policeman's brief enjoyment of middle-class status is ended by his spurned girlfriend's violence. In an ironic turnabout, the vision is realized only by the servant girl, who stands at the very bottom of this hierarchy. After being seduced, impregnated, and abandoned—even after murdering her lover—she somehow succeeds in obtaining for herself a stable and provident mate.

Puig is unmistakably critical of this scenario, in which sex and courtship are made part of the politics of class standing. He offers a condemnatory portrait of this system, making his attitude clear by portraying popular culture as stressing the acquisition of an impressive lover or spouse. (At the height of the cross-class tangle of sexual alliances, the local movie theater is running a Hollywood film centered entirely on the concept of marrying for wealth and security.) The criticism is clear, but Puig has not begun to look at alternative arrangements that would remove sexuality from this very politicized framework. This missing factor does, however, appear in Puig's later work, when he turns to utopian speculations about the future of sex.

THE BUENOS AIRES AFFAIR

If Puig's first novel was substantially patterned on the modern "serious" novel and his second novel derived playfully from the serialized soap opera, his third work, *The Buenos Aires Affair*, offered a renovated version of the detective novel. Puig remained manifestly faithful to the idea of simplifying his novelistic form enough to allow easy reading, although this accessibility did not preclude subtlety and complexity.

The novel was confiscated in Buenos Aires and deemed obscene, although it contains little in the way of overwhelming erotic content. *The Buenos Aires Affair* would seem to have hit a sensitive spot because the pair of lovers, an art critic and an aspiring sculptress, clearly form a sadomasochistic team, and the man bears the burden of a very troubled homosexual past. In short, the theme of nonstandard sexuality, indirectly alluded to in the confusion of Toto in *Betrayed by Rita Hayworth*, now emerges as an overt theme.

The "affair" of the title refers to both a police case, in the sense of a mysterious set of circumstances requiring investigation, and a liaison between the protagonists. The two meanings of the word coalesce, for the police are called in to resolve an out-of-control situation between the lovers. The man, having lost his ability to keep his sexual expression from interfering with society, has kidnapped his girlfriend and is holding her in bondage.

This disruptive act, reported at the very beginning of the novel, eventually turns out to be merely the culmination of a torturous relationship that came to have such a grip on the hero that he was no longer able to refrain from destructive and self-destructive actions. The novel reconstructs the pressures that led this man, an educated and influential member of the arts community, to burst out in reckless, antisocial behavior. Intertwined is the story of the sculptress. The woman's history is less dramatic, for she does not succumb to any wild outbreak of deranged behavior; rather, she has gradually reached a point where she finds any purposeful action difficult to plan or execute, so that even her sculpting is largely the passive activity of presenting and "conceptualizing" found objects. A third direction in the novel's development is the unfolding of the events caused by the kidnapping. The police, far from solving the tangle of disturbing evidence, essentially go through various standard procedures until the hero brings the matter to an end by destroying himself in his panic; the ever-passive heroine is befriended by a sane, motherly neighbor woman. In effect, the total contribution of the authorities is to report as properly as possible on a set of circumstances that they can neither influence nor understand. If any detective work is accomplished, it is that performed by the reader in attempting to obtain some degree of insight into this disordered tale of unhappy sexual alliances and cultural fashions.

To provide an understanding of the protagonists' problems, Puig employs a number of narrative procedures that tend to place the characters on the psychiatric couch. Transcriptions of the hero's exchanges with his psychotherapist are included, as well as "case histories" of both the man and the woman. The histories of both characters' troubles are couched in a language of pseudo-scientific objectivity, again evoking concepts of psychiatric investigation of the past.

In utilizing these "psychoanalytical" narratives, Puig would seem to be lampooning classical psychotherapy yet making use of its theories. The man's psychiatrist is, in effect, as confused and helpless as any layperson as he watches his patient display increasingly muddled thinking and erratic behavior. The woman, though not undergoing any type of psychiatric treatment that is directly presented to the reader, has recently fallen into the hands of the medical establishment as a result of her sudden inability to function, with similarly unhelpful results. It is worth remarking that the two people in the novel who are best able to counsel and soothe the frantic protagonists are simply laypersons who have a calm and stable outlook. The hero enters into a series of telephone exchanges with an older, tradition-steeped sculptress who, unlike the classically trained psychiatrist, is willing to speak to the disturbed man in commonsense terms. Her ability to carry on a sensible, reasonable conversation with the man stands out in a novel full of fatuous, jargon-filled talk. Reinforcing this theme that steady, ordinary people can function successfully as therapists is the appearance of the neighbor woman who, at the end, cares for the heroine. This neighbor, a young woman clearly satisfied with her husband and baby, asks the heroine as little as possible about the circumstances leading to her current beleaguered state, instead concentrating on getting her to rest and feel comfortable.

While the novel shows professional therapists being outdone by concerned laypersons, it is essentially favorable to the notion, heavily associated with psychiatry, that early-childhood experiences may underlie troubles faced in adulthood. At the same time, Puig is concerned with expanding the narrowly psychological and individualistic view of childhood development. He moves beyond the particular—the workings of the child's family—to look at factors that potentially affect all children reared in a particular society. The effects of mass media and culture are, once more, subjected to detailed scrutiny. The heroine, for example, carries a permanent sense of unease as a result of constantly being compared with the media-propagated images of perfect womanhood.

Her case history dwells on her father's attempts to remake his daughter into a conventionally attractive, vivacious young woman and her resulting unhappiness over her failure to match this standard. The father's favored reading matter, the popular 1940's magazine *Rico tipo* (fancy guy), is singled out for particular denunciation for its tendency to promote a single image of acceptable femininity and to deride women who fail to adhere to this highly conventional pattern of attractiveness. Another spotlighted aspect of popular culture is the system of recreational clubs for young women. In *The Buenos Aires Affair*, these social organizations are seen as essentially concerned with questions of prestige and "connections." The heroine's childhood is further marred by her ambitious mother's attempts to attain upward mobility through this supposedly leisure-providing system.

In *The Buenos Aires Affair*, Puig is most critical of the distortion of artistic activity that allows conformity to the capitalist society's patterns of "product marketing." For example, although the hero is well read in the field of art criticism, he is seldom observed analyzing artistic work. His essential function is that of a publicist and impresario. His friends, with their incessant festival-going, see themselves as marketable commodities that must be kept in the art public's eye. In this unattractive panorama of self-packagers and self-promoters, only one exception stands out: the extraordinarily sane older woman who is able to counsel the troubled hero. All evidence points to her conscientious and principled practice of assemblage art; her steadfast and workmanlike approach strikes the art critic in his professional conscience. It is his realization that he has awarded a prize to his heavily "hyped," but inconsequential, sculptress-lover, rejecting the well-conceived work of the older woman, that precipitates his final round of deranged behavior.

Culture consumption as a search for prestige is another of the novel's motifs. An amusing example occurs on the night of the heroine's conception. Her parents have just seen a performance of a play by Eugene O'Neill that affords them theatergoing satisfaction, but they are inhibited in their later discussion of it by their extreme desire not to be "one-upped" by each other. Within the dynamics of this marriage, the wife can lay claim to some degree of superiority to her husband; while he tends to favor "easy reading" material, she has the time to maintain at least a superficial knowledge of the arts. The daughter continues this pattern of competence in the arts as a way of maintaining status. In addition, Puig points to the fact that the characters live in a mass-media culture by using excerpts from old Hollywood melodramas as epigraphs to the chapters. These film dialogues do not comment directly on the issue treated in the chapter, but rather suggest a world in which the hyperbolic "Hollywoodization" of life situations has altered people's expectations about the drama, suspense, and romance they should find in their own lives.

The Buenos Aires Affair thus continues the examination of mass culture, but it is also a study in the attitudes and actions of fine-arts consumers. In earlier Puig novels, the characters can be seen as suffering from cultural deprivation, because of their lack of education, their isolation, or both. *The Buenos Aires Affair* presents characters who are of a cultural level comparable to that of an educated reader of novels; Puig thereby holds up a mirror to his reader that reflects criticism of the characters onto the reader himself. The heroine, Gladys, reads fashionable serious authors and spends time as a prize-winning, if docile and eager-to-please, art student. Her choices as a consumer of culture are typically those of a trend-conscious, informed viewer or reader, from a preference for starkly functional decor to her favorite television fare, relatively "classy" examples of Hollywood cinema. The hero is an influential art critic. What is amiss is their approach to culture. The heroine's artistic career offers an extreme example of a creator so uncertain of her own expression that she depends slavishly on the academic standards of competence that will win praise and awards for her. Leaving the structured world of the art school, she is unable to produce and becomes so distraught over her relation to art that even going to museums becomes unbearably painful.

If Gladys represents the constraints of academically institutionalized art, her lover reveals the same pattern in antiestablishment art. He is a leading figure on the experimentalist scene. His favored artists use approaches originally designed to defy and astound the art orthodoxy—found objects, assemblages, works with a strong random element, and so on. The creators of this work, however, are not rebels but dedicated careerists, obsessed with the notion of making a name for themselves. Among the ridiculous, petty actions attributed to this cliquish group, the worst is its treatment of Gladys. The woman is clearly going through a period of instability, but the avant-garde group chooses to perceive her as wildly innovative rather than unbalanced. Her debris sculptures, more pathological indications than works of art, are gaudily exploited as the last word in assemblage art. The group's disregard for the well-being of the disoriented woman at the center of all this promotional hoopla is the surest indictment of a type of high culture wholly dominated by the need to market and sell novelties to a jaded public.

The overall effect is to bring home the problem of passive cultural consumption and production by featuring characters and settings not likely to be far removed from the readers' own set of experiences. Particularly in *Gladys*, the bright, industrious young person who finds both modern culture and sex perpetually mind-boggling, Puig has created a figure capable of reflecting the reader's and the author's own difficulties amid the confusions of the current cultural scene.

The transition from the early, literarily complex Puig to the more accessible author of the later novels is not even. *Betrayed by Rita Hayworth* is set apart from the subsequent novels by its structural complexity and the amount of work the reader must perform to extract a sense of what is going on in the work. *Heartbreak Tango* was deliberately written for a broad audience, and Puig has expressed disappointment that the novel did not reach a wider public than it did. While the work does not require laborious reading, its commentary on the phenomenon of mass culture is by no means simplistic. *The Buenos Aires Affair*, relatively accessible despite a degree of narrative experimentation, introduced a new set of issues as Puig turned his critical scrutiny to the fine-arts culture, its consumers and practitioners, and the author's concern with nonstandard forms of sexuality.

KISS OF THE SPIDER WOMAN

Kiss of the Spider Woman, although a fascinating work in many respects, marks a certain repetition of themes and structures already familiar to Puig's readers. Without denigrating this work, one may describe it as lending itself less to critical consideration than do others of Puig's works, for it appears designed for readers who are not literary analysts. To give only one example of this phenomenon, long citations from essays on homosexuality are included as footnotes, an inclusion having very little to do with the literary texture of the work and a great deal to do with Puig's desire to convey to lay readers a consciousness of this misunderstood phenomenon. The same process of "laicization"—of writing more and more for the reader who is not a literary specialist—was the most notable aspect of the evolution of Puig's writing after that time.

Puig accepted the courtship of such determinedly "lay" reader groups as science-fiction aficionados and cultural workers concerned with the presentation of alternatives in sexuality; at the same time, many academic readers were baffled by the evolution of Puig's work. It has yet to be determined whether Puig actually moved away from the typical high-culture, "literary" reader or whether this variety of reader simply learned new reading strategies to follow Puig.

Naomi Lindstrom

OTHER MAJOR WORKS

PLAYS: *Bajo un manto de estrellas*, pb. 1983 (*Under a Mantle of Stars*, 1985); *El beso de la mujer araña*, pb. 1983 (*Kiss of the Spider Woman*, 1986; adaptation of his novel); *Misterio del ramo de rosas*, pb. 1987 (*Mystery of the Rose Bouquet*, 1988).

SCREENPLAYS: *Boquitas pintadas*, 1974 (adaptation of his novel); *El lugar sin límites*, 1978 (adaptation of José Donoso's novel).

BIBLIOGRAPHY

Bacarisse, Pamela. *Impossible Choices: The Implications of the Cultural References in the Novels of Manuel Puig*. Calgary, Alberta: University of Calgary Press, 1993. Excellent critical study of Puig's work focuses on the references to American films and to other elements of popular culture in his work. Includes bibliography and index.

_____. *The Necessary Dream: A Study of the Novels of Manuel Puig*. Totowa, N.J.: Barnes & Noble Books, 1988. Provides a useful introduction to Puig's literary career and the themes of his work, with individual chapters devoted to the major novels. Includes notes and bibliography.

Colas, Santiago. *Postmodernity in Latin America: The Argentine Paradigm*. Durham, N.C.: Duke University Press, 1994. Puig is included in this study of postmodern literature, which also examines the writings of Julio Cortázar and Ricardo Piglia. Devotes two chapters to *Kiss of the Spider Woman*, placing the novel within the context of Argentine politics.

Craig, Linda. *Juan Carlos Onetti, Manuel Puig, and Luisa Valenzuela: Marginality and Gender*. Woodbridge, England: Tamesis, 2005. Presents analysis of works by Puig and two other Latin American writers. Asserts that these authors express a shared sense of "postcolonial emptiness" and continually question realism.

Kerr, Lucille. *Suspended Fictions: Reading Novels by Manuel Puig.* Urbana: University of Illinois Press, 1987. Explores the themes of tradition, romance, popular culture, crime, and sex in Puig's major novels and examines the design of the author's career. Includes detailed notes.

Lavers, Norman. *Pop Culture into Art: The Novels of Manuel Puig.* Columbia: University of Missouri Press, 1988. Provides a concise discussion of the close relationship between Puig's life and the themes, techniques, and materials of his first seven novels. Includes bibliographies.

Levine, Suzanne Jill. *Manuel Puig and the Spider Woman: His Life and Fictions.* Madison: University of Wisconsin Press, 2001. Biography by one of Puig's translators draws on personal knowledge of Puig as well as on research in examining the intersections of his life and his art.

Magnarelli, Sharon. "Betrayed by the Cross-Stitch." In *The Lost Rib: Female Characters in the Spanish-American Novel.* Toronto, Ont.: Associated University Presses, 1985. Close reading and feminist analysis of Puig's novel *Betrayed by Rita Hayworth* is included in a larger examination of how female protagonists are portrayed in Spanish American fiction.

Mobili, Giorgio. *Irritable Bodies and Postmodern Subjects in Pynchon, Puig, Volponi.* New York: Peter Lang, 2008. Discusses works by Puig and other postmodern writers, focusing on their representations of wounded, torn, or deformed bodies and how they employ these depictions to address societal issues.

Tittler, Jonathan. *Manuel Puig.* New York: Twayne, 1993. One of the best introductions to Puig's work available in English. Begins with an introduction that provides a useful survey of Puig's career and then devotes separate chapters to the novels. Includes detailed notes and an annotated bibliography.

JAMES PURDY

Born: Fremont, Ohio; July 17, 1914
Died: Englewood, New Jersey; March 13, 2009
Also known as: James Amos Purdy

PRINCIPAL LONG FICTION

Malcolm, 1959
The Nephew, 1960
Cabot Wright Begins, 1964
Eustace Chisholm and the Works, 1967
Jeremy's Version, 1970
I Am Elijah Thrush, 1972
The House of the Solitary Maggot, 1974
In a Shallow Grave, 1976
Narrow Rooms, 1978
Mourners Below, 1981
On Glory's Course, 1984
In the Hollow of His Hand, 1986
Garments the Living Wear, 1989

Out with the Stars, 1992
Gertrude of Stony Island Avenue, 1997

OTHER LITERARY FORMS

In addition to his novels, James Purdy wrote in a variety of genres, including poetry, the short story, and drama. The most important of these other works are *Sixty-three: Dream Palace* (1956); *Color of Darkness: Eleven Stories and a Novella* (1957); *Children Is All* (1961), a collection of ten stories and two plays; and a volume of poetry, *The Running Sun* (1971).

ACHIEVEMENTS

James Purdy is considered one of the most important of the postmodern American writers. Along with Thomas Pynchon, John Barth, and John Hawkes, Purdy is acknowledged as one of the best of the generation of post-Joycean experimental writers. His writing is unique and powerful, and his vision remains etched in the reader's mind. Like other postmodern writers, Purdy took delight in experimenting with the texts and subtexts of narratives and treated his themes with humor and irony. In essence, Purdy's characters are motivated by irrationality; his style is ornate and complex, and his themes are surreal. Purdy is a writer whose works must be examined if the textures and ideas of the postmodern novel are to be appreciated.

BIOGRAPHY

James Amos Purdy was born on July 17, 1914, near Fremont, Ohio. He attended the University of Chicago and the University of Puebla in Mexico. Later, he worked as an interpreter in Spain, Latin America, and France. From 1949 until 1953, he taught at Lawrence College in Appleton, Wisconsin. In 1953, he decided to devote himself to writing full time. Purdy received Guggenheim Fellowships in 1958 and 1962 and a Ford Fellowship in Drama in 1961. He took a teaching post at New York University and settled in Brooklyn Heights, New York. On March 13, 2009, Purdy died in New Jersey.

James Purdy. (Fabian Bachrach/Library of Congress)

ANALYSIS

Because James Purdy was so hesitant to make public the details of his private life, it is impossible to correlate any of his works with his personal experiences. His works are hermetically sealed from his life and must be examined as entities in themselves. Purdy's themes, styles, and ideas change, develop, and expand from novel to novel, so it is not possible to delineate any one particular aspect of his work that is found consistently throughout. Certain preoccupations, however, are found, in varying degrees, in most of his works, and certain characteristics that are typical of postmodern fiction.

The characters in Purdy's novels are bizarre, grotesque, and governed by abnormal impulses and desires. Purdy uses his characters for purposes of symbolic manipulation rather than for the purpose of character development in the traditional sense. Many of his characters are physically or mentally mutilated, or both: They are tattooed, wounded, stabbed, raped, and, in one case, crucified. One of the major characteristics of all of his novels is his use of "unreal" characters whose thinking processes are "nonrealistic."

A primary concern of Purdy is the relationship of children to their parents; most of his novels include a domineering phallic woman, the search for a father, and the interrelationships within a family matrix. Many of his characters are orphans, illegitimate children, or children who have been abandoned by their parents. Along with these motifs, Purdy is preoccupied with the idea of being "grown-up" or mature. Within the quest for a father figure, the idea of becoming mature is interwoven into the text, and within this framework Purdy usually parodies the search for identity and its resultant ambivalence.

The interplay of sex, love, and violence occurs frequently throughout Purdy's writing. Virtually no love between man and woman appears in Purdy's novels—male-female relationships are either those of a prostitute and a man or a man who rapes women. Purdy does include a number of sexual affairs between men in his works, but these usually end in obsession and violence. In addition, many of the novels involve incest.

Also interwoven in the stories are themes of tyranny, freedom, dominance, and obsessive love. Frequently, the female characters are aggressive and domineering, and often the male characters are passive and dominated. Many of the characters are attempting to find their "freedom" from dominance, but the nature of obsessive love does not permit this.

Finally, in some manner or another, Purdy's novels all involve a writer within the narrative. In some books, this figure takes on more importance than in others; this device, typical of self-conscious "metafiction," serves to emphasize the autonomous reality of the fictive world.

MALCOLM

Many of the themes, motifs, and preoccupations of his subsequent novels are found in Purdy's first novel, *Malcolm*. The orphan motif that occurs so frequently in Purdy's works plays a vital part in *Malcolm*. Malcolm (no last name given), the reader is told, belongs nowhere and to nobody. His father has disappeared, and Malcolm's search for him forms the central psychological structure of the book. The fifteen-year-old Malcolm is sitting on a park bench outside the hotel where he is staying when Mr. Cox, an astrologer, takes an interest in him. He gives Malcolm a series of addresses in order to interest him in "things," and the ensuing visits to the people who live at the respective addresses form the core of the action in the novel. Malcolm becomes a parody of the picaro, for instead of acting he is acted upon. His main concern is to find his father, but his actions are governed by the tyrannical Mr. Cox and his circle of friends.

Within Mr. Cox's circle are Madame Girard and Girard Girard, an eccentric billionaire. At one point in the novel, Malcolm is offered a chance to be Girard Girard's son, but Malcolm tells him he has only one father and Girard Girard cannot take his place. Later, after Malcolm marries Melba, a famous black singer, he believes that he sees his father at a restaurant. Malcolm follows this man into the restroom. The man, however, denies that he is Malcolm's father and throws Malcolm down, causing Malcolm to hit his head. After this incident, Malcolm, who has deteriorated physically since his marriage, becomes too weak to get out of bed and eventually dies.

Thus, in this first novel, Purdy reveals many of his recurring preoccupations. In addition to the orphan's search for the father (paralleling the search for identity), Purdy explores the topic of tyranny and the theme of the fatality of a loveless marriage. A concern with the maturation process is also found in *Malcolm*. Gus, one of Melba's former husbands, is chosen to help Malcolm mature before his marriage. Gus's solution to helping Malcolm "mature" is to have Malcolm tattooed and to have him visit a prostitute.

In *Malcolm*, the characters are constantly questioning the substantiality of their existence; they are two-dimensional, almost comic-book figures. Malcolm is given addresses, not names, and consequently, places and events take primacy over the development of the personality. Malcolm himself has no last name, and when he dies there is no corpse in his coffin. All that is left of Malcolm are three hundred pages of manuscript that he had written, which Madame Girard attempts to organize.

THE NEPHEW

In *The Nephew*, Purdy turns to the small town of Rainbow Center for his setting and tells a story that superficially resembles a slice of small-town life. Underneath the seemingly placid exterior of Rainbow Center, however, as beneath the surface of the novel, much is happening. The text is surcharged with meanings, and the experience of reading this novel is similar to that of watching a film with the sound track slightly off.

The plot is simple and straightforward. Alma Mason and her brother, Boyd, receive news that their nephew Cliff is missing in action during the Korean War. Cliff, another of Purdy's orphans, had lived with the Masons. In order to alleviate some of the grief of his death, Alma decides to write a memorial honoring Cliff. The novel focuses on Alma's attempts to gather material for the writing of Cliff's memorial. During this process, she discovers many facets of Cliff's existence of which she had been unaware—particularly that Cliff had hated the town and that he had had a homosexual affair—which lead her to some revelations about herself and her relationship to Boyd and others in the community.

One of Purdy's concerns that can be noted throughout the novel is the inadequacy of judging people by their actions and their words. Communication is always inadequate and misinterpreted. Alma never does finish her memorial to Cliff, another indication that one can never fully understand another person. By the end of the story, however, Alma does become much more tolerant in her attitude toward what she considers the foibles of others.

CABOT WRIGHT BEGINS

Like *The Nephew*, *Cabot Wright Begins* concerns the attempt to write about another person—in this case, a businessman and rapist named Cabot Wright. Instead of one narrative voice, as in *The Nephew*, many emerge in *Cabot Wright Begins*, and this blending and confusion of narrative voices further demonstrate the impossibility of learning the true story about another person.

Purdy's third novel is an extremely pessimistic indictment and extended meditation on modern American culture. In *Cabot Wright Begins*, people are controlled by media-think, big business, and popular culture and by all the superficial aspects of modern existence. Feelings, emotions, and actions are all superficial, and even the rape scenes involving Cabot Wright are narrated in a dispassionate manner—much like secondhand violence seen on television or in the cinema. People exist on the screen of the text, and their ability to function in normal human terms is questioned.

Cabot Wright, another orphan, is twenty-six years old during the time of the novel. He is a stockbroker turned rapist. Bernie Gladhart, a used-car salesman, has been cajoled by his wife into writing the great American novel and has decided that a life history of Cabot Wright would be the perfect subject matter. In fact, the tentative title of Bernie's novel is "Indelible Smudge," which indicates Purdy's judgment about American culture at this time. Princeton Keith, the owner of a large publishing house, however, has commissioned Zoe Bickle to write the story in terms of popular fiction. Through a skylight, Zoe literally falls upon Cabot Wright himself, and Cabot offers to help her ghostwrite his biography. In the process of turning his life into popular fiction, however, he becomes alienated from himself. To him, the story does not portray his real self.

Cabot Wright seems to symbolize the attempt of modern men and women to assert their identity through violence. Only through the act of rape can Cabot penetrate the surface of another, but even then he becomes increasingly alienated and less alive. For Cabot, there are no answers.

EUSTACE CHISHOLM AND THE WORKS

In *Eustace Chisholm and the Works*, Purdy presents his concept of the sacrificial, violent, and grotesque aspects of love. In many horrific scenes he shows the re-

sults of obsessional love. The story revolves around the sexual love Daniel Hawes has for seventeen-year-old Amos Ratcliff. Amos, an illegitimate son, has been rejected by his father and has had incestuous relationships with his cousin (later revealed to be his mother). Daniel attempts to repress his feelings for Amos, but they finally become so overwhelming that he reenlists in the Army to escape. Instead of escaping, however, he permits his love for Amos to be brought to the surface and projected upon his commanding officer, Captain Stadger. During the affair between these two, Captain Stadger becomes increasingly more sadistic until finally he kills Daniel by disemboweling him, then commits suicide. This incident is the first in a series of homosexual blood sacrifices found in Purdy's novels.

Once again, as in all of Purdy's previous works, there is an author involved in an attempt to write the story. In this case, Eustace Chisholm is the writer who is attempting to incorporate the story of Amos and Daniel within the context of a larger epic poem that he is writing.

JEREMY'S VERSION

Purdy's next novel, *Jeremy's Version*, was written as part 1 of a projected trilogy called *Sleepers in the Moon-Crowned Valleys*. Although Purdy had dealt with orphans, the search for a father figure, and interrelationships within families in his previous works, this was his first novel in which the family matrix formed the basis for the entire work.

Again, there is a writer—in this case, Jeremy Cready—narrating the story being told to him by Uncle Matt. The basic story (which actually occurred more than fifty years before) involves the battle of wills between two strong women, Elvira Summerlad and Winifred Fergus; a divorce case; and the interrelationships of the three sons with one another and with their mother and father. Elvira Summerlad and Wilders Fergus were married, much against the wishes of his sister, Winifred, who thought the marriage was doomed. In a sense, Winifred was right, because Wilders abandoned Elvira and their sons. Winifred, however, goes to Wilders and tells him that since his sons are almost grown, he is needed at home. When he arrives, Elvira starts divorce proceedings against him.

The basic conflict is between Elvira and Winifred for

custody of the children. Wilders is indifferent to the whole affair. One of Purdy's major themes—that of the son confronting the father—occurs during the divorce proceedings, when the gay oldest son, Rick, confronts Wilders. Rick demands that Wilders tell him the reason for his existence since his father has never been around before to teach him—he has only had his mother, who, he claims, has emasculated him. After Elvira wins the divorce case, her second son, Jethro, attempts to shoot her, but Matt saves her and is wounded. A similar shooting scene, between mother and son, occurs again in *The House of the Solitary Maggot.*

I Am Elijah Thrush

I Am Elijah Thrush is a dreamlike, ornate, and highly stylized book, populated with strange characters and filled with unusual events. More than any of Purdy's other novels, this book exists in the realm of allegory and symbols. Among the major characters are a famous mime, Elijah Thrush; his great-grandson, a mute, called the Bird of Heaven; Millicent De Frayne, a tyrannical old dowager who retains her youth by drinking the seminal fluid of young men; and Albert Peggs, the black memoirist who tells the story and who, himself, has a bizarre "habit." In addition, the novel incorporates many elements of mythology in a comic manner, suggesting the debasement of culture in modern America.

As in many of Purdy's previous novels, the plot in *I Am Elijah Thrush* involves a person (in this case, Albert Peggs) being hired by someone to write the story. Millicent De Frayne hires Albert to recount the story of Elijah Thrush. Once again, this story involves a clash of wills between two strong people—Millicent and Elijah. For more than fifty years, she has been trying to gain control of Elijah and marry him. Eventually, she succeeds by manipulating Albert, the Bird of Heaven, and Elijah onto her boat, where she finally marries him. Late in the novel, Albert's "habit" is discovered: He sustains the life of a golden eagle by permitting the eagle to feed upon him. At the wedding feast of Millicent and Elijah, the eagle is served as the entree. After this incident, Albert "becomes" Elijah Thrush.

One of Purdy's major themes is that of confirming, or finding, an identity. In his novels, there is a plethora of name-changes, mistaken identities, disguises, masquerades, and other such motifs. The dreamlike structure of the narrative suggests that Albert Peggs is attempting to discover his identity by telling this story.

The House of the Solitary Maggot

The House of the Solitary Maggot is part 2 of the series called *Sleepers in Moon-Crowned Valleys.* The story is reconstructed—this time on a tape recorder—by one of the characters, and, as in part 1 of the series, *Jeremy's Version,* the family matrix is the psychological focus in the novel. The story involves Mr. Skegg, the magnate (the "solitary maggot"); Lady Bythewaite; and their three illegitimate sons: Clarence, who is legally "acknowledged" by the father; Owen, who is acknowledged by the mother; and Aiken, who is not acknowledged by either parent until later in the book.

The novel takes place in a dying community called Prince's Crossing. Owen, the youngest son, hero-worships his brother, Clarence, who goes to New York to become a famous silent-film star. After Clarence leaves, Owen turns to the other older brother, Aiken, whom he also worships. The two become inseparable. Aiken, who himself has no acknowledged father or mother, serves as a father figure to Owen, helping him "mature" by giving him his first shave and taking him to visit a prostitute. After visiting her, Owen loses his sight. Aiken, who has finally been acknowledged by Lady Bythewaite as her long-lost son, buys the Acres, the showplace of the community. When Clarence returns and refuses to accept Aiken as his brother, Aiken, whose pride is hurt, burns down the house and marries the prostitute. This marriage is a failure, and Aiken decides to leave.

Although Aiken has been estranged from Owen, he loves him obsessively. When Aiken goes to say good-bye to Owen and their mother, Owen shoots him. Lady Bythewaite, one of Purdy's typical strong-willed, castrating women, then shoots Owen. In another of Purdy's characteristically grotesque scenes, Owen's eyeballs fall out and Aiken swallows them. While Aiken remains unconscious in the hospital, Clarence returns and wants to be acknowledged as Aiken's brother. When the unconscious Aiken cannot comply, Clarence slits his own throat. Eventually, Aiken comes to live with his mother. Mr. Skegg acknowledges him as his son and takes care of him in his illness. The story concludes with the death of Aiken, who, in a dreamlike sequence, tries to ride off on a horse with the dead Owen.

IN A SHALLOW GRAVE

The protagonist of Purdy's next novel, *In a Shallow Grave*, is Garnet Montrose, a war hero who has been so badly wounded that he is turned almost inside-out and is the color of mulberry juice. Garnet seeks "applicants" to take messages from him to the Widow Rance, whom he wishes to court, but the applicants are so appalled by Garnet's appearance that they cannot accept the job. Finally, Quintus, a black adolescent, shows up by accident at Garnet's house and accepts the position. Quintus's responsibilities are to read to Garnet and to rub his feet. Later, a man named Daventry shows up. Even though he is not an applicant, he takes the position of messenger to the Widow Rance. Within this narrative structure, Purdy pursues many of his recurring themes.

One of the primary scenes involves a communion among Garnet, Quintus, and Daventry. Garnet is about to have his property taken away, but Daventry says that he will save Garnet's land and property if Garnet will commune with him. Daventry takes his knife, slits open his chest, and the three of them drink his blood. Later, they discover that Garnet's property has been saved by the Veterans Administration, who heard of his plight and paid the mortgage. The wounding and shedding of blood, along with the religious connotations of the scene, seem to indicate that language is inadequate for portraying emotions, that the only way to "love" another person is to shed blood for him or her.

Again, homosexual love appears in the novel, for Daventry and Garnet fall in love. They consummate their love in the dance hall where Garnet goes to dance by himself and relive the moments in the past when he was "normal." With Garnet's permission, Daventry marries the Widow Rance, but on his wedding night, he is swept up by a strong wind, smashed against a tree, and killed.

NARROW ROOMS

Narrow Rooms is a story about the love-hate relationship between Roy Sturtevant (the renderer) and Sidney De Lakes. Roy Sturtevant had been in love with Sidney since the eighth grade, until Sidney slapped him publicly and humiliated him; from that time, Roy has been planning his revenge. The story opens after Sidney has returned from prison, where he served time for killing Brian McFee. He finds a job as keeper of Gareth Vaisey, who has been injured in a fall from a horse. Sidney and Gareth fall in love and have an affair, but Roy Sturtevant still exercises a strange power over them.

In the central scene in the novel, after Roy and Sidney have a sexual encounter, Roy commands Sidney to crucify him on the barn door and then bring the body of Brian McFee to view the crucifixion. Roy, still alive, is taken down from the barn door and carried into the house. Sidney and Roy then pledge their love for each other, and Gareth, jealous, shoots them both. Subsequently, Gareth also dies. Though the subject matter of *Narrow Rooms* is largely sensational, the novel continues Purdy's exploration of the destructive nature of obsessive love.

MOURNERS BELOW

In *Mourners Below*, Purdy returns to the theme of hero worship. Seventeen-year-old Duane Bledsoe is mourning the death of his two half brothers, Justin and Douglas, who have been killed in the war. Eugene Bledsoe, the father, with whom Duane lives, is aloof and psychologically distant. The central episode in the novel occurs when Duane goes to a fancy-dress ball at the mansion of Estelle Dumont (who had been Justin's lover), and Estelle seduces him. After the ball, another of Purdy's rape scenes occurs when Duane is sexually assaulted by two men along the roadside. During the brief affair between Duane and Estelle, Estelle conceives a child, also named Justin. At the end of the story, Duane is given the child to rear, and Eugene states that it is Duane's destiny to rear a son.

Although this novel incorporates many of Purdy's familiar conceptions, it appears to be much more optimistic about the human condition than his previous novels. For example, Eugene and Duane do become reconciled in many ways, and there are many indications that Duane will make a good parent for the child. Furthermore, many of the grotesque and sadistic aspects of love are absent in this book. The men and the women in the story are not the tyrannical types found in previous works; they exhibit much more normal motivation. *Mourners Below* seems to indicate a new phase in Purdy's development, for in this novel he emphasizes the hopeful qualities of love and human existence.

ON GLORY'S COURSE

The search for a lost son plays a crucial role in *On Glory's Course*. Adele Bevington, the main character in the novel, has had an illegitimate son taken away from her and placed for adoption. The rest of the novel revolves around her quest for her lost son. One of the wounded veterans living in Fonthill, the location of the novel, believes that he knows the identity of Adele's son—he is a soldier who has been gravely wounded in the war and is now residing at the Soldiers' Home, barely alive and unable to respond to any communication. Adele attempts to prove that this soldier, Moorbrook, is her son, but by the end of the novel, neither Adele nor the reader is certain about Moorbrook's identity. Once again, Purdy's recurring motif of the search for a father figure is woven into the text of the novel.

IN THE HOLLOW OF HIS HAND

In the Hollow of His Hand relates the kidnapping of a boy, Chad Coultas, by Decatur, an Ojibwa Indian. Decatur is actually the father of the boy and wishes to rear him as an Indian; however, Lew Coultas, the man who has brought up Chad, wishes to recapture him and take him "home." The mother of Chad, Eva Lewis, had not even realized that Decatur was the father until he returned home from the military and began taking Chad on rides after school. She then remembered that she had, indeed, had a one-day affair with Decatur years before the action in the novel begins.

During the attempt to find Chad, the town of Yellow Brook is awakened to its small-town foibles and provincial attitudes, and once again Purdy reveals the darker side of small-town life and values. This novel is darkly satiric and deals with Purdy's attempts to create an almost mythological construct of his obsession with the search for an identity within the context of the family. Yet *In the Hollow of His Hand* is also an extremely humorous novel, delving into the souls of small-town America and American culture.

GARMENTS THE LIVING WEAR

Set in Manhattan, *Garments the Living Wear* opens with Jared Wakeman, an actor and organizer of a theater group facing a desperate situation. Not only has his benefactor, Peg Shawbridge, almost run out of money, his actors have been decimated by acquired immunodeficiency syndrome (AIDS), which Purdy's characters refer to simply as the Plague. Even Des Cantrell, whom Jared refers to as his soul mate, shows the first signs of the illness. The situation radically changes when Ed-

ward Hennings, an aged financial wizard and Peg's former lover, arrives with his young androgynous bride, Estrallita. Edward desires Jared, luring him with the dual attractions of money for his theatrical endeavors and the mysterious Estrallita.

Purdy imbues the novel with an aura of myth and mystery as Edward seemingly cures Des. This atmosphere is reinforced by the appearance of Jonas Hakluyt, an ex-convict turned evangelist with messianic overtones. The novel combines humor and psychological realism, myth, and magic as Purdy's characters struggle to survive in a world where both people and events are unpredictable and reality is frequently overshadowed by illusion.

OUT WITH THE STARS

Out with the Stars revolves around a group of socially intertwined figures. Abner Blossom, with the support of his talented protégé, Val Sturgis, has emerged from his retirement to compose an opera based on a mysterious libretto that was found in a "parlor" where young men indulge in orgies. The libretto is based on the life of Cyrus Vane, a photographer who specialized in nude studies of young African American men. Vane's wife, Madame Petrovna, is bitterly opposed to production of the opera and will go to any lengths to stop it. A secondary theme in the novel deals with corruption and the loss of innocence of Sturgis and his roommate, Hugh, as they drift deeper into the exotic world of Vane and Blossom. Purdy vividly explores both racial and sexual prejudice in *Out with the Stars*.

GERTRUDE OF STONY ISLAND AVENUE

In *Gertrude of Stony Island Avenue*, Carrie Kinsella, an elderly woman who has lived a dull and uneventful existence, attempts to understand the life and death of her daughter, Gertrude, a famous and flamboyant artist. During this search, she encounters a series of eccentric characters who influenced and were influenced by Gertrude. Purdy explores the nature of love and relationships as Carrie struggles to accept the fact that she and Gertrude failed to love each other. Like most of Purdy's novels, *Gertrude of Stony Island Avenue* presents a shadowy world full of pretense and ambiguity. Purdy's language and symbolism mirror this world, which is often distorted, hiding more than it reveals.

Earl Paulus Murphy
Updated by Mary E. Mahony

OTHER MAJOR WORKS

SHORT FICTION: *Don't Call Me by My Right Name, and Other Stories*, 1956; *Sixty-three: Dream Palace*, 1956; *Color of Darkness: Eleven Stories and a Novella*, 1957; *The Candles of Your Eyes*, 1985; *The Candles of Your Eyes, and Thirteen Other Stories*, 1987; *Sixty-three: Dream Palace—Selected Stories, 1956-1987*, 1991; *Moe's Villa, and Other Stories*, 2000.

PLAYS: *Mr. Cough Syrup and the Phantom Sex*, pb. 1960; *Cracks*, pb. 1962; *Wedding Finger*, pb. 1974; *Clearing in the Forest*, pr. 1978; *True*, pr. 1978; *A Day After the Fair*, pb. 1979; *Now*, pr. 1979; *Two Plays*, 1979 (includes *A Day After the Fair* and *True*); *What Is It, Zach?*, pr. 1979; *Proud Flesh: Four Short Plays*, 1980; *Strong*, pb. 1980; *The Berry-Picker*, pb. 1981; *Scrap of Paper*, pb. 1981; *In the Night of Time, and Four Other Plays*, 1992 (includes *In the Night of Time*, *Enduring Zeal*, *The Paradise Circus*, *The Rivalry of Dolls*, and *Ruthanna Elder*); *The Rivalry of Dolls*, pr., pb. 1992.

POETRY: *The Running Sun*, 1971; *Sunshine Is an Only Child*, 1973; *She Came Out of the Mists of Morning*, 1975; *Lessons and Complaints*, 1978; *The Brooklyn Branding Parlors*, 1986.

MISCELLANEOUS: *Children Is All*, 1961 (stories and plays); *An Oyster Is a Wealthy Beast*, 1967 (story and poems); *Mr. Evening: A Story and Nine Poems*, 1968; *On the Rebound: A Story and Nine Poems*, 1970; *A Day After the Fair: A Collection of Plays and Stories*, 1977.

BIBLIOGRAPHY

Adams, Stephen D. *James Purdy*. New York: Barnes & Noble Books, 1976. Adams examines Purdy's major work from the early stories and *Malcolm* up through *In a Shallow Grave*. Of particular interest is Adams's discussion of the first two novels in Purdy's trilogy *Sleepers in Moon-Crowned Valleys*.

Canning, Richard. *Gay Fiction Speaks: Conversations with Gay Novelists*. New York: Columbia University Press, 2000. This book's extensive interview focuses primarily on Purdy's identity as a gay novelist. Purdy also discusses his plays, acknowledging his interest in and debt to the Jacobean theater of early seventeenth century England.

Chupack, Henry. *James Purdy*. Boston: Twayne, 1975. This introductory overview contains a biography, an introductory chapter on what Chupack terms the "Purdian trauma," and analyses of Purdy's works. Includes a bibliography and an index.

Guy-Bray, Stephen. "James Purdy. In *The Gay and Lesbian Literary Heritage: A Reader's Companion to the Writers and Their Works, from Antiquity to the Present*, edited by Claude J. Summers. New York: Henry Holt, 1995. In this short article, Guy-Bray tries to identify some of Purdy's most pervasive themes, including the betrayal of love, the use of violence to resolve inner conflict, and the malevolence of fate.

Lane, Christopher. "Out with James Purdy: An Interview." *Critique* 40 (Fall, 1998): 71-89. Purdy discusses racial stereotypes, sexual fantasy, political correctness, religious fundamentalism, gay relationships, and the reasons he has been neglected by the literary establishment.

Schwarzchild, Bettina. *The Not-Right House: Essays on James Purdy*. Columbia: University of Missouri Press, 1968. A collection of Schwarzchild's incisive essays on Purdy's work, primarily focusing on his novels.

Tanner, Tony. Introduction to *Color of Darkness* and *Malcolm*. New York: Doubleday, 1974. Tanner's introductory essay discusses Purdy's novel *Malcolm* and the short-story collection *Sixty-Three: Dream Palace*. It also compares Purdy's effects with those achieved by the Russian realist Anton Chekhov.

Whitaker, Rick. "James Purdy." In *The First Time I Met Frank O'Hara: Reading Gay American Writers*. Photographs by Iannis Delatolas. New York: Four Walls Eight Windows, 2003. Whitaker examines the lives and works of Purdy and other gay writers, focusing on how their literary styles and perspectives were influenced by their sexuality.

Woodhouse, Reed. "James Purdy's *Narrow Rooms*." *Unlimited Embrace: A Canon of Gay Fiction, 1945-1995*. Amherst: University of Massachusetts Press, 1998. Woodhouse devotes a chapter to Purdy in his evaluation of fifty years of fiction written for, by, and about gay men. He views Purdy's works as an exploration of the ethics of gay life.

ALEXANDER PUSHKIN

Born: Moscow, Russia; June 6, 1799
Died: St. Petersburg, Russia; February 10, 1837
Also known as: Alexander Sergeyevich Pushkin

PRINCIPAL LONG FICTION

Evgeny Onegin, 1825-1832, 1833 (*Eugene Onegin*, 1881)
Arap Petra velikogo, 1828-1841 (*Peter the Great's Negro*, 1896)
Kirdzhali, 1834 (English translation, 1896)
Kapitanskaya dochka, 1836 (*The Captain's Daughter*, 1846)
Dubrovsky, 1841 (English translation, 1892)
Yegipetskiye nochi, 1841 (*Egyptian Nights*, 1896)
Istoriya sela Goryukhina, 1857 (*History of the Village of Goryukhino*, 1966)

OTHER LITERARY FORMS

Although Alexander Pushkin (POOSH-kuhn) wrote in almost every genre a nineteenth century author could attempt, he was primarily a poet. In a literary career spanning twenty-four years, he published a rich and varied collection of verse. He wrote two important historical poems, three major comic poems, a half dozen verse narratives, four *skazki* (fairy tales in verse), and numerous lyric poems.

Pushkin's canon contains several dramatic works: *Boris Godunov* (pb. 1831; English translation, 1918) is a long play, written in the manner of William Shakespeare's historical plays, about a crucial period in Russian civilization, the "Time of Troubles." Four short plays make up Pushkin's "Little Tragedies": *Pir vo vryemya chumy* (pb. 1833; *The Feast in Time of the Plague*, 1925), *Motsart i Salyeri* (pr., pb. 1832; *Mozart and Salieri*, 1920), *Skupoy rytsar* (pr., pb. 1852; *The Covetous Knight*, 1925), and *Kamyenny gost* (pb. 1839; *The Stone Guest*, 1936); each of these plays concentrates on a crucial moment in an individual's life. Though cast as drama, all five works are more lyric than theatrical; they are more intent on presenting character than on keeping the stage busy.

In addition to his long fiction, Pushkin wrote several short stories. The most famous and skillful of these works is *Pikovaya dama* (1834; *The Queen of Spades*, 1858), a story of greed, murder, and revenge set among the gaming tables of the aristocracy. Nearly as good are five stories collected as *Povesti Belkina* (1831; *Russian Romance*, 1875; better known as *The Tales of Belkin*, 1947): They depict, both comically and seriously, the life of the rural gentry and townspeople. Pushkin's research for his novel *The Captain's Daughter* provided him with materials for the nonfictional work *Istoriya Pugacheva* (1834; *The Pugachev Rebellion*, 1966).

In addition to his published works, Pushkin wrote hundreds of letters to personal friends and fellow officials. The almost seven hundred surviving letters vividly chronicle both Pushkin's personal life and his literary development.

No complete, uniform, and authoritative English translation of Pushkin's work exists. Several volumes offer a selection of his verse, though translators agree that rendering Pushkin's lyricism is well nigh impossible. Translations that capture somewhat more of the original are readily available for Pushkin's plays and stories. *Alexander Pushkin: Complete Prose Fiction* (1983), translated and annotated by Paul Debreczeny, is a valuable edition for English-speaking readers. Pushkin's letters have been collected into a well-annotated edition by J. Thomas Shaw: *The Letters of Alexander Pushkin* (1963). The handiest compendium of Pushkin in all of his genres is still the Modern Library volume *The Poems, Prose, and Plays of Pushkin*, edited by Avram Yarmolinsky and first published in 1936.

ACHIEVEMENTS

Alexander Pushkin is Russia's poet as Homer is Greece's, Dante is Italy's, and John Milton is England's. The nation mourned when he died, and Nikolai Gogol, a writer of the next generation, called him a unique manifestation of the Russian spirit. Four decades later, Fyodor Dostoevski proclaimed Pushkin a prophetic phenomenon whose characters embodied the people Russians would become in the late 1800's. After the 1917

Revolution, Soviet scholars produced an extraordinary amount of research and criticism on Pushkin. Modern Russian readers still turn to Pushkin's poetry for a distillation of their hopes and fears and for its lyricism. Virtually every one of Pushkin's works is regarded as a classic by his admirers, and, for once, the idolaters are mostly correct.

Unlike Russian writers of the previous century who imitated Western classicism and produced mostly pale reflections, Pushkin used European literary models to discover—or even to create—a literary Russia. When he began to write in the first decade of the nineteenth century, Russian literature was at a turning point. For the previous sixty years, it had imitated the forms and themes of French classicism and English sentimentalism. A new sensibility was then sweeping Europe, the Romanticism of Johann Wolfgang von Goethe, Lord Byron, André-Marie Chénier, and Sir Walter Scott. Pushkin responded with amazing alacrity. Reading Pushkin's letters, one is struck by how aware he was of not only the literary currents of his own country but also those of the Continent.

Still, Pushkin brought into his country's literature places, characters, and themes unmistakably Russian. His reading of Byron inspired him to works as diverse as *Kavkazskiy plennik* (1822; *The Prisoner of the Caucasus*, 1895), which discovered primitive southern Russia as a backdrop, and *Eugene Onegin*, which delineated the upper-class soul in its sicknesses. His reading of Shakespeare and Scott led him to the presentation of Russian historical themes on a small scale of ordinary lives as well as on a grand scale of royal lives.

Pushkin's lyric verse, begun under the tutelage of Byron and Chénier, gradually grew freer as he experimented with the rhythms and rhymes of the Russian language as a tool for the recording of what it was like to live, love, and suffer as one who came of age in the 1820's. He gave folktales, proverbs, and native speech shelf space in literature's emporium. Whatever the genre or theme of the work, Pushkin's crowning achievement was his style. Though a contemporary of the great European Romantics, Pushkin owed more to their lean classical style than to their richness. His thoughts were always compressed, the scene or emotion always sketched with a few quick, apt words, the story told with pointed economy. The non-Russian reader, unfortunately, misses what the average Russian reader loves him for most: the interplay of sensuous sound and simple sense.

One of Pushkin's classical features is his authorial objectivity. Unlike other Romantics, whose works are often autobiographical, Pushkin was not a confessional writer. Neither was he the distanced, detached, and "official" observer that the neoclassical poet was. His works are, more specifically, objective renderings—parables almost—of the emotional, psychological, and social life of the sensitive and intelligent contemporary Russian.

In this regard, Pushkin's long narratives (one work in verse and two in prose) may be most valuable to the non-Russian reader. *Eugene Onegin*, *Dubrovsky*, and *The Captain's Daughter* form a useful introduction to the second half of Pushkin's life and career. They record in straightforward narratives the writer's hopes and fears for his society, both about the personal integrity of individuals and about society's path toward freedom and justice. In Pushkin's Russia, the burning question for individuals was the priorities of virtue (did individual love and honor outweigh obedience and social conformity?) and the burning question for the body politic was social progress (could it be achieved on the back of serfdom and autocracy?). Pushkin felt as if the answers were sometimes yes, sometimes no. In the latter moments, he seemed unsure whether to react to that realization with tears, laughter, or anger.

BIOGRAPHY

Alexander Sergeyevich Pushkin was born into a Moscow family that boasted a six-hundred-year lineage of nobility. Each parent contributed something to his makeup. From his mother, descended from an Abyssinian princeling who had served Peter the Great, Pushkin received his fierce, dark looks and a passionate nature. From his well-educated father, who wrote poetry, Pushkin inherited a love of literature and gained early access to a family library well stocked with European classics.

In 1811, Pushkin was one of thirty boys chosen for the first class of the *lycée* at Tsarskoe Selo, a new school designed to train administrators for Czar Alexander's government. Flourishing in a liberal arts curriculum, Pushkin rapidly became the poet among his peers and, by 1814, published his first poem. His work soon became known to established poets and to the literary societies that looked to Europe for literary models to make Russian writing as good as any in the world. Having seen their nation defeat Napoleon I in 1815, young Russians were eager to match France culturally and to improve their country by importing European political ideals that would eliminate what liberal-thinking Russians thought were the twin cancers of their society: serfdom and autocracy.

Appointed to undemanding work in the Ministry of Foreign Affairs after graduation in 1817, Pushkin combined his literary and political fervors by writing poems like the ode "Vol'most': Oda" ("Ode to Freedom") with revolutionary themes. For three years, he pursued liberal ideals—and actresses of liberal virtue—until his poems attracted the attention of St. Petersburg's military governor, who decided that the young firebrand needed the cooling discipline of service in remoter regions.

In 1820, Pushkin was officially transferred and unofficially exiled to southern Russia and spent time in the

Crimea and the Caucasus before settling in Kishinev. Here Pushkin met young army officers who dreamed of political change and primitive tribesmen who lived fiercely and independently. These experiences, combined with his reading of the English Romantic poet Byron, helped Pushkin create several Romantic verse narratives about men who lived on the frontier of civilization and lived passionately according to their own wills. Pushkin would repeat throughout his career the pattern established here: Forced by circumstances into isolation, he would combine his own passionate apprehension of European literary fashions with distinctive Russian settings, characters, and themes.

In 1823, Pushkin secured a transfer to the Black Sea port of Odessa, but his reluctance to perform official duties and a letter expressing his atheist sentiments again earned for him official disapproval. He was dismissed from the service and sent to the family estate at Mikhailovskoe (three hundred safe miles from the capital), where his father, a local abbot, and the secret police could keep his political and religious views under surveillance. Once again cut off from society, Pushkin turned to literature, writing more verse and composing a play, *Boris Godunov*, modeled on Shakespeare's histories.

The exile at Mikhailovskoe kept Pushkin safe while a group of army officers—a few of them his friends, most of them readers of his revolutionary verse—led the unsuccessful Decembrist Revolt to block the accession of Nicholas I, presumed unsympathetic to Western reforms. At liberty, Pushkin's temperament might have led him to join the coup and thus to share the officers' fate of death or Siberian exile. By May of 1826, Pushkin, eager to leave exile and hoping that Nicholas might prove progressive, petitioned for and received pardon. There was only one stipulation: Nicholas himself would censor Pushkin's writing.

For four years, Pushkin lived and worked in St. Petersburg but accomplished little, writing only one poem and continuing *Eugene Onegin*, his magnum opus begun in 1823. In 1830, he determined to wed and successfully wooed the beautiful and younger Natalia Goncharov. The

Alexander Pushkin. (Library of Congress)

marriage seemed to settle Pushkin's adherence to Nicholas's regime: His wife's beauty made the couple in demand at palace balls; Pushkin reentered government service as a historiographer. Later, Nicholas appointed Pushkin to a court post, but the poet's fiercely independent and proud spirit did not allow easy mingling with aristocrats whose main political virtue was subservience.

In 1830, Pushkin began a period of intense creativity. Isolated for three autumn months at Boldino (far from Moscow and St. Petersburg), Pushkin completed *Eugene Onegin*, wrote several short stories and plays, and composed verse. Returning to St. Petersburg, he used the position of historiographer to research the peasant rebellion led by Yemelyan Pugachov in the 1770's, an uprising so destructive and traumatic that it halted the enlightened ideals of Catherine the Great and convinced subsequent czars that only ironfisted rule prevented revolution from below. Another retreat to Boldino in the autumn of 1833 produced several works, including a history of the rebellion and the great poem *Medniy vsadnik* (1837; *The Bronze Horseman*, 1899). In 1836, Pushkin concluded six years of concentrated writing with a novel and a literary journal.

His uneasy relationship with Nicholas's court reached a critical point in late 1836 when an anonymous wit awarded Pushkin a diploma as a member in good standing of "The Order of Cuckolds," a reference to the flirtatious attentions by the young French officer Georges d'Anthès to Natalia. After two months of anger and hesitation, Pushkin issued the inevitable challenge to a duel that took place on January 29, 1837. Pushkin was shot first, was critically wounded, and died a week later.

ANALYSIS

Alexander Pushkin's three major works, *Eugene Onegin*, *Dubrovsky*, and *The Captain's Daughter*, reflect many dimensions of his literary achievement. They show his ability to adapt Western genres to a Russian context; they demonstrate his stylistic mastery that is simultaneously economical and rich. Finally, in their emotional variety, they chart Pushkin's attempts to reconcile himself to czarist society and politics.

Each of these three works owes a literary debt. *Eugene Onegin*, a novel in verse, takes its inspiration from

Byron's *Childe Harold's Pilgrimage* (1812-1818) and *Don Juan* (1819-1824) but tempers their exuberance with characterization and scene setting from the eighteenth century novel of manners. *Dubrovsky* is kin to the robber tales of German Romanticism, which paint a heroic picture of an outlaw who is really more a self-willed outcast in opposition to social tyranny than an ordinary brigand. *The Captain's Daughter* is a historical novel in the manner of Sir Walter Scott, using the life of an ordinary participant to witness and to interpret some crucial national event. Pushkin's debt to foreign models is not surprising, because his letters show that he read practically everything, not only what was being produced in Russian but also what was being written in French, German, and English.

Like the greatest writers, Pushkin is a master of styles rather than a master of style. His long fictions are as varied as his whole corpus with its poems, plays, and folktales. *Eugene Onegin* is a complexly organized poem: There are eight chapters, each composed of at least 40 fourteen-line stanzas (389 stanzas all told), and each stanza follows a rigorous and formal rhyme scheme that disciplines a wealth of characterization, authorial commentary, and social observation into a coherent narrative. *Dubrovsky* is a quick-paced, dark-spirited, third-person narrative built around a stark contrast of justice and tyranny. *The Captain's Daughter* is a more leisured, romantic, first-person story in which youth and honor triumph over various obstacles.

The most interesting thing about Pushkin's three major long fictional works is the thematic course they chart. They all seek to depict life as led by members of the gentry, that social class that lives with one foot in the urban corridors of power and one in the rural paths of peasant-filled estates. No two of these works offer exactly the same perspective. *Eugene Onegin*, almost ten years in the writing during a crucial period of Pushkin's life, is the most complex and ambiguous work. No one emotion sums it up; by turns it is comic, satiric, pathetic, and tragic. *Dubrovsky* is an angry book, ruthless in its depiction of the petty tyrannies that infect the gentry with devastating effects. *The Captain's Daughter* shows murderous rebellion and government blindness but offers some small hope for the individual to steer between these twin disasters. Taking these works in order, the reader can trace Pushkin's diagnosis of the sickness of Russian society and his prescription for its remedy.

EUGENE ONEGIN

Eugene Onegin is a unique work. It is a product of the Romantic imagination that delighted in experimenting with literary conventions; it is a novel in verse, an attempt to mix the lyric insight of poetry with narrative's opportunity for social observation. Most other nineteenth century novels in verse failed, but Pushkin succeeded in writing both a powerful poem and an important work of fiction. To the Russian reader, sensitive to the nuances of tone and the play of imagery, *Eugene Onegin* is primarily a narrative poem. To the non-Russian reader who must rely on translation, *Eugene Onegin* is more accessible as a lyric novel. Once past the first chapter (the least novel-like), in which Pushkin sketches the subtle strains of Negin's soul as molded by society, the reader of the translation begins an intriguing love story. Novel-like, this love story traces the evolution of a romance from a country estate to a city drawing room: It depicts both the private reveries of the lovers and their passionate, hurtful encounters, and evaluates their relationship as they understand it and as it mirrors the society at large.

Eugene Onegin is a fashionable young man of contemporary St. Petersburg. His wealth and social status allow him to play the game he knows best: the seduction of beautiful women amid the endless round of teas, tête-à-têtes, and palace balls. An unbroken string of romantic conquests, however, makes him bored with life in general. At his uncle's death, Eugene inherits a country estate and retires to it. Here, he meets Vladimir Lensky, an eighteen-year-old who has all of Onegin's passionate nature but who has not yet had the chance to indulge it. All of Lensky's attention is directed toward Olga Larin, whom he loves romantically and for whom he writes poems. Through Lensky, Onegin meets Olga's sister Tatyana, an introspective and withdrawn girl who is convinced at first sight that Onegin is her destined lover. After several days of self-inflicted torment, knowing love only through novels, Tatyana writes Onegin a letter proclaiming her devotion. Two days later, he responds by lecturing her about the impossibility of anyone impressing his heart. Tatyana's spirit is crushed, but her love lives on.

Afterward, at Tatyana's name-day party, Onegin flirts outrageously with Olga, who unthinkingly enjoys his attentions. Vladimir does not enjoy them, suspecting his friend of trying to steal Olga's affection. He challenges Onegin to a duel that neither especially wants but that both know society demands when there is a woman in dispute. Onegin kills Vladimir and quickly departs on a foreign tour; Olga remains grief-stricken until another suitor replaces Vladimir; Tatyana haunts the house Onegin recently vacated, searching for a clue to his character, until her mother takes her to Moscow for the winter social season and a prospective husband.

When the story continues two years later, Tatyana is the wife of an army general. Onegin, returning to the social round, meets her and immediately falls in love. Making himself an intimate of the general's circle, Onegin dotes on Tatyana: helping with her cloak, opening doors for her, making constant small talk. Thoroughly infatuated but unsure of her feelings, Onegin writes her several letters professing his love. She grants him an interview at which she confesses that, although she still loves him, she rejects his love because she now has a wife's duty. She did not marry for love; she married the general only because he was the least unattractive of bad choices, but she is determined to remain faithful to her role. The novel ends as the husband enters to reclaim Tatyana from a thunderstruck Onegin.

The story is told through a series of parallels and contrasts. The quick-paced, dissolute, and spiritually enervating life at St. Petersburg contrasts with the tedious, controlled, and unimaginative life of the country. Tatyana's letter to Onegin and his reply (chapters 3 and 4) are ironically reversed in his letters to her and the subsequent interview (chapter 8). Tatyana's notions of sentimental love derive from her reading of eighteenth century novelists in the same degree that Onegin's spiritual lethargy is an imitation of nineteenth century Romantic angst. Lensky and Olga are more fulsome lovers than Tatyana and Onegin, yet their affection dies more quickly. Eugene dispatches the troublesome jealousy of Lensky with as little conscience as he dispatches the jejune affection of Tatyana.

Complicating the story is the presence of an obtrusive narrator. He has known Onegin, in fact, has shared many of his attitudes. Like Onegin, he has missed the possibility for real passion by playing at too many imitations of it. Like Onegin, the narrator has a sharp eye for the absurdities of those people who live the social pattern without sensing its limitations.

Eugene Onegin is the novel's protagonist, but he is not a hero. If anything, he is an early version of the traditional Russian antihero, the "superfluous man." A superfluous man is one who possesses the creature comforts his society can offer but who does not have any reason to possess them. The ultimate superfluous man is Ivan Goncharov's Oblomov, who thinks long and hard at trying to discover a reason that would get him up from the couch. Pushkin's Onegin is less extreme, but the times and his temperament have combined to drain him of real sensation and passion. Only when Tatyana is out of reach (is it because she is out of reach?) does Onegin think to discover some motivation for participating actively in life, once again taking charge of his existence and seeking to connect with another human soul. Too often Onegin is content to follow the code of his social class: live as lord of the estate but take more notice of neighbors than of management; maintain honor over a trifle even at the expense of a friend's life; if one's emotions run too high or too seriously, become a poet as an outlet.

Tatyana is better than Onegin: She lives an imaginative life that is at least honest, although she succumbs in the end to the same social code that grips Onegin. Though superstitious about omens that signal a true love, she is at least anxious to know something about Onegin. Though her visits to his unoccupied house originate in simplistic devotion, they do lead to insights about his character. Though she partakes of St. Petersburg's fashionable whirl, she keeps aloof enough to remember her domestic commitment. On the outside, Tatyana is a lovely hoyden while Onegin is a work of fashion's art, but on the inside Tatyana draws two breaths and two heartbeats to every one of Eugene's.

The ending of the novel, in which Tatyana leaves the interview on her husband's arm while Onegin stands perplexed, is not a resolution. Though encouraged by friends to complete the story, Pushkin did not. Perhaps the tale ends appropriately as it stands, with the major characters etched in postures that represent their moral choices. Tatyana chooses sacrifice over happiness, and

Eugene is doomed to pursue the unpursuable woman. The dramatic ending offers readers none of the traditional comforts by which characters are parceled out some share of contentment.

DUBROVSKY

Dubrovsky is, like *Eugene Onegin*, an unfinished work. Unlike *Eugene Onegin*, it depicts oppression, violence, and death with only a few mitigating moments in which young love and honorable conduct win a momentary triumph. The story recounts the conversion of a young man, Vladimir Dubrovsky, from landowner to outlaw. Like Onegin, Dubrovsky is a member of the generation born around the end of the nineteenth century, but his family's relative poverty leaves little of the leisure allowed a young gallant of St. Petersburg. The novel's theme is political rather than social: the tyranny of the landowning class.

The elderly Andrey Dubrovsky owns a few serfs and the village of Kistenyovka; he is a mild and appreciative master. The neighboring landowner Kirila Troyekurov owns a much larger estate and is known to tyrannize his serfs. Though Dubrovsky and Troyekurov served together in the army and had become friends, two minor disputes over hunting dogs and hunting rights blossom into a full-scale animosity. Unaccustomed to having his will challenged in anything, Troyekurov plots to take over Dubrovsky's estate by filing a highly technical lawsuit under the guidance of a cunning lawyer. When Troyekurov's claim prevails, Dubrovsky goes mad at this outrage against justice. Invalided at home, Dubrovsky summons his son Vladimir from army service back to the estate. Vladimir sets to work to regain the estate legally, but before he can accomplish it, Troyekurov drives the elder Dubrovsky into a fatal seizure by riding insolently into the courtyard of the mansion he will soon occupy. On the day of the funeral, Troyekurov sends officers to seize control of the estate and the village before young Vladimir can claim his inheritance.

Galled by this triumph of tyranny, young Vladimir Dubrovsky and his peasants lock the officials in the occupied mansion and set the building afire. Disappearing into the forest, Vladimir's band begins to terrorize the neighborhood: robbing travelers, seizing the mail, torching manor houses. The only estate to escape attack belongs, oddly enough, to Kirila Troyekurov.

Meanwhile, Troyekurov has hired a French tutor, Deforges, for his daughter Masha. He decides to have fun with the handsome young foreigner by locking him in a room with a hungry bear. Much to the sadistic landlord's surprise, the tutor pulls a gun from his pocket and shoots the bear. Deforges proves as charming as he does forearmed, and soon Masha is in love with him.

On a festival day, all the neighboring gentry gather for a party at Troyekurov's estate. One of them arrives late: Anton Pafnutyich, the lawyer who directed the suit against Vladimir and who was recently robbed by him. His story sets the guests to comparing tales about the notorious robber who steals with pomp and grace from only the richest of the local ruling class. Pafnutyich refuses to leave the safety of the estate and stays for the night in Deforges's room, only to discover that the tutor is actually Vladimir in disguise.

His identity now dangerously compromised, Vladimir plans to leave the estate after confessing his love to Masha, revealing his identity, and securing her promise that she will call for him if she ever needs assistance.

The promise seems superfluous until the next summer, when Troyekurov makes plans to marry Masha to his neighbor, Prince Vereysky. Twice Masha's age and driven to ennui and dissipation by unrestricted indulgence, Vereysky is a repugnant suitor in Masha's eyes, but her father insists on the marriage. Masha secures Vladimir's assistance in case she cannot talk her father out of his determination. She even writes a letter to Vereysky frankly avowing her repugnance, but it simply whets both his appetite and her father's to exert their authority. Forced to attend the wedding ceremony, Masha expects any minute to be rescued by Vladimir Dubrovsky, but he fails to appear before the priest pronounces the vows over bride and groom. Not until Vereysky's carriage is homeward bound does Dubrovsky appear; he seizes the Prince and pronounces Masha free, but she insists that like it or not, she is now a wife. Though wounded in the shoulder by a bullet and to the heart by her reply, Dubrovsky withdraws without hurting anyone or stealing a thing. In revenge, the authorities send soldiers to track Dubrovsky down. As they besiege his forest fortress, Dubrovsky escapes into the woods. The robberies and attacks on the local gentry cease, and Dubrovsky is rumored to have gone abroad.

Dubrovsky has all the plot conventions of late eighteenth, early nineteenth century robber fiction. Its hero is young, dashing, handsome, and no ordinary criminal. There is a maiden in distress who is, of course, his beloved. Her distress arises from the tyranny of a cruel parent and a lustful suitor. There is adventure, violence, and death in dark and unexpected places. Characters are little more than cardboard figures, for the emphasis is on a fast moving plot filled with dramatic confrontations of innocence and guile, good and evil.

What is sensational about *Dubrovsky* is its theme. Pushkin creates a rebellious hero who wins the reader's sympathy; Vladimir Dubrovsky is after all, like Robin Hood, on the side of justice and true love. In the Russia of Nicholas I, where even verbal dissent quickly caught official notice, such an ennobling of a man in opposition to the political system was an act of heresy. In painting such a stark contrast between the tyranny of Troyekurov and the nobility of Dubrovsky, however, Pushkin seems to have written the story into a corner from which there is no escape. Commonly regarded as unfinished, *Dubrovsky* may have been abandoned where it stood because the author could think of no satisfactory conclusion. The heroine is cruelly married, the system has asserted an overwhelming power in defense of the local tyrant, and the pillaging by Dubrovsky's band is but an annoying hangnail on the strong fist of autocracy. Dubrovsky himself, as the manuscript ends, is in a hopeless situation. Like Eugene Onegin at the end of his novel, Vladimir Dubrovsky has lost his beloved to an older military man and has no means to extract any satisfying revenge to compensate for that loss. Pushkin wisely took leave of Onegin at that incomprehensible moment that Tatyana walks away with her husband. Similarly, Pushkin seems instinctively to have left Dubrovsky at that point because he has literally no future worth recounting; he is beaten. *Dubrovsky* may not be unfinished as much as it is unfinishable.

THE CAPTAIN'S DAUGHTER

Pushkin's final fictional work, *The Captain's Daughter*, offers thematic resolutions that *Dubrovsky* could not achieve. *The Captain's Daughter* is another tale of a young man of a gentry family who must oppose the system, but the hero of this novel is able to both fight for personal justice and remain (although with difficulty) in harmony with the political and social system. Perhaps by setting his story sixty years in the past, Pushkin was better able to see how an individual could control his own life and yet remain a part of society. The person who maintains his honor may in fact contribute to the betterment of the whole society.

The Captain's Daughter is set in the days of a peasant uprising, the Pugachov rebellion, which broke out in eastern Russia in the mid-1770's and was subdued in a few years after great difficulty by the armies of Catherine the Great. This uprising tempered Catherine's enthusiasm for bringing Western ways and ideas to Russia by showing precisely how fragile was the monarch's grip on the sprawling Russian landscape. Afterward, the Pugachov rebellion symbolized the autocracy's nightmare about the dangers that seethed under the surface of Russian civilization, that demanded constant vigilance; it was perhaps the one thing that made the ruling class reluctant to follow Europe's lead toward parliamentarian and constitutional government. In Nicholas I's Russia, where memories of the Decembrist coup were always fresh, to write about the Pugachov rebellion was practically to write about contemporary politics.

The Captain's Daughter tells how Peter Grinyov enters military service. Instead of sending his son Peter to elegant service with a St. Petersburg battalion, the elder Grinyov, who is a believer in the old-fashioned values of sacrifice and hard work, has Peter assigned to a regiment on the eastern frontier of the empire at Orenburg. In disgust, Peter sets off with his faithful serf Savelyich and meets with two adventures along the way: An army veteran gets him drunk and cheats him at pool; a peasant saves Peter and Savelyich when they become lost in a snowstorm, and Peter repays the man with an expensive coat.

At Orenburg, Peter is assigned to a small outlying fort; he is only one of three regular army officers overseeing a ragtag battalion of local men. The second of the three is Shvabrin, a young dandy who has been exiled from St. Petersburg for dueling. The third is the commandant of the fort, Captain Mironov, a somewhat comic figure who occasionally drills his troops in the distinctly unmilitary garb of nightshirt and nightcap. The only society for the three officers is provided by Mironov's wife, Vasilisa, and his maiden daughter Masha.

Rather quickly, Peter and Shvabrin become rivals for Masha and, in St. Petersburg-like manner, engage in a duel. Peter is seriously wounded, but the injury turns out favorably because his convalescence requires the constant attention of Masha. This intimacy quickly leads the young people to confess their love for each other. Peter writes home for permission to wed Masha but receives a stinging and firm letter of refusal from his father.

As the unhappy lovers ponder their next move, the peasant rebellion led by Yemelyan Pugachov begins, and its main army approaches the mud-and-wood fort. The defenders are quickly overwhelmed. The captain is killed, Shvabrin goes over to the enemy, Masha goes into hiding, and Peter is spared execution because the rebel leader Pugachov is the same peasant to whom Peter generously gave his coat.

Returning to his own fortress at Orenberg, Peter eagerly counsels an attack in order to free Masha, but the commander is reluctant to stir from the city's safety. When Peter learns that Masha has been discovered and given to Shvabrin, he sets out alone to rescue her. Captured by rebel sentries, Peter is brought before Pugachov. Impressed by Peter's bravery and honesty, Pugachov decides to let the young man take Masha away. Escaping from the rebel camp, the lovers meet with a Russian detachment. Peter sends Masha to his family estate while he continues to serve against the rebels.

By the uprising's end, Masha has won the hearts of Peter's parents so that they no longer object to the marriage. Peter, however, is arrested on the charge of having helped the enemy. Unwilling to explain his movements back and forth between enemy camp and duty post in order to protect Masha, Peter risks court trial. Masha travels to Moscow to beg for mercy from the empress herself. Telling her story to a woman she meets in the palace garden, Masha surprisingly discovers the next day that she had unknowingly spoken to Catherine herself. Catherine grants Peter pardon, and the lovers are free to wed.

In the character of Peter, Pushkin draws a composite of the young Russian of gentry class. Like others, Peter has to reconcile the conflicting claims of his European and Slavic heritages. It is not easy, because both heritages are mixtures of good and bad. The European inheritance has taught him to be an individual and to pursue Masha's love as a high good, but Europe is also the source of the dandyism and false honor represented by Shvabrin. The Slavic inheritance brings a high demand for loyalty to family and state, but its class structure hinges on oppression and cruelty. Peter tries to bring together the best of each heritage. He is a loyal subject of the empress, but he is sensitive enough to the humanity of the rebel peasants to wish that reform would do away with those conditions that breed revolution.

Pushkin makes in political terms a daring parallel. Peter and Masha each undertake a solitary journey to save the other: Peter goes to Pugachov and Masha goes to Catherine. The monarchs behave remarkably alike: They detect the honesty and honor within the petitioner, which justifies granting mercy to an apparent enemy. For Pushkin to suggest that Pugachov was anything less than a madman or a devil's henchman or the epitome of betrayal was political heresy. While Peter never condones Pugachov's taking up arms, he is impressed by the leader's sincerity and—amid the expected horrors of the war—comparative humaneness.

Masha herself emerges an emblem of Russia. Like her country in the eighteenth century, poised between a Slavic past and a European future, the maidenly Masha is about to determine her future. Wisely, she rejects the superficial Western ways of Shvabrin in favor of the cultured but natural impulses of Peter. Endangered by rebellion, Masha's future hangs in the balance until she is rescued by the bravery, even foolhardiness, of one who loves her. In turn, she repays love with love, risking public embarrassment to support the proposition that a man can talk to his country's enemy, even cooperate with him, and still be a patriot.

Peter's fate offers, then, a hope for autocratic, unchanging Russia. Horrified by the rapine and destruction, Peter is convinced that rebellion is no cure for what ails his country. He is living proof, however, that ideals and manners can change for the better. Peter is less class-conscious than his father; he rejects the cronyism and immoral ways of the aristocratic soldier; he learns to see the humanity of the peasant beneath the rough exterior. Peter escapes the consequences of his new attitudes only because of Catherine's intervention. Still she does intervene, and she sees what a progressive monarch ought to see: Firm rule is not incompatible with individual integrity and public morality.

Set in the reign of one ironfisted monarch, *The Captain's Daughter* speaks to another. It seeks to reassure Nicholas I that certain Western ideals (of love and personal honor) are not incompatible with traditional Russian virtues of obedience and loyalty. It suggests that a ruler can hasten national improvement by recognizing and cooperating with the heartfelt desire of others to improve the country. It reminds the monarch that statecraft is more than minding the jail so the prisoners do not escape. *The Captain's Daughter* is Pushkin's most positive fictional work because it suggests that although love will not overcome or solve all, love—personal and social—has a better chance than whatever is in second place to ameliorate the lot of the individual and consequently the nation.

Robert M. Otten

OTHER MAJOR WORKS

SHORT FICTION: *Povesti Belkina*, 1831 (*Russian Romance*, 1875; better known as *The Tales of Belkin*, 1947); *Pikovaya dama*, 1834 (*The Queen of Spades*, 1858).

PLAYS: *Boris Godunov*, pb. 1831 (wr. 1824-1825; English translation, 1918); *Motsart i Salyeri*, pr., pb. 1832 (*Mozart and Salieri*, 1920); *Pir vo vryemya chumy*, pb. 1833 (*The Feast in Time of the Plague*, 1925); *Rusalka*, pb. 1837 (*The Water Nymph*, 1924); *Kamyenny gost*, pb. 1839 (wr. 1830; *The Stone Guest*, 1936); *Skupoy rytsar*, pr., pb. 1852 (wr. 1830; *The Covetous Knight*, 1925); *Stseny iz rytsarskikh vryemen*, pr., pb. 1937 (wr. 1835); *Little Tragedies*, 1946 (includes *The Covetous Knight*, *The Stone Guest*, *Mozart and Salieri*, and *The Feast in Time of the Plague*).

POETRY: *Ruslan i Lyudmila*, 1820 (*Ruslan and Liudmila*, 1936); *Gavriiliada*, 1822 (*Gabriel: A Poem*, 1926); *Kavkazskiy plennik*, 1822 (*The Prisoner of the Caucasus*, 1895); *Bratya razboyniki*, 1824; *Bakhchisaraiskiy fontan*, 1827 (*The Fountain of Bakhchisarai*, 1849); *Graf Nulin*, 1827 (*Count Nulin*, 1972); *Tsygany*, 1827 (*The Gypsies*, 1957); *Poltava*, 1829 (English translation, 1936); *Domik v Kolomne*, 1833 (*The Little House at Kolomna*, 1977); *Skazka o mertvoy tsarevne*, 1833 (*The Tale of the Dead Princess*, 1924); *Skazka o rybake ir rybke*, 1833 (*The Tale of the Fisherman and the Fish*, 1926); *Skazka o tsare Saltane*, 1833 (*The Tale of Tsar*

Saltan, 1950); *Skazka o zolotom petushke*, 1834 (*The Tale of the Golden Cockerel*, 1918); *Medniy vsadnik*, 1837 (*The Bronze Horseman*, 1899); *Collected Narrative and Lyrical Poetry*, 1984; *Epigrams and Satirical Verse*, 1984.

NONFICTION: *Istoriya Pugacheva*, 1834 (*The Pugachev Rebellion*, 1966); *Puteshestviye v Arzrum*, 1836 (*A Journey to Arzrum*, 1974); *Dnevnik, 1833-1835*, 1923; *Pisma*, 1926-1935 (3 volumes); *The Letters of Alexander Pushkin*, 1963 (3 volumes); *Pisma poslednikh let 1834-1837*, 1969.

MISCELLANEOUS: *The Captain's Daughter, and Other Tales*, 1933; *The Poems, Prose, and Plays of Pushkin*, 1936; *The Works of Alexander Pushkin*, 1936; *Polnoye sobraniye sochineniy*, 1937-1959 (17 volumes); *The Complete Prose Tales of Alexander Pushkin*, 1966; *A. S. Pushkin bez tsenzury*, 1972; *Pushkin Threefold*, 1972; *Polnoye sobraniye sochineniy*, 1977-1979 (10 volumes); *Alexander Pushkin: Complete Prose Fiction*, 1983.

BIBLIOGRAPHY

Bethea, David M. *Realizing Metaphors: Alexander Pushkin and the Life of the Poet*. Madison: University of Wisconsin Press, 1998. Describes the relationship between Pushkin's life and his art and discusses why, more than two hundred years after the author's birth, his work remains relevant. Includes illustrations and index.

Binyon, T. J. *Pushkin: A Biography*. New York: Alfred A. Knopf, 2004. Winner of the Samuel Johnson Prize for British nonfiction, this biography chronicles Pushkin's literary success alongside his personal failures. Describes how the writer included small pieces of his life in *Eugene Onegin* and other works.

Debreczeny, Paul. *The Other Pushkin: A Study of Alexander Pushkin's Prose Fiction*. Berkeley: University of California Press, 1983. Encompassing study examines all of Pushkin's prose works, including a lengthy discussion of his short stories, drawing on the extensive scholarship on the subject.

_____. *Social Functions of Literature: Alexander Pushkin and Russian Culture*. Stanford, Calif.: Stanford University Press, 1997. Discussion of Pushkin is divided into three parts: the first is devoted to selected readers' responses to Pushkin, the second explores the extent to which individual aesthetic responses are conditioned by environment, and the third concerns the mythic aura that developed around Pushkin's public persona.

Evdokimova, Svetlana. *Pushkin's Historical Imagination*. New Haven, Conn.: Yale University Press, 1999. Focuses on Pushkin's fictional and nonfictional works on the subject of history, including the novels *The Captain's Daughter* and *Peter the Great's Negro*. Considers Pushkin's ideas on the relationship between chance and necessity, the significance of great individuals, and historical truth.

Feinstein, Elaine. *Pushkin: A Biography*. London: Weidenfeld & Nicolson, 1998. Biography draws on previously undiscovered documents to recount the events of Pushkin's life, describe his paradoxical personality, and provide new information about his death.

Kahn, Andrew, ed. *The Cambridge Companion to Pushkin*. New York: Cambridge University Press, 2006. Collection of essays by Pushkin scholars discusses a wide range of topics, including *Eugene Onegin* and Pushkin's other prose fiction; Pushkin and politics, history, and literary criticism; and Pushkin's position in Soviet and post-Soviet culture.

Lezhnev, Abram. *Pushkin's Prose*. Ann Arbor, Mich.: Ardis, 1974. In one of the rare examples of Russian scholarship translated into English, Lezhnev presents views of a native scholar on Pushkin's prose as seen in the thought and criticism of Pushkin's contemporaries.

Ryfa, Juras T., ed. *Collected Essays in Honor of the Bicentennial of Alexander Pushkin's Birth*. Lewiston, N.Y.: Edwin Mellen Press, 2000. Selection of scholarly essays examines various works by Pushkin and his influence on his literary descendants. Some of the essays discuss *Eugene Onegin* and *The Captain's Daughter* and compare Pushkin to Russian writers Leo Tolstoy and Anton Chekhov.

Terras, Victor. "Pushkin's Prose Fiction in an Historical Context." In *Pushkin Today*, edited by David M. Bethea. Bloomington: Indiana University Press, 1993. Discusses Pushkin's importance in the ascendancy of prose fiction in Russia in the nineteenth century and comments on the basic characteristics of Pushkin's prose style.

Tertz, Abram. *Strolls with Pushkin*. New Haven, Conn.: Yale University Press, 1994. Free-flowing and sometimes irreverent analysis critically contests the major works, artistic habits, and persisting cultural legacy of the prominent Russian poet and novelist.

Vitale, Serena. *Pushkin's Button*. Translated by Ann Goldstein and Jon Rothschild. New York: Farrar,

Straus and Giroux, 1999. Presents a cultural history and narrative of the last months of Pushkin's life before his fatal duel. Draws on new research and on information gleaned from secondary literature and the memoirs and letters of Pushkin's contemporaries to bring to life the world of St. Petersburg in the 1830's.

BARBARA PYM

Born: Oswestry, England; June 2, 1913
Died: Oxford, England; January 11, 1980
Also known as: Barbara Mary Crampton Pym; Tom Crampton

PRINCIPAL LONG FICTION

Some Tame Gazelle, 1950
Excellent Women, 1952
Jane and Prudence, 1953
Less than Angels, 1955
A Glass of Blessings, 1958
No Fond Return of Love, 1961
Quartet in Autumn, 1977
The Sweet Dove Died, 1978
A Few Green Leaves, 1980
An Unsuitable Attachment, 1982
Crampton Hodnet, 1985
An Academic Question, 1986

OTHER LITERARY FORMS

In 1984, a collection of the diaries and letters of Barbara Pym (pihm) was published by Hazel Holt and Hilary Pym under the title *A Very Private Eye: An Autobiography in Diaries and Letters*. In 1987, Holt edited a miscellany of Pym's writings, *Civil to Strangers, and Other Writings*, that contained mostly fiction but some nonfiction.

ACHIEVEMENTS

Barbara Pym was a writer of distinctive qualities who, having suffered discouragement and neglect for

fifteen years, was rediscovered toward the end of her life, to take her rightful place as a novelist of considerable originality and force. Often compared favorably with Jane Austen's novels, Pym's are essentially those of a private, solitary individual, employing precise social observation, understatement, and gentle irony in an oblique approach to such universal themes as the underlying loneliness and frustrations of life, culture as a force for corruption, love thwarted or satisfied, and the power of the ordinary to sustain and protect the men and women who shelter themselves under it. Also like Austen, Pym has no illusions about herself and very few about other people: "I like to think that what I write gives pleasure and makes my readers smile, even laugh. But my novels are by no means only comedies as I try to reflect life as I see it."

The story of Pym's early achievements, her long enforced silence, and her remarkable rediscovery perhaps says more about the publishing world than about either her books or her readers. Between 1949 and 1961, while working as an editorial assistant at the International African Institute, Pym wrote a novel every two years. As each manuscript was finished, she sent it off to Jonathan Cape. Her first six novels established her style, were well received by reviewers, and enjoyed a following among library borrowers. *Excellent Women*, her most popular novel, sold a little more than six thousand copies.

Then, in 1963, Pym put her seventh novel, *An Unsuitable Attachment*, in the mail. A short time later, it was returned: Times, she was told, had changed. The "swinging sixties" had no place for her gently ironic comedies about unconventional middle-class people leading outwardly uneventful lives. "Novels like *An Unsuitable Attachment*, despite their qualities, are getting increasingly difficult to sell," wrote another publisher, while a third regretted that the novel was unsuitable for its list.

Being a woman of determination with a certain modest confidence in herself, Pym went to work on an eighth novel, *The Sweet Dove Died*; when she sent it off to Cape, however, it too came back. She adopted a pseudonym—"Tom Crampton"—because "it had a swinging air to it," but twenty publishers turned down the novel. Humiliated and frustrated, she began to feel not only that her new books were no good but also that nothing she had ever written had been good. *No Fond Return of Love* was serialized by the British Broadcasting Corporation (BBC) and Portway Reprints reissued five others, Pym's books retained their popularity among library borrowers, and Robert Smith published an appreciation of her work in the October, 1971, issue of *Ariel*—but despite these signs of the continuing appeal of her work, Pym could not find a publisher, and by the mid-1970's, her name appeared to have been forgotten.

A renaissance in Pym's fortunes came with startling suddenness in 1977, when, to celebrate three-quarters of a century of existence, *The Times Literary Supplement* invited a number of well-known writers to name the most over- and underrated novelists of the century. Both Philip Larkin and Lord David Cecil—for years staunch admirers of hers—selected Pym as having been too long neglected, the only living writer to be so distinguished in the poll. Larkin praised her "unique eye and ear for the small poignancies and comedies of everyday life." Cecil called her early books "the finest example of high comedy to have appeared in England" in the twentieth century.

The publicity surrounding the article, not surprisingly, had positive effects on Pym's reputation. Macmillan published her new novel, *Quartet in Autumn*, near the end of 1977; later it was short-listed for the Booker Prize. Cape began to reissue her earlier books; Penguin and Granada planned a series of paperbacks; she was widely interviewed; finally, she appeared on the radio program *Desert Island Discs* as well as in a television film called *Tea with Miss Pym*. *The Sweet Dove Died* was published in 1978, followed by her last novel, the posthumously published *A Few Green Leaves* (1980). The manuscript of *An Unsuitable Attachment* was found among her papers after her death and published in 1982 with an introduction written by Philip Larkin. A book was prepared from her diaries and short stories.

Pym's novels are distinguished by an unobtrusive but perfectly controlled style, a concern with ordinary people and ordinary events, and a constant aim to be readable, to entertain in a world that is uniquely her own. They are also distinguished by a low-key but nevertheless cutting treatment of assumptions of masculine superiority and other sexist notions—all this well in advance of the women's movement, and without the rhetoric that mars so much feminist fiction. Although hers is a closed world—what Robert Smith called "an enchanted world of small felicities and small mishaps"—it is also real and varied in theme and setting, with its own laws of human conduct and values, its peculiar humor and pathos. Middle-aged or elderly ladies, middle-aged or elderly gentlemen, civil servants, clergymen, anthropologists and other academics—these are the people about whom Pym develops her stories.

The world in which Pym's characters live, whether urban or provincial, is also a quiet world—evoked in such detail as to make the reader feel that the action could not possibly take place anywhere else. Taken together, her novels constitute that rare achievement: an independent fictional world, rooted in quotidian reality yet very much the creation of Barbara Pym. Central characters from one novel appear in passing or are briefly mentioned in another; delightful minor characters turn up in unexpected places. This pleasure of cross-references is characteristic of Pym's art, in which formal dexterity and a marvelous sense of humor harmonize with a modest but unembarrassed moral vision. "I prefer to write about the kind of things I have experienced," Pym said, "and to put into my novels the kind of details that amuse me in the hope that others will share in this."

BIOGRAPHY

Barbara Mary Crampton Pym was born on June 2, 1913, in Oswestry, Shropshire, a small English town on the border of Wales. Like many of her characters, she led a quiet but enjoyable life among middle-class people with an Anglican background. Her father, Frederick

Crampton Pym, was a solicitor and sang in the church choir; her mother, Irena (Thomas), was of half Welsh descent and played the organ. Pym was given a good education (Huyton College, a boarding school near Liverpool; and St. Hilda's College, Oxford, from which she received a B.A. in English language and literature in 1934), saw some wartime service (Postal and Telegraph Censorship in Bristol, 1939, and the Women's Royal Naval Service in England and Italy, 1943-1946), and lived in various sections of London: Pimlico, Barnes, and Kilburn. She wrote down everything she saw in a series of little notebooks and later "bottled it all up and reduced it, like making chutney."

In 1948, Pym began working at the International African Institute, first as a research assistant and later as an assistant editor of the journal *Africa*. She was given the job of preparing the research for publication, and regretted that more of the anthropologists did not turn their talents to the writing of fiction. In their work, she found many of the qualities that make a novelist: "accurate observation, detachment, even sympathy." Needed was a little more imagination, as well as "the leavening of irony and humour." Several of her novels draw on her years at the Institute to study the behavior patterns and rituals of a group of anthropologists. In *Less than Angels*, for example, she portrays an anthropologist and his female coworkers, gently mocking the high seriousness with which they pursue their research among primitive African tribes and the shameless jargon in which they converse. No doubt the narrator is speaking for Pym herself when she concludes, "And how much more comfortable it sometimes was to observe [life] from a distance, to look down from an upper window, as it were, as the anthropologists did."

Although her first novel did not appear until 1950, Pym began writing when she was a schoolgirl, and even completed a novel when she was sixteen. After leaving Oxford, she started to write seriously and finished two more novels, but did not succeed in getting them published. By then, however, her literary tastes were well set. Above all, she was addicted to novels. Anthony Trollope and Jane Austen were her favorite novelists, and she knew their works intimately; but she read all the fiction she could, and listed among her favorites Ivy Compton-Burnett, Anthony Powell, and Iris Murdoch.

She was less tolerant of contemporary novels, and she viewed popular and sentimental fiction with the critical eye of the satirist. Nowhere in her own fiction does the reader find the sentimental excesses and sensational unrealities of much of the popular fiction that was being published in Pym's lifetime.

In 1971, Pym had a serious operation, and in 1974, she retired to live with her sister near Oxford. She died on January 11, 1980, at the age of sixty-six.

Analysis

Like most novelists, Barbara Pym was interested above all in human nature, and for most of her life she trained both eye and ear upon the exploration of that subject in its many fascinating dimensions. Her first published novel, *Some Tame Gazelle*, sets the tone and subject for what is to come as she casts her specialist's eye on British lower-class and lower-middle-class life and focuses on the quiet domestic lives of a few people. At the center are two unmarried women who have decided that, rather than seeking marriage, they will be happier living alone together. An all-pervasive influence of the Anglican Church, numerous references to anthropology and English literature, the weakness of men, realism, and a sometimes devastatingly comic tone are among the many distinctive features of not only this early novel but the later ones as well. Much the same judgment may be made for two posthumously published novels: *Crampton Hodnet*, which she had written in the 1930's but never intended to publish, and *An Academic Question*, for which she had written two drafts (one in first person, another in third person) but abandoned to write *Quartet in Autumn*. In 1986, Hazel Holt published an amalgamation of the two drafts. In spite of their thin plots and shallow characterization, both novels contain Pym's characteristically sharp observations and lively dialogue among the minor characters, as well as her concern with the elderly. Considered together, in all twelve of her novels Pym communicates her vision in an engaging, entertaining, and readable way. Her wit, her sense of style, her devotion to language and its revelation of character, and the richness of her invention all compel respect and critical attention.

"In all of her writing," Philip Larkin has written of Pym, "I find a continual perceptive attention to detail which is a joy, and a steady background of rueful yet courageous acceptance of things." In this statement, Larkin points to perhaps the single most important technique—and theme—in Pym's work. *Excellent Women*, *A Glass of Blessings*, and *Quartet in Autumn* develop their effects, as indeed do all of Pym's twelve novels, by exploiting the comedy of contemporary manners. Like her anthropologists, whom she quietly mocks for their esoteric detachment, Pym scrupulously notes and records the frustrations, unfulfilled desires, boredom, and loneliness of "ordinary people, people who have no claim to fame whatsoever." The usual pattern for the heroine is either retrenchment into her own world or, as a result of interaction with others, self-realization. By representing intensively the small world most individuals inhabit, it is Pym's method to suggest the world as a whole as well.

Usually Pym appoints a heroine to comment on the intimate details of social behavior. In *Excellent Women*, the assignment falls to Mildred Lathbury, who, as an observer of life, expects "very little—nothing, almost." Typical of Pym's "excellent women," Mildred is preoccupied with order, stability, and routine, but her special interest centers on the lives and crises of those around her—including her new neighbors, Rockingham and Helena Napier; the vicar, Julian Malory; and the anthropologist, Everard Bone. Faced with Mildred's honesty, diffidence, and unpretentiousness, the crises are resolved happily.

In Pym's fifth novel, *A Glass of Blessings*, the heroine is Wilmet Forsyth, a young and leisured woman bored with her excessively sober civil-servant husband. Her near romances with a priest, her best friend's husband, and Piers Longridge (in whose friend Keith she discovers a rival) are only some of the pairings in this intricate drama of romantic errors. When the possibility of a love affair fails to materialize, Wilmet finds a different kind of consolation in religion.

Finally, Pym's antiheroic view of life is particularly obvious in her most somber work, *Quartet in Autumn*, the first of her novels to be published after fifteen years of silence. Whereas her earlier work was a small protest against everyday life, *Quartet in Autumn* offered a formal protest against the conditions both of life itself and of certain sad civilities. The comedy is cold and the outlook is austere in this story of four people in late middle age who suffer from the same problem: loneliness. In its manipulation of the narrative among Edwin, Norman, Letty, and Marcia, the novel also represents Pym's greatest technical achievement.

EXCELLENT WOMEN

Excellent Women, described by one critic as the most "felicitous" of all of Pym's novels, explores the complications of being a spinster (and a religious one, at that) in the England of the 1950's. The setting is a run-down part of London near Victoria Station, but the very high Anglican Church of St. Mary's also provides the background for some of the events described. In the quiet comfort of this world, where everything is within walking distance and a new face is an occasion for speculation, the pleasantness and security of everyday life dominate. Only small crises—such as an argument between Winifred and Alegra over how to decorate the church altar—form the counterpoint to comfort. As the narrator says, "Life was like that for most of us—the small unpleasantnesses rather than the great tragedies; the little useless longings rather than the great renunciations and dramatic love affairs of history or fiction."

Mildred Lathbury, the narrator, is representative of one of Pym's favorite character types: the "excellent woman." She lives very much as she did growing up in a country rectory, working part time for the aid of impoverished gentlewomen and devoting herself to the work of the parish. As one who tends to get involved in other people's lives, she knows herself, she says, "capable of dealing with most of the stock situations or even the great moments of life—birth, marriage, death, the successful jumble sale, the garden fête spoilt by bad weather."

In all of Pym's novels, says Philip Larkin, "a small incident serves to set off a chain of modest happenings among interrelated groups of characters." In this instance, it is the entry into Mildred's life of Rockingham Napier. A flag lieutenant to an admiral, Rockingham has just returned from Italy, where he served his country by being charming to dull Wren officers. His wife Helena, an anthropologist, does not welcome his return. Scornful of his easy charm and lack of serious purpose, she has become infatuated with another anthropologist, Everard Bone, her coworker in Africa. As Helena pursues, however, Everard flees.

The reader depends on Mildred for ironic commentary. Helena leaves her husband, who then departs for a cottage in the country. Excellent woman that she is, Mildred is invited by Rockingham to send him the Napier furniture, by Helena to get it back, by both to effect their reconciliation, and by Everard to read proof and make the index for his forthcoming book. Because the vicar, Julian Malory, needs to be protected from designing women and Everard needs her help with the book, it seems to Mildred that she may look forward to a "full life." Then she remembers Rockingham's smile and reads from Christina Rossetti: "Better by far you should forget and smile,/ Than that you should remember and be sad." "It was easy enough to read those lines and be glad at his smiling," she acknowledges, "but harder to tell myself there would never be any question of anything else." Still, Everard's affection is genuine, if undemonstrative—and not unmixed with a pragmatic desire to find a suitable typist, indexer, and all-around "helpmate"—and the reader is happy to learn, in a subsequent novel, that Mildred and Everard do indeed go on to wed.

Again set in the 1950's, town and country are contrasted in *A Glass of Blessings*, which Larkin regarded as the "subtlest" of Pym's books. The novel opens in St. Luke's Church on the feast of its patron, the "beloved physician," as St. Paul called him. Celebrating the feast and her thirty-third birthday, Wilmet Forsyth, the narrator and heroine, is the well-to-do but aimless wife (subject to "useless little longings") of a typical Pym husband—hopelessly imperceptive, though well-intentioned and reliable. Like Jane Austen's Emma, whom Pym has in mind throughout the novel, Wilmet is unused and spoiled. A beautiful woman, always exquisitely dressed, Wilmet is childless, idle, and snobbish. She is also utterly unknown to herself, unable to imagine another life, and afraid to risk herself, even on the London buses, certain that any disturbance will be disillusioning. Bored, without training for a career, despising routine, she plans "to take more part in the life of St. Luke's, to try to befriend Piers Longridge and perhaps even go to his classes."

Piers Longridge is a sour, moody gay man, a fact Wilmet never quite seems to grasp until well into the novel. He has taken a seemingly useless degree and now teaches Portuguese in adult education classes. Believing that she might relieve his unhappiness, she forces herself on him, hoping for the grand passion of her life, another fact that she never really admits. Finally, in a scene of high comedy and bitter pain, exasperated by Wilmet's attentions and her naïveté, Piers confronts her with his secret lover, Keith, a model, and accuses Wilmet of being incapable of affection. It is the first time anyone has told her anything near the truth, and in response, she says to Mary Beamish, "sometimes you discover that you aren't as nice as you thought you were—that you're in fact rather a horrid person, and that's humiliating somehow."

When she witnesses the courtship and marriage of Mary Beamish, an orphan and ex-Anglican nun, and Father Marius Lovejoy Ransome, Wilmet begins to perceive the possibilities of being useful in the parish and even of passion. After she finds out that Rodney has had an innocent flirtation with his secretary, Wilmet sees him differently, thinking, "I had always regarded Rodney as the kind of man who would never look at another woman. The fact that he could—and indeed had done so—ought to teach me something about myself, even if I was not quite sure what it was." The truth of it is that Wilmet has failed to recognize her society, including the parish of St. Luke's, for what it is—an erotic conclave of beauty and variety, both dangerous and enlivening. It is like George Herbert's "glass of blessings," full of the "world's riches"—"beautie . . . wisdome, honour, pleasure."

QUARTET IN AUTUMN

In her first six novels, Pym treats her characters with warm compassion and gentle irony. With *Quartet in Autumn*, however, her tone becomes harsher, more bitter, as she examines with bleak detachment the lonely rejection of the retired. Letty Crowe, another of Pym's excellent women, is sixty-five and faces retirement from the unspecified office job she has shared for many years with her colleagues, Marcia, Norman, and Edwin. For Letty, life in a rooming house is "a little sterile, perhaps even deprived." Retirement gives her a feeling of nothingness, as if she had never existed. During sleepless nights, her life unrolls before her, like that of a person drowning: forty years wasted looking for love. Images of dead leaves drifting to the pavement in autumn and being swept away recur throughout the novel. Indeed,

Letty tries not to dwell on the image of herself lying among the autumnal leaves "to prepare for death when life became too much to be endured."

Her former colleagues are of no help to Letty. Norman is a scrawny, sardonic bachelor. Edwin is a widower preoccupied with "the soothing rhythms of the church's year." Marcia is gravely ill and at least slightly mad—collecting tins of food she never opens and milk bottles that she hoards in a shed. The only pleasures she knows are visits to the clinic for checkups and bus trips to look at the mansion of her adored surgeon. Incapable of thought, she is far more pathetic than Letty.

Unlike her colleagues, Letty does try to act bravely, reading books on sociology, participating in church activities, still taking caring with her hair and her clothes. "She told herself, dutifully assuming the suggested attitude toward retirement, that life was still full of possibilities." At the close of the novel, she is, like Mildred and Wilmet, where she was at the beginning. Yet, at the slightest change in the routine of her eventless days, she courageously assures herself, "At least it made one realize that life still held infinite possibilities for change."

In *Excellent Women*, *A Glass of Blessings*, and *Quartet in Autumn*, Pym relies neither on violence nor on the bizarre. Nothing outwardly momentous happens, but the frustrations of a half dozen or more characters emerge clearly and poignantly. Some critics have felt that the narrowness of her life inevitably imposed limitations on her work. Beneath the calm surface of her novels, however, the events of the day do make an imprint—to a degree appropriate to the lives of ordinary middle-class people. Each novel is a miniature work of art, distinguished by an air of assurance, an easy but firm control of the material, and the economy of means to achieve it.

Dale Salwak

OTHER MAJOR WORKS

NONFICTION: *A Very Private Eye: An Autobiography in Diaries and Letters*, 1984.

MISCELLANEOUS: *Civil to Strangers, and Other Writings*, 1987.

BIBLIOGRAPHY

Allen, Orphia Jane. *Barbara Pym: Writing a Life*. Metuchen, N.J.: Scarecrow Press, 1994. Extremely useful volume for both beginning students and advanced scholars. Part 1 discusses Pym's life and work, part 2 analyzes her novels, part 3 examines different critical approaches to her work and presents a bibliographical essay, and part 4 provides a comprehensive primary and secondary bibliography.

Burkhart, Charles. *The Pleasure of Miss Pym*. Austin: University of Texas Press, 1987. Very readable work discusses Pym's life and autobiographical writings as well as her fiction through *An Academic Question*. Focuses on her worldview, the unique nature of her comedy, her religion, her place within the history of the novel, and her insights into relationships between the sexes. Includes photographs and an index.

Cotsell, Michael. *Barbara Pym*. New York: Macmillan, 1989. Offers cogent analysis of all Pym's novels, paying particular attention to the characters' thoughts and feelings. Discusses also Pym's sense of language, her unpublished writings, and her creative process. Includes an index.

Donato, Deborah. *Reading Barbara Pym*. Madison, N.J.: Fairleigh Dickinson University Press, 2005. Critical work examines Pym's narrative technique by focusing on four novels: *Some Tame Gazelle*, *Quartet in Autumn*, *Excellent Women*, and *Jane and Prudence*. Also discusses reviews and criticisms of Pym's work and compares Pym's fiction with that of other writers who were her contemporaries.

Lenckos, Frauke Elisabeth, and Ellen J. Miller. *"All This Reading": The Literary World of Barbara Pym*. Madison, N.J.: Fairleigh Dickinson University Press, 2003. Collection of essays examines the roles of reading and libraries in Pym's work, including discussions of individual novels and of Pym's literary reputation. Includes an annotated bibliography of Pym criticism published from 1982 through 1998.

Liddell, Robert. *A Mind at Ease: Barbara Pym and Her Novels*. London: Peter Owen, 1989. Liddell draws on his fifty years of friendship with Pym to write a critical survey of her works through *Crampton Hodnet*. Considers the attention Pym gave to her characters' domestic and emotional lives, examines the reasons for her revival in popularity, and guides the reader through her novels, explaining which are most successful and why.

Long, Robert Emmet. *Barbara Pym*. New York: Frederick Ungar, 1986. Presents an informative treatment of Pym's novels, paying particular attention to her recurring themes and character types, her modes of social comedy and satire, and her pervasive concern with "unrealized" love and solitude. Includes chronology, notes, and index.

Nardin, Jane. *Barbara Pym*. Boston: Twayne, 1985. Provides an excellent introduction to Pym's life and career, noting the origins and development of her themes, character types, and style. Includes chronology, notes, bibliography of primary and secondary sources, and index.

Rossen, Janice, ed. *Independent Women: The Function of Gender in the Novels of Barbara Pym*. New York: St. Martin's Press, 1988. Collection of ten essays considers Pym's craftsmanship, the literary influences on her work, and her special use of language. The contributors use biographical, historical, and feminist approaches to explore Pym's unique creative process as it relates to events in her life. Includes notes and index.

Wyatt-Brown, Anne M. *Barbara Pym: A Critical Biography*. Columbia: University of Missouri Press, 1992. Fine narrative and analytical biography describes the influence of Pym's art on her writing. The introduction, "Creativity and the Life Cycle," is especially informative. Includes notes and bibliography.

THOMAS PYNCHON

Born: Glen Cove, New York; May 8, 1937
Also known as: Thomas Ruggles Pynchon, Jr.

PRINCIPAL LONG FICTION

V., 1963
The Crying of Lot 49, 1966
Gravity's Rainbow, 1973
Vineland, 1989
Mason and Dixon, 1997
Against the Day, 2006

OTHER LITERARY FORMS

Before his novels began to come out, Thomas Pynchon (PIHN-chuhn) published a handful of short stories: "The Small Rain" (1959), "Mortality and Mercy in Vienna" (1959), "Low-Lands" (1960), "Entropy" (1960), and "Under the Rose" (1961—an early version of what became chapter 3 of *V.*). With the exception of "Mortality and Mercy in Vienna," these stories appear in the 1984 collection *Slow Learner*, which also includes "The Secret Integration," originally published in 1964. Two magazine publications, "The World (This One), the Flesh (Mrs. Oedipa Maas), and the Testament of Pierce Inverarity" (1965) and "The Shrink Flips" (1966), are excerpts from *The Crying of Lot 49*.

Pynchon has also published some pieces in *The New York Times Book Review*, including a 1984 meditation on distrust of technology ("Is It O.K. to Be a Luddite?"), a 1988 review of Gabriel García Márquez's *Love in the Time of Cholera*, and a 1993 sketch, "Nearer, My Couch, to Thee," on the sin of sloth (included in the collection *Deadly Sins*, by Pynchon and other hands). He has penned introductions or forewords to several works by other authors, including a reissue of Richard Fariña's 1966 novel *Been Down So Long It Looks Like Up to Me* (1983); a posthumous collection of writings by Donald Barthelme, *The Teachings of Don B.: Satires, Parodies, Fables, Illustrated Stories, and Plays of Donald Barthelme* (1992); a reissue of Jim Dodge's 1990 novel *Stone Junction* (1998); and a 2003 edition of George Orwell's 1949 novel *1984*. Pynchon has also written liner notes for the albums *Spiked! The Music of Spike Jones* (1994) and *Nobody's Cool*, by the rock group Lotion (1995).

ACHIEVEMENTS

Among those contemporary novelists who enjoy both popular and academic followings, Thomas Pynchon stands out as a virtual cult figure. His novels and stories stand up to the most rigorous critical analysis; they prove, like all great works of art, to be the product of a gifted sensibility and careful craftsmanship. At the same time, Dr. Samuel Johnson's "common reader" cheerfully wades through much abstruse matter because this author never fails to entertain—with bizarre plots, incandescent language, anarchic humor, and memorable characters.

Pynchon has an enormous, diverse, and fanatically loyal following. Many books, critical essays, and scholarly journal articles have been written on his work. Some of the fascination he holds for readers is derived from his reclusive habits. He has refused to be interviewed, photographed, or otherwise made into a darling of the mass media. Thirty years after the publication of his first novel, it finally became known that Pynchon makes his home in New York City.

Pynchon has been honored with a number of literary awards. He received the William Faulkner Foundation Award for *V.*, the 1967 Rosenthal Foundation Award of the National Institute of Arts and Letters for *The Crying of Lot 49*, and the National Book Award for *Gravity's Rainbow* in 1974. Though the judging committee unanimously voted to award the Pulitzer Prize in fiction to Pynchon for *Gravity's Rainbow*, the committee was overruled by an advisory board that found the novel immoral and "turgid." The Howells Medal, awarded once every five years, was offered to Pynchon in 1975, but he declined it.

Pynchon occupies a place in the front rank of twentieth and twenty-first century American fiction writers, and more than one distinguished critic has declared him America's finest novelist.

BIOGRAPHY

Because of Thomas Pynchon's passion for privacy, little is known about his life. He was born Thomas Ruggles Pynchon, Jr., into a family that lived in Glen Cove, East Norwich, and Oyster Bay—all on Long Island in New York. His father, an industrial surveyor and a Republican, eventually served as town supervisor of Oyster Bay. Pynchon was sixteen when he graduated from Oyster Bay High School in 1953. He was class salutatorian and winner of an award for the senior attaining the highest grade average in English. With a scholarship at Cornell University, he first majored in engineer-

ing physics but, though he was doing well academically, abandoned that curriculum after the first year. A year later, he decided to do a hitch in the U.S. Navy before completing his baccalaureate degree. He attended boot camp at Bainbridge, Maryland, and did advanced training as an electrician at Norfolk, Virginia. His two years in the Navy, partly spent in the Mediterranean, provided Pynchon with a number of comic situations and characters that he later exploited in his fiction, such as in "Low-Lands," *V.*, *Gravity's Rainbow*, and *Mason and Dixon*. Pynchon finished at Cornell as an English major and graduated in 1959. While at Cornell, he took a class taught by Vladimir Nabokov; Nabokov's wife, Vera, who did her husband's grading, remembered Pynchon for his distinctive handwriting.

Pynchon lived briefly in Greenwich Village and in uptown Manhattan before taking a job with the Boeing Company and moving to Seattle. With Boeing for two and a half years (until September, 1962), he worked in the Minuteman Logistics Support Program and wrote for such intramural publications as the *Minuteman Field Service News* and *Aerospace Safety*. After leaving Boeing, he lived in California and Mexico and completed *V.*, which was published in 1963 and hailed as a major first novel.

Over the years Pynchon was rumored to be living in various places, including California, Mexico, and Oregon. In the late 1970's, he made a trip to England that mysteriously was noted in the national newsmagazines. For a long time the author eluded his pursuers, but in the 1980's he supplied a few tantalizing autobiographical facts in the introductory essays he wrote for his *Slow Learner* collection and for the 1983 Penguin reprint of *Been Down So Long It Looks Like Up to Me*, the 1966 novel by his Cornell classmate Richard Fariña.

In 1996, Nancy Jo Sales, writing for the magazine *New York*, traced Pynchon to the Manhattan apartment he shared with his wife, Melanie Jackson (also his agent), and their son. The following year a photograph of Pynchon taken by James Bone appeared in the *London Times Magazine*, and a camera crew from the Cable News Network (CNN) taped Pynchon walking down a street. In these instances, Pynchon fought unsuccessfully to suppress publication or broadcast of his likeness. In 2004, however, the author voiced depictions of himself in two episodes of the animated television series *The Simpsons*: season 15, episode 10, "Diatribe of a Mad Housewife,"which first aired on January 25, 2004; and season 16, episode 2, "All's Fair in Oven War," which first aired on November 14, 2004.

ANALYSIS

The quest would seem to be the one indispensable element in the fiction of Thomas Pynchon, for each of his novels proves to be a modern-dress version of the search for some grail to revive the wasteland. Pynchon's characters seek knowledge that will make sense of their unanchored lives and their fragmented times; Pynchon hints that questing has a value irrespective of the authenticity of that for which one quests. The quest lends purpose to life, enabling one to function, to see life as worthwhile. At the same time, however, Pynchon invites his more privileged reader to recognize that the ordering principle thus projected is factitious. What is real is the gathering dissolution, the passing of human beings and whole civilizations. All attempts to discover or create order and system are doomed.

Even so, as Pynchon's career has developed, one notes what may be a tendency to define some grail of his own, an inclination to search for a way out of the cul-de-sac of a metaphysics perhaps unduly in thrall to the principle of entropy (broadly defined as the gradual deterioration of the universe caused by irreversible thermodynamic equalization). Pynchon's critics disagree sharply on this point. Some maintain that the intimation of counterentropic orders in *The Crying of Lot 49* and *Gravity's Rainbow* is merely a hook by which to catch unwary readers, a means of seducing readers into system making as delusive as that of any of Pynchon's characters. Other critics, unwilling to believe that Pynchon's frequently noted affinity with modern science has been frozen at a point attained some time in the 1950's, suspect that Pynchon means to hint at transcendental alternatives implicit in the vast mysteries of contemporary astronomy and particle physics.

Regardless of whether Pynchon is on a grail quest of his own (with all the propensity for mysticism that seems indispensable to such a quester), he continues to create intricate labyrinths in which readers experience the paranoia that also figures as a prominent theme in his

work. Paranoia is the conviction that mighty conspiracies exist, that all things are connected "in spheres joyful or threatening about the central pulse of [one]self." Pynchon's protagonists come to believe in this infinite reticulation of conspiracy because it is preferable to the possibility that "nothing is connected to anything." Pynchon's readers, by the same token, encounter fictive structures that formally imitate the paranoid premise: All is connected in great, seamless webs of interdependent detail.

The dialectic between order and disorder is the dialectic between art and life, and it is with reference to this neglected commonplace that one should analyze Pynchon's artifice. In art, traditionally, humanity lays claim—sometimes piously, sometimes impiously—to the divine prerogative of creation, the establishment of order where all before was without form and void. Pynchon gives evidence, since the almost nihilistic *V.*, of a fascination with the religious belief that there are "orders behind the visible," orders analogous to those found beneath the surface in works of art ostensibly reflecting life in all its chaotic aspects. *Gravity's Rainbow*, for example, strikes one at first as a complete mishmash, a welter of all-too-lifelike confusion, but one subsequently discovers it to be as finely crafted as James Joyce's *Ulysses* (1922) or *Finnegans Wake* (1939). Perhaps Pynchon can best be imagined in the company of such literary predecessors as William Blake, William Butler Yeats, and D. H. Lawrence—visionaries who counter the smugness and complacency of a scientific age with a calculated antirationalism.

These remarks adumbrate the last major topoi in Pynchon's work—science and art. Pynchon knows and makes artistic use of science. He has, if nothing else, dispatched legions of humanists in search of information about modern physics, chemistry, engineering, and cartography—disciplines to which they had previously been indifferent. As suggested above, however, science serves vision, not the other way around. Pynchon's work does more than that of any other writer—scientific or literary—to reverse the widening "dissociation of sensibility" that poet T. S. Eliot noted as part of the intellectual landscape since the seventeenth century. In Pynchon, and in his readers to a remarkable extent, C. P. Snow's "two cultures" become one again.

V.

In his first novel, *V.*, Pynchon brilliantly interweaves two narratives, one in the present (mid-1950's), the other in the period 1880 to 1943. The historical narrative, presented obliquely, concerns an extraordinary woman who appears originally as Victoria Wren and subsequently under *noms de guerre* in which the letter *V* of the alphabet figures prominently: Veronica Manganese, Vera Meroving. This is V., who turns up whenever there is bloodshed in the course of the twentieth century. In 1898, for example, she appears at the periphery of the Fashoda crisis in Egypt, and the following year she gravitates to Florence, where the spies of several nations are jockeying for position, engaging in what Pynchon calls "premilitary" activity. In 1913, she is in Paris, involved in a bloody theater riot which, like the crises in Egypt and Florence earlier, proves an earnest of World War I—a kind of fulfillment for V. in her early phase. When World War I ends with Western civilization intact, though permanently altered, V. begins to be involved with those elements that will figure in the more satisfying carnage of the century's real climacteric, World War II. In 1922, she is in German southwest Africa, where the massacre of the native Hereros reenacts the even greater massacre of two decades earlier and anticipates the really accomplished genocide in Europe between 1933 and 1945. On and off after 1918, she is on Malta, consorting with a group sympathetic to Mussolini and his Fascists. V. dies in an air raid on Malta in 1943—just as the tide turns against the Fascist cause with which she has become increasingly identified.

V.'s affinity with Fascism complements a decadent religiosity, and she comes to personify the drift to extinction of Western culture and of life itself. She gradually loses parts of her body and becomes more and more the sum of inanimate parts: false eye, false hair, false foot, false navel. She is a brilliant metaphor for entropy and the decline of civilization, and her baleful influence is projected in the novel's present in the decadence of the contemporary characters, most of whom are part of a group called the Whole Sick Crew. The Crew is exemplified by its newest member, the winsome schlemiel Benny Profane. Profane is incapable of love and emotional involvement; he is also perennially at war with inanimate objects. His dread of the inanimate suggests that he intu-

its the cultural situation as the century wanes. Though he is no thinker, he realizes that he and his fellows are Eliot's hollow men, on the way to their whimpering end. His inability to love is presented in comic terms—though fat, he is doted on by various desirable women, including the Maltese Paola Maijstral and the beautiful Rachel Owlglass. The failure is that of his entire circle, for though there is much sex among the Whole Sick Crew, there is no commitment, no love, no hope. The one baby generated by all the sexual freedom is aborted.

The Whole Sick Crew is what Western civilization has become as a result of entropic processes that are utterly random and mindless. The meaninglessness of entropy is something difficult for the human mind to accept, however, and in Herbert Stencil, a marginal member of the Crew, Pynchon presents what becomes his standard character, a person who must discover conspiracy to deal with the fragmentation of life and culture. It is Stencil who does the mythmaking, the elevating of Victoria Wren from mere perverted adventuress to something awesome and as multifaceted as Robert Graves's White Goddess. Nor is Stencil alone, for the undeniable desire for connectedness is quintessentially human. It is also shared by the sophisticated reader, who, seeking to solve the literary puzzle, becomes *another* Stencil, a quester for meaning in the convoluted plot of *V.* and in the identity of the mysterious personage who gives the novel its name. Pynchon's genius manifests itself in his ability to keep his readers suspended between his two mutually exclusive alternatives: that the clues to V.'s identity are the key to meaning and that V. is nothing more than a paranoid fantasy, the product of a mind that cannot deal with very much reality.

The fascination with which readers have responded to *V.* indicates that Pynchon is himself a brilliant mythmaker. Even after one has "solved" the mystery of V. and arrived at an enlightenment that Stencil explicitly rejects as a threat to his emotional and mental stability, one still finds the myth trenchant, moving, even terrifying. The decline of the West is a theme that one has encountered before, but never has one encountered it so cogently as in this woman who loves death and the inanimate. The real conspiracy, then, is an artistic one; the connectedness is that of the novel, the cabal between author and reader.

THE CRYING OF LOT 49

Pynchon's second novel, *The Crying of Lot 49*, seems slight between *V.* and *Gravity's Rainbow*, and Pynchon himself seems to consider it something of a potboiler. Some readers, however, believe it to be his most perfect work of art. It is the story of Oedipa Maas, who is named "executor, or she supposed executrix" of the estate of a former lover, the millionaire Pierce Inverarity. In carrying out her duties, she stumbles upon evidence of a conspiracy to circumvent the U.S. Postal Service. She discovers Tristero, a sub-rosa postal system at war for centuries with all officially sanctioned postal services, first in the Old World, then in the New World. Tristero subsumes an extraordinary number of revolutionary or simply alienated groups. In its New World phase, it seems to bring together all those within the American system who are disfranchised, disaffected, or disinherited—all those defrauded of the American Dream.

Oedipa, like Herbert Stencil, finds that the harder she looks, the more connections to Tristero she discovers, until the connections start revealing themselves in such number and variety that she begins to doubt her sanity. Oedipa's mental condition, in fact, becomes the book's central conundrum. She first confronts the question in a flashback early in the story. She recalls visiting a Mexico City art gallery with Pierce Inverarity and seeing a disturbing painting by Remedios Varo. In the painting, a group of girls are imprisoned at the top of a circular tower and made to embroider *el Manto Terrestre*—the earth mantle. The tapestry they create, extruded through the tower's windows, contains "all the other buildings and creatures, all the waves, ships and forests of the earth," for "the tapestry was the world." Oedipa recognizes in the painting a representation of the fact that she—like any other human being—is imprisoned mentally and perceptually in the tower of her individual consciousness. External reality, in other words, may be nothing more than what one weaves or embroiders in one's cranial tower. Oedipa weeps at human isolation. Later, tracking down the clues to Tristero (which seems coextensive with Inverarity's estate and enterprises), she cannot free herself from the suspicion that the proliferating connections she is discovering all have their throbbing ganglion in her own mind. She realizes that she is becoming a classic paranoid.

Though Pynchon does not resolve the question of Oedipa's sanity, he hints that becoming sensitized to the problems of twentieth century American culture (and to the horrors of the spiritual void contingent on certain twentieth century habits of mind) involves a necessary sacrifice of sanity or at least serenity. At the end, Oedipa is faced with a harrowing choice: Either she is insane, or Tristero—with its stupendous reticulation—really exists. When Oedipa attempts to rephrase the dilemma, she finds that the paranoia is somehow inescapable:

> There was either some Tristero beyond the appearance of the legacy America, or there was just America and if there was just America then it seemed the only way she could continue, and manage to be at all relevant to it, was as an alien, unfurrowed, assumed full circle into some paranoia.

Pynchon implies that Tristero, whatever its status as literal reality, is in effect a necessary fiction, a metaphor for the idea of an alternative to a closed system.

Oedipa's experiences are almost certainly an imaginative version of Pynchon's own. At the time of the novel, 1964, Oedipa is twenty-eight years old—the same age as Pynchon was in that year. Like Pynchon, she has attended Cornell and then gravitated to the West Coast. Like Pynchon, too, she comes to view herself as an "alien," unable to fit into the furrow of American success, prosperity, and complacency. Thus, one can read the novel as Pynchon's account of why he has gone underground. He has made common cause with America's disadvantaged; in all of his fiction, not to mention his article "A Journey into the Mind of Watts," one notes an obvious sympathy with minorities and something like loathing for the mechanisms of corporate greed responsible for the spoilage of the American landscape, both literal and psychic. *The Crying of Lot 49*, then, is a fictional hybrid of the spiritual autobiography—in the same tradition as Saint Augustine's *Confessions* (397-401) and William Wordsworth's *The Prelude* (1850).

These speculations—the need for an alternative to a closed system, the hints of spiritual autobiography—are supported by Edward Mendelson's brilliant essay "The Sacred, the Profane, and *The Crying of Lot 49*" (the single most satisfying reading of the novel, this essay has been reprinted in Mendelson's *Pynchon: A Collection of*

Critical Essays, 1978). Mendelson points out the novel's high density of language with religious connotations; he argues that what Oedipa really searches for—and behind her twentieth century humankind—is a new species of revelation, a way out of the agnostic, positivistic cul-de-sac of contemporary rationalism. He also provides an explanation of the novel's odd title. "Lot 49" is a group of stamps—Tristero forgeries—to be sold as part of the settlement of Pierce Inverarity's estate. The novel ends as lot 49 is about to be "cried" or auctioned. Oedipa, present at the auction, expects to confront some representative of the mysterious Tristero, who will attempt to acquire the evidence of the secret organization's existence. Mendelson suggests that the number 49 refers obliquely to the forty-nine-day period between Easter and the descent of the Holy Spirit at Pentecost; the revelation that awaits Oedipa at the crying of lot 49 is symbolically the revelation awaited by the modern world, whose existence so tragically lacks a numinous dimension. Thus, Pynchon ends his novel on a note of expectation, a yearning for some restoration of mystery, some answer to what the narrator calls "the exitlessness, the absence of surprise to life" in the modern age.

GRAVITY'S RAINBOW

All of Pynchon's books are filled with bizarre characters and incidents, but *Gravity's Rainbow* is especially dense and demanding. The hero is Tyrone Slothrop, an American army lieutenant attached to an Allied intelligence unit in World War II. Slothrop's superiors become aware that the map of his sexual conquests (or his sexual fantasies; this is kept ambiguous) coincides with the distribution of German V-2 rockets falling on London. Significantly, the erection *precedes* the arrival of the rocket. This fact, which calls into question the usual mechanism of cause and effect (it complements the fact that the rocket, traveling faster than the speed of sound, is heard falling *after* it has exploded) is of central importance to the novel, for Pynchon means to pit two scientific models against each other. The older model, still seldom questioned, posits a mechanistic universe that operates according to the laws of cause and effect.

The character associated with this worldview is the sinister Dr. Pointsman, a diehard Pavlovian threatened by the new model, which posits a universe in which physical phenomena can be plotted and predicted only in terms of uncertainty and probability (Pynchon is on sound theoretical ground here; he is presenting the physics of Werner Heisenberg and Max Planck). The character who embraces the more up-to-date worldview is the sympathetic Roger Mexico, a statistician. Between these two, poor Slothrop—a kind of Everyman—tries to stay alive and if possible free. Pointsman and his minions concoct an experiment with Slothrop; they will provide him with the best information they have on the German rocket and then observe him closely for further revelations. Slothrop, aware that he is being used, goes AWOL to embark on a private quest to discover the truth of his personal destiny—and perhaps the destiny of his age as well.

Pynchon picks his historical moment carefully, for World War II was the moment when the technological world came of age. Technology offers humanity complete control of its environment and its destiny; technology offers something very like transcendence—or it offers annihilation. Pynchon's novel is a meditation on the choice, which is seen nowhere more clearly than in the new rocket technology. Will humanity use the rocket transcendentally, to go to the stars, or will people use it to destroy themselves? The answer has been taking shape since the German rocket scientists were sent east and west after World War II, and Pynchon concludes his great narrative with the split second before the ultimate cataclysm: The apocalyptic rocket plunges toward the "theatre" in which the film *Gravity's Rainbow* has unreeled before the reader. Critical opinion is split on the degree of bleakness in this ending. Figuratively, says Pynchon, the world is separated from its end only by "the last delta-t," the last infinitesimal unit of time and space between the rocket and its target. The delta-t, however, is a relative unit of measure. Modern human folly has indeed set in motion the process of his own destruction, but the process might still be arrested by a reordering of priorities, human and technological.

As for Slothrop, he simply fades away. Pynchon says he becomes "scattered," and the world reveals a characteristic aspect of Pynchon's genius. Just as Joyce forced religious and liturgical language to serve his aesthetic ends, Pynchon forces technological language to serve humanistic and spiritual ends. "Scattering," a trope from particle physics, refers to the dispersal of a beam of radiation, but it also evokes *sparagmos*, the ritual dismemberment and dispersal of the divine scapegoat. Slothrop has been associated all along with Orpheus, whose dismemberment became the basis of one of the many fertility cults in the Mediterranean and Near East. In a sense, Slothrop dies for the sins of the modern world, and his scattering coincides with the founding of the Counterforce, a group of enlightened, anarchic men and women devoted to reversing the technology of violence and death. The Counterforce, which has affinities with various countercultural movements waxing at the moment of this novel's composition, is not particularly powerful or effective, but it offers hope for a planet hurtling toward destruction.

After *Gravity's Rainbow*, Pynchon published no new fiction for seventeen years. During this period, the counterculture retreated as the forces of reaction, complacency, and materialism took over, and perhaps it was this frightening and disheartening development that was behind Pynchon's long silence. He may have abandoned a book or books that came to seem unattuned to the post-1960's zeitgeist. Yet when the novelistic silence was at last broken, it was with a meditation on the historical polarization of the 1960's and the 1980's.

VINELAND

In his long-awaited fourth novel, *Vineland*, Pynchon returns to the California setting of *The Crying of Lot 49*. As in *V.*, Pynchon sets up a dual historical focus. He imagines characters in the present—the portentous year 1984—trying to come to terms with the period, twenty years earlier, when they and the whole country underwent a searing passage. Broadly, then, Pynchon here reflects on the direction the country's history has taken—from anarchic but healthy self-indulgence to neo-Puritan repression. These poles are visible in the People's Republic of Rock and Roll, with its ethic of freedom, pleasure, dope, music, and self-expression, and in the Nixonian and Reaganite reaction that put an end to the polymorphous perversity of the 1960's and ushered in the return to materialism and political conservatism.

The novel is structured—somewhat more loosely than is usual with Pynchon—around the quest of a girl named Prairie for the mother, Frenesi Gates, who abandoned her shortly after her birth. Prairie's father, Zoyd Wheeler, still loves Frenesi, as does the man with whom

she was involved before him—the sinister Brock Vond, a federal agent who had used her to infiltrate and subvert PR3 and other radical causes. Zoyd accepts his misery, but Vond will stop at nothing to get Frenesi back in his clutches—not even at kidnapping Prairie, who could be made into an instrument of renewed control. Also involved in the action are female Ninja Darryl Louise—DL—Chastain, an old friend of Frenesi, and DL's companion, the "karmic adjuster" Takeshi Fumimota, a kind of Zen private eye.

The centrality of Prairie, Frenesi, and DL, not to mention the narrational attention to Frenesi's mother and grandmother (Sasha Gates and Eula Traverse), make this essay Pynchon's first in feminist fiction. (Though a woman, V., was central to his first novel, it was really a parody of the kind of matriarchal vision associated with Robert Graves and the White Goddess.) It is in terms of this feminism that he is able in *Vineland* to move beyond the apocalyptic obsession that characterizes all three of his previous novels, as well as the stories "Mortality and Mercy in Vienna" and "Entropy." *Vineland* ends with a vision of familial harmony that is nothing less than mythic—an augury of what an America-wide family might be. Here the reader sees Prairie reunited with her mother and half brother, as Zoyd and others are also integrated. Vond alone is excluded (his surname is an apocope of the Dutch word *vondeling*, a foundling—as if to hint at his inability to be integrated into family wholeness). The reunion of the Traverse-Becker clans, which seem to center in their women, is Pynchon's Kurt Vonnegut-like imagining of the millennium, the era of peace and harmony that ironically succeeds the apocalyptic disruptions everywhere expected in the novel.

Herein, too, is the meaning of Pynchon's setting, the imaginary community of Vineland that provides the novel with its title. Vineland is the name given to the American continent by the Vikings, its first European visitors, at the end of the first millennium. Pynchon's novel reminds American readers that their land has been known to history for one thousand years.

MASON AND DIXON

A more proximate past figures in *Mason and Dixon*. In this most massive of his novels, Pynchon ranges over the eighteenth century, with particular attention to the careers of Charles Mason and Jeremiah Dixon, who are sent by the Royal Society to the far corners of the earth to observe the 1761 and 1769 transits of Venus. Between these two assignments Mason and Dixon accept a commission to establish the much-contested boundary between Pennsylvania and Maryland. The central part of Pynchon's mammoth novel concerns this project, which occupies his protagonists from 1763 to 1767.

The dates are important: Mason and Dixon do their work on the very eve of the American Revolution. Pynchon looks at the America they traverse for the switching points of the great railroad called history. He sees colonial America as a place where Western civilization paused one last time before following its Faustian course toward more rationalism, greater dependence on technology, and the throwing out of spiritual babies with the bathwater of magic and superstition. The religious freedom it offered notwithstanding, America has always, Pynchon suggests, been a place of struggle between the spiritual and material energies of the West. By the latter part of the eighteenth century, with the Revolution in the offing, the secularizing tendencies of the Enlightenment (notably Deism) made America the conservator, merely, of a few "poor fragments of a Magic irreparably broken." No longer the setting of "a third Testament," the New World remained only sporadically the "object of hope that Miracles might yet occur, that God might yet return to Human affairs, that all the wistful Fictions necessary to the childhood of a species might yet come true." Though aware that popular religion would always figure prominently in the moral economy of the emergent American nation, Pynchon suggests that some more genuine and legitimate spirituality was elbowed aside by the less-than-idealistic interests that fostered revolution (and he offers largely unflattering sketches of figures such as Founding Fathers Ben Franklin and George Washington). In the end, America became merely "one more hope in the realm of the Subjunctive, one more grasp at the last radiant whispers of the last bights of Robe-hem, billowing Æther-driven at the back of an ever-departing Deity." Pynchon seems, in *Mason and Dixon*, to reconceptualize the hallowed myth of a quest for religious freedom.

Indeed, he rewrites more than one archetypal American narrative. Thus he intimates, as in *The Crying of Lot 49*, some betrayal of the original American Dream; thus his protagonists, who twin the American Adam, must like so many of their literary predecessors decide whether to reenact the Fall. Pynchon also revisits the captivity narrative, with emphasis not on the godless savagery of the captors but on the nefarious scheming of the Europeans they serve. When American Indians kidnap Eliza Fields of Conestoga, they do so on behalf of evil Jesuits who seek to staff a bizarre convent-brothel called Las Viudas de Cristo: the Widows of Christ. Even more bizarre, perhaps, is Fields's escape with Captain Zhang, a Chinese feng shui master who objects to the severely rationalistic mensuration (and cartography) of the arch-Jesuit Padre Zarpazo.

Presently joining the crew of lumberjacks, roustabouts, and hangers-on accompanying Mason and Dixon, Zhang provides an important non-Western perspective on their project. "Boundaries," he declares, should "follow Nature—coast-lines, ridge-tops, river-banks—so honoring the Dragon or *shan* within, from which the Land-Scape ever takes its form. To mark a right Line upon the Earth is to inflict upon the Dragon's very flesh a sword-slash, a long, perfect scar." Zhang characterizes the Visto (the unnaturally straight ten-yard-wide swath the surveyors cut through the wilderness) as a conductor of *Sha*, the "Bad Energy" that will bring in its train "Bad History." As Zhang subsequently observes, "Nothing will produce Bad History more directly or brutally, than drawing a Line, in particular a Right Line, the very Shape of Contempt, through the midst of a People—to create thus a Distinction betwixt 'em—'tis the first stroke—All else will follow as if predestin'd, unto War and Devastation." The American Civil War, half a century later, would validate Zhang's remark as prophecy.

Sir Francis Bacon, describing the Idols of the Theater, long ago recognized how received ways of knowing within a given historical period make certain kinds of thinking difficult, if not impossible. Mason, for example, aspires to membership in the Royal Society even as he desperately tries to believe that death—especially the death of his beloved wife Rebekah—is not final. Yet the scientific calling that he shares with Dixon affords little latitude for such hope. Pynchon ingeniously imagines his protagonists as imperfectly amphibious men of their age. Each struggles to reconcile a propensity for supernatural or magical thinking with professional obligations to the new, rationalist order. Whether in South Africa, on the island of St. Helena, in America, or at the North Cape, Dixon and Mason sense that they are the inconsequential pawns of forces indifferent or hostile to them. Servants of the powerful and remote Royal Society, the surveyors suffer from a paranoia somewhat different from the usual Pynchon article—or perhaps they simply show us, belatedly, the positive side of a putative psychopathology. Pynchon hints, that is, at something admirable, even redemptive, in the paranoia of his eighteenth century Rosencrantz and Guildenstern. Mason and Dixon resist the coercive intellectual forces of their age.

As brilliantly realized as that age is in these pages, Pynchon delights in anachronistic violation of his historical frame. At a number of points the reader realizes that some piece of elaborately rendered eighteenth century foolery actually mirrors a twentieth century counterpart, for Pynchon frequently circumvents historical constraint to offer droll glimpses of what America and American culture will become. Hilarious, lightly veiled allusions to Popeye, Daffy Duck, the Jolly Green Giant, and *Star Trek* abound, not to mention numerous clever periphrases of a later vernacular. There are no cheap shots here, only the occasional "inexpensive salvo." Characters do not get their backs up—they suffer "Thoracick Indignation." Those hoping to keep costs down are reminded that "*prandium gratis non est*" ("there's no such thing as a free lunch"). The reader smiles, too, at "teton dernier," "aviating swine," "coprophagously agrin," and (of Fenderbelly Bodine exposing his buttocks to a foe) "pygephanous."

Pynchon fills his pages with the imaginative conceits his readers have come to expect. There is, for example, a wonderful talking canine, the Learned English Dog. There is also a character who, at the full moon, turns into a were-beaver. An eighteenth century Valley Girl's every sentence features "as" rather than the "like" that would characterize the speech of her twentieth century sister. A chef with the punning name of Armand Allegre fends off the amorous attentions of a mechanical duck— part Daffy, part Frankenstein's Monster—invented by Jacques de Vaucanson. Such joking has its serious side: de Vaucanson's punch-card technology would be re-

fined in the Jacquard loom and other automated weaving machines that played an important role in the Industrial Revolution, centerpiece of the Enlightenment. Subsequently, punch cards would play their role in the Age of Information.

In *Mason and Dixon*, then, Pynchon characterizes the eighteenth century as the moment in Western history when rationalism became a cultural juggernaut, crushing spiritual alternatives to Enlightenment thinking. As in *V.*, *Gravity's Rainbow*, and the 1984 essay "Is It O.K. to Be a Luddite?" the author focuses on the reification of Faustian appetite in scientific and technological advance, here symbolized in the profoundly unnatural Line that, arrowing its way into the mythic American West, consecrates the New World to reason—and to its abuses.

AGAINST THE DAY

In his 2006 novel *Against the Day*, Pynchon renews his engagement with history. At more than one thousand pages, this longest of his works to date resists easy summarizing. Many would characterize it as Pynchon's most demanding fiction—not because they find it hard to understand (one follows the action here, however fanciful, much more readily than that of *V.* or *Gravity's Rainbow*) but because it concedes so little to the kind of propulsive plotting that keeps one turning pages in more popular novels. The reader impatient with a text so vast must understand that originality will not always present itself as entertainment—especially if a writer means to engage and reframe history in fresh and perhaps radical ways.

In *Against the Day*, Pynchon has written a kind of "secret history" of the decades in which the most powerful nations of the world competed for colonies, jockeyed for strategic position, entered into secret covenants, engaged in what Rudyard Kipling called the "Great Game" of espionage, and fanned the endless brushfire conflicts in the Balkans. The novel documents the political and cultural currents that swept Western humanity into and through its first world war, but it also suggests that twenty-first century readers might discern in that earlier era a dark mirror of their own historical moment—hence the title, a phrase that recurs often in the King James Version of the Bible, usually with reference to the coming "day" of divine vengeance against the godless (in 2 Peter 3:7, for example, the deity holds the apocalyptic fire in reserve "against the day of judgment and perdition of ungodly men"). Pynchon implies the imminence, again, of violence such as that which convulsed the world in 1914-1918.

One marvels, first, at *Against the Day*'s extraordinary geographic range. Pynchon undertakes to represent, in nothing less than global perspective, the historical events and imagined private experience of the years 1893-1923. He ranges all over the world, sending characters to Iceland, to the Arctic, and to great tracts of "inner Asia," including Siberia and a vast region subsuming parts of China, Kazakhstan, Tajikistan, Uzbekistan, and Kyrgyzstan. He escorts readers to remote corners of the moribund Austro-Hungarian Empire and even reproduces examples of the vernaculars spoken there. He anchors these flights in interwoven narratives centering in the United States (especially the West), in various parts of Mexico, and in London, Venice, Paris, Göttingen, and the other great cities of European civilization.

By way of providing shape to his vast narrative, Pynchon focuses on the Traverse family, ancestors of Frenesi and Prairie in *Vineland*. Indeed, the lifelong labor activist Jess Traverse, who so memorably declaims the words of Ralph Waldo Emerson in the closing pages of that novel, appears as a youth in *Against the Day*, which centers its vast narrative on the lifelong travail of his parents, aunt, uncles, and grandparents. Jesse, as he is called here, is the grandson of the Adamic Webb Traverse, a miner passionately at odds, late in the nineteenth century, with the owners who employ and exploit him. Webb may or may not be the terrorist dynamiter of mining installations known as the Kieselguhr Kid (kieselguhr is diatomaceous earth, an ingredient of blasting powder), but his outspoken labor sympathies bring him to the attention of the loathsome Scarsdale Vibe, a tycoon contemptuous of the working classes and willing to go to any lengths to preserve plutocratic perquisites.

The ruthless Vibe, who thinks of unions as havens of anarchy and enemies of civilized order, eventually orders Traverse murdered. Webb's wife, Mayva, and all but one of their children, including sons Reef, Frank, and Kit, shoulder the burden of bringing violent justice to Vibe and his hired thugs. Kit, however, allows Vibe to pay his way to Yale, and, in an even more unsettling development, the Traverse daughter, Lake, takes up

with and eventually marries Vibe's creature, the vicious Deuce Kindred. Pynchon describes not only the quest for vengeance on the part of Webb's survivors but also their fanning out into the world, their romantic and marital connections, their shifts for survival in an increasingly complex and dangerous era, and their keeping of the faith against what Emerson calls "all the tyrants and proprietors and monopolists of the world." Carried along on the tide of modernity, Pynchon's characters alternately conspire with and resist forces that will presently define a new era: the American century.

Pynchon rethinks both history and historiography here. Like Henry James or Joseph Conrad, he scrutinizes the growth of international anarchy as a means of resistance to the capitalist Leviathan. He also seeds the past with a host of fanciful and creative conceits that, however factitious, remain curiously faithful to history (for, by his own admission, Pynchon shares with John Ruskin "a capacity responsive to the claims of fact, but unoppressed by them"). Thus, readers of *Against the Day* encounter time travel, Theosophical cabals, Jules Verne-like vessels for traveling under desert sands in search of Shambhala (Buddhism's mythical holy city), and a band of perennially youthful aeronauts, the Chums of Chance, whose adventures and banter parody those prominent in the various boys' books that became popular in the first years of the twentieth century (the Rover Boys series began in 1899, Tom Swift in 1910, the Hardy Boys and the Ted Scott Flying Stories in 1927).

The inclusion of the Chums's antics and melodramatic adventures (all realized with artful burlesque of the "Victor Appleton" or "Franklin W. Dixon" style) is typical of Pynchon's refusal, however serious his theme, to be bound by the conventions of realistic narrative. Indeed, he evidently desires to remind readers of the storytelling that, in the first decades of the twentieth century, commanded a much vaster audience than the age's critically sanctioned realism, naturalism, and emergent modernism. The mixing of styles and repudiation of decorum, of course, are hallmarks of the postmodernism that Pynchon, more than any other, has established as literary dominant in the years after World War II. With the Chums of Chance, Pynchon provides his own novelistic airship with the opposite of ballast. They represent a literal puerility that soars above terrestrial events—even as they are imagined as taking some fanciful part in them. The reader may think of the Chums as the embodiment of an innocence that the Great War and the coercions of capital can never quite destroy. The fact that they are figures of romance, however, makes its own comment on the survivability, the real-world viability, of such innocence.

The Chums have counterparts in other countries, notably the Italian "Amici dell'Azzardo" and the Russian "Tovarishchi Slutchainyi." Such replications—they include doubled characters, places, events, and things—figure everywhere in this text. Pynchon recurs with particular emphasis to "the doubly-refracting calcite known as Iceland spar," a crystal through which objects appear dimly twinned (one sees the effect reproduced in the image on the cover of the hardback first editions of the novel published by Penguin and Jonathan Cape). This feature, variously reticulated, seems ultimately to reinforce Pynchon's theme of history itself doubled. *Against the Day* depicts, according to its dust jacket, "a time of unrestrained corporate greed, false religiosity, moronic fecklessness, and evil intent in high places." Readers may recognize in this era what Barbara W. Tuchman would call a "distant mirror" of their own time. Karl Marx famously observed (in *The Eighteenth Brumaire of Louis Bonaparte*, 1851-1852) that history transpires twice, "the first time as tragedy, the second as farce." Pynchon suggests, to the contrary, that there is little to amuse in what appears to be the world's appalling recapitulation of the international lunacy that precipitated one world war and may yet precipitate another.

David Cowart

OTHER MAJOR WORKS

SHORT FICTION: "Mortality and Mercy in Vienna," 1959; "The Small Rain," 1959; "Entropy," 1960; "Low-Lands," 1960; "Under the Rose," 1961; "The Secret Integration," 1964; *Slow Learner: Early Stories*, 1984.

NONFICTION: *Deadly Sins*, 1993.

BIBLIOGRAPHY

Bloom, Harold, ed. *Thomas Pynchon*. New York: Chelsea House, 1986. Collection of essays on all aspects of Pynchon's literary works provides a good introduction for first-time readers of Pynchon's prose.

Cowart, David. *Thomas Pynchon: The Art of Allusion*. Carbondale: Southern Illinois University Press, 1980. Examines Pynchon's allusions to art, music, cinema, and literature. Useful for beginning and advanced readers of postmodern fiction.

Grant, J. Kerry. *A Companion to "The Crying of Lot 49."* Athens: University of Georgia Press, 1994. Discusses the major themes of the novel and addresses the allusions it contains. Includes bibliographical references and index.

_____. *A Companion to "V."* Athens: University of Georgia Press, 2001. Provides a chapter-by-chapter close reading of *V.*, explicating Pynchon's allusions, summarizing critical interpretations, and providing a framework for understanding the work.

Gussow, Mel. "Pynchon's Letters Nudge His Mask." *The New York Times*, March 4, 1998. Discusses the insights into Pynchon's creative process and emotions revealed by more than 120 letters that he sent to his agent, Candida Donadio.

Herman, Luc, and John M. Kraft. "Fast Learner: The Typescript of Pynchon's *V.* at the Harry Ransom Center in Austin." *Texas Studies in Literature and Language* 49, no. 1 (2007): 1-20. Reveals and analyzes fascinating details about the writing and editing of Pynchon's first novel

Horvath, Barbara, and Irving Malin, eds. *Pynchon and "Mason and Dixon."* Newark: University of Delaware Press, 2000. Collection of essays devoted to Pynchon's fifth novel discusses, among other topics, the work's relation to the author's earlier works, Pynchon's attitudes toward religion, and his use of historical documents.

Hume, Kathryn. *Pynchon's Mythography: An Approach to "Gravity's Rainbow."* Carbondale: Southern Illinois University Press, 1987. Excellent study examines in detail Pynchon's use of myths and legends in *Gravity's Rainbow*, noting that the range of Pynchon's mythography extends from the Grail and Faust legends to non-Western myths.

McClure, John. *Partial Faiths: Postsecular Fiction in the Age of Pynchon and Morrison*. Athens: Georgia University Press, 2007. Makes a strong case for including Pynchon among the novelists who reaffirm spiritual possibility.

Mattessich, Stefan. *Lines of Flight: Discursive Time and Countercultural Desire in the Work of Thomas Pynchon*. Durham, N.C.: Duke University Press, 2003. Explores the ways in which Pynchon's critique of late capitalist society describes the emergence of a new conceptualization of time, which Mattessich calls "subjective displacement."

Schaub, Thomas, ed. *Approaches to Teaching Pynchon's "The Crying of Lot 49" and Other Works*. New York: Modern Language Association, 2008. Invaluable and long overdue collection of essays features contributions by noted Pynchon scholars. Focuses on techniques for presenting Pynchon's works in the classroom, including contextualization of the novels within their historical settings and the exploration of racial and gender politics through the novels.

Slade, Joseph. *Thomas Pynchon*. 1974. Reprint. New York: Peter Lang, 1990. The first book-length study of Pynchon's fiction is still one of the best. Balanced and readable, with especially strong discussion of Pynchon's uses of science.

Smith, Shawn. *Pynchon and History: Metahistorical Rhetoric and Postmodern Narrative Form in the Novels of Thomas Pynchon*. New York: Routledge, 2005. Focuses on Pynchon as a writer of historical fiction and examines his philosophy of history. Novels discussed include *Gravity's Rainbow* and *Mason and Dixon*.

Thomas, Samuel. *Pynchon and the Political*. New York: Routledge, 2007. Adduces theorists—Adorno, Horkheimer, Benjamin, and others (including Jameson)—who provide the terms with which to assay the political metal in the Pynchon ore.

Weisenburger, Steven C. *A "Gravity's Rainbow" Companion: Sources and Contexts for Pynchon's Novel*. 2d ed., rev. and expanded. Athens: University of Georgia Press, 2006. Extraordinarily detailed encyclopedia presents information on the sources for the allusions used in Pynchon's novel. Very useful for tracing the influence of the author's short stories on his novels, given that several of the characters from his stories reappear in *Gravity's Rainbow*.

Q

RAYMOND QUENEAU

Born: Le Havre, France; February 21, 1903
Died: Paris, France; October 25, 1976
Also known as: Sally Mara

Principal Long Fiction

Le Chiendent, 1933 (*The Bark Tree*, 1968)
Gueule de Pierre, 1934
Les Derniers Jours, 1936 (*The Last Days*, 1990)
Odile, 1937 (English translation, 1988)
Les Enfants du limon, 1938 (*Children of Clay*, 1998)
Un Rude Hiver, 1939 (*A Hard Winter*, 1948)
Les Temps mêlés: Gueule de Pierre II, 1941
Pierrot mon ami, 1943 (*Pierrot*, 1950)
Loin de Rueil, 1944 (*The Skin of Dreams*, 1948)
On est toujours trop bon avec les femmes, 1947 (*We Always Treat Women Too Well*, 1981)
Saint-Glinglin, 1948 (*Saint Glinglin*, 1993)
Journal intime, 1950
Le Dimanche de la vie, 1951 (*The Sunday of Life*, 1976)
Zazie dans le métro, 1959 (*Zazie in the Metro*, 1960)
Les Œuvres completes de Sally Mara, 1962
Les Fleurs bleues, 1965 (*The Blue Flowers*, 1967)
Le Vol d'Icare, 1968 (*The Flight of Icarus*, 1973)

Other Literary Forms

Raymond Queneau (keh-NOH) was a prolific writer in many forms in addition to long fiction. He published a dozen major collections of poetry and many opuscules published in private or limited additions. His poetry spoofs the seriousness of twentieth century poetry through the use of odd end-rhymes, slang, and invented forms; at the same time, he also manages to deal with serious subjects. One of Queneau's best-known works is the unclassifiable *Exercises de style* (1947; *Exercises in Style*, 1958). In this work, he takes the kernel of a narrative and in a dazzling series of ninety-nine variations investigates the limits of the possibilities of language. Queneau also wrote essays, criticism, and the dialogue for several of the film adaptations of his novels.

Achievements

Raymond Queneau is an unclassifiable author, which is just what he would have wished. His novels of the 1930's, when he was associated with the Surrealists, abound in wordplay and experiments with colloquial language, but they are generally set against a somber backdrop of war and working-class life. The characters seem to be controlled by the language that they speak, with the consequence that they are viewed from an ironic distance. In the 1940's, with his literary reputation firmly established, Queneau took some daring chances. He published *Exercises in Style*, which, if judged by its narrative content, is of no substance whatsoever; he also published a semiserious parody of the then-popular scandal novel under an assumed name. Yet these were precisely the sorts of risks that Queneau enjoyed taking and that, in turn, make him both so hard to pin down and such a source of invention for subsequent writers.

Queneau's novels of the 1950's brought him a wide popular audience for the first time, with their bright and zany depiction of ordinary people having the time of their lives. In 1960, along with François Le Lionnais, he founded l'Ouvoir de Littérature Potentielle, or Oulipo (the workshop of potential literature), a group of writers who met regularly to discuss the infinite potential of language for recombination and creative invention. His association with this group (which remains intact into the twenty-first century), along with the experimental quality of his work, is often mentioned as leading to

Queneau's strong influence over the practitioners of the *nouveau roman*, or New Novel, of the 1960's.

Overall, Queneau enjoyed a productive, highly varied, yet playful career as a writer, introducing slang and colloquial language into "serious" literature. In some ways, he is the most significant literary figure to provide a link between the Surrealists of the 1920's and 1930's and the more language-oriented writers of the 1960's and 1970's.

BIOGRAPHY

Raymond Queneau was born on February 21, 1903, in Le Havre, France. His family background was modest; his parents ran a haberdashery. Queneau took his *lycée* degree in Le Havre in 1920 and then went to Paris to study philosophy. During the following decade he associated with the Surrealists and helped to edit the journal *La Révolution surréaliste*. For two years, Queneau fulfilled his military service obligation in North Africa; he eventually wrote of the experience in *Odile*. After his discharge, in 1928, he gained employment at a bank and married Janine Kahn.

Queneau's career as a novelist received some initial impetus from a voyage to Greece in 1932. There he wrote most of his first novel, *The Bark Tree*. Once started in his career as a writer, Queneau began to publish frequently in several genres. His first collection of poetry, *Chêne et chien* (1937), plays off the ambiguous Norman etymology of the Queneau family name, Quêne/Chêne ("oak tree") and Quenot/Chien ("dog"). In like manner, throughout his career in letters, Queneau would continually seek to blend humor with noble literary aspirations.

The literary contacts Queneau cultivated in his early years led in part to a position with the prestigious French publishing house Gallimard. In 1945, he assumed the role of editor for the *Encyclopédie de la Pléiade*, a multivolume encyclopedia of history, natural sciences, and social sciences. Queneau's was never purely a literary mind to begin with, and his association with the encyclopedia allowed him to continue to develop his wide-ranging interests in mathematics and science. In 1947, his poem "Si tu t'imagines" (if you would think) was set to music and became the most popular song of the year. In the same year, Queneau published a parody of the scandal novel, under the pseudonym Sally Mara. Only several years later, when he published *Journal intime* under the same name, did he admit to being the author of both works.

The decade of the 1950's saw Queneau reach his greatest popularity as a novelist with two cheerful, funny, "popular" novels, *The Sunday of Life* and *Zazie in the Metro*. Both novels were turned into critically acclaimed, popular films—the former by Claude Chabrol and the latter by Louis Malle—with Queneau's assistance on both projects. The popularity Queneau enjoyed at first hampered the acceptance of his work as literature. With the rise of the New Novel in the 1960's, however, and the new emphasis given by criticism to the significance of language itself in literary works, Queneau eventually came to be seen as a forerunner of contemporary novelistic practice.

Toward the end of his life, a writer both popular and honored, Queneau continued to publish collections of poetry, as well as two more novels, *The Blue Flowers* and *The Flight of Icarus*. Queneau died in Paris, on October 25, 1976, at the age of seventy-three.

Raymond Queneau. (Roger Viollet/Getty Images)

ANALYSIS

Raymond Queneau's long fiction can be characterized by its wordplay, humor, and attentive concern with the lives of people living in ordinary circumstances. His pursuit of radical linguistic measures—such as that of James Joyce, who among other English-language authors served as his literary model—is almost always tied to a depiction of working-class and lower-middle-class conditions. In fact, the language experiments that most identify Queneau's originality are his various ways of representing colloquial and slang expressions, or how real people actually talk. Interwoven with the depiction of the lives of ordinary people are an extraordinary number of learned allusions, buried quotations, and philosophical statements. Paradoxical as it may seem, Queneau's work points to the level of what might be called metaphysical thinking even by characters who would not know the meaning of the word. For Queneau, philosophy is interesting and useful primarily as it reflects the insights of simple people, which are often of a startling profundity.

A HARD WINTER

Queneau's novels of the 1930's deal with a range of subjects, from the lives of ordinary people in Le Havre, his birthplace, to his war experience in North Africa, to some of the crazy artists he knew in part through his associations with the Surrealists. *A Hard Winter* may be taken as representative of Queneau's work from this decade. Set during World War I, the winter of 1916 specifically, the novel examines with cool and detached humor some of the contradictions in popular sentiment and the reality of wartime existence. Through a slowly developing romance seen through the perspective of the main character, Lehameau, the novel also investigates the repressed emotional lives of the people from this world.

The novel clearly incorporates elements of Queneau's background and family experience. Lehameau, the protagonist, enlisted, was wounded in action, and is now working as a liaison with the English armed forces stationed in Le Havre. At the opening of the book, a group of Chinese soldiers are marching through the streets to the general amusement of the population. Lehameau expresses his feelings to a young woman (Miss Weeds) in the uniform of the British Women's Army Air Corps.

—Zey lâffe, bicose zey dou notte undèrrstande [They laugh because they do not understand].

Il dit encore [He said]:

—Aïe laïe-ke zatt: you dou nott lâffe [I like that: You do not laugh].

Here Queneau's humor and wordplay are at the foreground of the passage, representing a Frenchman speaking accented English through the use of French orthography. Throughout Queneau's work, the way people speak reveals more about them than they know about themselves. The passage has a deeper meaning as well, concerning the necessary understanding of people from other cultures. The dialogue also serves to set up a relationship between Lehameau and Miss Weeds that the rest of the novel explores.

Lehameau's sentiments of universal understanding are placed in an ironic light. He is in fact a racist and a protofascist who, behind a pacifist ideology, harbors the belief in the necessity of a German victory to restore France to its true greatness. Queneau's underlying motive for portraying such a character in a book published in 1939 can only be guessed. It is clear from the work itself that the intended effect is one of ironic distancing. Lehameau's stunted emotional life becomes the amusing subject of the book, in spite of the antipathy his political views almost necessarily provokes in the reader.

The low level of Lehameau's emotional development is further explored in the book through the relationship he cultivates with an adolescent girl and her younger brother following a random encounter on a bus. Lehameau courts the two of them through an appeal to English regimental badges and an obviously phony patriotism. He also takes the two to the cinema, after receiving the benevolent blessing of the head of the household, Madeleine, their older sister, who runs a brothel. Annette, the young girl, is one of Queneau's typically precocious nymphets, and in this way she anticipates two of Queneau's most famous characters, Sally Mara and Zazie. The way in which Lehameau's relationship with Annette develops in parallel fashion with his relationship to Miss Weeds is the true core of the novel.

Lehameau and Miss Weeds gradually fall in love, but they are prevented from fulfilling their relationship by a mixture of ignorance and institutional prudery. Miss Weeds, in the service of the British armed forces, at first resists Lehameau's overtures. When she later gives in to her feelings and they are on the verge of consummating their relationship, Miss Weeds is abruptly transferred back to England, effectively ending their relationship. The double standard of British morality is clearly Queneau's target here: Miss Weeds is protected by the military bureaucracy from the morally dangerous Frenchman; at the same time, Madeleine's primary customers in her bordello are the English soldiers stationed in Le Havre. Lehameau temporarily overcomes his sorrow at losing Miss Weeds through a brief tryst with Madeleine, at which time he also loses his virginity. In a surprise ending, on the last page of the book Lehameau marries—Annette. The various levels of irony at work in the novel prevent the reader finally from making any rigorous moral judgments on the actions of the characters.

EXERCISES IN STYLE *and* WE ALWAYS TREAT WOMEN TOO WELL

Queneau's career as a novelist took a strange turn in 1947, when he published two very different works. *Exercises in Style* is not a novel at all, but there are many who regard it as Queneau's greatest achievement. In a dazzling series of ninety-nine variations, the writer tests language to the limits of its possibilities. The narrative kernel remains constant throughout the various treatments: The speaker sees a strangely dressed man on a bus; the man angrily accuses a fellow passenger of stepping on his toes, then quickly grabs a vacant seat; two hours later, the speaker sees the man again talking with a man near the Gare Saint-Lazare. From formal logical analysis to haiku, from street slang to Anglicisms to Italianisms, Queneau shows that the work of the literary imagination has as its primary material language itself.

Queneau's other work published in 1947 is his parody of the scandal novel, *We Always Treat Women Too Well*, which he published under the pseudonym Sally Mara. Ostensibly, the work is the translation into French by Michel Presle of a work originally written in Gaelic by Sally Mara, and it presents an account of the events in a post office taken over by Irish nationalist insurgents during the Easter Rising of 1916. The insurgents are inconvenienced when they find, after securing the post office and releasing the postal workers, that Gertie Girdle has been left behind, locked in a ladies room. Poking fun at the macho posturing of men during wartime (as the ti-

tle suggests), Queneau shows how the insurgents' freedom of speech and behavior are seriously constrained by this woman's presence. Gertie also turns out to be more than they bargained for when her long-repressed sexuality reaches full flower and she becomes a seducer. Queneau has great fun with the conventions of both the action novel and the pornographic novel and characteristically enjoys manipulating language and literary reference: The insurgents' password, for example, is "Finnegans wake!"

The reader is instantly alerted to the tongue-in-cheek nature of the book through its style. The doorman who guards the post office opens the novel with "God save the King!" but is quickly dispatched, as follows:

> He did no more than murmur, this time, for he had already manifested his loyalty to such an extent that Corny Kelleher had wasted no time in injecting a bullet into his noggin. The dead doorman vomited his brains through an eighth orifice in his head, and fell flat on the floor.

As the insurgents' names suggest, Queneau's Ireland owes more to a reading of the work of James Joyce than to the accounts of Irish history. By the conclusion of the first chapter, the insurgents have expelled the remaining postal employees—they think—and have secured the post office. From the perspective of one of the insurgents, Dillon, the chapter concludes, "No more virgins offended his view."

While spoofing the action-and-sex novel, Queneau also incorporates his more serious literary models, using the unreliable narrator associated with the work of Joseph Conrad and the interior monologue style of Joyce. When Gertie Girdle takes over the narrative in chapter 4, it is as though she had stepped straight from the pages of Joyce right into (where else?) the ladies' room. Her simple mind reviews its limited contents: the state of modern plumbing, her intended, whether she should fix her hair again. When she sees an armed insurgent, her mind follows its own logic: He is armed and dangerous, he must be a Republican, only the British can save me, I will wait in the ladies room, they cannot touch me in here, it is only proper. As in *A Hard Winter*, the French perspective on Anglo-Saxon prudishness gives the writer plenty of material for his humorous purposes.

The humor turns dark as the novel progresses. Gertie is initiated into sex in the prurient style that the novel parodies, then begins to take an active role. At the same time the military position of the insurgents deteriorates, and they come under direct attack from British gunboats. The two situations intertwine in the narrative. As the shelling begins, one shot takes off Caffrey's head as he makes love to Gertie: "The body continued its rhythmic movement for a few more seconds, just like the male of the praying mantis whose upper part has been half-devoured by the female but who perseveres in his copulation." After Gertie frees herself, she considers the situation and concludes, "That's one less." Though shaken by the violence and initiated into not only sex but also, strangely enough, tenderness, Gertie's deepest feelings remain those of patriotism. She even evinces her satisfaction when the post office finally falls and the remaining insurgents are summarily executed before her eyes. Throughout the book, humor and wordplay predominate, rendering the outrageous situations of the narrative pathetic and human in Queneau's unique way.

JOURNAL INTIME

Queneau returned to writing as Sally Mara and eventually admitted to his authorship of "her" works with the publication of her *Journal intime* (intimate diary) in 1950. Once again, Queneau plays off the supposed prudishness and simplemindedness of his characters in the Irish setting, but, as always, through the lens of language. *Journal intime* is set in 1934-1935, at which time Sally Mara is studying Gaelic in order to write a novel and is still an almost incredibly naïve late adolescent. *Journal intime* is the story of her initiation into sexual matters in spite of rampant simplicity and a total lack of knowledge at the outset. In the manner of the five blind men and the elephant, Sally slowly progresses in her knowledge of the male sexual organs through a long process of trial-and-error experimentation.

The journal opens with Sally on the pier lamenting the return to France of her French teacher, Michel Presle. Through his inspiration, she resolves to write her journal in French (with the accompanying humoristic possibilities this opens up for the author). As she makes her way back down the gangplank, someone identified only as "un gentleman" advises her to "Tenez bon la rampe, mademoiselle" ("Hang on tight, miss"). She recalls that "At the same time was placed effactually in my free hand an object which had both the rigidity of a steel bar and the softness of velvet." Sally retains from this experience an everlasting respect for the kind qualities of the "gentleman" and the beginnings of her inquiry into that object she had held.

Sally's Gaelic lessons with Padraic Baoghal plunge her at once into the ambience of Irish nationalism as well as into a fertile arena for contact and further knowledge of men. One of these is her fellow student, Barnabé Pudge, who admires Sally from a repressed distance, but with the tenacity required to succeed eventually. During a sequence of darkened seances conducted by Baoghal's wife, who is a spiritual medium, Sally conducts her researches, which she began that night on the pier and continued in the darkness of a motion-picture theater one afternoon with Barnabé. Meanwhile, Sally's home life reveals how she could be so ignorant in the first place.

Sally's mother is a simpleminded woman who awaits the return of her husband by knitting socks for him. Sally's father left the family one night, saying he needed to buy a box of matches, and has yet to return, though many years have passed. This suits Sally, whose memories of her father are dominated by his practice of administering prolonged bare-bottomed spankings to her on a daily basis. Her brother is another simpleton, who sees life through an alcoholic stupor but who nevertheless manages to father a child by the family cook, Mrs. Killarney. As the birth of the child approaches, Sally wonders how the conception could have taken place in the absence of a marriage ceremony, and Mrs. Mara denies that her son could have played any role at all. In short, Sally's family, like some primitive culture from the dawn of time, remains partially in ignorance of the connection between sex and reproduction. Almost like someone who must reinvent the alphabet, Sally is left to discover the connection on her own; and discover the connection she does.

Sally's curiosity is satisfied to some extent when her uncle takes her that summer to see the coupling of two goats (a neologism made from the word for "billy goat" remains her verb for intercourse throughout the book). She is also aided by the discovery of the mythological miniatures painted by Mrs. Baoghal, which show the heroes' full equipment. At this time she also has her first experience of sexual pleasure, with the Baoghal's lesbian housemaid, Mève. While Sally's researches continue, her brother makes an honest woman of Mrs. Killarney, her father returns for a time, and she loses her virginity to a tough named Tim. At the end of the book, she does indeed marry Barnabé Pudge. This time, however, as they are boarding the boat for their honeymoon and Barnabé urges her to hold on tight, she is disappointed: "I moved my hand in the darkness, but all I found was a damp, cold rope. I understood then that my conjugal life had begun." The verve and humor that Queneau brings to Sally's exploits gently mock conventional morality while constructing a sense of the contradictory nature of sexual wisdom and ignorance.

THE SUNDAY OF LIFE

Queneau took the title for his next novel, *The Sunday of Life*, from a celebrated passage by Georg Wilhelm Friedrich Hegel in which the philosopher is discussing the depiction of peasant life in Dutch painting. Queneau's understanding runs parallel to the philosopher's belief that there is something so bright, so cheery in the lives of simple people that it seems that they must by their very nature be closer to the Ideal. This understanding by Queneau informs all of his work and, whether the setting is Le Havre, Ireland, or the working-class sections of Paris, it is what keeps the humor in the work from simply demeaning the characters. Queneau would rather investigate the naïve wisdom of the common person than the pompous idiocies of the wise.

Valentin Brû, the protagonist of *The Sunday of Life*, is one of Queneau's most fascinating characters. From his speech and his reactions to other people, one would have to judge him a simpleton, yet his clear-sighted view of the large scale of world events enables him to prosper in even the most difficult circumstances. The reader first sees Valentin through the eyes of two sisters, Chantal and Julia, who watch him from the window of their mother's haberdashery. Chantal teases her sister that she should marry this attractive soldier. Valentin has just returned from a campaign in Madagascar and is being housed in one of the local barracks. Through the machinations of Chantal and her husband, Paul, Valentin is indeed discharged and marries Julia, though she is some fifteen years his senior.

As in all of Queneau's work, the main action of the novel is in the language itself. In this case the simplicity of the characters' thought processes actually regulates their subsequent actions. Here, Valentin and Julia discuss their honeymoon and whether they can afford to let it interrupt their shopkeeping.

> No, of course, not, said Valentin. You see, then, said Julia. And yet, said Valentin, and yet, it's obligatory, a honeymoon. . . . Maybe we could put the honeymoon off until our next vacation, suggested Valentin. And when will we take the vacation, then? Julia objected. And he had no answer to that.
>
> They ended up by adopting the only possible solution, the one and only, to wit that Valentin alone would go on the honeymoon alone.

So Valentin sets off on an uproarious trip that involves humorous encounters with taxi drivers, prostitutes, and hoteliers. His simplicity both gets him into trouble and keeps him from being affected by it. The next thing he knows, he is graveside at a funeral and is reunited with his spouse, by accident.

The very next chapter contains another funeral, that of the mother Nanette, who leaves her shop and money to Valentin. Besides the recriminations he faces from his wife's family, he must face one of his worst fears at the dinner that follows the funeral: oysters. The language gains in exuberance from the protagonist's fears. The oysters are referred to as *animaux ostréicultivés*, *glaviusque molleux*, *lamellibranches*, and *mollusques crus*. These coinages test the ingenuity of the translator, who rises to the occasion with "ostreicultivated animals," "goblike mollusk," "lamellibranchia," and "raw mollusks." Valentin defends his distaste with the claim that they are living animals.

> "They're only just alive," said Paul.
> "They're just as alive as you and me," said Valentin.
> "Funny comparisons you make," said Julia.
> "It's true, though," said Valentin. "An oyster, it's a living creature. Just as much as I am. Zno difference. Zonly one difference: between the living and the dead."
> "You aren't very tactful," said Chantal.

All this wordplay and ludicrous conversation does come in the context of a commemoration of a departed relative. Yet this is simply Queneau's way of dealing with the eternal mysteries of human existence. Behind the apparently subhuman intelligence of a character such as Valentin, there is a deeper understanding of human existence than that found in many other more portentous works of literature.

The Sunday of Life takes a final series of narrative turns when Julia becomes a fortune-teller under the name Madame Saphir. Valentin's failing business allows him plenty of time to gossip, which gossip he, in turn, feeds to Julia. When Julia suffers a stroke, Valentin must take her place, and with his simpleminded wisdom he enjoys a greater success than she ever did. As the outbreak of World War II approaches, the prophecies grow darker. Even war, however, cannot fundamentally affect Valentin's destiny. He is remobilized, made a prisoner of war, and released. When Julia finds him at last, he is helping three female refugees climb into a crowded train through the window: "Julia choked with laughter: it was so as to get his hand on their behinds." *The Sunday of Life* is buoyant with such good cheer.

ZAZIE IN THE METRO

Zazie in the Metro is probably Queneau's best-known work. From its celebrated opening word *Doukipudonktan* (or, "Howcanaystinksotho," in other words, "Who is it thus emitting such a stench?") through its full sequence of zany adventures and outrageous word creations, *Zazie in the Metro* is a tour de force of comic wit and invention. A spiritual sister of Annette and Sally Mara, Zazie is all street-smarts and foul language. In the novel, the title of which bears her name, the joke is on her: What she most looks forward to doing in Paris, riding the Metro, is the one thing she does not do in the book, since the Metro workers are on strike during her visit.

Zazie arrives in Paris for a visit with her uncle, Gabriel, so that her mother can spend some time with her lover. Uncle Gabriel fits the pattern of Queneau's male characters and is a bit of a simpleton. For the first part of the book, he hides the true nature of his nocturnal employment from Zazie; in fact, he is a male stripper in a gay bar. Gabriel and his even more simpleminded friend, Charles, who drives a taxi, meet Zazie at the train station and bring her back to the apartment that Gabriel shares with his wife, Marceline. Much of the action in the first half of the book takes place in the apartment or in the bar in the basement of the same building. The bar's owner is

named Turandot, and his only waitress is Mado (short for Madeleine), but he also has a parakeet to keep him company. The parakeet's name is Laverdure, and he has one comment that he makes throughout the book: "Tu causes, tu causes, c'est tout ce que tu sais faire" ("Talk, talk, that's all you can do"). Interestingly, his comment almost always rings true in context.

Zazie has trouble staying put, so on the morning of her second day, while Gabriel is still asleep after his night's work, she leaves the apartment. Charles tries to catch up to her and protect her from harm, but she accuses him of molesting her and, after an indignant crowd gathers, makes her escape. She then picks up the novel's other main character, at first only referred to as the *type* (guy). At first it appears that he is a child molester; later in the book he reappears as Trouscaillon, an undercover police officer; still later he appears as Bertin Poirée and Aroun Arachide. It is to the *type* that Zazie recounts the story of her life, particularly that her mother murdered her father. Her father, it seems, was a drunk who had sexual designs on the nubile Zazie. The mother is aware of this and borrows an ax from her lover, George (a fact that is revealed during Zazie's testimony at the trial). One day, the mother says that she is going to the store for some spaghetti, but she actually lies in wait for the father to make his move. Zazie recounts the events:

> "Just then, she opens the door, quiet as can be, and comes in calmly, my papa he had his mind on other things the poor slob, he wasn't paying attention you might say, and that's how he got his skull split open. You have to hand it to her, she made a good job of it, my mamma. It wasn't a pretty sight. Even sickening. Enough to give me a complex."

Yet Zazie, in fact, seems to be one of the least "complexed" characters in the book. Her cheerful, worldly-wise naïveté carries her through the book's events and situations with a casual aplomb.

An ill-starred trip to see the Eiffel Tower, their encounter there with a busload of tourists, a subsequent chase through the streets of Paris, Gabriel's treating everyone to an evening at his nightclub, a subsequent celebration, fracas, and shooting—all this and more finds Zazie cheerful and wisecracking as usual. She is a very tired girl, however, when her uncle Gabriel returns her to her mother the next day. Zazie's madcap adventures seem cinematic in their conception, and it is probably no accident that Louis Malle's film adaptation is one of the small gems of the French cinema.

Throughout his career as a novelist, Queneau brought a wise and compassionate concern to the lives of ordinary people. That he used sometimes brilliant humor and an always engaging sense of play with language are two reasons that his work is now seen as a forerunner to the successive generation of French New Novelists. No matter what tradition literary historians place him in, Queneau will remain a unique literary figure.

Peter Baker

OTHER MAJOR WORKS

PLAY: *En passant*, pb. 1944.

POETRY: *Chêne et chien*, 1937 (*Raymond Queneau's "Chêne et Chien": A Translation with Commentary*, 1995); *Les Ziaux*, 1943; *Foutaises*, 1944; *L'Instant fatal*, 1946; *Petite cosmogonie portative*, 1950; *Si tu t'imagines*, 1952; *Le Chien à la mandoline*, 1958; *Cent mille milliards de poèmes*, 1961 (*One Hundred Million Million Poems*, 1983); *Texticules*, 1961; *Courir les rues*, 1967; *Battre la campagne*, 1968; *Fendre les flots*, 1969; *Morale élémentaire*, 1975 (*Elementary Morality*, 2007); *"Pounding the Pavement," "Beating the Bushes," and Other Pataphysical Poems*, 1985 (includes partial translations of *Courir les rues* and *Battre la campagne*).

NONFICTION: *Bâtons, chiffres, et lettres*, 1950 (*Letters, Numbers, Forms: Essays, 1928-1970*, 2007); *Entretiens avec Georges Charbonnier*, 1962; *Bords: Mathématiciens, précurseurs, encyclopédistes*, 1963; *La Littérature potentielle*, 1973; *Journaux, 1914-1965*, 1996 (Anne Isabelle Queneau, editor); *Traité des vertus démocratiques*, 1993.

MISCELLANEOUS: *Exercices de style*, 1947 (*Exercises in Style*, 1958); *Contes et propos*, 1981 (*Stories and Remarks*, 2000).

BIBLIOGRAPHY

Bastin, Nina. *Queneau's Fictional Worlds*. New York: Peter Lang, 2002. An analysis of Queneau's novels, describing how he created and organized their imaginary worlds. Bastin examines individual novels, such as *The Flight of Icarus*, *The Blue Flowers*, and *The Skin of Dreams*, in addition to pointing out common elements in Queneau's works. Includes a bibliography and an index.

Hale, Jane Alison. *The Lyric Encyclopedia of Raymond Queneau*. Ann Arbor: University of Michigan Press, 1989. Discusses Queneau's works in all genres, focusing on his use of language and humor and comparing his work to that of James Joyce, Samuel Beckett, and François Rabelais. Includes a bibliography.

Shorley, Christopher. *Queneau's Fiction: An Introductory Study*. New York: Cambridge University Press, 1985. Provides a general introduction to Queneau's novels. Separate chapters examine his innovative literary style and use of language, his varied use of narrative form, and his creation of fictional worlds. Includes a bibliography and an index.

Stump, Jordan. *Naming and Unnaming: On Raymond Queneau*. Lincoln: University of Nebraska Press, 1998. Stump explores the political, literary, and epistemological implications of character names in Queneau's novels and examines how the characters and narrators address or refer to others.

Sturrock, John. "Raymond Queneau." In *The Word from Paris: Essays on Modern French Thinkers and Writers*. London: Verso, 1998. A discussion of Queneau's novels and other works as well as his ideas about literature. Part of a collection of essays about twentieth century French literature and philosophy.

Thiker, Allen. *Raymond Queneau*. Boston: Twayne, 1985. An introduction to Queneau with biographical information, analysis of his major literary works, and a useful bibliography.

Velguth, Madeleine. *The Representation of Women in the Autobiographical Novels of Raymond Queneau*. New York: Peter Lang, 1990. Velguth examines the depiction of women in Queneau's first six novels within the context of social and intellectual life in twentieth century France. Her study includes the women in Queneau's life and the representation of women in his autobiographical novels.

R

WILHELM RAABE

Born: Eschershausen, duchy of Braunschweig (now
in Germany); September 8, 1831
Died: Braunschweig, Germany; November 15, 1910
Also known as: Wilhelm Karl Raabe; Jakob
Corvinus

PRINCIPAL LONG FICTION

Die Chronik der Sperlingsgasse, 1856 (as Jakob
Corvinus)
Die schwarze Galeere, 1861 (novella; *The Black
Galley*, 1937)
Die Leute aus dem Walde, 1863
Der Hungerpastor, 1864 (*The Hunger-Pastor*,
1885)
*Abu Telfan: Oder, Die Heimkehr vom
Mondgebirge*, 1868 (*Abu Telfan: Or, The
Return from the Mountains of the Moon*, 1881)
Else von der Tanne, 1869 (novella; English
translation, 1972)
Der Schüdderump, 1870
Der Dräumling, 1872
Horacker, 1876 (English translation, 1983)
Alte Nester, 1880
Prinzessen Fisch, 1883
Pfisters Mühle, 1884
Villa Schönow, 1884
Unruhige Gäste, 1886
Im alten Eisen, 1887
Das Odfeld, 1889 (*The Odin Field*, 2001)
Stopfkuchen: Eine See-und Mordgeschichte, 1891
(*Tubby Schaumann: A Tale of Murder and the
High Seas*, 1983)
Gutmanns Reisen, 1892
Die Akten des Vogelsangs, 1896
Hastenbeck, 1899
Altershausen, 1911

OTHER LITERARY FORMS

Wilhelm Raabe (RAHB-uh) wrote almost exclusively in the form of prose narrative. A small number of verses represent his only known departure from storytelling. His narrative production was substantial, however, with thirty titles usually designated as novels, another nineteen that may be classed as novellas, and a third group, also numbering nineteen, which are more loosely termed "stories" or "tales." Altogether, thirty-one of the shorter works appeared between 1859 and 1879 in six collections authorized by Raabe. Many of his works, including novels, were first published serially by various popular literary magazines before their appearance in book form. The periodical *Der Illustrirten Deutschen Monatshefte* (published by G. Westermann), which printed thirty-two of Raabe's works, also distributed his work to the German-speaking immigrant population in the United States; translations into English have been few, and hardly representative of Raabe's full achievement: *The Hunger-Pastor*, *Abu Telfan*, and the novellas *The Black Galley* and *Else von der Tanne*.

ACHIEVEMENTS

Until about the middle of the twentieth century, Wilhelm Raabe was widely characterized as a creator of eccentric figures unappealing to a broad audience, and as the writer of a rather difficult, idiosyncratic style ill suited to any but the specialist's attention outside Germany. These perceptions among his German readers probably harmed more than fostered his reputation, and they kept his name from the commonly accepted pantheon of nineteenth century German prose masters.

Critical reevaluations have since shown that the structures of Raabe's works, while superficially disorganized, are purposeful and consistent below the surface. His characters' seclusion from the world is not merely an idyllic retreat, but rather a safe position from which the writer quietly seeks nothing less than to unhinge the world and his own times. As for Raabe's apparent role as dispenser of wisdom for the proper conduct of life, critics have generally discarded the bad habit of citing him out of context and have come to view the "quotable" pronouncement as only one of the more obvious parts in a literary-aesthetic scheme reminiscent of Bertolt Brecht's theory of education through alienation, the establishment of aesthetic distance. Raabe's humor, too, is now generally seen in broader definition, complex in its nature, informing the attitude and tone of the works, determining fundamentally the relationship of content to language. His humor is hardly conceivable, even in the most "optimistic" stories, without recognition of the bitterly serious questioning of life's ultimate values in some of his other, "tragic" works.

There is not general agreement that one should even call Raabe's major prose works novels. The question is not so much one of length, even though they scarcely exceed two hundred pages in modern editions. More at issue are definitions based on formal and thematic characteristics. Raabe himself used the term "novel" (German: *Roman*) more sparingly than some literary historians have done in referring to his books, probably in order to distinguish them from conventional nineteenth century models, which typically exhibited a more predictable, sequential narrative form and a less pronounced narrator presence than his; he may have also used the term sparingly in order to disassociate his "stories" from the then-current, narrower use of the term *Roman* to mean a "love story with obstacles." His reluctance to be thought of as merely a novelist, like his unconventional narrative style in general, thus suggests his refusal to accede to the popular preference for literary entertainment.

Raabe's narrative style, his conception of personality, and the issues he raises in portraying the human condition are all persuasive reasons for claiming his works as precursors of the twentieth century novel. That, however, should not detract from an understanding of the late nineteenth century context in which his art developed or from an appreciation of his formal, psychological, and ethical response to his own age. The years following the foundation of the Second German Empire in 1871 were a time of generally high optimism and satisfaction for the German middle class, but by no means for Raabe. His principal characters, especially in the works written after 1875, were often rather ordinary persons faced with profound and difficult choices of how best to balance their aspirations against realities. Even the characters in his historical novels of these later years can be considered contemporaries of their author, for the essential issues of their existence are the issues of his time, too: the pursuit of happiness and the striving for personal achievement and fulfillment in the face of impersonal, materialistic, and potentially compromising challenges to individual integrity. Seen in this light, their various eccentricities only underscore their exceptional individualism.

The post-1871 Wilhelminian Empire in Germany fostered two attitudes that are of crucial importance to understanding Raabe's response to his times: a sense of urgency to master life in the opportune present and a faith in the lessons of history as a source of answers to the questions of the present. Raabe met both attitudes skeptically. External threats to the good (and vulnerable) instincts of his heroes and heroines are all the greater, and their resolution all the more urgent, because the resolution of conflicts in a hereafter was not commonly entertained as a credible possibility. Raabe also doubted quite seriously humankind's ability to understand historical forces, or to meet them effectively in the present, armed with knowledge of the past. He wrote historical novels, but ones informed by pessimism and resignation, works in which the perennial struggles of the individual for a more humane existence overshadow the events and crosscurrents of history. His treatment of historical subject matter thus denied the reader any historical paradigm for anticipating the course of events in the present.

Raabe's quest for truth, and that of his characters, required diverse, even fragmented visions of reality, since the world he sought to comprehend was itself diverse and fragmented. Thus, as Horst Daemmrich points out in his study *Wilhelm Raabe* (1981), the author typically employs multiple narrative perspectives, apparent disjunctions of temporal and spatial relationships, and "alienation effects" that prevent the reader's too-close identification with characters and events in the novels. It is perhaps easy in the English-speaking world to overlook one further aspect of Raabe's narratives—namely, the range of his individuals' responses to society in transition. Before that relationship can be adequately appreciated, one must remember that the Industrial Revolution and the profound transformations it brought about in society were just overtaking Germany during Raabe's literary career, while England and France had experienced them considerably earlier in the century.

That career was fraught with difficulties in Raabe's reception by the German reading public. In 1884, *Der Illustrirten Deutschen Monatshefte* terminated its more than ten-year collaboration with Raabe, saying that his readership had "had enough for the time being" and that his works were "too similar the one to the other." Only a year before, the influential novelist-theoretician Friedrich Spielhagen had prepared the way for publisher Westermann's decision by stating editorially that Germany no longer had a homogeneous audience for individual authors (like Raabe) whom it could call its own. Spielhagen had called for "new blood" to counter the threat of skepticism and pessimism and to provide the nation with a generation of "happily writing authors and

comfortably enjoying readers." For Raabe, this kind of program amounted to what he termed "writing for the tastes of chambermaids and shop clerks," and he wished no part of it. It may be, then, that his awareness of his own innovative style and his prefigurations of a future literary form enabled him to write "outside" his own time, rather than slavishly for it.

BIOGRAPHY

Wilhelm Karl Raabe, born September 8, 1831, in the small town of Eschershausen, began and ended his life in the Braunschweig duchy of what is now Germany. Until his thirteenth year, the world of his experiences was bounded by the Weser River in the west and by the surrounding hills north, east, and south, a setting that was to figure importantly in many of his writings, either by explicit reference or by an unmistakable resemblance. Raabe's father was a local government official who had studied law and who gave the boy a sense of inquiry and an interest in local history. His mother was the greater influence; under her guidance, Raabe learned to read, and in her, he found a sensitive intellectual companionship for which he remained always grateful. A sister, Emilie, was two years younger than Raabe, and a brother, Heinrich, four years younger. Raabe's father was transferred twice, first to the county seat at Holzminden on the Weser, later to Stadtoldendorf, the next town due south from Eschershausen.

In 1845, Raabe's father died suddenly at the age of forty-four. "Had he lived longer and educated me," Raabe later wrote, "I might have become a mediocre jurist." For a short time, the boy became instead an undistinguished pupil in the town of Wolfenbüttel some distance away from the beloved Weser Hills. His mother moved the family there because she had two brothers who taught at the Wolfenbüttel *Gymnasium* (college-preparatory secondary school). Despite their best efforts, Raabe, whose schooling in Stadtoldendorf had evidently been deficient, made poor progress in all of his subjects but German and drawing. In 1849, he was withdrawn from the school and placed as apprentice to a book dealer in Magdeburg, where he worked for four years.

His preferences in literature, which so far had tended toward travel and adventure stories, broadened during his term in the bookshop to include French and espe-

Wilhelm Raabe. (Getty Images)

cially English novelists: Alexandre Dumas, *père*, Eugène Sue, Laurence Sterne, Henry Fielding, Sir Walter Scott, Charles Dickens, and his apparent favorite, William Makepeace Thackeray. He seems to have admired Heinrich Heine most among German writers. Historical literature accounted for another good part of his reading. The apprenticeship did not work out, however, and Raabe returned to Wolfenbüttel to make a second attempt at earning the *Gymnasium* diploma that would admit him to university studies. After failing again, he decided to move to Berlin and to enroll there as a university auditor. He took up residence in the capital and attended lectures in philosophy, literature, and history. He was twenty-two years old.

On November 15 of that same year, 1854, Raabe solemnly noted an even more important decision: "the day when pen was put to paper." The result, completed in the following year, was his first piece of fiction, *Die Chronik der Sperlingsgasse* (the chronicle of sparrow lane). The Berlin publisher Franz Stage brought the novel out in 1856, and Raabe could at last return to Wolfenbüttel with a modest claim to achievement. Encouraged by several positive reviews of the book, Raabe was hopeful that he could earn his livelihood by his writing and was ready to attempt it. In a short time, he was at work on the next in a succession of books that continued until 1902.

In the summer of 1859, the young writer made the tour south that, ever since Johann Wolfgang von Goethe's Italian journey of 1786 to 1788, had been considered indispensable to a young German's artistic education. Raabe's destination had also been Italy, but the outbreak of war between Austria and France prevented his continuing there. The itinerary thus went only as far south as Vienna. On his return by way of Stuttgart, he met a number of writers and publishers, an assembly of literary figures such as it would have been difficult to find in his native region of northern Germany. In 1862, he would return to the Swabian capital for an important eight-year stay.

Raabe's first significant political activity was his joining the Deutscher Nationalverein (German National Union Party) in 1860, the initial step in his development of a lifelong political consciousness. The party had been founded in the preceding year by liberals whose object was the unification of Germany and the elimination of its antiquated feudal fragmentation. Raabe quickly became an active member and attended party congresses in 1860 and 1861. In the same year of 1861, he became engaged to Bertha Leiste, the daughter of a respected Wolfenbüttel family, and the couple married in 1862. Between 1862 and 1876, they had four daughters.

The move from Wolfenbüttel to Stuttgart and the eight years Raabe spent there (1862-1870) were important for two reasons: The near isolation of the provinces was exchanged for a considerably more cosmopolitan city with a vigorous community of writers and intellectuals, and Raabe made the acquaintance there, in 1866, of the writer Wilhelm Jensen and his wife, Marie. Wilhelm Jensen's literary success far exceeded his talent and the durability of his writings, and Raabe probably had little to learn from him in these terms. His friendship with Marie Jensen, however (and it may well have been no more than that), a woman fourteen years younger than Raabe, was clearly an intellectual and psychological benefice. Raabe's decision to return to the north, even though not acted upon until 1870, was made in 1868, only six days after the Jensens announced that they would move to Flensburg on the German-Danish border. Through letters and visits, Raabe and Marie Jensen maintained their friendship for the remainder of the novelist's life.

The Stuttgart years had been the second major period in Raabe's literary career; his years at Braunschweig (1870-1910) constituted the third and longest phase of his writing life. From the family's arrival there until 1902, he produced thirty-two novels and narratives. The work was almost uninterrupted, and with the income it brought, Raabe was able to give his family the requisite comforts of middle-class existence. Braunschweig, though large enough and the residence of a ducal family, was virtually devoid of the cultural stimulation and intellectual exchange he had known in Stuttgart, but it seems to have met his needs. Raabe's professional life there was solitary, and his personal life became settled and convivial. When in 1892 his youngest daughter died of meningitis at the age of sixteen, Raabe found it difficult to continue writing with his former hope and conviction. Friends and well-wishers made a festive occasion of his seventieth birthday in 1901, and the Universities of Göttingen and Tübingen awarded him honorary degrees.

Raabe considered himself, on completion of *Hastenbeck* in the late 1890's a "writer, retired." The time remaining until his death in 1910 was entirely his own.

ANALYSIS

The conflict, most broadly stated, which Wilhelm Raabe saw as inherent in Wilhelminian Germany was that between individual idealism and collective materialism. In the prevailing order of things, individual aspirations came face-to-face with a system of external realities that were, in their essence, vulgar, insensitive, and apathetic. How decent human beings were to preserve their integrity in the face of such entrenched insensitivity became the vital question: whether it was possible to conquer life on one's own terms rather than to accommodate oneself to life at the expense of one's dignity. Raabe developed and tested his responses to the question from early in his career, but he engaged it with growing urgency and sophistication in the works of the Braunschweig period. It was in those years that Germany's new political and economic vigor nourished the vulgar self-satisfaction he found so offensive. Closer examination of several of his novels may help to chart the successive statements of the conflict and his replies to it.

Raabe installs a variety of "outsiders" in the role of exemplar, mentor, guardian, or benefactor to take up the challenge of the oppressive external world. It is important to understand these characters—for example, the schoolmaster Werner Eckerbusch in *Horacker* or Heinrich Schaumann in *Tubby Schaumann*—from both the common and the initiated perspectives. In the public view they are misfits, castoffs, or nonachievers, but in their ability to wrest small victories from the established order and its agents, they occupy a place above, rather than outside, the ordinary.

Life, in Raabe's view and in his writings, is complex, and its realities can be adequately grasped only through multiple perspectives of narration; by leaving intact the interdependent groupings of characters as life presents them to him; and, in fact, by allowing the stories to tell themselves, each one determining the form and techniques appropriate to itself. It is perhaps the mark both of Raabe's realism and of his affinity with the twentieth century that he eschewed the traditional, comfortable form of narration through successive events in favor of a

sometimes "confusing" simultaneity or "structureless" disorder. Barker Fairley has thus likened Raabe's formal patterns to paintings by Rembrandt: "The elements of his tale do not deploy themselves in linear succession, as in a [Gottfried] Keller or [Theodor] Fontane novel, but come through from behind one another out of a twilight."

DIE CHRONIK DER SPERLINGSGASSE

Writing about his first novel, *Die Chronik der Sperlingsgasse*, in 1861, Raabe said, "Before that I composed (and consigned to the flames) neither tragedies nor verses, and thus I spared myself many of the sins which other young poets commit with pen and ink." *Die Chronik der Sperlingsgasse* was an out-and-out beginning, and it has remained a source of astonishment to literary critics that the young university student's leap into a writing career was so confident, successful, and, above all, skillful in its handling of the techniques that would distinguish his mature writings.

Not the least of this novel's surprising qualities is that its twenty-three-year-old author so convincingly assumes the perspective and disposition of an old man, Johannes Wachholder, the story's chronicler-narrator. Wachholder, once a student in Berlin, lives in an apartment clearly identifiable as the one Raabe occupied during his Berlin student years, and the chronology of the book's events shows that Wachholder records his story during virtually the same time, 1854 and 1855. His first entry in the book bears the date November 15, the date on which Raabe himself began to write. That, however, is the extent of verifiable autobiographical connections.

On one level, Wachholder's story is a recollection of events and relationships, beginning with the childhood he enjoyed with two companions in a provincial town, their separate changes of residence to Sparrow Lane in the capital, the marriage of the other two, Marie and Franz, and Wachholder's acceptance of his role as close friend to the young couple. A daughter, Elise, is born to Marie and Franz, but both parents die before the child's coming-of-age, and she is adopted by Wachholder. Devotedly he follows Elise's growing up, sees her happily married, and finally rejoices in the letters he receives from her and her husband.

The story told through Wachholder's reminiscences is accompanied, broken through, and reconnected by episodes in the present. Wachholder goes about his daily routines, observes life on the street below and across the way, and is visited by others who themselves take an occasional hand in the task of remembering and telling—the artist Strobel, the journalist Wimmer, and the schoolteacher Roder. There are digressions as well into the retold experiences of these "assistant chroniclers" (for storytelling is contagious) and into the implications of historical events such as the billeting of French troops in Sparrow Lane during the 1813-1814 Wars of Liberation or the massive German emigration to America in the post-1848 years.

Die Chronik der Sperlingsgasse is Raabe's first, but by no means his least convincing, example of a story that tells itself. Its prominent use of reminiscence as a narrative device might be considered a reversion to Romantic yearnings for an earlier, innocent age, be it in the historical sense or in the desire to recover one's childhood. The past to which Wachholder returns, however, is an unromantic one of only partial validity. His reminiscences are constantly subject to interruption and interpretation by what transpires on the present narrative level and must be seen in relation to this narrative present. The remembered world is meaningful for not only itself but also and especially the narrator's ability to remember it.

This novel was for some twenty years the victim of public indifference and neglect, and later of misplaced admiration—even into the twentieth century—as a "heartwarming tale" reflecting banal middle-class ideals and a kind of vague "Germanness" of spirit. The figure of Johannes Wachholder might serve as a focus of these difficulties in the book's reception. By nature and by his narrative method, he is garrulous and disorganized, and one of the putative faults of Wachholder-Raabe's book was its prolixity and lack of coherent formal organization. Then again, he is an endearing character, the selfless, undeclared suitor of Marie Volkmann, the devoted surrogate father to Elise, the convivial old gentleman, the child at heart. It would be easy, therefore, to attribute much of the book's later sentimental appeal to Wachholder himself. One needs only to acknowledge his central function as the reminiscing narrator of the novel, however, and his other roles and attributes fall into place. *Die Chronik der Sperlingsgasse* is, above all, the story of its own writing. That story is its cohesive

structural member, and it is the only story in the book that need not compete for attention as the narrated past and the narrative present must, because the story of Wachholder the chronicler unfolds on its own, preeminent level.

STUTTGART TRILOGY

In early November, 1862, Raabe began work on *The Hunger-Pastor*, and in June, 1869, he finished the writing of *Der Schüdderump*. A middle work, *Abu Telfan*, was composed over a two-year span, from 1865 to 1867. These three works thus fit neatly into the eight Stuttgart years generally regarded as Raabe's second creative period.

Raabe's colleague, Wilhelm Jensen, was the first (in 1870) to refer to the three novels as Raabe's Stuttgart trilogy, and for better or worse, the name has stood. Jensen's apparent reason for this grouping was his idea that all three illustrate the vanity of human happiness. Raabe seems more to have tolerated than welcomed the trilogy idea, but in 1891, he obliged its adherents with the explanation that the three books could be thought of as representing the three stages of human life—youth, middle years, and old age. Raabe specialists have also suggested the author's social criticism as the connecting principle, based on similarities in narrative attitude and in thematic substructure, or upon three complementary class perspectives: those of the proletariat (in *The Hunger-Pastor*), the middle class (in *Abu Telfan*), and the feudal nobility (in *Der Schüdderump*).

In the narrow definition of the word, the three do not form a trilogy, since there are not common elements in their respective plots (characters, places, or events that reappear or experiences and developments that are followed from one work to the next). It is possible, however, to link the three novels by means of their intellectual and ethical import. They can be seen as "novels of education" or "development" (bildungsromans), even though imperfect ones. This function is at least better fulfilled by the three in combination than by each work singly, for when taken together they account both for Raabe's "three ages of human life" and for the three perspectives of the major social classes. Moreover, a combined reading reveals the full range of forces, differently emphasized in the individual books, which affect human development: the nurturing security of one's home and family; the civilizing and socializing forces; and what Raabe called the "forces of darkness"—the foreign, the rabble, death, and fate.

THE HUNGER-PASTOR

The Hunger-Pastor appears initially to stand at the point of new beginnings for Raabe. It is the first work of ambitious proportions from the Stuttgart years, and it signals a departure from the historical themes that typified the minor narratives of the Berlin and Wolfenbüttel period following *Die Chronik der Sperlingsgasse*. On the other hand, there is still a certain artistic naïveté about it that Raabe seems to have gained a better mastery of in *Abu Telfan*. He himself counted *The Hunger-Pastor* among his youthful efforts, at least from the distance of four decades and with another twenty or so major works to his credit. "The people are quite satisfied with my stale juvenilia: *Chronicle* and *Hunger-Pastor*, and leave me holding all the rest," he complained in 1902. In 1906, he observed that it was still the books from his first creative period, specifically including *The Hunger-Pastor*, that assured him a steady income. Until the middle of the twentieth century, Raabe's name was persistently associated by the vast majority of readers with one title and one only, *The Hunger-Pastor*.

The novel's greatest flaw (and quite possibly a major source of its popular success) is a narrative procedure to which the mature Raabe would never have subscribed. *The Hunger-Pastor* traces the lives, from infancy to adulthood, of a "good" hero, Hans Unwirrsch, and a "bad" villain, Moses Freudenstein. The novel contrasts the morally irreproachable idealist with the ambitious and opportunistic materialist. Both characters are born on the same day into poor families in the town of Neustadt: Hans, the son of a shoemaker, and Moses, the son of a secondhand dealer. The hunger motif thus has a literal, physical meaning for these two children of the proletariat, but it is also part of a larger and sometimes only too obvious metaphoric field signifying Hans's loftier hunger for truth, rectitude, and the affirmation of love, in contrast with Moses's base hunger for power and material success.

The Hunger-Pastor has a certain appeal on the strength of its unpretentious style, vivid character portrayals, humorous episodes, uncomplicated narrative flow, loving attention to detail, and promise of virtue re-

warded. It also reveals an underlay of democratic sentiment through Raabe's treatment of the economically and politically disadvantaged class. In the matter of its artistic quality, however, a sense of narrative presence and perspective is sacrificed to the fatal involvement of the storyteller in the minutiae of his story. The challenge of intellectual complexity is lost in the effort to state a clear, undifferentiated "message." One modern critic of the novel likened Hans Unwirrsch's career to the ride of a Hollywood cowboy, in which the star sits on a mechanical horse with the landscape passing by behind, painted and repetitive, on an endless canvas loop. The birth of Hans's son at the end of the novel is transparently reminiscent of Hans's own birth at its beginning.

ABU TELFAN

Raabe's first real attempt to come to terms with the phenomenon of philistine, midcentury German society, and with the individual's conflict with that society's values, is set down in *Abu Telfan*. The name is that of a fictitious African village that one might think of as the end of the world for a civilized European of Raabe's time. Leonhard Hagebucher, expelled from the university, takes up the life of a colonial adventurer, is sold into slavery in Abu Telfan, and manages only years later to return to Germany. His homecoming bears a certain resemblance to Raabe's own return from Magdeburg to the more provincial Wolfenbüttel in 1853. Hagebucher imagines that he has regained a place in the civilized world after the physical privations and hardships of African enslavement, but he discovers that narrow-mindedness and complacent pettiness in his hometown of Bumsdorf are a no less painful imprisonment. Hagebucher becomes one of those characters in fiction who makes his uneasy "arrangement" with life, a native son taking his place in the corrupt social order but also a "foreign" traveler condemned to seeing his own hypocrisy in doing so.

With this unresolved confrontation between antipathy and accommodation, *Abu Telfan* introduces a fundamental uncertainty into Raabe's treatment of the individual in society. It is this that sets the novel apart from the clearly defined allegiances of *The Hunger-Pastor* and marks the beginning of a new period in Raabe's career, the shift from youthful optimism to his much-discussed pessimism and attitude of resignation. Raabe in later years denied that this new direction in his writings was the result of his acquaintance with Arthur Schopenhauer's philosophy during the Stuttgart years. Biographical evidence from the time of the novel's composition suggests no connection between the work and the external circumstances of a generally happy existence in Stuttgart. It is more likely that Raabe was only beginning to test narrative means for dealing with the opposed social and individual forces. *Abu Telfan* found its thematic refinement in 1891 with the appearance of *Tubby Schaumann.*

DER SCHÜDDERUMP

It is an even more striking pessimism that *Der Schüdderump* introduces with the medieval death-symbol of its title, the wagon used to transport the corpses of plague victims to the burial pit. The wealthy speculator, Dietrich Häussler, who uses persons literally to death, is indelibly associated with the figure of death who drives the cart. It is his granddaughter, Antonie, on whose tragic exploitation the novel turns, an orphaned child taken from poverty into the tutelage of the provincial nobility and thence to her grandfather's opulent, ruinous world in Vienna. Her childhood playmate from the Lauenhof at Krodebeck, Hennig von Lauen, follows her to Vienna but fails to comprehend the cause of Antonie's despair, is distracted by life in Viennese society, and can do no more than retreat to the simpler existence of country gentleman. He and the others of his noble class fail in the crucial contest with the ruthless materialists, owing primarily to their idealism or to their inadequate grasp of realities in a new age.

HORACKER

Both chronologically and technically, *Horacker* is a pivotal work in Raabe's oeuvre. He had been living in Braunschweig for five years when he began writing it and had produced thirteen books since *Der Schüdderump. Horacker* is widely regarded as the first of his finely crafted, mature narratives. In its story, *Horacker* still exhibits something of the character relationships as they were found in *Der Schüdderump*, namely, the plight of mistreated and threatened young persons; but an important difference is that in *Horacker*, a new sort of protector is brought forward to defend and reinstate them. He is Dr. Werner Eckerbusch, teacher in the Latin school of a small town in the Weser district and emphatically

referred to as "the last assistant principal," one remaining relic of earlier times, member of a species threatened with the fate of the New Zealand kiwi. Eckerbusch is the prototype of several characters in later novels: Wendeline Cruse and Peter Uhusen in *Im alten Eisen* (scrap iron), Noah Buchius in *The Odin Field*, and Mother Wackerhahn in *Hastenbeck*. All have passed the time of their usefulness to the changing world and are only tolerated on the social fringes. At the same time, they all possess a rare ability to sense the fear their young protégées have of established authority and society at large.

Eckerbusch and the young drawing teacher, Windwebel, intend nothing more ambitious than to walk to the next village on what may be the last fine summer day before the new school term. They set out, unperturbed by rumors of a criminal at large in the countryside. The outlaw in question is Cord Horacker, a young man sent to the reformatory for petty theft and now escaped after hearing that his sweetheart has fled her employer in Berlin and returned to help Horacker in whatever way she might. Both young persons are hungry, weary, and desperate—both for relief and for acceptance by the townspeople. Eckerbusch and Windwebel do indeed meet Horacker in the woods and persuade him finally to come with them to Gansewinckel, and by evening all the story's participants are reunited in the village pastor's garden. The entire sequence of events occupies little more than eight hours, about the time required to read the book. It is one of Raabe's slenderest plots.

Horacker is perhaps most noticeably modest in terms of the reality it attempts to depict. In the Stuttgart trilogy, the geographical range extended from the duchy of Braunschweig to the Baltic coast, Paris, Vienna, and the African continent. *Horacker* is confined to events within a range of a few kilometers. The more important reduction in the novel, however, is that in its cast of characters. They range only from the near destitute upward to the level of schoolteachers, pastors, and small-town lawyers. Raabe narrows his field of vision from that in the earlier works, but deepens it in order to probe the more tellingly human relationships between the outcasts and their defenders, the individuals and their anonymous, self-righteous persecutors. Hence it is that he so prominently contrasts his use of the impersonal pronoun "one" with the personal, binding "I" and "thou" of Eckerbusch and Horacker's relationship.

In its technique, this work is both remarkable in its own right and significant for its anticipation of the masterful late novels. The narrator in *Horacker* is a figure who has come into his own, still an authorial third-person storyteller, but now one who plays a prominent role of the kind Raabe had not exploited in the Stuttgart novels. Insofar as he also provides insight into the making of the narrative, he is a successor to Johannes Wachholder of *Die Chronik der Sperlingsgasse*; but as a figure entirely without Wachholder's direct, first-person connections with the novel's other characters, the narrator in *Horacker* claims a new independence on a level exclusively his. This aspect of the novel does three important things: It makes possible the freedom of multiple perspectives; it allows for an important relationship between narrator and reader; and, as a consequence of these two possibilities, it supports the humorous attitude that is the aesthetic mainspring of *Horacker*.

TUBBY SCHAUMANN

Raabe called *Tubby Schaumann* his best novel and spoke of it in letters to the Magdeburg professor Edmund Sträter as his "truly subjective" book, and his "most outrageous." By the term "subjective," Raabe referred to the novel's autobiographical import, but not as a verifiable retelling of events in his own life. The principal character, Heinrich Schaumann, may call to mind Raabe's own situation as an unwilling, unsuccessful pupil in the school at Wolfenbüttel, but the far more important connection is between Schaumann's conquest of life and his author's conquest of "the art of writing a narrative comedy."

The story is—technically—told by Eduard, a German emigrant to South Africa who has, by all conventional standards, succeeded brilliantly at life. Eduard (his last name is not given) is a prosperous colonial farmer who has fathered a large family. On a trip back to Germany and a visit to his native town, he learns from Heinrich Schaumann, a childhood friend once nicknamed Stuffcake on account of his inordinate appetite and obesity, the story of Schaumann's life and the solution to a long-unsolved murder case. On shipboard during the return voyage to Africa, Eduard records all that he has heard—hence the story's narrative frame and osten-

sible reason for being. It happens that the murder in question has been surrounded by rumors, as was the case with Cord Horacker's reputed criminality, but in *Tubby Schaumann*, the one in possession of the facts has the satisfaction of putting the rumormongers in their place.

At the heart of this novel's ethical and aesthetic impulse is a "bipolar" structure that Raabe used to impressive effect in a number of the best late novels, but most effectively in *Tubby Schaumann* and *Die Akten des Vogelsangs* (the documents of the birdsong district). By this means, a first-person narrator (Eduard) and the story's principal character (Schaumann) represent opposed forces, and the author does not wholly take the side of either—although Schaumann enjoys a visible advantage. In the place of a fixed system of values, this more open form establishes a relativity that was not present, for example, in the earlier "homecoming" novel, *Abu Telfan*. The question of how one achieves self-fulfillment does not receive a clear, generally valid answer in *Tubby Schaumann*.

Eduard, the globetrotter and highly successful bourgeois, experienced and knowledgeable, takes on the normally commanding role of narrator of the story. Schaumann, overweight and slow on his feet, the stay-at-home who has always preferred lying under the hedges to joining in the adventures of his companions, is the intended subject of Eduard's report. The traveler walks to Schaumann's farmstead expecting to impress the indolent, provincial recluse with tales of exotic adventure and material success. What happens, however, is a reversal of roles and a reeducation of narrator to listener. Schaumann begins to talk, and the story is his from that moment on.

While Eduard has been making his mark in the "great world" outside, Schaumann has been steadily acquiring and assimilating—"ingesting," like his metaphorical ancestor, the giant sloth—until he commands both an astonishing knowledge and an enviable status in the town. Eduard's experience is vast but superficial by comparison; Schaumann's is narrow but profound, reaching back through eons of time, while Eduard knows only the present. Still, the final answer is not necessarily Schaumann's, for he embodies certain ambivalences. His success in life is measured in the material terms recognized by the "canaille," the village rabble he disdains.

He is at the same time still a misfit at odds with the community he surveys from the old fortifications of his farm.

When he called *Tubby Schaumann* his "most outrageous" book, Raabe had in mind not so much what the novel tells as how it tells it. What he offered the public was a reversal of the commonly accepted ranking of the important things in life. Seemingly the book is a murder mystery and asks the primary question of murder mysteries: Whodunit? Schaumann has known the answer long before Eduard's arrival. It is another of those bits of knowledge that he has assimilated and could spit out again at will, but, for the moment, he will not. He withholds this sensational and violent resolution while leisurely educating Eduard to the superior importance of modest achievement and steady, organic development—his own life history. So Raabe, too, disabuses his readers of any expectations that they will find here a tale of adventure and intrigue, as the ironic subtitle *Eine See-und Mordgeschichte* (*A Tale of Murder and the High Seas*) suggests. The apparently rambling, discursive, indiscriminate presentation of the story is both the method and the point of this novel. It is as Fairley says of *Die Chronik der Sperlingsgasse*, "Nothing in the book . . . is superfluous, everything fits." One realizes this fact only on a second reading, however, just as Eduard can realize it only in recording the story after its telling by Heinrich Schaumann.

The vital question of whether the individual can conquer life on his (or her) own terms rather than accommodate himself to it at the price of his dignity still confronted Raabe in novels that followed *Tubby Schaumann*. Schaumann masters his situation; others manage at least an acceptable accommodation; and some, like Velten Andres in *Die Akten des Vogelsangs*, fail abjectly. The fates of three such characters can be read as a philosophical summation of Raabe's mature view of life. To that vital question, he replied with a humorous "yes" in *Tubby Schaumann* and with a cruel "no" in *Die Akten des Vogelsangs*. In the last of his books, *Altershausen*, which he left unfinished in 1902, he tested and weighed the issue but did not follow through to a resolution for its autobiographical hero, Fritz Feyerabend. If Raabe indeed intended one final reply to his question, he failed—or refused—to give it.

Michael Ritterson

BIBLIOGRAPHY

Arnds, Peter O. *Wilhelm Raabe's "Der Hungerpastor" and Charles Dickens' "David Copperfield": Intertextuality of Two Bildungsromane*. New York: Peter Lang, 1997. Arnds compares the two novels and argues that Raabe borrowed the plot and characters from Charles Dickens's *David Copperfield* to write *The Hunger-Pastor*. Includes a bibliography and an index.

Burdekin, Hannah. "Wilhelm Raabe: The Master, the 'Schöne Semitische Zauberin,' and Her 'Krummnasige Verwandtschaft.'" In *The Ambivalent Author: Five German Writers and Their Jewish Characters, 1848-1914*. New York: Peter Lang, 2002. Burdekin examines the portrayal of Jewish characters in works by Raabe and other German authors, questioning why the fiction and nonfiction of these liberal-minded writers contained language and images of anti-Semitism.

Daemmrich, Horst S. *Wilhelm Raabe*. Boston: Twayne, 1981. An extremely helpful orientation to Raabe's life and works; one of the volumes in Twayne's World Authors series. Includes a bibliography and an index.

Downing, Eric. *Double Exposures: Repetition and Realism in Nineteenth-Century German Fiction*. Stanford, Calif.: Stanford University Press, 2000. An analysis of realist fiction by Raabe and other nineteenth century German authors, focusing on their use of "redundant" motifs about nature, gender, family, class, and aesthetics.

Massey, Irving. "Wilhelm Raabe: Jewish Women." In *Philo-Semitism in Nineteenth-Century German Literature*. Tübingen, Germany: Niemeyer, 2000. Massey's study of nineteenth century German literature focuses on the philo-Semitic works of Raabe and other non-Jewish authors, describing the feelings of guilt that are expressed in many of these texts.

Pizer, John. "The Alter Ego as Narration's Motive Force: Wilhelm Raabe." In *Ego-Alter Ego: Double and/as Other in the Age of German Poetic Realism*. Chapel Hill: University of North Carolina Press, 1998. Pizer examines the use of the doppelgänger in fiction by Raabe and other German realists, describing how these "doubles" reflect the movement's aesthetic philosophy.

_____. "Wilhelm Raabe and the German Colonial Experience." In *A Companion to German Realism, 1848-1900*, edited by Todd Kontje. Rochester, N.Y.: Camden House, 2002. Pizer's analysis of Raabe's work during the time of German colonialism is included in this collection on German realism.

Sammons, Jeffrey L. *The Shifting Fortunes of William Raabe: A History of Criticism as a Cautionary Tale.* Columbia, S.C.: Camden House, 1992. Sammons chronicles how the critical reaction to Raabe's work has changed over the years, describing Raabe's disappointment that his social criticism was largely overlooked. Includes a bibliography and an index.

_____. *Wilhelm Raabe: The Fiction of the Alternative Community.* Princeton, N.J.: Princeton University Press, 1987. Sammons analyzes Raabe's work and maintains that he is the major German-language novelist in the years between Johann Wolfgang von Goethe and Theodor Fontane. Includes an extensive bibliography.

FRANÇOIS RABELAIS

Born: La Devinière, near Chinon, France; c. 1494
Died: Paris, France; April, 1553

PRINCIPAL LONG FICTION

Pantagruel, 1532 (English translation, 1653)
Gargantua, 1534 (English translation, 1653)
Tiers Livre, 1546 (*Third Book*, 1693)
Le Quart Livre, incomplete 1548, complete 1552 (*Fourth Book*, 1694)
Le Cinquième Livre, 1564 (*Fifth Book*, 1694)
Gargantua et Pantagruel, 1567 (includes all previous titles; *Gargantua and Pantagruel*, 1653-1694, 1929)

OTHER LITERARY FORMS

In preparation for his doctoral degree, François Rabelais (RAHB-uh-lay) composed commentaries on the *Aphorisms* of Hippocrates and the *Ars medicinalis* of Galen in editions of these works that Rabelais published in 1532. After his first trip to Rome, he edited a *Topographia antiquae Romae*, based on a work by Bartolome Marliani, which was published by Sébastien Gryphe in 1534. *La Sciomachie et festins* (simulated combats and feasts), published in Lyons by Gryphe in 1549, also refers to Rabelais's journeys. It is also known that Rabelais composed poetry. Many of his letters, especially letters that he wrote while in Rome, are available in various editions.

ACHIEVEMENTS

With François Rabelais, French literature entered into a new phase. After the great medieval epics and romances of the twelfth and thirteenth centuries, there had been a steady decline until the sixteenth century. In France, the new learning brought about by the rediscovery of ancient Greek manuscripts, the invention of printing, and the great voyages of discovery found its first expression in Rabelais. *Gargantua and Pantagruel* breathes the spirit of enthusiasm, liberation, and discovery that inspired the rebirth of culture and learning.

Nevertheless, there is in Rabelais much of the medieval. In fact, he chose as his inspiration a book popular at the time, *Grandes et inestimables cronicques du grant et énorme géant Gargantua* (1532; great and inestimable chronicles of the great and enormous giant Gargantua), based on the story of a giant associated with King Arthur, Merlin, Morgan, and Mélusine. Rabelais proposed a sequel in which he continued the popular comic of the *cronicques*. He enriched his legend with notes on history, geography, local custom, and theater; his is a Renaissance interpretation of a medieval carnival.

As the critic Jean Plattard noted, Rabelais maintained the medieval spirit of the farces and fabliaux in his violent imagery, his vulgarity, and his preoccupation with sexual matters. At the same time, Rabelais introduced the spirit of the Renaissance with his rejection of Scholasticism, his confidence in antiquity, his faith in science, and his belief in human progress.

Rabelais did not write a novel in the modern sense of the word, nor did he intend to compose one. As Jacques Boulenger observed, Rabelais wanted to embroider a vast canvas both with fantasies and with scenes from real life; in his encyclopedic ambition, he was typical of the Renaissance. Rabelais's achievement lies above all in his style, in a remarkable exploitation of all the possibilities of language. His giants are polyglots, and so is their creator. He uses French and Latin with ease; he creates words in torrents. He is equally adept in dialect, patois, argot, and scientific terminology. Boulenger described Rabelais's styles as "verbal intoxication in the dionysiac sense," yet when the occasion demands, as in the description of Badebec's death, Rabelais is a master of economy. The first French prose writer with genuine artistic talent and one of the greatest examples of the *esprit gaulois* found in the *Roman de Renart* (c. 1175-1205), the fabliaux, Molière, and Voltaire, Rabelais was truly a turning point in French literature.

BIOGRAPHY

Much of François Rabelais's biography is lost in obscurity, but modern scholars have established the principal events of his life. The year of Rabelais's birth, believed to be 1494, is still uncertain, but it is known that his father, Antoine, was a lawyer at the royal court of Chinon and was associated with the most enlightened men of his day. Rabelais spent his childhood at Chinon, especially at the family's country home, La Devinière, often mentioned in his works, and at Angers, his mother's birthplace. He was probably educated at the Benedictine abbey of Seuillé, evoked in Friar John's monastery in *Gargantua and Pantagruel*.

By 1521, Rabelais was a Franciscan monk at Fontenay-le-Comte in Bas Poitou; it was there that he met Pierre Amy, one of the outstanding Hellenists of the time, and entered into correspondence with the eminent French Hellenist Guillaume Budé. Rabelais translated some of Herodotus from Greek into Latin, and also contributed to André Tiraqueau's treatise on the laws of marriage, "De legibus connubialibus," echoes of which appear in book 3.

In 1523, the Greek books of the monastery were confiscated under orders from the Sorbonne, and shortly afterward Rabelais transferred to the Benedictines of Saint-Pierre-de-Maillezain, where he came into contact with the scholarly bishop Geoffroy d'Estissac. In 1527, Rabelais left the monastery and toured the same universities his Pantagruel visits in book 2. In 1532, he received his bachelor's degree in medicine from the University of Montpellier and assumed a post in Lyons, at that time the capital of the Renaissance. He also continued his classical commentaries and the same year published *Pantagruel*, censured by the Sorbonne for obscenity. Jean du Bellay, bishop of Paris, became Rabelais's protector in 1534, taking him to Rome as his personal physician. It was upon Rabelais's return that he published *Gargantua*, likewise censured because of its unfortunate coincidence with the Affair of the Placards.

Rabelais attempted briefly the life of a secular priest; by 1537, he was a doctor of medicine in Lyons. In 1541, he published a new edition of *Gargantua and Pantagruel*, with the attacks against the Sorbonne expurgated. The publication of book 3 in 1546 still provoked censure, as did that of the complete book 4 in 1552. His later days included more travel in Italy, especially with du Bellay. It is fairly certain that Rabelais died in Paris, at the beginning of April, 1553.

ANALYSIS

François Rabelais is universally regarded as one of the major figures in the Western literary tradition, in the company of Dante, Geoffrey Chaucer, William Shakespeare, and Miguel de Cervantes, yet he is more often praised than read. Indeed, in the judgment of scholar Mikhail Bakhtin, "Of all the great writers of world literature, Rabelais is the least popular, the least understood and appreciated."

The difficulty of Rabelais, the quality that discourages many modern readers from making headway in his work, is not the strategic obscurity of a James Joyce or an Ezra Pound; rather, it resembles the difficulty that one experiences in "getting" a joke, the humor of which is not immediately apparent. To read Rabelais is essentially to laugh, but humor is notoriously elusive, dependent on a wide range of local cultural assumptions and linguistic practices and thus quick to be lost in time and in translation. Here, there is a comparison with Shakespeare: One vein of Shakespearean humor, closely related to the humor of Rabelais, is accessible to the modern reader only via scholarly explication of wordplay, allusions, implicit cultural assumptions, and so on, but Shakespeare remains highly readable even when many of his bawdy puns, for example, are entirely missed.

The difficulty in grasping the spirit of Rabelais's jokes, their underlying intent, is confirmed by ongoing critical debate. Even such a fundamental issue as Rabelais's attitude toward Christianity and the Church has been the subject of bitter controversy. Throughout *Gargantua and Pantagruel* there are frequent satiric jabs at the rites and institutions of the Church. While Rabelais ridicules monasticism and the Papacy, however, and while his parodies of Christian ritual could be deemed sacrilegious if not blasphemous, he stops short of the open atheism of the Enlightenment.

Critics such as Abel Lefranc have argued that Rabelais was in fact a thoroughgoing rationalist who, unable to express his convictions openly, presented them in a humorous guise. According to such critics, Rabelais thus anticipated the skepticism of the Enlightenment. On the other hand, critics such as Lucien Febvre, who devoted a massive volume to a refutation of Lefranc, have argued that Rabelais's satire was directed against institutional abuses of the Church, not against the heart of Christian belief.

Although such questions may never be definitively resolved, one helpful approach to Rabelais's humor is that taken by Bakhtin, who places Rabelais in what he calls the carnival tradition, a tradition of folk humor with roots in the ancient past, encompassing such festivities as the Roman Saturnalia and still vital in the Middle Ages: "Celebrations of a carnival type represented a considerable part of the life of medieval men, even in the time given over to them. Large medieval cities devoted an average of three months a year to these festivities."

Bakhtin suggests that it is Rabelais's indebtedness to this folk tradition, an expression of popular culture still largely unexplored by literary scholars, that accounts for the relative failure of modern readers to appreciate his work. In the carnival atmosphere, all of the sacred values of medieval society were parodied in a ritualistic manner—often with the full participation of the clergy. Ra-

François Rabelais. (Library of Congress)

belais's humor is thus characterized by the systematic inversion typical of carnival: parody, blasphemy, gross physical images, and so on.

By placing *Gargantua and Pantagruel* in this context, Bakhtin shifts the emphasis from an interpretation of Rabelais's values—that is, the personal beliefs informing his work—to the folk tradition of which his work was the supreme expression even as it marked the decisive break between the Renaissance and the Middle Ages.

GARGANTUA AND PANTAGRUEL

Rabelais's Renaissance spirit is nowhere more apparent than in his style, an overflowing fountain of verbal exuberance, a rich compound of slang, odd words, jargon of the various professions, interminable lists, and other heterogeneous elements. *Gargantua and Pantagruel* is full of puns that are difficult to translate: *service du vin/service divin* (the wine service/the divine service); Grandgousier's name, from *Que grand tu as (gosier)*

(What a big gullet you have); or Epistemon, who has *la coupe têtée* (his chop headed off).

This exuberance is also evident in Rabelais's characterizations. Although he created types rather than flesh-and-blood people, his characters are unforgettable. Grandgousier, the progenitor of the illustrious family of giants, is the most shadowy. He appears as the noble lord, just and forgiving after the Picrocholine Wars and a good father to Gargantua. His son is curious, witty, garrulous, and loving. After the beginning of book 2, Grandgousier appears rarely, but always with concern for his son. Pantagruel, Gargantua's son, is the real hero of the story. After a well-delineated education, he becomes a kind lord, and his earlier wit changes to wisdom. Perhaps the best-portrayed characters are Friar John and Panurge. Friar John is the garrulous monk who always has something of the cloister about him; kind, generous, and witty, he enlivens all the adventures from the Picrocholine Wars to the voyage for the Divine Bottle. Panurge, the perpetual trickster and inventor of farces, changes his character in book 3 to that of a man caught in a dilemma: to marry or not to marry? To choose action or inaction? There are few female characters in *Gargantua and Pantagruel*; they are limited to Gargamelle, Grandgousier's wife, and Badebec, Gargantua's wife, who dies as she is giving birth to Pantagruel. Basically, the story is a very masculine one; as in the medieval farces, women are little more than bearers of children and objects of sexual desire.

GARGANTUA

Although published two years after *Pantagruel*, in 1534, *Gargantua* is known as book 1 because of its chronology. Gargantua is the father of Pantagruel, and the book tells of his miraculous birth, adolescence, education, and maturity. The prologue describes a *silenus*, a little box for rare drugs, which Rabelais compares to Socrates, and indeed to his own work: ugly from the outside but precious on the inside.

After Rabelais has made a Genesis-like presentation of Gargantua's genealogy, birth, and naming, the reader learns his first words: *à boire* (drink), symbolic of the thirst of the Renaissance man for the new learning. Much of book 1 is concerned with education; the critic Thomas M. Greene considers its essential theme to be the process of development in the young giant as he progresses from

the "random equality of childhood experience . . . to poise and sophistication without losing his capacity for naïve joy." First educated in a haphazard manner by the Sophists, he is purged by Ponocrates and learns more by ear than by eye to integrate all activities—physical, mental, and spiritual—and grow from chaos to discipline and from ignorance to truth and justice.

A lengthy episode treats the wars between Picrochole, King of Lerné, and Grandgousier, Gargantua's father, a noble and peace-loving lord. Lefranc sees historical and biographical material in this unjust war, as it takes place around La Roche-Clamard, near Seuillé, in Rabelais's native Chinon. As the war progresses, Friar John of the Funnels, the vibrant and impetuous monk, becomes Grandgousier's staunch ally. In the words and actions of Friar John, one finds some of Rabelais's finest satire of the monastic life he knew so well.

In recompense for his help in the war won by Grandgousier, Friar John receives the Abbey of Thélème, Rabelais's ideal for an elite community. This semiutopian monastery, modeled on the château of Bonnivet, admits both men and women of outstanding physical and moral traits, inviting them to spend their time in pursuit of culture and eventually to leave and marry. It is governed by only one rule: "Fay ce que voudras" (do what you wish). An enigmatic inscription in poetry concludes the book and invites the reader to continue the search for truth in the Renaissance spirit.

PANTAGRUEL

Book 2, *Pantagruel*, is the least coherent of the first four volumes. It reveals the author's unmistakable style and wit and gives promise of more adventures in the future. As in *Gargantua*, Rabelais traces the genealogy of Pantagruel in a burlesque parody of the Bible and Pliny the Elder's *Natural History* (77 C.E.), as he emphasizes his hero's gigantic appetite and prodigious strength. Because Pantagruel will later liberate himself and others from the bonds of ignorance, he frees himself as a child from the constraint of his cradle.

Education plays an important role here also, especially in chapter 8, in which Gargantua tells his son Pantagruel to become "an abyss of knowledge." Pantagruel also tours the famous universities of his day: Toulouse, a center of dance and fencing; Montepellier, noted for its wine; Avignon, for its women; Bourges, for its poor laws; and Angers, which he avoids because it is infested with the plague. He visits libraries, which Rabelais uses to satirize many spiritual texts and the immoral lives of those who read them.

In book 2, Pantagruel meets Panurge, who is to become his friend for life. Panurge is one of a long line of picaros; he introduces himself in many languages, a performance typical of his pranks, which, as Greene observes, "mingle in various measures humor, cunning, perversity, creative inspiration and malice." Rabelais describes Panurge as proper-looking, a bit of a lecher, always short of money (which he always finds by cunningly perpetrated larceny), and a perpetual trickster. His clever and often crude tricks form much of the wit of books 2 and 4.

In the courtly tradition, Panurge and Pantagruel go off to battle in Utopia, where Gargantua has been transferred by the fairy Morgue. Rabelais seems to return to the spirit of the *cronicques* as he ends his disjointed but highly original portrayal of the giants.

In contrast to the looseness of book 2, book 3 is the most unified of the entire series. In the prologue, Rabelais compares himself to Diogenes, who, though physically unfit for war, rolled his tub so as not to appear lazy. In the first six chapters, Panurge appears as the traditional spendthrift; having inherited an estate, he rapidly squanders his inheritance on feasting. In the remainder of the book, he engages in lengthy discussions on whether to marry. Many critics trace Rabelais's treatment of marriage and cuckoldry in book 3 to the medieval farces; others, such as Greene, see the search for truth and the importance of action as forming the real subject of the book.

Panurge consults various sources to resolve his dilemma: the *sortes vergilianae* (a book of Vergil opened at random), a fortune-teller, the poet Raminagrobis, the magician Herr Trippa. All give him the same response: If he marries, he will be cuckolded, beaten, and robbed. The theologian Hippothadée encourages him to choose someone like Solomon's "valiant woman"; the doctor Rondibilis tells him of woman's foibles; the philosopher Trouillogan has no definite answer. After a final consultation with the fool Triboulet, no more satisfactory than all the others, Pantagruel convinces Panurge to consult the Oracle of the Divine Bottle in Cathay. Thus, the stage is set for the adventures that occupy books 4 and 5.

In book 4, inspired by the accounts of navigation so prominent at the time, especially those of Jacques Cartier, Rabelais composed the travelogue or odyssey of his heroes—a fantastic account of imaginary places and allegorical people, filled with the marvelous and touching on science fiction, such as the frozen words that melt and begin to speak. There are many realistic allusions to Rabelais's own day, such as the Decretals, the base of canonical jurisprudence; the officers of law and justice, portrayed in the Chicanous; and the wars between Protestants and Catholics, symbolized by the battle with the Andouilles.

Rabelais also satirizes perennial vices such as gluttony and its opposite, a sterile asceticism based on pride rather than on genuine piety. Panurge reassumes the character of the trickster and in a famous episode drowns the sheep of the avaricious merchant Dindenault. The travelers have not reached the Divine Bottle by the end of book 4, but Rabelais's imagination and invention are here at their height.

Originally published posthumously as *L'Isle sonante* in 1562, book 5 differs so radically from the preceding ones that critics today still question its authenticity; it is bitter, rambling, and far less creative than its predecessors. In it, the story of the navigation continues through many more fantastic islands.

The Isle Sonante (ringing island), with its perpetually clanging bells, is inhabited by birds that resemble men and women and whose names refer to the clergy and members of religious orders. The Chats-fourrés (furry cats) are the officers of the Parlement of Paris, who refused Michel de l'Hospital's proposal for an edict of toleration for the Protestants. The Apedeftes, or ignoramuses, are the tax collectors and clerks in the counting houses.

After many other such adventures, the travelers finally reach the Divine Bottle and admire the magnificent temple in which it is located. The priestess Bacbuc invites Panurge to hear the long-awaited pronouncement, which consists of one word: "Drink." The priestess has another word of wisdom: *in vino veritas* (in wine is truth). The enigmatic conclusion has as many interpretations as there are critics, for essentially it tells readers to interpret their own destinies for themselves.

Irma M. Kashuba

OTHER MAJOR WORKS

NONFICTION: *La Sciomachie et festins*, 1549.

EDITED TEXTS: *Aphorisms*, 1532; *Ars medicinalis*, 1532; *Topographia antiquae Romae*, 1534.

MISCELLANEOUS: *Pantagruéline Prognostication*, 1532 (occasional verses and letters).

BIBLIOGRAPHY

Berry, Alice Fiola. *The Charm of Catastrophe: A Study of Rabelais's "Quart Livre."* Chapel Hill: University of North Carolina, Department of Romance Languages, 2000. Analyzes *Le Quart Livre*, the last novel by Rabelais published in the author's lifetime, demonstrating how the work expresses the elderly writer's despair over failing to achieve his youthful dreams.

Bowen, Barbara C. *Enter Rabelais, Laughing.* Nashville: Vanderbilt University Press, 1998. Focuses on the humor in Rabelais's work, describing why it was funny to his sixteenth century contemporaries and placing him within the tradition of Renaissance comic writings. Includes notes and bibliography.

Carron, Jean-Claude, ed. *François Rabelais: Critical Assessments.* Baltimore: Johns Hopkins University Press, 1995. Selection and revision of papers concerning Rabelais that were delivered at a 1991 symposium at the University of California, Los Angeles. Among the topics addressed are realism, feminism, and cultural connections in Rabelais's works.

Chesney, Elizabeth A., and Marcel Tetel. *Rabelais Revisited.* New York: Twayne, 1993. Provides a good introduction to the novels, with an annotated bibliography of important studies on Rabelais. Examines the relationships between men and women in Rabelais's works.

Coleman, Dorothy Gabe. *Rabelais: A Critical Study in Prose Fiction.* New York: Cambridge University Press, 1971. Presents a meticulous analysis of Rabe-lais as a prose stylist and of the genres in which he wrote. Includes bibliography.

Frame, Donald M. *François Rabelais: A Study.* New York: Harcourt Brace Jovanovich, 1977. Detailed study of Rabelais's life and work includes several chapters on his major fiction and on topics such as obscenity, comedy, satire, fantasy, storytelling, giantism, humanism, evangelism, characters, and fortunes in Rabelais's writings. Supplemented with detailed notes and an annotated bibliography.

Gauna, Max. *The Rabelaisian Mythologies.* Madison, N.J.: Fairleigh Dickinson University Press, 1996. Rabelais described his novels as "mythologies," and this study analyzes the mythological elements in *Pantagruel*, *Gargantua*, *Tiers Livre*, and *Le Quart Livre*. Includes bibliography.

Greene, Thomas M. *Rabelais: A Study in Comic Courage.* Englewood Cliffs, N.J.: Prentice-Hall, 1970. Excellent analysis of Rabelais's works is often cited as the best introductory study of the writer. Includes bibliography.

O'Brien, John, and Malcolm Quainton, eds. *Distant Voices Still Heard: Contemporary Readings of French Renaissance Literature.* Liverpool, England: Liverpool University Press, 2000. Collection of paired essays on five major authors applies modern critical theories to French Renaissance literature. The two essays on Rabelais provide a structuralist reading of *Pantagruel* and examine the methodology of *Tiers Livre*.

Zegura, Elizabeth Chesney, ed. *The Rabelais Encyclopedia.* Westport, Conn.: Greenwood Press, 2004. Alphabetically arranged collection of articles covers a wide range of topics, including Rabelais's characters, references to Renaissance and historical figures in Rabelais's works, themes and allusions in his works, and key influences on his writing. Also features a chronology of major events in his life and literary career.

ANN RADCLIFFE

Born: London, England; July 9, 1764
Died: London, England; February 7, 1823
Also known as: Ann Ward

PRINCIPAL LONG FICTION

The Castles of Athlin and Dunbayne, 1789
A Sicilian Romance, 1790
The Romance of the Forest, 1791
The Mysteries of Udolpho, 1794
*The Italian: Or, The Confessional of the Black
     Penitents*, 1797
Gaston de Blondeville, 1826

OTHER LITERARY FORMS

In addition to her novels, Ann Radcliffe published *A Journey Made in the Summer of 1794 Through Holland and the Western Frontier of Germany* (1795). It recounts a continental journey made with her husband and includes copious observations of other tours to the English Lake District. The work became immediately popular, prompting a second edition, *The Journeys of Mrs. Radcliffe*, published the same year. Following a common practice of romance writers, Radcliffe interspersed the lengthy prose passages of her novels with her own verses or with those from famous poets. An anonymous compiler took the liberty of collecting and publishing her verses in an unauthorized edition titled *The Poems of Ann Radcliffe* (1816). This slim volume was reissued in 1834 and 1845. Radcliffe's interest in versifying was increasingly evident when her husband, in arranging for the posthumous publication of *Gaston de Blondeville*, included with it a long metrical romance, *St. Alban's Abbey* (1826). Radcliffe also wrote an essay, "On the Supernatural in Poetry," which was published in *New Monthly Magazine* (1826). The record of her literary achievement still remains available, as all of her novels and the poems are in print.

ACHIEVEMENTS

Ann Radcliffe's fame as a novelist in modern times in no way compares to the popularity she enjoyed in the 1790's. With the publication of her third novel, *The Ro-*

mance of the Forest, this relatively unknown woman established herself as the best-selling writer of the period, receiving rave reviews from the critics and increasing demand for her works from circulating libraries.

Radcliffe's five gothic romances, published between 1789 and 1797, owed a portion of their motivation to Horace Walpole's *The Castle of Otranto* (1765) and two earlier gothic writers, Sophia Lee and Clara Reeve. The gothic tale reached its full development with Radcliffe's ability to manipulate the emotions of love and fear in such a manner as to provoke terror in her characters and readers alike. Though managing an effective use of the little understood complexities of the imagination, she offered her readers stereotyped plots, characters, and settings. Her disguises of foreign characters and lands were as thin as the supernatural illusions that often seemed anticlimactic in their emotional appeal. These weaknesses did not deter Radcliffe's public, who remained fascinated by her distinctive brand of romanticism, which combined the gloomy darkening vale of the more somber poets of the graveyard school, the extremes of imaginative sensibility (as in Henry Mackenzie's *The Man of Feeling*, 1771), and the medieval extravagance of the Ossianic poems of James Macpherson, as well as the pseudoarchaic fabrications of Thomas Chatterton's Rowley poems (1777).

Radcliffe nurtured this cult of melancholy, primitivism, sentimentalism, exoticism, and medievalism in her novels, becoming the epitome of the gothic genre to her contemporaries. *The Mysteries of Udolpho*, her best-known work, was satirized by Jane Austen in *Northanger Abbey* (1818) as representative of the entire mode.

Radcliffe's later importance was seen in a number of major Romantic writers who read her romances in their childhood. Percy Bysshe Shelley's *Zastrozzi* (1810), an extravagant romance, was a youthful answer to the genre. Lord Byron's *Manfred* (1817) appears as a gothic villain committing spiritual murder in a landscape of "sublime solitudes." Matthew Gregory Lewis and Mary Wollstonecraft Shelley clearly benefited from Radcliffe's strengths as a novelist of suspense, mystery, and the picturesque. In America, Washington Irving's, Edgar Allan

Poe's, and Nathaniel Hawthorne's tales of terror, along with Charles Brockden Brown's *Edgar Huntly: Or, Memoirs of a Sleep-Walker* (1799), were suggested by Radcliffe's work.

As the most popular and perhaps most important novelist between the eighteenth century masters and Austen and Sir Walter Scott, Radcliffe continues to claim the attention of academicians. Psychological, feminist, folklorist, and the more traditional thematic studies have proved the strengths of her art. In 1980, Devendra P. Varma (*The Gothic Flame*, 1957) began serving as advisory editor for the Arno Press series Gothic Studies and Dissertations, which has published dozens of texts dealing with Radcliffe's literary output; of those texts, more than one dozen discuss Radcliffe's novels at length. It is clear that there is at present a remarkable revival of interest in the gothic and in Radcliffe's work.

BIOGRAPHY

Ann Radcliffe was born Ann Ward on July 9, 1764, in Holborn, a borough of central London, the only child of William Ward and Ann Oates Ward. Her father was a successful haberdasher who provided the family with a comfortable life, allowing Radcliffe access to a well-stocked library and the time to read the works of every important English author, as well as numerous popular romances.

This quiet, sheltered existence was enlivened by the visits of Radcliffe's wealthy and learned uncle, Thomas Bentley, who was the partner of Josiah Wedgwood, the potter. Bentley's London home was a center for the literati; there, among others, the pretty but shy girl met Hester L. Thrale Piozzi, the friend and biographer of Samuel Johnson; Elizabeth Montagu, "Queen of the Blue-Stocking Club"; and "Athenian" Stuart.

In 1772, Radcliffe joined her parents at Bath, where her father had opened a shop for the firm of Wedgwood and Bentley. She remained sequestered in this resort until her marriage to the young Oxford graduate, William Radcliffe, in 1788. William had first decided to become a law student at one of the Inns of Court but abandoned this for a career in journalism. The couple moved to London soon thereafter, where William subsequently became proprietor and editor of the *English Chronicle*. The marriage was happy but childless, and the couple's circle of friends were primarily literary, which added encouragement to William's argument that his wife should begin to write.

With her husband away on editorial business, Radcliffe spent the evenings writing without interruption. Her first book, *The Castles of Athlin and Dunbayne*, was unremarkable, but her next two novels established her reputation as a master of suspense and the supernatural. *A Sicilian Romance* and *The Romance of the Forest* attracted the public's voracious appetite for romances. Both works were translated into French and Italian, and numerous editions were published, as well as a dramatization of *The Romance of the Forest*, performed in 1794. Radcliffe's success culminated in the appearance of *The*

Ann Radcliffe.

Mysteries of Udolpho; her decision to rely less on external action and more on psychological conflict produced ecstatic reviews. The excitement created by the book threatened the relative solitude of the Radcliffes, but the publisher's unusually high offer of five hundred pounds freed them to travel extensively on the Continent.

In the summer of 1794, the Radcliffes journeyed through Holland and along the Rhine River to the Swiss frontier. On returning to England, they proceeded north to the Lake District. While traveling, Radcliffe took complete notes concerning the picturesque landscape and included detailed political and economic accounts of the Low Countries and the Rhineland. These latter observations were probably contributed by her husband, though both Radcliffes found the devastation of the Napoleonic Wars appalling. *A Journey Made in the Summer of 1794 Through Holland and the Western Frontier of Germany* appeared in 1795.

Radcliffe's interest in the human misery of these regions and the legends and superstitions of the great fortresses and Roman Catholic churches of the Rhineland suggested her next work, *The Italian: Or, The Confessional of the Black Penitents*. As a romance of the Inquisition, it explored character motivation in great detail, while action became a method of dramatizing personalities and not a simple vehicle for movement from one adventure to another. *The Italian*, though not as popular as *The Mysteries of Udolpho*, was translated immediately into French and even badly dramatized at the Haymarket on August 15, 1797.

At the age of thirty-three, Radcliffe was at the height of her popularity; though she had never decided on writing as a potential source of income, her means by this time had become quite ample. With the deaths of her parents between 1798 and 1799, she found herself independently wealthy. Whether it was because of her secure financial condition or her displeasure with the cheap imitations of her novels, Radcliffe withdrew from the public domain and refrained from publishing any more works in her lifetime. Innumerable reports surfaced that she was suffering from a terminal illness, that the terrors of which she had written in her novels had driven her mad, or that she had mysteriously died. These reports were without substance; in fact, she wrote another novel, a metrical romance, and an extensive diary.

After her death, Radcliffe's husband found among her papers a novel, *Gaston de Blondeville*, which he arranged to have published. Written after Radcliffe's visit to the ruins of Kenilworth Castle in 1802, it came near to comparing with the historical romances of Sir Walter Scott but lost itself in a preoccupation with historical precision, leaving action and character to suffer from a lack of emphasis. The narrative poem, *St. Alban's Abbey*, appeared posthumously with this last novel; though Radcliffe had been offered an early opportunity for publication, she broke off negotiations with the publisher.

Content with retirement and relative obscurity, Radcliffe wrote in her last years only diary entries concerning the places she and her husband had visited on their long journeys through the English countryside. From 1813 to 1816, she lived near Windsor and probably at this time began suffering from bouts of asthma. From all reports, she enjoyed the company of friends, maintained a ready wit and a sly humor, but insisted on delicacy and decorum in all things. Shortly before her final illness, she returned to London; she died there on February 7, 1823, in her sixtieth year. The "Udolpho woman" or "the Shakespeare of romance writers," as one contemporary reviewer called her, has achieved a secure place in the history of English literature.

ANALYSIS

The novels of Ann Radcliffe serve as a transition between the major English novelists of the eighteenth century and the first accomplished novelists of the nineteenth century. In the years between 1789 and 1797, her five novels established a style that profoundly affected English fiction for the next twenty-five years and had a considerable impact in translation as well. From the negligible first novel, *The Castles of Athlin and Dunbayne*, to the sophisticated romances, *The Mysteries of Udolpho* and *The Italian*, Radcliffe demonstrated an ability to enrich the motives, methods, and machineries of each succeeding work. Manipulating the conventions of the gothic while introducing new thematic concerns and experiments with narrative techniques, Radcliffe became a master of her craft.

Improved control over the complex atmosphere of the gothic romance proved an early factor in Radcliffe's success. She went beyond the traditional gothic devices of lurking ghosts and malevolent noblemen torturing innocent girls to an interest in natural description. This delight with nature's sublime scenery gave tone and color to her settings while emphasizing the heightened emotions and imagination that were produced in reaction to the landscape. A skillful use of numerous atmospheric factors such as sunsets, storms, winds, thunderclaps, and moonlight, intensified the romantic tendencies of her time.

A scene typifying the Radcliffe concept of landscape portraiture has a ruined castle in silhouette, arranged on a stern but majestic plain at nightfall. This view does not depend on precision of outline for effect but instead on an ominous vagueness, creating in the reader an odd mixture of pleasure and fear. Her delight in the architecture of massive proportions and in the picturesque derived in part from her reading of the nature poets and her study of the paintings of Claude Lorrain, Nicolas Poussin, and Salvator Rosa. She reflected a mid-eighteenth century English passion in cultivating an acute sensibility for discovering beauty where before it had not been perceived. While she made landscape in fiction a convention, it was her combining of beauty in horror and the horrible in the beautiful that reflected the Romantic shift away from order and reason toward emotion and imagination.

Radcliffe's novels rely not only on strategies of terror but also on the psychology of feelings. The novels of sensibility of the past generation offered her alternatives to the gothic trappings made familiar in Walpole's *The Castle of Otranto*; those gothic aspects now became linked to various emotional elements in a total effect. By drawing on the poetry of Thomas Gray and Edward Young or the fiction of Oliver Goldsmith and Henry Mackenzie, Radcliffe created a minority of characters with complex natures who exhibited not only melancholy and doubt, love and joy, but also hate and evil intentions. She was one of the first English novelists to subject her characters to psychological analysis.

Of particular psychological interest are Radcliffe's villains. Cruel, calculating, domineering, relentless, and selfish, they are more compelling than her virtuous characters. Since their passions are alien to the ordinary person, she dramatically explores the mysteries of their sinister attitudes. Radcliffe's villains resemble those created by the Elizabethan dramatists, and their descen-

dants can be found in the works of the great Romantics, Byron and Shelley.

At her best, Radcliffe manifested strengths not seen in her first two novels nor in her last. Her first novel, *The Castles of Athlin and Dunbayne*, exhibits the most obvious borrowings, from sources as well known as *The Castle of Otranto* to numerous other gothic-historical and sentimental novels. Though immature, the work offers her characteristic sense of atmosphere with the marvelous dangers and mysteries of feudal Scotland depicted to full advantage. Its weaknesses become evident all too soon, however, as stock characters populate strained, often confused incidents while mouthing rather obvious parables about morality. Didacticism seems the motivating principle of the work. As David Durant observes in *Ann Radcliffe's Novels* (1980), "The characters are so controlled by didactic interests as to be faceless and without personality." The rigid obligations of *The Castles of Athlin and Dunbayne* to the morality of sentimental novels, the uniformity of a neoclassical prose style, and the repetitious, predictable action of the romance plot, trap Radcliffe into a mechanical performance.

A SICILIAN ROMANCE

Radcliffe's second novel, *A Sicilian Romance*, has a new strategy, an emphasis on action and adventure while subordinating moral concerns. This approach, however, was not effective because of the obvious imbalance between the two methods, and characterization suffered before a mass of incident. The interest in fear was expanded throughout the tale as a long-suffering wife, imprisoned in the remote sections of a huge castle by a villainous nobleman (who has an attachment to a beautiful paramour), struggles helplessly until rescued, after much suspense, by her gentle daughter and the young girl's lover. The characters' shallowness is hidden by a chase sequence of overwhelming speed that prevents one from noticing their deficiencies. To dramatize the movement of plot, Radcliffe introduced numerous settings, offering the reader a complete vision of the Romantic landscape.

Though *A Sicilian Romance* lacks the sureness of technique of the later novels and remains a lesser product, it did establish Radcliffe's ingenuity and perseverance. It was followed by the three novels on which her reputation rests: *The Romance of the Forest*, *The Mysteries of Udolpho*, and *The Italian*. Radcliffe's last novel, the posthumous *Gaston de Blondeville*, which was probably never meant for publication, exhibits the worst faults of the two earliest romances. Lifeless characters abound in a narrative overloaded with tedious historical facts and devoid of any action. In reconstructing history, Radcliffe was influenced by Scott but clearly was out of her element in attempting to make history conform to her own preconceptions. The primary innovation was the introduction of a real ghost to the love story. This specter, the apparition of a murdered knight demanding justice, stalks the grounds of Kenilworth Castle at the time of the reign of King Henry III. Radcliffe detracts from this imposing supernatural figure when she resorts to explanations of incidents better left mysterious.

THE ROMANCE OF THE FOREST

With the publication of her third novel, *The Romance of the Forest*, Radcliffe moved from apprenticeship to mastery. Her technique had advanced in at least two important elements: The chase with its multitude of settings is scaled down to an exacting series of dramas set among a few extended scenes, and characterization of the heroine is improved with the reduction of external action. Though suspense is extended rather illegitimately in order to produce a glorious final surprise, the novel is a genuine exploration of the realm of the unconscious. This remarkable advance into modern psychology gave life to the standard situations of Radcliffe's stories, allowing the reader to create his own private horrors.

Radcliffe's new emphasis on internal action makes her protagonist, Adeline, more credible than the stock romantic heroines whom she in many ways resembles. Adeline suffers from a nervous illness after mysteriously being thrust upon the LaMotte family, who themselves have only recently escaped, under curious circumstances, from Paris. Soon the group discovers a Gothic ruin, which contains the requisite underground room, rotten tapestries, blood stains, and a general aura of mystery.

Instead of the familiar chase scenes, a series of unified set pieces portray the exploration of the ruin, the seduction of the heroine, and the execution of the hero. The entire plot depends on the actions of a vicious but dominating sadist, the Marquis Phillipe de Montalt, and his conspiratorial agent, Pierre de LaMotte, against the unprotected Adeline. Because of the uncertainty of her birth, the sexual implications of this situation involve the

risk of incest. Among contemporary readers, *The Romance of the Forest* became an immediate success, owing to its well-constructed narrative, the charm of its description of Romantic landscapes, and a consummate handling of the principle of suspense.

THE MYSTERIES OF UDOLPHO

Radcliffe's next novel, *The Mysteries of Udolpho*, remains her best-known work. The sublimity of her landscapes and the control that she demonstrates in this novel mark an important change from her earlier novels; Radcliffe's handling of action and character also reached new levels of subtlety and success, moving the novel a step beyond the rather strict conventions of the sentimental mode to one of psychological inquiry.

The period of the novel is the end of the sixteenth century. The principal scenes are laid in the gloomy enclave of the Castle of Udolpho, in the Italian Apennines, but many glances are directed toward the south of France—Gascony, Provence, and Languedoc—and the brightness of Venice is contrasted with the dark horrors of the Apennines. Emily St. Aubert, the beautiful daughter of a Gascon family, is the heroine; she is intelligent and extraordinarily accomplished in the fine arts. Though revealing all the tender sensibilities of the characters associated with a hundred sentimental tales, Emily emerges as a credible figure who seems aware of the connections between the scenery around her and the characters who inhabit it. As a painter, she sees and thinks of life as a series of pictures. As Durant explains in *Ann Radcliffe's Novels* (1980), "She does not merely feel fright, but conjures up imaginary scenes which elicit it. . . . scenery inhabits the inner life of the heroine, as well as locating her actions."

A further element of Emily's characterization that adds to her credibility is her internalizing of the suspense produced by the action in the narrative. Her heightened sensibility reacts to fear and terror in an all-inclusive way; this acuteness of sensibility makes her easy prey for the villain, Signor Montoni. This sinister figure marries Emily's aunt for her money, and then conveys Emily and her unhappy aunt to the "vast and dreary" confines of the castle.

This impossible castle becomes a superbly appointed stage for the playing of the melodrama. As the melodrama has hopes of communicating a real sense of mystery, its action and characters remain subordinate to the environment, which pervades the entire texture of the work. Description of landscape is a major part of the book's concept, and Radcliffe pays homage to Rosa and Lorrain in emphasizing pictorial detail. The somber exterior of the castle prepares the reader for the ineffable horrors that lie within the walls and adumbrates the importance of landscape and massive architecture in the novel.

There are certain shortcomings in Radcliffe's method: Landscape description strangles action; the visual aspects of the novel have been internalized; and the device of the chase over great stretches of land has been subordinated by mental recapitulation of past scenes—action becomes tableaux. This internal action is slow-moving, tortuously so in a novel of 300,000 words. Critics have also objected to Radcliffe's penchant for a rational explanation of every apparent supernatural phenomenon she has introduced; others, however, point out that Radcliffe's readers enjoyed terror only if they were never forced into surrendering themselves.

The Mysteries of Udolpho brought new energy to the picturesque, the sentimental, and the gothic novel. Radcliffe alternated effectively between the picturesque vagueness of the landscape and the castle's hall of terrors. Her deft handling of sexual feeling, shown as antagonism between Montoni and Emily, is characteristic of her refusal to acknowledge sex overtly except as a frightening nameless power. The artificial terror, heightened sensibility, and pervading air of mystery produced a powerful effect on her readers, yet many felt cheated by her failure to satisfy fully the intense imaginative visions awakened by the book. These readers would have to wait for *The Italian*, probably Radcliffe's finest work and the high-water mark of gothic fiction.

THE ITALIAN

The unity, control, and concentration of *The Italian* display a superb talent. Radcliffe's narrative technique is more sophisticated than at any previous time, particularly in the subtle revelation of the unreliability of feelings based on first impressions rather than on rational judgment. The dramatic pacing remains rigorous throughout and relatively free from digressions. The story's impulse depends on the Marchesa di Vivaldi's refusal to allow her young son, Vincentio, to marry the heroine, Ellena di

Rosalba, whose origins are in doubt. The Marchesa relies on the sinister machinations of her monk-confessor, Schedoni, who decides to murder Ellena. Radcliffe's antipathy to Roman Catholicism is evident in her account of the horrors of the Carmelite abbey and its order, including the labyrinthine vaults and gloomy corridors. A strange blend of fascination and disgust is evoked here and in the scenes of the trial in the halls of the Inquisition, the ruins of the Paluzzi, and in the prison of the Inquisition. Clearly, the gothic aspects of *The Italian* function as representations of a disordered and morally evil past.

The vividness continues through to the climax of the story, when Schedoni, dagger in hand, prepares to murder Ellena but hesitates when he recognizes the portrait miniature she wears. Believing the girl is his lost daughter, he tries to make amends for his crimes. Though the solution involves more complex developments, the excitement of the confrontation between these two figures remains exceptional. Ellena has been a paragon of virtue, displaying piety, sensibility, benevolence, constancy, and a love of nature. To this catalog, Radcliffe adds intelligence, courage, and ingenuity. As an idealized character, Ellena represents the strengths necessary to prevail in the Romantic conflict against external, malign forces.

Schedoni, the devil-priest, is a figure of strong and dangerous sexual desire, associated, as is often the case in Radcliffe's work, with incest. Radcliffe counters the passivity and weakness of Ellena's virtues with this masculine version of desire—the lust of unregulated ambition. She describes him thus:

> There was something terrible in his air, something almost superhuman. . . . His physiognomy . . . bore traces of many passions . . . his eyes were so piercing that they seemed to penetrate at a single glance into the hearts of men, and to read their most secret thoughts.

His pride, greed, and loneliness combine to form a demoniac figure vaguely suggesting John Milton's Satan.

Eino Railo, in *The Haunted Castle* (1964), believes *The Italian* and the central character, Father Schedoni, were created under the revivified Romantic impulse supplied by the tragic monastic figure in Matthew Gregory Lewis's *The Monk* (1796). According to Railo, the difference between Ambrosio and Schedoni is that the latter "is no longer a young and inexperienced saint preserved from temptations, but a person long hardened in the ways of crime and vice, alarmingly gifted and strenuous, hypocritical, unfeeling and merciless." Radcliffe was inspired by Monk Lewis to write a more impressive book than earlier conceived; her bias against sexual and sadistic impulses and toward heightened romantic effect wins out in *The Italian*. While Ambrosio's passions remain tangled and confused by his need for immediate satisfaction and his lack of any lasting goal, Schedoni has well-defined goals for power, wealth, and status. His Machiavellian inclinations blend with pride, melancholy, mystery, and dignity, making him Radcliffe's most fully realized character. Her protest against *The Monk* created a story of tragic quality that goes beyond the conventional gothic paraphernalia and toward the psychological novel.

Radcliffe remains the undisputed master of the gothic novel and a central figure in the gothic revival, beginning in the late 1950's, which has seen the resurrection of hordes of forgotten gothic novelists and their tales. The generous volume of Radcliffe criticism in the second half of the twentieth century has redefined her place in literary history, acknowledging the prodigious sweep of her influence. On first reading her works, one must remember to search behind the genteel exterior of the artistry to discover the special recesses of terror, subconscious conflict, and the psychology of feelings that played a major role in the evolution of dark Romanticism.

Paul J. deGatego

OTHER MAJOR WORKS

POETRY: *The Poems of Ann Radcliffe*, 1816; *St. Alban's Abbey*, 1826.

NONFICTION: *A Journey Made in the Summer of 1794 Through Holland and the Western Frontier of Germany*, 1795.

BIBLIOGRAPHY

Dekker, George. *The Fictions of Romantic Tourism: Radcliffe, Scott, and Mary Shelley.* Stanford, Calif.: Stanford University Press, 2005. Dekker examines novels and travel writing by Radcliffe, Mary Wollstonecraft Shelley, and Sir Walter Scott, showing the connections between the two genres within the broader context of English Romantic literature.

Gordon, Scott Paul. "Ann Radcliffe's *The Mysteries of Udolpho* and the Practice of Quixotism." In *The Practice of Quixotism: Postmodern Theory and Eighteenth-Century Women's Writing.* New York: Palgrave Macmillan, 2006. Radcliffe's novel is included in this study of how eighteenth century British women writers used quixotic motifs in unexpected ways. Includes bibliographical references and an index.

Kickel, Katherine E. "Seeing Imagining: The Resurgence of a New Theory of Vision in Ann Radcliffe's *The Mysteries of Udolpho.*" In *Novel Notions: Medical Discourse and the Mapping of the Imagination in Eighteenth-Century English Fiction.* New York: Routledge, 2007. Kickel describes how fiction by Radcliffe and other eighteenth century English writers reflected new medical discoveries about the area of the brain that spurred the imagination. Kickel argues that these authors similarly sought to map the area of the brain that was responsible for imagination by creating narrators who reflect on the process of writing.

McIntyre, Clara Frances. *Ann Radcliffe in Relation to Her Time.* 1920. Reprint. New York: Archon Books, 1970. A dated but still useful study of Radcliffe that reviews the facts of her life and surveys her work. Presents contemporary evaluations of her novels, considers their sources, and lists translations and dramatizations of them.

Miles, Robert. *Ann Radcliffe: The Great Enchantress.* New York: St. Martin's Press, 1995. Explores the historical and aesthetic context of Radcliffe's fiction, with separate chapters on her early works and mature novels. Miles also considers Radcliffe's role as a woman writer and her place in society. Includes notes and a bibliography.

Murray, E. B. *Ann Radcliffe.* New York: Twayne, 1972. Surveys Radcliffe's life, drawing from *A Journey Made in the Summer of 1794 Through Holland and the Western Frontier of Germany* to illustrate her novels' geography. Examines the background of the gothic, with its supernatural elements, sentiment and sensibility, and sense of the sublime and the picturesque. Includes notes, a selected annotated bibliography, and an index.

Norton, Rictor. *Mistress of Udolpho: The Life of Ann Radcliffe*. London: Leicester University Press, 1999. Norton provides a comprehensive account of Radcliffe's life, including her background as a dissenting Unitarian, and places her novels within the context of her life. Includes a bibliography, notes, an index, and illustrations.

Rogers, Deborah D., ed. *The Critical Response to Ann Radcliffe*. Westport, Conn.: Greenwood Press, 1994. A compilation of contemporary criticism of Radcliffe's individual novels, as well as general criticism published from 1798 until 1899 and written by such authors as Samuel Taylor Coleridge, William Hazlitt, and Sir Walter Scott. Also includes fourteen critical articles published during the twentieth century, including pieces by William Dean Howells and Virginia Woolf.

Smith, Nelson C. *The Art of the Gothic: Ann Radcliffe's Major Novels*. New York: Arno Press, 1980. Contains a valuable introduction that reviews the scholarship on Radcliffe between 1967 and 1980. Analyzes the narrative techniques used to craft the gothic tale and surveys the gothic writers who followed Radcliffe. Includes end notes for each chapter and a bibliography.

Tooley, Brenda. "Gothic Utopia: Heretical Sanctuary in Ann Radcliffe's *The Italian*." In *Gender and Utopia in the Eighteenth Century: Essays in English and French Utopian Writing*, edited by Nicole Pohl and Brenda Tooley. Burlington, Vt.: Ashgate, 2007. Tooley's analysis of Radcliffe's novel is included in a study of the representation of women in eighteenth century utopian literature. Includes a list of works cited and an index.

AYN RAND

Born: St. Petersburg, Russia; February 2, 1905
Died: New York, New York; March 6, 1982
Also known as: Alisa (Alice) Zinovievna Rosenbaum

PRINCIPAL LONG FICTION

We the Living, 1936
Anthem, 1938 (revised 1946)
The Fountainhead, 1943
Atlas Shrugged, 1957
The Early Ayn Rand: A Selection from Her Unpublished Fiction, 1984 (Leonard Peikoff, editor)

OTHER LITERARY FORMS

In addition to her three novels and one novelette, Ayn Rand published a play and several philosophical disquisitions. An early critique, *Hollywood: American Movie City*, was published in the Soviet Union in 1926 without Rand's permission.

ACHIEVEMENTS

Ayn Rand won the Volpe Cup at the Venice Film Festival in 1942 for the Italian motion-picture dramatization of *We the Living*, a novel about the failures of the Soviet system. She was awarded an honorary degree, a doctor of humane letters, by Lewis and Clark College in Portland, Oregon, in 1963, but this sole award does not reflect the significance of her influence on America's philosophical and political economic thought.

BIOGRAPHY

Ayn Rand was born Alisa (Alice) Zinovievna Rosenbaum, the eldest of three children, into a Russian Jewish middle-class family in czarist Russia. When her father's pharmacy was nationalized following the Bolshevik Revolution of 1917, Rand, who had been writing stories since she was nine, found a calling: She turned against collectivism, and she elevated individualism—personal, economic, political, and moral—into a philosophy that eventually attracted a large, occasionally distinguished, following. Early in her career she declared herself to be an atheist.

At the University of Petrograd (now St. Petersburg), Rand studied philosophy, English, and history, graduating with highest honors in history in 1924. By then the works of French writers Victor Hugo and Edmond Rostand, and of Polish writer Henryk Sienkiewicz, had inspired her passion for the heroic and the ideal. Fyodor Dostoevski and Friedrich Nietzsche also left their mark.

Unhappy because the Soviet system was not moving in the direction of her republican ideals and because she had a dead-end job, Rand accepted an invitation from relatives and went to Chicago in 1926. It was while in the United States that she restyled herself Ayn Rand, and within a few months moved to Hollywood, California.

Working as a film extra, a file clerk, and a waiter and doing other odd jobs from 1926 to 1934, Rand perfected her language skills and became a screenwriter at various motion-picture studios. In 1937, she worked as an unpaid typist for Eli Jacques Kahn, a well-known New York architect, in preparation for her first major novel, *The Fountainhead*. Given her early experience in totalitarian Russia, Rand soon became known as the most driven of American anticommunists. She had acquired U.S. citizenship in 1931. In 1947, she appeared as a "friendly witness" before the House Committee on Un-American Activities (HUAC) during the period of the communist witch-hunts—an action she later admitted regretting. Along the way, in 1929, Rand married Charles Francis (Frank) O'Connor, a minor actor and amateur painter. He died in 1979.

After her major literary successes, Rand devoted herself exclusively to philosophizing, writing, and lecturing. She spoke on numerous Ivy League university campuses. She became a regular at the Ford Hall Forum and a columnist for the *Los Angeles Times*. She was coeditor or contributor to several philosophical publications. She was active in the Nathaniel Branden Institute, created to spread her philosophy of objectivism, until her personal and professional break with Nathaniel and Barbara Branden in 1968. This triangular relationship had played an important part in Rand's life, because the Brandens formed the nucleus of a close group of followers, ironically known as the collective.

Rand, a chain smoker whose loaded cigarette holder had become a symbol of her persona, was diagnosed with lung cancer in her seventies. She died in March, 1982, in the New York City apartment in which she had lived since 1951. Her wake was attended by hundreds of people, including Alan Greenspan, an early Rand devotee and later chair of the Federal Reserve Board Bank. Philosopher Leonard Peikoff, Rand's intellectual and legal heir, also was present.

Rand's publications have sold well over twenty million copies in English and in translation even as literary critics generally dismissed her ideas as reactionary propaganda or pop philosophy. Rand was a paradox. She was a writer of romantic fiction whose ideas were often taken seriously, but she was also a controversial individualist and a contrarian who defied the moral, political, social, and aesthetic norms of her times.

ANALYSIS

In her two major works of fiction, Ayn Rand explicated her philosophy of objectivism in dramatic form. Thus, in *The Fountainhead* and especially in *Atlas Shrugged*, Rand argues that reality exists independent of human thought (objectively), that reason is the only viable method for understanding reality, that individuals should seek personal happiness and exist for their own sake and that of no other, and that individuals should not sacrifice themselves or be sacrificed by others. Furthermore, unrestricted laissez-faire capitalism is the political economic system in which these principles can best flourish. Underlying this essence is the philosophy of unadulterated individualism, personal responsibility, the power of unsullied reason, and the importance of Rand's special kind of morality.

In her long fiction, the philosopher-novelist spells out her concept of the exceptional individual as a heroic being and an "ideal man," with "his" happiness as the highest moral purpose in life, with productive achievement the noblest activity, and reason the only absolute. Rand advocates minimal government intrusion and no initiation of physical force in human interactions. She represents such a system as enshrining the highest degree of morality and justice.

Because Rand also focuses on the denial of self-sacrifice and altruism, a staple of conventional morality and welfarism, she opposes both Christianity and communism. She finds it irrational to place the good of others ahead of one's own rational self-interest. Likewise, she denies mysticism and promotes the Aristotelian view that the world that individuals perceive is reality, and there is no other. Both her major novels can be considered elitist and antidemocratic in that they extol the virtues of a few innovative, far-thinking individuals over the mediocre majority, which is either ignorant and uncaring or, even worse, actively striving to destroy the brilliant individuals of great ability. Besides disparaging mediocrity, Rand also decried the power of connections, conformity with what has been done before, a trend she found far too evident in the American welfare state, and the intellectual bankruptcy she deemed it to have fostered.

Rand considered herself a practitioner of Romanticism, who was concerned with representing individuals "in whom certain human attributes are focused more sharply and consistently than in average human beings." Accordingly, in both these novels the characters of the heroes, sharply drawn, are idealized creations—not depictions of real individuals—who are in control of their own destinies despite major odds.

THE FOUNTAINHEAD

The Fountainhead is the story of Howard Roark, Rand's ideal man, an architect who has a vision of how buildings should really be designed. He is innovative and efficient; he also has a strong aesthetic sense and has integrity—in short, he is a man of principle and artistic individuality. Roark is contrasted with Peter Keating, a former classmate and fellow architect but a "second-hander," constantly replicating conventional styles because he has no originality of his own. He achieves a seeming success by manipulating others. Unlike Roark, whom he envies, Keating does not know who he really is.

Another of Roark's adversaries is Ellsworth Toohey. He writes a column for the *Banner*, arguing that architecture should reflect the art of the people. Gail Wynand is the *Banner*'s owner and newspaper magnate; he appreciates Roark's creativity but buckles under societal pressures, disregards his vision, and thereby engineers his own downfall as a worthy human being.

The love interest is embodied in Dominique Francon, the daughter of Guy Francon, the principal owner of the architectural firm that employs Peter Keating. She is a typical Rand heroine, a self-reliant idealist alienated by

Ayn Rand. (Library of Congress)

the shallow conventions of her day in interwar America and convinced that a life of principle is impossible in a world ruled by mediocrity. Her affair with Roark is motivated not by physical or emotional passion but by the recognition that he is a man of great worth. Along the way, in between and sometimes during other affairs, she marries Keating and then Wynand before finally marrying Roark. Dominique seems inconsistent in her ideals, attitudes, and critiques of architectural designs, but the inconsistencies are all part of her effort to spare Roark from ultimate destruction.

Roark, long professionally unsuccessful because he is unwilling to compromise the integrity of his creations, preferring not to work at all or to do menial tasks, eventually overcomes not only financial difficulties but also numerous intrigues by the likes of Keating. For instance, through the mean-spirited Toohey, Roark is assigned to build an interdenominational temple for a patron, Hopton Stoddard, a traditionalist who is abroad at the time. Toohey knows that Stoddard will hate Roark's radically innovative design. Roark makes the building's centerpiece Dominique's nude figure. Toohey incites public condemnation and persuades the patron to sue Roark for breach of contract. Stoddard wins the case, as Roark fails to defend himself in court.

Paradoxically, a friendship develops between Roark and Wynand, attracted to each other for different reasons. Wynand helps Roark in his defense at a second trial, which follows Roark's dynamiting a low-income housing project that Keating had commissioned. The latter had agreed not to alter Roark's design in any way in exchange for Roark's allowing Keating to claim credit for the former's innovative and cost-effective blueprint. When Keating fails to keep his promise and adulterates the design, Roark, with Dominique Francon's assistance, destroys the structure. The trial gives Roark the opportunity to spell out his—that is, Rand's—defense of ethical egoism and opposition to a world perishing from an "orgy of self-sacrifice" and conventional morality. After Roark's exoneration, Wynand commissions him to build the tallest skyscraper in New York City despite Wynand's losing Dominique to Roark.

Ultimately, *The Fountainhead* is a novel of ideas, of heroic characters who are the fountainhead of human progress and of their opposites, who live secondhand, second-rate lives and constantly seek social approval for their beliefs. The philosophy in the novel alternates with the action, and neither can be understood without the other.

ATLAS SHRUGGED

Rand's philosophy extolling the myth of absolute, rugged individualism and its relationship to society is most fully explicated in what proved to be her last work of fiction, several years in the making: the twelve-hundred-page *Atlas Shrugged*. In this novel, Rand tries to answer the question raised by one of her earlier heroes: "What would happen to the world without those who do, think, work, produce?" In this apocalyptic parable, it is John Galt of Twentieth Century Motors, a physicist, engineer, inventor, and philosopher, who is Rand's ideal man and leads the other "men of the mind" on a strike against the exploitation of the genuine creators of wealth by all the leeches and parasites—the nonproducers—whom they had been sustaining.

Rand's philosophy is played out through the stories

of the four heroes, the authentic moneymakers. They are the Argentine Francisco d'Anconia, heir to the world's leading copper enterprise; the Scandinavian Ragnar Danneskjold, a onetime philosopher who turns pirate in order to steal wealth back from the looters and return it to the producers of legitimate values; Henry (Hank) Rearden, an American steel magnate and inventor of a metal better than steel; and finally, the other American, John Galt, who, with the others, stops the ideological motor of the world in a strike before rebuilding society. The heroine, rail heir Dagny Taggart, wonders where the individuals of ability have gone.

Confronting them is an array of villains, manipulative appropriators, enemies of individualism and free enterprise, scabs, and moochers profiting from the achievements of the producers and united by their greed for unearned gains. Especially, there is Dr. Robert Stadler, the counterpart of Gail Wynand in *The Fountainhead*. Stadler, once the greatest physicist of his time, fully cognizant of the value of the human mind, fails to stand up for his principles. The progressive decay of James Taggart, Dagny's brother and the titular president of Taggart Transcontinental Railroad, parallels that of the society in which he lives.

In the novel, set some time in the vaguely defined future, the United States is following Europe down the long, hopeless path of socialism, government regulation, and a predatory state into a new Dark Age. The heroes join forces with other intelligent, freedom-loving leaders of commerce, industry, science, and philosophy to reverse the slide. They do this as Atlas may have done had he grown tired of holding the world on his shoulders without reward.

Eventually, the heroes repair to a secret Colorado mountain citadel, where they wait for their time to rebuild the decaying collectivist society whose end their "strike of the mind" against productive work is hastening. Galt, arrested and tortured by the looters but finally freed by the other heroes, delivers a thirty-five-thousand-word oration via a commandeered radio, epitomizing Rand's objectivism and views of the ideal man. Galt's (Rand's) philosophy then becomes that of the new society: "I swear by my life and my love of it that I will never live for the sake of another man, nor ask another man to live for mine." By the end of the novel, socialism has produced a bankrupt world pleading for the return of the men of the mind, who, after a confrontation with the parasites, start to rebuild society. *Atlas Shrugged* is Rand's most thorough exploration of the social ramifications of politics, economics, psychology, metaphysics, epistemology, aesthetics, religion, and ethics.

Peter B. Heller

OTHER MAJOR WORKS

PLAYS: *Night of January 16th*, pr. 1934 (also known as *Woman on Trial* and *Penthouse Legend*); *The Unconquered*, pr. 1940 (adaptation of her novel *We the Living*).

SCREENPLAY: *The Fountainhead*, 1949.

NONFICTION: *For the New Intellectual: The Philosophy of Ayn Rand*, 1961; *The Virtue of Selfishness: A New Concept of Egoism*, 1964; *Capitalism: The Unknown Ideal*, 1966; *Introduction to Objectivist Epistemology*, 1967, second enlarged edition, 1990 (Harry Binswanger and Leonard Peikoff, editors); *The Romantic Manifesto*, 1969; *The New Left: The Anti-Industrial Revolution*, 1971; *Philosophy: Who Needs It?*, 1982; *The Ayn Rand Lexicon: Objectivism from A to Z*, 1984 (Peikoff, editor); *The Voice of Reason: Essays in Objectivist Thought*, 1988 (Peikoff, editor); *The Ayn Rand Column*, 1991; *Letters of Ayn Rand*, 1995 (Michael S. Berliner, editor); *Journals of Ayn Rand*, 1997 (David Harriman, editor); *The Art of Fiction: A Guide for Writers and Readers*, 2000 (Tore Boeckmann, editor); *The Art of Nonfiction: A Guide for Writers and Readers*, 2001 (Robert Mayhew, editor); *Ayn Rand Answers: The Best of Her Q and A*, 2005 (Mayhew, editor).

MISCELLANEOUS: *The Objectivist Newsletter*, 1962-1965 (later known as *The Objectivist*, 1966-1971, edited by Rand); *The Ayn Rand Letter*, 1971-1976 (published by Rand).

BIBLIOGRAPHY

Baker, James T. *Ayn Rand*. Boston: Twayne, 1987. A brief introductory overview of Rand's life and work, written in an objective and highly readable style. Includes a chronology, references, a bibliography, and an index.

Branden, Nathaniel. *My Years with Ayn Rand*. Reprint. San Francisco, Calif.: Jossey-Bass, 1999. A personal account by Rand's disciple, organizer, spokesman, lover, and, ultimately, enemy. Includes photographs and an index. Originally published in 1989 as *Judgment Day: My Years with Ayn Rand*.

Branden, Nathaniel, and Barbara Branden. *Who Is Ayn Rand?* New York: Random House, 1962. This book contains three essays on objectivism's moral philosophy, its connection to psychological theory, and a literary study of Rand's methods in her fiction. It contains an additional biographical essay, tracing Rand's life from birth to her mid-fifties.

Britting, Jeff. *Ayn Rand*. Woodstock, N.Y.: Overlook Press, 2005. A readable biography of Rand's literary and personal life but lacking in scholarly analysis.

Gladstein, Mimi Reisel. *The New Ayn Rand Companion*. Rev. and expanded ed. Westport, Conn.: Greenwood Press, 1999. Provides biographical information, a summary of Rand's fiction and nonfiction, information about her characters, criticism of her writing, and a comprehensive bibliography. This revised edition contains newly discovered information about Rand's posthumous publications, updated biographical data, and summaries of books and articles published since her death.

Gladstein, Mimi Reisel, and Chris Matthew Sciabarra, eds. *Feminist Interpretations of Ayn Rand*. University Park: Pennsylvania State University Press, 1999. Collection of essays examining Rand's life and work from a feminist perspective. Includes pieces by cultural critics Susan Brownmiller and Camile Paglia and analysis of *Atlas Shrugged*.

Peikoff, Leonard. *Objectivism: The Philosophy of Ayn Rand*. New York: Dutton, 1991. A comprehensive overview of objectivist philosophy, written by the philosopher who was closest to Rand during her lifetime. Includes a discussion of Rand's ideas about reason, the good, virtue, happiness, government, art, and capitalism.

Pierpont, Claudia Roth. *Passionate Minds: Women Rewriting the World*. New York: Alfred A. Knopf, 2000. Evocative, interpretive essays on the life paths and works of twelve women, including Rand, connecting the circumstances of their lives with the shapes, styles, subjects, and situations of their art.

Sciabarra, Chris M. *Ayn Rand: The Russian Radical*. University Park: Pennsylvania State University Press,

1995. Sciabarra charts the evolution of the author as a philosopher, of her dialectics, and of her philosophy, beginning with her early years. Includes a bibliography and photographs.

Younkins, Edward W., ed. *Ayn Rand's "Atlas Shrugged": A Philosophical and Literary Companion.* Burling-ton, Vt.: Ashgate, 2007. Collection of essays discussing *Atlas Shrugged* as a work of literature and philosophy. Includes discussions of the novel's ideas about aesthetics, economics, and human relationships, the novel as a work of science fiction, and its characterization.

RAJA RAO

Born: Hassan, Mysore, India; November 8, 1908
Died: Austin, Texas; July 8, 2006

PRINCIPAL LONG FICTION

Kanthapura, 1938
The Serpent and the Rope, 1960
The Cat and Shakespeare: A Tale of India, 1965
Comrade Kirillov, 1976
The Chessmaster and His Moves, 1988
On the Ganga Ghat, 1989

OTHER LITERARY FORMS

For his first efforts as a writer, Raja Rao (row) wrote in Kannada, his mother tongue. From 1931 through 1933, he published three essays and a poem in Kannada in the journal *Jaya Karnataka*. Around that time, he also began to publish his earliest stories in English. These and others were collected and published as *The Cow of the Barricades, and Other Stories* in 1947. A later collection, *The Policeman and the Rose* (1978), includes seven stories published in the earlier volume and three new ones written chiefly during the 1960's. In addition to novels and short stories, Rao published essays, travelogues, and biographical sketches in various journals and popular magazines, some of which were collected in *The Meaning of India* (1996). Rao also coedited, with Iqbal Singh, two anthologies of essays on India: *Changing India* (1939) and *Whither India?* (1948). In addition, after more than a decade of work, he completed a towering spiritual biography of Mohandas Gandhi, *The Great Indian Way: A Life of Mahatma Gandhi* (1998).

ACHIEVEMENTS

Raja Rao, with Mulk Raj Anand and R. K. Narayan, is generally regarded as one of the most important modern Indian English novelists. The reasons for his preeminence are both historical and artistic. Rao is important historically because his first novel, *Kanthapura*, was published during the decade of the 1930's, when Indian English fiction first began to gain recognition. Although the Indian English novel is considered to have begun in 1878 with Toru Dutt's incomplete romance *Bianca: Or, The Young Spanish Maiden*, it was in the 1930's that Indian English fiction began to demonstrate maturity and accomplishment with the publication of Anand's *Untouchable* (1935), Narayan's *Swami and Friends* (1935), and Rao's *Kanthapura*.

Artistically, Rao is important because of his unique formal and thematic accomplishments. Although his productivity may seem meager in comparison to Anand's or Narayan's, Rao's achievement was considerable. Formally and stylistically, he was the most adventurous of the three. As M. K. Naik has noted, Rao consistently tried to adapt the Western form of the novel to suit his Indian subject matter. He used traditional Indian genres such as Purana, *sthalakatha*, and the Indian beast fable to structure his works. Thus, formally, his novels are based on Indian models. Furthermore, they are written in an English that is uniquely Indian in style, tone, mood, and rhythm. This Indianness of style is achieved through heavy reliance on translation, quotation, and the use of Indian proverbs, idioms, and colloquial patterns. Rao adroitly manipulates vocabulary and syntax to enhance the Indian flavoring of his English. The result is a style that, although distinctly Indian, is evocative and perfectly intelligible to Western readers as well.

Thematically also Rao is somewhat different from the other two major Indian English novelists, Anand and Narayan. Rao is a metaphysical novelist whose concerns are primarily religious and philosophical. *Kanthapura*, for example, shows a strong Gandhian influence as it documents the progress of a nonviolent agitation against the British in a remote South Indian village. *The Serpent and the Rope* and its sequel, *The Cat and Shakespeare*, are expositions of the ancient Indian philosophical outlook Vedanta. *Comrade Kirillov* is an evaluation of the efficacy of communism. In Rao's works there is thus an ongoing discussion of major philosophical systems, chiefly of India but also of the West.

Both stylistically and thematically, then, Rao succeeds in capturing the spirit of India in his works. His formal and stylistic innovations have expanded the expressive range of English and have influenced other writers who share Rao's predicament: the task of writing about a culture in a language that is not native to it. Rao was awarded the Sahitya Akademi Prize for 1964 by the Academy of Indian Literature. In 1969, he received the Padma Bhushan from the Indian government. In 1988, at the age of seventy-nine, Rao was awarded the tenth Neustadt International Prize for Literature, a $50,000 prize given biennially by the University of Oklahoma's prestigious international literary quarterly, *World Literature Today*, to recognize a body of work and a lifetime of literary excellence by a writer of any genre from any culture. Rao was the first Asian so honored. In January, 2007, Rao was awarded posthumously the Padma Vibhushan, India's second-highest civilian award, given for exceptional service to the Indian people.

BIOGRAPHY

Raja Rao was born into a respected Brahman family in Hassan, South India, the eldest son in a family of two brothers and seven sisters. His father taught Kannada at Nizam's College in the neighboring state of Hyderabad. The earliest influence on young Rao was his grandfather, with whom he stayed both in Hassan and in Harihalli while his father was in Hyderabad. Rao inherited a spiri-

tual orientation from his grandfather; his preoccupation stayed with Rao throughout his life and is evident in all his work.

Rao joined his father in Hyderabad when it was time for him to attend high school. After high school, he was sent to Aligarh Muslim University in North India. These Aligarh days proved to be crucial in shaping Rao's intellectual growth. Under the influence of Eric Dickinson, a minor poet and a visiting professor from Oxford, Rao's literary sensibility was awakened. He met other interesting students at Aligarh, such as Ahmed Ali, who became a famous novelist, and Chetan Anand, who became an influential film producer. Rao also began learning French at Aligarh, which contributed to his decision to go to France a few years later. After matriculating in 1927, he returned to Hyderabad to enroll as a student for the B.A. at Nizam's College. Two years later, he graduated, having majored in English and history.

In 1929, two other important events occurred in Rao's life. First, he won the Asiatic Scholarship of the Government of Hyderabad for study abroad. This marked the beginning of a new phase in his life; he left India for the first time to study at the University of Montpellier in France. In that same year, Rao married Camille Mouly, who taught French at Montpellier. Camille was undoubtedly the most important influence on Rao's life during the next ten years. She not only encouraged him to write but also supported him financially for several years. In 1931, his early Kannada writing began to appear in the journal *Jaya Karnataka*. For the next two years, Rao researched the influence of India on Irish literature at the Sorbonne. His short stories were published in journals such as *Asia* (New York) and *Cahiers du Sud* (Paris). In 1933, Rao abandoned research to devote himself completely to writing.

Although he never settled permanently in India, Rao's awareness of Indian culture grew during his stay abroad. He became a compulsive visitor, returning to India again and again for spiritual and cultural nourishment; indeed, in a sense, Rao never completely left India. In 1933, he visited Pandit Taranth's ashram in his quest for self-realization. In 1938, his small masterpiece, *Kanthapura*, although written earlier, was published from London. One year later, Rao's marriage disintegrated; he found himself back in India, his spiritual search renewed. In the next few years, Rao visited a number of ashrams and religious teachers, notably Ramana Maharshi of Tiruvannamalai, Narayana Maharaj of Kedgaon, and Mahatma Gandhi at Sevagram.

Around this time, Rao also became active in several social and political causes. He edited, with Singh, *Changing India*, an anthology of modern Indian thought from Ram Mohan Roy to Nehru that was published in 1939. He participated in the underground Quit India movement of 1942, boldly associating with a group of radical Socialists. In 1943-1944, he coedited with Ali a journal from Bombay (now known as Mumbai) called *Tomorrow*. He was the prime mover in the formation of a cultural organization, Sri Vidya Samiti, devoted to reviving the values of ancient Indian civilization; this organization failed shortly after its inception. In Bombay, Rao was also associated with Chetana, a cultural society for the propagation of Indian culture and values. Finally, in 1943, Rao's quest appears to have been fulfilled when he met his spiritual preceptor in Atmananda Guru of Trivandrum. Rao even thought of settling down there, but he returned to France following the death of his guru.

In 1960, twenty-two years after *Kanthapura*, Rao's masterpiece *The Serpent and the Rope* was published. Its sequel, *The Cat and Shakespeare*, came relatively soon thereafter, in 1965. Eleven years later, *Comrade Kirillov* was published in English, although it had appeared in a French translation, *Le Comrade Kirillov* (1965), much earlier. From 1965 until his retirement in 1980, Rao was professor of philosophy at the University of Texas at Austin, living, despite his growing international reputation as one of the most influential metaphysicians and philosophers of his era, in simplicity in a modest apartment near campus. During his two decades of teaching, Rao relished the challenges of the classroom, introducing students with self-effacing understatement to the complicated vision and sensibilities of the religious temperament. He was known for taking long looping walks with eager students along the campus's miles of bike trails.

In 1965, Rao married Katherine Ann Jones, an American stage actor. They had one son, Christopher Rama. After divorcing Jones in 1984, Rao married Susan Vaught, a former student. That marriage sustained Rao during his postteaching years, which were among his most productive. Despite frail health after several heart attacks, Rao worked until his death at the age of ninety-seven. He left behind a considerable body of manuscripts that—under the editorial direction of the Raja Rao Publication Project of the University of Texas Linguistics Research Center—promises significant works for some time to come, including five novels, a collection of stories, and a vast collection of speeches and correspondence. Perhaps most anticipated is the completion of Rao's massively conceived trilogy that began with the dense and labyrinthine *The Chessmaster and His Moves*. The manuscripts for the two concluding volumes, with the planned titles "The Daughter of the Mountain" and "A Myrobalan in the Palm of Your Hand," are among those under preparation by the Raja Rao Publication Project.

ANALYSIS

An understanding of Raja Rao's art is enhanced by a contextualization of his novels. Although Rao admitted to several Western influences, his work is best understood as a part of the Indian tradition. Rao regarded literature as *Sadhana*, or spiritual discipline; for him, writing was a consequence of his metaphysical life. His novels, hence, essentially represent a quest for the Absolute. From *Kanthapura* to *Comrade Kirillov*, Rao's protagonists grapple with the same concerns: What is Truth? How is one to find it? Their methods vary, as do their results, but they share the same preoccupation. The novels, thus, become chronicles of this archetypal search. Formally, all of his first four novels share certain features. Plot is de-emphasized; the narrative is generally subjective—even idiosyncratic—and episodic. The progression of the narrative is not linear but circular; in the Puranic manner of storytelling, which Rao adapts to the form of the Western novel, there are digressions, stories within stories, songs, philosophical disquisitions, debates, and essays. Characters are also frequently symbolic figures; often, the motivations for their actions might seem puzzling or insufficient. Finally, because the narration is subjective, the language of the narrator also tends to be unique, reflecting the narrator's peculiarities—his or her social, regional, and philosophical makeup.

KANTHAPURA

Rao's first novel, *Kanthapura*, is the story of how a small, sleepy, South Indian village is caught in the whirlpool of the Indian freedom struggle and comes to be completely destroyed. In the foreword, Rao himself indicates that the novel is a kind of *sthala-purana*, or legendary history, which every village in India seems to have. These local *sthala-puranas* are modeled on the ancient Indian Puranas—those compendia of story, fable, myth, religion, philosophy, and politics—among which are the Upa Puranas, which describe holy places and the legends associated with them. Hence, several features of *Kanthapura* are in keeping with the tradition of *sthala-puranas*. The detailed description of the village at the opening of the novel is written in the manner of a *sthala-purana*, wherein the divine origin or association of a place is established.

The village is presided over by Goddess Kenchamma, the *Gramadeveta* (village deity), and the novel provides a legend explaining her presence there, recalling several similar legends found in the Puranas. Like the place-Gods of the Puranas, Kenchamma operates within her jurisdiction, where she is responsible for rains, harvests, and the well-being of the villagers. She cannot extend her protection to other villages or to outsiders. The village deity thus symbolizes local concerns such as famine, cholera, cattle diseases, and poor harvests, which may have little to do with the world outside the village. Like Kenchamma, the river Himavathy also has a special significance in the novel and recalls passages describing famous rivers in the Puranas, such as the description of the river Narmada in Matsya Purana and the Agni Purana.

Similarly, *Kanthapura* shares certain narrative techniques with the Puranas. The story is told rapidly, all in one breath, it would seem, and the style reflects the oral heritage also evident in the Puranas. Like the Puranas, which are digressive and episodic, *Kanthapura* contains digressions such as Pariah Siddiah's exposition on serpent lore. The Puranas contain detailed, poetic descriptions of nature; similarly, *Kanthapura* has several descriptive passages that are so evocative and unified as to be prose poems in themselves. Examples are the coming of Kartik (autumn), daybreak over the Ghats, and the advent of the rains. Finally, the narration of *Kanthapura*

has a simplicity and lack of self-consciousness reminiscent of the Puranas and quite different from the narrative sophistication of contemporary Western novelists such as Virginia Woolf or James Joyce.

Kanthapura is also imbued with a religious spirit akin to that of the Puranas. The epigraph of the novel, taken from the sacred Hindu scripture the Bhagavad Gita (c. fifth century B.C.E.), is the famous explanation of the Hindu notion of incarnation: "Whensoever there is misery and ignorance, I come." The doctrine of incarnation is also central to the Puranas, most of which are descriptive accounts of the avatars of Vishnu. The avatar in *Kanthapura* is Gandhi, whose shadow looms over the whole book, although he is himself not a character. Incarnation, however, is not restricted to one Great Soul, Gandhi, but extends into Kanthapura itself, where Moorthy, who leads the revolt, is the local manifestation of Gandhi and, by implication, of Truth.

Although the form of *Kanthapura* is closely modeled on that of the *sthala-purana*, its style is uniquely experimental. Rao's effort is to capture the flavor and nuance of South Indian rural dialogue in English. He succeeds in this through a variety of stylistic devices. The story is told by Achakka, an old Brahman widow, a garrulous, gossipy storyteller. The sentences are long, frequently running into paragraphs. Such long sentences consist of several short sentences joined by conjunctions (usually "and") and commas; the effect is of breathless, rapid talking. The sentence structure is manipulated for syntactic and rhythmic effect, as in the first sentence of the novel: "Our village—I don't think you have ever heard about it—Kanthapura is its name, and it is in the province of Kara." Repetition is another favorite device used to enhance the colloquial flavor of the narrative. In addition to these techniques, translation from Kannada is repeatedly used. Nicknames such as "Waterfall Venkamma," "Nose-scratching Nanjamma," "Cornerhouse Moorthy" are translated; more important, Kannada idioms and expressions are rendered into English: "You are a traitor to your salt-givers"; "The Don't-touch-the-Government Campaign"; "Nobody will believe such a crow and sparrow story"; and so on. The total effect is the transmutation into English of the total ethos of another culture. *Kanthapura*, with its "Kannadized" English, anticipates the lofty "Sanskritized" style of *The Serpent and the Rope*, which, stylistically, is Rao's highest achievement.

Kanthapura is really a novel about a village rather than about a single individual; nevertheless, Moorthy, the Brahman protagonist of the villagers' struggle against the government, is a prototypal Rao hero. Moorthy is the leader of a political uprising, but for him, as for Gandhi, whom he follows, politics provides a way of life, indistinguishable from a spiritual quest. In fact, for Moorthy, Action is the way to the Absolute. In Gandhi, he finds what is Right Action. Thus, for him, becoming a Gandhi man is a deep spiritual experience that is appropriately characterized by the narrator as a "conversion." At the culmination of this "conversion" is Sankaracharaya's ecstatic chant, "Sivoham, Sivoham. I am Siva. I am Siva. Siva am I," meaning that Moorthy experiences blissful union with the Absolute. Indeed, the chant, which epitomizes the ancient Indian philosophical school of Advaita or unqualified nondualism, is found in all Rao's novels as a symbol of the spiritual goal of his protagonists. Moorthy, the man of action, thus practices Karma Yoga (the Path of Action), one of the ways of reaching the Absolute as enunciated in the Bhaghavad Gita. In the novels after *Kanthapura*, Rao's protagonists, like Moorthy, continue to seek the Absolute, although their methods change.

THE SERPENT AND THE ROPE

Published twenty-two years after *Kanthapura*, *The Serpent and the Rope* is Rao's most ambitious work. If the former is modeled on an Upa Purana (minor Purana), the latter is a kind of Maha Purana (major Purana) or epic; geographically, historically, philosophically, and formally, its sweep is truly epical. The novel includes a variety of settings, ranging from Paris to Ramaswamy's ancestral home in a South Indian village, from European locales such as Aix, Montpalais, Pau, Montpellier, Provence, Cambridge, and London to Indian locales such as Hyderabad, Delhi, Lucknow, Bombay, Bangalore, and Beneras. Rao delves into almost the whole of Indian history, from the invasion of the Aryans to the advent of British rule; European history, chiefly the Albigensian heresy; Chinese history—all of these come under discussion as the protagonist, Rama, a historian by training, expounds his theories in conversations with the leading characters. Philosophically, too, the novel's sweep is formidable: Rao discusses Hinduism, Buddhism, Catholicism, Islam, Daoism, Marxism, Darwinism, and Nazism.

Hence, it is not surprising to find *The Serpent and the Rope* extremely diverse in form as well. Rao quotes from an array of languages, including Sanskrit, Hindi, French, Italian, Latin, and Provençal; only the Sanskrit quotations are translated. There are long interludes and stories, such as Grandmother Lakshamma's story of a princess who became a pumpkin and Ishwara Bhatta's "Story of Rama." In addition, the novel contains songs, myths, legends, and philosophical discussions in the manner of the Puranas. The main narrative, the gradual disintegration of Rama's marriage with his French wife, Madeleine, is thus only a single strand holding a voluminous and diverse book together.

The Serpent and the Rope is an extremely challenging work thematically as well; Savithri's words in the novel sum it up well: It is "a sacred text, a cryptogram, with different meanings at different hierarchies of awareness." It may be approached on at least two different levels, the literal and the symbolic, although the two usually operate simultaneously. On the literal level of plot, the novel may appear puzzling and unsatisfying. The crux is: Why does the marriage of Rama and Madeleine disintegrate? Critics have attempted various answers, ranging from incompatibility between the Indian Rama and the French Madeleine to Rama's infidelity. Although such answers are plausible, they do not satisfy completely because these reasons are not perceived by the characters themselves. Rama and Madeleine are both aware of the growing rift between them, but they do not attempt to bridge it on a practical level. Instead, both watch the dissolution of the union with an almost fatalistic helplessness. Similarly, it is hard to understand why Rama seeks fulfillment in other women while averring his love for Madeleine at the same time, or why he never tells her of his affairs in spite of his claim that he keeps no secrets from her.

Rama, the narrator, does not answer such questions; he only chronicles the breakdown of the relationship, almost impersonally, as if there were little he could do to save it. He also does not feel himself responsible for having affairs with other women, one of which involves a ritual second marriage, while being married to

Madeleine at the same time. What is lacking, then, is an adequate motivation for the actions of the characters, something that most readers are conditioned to expect from a novel. Perhaps a better approach, however, instead of asking of the novel something that it did not intend to give, is to consider what it does clearly provide; indeed, questions that appear unresolved on the literal level are resolved more satisfactorily on the symbolic level.

Rama, the Brahman hero, is a seeker of Truth both by birth and by vocation (a Brahman is one who seeks Brahma, or the Absolute). As an Indian scholar in France, Rama is seeking Truth in the form of the missing link in the puzzle of India's influence on the West. According to Rama, this missing link is the Albigensian heresy: He thinks that the Cathers were driven to heresy by the influence of Buddhism, which had left India. Rama's quest for Truth is also manifested in his search for the ideal woman, because in the Hindu tradition, the union of husband and wife is symbolic of the union of man and God. The marriage of Siva and Parvathi is one such paradigmatic union in which Siva, the Absolute, the abstract, the ascetic, is wedded to Parvthi, the human, the concrete, the possessor of the earth. Another such union is that between the mythical Savithri and her husband Satyavan (*Satya* means "Truth"); Savithri, through her devotion, restores her dead husband to life.

In keeping with these paradigms, Rama—the thinker, the meditator, the seeker of Truth—can find fulfillment only in a Parvathi or a Savithri, who can bring him back to earth by her devotion. Madeleine, however, who has given up her Catholicism for Buddhism, becomes an ascetic, renouncing the earth, denying her body through abstinence and penance. Significantly, her union with Rama is barren: Both their children are stillborn. Madeleine also regards Truth as something outside herself, something that has to be striven for in order to be realized. Her dualism is the philosophical opposite of Rama's nondualism; Rama believes, following the Advaita Vedanta, that the self is a part of Truth, as the wave is a part of the sea, and that all separateness is illusion, like the illusion in which a rope is mistaken for a serpent.

Rama's true mate is an Indian undergraduate at Cambridge named, interestingly, Savithri. Savithri, despite her modishness—she dances to jazz music, smokes, wears Western clothes, and so on—is essentially an Indian. Unlike Madeleine, Savithri does not seek Truth; rather, instinctively and unselfconsciously, she *is* Truth. Her union with Rama is thus a natural and fulfilling one. Savithri, however, like Rama's sister Saroja, opts for an arranged marriage in the traditional Indian manner with someone else; hence, her relationship with Rama is never consummated. At the end of the book, Rama, divorced from Madeleine, sees a vision of his guru in Travancore and plans to leave France for India.

Rama's path to Truth, unlike Moorthy's Karma Yoga, is Jnana Yoga (the Path of Knowledge), also enunciated in the Bhaghavad Gita. Rama is not a man of action but an intellectual. Although he has accumulated knowledge, he still does not apprehend Truth clearly; like the deluded seeker in the fable, he mistakes the rope for the serpent, failing to see himself already united with Truth as Savithri is. Traditionally, a guru is necessary for the Jnana Yogi because only a guru can cure his delusion by *showing* him that what appears to be a serpent is really a rope. Thus, in the end, Rama resolves to seek his guru to be cured of his delusion.

THE CAT AND SHAKESPEARE

The Cat and Shakespeare, described by Rao as "a metaphysical comedy," clearly shows a strong formal Upanishadic influence. The spiritual experiences of its narrator, Ramakrishna Pai, are reminiscent of the illuminative passages in the Chandogya Upanishad that describe the experience of the Infinite. The dialogues in the novel are also Upanishadic in their question-and-answer patterns; the best example is the conversation between Govindan Nair and Lakshmi in the brothel. Nair's metaphysical speculations—such as "Is there seeing first or the object first?"—seem to be modeled on philosophical queries in the Upanishads. The cat links the novel to the Indian beast fable, and Nair's comic roguery shows similarities to the rogue fable in the Panchatantra. The major Western debt is to William Shakespeare, who is acknowledged in the title. Shakespeare is a symbol for the universal; according to Rao, Shakespeare's vision transcends duality and arrives at a unified view of the universe. There are numerous allusions to Shakespeare's play *Hamlet, Prince of Denmark* (pr. c. 1600-1601) in the novel, culminating in the "rat-trap episode" in which a cat is trapped in a large rat trap; this prompts

Nair to deliver a parody of *Hamlet* that begins: "A kitten sans cat, that is the question."

The Cat and Shakespeare is Rao's sequel to *The Serpent and the Rope* in that it shows what happens after a seeker's veil of illusion has been removed by the guru. Its theme may be summed up in Hamlet's words to Horatio toward the end of the play: "There's a divinity that shapes our ends,/ Roughhew them how we will." A similar view of grace is embodied in the novel in what Nair, the man who is united to Truth, calls "the way of the Cat." The "way of the Cat" is simply the notion that just as the kitten is carried by the scruff of its neck by the mother cat, the human being is completely at the mercy of the divine; consequently, the only way to live is to surrender oneself totally to divine grace, as the helpless kitten surrenders itself to the mother cat. Nair lives this philosophy and is responsible for teaching it to his ignorant neighbor, the narrator Pai. Pai is like the innocent hunter in the story who unknowingly heaped leaves on Siva and was rewarded with a vision.

Between Pai's house and Nair's is a wall over which Nair leaps every time he visits Pai. The wall is an important symbol because it represents the division between illusion and Truth. Nair crosses it easily, but Pai has never gone across. Toward the end of the novel, following Nair's cat, Pai accidentally crosses the wall. Like the lucky hunter, he also is vouchsafed a divine vision: For the first time, Pai sees the whole universe as a unity. The novel ends with Pai's spiritual as well as material fulfillment, as he has partially realized his lifelong ambition of owning a three-story house. *The Cat and Shakespeare*, although not as ambitious as *The Serpent and the Rope*, is as successful on its own terms. The novel is an elaborate puzzle that the author challenges the reader to solve; a solution is not only possible at all levels, but is completely satisfying as well. The way to the Absolute here is not the Karma Yoga or Jnana Yoga of the two previous novels, but Bhakti Yoga, or the Path of Devotion. The seeker recognizes himself as completely dependent on divine grace for his salvation and surrenders himself to the Benevolent Mother like a trusting kitten.

COMRADE KIRILLOV

Comrade Kirillov, published in English in 1976, is generally recognized as Rao's least ambitious novel; it is clearly a minor work compared with its three illustrious predecessors. Formally, it is an extended *vyakti-chitra*, or character sketch, a popular genre in Indian regional literature. The main story, narrated by one "R," is a mere ninety-three pages in large type, to which are appended twenty-seven pages of the diary of Kirillov's wife, Irene, and a concluding seven pages by the narrator; the effect is of a slight, sketchy novella.

Kirillov, alias Padmanabha Iyer, leaves India for California to propagate Theosophy but, after a period of disillusionment, becomes a Communist. From California, he moves to London, where, marrying a Czech immigrant, Irene, he settles down to the life of an expatriate intellectual. Like Rao's other protagonists, Kirillov starts as a seeker of Truth, but after he becomes a Communist he is increasingly revealed by the narrator to be caught in a system that curtails his access to Truth. Kirillov thus continuously rationalizes the major events in the world to suit his perspective. Nevertheless, following a visit to India several years after he has left, he realizes that his Communism is only a thin upper layer in an essentially Indian psyche. Irene also recognizes in her diary that he is almost biologically an Indian Brahman, and only intellectually a Marxist. By the end of the book, Kirillov is shown to be a man of contradictions: attacking and worshiping Gandhi simultaneously, deeply loving traditional India but campaigning for a Communist revolution, reciting Sanskrit *shlokas* but professing Communism.

The narrator is Kirillov's intellectual opposite, an adherent of Advaita Vedanta. There are numerous interesting discussions on Communism in the book, which has great value as a social document, capturing the life of an Indian expatriate intellectual between 1920 and 1950. Also of interest is Kirillov's relationship with Irene, which recalls Rama's relationship with Madeleine. Numerous similarities aside, this relationship is more successful: This marriage lasts, and the couple has a child, Kamal. Soon after Kirillov's return from India, however, Irene dies in childbirth, followed by her newborn daughter. Kirillov leaves for Moscow and is last heard of in Peking. The novel ends with the narrator taking Kamal, now in India, to Kanyakumari. Despite its humor, pathos, and realism, *Comrade Kirillov* falls short of Rao's three previous novels.

It is interesting to note that *Comrade Kirillov*, first

published in a French translation in 1965, was written earlier. Thematically, it represents the stage of negation before the spiritual fulfillment of *The Cat and Shakespeare*. Kirillov, as a Communist and atheist, has negated the Karma Yoga of *Kanthapura* and the Jnana Yoga of *The Serpent and the Rope* by denying the existence of the Absolute; thus, his quest results in failure. The Bhakti Yoga of *The Cat and Shakespeare*, especially in the character of Nair, is the culmination of the various stages of spiritual realization in the earlier novels. Nair is the first character in Rao's novels who does not merely seek Truth but who has found it and actually practices it.

THE CHESSMASTER AND HIS MOVES

The Chessmaster and His Moves, with its ambitious, daunting scale (it is actually three interrelated novellas that combined have more than one hundred named characters, take place on three different continents, and draw on both Eastern and Western religious philosophies), uses the apparatus of fiction to serve as occasion for a metaphysical investigation into the pilgrim road to Absolute Truth itself. Although during the last years of his life Rao completed the manuscripts of the other two volumes of the planned trilogy of which this novel is the beginning, *The Chessmaster and His Moves* can serve as a fitting capstone to Rao's lifelong investigation into the meaning of Truth in a world obsessed with the satisfactions of the carnal and the contentment of self. That intricate play of ideas inevitably recalls the towering novels of ideas of earlier philosopher-writers such as Fyodor Dostoevski, Thomas Mann, and particularly Herman Hesse. Indeed, it was on the strength of this work that Rao received the Neustadt Prize.

What plot Rao offers here—a series of relationships between an Indian academic and a succession of women—serves to test alternate visions of Truth, each of the women representing a facet of humanity's struggle to move beyond the limits of the flesh and the immediate (and its inevitable dissatisfactions and devastating pain) and to begin the difficult exploration of the interior that alone leads to Truth. Rao tests physical love and emotional love but ultimately endorses spiritual love—that is, love that rejects the compelling urge of others to set about deepening the perception of the soul. Rao uses the metaphor of chess (itself an Indian game) to suggest this

movement—within Rao's spiritualism, the travails of humanity are the subtle game moves of the Brahman-God, the Creator, designed to enable humanity to grow inwardly.

Sivarama (Siva) Sastri, the book's central character, is a brilliant if spiritually shallow mathematician living in Paris. Like Rao, Siva is a Brahman, part of the Indian diaspora, and struggles in vain to achieve Truth largely because he is seeking truth in his fascination with numbers (which appear to him reliable in their objectivity) and in his need for women (most notably a tumultuous affair with Jaya, a married woman, and his eventual marriage to a mysterious Frenchwoman, Suzanne Chantereux, who has apparently cured herself of tuberculosis through meditation but whose only child, developmentally disabled, died young). There is also Siva's sister, Uma Ramachandra, unable to have children and desperately unhappy about it.

Rao clearly develops the tension between the troubles and disappointments of the horizontal and the call of the spiritual. Amid this exploration of the troubling world of the immediate is an ongoing discussion Siva conducts with a friend, Michel, a learned rabbi, conversations that represent Rao's complex anatomy of the horrific reality of the Jewish Holocaust and the implications of its legacy for those who seek the path to Absolute Truth. It is under the tutelage of Michel, a survivor of a Nazi concentration camp, that Siva first begins to perceive the inadequacies of his own suppositions about the Truth. With the gradual evolution appropriate to a pilgrim character setting out to achieve a most comprehensive transcendent state, Siva comes in turn to see the thinness of the sensual, specifically his own pursuit of beautiful, intelligent women and ultimately the deceptive faux absolutes of numbers themselves.

The underlying philosophy here is that a novel is a powerful assertion in a spiritually empty postmodern world of the ancient privilege of wisdom writing to help direct the difficult attainment of spiritual fulfillment: Only through words, Rao suggests, can the Word be attained. Unlike trendy New Age literature, among which this novel has often been categorized, Rao does not pretend that mysticism is readily available or cheaply purchased. Siva struggles to perceive the necessary abolition of contradiction, the movement beyond the tension of flesh and spirit, illusion and reality, immediate and eternal as a first stage in what, given the dimension of Rao's projected trilogy, promises to become a most intricate awakening into Truth for both Siva and Rao's pilgrim reader.

ON THE GANGA GHAT

On the Ganga Ghat, Rao's last fiction published before his death, is a collection of short narratives so intricately bound together, so tightly arranged that Rao insisted they could only be read as a novel. Rao's two earlier collections of stories were just that—gatherings of individual stories, most previously published, and thus discrete and each able to be read (and explicated) independent of the others. Here, Rao, using the premise of examining the rich street life of Benaras (also known as Varanasi), the holiest city in the Hindu religion, examines in a cycle of ten stories (with a concluding chapter) a variety of characters who populate the teeming sacred city. The stories are, to borrow Rao's own description of its structure, like beads of the same necklace.

Rao juxtaposes the often morally compromised life of a modern urban center against the pilgrims who have come for centuries to bathe in the holy waters of the Ganges (or Ganga). He casts his often critical eye on the characters who approach the sacred river via the city's numerous ancient elaborately carved stairways, or ghats, leading down to the river's edge. In examining the lives of a variety of types, Rao creates a narrative trajectory upward, story to story, a movement toward illumination, a journey toward Truth that threads the stories/chapters and culminates in Rao's own conclusion in which he acknowledges the difficult struggle to leave behind the attractive complications of the material world (critics have suggested the work is a product of Rao's own spiritual life in postmodern America).

In juxtaposing the common people of the city's streets and their yearning for spiritual elevation, Rao's collection recalls one of his frequently acknowledged influences, the modernist James Joyce, and specifically the structure of Joyce's *Dubliners* (1914). *On the Ganga Ghat* brings together the preoccupations of Rao's two earlier collections of stories: the gritty social realism of *The Cow of the Barricades*, with its often grim depiction of the brutal conditions of India's impoverished population against the hypocrisy and indifference of its most

affluent, and *The Policeman and the Rose*, with its far more spiritual argument using parables and allegories in which pilgrim characters struggle to achieve the sublime affirmation of Truth against the temptations of the worldly and the stubborn fallibility of humanity.

What is most remarkable, however, is this book's unexpectedly comic tone, given the gravitas with which spiritual evolution is treated in Rao's other works. Here Rao indulges tongue-in-cheek satire that is never caustic in a style that, unlike his more elaborate and often dense abstract writings, is direct, uncomplicated by meditative speculations. With a kind of world-weary wisdom, Rao exposes with a generous sensibility humanity's inability to accept the responsibility of a spiritual education by telling of traveling princes, dignified beggars, noble urchins, big-hearted prostitutes, sharp-eyed ascetics, and unrepentant street thieves. Rao captures the irreverent, the morally bankrupt, and the hypocritical. Much as in traditional wisdom literature, Rao gives to animals the most profound insights into spirituality and the search for Truth, specifically a wise parrot and a shrewd cow. Without condescension and with a forgiving heart for the foibles of those who seek enlightenment that is often difficult to discern in Rao's other, longer works, *On the Ganga Ghat* suggests that Rao, himself edging toward death, wants to reassure his pilgrim readers that their struggles with their own imperfections are part of the narrative of their spiritual reclamation.

Makarand Paranjape
Updated by Joseph Dewey

OTHER MAJOR WORKS

SHORT FICTION: *The Cow of the Barricades, and Other Stories*, 1947; *The Policeman and the Rose*, 1978.

NONFICTION: *The Meaning of India*, 1996; *The Great Indian Way: A Life of Mahatma Gandhi*, 1998.

EDITED TEXTS: *Changing India*, 1939 (with Iqbal Singh); *Whither India?* (1948; with Singh).

BIBLIOGRAPHY

Bhattacharya, P. C. *Indo-Anglian Literature and the Works of Raja Rao*. Delhi: Atma Ram, 1983. Focuses on Rao's work within the context of Indian literature written in English. Includes primary and secondary bibliographies.

Hardgrave, Robert L., Jr., ed. *Word as Mantra: The Art of Raja Rao*. Austin: University of Texas Press, 1998. Collection of essays provides informative and accessible explication of Rao's religious argument.

Mittapalli, Rajeshwar, and Pier Paolo Piciucco, eds. *The Fiction of Raja Rao: Critical Studies*. New Delhi: Atlantic, 2001. Collection of essays covers a wide range of topics, including Rao's philosophy, his Indian voice, and his use of myth in his fiction.

Narasimhaiah, C. D. *Raja Rao: A Critical Study of His Work*. New Delhi: Arnold-Heinemann India, 1973. Early study provides among the most perceptive and significant assessments of Rao's fiction available.

Sankaran, Chitra. *Myth Connections: The Use of Hindu Myths and Philosophies in R. K. Narayan and Raja Rao*. 2d rev. ed. New York: Peter Lang, 2007. Presents comparative analyses of four novels by each of the two authors, focusing on similarities in themes and Hindu motifs in the works.

Sarang, Jaydeep, ed. *Raja Rao: The Master and His Moves*. Delhi: Authorspress, 2007. Wide-ranging collection of essays generally examines Rao's fictional techniques (using the metaphor of the chessmaster) as an expression of his spirituality.

Sharma, Kaushal. *Raja Rao: A Study of His Themes and Techniques*. Delhi: Sarup & Sons, 2006. Analysis of Rao's fiction places particular emphasis on the works' place within the tradition of the novel of ideas.

Sharrad, Paul. *Raja Rao and Cultural Tradition*. New Delhi: Sterling, 1987. Focuses on the influence on Rao's work of the decline of the British Empire and the end of the British Raj. Includes bibliographies and index.

Venkata Reddy, K. *Major Indian Novelists: Mulk Raj Anand, R. K. Narayan, Raja Rao, Bhabani Bhattacharya, Kamala Markandaya*. New Delhi: Prestige Books, 1990. Examines the work of Rao as well as other important twentieth century Indian authors who wrote in English. Includes index.

World Literature Today 62, no. 3 (1988). Special issue devoted to Rao's work, with emphasis on his early novels, is designed to introduce Rao to an American audience. Includes a particularly informative introduction and a bibliography.

MARJORIE KINNAN RAWLINGS

Born: Washington, D.C.; August 8, 1896
Died: St. Augustine, Florida; December 14, 1953
Also known as: Marjorie Kinnan

PRINCIPAL LONG FICTION

Blood of My Blood, wr. 1928, pb. 2002
South Moon Under, 1933
Golden Apples, 1935
The Yearling, 1938
The Sojourner, 1953

OTHER LITERARY FORMS

Although she is best known for one novel, *The Yearling*, Marjorie Kinnan Rawlings produced three other full-length novels and two novellas, the award-winning *Jacob's Ladder* and the undistinguished *Mountain Pre-* *lude*, which was serialized in 1947 in *The Saturday Evening Post* but never appeared in book form. She also wrote numerous shorter pieces for periodicals, beginning with a series of sketches about life in Cross Creek, Florida, which were printed in *Scribner's Magazine* under the title "Cracker Chidlings." During her lifetime, Rawlings brought out only one book-length volume of short stories, *When the Whippoorwill* (1940). However, virtually all of the short fiction that she published in magazines was collected in Rodger L. Tarr's edition of *Short Stories by Marjorie Kinnan Rawlings* (1994). Rawlings was also the author of a notable autobiographical work, *Cross Creek* (1942), and an anecdotal cookbook, *Cross Creek Cookery* (1942). A children's book, *The Secret River*, was published posthumously in 1955. The author's versatility is evident in *The Mar-*

jorie Kinnan Rawlings Reader (1956), edited by Julia Scribner Bigham. *Selected Letters of Marjorie Kinnan Rawlings* (1983) was edited by Gordon E. Bigelow and Laura V. Monti.

ACHIEVEMENTS

During the 1930's and the 1940's, Marjorie Kinnan Rawlings's fiction was popular with the general public and acclaimed by critics. Her novella *Jacob's Ladder* placed second in the 1931 Scribner Prize Contest, and two of her short stories, "Gal Young Un" in 1933 and "Black Secret" in 1946, won O. Henry Awards. Her first published novel, *South Moon Under*, was a Book-of-the-Month Club selection, as was *The Yearling*, which brought Rawlings a national reputation, a motion-picture contract, membership in the National Institute of Arts and Letters, and the 1939 Pulitzer Prize in fiction. Her autobiography *Cross Creek* was also a best seller and a Book-of-the-Month Club selection.

After her death, however, Rawlings was remembered either as a local colorist or as the author of two books for children, *The Secret River*, which in 1956 was selected as a Newbery Honor Book, and *The Yearling*, which in 1963 won the Lewis Carroll Shelf Award. The classification of *The Yearling* as a children's book was ironic, since Rawlings had written it with Mark Twain's *Adventures of Huckleberry Finn* (1884) in mind, intending to appeal at least as much to adults as to children.

The ongoing efforts of a few scholars to call attention to a writer they felt had been both inappropriately classified and unjustly neglected, along with the new emphasis on the relationship between human beings and the natural environment, resulted in the 1980's and the 1990's in an upsurge of interest in Rawlings, her novels, her short stories, and her compelling autobiography. Rawlings is now valued for not only her precision in describing a vanished way of life but also her lyrical prose, her mystical feelings about nature, and her insistence that there are truly noble people who spend their lives in poverty and obscurity.

BIOGRAPHY

Marjorie Kinnan Rawlings was the older of two children born in Washington, D.C., to Ida May Traphagen Kinnan and Frank R. Kinnan, a patent attorney. Raw-

lings read widely and began writing early. By the time she was six years old, she was submitting stories to area newspapers. At the age of eleven, she won a two-dollar prize in a contest sponsored by *The Washington Post*; at age fifteen, she placed second in *McCall's* Child Authorship Contest and saw her story published in that magazine.

Rawlings's father died in 1913, and the next year, the family moved to Madison, Wisconsin. That fall, Rawlings entered the University of Wisconsin, where she majored in English and was active in college publications and in the drama society. As a junior, she was elected to Phi Beta Kappa. After graduation, she moved to New York City and worked for a year for the Young Women's Christian Association. In 1919, she married Charles A. Rawlings, Jr., a journalist whom she had met at the university, and they moved to his hometown, Rochester, New York. During the next nine years, Rawlings wrote features for newspapers, advertising copy, and a syndicated column. However, all the short stories she submitted to magazines were rejected.

After visiting central Florida in 1928, the couple decided to move to the area. Purchasing an orange-grove property at Cross Creek, they settled down in their new home, and Rawlings began using Florida settings for her fiction. Within a year, she was a regular contributor to *Scribner's Magazine*, working closely with the influential editor Maxwell Perkins. Rawlings's first novel, *South Moon Under*, appeared in 1933. That same year, Charles and Marjorie were divorced.

For the next eight years, Rawlings lived alone at Cross Creek, ran her business and her household, and wrote short stories and two more novels, the disappointing *Golden Apples* and *The Yearling*. She enjoyed cooking and entertaining, going on outdoor expeditions, corresponding with interesting people, and visiting with her neighbors. One of her closest friends was Norton Sanford Baskin. In 1941, she married him and went to live at the Castle Warden Hotel in St. Augustine, which Baskin owned and managed. However, she continued to write stories and books about Cross Creek, including an autobiography titled *Cross Creek* and an anecdotal cookbook, *Cross Creek Cookery*. Ironically, it was this autobiography, which critics consider one of her best, that cost the author four years of constant worry. In 1943,

Zelma Cason filed a libel suit against Rawlings, based on the author's description of her in *Cross Creek*. The suit dragged on until 1947, when Rawlings was charged a nominal sum for damages.

Rawlings had decided that her next novel would have a different setting, upstate New York, where she spent her summers, as well as a more "serious" theme. Though it had been ten years in the making, *The Sojourner* lacked the vitality of the Florida works. Despite failing health, Rawlings now began research for a biography of her friend and fellow writer Ellen Glasgow. It would never be completed. On December 10, 1953, while Baskin and Rawlings were at their beach cottage, she suffered a cerebral hemorrhage. She died in a St. Augustine hospital on December 14 and was buried in Antioch Cemetery at Island Grove, near Cross Creek.

ANALYSIS

Whether they first encounter *The Yearling* as children or as adults, few readers can remain dry-eyed during the scene at the end of the book when the young protagonist, Jody Baxter, is forced to kill his pet deer. However, that memorable episode is just one of many incidents in Marjorie Kinnan Rawlings's fiction that illustrate her uncompromisingly realistic view of life. Indeed, it is ironic that for so long Rawlings was thought of as a children's writer, for in fact her rural world is as grim as that of Victorian author Thomas Hardy. Penny Baxter, Jody's father, describes growing up as learning that life is hard, that human beings can be malicious, and that feelings of insecurity and desperate loneliness are just part of being human. Though Rawlings and many of her characters display a mystical appreciation of nature, she never permits us to forget that living in a natural environment means accepting ugliness as well as beauty, suffering as well as joy, and death as a part of the daily routine.

SOUTH MOON UNDER

In *Jacob's Ladder*, Florry and Mart wandered from the piney woods and the Florida scrub to the Gulf Coast and back to the woods. By contrast, *South Moon Under* and *The Yearling* are set entirely in the "Big Scrub," a plateau bounded on the east by the St. John's River and on the west by the Ocklawaha. Before beginning *South Moon Under*, Rawlings spent several weeks in this wil-

Marjorie Kinnan Rawlings. (Library of Congress)

derness area. Piety Fiddia, with whom she stayed, became the model for Piety Jacklin in the novel, and her moonshiner son became the character of Lant Jacklin.

Like Mart and Florry, old Lantry has had difficulty putting down roots, but he is propelled by fear. As he tells his daughter, Piety, when he was making moonshine in North Carolina he killed a federal revenue agent, and he has been on the run ever since. However, the scrub is so remote, and his home there so isolated, that Lantry's worst fears are never realized. It is true that every season brings its own problems, drought or rain, insects or blight, but nevertheless Lantry and his family prosper. After his sons move on, Lantry persuades Piety to marry Willy Jacklin, who is a hard worker, if none too bright. Their son Lantry, or Lant, gives his grandfather great pleasure during the old man's last years. However, on his deathbed old Lantry once again succumbs to terror; only in death, it seems, can he escape from fear.

Old Lantry's story could be read simply as a morality tale. However, both in *Jacob's Ladder* and in *South Moon Under*, the author clearly sides with these hardworking, self-sufficient people who do not understand why there should be restrictions on such normal activities as hunting, fishing, whiskey-making, and letting livestock range freely, or why the government should constantly seek to block their efforts to support their families, even send them to prison, leaving those families destitute. As the fence-raising at the beginning of the novel illustrates, those who live in the Big Scrub rely on themselves and on each other, not on the government. One could almost justify Lant's killing his shiftless cousin Cleve as a service to the community, for Cleve is a spy and an informer, but in fact Lant was defending himself. Unlike Cleve's widow, who believes Lant and promptly marries him, outsiders would never understand. Like his grandfather, Lant will always have to live in fear of the law.

THE YEARLING

Although the setting for *The Yearling* is the same as that of *South Moon Under*, in this novel all of the action takes place within a single year, and instead of focusing on the conflict between two codes and two societies, *The Yearling* describes a boy's initiation into the natural world. It begins one April, with Jody Baxter so overwhelmed by nature's beauty that he cannot sleep; it ends the following April, with a revelation of nature's indifference. In all his hunting and fishing, Jody has never realized that the survival of one creature depends on the death of another. Then Jody's pet fawn, Flag, destroys the newly planted corn crop, and Penny tells his son the deer must be shot. Jody will never again view nature as he had the previous spring.

Now he knows too much, including the inevitability of loneliness, and only his father's understanding makes his discoveries endurable. Though, like young Jody, Rawlings responded to the breathtaking beauty of the Florida backwoods, she found even more to admire in many of the people who lived there. Her most memorable characters are those who, like Jody and Penny, have the courage to confront life and accept all that it holds for them, even the death of innocence.

Rosemary M. Canfield Reisman

OTHER MAJOR WORKS

SHORT FICTION: *When the Whippoorwill*, 1940; *Short Stories*, 1994 (Rodger L. Tarr, editor).

POETRY: *Poems by Marjorie Kinnan Rawlings: Songs of a Housewife*, 1997 (Tarr, editor).

NONFICTION: *Cross Creek*, 1942 (sketches); *Max and Marjorie: The Correspondence Between Maxwell E. Perkins and Marjorie Kinnan Rawlings*, 1999 (Tarr, editor).

CHILDREN'S LITERATURE: *The Secret River*, 1955.

BIBLIOGRAPHY

Bellman, Samuel I. *Marjorie Kinnan Rawlings*. New York: Twayne, 1974. An introduction to Rawlings, containing some biographical data but focusing on an analysis of her works. Includes copious notes, a bibliography, and an index.

Bloom, Harold, ed. *American Women Fiction Writers, 1900-1960*. Philadelphia: Chelsea House, 1997. Volume 3 includes brief biographies of Rawlings and ten other authors and critical essays about their work, including analyses of individual books and broader discussions of the authors' place in literary history.

Howard, Hugh. *Writers of the American South: Their Literary Landscapes*. Photographs by Roger Straus III. New York: Rizzoli, 2005. Collection of essays that discuss the relationship between southern geography and the work of southern writers, illustrated with photographs of the writers' homes and environs. The essay on Rawlings describes how she drew inspiration from the landscape of central Florida.

Morris, Rhonda. "Engendering Fictions: Rawlings and a Female Tradition of Southern Writing." *Marjorie Kinnan Rawlings Journal of Florida Literature* 7 (1996): 27-39. Argues that although Rawlings used the male voice in order to be taken seriously by the establishment, her works reveal a feminist perspective. Well documented.

Parker, Idella, and Mary Keating. *Idella: Marjorie Rawlings' "Perfect Maid."* Gainesville: University Press of Florida, 1992. The employee described by Rawlings in *Cross Creek* as the "perfect maid" recalls her life with Rawlings and comments on the author's feelings about race. Includes photographs and an index.

Rieger, Christopher. "Don't Fence Me In: Nature and Gender in Marjorie Kinnan Rawlings's *South Moon Under*." *Mississippi Quarterly* 57, no. 2 (Spring, 2004): 199-214. An analysis of the metaphorical meaning of fences in the novel. For Rawlings, fences symbolized modern society's threat to subjugate women and the then-uninhabited region of north-central Florida.

Silverthorne, Elizabeth. *Marjorie Kinnan Rawlings: Sojourner at Cross Creek*. Woodstock, N.Y.: Overlook,

1988. The standard biography, based on a close study of the author's papers, her unpublished works, and numerous interviews. Includes a helpful list of reviews, illustrations, and an index.

Tarr, Rodger L. *Marjorie Kinnan Rawlings: A Descriptive Bibliography*. Pittsburgh, Pa.: University of Pittsburgh Press, 1996. Lists all of Rawlings's publications but contains very few secondary sources. Includes useful information about her film involvements.

ISHMAEL REED

Born: Chattanooga, Tennessee; February 22, 1938
Also known as: Ishmael Scott Reed; Emmett Coleman

PRINCIPAL LONG FICTION

The Free-Lance Pallbearers, 1967
Yellow Back Radio Broke-Down, 1969
Mumbo Jumbo, 1972
The Last Days of Louisiana Red, 1974
Flight to Canada, 1976
The Terrible Twos, 1982
Reckless Eyeballing, 1986
The Terrible Threes, 1989
Japanese by Spring, 1993

OTHER LITERARY FORMS

Ishmael Reed may be best known as a satiric novelist, but he also gained a reputation as a respected poet, essayist, and editor. His poetry collections, which include *Catechism of D Neoamerican Hoodoo Church* (1970), *Conjure: Selected Poems, 1963-1970* (1972), *Chattanooga* (1973), *A Secretary to the Spirits* (1977), and *New and Collected Poems* (1988), established him as a major African American poet, and his poetry has been included in several important anthologies. In well-received collections of essays, including *Shrovetide in Old New Orleans* (1978), *God Made Alaska for the Indians* (1982), and *Writin' Is Fightin'* (1988), Reed forcefully presented his aesthetic and political theories.

Reed also proved to be an important editor and publisher. *Nineteen Necromancers from Now* (1970) was a breakthrough anthology for several unknown black writers. *Yardbird Lives!* (1978), which Reed edited with novelist Al Young, includes essays, fiction, and graphics from the pages of the *Yardbird Reader*, an innovative periodical that published the work of minority writers and artists. Reed's most ambitious editing project resulted in *Calafia: The California Poetry* (1979), an effort to gather together the forgotten minority poetry of California's past.

ACHIEVEMENTS

Ishmael Reed earned a place in the first rank of contemporary African American authors, but such recognition did not come immediately. Most established reviewers ignored Reed's first novel, *The Free-Lance Pallbearers*, and many of the reviews that were written dismissed the novel as offensive, childish, or self-absorbed. Although *Yellow Back Radio Broke-Down* was even less traditional than its predecessor, it received much more critical attention and became the center of considerable debate. Some reviewers attacked the novel as overly clever, bitter, or obscure, but many praised its imaginative satire and technical innovation. Moreover, the controversy over *Yellow Back Radio Broke-Down* stirred new interest in *The Free-Lance Pallbearers*. Reed's increasing acceptance as a major African American author was demonstrated when his third novel,

Mumbo Jumbo, was reviewed on the front page of *The New York Times Review of Books*. Both *Mumbo Jumbo* and *Conjure*, a poetry collection published in the same year, were nominated for the National Book Award.

Subsequent novels maintained Reed's position in American letters. In 1975, his *The Last Days of Louisiana Red* received the Rosenthal Foundation Award, and some reviewers viewed *Flight to Canada* as Reed's best novel. Yet his work proved consistently controversial. His novels have, for example, been called sexist, a critical accusation that is fueled by comparison of Reed's novels with the contemporary powerful fiction written by African American women such as Alice Walker and Toni Morrison. The charge of sexism is further encouraged by Reed's satiric attack on feminists in *Reckless Eyeballing*. Reed has also been called a reactionary by some critics because of his uncomplimentary portrayals of black revolutionaries. His fiction has been translated into three languages, and his poetry is included in *Poetry of the Negro*, *New Black Poetry*, *The Norton Anthology of Poetry*, and other anthologies. In 1998, Reed was awarded the MacArthur "genius" fellowship, a fitting recognition for a writer who consciously attempted to redefine American and African American literature.

BIOGRAPHY

The jacket notes to *Chattanooga* glibly recount the life of Ishmael Reed with the following: "born in Chattanooga, Tennessee, grew up in Buffalo, New York, learned to write in New York City and wised up in Berkeley, California." Each residence played a crucial role in his development.

Reed was given the name Emmett Coleman at birth. He was born to Henry Lenoir and Thelma Coleman, but before he was two years old, his mother remarried, this time to auto worker Bennie Reed. When the young Reed was four years old, his mother moved the family to Buffalo, New York, where she found factory work. Reed graduated from Buffalo's East High School in 1956 and began to attend Millard Fillmore College, the night division of the University of Buffalo, supporting himself by working in the Buffalo public library. A satiric short story, "Something Pure," which portrayed Christ's return as an advertising man, brought Reed the praise of an English professor and encouraged him to enroll in day classes. Reed attended the University of Buffalo until 1960, when he withdrew because of money problems and the social pressures that his financial situation created.

Reed married Priscilla Rose Thompson and moved into the notorious Talbert Mall projects. The two years he spent there provided him with a painful but valuable experience of urban poverty and dependence. His daughter, Timothy Bret Reed, was born there. During his last years in Buffalo, Reed wrote for the *Empire Star Weekly*, moderated a controversial radio program for station WVFO, and acted in several local stage productions.

From 1962 to 1967, Reed lived in New York City. As well as being involved with the Civil Rights movement and the Black Power movement, Reed served as editor of *Advance*, a weekly published in Newark, New Jersey. His work on *Advance* was admired by Walter Bowart, and together they founded the *East Village Other*, one of the first and most successful underground newspapers. An early indication of Reed's commitment to encouraging the work of minority artists was his organization in 1965 of the American Festival of Negro Art.

In 1967, Reed moved to Berkeley, California, and began teaching at the University of California, Berkeley. In 1970, he and his first wife divorced (after years of separation), and he married Carla Blank. In 1971, with Al Young, Reed founded Yardbird Publishing Company, which from 1971 to 1976 produced the *Yardbird Reader*, an innovative journal of ethnic writing and graphics. The Reed, Cannon, and Johnson Communications Company, which later became Ishmael Reed Books, was founded in 1973 and has published the work of William Demby, Bill Gunn, Mei Mei Bressenburge, and other ethnic writers. In 1976, Reed and Victor Cruz began the Before Columbus Foundation. Reed's daughter, Tennessee, was born in 1977.

Reed was denied tenure in the English Department at Berkeley, but he continued to serve as a lecturer at there. He also taught at Yale, Harvard, Columbia, Dartmouth, and a number of other colleges and universities. In 1995, he was awarded an honorary doctorate in letters from the State University of New York at Buffalo.

Reed made important contributions as a poet, novelist, essayist, playwright, and as an editor and publisher. He stated that he considers himself a global writer, and his success at writing poetry in the African language of Yoruba and his study of Japanese language and culture for his novel *Japanese by Spring* support this assertion. He also extended his literary range to include plays, such as *The Preacher and the Rapper* (published in 1997), and jazz albums, such as *Conjure I* (1983) and *Conjure II* (1989), and he even completed a libretto and served as the executive producer for a paid-television soap opera called *Personal Problems* (1981).

In the early 1990's, Reed was best known for his controversial essays on such issues as the beating of Rodney King by Los Angeles Police Department officers, the criminal and civil trials of O. J. Simpson,

Ishmael Reed. (James Lerager)

and the hearings on U.S. Supreme Court nominee Clarence Thomas. Some of these essays were collected in *Airing Dirty Laundry* (1993). However, Reed's most important contribution to American letters may well be his work as an editor and publisher for other ethnic writers. In all of his publishing ventures, Reed tries to expose readers to the work of Asian Americans, African Americans, Chicanos, and Native Americans in an effort to help build a truly representative and pluralistic national literature.

ANALYSIS

Ishmael Reed is consciously a part of the African American literary tradition that extends back to the first-person slave narratives, and the central purpose of his novels is to define a means of expressing the complexity of the African American experience in a manner distinct from the dominant literary tradition. Until the middle of the twentieth century, African American fiction, although enriched by the lyricism of Jean Toomer and Zora Neale Hurston, concentrated on realistic portrayals of black life and employed familiar narrative structures. This tendency toward social realism peaked with Richard Wright's *Native Son* (1940) and *Black Boy* (1945), but it was continued into the late twentieth century by authors such as James Baldwin. Reed belongs to a divergent tradition, inspired by Ralph Ellison's *Invisible Man* (1952), a countertradition that includes the work of Leon Forrest, Ernest J. Gaines, James Alan McPherson, Toni Morrison, and Alice Walker.

Believing that the means of expression is as important as the matter, Reed argues that the special qualities of the African American experience cannot be adequately communicated through traditional literary forms. Like Amiri Baraka, Reed believes that African American authors must "be estranged from the dominant culture," but Reed also wants to avoid being stifled by a similarly restrictive countertradition. In *Shrovetide in Old New Orleans*, Reed says that his art and criticism try to combat "the consciousness barrier erected by an alliance of Eastern-backed black pseudo-nationalists and white mundanists." Thus, Reed works against the stylistic limitations of the African American literary tradition as much as he works with them. Henry Louis Gates, Jr., compared Reed's fictional modifications of African American literary traditions to the African American folk custom of "signifying," maintaining that Reed's novels present an ongoing process of "rhetorical self-definition."

Although Reed's novels are primarily efforts to define an appropriate African American aesthetic, his fiction vividly portrays the particular social condition of black Americans. In his foreword to Elizabeth and Thomas Settle's *Ishmael Reed: A Primary and Secondary Bibliography* (1982), Reed expresses his bitterness over persistent racism and argues that the personal experience of racism that informs his art makes his work inaccessible and threatening to many readers:

> I am a member of a class which has been cast to the bottom of the American caste system, and from those depths I write a vision which is still strange, often frightening, "peculiar" and "odd" to some, "ill-considered" and unwelcome to many.

Indeed, "Ishmael" seems to be an ironically appropriate name for this author of violent and darkly humorous attacks on American institutions and attitudes, for the sharpness and breadth of his satire sometimes make him appear to be a person whose hand is turned against all others. His novels portray corrupt power brokers and their black and white sycophants operating in a dehumanized and materialistic society characterized by its prefabricated and ethnocentric culture. Yet Reed's novels are not hopeless explications of injustice, for against the forces of repression and conformity he sets gifted individuals who escape the limitations of their sterile culture by courageously penetrating the illusions that bind them. Moreover, in contrast to many white authors who are engaged in parallel metafictive experiments, Reed voices a confident belief that "print and words are not dead at all."

Reed's narrative technique combines the improvisational qualities of jazz with a documentary impulse to accumulate references and allusions. In his composite narratives, historical and fictional characters coexist in a fluid, anachronistic time. In an effort to translate the vitality and spontaneity of the oral, folk tradition into a literature that can form the basis for an alternative culture, Reed mixes colloquialisms and erudition in novels that are syncretized from a series of subtexts. The literary equivalent of scat singing, his stories-within-stories parody literary formulas and challenge the traditional limits of fiction.

Reed claims that his novels constitute "an art form with its own laws," but he does not mean to imply that his work is private, for these "laws" are founded on a careful but imaginative reinterpretation of the historical and mythological past. The lengthy bibliography appended to *Mumbo Jumbo* satirizes the documentary impulse of social realist authors, but it also underscores Reed's belief that his mature work demands scholarly research to be decoded. This artistic process of reinterpretation often requires the services of an interlocutor, a character who explicitly explains the events of the narrative in terms of the mythological past. Reed's novels describe a vision of an Osirian/Dionysian consciousness, a sensuous humanism that he presents as an appropriate cultural alternative for nonwhite Americans. His imaginative reconstructions of the American West, the Harlem Renaissance, the American Civil War, and contemporary U.S. politics, interwoven with ancient myths, non-European folk customs, and the formulas of popular culture, are liberating heresies meant to free readers from the intellectual domination of the Judeo-Christian tradition.

THE FREE-LANCE PALLBEARERS

Reed's first novel, *The Free-Lance Pallbearers*, takes place in a futuristic America called HARRY SAM: "A big not-to-be-believed out-of-sight, sometimes referred to as O-BOP-SHE-BANG or KLANG-A-LANG-A-DING-DONG." This crumbling and corrupt world is tyrannized by Sam himself, a vulgar fat man who lives in Sam's Motel on Sam's Island in the middle of the lethally polluted Black Bay that borders HARRY SAM. Sam, doomed by some terrifying gastrointestinal disorder, spends all of his time on the toilet, his filth pouring into the bay from several large statues of Rutherford B. Hayes.

The bulk of the novel, although framed and periodically informed by a jiving narrative voice, is narrated by Bukka Doopeyduk in a restrained, proper English that identifies his passive faith in the establishment. Doopeyduk is a dedicated adherent to the Nazarene Code, an orderly in a psychiatric hospital, a student at Harry Sam College, and a hapless victim. His comically futile efforts to play by the rules are defeated by the cynics, who manipulate the unjust system to their own advantage. In the end, Doopeyduk is disillusioned: He leads a successful attack on Sam's Island, uncovers the conspiracy that protects Sam's cannibalism, briefly dreams of becoming the black Sam, and is finally crucified.

The Free-Lance Pallbearers is a parody of the African American tradition of first-person, confessional narratives, a book the narrator describes as "growing up in soulsville first of three installments—or what it means to be a backstage darky." Reed's novel challenges the viability of this African American version of the bildungsroman, in which a young protagonist undergoes a painful initiation into the darkness of the white world, a formula exemplified by Wright's *Black Boy* and Baldwin's *Go Tell It on the Mountain* (1953). In fact, the novel suggests that African American authors' use of this European form is as disabling as Doopeyduk's adherence to the dictates of the Nazarene Code.

The Free-Lance Pallbearers is an unrestrained attack on U.S. politics. HARRY SAM, alternately referred to as "Nowhere" or "Now Here," is a dualistic vision of a United States that celebrates vacuous contemporaneity. The novel, an inversion of the Horatio Alger myth in the manner of Nathanael West, mercilessly displays American racism, but its focus is the corruptive potential of power. Sam is a grotesque version of Lyndon B. Johnson, famous for his bathroom interviews, and Sam's cannibalistic taste for children is an attack on Johnson's Vietnam policy. With *The Free-Lance Pallbearers*, Reed destroys the presumptions of his society, but it is not until his later novels that he attempts to construct an alternative.

YELLOW BACK RADIO BROKE-DOWN

Yellow Back Radio Broke-Down is set in a fantastic version of the Wild West of popular literature. Reed's protagonist, the Loop Garoo Kid, is a proponent of artistic freedom and an accomplished Voodoo *houngan* who is in marked contrast to the continually victimized Doopeyduk. Armed with supernatural "connaissance" and aided by a white python and the hip, helicopter-flying Chief Showcase, the Kid battles the forces of realistic mimesis and political corruption. His villainous opponent is Drag Gibson, a degenerate cattle baron given to murdering his wives, who is called upon by the citizens of Yellow Back Radio to crush their rebellious children's effort "to create [their] own fictions."

Although *Yellow Back Radio Broke-Down* satirizes Americans' eagerness to suspend civil rights in response to student protests against the Vietnam War, its focus is literature, specifically the dialogue between realism and modernism. The Loop Garoo Kid matches Reed's description of the African American artist in *Nineteen Necromancers from Now*: "a conjurer who works JuJu upon his oppressors; a witch doctor who frees his fellow victims from the psychic attack launched by demons." Through the Loop Garoo Kid, Reed takes a stand for imagination, intelligence, and fantasy against rhetoric, violence, and sentimentality. This theme is made explicit in a debate with Bo Shmo, a "neo-social realist" who maintains that "all art must be for the end of liberating the masses," for the Kid says that a novel "can be anything it wants to be, a vaudeville show, the six o'clock news, the mumblings of wild men saddled by demons."

Reed exhibits his antirealist theory of fiction in *Yellow Back Radio Broke-Down* through his free use of time, characters, and language. The novel ranges from the eighteenth century to the present, combining historical events and cowboy myths with modern technology and cultural detritus. Reed's primary characters are comically exaggerated racial types: Drag Gibson represents the whites' depraved materialism, Chief Showcase represents the American Indians' spirituality, and the Loop Garoo Kid represents the African Americans' artistic soul. Reed explains the novel's title by suggesting that his book is the "dismantling of a genre done in an oral way like radio." "Yellow back" refers to the popular dime novels; "radio" refers to the novel's oral, discontinuous form; and a "broke-down" is a dismantling. Thus, Reed's first two novels assault America in an attempt to "dismantle" its cultural structure.

MUMBO JUMBO

In *Mumbo Jumbo*, Reed expands on the neohoodooism of the Loop Garoo Kid in order to create and define an African American aesthetic based on Voodoo, Egyptian mythology, and improvisational musical forms, an aesthetic to challenge the Judeo-Christian tradition, rationalism, and technology.

Set in Harlem during the 1920's, *Mumbo Jumbo* is a tragicomical analysis of the Harlem Renaissance's failure to sustain its artistic promise. Reed's protagonist is PaPa LaBas, an aging hoodoo detective and cultural diagnostician. LaBas's name, meaning "over there" in French, reveals that his purpose is to reconnect African Americans with their cultural heritage by reunifying the

Text of Jes Grew, literally the Egyptian Book of Thoth. Reed takes the phrase Jes Grew from Harriet Beecher Stowe's Topsy and James Weldon Johnson's description of African American music's unscribed development, but in the novel, Jes Grew is a contagion, connected with the improvisational spirit of ragtime and jazz, that begins to spread across America in the 1920's. Jes Grew is an irrational force that threatens to overwhelm the dominant, repressive traditions of established culture. LaBas's efforts to unify and direct this unpredictable force are opposed by the Wallflower Order of the Knights Templar, an organization dedicated to neutralizing the power of Jes Grew in order to protect its privileged status. LaBas fails to reunify the text, a parallel to the dissipation of the Harlem Renaissance's artistic potential, but the failure is seen as temporary; the novel's indeterminate conclusion looks forward hopefully to a time when these artistic energies can be reignited.

The novel's title is double-edged. "Mumbo jumbo" is a racist, colonialist phrase used to describe the misunderstood customs and language of dark-skinned people, an approximation of some critics' description of Reed's unorthodox fictional method. Yet "mumbo jumbo" also refers to the power of imagination, the cultural alternative that can free African Americans. A text of and about texts, *Mumbo Jumbo* combines the formulas of detective fiction with the documentary paraphernalia of scholarship: footnotes, illustrations, and a bibliography. Thus, in the disclosure scene required of any good detective story, LaBas, acting the part of interlocutor, provides a lengthy and erudite explication of the development of Jes Grew that begins with a reinterpretation of the myth of Osiris. The parodic scholarship of *Mumbo Jumbo* undercuts the assumed primacy of the European tradition and implicitly argues that African American artists should attempt to discover their distinct cultural heritage.

THE LAST DAYS OF LOUISIANA RED

In *The Last Days of Louisiana Red*, LaBas returns as Reed's protagonist, but the novel abandons the parodic scholarship and high stylization of *Mumbo Jumbo*. Although LaBas again functions as a connection with a non-European tradition of history and myth, *The Last Days of Louisiana Red* is more traditionally structured than its predecessor. In the novel, LaBas solves the murder of Ed Yellings, the founder of the Solid Gumbo

Works. Yellings's business is dedicated to combating the effects of Louisiana Red, literally a popular hot sauce but figuratively an evil state of mind that divides African Americans. Yelling's gumbo, like Reed's fiction, is a mixture of disparate elements, and it has a powerful curative effect. In fact, LaBas discovers that Yellings is murdered when he gets close to developing a gumbo that will cure heroin addiction.

In *The Last Days of Louisiana Red*, Reed is examining the self-destructive forces that divide the African American community so that its members fight one another "while above their heads . . . billionaires flew in custom-made jet planes." Reed shows how individuals' avarice leads them to conspire with the establishment, and he suggests that some of the most vocal and militant leaders are motivated by their egotistical need for power rather than by true concern for oppressed people. Set in Berkeley, *The Last Days of Louisiana Red* attacks the credibility of the black revolutionary movements that sprang up in the late 1960's and early 1970's.

FLIGHT TO CANADA

Flight to Canada, Reed's fifth novel, is set in an imaginatively redrawn Civil War South, and it describes the relationship between Arthur Swille, a tremendously wealthy Virginia planter who practices necrophilia, and an assortment of sociologically stereotyped slaves. The novel is presented as the slave narrative of Uncle Robin, the most loyal of Swille's possessions. Uncle Robin repeatedly tells Swille that the plantation is his idea of heaven, and he assures his master that he does not believe that Canada exists. Raven Quickskill, "the first one of Swille's slaves to read, the first to write, and the first to run away," is the author of Uncle Robin's story.

Like much of Reed's work, *Flight to Canada* is about the liberating power of art, but in *Flight to Canada*, Reed concentrates on the question of authorial control. All the characters struggle to maintain control of their stories. After escaping from the plantation, Quickskill writes a poem, "Flight to Canada," and his comical verse denunciation of Swille completes his liberation. In complaining of Quickskill's betrayal to Abraham Lincoln, Swille laments that his former bookkeeper uses literacy "like that old Voodoo." In a final assertion of authorial control and the power of the pen, Uncle Robin refuses to sell his story to Harriet Beecher Stowe, gives the rights to

Quickskill, rewrites Swille's will, and inherits the plantation.

THE TERRIBLE TWOS

In *The Terrible Twos*, Reed uses a contemporary setting to attack Ronald Reagan's administration and the exploitative nature of the U.S. economic system. In the novel, President Dean Clift, a former model, is a mindless figurehead manipulated by an oil cartel that has supplanted the real Santa Claus. Nance Saturday, another of Reed's African American detectives, sets out to discover Saint Nicholas's place of exile. The novel's title suggests that, in its second century, the United States is acting as selfishly and irrationally as the proverbial two-year-old. The central theme is the manner in which a few avaricious people seek vast wealth at the expense of the majority of Americans.

RECKLESS EYEBALLING

Reckless Eyeballing takes place in the 1980's, and Reed employs a string of comically distorted characters to present the idea that the American literary environment is dominated by New York women and Jews. Although *Reckless Eyeballing* has been called sexist and anti-Semitic by some, Reed's target is a cultural establishment that creates and strengthens racial stereotypes, in particular the view of African American men as savage rapists. To make his point, however, he lampoons feminists, using the character Tremonisha Smarts, a female African American author who has written a novel of violence against women. Reed's satire probably is intended to remind readers of Alice Walker's *The Color Purple* (1982).

Because the novel's central subject is art and the limitations that society places on an artist, it is appropriate that Reed once again employs the technique of a story-within-a-story. Ian Ball, an unsuccessful African American playwright, is the novel's protagonist. In the novel, Ball tries to succeed by shamelessly placating the feminists in power. He writes "Reckless Eyeballing," a play in which a lynched man is posthumously tried for "raping" a woman with lecherous stares, but Ball, who often seems to speak for Reed, maintains his private, chauvinistic views throughout.

THE TERRIBLE THREES

The Terrible Threes, a sequel to *The Terrible Twos*, continues Reed's satiric attack on the contemporary capitalist system, which, he argues, puts the greatest economic burden on the least privileged. (Reed also was planning a third book in the series, *The Terrible Fours*.) In the first book, there appears a character named Black Peter—an assistant to St. Nicholas in European legend. This Black Peter is an impostor, however, a Rastafarian who studied and appropriated the legend for himself. In *The Terrible Threes*, the true Black Peter emerges to battle the false Peter but is distracted from his mission by the need to do good deeds. Black Peter becomes wildly popular because of these deeds, but a jealous St. Nick and concerned toy companies find a way to put Santa Claus back on top. Capitalism wins again.

JAPANESE BY SPRING

Japanese by Spring is postmodern satire. Like much of Reed's imaginative work, the book mixes fictional characters with "fictionalized" ones. Reed himself is a character in the book, with his own name. The protagonist of *Japanese by Spring* is Benjamin "Chappie" Puttbutt, a teacher of English and literature at Oakland's Jack London College. Chappie dabbled in activist politics in the mid-1960's, but his only concern in the 1990's is receiving tenure and the perks that accompany it. He will put up with virtually anything, including racist insults from students, to avoid hurting his chances at tenure. As in many of Reed's books, Chappie is passive in the face of power at the beginning of his story. He is a middle-class black conservative, but only because the climate at Jack London demands it. Chappie is a chameleon who always matches his behavior to the ideology of his environment. However, when he is denied tenure and is about to be replaced by a feminist poet who is more flash than substance, Chappie's hidden anger begins to surface.

Chappie also has been studying Japanese with a tutor named Dr. Yamato. This proves fortuitous when the Japanese buy Jack London and Dr. Yamato becomes the college president. Chappie suddenly finds himself in a position of power and gloats over those who denied him tenure. He soon finds, however, that his new bosses are the same as the old ones. Dr. Yamato is a tyrant and is eventually arrested by a group that includes Chappie's father, a two-star Air Force general. Dr. Yamato is released, though, and a surprised Chappie learns that there is an "invisible government" that truly controls the United States. Chappie has pierced some of his illusions, but there are others that he never penetrates, such as his blindness to his own opportunism.

The novel's conclusion moves away from Chappie's point of view to that of a fictionalized Ishmael Reed. This Reed skewers political correctness but also shows that the people who complain the most about it are often its greatest purveyors. Reed also lampoons American xenophobia, particularly toward Japan, but he does so in a balanced manner that does not gloss over Japanese faults. Ultimately, though, Reed uses *Japanese by Spring* as he used other novels before, to explore art and politics and the contradictions of America and race.

Carl Brucker
Updated by Charles A. Gramlich

OTHER MAJOR WORKS

POETRY: *Catechism of D Neoamerican Hoodoo Church*, 1970; *Conjure: Selected Poems, 1963-1970*, 1972; *Chattanooga*, 1973; *A Secretary to the Spirits*, 1977; *Cab Calloway Stands In for the Moon*, 1986; *New and Collected Poems*, 1988; *New and Collected Poems, 1964-2006*, 2006.

NONFICTION: *Shrovetide in Old New Orleans*, 1978; *God Made Alaska for the Indians*, 1982; *Writin' Is Fightin': Thirty-seven Years of Boxing on Paper*, 1988; *Airing Dirty Laundry*, 1993; *Conversations with Ishmael Reed*, 1995; *Another Day at the Front: Dispatches from the Race War*, 2002 (essays); *Blues City: A Walk in Oakland*, 2003; *Mixing It Up: Taking on the Media Bullies and Other Reflections*, 2008.

EDITED TEXTS: *Nineteen Necromancers from Now*, 1970; *Yardbird Lives!*, 1978 (with Al Young); *Calafia: The California Poetry*, 1979 (with Young and Shawn Hsu Wong); *The Before Columbus Foundation Fiction Anthology: Selections from the American Book Awards, 1980-1990*, 1992 (with Kathryn Trueblood and Wong); *MultiAmerica: Essays on Cultural Wars and Cultural Peace*, 1997; *From Totems to Hip-Hop*, 2003.

MISCELLANEOUS: *The Reed Reader*, 2000.

BIBLIOGRAPHY

Boyer, Jay. *Ishmael Reed*. Boise, Idaho: Boise State University Press, 1993. A brief, fifty-two-page overview of Reed's life and works. Includes a bibliography. One of the volumes in the Western Writers series.

Dick, Bruce Allen, and Amritjit Singh, eds. *Conversations with Ishmael Reed*. Jackson: University Press of Mississippi, 1995. A compilation of twenty-six interviews with the author that were conducted from 1968 until 1995. Includes one self-interview and a chronology of significant events in Reed's life.

Dick, Bruce Allen, and Pavel Zemliansky, eds. *The Critical Response to Ishmael Reed*. Westport, Conn.: Greenwood Press, 1999. Discusses Reed's novels in chronological order. Contains book reviews, essays, an interview in which Reed discusses works in progress, a chronology of his life, and bibliographical information.

Fox, Robert Elliot. *Conscientious Sorcerers: The Black Post-Modern Fiction of LeRoi Jones/Amiri Baraka, Ishmael Reed, and Samuel R. Delaney*. New York: Greenwood Press, 1987. A comparison of works by three African American writers who emerged in the 1960's. Fox situates Reed within both the tradition of black fiction and the self-conscious style of contemporary postmodernist fiction.

Gates, Henry Louis, Jr. *The Signifying Monkey: A Theory of Afro-American Literary Criticism*. New York: Oxford University Press, 1988. The section on Reed examines his fiction, especially the novel *Mumbo Jumbo*, as an extension of the tendency of black English to play deliberately with language.

McGee, Patrick. *Ishmael Reed and the Ends of Race*. New York: St. Martin's Press, 1997. McGee looks at Reed's refusal to meet expectations associated traditionally with African American writers, and he examines Reed's use of satire and his antagonism toward political correctness.

Mvuyekure, Pierre-Damien. *The "Dark Heathenism" of the American Novelist Ishmael Reed: African Voodoo as American Literary Hoodoo*. Lewiston, N.Y.: Edwin Mellen Press, 2007. Mvuyekure defines Reed's nine novels as postcolonial writings characterized by "neohoodoism," an aesthetic derived from African voodoo. He demonstrates how Reed transforms the English language and debates about colonialism into discourses about self-empowerment and self-representation, reconnecting African Americans with Africa.

_____, ed. *A Casebook Study of Ishmael Reed's "Yel-*

low Back Radio Broke-Down.* Chicago: Center for
Book Culture, 2003. A collection of four essays that
analyze Reed's novel from several perspectives, including that of African voodoo and American jazz.
Weisenburger, Steven. *Fables of Subversion: Satire and*

the American Novel, 1930-1980. Athens: University
of Georgia Press, 1995. A discussion of Reed's use of
encyclopedic Menippean satire in his novel *Mumbo
Jumbo* is included in this study of satire in thirty postmodern American novels.

ERICH MARIA REMARQUE
Erich Paul Remark

Born: Osnabrück, Germany; June 22, 1898
Died: Locarno, Switzerland; September 25, 1970
Also known as: Erich Paul Remark

PRINCIPAL LONG FICTION

Die Traumbude, 1920
Station am Horizont, 1927-1928 (serial), 1998
  (book)
Im Westen nichts Neues, 1928 (serial), 1929
  (book; *All Quiet on the Western Front*, 1929)
Der Weg zurück, 1931 (*The Road Back*, 1931)
Drei Kameraden, 1938 (*Three Comrades*, 1937)
Liebe Deinen Nächsten, 1941 (*Flotsam*, 1941)
Arc de Triomphe, 1946 (*Arch of Triumph*, 1945)
Der Funke Leben, 1952 (*The Spark of Life*,
  1952)
Zeit zu leben und Zeit zu sterben, 1954 (*A Time to
  Love and a Time to Die*, 1954)
Der schwarze Obelisk, 1956 (*The Black Obelisk*,
  1957)
Der Himmel kennt keine Günstlinge, 1961
  (*Heaven Has No Favorites*, 1961; also known
  as *Bobby Deerfield*, 1961)
Die Nacht von Lissabon, 1962 (*The Night in
  Lisbon*, 1964)
Schatten im Paradies, 1971 (*Shadows in
  Paradise*, 1972)

OTHER LITERARY FORMS

Poetry, adventure stories, and articles by Erich Maria
Remarque (ruh-MAHRK) appeared in the 1920's in
German newspapers and magazines before the young

author had assumed his pen name, and the novel *Die
Traumbude* was succeeded by *Station am Horizont*, a
novel that first appeared in installments in the journal
Sport im Bild. In the United States, several novels by
Erich Maria Remarque reached mass circulation in magazines such as *Collier's* and *Good Housekeeping* before
being published as single titles.

The film *The Other Love* (directed by André De Toth
and released in 1947) was based on Remarque's unpublished story "Beyond," and the story "Der letzte Akt"
(1955) was based on his screenplay of the book *Ten
Days to Die* (1955) by Michael A. Musmanno, concerning the Nuremberg Trials of Nazi war criminals. Questions of guilt and moral responsibility in wartime, dominant themes in Remarque's works, are treated also in
his two-scene play *Die letzte Station*, which was produced in Germany in 1956 and was adapted in 1974 as
Full Circle.

ACHIEVEMENTS

All Quiet on the Western Front is one of the world's
most successful novels. Within months after its appearance, it was widely translated and distributed, and some
four decades later its author observed that the work had
been translated into almost fifty languages and had a circulation of twenty to thirty million copies, including so-
called pirated editions. Only in the degree of its popularity, however, was this book exceptional among Erich
Maria Remarque's works, for *Arch of Triumph* and *The
Night in Lisbon* were also best sellers, and more than half
of his novels, as well as a short story, have been adapted
into films.

Remarque's choice of subject matter explains the primary reason for his appeal. In his novels set against the background of the world wars, issues such as personal moral responsibility and military subordination, war guilt, and pacifism are treated from the perspective of the soldier. His novels set in the Weimar Republic depict the dislocation and disorientation of that era, a time of inflation, unemployment, and political unrest. Finally, his exile novels depict the fate of emigrants and exiles from Hitler's Third Reich.

The interest evoked by Remarque's choice of subject is heightened by a streamlined, uncomplicated style that moves quickly and lends itself with an objective, semidocumentary tone to the excitement of automobile racing, the suspense of chase and pursuit, the stark horror of war, or the brutalities of a concentration camp. Consistent with the author's technique are characters drawn with such simplicity that they appear without betraying any insight into their internal lives or psychological motivations.

The ease with which Remarque's works can be read has influenced his critical reception in Germany, as has the magnitude of his commercial success. In Germany, his novels are classified as *Unterhaltungsliteratur* (entertainment literature), a rubric with pejorative aesthetic connotations. Nevertheless, critics are uneasy with such an evaluation, for the author's style is not banal, and moral issues are not trivialized in his work. Among readers not bound by critical predispositions, such as his English-language audience, for example, Remarque's work is more highly regarded.

BIOGRAPHY

Erich Maria Remarque was born Erich Paul Remark in Osnabrück, Germany, on June 22, 1898, the son of a bookbinder. While he was still a schoolboy, his life was interrupted by service in World War I. Like Paul Bäumer and Ludwig Bodmer, his personas in the novels *All Quiet on the Western Front* and *The Black Obelisk*, Remarque left the classroom to fight in the west, from which he returned with war injuries.

During the postwar years, Remarque tried his hand at various pursuits, including teaching, sales work, and automobile racing. As a journalist, he wrote articles on such subjects as automobiles, travel, and liquors, as well

as poetry and prose. His novel *Die Traumbude* appeared in 1920.

Reverting to the original French spelling of his surname, the author assumed the name Remarque and in 1925 moved to Berlin, where his writing appeared in the metropolitan press during the Weimar Republic. In the same year, he married Jutta Ilse Zambona, from whom he was divorced only a few years later. In 1927 and 1928, the novel *Station am Horizont* appeared in installments in a popular magazine; generated by a sketch of 1924, "Das Rennen Vanderveldes," this work depicted an unhappy love affair played out against a background of horse racing and auto sports.

Remarque moved to Switzerland in the early 1930's, taking with him his considerable wealth and acquiring a luxurious villa on the Italian border in Tessin. The villa was located at Porto Ronco near Ascona on Laggo Maggiore, and Remarque maintained it all of his life. The conditions of the author's residence there and the voluntary nature of his absence from Germany were radically altered in 1933, when the Third Reich prohibited the publication and distribution of his work by consigning it to the blacklist for the crime of literary treason committed against the soldiers of World War I.

Three Comrades appeared in 1937 in the United States, and in 1938 it was published in German by the exile press Querido, in Holland. At that time, Remarque remarried his former wife in Saint Moritz. Deprived of his German citizenship, he was consigned to the fate of an estimated four hundred thousand emigrants from Nazi Germany, including some fifty thousand political and literary exiles. Many of them employed desperate means to flee an unknown fate, moving throughout the countries contiguous to Germany without legal status and therefore under the threat of apprehension by authorities of those professed democracies. Such a life in exile is the subject of *Flotsam*, a theme that would become familiar in Remarque's works.

The author himself remained luxuriously ensconced in Switzerland until 1939, at which time he departed for the United States and traveled to Hollywood to see acquaintances, including Marlene Dietrich and members of the German exile community. Unlike other writers in exile, many of whom were unknown outside their native countries and therefore were forced to accept

Erich Maria Remarque. (Library of Congress)

whatever work was available, Remarque enjoyed an international reputation. His fame, moreover, was matched by his wealth, which was augmented by the revenue from books, magazine serials, and several films. A film version of *The Road Back* in 1937 was followed by one of *Three Comrades* in 1938, the screenplay for the latter written by F. Scott Fitzgerald. The success of both was, however, dwarfed in 1930 by that of the film version of *All Quiet on the Western Front*, which won several Academy Awards and enjoyed box-office success.

Remarque was joined in the United States by his wife shortly after his arrival there. This time the marital union was maintained until 1951; seven years later, Remarque married the film actor Paulette Goddard, to whom he remained married for the rest of his life. Darkly handsome, a bon vivant and ladies' man, Remarque pursued his tastes for beautiful women, art (especially Impressionist works), and wines and liquors—interests shared by his characters (who, however, lack the financial means to enjoy them fully). These characters, moreover, have usually gained their knowledge of art in museums, during long hours of concealment from the police.

Arch of Triumph, in 1945, became Remarque's second great success, a novel of exile that reached several million copies in translation and remained in its popularity unrivaled by the author's succeeding four novels. In 1963, Remarque again successfully captured the imagination of his readers with a best-selling novel, *The Night in Lisbon*. The threads of these works set in France and Portugal were then brought together in the posthumous novel *Shadows in Paradise*, which unfolds in the United States. Here, the exile Ross arrives from Lisbon, last seen as the port of departure in *The Night in Lisbon*; Ravic, who lived through the last days in Paris before the outbreak of hostilities—as did the figures in *The Night in Lisbon*—returns from *Arch of Triumph*, now permitted in the United States to practice surgery once again.

During his later years, Remarque divided his time between New York City and the site of his villa in Switzerland; shortly after attaining U.S. citizenship, he returned to Germany in 1948 for the first time since he had emigrated. He made no attempt to regain that citizenship of which he had been deprived, and with some irony he noted the experience of the central figures in his last two novels upon their own postwar return to Germany. The man who, in *The Night in Lisbon*, has assumed the name Schwarz seeks to reestablish his identity at a time when hundreds of members of the "master race" are attempting to lose theirs; Ross in *Shadows in Paradise*, believing that war crimes should not go unpunished, is confronted by a wall of feigned ignorance and innocence regarding those who might be guilty.

Germany awarded Remarque a signal honor in 1967 by granting him the Great Service Cross of the Federal Republic. On September 25, 1970, he died in a hospital in Locarno, Switzerland.

ANALYSIS

In *All Quiet on the Western Front*, Erich Maria Remarque's most famous novel, the reader experiences events during World War I, from summer to fall, 1917, that reduce a military company of 150 men to only 32. Without purporting to be authentic, the account nevertheless compels credibility. The war is portrayed in a factual style with such immediacy and force that, however impartial, the report shocked Remarque's readership and provoked a strong pacifist response.

ALL QUIET ON THE WESTERN FRONT

One scene in the work is representative of many. It illustrates the undercurrent that awoke such a reaction and provides an insight into attitudes characteristic of Remarque's novels generally. When the teenage recruit Paul Bäumer takes refuge in a shell crater from which there is no retreat under fire, he finds himself unexpectedly forced to share the site with a Frenchman, whom he stabs. Forced to share cover with the corpse of his anonymous enemy during the long wait until the firing should cease, Bäumer familiarizes himself with the man's identity and background by examining his papers—those of a simple typesetter. Bäumer promises himself that he will thereafter support the man's family and oppose the war.

Such a scene, as well as the expressions of antimilitarism with which the work is rife, provoked a violent response from the political right, including public disturbances at the showing of the film version in Berlin in 1930. Zealots dedicated to avenging the perceived outrages perpetrated by the Treaty of Versailles were infuriated by the direct contradiction of National Socialist dogma: The defeat of the German army was portrayed not as the consequence of a perfidious "stab in the back" but as the result of an Allied advantage gained by fresher, more numerous troops with adequate matériel and support; Russians, a species relegated by National Socialist genetics to a subhuman order, behave in a more brotherly fashion to one another in captivity than do Germans to their comrades in arms.

Written in the style of the 1920's known as *Neue Sachlichkeit* (New Objectivity), *All Quiet on the Western Front* treats in simply constructed, precise, and quickly moving prose a theme current in the literature of that time. Coincidentally, it breaks sharply with another fashion then in vogue.

During the age of Bismarck and the kaisers, politics, society, and familial affairs were dominated by the authoritarian father figure, who brooked no dissent. A variant of this type was the tyrannical pedagogue, a familiar character in German literature since before the end of the nineteenth century. This figure intimidated his hapless subjects in an attempt to demean them and break their

spirits; at the same time, however, he fostered a streak of antiauthoritarianism in the more hardy of them. In *All Quiet on the Western Front*, the attitudes engendered by such experiences are represented among boys who are marched out of the classroom as a body by their teacher to enlist for military service at the front. There, the teacher is succeeded by sergeants and other (interchangeable) figures of authority who provoke reactions of slavishness and insubordination known to the members of an entire generation.

All Quiet on the Western Front appeared during a time when works dealing with World War I enjoyed considerable popularity in Germany. Unlike Remarque's novel, however, most of these works presented a justification or rationalization, from the German point of view, of this terrible European tragedy. The fiction of Ernst Jünger, for example, glorifies the ennobling effects of war—its intensification of the manly virtues and the strength of the race.

Purporting to be "neither an accusation nor a confession" but rather a report on "a generation which was destroyed by the war even though it escaped the grenades," Remarque's work assumes the role of documentary journalism. No attempt is made, however, to preserve objective distance; the reader is induced to identify with Paul Bäumer and his comrades from the outset. Nineteen years old and neither men nor boys, the former classmates are tragically out of place at the front, members of a company whose numbers have been reduced from 150 to 80 in only two weeks. Daily encounters with death have endowed the adolescents with precious wisdom, cynicism regarding the pronouncements of the older generation, self-reliance, and a sense of camaraderie. The fate of their classmate Josef Behm conveyed a lesson for their generation. Behm had been reluctant to serve. Shot in the eyes during battle, he crawled around blindly, unable to find cover, and was picked off by gunfire—one of the first to be killed.

The message of the novel is written in the experience of Bäumer and his comrades. What has been learned in school is useless; the knowledge they need was never entrusted to them—for example, the trick of making fire from wet wood or the advantage gained by stabbing one's bayonet into the opponent's belly rather than into his ribs. The prospect of civilian life looms as a void on the horizon. No occupational skills were learned in the military, and the resumption of study seems purposeless. The war has ruined men for everything. On leave from the front, Bäumer is unable to find his way about in the strange civilian world.

The impartiality conveyed by the objective tone of a military report is dispelled by the horror that the novel depicts. Thrust and parry, attack and counterattack follow mindlessly under a netlike arch of hand grenades as men forge forward over the trenches with spades and bayonets; wounded horses scream horribly until put to death after the last injured soldiers are retrieved. A wretched death is spread by poison gas, and even its survivors are nearly suffocated by repeated inhalation of nothing but their own warm breath under the gas mask. Young, inexperienced recruits, ignorant of the uses of cover or the sound of shells, appear, only to be immediately shot down in scene after scene.

Remarque's literary characters move quickly along the hazardous course that traces the path of their lives. *All Quiet on the Western Front* is composed of a number of episodes collected into chapters that illustrate how chance, ingenuity, and determination are employed by a handful of soldiers to prevail against peril. As the novel progresses, the number of men diminishes until, finally, only one remains, Paul Bäumer, who himself dies on a day when the military dispatch reports that on the western front all is quiet, or, more accurately that there is "nothing new" (*nichts neues*): That is, the killing continues unabated; another death is not extraordinary.

The precariousness of survival—and its importance—is illustrated by the role that ordinary, but essential, objects play. A soldier whose leg had been amputated leaves his much-envied boots to a comrade, and shortly before each man's death, the boots are passed symbolically to the next man until Bäumer dies with them on his feet as the last of the seven classmates.

Respite from continuous struggle to survive and from exposure to danger presents itself when eight men remove themselves from the chaos about them. Isolation from events and the passage of time is achieved as in a return to the womb. On patrol in an empty village under fire, the soldiers collect all the provisions found there—suckling pigs, wine and spirits, sausage, canned goods, tobacco, and mattresses—and occupy the cellar and first floor of an empty house. For two weeks, they luxuriate there with drink, piano and song, and various pastimes, on an island of self-indulgent contentment and oblivion amid the continuing holocaust.

ARCH OF TRIUMPH

The uncertainties and hazards of life and the exigencies of survival are revealed nowhere more markedly than in Remarque's exile novels, the most successful example of which is *Arch of Triumph*. The work provided a formula to which the author returned: France in 1939, when German aliens concealed themselves in a sordid world consisting of seedy hotels and illegal activities and counted themselves lucky as long as they could evade the authorities who sought them for deportation to Switzerland. The central figure is pursued by a Gestapo agent from his past, whom he murders; the murderer then recklessly compounds his danger by returning illegally to Germany before he is finally detained and interned by French authorities upon the outbreak of war.

As the novel contains certain factual episodes or themes that reappear in other works, so, too, it brings together in the characters a complex of personality traits that can be found elsewhere in Remarque's fiction. From the earliest sketches originates the woman who suffers from cancer: in *Arch of Triumph*, Kate Hegström; in *Shadows in Paradise*, Betty Stein. The disease assumes tragic significance when it is recognized as terminal in the case of Helen Baumann in *The Night in Lisbon*, as it is with her predecessor, Pat Hollmann, in *Three Comrades*. In *Arch of Triumph*, too, Joan Madou, will be found, beautiful and amoral, infatuated by the attention of men and a captive of their devotion; she is distinguished from Helen Baumann only by her possessiveness.

The protagonist of *Arch of Triumph* is the German exile Ravic, once a soldier on the western front with Bäumer, it is suggested; thereafter a respected chief surgeon; and now, as an alien, an illegal medical practitioner. When faith and ideals are no longer sacrosanct, he observes, everything becomes more sacred in a human way; one reveres the spark of life in its lowest living form.

The significance attributed to coincidence in *All Quiet on the Western Front*, where chance alone enables the soldier to survive, plays a no less weighty role in *Arch of*

Triumph. Here it explains the fateful encounter of Ravic and Joan, as well as his subsequent deportation. Ravic's identity is established after he has been detained by the police as a witness, having passed a construction site as another pedestrian was injured there.

The couple's troubled love affair is threatened by insurmountable barriers, and their reaction to these threats is typical of Remarque's characters. Permanently paralyzed by a revolver shot from another lover and suffering unbearable pain, Joan easily persuades Ravic to administer to her a fatal injection as a means to escape the fate that lies ahead of her. Ravic himself, interned by French authorities as an enemy alien after the outbreak of war, awaits his end fatalistically with the comfort and sustaining strength provided by the knowledge of poison hidden in a hollow locket on his person, the thought of which enabled him once before to survive the ordeal of imprisonment in a German concentration camp.

THE NIGHT IN LISBON

The Night in Lisbon unfolds in a flashback set in France immediately prior to and during the war, a time when illegal immigrants, once mathematics professors or doctors, turned to passport forgery or the sale of stockings or of their valued Impressionist paintings to survive. It is the tale of a German immigrant, Josef Schwarz, told to an acquaintance, who listens patiently in return for two tickets on a passenger ship leaving the last point of departure from occupied Europe. Schwarz and his wife, Helen, were fleeing across Europe in the attempt to escape to the United States when Helen suddenly died. Schwarz relinquishes those passports and visas for which the couple no longer has any use, thus enabling the listener and his wife to find refuge in America themselves.

The exile phenomenon is associated in Remarque's works with religious imagery, which in *The Night in Lisbon* reaches its most highly developed form. The refugees are compared to the Israelites who departed from Egypt through the Red Sea—behind them, the German army and the Gestapo; to both sides, French and Spanish police; before them, the promised land of Portugal. The path of flight from Belgium to the Pyrenees and the suffering endured thereon are called to mind by the *via dolorosa*, Christ's route to the Crucifixion; America appears as Mount Ararat, a refuge from the Nazi flood, to be reached by ark from Lisbon.

In Remarque's work, a character whose daily existence is not exposed to inordinate risk lives in a most self-indulgent manner—as, indeed, the author did himself. Occasionally a person finds a den of refuge for concealment, a capsule within which he can withdraw to isolate himself from the unrelenting dangers of life. Oblivious to the world without, he exists as in another dimension, surrendering himself to the primary physical pleasures, as do the eight men in *All Quiet on the Western Front*.

In *The Night in Lisbon*, Helen and Schwarz interrupt their frantic flight from the Germans and police across several national boundaries when they discover an unoccupied mansion in France. There the two isolate themselves in a self-contained never-never land; with plentiful supplies of wine, potatoes, bread, honey, and firewood, they amuse themselves with abandoned masquerade costumes in a fool's paradise, undisturbed by the occasional drone of planes passing overhead.

When a central figure in Remarque's work sees his ultimate survival threatened by an insurmountable obstacle—such as cancer or the Gestapo—then he ends his own life, usually by poison, as in *Arch of Triumph*. The last days are played out with increasingly feverish enjoyment at an accelerating tempo to the discernibly approaching end. Helen's secret knowledge of her incurable malignant cancer heightens her frantic desire to enjoy herself, but the imminent threat of capture by the Germans, a prospect equivalent to death, requires an alternative sufficiently radical, and for this reason both Helen and Schwarz carry poison on their persons. The ultimate obstacle posed by Helen's terminal illness is surmounted by this means.

Remarque's individualism, his humanism, and his democratic instincts (however apolitical he was in practice) are the common threads that run throughout his work, linking *All Quiet on the Western Front* with his exile novels of the post-World War II years. It is, however, for a single book, his great novel of World War I, that Remarque will be remembered. In *All Quiet on the Western Front*, he gave voice to a lost generation—not metaphorically lost in the Paris of the 1920's but lost in battle by the hundreds of thousands.

Ward B. Lewis

OTHER MAJOR WORKS

PLAY: *Die letzte Station*, pr. 1956 (adapted by Peter Stone as *Full Circle*, 1974).

SCREENPLAY: *Der letzte Akt*, 1955.

BIBLIOGRAPHY

Barker, Christine R., and R. W. Last. *Erich Maria Remarque*. New York: Barnes & Noble Books, 1979. Provides an excellent introduction to Remarque's career, covering all of his major fiction. Includes bibliography and index.

Firda, Richard Arthur. *"All Quiet on the Western Front": Literary Analysis and Cultural Context*. New York: Twayne, 1993. Useful resource for students contains information on Remarque's life and career as well as discussion of the novel's autobiographical elements, style, and characterizations.

_____. *Erich Maria Remarque: A Thematic Analysis of His Novels*. New York: Peter Lang, 1988. Provides a good deal of helpful biographical material, relating Remarque's life to his novels. Firda's interpretation of Remarque's later novels is especially interesting.

Gilbert, Julie. *Opposite Attraction: The Lives of Erich Maria Remarque and Paulette Goddard*. New York: Pantheon, 1995. Combination biography and love story recounts the couple's meeting in the 1950's, their marriage in 1958, and their lives up to Remarque's death in 1970. Includes detailed notes and an excellent bibliography.

Gordon, Haim. *Heroism and Friendship in the Novels of Erich Maria Remarque*. New York: Peter Lang, 2003. Focuses on Remarque's depiction of ordinarily people who are capable of performing acts of heroism and of establishing genuine friendships in even the harshest circumstances. Includes bibliography and references.

Murdoch, Brian. *The Novels of Erich Maria Remarque: Sparks of Life*. Camden House, Rochester, N.Y.: 2006. Examines Remarque's entire body of writing, including his lesser-known novels, paying attention to recurring themes and motifs. Portrays Remarque as an artist, shedding light on his personal life and his reputation as a playboy.

Taylor, Harley U., Jr. *Erich Maria Remarque: A Literary and Film Biography*. New York: Peter Lang, 1989. Provides detailed background information on Remarque's family origins, his early years, his military service, and the making of the film adaptation of *All Quiet on the Western Front*. Includes bibliography, chronology, filmography, and index.

Tims, Hilton. *Erich Maria Remarque: The Last Romantic*. New York: Carroll & Graf, 2003. Biography focuses primarily on the events of Remarque's life, including his many relationships with women, rather than on his writings. Includes notes, bibliography, and index.

Wagener, Hans. *Understanding Erich Maria Remarque*. Columbia: University of South Carolina Press, 1991. Separate chapters examine individual major works, interweaving biographical background with literary analysis. Includes chronology, notes, and annotated bibliography.

MARY RENAULT
Mary Challans

Born: London, England; September 4, 1905
Died: Cape Town, South Africa; December 13,
1983
Also known as: Mary Challans

PRINCIPAL LONG FICTION

Purposes of Love, 1939 (also known as *Promise
of Love*, 1940)
Kind Are Her Answers, 1940
The Friendly Young Ladies, 1944 (also known as
The Middle Mist, 1945)
Return to Night, 1947
North Face, 1948
The Charioteer, 1953
The Last of the Wine, 1956
The King Must Die, 1958
The Bull from the Sea, 1962
The Mask of Apollo, 1966
Fire from Heaven, 1969
The Persian Boy, 1972
The Praise Singer, 1978
Funeral Games, 1981
The Alexander Trilogy, 1984 (includes *Fire from
Heaven*, *The Persian Boy*, and *Funeral
Games*)

OTHER LITERARY FORMS

All but two of the works published by Mary Renault
(rehn-OHLT) are novels. *The Lion in the Gateway: Heroic Battles of the Greeks and Persians at Marathon, Salamis, and Thermopylae* (1964) is a children's history of
ancient Greek battles. *The Nature of Alexander* (1975) is
a heavily documented biography placing the charismatic
leader in the context of his time and customs, a book that
also defines the two abiding preoccupations of Alexander's life and Renault's art. "Outward striving for honor,"
the Greek *to philotimo*, balances *arete*, the profound inward thirst for achievement knowingly made beautiful.
Together, as Alexander himself wrote, they win immortality: "It is a lovely thing to live with courage,/ and die
leaving an everlasting fame."

ACHIEVEMENTS

Critics praised Mary Renault's first five novels, written and set around World War II, for their realism, psychological depth, and literary technique. In 1946, one
year prior to its publication, *Return to Night* won the
MGM Award, $150,000, then the world's largest liter-
ary prize. Although this novel was never made into a motion picture, the award brought Renault American acclaim, augmented later by the success of her Greek
novels, but her work has never gained the academic attention it deserves. Renault received the National Association of Independent Schools Award in 1963 and the
Silver Pen Award in 1971, and she was a fellow of the
Royal Society of Literature.

BIOGRAPHY

Mary Renault (the pen name of Mary Challans), a
physician's daughter, was born on September 4, 1905, in
London. At eight, she decided to become a writer, and
she read English at St. Hugh's College, Oxford, from
1924 to 1927, where she preferred to study the Middle
Ages, the setting of an attempted historical novel she destroyed after several rejections. She had once thought of
teaching, but after graduation she entered nurses' training at Radcliffe Infirmary, Oxford, where she received
her nursing degree in 1937. She dated her literary career
from 1939, though she continued as a neurosurgical
nurse at Radcliffe Infirmary throughout World War II,
writing in her off-duty hours. Her first novels were
widely popular, but she claimed, according to Bernard F.
Dick, that "if her early novels were destroyed irrevoca-
bly, she would feel absolutely no loss."

Renault's postwar travels in the eastern Mediterranean
provided the impetus for a new literary phase marked by
her emigration to South Africa in 1948. After this move,
her exhaustive self-taught knowledge of ancient Greek
history and philosophy made her a mesmerizing novelist
able to re-create a lost world. In the estimation of Dick,
Renault was "the only bona fide Hellenist in twentieth
century fiction." Renault remained a resident of South
Africa until her death on December 13, 1983.

ANALYSIS

Mary Renault's novels celebrate and eulogize people's potential but transitory glory, a combination difficult for a world that has relinquished its acquaintance with the classics. Critic Peter Wolfe has described Renault's first five novels as her literary apprenticeship, "1930's novels" marked by then-fashionable themes of political engagement and sexual liberation. Bernard F. Dick has argued that her early fiction was influenced by the restrictive, pain-filled atmosphere of a World War II surgical hospital. Both are partly correct; Renault's early work deals with the individual's freedom from contemporary power structures and stifling social conventions.

Such topical concerns, however appealing to modern readers, are nevertheless peripheral to the core of Renault's art, the Platonism that she followed to the mythic depths in her later novels. When she began to write, Renault was already familiar with the Theory of Ideas developed in Plato's dialogues, wherein everything perceptible by human senses is imitative of changeless perfect Ideas beyond time and space. Each Idea corresponds to a class of earthly objects, all of which must inevitably change, leaving the Ideas the only objects of true knowledge in the universe. A transitory earthly object, however, may remind people of the Idea it represents. Plato theorized that before entering the body, the soul had encountered the infinite Ideas, and that, once embodied, the soul might vaguely remember them. Renault often convincingly incorporates Plato's anamnesis, the doctrine that "learning is recollection," in her fiction. Plato also believed that human recognition of such natural truths as the mathematically perfect circle could lead people stepwise to the contemplation of Absolute Truth, which he equated with Absolute Goodness and Absolute Beauty. He taught that the immortal human soul may be reborn through metempsychosis, or transmigration, another concept found throughout Renault's work.

Renault's novels are also informed by Plato's theory of love as defined by Socrates in *The Symposium* (c. 388-368 B.C.E.): Love is the desire for immortality through possession of or union with the Beautiful. Love manifests itself on its lowest levels by human sexuality, proceeds upward through intellectual achievement, and culminates in a mystical union of the soul with the Idea of Beauty. That Renault's heroes aspire to such union is their glory; that being mortal they must fail is the fate she eulogizes.

Plato, like most classical Greeks, allowed heterosexual love only the lowest rung on his ladder of love, as the necessary element for reproduction. Only the homosexual relationship was considered capable of inspiring the lifelong friendships that offered each partner the ideal of *arete*. All of Renault's novels illustrate some aspect of Platonic love; in the first, *Promise of Love*, she shows Vivian, a nurse, and Mic, who loves her because she resembles her brother Jan, achieving self-knowledge not through sexual passion but by affection, the ultimate stage of Platonic love, which at the close of the novel "recalls the true lover of [Plato's dialogue] the *Phaedrus* who is willing to sleep like a servant at the side of his beloved."

Renault's other early novels also have strong Platonic elements. *Kind Are Her Answers* foreshadows her interest in theater as mimetic form, Plato's first literary love, which she realized more fully in *The Mask of*

Mary Renault. (The Granger Collection, New York)

Apollo. Her third novel, *The Middle Mist*, concludes with references to Plato's *Lysis*, his dialogue on friendship that claims that erotic satisfaction destroys *philia*, the more permanent nonphysical union promised by Platonic love, a theme to which Renault returned more successfully in *The Last of the Wine*. Renault attempted unconvincingly in *Return to Night* and *North Face* to state the *amor vincit omnia* tradition of "women's fiction" in mythological metaphors, and found that she had to develop a new fictional mode capable of expressing her archetypal themes with Platonic concepts.

THE CHARIOTEER

Not published in the United States until 1959 because of its forthright treatment of homosexuality, *The Charioteer* is the only Renault novel to incorporate a systematic development of Platonic philosophy as the vehicle for commentary on contemporary life. In the *Phaedrus* (c. 388-368 B.C.E.), Plato depicted reason as a charioteer who must balance the thrust of the white horse of honor against the unruly black horse of passion. The image unifies Renault's tale of Laurie Odell, wounded at Dunkirk, who must come to terms with his homosexuality. After his friendship with the sexually naïve conscientious objector Andrew Raines dissolves, Laurie finds a lifelong partner in Ralph Lanyon, who brought him back wounded after they had fought at Dunkirk. Laurie attains an equilibrium between the two conflicting halves of his nature in a Platonic denial of sexual excess. As Renault comments in the epilogue, a Greek device she favors, "Now their [the horses'] heads droop side by side till their long manes mingle; and when the charioteer falls silent they are reconciled for a night in sleep."

In the ideal Platonic pattern, the older man assumes a compassionate responsibility for the honor of the younger, altogether transcending physical attraction and cemented by shared courage in battle. Renault's efforts at an entirely convincing presentation of such friendship are hindered by the intolerance with which homosexual relationships were usually viewed in the society of her time and the often pathetic insecurity it forced upon them. Despite these handicaps, Renault sympathetically portrays Laurie as "a modern Hephaestus, or maimed artist," as Wolfe notes, a character who wins admiration through striving to heal his injured life and nature and make of them something lasting and beautiful.

From roots far deeper than Plato's philosophy, Renault developed the vital impulse of her eight Greek novels, her major literary achievement. Central is the duality of Apollo and Dionysus, names the Greeks gave to the forces of the mind and of the heart, gods whose realms the mythologist Walter F. Otto has described as "sharply opposed" yet "in reality joined together by an eternal bond." In Greek myth, Zeus's archer son Apollo, wielder of the two-sided weapon of Truth, endowed people with the heavenly light called Art, by which he admonished humankind to self-knowledge and moderation through his oracle at Delphi. Paradoxically, Apollo shared his temple and the festival year at Delphi with his mysterious brother Dionysus, god of overwhelming ecstasy, born of mortal woman and all-powerful Zeus, torn apart each year to rise again, offering both wine's solace and its madness to humankind. Thought and emotion were the two faces of the Greek coin of life—in Otto's words, "the eternal contrast between a restless, whirling life and a still, far-seeing spirit."

Each of Renault's Greek novels focuses on a crucial nexus of physical and spiritual existence in Greek history. The age of legendary heroes such as Theseus of Athens, subject of *The King Must Die* and *The Bull from the Sea*, was followed by the Trojan War, 1200 B.C.E., the stuff of classical epic and tragedy and the harbinger of Greece's Dark Age, when only Athens stood against the Dorian invasion. By the sixth century B.C.E., the setting of *The Praise Singer*, Athens, under the benevolent tyrant Pisistratus, had become the model *polis* of the Greek peninsula, building a democracy that repelled imperial Persia and fostered the world's greatest tragedies in their Dionysian festivals. *The Last of the Wine* treats the fall of Athens to Sparta in the Peloponnesian Wars, 404 B.C.E., torn by internal strife and bled by foreign expansion. The restored Athenian democracy of a half-century later is the milieu of *The Mask of Apollo*. Shortly after Plato's death, his pupil Aristotle taught a prince in Macedon who dreams of Homeric deeds in *Fire from Heaven*, accomplishes them in *The Persian Boy*, and leaves an empire to be shattered by lesser men in *Funeral Games*—Alexander the Great.

THE LAST OF THE WINE

The Last of the Wine, like most of Renault's Greek fiction, is ostensibly a memoir, a form favored by classical authors. Its fictional narrator, a young and "beautiful" Athenian knight named Alexias, endures the agonizing aftermath of Athens's ill-fated Sicilian venture under Alkibiades, the magnetic but flawed former student of Sokrates. With Lysis, the historical figure on whom Plato modeled his dialogue on ideal friendship, Alexias begins the idealistic attachment they learned together from Sokrates, but physical passion, handled with sensitivity by Renault, overcomes them, and they ruefully must compromise their ideal. Sacrificing his honor for Lysis during the famine caused by the Spartan siege of Athens, Alexias models for sculptors, at least one lascivious, to feed his wounded friend, and in the battle to restore Athenian democracy, Lysis falls gloriously with Alexias's name upon his lips.

The novel's title, an allusion to the Greek custom in which the wine remaining in a cup is tossed to form the initial of a lover's name, metaphorically represents Athens's abandonment of the ideals of its Golden Age. Renault poignantly shows Lysis, a gentleman athlete in pursuit of *philotimo*, the hero's struggle for outward glory to emulate his ideal, beaten sadistically in the Isthmian Games by a monstrous professional wrestler, just as Athenian democracy is becoming warped by politicians such as the vicious Kritias and the cold-blooded Anytos, who will help condemn Sokrates. Alkibiades' personal disaster, abandoning Athens for its Spartan enemies, is an exemplary case of a leader who cannot resist abusing his charismatic gifts.

The Greek ideal of democracy learned at Sokrates' side and based on individual *arete*, inward pursuit of honor, still allows Lysis a moral victory often overlooked in this splendidly elegiac novel of the death of an era. "Men are not born equal in themselves," Lysis tells Alexias over wine one evening in Samos. "A man who thinks himself as good as everyone else will be at no pains to grow better." Lysis fights and dies for "a City where I can find my equals and respect my betters . . . and where no one can tell me to swallow a lie because it is expedient." At the end of the novel, as he listens to the distorted minds of bureaucrats, Alexias remembers the lamps of Samos, the wine-cup on a table of polished wood, and Lysis's voice: "Must we forsake the love of excellence, then, till every citizen feels it alike?"

The King Must Die *and* The Bull from the Sea

Renault analyzes the ideal of kingship in *The King Must Die* and *The Bull from the Sea*. In the earlier novel, she traces Theseus's early life from Troezen and Eleusis, where with the bard Orpheus he establishes the Sacred Mysteries, to the labyrinthine palace of Crete, where he destroys the brutal son of King Minos, who oppresses Athens. In the second, she pursues Theseus's progressive rule in Athens through his abandonment of Ariadne to Dionysus's bloody cult and his capture of the Amazon Hippolyta to the great tragedy of his life, his fatal curse on their son Hippolytus. Stylistically more evocative of Homer's mighty simplicity than the Attic cadences of *The Last of the Wine*, Renault's Theseus novels treat kingship as a manifestation of the divine inner voice that chooses the moment of willing consent when the monarch sacrifices himself for his people.

Both novels discuss a past so dim that its events have become the raw material of myth. Theseus's birth meshes the earthly with the supernatural, since it results from the divinely inspired compassion of the Athenian King Aigios for the stricken land of Troezen; the reader is left, as is customary in Renault's fiction, to decide where history ends and metaphysics begins. Until his son's death, Theseus practices the lesson learned from his grandfather's ritual sacrifice of the King Horse, one of the shocking joys hidden in pain that opens much of Renault's fiction: "The consenting . . . the readiness is all. It washes heart and mind . . . and leaves them open to the god."

By closing himself to the speaking god, however, obeying not his reason but his emotional reaction to his wife Phaedra's false accusations of Hippolytus, Theseus is lost. Only two bright moments remain to him: an anamnetic dream of Marathon where he fights beside the Athenians defending their city, his name their stirring war cry, and a glimpse before he dies of the boy Achilles, "as springy and as brisk as noonday, his arm round a dark-haired friend." Prescient, Theseus watches tragedy in the making: "The god who sent him that blazing pride should not have added love to be burned upon it," but— consoled that his own reputation has become Achilles' "touchstone for a man"—Theseus for the last time consents to the god of the sea.

THE MASK OF APOLLO

By the mid-fourth century B.C.E., late in Plato's life, sophisticated Athenians had accepted the gods as metaphysical forces within the human personality. In *The Mask of Apollo*, Renault poses the primal duality of Apollo and Dionysus in Greek culture, the calm, farseeing force of reason and art balanced against the irresistible force of ecstasy. An old mask of Apollo, reputedly from the workshop of the Parthenon's architect Phidias, accompanies Renault's narrator Nikeratos through his successful acting career, the fascinating backdrop to the political career of Dion of Syracuse, Plato's noble friend, who might have become the ideal philosopher-king Plato postulated in *The Republic*.

Though Dion is a model soldier and a principled statesman, circumstances force him to abandon his philosophical ideals to save Syracuse from devastation. Renault parallels his fall with Nikeratos's performance in Euripides' *The Bacchae* (405 B.C.E.), the enigmatic masterpiece named for the followers of Dionysus. As he meditates before Apollo's mask, Nikeratos hears his own voice: "With *The Bacchae* he [Euripides] digs down far below, to some deep rift in the soul where our griefs begin. Take that play anywhere, even to men unborn who worship other gods or none, and it will teach them to know themselves."

Plato's tragedy, acted out by Dion, was the "deep rift" that made people unable to follow him with united minds and hearts: "No one would fight for Dion, when he gave, as his own soul saw it, his very life for justice." By serving Apollo and Dionysus equally, however, Nikeratos the artist earns his gifts, one a Platonic dream of acting in a strange revenge drama, speaking lines beside an open grave to a clean skull in his hand. Through his love for his protégé Thettalos, whom he frees for achievements he knows will be greater than his own, Nikeratos plays Achilles in Aeschylus's *The Myrmidons* in a performance viewed by Alexander, a boy for whom men will fight and die, "whether he is right or wrong," a prince who "will wander through the world . . . never knowing . . . that while he was still a child the thing he seeks slipped from the world, worn out and spent." Had he encountered Plato's Ideals, which he instinctively sought, Renault proposes as the curtain falls on *The Mask of Apollo*, the Alexander of history might have made the philosopher-king Plato's Dion never could have been; but Nikeratos observes that "no one will ever make a tragedy—and that is well, for one could not bear it—whose grief is that the principals never met."

FIRE FROM HEAVEN

Renault's Alexander grows from boy to king in *Fire from Heaven*, in which she abandons the memoir form for more objective narration, as though no single point of view could encompass Alexander's youthful ideals, fired by the blazing Homeric *philotimo* in Achilles' honor he learned at the epic-conscious Macedonian court. Modern archaeology supports Renault's conviction that Alexander deliberately patterned his actions, even his father Philip's funerary rites, on the *Iliad* (c. 750 B.C.E.; English translation, 1611), which he read as though returning home, recognizing in his mutual love with Hephaistion the tragic bond of Achilles and Patroclus, the basis of the Western world's first, perhaps greatest, poem.

Arete, which cloaks the heavenly Idea of excellence in earthly beauty, came to Alexander less from Aristotle than through his instinctive attraction to Sokrates through Plato's works, which he read as a boy in Macedon. After defeating Thebes's Sacred Band at Cheironeia, where Philip's Macedonians secured the domination of all of Greece, Alexander stands "with surmise and regret" at Plato's tomb in Athens, listening to his disciple Xenokrates: "What he [Plato] had to teach could only be learned as fire is kindled, by the touch of the flame itself."

THE PERSIAN BOY

The novel in which Renault most precariously treats the question of homosexuality, *The Persian Boy*, is narrated by Bagoas, the handsome eunuch once King Darius's favorite and now the lover of Alexander. Renault's choice of Bagoas's point of view reflects her belief that Alexander was not corrupted by Persian luxury and imperial power, as many historians from classical times to the present have asserted, but that he sought to assimilate Eastern ways as a means of uniting his realm in spirit as well as military fact. Just as Alexander's "passionate capacity for affection" could allow him to accept affection wherever it was sincerely offered from the heart and yet remain wholly true to Bagoas's "victor now, forever," Hephaistion (who Renault feels is the most underrated man in history), Alexander felt "Macedon was my father's country. This is mine"—meaning the empire he had won for himself.

Renault believes that Alexander's eventual tragedy was that he was humanly unable to achieve equilibrium between his followers' personal devotion to him and their pragmatic selfish desires. Through Alexander's complex relationship with his dangerous mother Olympias, herself a devotee of Dionysus, Renault exemplifies the peril of neglecting the god of ecstasy basic to *The Bacchae*, in which Olympias herself had acted during Alexander's youth as a shocking challenge to Philip's authority. Toward the end of Alexander's own life, Dionysus's cruelty touches even him. Renault shows his purported deterioration as less his own fault than his men's when he must hold them by force as well as by love, even violating Macedon's dearest law, killing before their Assembly had condemned a man to death. The powerful god leads Alexander to excess; Bagoas sees that "his hunger grew by feeding." The Roman historian Arrian, following the memoir of Alexander's only faithful general Ptolemy, commented, "If there had been no other competition, he would have competed against himself."

Bagoas better than any also sees that "great anguish lies in wait for those who long too greatly." Alexander loses Hephaistion and with him nearly abandons his own senses, emerging only after his friend's funeral, in which he watches Thettalos, without Nikeratos for the first time, perform *The Myrmidons* one last time; "'Perhaps,' Bagoas thought, 'the last of the madness had been seared out of him by so much burning.'"

At the close of *The Persian Boy*, Renault notes in her afterword, "When his [Alexander's] faults (those his own times did not account as virtues) have been considered . . . no other human being has attracted in his lifetime, from so many men, so fervent a devotion. Their reasons are worth examining." In her two novels of Alexander's life, Renault not only examines the reasons but also brilliantly probes to the heart of one of the greatest human mysteries: how one person can ask, as did Homer's Achilles, "Now as things are, when the ministers of death stand by us/ In their thousands, which no man born to die can escape or even evade,/ Let us go"— and how other people, with all their hearts, can answer.

Such "true songs are still in the minds of men," according to the aged bard Simonides, narrator of *The Praise Singer*, recalling the "lyric years" when tragedy was being born of song and Athens was becoming the center of the earth. "We die twice when men forget," the ghosts of heroes seemed to tell him as a boy, and he has spent his life in "the bright and perilous gift of making others shine." In this novel, where Renault's heroic epitaph for *philotimo* and her noble elegy for people's hope of *arete* have given place to a gentler, less exalted nostalgia, she recognizes that "praising excellence, one serves the god within it." Renault also notes in her afterword that "the blanket generalization 'absolute power corrupts absolutely' is a historical absurdity," and she demonstrates that the respected rule of Pisistratus, nominally a "tyrant," formed the solid foundation on which Pericles erected Athenian democracy, even presaging through a discredited seer "a lightning flash from Macedon."

In Alexander's time, Renault observed, "the issue was not whether, but how one made [war]." At his death, brought about at least in part by his self-destructive grief for Hephaistion, Alexander's generals embarked on a cannibalistic power struggle—only Ptolemy, his half brother, emerging with any of the dignity Alexander had worn so easily in conquering his empire. Renault's *Funeral Games* is "the ancestral pattern of Macedonian tribal and familial struggles for his throne; except that Alexander had given them a world stage on which to do it."

FUNERAL GAMES

The most violent of Renault's Greek novels, *Funeral Games* contains a darkness that is alleviated only by flashes of Alexander reflected through the decency of the few who knew him best—Ptolemy, Bagoas, and Queen Sisygambis, who looked upon Alexander, not Darius, as her son. In them, something of Alexander's flame lingers a little while, a heavenly light extinguished at last in the wreckage of his empire in human depravity that Alexander could not prevent nor Renault fail to record.

In her eight novels of ancient Greece, Renault far surpasses conventional historical fiction. She achieves a mythic dimension in her balance of Apollonian and Dionysian psychological forces and philosophical precision in her treatment of Platonic doctrines. Her style is adapted to the Greek literature of each period she delineates, Attic elegance for *The Last of the Wine* and *The Mask of Apollo*, Hellenic involution counterpoised against Alexander's Homeric simplicity of speech. Renault links all eight novels with a chain of works of art, a finely crafted touch the classical Greeks would have applauded: The great tragedies, *The Myrmidons* and *The Bacchae*, Polykleitos's sculpture of Hermes modeled on Alexias, and the bronze of the liberator Harmodios in Pisistratos's day all serve as shaping factors in the portrait of her ultimate hero, Alexander. Mastering time, space, and modern ignorance of the classical world, Renault captures the "sadness at the back of life" that Virginia Woolf so aptly cited as the essence of Greek literature, the inevitable grieving awareness of people at the impassable gulf between their aspirations and their achievement. In the face of the eternal questions of existence, Renault's novels offer a direction in which to turn when, in Woolf's words, "we are sick of the vagueness, of the confusion, of the Christianity and its consolations, of our own age."

Mitzi M. Brunsdale

OTHER MAJOR WORKS

NONFICTION: *The Nature of Alexander*, 1975.

CHILDREN'S LITERATURE: *The Lion in the Gateway: Heroic Battles of the Greeks and Persians at Marathon, Salamis, and Thermopylae*, 1964.

BIBLIOGRAPHY

Abraham, Julie. "Mary Renault's Greek Drama." In *Are Girls Necessary? Lesbian Writing and Modern Histories*. New York: Routledge, 1996. Chapter on Renault's work is part of a larger study of lesbian writers. Discusses *The Last of the Wine*, *The Mask of Apollo*, *The Charioteer*, and other works.

Conrath, Alan Brady. "Something About Mary." *Gay and Lesbian Review Worldwide* 11, no. 3 (May/June, 2004): 15-17. Discusses why Renault is not considered a top-rank writer, attributing her literary reputation to the current critical bias against historical fic-

tion and the fact that Renault was a woman writer in the 1950's and 1960's.

Dick, Bernard F. *The Hellenism of Mary Renault*. Carbondale: Southern Illinois Press, 1972. Excellent introduction to Renault's work examines her entire literary output through *Fire from Heaven*. Dick places Renault in the mainstream of fiction and applauds her as one of the most creative historical novelists of the twentieth century.

Hoberman, Ruth. *Gendering Classicism: The Ancient World in Twentieth-Century Women's Historical Fiction*. Albany: State University of New York Press, 1997. Presents a feminist interpretation of historical fiction set in ancient Greece and Rome. Examines works by Renault and five other women writers, describing how these writers challenged the misogynist classical tradition.

Moore, Lisa L. "Lesbian Migrations." *GLQ: A Journal of Lesbian and Gay Studies* 10, no. 1 (2004): 23-46. Discusses Renault's place within gay and lesbian literature, evaluating the work of the pioneer lesbian writer, who disavowed gay rights, deemed male artists to be superior to women, and benefited from South African apartheid.

Sweetman, David. *Mary Renault: A Biography*. New York: Harcourt Brace, 1993. Explores Renault's life in England, including her education at Oxford, and then describes her years in South Africa. Offers a fascinating study of Renault's sexuality as it relates to her historical novels. Includes bibliography.

Wolfe, Peter. *Mary Renault*. New York: Twayne, 1969. First book-length examination of the writer is both a plea for Renault's recognition by the critics as an important twentieth century writer and a critical analysis of her work.

Zilboorg, Caroline. *The Masks of Mary Renault: A Literary Biography*. Columbia: University of Missouri Press, 2001. Analyzes Renault's novels from the perspective of queer theory, arguing that the depiction of transgressive sexual identities is a common feature of Renault's fiction. Includes bibliography and index.

WŁADYSŁAW REYMONT

Born: Kobiele Wielkie, Poland; May 7, 1867
Died: Warsaw, Poland; December 5, 1925
Also known as: Władysław Stanisław Reymont;
Władysław Stanisław Rejment

PRINCIPAL LONG FICTION

Komediantka, 1896 (*The Comedienne*, 1920)
Fermenty, 1897
Ziemia obiecana, 1899 (*The Promised Land*, 1927)
Chłopi, 1904-1909 (4 volumes; *The Peasants*, 1924-1925)
Marzyciel, 1910
Wampir, 1911
Rok 1794, 1913-1918 (3 volumes)

OTHER LITERARY FORMS

Although Władysław Reymont (RAY-mahnt) is remembered and celebrated chiefly as an epic novelist, his contribution to Polish literature includes a number of volumes of novellas and short fiction. Many of the scenes and characters that appear in the longer works, notably in *The Comedienne* and *The Peasants*, find their origins—in far cruder, less refined form—in the earlier short pieces. The most important collections and single editions of these works that significantly shaped the author's later masterpieces are "Pielgrzymka do Jasnej Góry" (1895; a pilgrimage to Jasna Góra), *Spotkania* (1897; meetings), "Lili" (1899), *Burza* (1907; the storm), *Z ziemi chełmskiej* (1910; from the Chełm territory), and *Za frontem* (1919; beyond the front).

There is evidence (confirmed in the author's correspondence and other sources) that Reymont attempted a number of plays, including a dramatization of *The Peasants*. A drama titled *Za późno* (too late) was staged in Paris and Warsaw in 1899, but no texts of these dramatic works have survived. Reymont's letters, particularly his impressions of travels abroad, have been published in uncollected editions.

ACHIEVEMENTS

During his lifetime, Władysław Reymont achieved a reputation of some note among Polish readers. After the publication of *The Comedienne*, his subsequent works were anticipated with great interest and even impatience, particularly the long-awaited final volumes of *The Peasants*. The long works, once they did appear, were not always met with unanimous accolades. Some reviewers complained that the author lacked a solid ideological point of view; others found the characterizations insufficiently developed, stereotyped, and unconvincing. Reymont's prominence, however, is not a result of the political content of his oeuvre or the paradigms of Polish society he chose to depict in his fiction; rather, his contribution stems from the epic, panoramic overview of the particular social class or professional milieu he so ably described. Reymont's most rewarding scenes present crowds: masses of peasants, underpaid laborers, or impoverished traveling actors. His keen attention to detail, together with his photographic memory (which captured not only visual but also all encompassing sensual images), served to portray accurately not specific heroes but heroic classes, not the greatness of individuals but the grandeur of universals.

This ability to present lucid, descriptive accounts of the essence of Polish national character, pastimes, and traditions led to Reymont's quick acceptance by an international audience. Translations of the major works (notably *The Promised Land* and parts of *The Peasants*) into Russian, German, and Swedish appeared soon after the original, prompting the author's candidacy for the Nobel Prize in Literature as early as 1918. Because of external political considerations, however, Reymont was not awarded the world's highest literary honor until 1924, at which time—according to the Swedish press—the Nobel was bestowed on the author ostensibly for *The Peasants* but also as an expression of "the sympathy of the Swedish people for the spiritual culture of that highly gifted Polish nation in the moment of triumph of a resurrected Poland."

BIOGRAPHY

Władysław Stanisław Reymont was born Władysław Stanisław Rejment, the fifth of nine children and the second son of Józef and Antonina (née Kupczyńska)

Rejment. The author's parents were petty landowners; the Rejments were a family in which, as biographer Barbara Kocówna has stated, "noble and peasant traditions intertwined." Reymont was born only four years after the unsuccessful January, 1863, uprising against the Russian occupiers of Poland. His early years were characterized by an atmosphere of patriotism and hard work, together with a strong devotion to cultural needs.

Once Reymont had achieved literary fame, he attempted to embellish or even alter his actual biography, often creating contradictory versions of his upbringing. There are, however, certain facts that require confirmation and others that appear indisputable.

Reymont was a rebellious youth who wanted no part of his family's agricultural livelihood. Similarly, he rejected his father's insistence on an education, even refusing to learn his father's profession of church organist. When Reymont failed his school entrance examinations, he was sent to Warsaw to live with his sister and brother-in-law and to learn the tailoring trade. Although he served his apprenticeship to the end, he did not take up his craft. Instead, he joined a traveling dramatic troupe (in 1884) and toured the provinces as a sometime actor. From all accounts, it appears that Reymont did not have acting abilities. Nevertheless, his experiences in the theater provided him with the subject matter for *The Comedienne* and its sequel, *Fermenty* (ferments).

Reymont sporadically held down a number of other jobs in trade and industry (even spending a short term as part of a circus group), interspersing these with equally brief stays with his family in the rural countryside. Ultimately, in the mid-1890's, he found steady employment at a small train station on the Warsaw-Vienna line, but this career was also short-lived.

Reymont, a self-taught man of letters, began writing seriously around this time and achieved his first literary success with the 1895 short story "Pielgrzymka do Jasnej Góry." He abandoned his railway job and returned to Warsaw to become a full-time writer. Living rather hand-to-mouth for the next five years, he managed to publish his theater novels and to become involved in spiritualist circles, which enabled him to travel to Paris and London. Reymont would maintain his interest in "life beyond the grave" for the rest of his life.

In 1898, Reymont accepted an advance from a Warsaw newspaper to write a novel on the industrial city of Lodz. He spent several months in this city of central Poland, producing his first epic, *The Promised Land*. In 1900, the author was injured in a railway accident outside Warsaw. His health would never again be the same. Compensation for injuries suffered in the mishap enabled Reymont to live independently, though not extravagantly, for the remainder of his life. In 1902, he married Aurelia Szacsznajder Szabłowska. They had no children.

During the first decade of the twentieth century, Reymont drew on his knowledge of rural life in Poland for the setting and inspiration of his greatest work, *The Peasants*. He then undertook to write a historical epic, but the intellectual implications and political context proved somewhat overwhelming for the autodidact. *Rock 1794* (the year 1794), a historical trilogy, was not favorably received.

In 1919 and 1920, Reymont, at the request of the Polish government, traveled to the United States to establish closer ties with immigrants settled there. These voyages produced a few short stories and several references in the author's correspondence to plans for another epic work—on the Polish émigré population in America.

Reymont spent the latter years of his life between his estate at Kołaczkowo and an apartment in Warsaw, writing short stories and contemplating his next novel. His last published work was a short piece titled "Bunt" (1924; the rebellion). Although he was aware of his candidacy for the Nobel Prize, he stated in his letters that this international recognition came as a surprise to him. Because of his ill health, he was unable to attend the 1924 ceremonies in Stockholm. Reymont died in Warsaw in 1925.

ANALYSIS

Władysław Reymont was a writer of large novels, as there are painters of broad landscapes. His works can be compared to the paintings of Pieter Brueghel, bustling with activity and replete with detail. This comparison with the sixteenth century Flemish artist can be extended even further: Both Brueghel and Reymont present panoramic scenes without specific heroes, yet they manage to convey precisely an ambience that immediately renders their works heroic and classic in composition.

Władysław Reymont. (© The Nobel Foundation)

Reymont's critics have charged that his novels suffer because of a lack of concentration on particular "heroic" personages. They assert that his overattention to detail in the descriptions of routines, customs, and other everyday realities surrounding his characters in fact detracts from their presentation and even distances the reader from identification and sympathy with potential heroes. It appears, however, that the author deliberately chose to emphasize the general, the sweeping nature of his vision, rather than encapsulate or incarnate it in the *dramatis personae* of his works. A catalog of the titles of his major works will confirm such an assumption: Excluding the first novel, *The Comedienne*, all subsequent titles indicate that Reymont was more interested in and intent on a presentation of—respectively—an urban milieu, the peasant class, and a historical era in *The Promised Land*, *The Peasants*, and *Rok 1794*. In this conscious election

of panorama over personage, Reymont recalls the epic nature of Leo Tolstoy's *Voyna i mir* (1865-1869; *War and Peace*, 1886).

Reymont was also accused by his contemporaries of a neglect of particular historical reference and ideological direction in his novels. There is some truth in this charge, but it must be remembered that the author was essentially uneducated. His intellectual limitations are most evident in the historical trilogy, for which the author conducted extensive research, but the result is an enumeration or regurgitation of textbook facts with no analysis or consideration of political implications. As a self-taught writer, however, Reymont was able to impart his knowledge and observations through his other literary works. What marks his greatness is not a lack of ideology but a keen awareness of feeling and attention to detail, a rich, emotional attachment to his subject, an affinity for the language, and a dedication to represent, as Reymont himself stated in his diary, life "as it is, not as it should be."

Reymont's early novels, like the short stories that anticipated them, depict the poverty and purposelessness of the lives of a troupe of traveling actors. As literary historian Julian Krzyżanowski has stated, the ordeals of Janka Orłowska in *The Comedienne* and *Fermenty* are important as a social document, "not for psychological depth, nor for sociological importance, but for their vital truth." The character of Janka, a would-be actor, is traced from her life in the theater, through the vicissitudes of such a peripatetic existence, to her return home (in the second novel) to resume a more stationary way of life on her father's estate. These debut novels are already characterized by their lengthy descriptions (here, of the drama troupe), Reymont's unique representation of characters through linguistic peculiarities, and his vivid depictions of nature and manorial life. Here, too, there is evidence of the author's predilection for the presentation of a human group as opposed to the potential heroic nature of an individual, in this case his leading lady. This tendency led in later works to a portrayal of an entire group as a heroic class.

THE PROMISED LAND

Reymont's *The Promised Land* is as much an anti-urban novel as it is a cinematic panorama of the rapidly growing industrial city of Lodz. Set in what Czesław

Miłosz has called "a kind of Manchester of eastern Europe," the novel centers on three young men, each a representative of one of the ethnic groups that have invaded the city to capitalize on its overnight boom. Karol Borowiecki, a Pole; Max Baum, a German; and Moryc Welt, a Jew, join forces for their mutual benefit to erect their own textile plant. These are the *Lodzermenschen*, a unique breed of ruthless capitalists, technologically superior but morally inferior to their parents and predecessors.

Surrounding the activities of this troika of would-be tycoons, there is an abundance of minor (and not so minor) characters whose presence serves to complete and particularize the ambitiously seething center for business and exploitation: Bucholc, the uncrowned king of Lodz and Borowiecki's former boss, whose life and death have meaning only as extensions of the machinery in his plant; Kessler, the abuser of young female employees who falls victim to one of his machines as he struggles with the father of one of the girls; Müller, the millionaire with the floridly decorated mansion in which he refuses to live; or his unappealing daughter, whom Borowiecki eventually marries (forsaking the woman who truly loved him and stood by him but who had no capital).

The Promised Land is also filled with descriptions of poverty, utter destitution, and injustice, as the laborers and peasants are abused and violated by their merciless employers. These people have traveled from their rural homesteads, abandoning their meager plots of land in search of "the promised land." They, too, like the *Lodzermenschen*, migrated to the city to find security and happiness; there is no happiness in this Polish Manchester, for, to Reymont's mind, there is no inherent good in the machines and machinations of urban industrialization. It is no accident, then, that the author depicts Lodz with repeated references to the animal and insect worlds. In the closing pages of the novel, Reymont, illustrating his antagonism toward the city and his despair for the nation that blindly marches toward industrialization, writes,

> For that "promised land," for that octopus, the villages have been deserted, the forests have disappeared, the land has been despoiled of its treasures, the rivers

dried out. For that land people were born. And it sucked everything in, crushed it in its powerful jaws, and chewed people and objects, the sky and the earth, in return giving useless millions to a handful of people and hunger and hardship to a whole throng.

From such a pessimistic, bleak description of city life, with its moral depravity, class exploitation, and antihuman environment, it was perhaps inevitable that Reymont should turn to a more edifying, positive theme, an affirmation of life at its roots, a portrait of a people in accord with nature.

THE PEASANTS

Reymont worked on the complete version of *The Peasants* for almost ten years. In fact, he had one volume written prior to his train accident in 1900; when he was well enough to return to work, he destroyed the first draft and began his manuscript again.

The Peasants is a truly epic novel, in both length and depth. Structured according to nature's cycle of seasons, its four volumes (*Autumn, Winter, Spring, Summer*) are a rich encyclopedia of rural and Polish customs, activities, beliefs, and superstitions. Reymont surpassed his previous efforts in the abundance of detail and nuance that fills the pages of the tetralogy. Of particular note is the language of the novel: The author was able to create a means of communication easily identifiable with the Polish countryside. Linguistic purists have countered that the dialect used in the novel is inauthentic, that no one in Poland speaks exactly as Reymont's characters do. This is not the point. The significance of *The Peasants* lies in the fact that the author consciously chose and crafted an idiom other than standard literary Polish—for not only his players but also the narrative itself. The result is a finely textured work, a tapestry of unique yet universal characters and episodes woven into the greatest Polish novel of the peasantry of all time.

The plot of *The Peasants* functions on two levels: First there is the motif of incest. Maciej Boryna, a twice-widowed peasant, marries the promiscuous, free-spirit Jagna, some thirty years his junior, with whom Maciej's son, Antek, is having an affair. The conflict of these characters, which occupies the first two volumes of the novel (*Autumn* and *Winter*), quickly takes on broad implications for the village of Lipec. The struggle is more than a moral one; it is generational and social, and its repercussions echo in the work's second motif: the changing social structure of the Polish village, particularly the conflicts that arise between the village and the manor. The peasants have lived on and worked their land for many generations, drawing needed resources from a nearby forest. When the landowner decides to sell and clear the forest, the peasants stage an uprising whose climax closes the second volume of the work in a moving and dramatic scene that signals the reconciliation between Boryna father and son.

The later volumes of *The Peasants* (*Spring* and *Summer*), less intense than the first two, focus more on village life and the antagonism between Jagna and Antek's wife, Hanka. Maciej Boryna, severely injured during the peasants' revolt, is bedridden through most of volume 3. At the close of *Spring*, he rises from his sickbed and, in a most symbolic scene, makes his way to his pasture to perform his final rite of spring and return his body to nature. The other men of the village, imprisoned for their rebellious activities, do not figure in these episodes. When they are finally released, the village of Lipce takes the judgment of Jagna into its own hands. The novel closes with the banishment of Jagna—the victory of the moral over the immoral, the triumph of the traditions of the collective over the vagaries of the individual.

The Peasants is a novel of the collective. Although the love intrigue is an important element in the development of the action, it is the entire village of Lipce that functions as hero. With the novel structured according to natural rhythms, village life is accurately depicted in a host of activities—natural, Christian, pagan—occurring as they do throughout a span of 365 days. Nature itself can be considered a complementary hero. Indeed, it is the human relationship with nature, its existence in accord with all of its forces, which then renders humanity heroic, symbolic, significant.

In *The Peasants*, Reymont affirms his belief in elemental life, in the tradition of "organic work" that had been promulgated by the positivists a generation earlier. For Reymont, the notion of life at its roots was meaningful not only symbolically but also in the most literal sense. His portrait of the peasants of Lipce was especially timely because the author rightly perceived that the centuries-old way of life in rural Poland was slowly

passing into history: Peasants were migrating to cities or emigrating to America "after bread"; estates were being sold or parceled; there was no future for the traditions of yesterday. In this sense, too, Reymont's *The Peasants* is a classic, marking the passing of the rural class in much the same way that Adam Mickiewicz had done for the gentry of Poland in his epic poem *Pan Tadeusz* (1834; English translation, 1917).

Wojtek Stelmaszynski

OTHER MAJOR WORKS

SHORT FICTION: "Pielgrzymka do Jasnej Góry," 1895; *Spotkania*, 1897; "Lili," 1899; *Burza*, 1907; *Z ziemi chełmskiej*, 1910; *Za frontem*, 1919; "Bunt," 1924.

PLAY: *Za późno*, pr. 1899.

NONFICTION: *Reymont we Francji: Listy do tłumacza "Chłopów" F. L. Schoella*, 1967 (letters); *Listy Władysława Stanislawa Reymonta do brata*, 1969 (letters); *Reymont w Ameryce: Listy do Wojciecha Morawskiego*, 1970 (letters); *Miłość i katastrofa: Listy do Wandy Szczukowej*, 1978 (letters); *Listy do rodziny*, 1980 (letters).

MISCELLANEOUS: *Pisma*, 1921-1925, 1930-1932 (32 volumes).

BIBLIOGRAPHY

Bechtel, Delphine. "Urbanization, Capitalism, and Cosmopolitanism: Four Novels and a Film on Jews in the Polish City of Lodz." *Prooftexts* 26, no. 1-2 (Winter, 2006): 79-106. Bechtel analyzes representations of Jewish life in Lodz, Poland, in *The Promised Land* and novels by three other writers, describing how these books present Jewish protagonists operating within a multilingual city. She also discusses the 1974 film adaptation of Reymont's novel.

Gregory, A. *Ladislas Reymont, Romain Rolland, Bertrand Russell*. Del Mar, Calif.: CRM, 1971. This study about three recipients of the Nobel Prize in Literature examines Reymont's life and work and includes a discussion of and an excerpt from his novel *The Peasants*.

Krzyżanowski, Jerzy R. *Władysław Stanisław Reymont*. Boston: Twayne, 1972. An introductory guide to Reymont's life and work. Part of the Twayne World Authors series. Includes a bibliography.

Mikos, Michael, and David Mulroy. "Reymont's *The*

Peasants: A Probable Influence on *Desire Under the Elms*." *Eugene O'Neill Newsletter* 10, no. 1 (Spring, 1986). A comparative study that emphasizes Reymont's wide influence on other writers, including Eugene O'Neill.

Miłosz, Czesław. *The History of Polish Literature.* 2d ed. Berkeley: University of California Press, 1983. Miłosz, a Polish poet and winner of the Nobel Prize in Literature, pinpoints Reymont's importance to Polish literature.

JEAN RHYS
Ella Gwendolen Rees Williams

Born: Roseau, Dominica Island, West Indies; August 24, 1894
Died: Exeter, England; May 14, 1979
Also known as: Ella Gwendolen Rees Williams

PRINCIPAL LONG FICTION

Postures, 1928 (also known as *Quartet*, 1929)
After Leaving Mr. Mackenzie, 1930
Voyage in the Dark, 1934
Good Morning, Midnight, 1939
Wide Sargasso Sea, 1966

OTHER LITERARY FORMS

Although Jean Rhys (rees) is now remembered primarily for her novels, her first published book was a collection of short stories, *The Left Bank, and Other Stories* (1927). As Ford Madox Ford points out in the preface to the collection, Rhys's heroines are geographically, psychologically, and emotionally of "the Left Bank," not only of Paris—although Rhys captured the Paris of the 1920's as well as anyone—but also of all of the cities of the world. They are underdogs, alone, betrayed, on the edge of poverty; they are women in a man's world.

In addition to *The Left Bank*, Rhys published two other collections of stories: *Tigers Are Better-Looking* (1968) and *Sleep It Off, Lady* (1976). In 1987, *The Collected Short Stories* brought together her work in this genre. At her death, she left an essentially completed first section of an autobiography with Diana Athill, who had edited *Wide Sargasso Sea* and *Sleep It Off, Lady*. Athill published this section and a less complete second section as *Smile Please: An Unfinished Autobiography*

in 1979. A collection of Rhys's letters was published in 1984.

ACHIEVEMENTS

When *Wide Sargasso Sea*, her last novel, was published, Jean Rhys was described in *The New York Times* as the greatest living novelist. Such praise is overstated, but Rhys's fiction, long overlooked by academic critics, began in the late twentieth century to undergo a revival, spurred by feminist studies. Rhys played a noteworthy role in the French Left Bank literary scene in the 1920's, and between 1927 and 1939, she published four substantial novels and a number of jewel-like short stories. Although she owes her current reputation in large measure to the rising interest in female writers and feminist themes, her work belongs more properly with the masters of literary impressionism: Joseph Conrad, Ford Madox Ford, Marcel Proust, and James Joyce. She began to publish her writing under the encouragement of her intimate friend Ford Madox Ford, and she continued to write in spite of falling out of favor with his circle. As prizes and honors came to her in her old age after the publication of *Wide Sargasso Sea*, it must have given her grim satisfaction to realize that she had attained entirely by her own efforts a position as a writer at least equal to that of her erstwhile friends.

BIOGRAPHY

Jean Rhys was born Ella Gwendolen Rees Williams in the West Indies on the island of Dominica in 1894, the daughter of a Welsh father and a part-Creole mother. English society classified her as "colored." Her childhood associates were often Creole, and she was surrounded by ideas peculiar to their culture, such as voodoo and witchcraft. At the same time, she attended a convent school and seriously considered the life of a nun. The colonial mentality was strong in Dominica, and the "proper" role for a well-bred young woman was sharply defined: passive, obedient, submissive.

In 1910, Rhys left Dominica and went to live in Cambridge, England, with her aunt, Clarice Rhys Williams. After a short term in a local school, she enrolled in the Royal Academy of Dramatic Art in London. Her father died soon after she arrived in England, and she found herself short of money. The transition from the West Indies to England must have been extremely painful for the sixteen-year-old girl: the climate harsh, the people cold, the social and economic situation threatening. Those who knew her as a young woman testified that she was strikingly beautiful. After a term at the Royal Academy of Dramatic Art, she toured as a minor actor or chorus girl with provincial theater troupes and did modeling. A young woman alone under these circumstances would have seen at first hand how male dominance and financial control in British society combined to exploit the female. Many of Rhys's stories and novels reflect scenes from her career on the stage, and most of them hinge on the theme of male exploitation of women through financial domination.

Near the end of World War I, Rhys married Jean Lenglet (alias Edouard de Neve), an adventurer who had served in the French Foreign Legion and who was probably employed by the French secret service during the war. The newlywed couple lived in Paris, constantly moving from one cheap hotel to another, although de Neve secured temporarily a position with the international mission administering Vienna. A son was born to them in 1919, but he lived only three weeks. A daughter born in 1922 lived but required special medical care.

Rhys tried to earn a living in Paris by modeling and writing. Pearl Adam, the wife of a correspondent for *The Times* of Paris, took an interest in some of Rhys's sketches and introduced her to Ford Madox Ford, then editor of *The Transatlantic Review*. Through him, she entered into the expatriate community of the early 1920's, meeting James Joyce, Ernest Hemingway, and other prominent writers. Shortly after Rhys met Ford in the au-

tumn of 1924, her husband was sent to prison for illegal dealing in antiques. Ford was living at the time with the artist Stella Bowen. Rhys, penniless, moved in with them and soon formed an intimate relationship with Ford. A casual episode in Ford's generally messy life was something much more serious for the young woman; Rhys treats this affair in her first novel, *Quartet*. De Neve never forgave Rhys for her involvement with Ford.

After her divorce from de Neve, Rhys became closely involved with a literary agent, Leslie Tilden Smith. They were eventually married and lived together until his death in 1945. Subsequently, Rhys married her late husband's cousin, Max Hamer, who later served time in prison for mismanagement of his firm's funds. Throughout the 1940's and 1950's, Rhys suffered greatly from poverty, poor health, and family problems. Her books were all out of print. She was not, however, entirely forgotten. The actor Selma Vaz Diaz adapted a dramatic monologue from *Good Morning, Midnight* for stage use in 1949, and eight years later, the British Broadcasting Corporation's third program presented the monologue, which received excellent notices. The publication of *Wide Sargasso Sea* in 1966 and the rapid growth of feminist studies led to a Rhys revival, and the reprinting of all her works followed. Rhys died in May, 1979, in Exeter, England.

ANALYSIS

Jean Rhys's first novel, *Quartet*, reflects closely her misadventures with Ford Madox Ford. The heroine, Marya Zelli, whose husband is in prison, moves in with the rich and respectable Hugh and Lois Heidler. Hugh becomes Marya's lover, while Lois punishes her with petty cruelties. The central figure is a woman alone, penniless, exploited, and an outsider. In her next novel, *After Leaving Mr. Mackenzie*, the central figure, Julia Martin, breaks off with her rich lover, Mr. Mackenzie, and finds herself financially desperate. *Voyage in the Dark* tells the story of Anna Morgan, who arrives in England from the West Indies as an innocent young girl, has her first affair as a chorus girl, and descends through a series of shorter and shorter affairs to working for a masseuse. In *Good Morning, Midnight*, the alcoholic Sasha Jensen, penniless in Paris, remembers episodes from her past that have brought her to this sorry pass.

All four of these novels show a female character subject to financial, sexual, and social domination by men and "respectable" society. In all cases, the heroine is passive, but "sentimental." The reader is interested in her feelings rather than in her ideas and accomplishments. She is alienated economically from any opportunity to do meaningful and justly rewarding work. She is an alien socially, either from a foreign and despised colonial culture or from a marginally respectable social background. She is literally an alien or foreigner in Paris and London, which are cities of dreadful night for her. What the characters fear most is the final crushing alienation from their true identities, the reduction to some model or type imagined by a foreign man. They all face the choice of becoming someone's gamine, *garçonne*, or femme fatale, or of starving to death, and they all struggle against this loss of personal identity. After a silence of more than twenty years, Rhys returned to these same concerns in her masterpiece, *Wide Sargasso Sea*. While the four early novels are to a large degree autobiographical, *Wide Sargasso Sea* has a more literary origin, although it, too, reflects details from the author's personal life.

WIDE SARGASSO SEA

Wide Sargasso Sea requires of the reader a familiarity with Charlotte Brontë's *Jane Eyre* (1847). In Brontë's novel, Jane is prevented from marrying Rochester by the presence of a madwoman in the attic, his insane West Indian wife, who finally perishes in a fire that she sets, burning Rochester's house and blinding him, but clearing the way for Jane to wed him. The madwoman in *Jane Eyre* is depicted entirely from the exterior. It is natural that the mad West Indian wife, when seen only through the eyes of her English rival and of Rochester, appears completely hideous and depraved. Indeed, when Jane first sees the madwoman in chapter 16 of the novel, she cannot tell whether it is a beast or a human being groveling on all fours. Like a hyena with bloated features, the madwoman attacks Rochester in this episode.

Wide Sargasso Sea is a sympathetic account of the life of Rochester's mad wife, ranging from her childhood in the West Indies, her Creole and Catholic background, and her courtship and married years with the deceitful Rochester to her final descent into madness and captivity in England. Clearly, the predicament of the West Indian wife resembles that of Rhys herself in many ways. In order to present the alien wife's case, Rhys writes a "countertext," an extension of Brontë's novel that fills in the "missing" testimony, the issues over which Brontë glosses.

Wide Sargasso Sea consists of two parts. Part 1 is narrated by the girl growing up in Jamaica who is destined to become Rochester's wife. The Emancipation Act has just been passed (the year of that imperial edict was 1833), and the blacks on the island are passing through a period of so-called apprenticeship that should lead to their complete freedom in 1837. This is a period of racial tension and anxiety for the privileged colonial community. Fear of black violence runs high, and no one knows exactly what will happen to the landholders once the blacks are emancipated. The girlish narrator lives in the interface between the privileged white colonists and the blacks. Although a child of landowners, she is impoverished, clinging to European notions of respectability, and in constant fear. She lives on the crumbling es-

Jean Rhys. (The Granger Collection, New York)

tate of her widowed mother. Her closest associate is Christophine, a Martinique *obeah* woman, or Voodoo witch. When her mother marries Mr. Mason, the family's lot improves temporarily, until the blacks revolt, burning their country home, Coulibri, and killing her half-witted brother. She then attends a repressive Catholic school in town, where her kindly colored "cousin" Sandi protects her from more hostile blacks.

Part 2 is narrated by the young Rochester on his honeymoon with his bride at her country home. Wherever appropriate, Rhys follows the details of Brontë's story. Rochester reveals that his marriage is merely a financial arrangement. After an uneasy period of passion, Rochester's feelings for his bride begin to cool. He receives a letter of denunciation accusing her of misbehavior with Sandi and revealing that madness runs in the family. To counter Rochester's growing hostility, the young bride goes to her former companion, the *obeah* woman Christophine, for a love potion. The nature of the potion is that it can work for one night only. Nevertheless, she administers it to her husband. His love now dead, she is torn from her native land, transported to a cruel and loveless England, and maddeningly confined. Finally, she takes candle in hand to burn down Rochester's house in suicidal destruction.

In Brontë's novel, the character of the mad wife is strangely blank, a vacant slot in the story. Her presence is essential, and she must be fearfully hateful, so that Jane Eyre has no qualms about taking her place in Rochester's arms, but the novel tells the reader almost nothing else about her. Rhys fills in this blank, fleshing out the character, making her live on a par with Jane herself. After all, Brontë tells the reader a great deal about Jane's painful childhood and education; why should Rhys not supply the equivalent information about her dark rival?

It is not unprecedented for a writer to develop a fiction from another writer's work. For example, T. H. White's *Mistress Masham's Repose* (1946) imagines that some of Jonathan Swift's Lilliputians were transported to England, escaped captivity, and established a thriving colony in an abandoned English garden, where they are discovered by an English schoolgirl. Her intrusion into their world is a paradigm of British colonial paternalism, finally overcome by the intelligence and good

feeling of the girl. This charming story depends on Swift's fiction, but the relationship of White's work to Swift's is completely different from the relationship of Rhys's work to Brontë's. Rhys's fiction permanently alters one's understanding of *Jane Eyre*. Approaching Brontë's work after Rhys's, one is compelled to ask such questions as, Why is Jane so uncritical of Rochester? How is Jane herself like the madwoman in the attic? Rhys's fiction reaches into the past and alters Brontë's novel.

Rhys's approach in *Wide Sargasso Sea* was also influenced by Ford Madox Ford and, through Ford, Joseph Conrad. In the autumn of 1924, when Rhys first met Ford, he was writing *Joseph Conrad: A Personal Remembrance*, which was published later that year. Some thirty years earlier, when Conrad was just beginning his career as a writer, his agent had introduced him to Ford in hopes that they could work in collaboration, since Conrad wrote in English (a language he had adopted only as an adult) with great labor. Ford and Conrad produced *The Inheritors* (1901) and *Romance* (1903) as coauthors. During their years of association, Ford had some hand in the production of several works usually considered Conrad's sole effort, although it has never been clear to what degree Ford participated in the creation of the fiction of Conrad's middle period.

About 1909, after Ford's disreputable ways had become increasingly offensive to Conrad's wife, the two men parted ways. Immediately after Conrad's death in 1924, however, Ford rushed into print his memoir of the famous author. His memoir of Conrad is fictionalized and hardly to be trusted as an account of their association in the 1890's, but it sheds a great deal of light on what Ford thought about writing fiction in 1924, when he was beginning his powerful Tietjens tetralogy and working for the first time with Rhys. Ford claimed that he and Conrad invented literary impressionism in English. Impressionist fiction characteristically employs limited and unreliable narration, follows a flow of associated ideas leaping freely in time and space, aims to render the impression of a scene vividly so as to make readers see it as if it were before their eyes, and artfully selects and juxtaposes seemingly unrelated scenes and episodes so that readers must construct the connections and relationships that make the story intelligible. These are the stylistic features of Rhys's fiction as well as of Ford's *The Good Soldier* (1915), Conrad's *Heart of Darkness* (1902), Henry James's *The Turn of the Screw* (1898), and Joyce's *Ulysses* (1922).

An "affair"—the mainspring of the plot in an impressionist novel—is some shocking or puzzling event that has already occurred when the story begins. The reader knows what has happened but does not understand fully why and how it happened. The story proceeds in concentric rings of growing complication as the reader finds something that appeared at first to be clear-cut becoming more and more intricate. In Conrad's *Lord Jim* (1900), the affair is the scandalous abandonment of the pilgrim ship by the English sailor. In *The Good Soldier*, it is the breakup of the central foursome, whose full infidelity and betrayal are revealed only gradually. Brontë's *Jane Eyre* provided Rhys with an impressionist "affair" in the scene in which the mad West Indian wife burns Rochester's house, blinding him and killing herself. Like Conrad's Marlow, the storyteller who sits on the veranda mulling over Jim's curious behavior, or *The Good Soldier*'s narrator Dowell musing about the strange behavior of Edward Ashburnham, Rhys takes up the affair of Rochester and reworks it into ever richer complications, making the initial judgments in *Jane Eyre* seem childishly oversimplified. "How can Jane simply register relief that the madwoman is burned out of her way? There must be more to the affair than that," the secondary fiction suggests.

One of the most important features of literary impressionism is the highly constructive activity that it demands of the reader. In a pointillist painting, small dots of primary colors are set side by side. At a certain distance from the canvas, these merge on the retina of the eye of the viewer into colors and shapes that are not, in fact, drawn on the canvas at all. The painting is constructed in the eyes of each viewer with greater luminosity than it would have were it drawn explicitly. In order to create such a shimmering haze in fiction, Ford advises the use of a limited point of view, which gives the reader dislocated fragments of remembered experience. The reader must struggle constantly to fit these fragments into a coherent pattern. The tools for creating such a verbal collage are limited, "unreliable" narration, psychological time shifts, and juxtaposition. Ford observes that

two apparently unrelated events can be set side by side so that the reader will perceive their connection with far greater impact than if the author had stated such a connection openly. Ford advises the impressionist author to create a verbal collage by unexpected selection and juxtaposition, and *Wide Sargasso Sea* makes such juxtapositions on several levels. On the largest scale, *Wide Sargasso Sea* is juxtaposed with *Jane Eyre*, so that the two novels read together mean much more than when they are read independently. This increase of significance is what Ford called the "unearned increment" in impressionist art. Within *Wide Sargasso Sea*, part 1 (narrated by the West Indian bride) and part 2 (narrated by Rochester) likewise mean more in juxtaposition than when considered separately. Throughout the text, the flow of consciousness of the storytellers cunningly shifts in time to juxtapose details that mean more together than they would in isolation.

Because *Wide Sargasso Sea* demands a highly constructive reader, it is, like *The Good Soldier* or *Heart of Darkness*, an open fiction. When the reader completes *Jane Eyre*, the mystery of Rochester's house has been revealed and purged, the madwoman in the attic has been burned out, and Jane will live, the reader imagines, happily ever after. *Jane Eyre* taken in isolation is a closed fiction. Reading *Wide Sargasso Sea* in juxtaposition to *Jane Eyre*, however, opens the latter and poses questions that are more difficult to resolve: Is Jane likely to be the next woman in the attic? Why is a disabled man a gratifying mate for Jane? At what price is her felicity purchased?

The doppelgänger, twin, or shadow character runs throughout Rhys's fiction. All of her characters seem to be split personalities. There is a public role, that of the approved "good girl," that each is expected to play, and there is the repressed, rebellious "bad girl" lurking inside. If the bad girl can be hidden, the character is rewarded with money, love, and social position. The bad girl will sometimes put in an appearance, however, when the character drinks too much or gets excited or angry. When the dark girl appears, punishment follows, swift and sure. This is the case with Marya Zelli in *Quartet*, Julia Martin in *After Leaving Mr. Mackenzie*, Anna Morgan in *Voyage in the Dark*, and Sasha Jensen in *Good Morning, Midnight*. It is also the case in Brontë's *Jane*

Eyre. The education of Jane Eyre consists of her learning to repress those dark, selfish impulses that Victorian society maintained "good little girls" should never feel. Jane succeeds in stamping out her "bad" self through a stiff British education, discipline, and self-control. She kills her repressed identity, conforms to society's expectations, and gets her reward—a crippled husband and a burned-out house. Rhys revives the dark twin, shut up in the attic, the naughty, wild, dark, selfish, bestial female. She suggests that the struggle between repressed politeness and unrepressed self-interest is an ongoing process in which total repression means the death of a woman's identity.

Todd K. Bender

OTHER MAJOR WORKS

SHORT FICTION: *The Left Bank, and Other Stories*, 1927; *Tigers Are Better-Looking*, 1968; *Sleep It Off, Lady*, 1976; *The Collected Short Stories*, 1987.

NONFICTION: *Smile Please: An Unfinished Autobiography*, 1979; *The Letters of Jean Rhys*, 1984 (also known as *Jean Rhys: Letters, 1931-1966*).

BIBLIOGRAPHY

Angier, Carole. *Jean Rhys*. New York: Viking Press, 1985. Biography treats Rhys's fiction as essentially autobiographical. Far from viewing the author as a feminist, Angier presents Rhys as an intensely lonely individualist and solipsist without a program or external loyalties. Depicts her lifelong attempt to understand herself as being governed by a tragic and pessimistic view of human nature and the world.

_____. *Jean Rhys: Life and Work*. Boston: Little, Brown, 1990. Major work of Rhys scholarship combines detailed biographical study with sections devoted to interpretations of the novels. Includes voluminous notes and an extensive bibliography.

Davidson, Arnold E. *Jean Rhys*. New York: Frederick Ungar, 1985. Draws heavily on a number of critical sources to support a feminist interpretation of Rhys's fiction and provides a useful approach to the major works. Includes bibliography and index.

Dell'Amico, Carol. *Colonialism and the Modernist Movement in the Early Novels of Jean Rhys*. New York: Routledge, 2005. Describes how Rhys's novels published before *Wide Sargasso Sea*, or the so-called European texts, address issues of colonialism and imperialism. Argues that Rhys viewed imperialism as a condition of homelessness for both the colonized and the urban colonizers.

James, Louis. *Jean Rhys*. London: Longman, 1978. Focuses primarily on *Wide Sargasso Sea* but also provides an informative short introduction to Rhys's life and the full range of her work. Includes bibliography.

Lonsdale, Thorunn. "Literary Allusion in the Fiction of Jean Rhys." In *Caribbean Women Writers*, edited by Mary Condé and Thorunn Lonsdale. New York: St. Martin's Press, 1999. Focuses on the many critically neglected intertextual references to nineteenth and twentieth century European and American literature in Rhys's novels and short stories.

Maurel, Sylvie. *Jean Rhys*. New York: St. Martin's Press, 1998. Examines Rhys's writings from the perspectives of feminist criticism and literary theory while providing close readings of the texts and of their language. Includes bibliography and index.

Savory, Elaine. *Jean Rhys*. New York: Cambridge University Press, 1998. Presents critical readings of all of Rhys's works, drawing on previously unpublished sources. Argues that Rhys's writings should be approached from a Caribbean perspective and discusses Rhys's representation of race, gender, social class, and nationality.

Simpson, Anne B. *Territories of the Psyche: The Fiction of Jean Rhys*. New York: Palgrave Macmillan, 2005. Offers a psychoanalytic reading of Rhys's novels and short stories, describing how these works explore the dynamics of the human psyche. Includes bibliography and index.

Thomas, Sue. *The Worlding of Jean Rhys*. Westport, Conn.: Greenwood Press, 1999. Views Rhys's works as "Dominican autoethnography" and emphasizes how Rhys's Creole background is reflected in her writings. Includes analyses of all five novels.

ANNE RICE

Born: New Orleans, Louisiana; October 4, 1941
Also known as: Howard Allen Frances O'Brien;
Anne Rampling; A. N. Roquelaure

PRINCIPAL LONG FICTION

Interview with the Vampire, 1976
The Feast of All Saints, 1979
Cry to Heaven, 1982
The Claiming of Sleeping Beauty, 1983 (as A. N.
    Roquelaure)
Beauty's Punishment, 1984 (as Roquelaure)
*Beauty's Release: The Continued Erotic
    Adventures of Sleeping Beauty*, 1985 (as
    Roquelaure; collective title for previous 3
    novels, *Sleeping Beauty Trilogy*)
Exit to Eden, 1985 (as Anne Rampling)
The Vampire Lestat, 1985
Belinda, 1986 (as Rampling)
The Queen of the Damned, 1988
The Mummy: Or, Ramses the Damned, 1989
The Witching Hour, 1990
The Tale of the Body Thief, 1992
Lasher, 1993
Taltos: Lives of the Mayfair Witches, 1994
Memnoch the Devil, 1995
Servant of the Bones, 1996
Violin, 1997
Pandora: New Tales of the Vampires, 1998
The Vampire Armand, 1998
Vittorio the Vampire: New Tales of the Vampires,
    1999
Merrick, 2000
Blood and Gold: Or, The Story of Marius,
    2001
Blackwood Farm, 2002
Blood Canticle, 2003 (together with *Interview
    with the Vampire*, *The Vampire Lestat*, *The
    Queen of the Damned*, *The Tale of the Body
    Thief*, *Memnoch the Devil*, *The Vampire
    Armand*, *Merrick*, *Blood and Gold*, and
    Blackwood Farm known collectively as the
    Vampire Chronicles)

Christ the Lord: Out of Egypt, 2005
Christ the Lord: The Road to Cana, 2008

OTHER LITERARY FORMS

Anne Rice is known primarily for her novels. In addition to her historical fiction and her well-known vampire and witch novel series, Rice has published several erotic novels. *The Claiming of Sleeping Beauty*, *Beauty's Punishment*, and *Beauty's Release* appeared under the pseudonym A. N. Roquelaure, while Rice used the pen name Anne Rampling for *Exit to Eden* and *Belinda*. Rice also wrote the screenplay for the 1994 film adaptation of her novel *Interview with the Vampire*.

ACHIEVEMENTS

For most of her career, Anne Rice has experimented with several different literary genres and has acquitted herself well in each: gothic horror, historical fiction, erotica, romance. The conventions of gothic fiction, however, best conform to Rice's early obsessions with eroticism, androgyny, myth, and the nature of evil. For critics and fans alike, the novels that constitute the Vampire Chronicles are her greatest achievement thus far. Gothic horror, like all popular fiction, is customarily slighted by commentators, who peg it as nothing more than a barometer of its own time, devoid of resonance. Paradoxically perhaps, Rice's success grew out of her ability to revamp the vampire, to update the hoary edifice first built by Horace Walpole in 1765 in *The Castle of Otranto*. She did more, however, than merely put her archetypal hero, the vampire Lestat, in black leather on a motorcycle; she made him, in all his selfishness and soul searching, emblematic of the waning days of the twentieth century.

With the publication in 2005 of the first of a projected four-part re-creation of the life of Jesus, Rice began mining a new literary vein. *Christ the Lord: Out of Egypt* and its sequel, *The Road to Cana*, draw on Rice's research into the Gospels and New Testament scholarship, but they also benefit from Rice's past experiments with historical fiction and—perhaps more surprising—her dexterity in creating fiction out of the supernatural.

BIOGRAPHY

Anne Rice was born Howard Allen Frances O'Brien on October 4, 1941, in New Orleans, Louisiana, to Howard O'Brien and Katherine Allen O'Brien. Howard O'Brien's reasons for bestowing his own name on his daughter remain obscure, but bearing a masculine name clearly had a profound effect on her. When she entered first grade, the little girl christened herself Anne. The name stuck, as did a lifelong obsession with androgyny.

The exotic, decadent, intoxicating atmosphere of her hometown must also be counted among Anne Rice's early influences—as must her mother's alcoholism. As she approached puberty, Anne devoted much of her time to reading in a darkened bedroom to the increasingly incapacitated Katherine. It was there, perhaps, that she acquired an affinity for vampires. She would later recall how her mother first explained alcoholism as a "craving in the blood" and then asked her to say the rosary. Anne watched her mother alternate between wild exhilaration and collapse and finally waste away, her body drained by addiction and an inability to eat. When Katherine died in 1956, the nexus of blood, religion, and death must have taken root in her young daughter's psyche.

Anne's father remarried when she was sixteen, and, after Anne's sophomore year in high school, he moved the family to Richardson, Texas, where Anne met Stan Rice. Stan was a year younger than Anne, and at first he did not seem to share her romantic feelings about their relationship. It was not until after Anne graduated and moved away to San Francisco that Stan finally realized his feelings. They were married on October 14, 1961, when Anne was twenty.

The couple took up residence in the San Francisco Bay Area, where they would remain for the next twenty-seven years. Stan, a poet, completed his undergraduate education and began teaching creative writing. Anne, too, completed her B.A., majoring in political science. After receiving a master's degree in creative writing in 1972, she devoted herself full time to her writing career.

In the meanwhile, however, a momentous event had occurred in the Rices' lives. Their daughter, Michele, who was born in 1966, devel-

oped a rare form of leukemia and died two weeks before her sixth birthday. The trauma of this loss seems to have plunged Anne Rice into depression. The old association between blood and death had returned to haunt her, but she fought off her demons by submerging herself in her writing. The result was her first published novel, *Interview with the Vampire*.

In 1978, the Rices had a son, Christopher, and a decade later they moved to New Orleans. With the proceeds of many best-selling books and the lucrative sale of film rights, Anne Rice purchased a mansion in the Garden District, which later became the setting of one of her novels and the scene of such memorable parties as the 1995 Memnoch Ball. During the 1990's, the Rices purchased and restored a number of other New Orleans properties, including Anne's childhood home on St. Charles Avenue and St. Elizabeth's Orphanage.

Anne Rice. (Christine Bocchiaro)

In 1996, after decades of self-declared atheism, Anne returned to the Roman Catholic Church. Her husband's death in 2002 from brain cancer may have contributed to Rice's decision that year to write from that time forward only for and about Jesus Christ. In 2005, after completing *Christ the Lord: Out of Egypt*, Rice moved to southern California to be nearer her son, eventually settling in Rancho Mirage. *Christ the Lord: The Road to Cana*, a sequel to *Out of Egypt*, was published in 2008.

ANALYSIS

Anne Rice discovered her strong suit early. Written in five weeks, *Interview with the Vampire* introduced the themes of compulsion, exoticism, and eroticism that would inform her later works. Although she has explored these themes against a wide variety of backdrops, it is her revival of the gothic—and of the vampire in particular—that both brought her critical attention and transformed her into a popular cultural icon. In 2005, Rice took on a dramatically new approach in her work as she dedicated herself to explication, through historical fiction, of the life of Jesus.

VAMPIRE CHRONICLES

Interview with the Vampire is the first of the books that Rice produced in her series known as the Vampire Chronicles. The books in the series shift back and forth in time, from the prevampire life of Lestat in eighteenth century rural France to his escapades in twentieth century New Orleans and then, in *Memnoch the Devil*, to the time of the creation of heaven and hell.

Interview with the Vampire introduces Lestat through the narrative of Louis, a vampire Lestat has "made." Louis relates his story to Daniel, a young reporter. Even as Louis grieves for his mortal life, Daniel craves Louis's power and immortality. Daniel has to overcome his initial horror and skepticism before he can accept the truth of what Louis says, but by the end of Louis's long story, Daniel is begging to be made a vampire too.

In *The Vampire Lestat*, Lestat relates his own version of his life. Lestat's narrative, like Louis's, is published as a book. (Indeed, Lestat has written his in order to correct several errors he perceives in Louis's earlier account.) Lestat, always a show-off, revels in publicity, and he uses the book to launch his career as a rock star. Like so many of Lestat's grand schemes, however, this plan

crashes, ending when Lestat barely escapes his fellow vampires' murderous attack as they seek revenge for his unpardonable publication of a book that reveals their secrets.

In *The Queen of the Damned*, Lestat becomes the consort of Akasha, the Egyptian ruler who became the mother of all vampires when a demon wounded and invaded her body, giving her immortality. Marius, an old Roman sage and vampire, has kept Akasha intact for more than two thousand years, but it is Lestat's energetic wooing that brings her out of her long stupor. She revives determined to rid the world of men, whose violence has made them unfit to survive. Only a remnant will endure for breeding purposes, she declares. Having partaken of her blood and fallen deliriously in love with her, Lestat nevertheless struggles against her insane project. He is finally saved from Akasha's wrath by Maharet and Mekare, witches who are also twin sisters and who destroy Akasha.

In *The Tale of the Body Thief*, Lestat, suffering from ennui, succumbs to the temptations of a body thief, Raglan James. The body thief offers Lestat a day of adventure in a mortal body in exchange for his own. Stupidly, Lestat accepts, even paying James twenty million dollars for the privilege of enjoying one day of mortality. James then absconds with both the money and Lestat's body, which Lestat is able to repossess only with the help of David Talbot, head of the Talamasca, a society dedicated to investigating the occult. Lestat, who is in love with David, then makes the resistant David into a vampire.

In *Memnoch the Devil*, a terrified Lestat discovers that he is being stalked by Satan, who calls himself Memnoch because he does not regard himself as a rebel angel or as God's accuser. Memnoch invites Lestat to become his lieutenant—not to gather souls for hell, but to redeem those awaiting enlightenment and salvation. Memnoch's argument is that he is offering God a grander creation, a purer vision of humankind, than God himself has conceived. In the end, Lestat repudiates Memnoch, doubting the devil's word and wondering if what he has "seen" is only what he has imagined.

With the Vampire Chronicles, Rice rejuvenates the conventions of gothic romance and the horror novel. Like earlier heroes, Lestat is a nobleman of surpassing courage and physical attractiveness. Indeed, the vampire elder Magnus makes him into a vampire because he has seen the handsome Lestat on the stage in Paris and admired his indomitable spirit. As in William Godwin's novel *Things as They Are: Or, The Adventures of Caleb Williams* (1794), Lestat is an insatiably curious protagonist attached to an older hero who represents both good and evil. Lestat must know the origins of vampirism, and he must follow his desires regardless of the cost to himself and others.

Lestat's eroticism also partakes of the gothic tradition. Reflecting Rice's abiding interest in androgyny, he finds himself attracted to both men and women—to the goddess Akasha and to the head of the Talamasca, David Talbot. Deeply devoted to his mother, Gabrielle, he takes her as his vampire lover. Incestuous and homoerotic elements that are veiled or only hinted at in earlier gothic fiction explode in Rice's chronicles. Rice also succeeds in making gothicism contemporary by making Lestat into a rock star, thus underscoring parallels between the cult of celebrity and the allure of the vampire.

MAYFAIR WITCHES SERIES

Rice conceived the first installment of the Mayfair Witches cycle, *The Witching Hour*, in 1985 after she finished writing *The Vampire Lestat*. She had generated some new characters that she at first envisioned as playing parts in the next volume of the Vampire Chronicles, but she soon reached the conclusion that these characters—a family of witches and their presiding spirit—deserved an entirely separate book, one set in New Orleans.

The protagonist of *The Witching Hour*, Michael Curry, is a successful forty-eight-year-old businessman who has his life blighted by a near-death experience. After nearly drowning in San Francisco Bay, he is rescued by a mysterious woman in a passing boat. He then discovers that simply by touching objects and people with his hands he has access to other lives and events. His insights, however, are fragmentary—as is his memory of an encounter with otherworldly beings during his drowning episode, when he promised to fulfill a mission for them.

One of Michael's doctors puts him in touch with his rescuer, who Michael believes will help him understand

what he is meant to do. When he meets Dr. Rowan Mayfair, a thirty-year-old blond beauty and a superb surgeon, Michael falls in love with her. Like Michael, Rowan is searching for answers. She has the power both to hurt and to heal people. She can stop a patient's bleeding simply by a laying on of hands; she can also cause a heart attack or stroke if she does not control her rage. Her obsession with saving people is her effort at self-redemption. Just as Michael hopes that touching Rowan and her boat will bring back his sense of mission, Rowan hopes that Michael will help reveal her past, which remains a mystery to her.

Rowan and Michael realize that their fates are linked to New Orleans, where as a boy Michael developed a fixation on a Garden District mansion that turns out to be Rowan's ancestral home. There he saw a spectral man, the Mayfairs' presiding spirit. Michael's intense memories of his childhood are connected, he is sure, with his near-death experience. When Rowan's birth mother dies, Rowan is visited by a spectral man, and she decides that she must return to the Crescent City.

Hovering around this couple is Aaron Lightner, an agent of the Talamasca. Through Aaron, Michael learns that Rowan is the descendant of a matriarchal family of witches that has fascinated the Talamasca for nearly three hundred years. A strong woman, Rowan believes she can destroy Lasher, the spectral man who has maddened the Mayfairs in an attempt to possess them. Like the others, however, Rowan loses control of Lasher, who invades the cells of the fetus growing within her and emerges as a powerful boy-man.

Rowan is rather like a female Dr. Faustus, determined to conquer the secrets of nature. She wants to heal, but the extremity of her desire cuts her off from her own humanity. Like Faust, she risks damnation. She is in thrall to her Mephistopheles, Lasher. When Michael playfully calls his lover Dr. Mayfair, the epithet suggests not only Dr. Faustus but also Dr. Frankenstein. Indeed, although Rowan finds Lasher's proposal that they create a super-race seductive, once their offspring is born, she plans to submit its cells to laboratory tests, thus reducing it to the status of a research subject.

In *Lasher*, the second installment in the series, Rowan has begun to help Lasher fulfill his desire. Together they have a girl child, Emaleth. The central revelation of the book is that the Mayfairs can, by interbreeding, produce a genetic aberration—a legendary race of nearly immortal giants known as Taltos, of which Lasher is a member. The Talamasca believe that Lasher is possessed of a unique genome, so when at the end of the book Michael Curry destroys him and Rowan does away with her demoniac girl child, it seems that Lasher's kind is no more.

However, *Taltos*, the third installment of the series, features another Taltos, Ashlar Templeton, an eccentric and reclusive billionaire toy maker. Ashlar's profession indicates that his nature is far more benign than Lasher's. Indeed, he more closely resembles Rice's vampires than his own protean kind. Unlike Lasher, he is not devoured by a need to propagate his supernatural breed; instead, he yearns—as much as Louis and, in his weaker moments, Lestat—for integration with humanity.

CHRIST THE LORD SERIES

When asked about her motivations for writing *Christ the Lord: Out of Egypt*, Rice has answered with winning directness and simplicity: "I wrote this book to make Christ real to people who had never thought about Him as real." Similarly, one of the hallmarks of the first installment of her projected series about Jesus is Rice's unadorned prose. In fact, it could not be otherwise. *Out of Egypt* concerns one year in the life of the seven-year-old Jesus, and it is written in the first person. This approach to storytelling is one that Rice has employed to good effect before, but while taking readers into the mind of a vampire is a good trick, adopting the perspective of a young boy who is only beginning to understand what sets him apart from humanity requires remarkable skill.

Rice claims that she has taken few liberties when writing her life of Jesus, and to that end she concludes *Out of Egypt* with a lengthy author's note in which she sets forth the extensive historical and biblical research she conducted before writing the book. She has been obliged to cast her net widely in order to move in her subject's world, however. There is, for example, no real historical support for the novel's opening, which situates Jesus, Mary, and Joseph in Alexandria, Egypt, and Rice makes liberal use of apocryphal sources throughout the book. She does so with considerable success, creating a whole world for this extraordinary boy to inhabit. Jesus is pictured surrounded by an extended, very Orthodox Jewish family that includes not only his mother and father but also an array of aunts, uncles, and cousins. The city they inhabit is rich with detail and situated squarely within the larger framework that was the Roman Empire. Rice's historical accuracy might seem to be her paramount concern were it not for her protagonist's still inchoate sense of otherness.

Rice is not coy about Jesus' supernaturalness: The book opens with a scene in which his animosity kills another boy, who is then resurrected by Jesus' remorse. This seven-year-old, however, knows little and understands less about where he came from. He begins to understand more after Joseph (who Jesus knows is not his father) declares that now that Herod is dead, the family should go home to Nazareth. Once there, Jesus begins to discover what happened in Bethlehem the night he was born and to understand the meaning of his miraculous gifts. Although *Out of Egypt* is not on a par with James Joyce's 1916 novel *A Portrait of the Artist as a Young Man*, Rice's first-person rendition of Jesus' dawning self-awareness is itself something of a miracle.

The sequel to *Out of Egypt*, *The Road to Cana*, is arguably even more masterful in its realization of Jesus' dual nature. This second installment concerns the "lost" young adulthood of Jesus, about which the Bible is largely silent. Rice is concerned with filling in the particulars Jesus encounters along the way to becoming a public man. That concern takes the form of concentration on the human aspect of Jesus (or Yeshua, as he is called), as revealed, once more, in first-person narrative. In this book Jesus is a thirty-year-old, unmarried man who knows he will not marry and who is surrounded by a society that expects him to do so. Around him swirl both parochial rumors of the virgin birth and political tensions with Rome; within him, the all-too-human desire for the beautiful Avigail wars with his desire to do God's will. Rice's goal in this novel is to make this counterpoint sing while keeping it faithful to what is known about the historical Jesus and believed about the biblical son of God. Largely, she succeeds in making Jesus' transformation into a man capable of turning water into wine during the festival at Cana believable to his public and to her readers.

Lisa Paddock

OTHER MAJOR WORK

SCREENPLAY: *Interview with the Vampire*, 1994.

BIBLIOGRAPHY

Badley, Linda. *Writing Horror and the Body: The Fiction of Stephen King, Clive Barker, and Anne Rice.* Westport, Conn.: Greenwood Press, 1996. Examines horror fiction as a fantastic genre that distorts images of the body and the self. Argues that the approaches to horror taken by the three authors discussed constitute a dialogue on the anxieties of American culture.

Hoppenstand, Gary, and Ray B. Browne, eds. *The Gothic World of Anne Rice.* Bowling Green, Ohio: Bowling Green State University Press, 1996. Collection of essays by a number of important Rice critics addresses all aspects of her fiction, including the Vampire Chronicles and her other stories of the supernatural.

Keller, James R. *Anne Rice and Sexual Politics: The Early Novels.* Jefferson, N.C.: McFarland, 2000. Addresses Rice's early works in terms of the author's approaches to issues of gender identity and sexual matters. Includes bibliographical references and index.

Ramslund, Katherine M. *Prism of the Night: A Biography of Anne Rice.* New York: Dutton, 1991. One of the most complete sources of information about Rice available, written with her cooperation. Offers the first serious attempt to assess her work critically and in a broad context.

_____, ed. *The Anne Rice Reader.* New York: Ballantine, 1997. Comprehensive volume provides interviews with Rice, her personal essays, and articles about her life and career as well as literary critiques of her works, assessment of her contribution to the literature about vampires, and discussion of her relationship to the gothic tradition.

Riley, Michael. *Conversations with Anne Rice: An Intimate, Enlightening Portrait of Her Life and Work.* New York: Ballantine Books, 1996. In an extended interview format, Rice discusses her writing career, her emotional involvement with her work, and many other topics, including the various forms of literature to which she has contributed.

Roberts, Bette B. *Anne Rice.* New York: Twayne, 1994. Solid introductory study includes chapters on Rice's life and art, her relationship to the gothic tradition, her vampire series, her historical novels, and her erotic fiction.

Smith, Jennifer. *Anne Rice: A Critical Companion.* Westport, Conn.: Greenwood Press, 1996. Provides criticism and interpretation of Rice's work in the context of women and literature, fantasy fiction, horror tales, the gothic revival, witchcraft in literature, and vampires in literature. Includes bibliography and index.

Tomc, Sandra. "Dieting and Damnation: Anne Rice's *Interview with the Vampire.*" In *Blood Read: The Vampire as Metaphor in Contemporary Culture*, edited by Joan Gordon and Veronica Hollinger. Philadelphia: University of Pennsylvania Press, 1997. Relates the vampire's transformation to contemporary female preoccupations with body image and self-abnegation.

Waxman, Barbara Frey. "Postexistentialism in the Neogothic Mode: Anne Rice's *Interview with the Vampire.*" *Mosaic* 25, no. 3 (Summer, 1992): 79-97. Explores the interrelationship of existentialism, postmodernism, and gothic fiction in Rice's Vampire Chronicles.

DOROTHY RICHARDSON

Born: Abingdon, Berkshire (now in Oxfordshire),
England; May 17, 1873
Died: Beckenham, Kent, England; June 17, 1957
Also known as: Dorothy Odle; Dorothy Miller
Richardson

PRINCIPAL LONG FICTION

Pointed Roofs, 1915
Backwater, 1916
Honeycomb, 1917
Interim, 1919
The Tunnel, 1919
Deadlock, 1921
Revolving Lights, 1923
The Trap, 1925
Oberland, 1927
Dawn's Left Hand, 1931
Clear Horizon, 1935
Dimple Hill, 1938
March Moonlight, 1967
Pilgrimage, 1938, 1967 (includes all previous
titles)

OTHER LITERARY FORMS

Dorothy Richardson's literary reputation rests on the
single long novel *Pilgrimage*. She referred to the parts
published under separate titles as "chapters," and they
were the primary focus of her energy throughout her
creative life. The first appeared in 1915; the last—
unfinished and unrevised—was printed ten years after
her death. Before 1915, she wrote some essays and reviews for obscure periodicals edited by friends and also
two books growing out of her interest in the Quakers.
She contributed descriptive sketches on Sussex life to
the *Saturday Review* between 1908 and 1914. During
the years writing *Pilgrimage*, Richardson did an enormous amount of miscellaneous writing to earn money—
columns and essays in the *Dental Record* (1912-1922),
film criticism and translations as well as articles on
various subjects for periodicals including *Vanity Fair*,
Adelphi, *Little Review*, and *Fortnightly Review*. She also
wrote a few short stories, chiefly during the 1940's.

None of this material has been collected. A detailed bibliography is included in *Dorothy Richardson: A Biography* by Gloria G. Fromm (1977).

ACHIEVEMENTS

The term "stream of consciousness," adapted from
psychology, was first applied to literature in a 1918 review of Dorothy Richardson's *Pointed Roofs*, *Backwater*, and *Honeycomb*. In the twentieth century, novels
moved from outward experience to inner reality. The experiments that marked the change were made almost simultaneously by three writers unaware of one another's
work: The first volume of Marcel Proust's *À la recherche du temps perdu* (1913-1927; *Remembrance of Things
Past*, 1922-1931) appeared in 1913, James Joyce's *Portrait of the Artist as a Young Man* began serial publication in 1914, and Richardson's manuscript of *Pointed
Roofs* was finished in 1913.

Richardson was the first novelist in England to restrict the point of view entirely to the protagonist's consciousness, to take for content the experience of life at
the moment of perception, and to record the development of a single character's mind and emotions without
imposing any plot or structural pattern. Her place in literature (as opposed to literary history) has been less certain; some critics feel that her work is interesting only
because it dates the emergence of a new technique. The
absence of story and explanation make heavy demands
on the reader. Since the protagonist's own limited understanding controls every word of the narrative, readers
must also do the work of evaluating the experience in order to create meaning.

Richardson wrote what Virginia Woolf called "the
psychological sentence of the feminine gender"; a sentence that expanded its limits and tampered with punctuation to convey the multiple nuances of a single moment.
She deliberately rejected the description of events, which
she thought was typical of male literature, in order to
convey the subjective understanding that she believed
was the reality of experience. The autobiographical basis
of *Pilgrimage* was not known until 1963. Richardson,
like her protagonist and like other women of her period,

broke with the conventions of the past, sought to create her own being through self-awareness, and struggled to invent a form that would communicate a woman's expanding conscious life.

BIOGRAPHY

Dorothy Richardson, born on May 17, 1873, was the third of four daughters. Her father, Charles Richardson, worked in the prosperous grocery business that his father had established, but he wanted to be a gentleman. He abandoned Nonconformity for the Church of England and, in 1874, sold the family business to live on investments. During Dorothy's childhood, periods of upper-middle-class luxury (a large house, servants, gardens, membership in a tennis club) alternated with moves arising from temporarily reduced circumstances.

Charles had hoped for a son, and he took Dorothy with him to lectures in Oxford and meetings of scientific associations. She was sent at age eleven to a private day school for the daughters of gentlemen. It was late enough in the century for the curriculum to emphasize academic subjects; her studies included logic and psychology. In 1890, realizing that her family's financial condition had become seriously straitened, Dorothy looked to the example of Charlotte Brontë and *Villette* (1853) and applied for a post as pupil-teacher in a German school. Six months in Hanover were followed by two years teaching in a North London private school and a brief spell as governess for a wealthy suburban family.

By the end of 1893, Richardson's father was declared bankrupt; in 1895, two of her sisters married. Her mother, Mary Richardson, was troubled by an unusually severe bout of the depression that had gripped her for several years. Richardson took her mother to stay in lodgings near the sea and found that she required almost constant companionship and supervision. On November 30, 1895, while her daughter was out for a short walk in the fresh air, Mary committed suicide.

At the age of twenty-two, responsible for her own support and severely shaken by the past two years' events, Richardson moved to an attic room in a London lodging house and took a job as secretary and assistant to three Harley Street dentists. For young women at that time, such a step was unusual; by taking it Richardson evaded the restraint, protection, and religious supervi-

sion that made teaching an acceptable profession for young women of good family. The nineteenth century was drawing to a close and London was alive with new ideas. Richardson explored the city, made friends with women who worked in business offices, and lived on eggs and toast so that she could afford concert tickets.

Soon after moving to London, she was invited for a Saturday in the country by an old school friend, Amy Catherine Robbins, who had married her science instructor at London University: That instructor's name was H. G. Wells. He had just published *The Time Machine* (1895). Richardson was fascinated by Wells and by the people and ideas she encountered at his house but angered by his way of telling her what to do. She was aware that she stood outside the class system and between the Victorian and modern worlds. She was drawn both to picnics with cousins at Cambridge and to anarchist and Fabian meetings. She sampled various churches (including Unitarian and Quaker) but refrained from committing herself to any group or cause.

In 1902, Richardson began contributing occasional articles and reviews to *Crank* and other magazines edited by a vegetarian friend. She refused a proposal from a respectable physician and broke her engagement to a Russian Jew, Benjamin Grad. Her friendship with Wells passed at some point into physical intimacy, but she continued to struggle against being overwhelmed by his ideas and personality. In 1906, finding herself pregnant, she brought the affair to an end; she looked forward to raising the child on her own and was distressed when she suffered a miscarriage.

Exhausted physically and mentally, Richardson left her dental job and went to Sussex to recover and think. In 1908, she began writing sketches for the *Saturday Review*. Then, as her fortieth year approached, she began deliberately searching for the form that would allow her to create what she called "a feminine equivalent of the current masculine realism."

Pointed Roofs was at first rejected by publishers. When it was published in 1915 it puzzled readers, distressed some reviewers, and failed to make money. Richardson persisted, however, on the course she had set, even while living an unsettled life in YWCA hostels and borrowed rooms and earning a minimal income by proofreading and by writing a monthly column for the

Dental Record. In 1917, she married artist Alan Odle, who was fifteen years younger than she and had been rejected for military service by a doctor who told him he had six months to live.

Richardson's books attracted some critical recognition in the years after World War I, but they never earned money; she was usually in debt to her publishers. She supported herself and Odle (who lived until 1948) and also coped with all the practical details of their life—housekeeping, paying taxes, writing checks, doing his business with publishers and exhibitors. The couple moved frequently, spending the off-season (when lodgings were less expensive) in Cornwall and going to rooms in London for the summer. During the early 1930's, Richardson took on the burden of five full-length translations from French and German. Returning to *Pilgrimage* and the state of mind in which it was begun became increasingly difficult for Richardson; the later volumes were weakened by extraliterary distractions and also by the psychological difficulty for the author in concluding the work that was based on her own life. The final segment, *March Moonlight*, was found unfinished among her papers after she died on June 17, 1957, at the age of eighty-four.

ANALYSIS

Pilgrimage is a quest. The novel's protagonist, Miriam Henderson, seeks her self and, rejecting the old guideposts, makes her own path through life. The book remains a problem for many readers, although since 1915 most of Dorothy Richardson's technical devices have become familiar: unannounced transitions from third-person narration to the first person for interior monologue, shifts between present and past as experience evokes memory, and disconnected phrases and images and fragmentary impressions representing the continuous nonverbal operations of the mind.

Looking back on the period when she was trying to find a way to embody Miriam Henderson's experience, Richardson described her breakthrough as the realization that no one was "*there* to *describe* her." Impressed by Henry James's control of viewpoint, she went one step further. The narrator and the protagonist merge; the narrator knows, perceives, and expresses only what comes to Miriam's consciousness. Furthermore, the narrator does not speak to any imagined reader and therefore does not provide helpful explanations. The scenes and people are presented as they impinge on Miriam's awareness—thus the most familiar circumstances are likely to be undescribed and the most important people identified only by name, without the phrases that would place them or reveal their relationship to Miriam.

Many readers are discouraged by the attempt to follow the book and make meaning of it; some are tempted to use Richardson's biography to find out what "really" happened and others prefer to read isolated sections without regard to sequence, responding to the feeling and imagery as if it were poetry. Because there is no narrative guidance, meaning is continually modified by the reader's own consciousness and by the extent of identification.

MIRIAM HENDERSON NOVELS

The first three titles show Miriam Henderson in the last stages of her girlhood and form the prelude to her London life. *Pointed Roofs* covers her experience in Hanover; in *Backwater*, she is resident teacher in a North London school and still drawn to the possibility of romance with a young man from her suburban circle; in *Honeycomb*, she briefly holds a post as governess before her sisters' weddings and her mother's death complete the disintegration of her girlhood family.

The Tunnel begins Miriam's years in London and introduces situations and characters that reappear in the next several volumes: the dental job; the room at Mrs. Bailey's lodging house; the new women, Mag and Jan; and the dependent woman, Eleanor Dear; and a visit to her school friend, Alma, who has married the writer Hypo Wilson. In *Interim*, Miriam perceives the difficulty of communicating her current thoughts and experiences to her sister and other old friends. *Deadlock* treats her acquaintance—growing into an engagement—with Michael Shatov. In *Revolving Lights*, she has decided not to marry Shatov and becomes increasingly involved with Wilson.

The Trap shows her sharing a cramped flat with a spinster social worker and growing despondent about the isolation that, she realizes, she imposes on herself to avoid emotional entanglements. *Oberland* is a lyrical interlude about a holiday in Switzerland. In *Dawn's Left Hand*, Miriam has an affair with Wilson and an intense friendship with a young woman (Amabel) who becomes a radical suffragist. *Clear Horizon* concludes much of the practical and emotional business that has occupied Miriam for several years; she disentangles herself from Wilson, Shatov, and Amabel and prepares to leave London. In *Dimple Hill*, she lives on a farm owned by a Quaker family, absorbs their calm, and works at writing. *March Moonlight* rather hastily takes Miriam up to the point of meeting the artist who would become her husband and to the beginning of her work on a novel.

This summary of events is the barest framework. Life, for Miriam Henderson, exists not in events but in the responses that create her sense of awareness. The books are made up of relatively independent sections, each treating a single segment of experience or reflection. Because of the depth with which single moments are recorded, the overall narrative line is fragmentary. Despite *Pilgrimage*'s length, it embodies isolated spots of time. Frequently, neither narration nor the memories evoked by subsequent experience indicate what events may have taken place in the gaps between. Furthermore, the book concentrates on those moments important to Miriam's interior experience, and it leaves out the times when she acts without self-awareness—which may include significant actions that take place when Miriam is so engrossed by events that she does not engage in thought or reflection.

Richardson disliked the phrase "stream of consciousness" because it implies constant movement and change. She preferred the image of a pool—new impressions are added, and sometimes create ripples that spread over the previously accumulated consciousness. Thus, Miriam's interior monologue becomes steadily more complex as she grows older. Her consciousness widens and deepens; fragmentary phrases show her making connections with her earlier experiences and perceptions; her understanding of past events alters with later awareness. The earlier volumes have more sensory impression and direct emotion; later, as Miriam grows more self-aware, she has greater verbal skill and is more likely to analyze her responses. Because of her more sophisticated self-awareness, however, she also grows adept, in the later volumes, at suppressing impressions or fragments of self-knowledge that she does not want to admit to consciousness.

In many ways, Miriam is not likable—readers are sometimes put off by the need to share her mind for two thousand pages. In the early books, she is a self-preoccupied, narrow-minded adolescent, oppressively conscious of people's appearance and social class, annoyingly absorbed in wondering what they think about her, defensively judgmental. The wild swings in mood and the ebb and flow of her energies during the day appear to have little cause and to be unworthy of the attention she gives them. Most people, however, would appear unpleasantly selfish if their minds were open for inspection. Miriam creates her self by deliberate consciousness. The danger is that she tends to withdraw from experience in order to contemplate feeling.

PILGRIMAGE

The events of *Pilgrimage* span the decades at the turn of the century but, because of the interior focus, there is relatively little physical detail or explicit social history to create an objective picture of the era. Women's developing self-awareness, however, must be seen as one of the period's significant events. Miriam reflects the mental life of her times in her range of responses to religion, the books she reads, and the people, ideas, and movements she encounters.

A good deal of life's texture and even its choices take place at levels that are not verbalized. Richardson's first publisher described her work as "female imagism." Miriam responds particularly and constantly to the quality of light. Readers are also aware of her reaction to places, objects, and physical surroundings; ultimately, it is through mastering the emotional content of this response that she is able to discover what she needs to have in her life.

Another continuing thread is created by Miriam's thoughts about men, about men and women together, and about the roles of women in society. Her basic animosity toward men gives shape to a series of statements on their personal, emotional, social, and intellectual peculiarities that falls just short of a formal feminist analysis. Each possible romance, each rejected or forestalled proposal amounts to a choice of a way of life. The matter is, however, complicated by Miriam's sexual reticence. Even though she can talk about free love, she is not conscious—or perhaps will not permit herself to become conscious—of overt sexual urges or of physical attraction to men or to women. She struggles not to let her feeling for certain women lead her to be absorbed by their lives or roles. In *Backwater*, Miss Perne's religion is dangerously comfortable; Eleanor Dear's passive feminine helplessness forces Miriam to become her protector; Amabel's possessiveness is as stifling as Hypo Wilson's. At the end—in *March Moonlight*—there is a hint of emotional involvement with the unidentified Jane. Struggling to know herself, Miriam is constantly faced with the problem of knowing other women.

POINTED ROOFS

Pointed Roofs comes close to being a structural whole—it begins with Miriam Henderson's journey to Hanover and ends with her return home six months later. She is on her first trip away from home, looking at new scenes, anxious about her ability to do her job and earn her wages, having her first taste of independence. Since Miriam is seventeen years old—and, as a Victorian daughter, a relatively innocent and sheltered seventeen—the reader often understands more than Miriam does and can interpret the incidents that develop her sense of who she is and where she fits in the world. Some of Miriam's reactions are cast in the form of mental letters home or imaginary conversations with her sisters, which provide a structured way to verbalize mental processes. Miriam pays attention to the sights and sounds and smells of Hanover because they are new, giving readers a sense of the physical setting absent in many of the later books.

Miriam's moods are typically adolescent. An incident or object can set off a homesick reverie or a bout of self-recrimination; the sound of music or the sight of rain on paving stones can create an inexpressible transport of joy. She is alternately rebellious and anxious for approval; she is glad to learn that her French roommate is Protestant (because she could not bear living with a Catholic), proud of the skill in logic that allows her to criticize the premises of a sermon, moved by the sound of hymns in German. She worries about her plainness, her intellectual deficiencies, her inability to get close to people. Observing class and cultural differences lets her begin to understand that she has unthinkingly absorbed many of her tastes and ideas; she starts to grow more deliberate. This portrait of Miriam at the age of seventeen—which forms the essential background for

the rest of *Pilgrimage*—is also interesting for its own sake.

Because the narrative is limited to Miriam's consciousness, the reader is able to supply interpretation. In one key scene, the middle-aged Pastor Lahmann, chaplain to the school, quotes a verse describing his ambition for "A little land, well-tilled,/ A little wife, well-willed" and then asks Miriam to take off her glasses so that he can see how nearsighted her eyes really are. Miriam, who is both furious at being "regarded as one of a world of little tame things to be summoned by little man to be well-willed wives" and warmed by the personal attention that makes her forget, for a moment, that she is a governess, is oblivious to the sexual implications of Pastor Lahmann's behavior, and she cannot understand why the headmistress is angry when she walks in upon the scene. Although Miriam's consciousness will develop in subsequent volumes, her combination of receptivity to male attention, anger at male assumptions, and blindness to sexual nuance will remain.

DEADLOCK

Deadlock contains a greater proportion of direct internal monologue than the earlier books. Miriam has grown more articulate; she interprets her emotional states and examines the premises underlying her conflicts. During her first years in London, she had cherished the city for the independence it gave her. By such acts as smoking, eating alone in restaurants, and dressing without regard to fashion, she deliberately rejected Victorian womanhood. In *Honeycomb*, she refused a marriage that would have satisfied her craving for luxuries because she could not accept a subordinate role. In *Deadlock*, Miriam is faced by the loneliness that seems inextricably linked to independence. Her work has become drudgery because she no longer has the sense of a social relationship with her employer. A Christmas visit to her married sister reveals the distance that has grown between them; Miriam had not even realized that Harriet's marriage was unhappy.

Deadlock is shaped by the course of Miriam's relationship with Michael Shatov. The romance forces her conflicts to the surface. Shatov is a young Jew recently arrived from Russia; a lodger at Mrs. Bailey's arranges for Miriam to tutor him in English. As she shows Shatov London, tired scenes recapture their original freshness.

Miriam is excited by her ability to formulate ideas when she argues about philosophy or works on a translation. Yet, although Miriam is buoyed by the joy of sharing her thoughts with another person, Shatov's continual presence comes between her and the life that was her own. Her love has a maternal quality: Though Shatov is only three years younger than Miriam, he is a foreigner and also, Miriam finds, rather impractical; she feels protective. She is also sexually reticent: Because she has despised traditional femininity, she does not know how to behave as the object of a courtship. The romance ends when Miriam deliberately engages Shatov in an argument that reveals his views of woman's limited nature. (The final scene restates the problem more concretely when Miriam visits an Englishwoman married to a Jewish man.)

Beneath these specific difficulties lies the friction between Miriam's individualism and Shatov's tendency to see problems in the abstract—she talks about herself, he dwells on the future of the race. For Richardson, the conflict reflects the irreconcilable difference between masculine objectivity (or materialism) and feminine subjectivity. The images of darkness accumulate as Miriam realizes the extent of her deadlock; unable to be a woman in the sense that men see women, she seems to have no path out of loneliness and alienation.

DAWN'S LEFT HAND

Dawn's Left Hand is a prelude to the deliberate detachment and observation that would turn Miriam into a writer. *Oberland* (the preceding book) vibrates with the sensory detail of a two-week holiday in Switzerland that makes London complications seem far away; returning, Miriam sees people objectively even when she is with them. The transitions between third-person narrative and internal monologue are less noticeable; Miriam and the narrator have virtually merged. The visual content of scenes reveals their meaning. Miriam looks at pictorial relationships and examines gesture and tone for the nonverbal communications that, to women, are often more meaningful than words. (During the years that she worked on *Dawn's Left Hand*, Richardson wrote regularly about films—which were still silent—for the magazine *Close Up*.)

Images of light carry emotional and symbolic content throughout *Pilgrimage*. When Miriam visits Densley's

medical office early in *Dawn's Left Hand*, the drawn shades are keeping out the light; she refuses his proposal—one last offer of conventional marriage—with a momentary wistfulness that is immediately replaced by a great sense of relief. She is increasingly aware of herself as an actor in the scenes of her life. Self-observation allows physical compositions to reveal power relationships: When Wilson comes into Miriam's room, she notices that he stands over her like a doctor, and when he embarks on a program of seduction to the music of Richard Wagner, she disputes his control by rearranging the chairs. On another occasion, in a hotel room, Miriam looks in the mirror to observe herself and Wilson. Her own position blocks the light and thus the scene is chilled even before she begins to see him as a pathetic naked male.

During the final stages of the Wilson affair, Miriam is increasingly preoccupied by a beautiful young woman—soon to be a radical suffragist—who pursues her ardently and pays homage to her as a woman in ways that bring home to Miriam the impossibility of real communion with men. Yet the deep commitment demanded by Amabel is frightening; her intense adoration forces Miriam into a role that threatens her independence more crucially than Wilson's overt attempts at domination. The advantage of being with people who interact only on superficial levels, Miriam realizes, is that she can retain her freedom.

MARCH MOONLIGHT

Although Richardson struggled to bring the events in *March Moonlight* up to 1912, the year that she began writing *Pilgrimage*, her form and subject virtually required the book to remain without conclusion. The narrative techniques of *March Moonlight* grow more deliberate; when Miriam begins to write, she thinks and sees differently and is aware of selecting and arranging details. Thus, the book's ending is only a middle: Miriam's sense of self would inevitably change as she reexamined and re-created her experiences in order to write novels. Once traditional formulas are rejected and *being* itself becomes the subject, there can be no ending; there is no epiphany, no coming-of-age, no final truth but rather a continuous process of self-making through self-awareness.

Sally Mitchell

OTHER MAJOR WORKS

NONFICTION: *Gleanings from the Works of George Fox*, 1914; *The Quakers Past and Present*, 1914; *John Austen and the Inseparables*, 1930.

BIBLIOGRAPHY

Bloom, Harold, ed. *British Women Fiction Writers, 1900-1960.* 2 vols. Philadelphia: Chelsea House, 1997. A brief biography and critical essays about Richardson's work and place in literary history is included in volume 2 of this survey of British women writers.

Bluemel, Kristin. *Experimenting on the Borders of Modernism: Dorothy Richardson's "Pilgrimage."* Athens: University of Georgia Press, 1997. The first chapter assesses Richardson and previous studies of her. Subsequent chapters explore Richardson's handling of gender, the problems of the body, science in *Pilgrimage*, and the author's quest for an ending to this long work. Includes notes and a bibliography.

Fromm, Gloria G. *Dorothy Richardson: A Biography.* Champaign: University of Illinois Press, 1977. An objective biography, which carefully draws distinctions between the events of Richardson's life and those of her fictional characters, but also identifies clear correlations between the two. Extensively researched and well written and supplemented by illustrations, chapter endnotes, a comprehensive bibliography, and an index.

Garrity, Jane. "'Neither English nor Civilized': Dorothy Richardson's Spectatrix and the Feminine Crusade for Global Intervention." In *Step-Daughters of England: British Women Modernists and the National Imaginary.* New York: St. Martin's Press, 2003. Garrity examines works by Richardson and three other modernist women writers to demonstrate how these works express the writers' ambivalent and complex feelings about English national culture.

Gevirtz, Susan. *Narrative's Journey: The Fiction and Film Writing of Dorothy Richardson.* New York: Peter Lang, 1996. A probing discussion of Richardson's aesthetic. This is a challenging study for advanced students. *Pilgrimage* receives detailed discussion throughout the book. Includes an extensive bibliography not only on Richardson but also on feminist theory, literary and cultural theory, poetics and phenomenology, theology and spirituality, travel and travel theories, and narrative.

McCracken, Scott. "Editorial." *Pilgrimages: The Journal of Dorothy Richardson Studies* 1, no. 1 (2008). Richardson scholar Scott McCracken introduces the first issue of a new academic journal focusing on Richardson's life and works.

Parsons, Deborah L. *Theorists of the Modernist Novel: James Joyce, Dorothy Richardson, Virginia Woolf.* New York: Routledge, 2007. A study of the aesthetic theories of Richardson and two other modernist writers. Parsons examines realism, characterization, gender representation, and other elements of Richardson's work.

Radford, Jean. *Dorothy Richardson.* Bloomington: Indiana University Press, 1991. An excellent introductory study, with chapters on reading in *Pilgrimage*, the author's quest for form, London as a space for women, and Richardson as a feminist writer. Includes notes and a bibliography.

Randall, Bryony. "Dailiness in Dorothy Richardson's *Pilgrimage.*" In *Modernism, Daily Time, and Everyday Life.* New York: Cambridge University Press, 2007. Argues that the temporal notion of "the day" partly structures Richardson's fiction. Also examines Richardson's attempts at rendering time without beginnings and endings.

Rosenberg, John. *Dorothy Richardson, the Genius They Forgot: A Critical Biography.* New York: Alfred A. Knopf, 1973. The strength of Rosenberg's biography lies in his scholarly credibility, as he aptly parallels events in *Pilgrimage* to Richardson's life. His concluding analysis of Richardson's pioneering impact upon the development of the novel, however, lacks the impact of his earlier writing but is still perceptive. Includes an index and a bibliography.

Winning, Joanne. *The Pilgrimage of Dorothy Richardson.* Madison: University of Wisconsin Press, 2000. Winning argues that Richardson's thirteen-volume novel contains a subtext of lesbian desire and sexuality, and she compares this novel to works by other lesbian modernist writers.

SAMUEL RICHARDSON

Born: Mackworth, Derbyshire, England; August 19,
　1689 (baptized)
Died: London, England; July 4, 1761

PRINCIPAL LONG FICTION

Pamela: Or, Virtue Rewarded, 1740-1741
Clarissa: Or, The History of a Young Lady,
　1747-1748
Sir Charles Grandison, 1753-1754

OTHER LITERARY FORMS

In addition to the three novels on which his fame and
reputation rest, Samuel Richardson's best-known work
is a collection of fictitious letters that constitutes a kind
of eighteenth century book of etiquette, social behavior,
manners, and mores: *Letters Written to and for
Particular Friends, on the Most Important Occasions* (1741), customarily referred to as *Familiar Letters*. It had been preceded, in 1733, by
a handbook of instruction concerning the relationship between apprentices and master print-
ers, which grew out of a letter Richardson had
written to a nephew in 1731, *The Apprentice's
Vade Mecum: Or, Young Man's Pocket Companion* (1733). Throughout his life, Richardson, like so many of his contemporaries, was a
prolific letter writer; notable selections of his
correspondence include six volumes edited by
his contemporary and early biographer, Anna
L. Barbauld, the first of which was published in
1804, and his correspondence with Johannes
Stinstra, the Dutch translator of his novels to
whom Richardson had sent a considerably important amount of autobiographical material.
Of only minor interest is Richardson's *A Collection of the Moral and Instructive Sentiments,
Maxims, Cautions, and Reflexions, Contained
in the Histories of Pamela, Clarissa, and Sir
Charles Grandison*, published anonymously in
1755, a series of excerpts emphasizing his conviction that "instruction was a more important
obligation to the novelist than entertainment."

ACHIEVEMENTS

Perhaps Samuel Richardson's most important contribution to the development of the novel was his concern
for the nonexceptional problems of daily conduct, the relationships between men and women, and the specific
class and caste distinctions of mid-eighteenth century
England. He sought and found his material from life as
he had observed and reflected on it from childhood and
youth as a member of the working class in a highly socially conscious society to his position as an increasingly
successful and prosperous printer and publisher. He contemplated this material with passionate interest and recorded it with a kind of genius for verisimilitude that sets
him apart from most of his predecessors. What one critic
has called Richardson's "almost rabid concern for the

Samuel Richardson. (Library of Congress)

details" of daily life and his continuing "enrichment and complication" of customary human relationships account in large measure for his enormous contemporary popularity: In *Pamela*, for example, the relationships between Pamela and Squire B. are so persistently grounded in the minutiae of ordinary life as to create a sense of reality seldom achieved in prose fiction prior to Richardson; at the same time, the outcome of the emotional and physical tug-of-war between the two main characters and the happy outcome of all the intrigue and sensationalism have about them the quality of conventional romantic love.

Richardson learned to know his characters so intimately, so thoroughly, as to triumph over his prolixity, repetitiveness, moralizing, and sentimentality. Equally important was his development of the epistolary novel. Other writers had used letters as a storytelling device, but few if any of Richardson's predecessors had approximated his skill in recording the external events and incidents of a narrative along with the intimate and instant revelation of a character's thought and emotions in the process of their taking place, a method so flowing, so fluid, so flexible, as almost to anticipate the modern technique of stream of consciousness. Richardson's works, along with those of his three great contemporaries—Henry Fielding, Tobias Smollett, and Laurence Sterne—prepared the way for the great achievements of the nineteenth century English novel.

BIOGRAPHY

The exact date of Samuel Richardson's birth is uncertain, but it is known that he was born in Derbyshire, probably on July 31, 1689; the record of his baptism is dated August 19, 1869. His father was a joiner and, according to Richardson, a "good draughtsman" who "understood architecture" and whose ancestors had included several generations of small farmers in Surrey; of his mother, the second wife of Richardson *père*, little is known. The family returned to London, where Richardson may have attended the Merchant Taylor's School in 1701 and 1702, at which time his formal education ended. In 1706, he was apprenticed to the Stationers' Company, and in 1715, he became a "freeman" of the Company. He married his former employer's daughter, Martha Wilde, in November 23, 1721, set up his own

business as a printer, was admitted to the Stationers' Company in 1722, and soon became what his major biographers—T. C. Duncan Eaves and Ben D. Kimpel—term a "prosperous and respected" tradesman. Six children, none of whom survived infancy or early childhood, preceded their mother's death in January, 1731. Two years later, on February 3, 1733, Richardson remarried, this time to Elizabeth Leake, also the daughter of a printer; four of their six children survived.

Richardson's career as an editor continued to prosper—among other distinctions, he was eventually awarded the lucrative contract to print the journals of the House of Commons—and by the mid-1730's, he had moved into a large house in Salisbury Court, where the family would live for the next two decades and where he would write the three novels on which his reputation rests.

For some time, two of Richardson's "particular friends," both of them London booksellers, had been urging him to compile a "little book . . . of familiar letters on the useful concerns of common life." An almost compulsive letter writer since early childhood—before he was eleven he had written to an elderly widow, reprimanding her for her "uncharitable conduct"—Richardson began the undertaking, one letter of which was an actual account he had heard some years before, the story of a virtuous servant who eventually married her master. The recollection of the incident stimulated his imagination, and so, at the age of fifty, he temporarily abandoned the letters project. In two months, writing as much as three thousand words a day, he completed the novel that, on November 6, 1740, without the author's name on the title page, was to explode upon the English scene:

Pamela: Or, Virtue Rewarded. In a Series of Familiar Letters from a beautiful Young Damsel, to her Parents. Now first published in order to cultivate the Principles of Virtue and Religion in the Minds of the Youth of both Sexes. A Narrative which has its Foundation in Truth and Nature; and at the same time that it agreeably entertains, by a Variety of Curious and affecting Incidents, is entirely divested of all those Images, which, in too many Pieces calculated for Amusement only, tend to inflame the Minds they should instruct.

Pamela was an instant success, going through five editions in less than a year and inspiring numerous burlesques, imitations, and parodies, including *An Apology for the Life of Mrs. Shamela Andrews* (1741, probably the work of Henry Fielding and the only parody of interest today) and serving as the impetus for Fielding's *The History of the Adventures of Joseph Andrews, and of His Friend Mr. Abraham Adams* (1742). *Pamela* was also dramatized in several forms and translated into German, French, and Dutch; its success, for the worse rather than the better, led Richardson to write a sequel, centering on his heroine's life after her marriage.

Meanwhile, Richardson continued to combine the roles of successful and prosperous businessman and author. Exactly when he began the novel that was to be his masterpiece is uncertain—one of his biographers thinks he was considering it as early as 1741—but he had the concept of *Clarissa* "well in mind" before 1744, began the actual writing in the spring or summer of that year, and by November was ready to send parts of the manuscript to his old friend Aaron Hill. Unlike *Pamela*, *Clarissa* did not have its origins in "real life"; Clarissa and Miss Howe, Richardson insisted, were "entirely creatures of his fantasy." The novel, almost a million words in length, was three years in the writing, including two "thorough" revisions, and published in seven volumes between December 1, 1747, and December 7, 1748; a subsequent eight-volume edition, "with Letters and passages restored from the original manuscript," was published between 1749 and 1751.

Though *Clarissa* was somewhat less controversial than *Pamela*, its reception was tumultuous; among other things, the author was accused of indecency because of the dramatic fire scene, and Richardson took the charges seriously enough to write an eleven-page pamphlet defending it. Sarah Fielding wrote what has been called an "ambitious defense" of the novel, and her brother Henry, whose masterpiece *The History of Tom Jones, a Foundling* was published soon after the last volumes of *Clarissa* in 1749, lavishly praised Richardson's work, although Richardson's dislike of what he considered Fielding's improprieties, along with the opening sections of *Joseph Andrews* and Fielding's possible authorship of *Shamela*, made any friendship between the two impossible (indeed, their relationship—or, more accurately, the lack of it—reflects little credit on Richardson).

One of Richardson's closest friends, Lady Bradshaigh, had written him soon after publication of the

fourth volume of *Clarissa*, entreating him not to let his heroine die, and subsequently urged him to write a "novel about a Good Man." How much this influenced Richardson, if at all, is purely conjectural, but early in 1750, he had begun what was to be his last novel. Despite his stated intention not to publish this "new work," the first six volumes of *Sir Charles Grandison* were published late in 1753 (November 13 and December 11), and the concluding volume on March 14, 1754. As had been the case with *Pamela* and *Clarissa*, Dutch, German, and French translations soon followed.

In his preface to *Sir Charles Grandison*, Richardson, in his guise as the "editor" of the manuscript, announced that after this third novel he would write no more. He had, however, been in the process of compiling a series of selections from his novels that was published in March, 1755, as *A Collection of the Moral and Instructive Sentiments, Maxims, Cautions, and Reflexions, Contained in the Histories of Pamela, Clarissa, and Sir Charles Grandison*. He continued to be active as a printer and to make minor revisions in his novels, particularly *Pamela*, but his "dislike to the pen" continued. During his last years, he devoted more and more time to his correspondence—since the early 1740's, he had kept copies of all or most of his letters—apparently with the idea of eventual publication. On June 28, 1761, he suffered a stroke that resulted in his death a few days later on July 4, 1761.

ANALYSIS

"Why, Sir, if you were to read Richardson for the story, your impatience would be so much fretted that you would hang yourself. But you must read him for the sentiment, and consider the story as only giving occasion to the sentiment." This comment by Samuel Johnson is only partly relevant. As James E. Evans states in his introduction to Samuel Richardson's series of excerpts, the revival of Richardson's reputation in recent decades has grown out of the assertion that he "remains a great writer in spite of his morality" and must be read "'for the story' (psychological realism and conscious artistry), because we no longer read 'for the sentiment.'"

Richardson himself stated quite clearly, in his prefaces to *Pamela* and *Clarissa*, and in his letters, that his purpose as an author was to depict "real life" and "in a manner probable, natural, and lively." At the same time, however, he wanted his books to be thought of as instruments of manners and morals intended to "teach great virtues." Fiction, he insisted, should be useful and instructive; it should edify readers of all ages, but particularly should be relevant and appealing to youth. Richardson observed with passionate interest and recorded with a genius for infinite detail the relationships between men and women; the concerns of daily life; and the particular class and caste distinctions of mid-eighteenth century England. This intense interest in the *usual* sets him apart from such predecessors as Daniel Defoe or the seventeenth century writers of prose romances. In all of his novels, and particularly, perhaps, in *Pamela*, the relationship between his main characters has about it the quality of traditional romantic love; at the same time, the novels are so realistically grounded in the accumulation of a mass of day-to-day realistic details as to create a remarkable sense of authenticity. Characteristic of this creation of the illusion of real life is the account, possibly apocryphal, of *Pamela*'s being read aloud by the local blacksmith to a small group of the village's inhabitants on the village green; finally, when Pamela's triumph by her marriage to Squire B. was assured, the villagers indulged in a spree of thanksgiving and merrymaking; it was *their* Pamela who had conquered.

Richardson, then, was both a conscious, self-avowed realist, and also an equally conscious, self-avowed teacher and moralist. This dualism permeates all three of his novels and is perhaps most apparent—and transparent—in *Pamela*. It is, indeed, Richardson's hallmark, and is the source both of his strength and weakness as a novelist.

PAMELA

Reduced to its simplest terms, the "story" or "plot" of the first volume of *Pamela* is too well known to warrant more than the briefest summary. The heroine, a young servant girl, is pursued by her master, Squire B., but maintains her virginity in spite of his repeated and ingenious efforts, until the would-be seducer, driven to desperation, marries her. Thus is Pamela's virtue rewarded. The continuation of the novel in volume 2, a decided letdown, is virtually plotless, highly repetitive, and highlighted only by Squire B.'s excursion into infidelity. Volumes 3 and 4, written partly because of Richardson's indignation with the various parodies of the first

volume of *Pamela*, have even less to recommend them. Labeled as "virtually unreadable" by one modern commentator, even Richardson's most understanding critic-biographers, T. C. Duncan Eaves and Ben D. Kimpel, have dismissed them as "Richardson at his worst, pompous, proper, proud of himself, and above all dull."

Despite his frequent excursions into bathos and sentimentality, when he is not indulging in sermonizing on ethics and morality, the Richardson of the first volume of *Pamela* writes vigorously, effectively, and with keen insight and intimate understanding of his characters. *Pamela* contains many powerful scenes that linger long in the reader's memory: the intended rape scene, the sequence in which Pamela considers suicide, even parts of the marriage scene (preceded by some prodigious feats of letter writing to her parents on the day prior to the wedding, from six o'clock in the morning, half an hour past eight o'clock, near three o'clock [ten pages], eight o'clock at night, until eleven o'clock the same night and following the marriage) are the work of a powerful writer with a keen sense for the dramatic.

In the final analysis, however, the novel succeeds or fails because of its characters, particularly and inevitably that of Pamela herself. From the opening letter in which she informs her parents that her mistress has died and Squire B., her mistress's son, has appeared on the scene, to the long sequence of her journal entries, until her final victory when her would-be seducer, worn out and defeated in all his attempts to have her without marriage, capitulates and makes the "thrice-happy" Pamela his wife, she dominates the novel.

In effect, and seemingly quite beyond Richardson's conscious intent, Pamela is two quite different characters. On one hand, she is the attractive and convincing young girl who informs her parents that her recently deceased mistress left her three pairs of shoes that fit her perfectly, adding that "my lady had a very little foot," and, having been transferred to Squire B.'s Lincolnshire estate, laments that she lacks "the courage to stay, neither can I think to go." On the other hand, she is at times a rather unconvincing puppet who thinks and talks in pious platitudes and sees her "honesty" as a very valuable commodity, a character—in Joseph Wood Krutch's words—"so devoid of any delicacy of feeling as to be inevitably indecent."

Squire B. is less interesting than Pamela, and his efforts to seduce Pamela tend to become either boring or amusing. Her father, the Old Gaffer, who would disown his daughter "were she not honest," similarly frequently verges on caricature, although one distinguished historian of the English novel finds him extremely convincing; and Lady Davers, Squire B.'s arrogant sister, tends to be more unbelievable than convincing, as do Pamela's captors, the odious Mrs. Jewkes and the equally repulsive Colbrand.

In spite of its shortcomings, *Pamela* cannot be dismissed, as one critic has commented, as "only a record of a peculiarly loathsome aspect of bourgeois morality." *Pamela* has great moments, scenes, and characters that pass the ultimate test of a work of fiction, that of *memorableness:* scenes that remain in the reader's consciousness long after many of the events have become blurred or dimmed. It is equally important historically: Among other things, its popularity helped prepare the way for better novelists and better novels, including what Arnold Bennett was to call the "greatest realistic novel in the world," Richardson's *Clarissa.*

CLARISSA

Unlike *Pamela, Clarissa* did not have its origins in "real life"; his characters, Richardson insisted, were "entirely creatures of his fantasy." He commenced the novel in the spring or summer of 1744; it was three years in the making, two of which were primarily devoted to revision (it has been said that when his old friend Aaron Hill misread *Clarissa,* Richardson devoted a year to revising the text for publication). Almost a million words in length, the plot of *Clarissa* is relatively simple. Clarissa Harlowe, daughter of well-to-do, middle-class parents with social aspirations, is urged by her family to marry a man, Solmes, whom she finds repulsive. At the same time, her sister Arabella is being courted by an aristocrat, Robert Lovelace. Lovelace, attracted and fascinated by Clarissa, abandons his lukewarm courtship of Arabella and, after wounding the girl's brother in a duel, turns his attention to Clarissa, in spite of her family's objections. Clarissa lets herself be persuaded; she goes off with Lovelace, who imprisons her in a brothel, where he eventually drugs and rapes her; she finally escapes, refuses the contrite Lovelace's offers of marriage, and eventually dies. Lovelace, repentant and haunted by his

evil act, is killed in a duel by Clarissa's cousin, Colonel Morden.

Counterpointing and contrasting with these two major characters are Anna Howe, Clarissa's closest friend and confidant, and John Belford, Lovelace's closest friend. Around these four are a number of contrasting minor characters, each of whom contributes to the minutely recorded series of events and climaxes, events that in their barest forms verge on melodrama and at times even farce. Even so, the novel in its totality is greater than the sum of its parts: It has about it the ultimate power of Greek tragedy, and Clarissa herself, like the major characters of Greek drama, rises above the occasionally melodramatic or improbable sequences to attain a stature not seen in English prose fiction before and seldom surpassed since.

Much of the power and the drama of *Clarissa* grows out of the author's effective use of contrast—between Clarissa and Anna Howe; between Lovelace and Belford; and between the country life of the upper middle class and the dark, rank side of urban England. This and the richness and variety of incident redeem the sometimes improbable events and lapses into didacticism and give the novel a sense of reality larger than life itself.

In the final analysis, the great strength of the novel is the creation of its two main characters. Clarissa, with her pride and self-reliance, "so secure in her virtue," whose feelings of shame and self-hatred are such that she begs Lovelace "to send her to Bedlam or a private madhouse" (no less a master than Henry Fielding praised Clarissa's letter after the rape as "beyond anything I had ever read"), could have degenerated into bathos or caricature but instead attains a level of intensity and reality unique in the novel prior to 1740.

Although Clarissa dominates the novel, Richardson is almost as successful with Lovelace, despite the fact that in the early portions of the novel he seems for the most part like Squire B., just another Restoration rake. His transformation, following his violation of Clarissa, grows and deepens: "One day, I fancy," he reflects, "I shall hate myself on recollecting what I am about at this instant. But I must stay till then. We must all of us have something to repent of." Repent he does, after his terse letter announcing the consummation of the rape: "And now, Belford, I can go no further. The affair is over. Clarissa lives."

Belford, like the reader, is horror-stricken. In committing the rape, Lovelace has acted not as a man but as an animal, and his expiation is, in its own way, much more terrible than Clarissa's, who at times somewhat complacently contemplates her own innocence and eventual heavenly reward. Lovelace remains a haunted man ("sick of myself! sick of my remembrance of my vile act!") until his death in a duel with Colonel Morden, a death that is really a kind of suicide. The final scene of the novel and Lovelace's last words, "Let this Expiate!," are among the most memorable elements of the entire novel, and Richardson's portrayal of a character soiled and tarnished, an eternally damaged soul, is unforgettable.

SIR CHARLES GRANDISON

As early as February, 1741, an anonymous correspondent had asked Richardson to write the "history of a Man, whose Life would be the path that we should follow." By the end of the decade, with *Pamela* and *Clarissa* behind him, and influenced by old friends, including Lady Bradshaigh, Richardson began thinking seriously about such a novel. Despite increasing ill health and the continuing demands of his business, he was soon immersed in the project, a novel designed to "present" the character of a "Good Man," and to show the influence such a character exerted "on society in general and his intimates in particular." Although he had at one time decided not to publish the novel during his lifetime, the first volumes of *Sir Charles Grandison* came out in 1753. Even before the seventh and last volume was in print the following year, some critics were stating their dissatisfaction with Sir Charles's "Unbelievable Perfection," a criticism Richardson repudiates in a concluding note to the last volume: "The Editor [that is, Richardson himself] thinks human nature has often, of late, been shown in a light too degrading; and he hopes from this series of letters it will be seen that characters may be good without being unnatural."

Subsequent critical opinion of the novel has varied widely; a few critics consider it Richardson's masterpiece, while many regard it as his least successful novel. *Sir Charles Grandison* differs dramatically from its predecessors in its concern with the English upper class and aristocracy, a world that Richardson freely acknowledged he had never known or understood: "How shall a man obscurely situated . . . pretend to describe and enter into

characters in upper life?" In setting, too, the novel was a new departure, ranging as it does from England to Italy and including a large number of Italians, highlighted by Clementina, certainly the most memorable character in the novel. The conflict in Clementina's heart and soul, her subsequent refusal to marry Sir Charles because he is a Protestant, and her ensuing madness are as effective as anything Richardson ever wrote, and far more convincing than Sir Charles's rescue of Harriett Byron following her abduction by Sir Hargrove Pollexfen and their eventual marriage. Harriett, though not as interesting a character as either Pamela or Clarissa, shares with them one basic habit: She is an indefatigable letter writer, perhaps the most prolific in the history of English prose fiction, at times sleeping only two hours a night and, when not admiring Grandison from afar, writing letters to him. (Not uncharacteristic of her style is her appeal to the clergyman who is supposed to marry her to Sir Hargrove: "Worthy man . . . save a poor creature. I would not hurt a worm! I love everybody! Save me from violence!")

Sir Charles himself is similarly less interesting than either Squire B. or Lovelace, and it is difficult today for even the most sympathetic reader to find a great deal to admire in the man who is against masquerades, dresses neatly but not gaudily, is time and time again described as a "prince of the Almighty's creation," an "angel of a man," and "one of the finest dancers in England." Most of the other characters, including the Italians (with the notable exception of Clementina), are similarly either unconvincing or uninteresting, except for two small masterpieces of characterization: Aunt Nell, Grandison's maiden aunt; and Lord G., Charlotte Grandison's husband, a gentle and quiet man, in love with his temperamental wife, often hurt and bewildered by her sharp tongue and brusque actions.

Horace Walpole is said to have written off *Sir Charles Grandison* as a "romance as it would be spiritualized by a Methodist preacher"; and Lord Chesterfield also dismissed it, adding that whenever Richardson "goes, *ultra crepidem*, into high life, he grossly escapes the modes." On the other hand, Jane Austen specifically "singled . . . [it] out for special praise," and Richardson's major biographers believe that in *Sir Charles Grandison*, his "surface realism and his analysis of social situations are at their height."

Whatever his weaknesses, Richardson was one of the seminal influences in the development of the novel. His impact on his contemporaries and their immediate successors was profound, not only in England but on the Continent as well, and eventually on the beginnings of the novel in the United States. He popularized the novel of manners as a major genre for several decades, and his use of the epistolary method added another dimension to the art of narrative. Although his novels have frequently suffered in comparison with those of his major contemporary, Henry Fielding, in recent years a renewed interest and appraisal of Richardson and his work have placed him securely in the ranks of the major English novelists.

William Peden

OTHER MAJOR WORKS

NONFICTION: *The Apprentice's Vade Mecum: Or, Young Man's Pocket Companion*, 1733; *Letters Written to and for Particular Friends, on the Most Important Occasions*, 1741; *A Collection of the Moral and Instructive Sentiments, Maxims, Cautions, and Reflections, Contained in the Histories of Pamela, Clarissa, and Sir Charles Grandison*, 1755; *The Correspondence of Samuel Richardson*, 1804 (Anna Barbauld, editor).

BIBLIOGRAPHY

Blewitt, David, ed. *Passion and Virtue: Essays on the Novels of Samuel Richardson*. Toronto, Ont.: University of Toronto Press, 2001. Collection of essays examines various aspects of Richardson's three novels, including such topics as the politics of virtue in *Pamela, Clarissa* and scripture, and Richardson on body and character in *Sir Charles Grandison*.

Bloom, Harold, ed. *Samuel Richardson*. New York: Chelsea House, 1987. Presents an informative editor's introduction followed by six essays devoted to *Clarissa* and two each to *Pamela* and *Sir Charles Grandison*. Includes a chronology of Richardson's life and a brief bibliography.

Brophy, Elizabeth Bergen. *Samuel Richardson*. Boston: Twayne, 1987. Provides a good introduction to Richardson, containing biographical information as well as analyses of his writings. Includes bibliography and index.

_____. *Samuel Richardson: The Triumph of Craft*. Knoxville: University of Tennessee Press, 1974. Rejecting the notion that Richardson's unconscious produced great novels in spite of the author, Brophy determines his theories about fiction and then compares these ideas with Richardson's practice.

Eaves, T. C. Duncan, and Ben D. Kimpel. *Samuel Richardson: A Biography*. Oxford, England: Clarendon Press, 1971. Definitive biography is based on fifteen years of research. Devotes three chapters to each of the novels and concludes with four excellent chapters on Richardson's personality, thoughts, reading, and achievements.

Keymer, Thomas, and Peter Sabor. *"Pamela" in the Marketplace: Literary Controversy and Print Culture in Eighteenth-Century Britain and Ireland*. New York: Cambridge University Press, 2005. Recounts the cultural impacts of *Pamela*, which became the best-selling novel of its time and was the subject of numerous critiques, parodies, sequels, comedies, and operas.

Lams, Victor J. *Anger, Guilt, and the Psychology of the Self in "Clarissa."* New York: Peter Lang, 1999. Examination of *Clarissa* focuses on Lovelace as a narcissistic personality and on Clarissa's forced change of philosophical stance in reaction to his actions. Includes bibliography and index.

_____. *Clarissa's Narrators*. New York: Peter Lang, 2001. Argues that the novel's structure consists of five movements resembling the acts in a play; these movements emerge from the round-robin transfer of three narrators. Includes bibliography and index.

Rivero, Albert J., ed. *New Essays on Samuel Richardson*. New York: Palgrave Macmillan, 1996. Contributors to this collection of scholarly essays approach Richardson's three novels from a variety of theoretical perspectives. Includes index.

Watt, Ian. *The Rise of the Novel: Studies in Defoe, Richardson, and Fielding*. 2d American ed. Berkeley: University of California Press, 2001. Contains excellent chapters on *Pamela* and *Clarissa*, praising the psychological depth of the characters. Analyzes Richardson's contribution to the development of English prose fiction and relates the novels to the social situation of their day.

MORDECAI RICHLER

Born: Montreal, Quebec, Canada; January 27, 1931
Died: Montreal, Quebec, Canada; July 3, 2001

PRINCIPAL LONG FICTION

The Acrobats, 1954 (also known as *Wicked We Love*)
Son of a Smaller Hero, 1955
A Choice of Enemies, 1957
The Apprenticeship of Duddy Kravitz, 1959
The Incomparable Atuk, 1963 (also known as *Stick Your Neck Out*)
Cocksure: A Novel, 1968
St. Urbain's Horseman, 1971
Joshua Then and Now, 1980
Solomon Gursky Was Here, 1989
Barney's Version, 1997

OTHER LITERARY FORMS

As a professional writer, spurning academic life for wider creative possibilities, Mordecai Richler (RIHCH-lur) was known for producing short stories, essays, articles, film scripts, television plays, and children's literature. Much of his work first appeared in prestigious magazines such as *The Atlantic Monthly*, *The New Yorker*, *New Statesman*, and *Encounter*. Some of his individual stories, many of which became chapters in his novels, have been collected in *The Street: Stories* (1969). A children's book, *Jacob Two-Two Meets the Hooded Fang* (1975), and two novels, *Joshua Then and Now* and *The Apprenticeship of Duddy Kravitz*, have been adapted into motion pictures. The film version of *The Apprenticeship of Duddy Kravitz*, directed by Ted Kotcheff, received the Golden Bear Award at the Berlin Film Festival in 1974; in addition, Richler's screenplay for the film was nominated for an Academy Award, and it won a Screenwriters Guild of America Award. The motion-picture adaptation of *Joshua Then and Now*, also directed by Kotcheff from a screenplay by Richler, was released in 1985.

ACHIEVEMENTS

Forsaking Canada for the more exciting atmosphere of Paris, Mordecai Richler struggled with his work and lived in poor circumstances, publishing very few stories. Here, however, he met some significant figures of the new literary set who reacted favorably to his work; among them were Allen Ginsberg, Herbert Gold, and Terry Southern. After returning to Canada for a short while, Richler finished his first novel, *The Acrobats*. As is often the case with Canadian writers, Richler preferred to publish outside his own country, where he felt more appreciated. His first effort was accepted by André Deutsch in London. In later years, with his reputation secure, he decided to publish with the Canadian publishing house McClelland & Stewart.

In order to make a living exclusively as a writer, Richler left Canada again. Still using his Canadian experience as the substance of his work, Richler was very productive in England, publishing stories and novels that met with much acclaim. Even his film scripts for *No Love for Johnnie* (1961), *Young and Willing* (1964), and *Life at the Top* (1965), which Richler considered inferior work for an often superficial medium, were positively reviewed. Richler twice won Canada's foremost literary prize, the Governor-General's Award, for *Cocksure* and *St. Urbain's Horseman*. Although he achieved a certain notoriety for his searing portraits of Canadian life, he finally gained acceptance as one of Canada's most distinguished novelists. In 2001, not long before his death, he was made a Companion of the Order of Canada.

BIOGRAPHY

Mordecai Richler was born in Montreal, Canada, in 1931, in the heart of the Jewish ghetto. His father was a junk dealer and his mother was a housewife (in later years, she wrote a book about her life). Her father was a rabbi whose influence ensured an Orthodox household. By turning away from Orthodoxy at a young age, however, Richler ran into trouble at home, which perhaps accounts for some of his perceptive but acerbic reflections on family life. Further compounding his problems as a youth, his parents divorced when he was thirteen years old. As a response to the breakdown at home, Richler joined a Zionist labor group called Habonim and dreamed of settling in Palestine. Only later did he go to Israel as a journalist.

In his adolescent years, Richler attended Baron Byng High School, a predominantly Jewish school even though it was part of the Protestant school system. In his stories and novels it is transformed into Fletcher's Field High School and peopled with characters known to Richler in his youth. After high school, Richler attended Sir George Williams University in Montreal (now Concordia University) because his high school grades were not good enough to gain him admittance to McGill University. Although he later returned to Sir George as writer-in-residence, the academic life did not appeal to him. He once remarked that "academe, like girls, whiskey, and literature, promised better than it paid." Rejecting a life of scholarship, Richler decided on the uncertain life of a freelance writer in Europe, where he could develop his own style and not merely put a stamp of approval on someone else's.

After living in Paris for two years, where he published his first story in a magazine called *Points* and got his first taste of expatriate life, Richler returned to Montreal. There he joined the Canadian Broadcasting Company for a short time, earning enough money to complete his first novel, *The Acrobats*. The novel aroused more attention in England than in Canada, which perhaps convinced him that the richer literary heritage there would fuel his talents. For the best part of twenty years, then, Richler lived in England, producing many novels, short stories, and film scripts.

Although Richler needed this geographical and cultural change to gain an ironic and critical distance in his work, he used his Canadian experience as the basis of his fiction; he once said that the first twenty years of a writer's life determine the character of his writing and inform his imaginative vision. Even after many years in England, Richler never felt sufficiently integrated into English society to capture the essence of that particular culture. Feeling himself an outsider in England and cut off from the social context of Canada, Richler returned in 1972 to settle with his wife and five children in Montreal. He died there on July 3, 2001.

ANALYSIS

In an article titled "Why I Write," Mordecai Richler repeats the honest answer given by George Orwell to the same question: sheer egotism, aesthetic enthusiasm, po-litical purposes, and historical impulse. These reasons, modified by Richler's unique perception, are clues to the form and content of his work.

Richler's egotistical desire to be talked about was, no doubt, fulfilled, as he was the victim of attacks from both Jews and Protestants for what they considered to be unjust satiric portraits of their respective communities. He even said that to be a Jew and a Canadian is to emerge from the ghetto twice, as a sense of self-consciousness and envy pervades both societies. His satire, however, even when confined by the geography of Montreal, is more universal than some critics have assumed, and this element has enhanced his status as a significant writer. Although Richler never wanted to acquire the role of writer as personality (avoiding the talk-show circuit as much as possible and loathing being cast as the kind of figure Norman Mailer became), his fierce attacks on provincialism, pretension, community arrogance, envy, and class economic superiority marked him as a highly visible, eccentric, and often vicious outsider.

While there is a great deal of harshness in Richler's writing, it is not merely personal vindictiveness; rather, it is a narrative strategy of accurate observation informed by imagination. It is a grotesque comic style designed to emphasize the absurdity of the human condition and to mock those whose misdirected values merely cause suffering. In *The Acrobats*, Richler dissects a generation of hollow men who infest the corrupt world of Spain's festival time, in which a loss of belief is symbolized by *fallas*, empty wood and papier-mâché dolls. It is a nightmare world of confusion and fantasy that culminates in the death of antihero André Bennett. Without capturing the flavor and intensity of Ernest Hemingway's lost generation, Richler, in a limited way, sets the themes for his later novels by attacking all attitudes that he thinks are essentially destructive.

Richler admitted to a certain sense of guilt prompted by the discrepancy between his life at home facing a blank page and the memory of his father going to work in his junkyard in subzero weather. Perhaps this recognition of the severity of ordinary life gave him the focus of his work, the precisely observed but critically and ironically rendered life of the common man fighting circumstances greater than himself.

Richler's intelligence, however, did not allow him to

glorify his protagonists uncritically. The tension between what is and what ought to be is always present in Richler's fiction; the result is a controlled realism balanced by a satiric distance that allows fantasy, nightmare, and a morally grounded sense of the ridiculous. As George Woodcock observed, Richler was influenced by the realism of André Malraux, Albert Camus, and Louis-Ferdinand Céline, but Richler himself praised Evelyn Waugh as the greatest novelist of his time, and there is in Richler's work much of the energy, sensibility, and bawdiness of American writers such as Philip Roth.

When Richler spoke of a political purpose, he followed Orwell's idea that a novelist should push the world in a certain direction, that in fact any serious novelist is therefore a moralist. Although many of his stories end tragically, there is still a sense that his characters exist not as victims of a cruel, impersonal fate but as victims of their own and others' actions. The choices they make are important ones and often lead to disaster when they are not based on a consistent moral viewpoint. Norman Price in *A Choice of Enemies* recognizes that choices are significant but no longer has the courage to make the difficult ones that confront his modern generation. He ends up complacently accepting values from his friends. In *The Apprenticeship of Duddy Kravitz*, Richler succeeds in making Duddy a partially sympathetic character, often a victim of powerful people even more ruthless than he is, but Duddy, blinded by ambition, is the indirect cause of his friend Virgil's paralysis from a motor accident. In his enthusiasm for the direct, specific attack, however, Richler takes a moral position that often seems diffuse or simply confusing. Two of his novels, *St. Urban's Horseman* and *Joshua Then and Now*, manifest a more coherent intention that makes the satire even more meaningful.

Much of the force of Richler's work comes from his observation and memory of life in the Montreal ghetto of his youth. Even novels such as *Cocksure* and *The Acrobats* are distilled through the experience of the expatriate Canadian trying to make sense of a less provincial foreign world. Richler said that he felt rooted in Montreal's St. Urban Street, and, because that was his time and place, he elected to get it right. To that end, Richler's fiction often concerns the same characters from Fletcher's

Mordecai Richler. (Christopher Morris)

Field High School as they experience life at different stages of intellectual and emotional growth. A peripheral character such as Jake Hersh, for example, in *The Apprenticeship of Duddy Kravitz* and *The Street*, becomes the focus of *St. Urban's Horseman*.

THE APPRENTICESHIP OF DUDDY KRAVITZ

There is so much comic energy in *The Apprenticeship of Duddy Kravitz* that the reader can easily underestimate the social and moral implications of the work. Richler stated that to a certain extent the reader should sympathize with Duddy, who must rise above the poverty of the St. Urban ghetto to challenge and defeat powerful manipulators such as Jerry Dingleman, the Boy Wonder. The ambiguity of Duddy's character creates a problem of moral focus, however, in that some of his victories are at the expense of truly kindhearted people, such as Virgil Roseboro and Yvette.

There are certainly many reasons for Duddy's aggressive, almost amoral behavior. His mother died when

Duddy was very young, leaving him without the female stability he needed at the time. His father, Max the Hack, who drives a Montreal cab and pimps on the side, lets Duddy fend for himself, as most of his affection and attention goes to his elder son, Lenny. Duddy remembers that his father wrote many letters to Lenny when he worked at a resort, but Max refuses to write to Duddy. Max also encourages Lenny to go to medical school and is proud of his achievements; he makes it obvious that he expects little from Duddy and does not perceive the extent of Duddy's ambition or his loyalty to his family. Duddy is also often humiliated by the affluent university students with whom he works as a waiter at the Hotel Lac des Sables. Irwin Shubert, for instance, considers Duddy a social inferior and, using a rigged roulette wheel, cheats him out of three hundred dollars.

Although Richler elicits sympathy for Duddy by explaining his situation, he undercuts a completely sympathetic attitude toward Duddy by detailing the results of the character's actions. Duddy's exploitation of the other students of Fletcher's Field High School leads even his friend Jake Hersh to believe that Duddy makes everything dirty. Duddy's schemes to make money are clever enough; he works out a system to steal hockey sticks from the Montreal Canadiens, but he does not realize that the blame rests on the stick boy, who is trying to earn money through honest, hard work. More seriously, Duddy, through a cruel practical joke, is responsible for the death of Mrs. Macpherson, the wife of one of his teachers. Later, as he tries to make his dream of owning land come true, Duddy rejects his lover, Yvette, causes the paralysis of his friend Virgil, from whom he also steals money, and alienates his grandfather, Simcha, who cares for him more than anyone else.

Duddy's relationship with Simcha provides both the moral tone and the narrative drive of the novel. Simcha, a man trusted but not loved by the elders of the St. Urbain ghetto for his quiet, patient integrity, is loved by his favorite, Duddy. Like many others of his generation, Simcha feels the weight of the immigrant's fear of failure and instills in Duddy the idea that a man without land is a nobody. For Simcha, this cliché is a more complex concept associated with the traditional struggles of the Jews and presupposes a sense of responsibility. Duddy misinterprets the implications of his grandfather's advice and

perceives it as a practical imperative. He determines to gain land at any cost, involving himself in many schemes—from importing illegal pinball machines to filming Bar Mitzvahs with a bizarre, alcoholic documentary director—in order to purchase land for commercial development.

For a short time, Duddy's plans misfire; he goes bankrupt and is unable to pay for the land he wants so badly. Upon hearing that the Boy Wonder, the ghetto "miracle" who has escaped his environment by drug peddling and other corrupt means, covets the same land, Duddy forges checks in Virgil's name to get enough money to make the purchase. In a closing scene, Duddy brings his family to see his property. By coincidence, the Boy Wonder arrives, and Duddy drives him away with verbal abuse. His father is more impressed with this act of defiance than with Duddy's achievement, and later, among his circle of friends, Max begins to create a legend about Duddy in much the same way he created the legend of the Boy Wonder. Although his victory has been effected through deceit and victimization, Duddy's behavior seems vindicated; he smiles in triumph, unaware that he continues only under the spell of a shared illusion. The reader is left elated to a certain extent at the defeat of the Boy Wonder, yet sobered by the figure of Simcha crying in the car after Yvette has informed him of Duddy's method of acquiring the land.

ST. URBAIN'S HORSEMAN

Unlike Duddy Kravitz, whose life is defined by the wealth he acquires, Jake Hersh of *St. Urbain's Horseman* is defined by the exploits of his cousin Joey, the "Horseman" of the title. In his quest for certainty and identity in a world of confusion and moral ambiguity, Jake chooses a dubious model of behavior that eventually becomes an obsession. Much of the comedy and much of the human drama in the book come from the discrepancy between Jake's illusions of the Horseman and the reality of his own life.

In this work Richler experiments with a cinematic style of flashbacks and flash-forwards, not only to create a sense of suspense but also to show the role memory plays in developing a character. It is obvious that Jake is involved in some sort of sex scandal that threatens his married and professional life. As the trial progresses, the narrative is punctuated by the events in Jake's life that have led him to this degradation. In his youth, he wanted to escape the St. Urbain ghetto and the provincial nature of Canada itself. Typically, however, he leaves Canada to escape boredom only to find it everywhere.

Although Jake's loving relationship with his wife offers the promise of real stability, Jake seems to believe that only his cousin Joey leads a meaningful life, fighting injustice wherever he can find it. Specifically, he thinks Joey is the lone avenger riding after Josef Mengele, the feared *Doktor* of the Nazi extermination camps. At first, Joey is simply the black sheep of the Hersh family, leaving home at a young age and returning periodically to disrupt the mundane lives of his relatives. Jake, who is eleven years younger than Joey, perceives him to be a hero and dismisses the accusations that he is just a criminal taking advantage of others for his own gain. Uncle Abe even tells Jake that the famed Horseman is more likely to blackmail Mengele than kill him.

By the time Jake reaches adulthood, his fantasies and nightmares about his cousin assume mythic proportions, and he incorporates this mythology into his daily concerns, measuring himself against the Horseman he has created. Jake's consequent search for Joey in Israel and Germany uncovers the grim reality of Joey's fraud, drug smuggling, and disastrous love affairs, but Jake only rationalizes his negative impression; he places the Horseman's quest for "justice" beyond the sphere of ordinary moral culpability or human responsibility.

Jake reasons that he is a product of his generation, conceived in the Great Depression. He and others like him lived through the Spanish Civil War, World War II, the Holocaust, the Israeli War of Independence, McCarthyism, the Korean War, and finally the Vietnam War. They were always the wrong age to be involved; they were merely observers, moral bystanders who could protest and give advice, but who were fundamentally impotent. Jake wants answers to his plight but feels even more alienated from the important issues of his time because he is a case history of the Jewish intellectual born into the Canadian working class. He finds his generation and its concerns trivial and peripheral, easily susceptible, in his thinking, to the guilt induced by the "injustice collectors"—the prison camp survivors and the starvelings of Africa.

These issues, these betrayals of age, are contrasted with the more personal betrayals of life: Jake's father rejects his marriage to a non-Jew; Luke Scott decides to choose a British director instead of Jake, his best friend, for his first major script; Jenny dismisses Jake as a lover because he is too young; and Harry Stein implicates Jake in the rape of a young woman. Jake is no more capable of understanding these events than he is capable of understanding historical events of more significant import.

After the trial, in which Jake is found guilty of indecent assault and fined, he receives word that the Horseman has been killed in a plane crash while smuggling cigarettes. He retreats to his attic and finds a gun hidden in the Horseman's saddle. It fires only blanks, its efficacy as illusory as the Horseman's exploits. Upon discovering this, Jake seems to return to reality, but later he dreams that he is the Horseman extracting gold fillings from Mengele's teeth with pliers. He wakes up and changes the Horseman's journal to read "presumed dead." The irony is that Jake will probably continue to search for certitude and will live a tolerable life based on illusion; he does not realize that the love of his wife is the stable point that will exist despite the illusion.

JOSHUA THEN AND NOW

There are many similarities between *St. Urbain's Horseman* and *Joshua Then and Now*: The time schemes of both works are not linear but rather shift backward and forward in a search for meaning that takes precedence over simple historical considerations; the characters are graduates of Fletcher's Field High School who gain obvious material success but are not immune to even the minor ravages of time; the major issues of the world are always present, but private and personal issues dominate; and Joshua Shapiro, like Jake Hersh, tries to make sense of his own life in terms of facing the past. The important difference between the two novels is that Richler's attitude toward life in *Joshua Then and Now* is much more humane, and love is seen as the moral imperative that makes all other attitudes seem trivial.

Joshua Then and Now begins close to the present with Joshua in a cottage retreat suffering from multiple fractures incurred in a car accident. Because of hints of a sex scandal, he is guarded from the press by his father, Reuben, and his father-in-law, Senator Stephen Hornby. Joshua reads many letters from his fans and colleagues who have scorned him for what they think is his atrocious behavior, but he is able to put this criticism into perspective. He believes this public display of disapproval is what he deserves for the roguish behavior of his youth. Reflecting on his life, he now is able to see clearly what was of real importance.

Joshua's background seems almost surreal; certainly it is more colorful than the lives of his friends in St. Urbain. Joshua's aspiration to be a sportswriter derived from his father, who was a Canadian boxing champion. After his retirement from the ring, Reuben became an enforcer for a gangster named Colucci. As a youngster, Joshua had to suffer both his father's long absences and the resentment of the neighborhood over Reuben's involvement with Colucci. Joshua's mother, Esther, is an eccentric who bewilders him even more than his father. At Joshua's Bar Mitzvah, Esther has too much to drink and decides to let the young boys see her perform as an exotic dancer. She shocks them with the explicitness of her movements and even lets them fondle her. Later in life, she gets involved in pornographic films and in running a massage parlor. It seems that Joshua's independent and sometimes improbable behavior is the logical result of his upbringing.

In trying to prolong his adolescence, Joshua becomes as ridiculous as his parents, and although his exploits seem harmless, they do have consequences; Joshua's fake letters about the novelist Iris Murdoch's homosexuality, written to make money at the expense of the University of Texas, end up being made public, to Joshua's disgrace. The pranks that he plays to gain revenge on his enemies—taking labels off Pinsky's valuable wine bottles, defacing Jonathan Coles's original painting, and planting illegal currency at Eli Seligson's house—conclude with Joshua's injuring himself in a high-speed car chase. For Joshua, at least, these episodes are a learning experience; they are stages on his way to maturity.

Joshua has many friends from his youth who still get together as the "Mackenzie King Memorial Society," the name being an ironic comment on a prime minister whom they consider a fraud. As successful as they are, however, in their middle age they are susceptible to lawsuits, tax-evasion inquiries, bypass operations, hair transplants, and cancer. The struggle for material wealth and its attainment now seem inadequate as values. More

important is Joshua's involvement with the country-club circle. After marrying Pauline, Joshua is introduced to Jane and Jack Trimble and Pauline's brother Kevin. Joshua marries above his social class, but he takes a resentful and superior attitude to his wife's friends and relatives. He does as much as he can to sabotage a group that he believes has all the advantages. Through the years, however, he sees the disintegration of the Trimble marriage, the dashed hopes of the senator, and the death of Pauline's dependent brother, which precipitates her madness, and realizes that, even with their pretensions, they were only trying to survive.

The echoes of the past are most vividly sounded when Joshua returns to Ibiza, Spain, to confront Mueller, a German, who had disgraced him more than twenty-five years before. To gain revenge on Mueller, Joshua leaves his wife at a crucial time in her life, when she needs his comfort to fight off impending madness. In Spain, he notices remarkable changes: The friends he had are gone; many of his former haunts have been destroyed; the road to Almeria, the route of the retreating Republican army, is now dotted with hotels, condominiums, and commercial signs; and more significantly, Mueller is dead, a victim of cancer. To cleanse himself of the past, however, Joshua pays a price. His wife is institutionalized; then, after a prolonged stay at the hospital, she disappears. The novel ends with a loving reconciliation that suggests a change in Richler's perspective. Still on crutches as a result of his accident, Joshua recuperates at Hornby's cottage, accompanied by his children, the senator, and Reuben. In the final scene, Pauline returns, and Reuben sees Joshua in the vegetable garden without his cane, being supported by Pauline.

SOLOMON GURSKY WAS HERE

Solomon Gursky Was Here is Richler's richest and most complex work, a 150-year chronicle of the ambitious and conniving Gursky family (loosely based on the real-life liquor kings of Montreal, the Bronfmans), weaving back and forth in time from the ill-fated Franklin Expedition in the Arctic to the political uncertainties of modern times. Beneath the surface of what is essentially a mystery story, a search for the elusive but seemingly ubiquitous Solomon Gursky, Richler examines the greed and corruption of society, the nature of the Jewish and Canadian peoples, mythological forces of the past, and the tenuous but compelling hold of love. Although uncompromising in his satiric portrait of the characters, Richter nevertheless alludes to the positive creative power of those who strive for understanding, however difficult the quest may be.

At the center of the novel stands writer Moses Berger, son of failed poet L. B. Berger, who has sold out to the Gurskys. Because of his father, Moses hears of Solomon Gursky at an early age and becomes obsessed with the almost mythical nature of this character. The alcoholic Moses, more a follower than the leader that his name suggests, investigates stories and documents and uncovers clues about why Solomon decided to resist the purely materialistic interests of his brothers Bernard, the ruthless businessman who has built his fortune by bootlegging, and Morrie, his unctuous partner. Moses discovers that Solomon's enigmatic grandfather, Ephraim, was a criminal once imprisoned on Botany Bay, by incredible ingenuity the only survivor of the Franklin Expedition, a shaman of Eskimos who taught them Yiddish, and an energetic profligate perplexing in his moral ambiguity. Ephraim is, however, both a comic manifestation and a serious vital force of Judaism, instilling imagination and realism in Solomon, his spiritual heir.

Moses' search for the "real" Solomon, then, is an attempt to reclaim his past as a Jew and participate in the redemptive value of this figure, who takes on the mythic qualities of the raven that insinuates itself into a diversity of situations to provoke the apathetic and the misguided. Although Moses cannot quite verify all the incarnations of the mysterious Solomon, he suspects that Solomon has influenced many of the nobler acts that occur: the attempt to take over Bernard's McTavish distillery, the creation of the Israeli Air Force, and the success of the raid on Entebbe. By trying to restore order in his own life, through research and the dogged pursuit of the truth concerning Solomon, Moses begins to understand that honest engagement, not exploitation of life, is a source of value and meaning. No one is spared in Richler's caustic view, but some can glimpse hope, however concealed it may be.

BARNEY'S VERSION

In some respects, Moses' search for truth extends into *Barney's Version*, published almost a decade after *Solomon Gursky Was Here*. In this novel, however, Richler creates a character who risks becoming a parody not only of the author's earlier characters but also of the author himself. Barney Panofsky—"trash" television producer, lifelong Montrealer, and rabid hockey fan—is a man whose passions have often been too strong for his own good. Among other fiascoes, he drinks too much, smokes cigars obsessively, bungled three marriages, and potentially committed murder. His faults become an issue, however, only when he learns that Terry McIver, a friend from his youthful years in Paris, is about to publish an autobiography. Rightfully afraid of what Terry has to say about him, Barney immediately sets to penning his memoirs, his version of past events from which the novel's title is born.

The central action of *Barney's Version* is at turns poignant and hilarious. As expected, Barney recounts history much to his own benefit, including scorching depictions of his first two wives, a "martyred" feminist icon and a stereotypical Jewish princess. He rarely offers conscious insight into his own shortcomings and, in fact, often forgets or revises details of his life at its most crucial moments. Still, Barney manages to make his audience feel sympathy for him, especially in recalling his, Barney's "heart's desire," and his likely soul mate. What ultimately emerges from Barney's memoir is a credible protagonist—foul-mouthed, hedonistic, sometimes oblivious, infrequently accepting blame—who manages to retain his desire for "true love" and for a creative outlet beyond the shallow commercialism of his television production company. As with Richler's other works, Barney becomes an enigmatic hero, tainted by his world experiences, yet still not devoid of hope.

Nevertheless, Barney's hope feels less substantial than the kind exhibited by characters in Richler's earlier fiction. One wonders if Barney truly longs for a better world, or simply for one in which people like Terry McIver do not threaten to reveal his secrets. This question is reinforced by the vitriol that Barney occasionally heaps on some of Richler's most familiar targets (feminists, Quebecer separatists, pretentious Jews, pseudointellectuals, vegetarians, antismoking zealots, and just about any other standard-bearer of political correctness). Despite the ongoing matter of whether Barney did or did not kill his former friend Boogie, the momentum of the novel sometimes lags, feeling less like a well-plotted story than like a meandering path between Barney's occasional rants. Though unequivocally humorous, such tirades sometimes feel more like a lecture from Barney (or perhaps straight from Richler himself) in which the protagonist's own foibles are tragically overlooked in his attempt to decimate his targets.

Whether he is a narrow-minded curmudgeon or a keen social satirist, Barney does extend Richler's quirky vision of the world with undeniable force. Perhaps it is a mistake to ask for moderation from a writer like Richler. His work has always been effective because of its raw power, its unsparing depiction of any character type that happened to drift beneath the author's lens. Richler was praised widely for the richness of his comic vision and for his keenly observed, unsentimental portrait of Montreal's inhabitants (Jew and non-Jew alike). Through an imaginative extension of this vision, Richler developed into a novelist of importance, with his message transcending the limited boundaries of St. Urbain Street to assume universal significance.

James C. MacDonald
Updated by J. David Stevens

OTHER MAJOR WORKS

SHORT FICTION: *The Street: Stories*, 1969.

SCREENPLAYS: *No Love for Johnnie*, 1961 (with Nicholas Phipps); *Young and Willing*, 1964 (with Phipps); *Life at the Top*, 1965; *The Apprenticeship of Duddy Kravitz*, 1974 (adaptation of his novel); *Joshua Then and Now*, 1985 (adaptation of his novel).

NONFICTION: *Hunting Tigers Under Glass: Essays and Reports*, 1968; *Shovelling Trouble*, 1972; *Notes on an Endangered Species and Others*, 1974; *The Great Comic Book Heroes, and Other Essays*, 1978; *Home Sweet Home*, 1984; *Broadsides: Reviews and Opinions*, 1990; *Oh Canada! Oh Quebec! Requiem for a Divided Country*, 1992; *This Year in Jerusalem*, 1994; *Belling the Cat: Essays, Reports, and Opinions*, 1998; *Dispatches from the Sporting Life*, 2001; *On Snooker: The Game and the Characters Who Play It*, 2001.

CHILDREN'S LITERATURE: *Jacob Two-Two Meets the Hooded Fang*, 1975; *Jacob Two-Two and the Dinosaur*, 1987; *Jacob Two-Two's First Spy Case*, 1997.

EDITED TEXTS: *Canadian Writing Today*, 1970; *Writers on World War II: An Anthology*, 1991.

BIBLIOGRAPHY

Benson, Eugene, and William Toye, eds. *The Oxford Companion to Canadian Literature*. Toronto, Ont.: Oxford University Press, 1998. Collection of essays is useful not only for general information on Richler but also for placing the author's work within context with a solid cross-index to related writers and literary movements in Canada.

Brenner, Rachel Feldhay. *Assimilation and Assertion: The Response to the Holocaust in Mordecai Richler's Writings*. New York: Peter Lang, 1989. Examines the portrayal of the Holocaust in Richler's fiction. Maintains that Richler's work reflects the powerlessness that Canadian Jews felt about the European tragedy, a feeling that was intensified by their experiences of anti-Semitism in the 1930's and 1940's.

Craniford, Ada. *Fiction and Fact in Mordecai Richler's Novels*. Lewiston, N.Y.: Edwin Mellen Press, 1992. Devotes separate chapters to analyses of Richler's first nine novels, through *Solomon Gursky Was Here*. Also offers informative discussion of Richler's Jewishness and his identity as a Canadian. Includes bibliography and index.

Darling, Michael, ed. *Perspectives on Mordecai Richler*. Toronto, Ont.: ECW Press, 1986. Eight essays by different writers present analyses of Richler's craft and the moral vision expressed in his fiction. Some of the articles provide illuminating overviews of Richler's themes.

Kramer, Reinhold. *Mordecai Richler: Leaving St. Urbain*. Montreal: McGill-Queen's University Press, 2008. Demonstrates how Richler's life was the source of his fiction and argues that his Jewishness, "Canadianness," and secularism were central to both his life and his work. Includes notes, bibliography, and index.

McSweeney, Kerry. "Mordecai Richler." In *Canadian Writers and Their Works*, edited by Robert Lecker, Jack David, and Ellen Quigley. Vol. 6. Toronto, Ont.: ECW Press, 1985. Provides an orderly, lucid, and insightful analysis of Richler's fiction through *Joshua Then and Now*. Includes notes and select bibliography.

Posner, Michael. *The Last Honest Man: Mordecai Richler, an Oral Biography*. Toronto, Ont.: McClelland & Stewart, 2004. Recounts Richler's life through interviews with family members, friends, colleagues, editors, drinking and snooker companions, and others who discuss their experiences with and impressions of the author.

Ramraj, Victor J. *Mordecai Richler*. Boston: Twayne, 1983. Good introductory study of Richler's fiction (up to *Joshua Then and Now*) is enriched by an informative preface, a useful chronology of Richler's writing life, and a thorough select bibliography.

Woodcock, George. *Mordecai Richler*. Toronto, Ont.: McClelland & Stewart, 1970. Concise discussion of Richler's fiction presents analyses in a down-to-earth prose style accessible to student readers. Includes a bibliography.

CONRAD RICHTER

Born: Pine Grove, Pennsylvania; October 13, 1890
Died: Pottsville, Pennsylvania; October 30, 1968
Also known as: Conrad Michael Richter

PRINCIPAL LONG FICTION

The Sea of Grass, 1936
The Trees, 1940
Tacey Cromwell, 1942
The Free Man, 1943
The Fields, 1946
Always Young and Fair, 1947
The Town, 1950
The Light in the Forest, 1953
The Lady, 1957
The Waters of Kronos, 1960
A Simple Honorable Man, 1962
The Grandfathers, 1964
The Awakening Land, 1966 (includes *The Trees*, *The Fields*, and *The Town*)
A Country of Strangers, 1966
The Aristocrat, 1968

OTHER LITERARY FORMS

Conrad Richter (RIK-tur) wrote fourteen novels, all of which were published by Knopf, but in addition to the longer fiction that Richter produced between 1937 and 1968, he also wrote short stories and a variety of nonfiction. He was nearly as prolific a short-story writer as he was a novelist, his earliest published story appearing in 1913. His first volume of collected short stories includes twelve stories under the title *Brothers of No Kin, and Other Stories* (1924); nine more stories were collected in *Early Americana, and Other Stories* (1936). Richter wrote short fiction throughout his career, producing more than thirty-one stories, most of which appeared in *The Saturday Evening Post*. Many of Richter's stories still remain uncollected, but a number were gathered in *The Rawhide Knot, and Other Stories* (1978). Richter's nonfiction includes four book-length essays on his eclectic personal philosophy: *Human Vibration: The Mechanics of Life and Mind* (1925), *Principles in Bio-Physics: The Underlying Process Controlling Life Phenomena and Inner Evolution* (1927), *The Mountain on the Desert* (1955), and *A Philosophical Journey* (1955). Six of Richter's novels have been adapted for motion pictures and television, and Richter himself worked periodically as a writer for Metro-Goldwyn-Mayer in Hollywood between 1937 and 1950, but found that writing for motion pictures was not his forte.

ACHIEVEMENTS

Conrad Richter did not achieve widespread recognition during his long career as a writer despite his receiving the Pulitzer Prize in fiction in 1951 for *The Town* and the National Book Award for fiction in 1960 for *The Waters of Kronos*, beating out Harper Lee's *To Kill a Mockingbird* and John Updike's *Rabbit Run* among the competition. A reclusive man who spent much of his life in rural Pennsylvania and in the isolated mountains of New Mexico, Richter was not a colorful figure whose life drew attention to his work. Because much of his work appeared in serial form for popular and pulp magazines, he has been too hastily dismissed by academic critics. At his best, Richter is a historical novelist of the first rank. He re-creates the past not as a historian would, but rather by reproducing the actualities of frontier experience, conveying them through fidelity to details and local expression. When Richter's purposes as an artist are more fully understood, it seems certain that critical assessments of his work will acknowledge the judgment of the general reader, with whom Richter continues to be popular.

BIOGRAPHY

Conrad Michael Richter was born in Pine Grove, Pennsylvania, on October 13, 1890, the eldest of three sons of a Lutheran minister. Richter grew up in several small rural Pennsylvania towns where his father had congregations. He came from mixed German, French, and Scotch-Irish blood. One of his forebears served with George Washington's Continental Army and another fought as a Hessian mercenary for the British. His grandfather, uncle, and great-uncles were preachers. Richter was brought up in bucolic surroundings, and he passed a happy boyhood in a score of central and northern Pennsylvania villages. In 1906, he graduated from Tremont High School and during the next three years took a number of odd jobs—clerking, driving teams, pitching hay, and working as a bank teller. His first permanent job was as a reporter for the *Johnstown* (Pennsylvania) *Journal*, a job he started at the age of nineteen.

Richter's first published story, "How Tuck Went Home," was written in 1913 while he was living in Cleveland, Ohio. In 1914, a second story, "Brothers of No Kin," was awarded a twenty-five-dollar prize for being one of the best stories of the year. In 1915, Richter was married to Harvena Maria Achenbach. Moving West to find his fortune in a silver mine venture at Coeur d'Alene, Idaho, he made a short sojourn as a speculator in the mine fields. After returning East, where the couple's daughter was born in 1917, Richter started writing children's literature and published a periodical for juveniles called *Junior Magazine Book*. Meanwhile, his short stories had been appearing in magazines such as *Ladies' Home Journal* and *Saturday Review*.

Richter's early work as a newspaper reporter and editor influenced his literary style. His sparse method of ex-

pression was a product of his journalism training, and the typical length of his novels is about two hundred pages. In lieu of formal education, Richter, like many self-taught people, became a voracious reader. In an interview, he said, "All my life I have been a reader and one of my joys as a boy and young man was a good book in which I could lose myself." His reading was eclectic, ranging from the adventure writer W. H. Hudson to scientific authors such as Michael Faraday and G. W. Crele, whose theories of chemistry and physics influence Richter's later philosophical works. Ralph Waldo Emerson, Henry David Thoreau, and John Burroughs also helped shape his idealistic views on nature. The most important influence on his own writing came, however, from Willa Cather, whose pioneer characters and Western backgrounds provided the model for much of Richter's fiction.

In his early short fiction, Richter used the formulas of the popular literature of the period, which still abided by the conventions of the genteel tradition. The typical tale revolved around stock plots such as a case of mistaken identity, a rich youth's rehabilitation through hardships shared with the common people, a city girl coming to terms with country life, and so on. As might be expected, these stories used cardboard characters and were tailored to readers' moral and social assumptions. Richter's first stories were self-admitted "potboilers" from which he only expected to get a bit of money for his family. During the period between 1917 and 1928, when Richter was engaged in hackwriting (freelancing) and publishing for a living, he started to develop his ideas on psychoenergics, as he called his theory of human personality. This theoretical interest led to three works—*Human Vibration*, *Principles in Bio-Physics*, and a privately printed monograph, *Life Energy*. These essays contained the germ of another book-length essay that he published twenty-eight years later as *The Mountain on the Desert*, his fullest attempt to articulate his personal philosophy.

In 1928, Richter's wife's illnesses caused a move to the Southwest, an event that would have a major effect on his career as a writer and mark a turning point in his life. What had started as a misfortune would turn out otherwise. Stimulated by the culture and climate of New Mexico, Richter published a second volume of stories, *Early Americana, and Other Stories*, and his first novel,

Conrad Richter.

The Sea of Grass. The writer's material was enlarged. He had always taken the ingredients of his fiction from family memories and observations; when he moved to New Mexico, as he later wrote in his unpublished *A Few Personal Notes*, "The backlog of my material still came from first sources, fine old-time men and women, chiefly from New Mexico and Arizona, Texas and Indiana territory, who lived through many of the early days."

In 1940, Richter published *The Trees*, the first volume of a trilogy that would be completed with *The Fields* in 1946 and *The Town* in 1950. After the publication of his southwestern novel *Tacey Cromwell* in 1942, Richter received his first literary award, the gold medal for literature given by the Society of Libraries of New York University. In 1944, an honorary doctorate degree in literature was conferred upon him by Susquehanna University in Selinsgrove, Pennsylvania, in recognition of his attainments as a native son. During the decade of the 1940's, Richter also received the Ohio Library Medal Award for literature.

In 1950, Richter returned to his native heath, Pine Grove, Pennsylvania, where he would remain for the rest of his life except for return trips to the Southwest and winters in Florida. In 1951, he won the Pulitzer Prize in fiction for *The Town*. Although he wrote one more

novel, *The Lady*, about the West, most of Richter's remaining career was given over to the subjects with which he had started as a writer—the people and land of his birthplace. He completed his best-selling novel *The Light in the Forest* after his return home; like his later novel, *A Country of Strangers*, it was inspired by the beauty of the Eastern landscape and by the deeper sense of history one feels in the East. At the close of the 1950's, Richter was awarded his second honorary doctorate, this time by the university of his adopted state, New Mexico. In the early 1960's, he completed two volumes of his projected Pennsylvania trilogy—*The Waters of Kronos* and *A Simple Honorable Man*. Richter won the National Book Award for the former; he was at work on the third volume of the trilogy when he died in 1968 at the age of seventy-eight. Since his death, two works have appeared: the novel *The Aristocrat* and a book of stories, *The Rawhide Knot, and Other Stories*.

ANALYSIS

Conrad Richter's qualities as a writer are partly described by the title of one of his late novels, *A Simple Honorable Man*. Although the book is about his father, the same terms might be used to characterize Richter's fiction, which is simple, concise, and concerned with basic virtues. Thus, it is something of a paradox that Richter's novels and stories are underpinned by a rather complex theory of human life and history, and that these philosophical, quasi-scientific ideas provide a conceptual framework over which the characters, plots, and settings of his fiction are stretched like a covering fabric. Another major tendency of Richter's fiction is that it is intensely autobiographical, deriving from family traditions and experience. In his youth, Richter heard stories of frontier experiences from relatives who had been pioneers themselves. It was his fascination with the way things had been and his conviction that he could inspire his readers to cope with modern problems by showing how ordinary people in the past had overcome the adversities of their frontier that prompted him to become a historical novelist.

Equally important to Richter's development as a novelist, however, were the quasi-scientific philosophical principles that he developed long before his first novel was published. Thus, Richter is unlike most writers in that his fiction does not represent the developing and unfolding of a philosophy, but rather the extension of a belief system that was essentially static after being established. This being the case, it is important to grasp some of the rudiments of Richter's philosophy before discussing his longer fiction, for his themes as a novelist grow out of his philosophical notions.

It must be pointed out that despite their would-be scientific titles and vocabulary (*Human Vibration* and *Principles in Bio-Physics*), Richter's book-length essays lack the rigor of scientific methodology. At first glance, his theory of life seems to be based on an odd merging of materialism and idealism. His first premise is that humans function in response to bodily cellular vibrations, or vibes, that are regulated by reserves of psychical or physical energy. If energy abounds, people are in harmony with life. The ultimate expression of human harmony is compassion for fellow humans. Other signs are charity, fortitude, and the confidence to prevail against hardship, a sense of unity with nature, a tendency toward betterment in history, and a quest for freedom. On the other hand, if energy sources are low, there is a lack of harmony in life. Conflict with nature, with other people, and with oneself all signify a deficiency of energy; other such manifestations are restless wandering, fruitless searching for intangibles, and historic change for the worse. Thus, as Richter explains it, human life and history are governed by mechanical laws.

Richter's second premise is based on what can best be described as quasi-scientific ideas. He holds that people respond in mind and body with "cellular energy" to outside stimuli. Activity causes the cells in one's body to overflow, revitalizing the weak cells. The process is like that of an electrical circuit in which there is a constant reenergizing while the operation continues. Therefore, constant use ensures a steady power source, whereas disuse can cause the source to decline and lose power. In human terms, mental and physical exertion stimulates the release of energy and speeds up energy transfer through the cell structure.

Like many American autodidacts, Richter combined Yankee know-how and practicality with the visions of the crank philosopher. His biophysics serves as a point of departure for accurate historical fiction about the actualities of pioneer life. By Richter's own admission, much of what he produced before he moved to New Mexico in 1928 was hack writing for the pulp magazines, but while there he was led to new literary subjects. He launched his career as a serious author with a series of stories and novels. Inspired by the grand surroundings of his Western residence and informed by extensive research and the philosophical themes that would run through his subsequent fiction, he produced his first novel, *The Sea of Grass*.

THE SEA OF GRASS

The Sea of Grass was well received on publication and remains highly regarded by readers and critics. The similarities between Richter's story of a strong-willed southwestern pioneer woman and Cather's *A Lost Lady* (1923) were quickly noted. The central idea of *The Sea of Grass* was sounded in a short story titled "Smoke over the Prairie," published two years earlier in *The Saturday Evening Post*. The novel is set in New Mexico during the last decades of the nineteenth century. It revolves around a feud between cattle ranchers (led by Colonel James Brewton) who use the open grasslands for grazing and growing numbers of farmers, called "nesters" by the cattlemen, who are supported by Brice Chamberlain, a federal judge. A subplot concerns a love triangle between Brewton, his wife, Lutie, and Chamberlain, which ends with the tragic death of the son of Brewton and Lutie, whose paternity is uncertain, since it is implied that Chamberlain might well have been the boy's father.

The major theme is the decline of the grasslands, a historic change for the worse. The story is narrated as a reminiscence by Hal Brewton, a nephew of Colonel Brewton. He tells the story of an era that has already passed and thus conveys an aura of nostalgia that Richter himself apparently felt for these bygone days. In fact, Hal Brewton is actually a persona for the author and reflects his attitudes toward events. For this reason, Hal remains a one-dimensional character, yet his role as narrator serves to create an objective view of the material. Hal is involved in the events he describes but not so closely as to have his judgment obscured. He is a boy when the story starts and is the town doctor when the story ends twenty-five years later. The first part of the book is devoted to Lutie, a lively and lovely belle from St. Louis, who comes to Salt Fork, New Mexico, to marry the cattle baron Jim Brewton. The Colonel, as he is called, has a battle going on with the nesters because he believes that the dry lands are doomed to be blown away if they are plowed. The marriage results in three children, but Lutie grows tired of her life as a rancher's wife and simply walks out, staying away for fifteen years. She had left thinking that her lover, Chamberlain, would come with her, but he remains to support the cause of the farmers.

The title of the book implies that it is a story about the land, and it is indeed, for the basic conflict of the novel arises from how the land will be used. *The Sea of Grass* also introduces the typical Richter hero and heroine in Colonel and Lutie Brewton. The Colonel embodies the best combination of idealism and pragmatism, but he is not complex. He reflects the virtues Richter admires—integrity and courage—and he exercises his control over his world with sure authority. Lutie, in contrast, is the first in a line of female characters in Richter's fiction who are not in harmony with their existence, and who achieve maturity only through hardship and suffering. When she returns to the Southwest, she has finally learned that she needs the sense of fulfillment that comes from the exertion required to survive on the sea of grass. *The Sea of Grass* is ultimately a novel in which the triumph belongs to the earth, for it is the land itself that finally, through a drought, defeats the persistent nesters and subdues Lutie's willful romanticism when her son is destroyed by the violence of the Southwest. Although *The Sea of Grass* is a lasting achievement, it has some of Richter's characteristic flaws as well. There is a thinness to the writing that gives the impression of a screenplay or an extended short story rather than a fully realized novel, a charge leveled with even more justification against Richter's next novel, *Tacey Cromwell*.

TACEY CROMWELL

Tacey Cromwell was generally not as well received as *The Sea of Grass*, perhaps because the heroine is a prostitute and the hero a gambler. Recalling his Idaho experience, Richter sets the plot of *Tacey Cromwell* in a mining town called Bisbee; his treatment of this setting reflects extensive research concerning life in early Western mining towns. He shows the ethnic diversity of the miners and the pretensions of the leading townsmen, who have risen from humble origins to positions of wealth and power. The plot of the novel is built around the conflict between the rough-and-ready immigrants

and the new rich ruling class in town. The narrator is again a small boy, Wickers Covington, who is both an observer and a partial participant in the action, about which he reminisces as he tells the story after the fact.

The book begins with the runaway boy Wickers escaping from an uncle in Kansas who has mistreated him. Changing his name to Nugget Oldaker, he heads to Socarro, New Mexico, where his half brother, Gaye Oldaker, is living. He finds his kinsman in a house of tolerance called the White Palace, which is ironically named, for it is a place of prostitution. His brother's mistress is a prostitute named Tacey Cromwell. Fearing that an upbringing in a bordello would prejudice the lad's morals, the couple moves away to give Nugget a decent home. They relocate in a mining town in Arizona, where they settle down and start the climb to success. Tacey and Gaye never marry, but they remain something of a team. She shows incredible altruism toward her former lover, even after he leaves her and marries the richest woman in town. Tacey's conversion to respectability is hastened by the adoption of two children of a neighbor killed in a mine accident. The good women of the town, however, take umbrage at the children being reared by even a reformed prostitute, and they bring legal action against Tacey, which results in her losing the children.

Undaunted by disappointment in love, community treachery, and sickness, Tacey starts a business as a dressmaker. At first she is boycotted by the priggish ladies, but one of her creations is worn at an annual ball by a lady who did not know or care about Tacey's reputation. The dress is a sensation, and her future as a dressmaker and designer is made overnight. Meanwhile, Gaye has been appointed territorial treasurer, a position he sought after being encouraged by Tacey. His wife, the haughty and puritanical Rudith Watrons, is drenched in a rainstorm that leads to a long illness and finally to her death. Nugget, who has grown up and become a mining engineer, returns to Bisbee, and one of the foster children taken from Tacey is restored to her. Thus, the novel ends with things returned to their original condition, but with the new harmony that hardship always hands to those who accept it in Richter's fictional worlds.

The novel also illustrates the concept of "westering," the process of evolution in which a region goes from frontier to community. Such a process, in Richter's conception, involves more than historic change. On the physiological and psychological levels, *Tacey Cromwell* depicts Richter's theory of altruism. Tacey's selfless assumption of guilt, both hers and her gambler-lover's, so that Gaye and his children might prosper, is close to the formula plot of the prostitute with a heart of gold used by Bret Harte in his Western fiction. Richter, however, has Tacey's sacrifice pay off, and she finally rises to respectability and eventual reunion with her lover and loved ones.

THE LADY

The Lady, Richter's ninth novel and his third with a southwestern setting, was published fifteen years later in 1957. *The Lady* was better received by the critics and evidences Richter's increased competence as a writer. It is a stronger novel because the central character, Doña Ellen Sessions, is more fully developed than Tacey Cromwell. The plot is partly based on an actual case, an unsolved New Mexico mystery of the frontier period, that involved the disappearance and probable murder of a judge and his young son. The conflict in this book centers on the struggle between Spanish American sheepherders and Anglo-American cattle ranchers.

The story is told by a narrator named Jud, who tells of events that happened sixty years before, when he was ten years old. He, like the juvenile narrators of *The Sea of Grass* and *Tacey Cromwell*, is both a participant and a witness. Jud is taken in by his cousin, the territorial judge Albert Sessions, after his own father has abandoned him. The judge's wife is the charming and arrogant Doña Lady Ellen, as she is styled because of her noble Spanish and English bloodlines. She is the owner of a giant sheep spread, inherited from her parents. In addition to breeding and wealth, she has acquired skills as a horseback rider and markswoman. The villain of the piece is her brother-in-law, a mercenary and unethical lawyer, Snell Beasley. The violent feud that is the focus of the book is begun when Beasley drives a cattle herd through Doña Ellen's ranch. A shoot-out results in the death of some of the cattlemen.

The chain of events that leads to the disappearance of Judge Sessions and his young son, Wily, is set in motion. Thinking Doña Ellen is now vulnerable, Snell Beasley sets out to destroy her completely. Doña Ellen is forced to sell her once great ranch, and it seems that her humiliation is complete, yet in the final scene of the novel, poetic justice is served. A buggy race between Doña Ellen and Snell ends with an accident, and her adversary is killed; thus, the heroine gets her revenge in a somewhat melodramatic ending. Her victory underscores Richter's central themes of endurance in the process of westering and the mystic bond between people and landscape. It is fitting that Richter's last book about his adopted Southwest should be concluded with a glorification of the land that had inspired him to write the type of fiction that would be his forte—historical romances.

THE TREES

While working on his southwestern novels, Richter began in the early 1940's his trilogy, *The Awakening Land*, about the Pennsylvania-Ohio frontier, which was conceived from the first as a whole. The first novel of the trilogy, *The Trees*, is set in the late eighteenth and early nineteenth centuries. The novel unfolds the story of a typical pioneer family, the Luckett clan, whose frequent migrations through the great sea of woods that covers the Ohio Valley and the Allegheny Mountains is the basis of the plot. In this novel, Richter vividly depicts the darkness of the forest floor as well as the moral darkness in the heart of people. The protagonist of *The Trees* is a woodswoman named Sayward Luckett, a larger-than-life figure who is the focal character of the entire trilogy. She is married to Portius Wheeler, who, for reasons never explained, has abandoned his native New England, where he was educated as a lawyer, and has become a loutish and drunken backwoodsman. Although nearly all traces of culture and civilization have been erased from him by the time he is married to Sayward, she nevertheless prevents him from further decline, and he honors her by making a reformation.

In addition, *The Trees* tells how Sayward as a girl had wandered with her nomadic family, breaking away from that way of life to marry Portius and settle down. Richter intended that Sayward's experiences should reflect the whole pioneer experience of movement, settlement, and domestication. Using the span of one woman's life, the novel reflects the process of historical change in the Ohio Valley from hunters to farmers to town dwellers. Thus, like Richter's southwestern novels, *The Trees* traces social evolution; it also resembles his southwestern novels in being episodic, in having a strong heroine, and in its themes of hardship and endurance, ending in ultimate triumph. It differs most from the earlier books in that there is no boy narrator. Richter's point of view is omniscient in the trilogy, and he uses more dialect in the dialogue. Furthermore, in an effort to make his depiction of pioneer life more convincing, he uses folktales and superstitions to reflect the primitive way of life on the frontier.

THE FIELDS

The final two volumes of the trilogy, *The Fields* and *The Town*, continue the portrait of Sayward and depict the conquering of the land through the process of civilization. *The Fields* tells of Sayward's ten children and her husband's affair with the local schoolteacher. The affair leads to an illegitimate daughter. Sayward is devastated by Portius's unfaithfulness, yet she recovers from this crushing experience when she hitches a pair of oxen to a plow and begins to till the fields. She sees in the great brutes' tolerance and strength and in the permanence of the earth a prescription for her own survival.

THE TOWN

The Town, though not any more successful artistically than the first two parts of the trilogy, was awarded the Pulitzer Prize in 1951, more for the entire series than for its concluding volume. *The Town*, which is set in pre-Civil War Ohio, deals mostly with the romance between Sayward's youngest son, Chancey, and her husband's illegitimate daughter, Rosa Tench. The love between the half brother and sister is marked by tragedy; she commits suicide following a balloon accident. The rest of the book completes Sayward's story. The conflict that fills out the plot is between mother and son: Sayward tries to make a pioneering man out of Chancey, but he refuses to accept her value system and goes off to edit a liberal newspaper in Cincinnati. The newspaper, which is supported by an unknown patron, publishes Chancey's socialist views, which are an affront to his mother. Just before her death, he learns that she was the secret benefactor who had supported his career over the years. Chancey has to reexamine his philosophy in the light of this revelation. He concludes that his mother's doctrine of hard work and self-reliance is a better one than his own. Thus, Sayward dies at the age of eighty, having won her last victory, rescuing her son from the heresy of socialism; the puritan faith in work of the older generation remains superior to modern liberal social theory.

Thus, in his trilogy, Richter brings full circle the westering process in which wilderness gives way to farms and farms become towns—historic change for the better; that is the essence of the American experience. Yet as civilization eradicates the wilderness, something is lost as well as gained. The frontier's hardships had tested people and honed their character. Modern Americans lack hardiness, vigor, and self-reliance, those qualities of mind and spirit that their ancestors had in abundance, as the heroine of Richter's Ohio trilogy so amply shows.

Richter produced some half dozen minor novels on various historical subjects and themes, but the major achievements of his later career are *The Waters of Kronos* and its sequel, *A Simple Honorable Man*, the first two volumes of a projected trilogy that he did not live to complete. The former is regarded as one of Richter's highest artistic successes and won wide critical acclaim, earning a National Book Award in 1960. The book is one of Richter's most autobiographical.

Richter's main character, a man named John Donner, resembles Richter himself; the character's parents are very much like his family as well. *The Waters of Kronos* is an almost mystical story in which Donner, an ill and aged man, returns from the West to his Pennsylvania hometown, which is covered by a human-made lake, to visit the graves of his ancestors. At the cemetery, he meets an old man, who takes Donner down a steep hill where, to his incredulous eyes, he finds his town just as it looked sixty years ago. The remainder of the plot is a reexamination of the scenes of his childhood and a reunion with friends and relatives. The journey into the past enables him to learn that what he has always feared is not true—that the gap between his faith and that of his father is not as wide as he once thought. He discovers that he is his father's spiritual son. His final realization from his return to the past is that they have both worshiped the same god in different ways. Having come to terms with his father's god in his novel, Richter's next book shows how he gains further understanding of his parents as a person.

A SIMPLE HONORABLE MAN

A Simple Honorable Man describes the life of Donner's father, Harry, who at age forty gives up a career in business for a lifetime of service to the Lutheran Church. Like *The Waters of Kronos*, this book is clearly autobiographical, but it is more than a nostalgic family history, for in this novel as in the previous one, Richter tries to come to grips with a number of philosophical problems. The novel emphasizes that the most important things in life are not social status or power of office or money but altruistic service to others. Harry Donner's greatest satisfaction is not in putting money in the bank but in helping those who are in need.

The third volume of the trilogy, on which Richter was at work when he died, was intended to show, as the first two books had done, his reconciliation with his actual father and his final reconciliation with his spiritual father. The two volumes that he did complete are a fitting capstone to Richter's career as a writer. His personal struggles, reflected through those of the Donners, show him to be a man of spiritual and intellectual integrity. The order and lucidity of the narrative reveal his artistry; the restrained realism that characterizes his fiction mutes the sentimentality inherent in such materials, and even though dealing with personal subject of a moral nature, he never lapses into overt didacticism.

Except for *The Sea of Grass*, Richter's reputation will rest most firmly on the books written in the last stages of his career, especially *The Waters of Kronos*; nevertheless, he will probably continue to attract readers who admire exciting, concise, sometimes lyrical stories and novels about the early history of the United States and the common people who experienced it.

Hallman B. Bryant

OTHER MAJOR WORKS

SHORT FICTION: *Brothers of No Kin, and Other Stories*, 1924; *Early Americana, and Other Stories*, 1936; *The Rawhide Knot, and Other Stories*, 1978.

NONFICTION: *Human Vibration: The Mechanics of Life and Mind*, 1925; *Principles in Bio-Physics: The Underlying Process Controlling Life Phenomena and Inner Evolution*, 1927; *The Mountain on the Desert*, 1955.

CHILDREN'S LITERATURE: *Over the Blue Mountain*, 1967.

BIBLIOGRAPHY

Barnes, Robert J. *Conrad Richter*. Austin, Tex.: Steck-Vaughn, 1968. Presents discussion of Richter's writing, focusing on three of his novels and nine short stories that are set in the Southwest. Includes a brief biography.

Edwards, Clifford D. *Conrad Richter's Ohio Trilogy: Its Ideas, Themes, and Relationship to Literary Tradition*. The Hague, the Netherlands: Mouton, 1970. Good discussion of Richter's Ohio trilogy—*The Trees*, *The Fields*, and *The Town*—includes a detailed analysis of the writer's philosophical and psychological themes.

Gaston, Edwin W., Jr. *Conrad Richter*. Rev. ed. Boston: Twayne, 1989. Provides an excellent introduction to Richter, his life, and his work. Surveys Richter's life and philosophy to examine how they resonate in all of his writings. Includes comprehensive notes, references, a bibliography, and an index.

Johnson, David R. *Conrad Richter: A Writer's Life*. University Park: Pennsylvania State University Press, 2001. Johnson, aided by access to Richter's private papers, describes Richter's creative process. Places Richter's work within the context of America's golden age of mass-market magazine and novel publishing, which lasted from the 1920's to the 1960's. Includes illustrations, a bibliography, and an index.

Lahood, Marvin J. *Conrad Richter's America*. The Hague, the Netherlands: Mouton, 1975. An appreciative, if not critical, summary of Richter's literary work. Avoids a chronological approach, instead devoting separate chapters to discussions of thematic subject matter.

Richter, Harvena. *Writing to Survive: The Private Notebooks of Conrad Richter*. 1988. Rev. ed. Lincoln, Nebr.: Backinprint.com, 2001. This book was formed out of the curiosity of Richter's daughter, Harvena, who gathered his voluminous collection of novel notebooks, journals, personal critiques, and other unpublished writings into this unique work. A study of Richter's writing styles and his approach to writing in general.

ALAIN ROBBE-GRILLET

Born: Brest, Finistère, France; August 18, 1922
Died: Caen, France; February 18, 2008

PRINCIPAL LONG FICTION

Les Gommes, 1953 (*The Erasers*, 1964)
Le Voyeur, 1955 (*The Voyeur*, 1958)
La Jalousie, 1957 (*Jealousy*, 1959)
Dans le labyrinthe, 1959 (*In the Labyrinth*, 1960)
La Maison de rendez-vous, 1965 (English
 translation, 1966)
Projet pour une révolution à New York, 1970
 (*Project for a Revolution in New York*, 1972)
La Belle Captive, 1975 (René Magritte,
 illustrator; English translation, 1995)
Topologie d'une cité fantôme, 1976 (*Topology of
 a Phantom City*, 1977)
Souvenirs du triangle d'or, 1978 (*Recollections
 of the Golden Triangle*, 1984)
Un Régicide, 1978
Djinn, 1981 (English translation, 1982)
Le Miroir qui revient, 1984 (*Ghosts in the
 Mirror*, 1988)
Angélique: Ou, L'Enchantement, 1987
Les Derniers Jours de Corinthe, 1994
La Reprise, 2001 (*Repetition*, 2003)
Un Roman sentimental, 2007

OTHER LITERARY FORMS

In addition to his novels, Alain Robbe-Grillet (rawb-eh-gree-YAY) wrote short fiction, nonfiction works on the New Novel, photo-essays, and screenplays.

ACHIEVEMENTS

After the mid-1950's, Alain Robbe-Grillet endeavored to explain and demonstrate the meaning of the innovative brand of fiction known as the *nouveau roman*, or New Novel. To him, the New Novel was a constantly evolving genre. Its form is not ready-made. Rather, it explores the human way of experiencing, understanding, and coping with the constantly changing realities of the age; it moves forward, beyond dogmas established for previous ages.

The New Novel centers on individuals and their subjective reactions and relationships to the objects or things in the world around them. It reports humankind's limited experiences: how people see, feel, and imagine their lives. Thematic significance or meaning is given to objects or relationships only when they come into *temporary* existence with people. What Robbe-Grillet first called "supports"—thought-related objects and visual motifs representing part of a character's experience—were what T. S. Eliot called "objective correlatives." By using objects, people, and patterns of things as temporary objective correlatives, Robbe-Grillet achieves high levels of character-reader subjectivity. He forces the reader to collaborate in the work by connecting dislocated objects, experiences, and scenes and by accepting and understanding paradoxical similarities and themes.

With his first *ciné-roman* (film-novel), *L'Année dernière à Marienbad* (1961; *Last Year at Marienbad*, 1962), Robbe-Grillet began a second career as a writer and director of several screenplays. Additionally, he helped establish the original *ciné-roman* as a genre distinct from either novel or film. Usually a simplified rendering of a script with stills from the film already made, Robbe-Grillet's film-novels contain imagery and story elements similar to those found in his novels, yet they are independently conceived and have a structural integrity uniquely their own.

In his second phase, in the 1960's and 1970's, Robbe-Grillet wrote his militant and sexually violent *Project for a Revolution in New York*. He also produced films with aberrant sexual behavior clearly depicted, such as *Trans-Europ-Express* (1966) and *Glissements progressifs du plaisir* (1974; *The Successive Slidings of Pleasure*, 1974).

The three books that are termed Robbe-Grillet's "romanesques," *Ghosts in the Mirror*, *Angélique: Ou, L'Enchantement* (Angelique: or, enchantment), and *Les Derniers Jours de Corinthe* (last days of Corinthe), began a third cycle. Since these works integrate personal memories with artistic theories and invented obsessions, some critics have called them "autofictions" or "autobiographical fictions."

Robbe-Grillet is known in the United States as an

iconoclastic breaker of traditions as well as for the novels *The Voyeur* and *Jealousy* and the film *Last Year at Marienbad*. None of these early works, however, offers more than a suggestion of the full extent of the experimentations of his third phase.

BIOGRAPHY

Alain Robbe-Grillet was born August 18, 1922, in Brest, France. He studied at the Institut National Agronomique in 1941-1942. During the World War II German occupation of France, his institute class was taken to a factory in Nuremberg and forced to work on lathes and milling machines. In 1943, ill with infectious rheumatism, he was sent for recovery to a French hospital. Later, he returned to the institute, graduating in 1946. He also served as *charge de mission* with the Institut National des Statistiques, 1945-1948.

From 1949 to 1951, Robbe-Grillet was an agronomist with the Institut des Fruits el Agrumes Coloniaux, traveling extensively in Morocco, Guinea, Guadeloupe, and Martinique. His novel *Un Régicide*, unpublished until 1978, was completed in 1949. Robbe-Grillet's second novel, *The Erasers*, was published in 1953 by Editions de Minuit in Paris. In 1955, he became a literary adviser to Minuit. In 1960, he accepted membership in the Television Programming Committee. During this decade he also married Catherine Rstakian (1957).

Robbe-Grillet and his literary work have received many honors. *The Voyeur* won the Prix des Critiques in 1955; the film *Last Year at Marienbad* won both the Prix du Lion d'or and the French Melies Prize. In 1964, he made his first trip to the United States for a lecture tour at several universities. Additionally, he was a term lecturer at New York University in 1972, 1975, and 1979; at University of California in 1978; at Columbia in 1989, and also at Washington University in St. Louis. In 1975, a ten-day colloquium on Robbe-Grillet was presented at Cerisy-la-Salle. He was guest of honor, in 1986, at the Writers' Week-Long Festival in New Zealand.

Robbe-Grillet was a center of critical controversy from the late 1950's onward. Few movements have sparked such acrimonious debates as his literary innovations. Notably controversial have been his depictions of racism, chauvinism, and women as victims, and his apparent fascination with sadomasochism. In 1974, when the film *The Successive Slidings of Pleasure*, for which he wrote the screenplay, was shown in Italy, the theater was shut down; Robbe-Grillet was accused of being a pornographer. Conversely, in 1975, the French government accepted him into the French Legion of Honor. He died on February 18, 2008, in Caen, France.

ANALYSIS

The newcomer to the New Novel should read Alain Robbe-Grillet's books in the sequence in which they were written, because each work employs new elements developed in its predecessor. The temporal device of a stopped wristwatch in *The Erasers*, for example, parallels the suppression of a political investigator's childhood memory; the main character of *The Voyeur* is a wristwatch salesman who is obsessed with liquidating his timepieces while escaping apprehension for his crime; the narrator of *Jealousy* almost destroys his own and

Alain Robbe-Grillet. (Roger Viollet/Getty Images)

the reader's concept of time through his suspicion and obsessive fear.

Robbe-Grillet's narrators are characterized by their obsessions, ranging from an obsession to discover, to an obsession to remain undiscovered, to an obsession to disassemble time, and finally to suppressed and then blatant sexual obsessions. Aligning himself with Jean-Paul Sartre, who advised against the objective and the omniscient point of view, Robbe-Grillet's pronounced intention has been to produce a viewpoint that—like real, immediate experience—is entirely subjective, always taking place in the mind of an obsessive narrator. Thus, events from an overimaginative, sometimes delirious point of view can be shaped into a highly structured narration. Again, form is all-important.

THE ERASERS

Robbe-Grillet wrote a brief synopsis for the dust jacket of his first novel, *The Erasers*. He called the novel a conventional detective story involving a murder and a solution of the crime, but one in which the relationship between victim and detective becomes clear only as the story ends. Because of the narrative's symmetrical time structure—twenty-four hours, beginning and ending with a gunshot—everything that the detective realizes has happened takes place, the author explains, during the flight of the bullet. To reinforce this structure, the detective's wristwatch stops ticking for the same twenty-four-hour period and begins again when he kills the very man whose murderer he was supposed to find.

Prior to this moment of discovery, immediate recollection of past events and anticipation of future ones—as well as imagined scenes that are, in fact, hypothetical reconstructions of a falsely reported crime—combine to form the circular plot. During this time, the detective attempts to deal with his faltering mind by buying gum erasers from attractive female stationers. His inexplicable behavior eventually, at the final moment, brings to the surface of his subconscious mind a significant memory. The thoughts and views of the investigator are not the only ones the reader shares; the viewpoint shifts from detective to assassin, to the assassin's superior, to the local police chief, to the would-be victim. These shifting viewpoints create a severe narrative weakness: The reader is thus kept aware that whatever the psychological state of the detective may be, he is but one of several characters under the control of an omniscient intelligence.

The plot structure of *The Erasers* is a departure from the conventional dramatic form of Greek tragedy; Robbe-Grillet reshapes the familiar dramatic curve into a closed loop. Critics have identified elements common to both *The Erasers* and Sophocles' *Oedipus Rex* (c. 420 B.C.E.). Among them are the novel's five-act structure, the significance of the riddle of the sphinx, connective images, and most obviously the themes of patricide and incest. Yet this dramatic understructure also calls attention to the author's presence and fixed plan. Early critics suggested that the author had rejected plot in favor of the depiction of objects by a protagonist whose view the reader shares. In fact, however, plot is very important to Robbe-Grillet. Plot is a formal element, and circular plot is more intricate than linear plot. With all the cycles observable in nature and human experience, it is the traditional plot line that appears unnatural and fragmented—an arc without closure.

THE VOYEUR

While in *The Erasers* a detective gropes toward discovery of a suppressed childhood memory, the lone viewpoint character of *The Voyeur*, Mathias, struggles to suppress the memory of his recent crime and thus his guilt. The viewpoint character is now on the other side of the law and normal thought. Eventually, the reader is able to determine what has taken place from the reappearances of objects that Mathias sees, remembers, or imagines.

The character Mathias has been compared to William Faulkner's Mink Snopes, but while Faulkner elevates the bad man Snopes, Robbe-Grillet coolly treats Mathias as a devious criminal whose furtive thoughts are also the reader's thoughts. Ultimately, the result of Mathias's suppression is what Robbe-Grillet labels "a void" in the narrative, a void that represents the unspeakable missing segment of the action that becomes obvious simply by its absence. Also, the void represents the obscenity that the reader may be unwilling to imagine, yet will imagine, thanks to meaningful objects observed.

Skulking about, the psychotic salesman supplies the novel's plot in the form of his movement, thinking ahead as he goes. He repeatedly anticipates his approaching business call at the home of the girl for whom he lusts.

Having learned earlier that she is rumored to be promiscuous, he anticipates his reception—as a good salesman will—and the family's possible responses to his pitch; when near the end of part 1 he actually enters the house, the reader knows he is planning to do much more than pitch his wristwatches. Meanwhile, the suggestive objects he sees (knives, film posters depicting violence) and hears (sirens, the repeated slapping of water against rock), as well as his preparations (he buys candy to lure the girl and cigarettes with which to torture her), build toward the criminal acts the reader will not see but will know to have happened. These plot fragments, the views of a distorted, obsessive mind, gradually align until the sequence of events as they have really occurred becomes clear.

The title of the novel presents the reader with a puzzle: Which of the characters is the voyeur? Most analysts agree that it is not Mathias—he commits crimes separate from and in excess of Peeping Tomism. A more likely voyeur is young Julien Marek; Julien witnesses the rape and murder, but he seems willing to condone it, even to help cover it up by not reporting what he has seen and knows to be true, as if he is either ashamed to admit that he watched the crime without trying to stop it or is— through the guilt of his passivity—a collaborator. That the reader is the voyeur is a stronger possibility, and most likely the author's design, for the reader could not be involved more intimately. This participation of the reader operates through the narrator's view of certain objects and his repeated description of these objects. The reader-voyeur, then, collaborates both with Mathias and with his creator.

JEALOUSY

In *Jealousy*, events first imagined overlie events later realized, and objects seen overlie objects remembered. Driven by suspicion and fear, the narrator sees a montage of objects that represent recent, then immediate, then imagined future events. This use of montage in fiction comes directly from Gustave Flaubert, who compared his work to that of a composer of music, especially orchestrations, which are vast, complex montages of individual sounds. In such music and in *Jealousy*, form is part of the content. *Jealousy*'s narrator is not incoherent; the novel derives its dramatic energy from the narrator's attempts to restructure his experience. The narrator's

stress provides the mainspring that powers his mental clock and the reader's sense of the time that constitutes the narrative.

Three characters form a typical love triangle: The narrator is the husband, who is jealous of "A." (his wife) and Franck, the neighboring husband whose own wife remains ill at home. The story takes place on a tropical plantation; that is, the story takes place in the mind of the jealous husband, who remains in the plantation house to sulk and suspect the worst, while A. and Franck take a trip together into town, returning very late, their relationship apparently less intimate than it had been. Within the story is a parallel text (the plot of a novel Franck has given A.) and several clockless time coordinates: various stages of a bridge that is being built near the house, the pruning and harvesting of banana trees, and shadows cast by columns of the veranda. A logistical reference point inside the house is the outline of a centipede squashed by Franck on the wall of the dining room. The image of the centipede forms a thematic and physical centrality to which the narrator repeatedly returns; it becomes the narrative's most visible objective correlative.

In *Jealousy* more than in his previous two novels, Robbe-Grillet places the reader in the narrator-observer's mind to see exactly what he sees. The story *is* what is seen. The story's closure results from increased distance between the narrator and the reader as his worst fears recede. As the narrator's stress decreases, plot-related tension decreases. There has been no final resolution, only an end, however temporary, to the narrator's jealousy.

IN THE LABYRINTH

Unique among Robbe-Grillet's early novels, *In the Labyrinth* makes visible a narrator in the process of creating a narrative. He identifies himself by framing his narrative with personal pronouns: "I" is the first word of the story and "me" the last. The story's main events are as follows: A soldier has come to a strange city following a disorienting and controversial military retreat; determined to return the personal effects of a comrade in arms to an unidentified member of his family, the ill and feverish soldier tries unsuccessfully to find the meeting place, is helped on his way by a young boy and his mother, and is treated by a physician who later identifies himself as the narrator; but the soldier leaves the barracks to keep his rendezvous, is wounded by a motorcycle patrol, and eventually dies.

For the viewpoint character, the soldier, this city in which he finds himself is the labyrinth. Two other labyrinths are evident: the labyrinth of the novel-information, through which the narrator progresses, imagining the experience of the soldier, and the labyrinth of the completed story, through which the reader must progress with object-related authorial guidance. The novel's form is at once all three labyrinths.

The narrator's methods of guiding the reader are also three: clockless time references, objects that interconnect events, and parallel scenes. Time references are established through description of snow accumulated on the street, the presence of darkness or daylight, and the growth of the soldier's beard. The reader is thereby able to locate linear events in nonlinear time. The second method of guiding the reader is the description, in precise geometric detail, of objects that interconnect events so that the reader can recognize these objects in the narrator's room and in the scenes the narrator imagines: Circles of light are cast by the narrator's lamp and by exterior street lamps, while marks in the surface dust of the room suggest marks in the snow outside, and the shape of a cross appears as a souvenir bayonet, a string tied around a box, the intersections of streets, hallways, and so forth.

The third way in which the narrator guides the reader through the labyrinth shows the narrator's imagination at work. One wall of his room is entirely curtained, suggesting a proscenium arch beyond which could be a stage or an audience. Also, an engraving hung on one wall of the narrator's room depicts a one-room café and shows three walls, the fourth being open to the viewer—the narrator, an audience of one, and all his readers. Present in the pictured café are doubles of objects and characters that will appear in the narrative: the boy who guides the soldier through the snow to his barrack room, the box tied with string that the soldier carries, the soldier seated at a table similar to a table in the narrator's room, the boy's mother working in the café as a waitress, and nondescript figures who will question the legitimacy of the soldier's retreat from battle. Thus, the reader in the labyrinth shares both the soldier's disoriented wandering and the narrator's creative exploration.

Although *In the Labyrinth* retains key elements of the author's continually evolving style, this novel is most striking in the visibility of its formation. In *The Voyeur*, imagined scenes occur in the mind of only one character but are related to his compulsion to escape, both mentally and physically. In *Jealousy*, the viewpoint character and the narrator are the same, and his obsessive emotions trigger imagined scenes. In *In the Labyrinth*, the narrator imagines everything except the room in which he sits, creating scenes deductively from objects at hand and a picture on the wall. These works represent Robbe-Grillet's early novels, and *In the Labyrinth* is the most important in terms of narrative invention and form.

La Maison de rendez-vous

The setting of *La Maison de rendez-vous* is the Blue Villa of Lady Ava in the British Crown Colony of Hong Kong. One of two principal characters, Lady Ava is the purveyor of entertainment, drugs, and women for a nebulous group of people, a sensual elite. Lady Ava's bordello replaces the solitary room of the narrator of *In the Labyrinth*; as the story's physical center, Blue Villa houses stage properties that are used to create narrative links with objects and events elsewhere.

Three principal devices are used to construct these links: statuary, the "freeze-frame," and the stage-curtain motif from *In the Labyrinth*. The statuary in the garden of Blue Villa is painted and life-size, and a variant of that statuary is a mannequin seen in a downtown store window; mannequins become a frequent device of Robbe-Grillet from this point on, allowing scene-doubling as well as character-doubling. The cinematic freeze-frame is used frequently in all Robbe-Grillet's fiction. This technique is used not merely to emphasize, as it usually is used in films, but also to signal the beginning of a new sequence of events, just as the onset of a new sequence of thoughts, in ordinary experience, often appears to be triggered by a personal gesture—stopping short and turning around, for example, or reaching for some object and seeing in startling detail for a frozen instant one's own outstretched hand. Robbe-Grillet uses street signs, posters, photographs, and engravings as thematic two-dimensional objects that trigger turns of thought in a similar manner.

The third device, at first the curtain covering the wall of the room of *In the Labyrinth*'s narrator, becomes in *La*

Maison de rendez-vous a real curtain and stage at Blue Villa, a stage on which are performed erotic tableaux whose actions connect via statuary and freeze-frames to scenes elsewhere in Hong Kong or on the mainland. Additional doublings are derived from two characters who are twins and from other characters who have alternate identities with similar names.

Analysts have balked at this novel because its plot has no clear purpose save the display of cinematic motifs that seem to have evolved from Robbe-Grillet's early novels and film work. Indeed, if one looks beyond this novel's sensual imagery and erotic content, beyond its visual structure and descriptive techniques, only the simplest story remains: In a locale of mystery and intrigue, an American client of Lady Ava wants to buy one of her employees—a young Eurasian woman whose fiancé either kills himself or is killed. Meanwhile, the American murders the drug vendor, who refuses to lend him money to buy the object of his lust, and when he returns to Blue Villa to steal his prize, he finds Lady Ava dying and the police awaiting him. The plot has been doubled too; a second story is to be found, parallel to the first.

To make appropriate an object-oriented narration of their subjective views, Robbe-Grillet employs characters who experience great physical stress and mental disunity: suppression, perversion, obsession, and feverish imaginings. In *La Maison de rendez-vous*, he presents some of each as well as the effects of drugs. Some of these characters experience memory, imagination, and immediate existence indiscriminately—and that is how the first five novels are alike. An important difference between the first three novels and the two following is the presence of a narrator who forms the story as he goes along. In *La Maison de rendez-vous*, however, the second plot is provided by a second narrator, and it is the reader's challenge to find the two narrators.

PROJECT FOR A REVOLUTION IN NEW YORK

Project for a Revolution in New York contains descriptive and formal elements that recall Robbe-Grillet's early work: circular plot, parallel texts, object indicators of time or scene-shifting, and visual projections of the narrator's imagination. At one surrealistic juncture, a vacant city lot surrounded by a demolition fence and paved with flat stones suggestive of a chessboard contains props from other Robbe-Grillet fictions, objects that lie abandoned and waiting in the weeds to be discovered and pondered by the narrator. This device produces a cross-textual consciousness that interconnects the various novels like a composer's favorite elemental themes that are developed further in successive compositions. Playfully esoteric authorial intrusion also occurs during plot-related interrogative dialogues that double as lines of critical questioning about the worth and purpose of this novel; the reader who finds *Project for a Revolution in New York* revolting is thus anticipated. Yet by accepting these devices as viable narrative elements, the reader will recognize in this novel a startling coherence.

In *Project for a Revolution in New York*, a narrative viewpoint like that of *In the Labyrinth* and *La Maison de rendez-vous* becomes the vision of a character like Mathias of *The Voyeur*. This narrator does not enter the fiction; the fiction enters him—and the context is different. Whereas Mathias is sexually aberrant in a normal social setting, the narrator of *Project for a Revolution in New York* behaves normally within a peer group that is itself contained in an abnormal society. Abandoned buildings and the subways of the city are filled with a decadent revolutionary madness that culminates in politically motivated assaults on the young daughters of establishment families. This premise frees the willful cruelties of the Mathias figure, now a describer rather than a concealer of atrocity, who does not suppress, but reveals in detail, the gruesome machinations of members of the group.

Readers unacquainted with Robbe-Grillet's earlier novels will be surprised by the content as well as the form of *Project for a Revolution in New York*. Unlike *The Voyeur*, in which Mathias's crime occurs offstage to create the "void" better imagined by the reader, or *La Maison de rendez-vous*, in which sexual aberrance is largely suggestive, here violent sexual behavior is set forth in such a way that the reader need not imagine anything. Critical discussions about this work have related its content to sadistic themes of works now within the modern literary tradition and to archetypal literature containing mythic or acultural themes. Robbe-Grillet himself asserts a need for audience catharsis and here makes use of the masks and deus ex machina of Greek drama. He has used such elements before—*The Erasers* builds on plot elements from *Oedipus Rex*—but the fact remains that this novel describes cruel and deadly perversions performed by adult men on adolescent girls. This device involves readers in a new way: The story's perverse content encourages the reader to see the characters and their actions metaphorically as social satire. The violence of the age, whether it be sexual, political, or civil, is pervasive yet habitually ignored. Shutting real violence out of view may ultimately create the absurd world of *Project for a Revolution in New York*, just as the novel's narrator creates a world of absurdities.

TOPOLOGY OF A PHANTOM CITY

In his 1954 essay "A Novel That Invents Itself," Robbe-Grillet refers to characters who "make themselves" and who, in turn, create their "own reality . . . a kind of living tissue, each cell of which sprouts and shapes its neighbors." The first narrative section of *Topology of a Phantom City* is titled "In the Generative Cell." Although more than twenty years of writing separate the early statement from this 1975 novel, the connection remains fast. Underlying *Topology of a Phantom City* is the author's concept of cellular growth: Like life, fiction creates itself through a process of mitosis.

Robbe-Grillet consistently uses mathematical description to create the freeze-frame effect that usually signifies a shift of scene or viewpoint. At such a point in the narrative, objects are described in terms of their planes and angles, their shapes and configurations. The word "topology," moreover, is a mathematical term that refers to the properties of geometric forms that remain constant even when the forms change. In other words, topological elements carry over from one state of being to the next. Like *In the Labyrinth*, this story grows out of itself as the narrator discovers the final shape it should take.

The narrator of *Topology of a Phantom City* begins his story by describing a single cell—a white room—that contains several young women who are being held captive. Some of the women are playing with tarot cards, and an illustrated notice of some kind is visible on one wall. From these stark details, the story grows, each scene a subdivision of the preceding scene, until the narrator has invented not only the lost city but also its recent history, its contemporary rebirth as a historical restoration, and an ancient mythology that includes timeless scenes of hermaphroditic ritual and tragic carnage. The phantom city thus grows backward from the single gen-

erative cell to its own mystical origin, while the novel grows forward into its ultimate form.

The narrative of *Topology of a Phantom City* has been reinforced with numerous cross-textual references. As in *Project for a Revolution in New York*, motifs from the author's other works appear in this text. The eye motif (now the eye of a camera) and parts of Mathias's bicycle from *The Voyeur* appear, for example, as do the mannequin and the iron bed from *Project for a Revolution in New York*. The narrator even refers overtly to the author's work, mentioning Lady Ava's Blue Villa and the eraser idea from the first novel. Extratextual references are also made: During one descriptive sequence, a character identified as D. H. and then as David H. photographs young women who assume sensual attitudes and mirrored poses that the reader may see in the photo-essay titled *Rêves de jeunes filles* (1971; *Dreams of a Young Girl*, 1971), a collaborative production of Robbe-Grillet and photographer David Hamilton. Again and again, Robbe-Grillet, the author, superimposes his consciousness on that of his narrator and, through playful intrusions, refocuses the reader's attention on the inventive process, rather than on the product, of his narrative search.

Most obviously, the letter *V* carries blatant significance. The goddess Vanade (suggestive of a species of butterfly, a flying *vee*), the city of Vanadium, the obliteration of the inhabitants by gases from a *v*olcano, the narrative attention given the words "Da*v*id," "di*v*an," "gra*v*id," "*v*agina," and several more—all interconnect with triangular shapes such as the profile of the *v*olcano, the city's wedge-shaped plaza, the pointed portico of the temple, the spread legs of sacrificial *v*irgins, and so forth. Since *V* is also the Roman numeral five, many objects appear in this exact quantity, the symbolism of which is also significant: In occult numerology, the value five is located in the center of the human personality "cell," or matrix, representing feminine qualities traditionally exploited by men and—in medieval Christian symbol systems—the combined senses, thereby the corporeal life, the flesh. None of these references is subtly made, which is to say that the author repeatedly asserts what he is doing. He is generating a narrative, simultaneously inventing both content and form. The images he chooses are not symbolic allusions but cellular parts of the formal development, organic fictive growth.

DJINN

Robbe-Grillet's novel *Djinn* appears to be a transitional work. Gone are the erotic and the sadistic elements. Sly intertextual references have been replaced with wry and humorous ones, although the structure of this novel is far more complex than that of *In the Labyrinth*. Children are involved in the story not as objects but as clever protagonists who influence the narrator's method of telling and help lead him through an invisible labyrinth of his own making. *Djinn* is encoded with sudden shifts in viewpoint and verb tense that indicate the presence of double characters with double motives. There are also overtones of the Oedipus myth, with its psychological implications, but of the old, blind Oedipus at Colonus being led by a child.

Having written a French primer for intermediate language students (*Le Rendez-vous*, 1981), Robbe-Grillet employed the idea here as a framing device: A French teacher disappears, leaving behind a mysterious manuscript, the story of Simon Lecoeur and Djinn. Their narrative progresses with increasing intricacy as Simon's identity changes, by his own inclination and by the intrusion of an unclearly identified narrator who usurps both manuscript and viewpoint. Is Djinn male, female, or androgynous? The novel is a puzzle with pieces that are shaped alike: Simon is known to his students as Yann, spelled Ján; his young friend is named Jean, and Jean's sister is named Jeannie. Other Jeans and Jeannies surface, too. (A "djinn," or jinni, is a mythical Islamic spirit that can enter bodies at will for good or evil.) A novel that is this much a puzzle must be brief—128 pages—but its brevity heightens its complexity. Repeated readings lead to a fuller understanding of its manifold story; the structure of earlier works becomes clear by the second reading.

AUTOBIOGRAPHICAL FICTION

In the third phase of Alain Robbe-Grillet's career, *Ghosts in the Mirror*, *Angélique*, and *Les Derniers Jours de Corinthe* present his autobiographical fiction. *Ghosts in the Mirror* provides the oval mirror that the quasimythical Comte de Corinthe struggled to retrieve from the sea. Through this mirror's oval eye, the "I" of Robbe-Grillet, the sole narrator, directs or misdirects the readers while he spins his fictions. He describes his plot structure as a work progressing in a linear fashion through his life, from "critical essay to novel, from book to film, continually questioning," and including the sea and fear, two things giving theme or structure to previous works. His actual method, however, shows his usual scorn for traditions. An achronological approach dominates. Time sequences alter when dislocated descriptions, tangential ideas, critical theories, and subjective fantasies are incorporated where they neither belong nor seem to fit.

Robbe-Grillet's fictional characters reappear in fragmented or altered forms in these works. Angélique has many incarnations. She may be the living model for Violet or Jacqueline in *The Voyeur*. Other shifting images depict her as not only Corinth's fiancé but also mysterious washerwomen fairies or even a vampire bat. (This last pairs her with the author's mother, who shelters a bat in her blouse.) At her death, she becomes an Ophelia floating on the waters.

Cross-textual references to key objects and parallel scenes are again used as linking devices. Allusions to torn, bloodstained clothing and broken glass link related objects to previous sequences of sexual activity or interests to many scenes in *Angélique*. Childhood memories of Robbe-Grillet's red-curtained bedroom parallel one curtained room from *In the Labyrinth*. Robbe-Grillet creates an imaginary, isolated white cell in which his fantasized captivity recalls women prisoners in another white room in *Topology of a Phantom City*. This depiction illustrates one of Robbe-Grillet's favorite concepts: generators, starting points for evolutionary growth. Here, Mersault's prison cell is a "generative cell" able to create its own cellular growth and shape other organic fictive growth such as the fantasy cell in *Ghosts in the Mirror*.

Another significant element is the sly, playful humor that surfaces. Repeatedly, Robbe-Grillet refocuses the reader's attention on the inventive process rather than on the product of his narrative search. In *Ghosts in the Mirror*, Robbe-Grillet admits, "I don't believe in truth," but he adds, "I'm not a truthful soul but nor do I tell lies." Further, according to Robbe-Grillet, "an author is a being without a face." If the author is writing his (or her) autobiography, not fiction, his query should be, "Who is Alain Robbe-Grillet?" rather than "Who was Henri de Corinthe?"—the first question in *Ghosts in the Mirror*. That confusing situation is at the heart of Robbe-Grillet's autofictions. Are these works fact or fiction? How much real biographical information does the author provide for the reader? Are his childhood memories real or false? In autobiography, a reader expects to discover more information about the author than has previously been known. Here, there are few documentable facts revealed that are not already known about Robbe-Grillet's personal and public life. The autofictions could be skillful and sly efforts to reject the familiar conventions of form by creating a new one. Indeed, without telling their readers, writers have been telling lies for centuries.

Joseph F. Battaglia
Updated by Betsy P. Harfst

OTHER MAJOR WORKS

SHORT FICTION: *Instantanés*, 1962 (*Snapshots*, 1965).

SCREENPLAYS: *L'Année dernière à Marienbad*, 1961 (*Last Year at Marienbad*, 1962); *L'Immortelle*, 1963 (*The Immortal One*, 1971); *Trans-Europ-Express*, 1966; *L'Homme qui ment*, 1968 (*The Man Who Lies*, 1968); *L'Éden et après*, 1970 (*Eden and Afterwards*, 1970); *N a pris les dés*, 1971; *Glissements progressifs du plaisir*, 1973 (*The Successive Slidings of Pleasure*, 1974); *Le Jeu avec le feu*, 1975 (*Playing with Fire*, 1975); *La Belle Captive*, 1983 (*The Beautiful Prisoner*, 1983); *Taxandria*, 1994; *Un Bruit qui rend fou*, 1995 (*The Blue Villa*, 1995); *C'est Gradiva qui vous appelle*, 2002 (*It's Gradiva Who Is Calling You*, 2006).

NONFICTION: *Pour un nouveau roman*, 1963 (criticism; *For a New Novel: Essays on Fiction*, 1965); *Rêves de jeunes filles*, 1971 (photographs by David Hamilton; *Dreams of a Young Girl*, 1971); *Les Demoiselles d'Hamilton*, 1972 (photographs by Hamilton; *Sisters*, 1973); *Construction d'un temple en ruines à la Déesse Vanadé*, 1975 (etchings by Paul Delvaux); *Le Rendez-vous*, 1981.

MISCELLANEOUS: *Le Voyageur: Textes, causeries, et entretiens, 1947-2001*, 2001 (with Olivier Corpet, editor).

BIBLIOGRAPHY

Angelini, Eileen M. *Strategies of "Writing the Self" in the French Modern Novel: C'est moi, je crois*. Lewiston, N.Y.: Edwin Mellen Press, 2001. Analyzes three novels by Robbe-Grillet—*Ghosts in the Mirror*, *Angélique*, and *Les Derniers Jours de Corinthe*—and works by Nathalie Sarraute and Marguerite Duras, focusing on how the three writers use various genres to create autobiography.

Fletcher, John. *Alain Robbe-Grillet*. New York: Methuen, 1983. This short study is by one of the best critics of French twentieth century fiction, who takes a thematic approach. Fletcher concludes that Robbe-Grillet has hastened the demise of modernism even though Robbe-Grillet felt that he had championed it.

Harger-Grinling, Virginia, and Tony Chadwick, eds. *Robbe-Grillet and the Fantastic*. Westport, Conn.: Greenwood Press, 1994. Collection of essays by critics and former students of Robbe-Grillet who focus on the themes of fantasy and the use of experimental methods in his work.

Hellerstein, Marjorie H. *Inventing the Real World: The Art of Alain Robbe-Grillet*. Selinsgrove, Pa.: Susquehanna University Press, 1998. A study of Robbe-Grillet's work in film includes discussions of his fiction, a good bibliography, and an index.

Jefferson, Ann. *The Nouveau Roman and the Poetics of Fiction*. New York: Cambridge University Press, 1980. A survey of the French New Novel that covers Robbe-Grillet in several chapters, including two on *The Erasers* and *Jealousy*. Jefferson describes his narratives as "unnatural." This study, although it covers novelists other than Robbe-Grillet, is useful for setting his writing into perspective and seeing Robbe-Grillet as a part of a French literary movement of the 1950's and 1960's.

Leki, Ilona. *Alain Robbe-Grillet*. Boston: Twayne, 1983. Leki takes each of Robbe-Grillet's major novels and discusses it in turn, finishing with *Un Regicide*. She concludes that after the debate on Robbe-Grillet's subjectivity and objectivity diminished, discussion focused on his use of narrative strategies. An excellent study for a general survey of this work. Includes a solid bibliography.

Morrisette, Bruce. *The Novels of Robbe-Grillet*. Ithaca, N.Y.: Cornell University Press, 1975. A translation of a French-language work by an American expert on Robbe-Grillet. Morrisette is, along with John Fletcher (above), the dean of criticism on Robbe-Grillet, and in this study he takes the reader through the major novels by examining such themes as the maze, the narrator and his doubles, and the cinematic novels.

Ramsay, Raylene L. *Robbe-Grillet and Modernity: Science, Sexuality, and Subversion.* Gainesville: University Press of Florida, 1992. Ramsay discusses modernity, complementarity, myth, and sado-eroticism, all elements of Robbe-Grillet's narrative. The study also includes interviews with Robbe-Grillet, which shed light on his creative process. Includes a bibliography.

Roland, Lillian Dunmars. *Women in Robbe-Grillet: A Study in Thematics and Diegetics.* New York: Peter Lang, 1993. Roland focuses on the representation of women in Robbe-Grillet's novels, describing how the writer provides perspectives on women through narrators, narrative, and characters. Includes a bibliography and an index.

Smith, Roch C. *Understanding Alain Robbe-Grillet.* Columbia: University of South Carolina Press, 2000. An introductory guide to Robbe-Grillet's work and theories that aims to make him less bewildering to readers. Smith discusses the characterization, narration, plots, and other elements of Robbe-Grillet's fiction.

Stoltzfus, Ben. *Alain Robbe-Grillet: The Body of the Text.* London: Associated University Presses, 1985. Stoltzfus contends that Robbe-Grillet exaggerates images of sex and violence in his novels in order to expose and undermine them. Includes a bibliography and an index.

ELIZABETH MADOX ROBERTS

Born: Perryville, Kentucky; October 30, 1881
Died: Orlando, Florida; March 13, 1941

PRINCIPAL LONG FICTION
The Time of Man, 1926
My Heart and My Flesh, 1927
Jingling in the Wind, 1928
The Great Meadow, 1930
A Buried Treasure, 1931
He Sent Forth a Raven, 1935
Black Is My Truelove's Hair, 1938

OTHER LITERARY FORMS

Before Elizabeth Madox Roberts was a novelist, she wrote poetry, including children's verse—facts that explain much about her work as a novelist—and she continued to produce some poetry throughout her career. Her first collection of verse, privately printed in 1915, was *In the Great Steep's Garden*, a pamphlet consisting of a few short poems accompanying photographs. A second collection of poetry, *Under the Tree*, appeared in 1922, published by Huebsch, which soon became the Viking Press and the publisher of Roberts's subsequent work. A revised edition of *Under the Tree* appeared in 1930, and a third collection of Roberts's poetry, *Song in the Meadow*, came out in 1940.

In addition, Roberts wrote short stories, which, like her poetry, found a ready market in leading magazines of the day. Her short fiction was collected in *The Haunted Mirror* (1932) and *Not by Strange Gods* (1941).

ACHIEVEMENTS

Elizabeth Madox Roberts's reputation as a writer furnishes an interesting case study in literary fashions and critical evaluation. Few novelists have begun their careers to such popular and critical acclaim as Roberts achieved with *The Time of Man* in 1926, acclaim that was renewed and confirmed by *The Great Meadow* four years later. With the 1935 publication of *He Sent Forth a Raven*, however, Roberts's literary reputation went into a precipitous decline. By her death in 1941, it had struck bottom. Since then, there have been intermittent attempts, including several book-length studies, to resurrect her reputation, frequently with highly inflated praise. Claims that she is among the half dozen or so great American novelists of the twentieth century do her as much disservice as does the vague "regionalist" label that her special pleaders decry.

Perhaps as a result of her early success and her relative isolation in Kentucky, Roberts seems likewise to have overestimated her powers: With talents along the lines of a May Sarton, Roberts was apparently encouraged to think of herself as another William Faulkner, with a little Herman Melville and Thomas Mann thrown in for good measure. Her style, so often termed "poetic," achieves some fine effects indeed, but at immense cost to the narrative flow of her novels. Her style is allied to her narrative focus, almost invariably the novel's female protagonist, whose perceptions and sentiments are spun out at length while the reader waits for something to happen. Little does happen, except that the heroines take long walks. The effect is somewhat reminiscent of an agrarian Virginia Woolf. Perhaps the reader is treated to such a subjective focus because Roberts's protagonists, however different, are to some extent alter egos of their author, whose own comments blend imperceptibly into their observations.

The results of all this are slow-moving and sometimes flimsy plots, dimly realized characters (except usually for the protagonist), loss of authorial perspective, and tedium. As if these results were not unhappy enough, Roberts also had trouble dealing with ideas and with the overall plans for her novels.

Despite all these limitations and failings, Roberts deserves a revival. Most readers will find her lighter novels, *A Buried Treasure* and *Black Is My Truelove's Hair*, still entertaining, and *The Great Meadow* possesses some epic qualities. All of Roberts's novels involve significant themes, and all deal incidentally with significant social issues, such as economic conditions, racism, and sexism. In particular, both feminists and antifeminists will find much of interest in Roberts's depiction of her female protagonists, in her treatment of male-female relationships, and in Roberts's own biography.

BIOGRAPHY

Elizabeth Madox Roberts's life was marked by a few salient facts. Descended from early settlers of Kentucky, she was the second of eight children born to Mary Elizabeth Brent and Simpson Roberts, Confederate veteran, teacher, grocer, and occasional surveyor-engineer. Rob-

erts lived most of her life in Springfield, a small county-seat town on the southwestern edge of the Kentucky bluegrass region. She attended high school in Covington, Kentucky (1896-1900) and college at the University of Chicago (1917-1921), where she received the David Blair McLaughlin Prize for prose and the Fiske Poetry Prize, served as president of the poetry club, and became a member of Phi Beta Kappa before graduating with a doctorate in English. She began college at the age of thirty-one because limited finances and ill health delayed her. She suffered from poor health much of her life.

From 1910 to 1916, Roberts made various stays with a brother and a sister in Colorado, in part to recuperate from what was possibly tuberculosis. At the height of her literary career, she experienced severe headaches and a skin rash, both possibly nervous in origin. During her last years, when she wintered in Florida for her health, she suffered severely from Hodgkin's disease (cancer of the lymphatic system), the eventual cause of her death.

Because of her ill health and perhaps her own disposition, Roberts led a quiet personal life, at times almost reclusive. She never married, though she always enjoyed a circle of friends, including friends from her Chicago years whom she later wrote and sometimes visited. In a sense, she never left the family circle, building her own house onto her parents' Springfield home when she came into money from her writing. She also enjoyed contacts and visits with her brothers and sisters. At heart, she was a solitary, introspective individual who guarded her privacy, growing a hedge around her backyard garden. Besides reading and writing, her favorite activities included listening to music, gardening, sunbathing, and taking long walks into secluded areas of the countryside (from which she returned to make voluminous notes).

These conditions of Roberts's life exercised strong influences, both positive and negative, on her writing career. Her family's proud pioneer heritage not only stimulated her imagination but also encouraged her to paint an idyllic picture of Kentucky's past and present. The sleepy farming region around Springfield was also a rich source of material—indeed, her prime source—but at the same time it effectively isolated her from literary circles that might have served to encourage, temper, and appreciate her efforts. These functions were served briefly by her stay at the University of Chicago. Her heady experience of Chicago, where literary circles flourished both inside and outside the university, filled her with ideas and propelled her into sustained literary production, but perhaps this hothouse experience also encouraged her to overreach herself as a writer.

The effects of Roberts's circumscribed personal life can also be detected in her fiction, particularly in her efforts to depict character and to describe male-female relationships, possibly also in her habitual narrative focus. To a great extent, Roberts's fiction provides an ironic counterpoint to her personal life. In most of her novels, the main narrative interest is her heroines' search for identity, worked out through the rituals of courting and mating: Her heroines suffer their shipwrecks but eventually find safe harbor in marriage. The men in their lives are either grandfatherly, brutish, bucolic, or childishly vengeful; the heroines get advice from the grandfatherly ones, are hurt by the brutish ones, and marry either the bucolic or childishly vengeful ones. Fathers are frequently possessive, obstructing their daughters' paths to marriage; one can only wonder about Roberts's relationship with her father, who refused her money for college and then had her underfoot for the rest of his life. To Roberts's credit, it must be said that in her novels, men, however unpromising, are absolutely vital to the scheme of things.

On the other hand, too, if Roberts's personal life had been less circumscribed, she might not have taken up writing at all. Writing became her means of achieving identity—and against stronger odds than any of her heroines had to face. However sickly and easily demoralized Roberts might seem, she had a vein of iron in her character that also came out in her heroines and in her themes. Even Roberts's ill health furnished her with potent material. Her heroines frequently develop by means of long illnesses and convalescence, from which they emerge born again, like a butterfly from its pupa. It was perhaps toward such a rebirth that Roberts was aiming in her writing.

ANALYSIS

Although commentators on Elizabeth Madox Roberts like to describe her main theme in such terms as "the ordering of chaos" or "the triumph of spirit over matter,"

Elizabeth Madox Roberts. (National Archives)

one need not be so high-minded and vague. A hard-headed Kentucky version of her major theme would be more specific: ownership of the land. This theme reflects an old, revered attitude in Kentucky, where in some parts even today one can be shot for trespassing. The theme also reflects an old, revered American (even Anglo-Saxon) attitude, a pioneer urge to settle and possess, if necessary by violence—an urge that today achieves its debased avatar in the mass media and advertising.

In its gentler, more settled aspects, however, Roberts's theme embodies a Jeffersonian, agrarian vision of American democracy, the American Dream of independence through ownership of the land. The theme eventually embodies a more universal vision, a vision of harmony with the land, a realization, serenely accepted, that those who possess the land are also possessed by it. Unhappily, whether expressed by Roberts or by other American writers whose characters want to own chicken farms or raise rabbits, the theme is a poignant reminder that many Americans have in actuality been vagabonds, whether the pioneer variety or today's rootless variety.

In this sense, then, the theme embodies an idyllic but unrealized American Dream; it was apparently Roberts's conviction, however, that this dream came very close to being realized in Kentucky.

In developing her theme, Roberts reveals the influence of her favorite philosopher, George Berkeley, the eighteenth century bishop who denied the existence of matter, holding that "things" exist only as "ideas" or "spirits" in the minds of God and people. Such a philosophy would seem, at first, to preclude any relationship with the land; on the contrary, it points to a divine immanence, to the spiritual nature of all things, including the land. The philosophy also implies the worth of "subjective" truth, justifying Roberts's narrative focus on the lengthy observations of her protagonists. As a result of this focus, her novels are full of loving descriptions of the land, the flora and fauna, and the weather. Held constantly before the reader, the land forms an immense backdrop or tableau against which human action is played out, a background so overwhelming at times that the characters seem to emerge out of it and then sink back into it.

Because of their closeness to the land, many of Roberts's characters exhibit a sameness: Mostly simple farmers, their lives governed by the imperatives of the seasons, crops, animals, they identify with the soil in their talk and in their impulses. Rather inarticulate, they have a blood-knowledge of the earth that requires little discussion. The continuity of their lives with the land is also reflected in their impulses to create life, to mate and procreate. To Roberts, these characters represent an ideal, a settled state, though to her readers they might seem too bucolic to be interesting.

The state of health represented by such characters is what Roberts's protagonists aspire to and her maladjusted characters lack. Like the bucolic characters, Roberts's protagonists seek to mate and procreate. The protagonists do not achieve their aims easily, though, having to reenact the archetypal struggle of their pioneer ancestors before they reach a settled state. When misfortune frustrates their desires, they get back in touch with the earth through the simple therapies of raising chickens, growing a garden, sunbathing, or taking rides in the country. Some end up marrying farmers. Such is the ultimate salvation of Theodosia, the highbred protagonist of

My Heart and My Flesh, whose alienation from the land is an index of her initial maladjustment. Other unhappy characters in Roberts's novels are similarly out of touch with the land, such as Stoner Drake in *He Sent Forth a Raven* and the evil Langtry in *Black Is My Truelove's Hair*.

These patterns of behavior exhibited by her characters are the prime means through which Roberts develops her theme, with examples of each pattern generally to be found in each of her novels. To some extent, however, each novel emphasizes a particular aspect of her theme, with *He Sent Forth a Raven* being Roberts's most ambitious effort to pull all her characteristic motifs together in a single work.

THE GREAT MEADOW

Although *The Great Meadow* was Roberts's fourth novel, it was apparently the first conceived. This is appropriate, since thematically *The Great Meadow* comes first among her novels. Set around the time of the American Revolution, it celebrates the early settlement of Kentucky, that other Eden, that paradise, that promised land. The epic qualities of this novel have led some commentators to compare it to Homer's *Odyssey* (c. 725 B.C.E.; English translation, 1614), though it could more appropriately be compared to Vergil's *Aeneid* (c. 29-19 B.C.E.; English translation, 1553). Like Latium, Kentucky has to be wrested from the "aborigines." The novel even has its epic heroine with a noble name, Diony, and noble progenitors, sturdy Pennsylvania Methodists and Quakers on her mother's side and Virginia Tidewater gentry on her father's. Diony is, in truth, the founder of "a new race," though before she marries and sets out for Kentucky, she has to get her father's permission (in typical fashion for Roberts's possessive fathers, he at first denies her).

After a slow start in Albemarle County, Virginia, the novel follows Diony, her husband, and a small party of settlers as they trek across the rugged Appalachians to Harrod's Fort, where they proceed to fight off Native Americans and establish farms. The growth of their settlement corresponds to Diony's growth as a person, largely a development of awareness. A convinced Berkeleian who frequently quotes from the philosopher's works, she receives a real challenge to her beliefs when she is banged in the head with a tomahawk, but the tomahawk incident and the scalping of her mother-in-law are only smaller parts of the overall challenge represented by the alien wilderness. In the beginning, Diony had imagined God as a benevolent deity creating "a world out of chaos," but since everything that exists is a thought of God's, God must also have created the wilderness, where wolves howl and savages prowl. Unlike Daniel Boone—or for that matter the Native Americans—Diony cannot feel at home in the wilderness; instead, she must remake the wilderness into her vision of home, a vision of a settled, orderly, agrarian society where the land is "owned."

Although Diony clings stubbornly to her vision of order, the wilderness does make her more tolerant of disorder. Even before she leaves for Kentucky, she has a "wilderness marriage . . . without law" (performed by a Methodist minister). Later, her experiences of hardship and deprivation at Harrod's Fort lead her to observe that "men wanted law to live by" but that women and babies "followed a hidden law"—that is, a law based on concrete, immediate human needs. This frontier tradition of making do the best one can, without too much scrupling about moral and legal niceties, serves Diony well at the end of the novel. Her husband, Berk Jarvis, goes into the wilderness to seek revenge against the Native American, Blackfox, who has his mother's scalp. When Berk does not return in a year or so, he is presumed dead, and Diony marries Evan Muir, who had helped provide for her after Berk left. Then, three years after he left, Berk shows up. Faced with two husbands and a child by each, Diony exercises the frontier woman's option: She sends Evan away, takes Berk back, and then goes to bed for a good, sound sleep.

The same spirit of make-do morality also characterizes the settlers' relations with the Native Americans. Diony's mother, Polly, influenced by Quaker thought, not only opposes the slaveholding favored by the Tidewater gentry but also opposes taking land from the American Indians. At the dinner table where the men are enthusiastically discussing "the promise land" of Kentucky, Polly angrily announces that Kentucky "belongs to the Indians" and that white trespassers there will get "skulped." Quiet reigns while the men contemplate images of "battle, fire . . . rapine, plunder." These thoughts, however, dampen their enthusiasm only momentarily. Striking the table for emphasis, they argue that Ken-

tucky, "a good country," belongs to those strong enough to take and hold it—that is, "the Long Knives." Later, the last term is revised to "civilized man." Apparently, the latter argument is the one Roberts favors, since the rest of her novel eulogizes the settlers' taking of Kentucky. For example, as Diony's party breaks through Cumberland Gap, Roberts describes them as marching forward, "without bigotry and without psalm-singing," to take "a new world for themselves . . . by the power of their courage, their order, and their endurance." Thus is a time-honored Kentucky tradition established.

If *The Great Meadow* celebrates the vision of this other Eden, *A Buried Treasure* and *Black Is My True-love's Hair* celebrate the realization of the vision. Like all of Roberts's novels except *The Great Meadow*, they are set in early twentieth century Kentucky, roughly contemporaneous with the period of their composition. Both novels were expanded from shorter pieces and show the effects of padding and lengthening, but at the same time they are Roberts's most entertaining novels and exhibit, in its purest form, her theme of living on the land. Generally light and pleasant works, they depict a pastoral scene where the land is the source of happiness and renewal.

A BURIED TREASURE

A Buried Treasure differs from other novels in its comic tone and in its older protagonist, Philadelphia Blair. Philly's farmer husband, Andy, finds a pot of old gold and silver coins under a stump on their land, and the rest of the novel concerns their efforts to announce their find and at the same time protect it from thieves. The flimsy plot is complicated somewhat by Philly's machinations to slip away her cousin's daughter, Imogene (whose possessive father, Sam Cundy, will not let her wed), and marry her to Giles Wilson. In addition, a subplot, introducing experimentation with point of view and synchronous time, treats seventeen-year-old Ben Shepherd's search for his ancestors' graves. To a great extent, the whole novel is an extended pun on the meanings of "buried treasure."

Ben Shepherd finds the graves of his ancestors, who naturally go all the way back to the pioneer settlers of Kentucky. Imogene marries her beau, a jolly young farmer who wears horseshoes. Philly becomes more aware of her deep love for Andy, particularly when he loans the widow Hester Trigg (who gives him cherry pie) two pearls that he got from the treasure pot and normally wears in a small sack tied around his lower abdomen. Both Philly and Andy become more aware of their love for the land, from whence the treasure pot came, put there perhaps by some ancestor. Despite an evil old hen that eats her own eggs, and the threat of two itinerant house painters who are thieves, the novel ends happily in a communal ring dance out in the pasture under the moonlit sky of the summer solstice.

BLACK IS MY TRUELOVE'S HAIR

Compared to *A Buried Treasure*, *Black Is My Truelove's Hair* is somewhat less satisfactory. Its title drawn from an Appalachian ballad containing the line "I love the ground whereon he stands," *Black Is My Truelove's Hair* concerns a young woman, Dena Janes, who "loved too much" and whose first lover, the black-hearted Langtry, is untrue. A truck driver who brags that he has no home, Langtry takes Dena on the road, refuses to marry her, treats her brutally, and threatens to kill her if she ever loves another man. After six days, Dena flees home, walking most of the way. Beginning at this point (the affair with Langtry is told through brief flashbacks), the novel treats Dena's gradual rehabilitation in the rural community and her eventual engagement to marry the miller's son, Cam Elliot. Although received at first with leering remarks and invitations, Dena is not given the Hester Prynne treatment. Even on her way home from the Langtry affair, the distraught Dena maintains she has "a right to a life that makes good sense." Apparently the people of the community agree.

Dena restores herself with the help of time, a sympathetic sister, routine chores of gardening and tending animals, sunbathing, and the advice of the local oracle, the apple-grower Journeyman, who observes that Dena is like one of his overburdened apple trees, "destroyed by its own abundance." As Dena recovers, the passage of time is marked by great to-dos over a strayed gander and a lost thimble; these comic commotions are supposed to be highly symbolic, but to the reader they may seem merely silly. The reader is also likely to find the ending anticlimactic. The fearsome Langtry shows up, gun in hand, but when he chases Dena into Journeyman's moonlit orchard and views her abundance, he shoots to miss. The story is resolved when Journeyman appears, de-

stroys the gun, and buries it in the earth, leaving Dena free to go her own way.

THE TIME OF MAN

While *The Great Meadow* and the pastoral novels emphasize the positive aspects of Roberts's theme, *The Time of Man* and her other novels emphasize negative aspects. Dealing with poor tenant farmers who move from place to place, *The Time of Man* shows the plight of people who live on the land but do not own it. They have, in effect, been reduced to beasts of burden. Laboring mainly for others, they receive only enough from their labors to ensure their continuing usefulness, their subsistence. Their inability to escape from this cycle probably means that their children will continue it.

Although Roberts's subject raises weighty social issues, suggesting a novel along the lines of John Steinbeck's *The Grapes of Wrath* (1939), *The Time of Man* is not a novel of social protest. Instead, with Roberts's narrative focus on the mind of her protagonist, *The Time of Man* is more a bildungsroman, tracing the development of Ellen Chesser from a girl of fourteen to a woman in her mid-thirties.

The reader follows Ellen as she bounds about the woods and fields, joins a group of other teenagers, gets a boyfriend, loses her boyfriend, withdraws into her hurt, meets another man, marries him, has four children, is estranged from her husband when he is unfaithful, experiences the death of her fifth child, and is reconciled with her husband. In short, whatever her social status, Ellen's experience of life over a generation is typical of most people's; in this sense, then, her experience is representative of "the time of man"—experiences of beauty and love, disappointment and tragedy, all within the context of passing time. Her ability to hold her experiences within this context is the key to her appreciation of beauty and love and her endurance of disappointment and tragedy. This ability derives from her closeness to the land, her sense of the seasons and participation in the rhythms of the earth: her jaunts through the woods, her work in the fields and garden, her courtship and marriage, her children.

Ellen illustrates what the Native Americans knew—that one can live in harmony with the land without owning it. To this extent, the several moves she makes from farm to farm, first with her parents and then with her husband, are almost irrelevant. Still, Ellen is aware of the inequities and injustices of the landowner-tenant system, a carryover from slave plantations, with some landowners continuing to act as if they own their tenants. She is incensed when her husband, while she and the children starve, identifies with, even takes pride in, the richness and show of their arrogant landlord. Both she and her husband carry around a vision of having their own farm someday, in "some better country." Perhaps they are headed toward this vision when, at the end of the novel, after her husband has been wrongly accused of barnburning and run out of the country, they are on the road again.

Roberts's first novel, *The Time of Man* is judged by some critics to be her best. Her exposition of her heroine's mind and development is a consummate job, and the novel does include some recognition of social problems in "the great meadow" of Kentucky; many readers, however, will feel that Roberts dwells too long on Ellen's early years, so that the first part of the novel drags.

JINGLING IN THE WIND

Roberts's other novels could all be called "novels of maladjustment," since they all show, in one manner or another, people who are out of touch with the land. Of these, *Jingling in the Wind*, which includes Roberts's only depiction of an urban setting, presents the most extreme case. There is much that Roberts finds artificial, even bizarre, in the city, such as neon advertisements that usurp the stars. In short, *Jingling in the Wind*, sometimes described as a satiric fantasy, is an outright attack on many trends of modern civilization. The loose plot concerns a couple of rainmakers, Jeremy and Tulip, who give up their unnatural profession in order to marry and have children. Usually considered Roberts's worst novel, *Jingling in the Wind* is interesting for its contribution to her grand theme.

MY HEART AND MY FLESH

Another novel of maladjustment is *My Heart and My Flesh*, centering on Theodosia Bell, a neurasthenic product of the wealthy landowning class. In this Faulknerian work exhibiting the results of southern decadence, the protagonist gradually loses everything that has insulated her from contact with the land—her wealth, her boyfriends, her home, her grandfather and sottish father, even her feelings of racial superiority (she discovers she

is a half sister to three mixed-race people in town). As a child, Theodosia is so out of place in the countryside that a pack of hounds attack her. As an adult, when disillusionment, poverty, and sickness have brought her down to earth, she moves in with the pack, even eats their food. Later she finds health and happiness by teaching in a country school, living in her pupils' homes, and marrying a farmer. Thus, the pattern of rebirth through contact with the land is perfectly illustrated by Theodosia.

HE SENT FORTH A RAVEN

Conversely, a negative example is provided by Stoner Drake, the monomaniacal old man in *He Sent Forth a Raven*. The title's biblical reference to Noah, who trusted in God, provides a lucid contrast to Drake's blasphemous behavior. When his second wife dies, Drake vows never to set foot on God's green earth again. His anger hardening into inflexible principle, he keeps his word, never venturing from the house and managing his farm from a rooftop observatory, summoning workers and family members with blasts on a hunting horn or conch shell. The blasts symbolize not only his pathetic defiance of God but also his alienation from other people and the land. To Drake, of course, they symbolize command, and in his house he is an absolute dictator.

Drake's rancorous behavior is self-punishing, but it also takes a toll on the people around him. For example, he prevents his daughter, Martha, from entertaining suitors. When one finally ventures a polite visit as a guest, Drake confronts him and Martha with loud, vile charges of fornication. The young man leaves, and Martha, thunderstruck, falls into fever and delirium, temporarily losing her hearing; when after some weeks it returns, the first things she hears are "the loud horn and the screaming of the swine." She thereafter reconciles herself to being a spinster and to banking the fires at night (so the house will not catch fire and her father burn up with it).

Standing in contrast to Drake is his granddaughter, Jocelle, the novel's heroine, who takes a lesson from her aunt's fate. Growing up in the house with Drake and Martha, Jocelle manages to live a relatively normal life because she is free to roam the fields, sometimes even beyond the range of the horn. Like all of Roberts's female protagonists, Jocelle does suffer her traumas, but she is strong enough to bounce back. For example, when Drake's nephew, Walter, rapes her, Drake renews his ridiculous vow, but Jocelle eventually recovers from her shock. At the end of the novel, she is happily married and a mother, her husband the manager of the farm, while Drake sits before the fireplace and hardens into brittle senility, unable to remember the reason for his vow.

Harold Branam

OTHER MAJOR WORKS

SHORT FICTION: *The Haunted Mirror*, 1932; *Not by Strange Gods*, 1941.

POETRY: *In the Great Steep's Garden*, 1915; *Under the Tree*, 1922, 1930; *Song in the Meadow*, 1940.

BIBLIOGRAPHY

Campbell, Harry Modean, and Ruel E. Foster. *Elizabeth Madox Roberts: American Novelist*. Norman: University of Oklahoma Press, 1956. A biographical and critical study containing analyses of Roberts's novels and short stories.

McDowell, Frederick P. W. *Elizabeth Madox Roberts*. New York: Twayne, 1963. A basic introduction to Roberts's life and work, featuring analyses of her novels and short stories. Includes a bibliography and an index.

Nicolaisen, Peter. "Rural Poverty and the Heroics of Farming: Elizabeth Madox Roberts's *The Time of Man* and Ellen Glasgow's *Barren Ground*." In *Reading Southern Poverty Between the Wars, 1918-1939*, edited by Richard Godden and Martin Crawford. Athens: University of Georgia Press, 2006. Collection of essays in which contributors maintain that many southern writers, social scientists, and activists who professed to be progressive actually upheld the traditional economic and social systems that maintained poverty. The essay on Roberts discusses how her novel, *The Time of Man*, fits the contributors' claims.

Perry, Carolyn, and Mary Louise Weaks, eds. *The History of Southern Women's Literature*. Baton Rouge: Louisiana State University Press, 2002. Roberts is one of the authors included in this examination of southern women writers. Part 3, "Renaissance in the South, 1900-1960," contains an essay on Roberts's work.

Rovit, Earl H. *Herald to Chaos: The Novels of Elizabeth Madox Roberts*. Lexington: University Press of Kentucky, 1960. Rovit provides a thorough analysis of Robert's style. He discusses Roberts's presentation of heroic characters engaged in epic struggles against the forces of nature, her critical neglect, and her role in American literature.

Simpson, Lewis P. "History and the Will of the Artist: Elizabeth Madox Roberts." In *The Fable of the Southern Writer*. Baton Rouge: Louisiana State University Press, 1994. This analysis of Roberts's work and her relationship to the South is one of eleven essays in Simpson's examination of southern writers. Includes a bibliography and an index.

_____. "The Sexuality of History." *Southern Review* 20 (October, 1984): 785-802. In this special issue of memoirs, reminiscences, and essays on Roberts, Simpson discusses her as a particularly modern writer whose struggle to repudiate the philosophy of idealism is the major theme of her work. He compares Roberts to William Faulkner in their awareness of the inwardness of history.

Spivey, Herman E. "The Mind and Creative Habits of Elizabeth Madox Roberts." In *All These To Teach*, edited by Robert A. Bryan, Alton C. Morris, A. A. Murphree, and Aubrey L. Williams. Gainesville: University of Florida Press, 1965. Spivey argues that although Roberts's achievements were greater than realized by her contemporaries, her handicaps as an artist were more than she was able to overcome. He claims that Roberts is too much concerned with people in general and too little with particular individuals, that there is not enough external action in her work, and that her unmastered technical experiments prevent reader understanding.

Tate, Linda. "Elizabeth Madox Roberts: A Bibliographical Essay." *Resources for American Literary Study* 18 (1992): 22-43. A summary and critique of previous criticism of Roberts's work. Tate argues that Roberts's role in the Southern Renaissance has not been sufficiently explored and claims that the highest untapped appeal of her work is feminist criticism.

_____. *A Southern Weave of Women: Fiction of the Contemporary South*. Athens: University of Georgia Press, 1994. This examination of southern women 's fiction published in the late twentieth century discusses Roberts's novels as background for the work of the later writers.

MARILYNNE ROBINSON

Born: Sandpoint, Idaho; November 26, 1943

PRINCIPAL LONG FICTION

Housekeeping, 1980
Gilead, 2004
Home, 2008

OTHER LITERARY FORMS

Although Marilynne Robinson's novels have been her most acclaimed works, her critical essays on topics ranging from environmental disaster to religion have been praised as valuable contributions to life and letters in the United States. Her book *The Death of Adam: Essays on Modern Thought* (1998) explores the contours of modern culture as its ideas have been shaped by thinkers as diverse as John Calvin, Charles Darwin, and Sigmund Freud. In an earlier book, *Mother Country* (1989), Robinson examines the significant physical and environmental damage caused by Sellafield, a nuclear reprocessing plant in Britain. In addition to writing fiction, Robinson frequently contributes essays and reviews to such periodicals as *The Paris Review*, *Harper's*, and *The New York Times Book Review*.

ACHIEVEMENTS

Many critics have called Marilynne Robinson a "writer's writer" for her elegant and hauntingly evocative use of language and for the spiritual force of her stories. Her first novel, *Housekeeping*, appeared to great critical acclaim in 1980, and writers from Walker Percy to Mary Gordon and Doris Lessing praised it for its richness and variety of tone, its delightful sentences, and its haunting dream of a story. *Housekeeping* was nominated for a Pulitzer Prize, and it won the Hemingway Foundation/PEN Award for best first novel for 1980 as well as the Richard and Hinda Rosenthal Award of the National Institute of Arts and Letters.

Although Robinson produced two books of nonfiction between her first and second novels, twenty-four years passed before she turned her pen to fiction again. In 1989, *Mother Country*, Robinson's nonfiction examination of the consequences of pollution at the British nuclear reprocessing plant Sellafield, was a finalist for the National Book Award. When *Gilead* appeared in 2004, Robinson's loyal cadre of readers gladly welcomed her return. Critics once again heaped praise on Robinson's writing, and the novel won the 2005 Pulitzer Prize for fiction as well as the 2004 National Book Critics Circle Award for Fiction. In 2008, her third novel, *Home*, was named a finalist for the National Book Award and the National Book Critics Circle Award for fiction.

BIOGRAPHY

The younger of two children, Marilynne Robinson was born on November 26, 1943, in Sandpoint, Idaho. As a child, Robinson moved around quite a bit in the northwestern United States, living in the towns of Sagle, Sandpoint, and Coolin and several smaller towns. In 1962, she graduated from Coeur d'Alene High School and then entered Pembroke College, the former women's college at Brown University, where she joined her brother, who was already a senior. Her college studies in religion and creative writing prepared the ground for her later novels, for religion plays a key role in all three of her novels.

After she graduated from Brown, Robinson taught for a year in France at the Université de Haute-Bretagne before returning to the United States to pursue graduate work in English at the University of Washington. She completed her Ph.D. with a dissertation on William Shakespeare in 1977, but she began writing her first novel, *Housekeeping*, while she was working on her dissertation. During graduate school she also married and began to raise a family. In 1989, she and her husband separated, leaving Robinson to raise her children alone.

Housekeeping was published to great acclaim in 1980, winning major awards and becoming an American classic almost instantly, yet twenty-four years passed before Robinson published her next novel, *Gilead*. During the years between novels, Robinson continued to write, producing two nonfiction books, *Mother Country* and *The Death of Adam*. During these years she also started teaching. Robinson has been a visiting professor at numerous universities, including the University of Kent and Amherst, and she has also taught in the University of Massachusetts M.F.A. Program for Poets and Writers and the New York State Writers' Program at Skidmore College. In 1991, Robinson became a member of the faculty at the University of Iowa's Writers' Workshop.

ANALYSIS

Like Willa Cather, Sarah Orne Jewett, and other novelists of the Midwest before her, Marilynne Robinson elegantly draws evocative settings in which her characters must cope with the loneliness and the isolation of their settings. Although her first novel, *Housekeeping*, is set in a little town in the Northwest, the two young girls at the novel's center must discover strategies either to embrace the forbidding loneliness of the glacial plain on which they live or to reject its haunting isolation and the ghostly memories that inhabit the town. Robinson effectively re-creates the social and physical challenges that life in often inhospitable environments can bring. Although her novels rarely focus on community, they do explore the ways in which individuals must navigate the rough waters of their lives in the larger world.

Many critics have called Robinson a feminist writer and have often spoken of her in the same breath with Toni Morrison and Margaret Atwood, among others. While Robinson's novels certainly feature lyrical prose, as do the works of these other writers, only *Housekeep-*

ing focuses on women and their role in society. That novel does ask questions about the nature of women and what it might be like to live in a society populated exclusively by women. The only men in the novel are either deceased or ineffectual, and the two young girls and the aunt with whom they live must decide how they want to define themselves as women. Do they define themselves in the light of men, dressing for them and becoming a part of their society, or do they define themselves by their tasks—"housekeeping," for example—and construct their own society apart from the world around them? Can they define themselves simply by the ways in which they construct their own community of women and the codes they enact to provide structure to that community? In the novels published since *Housekeeping*, however, Robinson has focused specifically on the lives of men who must come to terms with their harsh environments as well as their spiritual roles in their communities, in their families, and in their own lives.

Above all, Robinson's novels meditate on religious questions, and they are imbued with an almost mystical quality in which even the bleakest landscape or most mundane social situation is shot through with rays of transcendence and spirituality. Both *Gilead* and *Home* deal explicitly with a family of preachers and their attempts to understand their calling and the power of grace and mercy. Although *Housekeeping* does not feature religion in the same explicit fashion, it nevertheless raises questions about incarnation, revelation, grace, the nature of faith, and mystery.

HOUSEKEEPING

After their mother dies by driving her car off a cliff into a lake, Ruth and Lucille, the two young sisters at the center of *Housekeeping*, grow up in the family house under the guidance of a variety of women. Set in the small Far West town of Fingerbone, the novel revolves around these two young girls' coming-of-age in a town where everyone knows everyone else's business and where the glacial lake that borders the town has swallowed up both their

Marilynne Robinson. (AP/Wide World Photos)

grandfather and their mother.

After their mother dies, the girls first live in the family house with their grandmother, Mrs. Sylvia Foster. When she dies, two bumbling great-aunts, Lily and Nona Foster, take over responsibility for the girls. Since these women are never sure what to do with the children and never sure how to respond to their questions or their behavior, they soon flee, but not before they ask the girls' aunt, Sylvie Fisher, if she can come live with the girls. While Lily and Nona debate whether or not Sylvie, the prodigal daughter of Sylvia Foster, who has run away to get married and never looked back, will even show up, Ruth and Lucille try to take care of themselves and explore the town and the woods surrounding it. Sylvie Fisher does indeed show up one day, and Lily and Nona gladly flee from their child-rearing tasks.

The girls soon discover that Sylvie is an eccentric who lives by her own rules and in her own time. When the house floods, she simply moves the family to the second floor, visiting the first floor sometimes to grab a piece of coal for the stove. Although Sylvie appears to be committed to staying with the girls, the two sisters are constantly afraid that she will leave silently one night, never to return. Sylvie's odd behavior begins to drive a wedge between Ruth and Lucille, who had once been close-knit as they tried to navigate the choppy channels of a world full of loss. Eventually, through a number of incidents, Lucille decides to leave home and to live with one of her schoolteachers. She makes some new friends, goes shopping for clothes, and begins to fit in with her classmates at school. Ruth, on the other hand, becomes more and more like Sylvie. One night, the two of them row out onto the lake and spend the night there. The next morning they hop a freight train back into town. When the local sheriff appears at the door later that morning to try to remove Ruth from Sylvie's custody, Ruth decides in that moment that she prefers a life of transience with her aunt Sylvie to a settled life in Fingerbone. The novel's dramatic ending follows them to their own ends as they burn down the family house and vanish into the woods.

Several themes emerge in *Housekeeping* that appear in Robinson's later fiction as well. The novel emphasizes the nature of place. Fingerbone, a haunting skeletal name that symbolizes death as well as a pointer of new directions, is physically isolated, and its isolation is made even harsher by the periodic flooding of the glacial lake. This small town is not only the ancestral home where Ruth's and Lucille's identities are shaped by their family natures but also the place where they can choose to remain rooted or from which they can pull up their roots. In some ways, living in Fingerbone is destiny, for the town itself shapes the girls and their decisions.

Housekeeping also deals with the idea of grace. Eccentric as she is, Sylvie Fisher loves Ruth and Lucille as deeply as she might love her own children. She understands that love means allowing individuals freedom to find their own ways, to succeed or to fail in the choices they make. Although she expresses her love and grace in her own peculiar way, she provides the girls the freedom they need to decide for themselves which directions they will choose. The novel also deals with loss and survival, illustrating through Ruth's and Lucille's choices the ways in which individuals cope with loss.

The names of the characters in the novel are also symbolic. The Fosters, of course, are a foster family for the girls, enabling them and fostering a certain kind of attitude toward life. Sylvie Fisher operates differently. Like Jesus, she is a fisher of people who tries to get the girls to follow her and, like her, to develop their own strategies for coping with loss. She refuses to give them pat answers, preferring instead to let Ruth and Lucille do a bit of their own fishing for answers. Like her biblical counterpart, Ruth goes off into a strange country with her kinswoman in search of a new life. Finally, the opening of *Housekeeping*, in which the narrator proclaims that her name is Ruth, echoes that of Herman Melville's *Moby Dick* (1851), which begins, "Call me Ishmael." With such an opening, readers know quickly that they will soon find themselves on a journey with a character in search of herself.

GILEAD

Twenty-four years after the publication of *Housekeeping*, Robinson published a very different kind of novel in *Gilead*. The evocative and haunting prose of this work hones in on one central character and his struggles to come to terms with his past, his present, and his future. Set in the small midwestern town of Gilead, Iowa, the novel takes the form of a letter written in 1956 by seventy-seven-year-old pastor John Ames, who is seriously ill with angina and who feels death approaching, to his seven-year-old son. The letter provides a chronicle of the Ames family history as well as a theological meditation on living a life focused on forgiveness and grace.

Ames comes from a long line of preachers. In the story he relates, his grandfather, living in Maine in the mid-nineteenth century, has a vision of Christ in chains that drives him to move west to Kansas to preach against slavery. He eventually becomes a chaplain in the American Civil War and loses his right eye in battle, but he believes that his struggle in the war will help lead to freedom for the slaves. Ames's preacher father, an ardent pacifist, clashes often with his own father, the Civil War chaplain. Ames himself marries young, but his first wife dies in childbirth. For the next forty years, Ames lives in solitude, preaching on mundane topics such as baptism and confirmation. At sixty-seven, Ames remarries; his second wife is thirty years younger than he, and the young son to whom Ames is writing is their child.

Ames estimates that during his pastorate he must have preached enough sermons to fill 255 volumes. His most enduring sermon is one on World War I and the great influenza epidemic of the same time. In that sermon, he observes that the young men dying of influenza are escaping a far worse fate. He never preaches it, however, because he thinks that the only people it might reach are those opposed to the war already. During his forty years of solitude, his best friend, the Reverend Robert Boughton, has a son and names him John Ames Boughton. The boy, known as Jack, brings Ames little joy, however, for he is forever playing hurtful pranks on Ames. In his long letter to his own young son, however, Ames says that people can change, so we must be prepared to forgive them.

Gilead offers an extended theological meditation on the nature of forgiveness and the nature of grace. In the Bible, Gilead is a mountainous territory whose trees produce a soothing balm that the prophet Jeremiah compares to the healing power of God. In his letter to his young son, Ames offers his own balm as he strives to forgive young Jack Boughton for his prodigal and hurtful ways. The balm is meant not only for Jack but also for Ames and his son. Ames adopts Jack as his spiritual son and works to overcome any resentment he feels toward Jack for his profligate ways.

Much as she does in *Housekeeping*, in *Gilead* Robinson chronicles the struggles between children and their parents or their elders. In this case, Ames must come to terms with the conflicts between his father and grandfather as well as those between himself and Jack. By the end of the novel, Ames has accepted his coming death, and, in a breathtaking moment toward the end of the book, he graciously blesses Jack while the two are sitting on a bus-stop bench in the city.

HOME

In the sequel to *Gilead*, Robinson once again takes up questions of grace and forgiveness, redemption and hope. *Home* also involves two men who are struggling to reconcile themselves to each other. In *Home*, John Ames's closest friend, the Reverend Robert Boughton, is dying. His daughter Glory, the youngest of his eight children, has returned to Gilead to take care of her dying father. Soon, her prodigal brother, Jack, the spiritual son of John Ames, returns to Gilead as well. A miscreant, an alcoholic who has spent time in jail for various crimes, Jack is at once the black sheep of the family and Robert Boughton's most beloved child.

After being gone for twenty years, Jack arrives in Gilead seeking to be reconciled with his father; he forms a strong bond with his sister, Glory, and he seeks forgiveness and mercy from John Ames as he painfully confesses his old misdeeds and the ways he has hurt Ames. The novel follows the Boughton family members day by day as they try to overcome past failures and shortcomings and to come to terms with the reality of Robert's dying and their attempts to bond anew as a family. Glory patiently endures the barbs that her father and her brother throw at each other as they try to forge a new bond of love. Toward the end of the novel, Jack's son meanders into the house and his mother, Della, declares that her son thinks he wants to be a preacher. As the novel draws to a close, Glory reflects that she has been waiting a lifetime for this moment and declares that God works in mysterious and wonderful ways.

Home is a retelling of the prodigal son story from the New Testament. Robinson's story differs a little in that the older son is the prodigal while the younger child is the one who remains stable and close to home. In the Bible story (Luke 15:11-32), the younger son is the prodigal and the older feels betrayed by the father's love for the prodigal. Robinson demonstrates the great anguish that accompanies homecomings, especially in cases involving a coming death. The strongest themes here are redemption and reconciliation. No matter what misdeeds Jack has committed in the past, his father and his sister love him enough to be reconciled to him. He can be redeemed from his past life and start anew with those he has wronged because in their gracious love for him they open their arms wide and welcome him back into their family. As Glory declares at the end of the novel, the Lord is merciful and loving, and the future of this family opens into that love and mercy as Jack's son enters the ministry. In *Home*, Robinson once again shows the ways in which the mysteries of God enter the mundane and ordinary world of men and women.

Henry L. Carrigan, Jr.

OTHER MAJOR WORKS

NONFICTION: *Mother Country*, 1989; *The Death of Adam: Essays on Modern Thought*, 1998.

BIBLIOGRAPHY

Burke, William. "Border Crossings in Marilynne Robinson's *Housekeeping*." *Modern Fiction Studies* 37, no. 4 (Winter, 1991): 716-725. Explores the dramatic tension that arises from the manner in which various characters in Robinson's novel define themselves either by their rootedness to place or by their rootlessness.

Carver, Christine. "Nothing Left to Love: *Housekeeping* and Strange Freedoms." *American Literature* 68 (March, 1996): 111-137. Focuses on Robinson's treatment of the exhilarating yet mournful freedom that comes with loss.

Gernes, Sonia. "Transcendent Women: Uses of the Mystical in Margaret Atwood's *Cat's Eye* and Marilynne Robinson's *Housekeeping*." *Religion and Literature* 23 (1991): 143-165. Examines images of transcendence in the two novels, with particular focus on the ways in which the women in Robinson's novel forge spiritual bonds with one another and the world around them.

Greiner, Donald. "Revising the Paradigm: Female Bonding and the Transients of *Housekeeping*." In *Women Without Men: Female Bonding and the American Novel of the 1980's*. Columbia: University of South Carolina Press, 1993. Discusses how the main characters in *Housekeeping* devise ways of coping with loss and alienation.

Hubbard, Stacy Carson. "The Balm in *Gilead*." *Michigan Quarterly Review* 44, no. 3 (Summer, 2005): 541-544. Provides discussion of Robinson's novel *Gilead*, with an emphasis on the comfort and mercy that the protagonist, John Ames, offers his antagonist, Jack Boughton.

Leah, Gordon. "'A Person Can Change': Grace, Forgiveness, and Sonship in Marilynne Robinson's Novel *Gilead*." *Evangelical Quarterly* 80, no. 1 (2008): 53-58. Examination of *Gilead* focuses on the novel's central themes of forgiveness and mercy.

Robinson, Marilynne. "At Home with Marilynne Robinson." Interview by Claire Kirch. *Publishers Weekly*, July 14, 2008. Robinson discusses her novel *Home*, her writing habits, and her life of teaching at the Iowa Writers' Workshop.

ROMAIN ROLLAND

Born: Clamecy, France; January 29, 1866
Died: Vézelay, France; December 30, 1944
Also known as: Romain Edmé Paul-Émile Rolland

PRINCIPAL LONG FICTION

L'Adolescent, 1904
L'Aube, 1904
Le Matin, 1904
Jean-Christophe, 1904-1912 (*John-Christopher*, 1910-1913; better known as *Jean-Christophe*, 1913; includes the following 10 novels)
La Révolte, 1906-1907
Antoinette, 1908
La Foire sur la place, 1908
Dans la maison, 1909
Les Amies, 1910
Le Buisson ardent, 1911
La Nouvelle Journée, 1912
Colas Breugnon: Bonhomme vit encore!, 1919 (*Colas Breugnon*, 1919)
Clérambault: Histoire d'une conscience libre pendant la guerre, 1920 (*Clerambault: The Story of an Independent Spirit During the War*, 1921; initially serialized as *L'Un contre tous*, 1917 [incomplete version])
Pierre et Luce, 1920 (*Pierre and Luce*, 1922)
L'Âme enchantée, 1922-1933 (7 volumes; *The Soul Enchanted*, 1925-1934)

OTHER LITERARY FORMS

In addition to his novels, Romain Rolland (raw-LAHN) is known for his biographies, including *François Millet* (1902), which was published only in English; others include *Beethoven* (1903; English translation, 1907), *Michel-Ange* (1905; *Michelangelo*, 1915), *La Vie de Michel-Ange* (1906; *The Life of Michelangelo*, 1912), *Haendel* (1910; *Handel*, 1916), *Vie de Tolstoï* (1911; *Tolstoy*, 1911), and *Mahatma Gandhi* (1924; *Mahatma Gandhi: The Man Who Became One with the Universal Being*, 1924). Among his musicological works, *Goethe et Beethoven* (1927; *Goethe and Beethoven*, 1931) and the comprehensive work *Beethoven: Les Grandes*

Époques créatrices (1928-1945)—part of which was translated as *Beethoven the Creator* (1929)—are of general interest.

The genre that Rolland embraced initially, without much recognition, was drama. He later grouped several of his plays into cycles. These are *Les Tragédies de la foi* (1913), consisting of his first published play, *Saint Louis* (1897)—together with *Aërt* (1898) and *Le Triomphe de la raison* (1899)—and the cycle *Théâtre de la révolution* (1909), originally consisting of *Les Loups* (pb. 1898; *The Wolves*, 1937), *Danton* (pr., pb. 1900; English translation, 1918), and *Le Quatorze Juillet* (pr., pb. 1902; *The Fourteenth of July*, 1918), and later including *Le Jeu de l'amour et de la mort* (pb. 1925; *The Game of Love and Death*, 1926), *Pâques fleuries* (pb. 1926; *Palm Sunday*, 1928), *Les Léonides* (pb. 1928; English translation, 1929), and *Robespierre* (pb. 1939). Editions that appeared during Rolland's lifetime show different or incomplete groupings.

Among Rolland's other important writings for and about the theater are the satire *Liluli* (pb. 1919; English translation, 1920) and *Le Théâtre du peuple: Essai d'esthétique d'un théâtre nouveau* (1903; *The People's Theater*, 1918). Of Rolland's extensive correspondence, thirty volumes have been published in *Cahiers Romain Rolland* (1948-1996). Autobiographical works and published diaries include *Le Voyage intérieur* (1942; *The Journey Within*, 1947) and *L'Inde: Journal 1915-1943* (1949), as well as *Journal des années de guerre, 1914-1919* (1952). Rolland commanded international attention with his political, polemical, and pacifist writings. Among them are *Au-dessus de la mêlée* (1915; *Above the Battle*, 1916) and *Les Précurseurs* (1919; *The Forerunners*, 1920), which reappeared together in *L'Esprit libre* (1953). This collection of essays and open letters is essential for an understanding of Rolland's position within the post-World War I European intellectual elite.

ACHIEVEMENTS

Romain Rolland remained a relatively obscure figure until he was almost fifty years old. His education prepared him for a career in teaching the history of art and music, and he was on the faculty of the École Normale Supérieure and the Sorbonne until 1912 while maintaining a correspondence with various European intellectuals. Although Rolland had the support of some devoted friends, notably his former teacher, Gabriel Monod, and the aged German writer Malvida von Meysenbug, his early literary endeavors met with little success. In 1903, Charles-Pierre Péguy, his friend from the École Normale Supérieure with whom he shared both idealism and literary talent, published Rolland's work in his *Cahiers de la Quinzaine*, which had a relatively small but international intellectual readership. In this periodical, the ten volumes of Rolland's novel *Jean-Christophe* appeared in segments dating from February 2, 1904, to October 20, 1912. These publications proved to be the foundation of his fame. In 1905, Rolland received the Vie Heureuse prize; in 1909, the award of the Légion d'Honneur; in 1913, the Grand Prix de la Littérature of the French Academy; and in 1915, the Nobel Prize in Literature.

The basis of Rolland's philosophy was the achievement of a Pan-European unity and the social and intellectual emancipation of the masses through the efforts of an international elite—a goal that he perceived as attainable. His hopes were temporarily shattered by the outbreak of World War I and the ensuing spirit of nationalism and patriotism, which created political chasms between former friends. Some of Rolland's most polemical writings date from that period. He had, however, attained a faithful international following among the world's intellectual leaders. Among them were Albert Einstein, Maxim Gorky, Sigmund Freud, Richard Strauss, Ernst Bloch, and many others who honored him with contributions to the volume *Liber amicorum* (1926) for his sixtieth birthday. Although he favored the revolution in Russia, he decried the ensuing bloodshed that established the Communist regime. True progress, he claimed, could not be achieved by unprincipled means.

Rolland then turned to the inspiration of Mahatma Gandhi's movement of passive resistance, which sought political freedom and self-government by nonviolent means. Rolland's vision of a Pan-European unity broadened to include an international humanist movement of global extent and the establishment of a European Shantiniketan, an international House of Friendship and Archives for pertinent publications of global interest and

origin. He became disenchanted with the Indians when he perceived their lack of a sense of urgency. The rise of National Socialism; his marriage to a Russian woman, Marie Koudachev, in 1934; and a 1935 trip to the Soviet Union, where he visited Gorky, convinced him, in the face of the seeming impotence of the European alliance he had supported, that the international Communist movement offered the only alternative to Nazi Germany's power politics. He presided in absentia over the International Congress Against War and Fascism held in Amsterdam in 1932, refused the Goethe Prize offered him by Germany in 1933, and commenced writing polemical essays and open letters against fascist propaganda in Germany and Italy. He witnessed the German invasion of France but died before the end of World War II.

While Rolland has been variously called a pacifist, an activist, a communist, an idealist, a humanist, a nationalist, a mystic, and a rationalist, he was, in effect, all of these. He is recognized for his undaunted attempts to promote the cause of peace in war-torn Europe, for his desire to unite the world's intellectual elite to achieve these goals, for his belief in the ultimate prevalence of reason, and for his fiction, which contains a didactic base for the dissemination of these beliefs.

BIOGRAPHY

Romain Rolland was born Romain Edmé Paul-Émile Rolland in Clamecy (Nièvre), France, on January 29, 1866. His father, Émile, a fourth-generation notary, and his deeply religious and musically talented mother, Antoinette-Marie (née Courot), were financially secure and respected in the Burgundian borderland in which their families had lived since before the Revolution. One of his lasting early memories was the death of his younger sister, Madeleine, while the family was vacationing at Arcachon, near Bordeaux. The experience left the then five-year-old Rolland with a fear of death and a preoccupation with respiratory ailments. In later life, he included in his works images of suffocation, such as in the opening passages of *Beethoven*, and the frailty of his health, with which he struggled to the end of his life, contained a strong neurotic element.

To facilitate Rolland's schooling, the family moved to Paris in the fall of 1880. The impression he gained of the city, described in his *Mémoires et fragments du journal* (1956), is that of an unwholesome, immoral, feverish, sickening, godless abyss, breathing death and decay. The coarseness of literature, vice on the streets, and the sexual brutality expressed by the young imbued him with a belief that this decadence foreshadowed the death of Western civilization, a theme that dominates the fifth (*La Foire sur la place*) and tenth (*La Nouvelle Journée*) volumes of his novel *Jean-Christophe*. After his years at the *lycée*, where he became friends with Paul Claudel and André Suarès, he studied art and music at the École Normale Supérieure from 1886 to 1889. The following two years he spent in Rome on an appointment to the École Française. While studying feverishly, he also fell passionately in love with a young woman, Sofia Guerrieri-Gonzaga; found a friend and confidant in the aged German writer Malvida von Meysenbug, who had enjoyed the friendship of Friedrich Nietzsche and Richard Wagner; and wrote his first plays: "Empédocle"

Romain Rolland. (© The Nobel Foundation)

(1890), which remained a fragment, and "Orsino" (1890), which was finished but not published. The two years in Rome were to be among the happiest of his life.

After his return to Paris, Rolland married Clotilde Bréal, daughter of a philology professor, on October 31, 1892. This marriage lasted until May, 1901. During the years from 1892 to 1900, he wrote numerous plays that met with minimal success. Among them are *Les Baglioni* and *Niobé* (both written in 1892), *Caligula* (wr. 1893), *Le Siège de Mantoue* (wr. 1894), and *Savonarole* and *Jeanne de Pienne* (both written in 1896). His first published play was *Saint Louis* (pb. 1897), and on May 3 and May 18, 1898, respectively, his *Aërt* and *The Wolves* were staged. In the meantime, he had also finished his dissertation in 1895 and had begun teaching the history of art at the École Normale Supérieure. Rolland's dramatic work contains a strong didactic element. Frequently based on historical figures or events, the protagonists often show a moral fortitude and spiritual strength that permits them to be emotionally "victorious" even in defeat. After outlining his ideas for a revitalization of the theater in *Le Théâtre du peuple*, he abandoned the dramatic genre for some time and turned to the production of novels and biographies.

The monumental work *Jean-Christophe*, its ten volumes written over a period of eight years, established Rolland as a writer. He wrote for and was acknowledged by an intellectual elite across Europe and beyond, among whom he developed a faithful following of friends. They were keenly aware of the political unrest that Rolland describes at the end of the novel as a smoldering fire ready to break into a full-fledged conflagration. After an automobile accident in October, 1910, which nearly killed him, he took two years' leave of absence from the Sorbonne, where he had been teaching since November, 1904, and he resigned altogether in 1912. Despite his political forebodings, news of the outbreak of World War I came as a surprise to him while he was vacationing with an American, Helena Van Brugh De Kay, in Switzerland. After the assassination of the Austrian archduke Ferdinand, he decided to remain in this political refuge. From 1914 to 1915, he worked at the Agence Internationale des Prisonniers de Guerre. His political essays became increasingly scathing in their denunciation of the war and in their call for reason among the warring nations. His satire *Liluli*, unmasking the treachery of "illusion," had its conception in the early war years. In the spring of 1919, he wrote "Déclaration de l'indépendance de l'esprit," in which he blamed the intellectual elite for succumbing to petty nationalism and political party interests.

This led to a controversy with Henri Barbusse, who denounced what he called Rollandism in *Light* (1919). Rolland, in an open letter to Barbusse in *L'Art libre*, published in January, 1922, harshly denounced the doctrine of neo-Marxist communism. By then, Rolland was an internationally known figure, had received several important awards for his work (including the Nobel Prize), and, after a brief return to France shortly before the death of his mother in 1919, had moved permanently to Switzerland; he established himself, his father, and his sister in the Villa Olga in Villeneuve in 1922. His three shorter novels, *Colas Breugnon*, *Clerambault*, and *Pierre and Luce*, were followed here by another monumental novel divided into four books published in six volumes. *The Soul Enchanted*, published between 1922 and 1933, is feminist in its thrust and criticizes established social structures and concepts.

Having established contact with the Indian liberation movement, Rolland wrote Gandhi's biography and received a visit in June, 1926, from the Indian writer Ribindranath Tagore. Shortly after Gandhi visited Rolland in December, 1931, Rolland became disenchanted with the Indian philosophy. Although he was by then an old man, he was pervaded by a sense of urgency to combat the new global confrontation that he perceived to be gathering force. It was at this point that he turned to communism's proclaimed international peace movement as an alternative to fascism. In 1932, he accepted the presidency of the International Congress Against War and Fascism and became an honorary member of Leningrad's Academy of Sciences. Marie Koudachev, daughter of a Russian father and a French mother, became Rolland's second wife in the summer of 1934. A year later, he visited the Soviet Union and Gorky, returning convinced that the Russian Revolution had been a good thing.

Rolland continued his polemics against the National Socialist regime and against Benito Mussolini at every level. In 1938, he moved to Vézelay, only a short distance from his birthplace, and took up work, once more, on a play about the Revolution (*Robespierre*), on his *Mémoires et fragments du journal* (published unfinished, after his death), and on his last biography, *Péguy*. He also worked on the final volumes of *Beethoven: Les Grandes Époques créatrices*. Shortly after the publication of the autobiographical work *The Journey Within*, he became seriously ill and had three "visions" of a religious nature. Although he recovered sufficiently to continue working, his health remained precariously poor until his death on December 30, 1944.

ANALYSIS

The novel with which Romain Rolland established his fame, a work translated into numerous languages, was *Jean-Christophe*. Its inception dates at least to 1890—to the years in Rome and the friendship with Malvida von Meysenbug. She had, he insisted, "created" him, and he honored her memory in two of the novel's characters. With her, he also shared a veneration of Beethoven, on whom, according to Rolland, the protagonist is modeled. The hero, a great German musician, is forced by circumstance to live outside Germany in Paris, Italy, and Switzerland, and his experiences and perspectives are recounted and analyzed.

JEAN-CHRISTOPHE

While Romain Rolland admits that the protagonist is not the historical Beethoven but a Beethoven of Rolland's own times, he also refers to the novel as the "history of my soul transposed into one greater than I." It is true that the parallels between Beethoven and Jean-Christophe are quickly exhausted and that many of Jean-Christophe's experiences and characteristics have their foundation in those of Rolland himself. Just as the novel's hero crosses the Rhine River, transcending in a symbolic gesture the boundaries between Germany and France, so Rolland attempted to overcome geographical and political barriers by uniting the intellectual elite of Europe's nations. The fifth book of *Jean-Christophe*, *La Foire sur la place*, not only shows Rolland's talents of critical evaluation but also is strongly reminiscent of his initial impression of Paris. Jean-Christophe finds the cultural life, particularly the world of theater and music, superficial and governed by the principles of economics; its representatives are without idealism, talent, or proficiency and merely court fame and money. Above the noise and the luxury, there is an all-pervasive smell of death and decay.

This, however, is only one side of France. Jean-Christophe finds the "real" France in his encounter with the "real" artist Olivier and his sister, Antoinette. The distinction between what is the apparent and what is the true face of a nation is evident in his communication with European intellectuals from his early correspondence into the times of war: Germans per se are not the enemies of France; rather, the enemies are the nationalistic and corrupt elements in the German political hierarchy. The title of the fourth book, *La Révolte*, could accurately describe the action of the first nine. Jean-Christophe's mystical experience in book 9, *Le Buisson ardent*, where he claims defeat but is strengthened and encouraged by an indefinable but possibly divine being, is the upbeat prelude to the prophetic tenth book, *La Nouvelle Journée*. Conflict is eternal; thus, the river's mysterious voices echo Jean-Christophe's hope of resurrection in the death scene and praise the "divine union" of love and hate, life and death.

Sigmund Freud, whom Rolland visited in Vienna in 1924, was intrigued by the water symbolism Rolland used in many of his works. In Rolland's personal symbolism, the river and the ocean are not merely conventional figures for the passage of life or the venture into eternity and death; they express the origin of religious energy. Others of the four elements of ancient philosophy (earth, air, fire, water) are also used frequently for dramatic value and symbolic interest. The storm or thunderstorm reveals to Jean-Christophe the nature of God in the third book, *L'Adolescent*, but it is an equally important and powerful motif in *Beethoven*, *The Life of Michelangelo*, and *Tolstoy*. Fire in the forest becomes a symbol in the tenth book of *Jean-Christophe* for the political chaos and destruction threatening Europe from all sides. Mystical experiences and visions clarify the path the protagonist is to take, as Rolland himself was guided by such phenomena. Finally, the motif of conflict and strife—central to *Jean-Christophe*—is apparent in almost every other work by Rolland. Rolland's protagonists are characteristically vanquished victors, suffering martyrs with a mission. Whether they preach the gospel of religious conviction or belief in that primal creative

power many associate with God (*Saint Louis*, *Jean-Christophe*), the power of art (*Beethoven*, *The Life of Michelangelo*), or the doctrines of freedom, justice, and peace (*The Soul Enchanted*, *Clerambault*, *Pierre and Luce*), Rolland's heroes are aggressive spirits whose intellectual stamina overcomes their physical frailty. They single-handedly lead the fight against the world's iniquity and broadcast their message with the example of their death. To that extent, much of Rolland's fiction is didactic.

COLAS BREUGNON

A novel of a somewhat different character is *Colas Breugnon*. Revisiting his birthplace, Clamecy, Rolland was inspired in April, 1913, to sketch the robust, merry, occasionally malicious, always talkative people of his ancestral town. The novel was finished before the war but not published until after it. Perhaps because of its humorous style and the colorful and intriguing depiction of life in the provinces, *Colas Breugnon* is one of Rolland's most popular novels. Besides personifying the vitality and courage inherent in the local population, the character Colas Breugnon portrays some of the more somber aspects of existence.

Rebuilding from the ravages of war, marrying a woman other than the one he loved, rearing sons with whom he is not compatible, protecting life and property from marauding soldiers, the carpenter grapples with crises and disappointments without losing his innate sense of humor. Rolland cannot resist adding a sprinkling of metaphysics in the guise of Breugnon's jovial philosophy: Every person, Breugnon declares, has twenty different persons within him, and thus a single god is insufficient. He believes in many gods, pagan and Christian, and within him they "all get along together very well, each with his job and his home."

CLERAMBAULT

Clerambault, published originally in 1917 in a serialized version under the title *L'Un contre tous*, appeared three years later in book form. Toward the end of 1916, Rolland spoke of his own "liberation" from the dominance of collective passions and the mysticism evident in *Jean-Christophe*, and of the subsequent maturation of his critical faculties.

Clerambault, a member of the French middle class and an intellectual, undergoes a similar change in his emancipation from and criticism of the fanatic nationalism and anti-German hysteria during World War I. Initially, Clerambault questions the fervor of his son, Maxime, who perceives in the outbreak of war the rebirth of the Revolution: "Are you quite certain?" he asks him. His own patriotism is inflamed, however, while Maxime experiences a change of heart when confronted with the horrors of war at the front. When Maxime briefly returns home on furlough, Clerambault reads to his son hymns and marching songs that he has composed, expecting Maxime's approval. "Are you quite certain, father?" is Maxime's unspoken reaction, and he returns to the front and his death.

When Clerambault recognizes that war is no solution to international conflict and that the mass hysteria fanned by fanatic patriots merely plays into the hands of unscrupulous politicians, he courageously voices his opinion and, like Rolland himself, is branded as a traitor and pacifist. Like the Socialist leader Jean Jaurès, Clerambault is assassinated for his convictions. Rolland goes so far as to liken his protagonist to an apostle of Christ, whose agony reaches "the ends of the earth." The novel is a highly tendentious expression of Rolland's pacifism. Its theme is aptly stated in the introductory passage: Humanity is not served by those who betray their conscience, their intelligence, and their integrity in order to conform, but by those who oppose the misuse of power and rebel against an unjust authority, even if it leads to conflict with the majority. *Clerambault* and its successor, *Pierre and Luce*, written under the vivid impressions left by World War I, were superseded by another monumental novel published in six volumes, *The Soul Enchanted*.

THE SOUL ENCHANTED

The Soul Enchanted breathes the spirit of a new age of progress, hope, and emancipation. Like *Jean-Christophe*, it traces the emotional development of the protagonist through the battles of a lifetime; as in the earlier novel, the passage of time is symbolically connected to the image of the river—in conjunction with historical events, in Annette Rivière's name, and in the progressive intellectual and material emancipation she personifies, which Rolland perceived as a social phenomenon during his lifetime. Unlike *Jean-Christophe*, *The Soul Enchanted* has a female protagonist, renders a view of

life's difficulties from the woman's perspective, and is frequently feminist in its approach. In a sense, Rolland's expressed desire, voiced as late as 1913, that he often "would have liked to be a woman," was fulfilled through the execution of this novel. His portrayal of Annette shows his penetrating insight into the social conditioning affecting women's self-perception, role modeling, and heterosexual relationships, as well as the political and materialistic consequences of these behavior patterns. Rarely has a male author so accurately portrayed woman on this dual level: her development in the context of external (social and material) influences, and in relation to her intellectual, emotional, and moral life. Annette is a woman of courage, strength, and motherliness who exhibits at the same time the instincts of a creature of nature.

Annette is the daughter of a Parisian architect. She is intelligent, educated, self-assured, and financially independent. Two occurrences drastically change the course of her future: She breaks her engagement to a promising young man of a wealthy family because she perceives that to be his wife means complete subordination to the point of self-abnegation, and she persists in her refusal to marry him even after she finds herself pregnant; after the death of her father, she loses her money through the unfortunate speculations of the curator. Annette's situation is considerably more traumatic than that of a lower-class girl in similar circumstances, for she has not been reared to compete for her daily bread in a world where hunger, poverty, illness, and unemployment are constant companions. Ostracized by the members of her social class because of her "immoral conduct" (she gives birth to a son and decides to rear him alone) and lacking marketable skills to earn a living, Annette experiences the full force of discrimination and prejudice against independent women. The novel follows Annette through the early stages of her new life, the building of a career, the joys and tribulations of motherhood, and the relative serenity of her mature years.

Rolland's purpose is not solely the depiction of the struggle for emancipation of France's women, although some sententious proclamations in the text certainly promote this cause. Male characters such as Philippe Villard are also engaged in a bitter struggle for survival. Rolland's protagonist is female because the difficulties encountered by the lower classes in general in a struggle for basic freedoms, rights, and equality are much more pronounced in that gender. Women, Rolland contends, are the last segment of the population still enslaved in the twentieth century. They have not yet recognized the advantage that lies in their numbers, they have not yet learned to organize their struggle on the model of communism, and they are still fighting the primitive war on a one-to-one basis: not a struggle against fate or nature or the ruling class, but a war of worker against worker for the daily meager subsistence. The novel proclaims the need for a concerted effort in the manner of a class struggle to bring about change and the dawning of a new day of social equality.

The Soul Enchanted shows conflict as a necessary part of life, for it builds strength of character and is the foundation of great societies. Thus, Rolland returned in his mature years to an intellectually refined version of his earlier idealism, stripped of any religious overtones: "Peace is not the absence of war," he notes in *The Soul Enchanted*. "It is virtue born of the powers of the spirit."

Helene M. Kastinger Riley

OTHER MAJOR WORKS

PLAYS: *Saint Louis*, pb. 1897; *Aërt*, pr., pb. 1898; *Les Loups*, pb. 1898 (*The Wolves*, 1937); *Le Triomphe de la raison*, pr. 1899; *Danton*, pr., pb. 1900 (English translation, 1918); *Le Quatorze Juillet*, pr., pb. 1902 (*The Fourteenth of July*, 1918); *Le Temps viendra*, pb. 1903; *La Montespan*, pb. 1904 (*The Montespan*, 1923); *Théâtre de la révolution*, 1909 (includes *Les Loups*, *Danton*, and *Le Quatorze Juillet*); *Les Tragédies de la foi*, 1913 (includes *Saint Louis*, *Aërt*, and *Le Triomphe de la raison*); *Liluli*, pb. 1919 (English translation, 1920); *Le Jeu de l'amour et de la mort*, pb. 1925 (*The Game of Love and Death*, 1926); *Pâques fleuries*, pb. 1926 (*Palm Sunday*, 1928); *Les Léonides*, pb. 1928 (English translation, 1929); *Robespierre*, pb. 1939.

NONFICTION: *François Millet*, 1902 (published only in English); *Beethoven*, 1903 (English translation, 1907); *Le Théâtre du peuple: Essai d'esthétique d'un théâtre nouveau*, 1903 (*The People's Theater*, 1918); *Michel-Ange*, 1905 (*Michelangelo*, 1915); *La Vie de Michel-Ange*, 1906 (*The Life of Michelangelo*, 1912); *Musiciens d'aujourd'hui*, 1908 (*Musicians of To-day*, 1914); *Musiciens d'autrefois*, 1908 (*Some Musicians of Former Days*, 1915); *Haendel*, 1910 (*Handel*, 1916); *Vie de Tolstoï*, 1911 (*Tolstoy*, 1911); *Au-dessus de la mêlée*, 1915 (*Above the Battle*, 1916); *Les Précurseurs*, 1919 (*The Forerunners*, 1920); *Mahatma Gandhi*, 1924 (*Mahatma Gandhi: The Man Who Became One with the Universal Being*, 1924); *Goethe et Beethoven*, 1927 (*Goethe and Beethoven*, 1931); *Beethoven: Les Grandes Époques créatrices*, 1928-1945 (partial translation *Beethoven the Creator*, 1929); *Essai sur la mystique et l'action de l'Inde vivante*, 1929-1930 (*Prophets of the New India*, 1930; includes *La Vie de Ramakrishna*, 1929 [*Ramakrishna*]); *La Vie de Vivekananda et l'Évangile universel*, 1930 (*Vivekananda*); *Empédocle d'Agrigente, suivi de l'éclair de Spinoza*, 1931; *Quinze ans de combat, 1919-1934*, 1935 (*I Will Not Rest*, 1936); *Compagnons de route, essais littéraires*, 1936; *Le Voyage intérieur*, 1942 (*The Journey Within*, 1947); *Péguy*, 1944 (2 volumes); *L'Inde: Journal 1915-1943*, 1949; *Journal des années de guerre, 1914-1919*, 1952; *L'Esprit libre*, 1953 (includes *Au-dessus de la mêlée* and *Les Précurseurs*); *Mémoires et fragments du journal*, 1956.

MISCELLANEOUS: *Cahiers Romain Rolland*, 1948-1996 (30 volumes).

BIBLIOGRAPHY

Fisher, David James. *Romain Rolland and the Politics of Intellectual Engagement*. 1988. Rev. ed. New Brunswick, N.J.: Transaction Books, 2004. Divided into the following sections: Rolland's ambiguous position in the 1920's, his involvement in left-wing politics in the 1930's, and a concluding chapter on "pessimism of the intelligence, optimism of the will." This revised edition contains a new introduction by Fisher. Includes detailed notes and a bibliography.

Francis, R. A. *Romain Rolland*. Oxford, England: Berg, 1999. A study of Rolland's life and the influences on his art. Francis analyzes all of Rolland's works to chart the development of his thought. Includes a bibliography and an index.

Gossman, Lionel. "Portrait of a City from Romain Rolland's *Jean-Christophe*." In *Basel in the Age of Burckhardt: A Study in Unseasonable Ideas*. Chicago: University of Chicago Press, 2000. Gossman's study of the intellectual climate in nineteenth century Basel, Switzerland, includes a brief discussion of how Rolland depicted the city-state in his novel *Jean-Christophe*.

March, Harold. *Romain Rolland*. New York: Twayne, 1971. An introductory study, with chapters largely built around the places where Rolland lived and worked. Includes a chronology, notes, and a bibliography.

Parsons, William B. *The Enigma of the Oceanic Feeling: Revisioning the Psychoanalytic Theory of Mysticism*. New York: Oxford University Press, 1999. Explores the psychoanalytic theory of mysticism as conceived by Rolland and Sigmund Freud. Rolland thought that mysticism was an "oceanic feeling," and he and Freud discussed this concept in their correspondence. Parsons analyzes their letters and examines other correspondence and texts by Rolland to discuss the writer's personal sense of mysticism.

Starr, William Thomas. *Romain Rolland: One Against All—A Biography*. The Hague, the Netherlands: Mouton, 1971. Starr provides a study of Rolland based on his letters, his other writings, and the impressions of others, arguing that these strands cannot be separated in discussing the writer. Includes a chronology and an index.

Zweig, Stefan. *Romain Rolland: The Man and His Work*. New York: Thomas Seltzer, 1921. Zweig, a veteran biographer, provides a comprehensive, lively account, divided into sections on biography, Rolland's early work as a dramatist, the heroic biographies, and *Jean Christophe*, among others. The book captures the complexity of the public intellectual, political activist, and major literary figure, although Zweig, a friend of Rolland, tends to eulogize his subject.

JULES ROMAINS

Born: Saint-Julien-Chapteuil, France; August 26, 1885

Died: Paris, France; August 14, 1972

Also known as: Louis-Henri-Jean Farigoule

PRINCIPAL LONG FICTION

Mort de quelqu'un, 1911 (*Death of a Nobody*, 1914)

Les Copains, 1913 (*The Boys in the Back Room*, 1937)

Sur les quais de la Villette, 1914 (reprinted as *Le Vin blanc de la Villette*, 1923)

Psyché, 1922-1929 (*The Body's Rapture*, 1933; includes *Lucienne*, 1922 [*Lucienne's Story*]; *Le Dieu des corps*, 1928 [*The Body's Rapture*]; *Quand le navire . . .* , 1929 [*Love's Questing*])

Les Hommes de bonne volonté, 1932-1946 (*Men of Good Will*, 1933-1946; includes *Le 6 Octobre*, 1932 [*The Sixth of October*, 1933];

Crime de Quinette, 1932 [*Quinette's Crime*, 1933]; *Les Amours enfantines*, 1932 [*Children's Loves*, 1934]; *Éros de Paris*, 1932 [*Eros in Paris*, 1934]; *Les Superbes*, 1933 [*The Proud*, 1934]; *Les Humbles*, 1933 [*The Meek*, 1934]; *Recherche d'une église*, 1934 [*The Lonely*, 1935]; *Province*, 1934 [*Provincial Interlude*, 1935]; *Montée des perils*, 1935 [*Flood Warning*, 1936]; *Les Pouvoirs*, 1935 [*The Powers That Be*, 1936]; *Recours à l'abîme*, 1936 [*To the Gutter*, 1937]; *Les Créateurs*, 1936 [*To the Stars*, 1937]; *Mission à Rome*, 1937 [*Mission to Rome*, 1938]; *Le Drapeau noir*, 1937 [*The Black Flag*, 1938]; *Prélude à Verdun*, 1938 [*The Prelude*, 1939]; *Verdun*, 1938 [*The Battle*, 1939]; *Vorge contre Quinette*, 1939 [*Vorge Against Quinette*, 1941]; *La Douceur de la vie*, 1939 [*The Sweets of Life*, 1941]; *Cette grand lueur à l'Est*, 1941 [*Promise of*

Dawn, 1942]; *Le Monde est ton aventure*,
1941 [*The World Is Your Adventure*, 1942];
Journées dans la montagne, 1942 [*Mountain
Days*, 1944]; *Les Travaux et les joies*, 1943
[*Work and Play*, 1944]; *Naissance de la
bande*, 1944 [*The Gathering of the Ganges*,
1945]; *Comparutions*, 1944 [*Offered in
Evidence*, 1945]; *Le Tapis magique*, 1946
[*The Magic Carpet*, 1946]; *Françoise*, 1946
[English translation, 1946]; *Le 7 Octobre*,
1946 [*The Seventh of October*, 1946])
Le Moulin et l'hospice, 1949
Le Fils de Jerphanion, 1956
Une Femme singulière, 1957 (*The Adventuress*,
1958)
Le Besoin de voir clair, 1958
Mémoires de Madame Chauverel, 1959-1960
Un Grand Honnête Homme, 1961

OTHER LITERARY FORMS

Jules Romains (ROH-man) began his literary career
with poetry: His first published work was *L'Âme des
hommes* (1904; the soul of men). *La Vie unanime* (1908;
the unanimist life), his most popular collection of poems,
is written in the unanimist vision, the theory that those
principles unifying humanity take precedence over individual differences in literary representation. *Un Être en
marche* (1910; a being in march) takes as its theme a
walk in Paris. *Odes et prières* (1913; odes and prayers) is
Romains's least unanimist volume of poetry. *Le Voyage
des amants* (1920; the lovers' voyage) is an extended
poem to his first wife, Gabrielle. *Europe* (1916) and *Ode
Génoise* (1925) are on the theme of war. *Chants des dix
années* (1928; songs of ten years) is a recapitulation of
earlier poems with some new additions. *L'Homme blanc*
(1937; the white man) is Romains's most ambitious poetic project, a kind of *La Légende des siècles* (1859-
1883; a five-volume work by Victor Hugo). *Pierres
levées* (1957; lifted stones), written during World War II,
returns to the theme of war. *Choix de poèmes* (1948; selection of poems) and *Maisons* (1953; homes) conclude
Romains's poetic works. Although most of his poetry
has not been translated into English, Romains is a respected poet in the French literary tradition.

Romains gained his fame through the theater. He

began his drama career in 1911 with the production and
publication of *L'Armée dans la ville* (the army in the
city) and continued it with one of his best plays,
Cromedeyre-le-Vieil, written between 1911 and 1918.
This verse play, set in the Velay, was produced by
Jacques Copeau in 1920 and published the same year.
Another dramatic work, *Donogoo-Tonka: Ou, Les Miracles de la science* (pb. 1920; *Donogoo*, 1937) and performed at the Théâtre Pigalle in 1930, is "a heroic comic
epic of modern publicity." The play, first conceived as a
film, was made into a film in 1936 (*Donogoo Tonka*,
with Reinhold Schünzel). Published in 1921 was the
play *M. Le Trouhadec saisi par la débauche* (Monsieur
de Trouhadec seized by debauchery), which was followed by his greatest success, *Knock: Ou, Le Triomphe
de la médecine* (pr. 1923; *Dr. Knock*, 1925), produced by
Louis Jouvet. *Amédée et les messieurs en rang* (pr. 1923;
Six Gentlemen in a Row, 1927) and *La Scintillante* (pr.
1924; *The Peach*, 1933) were written as companion
pieces to *Dr. Knock*. *Le Mariage de Le Trouhadec* (pr.,
pb. 1925) and *Boën: Ou, La Possession des biens* (pr.
1930) were failures on the stage; *Le Dictateur* (pr., pb.
1926; wr. 1911-1925) was a partial success. *Volpone* (pr.
1928) is a French version of Stefan Zweig's adaptation
of Ben Jonson's *Volpone: Or, The Fox* (1605-1606). *Le
Roi masqué* (pr. 1931; the masked king) is a lighthearted
boulevard farce. After writing this play, Romains abandoned the theater for a decade, thereafter writing only
Grâce encore pour la terre (pr., pb. 1941), published
in New York but never performed in France; *L'An mil*
(pr., pb. 1947; the year 1000), written in Mexico; and
Barbazouk (pr., pb. 1963; wr. 1956), also written in
Mexico and performed only in Germany. With the exception of *Dr. Knock*, few of these plays are available in
translation.

Romains also wrote several short stories. *Le Bourg
régénéré* (1906; the regenerated village) inaugurated his
unanimist vision in prose. *Nomentanus le réfugié* (1943)
and *Bertrand de Ganges* (1944) are popular stories on a
medieval theme. *Violations de frontières* (1951; *Tussles
with Time*, 1952) and *Portraits d'inconnus* (1962), a series of unconnected sketches, were written after World
War II.

Throughout his life, Romains wrote a great number
of essays, articles, and journalistic works. Many were

later collected and published in book form. His early journalistic works were literary, including those found in *Manuel de déification* (1910), a manual of precepts on the order of André Gide's *Nourritures terrestres* (1897; *Fruits of the Earth*, 1949), and *Puissances de Paris* (1911), a collection of prose poems about Paris. *Problèmes d'aujourd'hui* (1931) reveals Romains's attitude toward World War I. In 1920, he published *La vision extra-rétinienne et le sens paroptique* (*Eyeless Sight*, 1924), the only work bearing his real name, Louis Farigoule—a scientific treatise never accepted in scientific circles. *Problèmes européens* (1933) contains revisions of earlier essays and an important new essay on Marxism. *Pour l'esprit et la liberté* (1937; for the spirit and freedom), *Cela dépend de vous* (1938; that depends on you), and *Sept mystères du destin de l'Europe* (1940; *The Seven Mysteries of Europe*, 1940) concern the threat of World War II. *Une Vue des choses* (1941) was first published in English in a collection titled *I Believe* (1939). *Salsette découvre l'Amérique* (1942; *Salsette Discovers America*, 1942) contains comic overtones. Postwar essays include *Le Problème no. 1* (1947), on how to avoid a third world war; *Saints de notre calendrier* (1952), an attempt at systematic literary criticism; *Confidences d'un auteur dramatique* (1953) and *Souvenirs et confidences d'un écrivain* (1958), containing valuable personal and literary memoirs; *Examen de conscience des français* (1954; *A Frenchman Examines His Conscience*, 1955), an indictment of the Fourth Republic; and *Situation de la terre* (1958; *As It Is on Earth*, 1962).

During the last decade of his long life, Romains continued to write essays and articles, the best of which is *Lettre ouverte contre une vaste conspiration* (1966; *Open Letter Against a Vast Conspiracy*, 1967). His last book, *Amitiés et rencontres* (1970), recalls people whom he met during his life.

ACHIEVEMENTS

Known for the sheer volume of his work, Jules Romains is one of the most impressive figures of twentieth century French literature. He excelled in all literary domains: poetry, drama, fiction, and the essay. Although he worked at all four simultaneously, each genre dominated a given decade of his life: poetry, from 1908 to 1916; drama, from 1920 to 1930; fiction, from 1932 to

1946; the essay, from 1952 to 1966. As a poet, Romains is noted especially for *La Vie unanime*; as a dramatist, for *Dr. Knock*, a satire on imaginary invalids; and as an essayist, for his attitude toward war, before and during World War II.

Romains's novels, however, are most likely to assure his immortality. *Men of Good Will*, consisting of twenty-seven volumes and more than eight thousand pages, is impressive for its bulk alone; it is one of the longest novels in all Western literature. Intended as the portrayal of an age and the study of modern, as opposed to traditional, values, it remains one of the most detailed documentaries of the period between 1908 and 1933. At the same time, it contains reflections on the great questions that tormented Western Europe at the turn of the twentieth century—a continent on the verge of an impending cataclysm that was to erupt as a world war. Immensely popular, the twenty-seven volumes assured the author's fame and financial independence.

Romains excelled in short fiction as well. His early stories, written from a unanimist viewpoint, show the growth of collective consciousness from an idea. In *Le Bourg régénéré*, for example, a scribbled piece of graffiti returns a lethargic town to a vigorous existence; in *Death of a Nobody*, the death of a relatively unknown man creates a number of unanimist communities. Romains was equally gifted in burlesque humor, as in his novel *The Boys in the Back Room*, and in the idealistic portrayal of love, as in his trilogy, *The Body's Rapture*, in which a couple is really one soul.

Romains traced the beginning of his unanimist vision to a walk he took in October, 1903, along the rue d'Amsterdam with his friend Georges Chennevière. Not unlike René Descartes's vision in his stove-heated room and Paul Valéry's "nuit de Gênes," Romains's revelation was a sudden awareness of his literary vocation and of its direction. He perceived the street and the city as a vast unity, with a soul and spirit of its own. All was suspended in an eternal present, such as that which Henri Bergson describes. The duty of the unanimist poet or novelist was to bring to light such collective forces hidden in solitude. The critic André Cuisinier sees this "collective spirit" as related to the growing interest in sociology during Romains's day, and especially to the work of Émile Durkheim. Thus, Romains provides many glimpses of groups in his early plays, poetry, and stories, bringing collective consciousness to life, especially in the city of Paris.

Romains, like Charles Baudelaire, whom he both admired and opposed, is a poet of Paris, of its anonymous crowds and its burgeoning mechanization. Scenes of Paris at five o'clock in the evening or on Bastille Day (July 14) in *Men of Good Will* are both lyric and unanimist. Romains is able to create a composite picture of the Paris that he knew so well, from its monuments, its zigzagging streets with newly invented automobiles, its rich and its poor, its proud and humble, its people of goodwill and its criminals. Thus, he echoes Hugo's "Paris à vol d'oiseau" in *Notre-Dame de Paris* (1831; *The Hunchback of Notre Dame*, 1833), with its almost ecstatic delight in the spirit of the city.

At a time when Surrealism had shattered the traditional literary viewpoints of order and reason and when avant-garde writers everywhere were eroding the traditions of plot, sequential time, and the omniscient narrator, Romains rejected innovation. Although he wrote burlesque parody and used naturalistic overtones in the manner of Émile Zola, his style is worthy of the best in the classical tradition. In prose, the speech of his characters simulates the best of contemporary French, although maintaining the peculiarities of a given social class. His vocabulary is as rich as the variety of his themes, and the music of his prose shows the fruits of an apprenticeship to the best of poetic models.

BIOGRAPHY

Jules Romains was born Louis-Henri-Jean Farigoule on August 26, 1885, in Saint-Julien-Chapteuil in the Velay. He was to maintain a deep attachment to his native soil and would return to its mountains and valleys in prose and poetry. The only son of Henri Farigoule and Marie Richier, both from long-standing Velay families, Romains came to know Paris intimately, for his father was a schoolteacher there. The family lived on the northern slope of Montmartre, and in the fantasy of Louis Bastide rolling his hoop in *Men of Good Will*, one can imagine the author's childhood. Thanks to a government policy on education, the young Romains was able to attend the

Jules Romains. (Time & Life Pictures/Getty Images)

Lycée Condorcet and later the prestigious École Normale Supérieure. Pleasant experiences of both are echoed in *The Boys in the Back Room* and *Men of Good Will*.

Like Jallez in *Men of Good Will*, Romains (he adopted the pseudonym in 1904) underwent a religious crisis in his early teens. In 1903, a semimystical experience on the rue d'Amsterdam swept him into unanimism, which became for him a quasi religion and inspired especially his earlier works. After his brilliant scholastic achievements, he embarked immediately upon a literary and teaching career. He began with poetry, becoming familiar with the Abbaye group of poets, among them Georges Duhamel and Charles Messager Vildrac. While teaching at Laon from 1910 to 1914, Romains associated with Jean Moréas, Gide, Guillaume Apollinaire, Max Jacob, and Pablo Picasso. He also maintained close ties of friendship with his companions at the Lycée Condorcet and the École Normale Supérieure, especially Georges Chennevière, who died in 1927.

During the years before World War I, Romains renewed his bond with Gabrielle Gaffé, whom he married in 1912 after her divorce. Despite many literary evocations of Gabrielle, the marriage had an inauspicious beginning and was not to last; in 1936, the two were divorced. Romains was mobilized at the beginning of the war, but because of health problems he was discharged in 1915. His previous year of military service, in 1905, in the infantry at Pithiviers, had left him with a strong distaste for the military, and for the horrors of war in general, reflected especially in two books of *Men of Good Will*, *The Prelude* and *The Battle*; in the articles of *Problèmes d'aujourd'hui*; and in the poetry of *Europe*.

By 1918, Romains was already a recognized leader of a literary movement and had a permanent publisher, Gallimard, although later he transferred to Flammarion. He was living then in Nice and abandoned teaching for a literary career, working principally in drama from 1919 to 1931. The triumph of *Dr. Knock* in 1924 brought him even greater fame and made him financially independent. During this time, he traveled widely in Europe and the Middle East, living in Hyères, near Toulon, or in Paris. He was the poetry critic for *L'Humanité* until that periodical came under communist control, and a correspondent for *La Dépêche de Toulouse*. With a university degree in science as well as in letters, he claimed to have discovered "extraretinal" vision. Scientists, however, remained skeptical of Romains's theory, leaving him embittered by his failure to establish himself in the world of science.

After 1930, Romains's travels took on a semipolitical character; he lectured in London, Madrid, Germany, and the United States, preaching the necessity of Franco-German rapprochement and understanding, as did his character Gurau in *Men of Good Will*. In 1936, Romains married his former secretary, Lise Dreyfus. Because of the growing hostilities to the Jews, as a result of which Lise's mother perished, Romains and his wife left France in 1940. He continued to support Charles de Gaulle and to denounce the Vichy government through numerous radio broadcasts, published in *Messages aux français* (1941). Thereafter, he settled in the United States and then moved to Mexico City, where he lived from 1942 to 1945.

In 1946, Romains returned to France for his official reception into the French Academy. With a sumptuous apartment in Paris and an estate in Touraine, he became something of a literary aristocrat, maintaining a lofty distance from artistic innovations and insisting on traditional values in literature. Many of his earlier allies, such as Gide and Duhamel, fell victim to his incisive pen. Romains continued to write until 1970, traveling widely, including a visit to Asia. His writing during the 1950's and 1960's adds little to the literary stature he gained before 1946. His main work during his last two decades took the form of essays, personal memoirs, and literary criticism. Increasingly self-sufficient and rather egotistical, he was both shunned and respected. He died in Paris on August 14, 1972, one of the giants of modern literature.

ANALYSIS

With the appearance of *Men of Good Will*, Jules Romains became an overwhelmingly popular novelist, with each of the work's twenty-seven volumes selling thousands of copies. A popular writer must first of all hold the interest of his readers. This Romains does, not only in his massive *roman-fleuve* but in his shorter novels as well. His plots are fast-moving, and even the longer works contain satisfying and immediate subplots. He generally begins in medias res, without a great deal of preparation, unlike Honoré de Balzac, whom he greatly admired. His ability to treat a number of subjects, both within his multivolume works and within the range of his shorter novels, provided an appeal to a broad public.

The shorter works, however, as well as the trilogy *The Body's Rapture*, are relatively weak in plot. *The Boys in the Back Room*, although entertaining, is an adolescent *canular*, while *The Body's Rapture* is a superficial idealization of sexual love. These works were intended to develop a unanimist vision: camaraderie, or the one soul of the couple. Thus, a single idea takes on a mystical dimension in a couple or a group. In his later works, Romains indulged himself in many digressions on the important questions of the day and on his personal preoccupations; this material wearies the reader and detracts from story development.

In his portrayal of characters, Romains likewise departed from the Balzacian tradition. Particularly notable is the paucity of physical description of the characters.

Jallez, one of the principal characters in *Men of Good Will*, is never described physically throughout the entire work. Romains limits his character analysis to moral and psychological portrayal. Since interior monologue is his main tool, the reader knows only how his characters see themselves and is seldom aware of how they are perceived by others.

Even a sympathetic reader will concede that there is a certain lack of substance in Romains's characters (especially the female characters, which are far less convincing than the males). To Romains, the collective mattered more than the individual. Thus, the effect of Godard's death is more important than Godard himself, and Paris is more important than the men of goodwill—and not-so-goodwill—who live there.

Romains's narrative technique consists in the use of interior monologue first, then dialogue, and last narration, much of which is hard to distinguish from interior monologue. Romains also uses a great deal of first-person narration. *Lucienne's Story* and *The Body's Rapture* are both told in this manner, by Lucienne and Pierre respectively. In the Balzacian tradition, Romains uses a pseudo-omniscient narrator, sometimes in combination with the first-person narrator. This technique results in an impression of great immediacy and dramatic intensity—without, however, fully concretizing the characters.

Like his hero Jallez, Romains became disillusioned with religion in his early teens yet sought a substitute in unanimism, which always contained mystical overtones. The subject of religion is prominent in his novels, from the parody of the priest's sermon in *The Boys in the Back Room* to Abbé Jeanne's genuine spirituality. Like his main characters in *The Lonely* (book 7 of *Men of Good Will*, Romains was always searching for a community, be it the Catholic Church, socialism, Freemasonry, or the communist revolution. In his own life and writings, he illustrated the fundamental solitude of the human condition and the search for identification with a group.

Both as a reflection of his own tensions and as a reaction to Victorian prudishness, Romains dwelt on sexuality. His themes run from eroticism to reverence to idealism, from friendship to love in marriage to sexual perversion. Naturalistic in style, his works incorporate

frank descriptions of these themes, often blending them with delicate poetry, as in the rapture of Lucienne and Pierre on their wedding night in *The Body's Rapture*. Romains's style is varied, ranging from parody in the sermon delivered by Bénin in *Les Copains* to the purity of courtly love in Jallez's admiration for Hélène Sigeau and Françoise, the perversions of *Vorge Against Quinette* and *The Magic Carpet* in *Men of Good Will*, the prostitution of Isabelle Maillecottin, and the various liaisons throughout the work. Romains also shows the link between violence and passion, as in Quinette and the poet Vorge. Romains's treatment of sexual themes is didactic, directed against the stereotyped Catholic teachings on marriage and procreation. His naturalistic descriptions of Marie de Champcennais's crude abortion, for example, point up his belief in the need for more tolerant legislation.

The burlesque style of Romains's earlier works and the optimistic beginning of *Men of Good Will* ultimately gave way to pessimistic portrayals of war and confusion. Romains's later works are less positive and less unanimist. In them, unanimism exists as a backdrop for painting individual characters. Romains poses problems with ever-increasing intensity: the war, technology, economic gains and rivalry, the difficulties of personal relationships. He sees no solutions to these problems other than to live as persons of goodwill.

DEATH OF A NOBODY

Death of a Nobody, Romains's first critically acclaimed novel, was inspired by its author's unanimist vision of life and death. In it, Jacques Godard, a humble but honest retired engineer and a childless widower, dies of a chill contracted while he was mounting the dome of the Panthéon. This death soon produces a positive reaction in many characters: the concierge, who carefully performs the necessary arrangements for the funeral; neighbors, who come to view the body and who collect money for a wreath; the villagers who live near Godard's aged parents in the Velay. His father makes the long trip to Paris and fellowships with the travelers in the stagecoach and on the train—here Romains evokes a unanimist collective consciousness. The story ends with a eulogy of life by an anonymous young man.

Although definitely animated by Romains's unanimist vision, *Death of a Nobody* is not contrived; rather, it is a picture of the various groups that form around the memory of Godard. It differs from ordinary portrayals of death in that the physical aspects of death are hardly noted; the emphasis is, rather, on its spiritual effects. Here, as in his short story *Le Bourg régénéré*, Romains used the technique of "simultaneity," presenting the various reactions to Godard's death that take place at the same time.

THE BOYS IN THE BACK ROOM

The next of Romains's short novels to attain popularity was *The Boys in the Back Room*, which was made into a film in 1964. Very different from the delicately simple *Death of a Nobody*, this book is a farcical and witty portrayal of seven young men who travel through France and impersonate a number of serious and important people on their way to "avenge" Ambert and Issoire, towns they have picked at random on a dusty map of France. At a railway station, Bénin, the principal member of the group—modeled on Romains himself—passes himself off as a Russian official; at Ambert, Broudier masquerades as a minister, and Bénin, as "the illustrious Père Lathuile," delivers a magnificent sermon on sexuality. Finally, in Issoire, a statue, supposedly of Vercingetorix, is unveiled, proving to be the nude figure of Bénin.

Although totally different in tone from *Death of a Nobody*, *The Boys in the Back Room* is also a unanimist text, closely related to *Le Bourg régénéré* and *Donogoo*, showing the collectivity aroused to dynamic activity. In *The Boys in the Back Room*, before Gide, Romains makes use of the term *acte gratuit*, and shows it in operation in the pranks of the seven young men. The parody of the clergy, of the provincial bourgeoisie, and of the military, though traditional in the French comic genre, is incorporated into a highly entertaining comic piece, of which there are relatively few in French literature.

THE BODY'S RAPTURE

Romains's last major work of sustained fiction before *Men of Good Will* was the trilogy *The Body's Rapture*. The first volume, *Lucienne's Story*, portrays the ideal courtship between the narrator and the main character, Lucienne, and Pierre Febvre, a cousin of the Barbelenet family, to whose two girls Lucienne gives music lessons. Lucienne is modeled on Romains's first wife, Gabrielle, especially in her love of music and culture and in her sensitivity. This volume, though the best

of the trilogy, is relatively weak in plot, and the character of Lucienne, while delicately analyzed from a psychological rather than physical point of view, is nevertheless unconvincing.

In the second volume, *The Body's Rapture* (the English version bears the title of the trilogy as a whole), the couple prepares for marriage, and the story is told from Pierre's viewpoint. Romains's frank and detailed account of the couple's wedding night shocked many readers when the book was published, although his point was simply to glorify the physical union of man and woman as a kind of religious rite with marriage as the initiation. He wished to show the attainment of a spiritual unanimism of the couple through their physical love, and to sing the glories of the flesh.

The final volume, *Love's Questing*, is generally acknowledged to be the weakest. It lacks credibility in its supposition that material distance can be surmounted by a kind of self-projection. While Pierre is on duty on his ship, he feels Lucienne's physical presence with him; Lucienne, likewise, "sees" Pierre's ship from her apartment at Marseilles. For Romains, such a union was possible through the unanimist vision. The lengthy trilogy has an improbable and rather commonplace ending: The average couple "lives happily ever after," probably because Romains's own marital difficulties caused him to become weary of the project.

Often dismissed as too idealistic, the trilogy pales in comparison with the great twenty-seven-volume work that Romains was already preparing. *Lucienne's Story*, however, almost won for him the Prix Goncourt in 1922. That year's winning book, *Le Martyre de l'obèse* (1922), by Henri Béraud, has failed to survive, while *Lucienne's Story* is still read and appreciated. On the whole, *The Body's Rapture* shows a shift in Romains's technique, from unanimism to a more personal and traditional type of work with deeper psychological analysis than in Romains's earlier works. It therefore sets the stage for *Men of Good Will*.

MEN OF GOOD WILL

Men of Good Will is more than a novel; it is a *roman-fleuve*, a *roman-somme*. Imposing in its length—twenty-seven volumes of more than eight thousand pages—it is Romains's greatest accomplishment, undoubtedly the primary reason for his reception into the French Academy in 1946. Romains had initiated the project in 1923 but did not begin publication until 1932, when the first two volumes appeared simultaneously, subsequent volumes appearing at the rate of two volumes a year. Books 19 through 24 were published in New York, because of the war, and in 1946, Flammarion published the remaining three. The work was extremely popular; at the time of Romains's death, more than two million copies had been sold.

In a preface that ranks among the important literary prefaces in history, Romains compares his project with Zola's *Les Rougon-Macquart* (1871-1893) and Balzac's *La Comédie humaine* (1829-1848; *The Human Comedy*, 1895-1896) but charges that the individual novels of their cycles do not make up a unified whole. He also rejects the single hero that characterizes the works of Marcel Proust and Thomas Mann. His aim, he states, is to portray society and the modern world. He wishes to paint a number of people and scenes, allowing characters and ideas to appear and disappear spontaneously. As in life, some will have a future; others will be doomed to oblivion. Above all, Romains wished to write a book accessible to the greatest possible number of people. In the unanimist spirit, he wished to create "a vast human communion, an immense camaraderie."

Despite his claims to have written "a new novel," most critics find Romains's work fairly traditional, much in the style of Guy de Maupassant and Anatole France. Not unlike Proust and Mann, he does have a central hero—rather, two who express different facets of Romains's personality. The peasant-born Jean Jerphanion, like the Velay-born Romains, comes to Paris to study at the École Normale Supérieure. Practical and direct, he is attracted by politics and has a strong desire for social justice. After several trivial sexual encounters, he marries the sedate and intelligent Odette, serves in the army at Verdun, and embarks upon a political career. The introspective Pierre Jallez represents the more intimate side of Romains, with his religious, moral, and sentimental crises. Jallez is a Parisian, and in his love of the city he initiates Jerphanion into his favorite haunts. His search for an ideal leads him from a childhood love for Hélène Sigeau through many empty flirtations, including a disappointing liaison with Juliette Ezzelin, not unlike Romains's first marriage. It culminates in his eventual marriage to Françoise Maïeul, modeled on Romains's second, younger wife, Lise Dreyfus. Jallez, like Romains, becomes a journalist, a writer, and a seeker for the meaning of life.

True to his aim of portraying society, Romains does not let the two main characters of his work dominate it completely. He brings them into contact, often rather gratuitously, with various segments of society. As Cuisinier has noted, Romains's characters fall into all the essential categories of the period, rendering the epoch itself the main character. At the bottom, there is the world of the poor, illustrated by Louis Bastide and his family. They, like Romains's own family, live in Montmartre. The father loses his job, and little Louis—the single convincing portrait of a child in the entire work—takes on odd jobs to support the family. The milieu of the schoolteacher, so important in the early days of the Third Republic, is represented by the circle gathered around Sampeyre, the retired history professor. They include Legraverend, who toys with Marxism, Louis Argellati, Mathilde Cazalis, courted by both Clanricard and Jerphanion, Laulerque the rabid individualist, and Clanricard the Socialist and the Freemason, who befriends Louis Bastide and marries Mathilde but loses his happiness with her and his idealism.

Jallez and Jerphanion represent the world of "Normalien" students at the École Normale Supérieure, a world that Romains knew well. The middle class is present in the actor Germaine Baader, originally the mistress of the idealistic Gurau, who, like Jerphanion, aspires to a political career, and the untalented writer Georges Allory. Gurau and Germaine are drawn into the world of big business and concomitant dishonesty when Gurau tries to uncover the intrigues of a great oil cartel, led by Sammécaud and de Champcennais. The latter, in turn, furthers his business affairs by collaborating with the automobile manufacturer Bertrand.

The world of growing technology and the economic development in modern society is reflected in the complex intrigues of the oil cartel and the automobile industry, as well as in the enormous real estate transactions of Haverkamp, symbolized in his voracious devouring of a huge, rare steak. All of these industrialists profit from the war, which increases the stock of the oil cartel and eventually brings about the ruin of Haverkamp. The war takes on various meanings for different individuals and groups: It is a source of income for Haverkamp and de Champcennais, as well as an economic advantage for the small workers; a political rallying point for Gurau and Jerphanion; and a symbol of power to the Marxists and the striking union members.

Among the many subcultures depicted in the novel, one of the most striking is that of the criminal world, represented by Quinette, who is modeled on Henri Landru, the notorious modern-day bluebeard who was a neighbor of Romains. By contrast, there is the spiritual world of the humble parish priest, Abbé Jeanne, who regulates his actions by the single law of love. There is the world of ecclesiastical ambition in the former graduate of the École Normale Supérieure, Abbé Mionnet, who meets the illustrious Cardinal Merry Del Val and diplomatically handles many scandals, to become at the end Archbishop of Tours. There is the real world of actual historical figures, Aristide Briand, Jean Léon Jaurès, and the circle of poets, among them Romains himself, whom Jallez meets at the Closerie des Lilas. There is even the animal world, represented by the dog Macaire, whose amorous expeditions through Paris recall those of his human counterparts.

The female world pales in comparison to this vast masculine panorama. In Romains's fiction, women seem to exist only as stimulants to men's sexual desires or as ideals of purity, not unlike the traditional Eve/Virgin Mary dichotomy. The idealistic women—Hélène Sigeau, Françoise Maïeul, and Odette Jerphanion—are shadowy figures in their transparent purity. The more seductive female characters—Juliette Ezzelin, Germaine Baader, and even the unwilling Marie de Champcennais—are more credible and human. With the strong emphasis on erotic and sentimental scenes in the novel, it is somewhat surprising that a strong female character does not emerge.

By consensus, the best books in the series are the first four, in which Romains draws rapid flashes of characters and scenes, especially of Paris and the meeting of Jallez and Jerphanion. The sixth book, *The Meek*, the story of Louis Bastide and his family, and the seventh book, *The Lonely*, the search for human community and an ideal among the various principal characters, are also excellent. Books 15 and 16, *The Prelude* and *The Battle*,

which deal with World War I as seen through the battle at Verdun, are also acknowledged as superior. In them, Romains's antiwar attitude is very strong, yet his admiration for Pétain and his appreciation of the camaraderie produced by the war are equally powerful. The fact that these two volumes were published in 1938, on the eve of a second worldwide clash, made them even more highly appreciated.

Like Balzac, Zola, and Leo Tolstoy, and his contemporaries Proust and Romain Rolland, Romains created a vast panorama of an age, yet Jerphanion on the roofs of the École Normale Supérieure does not climb to the height of Balzac's Rastignac at Père Lachaise in his wager with Paris; nor, fighting at Verdun, does Jerphanion equal Tolstoy's Prince Andrei Bolkónsky at Borodino. There is no female character that approaches Tolstoy's Natasha. Although Romains states his preference for nonviolence and his hatred of war in *The Battle*, he reaches neither Tolstoy's exuberance of national pride in the portrayal of the invasion of Moscow nor his discovery of the role of chance in Napoleon's downfall.

Romains poses many questions—too many, perhaps—but does not explore them with the intensity of a Balzac or a Tolstoy. He portrays crime but not vice; he depicts society but not the enigmatic forces that control an individual through power and desire. He explores the inner depths of Jallez, examines the forces of eros and ambition, but lacks the intuitive perceptions of Proust and Balzac. Length and order seem to replace depth and spontaneity; unanimism masks individual freedom. What will remain of Romains and his vast novel is perhaps what he worked on least: the portraits of Paris, the humiliated, and the poor, and the two friends who, like the pilgrims of Emmaus, trudge along the paths of life to bear witness to an event, a vision, which only they have seen.

Irma M. Kashuba

OTHER MAJOR WORKS

SHORT FICTION: *Le Bourg régénéré*, 1906; *Nomentanus le réfugié*, 1943; *Tu ne tueras point*, 1943 (*Thou Shalt Not Kill*, 1943); *Bertrand de Ganges*, 1944; *Violations de frontières*, 1951 (*Tussles with Time*, 1952); *Portraits d'inconnus*, 1962.

PLAYS: *L'Armée dans la ville*, pr., pb. 1911 (verse play); *Cromedeyre-le-Vieil*, pr., pb. 1920 (wr. 1911-

1918; verse play); *Le Dictateur*, pr., pb. 1926 (wr. 1911-1925); *M. Le Trouhadec saisi par la débauche*, pb. 1921; *Knock: Ou, Le Triomphe de la médecine*, pr. 1923 (*Dr. Knock*, 1925); *Amédée et les messieurs en rang*, pr. 1923 (*Six Gentlemen in a Row*, 1927); *La Scintillante*, pr. 1924 (*The Peach*, 1933); *Le Mariage de Le Trouhadec*, pr., pb. 1925 (music by Georges Auric); *Démétrios*, pr. 1925; *Jean le Maufranc*, pr. 1926; *Volpone*, pr. 1928 (adaptation of Stefan Zweig's adaptation of Ben Jonson's play *Volpone*; music by Auric); *Le Déjeuner marocain*, pr., pb. 1929; *Boën: Ou, La Possession des biens*, pr. 1930; *Donogoo-Tonka*, pr. 1930; *Musse: Ou, L'École de l'hypocrisie*, pr. 1930 (revision of *Jean le Maufranc*); *Le Roi masqué*, pr. 1931; *Grâce encore pour la terre*, pr., pb. 1941; *L'An mil*, pr., pb. 1947; *Barbazouk*, pr., pb. 1963 (wr. 1956; radio play).

POETRY: *L'Âme des hommes*, 1904; *La Vie unanime*, 1908; *Un Être en marche*, 1910; *Odes et prières*, 1913; *Europe*, 1916; *Le Voyage des amants*, 1920; *Ode Génoise*, 1925; *Chants des dix années*, 1928; *L'Homme blanc*, 1937; *Choix de poèmes*, 1948; *Maisons*, 1953; *Pierres levées*, 1957.

SCREENPLAY: *Donogoo-Tonka: Ou, Les Miracles de la science*, pb. 1920 (*Donogoo*, 1937).

NONFICTION: *Manuel de déification*, 1910; *Puissances de Paris*, 1911; *Au-dessus de la mêlée*, 1915; *La Vision extra-rétinienne et le sens paroptique*, 1920 (*Eyeless Sight*, 1924); *Problèmes d'aujourd'hui*, 1931; *Problèmes européens*, 1933; *Pour l'esprit et la liberté*, 1937; *Cela dépend de vous*, 1938; *Sept mystères du destin de l'Europe*, 1940 (*The Seven Mysteries of Europe*, 1940); *Messages aux français*, 1941; *Une Vue des choses*, 1941 (first published in English in *I Believe*, 1939); *Salsette découvre l'Amérique*, 1942 (*Salsette Discovers America*, 1942); *Le Problème no. 1*, 1947; *Saints de notre calendrier*, 1952; *Confidences d'un auteur dramatique*, 1953; *Examen de conscience des français*, 1954 (*A Frenchman Examines His Conscience*, 1955); *Passengers de cette planète, où allons nous?*, 1955; *Situation de la terre*, 1958 (*As It Is on Earth*, 1962); *Souvenirs et confidences d'un écrivain*, 1958; *Hommes, médecins, machines*, 1959; *Ai-je fait ce que j'ai voulu?*, 1964; *Lettre ouverte contre une vaste conspiration*, 1966 (*Open Letter Against a Vast Conspiracy*, 1967); *Amitiés et rencontres*, 1970.

BIBLIOGRAPHY

Boak, Denis. *Jules Romains*. New York: Twayne, 1974. Widely acclaimed as the definitive biographical and literary source on Romains, Boak's study comprehensively covers the life and work of the writer. Includes a bibliography.

Madden, David. "David Madden on Jules Romains's *Death of a Nobody*." In *Rediscoveries II: Important Writers Select Their Favorite Works of Neglected Fiction*, edited by Madden and Peggy Bach. New York: Carroll & Graf, 1988. Madden discusses Romains's novel *Death of a Nobody* as the work exemplifying the roots of Romains's ideas of unanimism.

Stansbury, Milton H. *French Novelists of Today*. Port Washington, N.Y.: Kennikat Press, 1966. Choosing Romains in part for his "colorful personality," Stansbury offers a condensed biography and survey of Romains's most recognized writings.

SINCLAIR ROSS

Born: Near Shellbrook, Saskatchewan, Canada;
   January 22, 1908
Died: Vancouver, British Columbia, Canada;
   February 29, 1996
Also known as: James Sinclair Ross

PRINCIPAL LONG FICTION

As for Me and My House, 1941
The Well, 1958
Whir of Gold, 1970
Sawbones Memorial, 1974

OTHER LITERARY FORMS

In addition to his novels, Sinclair Ross wrote short stories, ten of which are collected in *The Lamp at Noon, and Other Stories* (1968). A later collection, *The Race, and Other Stories*, appeared in 1982. In addition to their intrinsic merit, the short stories are important as proving grounds for many of the plots, themes, and characters of Ross's novels. A memoir, *Just Wind and Horses*, was published in 1988.

ACHIEVEMENTS

The fact that *As for Me and My House*, Sinclair Ross's first novel and the one on which his reputation rested for many years, was published in 1941 in the United States and not in his native Canada is indicative of the author's early struggle for recognition in his home country. Previously, he had published several short stories that gained little attention, perhaps because of their rather somber view of the human condition as reflected in the lives of the characters: Canadian prairie dwellers during the Great Depression. A few copies of *As for Me and My House* sold in Canada, but the reading public there was not interested in the Canadian West, a region apart from the rest of the world, and the merits of the novel went largely unappreciated until publication of the New Canadian Library paperback edition in 1957. Today, *As for Me and My House* holds a secure place among the classics of Canadian fiction. Like Mark Twain's *Adventures of Huckleberry Finn* (1884) and F. Scott Fitzgerald's *The Great Gatsby* (1925), it is a parable by which a

country can measure its imaginative life. In its complex rendering of humans struggling with inner conflict and the psychological effects of landscape and the elements, and in its richly resonant language, it surpasses the best of Frederick Philip Grove, the leading prairie realist before Ross, and it maps a fictional terrain that continued to be explored by Margaret Laurence, Rudy Wiebe, Robert Kroetsch, and others. Though Ross's next two novels, *The Well* and *Whir of Gold*, fail to match the achievement of *As for Me and My House*, a renewing fourth novel, *Sawbones Memorial*, is of high quality.

In his best fiction, a sentence or two of Ross's lean, spare, honest prose can illuminate the life of an entire community. In his best fiction, too, Ross has the ability to identify with his characters and with their time and place. Margaret Laurence once said that "he got his time and place in the prairies exactly right." Ross could not have asked for a more satisfying tribute.

BIOGRAPHY

A very private man, Sinclair Ross was reticent about his personal life and preferred to let his art speak for him. It is possible, however, to piece together at least the outward facts of his life. Born January 22, 1908, in northern Saskatchewan, James Sinclair Ross was the third child of Peter and Catherine Ross, who met and married in Prince Albert, Saskatchewan, in 1897. Peter had been born on an Ontario farm to Scottish parents, and Catherine had been born in Scotland. When he was three, Ross's parents separated, his mother taking custody of him, and his father taking the two older children. After the separation, Mrs. Ross found employment as a housekeeper on several farms. Ross assisted with farm chores and learned the vagaries of horses and men as well as the daunting effects of landscape and climate on the prairie dwellers. He retained strong memories of his isolation in those years.

After he graduated from high school in 1924, Ross went to work for the Royal Bank of Canada, his sole employer until his retirement in 1968. In 1933, the bank rewarded Ross's stints in several small Saskatchewan towns by sending him to Winnipeg, Manitoba, where he remained until 1946, except for World War II military service, and finally to Montreal. Upon retirement from the bank, he lived in Greece for three years and then moved to Spain in 1971. Culture and climate (he suffered from arthritis) influenced Ross's decision to live by the Mediterranean Sea. Competent in Spanish and French, somewhat less so in Greek, Ross read the original versions of the literatures of these languages. Living abroad, he noted, gave him a stronger sense of his Canadian identity. Although the pattern of Ross's life was one of gradual withdrawal eastward from the pioneer prairies toward older, more cosmopolitan cultures, his true subject and setting remained the Canadian prairies, specifically rural Saskatchewan and its people.

Few of Ross's colleagues at the bank knew him as a writer, though he was always a self-described "compulsive scribbler," despite having had "so little success." Given his isolation from any real literary community, some of Ross's determination to write, mostly at night after long days at the bank, must be credited to his mother, the strongest influence in his life and a model for some of the women in his fiction. Ever conscious of her moral and intellectual refinement (her father had studied theology at the University of Edinburgh, taught at Oberlin College in Ohio, and eventually been ordained a Unitarian minister), Catherine encouraged her young son to take piano lessons, experiment with oil painting, and read widely. In particular, Ross remembered reading Sir Walter Scott, Charles Dickens, and Thomas Hardy, whose *The Return of the Native* (1878) may well have influenced him, though he noted that he was never aware of any literary influences. For many years Ross had to support his mother as well as himself in the succession of small towns and cities to which she followed him, making it impossible for him to resign from the bank to devote his full energy to writing.

Ross's most productive period was the 1930's. Many of his best short stories were published then; one of them, "No Other Way," won third prize in a competition for unpublished writers. In 1941, *As for Me and My House* appeared. Ross had already destroyed the manuscripts of two earlier, unsatisfactory novels, and he would later destroy another, a possibly autobiographical story of a Canadian soldier from Manitoba written during World War II.

Discouraged by the reception of *As for Me and My House*, Ross did not publish his second novel, *The Well*, until 1958, but it was greeted with even less enthusiasm than his first. *The Well* was influenced by his negative reaction to Montreal, where for twenty-two years the ascetic Ross lived largely within himself, avoiding the "literary swim," as he called it. Much of his third novel, *Whir of Gold*, was also written in Montreal, then completed after his retirement. Written in Europe, his last published novel, *Sawbones Memorial*, is a forgiving reminiscence of the prairies as Ross knew them in the 1930's and 1940's. Bearing an obvious kinship to its predecessors, it is nevertheless a more mellow novel, striking a better balance between humorous detachment and bitterness, rejection, and grudging nostalgia.

In 1992, Ross's work was recognized by his home nation when he was made a Member of the Order of Canada. In 1996, he died in Vancouver, British Columbia, where he had lived in a nursing home for many years.

Analysis

Despite his relatively small output and rather limited fictional world, Sinclair Ross succeeded in universalizing the human concerns of his novels. Drought, poverty, and the hardship and anxiety they cause are universal concerns, but life on the Canadian prairies in the 1930's and 1940's becomes in Ross's works a paradigm of the human condition everywhere. Moreover, at its most intense Ross's fiction evokes a characteristic mood, a synthesis of human isolation, claustrophobia, and threatening nature that serves as his trademark, making his writing as distinctive and recognizable as that of his contemporaries Ernest Hemingway and William Faulkner.

As Ross once noted, "Most writers have only one or two themes that they constantly develop in their work." Ross, in contrast, has three: communication, or more often the failure of communication, in human relationships; the struggle to find an authentic self and live a fulfilled existence; and humankind's struggle against the land and the elements. In Ross's novels, man-woman relationships, in particular, are vitiated by a failure to communicate, or even a failure to attempt communication. In *As for Me and My House*, the Bentleys are isolated from each other by their emotional and psychological shortcomings. In *The Well*, a generation gap of attitudes and values separates the old farmer, Larson, and his young wife, Sylvia. In *Whir of Gold*, Sonny McAlpine's emotional immaturity and prairie Calvinist attitudes destroy his chances of happiness with the good-hearted prostitute Madelaine. Among the prairie homesteaders, poverty, climate, physical toil, pessimism about the future, and a repressive Puritan morality are hardly conducive to romance.

Writing about women in Canadian and American prairie fiction, the novelist Robert Kroetsch asks, "How do you establish any sort of *close* relationship in a landscape—in a physical situation—whose primary characteristic is distance?" Thwarted in their attempts at closeness, Ross's women become domineering and manipulative (Mrs. Bentley), sexually aggressive (Sylvia), or maternal and possessive (Madelaine). Love becomes a power struggle. The women's superior social and intellectual backgrounds, or their emotional needs, cause them to treat their men as sons rather than as lovers. As for the men in Ross's novels, Oedipal overtones—their failure in heterosexual love, their need for mothering women, the lack of adequate father figures in their youth, for example—are present in the principal male characters and may conceal a homosexuality that Ross does not overtly confront until *Sawbones Memorial*. Indeed, Ross's men seem to have better rapport with animals than with other people, and the best-written passages in his later novels are those involving animals, especially horses. Horses serve as companions or as daring symbols of sexuality, independence, and the imaginative life.

For the artist, a recurrent figure in Ross's world of outsiders and misfits, the failure of communication is especially acute. The aspirations of the artist find little nourishment in prairie society, or—by implication—in Canada and North America as a whole. The failure of Ross's struggling painters and musicians to communicate their vision is symptomatic of the larger failure of the national imagination. In *As for Me and My House*, Philip Bentley's paintings are as stillborn as his first child. In *Whir of Gold*, Sonny McAlpine's musical ambition is blunted by prairie attitudes that burden him even in distant Montreal. In this respect, Sonny, like Philip, is a typical Canadian literary protagonist, incapable of great art or memorable literary heroism on account of the

domination of a persistent puritanism. The failed artist as modern literary hero is a familiar type, best exemplified perhaps by James Joyce's Stephen Dedalus, but when the Canadian protagonist discovers he or she is in disagreement with the dictates of the system, whether religious, social, or other, a peculiar Calvinist-Puritan conditioning causes the individual to blame him- or herself, internalizing the tension and engaging in painful and destructive soul-searching in an attempt to discover personal deficiencies.

Philip Bentley's self-absorption and his unfinished pictures of headless figures and the false fronts of the town are a measure of the frustration of his search for meaning and significance in life. In this respect, Philip and the other artist-protagonists in Ross's fiction represent humankind's search in modern North America for an authentic existence, either by coming to terms with a repressive social, cultural, and natural environment (the Canadian way) or by overthrowing it entirely (formerly the American way). Ross's characters are locked into themselves and unable to find any means of escape. This in turn leads to a withholding of emotion and strained relationships devoid of real communication. Canadian literary critic Northrop Frye called the trap preventing self-realization in Canada the "garrison mentality," the tendency of frontier societies to barricade themselves psychologically and culturally against the alien wilderness behind the ordered "civilized" propriety of a transported Eastern culture rather than adapt to the new environment. The superficial Christianity that Bentley practices, for example, is inadequate to reconcile human beings with nature on the prairie; there are hints in *As for Me and My House* that a natural, pastoral paganism would be more helpful. Frozen in its own negations and reinforced in the Depression by an overwhelming sense of failure, Christianity engenders guilt and self-destructive behavior (in the turning to crime of the protagonists of *Whir of Gold* and *The Well*, for example) rather than encouraging self-realizing ambition, individualism, and instinct.

Indeed, by the time Ross came to write *The Well* and *Whir of Gold*, he felt that the real wilderness is in the human chaos of the modern city. The true prairie, as opposed to the garrison, is regenerative; it is the way to redemption and self-realization. Completely alienated from society, the criminal is the ultimate outsider, but in

The Well, Chris Rowe, the small-time Montreal thug hiding out on a prairie farm, does find regeneration in nature, the courage to face punishment for his crimes, and probably an authentic existence within the community of prairie dwellers. Whereas in *The Well* a life in nature regenerates a young criminal, in *Whir of Gold*, Sonny McAlpine's experience in the city almost destroys him. The keys to his survival are his nostalgic recollections of his prairie upbringing, especially those involving his horse, which serve as an anchor of self and identity amid the disorientation and venality of Montreal.

Ross's third major theme, humankind's struggle with the land and the elements, probably derives from experience and observation as well as from his reading of the literary naturalists, especially Thomas Hardy. Moods are known to be affected by climate and geography, but on the prairies of Ross's novels, as on Hardy's moors, characters and their relationships seem to be deterministically influenced by wind, heat, drought, dust, rain, snow, and ice. The psychological and emotional toll these elements exact leads characters to regard nature as part of an indifferent, even hostile universe. Ross was also, however, the first of the Canadian prairie realists to go beyond this naturalistic treatment of the landscape; his characters are psychologically conditioned by the prairie, but they also project their own subjectivity onto the external environment. In effect, they interact with it, so that not only is character determined by external environment, but environment also becomes an extension of the mind. Its challenge can test and strengthen the endurance of those who survive, uniting them in the common struggle against it; it can be a regenerative sanctuary for an urban fugitive such as Chris Rowe.

The defeated ones find little in religion to sustain the human spirit, at least the version of it proffered by prairie Christianity. One of Philip Bentley's redeeming qualities is precisely that he cannot believe in deliverance through a faith reduced to hollow forms and meaningless rituals that hypocritically ignore the Christian virtues of charity and compassion. In a deeper sense, however, Ross is a religious writer in that the underlying concern of his fiction is humankind's struggle "with the implacable blunderings of Nature" in an indifferent universe. In the face of this daunting situation, Ross holds up rationalists and humanists, such as Mrs. Bentley and Paul

Kirby in *As for Me and My House* and Doc Hunter in *Sawbones Memorial*, who stake their faith on human courage, reason, and idealism, "all the things that really are humanity," in Mrs. Bentley's words. Others, such as Sonny McAlpine and old Larson, find solace in the illusory world of the past, a youthful world of happiness and material and spiritual well-being, unthreatened by darker realities. If Ross's characters are escapist-dreamers, however, their dreams must sometimes be blown away, like the false fronts of Main Street in a windstorm, to reveal the reality in which a new, authentic self can be forged.

As for Me and My House

As a youth in Saskatchewan, Ross was encouraged by a United Church minister to enter the ministry rather than banking. Already skeptical about organized religion, although he taught Sunday school and played the organ in church, Ross "was not tempted in the least. But I began to think, 'Suppose I did, or someone else did who did not really believe in it, and felt trapped in the ministry.' That was the origin of *As for Me and My House*." Ross has revealed also that he once knew a minister whose plight resembled Philip Bentley's. Mrs. Bentley appears to have been based, at least in part, on Ross's mother, to judge by his recollections of her.

Like Ross's next two novels, *As for Me and My House* is the story of an inner quest for the authentic self. It thus belongs to a literary genre that includes works as diverse as John Bunyan's *The Pilgrim's Progress* (1678, 1684), Johann Wolfgang von Goethe's *Wilhelm Meisters Lehrjahre* (1795-1796; *Wilhelm Meister's Apprenticeship*, 1824), Henry David Thoreau's *Walden: Or, Life in the Woods* (1854), and Walt Whitman's *Leaves of Grass* (1855). It is also kindred to a large number of Canadian works in which the search for personal and national identity is a dominant theme. Ross's ironic vision is nowhere better illustrated than in the fact that Bentley's search for an authentic self compels him to reject the church's way, which is to follow the teachings of Jesus Christ. Finally, he tears down the facade of his old self, but the new, authentic self must be forged in the secular, humanist crucible of art rather than in the empty chalice of the church. Sandra Djwa's perception of the "latter-day Puritanism of the psychological search for self," in a world where "Christianity has become a meaningless form without spirit, where people must learn to reject the false gods without before it is possible to find the true God within and an authentic sense of direction," suggests the continuing contemporaneity of the book, if one thinks of the self-realization movements of the 1960's and 1970's.

As for Me and My House is a taut, intense, and bitter record of repressed, static lives in rural Saskatchewan in the 1930's. It deals with the Bentleys' year in Horizon, the fourth small-town prairie residence in twelve years for the thirty-five-year-old minister and his wife. Told in journal form by Mrs. Bentley, the book is an indictment of puritanical moral attitudes and cultural sterility. It is also bleakly pessimistic about the possibility of communication in human relationships, especially marriage. Outsiders by virtue of their position in the community and their parishioners' awareness that to them Horizon is merely a way station in a stultifying series of prairie pastorates, the Bentleys are estranged from the townsfolk as well as from each other. With no real vocation as a minister of the Gospel, Bentley wants to believe he has some talent as a painter, but his daubing shows little evidence of this, mainly because his creativity is frozen by self-lacerating guilt arising from his clerical charade.

Embittered by his failure as a minister and twelve years of entrapment in drought and depression-ridden prairie towns, Philip seeks consolation through an adopted son whose natural father had abandoned him, but—in keeping with the melancholy pattern of discontinuity between the generations in Ross's works—societal pressure (the boy's Catholicism is unacceptable, as is his parental background) forces the Bentleys to give up their son. Philip lacks a natural father as well as a son. Having sired Philip illegitimately, his father died before he was born; Philip's own child was stillborn. Despite, or on account of, the scorn to which his illegitimacy subjected him, Philip followed his father's path, first into the ministry and then into art. He saw the church's offer of an education in return for a commitment to the ministry as a means of escaping humiliation, but he had planned to leave it quickly for a painting career. He is prevented from doing so by an inanition of the soul that arises from marital responsibilities, economic conditions, and guilt over abandoning his flock. Adultery seems briefly to offer a way out for Philip, but Mrs. Bentley soon learns of

it, and the other woman dies giving birth to Philip's child. In what can be interpreted as a hopeful conclusion, however, the Bentleys adopt this child, and, with the money Mrs. Bentley has saved, they leave Horizon for a city life as owners of a used-book store. Their hope is that running the store will allow Philip time to pursue his painting without the crippling emotional and psychological burdens of the past.

The essence of Ross's achievement in *As for Me and My House* lies in the rich complexity of character and theme realized through brilliant manipulation of point of view and language. For almost three decades after the book's publication, it was assumed that Mrs. Bentley's reporting was accurate and that her point of view was reliable. Certainly, if the reader accepts the point of view of her journal, then the town and her husband both fail her. She is the long-suffering, supportive wife, the superior woman languishing in a cultural and domestic wasteland. As late as 1957, in his introduction to the New Canadian Library edition of the book, Roy Daniells called her "pure gold and wholly credible." If the reader accepts Ross's implicit invitation to read between the lines, however, Mrs. Bentley's self-indulgent meanness, her lonely pride, and her manipulation of Philip to satisfy her own ego are the reasons for her defeat and, to some extent, her husband's.

The many inconsistencies and outright contradictions in Mrs. Bentley's journal suggest that her single perspective is actually a source of considerable ambiguity in the book and of ambivalence on the reader's part. Several questions are raised: How accurate are her perceptions and assessments of her husband and the townspeople? How accurate are her perceptions of her own behavior and attitudes? Is the fact that the reader never learns her first name a clue to how *non*revealing her journal is? In 1969, William H. New argued that the reader's ambivalence toward Mrs. Bentley arises not so much from uncertainty about her credibility as from Ross's ironically pitting the reader's viewpoint against hers in such a way that the reader comes to appreciate the depth and complexity of the narrator's situation as well as Ross's control of his material. Through ironic use of symbols such as lamps, moths, Philip's study door, railroad tracks, and the false fronts of Horizon's main street, and through imagery involving gardens, horses, heat, dust, rain, snow, and the prairie itself, Ross reveals Mrs. Bentley's journal to be an exercise in self-deception and evasiveness. In the final analysis, this book about communication and its failure informs the reader of the impossibility of taking sides, despite the human inclination to do so.

THE WELL

When *The Well* was published in 1958, Ross had been living in Montreal for twelve years. The new urban environment awakened his interest in the motivations of the criminal mind, and remoteness from the prairie prompted a realization of its regenerative potential. In *As for Me and My House*, Philip Bentley leaves the prairie to seek an authentic self in the city; in *The Well*, Chris Rowe flees the city and achieves authentic selfhood through his moral regeneration on the prairie. Apart from this about-face, the two novels bear a close kinship. The setting of *The Well* is once more rural Saskatchewan; once more the characters fail to communicate and are claustrophobically trapped by the past as well as the present; once more they are psychologically conditioned by the prairie environment while projecting their own subjectivity onto it; and once more there is discontinuity between the generations.

The Well is a story of three barren misfits whose lives converge in the little prairie community of Campkin in the 1940's. The central character, Chris Rowe, is a fatherless twenty-year-old criminal from Montreal whose petty larcenies have culminated in the shooting of an intended robbery victim whose fate the novel leaves in doubt. Handsome, tough, and arrogant, Chris nevertheless has a potentially sensitive, gentle, nature that has been brutalized by his urban upbringing. Fleeing on westbound trains to escape arrest, Chris accepts an offer of farmwork in Campkin, his intention being to maintain a low profile for a while before resuming his westward flight. He soon finds himself enmeshed, however, in a conflict for domination over him between Larson, his employer, and Larson's wife, Sylvia.

Like Chris, Larson is pursued by the past. Ten years before, Larson's first wife had died; his son, also named Chris, died soon after. Grief has warped Larson's mind several degrees beyond eccentricity, despite outward symbols of material success such as his Cadillac and new young wife. Pathetically trying to relive the past, Larson

makes a virtual shrine of the old homestead he began with his first wife. Its chief icon is the well they dug together, a symbol of their shared achievement and happy union. Larson also keeps a horse with the same name as his dead son's horse, and he even imagines that Chris Rowe is the dead son returned. He treats Chris as a surrogate son, assuming he will take over the farm eventually and reestablish continuity with the edenic past.

To the extent that Larson's aversion to the present stems from his longing for the pretechnological past, when farming offered pride of individual accomplishment and close identity with the soil, Ross is sounding a theme found in the work of other prairie realists such as Grove and Laurence: the human costs of increasing technology on the prairie farms. As usual, Ross's focus is on the dynamics of one or two human relationships, but *The Well* can be read as a work of social criticism that probes, as Robert D. Chambers has put it, "some neglected side effects of that new prairie trinity: mechanization, mobility, and money."

Larson's wife, the voluptuous, ambitious Sylvia, had married Larson five years earlier to escape the poverty and drudgery of life as a waitress in Campkin. Partly because of a thirty-year age difference, there is neither love nor communication between them; in fact, Sylvia's plan is to kill Larson and abscond with his money. If Mrs. Bentley's designs for Philip are manipulative, those of Sylvia for Chris are evil and predatory. Her fantasy is that the adulterous relationship that quickly develops between them will make it easier for her to coerce Chris into helping her murder Larson, stuff his body down the well, and persuade the townspeople that he suddenly left on a train, as he often talked of doing. After a judicious interval, the two would marry and retire to California. In a lurid climax, Sylvia shoots her husband after wresting the gun from Chris, whose loyalty to his new surrogate father prevents him from doing so. Sylvia is eventually forced out of the house, never to be seen again. Larson expires, but not before he writes a note indicting Sylvia and exculpating Chris, leaving the farm to him as well. Chris still faces uncertain punishment for the Montreal shooting, but the important thing is that he now has the courage to do so. His refusal to be tempted further into crime by Sylvia, coupled with his loyalty to Larson, is redemptive. Once free of the trap of his past, his best instincts released by the regenerative powers of nature and the rhythms of farm life, Chris will have a chance to achieve authentic selfhood, an end to alienation, and even community with the prairie dwellers.

If *As for Me and My House* is Ross's best novel, *The Well* is in many ways his weakest. Ross admitted his failure to "get inside" the criminal mind to make Chris Rowe a sympathetic character. The ending is wildly melodramatic, as Ross also acknowledged. "I would like to do it again and give it a different ending," he stated. "I see now how it should be done." The book suffers also from a thinness of texture, a lack of intensity and power, attributable to Ross's decision to substitute the flat, banal language of barely literate characters for the richly metaphorical prose of *As for Me and My House*, and to the general lack of complexity of character, theme, and point of view. In view of these flaws, the book's cool reception seems justified.

WHIR OF GOLD

In two important ways, *Whir of Gold*, Ross's third novel, is a reverse image of *The Well*. The latter is a Rousseauistic study of a victim of urban corruption in Montreal whose innate goodness is brought out by the morally regenerative life in nature; the former is a Hobbesian study of the nasty and brutish life of a prairie youth in the same city. Again, a man and a woman compete for domination of the young hero, but whereas in *The Well* the man is basically decent, despite his misfortunes in life, and the woman grotesquely evil, in *Whir of Gold* the reverse is true. In other ways, *Whir of Gold* resembles *The Well* quite closely. Like Chris Rowe, Sonny McAlpine is arrogant, alienated, and female-dominated. Like Chris, Sonny is drawn into crime. In common with both of the earlier novels, *Whir of Gold* is concerned with entrapment, the failure of communication, and the baneful influence of the past. Its conclusion is more pessimistic than those of Ross's previous novels. Indeed, Sonny McAlpine's struggle and eventual defeat as a musician may represent Ross's pessimistic answer to the question of whether Philip Bentley's move to the city will really enable him to develop an authentic self. In the thirty years between *As for Me and My House* and *Whir of Gold*, Ross seems to have concluded that neither the rural nor the urban environment in Canada is capable of nourishing the artistic imagination.

The plot is simple and familiar, sometimes to the point of cliché. Determined to prove his superior musical talent and plagued by guilt over his sensible choice of a career in popular rather than classical music in the Saskatchewan farm community where he was reared, the young, innocent Sonny takes his clarinet to Montreal, but competition and commercialism in the wicked city combine to thwart his ambitions. Out of money and hope, he is contemplating retreat to the West when he meets Madelaine, a good-hearted nightclub floozie as lonely as he. Mad, as she is called, is from Nova Scotia, a place as remote in spirit from Montreal as is Saskatchewan. Comrades in alienation, the two decide to live together in Sonny's skid-row rooming house immediately after a first-night sexual encounter. More spontaneous and generous than other female characters in Ross's works, Mad nevertheless has comparable plans for her man. Once he is sexually involved with her, her idea is to return with him to Nova Scotia, where they will manage a restaurant and live a simple, healthy life far from the psychological rat race and moral wasteland of Montreal. In effect, she tries to trap Sonny into domesticity, as Sylvia tries to trap Chris Rowe through her plot to kill Larson.

As Mad sees it, the chief obstacle to this scheme is Sonny's neighbor, Charlie, the only other character of consequence in the small, claustrophobic world of the novel. A small-time, street-mean crook, Charlie exploits Sonny's weaknesses (primarily, a self-destructive urge arising from the guilt he feels about wasting his musical talent) to involve him, against the vehement opposition of Mad, in robbing a jewelry store. In the robbery, Sonny is shot and is himself robbed of his share of the loot by Charlie. The relationship between Sonny and Mad is likewise doomed, as are most male-female relationships in Ross's novels. The protagonist's emotional immaturity causes him unconsciously to seek an Oedipal relationship, which Mad's need to mother conveniently satisfies. Because of his insecurity, however, Sonny is unwilling to risk commitment, reacting to Mad's mothering as a smothering possessiveness and to her praise of his sexual prowess as proof of his limited talent. Ross implies that Sonny's background—specifically, his repressive prairie puritanism—is largely responsible for both his lack of feeling for Mad and his guilt over his shabby treatment of her.

Sonny, it appears, was Mad's "whir of gold," a fleeting vision of happiness, beauty, and self-fulfillment. The book's title and central symbol derives from an incident in Sonny's childhood. Out of curiosity and cruelty, he once pursued and killed a flicker bird in an attempt to capture it. The bird's wings "flashed like a whir of gold, a gust of feathered light," before the bird died. Years later, Sonny's pursuit of a musical career leads to the deathly alienation of the criminal world, and his aborted relationship with Mad to the bleak realization, once she leaves, that he has rejected probably the best chance for happiness he will ever have. The whir of gold is a fragile thing, impossible to capture. To attempt to do so is to destroy it, and also to destroy oneself through its false promise of permanence.

Ross's deep pessimism about human relationships in *Whir of Gold* is presaged in much of his earlier fiction, where puritanical constraints conflict with the human instinct for beauty, imagination, freedom, and daring. Sonny has an innate predilection for these, but his farm upbringing and moral background have indoctrinated him with practicality, restraint, discipline, and caution, values dictated also by a prudent regard for the often hostile natural elements of the prairie. Not that beauty, imagination, freedom, and daring flourish in Montreal, but Sonny's failure there is partly a deterministic result of his projection of prairie attitudes onto the city, just as earlier Ross characters project their fears onto the external prairie environment.

Unfortunately, *Whir of Gold* is not a powerfully realized novel. It does not make a profound or relevant statement about psychological repression and cultural alienation. In deferring to trends in popular fiction—inarticulate characters, limited lives, disjointed language, sordid settings—Ross denies it depth of meaning. Referring to the novel's "desperate brand of naturalism," Chambers has pointed out that "Ross's pages are covered with mundane and trivial things, as though the endless plates of bacon and eggs and all those nice hot cups of coffee will somehow cohere to underpin a work of art."

The use of Sonny's first-person point of view weakens the novel further. Sonny is a vapid Candide, a vacuous Ulysses, and the other characters are mere literary extensions of his personality. Ross professed an interest in the motivations of the criminal mind (though he admitted he probably lacked sufficient insight), but Sonny is incapable of understanding Charlie's character or his own drift toward crime. Similarly, the forays into metaphorical language, so successful in *As for Me and My House*, seem artificially literary because they are inappropriate to Sonny's character. In contrast with the richness of symbols found in *As for Me and My House*, *Whir of Gold* has only two symbols of any significance: the whir of gold and Sonny's horse, Isobel. Finally, the structure of the book is poorly balanced, with the central Sonny-Mad relationship starved for development in the second half because of Ross's increasing preoccupation with the robbery.

Apart from its successful interweaving of several perspectives in time, *Whir of Gold* did not advance Ross's reputation as a novelist any more than did *The Well*. In fact, it confirmed the uneasy doubts of some that Ross was a one-book author who had reached his peak in his first novel. Perhaps he was essentially a short-story writer, albeit a good one, lacking the technical resources or sustaining vision required of the novelist.

SAWBONES MEMORIAL

Sawbones Memorial reassured the doubters by proving convincingly that Ross was more than a one-book novelist, although its success is attributable in part to a form that utilizes the economy and precision of the short story. It succeeds also because in it Ross returns to the time and place he knows best, the Canadian prairie during the 1930's. Like *As for Me and My House*, it has a central intelligence who is perceptive and ironically detached. Unlike the two- or three-person relationships he minutely dissects in earlier novels, Ross creates a large, diverse cast of thirty characters in *Sawbones Memorial*, and while the townspeople seem no less petty and narrow-minded than before, those on the side of life, a generous and enlightened few, dominate the action in the novel. If, as Ronald Sutherland has insisted, a new Canadian literary hero has replaced the old, Doc Hunter must be counted a member of the new breed. Certainly his self-reliance, independence, and acceptance of life are preferable to Philip Bentley's intense struggle with his demons of guilt and self-doubt. Perhaps, as one reviewer stated, Ross himself "has stopped fighting life and come to terms with it." Perhaps the fact that the book was written in Europe during Ross's retirement, at several removes in time and space from Ross's Saskatchewan of the 1930's, explains the mellow, often humorous tone. In any case, the book is more hopeful than any of its predecessors, despite its return to some of Ross's familiar, depressing themes.

Sawbones Memorial comprises a collection of reminiscent vignettes depicting life in Upward, the small town that Doc Hunter has ministered to through forty-five years of pioneering, drought, and depression. The raison d'être of the vignettes is a ceremony held in April, 1948, to mark the doctor's retirement and the opening of the new Hunter Memorial Hospital. Accordingly, both reminiscing and looking to the future are in order. Though the action is limited to a few hours of the present, by the end of the novel Ross has roamed back and forth through four generations and several decades to lay bare the attitudes and preoccupations, tensions and antagonisms, and hypocrisies and prejudices of Upward's citizens.

Representing the full diversity of the community, the characters include farmers, storekeepers, teachers, ministers, and housewives, people old and young, living and dead, absent and present. They do not develop psychologically so much as they show the effects of time. Through the episodes in which they appear and reappear, they comment on the action, on Doc Hunter, and on one another. Occasionally, the same incident is retold by different characters, the contrasting viewpoints giving rise to comic or tragic irony. Little by little, the reader comes to know the characters. Doc Hunter's is the unifying point of view for those of the thirty characters whose stories constitute the book; conversely, the reader comes to know him through his shamanlike role in the lives of the other characters. The central character and intelligence, Doc is also the focus of attention at the gathering, as he has been the focus of the town's hopes and fears for more than four decades. His own suffering, it is implied, broadens and deepens the efficacy of his mission as a doctor. It seems he was married too long to a frigid wife and thus shares with other Ross protagonists an unfulfilled emotional life, though his experience has neither embittered him nor lessened his philosophical tolerance of human imperfection, of which there is God's plenty in Upward.

As with many fictional studies of small towns, from Winesburg, Ohio, to Peyton Place and beyond, Upward's appearance of respectability, especially its straitlaced attitudes concerning sexual morality, conceals a closetful of skeletons: rape, abortion, incest, murder, euthanasia, to name only a few. As the town's sole physician for almost half a century, Doc Hunter knows the contents of the closet better than anyone, a fact that gives pause to those who would prefer to forget their past in order to gossip more self-righteously. The more admirable characters, on the other hand, are often outsiders, defined as anyone who deviates from Upward's conventional standards of moral and social behavior. More so than Ross's earlier outsider-protagonist, these are very human characters whose struggles and triumphs the readers can share.

Sawbones Memorial is also more ambitious in form and conception than Ross's earlier novels. The large number of characters, the experimentation with multiple points of view, the reliance on dialogue, monologue, speeches, and flashbacks to convey information, reveal personality, and establish mood (much as in drama and film), are all new. The dialogue is especially remarkable in that each character is individuated through diction, idiom, intonation, or rhythm. (Ross has said that the idea of using nothing but the speech of his characters to construct a novel came to him as he overheard fragments of reminiscences at the opening of the Royal Bank's new head office in Montreal.) It is true that the book turns against two familiar themes: the failure of communication and the stultification of the spirit in the small prairie towns of Ross's time. The roots of human alienation, whether personal or social, are still to be found in agonized confusion over sexuality, but Ross deals with a larger range of human experience than before, including such timeless concerns as the nature of human evil and the evil of human nature, birth and death, youth and age, courage and cowardice, cruelty and compassion. For one day in time, at least, in the spring of 1948, these are reconciled as Doc Hunter speaks of retirement and the continuity symbolized by the new doctor's arrival. It is all beginning again, "just as it was all beginning that day" when he first arrived.

John H. Ferres

Other major works

SHORT FICTION: *The Lamp at Noon, and Other Stories*, 1968; *The Race, and Other Stories*, 1982.

NONFICTION: *Just Wind and Horses*, 1988 (memoir).

Bibliography

Chambers, Robert D. *Sinclair Ross and Ernest Buckler*. Montreal: Copp Clark and McGill-Queen's University Press, 1975. Joint study of two of Canada's finest authors features close textual analyses of their respective styles. Includes bibliography.

Fraser, Keath. *As for Me and My Body: A Memoir of Sinclair Ross*. Toronto, Ont.: ECW Press, 1997. Revelatory reading of *As for Me and My House* emphasizes the novel's biographical basis, in particular its veiled acknowledgment of Ross's homosexuality. Also includes a frank portrait of Ross's later years, when the onset of Parkinson's disease and his growing sense of failure as a writer made his life very difficult.

Mitchell, Ken. *Sinclair Ross: A Reader's Guide*. Moose Jaw, Sask.: Coteau, 1980. Insightful overview, aimed at the general reader, presents an experienced author's response to the work of an older peer. Discussion of Ross's work includes analyses of all four of the novels.

Moss, John, ed. *From the Heart of the Heartland: The Fiction of Sinclair Ross*. Ottawa: University of Ottawa Press, 1992. Collection of scholarly essays includes feminist, postmodernist, semiotic, and narratological studies of Ross's major works. Although some of the contributors tend to wander off into the far reaches of literary theory, the variety of viewpoints presented makes this a stimulating and thought-provoking collection.

Stouck, David. *As for Sinclair Ross*. Toronto, Ont.: University of Toronto Press, 2005. Stouck, who knew Ross in the later years of the writer's life, draws on their acquaintanceship and on archival records to provide a detailed account of Ross's life. Maintains that Ross wrote about small towns and prairie farmers in order to make his readers feel uncomfortable with their racial, ethnic, and gender prejudices.

_____. "Continuing to Read Sinclair Ross." *American Review of Canadian Studies* 32, no. 4 (Winter, 2002): 695-702. Focuses on Ross's novels, interpreting *As for Me and My House* in terms of identity and self-construction and analyzing *Sawbones Memorial* from the perspective of postcolonialism. Also describes Ross's disappointment with *The Well* and the difficulties he confronted in publishing *Whir of Gold*.

_____, ed. *Sinclair Ross's "As for Me and My House": Five Decades of Criticism*. Toronto, Ont.: University of Toronto Press, 1991. Collection presents contemporary reviews and opinions of Ross's most accomplished novel as well as critical essays on the work published between 1957 and 1991. Includes bibliography and index.

Woodcock, George. *Introducing Sinclair Ross's "As for Me and My House": A Reader's Guide*. Toronto, Ont.: ECW Press, 1990. Introductory work aimed at first- and second-year university students discusses Ross's literary influences and numerous elements of the novel, including the symbolism of names, physical setting, characters, and the legacy of illegitimacy.

HENRY ROTH

Born: Tysmenica, Galicia, Austro-Hungarian
   Empire (now in Ukraine); February 8, 1906
Died: Albuquerque, New Mexico; October 13, 1995

PRINCIPAL LONG FICTION

Call It Sleep, 1934
Mercy of a Rude Stream, 1994-1998 (includes *A Star Shines over Mt. Morris Park*, 1994; *A Diving Rock on the Hudson*, 1995; *From Bondage*, 1996; and *Requiem for Harlem*, 1998)

OTHER LITERARY FORMS

In addition to his novels, Henry Roth wrote a number of essays, short stories, and fragments that editor Mario Materassi collected and published in 1987 as *Shifting Landscape: A Composite, 1925-1987*.

ACHIEVEMENTS

With *Call It Sleep*, Henry Roth created a masterpiece of American Jewish fiction and a classic novel of immigration, one that brilliantly adapts the insights associated with Austrian psychoanalyst Sigmund Freud and the techniques associated with Irish writer James Joyce in order to recount the traumatic experiences of an impressionable young foreigner in New York City. However, it was not until thirty years after its publication that the book began to be widely read, studied, and admired. Discouraged by neglect of his first novel, Roth abandoned the literary life and did not return to writing novels until a prodigious burst of creativity in his final years yielded 3,200 manuscript pages of disturbing autobiographical fiction, the tetralogy titled *Mercy of a Rude Stream*, half of which appeared after the author's death at the age of eighty-nine. The sixty-year gap between publication of *Call It Sleep*, in 1934, and *A Star Shines over Mt. Morris Park*, the first volume of the tetralogy, in 1994, repre-

sents the most remarkable instance in American literary history of writer's block and late artistic renewal.

BIOGRAPHY

Like David Schearl, the young protagonist of *Call It Sleep*, Henry Roth was born in 1906 in the Galician region of the Austro-Hungarian Empire (now in Ukraine) but was brought to New York City when only two years old. Like many other working-class Jewish immigrants, the Roths settled on the lower East Side of Manhattan but later relocated to Harlem. Roth manifested talent with a story in the student magazine of New York's public City College. Eda Lou Walton, a professor at New York University who befriended Roth and encouraged him to write, became his mentor and lover. Eventually, Roth moved into her Greenwich Village apartment, where he wrote *Call It Sleep*. Though Walton helped him find a publisher, the Depression year 1934 was not propitious for a literary debut, and, though the book received favor-

Henry Roth. (Harvey Wang)

able reviews, its publisher, Robert O. Ballou, was forced into bankruptcy.

Roth began a second novel but, convinced that it was unworthy of the Marxist ideals he then set for himself, he abandoned both it and the cosmopolitan ferment of New York. He married Muriel Parker, a composer he had met at the Yaddo artists' colony, and moved with her to rural Maine. Abandoning her own musical aspirations, Muriel supported him and their two sons by teaching school, while Roth helped by chopping wood, selling maple syrup, fighting forest fires, tutoring Latin and math, and serving as an attendant at a mental hospital. For most of a decade, he raised and slaughtered geese and ducks.

In 1964, *Call It Sleep* was rediscovered, and, at the age of fifty-eight, its obscure author suddenly found himself famous. Roth was plagued by persistent questions about his current projects. In 1968, after an abortive effort to write a novel set during the Spanish Inquisition, he and Muriel moved to Albuquerque, New Mexico. After Muriel's death in 1990, Roth attempted suicide but survived to complete his last great literary task at the age of eighty-nine. Despite agonizing rheumatoid arthritis, he managed to produce an enormous autobiographical fictional sequence, one that revisited its author's strained relationship with his abusive, embittered father and incestuous relationships with his sister and his cousin. Upon Roth's death in 1995, two of the four volumes of *Mercy of a Rude Stream* had been published, while the final two appeared posthumously, in 1996 and 1998, respectively. Enough material remained for two additional volumes, but Roth's publisher, St. Martin's Press, determined that they fell outside the *Mercy of a Rude Stream* cycle and remained uncertain about when or whether they would be published.

ANALYSIS

For much of the twentieth century, Henry Roth, the novelist who vanished for sixty years after a stunning debut, seemed a gloss on writer F. Scott Fitzgerald's quip that American lives lack second acts. Yet his long life offers enough acts to please the most garrulous of playwrights and challenge the most assiduous of biographers. He is at once salutatorian and valedictorian of twentieth century America, a contemporary of both William Faulkner and Don DeLillo. His pioneering use of

stream of consciousness captured a newly urbanized, industrialized society undergoing massive transformation, but Roth survived into a very different era to write his own requiem.

In retrospect, *Call It Sleep* seems so unequivocally a major artistic achievement that it is difficult to understand why it was neglected for thirty years. However, in 1934, American culture lacked a category for American Jewish literature. By 1964, Roth fulfilled the need to anoint a worthy ancestor to Saul Bellow, Bernard Malamud, and Philip Roth, to legitimate a newly canonized tradition. It was only after ethnicity became a crucial issue in American society that Roth's novel could be appreciated for its pioneering embodiment of multiculturalism and multilingualism.

Mercy of a Rude Stream is of a different order of accomplishment than *Call It Sleep*. The fictional sequence that Roth created in his final years is of compelling interest to those fascinated by a tormented author's representation of his own compulsions and his desperate attempt to find closure. If Roth's virtuosic first novel appeared ahead of its time, his parting tetralogy was a throwback—a fictional sequence that not only is set in the 1920's but also employs the naturalistic style common to that era. From *Call It Sleep* to *Requiem for Harlem*, Roth's frustrated literary career is itself the most remarkable narrative he created.

CALL IT SLEEP

Call It Sleep begins in May, 1907, with the arrival by ship from Europe of two-year-old David Schearl and his mother, Genya. They are met at Ellis Island by David's father, Albert, a surly, abusive man who is embittered by disappointment. Albert is forever falling out with fellow workers and forced to seek new employment, as a printer and then as a milkman. The family moves from modest lodgings in Brooklyn's Brownsville neighborhood to a crowded tenement on the lower East Side of Manhattan. Roth's book focuses on young David's troubling experiences during the years 1911-1913, as a stranger in a strange land. *Call It Sleep* is a coming-of-age novel about a hypersensitive Jewish boy who is forced to cope alone with the mysteries of sex, religion, and love.

After a brief prologue recounting David's arrival in America, Roth organizes his story into four sections, each defined by a dominant image: "The Cellar," "The

Picture," "The Coal," and "The Rail." What might otherwise seem casual details are magnified by refraction through the mind of an anxious child. Roth's use of stream of consciousness intensifies the sense of an unformed mind trying to assimilate the varied sensations that assault it. The family apartment is a haven for David, as long as his father, who even doubts his paternity of the boy, is not home and his doting mother can lavish her affections on him. When David ventures out into the clamorous streets, he encounters threats, from both rats and humans.

At the heder, the drab religious school where Jewish boys are given rote instruction in a Hebrew Bible they cannot understand, David is confused and inspired by Isaiah's account of the angel with a burning coal. Eavesdropping on a conversation between his mother and her sister, Bertha, he misconstrues an explanation for why Genya, disgraced after being jilted by a Gentile, married Albert. When Leo, an older Polish boy, persuades David to introduce him to his cousin, Esther, David is overwhelmed by incredulity and guilt over the sexual liberties that Leo takes. Fleeing his brutal father, David is shocked into unconsciouness after touching the live rail of a street car. Faced, like the reader, with sensory overload, David might as well call it sleep, embracing temporary oblivion as restoration after a long, disorienting day.

To explore the tensions among Albert, Genya, and David, a clanging family triangle rife with resentments and recriminations, Roth appropriates the theories of Freud, particularly in describing the powerful Oedipal bond between mother and son as well as the almost patricidal strife between Albert and David. The authority of Joyce asserts itself, not only in the fact that Roth's account of David Schearl, a surrogate for the author himself, is in effect another portrait of the artist as a young man but also in his lavish use of stream of consciousness and his meticulous deployment of recurrent imagery.

During the two decades surrounding the beginning of the twentieth century, massive, unprecedented migration from eastern and southern Europe was radically reshaping American society; more effectively than any other novel, *Call It Sleep* records the traumas experienced when the Old World met the New World. Many of Roth's immigrants are inspired by the American Dream of enlarged opportunity, while others are repulsed by an urban nightmare. Call *it*, too, sleep.

Though the Schearls are Polish Jews, the eclectic slum in which they live also serves as home to immigrants and natives from many other backgrounds. Not the least of Roth's accomplishments is his success at rendering the diversity of David's environs. Yiddish is the first language of the Schearls, but English, German, Hebrew, Italian, and Polish are also spoken, in varying registers, by characters in the story. In a novel designed for an Anglo reader, it would be misleading and demeaning to put fractured English into the mouths or minds of fluent Yiddish speakers when they are assumed to be using their native language. Instead, Roth fashions English prose supple enough to represent the varying speech and thoughts of those who speak and think in other tongues.

Call It Sleep is significant for reflecting a momentous phenomenon that transformed the United States but was ignored by many of Roth's literary contemporaries. In its vivid rendition of a child's-eye view, its dramatic exposure of family tensions, and its creation of a rich linguistic texture, Roth's first novel is an artistic triumph.

MERCY OF A RUDE STREAM

Though they were published separately and can be read independently and autonomously, the four novels that constitute *Mercy of a Rude Stream* are best understood together, as a single narrative sequence. The entire tetralogy follows the coming-of-age of Ira Stigman, a Jewish emigrant to New York, from 1914, when he is eight years old, until 1927, when he is twenty-one and a senior at City College. Despite the change in names and the addition of a younger sister, Minnie, Ira seems largely an extension of David Schearl from *Call It Sleep*. He is also a thinly disguised version of Roth himself. The autobiographical basis of the books is made even more apparent by interpolated sections in which an older Ira, an ailing octogenarian author living in Albuquerque, addresses his word processor, calling it Ecclesias. He comments on his own renewed, belated efforts at writing fiction. Ira as author poses the question that most readers will raise about Roth himself—Why, approaching death, does he struggle to record such lacerating memories?

In narrating his story, Ira forces himself to revisit an unhappy childhood and adolescence, in which he and his mother, Leah, are terrorized by his psychotic father, Chaim. When the family moves from the lower East Side to a largely Irish neighborhood in East Harlem, Ira feels rudely wrenched out of an organic, nurturing Jewish community. He recalls the painful details of broken friendships and of his public disgrace when he was expelled from high school for stealing fountain pens. The most agonizing recollections—and the element that has drawn the most attention to Roth's final books—concern Ira's sexual transgressions. The second volume, *A Diving Rock on the Hudson*, offers the startling revelation that, beginning when he was sixteen years old and she was fourteen years old, Ira regularly, furtively committed incest with his sister, Minnie. He also maintained covert sexual relations with his younger cousin, Stella. Recollections of incest continue through volumes 3 and 4 and fuel the author's suicidal self-loathing. The older Ira longs to die but feels compelled to tell his story first, as though narration might bring purgation and even redemption.

Unlike the bravura *Call It Sleep*, much of *Mercy of a Rude Stream* is written in undistinguished prose that is at most serviceable in evoking working-class, urban life during and after World War I. Ira offers details of jobs he held, including stock boy in an upscale food store, soda peddler at Yankee Stadium and the Polo Grounds, and salesman in a candy shop. His sentimental education is very much connected to his intellectual one, and, though his grades are mediocre, Ira thrives in college. Publication of a short story in the student magazine awakens literary ambitions; his friendship with affluent Larry Gordon enlarges Ira's life beyond his own squalid situation. He begins to acquire social graces and to strike on ideas. Ira becomes inebriated with reading, particularly after Edith Welles, the professor who was Larry's lover, becomes Ira's mentor and lover. Edith, who is modeled on Roth's own Eda Lou Walton, introduces Ira to the most influential books and people of New York's bohemian culture.

In the final pages of the cycle's final book, *Requiem for Harlem*, Ira bids farewell to his dysfunctional, debilitating family and his loathsome sexual compulsions by moving down to Greenwich Village to live with Edith. The apprentice artist is finally ready to write a novel very much like *Call It Sleep*. Finally, after disburdening himself of excruciating secrets, the eighty-nine-year-old Roth finished writing and prepared at last to call it sleep.

Steven G. Kellman

OTHER MAJOR WORKS

SHORT FICTION: "Broker," 1938; "Somebody Always Grabs the Purple," 1940; "Petey and Yorsee and Mario," 1956; "At Times in Flight," 1959 (parable); "The Dun Dakotas," 1960 (parable).

MISCELLANEOUS: *Shifting Landscape: A Composite, 1925-1987*, 1987 (Mario Materassi, editor).

BIBLIOGRAPHY

Adams, Stephen J. "'The Noisiest Novel Ever Written': The Soundscape of Henry Roth's *Call It Sleep*." *Twentieth Century Literature* 35, no. 1 (Spring, 1989). Adams analyzes the power and integral role of sounds in Roth's novel *Call It Sleep*.

Buelens, Gert. "The Multi-Voiced Basis of Henry Roth's Literary Success in *Call It Sleep*." In *Cultural Difference and the Literary Text: Pluralism and the Limits of Authenticity in North American Literatures*, edited by Winfried Siemerling and Katrin Schwenk. Iowa City: University of Iowa Press, 1996. An examination of Roth's famous novel, focusing on the ways in which he represents different languages and voices.

Halkin, Hillel. "Henry Roth's Secret." *Commentary* 97, no. 5 (May, 1994). A study of Roth's novels and his homosexual experiences, in which Halkin compares the lives and works of Roth and British writer T. E. Lawrence.

Kellman, Steven G. *Redemption: The Life of Henry Roth*. New York: W. W. Norton, 2005. An engaging, readable account of the writer's life, particularly good in examining the long interim between Roth's novels. According to Kellman, Roth deliberately stopped writing because he did not want to confront his adolescent experiences with incest.

Lyons, Bonnie. *Henry Roth: The Man and His Work*. New York: Cooper Square, 1976. The first book-length study to address Roth's early work. Includes an interview with Roth, some biographical information, and a detailed reading of *Call It Sleep*.

Rosen, Jonathan. "Writer, Interrupted." *The New Yorker*, August 1, 2005. In his review of Kellman's biography (above), Rosen provides a detailed description of Roth's life, literary career, personality, and novels, and he recalls visiting Roth in Albuquerque in 1993.

Sokoloff, Naomi B. *Imagining the Child in Modern Jewish Fiction.* Baltimore: Johns Hopkins University Press, 1992. Roth's David Schearl is linked to representations of the child by other Jewish writers, including Sholom Aleichem, Hayim Nachman Bialik, Jerzy Kosinski, Aharon Appelfeld, David Grossman, A. B. Yehoshua, and Cynthia Ozick.

Walden, Daniel, ed. *Studies in American Jewish Literature* 5, no. 1 (Spring, 1979). A special issue of this journal devoted to essays on Roth. Includes a bibliography and an interview with the author.

Weber, Myles. *Consuming Silences: How We Read Authors Who Don't Publish.* Athens: University of Georgia Press, 2005. Roth figures prominently in Weber's discussion of four American authors who stopped writing for long periods of time. He argues that for some writers the decision to defer authorship can be an intelligent career move.

Wirth-Nesher, Hana, ed. *New Essays on "Call It Sleep."* New York: Cambridge University Press, 1996. A collection of some of the most engaging and useful analyses of Roth's first novel. Includes an essay by literary critic Leslie Fielder on the "many myths" of Roth and analysis of "language, nostalgic mournfulness, and urban immigrant family romance" in the novel.

JOSEPH ROTH

Born: Brody, Austrian Galicia, Austro-Hungarian Empire (now in Ukraine); September 2, 1894
Died: Paris, France; May 27, 1939
Also known as: Moses Joseph Roth

PRINCIPAL LONG FICTION

Hotel Savoy, 1924 (English translation, 1986)
Die Rebellion, 1924 (*Rebellion*, 1999)
Die Flucht ohne Ende: Ein Bericht, 1927 (*Flight Without End: A Report*, 1977)
Das Spinnennetz, 1928 (*The Spider's Web*, 1988)
Zipper und sein Vater, 1928 (*Zipper and His Father*, 1988)
Rechts und Links, 1929 (*Right and Left*, 1991)
Hiob: Roman eines einfachen Mannes, 1930 (*Job: The Story of a Simple Man*, 1931)
Radetzkymarsch, 1932 (*The Radetzky March*, 1933)
Tarabas, ein Gast auf dieser Erde, 1934 (*Tarabas, a Guest on Earth*, 1934)
Beichte eines Mörders, erzählt in einer Nacht, 1936 (*The Confession of a Murderer, Told in One Night*, 1938)
Die Hundert Tage, 1936 (*Ballad of the Hundred Days*, 1936)

Das falsche Gewicht: Die Geschichte eines Eichmeisters, 1937 (*Weights and Measures*, 1982)
Die Kapuzinergruft, 1938 (*The Emperor's Tomb*, 1984)
Die Geschichte von der 1002. Nacht, 1939 (*The Tale of the 1002nd Night*, 1998; also published as *The String of Pearls*, 1998)
Der stumme Prophet, 1966 (*The Silent Prophet*, 1979)
Perlefter, 1978

OTHER LITERARY FORMS

Joseph Roth was a prolific writer in a variety of prose forms. As a journalist for several leading German newspapers, Roth displayed his wide-ranging interest in politics, society, art, and culture through a "feuilletonistic" style that he succeeded in elevating to an art form. Between 1922 and 1939, he completed a number of short stories in addition to his fifteen novels. Like many of his longer works of fiction, *Die Legende vom heiligen Trinker* (1939; *The Legend of the Holy Drinker*, 1943), the most famous of these shorter works, is a tale of love and misfortune expressed through the lives of simple people and social misfits. Essays, short prose pieces, travel impressions, portraits, and book reviews complete the four volumes of his collected works, edited and published by friend and fellow-author Hermann Kesten.

The lengthiest and most notable of Roth's many essays, *Juden auf Wanderschaft* (1927; *The Wandering Jews*, 2001) and *Der Antichrist* (1934; *Antichrist*, 1935), give unequivocal testimony to the author's sense of social justice and firm commitment to humanity. Under the influence of neo-Romanticism as a student of German language and literature at the University of Vienna, Roth experimented with political and satiric poetry and with fairy-tale motifs. Although a number of his early works have been lost, Roth's major novels have enjoyed enduring popularity; several have been made into films, and many of his major works have been translated into English. Roth's papers are housed at the Leo Baeck Institute in New York.

ACHIEVEMENTS

As an itinerant journalist and exiled Austrian author, Joseph Roth came into close contact with many of the principal writers and intellectuals of his day in the coffeehouses and hotels of Paris, where most of his later years were spent, and in those of other European cultural centers such as Vienna, Berlin, and Prague. Roth can best be described as a revolutionary conservative. He was influenced by French and Russian psychological realism, as exemplified by Gustave Flaubert and Leo Tolstoy, as well as by the Viennese impressionism of Hugo von Hofmannsthal and Arthur Schnitzler. Impulse, instinct, and emotion, rather than analytical thought and objective reflection, characterize Roth and his writings. He portrays individuals in the age-old search for identity, justice, and truth in a changing world scarcely equipped to provide the security and stability that they so eagerly seek. An existential quest for meaning, transposed to cultural, geographical, spiritual, and intellectual contexts, forms the core of his work.

Up to 1926, Roth's fiction discloses a political and social "revolutionary" orientation in a subjectively eclectic rather than ideologically activist fashion. After 1926, his conservative side becomes more pronounced. Roth is revolutionary in the etymological sense of the word: The ideal state that society strives to attain has its source in the past. In an age dominated by war, existential uncer-

tainty, and crumbling traditions, Roth's fiction articulated both the anxieties and the hopes of common people in characters such as Franz Tunda in *Flight Without End* and Mendel Singer in *Job*. Roth's friend, Kesten, has accurately described him as a Romantic with the eyes of a realist: Roth was a republican, rationalist, skeptic, friend of the Socialist proletariat, *révolteur*, Jacobin, and unbeliever, as well as a monarchist and faithful Catholic.

Roth's compact journalistic style, characterized by repetition, questions, parataxis, interjections, and short chapters, was not innovative, yet the purity and simple power of his technique have kept his novels readable while many of the radical, experimental works of the 1920's and the 1930's have faded into oblivion. Roth's novels are contemporary yet timeless tales of homelessness and exile, deeply embedded in the context of Imperial Austria, the Weimar Republic, and National Socialism, yet transcending their time and place.

BIOGRAPHY

Moses Joseph Roth was born on September 2, 1894, in Brody, then part of the Austrian province of Galicia on the Russian border. The only child of a Jewish family of very modest means, Roth was reared by his mother in her father's home. Roth's father, who had been traveling at the time of his son's birth, had to be committed to a mental institution before his return home and never knew of the child's existence. As a young boy, Roth attended the *Gymnasium* (college-preparatory secondary school) in Brody, rather than the heder, the Orthodox Jewish school. That Roth's upbringing as a Jew, though not Orthodox, greatly affected his attitudes is evident in his later writing.

Roth pursued his interest in literature early; he studied German language and literature, together with philosophy, in Lemberg and subsequently in Vienna. In the imperial city, he became associated with the Polish author József Wittlin and studied under the famous Germanist Walther Brecht and his assistant Heinz Kindermann at the university there. With Wittlin, Roth volunteered for military service in 1916 during World War I; after his release from Russia as a prisoner of war, he returned to Vienna in 1918 in dire financial straits.

In Vienna, Roth embarked on a career as a journalist, and his financial position temporarily improved, although financial difficulties continued to plague him throughout his life, as did his alcoholism. In 1919, Roth met his future wife, the Viennese Friedl Reichler, whom he married in 1922. Between 1923 and 1932, Roth served as a correspondent for the *Frankfurter Zeitung* and traveled almost continuously throughout Europe. Roth's trip to Russia in 1926 had an especially formative impact in developing his thoughts on the possibilities for societal and cultural rebirth. The deteriorating condition of his wife's schizophrenia, however, made the late 1920's especially taxing years for him. The author's growing despair, alienation from society, and sense of personal guilt during this period contributed to his alcoholism. Friedl was finally admitted to a sanatorium near Amstetten in Lower Austria in 1935, where she stayed until immediately before her death. Surviving her husband by a about a year, Friedl became a victim of the Nazi euthanasia program in 1940. Roth considered his wife's illness a personal curse and a punishment by God; he lent this personal tragedy literary expression in his works, most notably in *Job*.

During the last decade of Roth's life, the writers Kesten and Stefan Zweig were among his closest friends. These last years were also shared with a woman named Andrea Manga Bell, whom Roth first met in 1929 and to whom he became passionately attracted. On January 30, 1933, Roth fled Germany and began a life of official exile in Vienna, Salzburg, Marseilles, Nice, Amsterdam, Ostend, Brussels, Limburg, Warsaw, and Zurich before settling in Paris. Financially destitute, Roth died in a paupers' hospital in Paris on May 27, 1939.

ANALYSIS

Joseph Roth's novels fall into two basic periods, the first of which extends from 1922 to 1926, the second from 1926 until his death in 1939. Influenced considerably by his diverse journalistic activities, Roth's early published fiction reflects the themes of social justice and revolt against oppression and exploitation that were characteristic of German literature during the Weimar Republic. The expressionistic writings of Ernst Toller and the satiric pieces of Bertolt Brecht are but two examples illustrating the importance of social and political themes in the literature of the day. Although Roth was never a political thinker in the manner of Toller or

Joseph Roth. (The Granger Collection, New York)

Brecht, or even of the young Thomas Mann, a deep feeling of compassion for humanity and great frustration with the conditions in Europe directly following World War I evoked great social concern in him. The title of his 1924 novel *Rebellion* alludes to these themes. Like Franz Grillparzer, the famous nineteenth century Austrian dramatist, Roth viewed the resurging nationalism of his day as a stage between humanity and bestiality.

Gradually, Roth moved away from the larger questions of societal reform and concentrated more on the individual's fate and on the search for identity. Roth's personal search for a new homeland began to crystallize into literary expression, as in the factual story about his friend, Franz Tunda, in *Flight Without End*. During this second phase of his career, Roth drew heavily on personal memories of Eastern Europe, the landscapes and characters of which color his novels and stories. For example, Roth's birthplace, Brody, which was the center of a lively smuggling trade, is accurately described in *Weights and Measures*, as is the smuggler-type Kapturak, who appears in this and other novels.

Roth's tendency during this phase of his career to romanticize the past is revealed in his symbolic exploitation of both the Austro-Hungarian monarchy, as represented by Emperor Franz Joseph, and of his own Eastern European and Jewish background. Although Roth recognized the onset of decay and decline in the monarchy and the often harsh imperfections of society in his birthplace, he nevertheless relied on these experiences to develop a supranational ideal based on hope and essential human values. The reshaping of these models into representative symbols provided the focal point for his later work; the nonprogrammatic social changes Roth advocated in his first three novels, for example, were transformed into abstract conservative idealism in the later works. The conclusion of *The Emperor's Tomb* exemplifies Roth's melancholic reverence for the established institutions of the past, which have been so long in the making. Though imperfect, this heritage provides the necessary cornerstone for building a positive future. Thus, the significance of Austria-Hungary and the melting pot of Eastern Europe, which together embody the agony of contemporary reality and the vestiges of bygone greatness, lies not in their political or social structure per se, but in the suggestive impact of what they symbolize.

Even Roth's historical novels, such as *Ballad of the Hundred Days*, which in part recounts Napoleon's return from Corsica, by no means present historical material for its own sake but rather reconcile the author's personal idealistic message with temporal reality. Thus, Napoleon, like Franz Joseph, is transformed from a worldly hero into a mystical one. Roth's cosmopolitan attitude and antinationalist zeal transform history into a new reality. As Carl Steiner shows, Roth's growing love for France (underscored by his long stay there) and his inclination to Catholicism give further evidence of an ongoing search for a new and more perfect homeland. Roth established this position when he wrote in *Antichrist*, "The whole earth is temporarily our home. But our real home is the eternal bosom of God." The various experiences of exile (existential, spiritual, and geographical) confronted Roth throughout his life. Roth's biographer, David Bronsen, summarizes this experience when he writes, "Every external assimilation is a flight or the attempt at flight out of the sad association of the perse-

cuted; it is an attempt to balance contradictions, which nevertheless continue to exist."

JOB

Despite the large degree of thematic consistency in Roth's later years, *Job* and *The Radetzky March* perhaps best display the poignancy of his themes and the lucid style he mastered. Written in the early 1930's, both novels convey the experience of exile, alienation, and tradition so characteristic of Roth's writings. In contrast to his earlier works, however, these two novels seek to furnish answers and solutions, even if solely on an idealistic level. *Job* launches into metaphysical flight; *The Radetzky March* delves into the myth of old Austria.

Job marked a noticeable change in perspective in Roth's literary career; its metaphysical preoccupations stand in sharp contrast to the more earthly concerns of the earlier novels. Moreover, for the first time, a positive answer is provided as a means of resolving the human dilemma. Spiritual faith conquers despair, frustration, and pride. In the final analysis, Mendel Singer's struggle with metaphysics is just as pressing an attempt at escape from the ravages of modern-day life as is the earth-centered quest for meaning of Franz and Carl Trotta in *The Radetzky March*. Mendel, Franz, and Carl reflect Roth's own struggle. Viewed together, the two novels complement each other in that they respectively reflect the spiritual and temporal realms in an interrelationship akin to the medieval hierarchical system, in which church and state represented these respective values.

Job, bearing the subtitle *The Story of a Simple Man*, takes place primarily in the easternmost regions of Austria-Hungary along the Russian border. Roth's novel about the family of Mendel Singer, an actual name borrowed from this Eastern European locale, stands in sharp contrast to the biblical story of Job, whose test by God resulted in the loss of great wealth and power. Mendel has never possessed earthly riches, but his plight is just as severe and his fall from grace just as shattering as that of his biblical counterpart. Mendel has been blessed with four children, although the youngest, Menuchim, is epileptic. The long, painful agony suffered by Mendel and his wife, Deborah, because of Menuchim's condition, becomes the central concern in the novel.

The theme of illness and recovery in the lives of Menuchim and of his sister Mirjam, who goes insane after she immigrates with her parents to New York, is closely associated with the feelings of guilt, despair, and hope Roth experienced during his wife's mental illness. Mendel and Deborah's outlook is basically Hasidic, reflecting Roth's own inclination toward mysticism and Romanticism. Intuition, rather than rational thought, governs the lives of these simple people. Initially, Mendel is more inclined than is Deborah to let fate run its course. His faith and trust in God's will do not allow him to seek help for his son, yet he acquiesces to Deborah's desire to visit the *Wunderrabbi* (miracle rabbi) to receive guidance. The rabbi prophesies to Deborah that her son will one day be healed when he says

> Pain will make him wise, ugliness kind-hearted, bitterness charitable, and sickness strong. His eyes will see far and wide, his ears will be clear and receptive. His mouth will be silent, but when he parts his lips they will bring forth good tidings. Have no fear and return home!

Deborah is as persistent in following her motherly instincts to save her son as Mendel is in his spiritual resolve.

Gradually, the toll of eking out a meager existence by instructing young Jewish boys in religion alienates Mendel from his wife, from God, and from society at large. The fulfillment of the prophecy seems more and more remote. After these years of economic and spiritual stagnation, Mendel and Deborah decide to immigrate to New York, where their second son, Schemarjah, is prospering. Their oldest son, Jonas, has joined the Russian army, and Mirjam, still a young girl, has unacceptably fallen in love with a Cossack. With heavy hearts, Mendel and Deborah leave Menuchim behind to be reared by friends.

The opportunity for a new beginning in the new world is short-lived. Problems similar to those in Europe confront the Singers. Encouraging news from the family caring for Menuchim consoles Mendel and his wife at first, but new tragedies inevitably befall them. Jonas is reported missing; Schemarjah is killed while serving as an American soldier in World War I; Deborah dies of shock at the news; Mirjam becomes mentally ill and must be committed to an institution. Mendel turns increasingly against God and believes that Menuchim must also be dead by this time, yet the rabbi's prophecy

is miraculously fulfilled. Menuchim appears, having finally been healed in his native environment. After overcoming the serious illness that afflicted him as a child, he has become a famous musician. Mendel, too, is restored, as he repents for his lack of faith in God's healing power. His crippled son, who stayed behind in a seemingly barren homeland, is the one who prospers in the end.

The symbolism of this blossoming in an otherwise seemingly arid milieu emphasizes Roth's dependence on heritage and tradition. While avoiding the nationalistic and Zionist sentiments he opposed, Roth presents a picture of spiritual wholeness realized through acceptance of one's indigenous home. The rabbi's admonition to Deborah to "Have no fear and return home!" assumes symbolic significance. All members of the family except Menuchim abandoned their home and suffered because of it. Through spiritual rejuvenation, Mendel is afforded the opportunity to reverse his physical and spiritual abandonment of his "home," and further hope still exists that Mirjam and Jonas, whose fates are not yet sealed, will one day share their father's salvation. In Roth's view, Mendel has become the ideal religious seeker. Faith, despair, and superstition mingle in him, as in the nontraditional religious faith of Mendel's creator. Mendel experiences the miraculous glory of salvation on this earth, a fate that Roth did not himself share but could only idealize in his artistic creation.

THE RADETZKY MARCH

The history of a peasant family from Sipolje, an eastern province in the Austro-Hungarian Empire, provides the content for the most famous of Roth's novels, *The Radetzky March*. Spanning the years from the mid-nineteenth century to the end of World War I, the novel re-creates the nostalgic, melancholic mood of political, social, and cultural decline during Franz Joseph's reign. For the various ethnic groups the monarchy encompasses, the emperor stands as a patriarchal figure, ecumenical in his humanity, but just as the dual monarchy became an anachronism in Europe when revolution, social ferment, and expanding industrialization catapulted Europe into the twentieth century, so too do Roth's main characters, Franz Trotta and his son, Carl Joseph, symbolize the end of an era. Both father and son live in the glory that was once Austria's, but adherence to an antiquated value system isolates them from their own time.

Franz's father, Joseph Trotta, has been elevated to the nobility from his simple peasant background as a result of his having saved the emperor's life at Solferino, a battle fought between the Austrians and Franco-Sardinians in 1859. The Trotta legacy lives on in the next two generations. By becoming the hero's heirs, Franz and Carl Joseph share in their predecessor's glory in a land rich in tradition. Yet this tradition slowly crumbles, as symbolized by the aged emperor's progressive loss of touch with the past; he confuses the three generations of Trottas as senility blurs his recollection of the history he helped to form.

The story of Joseph Trotta is climaxed by his resignation from the army over the misrepresentation and romanticization of his heroic deed in a school textbook. He rears his son, Franz, not to serve in the military but rather to serve the state as a civil servant. Franz rises to the position of chief district commissioner within the empire and exhibits unwavering loyalty to Austria. His life centers on duty and reputation. Franz's greatest disappointment occurs when his son, Carl Joseph, temporarily resigns from the military at the rank of lieutenant. When the emperor dies, Franz himself can no longer continue living. In his later years, Franz actually begins to resemble physically the emperor to whom he was so intimately devoted. The world of stability and security as he knew it has now completely ceased to exist after the emperor's death. Carl Joseph, too, increasingly experiences the emptiness of life.

In contrast with the basically flat character of Franz, Carl Joseph is developed more fully. Much as the successive generations in Thomas Mann's *Buddenbrooks* (1900) become more passive, impotent, and indecisive, so too is Carl Joseph rendered ineffectual. His anxiety at the waning of a great heritage clashes with his resigned recognition of ongoing change. The result for Carl Joseph is a life devoid of meaning, as he hardly makes an effort to preserve the empire. Only his grandfather's portrait and a few remaining relics from friends afford his life some meaning. The immortal "Radetzky March" itself, a lively, exuberant piece of music written by Joseph Strauss the elder in honor of one of Austria-Hungary's greatest military heroes, Count Radetzky, serves as a reminder of this once glorious past. The baroque contrast between *Schein* and *Sein*, between appearance and essence, is seen in the main characters' futile attempts to maintain the shell of Franz Joseph's empire.

Stylistically, *The Radetzky March* reflects little of the stylistic experimentation of the early twentieth century. Roth's fluid style is apparently a throwback to late nineteenth century realism, especially to the psychological realism of Flaubert and Tolstoy. The restricted instances of free indirect style (*erlebte Rede*), interjection, and thought recollections reveal Roth's familiarity with current stylistic techniques but an unwillingness to exploit them. Traditional stylistic techniques provide a certain semblance of security and stability in an otherwise tumultuous world. Just as his characters seek refuge in the past, so does Roth look to the past for his literary forms of expression. Idealistic conservatism manifests itself both in content and in form.

A number of Roth's novels have been reissued in English translation. Furthermore, a small but steadily growing critical literature attests the continuing relevance of the works of this exemplary exile.

Paul F. Dvorak

OTHER MAJOR WORKS

SHORT FICTION: *April: Die Geschichte einer Liebe*, 1925 (*April: The Story of a Love Affair*, 2002); *Der blinde Spiegel*, 1925 (*The Blind Mirror*, 2002); *Ein kapitel Revolution*, 1929; *Stationschef Fallmerayer*, 1933 (*Fallmerayer the Station Master*, 1986); *Die Büste des Kaisers*, 1934 (*The Bust of the Emperor*, 1986); *Die Legende vom Heiligen Trinker*, 1939 (*The Legend of the Holy Drinker*, 1943); *Der Leviathan*, 1940 (*The Leviathan*, 2002); *The Collected Stories of Joseph Roth*, 2002.

NONFICTION: *Reise durch Galizien*, 1924; *Im mittäglichen Frankreich*, 1925; *Bericht aus dem pariser Paradies*, 1926; *Der Rauch verbindet Städte*, 1926; *Die russische Grenze*, 1926; *Artikel über Albanien*, 1927; *Juden auf Wanderschaft*, 1927 (*The Wandering Jews*, 2001); *Leningrad*, 1928; *Das moskauer jüdische Theater*, 1928; *Briefe aus Deutschland*, 1929; *Brief aus dem Harz*, 1930; *Panoptikum: Gestalten und Kulissen*, 1930; *Bekenntnis zu Deutschland*, 1931; *Der Antichrist*, 1934 (*The Antichrist*, 1935); *Aus dem Tagebuch eines Schriftstellers*, 1937; *Über das "Dokumentarische,"* 1938; *Rede über den alten Kaiser*, 1939; *Briefe, 1911-*

1939, 1970 (letters); *Der neue Tag: Unbekannte politische Arbeiten, 1919 bis 1927, Wien, Berlin, Moskau*, 1970; *Berliner Saisonbericht: Reportagen und jouranlistische Arbeiten, 1920-1939*, 1984; *Im Bistro nach Mitternacht*, 1999 (*Report from a Parisian Paradise: Essays from France, 1925-1939*, 2003; also known as *The White Cities: Reports from France, 1925-1939*, 2004).

MISCELLANEOUS: *Werke in drei Bänden*, 1956 (4 volumes; Hermann Kesten, editor); *Werke: Neue erweiterte Ausgabe in vier Bänden*, 1975-1976.

BIBLIOGRAPHY

Acocella, Joan. "European Dreams: Joseph Roth." In *Twenty-Eight Artists and Two Saints: Essays*. New York: Pantheon Books, 2007. Acocella, a dance critic for *The New Yorker*, profiles Roth in this collection of her magazine pieces.

Gordimer, Nadine. "The Empire of Joseph Roth." *The New York Review of Books*, December 5, 1991. Gordimer, a Nobel Prize-winning novelist, examines the social and political contexts of seven of Roth's books, including his novels *The Radetzky March*, *The Emperor's Tomb*, and *Flight Without End*.

Hughes, Jon. *Facing Modernity: Fragmentation, Culture, and Identity in Joseph Roth's Writing in the 1920's*. London: Modern Humanities Research Association and the Institute of Germanic and Romance Studies, University of London, 2006. Hughes focuses on Roth's early writing, which has traditionally been overshadowed by critical acclaim for *The Radetszky March*. He reassess Roth's fiction published in the 1920's, arguing that both the form and content of these works define Roth as a modernist writer.

Manger, Philip. "*The Radetzky March:* Joseph Roth and the Hapsburg Myth." In *The Viennese Enlightenment*, edited by Mark Francis. New York: St. Martin's Press, 1985. This collection of essays on intellectual and artistic activity in Vienna includes an analysis of Roth's well-known novel.

Rosenfeld, Sidney. "Joseph Roth." In *Major Figures of Modern Austrian Literature*, edited by Donald G. Daviau. Riverside, Calif.: Ariadne Press, 1988. Roth is one of fifteen writers included in this study of twentieth century Austrian literature, with the chapter on Roth recounting the events of his life and analyzing his work.

_____. *Understanding Joseph Roth*. Columbia: University of South Carolina Press, 2001. Rosenfield examines Roth's novels, including *Job* and *The Radetzky March*, arguing that Roth's own experience of rootlessness and exile shaped both his life and work.

Williams, Cedric E. "Joseph Roth: A Time out of Joint." In *The Broken Eagle: The Politics of Austrian Literature from Empire to Anschluss*. New York: Barnes & Noble Books, 1974. Williams places Roth within the context of twentieth century Austrian politics. Includes a bibliography, an index, and illustrations.

Wood, James. "Joseph Roth's Empire of Signs." In *The Irresponsible Self: On Laughter and the Novel*. London: Jonathan Cape, 2004. Wood, a prominent literary critic, includes an essay on Roth in this collection on "the comedy of forgiveness," a form of humor that is more disposed to sympathy than to the ridicule and moral strictness of satire.

Worsching, Martha. "Misogyny and the Myth of Masculinity in Joseph Roth's *Radetzkymarsch*." In *Gender and Politics in Austrian Fiction*, edited by Ritchie Robertson and Edward Timms. Edinburgh, Scotland: Edinburgh University Press, 1996. Worsching's analysis of the depiction of masculinity in *The Radetzky March* is included in this collection of essays examining the depiction of gender and politics in Austrian fiction.

PHILIP ROTH

Born: Newark, New Jersey; March 19, 1933
Also known as: Philip Milton Roth

PRINCIPAL LONG FICTION

Letting Go, 1962
When She Was Good, 1967
Portnoy's Complaint, 1969
Our Gang (Starring Tricky and His Friends),
    1971
The Breast, 1972 (revised 1980)
The Great American Novel, 1973
My Life as a Man, 1974
The Professor of Desire, 1977
The Ghost Writer, 1979
Zuckerman Unbound, 1981
The Anatomy Lesson, 1983
Zuckerman Bound, 1985 (includes *The Ghost
    Writer, Zuckerman Unbound, The Anatomy
    Lesson*, and *The Prague Orgy*)
The Counterlife, 1986
Deception, 1990
Operation Shylock: A Confession, 1993
Sabbath's Theater, 1995
American Pastoral, 1997
I Married a Communist, 1998
The Human Stain, 2000
The Dying Animal, 2001
The Plot Against America, 2004
Everyman, 2006
Exit Ghost, 2007
Indignation, 2008

OTHER LITERARY FORMS

Five of Philip Roth's short stories are collected along with his novella *Goodbye, Columbus* in a volume bearing that title (1959). A number of his essays, interviews, and autobiographical pieces appear in *Reading Myself and Others* (1975). Roth's unproduced screenplay *The Great American Pastime* was anthologized in 1968, and several of his works, including *Goodbye, Columbus, Portnoy's Complaint*, and *The Human Stain*, have been adapted to film by others. In 1975, Roth began editing a series called Writers from the Other Europe for Penguin Books, to which he contributed several introductions. *The Facts: A Novelist's Autobiography* appeared in 1988, and *Patrimony: A True Story*, a memoir of his father's life, was published in 1991. In 2001, Roth published *Shop Talk: A Writer and His Colleagues and Their Work*; seven of the ten chapters in this work are conversations that Roth had with other important authors, such as Primo Levi, Aharon Appelfeld, Milan Kundera, and Mary McCarthy.

ACHIEVEMENTS

Philip Roth emerged as a leading Jewish American writer when his first published book, *Goodbye, Columbus*, won the National Book Award in 1960. Many of his subsequent works have involved Jewish characters and specifically Jewish American dilemmas; novels such as *Portnoy's Complaint, The Counterlife*, and *Operation Shylock*, in particular, involve characters struggling to reconcile their desires to be fully American during the age of American triumphalism with their deeply ingrained sense of separateness. More than a touch of local color, Roth's depictions of Jewish communities form a base from which to spin—and unspin—national and personal narratives. Along with contemporary writers such as John Barth and Norman Rush, Roth has created some of American literature's most memorable and most self-conscious storytellers: the angst-ridden Alexander Portnoy, the irrepressible Nathan Zuckerman, and the outwardly controlled, inwardly crumbling Swede Levov.

Roth's special concern in his work is the relationship between writer and subject, which is often closely drawn from his own personal life. His fictional accounts of smothering Jewish mothers, harried Jewish fathers, and illicit love affairs involving Jews in his early work made him notorious among the conservative Jewish establishment during the 1970's. Subsequent depictions of family relationships bearing a close resemblance to his own drew fire from his ex-wife Claire Bloom, among others. In his later work, Roth has brilliantly presented the fascinating relationship between fiction and autobiography, using fictional surrogates, such as Nathan Zuckerman, to explore what he calls "counterlives," or the proliferation of possible lives one single person might have lived.

Throughout his fiction, Roth exhibits the abilities of a master comedian. His ear is arguably the best of any contemporary writer, capturing the spoken voice in a wide variety of accents, intonations, and cadences, but his facility with dialogue sometimes leads critics to miss the serious undercurrents of his work. Roth's fiction covers a variety of satiric modes, from the social (*Portnoy's Complaint*) to the political (*Our Gang*) to the literary and academic (*The Professor of Desire*). Whatever mode he adopts, he presents the objects of his satire or comedy in vivid and compelling fashion. Once referred to as preeminently a social realist (as in *Goodbye, Columbus*), he has transcended that mode successfully in such works as *The Counterlife* and *Deception*, which show him, as ever, both a consummate craftsman and a tireless experimenter with his medium.

Roth has won numerous prestigious awards for what constitutes one of the twentieth and twenty-first centuries' most impressive bodies of literary work in the English language. Among other honors, he received the National Book Critics Circle Award for *Patrimony*, the PEN/Faulkner Award for *Operation Shylock*, the National Book Award for *Sabbath's Theater*, the Pulitzer Prize for *American Pastoral*, and the Ambassador Book Award of the English-Speaking Union for *I Married a Communist*. He also received the Koret Jewish Book Award and awards from the *New York Times* and *Chicago Tribune*, the National Jewish Book Award, and the PEN/Faulkner Award for Fiction for *The Human Stain*. He won the Sidewise Award for Alternate History as well as awards from a number of periodicals for *The Plot Against America*, and he was honored with another PEN/Faulkner Award for *Everyman*. In 1998, he was presented the National Medal of Arts in a White House ceremony, and in 2002 he won the Gold Medal in Fiction from the American Academy of Arts and Letters, the highest award the academy gives. He received the United Kingdom's W. H. Smith Award, given for making a contribution of significance to literature, for *The Human Stain* and again for *The Plot Against America*; he was the first author ever to win that award twice. In 2005,

he became the third living author to have his works published in a comprehensive edition by the Library of America.

BIOGRAPHY

Born in the Weequahic section of Newark, New Jersey, on March 19, 1933, Philip Roth learned very early what it was like to grow up Jewish in a lower-middle-class neighborhood of a large metropolitan area. His parents were Beth Finkel Roth and Herman Roth; his father was a salesman for the Metropolitan Life Insurance Company. After he graduated from Weequahic High School in 1950, Roth worked for a while at the Newark Public Library and attended Newark College of Rutgers University. A year later, he transferred to Bucknell University. Although the family could ill afford the expense of a private college, Herman Roth determined that if his son wanted to go there, he would go. At Bucknell, Roth began writing stories and edited the school's literary magazine. He also had his first love affairs, from which

Philip Roth. (© Nancy Crampton)

he drew incidents (fictionally transformed) for his subsequent novels. He received his B.A. in English, magna cum laude, in 1954, and he accepted a teaching fellowship at the University of Chicago for graduate work in English.

After receiving his M.A. in English from Chicago, Roth enlisted in the U.S. Army, but a back injury suffered during basic training resulted in an early discharge. He returned to Chicago to pursue doctoral studies in English and continued writing short stories; he had begun to get stories published as early as the fall of 1954 in small literary journals such as the *Chicago Review* and *Epoch*. Several of his stories were anthologized in Martha Foley's *The Best American Short Stories* and in *The O. Henry Prize Stories*. These honors, the success of his first published volume, *Goodbye, Columbus*, a Houghton Mifflin Literary Fellowship, and a Guggenheim Fellowship persuaded Roth to abandon graduate work in English for a career as a creative writer.

While a graduate student and instructor at the University of Chicago, Roth met and later married his first wife, Margaret Martinson Williams. The relationship was never a happy one, and after a few years they separated, Margaret steadfastly refusing to agree to a divorce. Meanwhile, they spent one year of their marriage (1960) at the Writers' Workshop at the University of Iowa, where Philip served on the faculty. After his first full-length novel, *Letting Go*, was published in 1962, he became writer-in-residence at Princeton University. He later taught English literature at the University of Pennsylvania. His experiences as an academic provided much material for his later novels, many of which have university settings or are otherwise peopled by academics.

The publication of *Portnoy's Complaint* in 1969, a year after his estranged wife was killed in an automobile accident, launched Roth's greatest notoriety, especially among the conservative Jewish community in the United States, and assured his fame as a novelist. He became an increasingly prolific writer, spending part of the year in his Connecticut home and part in London in an apartment near his writing studio. For years he shared his life with the British stage and screen actor Claire Bloom, whom he married in April, 1990. Their difficult relationship and 1995 divorce became a subject of Bloom's memoir, *Leaving a Doll's House* (1996) and received

highly fictionalized treatment in Roth's 1998 novel *I Married a Communist*.

Around the end of the twentieth century, Roth began living alone in his house in the woods of northwest Connecticut. He continues to visit New York from time to time and has contact with other writers, including younger ones, but his main focus is on his writing.

ANALYSIS

While his early works clearly show the influence of his literary idols—Henry James, Leo Tolstoy, Gustave Flaubert, Thomas Wolfe, and Theodore Dreiser—Philip Roth came into his own as a novelist beginning with *Portnoy's Complaint*, which reveals a unique voice in American literature. His subsequent development parallels his growing interest in other Continental writers, such as Anton Chekhov, Franz Kafka, Fyodor Dostoevski, and particularly contemporary writers such as Milan Kundera, whom Roth assisted in getting his works published in the United States. Roth's first novels are set squarely in his native land: in Newark, where he was born and reared; in the great Midwest, where he went to graduate school; and in New York and Philadelphia, where he lived, wrote, and taught literature at several universities. The protagonists of his later fiction travel abroad to Western and Eastern Europe and as far as Hong Kong. Roth's development as a novelist is thus the development, in part, of a growing cosmopolitanism along with a deepening interest in basic human concerns and predicaments.

Chief among those predicaments is the endless struggle between the id and the superego, or, in less Freudian terms, between the drive for sensual gratification and the drive for moral uprightness. On one hand, pulling at his protagonists (most of whom are men) is the powerful desire for sexual conquest; on the other is the almost equally powerful desire to lead a morally self-fulfilling and decent life. These drives, conflicting at almost every turn, nearly tear his protagonists apart. Even when, as at the end of *The Professor of Desire*, a protagonist believes that he has at least achieved a reasonable equilibrium and found peace, a nagging unease enters the picture, upsetting his contentment and providing a presentiment of doom.

Indeed, Roth's heroes, if one can apply that term to

such unlikely characters, all seem doomed in one way or another. Their pervasive sense of disaster, however, does not destroy Roth's comedy; it deepens it. A sense of the absurd, of the incongruities of human experience, also pervades Roth's novels and is the source of much rich humor. Moreover, his protagonists usually are fully self-aware; they understand their predicaments with uncommon self-perception, even if (more often than not) they are utterly baffled in trying to find a solution to or resolution of their dilemmas. Again, their awareness and frustration combine to make the reader laugh, though the reader must be careful not to let the laughter obscure or nullify the compassion that is also the character's due.

LETTING GO

Roth's first full-length novel, *Letting Go*, sets out all these themes and influences. The principal character, Gabe Wallach, is the educated, sophisticated young son of well-off middle-aged easterners. After a brief stint in the Army, Gabe pursues graduate studies in the Midwest. His mother has recently died, leaving her son with a heavy moral burden: not to interfere in the lives of others as she, regretfully, has done. It is a legacy Gabe finds almost impossible to live up to, until the very end, after he has nearly ruined the lives of several people close to him. Before that, he succeeds, however, in remaining aloof from his widower father, who is lonely and adrift and tries to persuade Gabe to return home. This is Gabe's only success, however, as eventually his father meets and marries a widow who helps him rediscover life's pleasures.

Meanwhile, Gabe has his affairs, none of which works out happily, and his friendships, especially with Paul and Libby Herz, whom he meets during graduate school in Iowa. Paul is a hardworking, highly principled young man who married Libby while they were still undergraduates at Cornell. Their mixed marriage—Paul is Jewish, Libby Catholic—is mainly the result of Paul's misguided sense of devotion and responsibility. Although the passion has long since gone out of their relationship, owing to Libby's poor health and neurotic disposition, Paul remains loyal. Together, they struggle with financial and other problems, including opposition from both sets of parents.

Gabe's life and the life of the Herzes intersect at various points, invariably with well-intentioned but almost disastrous consequences. At Iowa, Gabe tries to befriend the couple, offers various forms of assistance to them, and finds an unusual attractiveness in Libby, which culminates in little more than a kiss. Their affair, such as it is, focuses partly on Henry James's novel *The Portrait of a Lady* (1881), which Gabe lends to Paul; Libby reads the book and finds tucked into its pages the last letter Gabe's mother had written him when she lay dying. Both the novel and the letter help to form a bond between Gabe and Libby that endures. Later, when Gabe is teaching at the University of Chicago, their relationship resumes when Gabe helps Paul get a job in his department.

Through Martha Reganhart, with whom Gabe has begun to live, Gabe finds someone who is willing to let her unborn baby be adopted by the Herzes. Paul and Libby have wanted a child and nearly had one, but poverty-stricken as they were, Paul persuaded Libby to have an abortion. The incidents surrounding that event are both comical and dreadful. Afterward, Libby's health never becomes robust enough for her to risk conceiving another child; hence, they hope to adopt one. The circumstances of trying to adopt a baby involve episodes best referred to as "deadly farce," including several in which Gabe intervenes on the couple's behalf. At the same time, Gabe's relationship with Martha, a divorcée with two young children, deepens and then falls apart, largely the result of his inability to make a full and lasting commitment.

Gabe and Paul thus represent contrasting studies in personality. At the end, Gabe finally learns to "let go," the lesson his mother tried to teach him from her deathbed, but letting go for him means abandoning lover, friends, family, and career to become a wanderer in Europe, whence he writes Libby a final letter. Forwarded many times, an invitation to her adopted daughter's first birthday party arrives with no other message in it. This Gabe takes as "an invitation to be forgiven" for his nearly catastrophic interference in their lives. Gabe, however, feels unable to accept forgiveness—not yet, anyway. He is not "off the hook," he says, and does not want to be let off it, not until he can make some sense of the "larger hook" he feels he is still on.

PORTNOY'S COMPLAINT

The larger hook on which Roth's later protagonists wriggle is precisely the dilemma between commitment and freedom that they all experience. Thus, Alexander Portnoy of *Portnoy's Complaint* finds himself torn between his desire to maintain his position as New York's assistant commissioner for human opportunity, a job of considerable responsibility as well as prestige, and his desire to enjoy the full sexual freedoms heralded by the 1960's. For a while he seems to manage both, until his affair with Mary Jane Reed develops into something else—Mary Jane's wish to get married. Her sexual adroitness—she is called "the Monkey"—has kept them together for more than a year, but this demand for full commitment proves too much for Alex, who abandons her in Athens during a trip to Europe in which they have experienced the ultimate of their sexual adventures. Alex flees to Israel, the land of his forefathers, only to find that when he tries to make love there he is impotent. The experience drives him to seek help from Dr. Otto Spielvogel, a New York psychiatrist.

The novel, in fact, is told as a series of confessions, or therapy sessions, and derives its title from the name Dr. Spielvogel gives to his patient's illness. "Portnoy's Complaint" is "a disorder in which strongly felt ethical and altruistic impulses are perpetually warring with extreme sexual longings, often of a perverse nature." The symptoms of the illness, Spielvogel believes, can be traced to the mother-child relationship, and indeed Portnoy's boyhood has been fraught with problems, often hilarious ones as he recounts them, occasioned by his stereotypical Jewish mother. Sophie Portnoy is a domineering, overprotective mother who frequently drives her young son to distraction as he tries in vain to understand her demands on him and her suffocating affection. Jack Portnoy, his father, long-suffering (mostly from constipation) and hardworking, seems unable to mitigate the family relationship, exacerbating Alex's quandary. No wonder he grows up as he does, afflicted with the dilemma, or the condition, that Dr. Spielvogel describes. By the end of the novel, after the long unfolding of his tales of woe, all Alex hears from his therapist is, "Now vee may perhaps to begin. Yes?"

My Life as a Man

In a sense, that *is* just the beginning. Roth tried hard to progress further in his next "family" novel, *My Life as a Man*, which took him years to write. Meanwhile, he wrote the pre-Watergate Nixon satire *Our Gang* and the satirical burlesque of American culture *The Great American Novel*, which takes the great American pastime, baseball, as its focus and its vehicle. Yet it was the fictionalized account of his marriage—or rather, the affair that turned into marriage through a masterful trick—that really preoccupied Roth in the years following *Portnoy's Complaint*. In *My Life as a Man*, Roth invents not one fictional surrogate but two: Peter Tarnopol, a writer, and Tarnopol's own fictional surrogate, Nathan Zuckerman. The two "useful fictions" that precede "My True Story," or the novel proper, are Roth's early experiments with "counterlives," which he developed at greater length and complexity in his later novel, *The Counterlife*. They provide alternative, "possible" accounts of Peter Tarnopol's early life—and, through Tarnopol's, Roth's.

Peter's problem is trying to discover how he ever got involved with Maureen, his wife of ten years, from whom he is finally separated but who refuses to grant him a divorce. Related to this problem is the current one he experiences with his beautiful and dutiful lover, Susan Seabury McCall, a young widow who provides Peter with apparently everything he wants; however, she is essentially too submissive, too dull. One part of Tarnopol misses the excitement—no, the frenzy—that Maureen brought into his life, while another part hates it. Though it does not follow a strict chronological sequence, the novel becomes an account of Peter's experience first with Maureen, then with Susan, whom he finally also leaves and determines to give up, despite her attempted suicide. Writing the novel in guarded solitude at an artist's colony called Quahsay, Tarnopol retrospectively tries to understand his plight.

The Breast

The Breast is another novel written during this period when Roth was trying to compose *My Life as a Man*. This book is the sequel to *The Professor of Desire*, written a few years later. Like Portnoy, Zuckerman, and Tarnopol, David Kepesh is a nice young Jewish man, brought up by caring parents in a sheltered Jewish environment, who early in life experiences the pleasures of emancipation and of the flesh, first as a Fulbright scholar living in London, then as a graduate student at Stanford University. Like Tarnopol, he becomes the victim of a femme fatale, a woman who, like Maureen, has "lived." Helen Baird is a striking beauty, but more than her beauty, her experience living abroad as the lover of a Hong Kong millionaire attracts Kepesh. They become lovers and later, disastrously, husband and wife. Gradually, Kepesh sinks into the condition of becoming Helen's servant, if not slave, until she flees once more to Hong Kong, hoping to reunite with her erstwhile lover. He will not have her, and David must rescue her, but in the process he becomes aware that their life together is over, and they get divorced.

David now moves back to New York, where he gets a job teaching comparative literature, meets Claire, a young schoolteacher, and falls in love with her. During this period he undergoes psychotherapy to "demythologize" his marriage to Helen; Dr. Klinger becomes Claire's advocate against David's brooding over Helen. During this period also, David's mother dies, and like Gabe Wallach in *Letting Go*, Kepesh has a widowed father on his hands. The elder Mr. Kepesh is by no means as demanding as Dr. Wallach, however; on the contrary, he is delighted with his son's liaison with Claire (as he was not with the marriage to Helen) and hopes that they will marry. The novel ends as the young couple, along with the elder Mr. Kepesh and a friend of his, a concentration camp survivor, spend a weekend in a bungalow in the Catskills, not far from where David grew up and where he now ponders his future. He seems to have everything he wants or needs, but somehow he feels dissatisfied, anxious, afraid that ennui will set in and destroy everything or that some other disaster will overtake him.

It does, but the disaster is hardly anything that David could anticipate. About a year later, as his lovemaking with Claire has almost ceased, he turns into a six-foot, 155-pound breast. In *The Breast*, Roth partly follows Franz Kafka's *Die Verwandlung* (1915; *The Metamorphosis*, 1936), an obvious, but not exact, source for this novella. Unlike Kafka, Roth tells the story from Kepesh's point of view, using the first-person narrator to convey something of the real anguish Kepesh feels and his amazement at his condition. If he was beset by a dilemma at the end of *The Professor of Desire*, his bafflement there is nothing to what he experiences now. Despite the aid and comfort that everyone—Claire, his father, Dr. Klinger—tries to give him, he remains at the end as bitterly confused and disturbed as ever, thoroughly unreconciled to his lot except as he vainly tries to persuade everyone that what has happened has not happened, that it is all a bad dream from which eventually he will awake, or that he has simply gone mad.

THE GHOST WRITER

Roth's next novels form a trilogy to which he has appended an epilogue, all under the title of *Zuckerman Bound*. Again, Roth borrows from autobiography to write his fiction, his own "counterlife." In *The Ghost Writer*, the first of the series that make up this portrait novel, Nathan Zuckerman is at the beginning of a promising career as a writer. He has published a few short stories and is now staying at an artist's colony (Quahsay again), trying to write more. Since he is not far from the home of E. I. Lonoff, a writer he much admires, he visits and is welcomed by the older writer and his wife. Zuckerman is surprised by them in many ways: first by Lonoff's austere life as a writer, spent endlessly turning his sentences around, and then by Hope Lonoff's conviction that her husband would be better off without her. By birth and upbringing far different from her husband— she is a New England Yankee as opposed to his immigrant origins—she is temperamentally unsuited to the kind of life they have led for many years. She is convinced, moreover, that Lonoff would be better off living with a younger woman, like Amy Bellette, a former student from the nearby women's college where Lonoff teaches, who obviously adores him. Lonoff refuses, however, to entertain any such thoughts of abandoning Hope or realizing his fantasy of living abroad in a villa in Italy with a younger woman.

Nathan is persuaded to stay the night, especially after he meets Amy Bellette, who is also staying there on a brief visit. Nathan has his own fantasy that evening, that Amy is really Anne Frank, author of the famous diary, who has miraculously survived the Nazi death camps. They fall in love, get married, and thus show his parents and other relatives that, despite what they may think from some of his stories, he is a good Jewish man, the worthy husband of the famous Jewish heroine. As a tribute to Roth's skill as a writer, the account of Amy's survival is quite credible; moreover, it shows Roth's understanding of compassion for the suffering in the death camps. At the same time, it supports Nathan Zuckerman's qualifications as a writer, justifying Lonoff's praise and encouragement of the young man.

ZUCKERMAN UNBOUND

Lonoff's belief in Nathan is borne out in *Zuckerman Unbound*, the second novel in the trilogy. By now Zuckerman is the author of several novels, including the notorious *Carnovsky*. This novel is to Zuckerman what *Portnoy's Complaint* is to Philip Roth, and *Zuckerman Unbound* recounts experiences similar to those Roth must have had, such as the notoriety that involved outsiders' mistaking his fictional characters for his real mother and father. Zuckerman is accosted in the streets, on the telephone, and apparently everywhere he goes by people who think they know him because they mistake his confessional novel for actual autobiography. Fiction and autobiography are at best distant relatives, however; for example, unlike Zuckerman's father, who is extremely upset by his son's novel and turns on him at his death, Roth's parents remained proud of their son's accomplishments and never took offense at what he wrote, notwithstanding the uproar in the Jewish community.

Zuckerman is beset by would-be hangers-on such as Alvin Pepler, the Jewish Marine, once a quiz-show winner but deprived of full fame by a scam reminiscent of the Charles Van Doren scandal. Zuckerman's brief affair (actually no more than a one-night stand) with the Irish actor Caesara O'Shea is a comic treatment of the adventures attributed to Roth by columnists such as Leonard Lyons, who insisted he was romantically involved with Barbra Streisand, though actually Roth at that time had not so much as met her. Finally, Zuckerman's trip to Miami with his brother, Henry, which ends with their estrangement on the way home after their father dies of a stroke, is totally different from actual events in Roth's life. All these incidents are, after all, "counterlives," imaginative renderings of what might have or could have happened, not what did.

THE ANATOMY LESSON

Similarly, in *The Anatomy Lesson*, the third novel in the series, Roth borrows from incidents in his own life but fictionalizes them so that no one-to-one equivalence can be made. Now, some years later, Zuckerman is afflicted with a strange ailment that causes him intense pain, from which he gets temporary relief only from vodka or Percodan. He can no longer write, but four different women tend to his other needs, including his sexual ones. Among them are a young Finch College student who also works as his secretary, his financial adviser's wife, an artist in Vermont who occasionally descends from her mountaintop to visit, and a Polish émigré whom Zuckerman meets at a trichological clinic (in addition to everything else, Zuckerman is losing his hair).

In despair of his life and his calling, Zuckerman decides to give up writing and become a doctor. He flies to Chicago, where he hopes his old friend and classmate Bobby Freytag will help him get admitted to medical school. En route on the plane and later from the airport, Zuckerman impersonates Milton Appel, a literary critic modeled on Irving Howe, who early praised Roth's work and then turned against it. In this impersonation, however, Zuckerman pretends that Appel is a pornography king, editor and publisher of *Lickety Split*, and an impresario of houses of pleasure. The impersonation is triggered by Appel's appeal, delivered through an intermediary, to Zuckerman to write an op-ed article on behalf of Israel.

Zuckerman as the porn king Appel provides plenty of material for those who like to see Roth as antifeminist but who thereby miss the point of his fiction. It is a tour de force, a persona adopting a persona—miles away from the real Roth. At his office in the hospital, Bobby Freytag reminisces with Zuckerman for a bit and then tries to talk him out of his scheme. Only the next day, when, under the influence of too much Percodan and vodka, Zuckerman falls and fractures his jaw does the healing begin, in soul as well as body. Zuckerman learns what real pain and loss are as he walks the corridors of the hospital watched over by his friend, who also weans him from his drug addiction. At the end, Zuckerman is a chastened and more altruistic individual, though still deluded into thinking he could change into a radically different person.

THE PRAGUE ORGY

The epilogue, *The Prague Orgy*, shows Zuckerman not as a doctor but as a famous novelist undertaking an altruistic mission on behalf of an émigré Czech writer whose father had written some excellent, unpublished stories in Yiddish. Unfortunately, the Czech's estranged wife holds the stories but will not release them. Zuckerman manages to fetch them without having to sleep with her, despite her pleas, but the stories are immediately confiscated by the police, who then escort him out of the country (this is pre-1989 Czechoslovakia). Zuckerman thus learns to accept his limitations and to become reconciled to them. He accepts that he will not become "transformed into a cultural eminence elevated by the literary deeds he performs."

THE COUNTERLIFE *and* DECEPTION

In *The Counterlife*, Nathan Zuckerman and his brother are briefly reunited, mainly so that Roth can explore alternative versions of a fate that first befalls one and then the other. The plot thus doubles back on itself more than once and is too complex for summary treatment. Despite its complexity, the novel is not difficult to follow and is full of surprises that intellectually stimulate as they also amuse the reader. Particularly interesting are the episodes in Israel, where Henry has fled to start a new life, bringing Nathan after him to discover what is going on. Much is going on, including a considerable amount of discussion from characters on the left and right of the political spectrum, with Nathan clearly in the middle. The latter part of the novel finds Nathan in London, married to an English divorcée with a child and trying to come to grips with British anti-Semitism, including some in his wife's family. Throughout the novel, Roth implicitly and sometimes explicitly raises questions about the nature of fiction and the characters that inhabit it.

He does so, too, in *Deception*, though in that novel, written almost entirely in dialogue, the experiment takes on a different form. Here, Roth drops his surrogate, Nathan Zuckerman; his main character, present in all the dialogue, is called Philip, who also happens to be a novelist who has written about a character named Zuckerman. Thus Roth seems here to speak in his own voice, though of course he does not, quite: He merely makes the partition separating him from his characters that much thinner, almost to the point of transparency, as when he takes on the critics who claim that when he writes fiction, he does autobiography, and vice versa. The novel is filled with discussions between "Philip" and his lover, who proves to be the woman Nathan married in *The Counterlife*; thus, much of the talk is naturally about fiction.

SABBATH'S THEATER

Roth turned away briefly from his various author personas to write the wickedly funny *Sabbath's Theater*, a novel about an aging pornographic puppeteer obsessed with death and socially proscribed forms of sex. Mickey Sabbath's perverse confessions and the absurd situations Sabbath creates for himself may remind some of Roth's early novel *Portnoy's Complaint*, but whereas Alexander Portnoy was tortured by his conflicting desires to be a model American and to satisfy his sexual longings, there is no such conflict in Sabbath. He revels in his capacity to break bourgeois mores, becoming a cause célèbre for defenders of the First Amendment in the 1950's, when running his randy street theater resulted in his arrest.

Since that time, he has lived in a small New England town, teaching college drama, until he is forced to resign for sexually harassing female students. Now he is locked in an acrimonious marriage with his wife Roseanna, a recovering alcoholic, and mourning the death of his sexually adventurous mistress Drenka. If *Portnoy's Complaint* revolves around Portnoy's confessions, *Sabbath's Theater* revolves around Sabbath's unapologetic reveling in nastiness. Through Sabbath's repellent diatribes against the Japanese, women, and self-help groups, Roth draws a figure for whom readers will find little sympathy. Because Sabbath himself seems so thoroughly jaded, many critics have decried the novel's sentimental turn toward Sabbath's past, into the death of his much-admired brother in World War II and the resulting demise of his mother, to contextualize Sabbath's bitterness.

AMERICAN PASTORAL

Roth portrays another bitter and obsessed character in *American Pastoral*, but in this novel the stakes are higher and the perspective a degree removed. Merry Levov is the stuttering teenage daughter of a beauty queen and a successful assimilated American Jew. She grows up in a prosperous New Jersey suburb in a loving home, the center of her father Swede's ideal, his "American pastoral." Then life changes. Merry's protests against the Vietnam War turn into ever more violent, clichéd complaints against American imperialism, capitalism, bourgeois complacency, and, finally, her family's own success story. She bombs the town's post office, killing a well-loved doctor and challenging her father's understanding of his life and his country. The story is told through her father's tortured pursuit of both his daughter and the reasons for her rage.

Roth deftly weaves social criticism into this compelling story for an insightful depiction of an entire generation blindsided by the great upheavals of the 1960's. Zuckerman reappears to interpret Swede Levov's story as an epic clash between the American innocent pursuing upward mobility and the return of the repressed violence inherent in that American Dream. Merry Levov, Zuckerman says, "transports him out of the longed-for American pastoral and into everything that is its antithesis and its enemy, into the fury, the violence, and the desperation of the counterpastoral—into the indigenous American berserk."

I MARRIED A COMMUNIST

Just as ambitious as *American Pastoral*, Roth's next book, *I Married a Communist*, takes the 1950's as its historical backdrop. Nathan Zuckerman again acts partly as interpreter and partly as scribe, this time to his former high school teacher, Murray Ringold. Murray tells the story of his brother Ira, a radio actor who was blacklisted during the era of McCarthyism. Ira becomes a populist hero to many, including young Nathan, until his actor wife, exasperated by Ira's repeated betrayals with other women, exposes him by publishing a tell-all book, *I Married a Communist*. The book destroys not only Ira's heroic profile but also his career, for he becomes blacklisted.

The plot of this novel once again alludes to events in Roth's own life, particularly to his divorce from Claire Bloom. Like the character Eve Frame, Bloom had a talented teenage daughter from an earlier marriage who caused friction in the marriage. Also like Eve Frame, Bloom published a memoir in which she, like Roth in several of his novels, exposed intimate details of their personal life. Ira's unthinking acceptance of the Communist Party and his subsequent devolution into an angry, bitter cynic give this political novel a decidedly conservative overtone.

THE HUMAN STAIN

The Human Stain is the final work in the group of novels known as Roth's American trilogy, which includes *American Pastoral* and *I Married a Communist*. Coleman Silk, an African American who passes for white, loses his job as dean at Athena College when he asks the students in his class whether two students who do not attend his class are "spooks." The two students,

who are African American, accuse Silk of having made a racist remark. Nathan Zuckerman, narrator of the tale, befriends Silk and guesses the secret of his true identity. Silk has a much younger mistress, Faunia Farley, whose husband kills both Faunia and Silk by forcing their car off an icy road. At Silk's funeral, faculty members who earlier distanced themselves from Silk finally speak in his defense. Zuckerman recognizes Silk's sister at the funeral and from her learns that many of his guesses about Silk's identity and about the irony of the accusations of racism are correct.

THE DYING ANIMAL

The narrator of *The Dying Animal* is David Kepesh, who also appears in *The Professor of Desire* and *The Breast*. Each year, David gets one student in the classes he teaches to become his mistress. Consuela Castillo is one of those mistresses. Years later, she returns to him and says that she faces a partial mastectomy. At the book's end, she calls him two weeks before she is scheduled for surgery and tells him the doctors have decided that they must remove the entire breast. She is alone and cannot eat. She needs David. At this point, the nameless person to whom David tells his tale advises David not to go. The reader does not know whether David goes. In this book, Roth challenges Kepesh's emphasis on the body alone while at the same time attacking what he considers to be American prudery.

THE PLOT AGAINST AMERICA

In *The Plot Against America*, Roth rewrites history, having Charles A. Lindbergh, the famous aviator and American hero, win the office of the U.S. presidency over Franklin D. Roosevelt in the election of 1940. The book focuses on seven-year-old Philip Roth and his family as they react to national events. An older Roth tells of the comfort he feels being an American Jew in Newark, New Jersey, and of the way that feeling changes to discomfort and fear as Lindbergh campaigns and wins the presidency.

During the 1930's, the historical Lindbergh sympathized with the Nazis, finding their air force especially admirable. While in Germany, he dined with Hermann Göring, Adolf Hitler's air marshal, who bestowed on Lindbergh the Commander Cross of the Order of the German Eagle. In Roth's novel, the Lindbergh administration has close ties to Nazi Germany. Even though

Lindbergh has as one of his advisers Philip's uncle by marriage, his mother's sister's husband, who is a rabbi and insists that Lindbergh means no harm to the Jews, Lindbergh institutes several anti-Semitic programs. One such program is intended to spread Jews throughout the country in order to dilute their voting power; another is to put Jewish children to work on farms, to make them more like other American children. Philip's brother Sandy goes to a farm and becomes a supporter of and spokesperson for the program. Philip's family comes further apart when his cousin Alvin, who lost a leg fighting for the Canadians against the Nazis, and Philip's father get into a fight because Alvin says he no longer has any concern for the Jews. Philip's parents are the real heroes of the novel. They protect and provide for their family, give love, and always try to do what they consider best and right in the face of tremendous chaos and evil.

Many critics have insisted that *The Plot Against America* is Roth's comment on the presidency of George W. Bush. Roth has denied this, but many critics have refused to accept what Roth says. In any case, Roth seems to have done his homework well. It is fact that in 1940 groups of Americans tried to get Lindbergh to oppose Roosevelt for the presidency, and Lindbergh did more than just flirt with Nazism and anti-Semitism. For many readers, however, the most horrifying fact of the book is not its historical background but that the events are related by a young child who reacts with immaturity and often terror to what is going on around him.

EVERYMAN

The nameless narrator of *Everyman* tells of a nameless protagonist who faces the deterioration of his body. This novel is loosely based on a fifteenth century English morality play also called *Everyman*, in which Death unexpectedly comes to call on Everyman. All worldly things desert him; only Good Deeds will accompany him beyond the grave. Similarly, Roth's nameless protagonist, who is largely dedicated to serving carnal lust, dies when he least expects it, apparently taking nothing with him beyond the grave.

Over the course of the novel, the protagonist inherits a store that he names Everyman's Jewelry Store. He marries three times; each of the second two times he marries the woman with whom he has been having an affair while still married to the previous wife. After separating from his third wife, he moves to a retirement home on the New Jersey shore, where he is lonely; he is estranged from his children, except for his daughter who lives in New York. He dies of cardiac arrest during what was supposed to be a minor, safe operation—an operation about which he did not inform his daughter. The book ends without the promise of the possibility of immortality and salvation offered by the medieval play.

EXIT GHOST

The title of *Exit Ghost* echoes stage directions in William Shakespeare's play *Hamlet, Prince of Denmark* (pr. c. 1600-1601). The words refer to the ghost of Hamlet's father, who was murdered by Hamlet's uncle. The ghost demands that Hamlet avenge the murder. Similarly, in Roth's book, ghosts from Nathan Zuckerman's past demand that he avenge the attempt of Richard Kliman to write a biography of one of Zuckerman's favorite authors, E. I. Lonoff, in which Kliman will expose to the world Lonoff's supposed incest with his half sister. The title also refers to Zuckerman himself, who is a kind of ghost. Having separated himself from the rest of the world by living in isolation in the Berkshires in Massachusetts and having hardly any relationship with the rest of humankind, he returns to New York for a procedure designed to end his incontinence from a prostate operation that has also rendered him impotent. At the book's end, he exits Manhattan to return to his rural retreat. The title also refers to Roth's earlier book *The Ghost Writer*, in which Zuckerman tells about a visit to Lonoff's house and his fantasy that Amy Bellette is really Anne Frank, the author of the famous diary.

Zuckerman, now a famous writer, meets a much older Amy Bellette, who is dying from a brain tumor. Zuckerman decides to protect her and the now-deceased Lonoff from Kliman but appears unable to succeed. He also meets Jamie Logon and Billy Davidoff, a married couple who know Kliman. In college, Jamie was Kliman's mistress, and Zuckerman fantasizes that she still is. Zuckerman finds her tremendously attractive but knows he is physically unable to do anything about his attraction. Finally, he invites Jamie to come to his hotel room, but she refuses. He then flees from New York—the final exit of a ghost from the novel.

Surveying the corpus of Roth's long fiction, one may conclude that he is a novelist who rarely repeats himself, even as he reworks ideas, issues, and dilemmas and reintroduces characters and locales. This is the essence of the "counterlife" motif that has been present in Roth's work from the start but became explicit only later on.

Jay L. Halio; Julie Husband
Updated by Richard Tuerk

OTHER MAJOR WORKS

SHORT FICTION: *Goodbye, Columbus, and Five Short Stories*, 1959; "Novotny's Pain," 1962 (revised 1980); "The Psychoanalytic Special," 1963; "On the Air," 1970; "'I Always Wanted You to Admire My Fasting': Or, Looking at Kafka," 1973.

NONFICTION: *Reading Myself and Others*, 1975 (expanded 1985); *The Facts: A Novelist's Autobiography*, 1988; *Patrimony: A True Story*, 1991; *Shop Talk: A Writer and His Colleagues and Their Work*, 2001.

BIBLIOGRAPHY

Brauer, David. *Philip Roth*. Manchester, England: Manchester University Press, 2007. Study of some of Roth's later novels presents discussion of the paradoxes and other difficulties the works present as a way of illustrating how rewarding it is to read the works.

Cooper, Alan. *Philip Roth and the Jews*. Albany: State University of New York Press, 1996. Carefully researched volume examines Roth's life and work, with particular focus on the author's political views, which are evident in his writing.

Halio, Jay L. *Philip Roth Revisited*. New York: Twayne, 1992. Provides some biographical information as well as a solid overview of the critical response to Roth's fiction up to the early 1990's.

Halio, Jay L., and Ben Siegel, eds. *Turning up the Flame: Philip Roth's Later Novels*. Newark: University of Delaware Press, 2005. Collection of essays provides a wide range of critical discussion of Roth's novels since the mid-1980's.

Milowitz, Steven. *Philip Roth Considered: The Concentrationary Universe of the American Writer*. New York: Taylor & Francis, 2000. Explores Roth's writings on the "concentrationary" world of the "camps" of the Holocaust, how this world keeps revealing itself through memories and other reminders, and how the "shadowy presence" of the Holocaust refuses forgetting.

Omer-Sherman, Ranen. *Diaspora and Zionism in Jewish American Literature: Lazarus, Syrkin, Reznikoff, and Roth*. Hanover, N.H.: University Press of New England, 2002. Discusses in depth how Emma Lazarus, Marie Syrkin, Charles Reznikoff, and Roth have addressed the issue of Jewish nationalism and the fate of the Jewish Diaspora.

Parrish, Timothy, ed. *The Cambridge Companion to Philip Roth*. New York: Cambridge University Press, 2007. Collection of eleven original scholarly essays critiques all of Roth's fiction, examining the themes of sexuality, cultural identity, and the Holocaust in the works. Serves as an excellent introduction to Roth's works. Includes a chronology.

Posnock, Ross. *Philip Roth's Rude Truth: The Art of Immaturity*. Princeton, N.J.: Princeton University Press, 2006. Shows how Roth uses immaturity and the loss of propriety as central ideas and forces in his works.

Royal, Derek Parker, ed. *Philip Roth: New Perspectives on an American Author*. Westport, Conn.: Praeger, 2005. Collection of astute essays discusses his work through *The Plot Against America*. Includes an extensive bibliography.

Safer, Elaine B. *Mocking the Age: The Later Novels of Philip Roth*. Albany: State University of New York Press, 2006. Treats Roth in some of his later works as a creator of humor and comedy with tears just beneath the surface. Focuses on the novels from *The Ghost Writer* to *The Plot Against America*.

JEAN-JACQUES ROUSSEAU

Born: Geneva (now in Switzerland); June 28, 1712
Died: Ermenonville, France; July 2, 1778

PRINCIPAL LONG FICTION

Julie: Ou, La Nouvelle Héloïse, 1761 (*Eloise: Or, A Series of Original Letters*, 1761; also known as *Julie: Or, The New Eloise*, 1968; better known as *The New Héloïse*)

OTHER LITERARY FORMS

Like many of the great figures of the Enlightenment, Jean-Jacques Rousseau (rew-SOH) wrote on a wide variety of topics and explored both literary and nonliterary forms. His first serious effort at writing—the one with which he hoped to launch his career upon his arrival in Paris in 1742—was a proposal for a new system of musical notation that he presented to the Académie des Sciences. Although his proposal did not win an overly enthusiastic reception, Rousseau was recognized as knowledgeable in music. Cardinal Richelieu asked him to adapt the verses and the music of a ballet by Voltaire and Jean-Philippe Rameau titled *Les Fêtes de Ramire* (1745). Rousseau's interlude *Le Devin du village* (pr. 1752; *The Cunning-Man*, 1766) met with much success at its first performance before King Louis XV at Fontainebleau. When the editors of *L'Encyclopédie* (1751-1780) were later soliciting authors for the various sections of this voluminous work, Rousseau was engaged to write the articles on music along with the article "Économie politique" ("Political Economy"). He also dabbled in theater, writing, among other plays, *Narcisse: Ou, L'Amant de lui-même* (1752). It was, however, particularly with his two anthropological essays, or discourses—*Discours sur les sciences et les arts* (1750; *The Discourse Which Carried the Praemium at the Academy of Dijon*, 1751; better known as *A Discourse on the Arts and Sciences*, 1913) and *Discours sur l'origine et les fondements de l'inégalité parmi les hommes* (1755; *A Discourse upon the Origin and Foundation of Inequality Among Mankind*, 1761)—that Rousseau established himself as an original writer of profound insight. The discourses set the stage for much of Rousseau's subse-

quent work: his epistolary novel, *The New Héloïse;* a retort to Jean d'Alembert's *L'Encyclopédie* article on Geneva, *Lettre à d'Alembert sur les spectacles* (1758; *A Letter to M. d'Alembert Concerning the Effects of Theatrical Entertainments*, 1759); a treatise on education, *Émile: Ou, De l'éducation* (1762; *Emilius and Sophia: Or, A New System of Education*, 1762-1763); a work of political theory, *Du contrat social: Ou, Principes du droit politique* (1762; *A Treatise on the Social Contract: Or, The Principles of Political Law*, 1764; commonly known as *The Social Contract*); and a short interpretive piece on language, *Essai sur l'origine des langues* (1781; *On the Origin of Languages*, 1967). In his later years, Rousseau turned to autobiographical writing and composed *Les Confessions de J.-J. Rousseau* (part 1, 1782; part 2, 1789; *The Confessions of J.-J. Rousseau*, 1783-1790), *Les Dialogues: Ou, Rousseau juge de Jean-Jacques* (first dialogue, 1780; complete edition, 1782), and, finally, *Les Rêveries du promeneur solitaire* (1782; *The Reveries of the Solitary Walker*, 1783).

ACHIEVEMENTS

With the publication of his first discourse, for which he won a prize at the Académie de Dijon, Jean-Jacques Rousseau vaulted to fame in the European world of letters. Montesquieu, Voltaire, and Rousseau rank as the seminal thinkers of the French Enlightenment. No one could ignore Rousseau's claim that civilization had corrupted humankind. The assertion gave new life to the quarrel between the ancients and the moderns.

As the debate over the contributions of the sciences and the arts raged on, Rousseau found himself increasingly isolated. His friends among the philosophes, who had championed the advancement of reason against intolerance and fanaticism, found themselves reluctant to accept the full implications of Rousseau's thesis once it was more amply elaborated in his second discourse. Ultimately, Rousseau was proposing a theory that would ensure human freedom from the undue constraints of society. As he wrote in *The Social Contract*, "Man is born free, and everywhere he is in chains."

In giving primacy to the individual's legitimate wants

and needs, Rousseau came to promote sensibility rather than reason as the characteristic feature of humankind. According to Rousseau, nowhere are human beings more capable of remaining in touch with themselves and their world than in nature, which provides a reflecting mirror for the human *état d'âme* (state of soul). By calling renewed attention to human sensibility and humankind's close ties with nature, Rousseau and his disciple Jacques-Henri Bernardin de Saint-Pierre were to influence profoundly the work of Romantic writers such as François-René de Chateaubriand and Alphonse de Lamartine.

Repercussions from Rousseau's oeuvre did not cease, however, in the early nineteenth century. The "Citizen of Geneva," as he was fond of calling himself, considerably reworked the tradition of confessional writing begun by Saint Augustine and continued by Michel Eyquem de Montaigne. His very self constituted the subject of *The Confessions of J.-J. Rousseau*, and he rightly concluded, in the opening lines of that work, that it was unique: "I am forming a project that has never had a precedent." As he composed his autobiographical pieces, Rousseau integrated his life's story by using sensation and feeling in a novel way to reinforce his memory. The modern reader finds in Rousseau's work not only many passages prefiguring Marcel Proust but also a generous introduction to the literature of the self.

BIOGRAPHY

Jean-Jacques Rousseau was born in Geneva, Switzerland, on June 28, 1712, to a Protestant family. His mother died nine days later. His father and his Aunt Suzanne reared him until Rousseau's father had to flee Geneva because of a quarrel with a military officer. The ten-year-old boy was placed in the Lambercier pension at Bossey, and it was there that Rousseau acquired a taste for country life that never left him. Once back in Geneva, Rousseau attempted an apprenticeship, first as a notary, then as an engraver, but considered the work boring and oppressive. Returning from a walk late one day in 1728, he found the gates to the city locked and decided to leave Geneva and seek his fortune elsewhere.

Rousseau's departure from the city of his birth marked the beginning of a life of constant roaming from one place to the next, a life of exile with relatively few

moments of tranquillity. One of these periods occurred, however, shortly after his flight from Geneva, when he met Madame de Warens in Annecy, France. This gentle and devout woman left a lasting impression on the young Rousseau. He would return to visit her several times during the next four years, before establishing residency at her home in Chambéry. Rousseau's brief but idyllic stay there—during which time he taught himself a variety of subjects—ended in disillusionment, however, when he discovered upon returning from one of his excursions that someone else had caught the eye of his "Maman." Not long thereafter, in 1742, he moved to Paris and met Thérèse Levasseur, a simpleminded girl with whom he would live almost continuously for the rest of his life. Their union produced five children, all of whom were placed in orphanages.

After the publication of Rousseau's second discourse, the couple moved to the area of Montmorency, where Rousseau was patronized at various times by Madame d'Épinay and the duc de Luxembourg. At the Ermitage, the lodge provided by Madame d'Épinay, Rousseau became an ardent admirer of his benefactor's sister-in-law, the Comtesse d'Houdetot. The passion he felt for this lovely woman no doubt influenced *The New Héloïse*, which he was writing at the time. The six years of solitude that Rousseau experienced in this area were extremely productive ones for him.

His serenity ended abruptly, however, in 1762. In that year, *The Social Contract* and *Emilius and Sophia* appeared in print. The condemnation heaped upon these works by political and religious institutions alike forced Rousseau henceforth to lead a life on the run. He was at first pursued by the police in France; his books were burned in Geneva. Moreover, at Môtiers, in the Prussian principality of Neuchâtel, his house was stoned. For a short time, Rousseau, offered asylum by the philosopher David Hume, lived in England, where he began preparing *The Confessions of J.-J. Rousseau*. His increasing sense of universal persecution, however, caused him to break off his friendship with Hume—as he had already done with many of his other friends—and leave England.

Rousseau returned to Paris in 1770 and remained there for eight years, until the Marquis de Girardin invited him to live on his property in Ermenonville. A few months after he had moved to his new residence, Rousseau died; he was buried on the premises in the restful setting of the Island of Poplar Trees. In 1794, during the French Revolution, Rousseau's remains were by special decree transferred to the Panthéon in Paris.

ANALYSIS

Man, according to Jean-Jacques Rousseau, is innately good. If he has become corrupt, it is society that has corrupted him. In the lace, frills, wigs, and pervasive artifice of the eighteenth century, Rousseau saw only a distortion of reality and an attempt to cover up the true nature of man. To peel away the accumulated layers of contact between man and society, Rousseau postulated for conceptual purposes a man of nature. Presumably, nature in this sense represented all that was furthest removed from the civilized world. In it, primitive men lived in relative isolation and enjoyed freedom in their simple, everyday activities.

When notions of property became widespread, however, the pure state of nature ceased to exist. Men moved into close contact with, and became dependent on, one another. Social classes established themselves, and inequities arose among them. A previous *amour de soi* (self-love)—based on self-preservation and giving rise to love and, concomitantly, pity of one's fellow human beings—yielded to *amour propre* (selfish love), a concern primarily with aggrandizement of oneself or one's possessions. Men's actions no longer came about spontaneously and from heartfelt emotions; they resulted, rather, from carefully contrived plots.

Notwithstanding his harsh attack on society, Rousseau did find in it some sources of hope. As long as man in society could feel pity, which Rousseau considered as perhaps the last vestige of primitive man, there remained the possibility of his self-betterment. Rousseau believed that man is a "perfectible" creature and predicated his educational and political theories on this belief. Sifting the various aspects of society, Rousseau came upon reason and government as key areas by which to reestablish morality. Reason, although not as reliable a guide as man's feeling or conscience, can ultimately lead him to enlightenment. As a young boy, Emilius, in the semi-fictional work named after him, receives an education in reason, but only after assimilating the full worth of his sensations and feelings. Moreover, the reason to which

his tutor introduces him takes on a "sensitive" character. Its content has essential meaning only insofar as it has the deeper cognitive backing of feeling. Government, in its turn, should also give full force to the individual's feeling and will. In his view of the state as seen in *The Social Contract*, Rousseau balanced the individual will with the general will by closely associating the one with the other. According to his scheme of things, each individual "uniting with all obeys, however, only himself and remains as free as before."

Rousseau's dogged pursuit of a virtuous individual freedom paralleled his search for truth and authenticity in his own life and in his works. He took as his motto a saying from Juvenal's *Saturae* (100-127 C.E.; *Satires*,1693): *vitam impendere vero* (to devote one's life to truth). When Rousseau criticized d'Alembert's article on Genevan theater, it was less out of any personal distaste for dramatic performances than out of his belief that

Jean-Jacques Rousseau. (Library of Congress)

the integrity of the spectators was being compromised. In the theater, they watched only feigned emotions and staged appearances without coming to any enhanced awareness of themselves or their fellow human beings. Rousseau countered this alienating experience with the public festival, or *fête*, in which participating members demonstrated what critic Jean Starobinski has called "transparency" in their behavior.

The privileged place that Rousseau granted simplicity, openness, and spontaneity in interpersonal relations led him not only to create in his fictional writing characters that illustrated these traits but also to attempt to exemplify them himself. In his autobiographical works, Rousseau established one of the closest rhetorical relationships yet seen in the history of literature between narrator and reader. While perusing the pages of *The Confessions of J.-J. Rousseau*, the dialogues, and *The Reveries of the Solitary Walker*, one comes to a new sense of realism in literature—almost able if not to touch then certainly to feel *intùs et in cute* (on the inside and under the skin) the writer of these works.

THE NEW HÉLOÏSE

In his only major novel, *The New Héloïse*, which bore the subtitle *Lettres de deux amants, habitants d'une petite ville au pied des Alpes, recueillies et publiées par J.-J. Rousseau* (*Letters of Two Lovers, Inhabitants of a Small Town at the Foot of the Alps, Collected and Published by J.-J. Rousseau*), Rousseau brought together many of his utopian ideas concerning humankind and society. The novel has a dreamlike quality; indeed, the subtitle reflects Rousseau's own predilection for an idyllic life in the country. Because he was composing *A Letter to M. d'Alembert*, *The Social Contract*, and *Emilius and Sophia* at the same time, echoes from these works found their way into *The New Héloïse*. They are particularly evident in the grape-harvest scene, the way of life, and the system of education chosen for Julie d'Étange's children at Clarens, the town in which she settles after turning away from the lover of her own choosing, Saint-Preux, and accepting her father's marital choice for her, Monsieur de Wolmar.

The grape harvest offers a positive example of the *fête* that Rousseau described to d'Alembert. It takes place outdoors in a public forum in which all members of the community can see one another. None of the theatrical devices or conventions that allow actors to hide behind masks and curtains and foster a mere representation of human feelings are operative there. The air of simple gaiety, combined with the industriousness of the event itself, conspires to effect an aesthetic and political ideal dear to Rousseau—an admixture of the pleasant (*l'agréable*) with the useful (*l'utile*).

The very house at Clarens has been modified to reflect the lifestyle of its inhabitants. Simple and practical furniture has replaced the former, richly decorated pieces. Another vegetable garden is cultivated where flower beds stood earlier. As for the community's society, however paternalistic it may be, its workers often act among themselves both independently and with one voice. When an individual's request agrees completely with the general will, it is automatically granted. The person's thanks, however, go not to another individual but to the group.

After Saint-Preux receives Wolmar's permission to join Julie and him at Clarens, he is charged with the instruction of their children. Although Saint-Preux no doubt possesses the requisite sensitivity to teach, Julie and Wolmar find it necessary to clarify with him their position on educating a child properly. Their system of education reflects Rousseau's own approach to this activity, which he felt was all too often preoccupied with making reason instead of nature the guiding force. Julie and Wolmar wish their children to be educated naturally, so that each step in the learning process follows the preceding one at an appropriate time and place. Should any outside factor disturb or rush this process, one ends up, as Julie notes, with "young doctors and old children." It is the tutor's foremost responsibility to develop rather than correct what nature has already given a child.

Despite some of its similarities to his other writings, *The New Héloïse* distinguishes itself in Rousseau's literary canon primarily by its subject matter. It is the one work in which the author, inspired by the correspondence between Abélard and Héloïse in the Middle Ages, integrates his thought around the central notion of love. In so doing, he not only accurately depicts the dialectics of desire but also offers an alternative to *amour-passion* in virtue. The book thus has a moralizing tone that Rousseau considered necessary for the society of his day. The vital struggle between a passionate love and a virtuous love—both of which inherently yield certain freedoms—underlies the entire novel.

Though very much in love, Julie and Saint-Preux must ultimately part company. Their separation, in conjunction with their intense feelings, lends aesthetic and dramatic plausibility to the novel's epistolary form. When Julie marries Wolmar, she undergoes a religious conversion that leads her to a new life of piety. In her letters to Saint-Preux, she attempts to tell him of the joys of virtue, which for him represents a renunciation of his desire for Julie. After several years and numerous trips, Saint-Preux, in the style of a bildungsroman character, is finally won over to virtue. What henceforth characterizes their relationship and, indeed, what has always characterized that between the novel's other major figures, Claire d'Orbe and Édouard Bomston, is a lasting friendship. Immune to the vagaries of passionate love, friendship becomes a source of peace and happiness. If Julie's death at the novel's end proves the intransmutability of passion, it does not altogether efface the intimate friendship among the remaining characters. In her absence, it is, by necessity, all that they have left as they hope to join Julie themselves.

John C. O'Neal

OTHER MAJOR WORKS

PLAYS: *Les Muses galantes*, pr. 1745 (opera); *Le Devin du village*, pr. 1752 (*The Cunning-Man*, 1766); *Narcisse: Ou, L'Amant de lui-même*, pb. 1752.

NONFICTION: *Dissertation sur la musique moderne*, 1743; *Discours sur les sciences et les arts*, 1750 (*The Discourse Which Carried the Praemium at the Academy of Dijon*, 1751; better known as *A Discourse on the Arts and Sciences*, 1913); *Discours sur l'origine et les fondements de l'inégalité parmi les hommes* (1755; *A Discourse upon the Origin and Foundation of Inequality Among Mankind*, 1761); *Lettre à d'Alembert sur les spectacles*, 1758 (*A Letter to M. d'Alembert Concerning the Effects of Theatrical Entertainments*, 1759); *Émile: Ou, De l'éducation*, 1762 (*Emilius and Sophia: Or, A New System of Education*, 1762-1763); *Du contrat social: Ou, Principes du droit politique*, 1762 (*A Treatise on the Social Contract: Or, The Principles of Politic Law*, 1764; commonly known as *The Social Contract*); *Le Sentiment des citoyens*, 1764; *Quatre lettres à M. le président de Malesherbes contenant le vrai tableau de mon caractère et les vrais motifs de toute ma conduite*, 1779; *Les Dialogues: Ou, Rousseau juge de Jean-Jacques*, 1780, 1782; *Essai sur l'origine des langues*, 1781 (criticism; *On the Origin of Languages*, 1967); *Les Confessions de J.-J. Rousseau*, 1782, 1789 (*The Confessions of J.-J. Rousseau*, 1783-1790); *Les Rêveries du promeneur solitaire*, 1782 (*The Reveries of the Solitary Walker*, 1783); *Political Writings*, 1915, 1954; *Religious Writings*, 1970.

MISCELLANEOUS: *The Works*, 1763-1773 (10 volumes); *The Miscellaneous Works*, 1767 (5 volumes); *Œuvres complètes*, 1780-1789 (33 volumes); *Œuvres complètes de Jean-Jacques Rousseau*, 1959-1969 (4 volumes).

BIBLIOGRAPHY

Coleman, Patrick. *Reparative Realism: Mourning and Modernity in the French Novel, 1730-1830*. Geneva, Switzerland: Librairie Droz, 1998. Examines *The New Héloïse* and novels by Abbé Prévost, Benjamin Constant, Madame de Staël, and Honoré de Balzac to describe how issues of grief and bereavement were handled in eighteenth and nineteenth century French fiction.

Cranston, Maurice William. *Jean-Jacques: The Early Life and Work of Jean-Jacques Rousseau, 1712-1754*. New York: W. W. Norton, 1982.

_____. *The Noble Savage: Jean-Jacques Rousseau, 1754-1762*. Chicago: University of Chicago Press, 1991.

_____. *The Solitary Self: Jean-Jacques Rousseau in Exile and Adversity*. Chicago: University of Chicago Press, 1997. Monumental three-volume biography has been hailed by some critics as the definitive account of Rousseau's life and work. Covers all of Rousseau's writings; chapter 9 in volume 2, titled "The Year of *Julie*," is devoted to *The New Héloïse*.

Damrosch, Leo. *Jean-Jacques Rousseau: Restless Genius*. Boston: Houghton Mifflin, 2005. Biography represents a useful addition to Rousseau scholarship, providing an incisive, accessible account of Rousseau's life and contributions to philosophy and literature. Includes illustrations, time line, bibliography, and index.

Dent, Nicholas. *Rousseau*. New York: Routledge, 2005. Provides an overview of the entire range of Rousseau's philosophy, paying particular attention to the theories of democracy and freedom outlined in *The Social Contract*. Also explains Rousseau's concept of the "general will."

Havens, George R. *Jean-Jacques Rousseau*. Boston: Twayne, 1978. Concise introductory account of Rousseau's life and career is coupled with analyses of his major works. Includes bibliography and index.

Howells, Robin. *Regressive Fictions: Graffigny, Rousseau, Bernardin*. London: Legenda, 2007. Analyzes *The New Héloïse* and works by two other writers to describe how the French novel changed in the mid-eighteenth century. Prior to that time, Howells maintains, novels reflected a worldly society, characterized by wit, social sophistication, and sexual experience; novels in the last half of the century were set in idealized, imaginary worlds characterized by originality, closeness to nature, and innocence.

Hulliung, Mark. *The Autocritique of Enlightenment: Rousseau and the Philosophes*. Cambridge, Mass.: Harvard University Press, 1994. Explains how Rousseau both reflected and departed from the main cur-rents in Enlightenment philosophy, particularly the ideas of Voltaire and Denis Diderot. Includes bibliography and index.

Morgenstern, Mira. *Rousseau and the Politics of Ambiguity: Self, Culture, and Society*. University Park: Pennsylvania State University Press, 1996. Analyzes Rousseau's political theory and its historical context, demonstrating how Rousseau's thought introduced notes of ambiguity that remain in current political life. Includes bibliography and index.

Riley, Patrick, ed. *The Cambridge Companion to Rousseau*. New York: Cambridge University Press, 2001. Collection of essays includes an overview of Rousseau's life and work, discussions of his philosophy, and a consideration of the images of authority in *The New Héloïse* and other works.

Wokler, Robert. *Rousseau: A Very Short Introduction*. 2d ed. New York: Oxford University Press, 2001. Provides a concise and lucid introduction to Rousseau's life and works, with information about his fiction and his educational and religious writings as well as discussion of his theories about politics, history, and music.

J. K. ROWLING

Born: Chipping Sodbury, Gloucestershire, England; July 31, 1965

Also known as: Joanne Kathleen Rowling; Kennilworthy Whisp; Newt Scamander

Principal long fiction

Harry Potter and the Philosopher's Stone, 1997 (also known as *Harry Potter and the Sorcerer's Stone*, 1998)
Harry Potter and the Chamber of Secrets, 1998
Harry Potter and the Prisoner of Azkaban, 1999
Harry Potter and the Goblet of Fire, 2000
Harry Potter and the Order of the Phoenix, 2003

Harry Potter and the Half-Blood Prince, 2005
Harry Potter and the Deathly Hallows, 2007

Other literary forms

In addition to her series of novels about the boy wizard Harry Potter, J. K. Rowling (ROHL-ihng) has composed the volumes *Fantastic Beasts and Where to Find Them* (2001) and *Quidditch Through the Ages* (2001); she has contributed all proceeds from sales of these works, more than fifty million dollars, to charity. Pretending to be volumes from the library at Rowling's fictional Hogwarts School of Witchcraft and Wizardry, these two works are brief, comic parodies of the kinds of informative books often written for children. For The

Children's Voice, a charity that she cofounded, Rowling handwrote and auctioned a book of fairy stories titled *The Tales of Beedle the Bard*, which sold for £1.95 million. One of the stories ("The Tale of the Three Brothers") appears in *Harry Potter and the Deathly Hallows*.

ACHIEVEMENTS

J. K. Rowling has received numerous awards for her writing. *Harry Potter and the Philosopher's Stone* won the Nestlé Smarties Book Prize as well as the British Book Award for Children's Book of the Year and the Children's Book Award. Other prizes for volumes in the Harry Potter series followed, including the Hugo Award and the Whitbread Children's Book of the Year Award, but all of these pale before Rowling's unprecedented achievement that, despite writing in a genre (children's literature) that was not expected to sell well, her Harry Potter series, particularly the last four volumes, so significantly broken sales records as to have changed the publishing industry and probably contributed to a renewed interest in reading for countless children. As millions of large books were put in print at once and delivered throughout the world for the parties that greeted their release, each new Harry Potter volume became a major news event and placed a strain on the avenues of parcel delivery, particularly because of the massive attempt to keep the details of the books secret until they were released. One reason for the popularity of the Harry Potter series is that through these works Rowling has subtly changed the nature of long fiction by showing how it can depict psychological development playfully yet insightfully, in great detail and with myriad interconnections.

BIOGRAPHY

The daughter of Peter James Rowling and Anne Rowling (who met at King's Cross railway station—a major location in the Potter series), Joanne Kathleen Rowling grew up in various Gloucester villages in England. Her best friend, Sean Harris, later served as one model for her character Ron Weasley. She studied classics at the University of Exeter and later became a researcher for Amnesty International, which pressures governments around the world to abandon the use of torture and other brutality.

J. K. Rowling. (© Richard Young/Courtesy, Allen & Unwin)

In 1990, much of the characterization and plot of the Harry Potter series occurred to Rowling as she was traveling by train. After the death of her mother that year, she deepened her sense of Harry's sorrow at his parents' demise. In 1992 in Portugal, where she was teaching, she married a television journalist. The marriage ended in divorce but left her with a baby daughter. She was living in poverty when she finished the first volume of her series, *Harry Potter and the Philosopher's Stone*, in 1995. Rowling has stated that this was a period when she suffered from depression and even thought of suicide. Eventually, however, she found an agent and then a publisher for the book.

As late as 1997, Rowling was able to spend her time writing only because she had received a monetary grant from the Scottish Arts Council. The next year, the American publisher Scholastic bid $105,000 for the right to publish the American edition of the first Harry Potter book—this was the first financial record for children's books that Rowling set. After that time, Rowling focused on completing the series, serving as an adviser on the very large-budgeted film adaptations that were made from the books, engaging in legal suits connected to the series, and raising funds for many charities.

ANALYSIS

In various interviews, J. K. Rowling has discussed her intention to furnish her child characters with increasingly complex abilities and mature emotions with each successive volume. Although various authors—for example, James Joyce in *A Portrait of the Artist as a Young Man* (1916)—have experimented with changing style to depict a protagonist's maturing consciousness, the Harry Potter series does so at extraordinary length and with considerable subtlety while alternating between comedy and adventure in a manner that prevents the author's psychological explorations and moralizing from being intrusive.

HARRY POTTER AND THE PHILOSOPHER'S STONE

Harry Potter and the Philosopher's Stone begins with its title character extremely isolated. He has no friends or sympathy from his foster parents, the Dursleys. He lives in a closet under the stairs, and the closest he comes to social life is playing with hand-me-down toys from his bullying cousin Dudley. Despite the fact that Harry is eleven, his psychological situation is typical of someone much younger, who has not yet fully bonded with parents and has not yet begun to have real companions. For Harry, growing up happens suddenly, as he is on the way to Hogwarts School of Witchcraft and Wizardry. He acquires the first of a number of benign parental figures in the person of the giant Hagrid as well as acquaintance with the two children who are to become his closest friends, Ron Weasley and Hermione Granger. For the first time, he is in the care of adults worthy of trust, but also of some (notably the potions professor, Snape) who arouse suspicion, so that Harry and friends fall into another of the normal activities of childhood, learning to break suspect rules. He meets his chief obstacle in Rowling's favorite chapter, "The Mirror of Erised," in which he resists the temptation to withdraw

from his friends and regress to being alone with his daydreams. His victory at the end of the book depends on aid he receives from the school's headmaster, Dumbledore, as well as from Ron and Hermione.

HARRY POTTER AND THE CHAMBER OF SECRETS

Whereas the first book in the series demonstrates the importance of finding one's group, the next three—each in a darker and more alarming way—show Harry the fallibility of groups despite the need for them. In *Harry Potter and the Chamber of Secrets*, betrayed by his best friend's sister, Ginny Weasley, he also finds less direct aid from Ron, Hermione, and Dumbledore than in the previous ending (although they contribute to the victory). At the climax, Harry fights as a sword-wielding hero against a dragonlike basilisk to save an imprisoned maiden. This is, of course, the realization of a typical adolescent fantasy, which teaches courage and self-reliance.

HARRY POTTER AND THE PRISONER OF AZKABAN

In *Harry Potter and the Prisoner of Azkaban*, these virtues (even when augmented with teamwork) turn out to be insufficient for total victory in a society where legal processes have become somewhat confused and corrupt. Near the opening, Harry is a fleeing criminal, expecting to be occupying a cell in the wizard's prison Azkaban for fighting back illegally against a viciously harassing aunt. His godfather, Sirius Black, despite being innocent of the mass murder for which he was convicted, has spent years in that prison, escaped, and now might lose his soul if caught.

In *Harry Potter and the Prisoner of Azkaban*, Rowling offers a special lesson in dealing with fears so intense that they lead toward depression, personified as Dementors. As one remedy for such fears, Professor Lupin (who has struggled with the terror that the beast within him will overpower him) teaches children to reimagine whatever they fear most into a ridiculous form. To counter Harry's vulnerability to despair, Lupin trains him to employ the even more powerful spell of the "Patronus" (a word derived from the Latin word *pater*, which means father). It requires Harry to remember an intense joy, in his case connected to his parents. It takes the form of the animal into which his father used to transform. Since the book is about overcoming depression by reconnecting with the past, its plot hinges on the manipulation of time itself via Hermione's magic amulet.

HARRY POTTER AND THE GOBLET OF FIRE

In the next volume, *Harry Potter and the Goblet of Fire*, the children are no longer as sheltered as they once were from the intricacies and machinations of the commercial world around them. The book starts with the massively merchandised sporting event the World Quidditch Cup. Although still at school, Fred and George, Ron's older brothers, keep attempting to collect a large wager on the tournament so that they can finance a business. Competition among three schools, conducted with repeated reference to prize money and betting, also involves publicity and a spying reporter, Rita Skeeter, who lies and twists facts to help her newspaper sell copies. This systematic distortion is worse than the occasional injustices exposed by the previous book.

The first books in the Harry Potter series thus present typical stages of human development that most modern people undergo: in the first book, the rise from isolation to companionship; in the second, the transition from dependence to independence; in the third, movement from defiance of law to learning how to deal with its inequities while preserving one's integrity; and in the fourth, the transition from innocence to understanding of the machinations of the modern, commercial world. The remaining books present still more complex visions of human development.

HARRY POTTER AND THE ORDER OF THE PHOENIX

In *Harry Potter and the Order of the Phoenix*, Harry, terrorized by nightmares that merge with the external world, must comprehend the intricate interrelationship of subjective and objective. He has reached an advanced developmental stage, recognizing that each person views the world through a unique subjective perspective, so people are not all experiencing precisely the same world but rather subtly different ones, shaped and colored by their viewpoints. Appropriate to this insight is appreciation of diversity. The Order of the Phoenix has a broad membership: a thief and members of the magical police, a magicless "squib" and professors of magic, a bureaucrat and a werewolf. This volume shows that cooperation among the members of this diverse group is essen-

tial if they are to avoid domination by the reactionary "purebloods"—the enemies of diversity. Both the sorting hat and Hermione preach this moral. The brightest of the group, she had already some signs of this stage in the previous volume, but now she campaigns for an alliance of all the school's houses, and her crusade for oppressed house elves intensifies. Agreeing with her, Dumbledore condemns the arrogance that results in the tyranny of one magical race over the others. Although not every character achieves this tolerant perspective, the last two books present even less common understandings.

HARRY POTTER AND THE HALF-BLOOD PRINCE

At the core of *Harry Potter and the Half-Blood Prince* is what Hermione calls Golpalott's Third Law: To counteract a mixture of poisons, an antidote must be more than a sum of antidotes to each poison; the cure must have something to catalyze the individual ingredients into a whole. This lesson in systems dynamics belongs to advanced studies that most of the students do not grasp at first—Harry among them—but it is the metaphor running throughout much of the book. As in the battle at the climax of *Harry Potter and the Order of the Phoenix*, members of that Order have been in individual duels with Voldemort's supporters—that is, have been separate antidotes. To counteract the figurative mixture of poisons with which Voldemort has been corrupting society, something more than such an accumulation is needed. Dumbledore's death becomes a catalyst, transforming the situation and (in the next book) inspiring his followers to equal self-sacrifice.

HARRY POTTER AND THE DEATHLY HALLOWS

The last book, *Harry Potter and the Deathly Hallows*, is the application of the complex teachings of the preceding book, as a way to make the wizarding community hale and whole again. To achieve this unification, each of the main characters must undergo some death-like loss of self, so that all can better meld with the community. Snape, Lupin, Dobby, and Fred Weasley are among those giving their lives. Hermione hides her parents and disappears from their memory, thus eradicating one foundation for her identity. In a baptism-like plunge, Ron, in dark, cold waters, purges his previous selfishness, a transformation completed only when he overcomes all the nagging fears of being second best that have limited him. Harry has a near-death experience in which he talks to Dumbledore (or imagines himself doing so) at King's Cross. He comes back from this with the authority and charisma of a self-sacrificing leader (group catalyst), ready to grant magnanimous forgiveness to any repentant enemy and thus to end the divisions of the society.

This final volume is an inconclusive conclusion built around the idea of the Elder Wand (which, at one point, Rowling considered mentioning in the book's title). Dumbledore admits to having wasted much of his life in dreams about possessing it, and Harry must also resist that temptation. It guarantees its rightful master victory in any duel, but this does not keep its possessors from losing—a fact that Voldemort ignores arrogantly, imagining himself somehow pure, immortal, and all-powerful: a personification of stasis. Rowling uses her paradox of the vulnerability of the seemingly unconquerable to show that no power, however magical, can control life, which is fluid, unpredictable, and constantly changing. This is a feature not only of this book's plot but also of the series—a vast river of words, flowing from one surprise to another and interconnected to a sea of publicity.

As she was writing the series, Rowling engaged with her readers through the Internet, giving clues to each future volume; fans of the books tried to guess what would happen next or wrote their own additional sections of the story. Thereby, they participated in Harry's education. The fans' interest intensified near the time of the publication of *Harry Potter and the Deathly Hallows*, and it did not stop after the book appeared. In interviews, Rowling continued to add to that book's epilogue, providing the further fates of characters as well as additional background information—for example, she revealed Dumbledore's homosexuality. Rowling thus significantly modified the closure that had long been assumed to be a characteristic of the novel genre.

James Whitlark

OTHER MAJOR WORKS

CHILDREN'S LITERATURE: *Fantastic Beasts and Where to Find Them*, 2001 (as Newt Scamander); *Quidditch* *Through the Ages*, 2001 (as Kennilworthy Whisp); *The Tales of Beedle the Bard*, 2008.

BIBLIOGRAPHY

Colbert, David. *The Magical Worlds of Harry Potter*. New York: Berkley Books, 2008. Provides explanations of the allusions to historical events and myths that Rowling employs throughout the Harry Potter series.

Granger, John. *Unlocking Harry Potter: Five Keys for the Serious Reader*. Allentown, Pa.: Zosima, 2007. Presents analysis of the themes found in the Harry Potter series, particularly that of alchemy.

Heilman, Elizabeth E., ed. *Critical Perspectives on Harry Potter*. New York: Routledge, 2008. Collection of essays addresses the Harry Potter books from the perspectives of various academic disciplines, including popular culture and anthropology.

Killinger, John. *God, the Devil, and Harry Potter: A Christian Minister's Defense of the Beloved Novels*. New York: St. Martin's Griffin, 2004. Offers thoughtful arguments defending the books against charges that they are un-Christian.

Nexon, Daniel H., and Iver B. Neumann, eds. *Harry Potter and International Relations*. Lanham, Md.: Rowman & Littlefield, 2006. Collection of essays by scholars in the field of international relations focuses on the connections made among various nations through the international success of the Harry Potter series.

Sexton, Colleen. *J. K. Rowling*. Minneapolis: Twenty-First Century Books, 2008. Brief, illustrated volume offers biographical information on Rowling.

Thomas, Scott. *The Making of the Potterverse: A Month-by-Month Look at Harry's First Ten Years*. Toronto, Ont.: ECW Press, 2007. Presents a history of the media coverage surrounding the Harry Potter series, with particular focus on the film adaptations. Includes interviews.

Trevarthen, Geo. *The Seeker's Guide to Harry Potter*. Ropley, England: O Books, 2008. Provides information on the various symbols that appear in the book series, particularly Celtic ones.

SUSANNA ROWSON

Born: Portsmouth, Hampshire, England; 1762
Died: Boston, Massachusetts; March 2, 1824
Also known as: Susanna Haswell; Susanna Haswell
Rowson

PRINCIPAL LONG FICTION

Victoria, 1786
The Inquisitor: Or, Invisible Rambler, 1788
Mary: Or, The Test of Honour, 1789
Charlotte: A Tale of Truth, 1791 (also known as
    Charlotte Temple, 1797)
Mentoria: Or, The Young Lady's Friend, 1791
The Fille de Chambre, 1792 (better known as
    Rebecca: Or, The Fille de Chambre, 1814)
Trials of the Human Heart, 1795 (4 volumes)
Reuben and Rachel: Or, Tales of Old Times, 1798
Sarah: Or, The Exemplary Wife, 1813
Charlotte's Daughter: Or, The Three Orphans,
    1828

OTHER LITERARY FORMS

Susanna Rowson (ROWZ-uhn) was a prolific, well-rounded writer. In addition to her ten works of long fiction, she produced three volumes of poetry: *Poems on Various Subjects* (1788), *A Trip to Parnassus* (1788), and *Miscellaneous Poems* (1804). Between 1794 and 1797, she wrote approximately seven dramatic works, most of which were probably performed but not published; the most popular of these was *Slaves in Algiers: Or, A Struggle for Freedom* (pr., pb. 1794). She also composed the lyrics for numerous songs and contributed to the production of at least two periodicals: the *Boston Weekly Magazine*, for which she wrote articles on a wide range of subjects and apparently also served as editor between 1802 and 1805, and the *New England Galaxy*, which was founded in 1817 and for which Rowson wrote chiefly religious and devotional prose pieces. Finally, she wrote and had published six pedagogical works: *An Abridgement of Universal Geography* (1805), *A Spelling Dictionary* (1807), *A Present for Young Ladies* (1811), *Youth's First Step in Geography* (1818), *Exercises in History* (1822), and *Biblical Dialogues* (1822).

ACHIEVEMENTS

Opinions of Susanna Rowson's achievements as a novelist have fluctuated widely since the nineteenth century. Earlier critics highly praised the moral tendency of her work and her storytelling skills, while later estimates have tended to disparage both and to find her writing limited and ordinary.

Among the handful of Americans who wrote novels in the late eighteenth century, Rowson was both the most prolific and the most coherent. As Dorothy Weil has shown, a well-developed system of aims and values emerges from all of Rowson's writings and gives her work notable unity and breadth. In particular, as Weil has demonstrated, Rowson's belief in gender equality and her concern with feminist issues and positive goals for women deserve wider recognition than they have received. In other respects, Rowson's novels are typical of the novelist's theory and practice in newly independent America and are interesting and revealing as a window on the nature of fiction in the late eighteenth century.

BIOGRAPHY

Susanna Haswell Rowson's remarkably full, active life began in Portsmouth, England, where she was born in 1762. Her mother died shortly after, and Rowson's first visit to America occurred when her father settled and married in Massachusetts and, in 1767, brought his daughter to join him, his new wife, and his three stepsons. Some of Rowson's experiences during this visit, including a shipwreck, appear later in *Rebecca*. By 1778, she was back in England, her father's apparently doubtful loyalty having led the fledgling American government first to confiscate his property and intern his family and him and then return them to England.

Rowson's initiative and independence soon revealed themselves. By the time she was in her twenties, she had secured a position as governess in the family of the duchess of Devonshire, beginning a life of service through teaching and writing; she also helped her father gain a pension, and she began publishing her fiction and poetry.

Rowson was twenty-four years old when her first novel, *Victoria*, appeared in London in 1786. The work's

Susanna Rowson. (Library of Congress)

Rowson's American period, during which she blossomed both as a performer and as an educator and moralist who attempted to serve others through many activities, including novel writing.

Rowson published her four-volume novel *Trials of the Human Heart* in 1795 and continued acting and writing in the theater until 1797. Then, once again, she turned her life and her career of service in a new direction. She opened the Young Ladies' Academy in Boston in 1797. Starting with only one pupil, she had one hundred and a waiting list within a year. She continued to instruct young women in her school until 1822, but she also continued to do so through her writing. She published the novels *Reuben and Rachel* and *Sarah* as well as another book of poetry, various songs and odes, and a theatrical piece. Her major works, however, were the six pedagogical books she wrote and published between 1805 and 1822 for use in her school.

All of this got done even as Rowson found time and energy for rearing several adopted children and for supporting church and charity, which included holding the presidency of Boston's Fatherless and Widow's Society. When she died on March 2, 1824, Rowson left in manuscript her final work, *Charlotte's Daughter*, the sequel to *Charlotte*; it was published posthumously in 1828.

ANALYSIS

Benjamin Franklin certainly had neither women nor novelists foremost in his mind when he published his "Information for Those Who Would Remove to America" in 1782. Susanna Rowson, who would remove to America a little more than a decade later, was exactly the sort of migrant Franklin would have embraced. America, he said, required useful members of society rather than persons "doing nothing of value, but living idly on the labour of others." Citizens of the new nation

> do not inquire concerning a stranger, *what is he?* but *what can he do?* If he has any useful art, he is welcome; and if he exercises it and behaves well, he will be respected by all that know him.

Rowson understood Franklin's kind of labor, and the years she spent in America as a writer and educator show that she cared about becoming a useful, respected mem-

subtitle, a sign of her aims and interests as a novelist, declared that *Victoria* was "calculated to improve the morals of the female sex, by impressing them with a just sense of the merits of filial piety." Later in 1786 she married William Rowson, and though he was apparently an ineffectual person, they shared an interest in music and theater and remained married for thirty-eight years.

Between Rowson's marriage and her immigration to America in 1793, she wrote prolifically, publishing five novels and two books of verse. In 1792, following the failure of her husband's hardware business, the couple, along with Rowson's sister-in-law, Charlotte, decided to join a theater company and tour the British Isles. The decision was fateful, because in 1793 they were seen by Thomas Wignell, an American who was recruiting players for the theater he was about to open in Philadelphia. Wignell took them to America in 1793, and thus began ber of society. Gaining this respect as a novelist was no easy task, for while fiction might have been popular with younger readers of the time, the "common verdict with respect to novels," as Noah Webster expressed it in 1788, was that "some of them are useful, many of them pernicious, and most of them trifling."

Rowson responded by producing novels that consistently stress Franklin's service ideal, especially for the young women she saw herself addressing. "We are not sent into the world to pass through it in indolence," says one of Rowson's wise widows to the heroine of *Trials of the Human Heart*. "Life which is not serviceable to our fellow creatures is not acceptable to our Creator."

Such was the ideal that Rowson held up to the women for whom she wrote. She herself sought to embody this ideal by writing novels that would be an honor to herself and a benefit to society. For many modern readers and writers of fiction, it may well be objectionable to regard novel writing as akin to the useful arts, namely of the kind Franklin mentions with approval in his prospectus—farming, carpentry, tanning, weaving, and shoemaking—but Rowson and some other scrupulous, early American novelists were in effect trying to do just that: produce fiction that would be of direct, lasting benefit to its readers by helping them live happy, fulfilled lives.

Rowson's novels typically exhibit a clear moral purpose and an unmistakable connection between virtue and happiness. The strong didactic element that modern readers may find distasteful in Rowson and her contemporaries was the essential finishing touch for many early American novelists. Of what use, these writers might have asked, was an uncultivated field or undeveloped talent? Almost from the outset, Rowson stressed that the moral purpose of her fiction and the well-being of her readers were more important to her than financial or critical success.

Rowson realized, of course, that too many novels had been published that were either trifling or pernicious, as Webster said, and did their readers no good. Her awareness was sharp enough that in *The Inquisitor* she offers a detailed summary of what she considers a typical "modern novel." To Rowson, the problem with such novels was that they were more likely to harm than aid the reader, and more inclined to mislead rather than enlighten. They often encouraged vice and error by show-

ing that the two lead to happiness rather than suffering, thus making them attractive instead of repugnant to the unwary reader. Novels such as these, and writers such as Jean-Jacques Rousseau and Johann Wolfgang von Goethe, were said to misuse the power of fiction by ennobling errant behavior such as suicide or adultery and charming the reader into accepting and even living by untruths made too attractive.

For Rowson and her contemporaries, fiction should never make error noble and vice fascinating, deluding the reader and ultimately causing him or her unhappiness; fiction should, instead, have the opposite psychological effect. Rowson would have agreed with what Columbia College student Daniel Tompkins, in 1794, called fiction's "true design and intent." Novels, he wrote in his journal, "are representations of men and things qualified to excite to the love of virtue and the detestation of vice." Such novels used the power of narrative and the feelings and imaginations of readers to move the reader away from vicious behavior and toward that which was virtuous and rewarding. As Rowson describes this process in her preface to *Trials of the Human Heart*, she hopes to "awaken in the bosoms of . . . youthful readers a thorough detestation of vice, and a spirited emulation to embrace and follow the precepts of Piety, Truth, and Virtue."

At the heart of Rowson's novels, then, is her concern with the "true felicity" of her readers and her belief that virtue leads to happiness as surely as vice and error do not. In changing the reader for the better, the novels seek to be both moral and affective. They work through the feelings and imagination and end in well-rooted, satisfying behavior. A closer look at three representative novels by Rowson will show how she tried to achieve these results.

CHARLOTTE

As Dorothy Weil observes in her study of Rowson, *In Defense of Women* (1976), *Charlotte* (titled *Charlotte Temple* in the American edition of 1797) is one of the wonders of American literature, primarily because of its immediate and long-lasting popularity. It was widely read upon its publication in America in 1797—about twenty-five thousand copies sold shortly after it appeared—and by the middle of the nineteenth century it had become the most frequently published popular novel in the United States. By 1905, it had gone through as many as two hundred editions, and in 1932, in his bibliographical study of Rowson, R. W. G. Vail claimed that more people had read *Charlotte* than any other work of fiction printed in America. Fueled by the novel's popularity, legends about the real-life identities of its main characters have flourished. In New York City's Trinity Churchyard, the grave of Charlotte Stanley, supposedly the model for the novel's heroine, now bears a slab with the inscription "Charlotte Temple."

The novel is also a revealing example of one kind of narrative by which Rowson tried to affect her readers as useful fiction was supposed to do. She does this by relating and having her readers imaginatively participate in one of the eighteenth century's favorite plots: the story of the causes and consequences of youthful error and delusion in which the heroine herself, and thus the reader, learns by bitter experience to love virtue and hate vice. Rowson also presents the heroine's learning process in a moral context of clearly stated values, thereby ensuring that the nature of virtue and vice is well defined throughout.

The main events of the novel are easily summarized. Charlotte Temple is a fifteen-year-old student at a boarding school in Chichester, England; the year is 1774. One day, she meets Lieutenant Montraville, who, finding Charlotte attractive and eventually deciding that he loves her, persuades her to see him and then to accompany him to America. Although she doubts herself the moment she decides to go, Charlotte nevertheless leaves her friends and her parents behind and, in the company of her lover, his deceitful friend, Belcour, and her evil teacher, Mademoiselle La Rue, sails to America. Once there, Montraville falls in love with another woman even as Belcour deceives him into believing that Charlotte has been unfaithful; Montraville abandons her, though she is now pregnant. Virtually alone and friendless, Charlotte has her baby and dies just after her distracted father has finally located her. Montraville kills Belcour in a duel and lives out his days married to the woman he loves but still sad and remorseful over his part in Charlotte's ruin. La Rue later dies in misery brought on by her life of dissipation.

This is the grisly narrative that Rowson attempts to make useful and instructive to the "young and thought-

less of the fair sex." She does this first by anchoring the events of the story in a context of contrasting values. In a novel designed to make virtue lovely and vice and error detestable, the reader should be very certain just what virtue and its opposites are. Among the important good people offered as attractive examples of the life of virtue are Charlotte's parents and Mrs. Beauchamp, her only real friend in America. These characters are distinguished by that active service to others that Rowson valued so highly. Each possesses a feeling heart and a generous hand, and each knows the exquisite satisfaction of comforting less fortunate fellow creatures. Moreover, these characters have given up fast-paced city life in favor of the simple, contented rural existence that befits men and women of feeling.

In contrast to such characters are the novel's bad people, especially La Rue and Belcour, who represent the false pleasures and values of selfishness. These clear contrasts between virtue and vice are established early in the novel and are regularly reinforced by a narrator who both relates and freely comments on the story. "Oh, my dear girls, for to such only am I writing," she says at one point in a typical utterance, "listen not to the voice of love unless sanctioned by parental approbation . . . pray for fortitude to resist the impulse of inclination when it runs counter to the precepts of religion and virtue."

The secret of fiction's power to further the happiness of readers lay not in static commentary and contrast, however, as much as in *process*—the learning process that the feeling reader would go through by participating imaginatively in the experience of the novel's heroine, Charlotte Temple. She is a poor deluded child who must learn by adversity that virtue leads to happiness, vice to misery. The novel is thus a psychological history of the causes and effects of error and vice, with Charlotte starting the novel as "an innocent artless girl" and ending "a poor forsaken wanderer" suffering "extreme agitation of mind" and "total deprivation of reason" as a result of her mistakes.

Rowson tries to show that Charlotte's basic problem is her inability to resist an impulse when it runs counter to the precepts of religion and virtue. Despite being reared by exemplary parents, Charlotte falls, and she does so, Rowson shows, because she allows herself to come under the influence of bad people who disable her power to resist dangerous, delusive inclinations in herself—just what was said to happen to weak, unwary readers of pernicious novels. Charlotte thus ends as "the hapless victim of imprudence and evil counsellors," the "poor girl by thoughtless passion led astray."

Like bad novels, the evil counsellors who overwhelm Charlotte's discretion and good sense are capable of using appearances—particularly the power of language and dress—to disable and deceive. A sorceress possessed of the "art of Circe," La Rue convinces Charlotte to meet, and later to continue seeing Montraville against her own better judgment. Thus does Charlotte "forsake the paths of virtue, for those of vice and folly." Eloping to America with Montraville, becoming pregnant and then left abandoned "to die with want and misery in a strange land," the very opposite of a useful and respectable member of society, Charlotte is "held up as an object of terror, to prevent us from falling into guilty errors." The reader, Rowson would hope, sees and feels that deviation from virtue is "an object of detestation," and vice and error themselves as detestable as their opposites, embodied in happy characters, are desirable. The ideal reader is the "reader of sensibility" who will "acutely feel the woes of Charlotte" and therefore behave so as to avoid them.

MENTORIA

Implicit in *Charlotte* is a pattern for a second type of useful novel that Rowson employed in *Mentoria*. As noted, the third-person narrator of *Charlotte* both relates and comments on the tale, making sure her readers understand its moral import and learn from it. In *Mentoria*, the nameless, wholly reliable preceptor of *Charlotte* becomes the story's main character. Her name is Helena Askham, and, in a series of letters to Lady Winworth's three daughters for whom she earlier was governess, Helena dispenses stories and lessons based on her own experience, which are designed to instruct young women on subjects of concern to them.

Like Charlotte, Helena combines humble origins with a good education. Unlike Charlotte, she is strong enough to resist impulses that run counter to the precepts of religion and virtue. She is able to do so because, sensitive and feeling though she is, she is also "endowed with discernment and sense far superior to the generality of young women of her age."

She shows her mettle early on when, placed in a situation very much like Charlotte's with Montraville, she is courted by Lady Winworth's son. Unlike Charlotte, who allowed the rhetoric and appearance of La Rue and Montraville to disable her judgment and excite errant, delusive hopes, Helena displays the control of feeling and pleasing inclination that is the mark of Rowson's strong women, and that enables her to stifle her rising passion for her suitor and reject him. Later, he does in fact marry someone closer to him in rank and fortune, and so does Helena, until her husband's death leaves her free to become governess and then mentor to the three Winworth children.

As this wise widow, a woman who, like the narrator of *Charlotte*, combines sensibility with strong good sense, Helena becomes the central character of *Mentoria*. The several stories she relates, therefore, are meant to do what the single story of Charlotte did: Use the power of narrative as a memorable, striking means of instruction for young women, a way of making "a lasting impression on the minds of fair readers" and thereby of advancing their happiness.

For example, the life of Helena's friend, Louisa Railton, is offered as "a model by which every young woman who wishes to promote her own felicity, will regulate her conduct." The beauty of the virtue of filial piety is illustrated by Louisa's choosing, after her mother's death, "a low roofed mansion, scanty meals, and attendance on a sick peevish father, to the lofty apartments, plenteous table, and variety of amusements she might have enjoyed with Lady Mary," her rich relative. She thereby gains, however, "a contented happy mind, [and] serenity dwelt in her heart and cheerfulness beamed in her eyes. . . . She lived beloved by all and died universally regretted." Made desirable and attractive, and distinguished as in *Charlotte* from its selfish opposite, the virtue of filial devotion should impress the reader and prompt her to imitation.

As Helena writes her pupils, "Be wise, my dear children, follow Louisa's example, so shall your lives be happy and your last moments peace." Helena continues to deal similarly with such topics as friendship, reputation, love, pleasure, and marriage, using the force of the striking instance to impress readers with the felicity of the virtuous life and the miseries of vice and error.

TRIALS OF THE HUMAN HEART

In *Trials of the Human Heart*, Rowson demonstrates a third type of "useful fiction." Her aim is to achieve the same effect as before—"to awaken in the bosoms of my youthful readers," as she says in the novel's preface, "a thorough detestation of vice, and a spirited emulation, to embrace and follow the precepts of Piety, Truth and Virtue." Like *Charlotte*, *Trials of the Human Heart* is a story of adolescent initiation, but rather than involving the reader in the misfortunes of a heroine such as Charlotte whose imprudence is her undoing, Rowson offers the character of Meriel Howard, who is the undeserving victim of the cruelty or caprice of others and as a result suffers through what one character calls "some of the heaviest trials to which the human heart is incident"— four volumes' worth, in fact, related through letters exchanged among the characters.

Like other Rowson heroines, Meriel is artless and innocent at the start—having indeed spent much of her childhood in a convent—and she possesses a generous heart as well. As she writes her convent friend, Celia, "I am weak as an infant, whenever a scene of distress or happiness meets my eye; I have a tear of sympathy for the one, and a smile of gratulation for the other." Thus endowed, Meriel leaves the convent and enters a world that ends up causing her far more distress than happiness.

The first incidents of the novel, when Meriel is about sixteen years old, are typical of the pattern of disappointed expectation that repeats itself in Meriel's life and occasions her learning and uttering many lessons about life. On her way home to Bristol, she thinks about the coming reunion with her parents, whom she has not seen for most of her childhood. "I pictured them to myself, as very amiable old people—and, in fancy, felt their embraces and kissed off the tears of joy I saw falling from their eyes." What she finds instead is a "suffering saint" of a mother, her settled melancholy the result of living with a husband who is cruel and unfeeling and a son notable for "frigid coldness."

Meriel soon discovers that her father—who much later in the novel turns out not to be her father—is a freethinker and a hypocritical villain, concealing under the "mask of integrity and honour every vice which can disgrace human nature." Indeed, it was because of her fa-

ther's vitiated morals that Meriel was originally placed in a convent. She now finds him ardently pursuing an adulterous affair; after she succeeds in breaking that up, she herself becomes the object of his amorous attention, an event one character describes as "too dreadful, too shocking to human nature, to wear even the face of probability."

Soon after, Meriel reflects that she no doubt has many more trials yet to endure, and she is absolutely right. In one episode after another, she—like her counterpart, Rebecca, the heroine of the novel of the same name—attracts the compromising notice rather than the solicitude of married men and the venom rather than the pity of other women. As Meriel remarks later, looking back over her life, "how hard is my fate. Possessed as I am of a heart moulded to compassion, glowing with universal affection toward my fellow creatures, I am constantly thrown among people, whose every feeling is absorbed in self."

For Meriel as for the reader of this and virtually every other Rowson novel, the purpose of the heroine's experiences is to teach about truth and error—what Meriel calls the "useful lessons taught me in the school of adversity." Born to be the sport of fortune, Meriel learns that "this is a sad—very sad world to live in.—For if we love anything we are sure to lose it." The truly important lesson, however, follows on this. Having so painfully discovered the error of her innocent belief that "every heart glowed with humanity, friendship and sincerity toward each other," Meriel periodically entertains the opposite error. "What a world this is," she writes to her enviably placid convent friend. "Were it not impious, I could wish I had never entered it."

Despair is indeed impious, and the heroine, like the reader, learns that such feelings run counter to the precepts of religion and virtue. Unlike Charlotte, however, Meriel is capable of pulling back from harmful vice and error. The proper response to misfortune is, first, to bear up under it; one's duty, as Meriel says, is "to submit without repining, to the will of Him, who never lays on his creatures the rod of affliction but for some wise purpose." Second, one must serve, not retreat: "We are not sent into the world to pass through it in indolence," Meriel is told. "Remember, that life which is not in some measure serviceable to our fellow creatures, is not acceptable to our Creator." As Meriel and the reader learn, the suicidal response in any form is never appropriate. At the end of the novel, Meriel anticipates a happy marriage and hopes both to deserve and preserve her good fortune "by exerting the abilities with which I am amply endowed to chear the desponding heart, sooth the afflicted spirits and soften the bed of pain."

Like other Rowson heroines, Meriel has found the secret of happiness. For her readers, Rowson wanted nothing less. Living happily in the real world of human folly and disappointment is the ideal embodied in her many novels and her own varied life. To have found so many ways to demonstrate that ideal is surely a tribute to her strength and her inventiveness.

Michael Lowenstein

OTHER MAJOR WORKS

PLAYS: *The Female Patriot*, pr. 1794 (no longer extant); *Slaves in Algiers: Or, A Struggle for Freedom*, pr., pb. 1794; *The Volunteers*, pr., pb. 1795; *Americans in England*, pr., pb. 1796 (revised as *The Columbian Daughter*).

POETRY: *Poems on Various Subjects*, 1788 (no extant copy); *A Trip to Parnassus*, 1788 (also known as *A Trip to Parnassus: Or, The Judgment of Apollo on Dramatic Authors and Performers*); *Miscellaneous Poems*, 1804.

NONFICTION: *An Abridgement of Universal Geography*, 1805; *A Spelling Dictionary*, 1807; *A Present for Young Ladies*, 1811; *Youth's First Step in Geography*, 1818; *Biblical Dialogues*, 1822; *Exercises in History*, 1822.

BIBLIOGRAPHY

Bontatibus, Donna R. *The Seduction Novel of the Early Nation: A Call for Socio-Political Reform*. East Lansing: Michigan State University Press, 1999. Bontatibus examines novels about seduction, intrigue, and scandal written by Rowson and other women in the years of the early American republic. She argues that these novels reflect the social and political concerns of middle-class women, whom the American Revolution failed to free from colonial oppression.

Brown, Herbert Ross. *The Sentimental Novel in Amer-*
ica: 1789-1860. New York: Farrar, Straus and Giroux, 1975. Rowson is included in a thorough discussion of the sentimental novel, with Brown explaining the reasons for the enduring popularity of *Charlotte*. Includes a bibliography and an index.

Castiglia, Christopher. "Susanna Rowson's *Reuben and Rachel*: Captivity, Colonization, and the Domestication of Columbus." In *Redefining the Political Novel: American Women Writers, 1797-1901*, edited by Sharon M. Harris. Knoxville: University of Tennessee Press, 1995. Rowson's novel *Reuben and Rachel* is examined as part of a collection analyzing political novels written by American women. The essays challenge the conventional belief that the political novel is solely a male province.

Davidson, Cathy N. *Revolution and the Word: The Rise of the Novel in America*. New York: Oxford University Press, 1986. Davidson's superb interdisciplinary study of the eighteenth century "reading revolution" highlights commonplace responses to the extraordinarily popular *Charlotte* and analyzes Rowson's complex characterization of the villain Montraville. Davidson argues that Rowson's plots of "sexual crime and feminine punishment" expose society's double standard of justice. Rowson's other novels are briefly discussed.

Derounian-Stodola, Kathryn Zabelle. "The Gendering of American Fiction: Susanna Rowson to Catharine Sedgwick." In *Making America, Making American Literature: Franklin to Cooper*, edited by A. Robert Lee and W. M. Verhoeven. Amsterdam: Rodopi, 1996. Collection of essays examining how early American literature helped shape a national identity for the newly created nation. Derounian-Stodola's essay focuses on works by Rowson and other women who were first-generation American writers.

Rust, Marion. *Prodigal Daughters: Susanna Rowson's Early American Women*. Chapel Hill: University of North Carolina Press, 2008. A critical biography, discussing the range of Rowson's works. Rust argues that Rowson's fiction and plays attracted female readers and theatergoers because her female characters, balanced between autonomy and submission, accurately reflected women's status in the early American republic.

Stern, Julia A. *The Plight of Feeling: Sympathy and Dissent in the Early American Novel*. Chicago: University of Chicago Press, 1997. Stern analyzes *Charlotte*, Hannah Webster Foster's *Coquette*, and Charles Brockden Brown's *Ormond* to show that these sentimental and melodramatic novels reflect the emotional history of the early American republic.

Weil, Dorothy. *In Defense of Women: Susanna Rowson (1762-1824)*. University Park: Pennsylvania State University Press, 1976. Weil defends Rowson from male critics who focus on the didactic nature of Rowson's writings. Rowson's contributions to the education of girls and women in the early republic are thoroughly discussed.

GABRIELLE ROY

Born: Saint-Boniface, Manitoba, Canada; March 22, 1909

Died: Quebec City, Quebec, Canada; July 13, 1983

PRINCIPAL LONG FICTION

Bonheur d'occasion, 1945 (*The Tin Flute*, 1947)

La Petite Poule d'eau, 1950 (*Where Nests the Water Hen*, 1950)

Alexandre Chenevert, 1955 (*The Cashier*, 1955)

La Montagne secrète, 1961 (*The Hidden Mountain*, 1962)

OTHER LITERARY FORMS

Gabrielle Roy was proficient in several literary forms. While never regarding herself as a major theorist, her essays on art, life, and the Canadian scene were thoughtful and well crafted. Especially noteworthy was her participation in Expo 67 in Montreal; her provocative essay "Terre des hommes" became the theme for the international expo: Man and His World.

Early in her career, Roy demonstrated her skills as a short-story writer. Several of her collections contain independent sketches, even mood pieces, united by central themes and characters. As a short-story writer she transmuted her own childhood, her early experiences as a teacher, and her reminiscences of family members into evocative fiction that celebrated the vast Canadian landscape and its diverse populations. Her themes are mainstays of Canadian literature: loneliness, the cold emptiness of vast spaces, the austere beauty of the landscape, and the endurance of a pioneering population. To this literature she added a compassion for animals and an awareness of their essential relationship to human beings.

Rue Deschambault (1955; *Street of Riches*, 1957) features a series of childhood memories, fictionalized sketches from Roy's youth. *La Route d'Altamont* (1966; *The Road Past Altamont*, 1966) is a collection of four stories made cohesive by their common themes. *Cet été qui chantait* (1972; *Enchanted Summer*, 1976) employs as its setting a place called Charlesvoix, in northern Quebec. Charlesvoix became Roy's summer home for several years. *Ces enfants de ma vie* (1977; *Children of My Heart*, 1979) includes short narratives and character sketches inspired by Roy's early teaching career. *Un Jardin au bout du monde* (1975; *Garden in the Wind*, 1977) draws fictional portraits from the human mosaic of Canada's immigrants—French and English settlers, Russian Doukhobors, Poles, Ukrainians, Italians, and Chinese—people new to a land that was found to be simultaneously welcoming and forbidding.

In addition to her adult fiction, Roy published two notable books for children: *Ma vache Bossie* (1976; *My Cow Bossie*, 1980) and *Courte-Queue* (1979; *Cliptail*, 1980). The juvenile volumes are linked thematically by their subjects: animals loved by humans. In *My Cow Bossie*, a young boy receives a cow as a birthday present. Though his family is ill equipped to deal with farm animals, the child develops responsibility in a year of caring for the cow and even learns a few basic lessons in economics. *Cliptail*, which earned a Canada Council Prize for best children's story of the year, detailed the misadventures of a cat. Early mishaps include the loss of her tail in an encounter with a canine and the deaths of her first litter of kittens. The cat's luck, however, changes when she adopts an orphan kitten and after she makes friends with a difficult human adult. Canadian writers' unique contribution to world literature has been their development of the realistic animal story, and Roy's children's books exemplify the genre.

In the last years of her career, Roy intended to write a full autobiography. Sadly, only the first volume was completed. *La Détresse et l'enchantement* (1984; *Enchantment and Sorrow*, 1987) covers the early years of her life, long before her artistic maturity. Sketches, fragments, and unfinished notes are all that now remain of the rest of this project. While she did not entirely resist the temptation to enhance personal drama for literary effect, Roy was more honest than many writers in recording her own story.

ACHIEVEMENTS

Gabrielle Roy is well established as one of Canada's leading writers—some would give her the first place in Québécois literature—and is a significant figure in international French letters. Her first novel, *The Tin Flute*, is frequently credited as an influence on the Quiet Revolution, an enlightenment movement that brought the province of Quebec into the mainstream of twentieth century life. When it was published in English, the book won the 1947 Governor-General's Award, the highest honor Canadians bestow on their writers. The book was then picked up by the Literary Guild in the United States, making Roy a figure on the international literary scene. The Royal Society of Canada followed with the Lorne Pierce Medal. Not to be outdone by the English-speaking establishment, Québécois critics bestowed the Prix Femina on the French edition of the novel.

A number of marks of recognition followed. In 1956, Roy was awarded the Prix Ludger-Duvernay of the Saint-Jean Baptiste Society of Quebec. The following year she won her second Governor-General's Award, for *Street of Riches*. In 1967, she was made a Companion of the Order of Canada and won a Canada Council Medal the following year. The Prix David from the Quebec provincial government came in 1971. The year 1978 was especially important for Roy as well, as she earned a

third Governor-General's Award, this time for *Children of My Heart*, and the Canada Council's Prize for Children's Literature for *Cliptail*. Roy's renown in Canada has been such that at least five schools have been named for her, schools in the provinces of Manitoba, Ontario, British Columbia, and Alberta. Her books have become required reading in many French- and English-speaking schools, and in 2004, the Bank of Canada issued a bank note featuring a brief quotation from her novel *The Hidden Mountain*.

As she became an international figure of letters, Roy's works were translated into more than one dozen languages, notably Japanese and Russian. She is recognized today as one of the most faithful writers depicting the unique Canadian landscape and its populations. Some critics have compared her novels to those of Honoré de Balzac, Selma Lagerlöf, Sigrid Undset, Thomas Hardy, and Willa Cather. She was the first woman elected to the Royal Society of Canada, and she has been one of the most important influences in the movement to establish an international reputation for Canadian fiction. Because her most memorable fictional characters have been strong women, Roy is noted by many as a feminist.

BIOGRAPHY

Born into a large Roman Catholic, French-speaking family in Manitoba, Canada, Gabrielle Roy was educated in the French language at a time when French Canadians were considered by many to be second-class citizens of their native land. She was a gifted student who also became proficient in English while in school. For a time she aspired to an acting career and participated in a French-speaking theater group in Manitoba. Having to earn a living, however, she chose to enroll in a teacher-training program at the Winnipeg Normal Institute. This led to appointments in several elementary schools, including one in the most remote region of the province. Whatever the hardships, this remoteness would prove invaluable for her second novel, *Where Nests the Water Hen*.

A youthful Roy began to feel that Canadian provincialism was a burden, so she left Canada for Europe, living in both France and England for extended periods of time. During this stage of her life, like many other gifted North American artists who lived for a time in Europe, she studied drama and wrote reflective sketches of Canadian life. When she returned to North America, she was ready to concentrate on her literary calling. At the age of thirty-eight, she married Marcel Carbotte. Although initially the couple appeared to have much in common, and though they spent three years together in France—where Carbotte acquired his medical specialization in gynecology—they spent the last years of their marriage living separately. They had no children, and Roy always referred to her books as her progeny.

By 1952, Roy established residence in Quebec City, which she regarded as the Francophone center of North America. She continued to write and took an active part in the English translation of her books. Frequently consulted on matters of Canadian culture, she was selected to serve on the panel that gave Expo 67 its central theme. It was her proposal, "Terre des hommes," which was inspired by the title of a 1939 book by French writer Antoine de Saint-Exupéry, that led to the exhibition's

Gabrielle Roy. (Courtesy, McGill University)

theme. Roy died in Quebec City in 1983 at the age of seventy-four.

ANALYSIS

One of Gabrielle Roy's major achievements was her international readership. Prior to the development of CanLit (the Canadian literature "movement"), both French and English writers in Canada faced severely limited circulation of their works around the world. The vast publishing industries of France, England, and the United States largely ignored Canada's finest writers. Roy was deserving of world attention with novels that reflected movements and trends in mainstream fiction while expressing the distinctive concerns of the Quebec milieu.

With novels set in both the Western wilderness of Canada and in Montreal, Canada's largest city, Roy can be studied as both a local colorist and a fictional-realist surveying the pathology of a great city. Her harsh depictions of the lives of impoverished families enduring economic depression in a metropolitan environment inspired comparisons to the greatest of French naturalistic writers, Émile Zola. Roy's fictional portrait of the middle-aged Montreal bank teller Alexandre Chenevert was praised for its psychological authenticity. Many of Roy's shorter works, which are often poetic sketches more than short stories, convey the sights, sounds, and even the pungent flavor of the Canadian prairies that she remembered from her childhood. These reminiscences were well within the tradition of continental French impressionist writing.

THE TIN FLUTE

This first novel is widely ranked as Roy's best. The first of Roy's urban novels, *The Tin Flute* certainly has been the most influential, with its detailed depiction of lower-class life in Montreal during the Great Depression. The shabbiness of household furnishings, the slush of winter snow, and the conversations of Montreal taxi drivers and waitresses are recorded in precise detail. Especially notable, even amusing, is the lively account of "moving day," a springtime tradition of the city's lower classes.

The narrative is sociologically significant in its demonstration of the ways in which World War II changed French Canada, providing opportunities for many to climb out of poverty. In the novel, World War II, which spreads carnage throughout Europe, actually comes as salvation to Canada's urban poor. The men in families enlist in the Canadian army, earn money, and thus provide material benefits for those at home. As war industries emerge, they, too, offer economic opportunities to many laborers for the first time.

The novel's English title, *The Tin Flute*, is taken from the name of a child's toy, which in the book symbolizes the repressed longings of deprived people. Not only did Roy tell the story of a French-Canadian family's life of both squalor and hope in the nation's largest city; she also provided insight into urban life generally. Critic Hugo McPherson believes the strength of the novel is in "its stunning documentary quality."

The female characters of the novel are especially engaging, particularly the mother, a woman who has seen better days. She holds her family together, though she must cope with the hopelessness of her husband and the selfishness of her son. Her daughter, whose earnings at a lunch counter are sometimes the family's sole support, becomes pregnant after a brief sexual encounter with a man who shuns responsibility. When the daughter feels compelled to marry another man, whose love she does not return, she accepts what she knows is only a second-hand happiness.

WHERE NESTS THE WATER HEN

Roy's second important novel may be classified as an idyllic interlude. If Roy's urban novels shock in their bleak details, this fictionalized account of the author's early experiences as a teacher in the Canadian hinterland, charmed by surrounding nature, expresses idealized memory.

The Tousignants are a large French-Canadian family on an isolated farm, with Métis Indians several miles away as their nearest neighbors. Only irregular mail service and the occasional visit from a priest, who says mass at their kitchen table, provide contact with the outside world. Once a year, Madam Tousignant makes an epic journey to the nearest equipped town, where she gives birth to her latest child. On these annual outings, she meets other folk: a Jew named Abe Zlutkin, the Icelandic Bjorgssons, a Ukranian, and a Scot. The Tousignants also share native festivals with the Métis, though they share no common language. Madam Tou-

signant's demands for a school for her growing family finally persuade the provincial government to send an interesting series of teachers into the wilderness to live with the family. Relations between this isolated French-Canadian family and the English-speaking government officials are described with humor.

THE CASHIER

Roy's portrait of Alexandre Chenevert, a middle-class Montreal bank teller, is regarded by some readers and critics as her best work. Though this "little man" is strongly particularized by Roy's art, he becomes also a modern Canadian Everyman, anonymous, lost in the masses and in the routine of the workaday world. Some critics read *The Cashier* as a modern tragedy.

Chenevert relates to his wife and daughter only on a superficial level. God Almighty seems equally elusive to him. Discontented, Chenevert acknowledges himself to be commonplace, his surroundings uncaring and dreary. However, he longs to be a citizen of the world. He reads about the life of Mahatma Gandhi, halfway around the world, and the Hindu activist and mystic becomes his personal hero.

Because of a mistake in balancing his books, Chenevert must work overtime, which harms his health. Persuaded by his friends to take a holiday, he vacations in the Laurentian Mountains, where he observes farmers seemingly content with their lot. He idealizes this retreat, far from the frantic, cluttered city, though for him it is only temporary. In the last section of the book, Chenevert discovers, as he has long feared, that he is dying of cancer. Only at the end does he achieve some reconciliation with life. As in classical tragedy, he finds that he has learned from his endurance as his life ends in suffering. Although Roy never aspired to be a philosophical novelist, Chenevert, her most memorable hero, is perplexed by some of the same existential questions that confront the heroes and antiheroes in novels by fellow francophone writers André Langevin and Albert Camus.

Allene Phy-Olsen

OTHER MAJOR WORKS

SHORT FICTION: *Rue Deschambault*, 1955 (18 linked stories; *Street of Riches*, 1957); *La Route d'Altamont*, 1966 (4 linked stories; *The Road Past Altamont*, 1966); *La Rivière sans repos*, 1970 (*Windflower*, 1970); *Cet été qui chantait*, 1972 (*Enchanted Summer*, 1976); *Un Jardin au bout du monde*, 1975 (*Garden in the Wind*, 1977); *Ces enfants de ma vie*, 1977 (*Children of My Heart*, 1979); *De quoi t'ennuies-tu, Éveline?*, 1982.

NONFICTION: *Fragiles lumières de la terre*, 1978 (*The Fragile Lights of Earth*, 1982); *La Détresse et l'enchantement*, 1984 (*Enchantment and Sorrow*, 1987); *Ma chère petite soeur: Lettres à Bernadette, 1943-1970*, 1988 (*My Dearest Sister: Letters to Bernadette, 1943-1970*, 1990).

CHILDREN'S LITERATURE: *Ma vache Bossie*, 1976 (*My Cow Bossie*, 1980); *Courte-Queue*, 1979 (*Cliptail*, 1980); *L'Espagnole et la pekinoise*, 1986 (*The Tortoise-shelle and the Pekinese*, 1989).

BIBLIOGRAPHY

Clemente, Bill. *Gabrielle Roy: Creation and Memory.* Toronto, Ont.: ECW Press, 1997. Relates the major themes and concerns of Roy's work to three pivotal phases of her life: the early years in Manitoba, her youthful two-year sojourn in France, and her later life in Quebec.

Coleman, Patrick. *The Limits of Sympathy: Gabrielle Roy's "The Tin Flute."* Toronto, Ont.: ECW Press, 1993. A comprehensive and favorable analysis of the novel generally regarded as Roy's masterpiece.

Everett, Jane, ed. *In Translation: The Gabrielle Roy-Joyce Marshall Correspondence.* Toronto, Ont.: University of Toronto Press, 2005. A compilation of the extensive correspondence between the author and her English translator. Of special focus are the musings on the art of translation and the problems involved in rendering French prose into English.

Hess, M. G. *Gabrielle Roy.* Boston: Twayne, 1984. A useful survey volume in the Twayne World Authors series, examining all of Roy's writings. Includes brief commentary and analysis of each of her works.

Knoller, Eva-Marie, ed. *Cambridge Companion to Canadian Literature.* New York: Cambridge University Press, 2004. Helpful, timely essays covering a range of topics, with especially pertinent chapters on Francophone writing and Canadian fiction.

New, W. H. *A History of Canadian Literature.* Montreal: McGill-Queen's University Press, 2003. A contemporary, comprehensive survey of Canadian fiction, from Inuit myths to contemporary novels, with insightful attention to recurrent themes related to the history and traditions of the country.

Richard, François. *Gabrielle Roy: A Life.* Translated by Patricia Claxton. Toronto, Ont.: McClelland & Stewart, 1996. A lengthy, well-documented study, and the only complete biography of Roy. Special attention is given to the struggles of Roy's life and the way they were transmuted into her fiction.

SALMAN RUSHDIE

Born: Bombay (now Mumbai), India; June 19, 1947
Also known as: Ahmed Salman Rushdie

PRINCIPAL LONG FICTION

Grimus, 1975
Midnight's Children, 1981
Shame, 1983
The Satanic Verses, 1988
Haroun and the Sea of Stories, 1990 (fable)
The Moor's Last Sigh, 1995
The Ground Beneath Her Feet, 1999
Fury, 2001
Shalimar the Clown, 2005
The Enchantress of Florence, 2008

OTHER LITERARY FORMS

In addition to his novels, Salman Rushdie (ROOSH-dee) has produced short stories and works of nonfiction. *The Jaguar Smile: A Nicaraguan Journey* (1987) is a book of travel and political observations written following Rushdie's visit to Nicaragua in July, 1986, as a guest of the Sandinista Association of Cultural Workers. Among his short stories; the best known is "The Prophet's Hair," which appeared originally in the *London Review of Books* in 1981 and has been reprinted in *The Penguin Book of Modern British Short Stories* (1987). A fable in the style of *The Arabian Nights' Entertainments*, *Haroun and the Sea of Stories* was published in 1990, and the collection of short stories *East, West: Stories* (1994) includes "The Prophet's Hair" and the dazzling "At the Auction of the Ruby Slippers." The essays in Rushdie's *Step Across This Line: Collected Nonfiction, 1992-2002* (2002) deal with a variety of subjects, including popular culture, politics, and soccer.

ACHIEVEMENTS

Although furor and indignation have followed the publication of a number of Salman Rushdie's novels, the works have also received critical praise and rave reviews. *Midnight's Children* won the James Tait Black Memorial Prize, the English Speaking Union Literature Award, and the Booker Prize; it has been translated into twelve languages. Although *Shame* was banned in Pakistan, as *Midnight's Children* had been in India, it too received critical plaudits for its seriocomic portrait of Pakistani life. No writer since English satirist Jonathan Swift has aroused as much ire from so many sources, notwithstanding the notoriety of *The Satanic Verses*, which won the Whitbread Award as best novel of 1988. On February 14, 1989, the Ayatollah Ruhollah Khomeini, the fundamentalist spiritual leader of Iran, issued a fatwa (a proclamation concerning a matter of Muslim faith) that called for Rushdie's death as an enemy of Islam and sanctioned similar reprisals against those who published or distributed *The Satanic Verses*. Rushdie became a Knight of the British Empire in 2007. Ironically, this royal honor served to rekindle the hatred and many of the threats that haunted him following publication of *The Satanic Verses*.

Rushdie's novels, actually modern picaresques, explore the tragicomic results of lost identity; they portray in exuberant, highly inventive, satirical style what the author considers to be the consequences of living in cultures that have become mixed, distorted, and diluted through combinations of expediency, political ineptitude, and exploitative religion.

BIOGRAPHY

Ahmed Salman Rushdie was born in Bombay (now Mumbai), India, on June 19, 1947, less than two months before the end of the British Raj. His father, Anis Ahmed Rushdie, and his mother, Negin Butt Rushdie, were Muslims with ties to the region that would become Pakistan. The family did not at first join the Muslim exodus to Pakistan that began after partition in September, 1947. Even so, they became increasingly aware of their minority status as Muslims in a predominantly Hindu state.

Although the Rushdies were nominally Muslim, they also identified with India and with Great Britain. Rushdie's father had been educated in England, at Cambridge University, and had determined to rear his son and three daughters to appreciate their multicultural background. As a result, Rushdie had, from boyhood, access to a variety of works in his father's library. It became a recurring argument between father and son, however, that the boy did not make adequate use of this wealth of books. His private reading during boyhood was generally limited to an English translation of the fifteenth century collection of stories known as *The Arabian Nights' Entertainments* (or *The Thousand and One Nights*). His mother, considered "keeper of the family stories," regaled young Rushdie and his sisters with a wealth of anecdotes on their family history; he remembered them all and would later adapt many of them in his writings.

Rushdie was sent to the Cathedral and John Connon School, a British-administered primary school with Anglican affiliation located in Bombay. As his sister Sameen has recalled, "He mopped up all the prizes," was not very adapt at games, read extensively in both serious and popular literature, and loved both American B films and Hindu hit films. In 1961, at the age of thirteen, he was sent to the prestigious Rugby public school in England. At Rugby, however, although the masters were generally fair-minded, Rushdie felt alienated from his classmates, the "old boys" from British established families, who subjected him to cruel pranks. Rushdie compensated for the pranks and racial taunts by excelling at debates, appearing in theatrical productions, and thriving in academic areas, winning the Queen's Medal for history and securing (but refusing) a scholarship at Balliol College, Oxford.

In 1964, the Rushdie family had emigrated to Kara-

Salman Rushdie. (© Jerry Bauer)

chi, Pakistan, and while Rushdie was not enthusiastic about returning to England, he had been offered a scholarship at his father's university, King's College, Cambridge, and amid the India-Pakistan war in 1965, his father literally pushed him onto an airplane bound for the United Kingdom. Rushdie's attitude toward his father was often argumentative, and there was a serious rupture in their relationship when he entered Cambridge. Shortly before the elder Rushdie's death in 1987, there was a rapprochement between the two men.

At Cambridge, Rushdie decided to read for a degree in history, and he eventually attained a 2.2 (that is, "second-rate") degree, but he thrived in the social atmosphere of the mid-1960's. "It was a very good time to be at Cambridge," he has stated. "I ceased to be a conservative snob under the influence of the Vietnam War and dope." He continued his involvement in theater, and upon his graduation in 1968, he attempted to work in the entertainment industry in Pakistan. He found that cen-

sorship was inescapable there, however, and returned to London, where he worked in amateur theatricals and supported himself as a copywriter at the J. Walter Thompson advertising agency. He had already begun to think of himself as a writer, however, and he completed a never-published novel in 1971, "The Book of the Pir," which he has described as "post-Joycean and sub-Joycean."

Grimus was Rushdie's first published novel, written while he was still working irregularly in advertising to earn an income. It was a commercial failure and never was published in the United States, but it was favorably reviewed in London's *The Times Literary Supplement* (January 21, 1975), and it attracted notice and the beginnings of an audience for Rushdie. It took several short stories and five years before Rushdie produced his next novel, *Midnight's Children*. This work won rave reviews on both sides of the Atlantic, but it also offended a great many people, among them the family of Indira Gandhi, then prime minister of India. Rushdie made a public apology for the cutting satirical references to her and specific members of her family in the novel, but he made no changes in subsequent editions. The affair was exacerbated by the fact that Rushdie's accusations coincided with the Indian army's assault on the Golden Temple of the Sikh Muslims. The assassination of Mrs. Gandhi in 1984 brought a tragic end to this series of events.

Having offended large numbers of Indians with *Midnight's Children*, Rushdie published *Shame*, his portrayal of the blood feuds that led to the deposing and execution of Pakistan's prime minister Zulfikar Ali Bhutto by his former protégé, Mohammad Zia-ul-Haq. The same pattern followed publication of this novel, but this time Rushdie had offended the Pakistanis, India's enemies. Again Rushdie had great commercial success and received critical plaudits, but *Shame*, which Rushdie has called *Midnight's Children's* "antisequel," was denied publication in Pakistan just as *Midnight's Children* had been banned in India.

By 1985, Rushdie was sought after by every major publisher. Viking Penguin offered him an advance of $850,000 for rights to his work then in progress, leading to a rancorous break with Liz Calder, an old friend trying to establish her own publishing firm. Everyone in publishing circles knew that the new book would cause a sensation, but no one, not even Rushdie, could have known that *The Satanic Verses* would make him a marked man.

After February 14, 1989, with the Khomeini decree of death, Rushdie's life came to resemble the plots of his novels. The threat of assassination forced him to close his London home and go into hiding. Viking Penguin received thousands of threatening letters. Bookstores that did not remove *The Satanic Verses* from their shelves were threatened with bombings. Riots related to the book broke out in Bombay; at least five people were killed and dozens injured in Islamabad, Pakistan; and two Muslim leaders were killed in Brussels, Belgium, after they expressed opposition to censoring the book. Two bookstores in Berkeley, California, were fire-bombed, and a bomb blast in London, which killed the terrorist who had placed the bomb, was attributed to the anti-Rushdie campaign. Rushdie's Japanese translator was murdered, his Italian translator was wounded in a knife attack, and his Norwegian publisher was almost killed in a shooting.

Although some members of the British political establishment expressed a personal distaste for Rushdie, and authors such as John le Carré and Roald Dahl (who called him a "dangerous opportunist") claimed that Rushdie deserved his predicament, Scotland Yard was assigned the task of protecting him.

The fatwa on Rushdie's life inevitably continued as the bane of his existence. Writers such as William Styron, Milan Kundera, and Norman Mailer called upon the governments of democratic nations to exert pressure on Iran, and, without making his position public, horror writer Stephen King insisted that any bookstore chain that gave in to threats and removed Rushdie's books from its shelves would have to remove King's as well. In 1990, Rushdie issued a statement that he had "converted" to Islam to show "people who viewed me as some kind of enemy that I wasn't one," but he realized that he had acted out of "despair and disorientation" and "made strenuous steps to get out of the false position."

When Rushdie made a secret trip to the United States in 1992, President George H. W. Bush's administration avoided contact with him, but in 1993 he was able to arrange a brief meeting in the White House with President Bill Clinton. The British government of Prime Minister

John Major was more supportive, albeit discreetly, than its predecessor. In the third year of his concealment, Rushdie began to write again, remarking "If I can't write, then, in a way, the attack has been successful." His fable *Haroun and the Sea of Stories*, written as a means of speaking to his son, whom he could not contact while in hiding, was published in 1990, and a collection of short fiction, *East, West*, was released in 1994. After five years of labor, *The Moor's Last Sigh* was published in 1995.

The fatwa and life in hiding ended Rushdie's marriage to his second wife, the American novelist Marianne Wiggins; they divorced in 1993 (his first marriage, to Clarissa Luard, with whom he had a son, ended in divorce in 1985). His third marriage, to Elizabeth West, produced one son and ended in divorce in 2004. Rushdie's *The Enchantress of Florence* was written even as his fourth marriage, to actor Padma Lakshmi, was unraveling (they divorced in 2007) and contains, amid much else, a meditation on an ideal wife conjured in dream.

During the mid-1990's, Rushdie appeared in public more often, unannounced but usually greeted with considerable enthusiasm, and was active in encouraging international resistance to the fatwa. In 1998, some more moderate members of the Iranian government moved toward a withdrawal of the fatwa, but Rushdie's safety was still not entirely guaranteed, and he remained cautious in terms of his movements into the early years of the twenty-first century.

ANALYSIS

Many Western readers, ignorant of Islam and Hinduism, the 1947 partition of the Indian subcontinent and the creation of Pakistan, the India-Pakistan war of 1965, and the Pakistani civil war of 1974, may tend to read Salman Rushdie's novels as bizarre entertainments. This is unfortunate, since each is a picaresque allegory into which the author has inserted details from his own life in order to prove that myth is history, today is yesterday, and the life of one person is integral to the history of nations. Rushdie masks events here and there and relentlessly mixes Persian and Hindu myths, but the hiatus in logic that this method creates is merely to prove his contention that an Anglo-Indian-Pakistani is a person with a hole in the body, a vital place in which there is a haunting void.

MIDNIGHT'S CHILDREN

Midnight's Children is Rushdie's allegorical picaresque on the history of the modern state of India. Its narrator, Saleem Sinai, is one of those whose birth coincided with the hour and day India achieved independence: midnight, August 15, 1947. He and many others, including Jawaharlal Nehru, India's first prime minister, considered these "midnight's children" singled out, privileged by the hopeful hour at which they began their lives. Saleem discovers that he does indeed have special powers; he can, in his mind, summon all the other children born during the midnight hour of August 15, 1947, and, when a boy, he does so nightly, establishing the "Midnight Children's Conference," a forum he hopes will augur well for organizing the leaders of the new state.

Saleem's family is prosperous; they reside in one of Bombay's more affluent sections on an estate of homes once owned by an Englishman, William Methwold, who left India on the very day the Raj ended. Through a bizarre series of events (an accident at school that reveals that his blood type corresponds to neither parent and the subsequent confession of Mary Pereira, a nurse who had worked at the hospital at which Saleem was born), Saleem's family discovers that Mary had intentionally switched children, giving the Sinais a child of one of Bombay's poorest families. Only Saleem, through his telepathic powers, knows that the Sinais's real son, reared as a street urchin named Shiva, is actually an illegitimate child of the Englishman Methwold. Though the Sinais make no attempt to locate their own boy and do accept Saleem as their own, Saleem recognizes Shiva as his nemesis and realizes that Shiva may well destroy him.

Each of the children of midnight has some special talent or ability by virtue of time and date of birth: Saleem's telepathic skills, Shiva's extraordinarily strong knees (which he uses to kill the Indian street entertainer he believes is his father), and the abilities of Parvati-the-witch, who seeks to use her talents only for good. All the children become caught up in the political machinations that follow upon India's independence and the creation of Pakistan. Saleem's family, aware that they are part of India's unwanted Muslim minority, immigrate to Pakistan.

This event, plus the fact that Saleem no longer wishes to have any contact with Shiva, the rightful heir of the Sinais, ends Saleem's nightly summoning of the Midnight Children's Conference. Once in Pakistan, Saleem discovers that his telepathic powers do not work. He tries, instead, to develop his exceptional power of smell, utilizing his huge nose to smell danger, injustice, unhappiness, poverty, and other elements of Pakistani life.

Saleem and his family become caught up in Pakistan's 1965 war with India. Saleem's former countrymen become his enemies, and all of his family are killed in the war, except his sister, who has taken the name Jamila Singer and has become famous as a singer of patriotic songs. When the east wing of Pakistan secedes in 1973 and declares itself the independent state of Bangladesh, Saleem enlists in Pakistan's canine patrol, the Cutia, performing the function of a dog to sniff out traitors. Pakistan's devastating loss in the war leaves Saleem without a country. Ultimately, it is Parvati-the-witch who uses her magic to make him disappear and return him to India.

Saleem marries Parvati but is unable to consummate the marriage. Whenever he tries to do so, he sees the decaying face of Jamila, the woman who had been reared as his sister. Saleem had loved Jamila, but he also had come to recognize that their nominal brother-sister relationship would not allow her to be his. Out of frustration, Parvati takes Shiva, now a major in India's army, as her lover. She gives birth to his child, named Aadam, whom Saleem acknowledges as his own son.

Shiva, the destroyer, supervises the slum clearance project that not only eliminates the Bombay quarter in which the magicians had lived but also kills Parvati and many of her magician colleagues who had refused to leave their homes. Saleem is one of those arrested and brought to Benares, the town of the widows. Here he is imprisoned, forced by Shiva to name and identify the skills of the children of midnight; he is released only after he has been forcibly sterilized. Oddly, those arrested as a result of Saleem's information do not blame him; they, too, are sterilized.

Much more happens in *Midnight's Children*. The novel is structured as a family history that reaches back to Saleem's grandparents and describes the political circumstances in India after World War I, through World

War II and the end of the Raj, to the war with Pakistan and the Pakistani civil war. It is also highly mythic. Sinai, the surname of the narrator, masks the name of the Arabian philosopher Avicenna (Abū ʿAlī al-Husain ibn ʿAbdallāh ibn Sīnā; 980-1037), who saw the emanations of God's presence in the cosmos as a series of triads of mind, body, and soul. The triads appear in the three generations of Sinais who appear in the novel, but the three religions of India—Hinduism, Islam, and Christianity—which also appear, do nothing to reverse the downward course of India's fortunes after 1947. Sin is the ancient moon god of Hadhramut, who acting at a distance can influence the tides of the world. He is represented by the letter *S* and is as sinuous as the snake. Appropriately, Saleem discovers his son Aadam in the care of a master snake charmer, Picture Singh. Sinai is both the place of revelation, of commandments and the golden calf, and the desert of barrenness and infertility that is Rushdie's view of modern India.

Saleem's nose resembles the trunk of the elephant deity, Kali, who is the god of literature, and the huge ears of Saleem's son Aadam carry the motif into India's future. Shiva is the Hindu god of destruction and reproduction, a member of the trinity that includes Brama and Vishnu. The closing chapters of the novel find Saleem the manager of a Bombay pickle factory owned by his former nurse, Mary Pereira, the woman who had originally exchanged him for the true son of the Sinais, underscoring the motif of absurd continuity, pickled history, and Saleem's huge nose, which is called a cucumber as often as it is an elephant's trunk.

The most savage satire of the book is reserved for Indira Gandhi, daughter of Nehru and, until her 1984 assassination, prime minister of India. Rushdie repeatedly cites a famous newspaper photograph in which her hair is white on one side and black on the other to symbolize her hypocrisy. He ridicules Sanjay Gandhi, her son, now also dead, as the mastermind of India's slum clearance and birth-control plans. Specific members of Gandhi's cabinet appear in the novel with appendages to their titles, such as "Minister for Railroads and Bribery." Gandhi's campaign slogan "Indira is India, and India is Indira," which Rushdie often quotes in these contexts, thus becomes a dire prophecy. It is little wonder that distribution of *Midnight's Children*, published during In-

dia's state of national emergency, was prohibited in India. The novel also made Rushdie persona non grata in the country of his birth.

SHAME

Rushdie has called *Shame* his "antisequel" to *Midnight's Children*. It has picaresque and seriocomic elements that resemble those of the earlier novel, but its characters are Pakistanis, members of the power elite that had its historical counterpart in the circle of deposed prime minister Zulfikar Ali Bhutto and Bhutto's protégé, the man who engineered the coup and Bhutto's trial and execution, Mohammad Zia-ul-Haq. *Shame* created as much consternation in Pakistan as *Midnight's Children* had in India, with precisely the same result: The novel was banned in Pakistan, and Rushdie was considered subversive.

The title of *Shame* derives from the Urdu word *Sharam*, and it contains an encyclopedia of nuance the English barely suggests: embarrassment, discomfiture, indecency, immodesty, and the sense of unfulfilled promise. Rushdie thus explores in this work themes that are similar to those of his first novel. All the characters experience shame in one or another of these forms as well as some its converse, shamelessness.

Shame also maintains the highly mythic, literary tone of *Midnight's Children*. Its unprepossessing hero, evocatively named Omar Khayyám Shakil, is a paunchy doctor of great promise with the name of the Persian poet known for the twelfth century *Rubáiyát*, the erotic lyric poems imitated in English by Edward FitzGerald in 1859. Rushdie's Omar is born in a crumbling house called Nishapur (also the town of the historical poet's birth), once the mansion of an Englishman, Colonel Arthur Greenfield, in a Pakistani backwater identified only as "Q," but perhaps Quetta.

The circumstances of Omar's birth are ambiguous. He has three mothers: Chhunni, Munnee, and Bunny Shakil. These three sisters all consider him their son, and none discloses which of them actually gave him birth, nor will they disclose the name of his father, though the reader learns that he is an Englishman. Omar's situation is thus a metaphor of the mixed cultural legacy Rushdie often describes. Indeed, Rushdie has often spoken of himself as a man with three mothers: India, Pakistan, and England. The house in which Omar is reared is a labyrinth, a relic of the British Raj; its corridors lead to rooms unoccupied for generations, and Omar, who in his early boyhood is prohibited from leaving the house at any time, is frightened out of his wits when he ventures too far and sees that the water-seeking roots of a tree have punctured the house's outer walls. All of this is Rushdie's metaphorical description of the state of mind of a person with mixed and hostile origins: alienated, loveless, relentlessly, fearfully traversing the labyrinth of the mind, and feeling shame. Omar's only glimpse of the world outside Nishapur is through his telescope, appropriately, given that the poet for whom he was named was also an astronomer.

The novel is filled with a wealth of characters whose backgrounds are similarly symbolic and complex. Rushdie draws them together both through family relationships and through their individually shameful actions as well as their capacity to feel shame. For example, Bilquìs Kemal Hyder is a woman reared in Bombay, India, by her father, Mahound "the Woman" Kemal, owner of a motion-picture theater. The epithet regularly applied to her father is simultaneously an indication of his motherly solicitude for his daughter and a jibe at his having lost his masculinity by assuming the burden of child rearing. After her father dies in a terrorist bomb blast that also destroys his theater, Bilquìs is rescued by Raza "Razor Guts" Hyder, Rushdie's version of Zia, an ambitious young military officer who takes her as his bride and returns to the family home in Karachi, Pakistan, the country created by partition of the Indian subcontinent. Thrust into an uncompromisingly Muslim environment, she finds herself shamed when she is unable to bear Hyder a son. Of their two daughters, Sufiya Zinobia Hyder and Naveed "Good News" Hyder, the first is perpetually childlike, the result of a mistreated case of meningitis. Bilquìs and Hyder's second daughter, "Good News," atones for her mother's relative infertility by bearing twenty-seven children.

The focus of *Shame* is the rise to power of Omar's companion in dissipation, Iskander "Isky" Harappa, based on Zulfikar Ali Bhutto. Isky gives up drinking and womanizing in middle age, adopts the veneer of a devout Muslim, and seizes power after the loss of Pakistan's east wing. For a time he remains popular, assisted by his beautiful unmarried daughter, Arjumand "Virgin Iron-

pants" Harappa, Rushdie's satiric depiction of Benazir Bhutto, who would later become prime minister of Pakistan. Isky's wife, Rani Humayun Hyder, remains out of the limelight on the family's isolated estate, where she weaves shawls that document all of her husband's acts of shame—a twist on the Penelope motif of Homer's *Odyssey* (c. 725 B.C.E.; English translation, 1614). By the time Isky is hanged in a military coup, Rani has completed eighteen of these shawls. (Rushdie enumerates the details of each in an angry excursus modeled on a Homeric epic catalog.)

When Hyder seizes power, he encourages the trial and conviction of Isky Harappa. After a curious combination of circumstances causes Harappa's death, Hyder orders the corpse hanged, ostensibly carrying out the court's sentence of execution. Hyder's increasing concern is, however, the deviant behavior of his daughter, Sufiya Zinobia. Though well past twenty, she has the mental age of less than ten. Hyder accepts Omar Shakil's offer to marry her, made out of shame for his past womanizing and platonic love for the young woman whose life he had saved. Sufiya Zinobia is, however, aware that some act about which she knows nothing regularly accompanies marriage. She twice escapes from the Hyder house, where she is literally imprisoned (recalling Shakil's own imprisonment in youth), allows herself to be raped at random by street-walking men, then decapitates the men who have raped her. The villagers who discover these decapitated corpses create the legend of a wild white panther to explain the murders, but Hyder knows that his daughter is the killer and fears that she will eventually decapitate him.

When Hyder's downfall appears imminent, he, his wife Bilquìs, and Shakil escape to the closed mansion of Shakil's youth, and Shakil's three mothers give them sanctuary. Shakil quickly realizes, however, that the three old women plan to kill Hyder in reprisal for his having ordered the death of their younger son, Babar Shakil, for his terrorist involvements. This they do, though not before the accidental death of Bilquìs. Shakil dies soon thereafter, shot by Talvar Ulhaq, Hyder's son-in-law and former state police chief. The pantherlike figure of Sufiya Zinobia observes the carnage, with Harappa's daughter Arjumand hovering as a vision of a future of "a new cycle of shamelessness."

Rushdie's point, developed through these and other complexities of plot, is that shame and shamelessness develop through religious and political failure; the images of Islam and Pakistan that he invokes are filled with parricide and cruelty, but never genuine and simple love. That those who destroy one another are related by family as well as national ties merely compounds the tragedy and the shame. Rushdie's Pakistan is presented as "a failure of the dreaming mind."

THE SATANIC VERSES

The Satanic Verses is Rushdie's strongest indictment of politicized religion, mixed cultural identity, and insensitive, arbitrary officialdom. Its tone is allegorical, picaresque, satiric, and irreverent. Those who know details concerning the founding of Islam, British politics, and contemporary London will recognize the objections made to the book; those unaware of these particulars will likely be puzzled by the novel's character and chronological shifts and may even wonder why the work has caused such consternation.

The novel begins with an explosion, a passenger airplane destroyed by a terrorist bomb as it flies over the English Channel. Only two passengers survive: Gibreel Farishta and Saladin Chamcha, two actors of Indian origin. Miraculously, they float to earth unharmed. Farishta, whose first name is the Indian form of that of the angel Gabriel, has made his reputation playing Krishna, Gautama Buddha, Hanuman, and other Indian deities in films known as theologicals. Chamcha, a complete Anglophile, has achieved fame by doing commercial voice-overs in England, though his face is unknown to his admiring audience. With this as background, Rushdie establishes the figure of the angel Gibreel (in Islam associated with bringing Allah's call to theProphet Muhammad) and the apparently diabolical Chamcha, who has traded his ethnic identity for a pseudo-British veneer.

When they land, Chamcha discovers that he has grown horns under his very English bowler, as well as cloven hooves and a huge phallus—this despite his mild demeanor, elegant manners, and proper British appearance. Farishta (whose surname means "sweet") finds that he has a halo, despite his being an unconscionable womanizer. His very trip to England was a pursuit of Alleluia Cone, the British "ice queen" of Polish refugee parents. Cone is an internationally famous mountain climber who has conquered Mount Everest. Rushdie thus mixes the imagery of good and evil, angel and demon; this is an exponential motif of the entire novel. It follows that the British police arrest Chamcha as an illegal immigrant and brutalize him terribly. Farishta, however, because of his angelic appearance, remains free, having charmed the police and having refused to identify Chamcha.

The narrative then abruptly shifts to introduce Mahound, a blasphemous name for Muhammad, the founder of Islam. Edmund Spenser used the name Mahound in *The Faerie Queene* (1590, 1596) to represent a heathen idol reserved for oaths sworn by the wicked. Rushdie's Mahound profanely re-creates Muhammad's call from Allah through the angel Gabriel. Mahound, like Muhammad, is a businessman; he climbs Mount Cone and looks down on the city of sand that Rushdie calls Jahilia, a fictive town that corresponds to Mecca. Mahound's pursuit of his destiny on Mount Cone corresponds to Gibreel's pursuit of mountain climber Alleluia Cone; his dream-filled sleeps as he awaits the angel Gibreel resemble the trancelike seizures, ever increasing in severity, of Gibreel Farishta.

Mahound's companions are described as the scum of Jahilia (Muhammad's companions were former slaves), and Rushdie puckishly names one of them Salman. They have the habit, dangerous in a city built entirely of sand, of constantly washing themselves (a parody of Muslim ritual purification). The twelve whores of Jahilia (which means "ignorance" or "darkness"), reminiscent of Muhammad's twelve wives and known as Mothers of the Believers, reside in a brothel called the Curtain. Translated as *hejab*, this can be associated with the curtainlike veil worn by pious Muslim women.

Abu Simbel, the name of the village flooded in the 1960's when Egypt constructed the Aswān High Dam, is the name given here to the ruler of Jahilia, a city also endangered by water. Because he recognizes Mahound as a threat to his power, Abu Simbel offers him a deal. If Mahound's Allah will accept a mere 3 of Jahilia's 360 deities into the new monotheistic religion, he will recognize it and give Mahound a seat on the ruling council. It will not be much of a compromise, Abu Simbel insists, since Mahound's religion already recognizes Gibreel as the voice of Allah and Shaitan (Satan) as the spirit the Qur'ān records would not bow before Adam.

Mahound decides to compromise. He climbs Cone Mountain, consults with his Gibreel, then returns to Jahilia to announce the new verses: "Have you thought upon Lat and Uzza, and Manat, the third, the other? . . . They are the exalted birds, and their intercession is desired indeed." These are the so-called Satan-inspired inclusions of the goddesses of motherhood (Lat), beauty and love (Uzza), and fate (Manat) as daughters of Allah, which the Qur'ān rejects as heresy. Mahound later publicly recants this heretical insertion and flees to Yathrib (the ancient name for Medina), corresponding to the historical account of the *hegira*, Muḥammad's flight from Mecca to Medina. Gibreel reappears to announce: "It was me both times, baba, me first and second also me." One can draw implications that Islam was founded by rationalizing good and evil, that its founder was both a sincere mystic and a power-hungry entrepreneur, and that Gibreel, an actor who specializes in impersonating deities, had given at least one bravura performance that changed history.

Rushdie goes on to recount a masked sardonic version of the holy war to establish Islam, continuing to blur the distinction between ancient and modern times. A bearded, turbaned imam in exile in London (which he considers Sodom) is in exile from his homeland, called Desh. When a revolution begins in Desh and overthrows the corrupt empress, named Ayesha (ironically also the name of Muḥammad's favorite wife), Gibreel (perhaps the angel, perhaps the actor Farishta, perhaps one and the same) flies the imam to Desh on his back in time to see the carnage. This episode can be interpreted as the recall to Iran of the Ayatollah Khomeini, who was in exile near Paris until the overthrow of the shah. When the revolution succeeds, Ayesha metamorphoses into the mother goddess, Al-Lat, she whom Mahound had falsely named a daughter of Allah in the satanic verses.

In a parallel sequence, an epileptic peasant girl, also named Ayesha, arouses the lust of a landowner named Mirza Saeed, whose wife is dying of breast cancer. As Moses led the Israelites out of Egypt, so Ayesha, who declares that her husband the archangel Gibreel has told her to do so, leads the entire village, including Saeed's wife, on a pilgrimage by foot to Mecca. She declares that the

Arabian Sea will open to admit them (recalling the parting of the Red Sea in Exodus); butterflies mark their privileged status, and they are Ayesha's only food (recalling the manna of the Israelites). All that the unbelievers see as they watch the pilgrims is their disappearance into the Arabian Sea. The implication remains that Ayesha parts the sea for those who believe; to everyone else, the entire enterprise ends as a cult suicide. This motif emphasizes the novel's focus on migration, which Rushdie has claimed is its central subject.

Much more happens in *The Satanic Verses*. London, called "Ellowen Deeowen" by Farishta, is beset by ethnic antagonisms. Its police and most whites are brutal racists; its Indians are rogues or displaced mystics. Still, nothing in Rushdie's novel is what it appears to be, and that is his point. Empires and religions alike arise from a combination of noble and sordid motives. It is impossible to admire or hate anything unreservedly; there is evil even in that which appears absolutely good, and, conversely, one can explain evil in terms of good gone awry. Such relativism is hardly new, but the notoriety *The Satanic Verses* has received has obscured the author's point. What is clear is that *The Satanic Verses* is the logical sequel to ideas Rushdie began to develop in *Midnight's Children* and *Shame*, as well as an allegory that strains narrative and religious sensibilities to the breaking point.

THE MOOR'S LAST SIGH

As a kind of permanent immigrant, a man who can neither return to a home country (India) nor feel really at home in any other land, Rushdie has, as Henry Louis Gates, Jr., has noted, presented a "vision of migrancy as the very condition of cultural modernity." A crucial aspect of this aesthetic position, however, has been an intense examination of the various homelands that formed—and continued to inform—the intellectual, spiritual, and political components of Rushdie's psychological being. Whereas *Midnight's Children* and *Shame* focus on India and Pakistan at specific, contemporary moments in their postcolonial history, *The Moor's Last Sigh* is an attempt to account for and understand the origins and evolution of the complex cultural matrix that Rushdie refers to as "Mother India." Its narrative combines the overall structure of the classic nineteenth century novel, projecting the epic sweep of history, with an episodic linkage of individual incidents and characters akin to the picaresque; it is also similar to Eastern story cycles.

The Moor of the title is Moraes Zogoiby, son of Aurora Da Gama, whose lineage is Indian Muslim, and Abraham Zogoiby, whose ancestors include Muslim and Jewish exiles who were banished from Spain in 1492. Through the course of the novel, Moraes tells the story of his family from the mid-nineteenth century to the present (the 1990's), where he, the lone survivor, has returned to Spain to continue a frustrating quest for his mother's legacy: the Moorish paintings that may reveal the essential truth and meaning of his life.

This intricate, swirling mix of history, myth, legend, personal feuds, ethnic rivalries, and disappointed love is the story of a man trying to make some sense of his life as well as the story of his fascinating, driven family. It is also the saga of a country with a long past, an interim as a semisubjugated colonial entity, and a turbulent, troubled present. While much of the narrative is written with the kind of vivid, detailed realism that is one of the marks of Rushdie's style—an abundance of descriptive images and evocative details—frequent infusions of mystic moments, almost hallucinatory states of being, apparent intrusions of the supernatural, and other features of Magical Realism contribute to a larger dimension than a historic record. This is especially apparent in the presentation of Aurora Zogoiby as a symbol for India itself, an equivalent to the *Mother India* (the name of a film released in 1957, the year of Moraes's birth) that represents all of the clashing, tempestuous qualities exerting an immense emotional pull on its inhabitants. It is also apparent in Moraes's (meaning Rushdie's) exhilarated response to and evocation of the city of Bombay, an urban masculine complement to the more pastoral, and historically traditional, feminine motherland.

Moraes states early in the novel that his account is one of regret, "a last sigh for a lost world," and the world that he re-creates or reimagines is a rich fusion of cultures, a hybrid set in sharp contrast to what Rushdie calls "the fundamentalist, totalized explanation of the world" that he has challenged throughout his work. The novel begins in the region of Cochin, where the West (Europe) and the East (India) met and mingled for the first time. It was the central site of the pepper crop, and among other

extended metaphors that are threaded through the novel, spice—the source of the Da Gama family wealth—stands for passionate love. The shift from commerce in the spice trade to the contemporary economics of currency and technology underscores the separation of the human from its most significant strengths and is one of the primary causes of the downward course that the Da Gama line takes.

For Rushdie, love begins as an irresistible rush of physical feeling that overwhelms the senses but then is complicated by circumstances of family, ambition, and cultural forces beyond individual control. While Moraes maintains that "defeated love would still be love," Rushdie has observed that "the central story of Aurora and Abraham in the book is a story of what happens when love dies." Moraes struggles to fill the "dreadful vortex" of its absence, and though his life in retrospect reveals his failure in all the realms where love matters (nation, parents, partner), his efforts to understand love's power and to use it in accordance with a set of human values redeem his failure.

The loss of Moraes's family foundation due to love's blindness and treachery is balanced by the restoring capacity of the love for a place and by the invigorating experience of artistic consciousness as a means of illumination. *The Moor's Last Sigh* is a paen to a special place, the vanishing (perhaps never existent) India of Rushdie's heart's core, the "romantic myth of a plural, hybrid nation," which he lovingly describes in Aurora's paintings.

A sense of loss permeates the narrative, as Moraes's three sisters, his treacherous lover Uma Sarasvati (possibly based on Marianne Wiggins), many acquaintances, and various semiadversaries die prematurely. Adding to this loss are his estrangement from his parents and his separation from the places he has known as home. As a compensation of sorts, India continues to glow in Moraes's mind, rendered indelibly in Rushdie's verbal paintings. It is the unifying concept for what Rushdie calls "the four anchors of the soul," which he lists as "place, language, people, customs." The sheer size of the India that Rushdie constructs, in addition to a palimpsest of its layers, makes it an elusive, almost chimerical country. *The Moor's Last Sigh*, laced with loss, disappointment, frustration, and anger, is not a pessimistic vision of existence, because even when place, peoples, and customs are removed, language remains, and Moraes—who exhibits all of the verbal virtuosity that is a feature of Rushdie's style—utilizes the powers of language in the service of truth, to his last breath.

THE ENCHANTRESS OF FLORENCE

The Enchantress of Florence is an ambitious work; though presented as a novel, it more closely resembles medieval romance. It is concerned with the storytelling process more than with telling a sustained story. Frame tales appear within frame tales, and the result is a work that resembles the fifteenth century collection of stories *The Arabian Nights' Entertainments* (also known as *The Thousand and One Nights*) or perhaps John Barth's *Chimera* (1972), his own resetting of the Scheherazade tales.

The central figure of *The Enchantress of Florence* is Akbar the Great, the liberal Mughal emperor of the sixteenth century, a historical figure. Akbar represents toleration of religion, no doubt an attractive symbol for Rushdie, given the precarious circumstances under which he has lived since publication of *The Satanic Verses*. Akbar sees the world in which he lives dissolving into hatred and violence. Though something of a philosopher king, he seems paralyzed by his inability to trust any of those around him, even his closest advisers.

A mysterious traveler from the West suddenly appears at Akbar's court. He too has a basis in history, though his identifications are several. The stranger is variously Agostino Vespucci (cousin of the explorer Amerigo Vespucci), though he also calls himself "Uccello." The immediate reference appears to be to Paolo Uccello, born Paolo di Dono (1397-1475), a Renaissance painter known for his application of mathematical principles to his art in conveying perfect perspective. It is also true, however, that this relatively common Italian surname, meaning "bird," implies someone wise but crafty and possibly untrustworthy. Vespucci-Uccello has a third identity, perhaps the most significant, that of Mogor dell'Amore, the "Mughal of Love." Vespucci-Uccello-Mogor dell'Amore claims kinship with Akbar and quickly becomes his closest adviser, though even Akbar is aware of the seductive quality of his new adviser's tale telling.

The Enchantress of Florence is a verbal arabesque

with an enormous number of characters. Many of these are historical figures fictionalized and reworked, such as the Medicis and Niccolò Machiavelli. There is also a variation on the Pygmalion myth. Despite his extensive harem, Akbar is able to conjure up only one, Jodha, who is perfect, and he has done this through a dream. Jodha's opposite is Qara Köz ("Black Eyes") whose androgynous sensuality fills Rushdie's romance. Rushdie channels this sensuality into aesthetics, however, for this is his abiding concern.

Robert J. Forman
Updated by Leon Lewis

OTHER MAJOR WORKS

SHORT FICTION: *East, West: Stories*, 1994; "The Firebird's Nest," 1997; "Vina Divina," 1999.

PLAY: *Midnight's Children*, pr., pb. 2003 (adaptation of his novel; with Simon Reade and Tim Supple).

NONFICTION: *The Jaguar Smile: A Nicaraguan Journey*, 1987; *Imaginary Homelands: Essays and Criticism, 1981-1991*, 1991; *The Wizard of Oz: A Short Text About Magic*, 1992; *Conversations with Salman Rushdie*, 2000 (Michael Reder, editor); *Step Across This Line: Collected Nonfiction, 1992-2002*, 2002.

BIBLIOGRAPHY

Appignanesi, Lisa, and Sara Maitland, eds. *The Rushdie File*. Syracuse, N.Y.: Syracuse University Press, 1990. Collection of essays surveys critical reaction to *The Satanic Verses*. Includes the text of the Khomeini fatwa.

Cundy, Catherine. *Salman Rushdie*. Manchester, England: Manchester University Press, 1996. Provides a good, readable introductory overview of Rushdie's fiction.

Dascalu, Cristina Emanuela. *Imaginary Homelands of Writers in Exile: Salman Rushdie, Bharati Mukherjee, and V. S. Naipaul*. Youngstown, N.Y.: Cambria Press, 2007. Examines how exile, voluntary and involuntary, has affected the work of these three quite different writers.

Goonetilleke, D. C. R. A. *Salman Rushdie*. New York: St. Martin's Press, 1998. Focuses on Rushdie's long fiction, examining the author's technique, autobiographical and historical elements in his work, and his position as a writer between cultures, among other topics.

Gurnah, Abdulrazak. *The Cambridge Companion to Salman Rushdie*. New York: Cambridge University Press, 2007. Provides a comprehensive introduction to Rushdie's work for the general reader.

Hamilton, Ian. "The First Life of Salman Rushdie." *The New Yorker*, December 25, 1995. Excellent, illuminating presentation of Rushdie's life before the fatwa, written with Rushdie's assistance and including accounts from interviews with many of Rushdie's friends and peers.

Hassumani, Sabrina. *Salman Rushdie: A Postmodern Reading of His Major Works*. Madison, N.J.: Fairleigh Dickinson University Press, 2002. Presents close readings of Rushdie's five major novels from *Midnight's Children* through *The Moor's Last Sigh*.

Pipes, Daniel. *The Rushdie Affair: The Novel, the Ayatollah, and the West*. New York: Birch Lane Press, 1990. Recounts the controversy attending publication of *The Satanic Verses*, but examines the question from the Muslim point of view. Suggests that valid arguments against publication of the novel were lost in the wake of the Khomeini fatwa that decreed Rushdie's death, in effect giving credence to the stereotype of Muslims held by many Westerners.

Rushdie, Salman. *Salman Rushdie Interviews: A Sourcebook of His Ideas*. Edited by Pradyumna S. Chauhan. Westport, Conn.: Greenwood Press, 2001. Handy selection of Rushdie's many interviews provides insight into his thinking, writing, and life experience.

Taneja, G. R., and R. K. Dhawan, eds. *The Novels of Salman Rushdie*. New Delhi: Indian Society for Commonwealth Studies, 1992. Wide-ranging compilation of essays by contributors from the Indian subcontinent covers all of Rushdie's writing through 1992 except *The Satanic Verses*. Provides a perspective beyond the criticism of Anglo-American authors.

RICHARD RUSSO

Born: Johnstown, New York; July 15, 1949

PRINCIPAL LONG FICTION

Mohawk, 1986
The Risk Pool, 1988
Nobody's Fool, 1993
Straight Man, 1997
Empire Falls, 2001
Bridge of Sighs, 2007

OTHER LITERARY FORMS

Although Richard Russo (REWS-oh) has published a number of short stories in various journals, he has always been primarily a novelist. In addition to his novels, he has written a variety of screenplays, most notably the neo-noir film *Twilight* (1998), cowritten with director Robert Benton; the film stars Paul Newman, Gene Hackman, and Susan Sarandon, among others. He also adapted author Scott Phillips's crime novel *The Ice Harvest* with Benton; the film, directed by Harold Ramis, was released in 2005. That same year, Russo wrote an adaptation of his own novel *Empire Falls* for a television miniseries that aired on the cable network HBO. In 2001 he contributed an introduction to *The Collected Stories of Richard Yates*. He has published one book of short stories, *The Whore's Child, and Other Stories* (2002).

ACHIEVEMENTS

Before he found success as a novelist, Richard Russo earned a fellowship from the Pennsylvania Council of Arts in 1983. In 1989, while living in Illinois, he received the annual prize from the Society of Midland Authors, awarded each year to a single author from one of twelve midwestern states, for *The Risk Pool*. Although it never earned any awards, his novel *Nobody's Fool* was met with unanimous critical acclaim and had healthy sales; the success of the film adaptation (written and directed by Robert Benton and released in 1994) helped solidify Russo's career, and some critics think that the Pulitzer Prize he received some years later could have been awarded to *Nobody's Fool. Straight Man* was also exceptionally well received and earned excellent notices. *Empire Falls* was named one of the Best Books of 2001 by *Library Journal* and earned the 2002 Pulitzer Prize for fiction.

BIOGRAPHY

Richard Russo was born in Johnstown, New York, and grew up in the upstate New York town of Gloversville. His father left the family when Russo was still a boy, and troubled relationships between fathers and sons haunt many of his novels. Gloversville was named, in part, because of the glove-making and leather-tanning factories that provided most of the work for residents (and polluted the nearby waterways). Many of Russo's novels are set in the fictional town of Mohawk, which also has an economy based on tanneries. The economics

and working lives that Russo saw as a boy, coupled with his work in construction and road crews in high school and college summers, would particularly inform the blue-collar aesthetic of much of his fiction.

Russo attended the University of Arizona, where he earned a bachelor's degree in 1971 and eventually a Ph.D. in literature in 1980. He realized while working on his dissertation that writing fiction appealed to him more than did literary criticism and academic writing, and he stayed on to earn a master of fine arts degree in 1981. Five years later, he published his first novel, *Mohawk.*

Russo has taught creative writing at various universities, including Southern Illinois University (Carbondale, Illinois), Colby College (Waterville, Maine), and the low-residency M.F.A. program for writers at Warren Wilson College (Ashville, North Carolina). Following the success of *Nobody's Fool* and its 1994 film adaptation, Russo was able to write full time. Additionally, he and Benton formed a friendship and a writing partnership during Benton's adaptation of *Nobody's Fool;* to-

Richard Russo. (© J. D.)

gether they have collaborated on screenplays for such films as *Twilight* and *The Ice Harvest*.

ANALYSIS

Several overarching thematic motifs connect a number of Richard Russo's novels, certainly owing in part to the author's own experiences. Five of his novels detail small-town life in places not so different from Gloversville, New York; *Mohawk*, *The Risk Pool*, and *Bridge of Sighs* are all set in or next to the fictional city of Mohawk, New York, a blue-collar factory city with unemployment and pollution problems stemming from its tannery industry. *Nobody's Fool* is set in the similar fictional city of North Bath in the same region of New York, and *Empire Falls* is set in a small, dying mill town in rural Maine. In all these novels, Russo is interested in the connection of small-town lives and the ripple effects of frustrated ambitions and disappointments. Characters in his novels often have to choose between self-interest on one hand and sacrifice and selfless responsibility on the other. Even as he is interested in fathoming nineteenth century essayist Henry David Thoreau's idea that most people live "lives of quiet desperation," Russo is also interested in another quality that has perhaps become less common in the American strain: integrity.

Parenthood is another abiding interest in these novels. Problematic or troubling relationships between fathers and sons haunt *Mohawk*, *The Risk Pool*, *Nobody's Fool*, and *Straight Man*. Donald "Sully" Sullivan in *Nobody's Fool*, Hank Deveraux in *Straight Man*, Miles Roby in *Empire Falls*, and Lou Lynch in *Bridge of Sighs* are also defined, their needs, ambitions, and hopes qualified, by their roles as fathers. Similarly, strong women—as mothers, wives, mentors, and employers—often occupy central roles in the lives of Russo's male characters. Despite the frequently dark or poignant subject matter of the novels, however, Russo's rendering of self-destructive characters and bleak circumstances is often wry and humorous; much of his success and his reputation stem from the laconic wit of his novels.

MOHAWK

Mohawk, New York, serves as a fictional stand-in for Gloversville. It, too, is a blue-collar town dependent on tanneries and factories to keep the town economically viable (if just barely). In *Mohawk*, Russo's first novel,

even as the tanneries die out and the city is made in some ways literally sick through the pollutants dumped into the town's waterways by the industry, the tensions of economic dissolution are played out on a more overt level by the animus between two aging men: Mather Grouse, an ailing retired leather worker, a man with integrity and ethics, and his onetime coworker and (mostly) unspoken enemy, Rory Gaffney, a man with few scruples. The battles affecting Grouse and Gaffney permeate into the next generation. Mather's daughter Anne, her husband Dallas, and her son Randall are products of the small-town cauldron that seeks both to forge them and to burn them out. Even as the older generation passes away, the younger generations have to decide between following their dreams or denying themselves

THE RISK POOL

The Risk Pool is also set in Mohawk, and some characters from the prior novel appear. Ned Hall's recondite and rebellious father, Sam, impregnated Ned's mother, Jenny, just after returning from World War II; within six months of Ned's birth, Sam has been kicked out of the house, never to return on a permanent basis. Ned does not see his father at all for many years, then he begins seeing him in short doses (as when his father kidnaps him for a weekend fishing trip that goes awry); these encounters serve to point out that his father is not appropriately responsible or suited for fatherhood. When Ned's mother suffers a breakdown, Ned lives for a while with his father and must learn to fend for himself and to go with the currents of an irregular life as easily as does the notorious Sam. Two-thirds of the way through the novel, the narrative abruptly shifts forward in time almost two decades. In debt and in trouble, seeming his father's son, Ned is summoned home to Mohawk after ten years away. He is faced with a choice similar to the one that his father made about Ned and his mother. Ned can either take responsibility for his ailing father and help him, or he can deny him.

NOBODY'S FOOL

One of Russo's most esteemed and beloved novels, *Nobody's Fool* tells the story of sixty-year-old Donald "Sully" Sullivan and a large supporting cast of characters, including Sully's still-angry ex-wife, his estranged son Peter, his grandsons, a surrogate mother in the form of elderly landlady Beryl Peoples, his rival (and in some ways good friend) Carl, Carl's wife Toby, and his slow-witted sidekick, Rub. Sully is at war with the world in a gently angry, archly wry kind of way. Like Ned Hall, he has had a difficult relationship with his now-deceased and abusive father and has unwittingly followed at least somewhat in his father's footsteps by being an aloof and distant father to his son.

Nobody's Fool is set in North Bath, New York, a city similar to Mohawk but one that had once been a rich and prosperous resort town and now is dying away. Sully is troubled throughout the novel by a sore and swollen knee; in many ways the knee is indicative of his own inability to move and to break free of both physical and emotional inertia. With the return of his son and grandsons, however, he has a chance to redeem himself—if he can at least refrain from punching a particularly irritating police officer.

STRAIGHT MAN

Straight Man, Russo's follow-up to *Nobody's Fool*, is a departure from the blue-collar framework established in his first three novels. *Straight Man* is a witty academic novel of manners in the vein of *Lucky Jim* (1954) by English author Kingsley Amis. Hank Deveraux, the narrator of *Straight Man*, is even referred to by an enemy as "Lucky Hank." Hank is a creative-writing professor and English Department chair at West Central Pennsylvania University, a small Rust Belt institution fallen on hard times. Hank and his wife live in a sparsely developed area, and throughout the novel he is resistant to the lots around their home being bought, sold, and developed; in a way this serves as a central metaphor for the book.

Hank is given any number of opportunities to sell out, but he refuses to do so, even when his own interest would be better served. Like other Russo protagonists, Hank is frequently his own worst enemy. His sense of independence and his integrity are put to the test when he is called upon to fire members of his department for budgetary reasons. Hank is as dry and droll as any of Russo's creations, and in a moment of pique he tells a television news crew, sent to cover the opening of a new campus building, that he will kill one duck a day until his budget is saved. Ironically, Hank is holding a goose, not a duck, when he makes this proclamation, and within days demonstrators are picketing the campus with pictures of the

goose in question on placards while they strive to save the endangered "duck."

Fatherhood plays a central role in the novel, as it does in other Russo novels. Hank has a distant relationship with his own cold and accomplished professor father. At the same time, he is involved, almost against his will, in saving his daughter's troubled marriage and straightening out his son-in-law. *Straight Man* is a wry send-up of modern academic culture, yet for all its differences from the greater body of Russo's work, it holds true to his basic themes and interests: the need to maintain integrity balanced against ambition and self-fulfillment, relationships between fathers and their children, and rebelliousness for the sake of rebelliousness.

EMPIRE FALLS

Although many critics have asserted that *Nobody's Fool* and *Straight Man* represent Russo's highest achievement, *Empire Falls* is his most lauded novel, having won the Pulitzer Prize in 2002. Set yet again in a small, blue-collar town (this time in Maine) with a failing industry (a textile mill instead of a tannery), the novel centers on Miles Roby, who runs the Empire Grill diner. Miles is an easygoing (if occasionally sardonic) man with many friends. Divorced from his wife Janine, he has a strong relationship with his daughter Tick and, like Sully in *Nobody's Fool*, a large supporting cast of characters who, in serving as foils, help the reader better understand Miles.

Miles is a man who in some ways feels trapped by the small town of Empire Falls, but each time he tries to devise a new way out, something occurs that keeps him home. He has a troubled relationship with the city's dowager heiress, Mrs. Francine Whiting, inheritor of the textile mill at the center of the Empire Falls economy. She is the silent owner of the Empire Grill and subtly seeks to control him, not allowing him any freedom or his own head of steam. Like most of Russo's other male characters, Miles has a problematic relationship with his father, but in some ways it is his father's streak of rebelliousness and wildness that Miles needs to emulate—before his daughter Tick is trapped just as Miles has been.

BRIDGE OF SIGHS

Russo's abiding motifs of fatherly love, blue-collar realities, strong mothers, honesty, and self-denial are all again displayed in *Bridge of Sighs*. The novel is built around a triangle composed of three protagonists: Lou C. Lynch (called "Lucy" by his friends); Lou's best friend, Bobby Marconi, who grows up to be a famous painter; and Lou's girlfriend and eventually his wife, Sarah. Although the narrative is filtered at times through the third-person perspectives of Bobby and Sarah, the central protagonist is Lou, who tells his part in the first person.

Unlike so many of Russo's protagonists, Lou is not saddled with a distant or absent father. Lou's father, Big Lou, is present and caring in every way; his only failure—at least according to Lou's mother, Tessa—is his simplistic and optimistic view of life. Throughout the novel, Lou has to chose between his mother's aggressive and sharp-eyed perspective on the one hand and his father's open-hearted approach to the world on the other. His friend Bobby, however, has a father who beats Bobby's depressive mother, and as a result Bobby's transition to manhood is defined by his defiance of his father. As the third leg of the triangle, Sarah is loved by both Lou and Bobby, and slowly the reader realizes that although she loves Lou's essential goodness and kindness, her heart is more excited by Bobby's abandon.

The novel is a study of giving in to self-indulgence, as demonstrated by Lou's uncle Dec and the middle-aged Bobby Marconi, who calls himself Robert Noonan (taking his mother's name), juxtaposed against sacrifice for the good of others, as shown by Big Lou, by Sarah, who lets Bobby go, and by Lou, who perhaps even denies his own sexuality. Although more uneven than comparable novels such as *Nobody's Fool*, *Bridge of Sighs* breaks new ground in terms of scope and structure for Russo.

Scott D. Yarbrough

OTHER MAJOR WORKS

SHORT FICTION: *The Whore's Child, and Other Stories*, 2002.

SCREENPLAYS: *Twilight*, 1998 (with Robert Benton); *The Ice Harvest*, 2005 (with Benton; based on Scott Phillips's novel); *Keeping Mum*, 2005 (with Niall Johnson).

TELEPLAYS: *The Flamingo Rising*, 2001 (based on Larry Baker's novel); *Brush with Fate*, 2003 (based on Susan Vreeland's novel *Girl in Hyacinth Blue*); *Empire Falls*, 2005 (based on his novel).

EDITED TEXTS: *The Book of Eros: Art and Letters from Yellow Silk*, 1995 (with Lily Pond); *A Healing Touch: True Stories of Life, Death, and Hospice*, 2008.

BIBLIOGRAPHY

McConkey, James. "Life with Father and Son." *Washington Post Book World*, November, 1988. Discusses *The Risk Pool* in the context of upstate New York cities such as Russo's own Gloversville.

McCulloch, Jamie. "Creating the Rogue Hero: Literary Devices in the Picaresque Novels of Martin Amis, Richard Russo, Michael Chabon, Jonathan Safran Foer, and Steve Tesich." *International Fiction Review* 34, nos. 1/2 (January, 2007): 13-26. Presents a detailed consideration of humor in contemporary fiction. Discussion of Russo's work focuses particularly on *Straight Man*.

Menand, Louis. "Upstate." Review of *Bridge of Sighs*, by Richard Russo. *The New Yorker*, October 15, 2007. Analytical review considers Russo's use of small industrial towns in the American Northeast in comparison to the use of Dublin by Irish writer James Joyce.

Montrose, David. "Fightin' an' Feudin'." *The Times Literary Supplement*, March 6, 1987. Insightful discussion addresses the themes appearing early in Russo's career that will prove to be hallmarks of his fiction.

Proulx, E. Annie. "What It Takes to Endure the Lost, Stubborn Citizens of Richard Russo's Upstate New York." *Chicago Tribune Books*, May 30, 1993. Novelist Proulx discusses *Nobody's Fool* and focuses in particular on Russo's recurring use of troubled father-son relationships.

Russo, Richard. "How 'I' Moved Heaven and Earth." *The New York Times Magazine*, October 17, 1999. The author discusses the genesis of *Straight Man* and the general role of art—and literature—in humankind's attempts to make sense of the universe.

Smith, Wendy. "Richard Russo: The Novelist Again Explores the Crucial Impact of Place on Individual Destinies." *Publishers Weekly*, June 7, 1993. Provides an overview of Russo's fiction and discusses the autobiographical context of his early novels.

S

ERNESTO SÁBATO

Born: Rojas, Argentina; June 24, 1911

PRINCIPAL LONG FICTION

El túnel, 1948 (*The Outsider*, 1950; also known
as *The Tunnel*)
Sobre héroes y tumbas, 1961 (*On Heroes and
Tombs*, 1981)
Abaddón, el exterminador, 1974 (revised 1978;
The Angel of Darkness, 1991)

OTHER LITERARY FORMS

In addition to his three novels, Ernesto Sábato (SAH-bah-toh) has published several volumes of essays. His career as a writer can be divided into two major periods. The first includes the publication of *The Outsider*, his first novel, and three volumes of essays: *Uno y el universo* (1945; one and the universe), *Hombres y engranajes: Reflecciones sobre el dinero, la razón, y el derrumbe de nuestro tiempo* (1951; men and gears: reflections on the money, the reason, and the collapse of our time), and *Heterodoxia* (1953; heterodoxy). The second period begins in 1961 with the publication of his novel *On Heroes and Tombs* and includes such collections of essays as *El escritor y sus fantasmas* (1963; the writer and his ghosts), *Tango: Discusión y clave* (1963; the tango: discussion and key), *Tres aproximaciones a la literatura de nuestro tiempo: Robbe-Grillet, Borges, Sartre* (1968; three approaches to the literature of our time: Robbe-Grillet, Borges, Sartre), *Itinerario* (1969; itinerary), and *La convulsión política y social de nuestro tiempo* (1969; political and social upheaval of our time).

During the time between these periods of major production, Sábato also produced two volumes largely devoted to political problems in Argentina: *El otro rostro del peronismo* (1956; the other face of Peronism) and *El caso Sábato* (1956; the case of Sábato), the last a collec-tion of documents gathered by his friends to account for Sábato's resignation of his post as editor of *Mundo Argentino*, an important weekly journal. Sábato had resigned to protest the policies of the provisional government that followed the overthrow of Juan Domingo Perón in 1955.

Metaphysical concerns are the subject of many of Sábato's essays. *Uno y el universo* contains the idea that humans must reject the reductivity of positivistic science and return to a balance that incorporates the intuitive, the irrational, and the subjective. In *Heterodoxia*, there is a discussion of Jean-Paul Sartre, while *Hombres y engranajes* includes an essay on "The Existential Reaction" that discusses Søren Kierkegaard, Friedrich Nietzsche, Fyodor Dostoevski, Sartre, and Albert Camus—the pantheon of literary existentialism.

ACHIEVEMENTS

Ernesto Sábato's reputation as one of Argentina's leading novelists is well established, both within his own country and abroad. His first novel, *The Outsider*, has been translated into a number of foreign languages and has an assured place in the history of modern fiction. His second novel, *On Heroes and Tombs*, while originally published in 1961, appeared in English twenty years later. His third novel, *The Angel of Darkness*, was translated into English in 1991. *The Outsider* has been acclaimed as a major contribution to the existential novel, following in the footsteps of Sartre and Camus. While Sábato's political writings have been primarily of interest to those who are most directly concerned—the people of Argentina—his defense of such fundamental principles as freedom of the press, free elections, and democratic processes, often endangering his livelihood as well as exposing him to physical danger, has justly created international sympathy for him. He has also written about his methods of work and the relationship of his experiences to his literary creations.

BIOGRAPHY

Ernesto Sábato was born on June 24, 1911, in the small Argentine town of Rojas in the territory of La Pampa. Rojas is located some 180 miles southwest of Buenos Aires. Both his father and his mother were Italian immigrants; his mother, with whom he had a close relationship, was from an old and distinguished Italian family. The family business was a small flour mill that earned for the Sábatos enough money to take care of their family of eleven children. This large group of children resulted in a family life that was characterized by discipline and obedience. In 1929, Sábato entered the National University of La Plata as a student of science. In 1934, he married Matilde Kusminsky, a fellow student. He obtained a doctorate in physics from the same school in 1937.

Sábato's university days also introduced him to the violent political controversies that are characteristic of Argentina. In 1934, Sábato went to an antifascist congress in Brussels as a representative of the Young Communists of Argentina. The plan for the trip included a stay in Moscow for the delegates in order for them to receive further instruction in Communist ideology. Disillusioned with the idea that Communism could solve social problems, Sábato left the group and went, alone and without resources, to Paris, where he was dependent on charity until some Venezuelan students took him in.

Sábato returned to the University in Argentina and, after completing his doctorate in 1937, took a job in Paris at the Curie Laboratory, where he worked with Irène Joliot-Curie. While occupied with his work on radiation theory, he was also intensely interested in the literary life of Paris and thoroughly explored the world of the Surrealists and other literary movements of the time. During this period, he began work on a novel that was to be called "La fuenta muda" (the mute fountain); the book, however, was never published, although Sábato used some of the material in the subsequent *On Heroes and Tombs*. Even though he was losing interest in his scientific career, Sábato next accepted, in 1939, an appointment at the Massachusetts Institute of Technology, so that he might continue his radiation studies.

Sábato went back to his native Argentina in 1940 to accept two posts, a part-time professorship of physics at the National University of La Plata and a similar appointment at a normal school in Buenos Aires. He not only carried on his teaching duties at the two schools but also began to write for the literary section of *La nación*, a large newspaper in Buenos Aires. His hostility to the restrictions on the freedom of the press, which he aired in the pages of *La nación*, resulted in a forced resignation from his two university posts after the military junta of Perón came to power in 1945. In 1947, Sábato became an executive for UNESCO with duties in Paris and Rome; he resigned from this post, which he described as a bureaucratic nightmare, in order to complete work on his first novel, *The Outsider*, which was published in 1948.

In 1955, Sábato became the editor of the popular magazine *Mundo Argentino* but was forced to resign in

Ernesto Sábato. (Time & Life Pictures/Getty Images)

1956 because of his opposition to the military dictatorship that followed the fall of the Perón government. Another appointment, as Director of Cultural Relations in the government of Arturo Frondizi in 1958, also ended with Sábato's resignation—again because of his disagreement with the policies of the government. His preoccupation with the social and political realities of modern Argentina is reflected in his novel *On Heroes and Tombs*, which was published in 1961. In the following year, Sábato went on an extensive lecture tour in Europe, where he spoke on the political and philosophical subjects that he has treated in several volumes of essays. In 1974, the Spanish-language edition of his book *The Angel of Darkness*, appeared. Thereafter, he lived in relative seclusion with his family in Santos Lugares, a suburb of Buenos Aires.

ANALYSIS

Ernesto Sábato's essays show that he is widely knowledgeable concerning the standard works in modern philosophy and aesthetics. Herbert Spencer, Charles Darwin, Émile Zola, Sigmund Freud, Carl Jung, Sartre, and Camus, as well as many others, have contributed to his intellectual background. Many of his essays deal with the application of ideas that have become the commonplaces of Western thought to the special problems that beset Argentina in its search for a stable government as well as for a national identity. Sábato's novels reflect his early interest in the Surrealist movement and in the existential experiments of Sartre and Camus. In addition, some critics discover in Sábato's work an affinity with the Magical Realism that characterizes a number of the recent novelists of Latin America.

In his novels, Sábato uses motifs and symbols that have led some critics to interpret his work in Freudian terms or through the identification of Jungian archetypes. In the way of many twentieth century writers, Sábato's work describes an alienated and indifferent world in which religion no longer provides a foundation for the values of society. It is a world dominated by positivism, reason, and science. Sábato's novels depict the pathos and terror of characters who are conscious of living in a materialistic chaos surrounded by the remnants of past glories. Each of his novels involves a quest or journey: In *The Outsider*, the protagonist is Juan Pablo

Castel, whose quest ends in madness and despair; in *On Heroes and Tombs*, it is Martín de Castillo, who finally discovers the inextinguishable hope of simple people, which permits the book to end on a note of cautious optimism; in *The Angel of Darkness*, Sábato himself is the principal spokesman for the idea that after the apocalyptic events at the end of the twentieth century, a new and more complete human being will arise. The quest theme in Sábato's fiction is complemented by the theme of existential isolation, which is perhaps best seen in *The Outsider*, in which the limited number of characters and relative simplicity of the plot lead to concentration on a single idea.

THE OUTSIDER

In *The Outsider*, Sábato develops the theme of the isolation of the individual and the impossibility of communicating with another person. His protagonist, Juan Pablo Castel, a painter, hates his own past, choosing to remember only the evil things that have happened to him; he also is more likely to emphasize the bad qualities of his fellow human beings than their redemptive ones. He is without friends or family and, at the point at which his story begins, without a lover. *The Outsider* has been compared, with some justice, to Camus's *L'Étranger* (1942; *The Stranger*, 1946) because of its existential treatment of the subject of human alienation.

The "tunnel" is a metaphor for the solitary awareness and isolation of each individual. Castel, an alienated artist, discovers or imagines that one other person, María, understands his work and may therefore provide a key to end his isolation. They become lovers, but Castel begins to realize that there are many facets of María with which he is unfamiliar. He hopes to overcome his isolation through love, which leads him to demand exclusive sexual possession, although he is aware that María is married. Her husband, Allende, is blind and has apparently decided to settle for the kind of relationship that María can provide for him without probing too closely into the aspects of her life that he cannot share. Castel is disappointed in his desire; María, as she must, remains a separate entity, and, as he comes to realize, he understands very little about her. Castel further discovers or imagines that María is unfaithful to him with another lover. The murder of María, reported to the reader in the first sentence of the novel, results, and Castel's isolation in a cell in a madhouse is complete, with his conviction that his paintings are now being laughed at as the work of a psychopath.

The technique of presentation in *The Outsider* is comparable to that of Camus's *The Stranger* and Sartre's *La Nausée* (1938; *Nausea*, 1949) in that none of the three narrators—Castel, Meursault, and Antoine Roquentin—seems to be in control of the materials of the story that he has elected to tell. In each of these books, the narrator implies that there is in reality no "story" to tell, because there are no stories—that is to say, no neatly arranged sequences of events that lead to an unanticipated though "correct" turn at the end to illustrate the author's concept of correct behavior or proper choice. There is only the awful confrontation of the individual self with his perceptions. In turn, these three protagonists resemble Kierkegaard's various personae as well as Nietzsche's Dionysian poet. Both of these nonsystematic philosophers used techniques more comparable to those of literature than to those of philosophical discourse. In a similar fashion, Sábato, as did Sartre and Camus, has divided his attention between fiction and the essay form. In the two novels that have followed *The Outsider*, Sábato has to an increasing extent worked "extraliterary" materials into his fiction.

ON HEROES AND TOMBS

In *On Heroes and Tombs*, as in *The Outsider*, the setting is modern Buenos Aires; one of the major happenings in the novel is the subject of a police report dated July 25, 1955. The chief characters consist of Martín de Castillo, a young man whose quest for meaning and coherence is an important element in the story; Alejandra Vidal Olmos, a strange young woman with whom he falls in love; Fernando Vidal Olmos, her father; and Bruno Bassán, who is connected with the other characters in several ways. Martín's father is an unsuccessful painter, and their relationship is strained and distant. His mother tells Martín that she had tried to abort him and gives every indication of continuing to hate him and to resent his presence. Estranged from his immediate family, lonely, and often sick, Martín grows up, and the story begins when he is nineteen years old. His quest is to seek some principle of order and coherence in the chaos of the megalopolis, but on his way he falls in love with Alejandra after a meeting that seems to have been fated.

Alejandra is a composite Argentine woman, by no means representative, according to Sábato, but nevertheless bearing some relationship to the Argentine character, which has a reputation for moodiness and contradictions.

Martín discovers that Alejandra is a descendant of an old family representing the glorious past of Argentina, largely through the heroic exploits of General Lavalle, an ancestor three generations in the past. She lives in a decaying house occupied by the eccentric or mad remaining members of the family. Martín is unable to understand Alejandra's strange moods, which she will not explain, or the strange company she sometimes keeps. He is aware that she has a number of male friends; some of her associates are frivolous or trivial people, such as Wanda of the boutique and Bobby, the social butterfly. Listening to the stories of her past that Alejandra tells him, Martín realizes that she rejects Christianity and its moral values but has found nothing to replace them. Through him, the reader is made to see the relationship between past injustices—the neglect of the majority of Argentines by the wealthy and powerful—and the continuing political struggles that have left the hopes of the nation unfulfilled. The dream of a just society for those who left Europe to find a better life has been shattered.

Throughout the novel, there is frequent opportunity for the introduction of themes that are pertinent to social and political conditions in Argentina. Bruno Bassán is a spokesman for some of Sábato's political ideas, and his conversations with Martín draw on Sábato's lifelong struggle against oppression and injustice. The thrust of the novel is not, however, partisan politics but rather the examination of a broader historical and philosophical perspective that connects Argentina and its problems with the plight of modern man. Sábato says in one of his lectures that there is something of Perón in every Argentine, suggesting that all are responsible to some degree for the oppressive reactionary forces that are loosed in a nation that fails to solve its pressing social and economic problems. It is Bruno in *On Heroes and Tombs* who calls for recognition of the individual life and who identifies the need for the solace and companionship of a true community that is lacking in the modern industrial city.

Martín, on his voyage of discovery through Buenos Aires, meets many strange people who leave him puzzled or confused about their lives and ambitions. His dream of possessing the haunting Alejandra is marred by his uneasy knowledge that there is still much he has to learn about her. He is particularly uneasy about her relationship with her father, Fernando, which is finally revealed to have been incestuous. The dream that the possession of María represented for Castel in *The Outsider* is repeated in *On Heroes and Tombs* through Martín's attraction to and subsequent loss of Alejandra. The attempt of both men to overcome their isolation and alienation through love ends in madness for Castel and in sorrow for Martín. Both women represent the "past" in that they have been formed by a sophisticated society that has lost direction and purpose. They and the society are contradictory and lacking in substance. Martín loses Alejandra, and her loss is also symbolic of the lost world of the past. The fire that destroys the old house, Mirador, killing both Alejandra and Fernando, signifies the purification by fire for which Alejandra had been calling.

The third part of *On Heroes and Tombs* is a lengthy document composed by Fernando titled "Informe sobre ciegos" (a report on the blind), which has survived the fire. While it presents a first-person account of Fernando's life and clears up many details not previously dealt with in the narrative, it is distorted by Fernando's conviction that the blind are the earthly agents of a malevolent deity who uses blind people and their dupes to spy on other people and to control their lives by black magic, drugs, and intrigues. He believes that the blind manipulate all other people through secret organizations, and he takes it upon himself to investigate their activities and write a long report on his findings. Though he pretends that his investigations are scientific and rational, it is clear that Fernando is unable to distinguish his fantasies or hallucinations from real events and that his paranoia regarding the blind is pathological. It is perhaps this aspect of the book—the equal presentation of the fantastic and the real—that has led some critics to include Sábato with the Magical Realists in Latin American literature. The third part of the book concludes with a symbolic journey (or Fernando's vision of one) through the sewers of Buenos Aires, converted in his imagination into a hideous underworld where he is tortured by scenes of horror.

The last section of the novel opens with the revelation of the fire in Barracas that has destroyed Alejandra and Fernando. Bruno Bassán, who has been connected with both Fernando and Alejandra and has also served as a mentor for Martín, is the chief subject of this section. It is made up of Bruno's recollections of his life amid the political turmoil of twentieth century Argentina. The end of the novel consists of scenes from the story of General Lavalle, which has been told to Martín earlier at Mirador. Lavalle, Fernando's ancestor, was a revolutionary who in 1830 was fleeing toward Bolivia with the remnant of his followers. These scenes are intercalated with an account of Martín's search for a new life after the death of Alejandra. The 175 survivors of General Lavalle's force support him while he is alive and transport his head after he is dead in order to avoid its being displayed in triumph by his enemies.

The loyalty of these men and their mistaken heroism and idealism contrast with Martín's attempt to find authenticity in his own life. The revolutionaries are fleeing north in a chivalric though futile gesture, while Martín is looking south toward Patagonia, Argentina's vast and potentially productive backcountry. He turns away from Buenos Aires and its sophistication, rationalism, and troubled past and concludes his journey with the discovery of a largely undeveloped world, the world of people who have a simple faith in themselves and in the future. He is first rescued by Hortensia Paz and is impressed by her faith and goodwill even in the face of poverty; then, he meets Bucich, a truck driver who also has hope and a sense of purpose. With these experiences, Martín begins a new life.

THE ANGEL OF DARKNESS

The Angel of Darkness, a difficult, experimental work, was published in 1974 and was not immediately published in an English translation. There are two indicated divisions in the work. The first, brief section, about fifteen pages, is labeled "Some events that occurred in the city of Buenos Aires at the beginning of the year 1973" and consists of a third-person narrative introducing many of the characters who will appear in the novel: Bruno, Schneider, Natalicio Barragán, Nacho, Agustina, Martín, Marcelo. Sábato is himself a character in the book, as are several characters from *The Outsider* and *On Heroes and Tombs*. The second division is introduced by the following:

Confessions, dialogues, and some dreams that preceded the previous facts but that are probably their antecedents although not always in a clear or unequivocal way. The first part takes place between the beginning and the end of 1972. Nevertheless, other, older episodes are included (ones that occurred in La Plata, in prewar Paris, in Rojas, and in Capita Olmos; the last two are small towns in the province of Buenos Aires).

Sábato has chosen to use a highly self-conscious form of fictional presentation that includes some depiction of the process of creation—that is, the conscious and unconscious mental activity that goes on in the mind of the creator as the novel is being written. He achieves multiple perspectives in the novel by frequent shifts in point of view and by the inclusion of material from other genres: poetry, the essay, reportage, and so on. The characters include people from real life and from his other novels; there are also newspaper clippings arranged to form an ironic commentary on the society, much in the manner of John Dos Passos's *U.S.A.* (1938). By these devices, Sábato produces a multidimensional structure intended to reflect the complexity of reality. In this way, the technique itself is a demonstration of one of the main theses of the novel.

A major theme in the novel is the apocalyptic condition of the modern world. The three key words in this apocalyptic vision are "sex," "destruction," and "death." These same words are reflected in the stories of the major fictional characters, Nacho, Barragán, and Marcelo. Sábato, in his comments as he appears in the novel, predicts the rise of a new man who, having plumbed the depths of his unconscious, will respond to his subjective and irrational aspects as well as to the rational and mechanical in his nature. The novel ends with a vision of the rise of this new man after the destruction of the old world with its crippling dependence on reason as a sole guide to human fate. The structure of this novel is loose, and the characters do not come to have any life independent of their role as carriers of ideas that Sábato has already developed in his essays.

Although Sábato has published only three novels, his oeuvre is an essential element in the extraordinary spectrum of postwar Latin American fiction. From the parabolic intensity and narrow focus of *The Outsider* to the rich narrative complexity of *On Heroes and Tombs* to the

outer limits of *The Angel of Darkness*, Sábato has traveled a great distance.

F. William Nelson

OTHER MAJOR WORKS

NONFICTION: *Uno y el universo*, 1945; *Hombres y engranajes: Reflecciones sobre el dinero, la razón, y el derrumbe de nuestro tiempo*, 1951; *Heterodoxia*, 1953; *El caso Sábato*, 1956; *El otro rostro del peronismo*, 1956; *El escritor y sus fantasmas*, 1963; *Tango: Discusión y clave*, 1963; *Tres aproximaciones a la literatura de nuestro tiempo: Robbe-Grillet, Borges, Sartre*, 1968; *Itinerario*, 1969; *La convulsión política y social de nuestro tiempo*, 1969; *Mitomagia: Los temos del misterio*, 1969; *Ernesto Sábato: Claves políticas*, 1971; *La cultura en la encrucijada nacional*, 1973; *Diálogos*, 1976; *El escritor y la crisis contemporánea*, 1976 (partial translation as *The Writer in the Catastrophe of Our Time*, 1990); *La robotización del hombre y otras páginas de ficción y reflexion*, 1981; *Entre la letra y la sangre: Conversaciones con Carlos Catania*, 1989; *Lo mejor de Ernesto Sábato*, 1989; *Antes del fin*, 1998; *La resistencia*, 2000; *Medio siglo con Sábato: Entrevistas*, 2000 (interviews).

EDITED TEXT: *Cuentos que me apasionaron*, 1999-2000 (2 volumes).

MISCELLANEOUS: *Obra completa*, 1997 (2 volumes).

BIBLIOGRAPHY

Bachman, Caleb. "Ernesto Sábato: A Conscious Choice of Words." *Americas* 43, no. 1 (January-February, 1991): 14-20. A look at Sábato's life and work. Addresses the dark tone of his novels, as well as comments by critics "who feel that his 'black hope' is several shades too dark."

Borchardt, Edith. "Criminal Artists and Artisans in Mysteries by E.T.A. Hoffmann, Dorothy Sayers, Ernesto Sábato, Patrick Süskind, and Thomas Harris." In *Functions of the Fantastic: Selected Essays from the Thirteenth International Conference on the Fantastic in the Arts*, edited by Joe Sanders. Westport, Conn.: Greenwood Press, 1995. Borchardt's study of the mystery fiction of Sábato and four other authors was one of the papers presented at a 1992 conference on the fantastic in literature and popular culture.

Busette, Cedric. *"La familia de Pascual Duarte" and "El t nel": Correspondences and Divergences in the Exercise of Craft.* Lanham, Md.: University Press of America, 1994. One of the few English-language analyses of Sábato's work. This study reveals some of his overall concerns, expressed also in *The Outsider*. Includes bibliographical references.

Cheadle, Norman. "Mise en abyme and the Abyss: Two Paintings in Ernesto Sábato's Trilogy of Novels." *Hispanic Review* 63, no. 4 (Autumn, 1995): 543-553. Cheadle discusses Sábato's use of iconic metaphors in his trilogy *The Outsider, On Heroes and Tombs*, and *The Angel of Darkness*.

Flores, Angel. *Spanish American Authors: The Twentieth Century.* New York: H. W. Wilson, 1992. Flores provides a good overall view of Sábato's work, offering a brief critical analysis of selected novels and common themes that thread through his fiction.

Kennedy, William. "William Kennedy on Ernesto Sábato." In *Mutual Impressions: Writers from the Americas Reading One Another*, edited by Ilan Stavans. Durham, N.C.: Duke University Press, 1999. Collection in which prominent writers from the Americas analyze the work of other writers, focusing on connections between North and South American literature. Kennedy, an American novelist, provides a critique of Sábato's work.

Oberhelman, Harley Dean. *Ernesto Sábato.* New York: Twayne, 1970. An excellent biography of Sábato. Oberhelman brings together the man and his works in one of the best biographies in the Twayne World Authors series.

Sábato, Ernesto. "The Great Arc of the Novel." In *The Oxford Book of Latin American Essays*, edited by Ilan Stavans. New York: Oxford University Press, 1997. An English translation of Sábato's essay about the novel is included in this anthology of essays by Latin American writers.

FRANÇOISE SAGAN
Françoise Quoirez

Born: Cajarc, France; June 21, 1935
Died: Honfleur, France; September 24, 2004
Also known as: Françoise Quoirez

PRINCIPAL LONG FICTION

Bonjour Tristesse, 1954 (English translation, 1955)

Un Certain Sourire, 1956 (*A Certain Smile*, 1956)

Dans un mois, dans un an, 1957 (*Those Without Shadows*, 1957)

Aimez-vous Brahms?, 1959 (English translation, 1960)

Les Merveilleux Nuages, 1961 (*Wonderful Clouds*, 1961)

La Chamade, 1965 (English translation, 1966)

Le Garde du cœur, 1968 (*The Heart-Keeper*, 1968)

Un Peu de soleil dans l'eau froid, 1969 (*Sunlight on Cold Water*, 1971; also known as *A Few Hours of Sunlight*)

Des bleus à l'âme, 1972 (*Scars on the Soul*, 1974)

Un Profil perdu, 1974 (*Lost Profile*, 1976)

Le Lit défait, 1977 (*The Unmade Bed*, 1978)

Le Chien couchant, 1980 (*Salad Days*, 1984)

La Femme fardée, 1981 (*The Painted Lady*, 1983)

Un Orage immobile, 1983 (*The Still Storm*, 1984)

De Guerre lasse, 1985 (*A Reluctant Hero*, 1987; also known as *Engagements of the Heart*)

Un Sang d'aguarelle, 1987 (*Painting in Blood*, 1988)

La Laisse, 1989 (*The Leash*, 1991)

Les Faux fuyants, 1991 (*Evasion*, 1993)

Un Chagrin de passage, 1994 (*A Fleeting Sorrow*, 1995)
Le Miroir égaré, 1996

OTHER LITERARY FORMS

A prolific novelist, Françoise Sagan (sah-GAHN) wrote many plays as well. These works, however, remain less well known in the United States than her novels, nearly all of which appeared in English translation very soon after their publication in France. The titles of Sagan's plays, such as *Château en Suède* (pr., pb. 1960; castle in Sweden), *Les Violons parfois* (pr. 1961; sometimes violins), and *La Robe mauve de Valentine* (pr., pb. 1963; Valentine's mauve dress), suggest the same themes of worldly love and disillusionment that are found in her novels.

In addition to the plays, Sagan wrote or collaborated on scripts for the films *La Chamade* (1969) and *Le Bal du Comte d'Orgel* (1970; the Count d'Orgel's ball), which is based on the novel by Raymond Radiguet, and a television script, *Le Sang doré des Borgia* (1977; the golden blood of the Borgias). She wrote the scenario for the ballet *Le Rendez-vous manqué* (pr. 1958; the broken date) with Michel Magne, and she directed a film for which she wrote the screenplay, *Les Fougères bleues* (1977; the blue ferns). Like many of the characters in her novels, Sagan moved in a world of celebrities; her book of autobiographical fragments, *Toxique* (1964; English translation, 1964), was illustrated by Bernard Buffet. She collaborated with Federico Fellini on the text of *Mirror of Venus* (1966), with photographs by Wingate Paine. In addition, she wrote commentary on New York City, lyrics for Juliette Greco, and a book on one of the most famous of France's "beautiful people," *Brigitte Bardot* (1975; *Brigitte Bardot: A Close-Up*, 1976), with photographs by Ghislain Dussart.

ACHIEVEMENTS

The reading public was astonished to discover, in 1954, that the author of the best-selling novel *Bonjour Tristesse* was an eighteen-year-old girl who had dashed off her sophisticated tale in several weeks during her summer vacation. Sagan's first novel was awarded France's Prix des Critiques, and after that time, her elegant prose continued to charm critics, earning for her comparisons with W. Somerset Maugham, Colette, and the best of France's classical stylists. What amazed admirers of her first novel was the fact that a teenager could so accurately portray the emotional lives of adults several decades older. Indeed, it is in her depiction of love in all of its psychological variations that Sagan made her mark. In her early novels, written during her twenties, she captures the mood of egocentric cynicism so characteristic of young adults who are world-weary before they have known the world. In later novels, her characters are wealthy, worldly, and disabused about the possibility of finding lasting happiness. Always coolly restrained, Sagan wrote of the fleeting, fragile joys of love, nearly always in the shadow of deception and disillusionment. The world she created is a stylish miniature, an urbane setting for the emotional entanglements of the idle rich.

BIOGRAPHY

Françoise Quoirez, who would later take on the pen name Françoise Sagan, was born in June, 1935, at Cajarc in the Lot department of France, on the property of her bourgeois Catholic family. Her father was pursuing a successful career with the Compagnie Générale d'Electricité, and her childhood was typical for a girl from a wealthy bourgeois family. Even World War II did not seriously disrupt the lives of the Quoirez family. In spite of the war, the children were expected to continue their studies, and Sagan was enrolled in school at Lyons. Already a free spirit, she was intelligent and quick to learn whatever she needed or wished to know. Intolerant of traditional methods of education, she began to read extensively at this time when she was languishing under the constraints of her schooling.

After Paris was liberated from German occupation in 1944, the Quoirez family returned to the city, where Sagan was enrolled in school again. She attended several schools and finally was expelled from the Couvent des Oiseaux for lack of *spiritualité*. At the same time, it was discovered that she was anemic and in poor health, and for the sake of her health she was sent away for a year to a school in the mountains. On her return to Paris, Sagan attended a more modern coeducational school, where discipline was not rigorous and it was possible for her to cut classes to spend afternoons reading or roaming the streets of Paris. It is said that she regularly failed her ex-

Françoise Sagan. (Time & Life Pictures/Getty Images)

aimless young adults. Her own life seemed to resemble that of her wealthy, restless characters. She was said to enjoy gambling, drinking, and driving sports cars very fast, with a bare foot on the accelerator. In 1956, *A Certain Smile* appeared and became a commercial success; in 1958, a film adaptation of the novel was released.

Sagan was clearly a naturally gifted stylist and the celebrated *enfant terrible* of her generation. A serious driving accident in 1957 may have slowed her pace for a time on the highway, but it did not slow the flow of her writing. Novels, plays, ballets, and songs continued to appear regularly from Paris or from the country, where Sagan sometimes preferred to work. Her first marriage, to Guy Schoeller in 1958, ended in divorce, as did her second marriage, to Robert James Westhoff in 1962. She had one son, Denis. Sagan died in 2004 in Honfleur, France, at the age of 69.

ANALYSIS

It is the task of a novelist to create a world that appears to be very close to life, so close that it resonates within the reader's own imagination. In fact, fictional worlds are much more consistent and formally structured than random lives. It is only the art of the novelist that creates the illusion of worlds resembling reality. By imposing a structure—a consistent artistic vision—on a realm of whatever scale he or she chooses, the novelist is able to reveal the significance (or insignificance) and the coherence (or absurdity) of human experience.

The world examined and transformed in the novels of Françoise Sagan has been so much of a piece that critics have been known to refer to it as "Saganland." It is a place where the idle rich amuse and torment themselves with the pleasures of love, dashing away in their sports cars when they need to feel the fresh wind in their hair. The backdrop for their existence is the Riviera, Paris, New York, or Hollywood. The mood is one of bored cynicism, sophisticated disillusionment. It is an essentially frivolous and trivial world that has caused many literary critics to begrudge Sagan serious consideration in spite of the classical elegance of her writing style.

BONJOUR TRISTESSE

Given the tendency of critics in the 1970's to greet each new Sagan novel with condescension, the success of her first novel, *Bonjour Tristesse*, turned out to be a

aminations in July and then made them up to be readmitted in October. In the end, she failed the examination that would have allowed her to continue her education at the Sorbonne. This time, there was no possibility of a makeup exam. It was this failure that turned her into a novelist.

In order to escape her mother's disapproval, Sagan returned alone from the family's vacation in the south of France to their apartment on the boulevard Malesherbes in Paris. There she wrote *Bonjour Tristesse* in a matter of weeks (the legend varies from three and a half weeks to two and a half months), submitting the manuscript to Éditions Julliard in early January, 1954. It was published in March of the same year.

Published under the Proustian pseudonym "Sagan," *Bonjour Tristesse* was a critical as well as a commercial success. Both public and critics were stunned by the blasé amorality of the precocious teenage author. Equally impressive was her elegant writing style in the lucid, classical French tradition. Sagan soon was hailed as a spokeswoman for a whole generation of cynical, decidedly mixed blessing. At the time of its publication, Sagan was a teenager who became an overnight celebrity; yet the novel, until Sagan's later writing, seemed to set the standards for and define the limits of Sagan's fictional world.

The story takes place on the Riviera near Cannes, where seventeen-year-old Cécile is spending an idyllic summer with her father, Raymond, who has been a widower for many years. The presence of Elsa, her father's current mistress, does not trouble Cécile, accustomed as she is to her father's sophisticated and liberal sexual mores. In any case, she is too busy having her own first fling to be troubled by her father's unconventional household. Instead, the shadow cast over her happiness is that of Anne, a refined and beautiful woman of her father's age whom he seems prepared to marry and who threatens to bring order and discipline to the cheerfully bohemian existence of father and daughter.

Sagan prefers to deal with triangular relationships; Elsa is thus quickly expelled from the household, not to reappear until Cécile arranges to dangle her as bait before her father's roving eye. Beneath Anne's cool self-control lies a highly developed sense of honor and commitment. When she happens upon Elsa and Raymond embracing in the pine woods, the denouement is swift. Anne drives off, her face a mask of grief and betrayal. Raymond and Cécile are waiting like two guilty children when the news arrives that Anne's car has plunged over a cliff. Although it appears to be an accident, Cécile will always think of it as suicide, Anne's perfect and magnanimous gift to the careless and irrepressible pair.

Anne's death brings to an end the affairs of summer. Father and daughter return to Paris, where, after a month's seclusion, their life begins again in its old way, with young men for her, young women for him, and the prospect of another summer on the Riviera. Only at dawn, alone in her bed, does Cécile sometimes feel troubled by the memory of Anne, unable to escape the knowledge of sadness beneath the gay laughter of her carefree existence.

A CERTAIN SMILE

In her second novel, Sagan transfers the same themes of love and commitment, youth and age from the sparkling sea and pine forests of the Riviera to the student cafés and lodgings of Paris. In *Bonjour Tristesse*, Anne

represents the stable, mature personality in confrontation with the youthful, changeable character of Cécile, still searching for herself, unwilling to risk being molded by any exterior discipline. The heroine of *A Certain Smile*, Dominique, resembles Cécile as she might have been two years after the fateful summer in Cannes.

Dominique is a student at the Sorbonne, and, although she has a faithful and dependable lover in Bertrand, a fellow student, she is vaguely bored and dissatisfied with her life without understanding why. As in *Bonjour Tristesse*, the interest of *A Certain Smile* lies in the psychological development of the characters rather than in action or physical description. As in all of Sagan's novels, the settings serve merely as backdrops to characterization. The café where Dominique meets Bertrand at the beginning of the novel is not described at all. The jukebox exists only for the psychological effect of its song on Dominique, and the glass Bertrand hands to her is there to demonstrate Bertrand's proprietary manner toward Dominique and her somewhat abstracted response.

Through Bertrand, Dominique meets his Uncle Luc, whose restless search for pleasure rouses Dominique from her languor. At the same time that she is becoming Luc's mistress, Dominique must deal with her feelings toward Luc's charming wife, Françoise, a warmer, more human version of Anne. Françoise begins to treat Dominique as a daughter, and Dominique, whose own mother has withdrawn from life psychologically, accepts her kind attention at the same time that she betrays their relationship. With the amorality that is typical of Sagan's characters, Dominique agrees to spend two weeks in Cannes with Luc.

In the end, Dominique recovers from her unrequited passion for Luc and accepts the episode as her sentimental education, no different from a thousand other love stories. She feels wiser than her pretentious student comrades but does not seem able to fill the vacuum with anything more positive than a cool indifference to emotional involvement. Henceforth, she will accept the pleasures of the sun, sports cars, and sex as they are offered, with no illusions that they will last beyond the present moment.

THOSE WITHOUT SHADOWS

The moral ennui seen in Luc and Dominique was to pervade Sagan's novels for the next twenty years. *Those*

Without Shadows, her third novel, introduces a group of characters that reappear from time to time in later novels. Structurally, the plot of *Those Without Shadows* proceeds as a series of interlocking triangles. The cast of characters consists of four couples of the Parisian artistic intelligentsia plus Édouard, the typical "young man from the provinces" who arrives in Paris seeking his fortune and his own sentimental education. Although, in comparison with her first two novels, *Those Without Shadows* comprises a greatly expanded cast of characters (as well as marking a shift in narrative perspective from the first to the third person), the focus at any given moment is on a particular three who form an amorous grouping.

It seems logical to refer to the characters as a "cast," because *Those Without Shadows* and Sagan's subsequent novels consistently depict bittersweet dramas played out on the stages of fashionable cafés, drawing rooms, and beaches where the idle rich play their parts. No longer students, these characters are actresses, writers, and producers. The line is blurred between theatrical illusion and reality; often there is nothing behind a character's mask, as though Sagan is duplicating in her characterizations the superficiality of the characters themselves.

The sensation of reading a script is accentuated in these novels by the lack of description, absence of color, and simplicity of detail. What counts are the relationships between characters, their conversations and their interior monologues. Although her restrained, spare style seems very modern, Sagan continues a nineteenth century novelistic tradition in her willingness to reveal the thoughts and emotions of her characters.

One of these figures, the attractive Josée, appears in three novels and seems to embody both affirmative values and entrenched dilemmas in Sagan's fiction. By following Josée's career, one can perceive themes and patterns that recur throughout the novels. In *Those Without Shadows*, Josée is a wealthy, rootless girl, vaguely uneasy about her lack of purpose in life. She feels completely adrift, spared as she is from even the necessity of earning a living. She is in love with Jacques and is loved by Bernard. The fact that Jacques is a serious medical student seems to provide an emotional anchor for Josée. Nevertheless, at the end of the novel, Bernard and Josée

note that only the passage of time is reliable; in a month, or a year (*dans un mois, dans un an*, as in the French title), Josée will probably no longer love Jacques, nor will Bernard love Josée. Nothing, however, will really have changed: "Plus ça change, plus c'est la même chose" (The more things change the more they are the same). When Bernard wonders what it all means, Josée's advice is that it is best not to think about it. Thus, life goes on in Saganland.

WONDERFUL CLOUDS

The next two novels in which Josée appears intensify Sagan's focus on the actions of those in love and particularly on the illogical twists and turns of the amorous psyche. *Wonderful Clouds* finds Josée in the United States, enmeshed in a peculiar marriage to Alan, a rich American who is handsome, neurotic, and obsessively jealous. Their perverse relationship has isolated Josée from her former social network in France and has all but extinguished her zest for life. The Florida sun is relentless rather than soothing and nurturing.

Beneath Josée's despairing cynicism, however, remains an unquenchable spark of spontaneous gaiety, an enduring joie de vivre that distinguishes all of Sagan's most sympathetic characters. If they are careless of others, irresponsible, and capricious in love, they are also capable of nostalgia for a lost innocence, a wistful longing for a paradise that has never been and that their worldly selves would assert could never be. They are soothed by the simple, sensual pleasures of the sun, the wind, a musical refrain, or the fragrance of spring. As long as these things can be felt, a naïve, basic joy in living remains. This childlike spirit responds to and believes in a friendship of a selfless nature, and while no fuss is made over friendship and fresh air, the possibility of rediscovering such wholesome joys is frequently all that prevents a character from giving up life altogether.

In Josée's case, it is Bernard's friendship that helps her break away from Alan's cruelly possessive spell. Unfortunately, her husband follows her to France, where the plot follows their psychological struggles set against the backdrop of Josée's old artistic and literary crowd. In the end, Josée and Alan reach an empty truce: Having killed their love, they are too exhausted to part from each other.

LOST PROFILE

Lost Profile, written more than a decade after *Wonderful Clouds*, offers an even more bizarre twist in the puzzle of freedom and bondage that threatens to overwhelm Josée in her relationship with Alan. At the beginning of *Lost Profile*, she is literally a prisoner in their Paris apartment, until she is forcibly rescued by a powerful businessman, Julius Cram. He then provides her with a job, an apartment, and designer clothes, arranging everything so that the credulous Josée is unaware of the source of her "good fortune." Julius makes no physical demands on her, and eventually she meets Louis, a handsome veterinarian who represents the wholesome, sane country life.

Julius's apparent disinterest turns increasingly menacing, even as he reveals his delight in Josée's lively spirit, the one thing that never bores him. At the same time, Josée has been growing more and more confident in what she believes is her new life as an independent woman. When Julius's masquerade disintegrates in an explosive scene that reveals him as a madman with delusions of absolute power over Josée's life, she flees to the country, to Louis and their dog, to their marriage and their baby. Her illusory freedom from Alan had been only another perverse gilded cage, a grotesque form of bondage, manipulated by the spiritually frozen Julius, who is as much a victim of his machinations as is Josée.

Sagan's other novels of this twenty-year period are essentially variations on the same theme. There is always a confrontation between youth and age, frequently between an attractive middle-aged woman and a younger man. The young man who pines for Paule in *Aimez-vous Brahms?* reappears in *The Heart-Keeper* as a Hitchcockian psychopath who kills anyone who annoys his adored mistress, a fact it takes her four murders to realize. In *La Chamade*, the Josée-like heroine returns to her older protector, unable to manage the realities of life without wealth. This group of novels ends with an affirmation of enduring love, however, as Béatrice and Édouard, who had an unhappy affair in *Those Without Shadows*, rediscover, in *The Unmade Bed*, what promises to be a lasting commitment to each other.

In 1972, Sagan published an unusual book, *Scars on the Soul*, in which she weaves bits of first-person narration within a sketchy fictional tale involving two characters from her play *Château en Suède*. The narrator, who resembles Sagan in almost every respect, discusses her craft of fiction and the state of her soul, carelessly picking up her story from time to time, occasionally dropping a character who bores her or whom she has simply forgotten. Eleanor and her brother Sebastian, the fictional protagonists, are a pair of elegant, insouciant freeloaders who care only for each other. In the beginning, they have arrived in Paris, penniless and seeking "patrons." At the end, they have joined the narrator for a respite from society at her country house near the Atlantic coast. Critics scarcely knew what to make of this perplexing text. Some accused Sagan of lazily combining her own woolgathering with a threadbare plot. Others took the novel as a shallow attempt to write a New Novel in the intellectual manner of modern French novelists such as Alain Robbe-Grillet, Nathalie Sarraute, or Michel Butor. Most agreed that *Scars on the Soul* seemed to reveal an author who had lost her taste for the glamorous, worldly society she had chronicled ever since her first best seller.

It is not surprising, then, to note that the novel following *Scars on the Soul* is *Lost Profile*, in which Josée turns her back on Parisian high society to follow her veterinarian to the country. For once, there is the suggestion of something to fill the emptiness. Where Lucile's experiment with love and commitment in *La Chamade* ends in abortion and defeat, Josée, pregnant by Louis, has at last discovered a plenitude, a purpose for her heretofore aimless existence.

THE UNMADE BED

In *The Unmade Bed*, Sagan's last novel of the 1970's, Béatrice and Édouard also return from a social life of changing partners and relationships based on ambition or proximity more often than on any real bonds. Their sensual hideaway, a repeated motif in Sagan's novels, becomes for the first time a positive symbol. Sagan's previous variations on the theme of the secluded love nest always implied a break in time after which the lovers return to the world and to inevitable separation. Dominique and Luc (in *A Certain Smile*) or Josée and Bernard (in *Those Without Shadows*) simply step out of their usual lives for a brief, idyllic tryst. Gilles and Nathalie (in *A Few Hours of Sunlight*) are tragically unsuccessful when they try to transfer their privileged moments of isolation in the provinces to the new setting of

Gilles's full life in Paris. Alan, of course, completely reverses the image in the perverse prison from which Josée barely escapes. In contrast to all of these novels, *The Unmade Bed* depicts a secret refuge in the heart of Paris where Béatrice and Édouard can renew their private commitment and where they may find lasting fulfillment.

SALAD DAYS

Having achieved a more positive view of the possibility for happiness between two individuals, Sagan published a startlingly different novel in 1980 that seemed intended as a reply to critics who wondered whether she was capable of writing about anything other than the gilded jet set. This novel, *Salad Days*, is set in a grimy working-class boardinghouse near Lille. As in Sagan's other novels, the structure of the plot is classically simple, although the novel is filled with descriptive detail. The focus is on the emotional relationship between a young man and an older woman. This man, however, is one of life's awkward losers, and she is his landlady, a well-worn former gangster's moll. The story is in the tradition of Guy de Maupassant. A young man finds a cache of jewels whose mere presence in his shabby room transforms his life. Believing that he murdered to gain possession of the jewels, his landlady gazes upon him in admiration. He responds by acting the part of an aggressive type, capable of sudden violence. They become lovers, their love nest a deliberate parody of all of those glamorous hideaways in Sagan's earlier novels. In the end, the young man proves his own worth, just as Sagan proves her ability to depict a shadowy underworld miles away from the sunny Riviera.

THE PAINTED LADY

With *The Painted Lady*, Sagan returned to the world of the very rich, but in this novel they are observed from a distance. No longer sharing the embrace of her two main characters, as in *Scars on the Soul*, the narrator here keeps an ironic and omniscient eye on her socialites, whom she sets forth on a luxury cruise ship aptly named *Narcissus*. In this more loosely structured novel, Sagan seems to have chosen the traditional novelist's way of combining an entertaining story with witty social commentary as she observes life in the luxury class aboard her ship of fools. A pure soul, reminiscent of Josée, is detached from her cruel spouse by her love for a happy-go-lucky con artist. An ambitious starlet is revealed as a foolish, heartless creature, while her director finds true friendship, and perhaps more, with an elegant, aging socialite. Each is revealed as flawed in some more or less amusing way, to the degree that each retains good humor and a passionate, spontaneous zest for life. In *Bonjour Tristesse*, these qualities made Cécile appealing instead of appalling. In *The Painted Lady*, these values remain, Sagan's true gold beneath the gilt. The former *enfant terrible* showed herself to be a perceptive chronicler of human nature, recounted with Gallic humor, charm, and elegance.

Jan St. Martin

OTHER MAJOR WORKS

SHORT FICTION: *Des yeux de soie*, 1976 (*Silken Eyes*, 1977); *Musiques de scènes*, 1981 (*Incidental Music: Stories*, 1983).

PLAYS: *Le Rendez-vous manqué*, pr. 1958 (ballet scenario; with Michel Magne); *Château en Suède*, pr., pb. 1960; *Les Violons parfois*, pr. 1961; *La Robe mauve de Valentine*, pr., pb. 1963; *Bonheur, impair, et passe*, pb. 1964; "*Le Cheval evanoui*," "*L'Echarde*," pr., pb. 1966 (2 plays); *Un Piano dans l'herbe*, pr., pb. 1970; *Il fait beau jour et nuit*, pb. 1979; *L'Exces contraire*, pr. 1987.

SCREENPLAYS: *Landru*, 1963 (with Alain Cavalier); *La Chamade*, 1969 (adaptation of her novel); *Le Bal du Comte d'Orgel*, 1970 (with Philippe Grumbach; adaptation of Raymond Radiguet's novel); *Les Fougères bleues*, 1977 (adaptation of her short story "Des yeux de soie").

TELEPLAY: *Le Sang doré des Borgia*, 1977 (with Jacques Quoirez and Étienne de Monpezat).

NONFICTION: *Toxique*, 1964 (English translation, 1964; illustrated by Bernard Buffet); *Mirror of Venus*, 1966 (with Federico Fellini; photographs by Wingate Paine); *Réponses: 1954-1974*, 1974 (*Responses: The Autobiography of Françoise Sagan*, 1979; also known as *Night Bird: Conversations with Françoise Sagan*, 1980); *Brigitte Bardot*, 1975 (photographs by Ghislain Dussart; *Brigitte Bardot: A Close-Up*, 1976); *Avec mon meilleur souvenir*, 1984 (*With Fondest Regards*, 1985); *Sarah Bernhardt: Le Rire incassable*, 1987 (*Dear Sarah Bernhardt*, 1988); *Et toute ma sympathie*, 1993; *Derrière l'épaule . . .*, 1998.

BIBLIOGRAPHY

Cismaru, Alfred. "Françoise Sagan: The Superficial Classic." *World Literature Today* 67, no. 2 (Spring, 1993): 291-294. Assesses Sagan's work in order to determine whether it makes an authentic contribution to literature.

Faulks, Sebastian. "Forever a Mistress." *The New Yorker* 74, no. 1 (April 27, 1998-May 5, 1998). Profile of Sagan presents information about her life, her literary career, and several of her books. Includes comments from Sagan, who expresses her continued hope to complete a "masterpiece."

Holmes, Diana. "Love in a Brave New World: Romance in the 1950's." In *Romance and Readership in Twentieth-Century France: Love Stories*. New York: Oxford University Press, 2006. Chapter within a history of French romantic fiction discusses the place of Sagan and her novels *Bonjour tristesse*, *A Certain Smile*, and *Those Without Shadows*.

Lloyd, Heather. *Françoise Sagan, "Bonjour tristesse."* Glasgow, Scotland: University of Glasgow French and German Publications, 1995. Study of Sagan's first novel includes discussion of the work's characters and values, setting, and literary style, among other elements.

_____. "'Starlette de la littérature': Françoise Sagan." In *Stardom in Postwar France*, edited by John Gaffney and Diana Holmes. New York: Berghahn Books, 2007. Profile of Sagan is included in a larger examination of mass culture in post-World War II France that focuses on the "stars" of film, literature, politics, and the intellectual community.

Miller, Judith Graves. *Françoise Sagan*. Boston: Twayne, 1988. Presents a solid critical assessment of Sagan's work along with biographical information. Includes bibliography and index.

Morello, Nathalie. *Françoise Sagan, "Bonjour tristesse."* London: Grant & Cutler, 1998. Reader's guide to Sagan's novel includes critical literature about the book.

ANTOINE DE SAINT-EXUPÉRY

Born: Lyons, France; June 29, 1900
Died: Near Corsica; July 31, 1944
Also known as: Antoine-Marie-Roger de Saint-Exupéry

PRINCIPAL LONG FICTION

Courrier sud, 1929 (*Southern Mail*, 1933)
Vol de nuit, 1931 (*Night Flight*, 1932)
Terre des hommes, 1939 (autobiography in novel form; *Wind, Sand, and Stars*, 1939)
Pilote de guerre, 1942 (*Flight to Arras*, 1942)

OTHER LITERARY FORMS

An original and accomplished prose stylist, Antoine de Saint-Exupéry (sahn-tayg-zew-pay-REE) published his first two or three volumes as novels before arriving at his definitive literary form, a combination of essay, memoir, fable, and prose poem that is difficult to classify. To this latter category belong his best-known volumes: an autobiography in the form of a novel, *Wind, Sand, and Stars*; the posthumously published *Citadelle* (1948; *The Wisdom of the Sands*, 1950), consisting of philosophical observations and reflections; and *Le Petit Prince* (1943; *The Little Prince*, 1943), which, published with the author's own watercolor illustrations, has since become an international children's classic.

ACHIEVEMENTS

Antoine de Saint-Exupéry drew critical attention early in his short life as perhaps the only pioneer aviator with the soul and talent of a poet. Although several other pilots, including Charles A. Lindbergh himself, had attempted to record on paper their impressions and reflections from the air, only "Saint-Ex," as his friends came to call him, had the literary skill and sensitivity to produce documents, at first fictionalized, that proved to be of lasting value. Since his plane disappeared off the coast of Corsica in 1944, presumably shot down by German fighters, Saint-Exupéry's writing has suffered somewhat from both critical and general neglect, perhaps in part because air travel has long since become commonplace. His style, however, remains as fresh and thought-provoking as when his works were first published. Reflective, unobtrusively "classical" in style, and showing erudition lightly worn, Saint-Exupéry's works appear destined to survive and to be remembered long after they have outlived their "historical" or documentary value.

Both at home and abroad, Saint-Exupéry is perhaps best remembered as the author of *The Little Prince*, a substantial prose work written and destined for children but one that has found a wide and appreciative audience among adults as well. Perhaps best summarized as an illustrated parable of relativity, or at least of relative importance (thereby recapitulating the author's major contributions as a writer-pilot), *The Little Prince* ostensibly recalls the author's chance encounter, while stranded in the desert, with the child-prince and sole inhabitant of the distant asteroid B-612. *The Little Prince* is emphatically not a work of science fiction, even in juvenile form: Harking back to the venerable literary tradition of the imaginary voyage, exemplified by such eighteenth century masterpieces as Montesquieu's *Lettres persanes* (1721; *Persian Letters*, 1722), Voltaire's *Le Micromégas* (1752; *Micromegas*, 1753), and Jonathan Swift's *Gulliver's Travels* (1726), *The Little Prince* invites the reader, young or old, to suspend preconceived judgments and view the universe through the oddly perceptive eyes of the ingenuous prince. Somewhat marred for today's audience (even among the young) by a certain preciosity and triteness of expression, *The Little Prince* has nevertheless earned the stature of a true classic in the genre, thanks to the genuine wisdom and mature insight only half concealed among its hundred-odd pages.

BIOGRAPHY

Scion of an old, distinguished, and noble Limousin family, Antoine-Marie-Roger de Saint-Exupéry was born in Lyons on June 29, 1900. It might reasonably be said of him, and without insult, that he was surely among the most successful failures of his generation, having experienced severe setbacks in most of his attempted ven-

tures, including aviation. Only his writing career appears to have developed and prospered without undue incident, yet few who knew him in his youth would have foreseen that he would become a writer. A notoriously poor student, Saint-Exupéry failed his entrance examination to the French École Navale (naval academy) and tried thereafter to apply himself to architecture, as he had earlier attempted music. Tempted by aviation ever since his first flight, as a passenger at about the age of twelve, "Saint-Ex" had the good fortune to emerge from his required military service some ten years later as a pilot-officer. Dissuaded from a career in aviation by the family of the woman to whom he was then betrothed, Saint-Exupéry obligingly turned to office work, spending most of his free time in the air. By 1925, he had begun to write about aviation for trade periodicals; the following year, he was engaged by Latécoère's aviation company, initially as a test pilot and soon thereafter to fly the mail between France and its African colonies.

Following the success of *Southern Mail*, which is based on his African experiences, Saint-Exupéry at last received a diploma in naval aviation and moved to South America, where he was placed in charge of airmail service for the government of Argentina. Soon after writing and publishing *Night Flight* in 1931, Saint-Exupéry found himself in charge of a new, reorganized mail route between France and South America; earlier in the same year, he had married Consuelo Suncin de Sandoval, widow of an Argentine journalist. Throughout the 1930's, despite documentably modest abilities as a pilot, Saint-Exupéry continued his attempt to forge new territories through the air; although frequently lost or injured, or both, he continued to draw comfort and perseverance from the simple fact of his survival, frequently eulogizing fallen aviators less fortunate than he.

To his credit, Saint-Exupéry established several new mail routes before deciding, in 1937, to cover the Spanish Civil War as a journalist; later in that year, however, he was seriously injured in his attempt to forge yet another air route, between New York and Tierra del Fuego. Commissioned a captain of air service during the "phony war" of 1939-1940, Saint-Exupéry repaired soon thereafter to New York, where he conducted experiments on jet propulsion and worked on his manuscripts while awaiting the opportunity for further military service. In

Antoine de Saint-Exupéry. (National Archives)

May, 1943, he rejoined his former squadron, by then under U.S. command, in North Africa. Hampered by advancing age and the cumulative result of his injuries, Saint-Exupéry was frequently discouraged from flying but chose to ignore the advice of superior officers, both French and American. On July 31, 1944, already well past the limit of flights that had been grudgingly allowed him, he took off from Corsica on "one last" reconnaissance flight over the Alps. At the time of his disappearance, returning toward Corsica, he was wearing the "oak leaves" of a major in the U.S. Army Air Corps.

ANALYSIS

"The airplane," wrote Antoine de Saint-Exupéry in *Wind, Sand, and Stars*, "has helped us to discover the true face of the earth; for centuries, the roads had kept us fooled." Throughout his career, at first in fictionalized narrative, later in such extended lyric essays as *Wind, Sand, and Stars* and *The Wisdom of the Sands*, Saint-

Exupéry would exploit the still rare perspective of the aviator for his memorable insights into life, death, and the human condition. Regardless of the original "packaging," Saint-Exupéry's work is, in fact, all of a piece, with little distinction visible between his mature essays and those earlier works initially conceived and marketed as novels. As scholar of French fiction Wilbur M. Frohock has observed, Saint-Exupéry's novels are indeed quite alike in theme and content: "An aviator is aloft in his plane exposed to danger by the very fact of flight itself, while another man, familiar with all the dangers the first is exposed to, anxiously awaits the outcome of the ordeal." *Southern Mail*, Saint-Exupéry's first published book, is the most novelistic of the lot, with a strong and memorable romantic subplot; thereafter, the stuff of adventure itself sufficed for the telling of a tale.

Characterization in Saint-Exupéry's fiction, although always plausible, depends primarily on basic human responses to the combined stimuli of discovery and danger, tending toward Ernest Hemingway's proclaimed ideal of "grace under pressure." Even more important, however, is the lucidity apparently made possible by flight; in Saint-Exupéry's strongest passages, solitude and altitude combine to form an epiphanic wisdom. From several thousand feet in the air, people and their buildings appear small indeed, the differences among them likewise diminished. Perceptive observations abound in Saint-Exupéry's work, both fictional and otherwise; the pilot's lucidity, once obtained, serves him admirably on the ground as well as in the air. One of his best-realized and most memorable reflections occurs at the end of *Wind, Sand, and Stars*, as the author recalls a recent train trip across Eastern Europe. Wandering from one end of his train to the other, Saint-Exupéry found himself walking through a third-class car filled with recently displaced laborers on their way back from France. On their faces, he claims, he could plainly read the dehumanizing effects of brutal, mindless work. Fixing his eyes on one particularly brutalized couple, he tries to reconstruct in his mind a time when either man or wife might have been attractive or might have found each other so. Unfortunately, he muses, "there is no gardener for men," who grow up and grow old as they must, without cultivation. As the author muses, his gaze falls at last upon a promising-looking little boy, asleep between his parents. For want of proper attention, the boy will doubtless soon become as dehumanized as they are, to society's ultimate loss. Looking around the car, he concludes, "It is as if, in each of these people, Mozart had been assassinated."

SOUTHERN MAIL

In his earliest published works, Saint-Exupéry intersperses his reflections with enough plot and characterization that the books might reasonably be classified as novels. *Southern Mail* presents the career and eventual death of the airmail pilot Jacques Bernis against the background of his feelings for Geneviève Herlin, a married woman two years his senior with whom he has apparently been in love since adolescence. Narrated by a nameless friend and fellow pilot who has known Geneviève as long as Bernis has, *Southern Mail* derives considerable effect from descriptions of Geneviève's troubled marriage and the death of her young son. The main function of such background, however, is to deepen the portrayal of Bernis as a man, not merely as a pilot; included also are brief glimpses of his and the narrator's youth, together with mention of the books that both boys were obliged to read in school. The challenge of aviation is thus related through the lives of two exemplary individuals who have chosen to accept it; the narrator, meanwhile, is careful to reveal somewhat less about himself than he does about Bernis.

In *Southern Mail*, Saint-Exupéry experiments frequently with narrative voice, seeking and occasionally finding the singular viewpoint of his later efforts. Couched initially in the first-person plural "we," suggesting the fraternity of fliers, the narration thereafter alternates between third-person exposition and first-person recollection, with occasional shifts into the second person as the narrator speaks directly to Bernis. Throughout his work, even after abandoning the novel form, Saint-Exupéry continued the practice of second-person narrative, addressing himself to fellow pilots both living and dead. Unlike the younger novelist Michel Butor, who, in *A Change of Heart* (1957), sought to revolutionize the genre through the use of second-person narration, Saint-Exupéry adopted the form quite naturally and unobtrusively, avoiding many of the pitfalls of omniscience commonly associated with asides or with abrupt changes in narrative voice. The author's style, for all of its classical correctness and even elegance, is unfailingly natural in its effect, as if the author were inviting the reader to peer over his shoulder as he searches for the most appropriate figure of speech.

NIGHT FLIGHT

Night Flight, based on the author's flight and management experience in South America, retains the structure and pacing of a novel while dispensing with many of the conventions employed in *Southern Mail*. Fabien's bride of six weeks admires his body while he sleeps and fears for his safety in the air, but far less is seen of her than of Geneviève Herlin in the earlier novel. In keeping with the author's recent experience, the ground manager Rivière rivals or exceeds in importance the pilot Fabien, yet little is revealed of him beyond the limits of his job. Narrated entirely in the third person, *Night Flight* focuses primarily on the challenge of flying the mail over long stretches of treacherous and often hostile territory. As in *Southern Mail*, Saint-Exupéry derives some of his appeal from the exotic setting of his narrative; his main concern, however, is the one later spelled out in *Wind, Sand, and Stars*: "The earth teaches us more about ourselves than do any books, because it resists us. Man discovers himself by measuring himself against an obstacle." The airplane, he maintains, serves the pilot as a useful tool toward the discovery of universal truth, much as a plow serves the farmer toward the same end. Throughout *Night Flight*, the elemental struggle of people against the elements recapitulates in each life the whole of human history, including the discovery of fire and the invention of the wheel.

As Frohock has pointed out, however, the vast majority of images in *Night Flight* are marine in origin, harking back to humankind's age-old struggle against the sea. To be sure, Saint-Exupéry did not single-handedly invent the use of marine imagery applied to aviation. In the early days of powered flight, common wisdom would refer as easily to "airships" as to "horseless carriages" and to the pilot of an airborne "vessel" as its "captain." Frohock is correct, however, in noting Saint-Exupéry's fondness, at times almost obsessive, for nautical simile and metaphor, conceding that the author's use of this imagery is highly skillful, never forced or hackneyed. The notion of night flight, indeed, readily suggests the solitude and dangers of sea voyage; as Frohock observes, the pilot flying without instruments loses a sense of the horizon at night and is likely to confuse ground lights with stars. The author's sustained use of marine imagery, however, appears more firmly established in his own mind than in its supposed referent, causing Frohock to conclude that Saint-Exupéry was, in fact, neither a novelist nor even an essayist but rather a poet who happened to express himself in prose, occasionally labeling his product as novels.

WIND, SAND, AND STARS

With *Wind, Sand, and Stars*, Saint-Exupéry abandoned all pretense of attempting a novel, writing candidly and anecdotally in his own person. Part memoir, part speculative essay, *Wind, Sand, and Stars* is nevertheless among the most successful and rewarding of his works, combining valuable insights with equally valuable eyewitness documentation. Somewhat more convincing in his own right than any of his previous fictionalized characters, Saint-Exupéry revisits, with fresh eyes and narrative voice, much of the same territory covered in the novels, recalling the thrills, dangers, and challenges of pioneer air travel. Among his more memorable recollections is one of being stranded in the Sahara after a forced landing early in 1936, an incident that would later form the basis of his speculative children's fantasy *The Little Prince*. Too personal and discursive to approach philosophy, *Wind, Sand, and Stars* nevertheless quite literally reaches toward new heights in the reflective essay form, with well-phrased ideas that remain challenging and valid long after powered flight has ceased to be a novelty.

Following his service as a military aviator before the fall of France in 1940, Saint-Exupéry wrote of his experience in *Flight to Arras*, a tightly written memoir that often resembles a novel, even though the names of its characters have not been changed from those of the real-life persons on whom they are modeled. Typically, *Flight to Arras* is rich in reflection and imagery; unlike *Wind, Sand, and Stars*, however, Saint-Exupéry's war narrative is neatly structured, with a beginning, a middle, and an end. *The Little Prince*, published in the following year, is perhaps the most openly "creative" of the author's published works, ostensibly re-creating a vision that occurred to him in his delirium while he was stranded in the desert. In thought and theme, however, *The Little Prince* hardly differs from those of Saint-

Exupéry's works originally intended for an adult audience. The posthumously published *The Wisdom of the Sands*, on which the author had begun work as early as 1936, is an extended speculative essay couched in a prose so dense and "poetic" that it often appears deliberately obscure. Perhaps indirectly influenced by Surrealism as by other post-Symbolist experiments in poetry, the work falls short of the philosophical statement toward which Saint-Exupéry seems to be striving and remains, even for his staunchest supporters, a difficult and baffling text.

It is difficult to say what direction Saint-Exupéry's work might have taken had he survived World War II to behold the nuclear age. The obscurity of *The Wisdom of the Sands* suggests strongly that, in any case, his best and most effective writing was probably behind him. By the end of World War II, moreover, aviation was long past the pioneer stage, and there were fewer potential readers who had not experienced air travel in some form. His early works, however, remain unchallenged for what they were and are: well-phrased expressions and illustrations of indomitable human dignity, rendered timeless by the observer's innate sense of poetry. As Frohock has wryly observed of Saint-Exupéry, "A survey of his imagery does not reveal a novelist. But a poet, even in the 1930's, did not need to be a novelist."

David B. Parsell

OTHER MAJOR WORKS

NONFICTION: *Citadelle*, 1948 (philosophical observations and reflections; *The Wisdom of the Sands*, 1950).

CHILDREN'S LITERATURE: *Le Petit Prince*, 1943 (*The Little Prince*, 1943).

BIBLIOGRAPHY

Breaux, Adele. *Saint-Exupéry in America, 1942-1943: A Memoir.* Madison, N.J.: Fairleigh Dickinson University Press, 1971. Covers the events of Saint-Exupéry's time in the United States during World War II.

Capestany, Edward J. *The Dialectic of "The Little Prince."* Lanham, Md.: University Press of America, 1982. Searching study focuses on Saint-Exupéry's use of myth. Presents a chapter-by-chapter analysis of the book.

Des Vallieres, Nathalie, comp. *Saint-Exupéry: Art, Writ-*

ing, and Musings. New York: Rizzoli International, 2004. Collection of Saint-Exupéry's photographs, letters, drawings, and private notebooks, which recount the writer's life in both words and images. Compiled by Saint-Exupéry's great-niece.

Higgins, James E. *"The Little Prince": A Reverie of Substance.* New York: Twayne, 1996. Provides information on the book's literary and historical contexts, including its critical reception, and an interpretation that emphasizes the "eye of innocence," "the landscape of metaphor," and explorations of the spirit and of responsibility. Includes an appendix on approaches to teaching the novel as well as notes and an annotated bibliography.

Robinson, Joy D. Marie. *Antoine de Saint-Exupéry.* Boston: Twayne, 1984. Unusually thorough study is perhaps the best resource for the beginning student of Saint-Exupéry's works. Opens with three chapters devoted to Saint-Exupéry's childhood, his student and soldier years, and his career as an aviator, with subsequent chapters following the development of both his life and his writing. Includes chronology, notes, and annotated bibliography.

Saint-Exupéry, Consuelo de. *The Tale of the Rose: The Passion That Inspired "The Little Prince."* Translated by Esther Allen. New York: Random House, 2001. Memoir by Saint-Exupéry's wife—the possible model for the Little Prince's coquettish flower—recalls her difficult marriage to the restless and irresponsible aviator and writer.

Schiff, Stacy. *Saint-Exupéry.* New York: Alfred A. Knopf, 1995. Contains substantial previously unavailable material on Saint-Exupéry's life and career, especially his experience as a war pilot. Draws on extensive interviews in considering the relationship between Saint-Exupéry the aviator and Saint-Exupéry the writer. Includes very detailed notes and a bibliography.

J. D. SALINGER

Born: New York, New York; January 1, 1919
Also known as: Jerome David Salinger

PRINCIPAL LONG FICTION

The Catcher in the Rye, 1951

OTHER LITERARY FORMS

Little, Brown published three collections of short fiction by J. D. Salinger (SAL-ihn-jur): *Nine Stories* (1953), *Franny and Zooey* (1961), and *"Raise High the Roof Beam, Carpenters"* and *"Seymour: An Introduction"* (1963). An unauthorized paperback collection of his stories in two volumes, *The Complete Uncollected Short Stories of J. D. Salinger,* apparently published by an unidentified source in Berkeley, California, was issued in 1974. It provoked Salinger's first public statement in some years, denouncing the collection, which was suppressed by the copyright holders. There has been one film adaptation of his work, produced by Samuel Goldwyn and adapted by Julius J. and Phillip G. Epstein from Salinger's "Uncle Wiggily in Connecticut," renamed *My Foolish Heart* (1950) and starring Susan Hayward and Dana Andrews. Salinger was so upset by the screen version that he banned all further adaptations of his work into any other medium.

ACHIEVEMENTS

In the post-World War II years, J. D. Salinger was unanimously acclaimed by both literate American youth and the critical establishment. His only novel has sold steadily since its publication, and it not only still generates high sales but also generates intense discussion as to its appropriateness for classroom use. Although not a prolific writer, Salinger's popularity in terms of both sales and critical articles and books written about him has continued unabated since the early 1950's.

The Catcher in the Rye is one of the most widely read and influential postwar novels, and it entered the culture as a statement of youth's view of the complex world. The novel has been translated into German, Italian, Japanese, Norwegian, Swedish, French, Dutch, Danish, Hebrew, Czechoslovakian, Yugoslavian, and Russian and has been highly successful. In Russia, possession of a copy of *The Catcher in the Rye* became something of a status symbol for young intellectuals. Although there have been problems in translating the particularly American idiom into foreign languages, the story touches a nerve that cuts across cultural and global lines. The novel has also been favorably compared to Mark Twain's *Adventures of Huckleberry Finn* (1884) in terms of its portrayal of the "phoniness" of society, the coming-of-age of a young man, and its use of colloquial language.

Salinger's reputation, paradoxically, has been aided by his refusal to give interviews or to be seen in public. Critics and magazine writers have pursued him relentlessly, trying to discover his thoughts, concerns, and approaches to literature and writing.

BIOGRAPHY

Jerome David Salinger was born in New York, New York, on January 1, 1919, the second child and only son of Sol and Miriam (Jillich) Salinger, although details on Salinger and his parents' life is clouded. Salinger's father was born in Cleveland, Ohio, and has been noted as being the son of a rabbi, but he drifted far enough away from orthodox Judaism to become a successful importer of hams and to marry a Gentile, the Scotch Irish Marie Jillich, who changed her name soon after to Miriam to fit in better with her husband's family. During J. D.'s early years the Salingers moved several times, to increasingly affluent neighborhoods.

Salinger attended schools on Manhattan's upper West Side, doing satisfactory work in all subjects except arithmetic. He probably spent most of his summers in New England camps like most sons of upper-middle-class New York families; he was voted the "most popular actor" in the summer of 1930 at Camp Wigwam in Harrison, Maine. When he reached high school age, he was placed in Manhattan's famed McBurney School, a private institution, where he was manager of the fencing team, a reporter on the *McBurnean*, and an actor in two

plays; however, he flunked out after one year. In September of 1934, his father enrolled him at Valley Forge Military Academy in Pennsylvania.

During his two years at Valley Forge, Salinger did satisfactory, but undistinguished, work. He belonged to the Glee Club, the Aviation Club, the French Club, the Noncommissioned Officers' Club, and the Mask and Spur, a dramatic organization. He also served as literary editor of the yearbook, *Crossed Sabres*, during his senior year. He is credited with writing a three-stanza poetic tribute to the academy that has since been set to music and is sung by the cadets at their last formation before graduation. Although not yet the recluse that he would later become, Salinger began to write short stories at that time, usually working by flashlight under his blankets after "lights out." Astonishingly, he also appeared interested in a career in the motion-picture business, as either a producer or a supplier of story material. He graduated in June of 1936.

It is unclear what Salinger did after graduation, but he enrolled at least for the summer session of 1937 at Washington Square College in New York. Salinger, in one of his rare interviews, mentioned that he spent some time in Vienna, Austria, and in Poland learning German and the details of the ham-importing business; it is not clear if his father accompanied him or not, but his trip probably occurred before Adolf Hitler's Anschluss, possibly in the fall of 1937.

On his return to the United States, Salinger enrolled at Ursinus College, a coeducational institution sponsored by the Evangelical and Reformed Church at Collegeville, Pennsylvania, not far from Valley Forge. Although he remained only one semester, he wrote a humorous and critical column, "The Skipped Diploma," for the *Ursinus Weekly*. He returned to New York and enrolled in Whit Burnett's famous course in short-story writing at Columbia University. It has been noted that Burnett was not at first impressed with the quiet youth who made no comments in class and seemed more interested in playwriting. However, Salinger's first story, "The Young Folks," was impressive enough to be published in the March, 1940, issue of *Story*, edited by Burnett.

After publishing in a magazine famous for discovering new talent, Salinger spent another year writing with-

J. D. Salinger. (National Archives)

papers in a ground school for aviation cadets. He applied for Officer Candidate School but was transferred to the Air Service Command in Dayton, Ohio, and wrote publicity releases. Finally, at the end of 1943, he was transferred to the Counter-Intelligence Corps. He also conducted a long correspondence with Eugene O'Neill's daughter, Oona.

Salinger continued to write whenever he found the opportunity, publishing again in *Collier's*, *Story*, and at last in the well-paying and highly celebrated *Saturday Evening Post*. One of the *Saturday Evening Post* stories marks the first mention of the character Holden Caulfield. Salinger also sent Whit Burnett two hundred dollars from his earnings from the "slicks" to be used to encourage young writers and be applied to future writing contests for college undergraduates, such as the contest won by Norman Mailer in 1941.

After training in Tiverton, Devonshire, Salinger joined the American Fourth Division and landed on Utah Beach five hours after the initial assault wave on D-Day. He served with the division through five European campaigns as a special agent responsible for security of the Twelfth Infantry Regiment. There is an unsupported story that Salinger had an audience with author and war correspondent Ernest Hemingway, who shot off the head of a chicken either to impress Salinger or to demonstrate the effectiveness of a German Luger. This incident has been used to explain why Salinger has written about Hemingway in a bad light in his stories and has Holden Caulfield in *The Catcher in the Rye* detest Hemingway's *A Farewell to Arms* (1929). There are also reports that during the war Salinger married a French woman, Sylvia, who was a doctor, possibly a psychiatrist. The two returned together to the United States after the war, according to biographer Ian Hamilton, but the marriage, which took place in September, 1945, lasted only eight months.

After the war, Salinger decided to make a living by selling stories to the so-called slicks, publishing again in *The Saturday Evening Post* and *Collier's*, which issued "I'm Crazy" in its Christmas issue. "I'm Crazy" featured the long-delayed debut of Holden Caulfield, who had been mentioned as missing in action in several of Salinger's wartime stories. *Mademoiselle, Good Housekeeping,* and *Cosmopolitan* also published Salinger's

out success until, at age twenty-two, he broke into the well-paying mass circulation magazines with a "short, short story" in *Collier's* and a "satire" in *Esquire*; he even had a story accepted by *The New Yorker*, which delayed publication of "Slight Rebellion off Madison" until after World War II. This story proved to be one of the forerunners to *The Catcher in the Rye*.

During 1941, Salinger worked as an entertainer on the Swedish ocean liner MS *Kungsholm*. Upon his return to the United States, he wrote to the military adjunct at Valley Forge, Colonel Milton G. Baker, to see if there was some way that he could get into the service, even though he had been classified as 1-B because of a slight cardiac condition. After Selective Service standards were lowered in 1942, Salinger was inducted and attended the Officers, First Sergeants, and Instructors School of the Signal Corps. He also reportedly corrected work. *Cosmopolitan* featured a short novelette, "The Inverted Forest," an involved, obscure allegory of an artist, his possible muses, and his fate. During part of this period, Salinger lived with his parents but also kept a Greenwich Village apartment to entertain various young women. He also, supposedly, began to develop an interest in Zen Buddhism that is illustrated in his stories, especially the Glass family saga, following publication of *The Catcher in the Rye*, but there is no suggestion that he actually became a Buddhist.

After the disastrous film version of "Uncle Wiggily in Connecticut" and stories in *Harper's* and *World Review*, Salinger settled down with a contract to produce stories solely for *The New Yorker* and thereafter published exclusively for that magazine. At that time, Salinger was also his most public: He lived in Tarrytown, New York, and even visited a short-story class at Sarah Lawrence College. Although he seemed to enjoy the conversation and interaction, he never repeated it. It was during that period that he decided to avoid all public appearances and concentrate his efforts on writing.

The Catcher in the Rye finally made its appearance on July 16, 1951, although years earlier Salinger submitted, accepted, and then withdrew a much shorter version. It was not the immediate hit that time suggests, but it did gain Salinger enormous critical praise and respect. The novel was successful enough to cause Salinger to have his picture removed from the dust jacket of the third edition and all subsequent editions; annoyed by the letters, autograph seekers, and interviewers that sought him, he apparently sailed to Europe to keep his composure and avoid publicity.

In 1952, Salinger settled in Cornish, New Hampshire, a small town across the Connecticut River from Windsor, Vermont. His first house in Cornish was a small saltbox on ninety acres with no furnace, no electricity, and no running water. In 1953, Salinger met his future wife, Claire Douglas, in Manchester, Vermont. The daughter of a well-known British art critic, she was then a nineteen-year-old Radcliffe student. During his first two years in Cornish, Salinger fraternized with high school students in the area, attended their basketball games, and entertained them in his home. In November of 1953 he granted Shirley Blaney an interview for the

high school page of the Claremont, New Hampshire, *Daily Eagle*. He became upset when the interview was printed prominently on the editorial page of the paper instead. Thereafter he ceased entertaining area students and built a fence around his home.

In January, 1955, he returned to print in *The New Yorker* with the publication of "Franny," the first of the Glass family series that occupied all of his forthcoming stories. He supposedly dedicated it to his new bride, whom he married in Barnard, Vermont, on February 17, 1955. On December 10 of that year, the Salingers became the parents of their first child, Margaret Ann; on February 13, 1960, their only son, Matthew, was born. Afterward, Salinger concentrated his efforts on rearing his family and documenting the Glass family. Little was heard or read from Salinger after the 1965 publication of "Hapworth 16, 1924" in *The New Yorker*. He was divorced from his wife in November, 1967.

The reclusive Salinger, dubbed "the Greta Garbo of American letters" by *People Weekly* in reference to another famous but hermitic figure, was thrust into the media limelight in the mid-1980's because of disputes over the content of a biography being published by Ian Hamilton. Thwarted in his quest for an interview with Salinger, Hamilton had nevertheless found two valuable, and hitherto untapped, research sources: collections of Salinger letters in Princeton University's Firestone Library and the library of the University of Texas. Galleys of Hamilton's book were slipped to Salinger by a book dealer in 1986, and Salinger immediately protested the use of his unpublished letters. Attempts at compromise failed, and Salinger filed suit against Hamilton and his publisher, Random House. Eventually, a U.S. Court of Appeals ruling decreed that the letters were indeed Salinger's property and could not be quoted, or even paraphrased, without his permission. The U.S. Supreme Court declined to hear an appeal, and Salinger returned to his seclusion. Hamilton's book *In Search of J. D. Salinger*, minus the content of the letters but filled out with a detailed account of the controversy, was finally published in 1988.

ANALYSIS

J. D. Salinger's characters are always extremely sensitive young people who are trapped between two dimensions of the world: love and "squalor." The central problem in most of his fiction is not finding a bridge between these two worlds but bringing some sort of indiscriminate love into the world of squalor: to find a haven where love can triumph and flourish. Some characters, such as the young, mixed-up Holden Caulfield, adopt indiscriminate love to aid them in their journey through the world of squalor, while others, such as Seymour Glass, achieve a sort of perfect love, or satori, and are destroyed, in Seymour's case by a bullet through his head. Each of these characters is metropolitan in outlook and situation and is introverted: Their battles are private wars of spirit, not outward conflicts with society. The characters' minds struggle to make sense of the dichotomy between love and squalor, often reaching a quiet peace and transcending their situation through a small act.

Frederick L. Gwynn and Joseph L. Blotner, in *The Fiction of J. D. Salinger* (1958), offer an analysis of Salinger that claims he is the first writer in Western fiction to present transcendental mysticism in a satiric mode, or simply to present religious ideas satirically. Although much has been made of Salinger's Zen Buddhism, the stories do not seem to be about applying Buddhist principles to modern life, nor do they present a clear and coherent statement of what these principles entail or signify. Holden Caulfield does not react as a Buddhist would, nor does he seek consolation from Buddhism. The Glass family may mention Buddhism, but because of their acquaintance with all religions and their high intelligence and hyperkinetic thirst for knowledge, Salinger suggests that they have picked and chosen aspects from various religions and created a composite of them all. If anything, Salinger's characters seem to move toward a "perfect" Christian ideology—indiscriminate love.

The normality of the characters in Salinger's stories is a primary attraction for readers. Holden Caulfield is no better or no worse than any young high school boy; he is merely a bit more articulate and honest in his appraisals, more open with his feelings. Even though the Glasses are brilliant, they are not cerebral or distanced from the reader because of their brilliance; and all the characters live in the same world and environment as the readers do. Their moments of pain and delight are the same as the readers', but Salinger's characters articulate these moments more naturally and completely.

Another element that draws readers into Salinger's world is his use of satire. The satire not only touches upon the characters' descriptions and reactions to the world but also touches on the characters themselves. Holden Caulfield's confrontation with Maurice, the brawny Edmont Hotel elevator operator-pimp, shows not only the ridiculousness of the antagonist but also Holden's stupidity for attempting to reason with him. Even if he does not realize it, Holden does many of the things that he tells readers he hates. He is critical enough, however, to realize that these things are wrong.

All of Salinger's work has also a strong focus on the family; it is held as an ideal, a refuge, and a raft of love amid a sea of squalor. Although the family does not provide the haven that Salinger suggests it might, it is through coming home that the characters flourish, not by running away. Holden, in *The Catcher in the Rye*, never realistically considers running away, for he realizes that flight cannot help him. At the critical moment his family may not be ready to grant him the salvation that he needs, but it is his only security. If the world is a place of squalor, perhaps it is only through perfect love within the family unit that an individual can find some kind of salvation. It is important to notice that the family unit is never satirized in Salinger's fiction.

THE CATCHER IN THE RYE

The basic story of *The Catcher in the Rye* follows the adventures of sixteen-year-old Holden Caulfield, an independent, self-indulgent, idealistic, and sentimental figure of adolescent rebellion, during a forty-eight-hour period after he has been expelled from Pencey Prep, the latest of three expulsions for Holden. After confrontations with some fellow students at Pencey, Holden goes to New York City, his hometown, to rest before facing his parents. During the trip he tries to renew some old acquaintances, attempts to woo three out-of-towners, hires a prostitute named Sunny, and copes with recurring headaches. Eventually, after two meetings with his younger sister, Phoebe, he returns home. At the beginning of the novel he has told readers that he is in California recovering from an illness and that he is reconciled with his family. The entire story of Holden's exploits comes to us through a first-person narration, one that contains youthful phrasing and profanity and has many digressions, but one that has a mesmerizing flow to it.

Holden is a confused sixteen-year-old, no better and no worse than his peers, except that he is slightly introverted, a little sensitive, and willing to express his feelings openly. His story can be seen as a typical growing process. As he approaches and is ready to cross the threshold into adulthood, he begins to get nervous and worried. His body has grown, but his emotional state has not. He is gawky, clumsy, and not totally in control of his body. He seeks to find some consolation, some help during this difficult time but finds no one. The school cannot help him, his peers seem oblivious to his plight, his parents are too concerned with other problems (his mother's nerves and his father's business activities as a corporate lawyer). His girlfriend, Sally Hayes, who has a penchant for using the word "grand" and whom Holden calls the "queen of the phonies," is no help, and his favorite teacher, Mr. Antolini, merely lectures him drunkenly. The only people with whom he can communicate are the two young boys at the museum, the girl with the skates at the park, and his younger sister, Phoebe: All of them are children who cannot help him in his growing pains but remind him of a simpler time, one to which he wishes he could return. Eventually, he does cross the threshold (his fainting in the museum) and realizes that his worries were unfounded. He has survived. At the end of the book, Holden seems ready to reintegrate himself into society and accept the responsibilities of adulthood.

Through Holden's picaresque journeys through New York City, he grows spiritually. He slowly begins to recognize the "phoniness" around him and the squalor that constantly presses down on him. Although he castigates himself for doing some of the phony things, lying especially, Holden does realize that what he is doing is incorrect: This understanding sets him above his fellows; he knows what he is doing. Holden never hurts anyone in any significant way; his lies are small and harmless. Conversely, the phony world also spins lies, but they are dangerous because they harm people. For example, Holden mentions that Pencey advertises that it molds youth, but it does not. He is angry with motion pictures because they offer false ideals and hopes, yet Holden's lies help a mother think better of her son. Like Huck Finn, Holden lies to get along, not to hurt, and, also like Huck, he tries to do good. Near the end of the novel, Holden dreams of fleeing civilization and building a cabin out West, something that belies his earlier man-about-town conduct.

By the end of the book, Holden has accepted a new position—an undiscriminating love for all humanity. He even expresses that he misses all the people who did wrong to him. Although not a Christ figure, Holden does acquire a Christlike position—perfect love of all humankind, good and evil. He is not mature enough to know what to do with this love, but he is mature enough to accept it. In this world, realizing what is squalor and what is good and loving it all is the first step in achieving identity and humanity: Compassion is what Holden learns.

Recalling all the suffering and pain that he has witnessed, Holden develops a profound sense of the human condition and accepts Christ's ultimate commandment. In the passage regarding Holden's argument with his Quaker friend Arthur Childs, Holden argues that Judas is not in hell because Jesus would have had the compassion and love not to condemn Judas to hell. Also, Jesus did not have time to analyze who would be perfect for his Disciples; thus, they were not perfect and would have condemned Judas if they had had the chance. In this discussion, Holden points out his own dilemma, not having time to analyze his decisions, and his belief in the perfect love that he embraces at the end of the book. Although not a would-be saint, Holden does become a fuller human being through his experiences.

The title symbol of the novel comes from Holden's misreading of a line from a song of Robert Burns. Holden's wish, as expressed to his sister, is to be a catcher in the rye, one standing beneath a cliff waiting to catch any child who falls over it: He seeks to spare children the pain of growing up and facing the world of squalor. He also hopes to provide some useful, sincere activity in the world. The catcher-in-the-rye job is one that Holden realizes is impractical in the world as it is. Only by facing the world and loving it indiscriminately can anyone live fully within it and have any hope of changing it.

In the novel, Holden is also constantly preoccupied with death. He worries about the ducks in Central Park's lagoon freezing in winter, about Egyptian mummies, and about his dead brother, Allie. He cries to Allie not to let him disappear. This symbolizes Holden's wish not to disappear into society as another cog in the great machine, and his desire not to lose what little of himself he feels that he has. To Holden, the change from childhood to adulthood is a kind of death, a death he fears because of his conviction that he will become other than he is. This fear proves groundless by the end of the book. His name also provides a clue: Holden—hold on. His quest is to hold on to his adolescent self and to save other children from the pain of growth. His quest fails, but his compassion and the growth of his humanity provide him with better alternatives.

Regarding sex, Holden tends to be puritanical. His trouble lies in the fact that he begins to feel sorry for the girls he dates, and he has too much compassion for them to defile their supposed virtue. This problem ties in with his compassion: He tries to see people as they are and not as types. He looks quickly and may make rash judgments, but once he talks to or acquaints himself with someone, he sees him or her as an individual. His mentioning of the boring boy he knew in school who could whistle better than anyone is the perfect example: Holden cannot help but confront people as individuals. Again, this shows his growing compassion and indiscriminate love. He sympathizes with the girl's position, which is a very mature quality for a teenager. At Pencey, for example, he wants to protect a childhood friend named Jane Gallagher from Ward Stradlater, remembering that she always kept her kings in the back row in checker games and never used them.

The Catcher in the Rye also reflects the art of a maturing author. Although there is no indication that Holden will become a novelist, there are clues scattered throughout the novel that he has an artistic sensibility. His sensitivity, his compassion, his powers of observation, and his references to himself as an exhibitionist are several such clues.

Later, Salinger more fully develops the contrast between squalor and love in the world and reintroduces various elements of his Caulfield family saga in his grand design of charting the story of the Glass family. The compassion, the satire, the heights of perfect love, the love of the family unit, and the use of brilliant conversational language that characterized Salinger's great novel, *The Catcher in the Rye*, will continue to set his fiction apart.

Domenic Bruni
Updated by James Norman O'Neill

OTHER MAJOR WORKS

SHORT FICTION: *Nine Stories*, 1953; *Franny and Zooey*, 1961; *"Raise High the Roof Beam, Carpenters"* and *"Seymour: An Introduction,"* 1963.

BIBLIOGRAPHY

Alexander, Paul. *Salinger: A Biography*. New York: Renaissance Books, 2000. An attempt to explain Salinger's reclusiveness, which the author relates to themes in Salinger's fiction.

Alsen, Eberhard. *A Reader's Guide to J. D. Salinger*. Westport, Conn.: Greenwood Press, 2003. Alsen offers an insightful analysis of *The Catcher in the Rye* and other works, as well as useful indexes and appendixes covering all of Salinger's fiction.

Bloom, Harold, ed. *J. D. Salinger*. New ed. New York: Bloom's Literary Criticism, 2008. Collection of essays, including several interpretations of *The Catcher in the Rye*, analyses of the novellas and short stories, and "Rhetoric, Sanity, and the Cold War: The Significance of Holden Caulfield's Testimony." Includes a chronology, a bibliography, and an index.

_____. *J. D. Salinger's "The Catcher in the Rye."* New York: Chelsea House, 2007. A guide to the novel, featuring a biographical sketch of Salinger, list of characters, summary and analysis, and essays providing critical interpretations. Includes an annotated bibliography and index.

French, Warren. *J. D. Salinger, Revisited*. Boston: Twayne, 1988. One of the most helpful and informative books on Salinger. French, who has written an earlier book on Salinger, explains here how he changed his perspective on some of Salinger's works. In addition to offering a useful chronology and bibliography, French discusses the New Hampshire area, where Salinger and French have lived. French also makes enlightening comparisons of the stories to films. Notes, references, index.

Graham, Sarah. *J. D. Salinger's "The Catcher in the Rye."* New York: Routledge, 2007. Discusses the text and context of the novel and its critical history; contains updated critical essays analyzing the book. Also includes a list of books and Web resources providing additional information.

Maynard, Joyce. *At Home in the World: A Memoir*. New

York: Picador USA, 1998. Maynard's memoir describes her year-long relationship with Salinger, revealing many details of his private life, which he struggled to suppress. An excellent biographical source.

Pinsker, Sanford. *"The Catcher in the Rye": Innocence Under Pressure.* New York: Twayne, 1993. Pinsker argues that *The Catcher in the Rye* has affinities with several great American novels told by a retrospective first-person narrator and that it is perhaps the best portrait of a sixteen-year-old American boy ever written.

Salinger, Margaret Ann. *Dream Catcher: A Memoir.* New York: Washington Square Press, 2000. Salinger's daughter describes her experience growing up in the shadow of her famous yet reclusive father.

Salzman, Jack, ed. *New Essays on "The Catcher in the Rye."* New York: Cambridge University Press, 1991. Provides an overview of the history of the writing and publication of *The Catcher in the Rye*, its critical reception, attempts at censorship, and its position in a postmodernist literary world. Individual essays examine the novel's ideology in the context of the Cold War, the subculture the book depicts, its treatment of adolescent crisis, and its narrative structure.

Steinle, Pamela Hunt. *In Cold Fear: "The Catcher in the Rye" Censorship Controversies and Postwar American Character.* Columbus: Ohio State University Press, 2000. A study of the impact of the novel when it was released during a nervous period in American social and political history. Includes a bibliography and an index.

JAMES SALTER

James Horowitz

Born: Passaic, New Jersey; June 10, 1925
Also known as: James Horowitz

PRINCIPAL LONG FICTION

The Hunters, 1957
The Arm of Flesh, 1961 (revised as *Cassada*, 2000)
A Sport and a Pastime, 1967
Light Years, 1975
Solo Faces, 1979

OTHER LITERARY FORMS

In addition to his novels, James Salter has published short fiction in the collections *Dusk, and Other Stories* (1988) and *Last Night* (2005). He has also written screenplays and works of nonfiction that include memoirs and travel writing.

ACHIEVEMENTS

James Salter is a novelist who has never reached a large or wide audience for his delicately plotted and precisely written novels, although the works have brought him much critical praise. The most noticeable aspect of his novels is the search for an edenic world or a perfect moment. His protagonists fail to achieve or sustain that moment, but they prove themselves worthy of the quest. Also noteworthy are Salter's careful observation and his polished and occasionally lyrical style.

Salter has been the recipient of several literary awards, including the PEN/Faulkner Award and the John Steinbeck Award. In 2000, Salter was inducted into the American Academy of Arts and Letters.

BIOGRAPHY

James Salter was born James Horowitz on June 10, 1925, in New York City. He attended Georgetown University and graduated from West Point. After graduation, he became a U.S. Air Force pilot and served on active duty from 1945 until 1957, when he resigned to devote his time to writing. Salter married Ann Altemus in 1951; they had four children before divorcing in 1975. He began living with Kay Eldredge in 1976, and in 1985 they had a son; Salter and Eldredge married in 1998.

With his first novel, *The Hunters*, Salter drew directly on his military experience in describing Air Force fighter pilots during the Korean War. In 1961, his next novel, *The Arm of Flesh*, returned to the milieu of fighter pilots, but its protagonists are a lost pair of pilots in peacetime in a troubled Germany. In 1967, Salter published *A Sport and a Pastime*, which is set in a very different world—that of the French bourgeoisie; it deals with two young lovers and stresses the inevitability of fate. In 1975, he published an ambitious and different type of novel: *Light Years* is an analysis of the breakup of a supposedly perfect marriage, done in the manner of F. Scott Fitzgerald. In *Solo Faces* Salter returned to his studies of aloof warriors who live by a very specific code, but this time the area of action is mountain climbing.

James Salter. (AP/Wide World Photos)

ANALYSIS

James Salter's primary concerns are the achievement of perfection and the integrity of the individual. He is more interested in how people live than in what success they achieve. Salter's novels stress that whatever perfection is achieved is in any case transitory. Age or death destroys skills and whatever grace his characters discover or embody. This reality does not mean that the struggle is useless; it is part of the human being's glory to struggle for something higher in the face of imperfect human nature.

THE HUNTERS

The Hunters, Salter's first novel, draws on his Air Force experience. The hero is Cleve Saville, a veteran pilot who has come to Korea to fly Air Force jets against the Russian MIGs. As an experienced pilot, Cleve is also called upon to train an unsuccessful flight of young pilots. Cleve's first conflict is with Lieutenant Sheedy.

Sheedy is good at self-promotion; he makes a number of dubious claims about shooting down Russian MIGs. His wingman is very cooperative, supporting claims that cannot be confirmed. The commander of the squadron, Colonel Dutch Imil, is eager to accept these dubious claims because they enhance his reputation and that of the group. The conflict comes to a head when Cleve overhears Sheedy rewriting the description of a kill in order to get the Distinguished Flying Cross rather than a lesser Air Medal. This represents a violation of the ode of the warrior by which Cleve lives: What is important is to strive for excellence within the group; any attempt to grab glory, deserved or not, is unacceptable. True glory is, for Cleve, within oneself.

In Korea Cleve meets an old friend, Captain Abbot, who was a very successful pilot in World War II but has now lost his nerve. He claims malfunctions with his plane and scrubs nearly every mission. As a result, Abbot is sent to Japan to an office job, where he can retain his rank if not his integrity. Cleve is sympathetic toward Abbot, but he knows that he cannot give him the courage he needs to continue to be a fighter pilot; it must come from within.

Cleve works at teaching young pilots the calm professionalism that is needed in a good pilot. He becomes a father figure to all these pilots but one: Lieutenant Pell. Though Pell is only newly trained as a fighter pilot, he has great confidence. Cleve has noticed that overconfidence in Pell's brash overtures to a Japanese woman while he waited to be shipped to Korea. Cleve reprimanded Pell at that time, but Pell had not paid much attention. The real problem comes when Pell begins to be successful in shooting down MIGs while his leader, Cleve, has yet to shoot down his first airplane. Pell's success comes because he often leaves the formation to go after Russian airplanes on his own. Cleve reprimands him and brings the matter to Imil, but Imil refuses to do anything that would jeopardize his "kill rate."

While Cleve is on leave in Tokyo, having an idyllic encounter with the daughter of a Japanese painter, he receives news that someone in his flight has been shot down. Upon returning, he finds that the pilot died because Pell left him unprotected and went off on his own to gain the glory of another kill. Imil, however, refuses to ground a man with five kills, an ace.

The climax of the book comes when Cleve shoots down the enemy's ace, "Casey Jones," while he and his wingman, Hunter, are very short of fuel. After this victory, Cleve barely manages to glide his airplane to a landing, but Hunter does not make it. Back at the base, Cleve is unable to support his claim of having downed Casey Jones, because the film in his plane's camera did not run; his dead wingman was the only witness. Suddenly, Cleve reverses the situation, claiming that Hunter shot down Casey Jones and that he was a witness to it. Cleve is proud of his accomplishment but does not need the recognition that would come with such a victory. He has kept a pledge to Hunter that he would get a MIG before he left Korea; for Cleve, meeting commitments and personal integrity are more important than public glory.

Cleve dies in the last chapter, but that is really a denouement rather than a climax, for he has succeeded in living by the code of the warrior. Salter's philosophy of heroism owes much to Ernest Hemingway. His style is also rather similar to Hemingway's, although Salter avoids the mannerisms of the earlier writer.

LIGHT YEARS

Light Years is a very different novel from *The Hunters*, more in the tradition of Henry James or F. Scott Fitzgerald than of Hemingway. Viri is a successful architect, but he longs for a greater creative achievement; he envies such great architects as Christopher Wren and Stanford White, but he realizes that their accomplishments are beyond him. His wife, Nedra, is the center of the marriage: She arranges the meals, parties, and outings that make their life outwardly enviable. There always seems to be an amusing friend at hand—Viri and Nedra are hardly ever alone—and the superb food and wine the couple and their friends consume are described in loving detail, as is Viri and Nedra's stately Victorian house on the Hudson River.

When Nedra must visit her dying father in Altoona, Pennsylvania, she observes there the broken windows and empty warehouses that signify a very different lifestyle. She does sincerely grieve at the death of her father, but her call to Viri is telling: She bemoans the badly designed hospitals of the area. Clearly, Nedra's life is more style than substance. The visit raises anxieties, reminding her of her very different origins; the good life she enjoys with Viri seems not a natural life but an invented one.

Soon the facade of Viri and Nedra's "perfect" marriage is peeled back further. Nedra is having an affair with Jivan, and Viri is attracted to another woman. Nedra does not seem to consider her affair a threat to the marriage, and Viri apparently accepts it, although he is not pleased by it. Nedra holds that the way one lives one's life is more important than traditional bonds and legal connections.

The turning point of the book seems to come near the middle rather than the end. Nedra and Viri's friend Arnaud is beaten and robbed in New York City. He recovers physically from the beating but not psychologically, for he has experienced the darkness outside Eden and can no longer participate in the rounds of parties and dinners, wine, chocolate, and pears. A cloud has fallen upon Eden.

Viri and Nedra go to Europe, a trip that should be the culmination of their perfect life but instead proves its destruction. Nedra suddenly announces, "I don't want to go back to our old life." Outwardly beautiful as their marriage may be, it has become a lifeless routine. They are divorced in the fall (another echo of a lost Eden) and go their separate ways.

Exhilarated by the possibilities of a new life, Nedra

returns to Europe and stays for a while at Davos, Switzerland. She meets a Mr. Pall there but does not stay; continuing her search for perfection, she feels a kind of "pagan happiness." The climax of that search is her attempt to join a theatrical company. She is rejected because of her age, but she has a brief affair with the director, Richard Brom. He assures her, "You'll find your new life." She knows, however, that "these are her last days. She will never find them again."

Viri decays very quickly after Nedra leaves. The house that once held a kind of perfection now feels dark and gloomy. He visits friends, but that is only a reminder of a better past. Finally, he sells the house and goes to Europe.

Nedra has taken an apartment and is serene although her health is failing. She talks often to her daughter Franca; she had earlier encouraged Franca to search for the life that has eluded her. Now she says that love is only an illusion; it does not last. She dies like her father did: "suddenly in the fall of the year."

The novel ends with Viri. He has married an Italian woman, but it is more a capitulation than a love match. Revisiting the house on the Hudson, he finds it "terrible." At the end he sums up the fall from Eden: "It happens in an instant. It is all one long day, one endless afternoon, friends leave, we stand on the shore."

SOLO FACES

Salter's fifth novel, *Solo Faces*, features another uncompromising protagonist: Rand, a mountain climber and a man of few words. He is involved with a woman, Louise, but she is less important to him than his quest to climb mountains. When he meets another climber, Cabot, he decides to leave his job and Louise and go to France.

In Chamonix, Rand—his first name, Vernon, is not mentioned at all until near the end of the book—waits for the weather to clear, although he does a few easy climbs with an Englishman, Bray. When Cabot arrives in Chamonix, the serious climbing and testing begin. Rand and Cabot decide to climb the Dru, a very difficult mountain. On the climb, Cabot is hurt when a rock slide smashes his face. Rand manages to reassure him and finally to drag him to the summit, where he can be rescued, but now Cabot cannot bear to climb with Rand, for Rand has seen his weakness. Cabot has used climbing as an attempt to achieve fame and fortune; Rand, on the other hand, sees climbing as an activity to be practiced for its own sake.

Soon after, Cabot is leading an assault on a famous mountain, the Eiger. Significantly, Rand is excluded, and the climb is like an attack on an enemy. Cabot takes camera crews along to record this event in order to profit from the climb—a complete violation of the code by which Rand lives. Cabot also drives his men beyond what they are capable of achieving; one of the party, Bray, falls to his death as a result of Cabot's ambition.

Rand's great moment in climbing is in direct contrast to that of Cabot. When he hears that an Italian climbing party is caught on the Dru with some injured climbers, he hastily collects a group and climbs the mountain under very difficult conditions to rescue them. The guides of Chamonix have taken an easier and more roundabout direction, and Rand's party arrives first. As a result of this heroic deed, he becomes famous. He resists for a while, refusing to talk to reporters, but finally the machine of publicity overcomes his reticence. He goes to Paris, where he lives with Catherin, but now he is noticed in restaurants; he is a celebrity. Celebrity, however, is a quickly passing state. Once more, Rand leaves a loving woman and returns to his quest in Chamonix.

Rand, now a legend, makes solo climbs on mountain after mountain. Rumors about his activities and accomplishment circulate, and his name is spoken reverently. Rand ignores all of this to concentrate on what he must do: climb as well as he can. He chooses the most famous climb of all, the Walker, for a solo ascent. The climb is difficult, but he continues until he reaches a limit, a line he cannot cross. There is a moment when he cannot go on, cannot climb higher. In this failure, "something had gone out of him."

The rest of the book is a long denouement after the climax on the Walker. Returning to the United States, Rand meets with Cabot, who has fallen from a mountain in the Tetons; Cabot is in a wheelchair, although there is nothing physically wrong with him. Rand attempts to get him out of the wheelchair by goading and pushing him. Rand knows that one cannot give up, even if one has lost the seemingly magical power one had previously possessed; it is as heroic to live well in defeat as it is to live well in victory.

In the last section of the novel, Rand is living in Mexico. Certain that man is only a "fake," no matter how strong or heroic he may seem, he struggles to maintain his integrity, to live out the time given to him. He returns to California and to Louise as the novel ends. Rand has taken his quest as far as he can and must now live in a diminished world.

Salter writes for the most part in a minimalist manner, with few adjectives or needless passages. He is fond of physical description, however, of places and, oddly, of characters' teeth. Lyrical, poetic passages mark important moments in each narrative. These passages are, perhaps, too frequent in *Light Years* and weaken the novel. In *Solo Faces*, Salter manages to reserve them for a few crucial moments; in that context, they are very effective.

Salter's most persistent theme is the quest for whatever perfection this earth holds. That flawless moment can be achieved only briefly, if at all, but each of his protagonists is compelled to take up the quest. The end may be death or despair, but that does not matter. What matters is the attempt, the uncorrupted quest.

James Sullivan

OTHER MAJOR WORKS

SHORT FICTION: *Dusk, and Other Stories*, 1988; *Last Night*, 2005.

SCREENPLAYS: *The Appointment*, 1969; *Downhill Racer*, 1969; *Three*, 1969; *Threshold*, 1981.

NONFICTION: *Still Such*, 1992; *Burning the Days: Recollection*, 1997; *Gods of Tin: The Flying Years*, 2004; *There and Then: The Travel Writing of James Salter*, 2005; *Life Is Meals: A Food Lover's Book of Days*, 2006 (with Kay Salter).

BIBLIOGRAPHY

Begley, Adam. "A Few Well-Chosen Words." *The New York Times Magazine*, October 28, 1990. Presents biographical information on Salter as well as an overview of his writing.

Dowie, William. "A Final Glory: The Novels of James Salter." *College English* 50 (January, 1988): 74-88. Explores the theme of glory in Salter's novels.

_____. *James Salter*. New York: Twayne, 1998. Comprehensive work provides the first book-length examination of Salter's life and career.

_____. "*Solo Faces:* American Tradition and the Individual Talent." In *Essays on the Literature of Mountaineering*, edited by Armand E. Singer. Morgantown: West Virginia University Press, 1982. Places Salter's novel within the literature of mountain writing.

Miller, Margaret Winchell. "Glimpses of a Secular Holy Land: The Novels of James Salter." *Hollins Critic* 19, no. 1 (1982): 1-13. Discusses the theme of the secular paradise as found in Salter's novels.

Salter, James. "James Salter: The Art of Fiction." Interview by Edward Hirsh. *The Paris Review* 127 (Summer, 1993): 54-100. Salter discusses many aspects of his life and career in this lengthy interview.

Smith, Dinitia. "A Fighter Pilot Who Aimed for Novels but Lives on Film." *The New York Times*, August 25, 1997. Focuses on Salter's film work.

Vernon, Alex. *Soldiers Once and Still: Ernest Hemingway, James Salter, and Tim O'Brien*. Iowa City: University of Iowa Press, 2004. Examines how service in the military and wartime experiences shaped the identities and the literary works of Hemingway, Salter, and O'Brien. Focuses in particular on gender identity and social dynamics in the works of the three authors.

GEORGE SAND

Amandine-Aurore-Lucile Dupin

Born: Paris, France; July 1, 1804
Died: Nohant, France; June 8, 1876
Also known as: Amandine-Aurore-Lucile Dupin;
Baronne Dudevant

PRINCIPAL LONG FICTION

Indiana, 1832 (English translation, 1833)
Valentine, 1832 (English translation, 1902)
Lélia, 1833, 1839 (English translation, 1978)
Mauprat, 1837 (English translation, 1870)
Spiridion, 1839 (English translation, 1842)
Le Compagnon du tour de France, 1840 (*The
Companion of the Tour of France*, 1976; also
known as *The Journeyman Joiner*, 1847)
Consuelo, 1842-1843 (English translation, 1846)
La Comtesse de Rudolstadt, 1843-1844 (*The
Countess of Rudolstadt*, 1847)
Jeanne, 1844
Le Meunier d'Angibault, 1845 (*The Miller of
Angibault*, 1847)
La Mare au diable, 1846 (*The Devil's Pool*,
1929; also known as *The Enchanted Lake*,
1850)
Lucrezia Floriani, 1846 (English translation,
1985)
Le Péché de M. Antoine, 1847 (*The Sin of
Monsieur Antoine*, 1900)
La Petite Fadette, 1848-1849 (*Fanchon the
Cricket*, 1864; also known as *Little Fadette*,
1850)
François le champi, 1850 (*Francis the Waif*,
1889)
Les Maîtres sonneurs, 1853 (*The Bagpipers*,
1890)
Elle et lui, 1859 (*She and He*, 1902)
Le Marquis de Villemer, 1861 (*The Marquis of
Villemer*, 1871)
La Ville noire, 1861
Mademoiselle la Quintinie, 1863
Mademoiselle Merquem, 1868 (English
translation, 1868)

Marianne, 1876 (novella; English translation,
1883)
Historic and Romantic Novels, 1900-1902 (20
volumes)

OTHER LITERARY FORMS

George Sand, who was famous during her lifetime primarily as a novelist, earned a living for many years as a journalist. Some of her essays on art, literature, politics, and social questions are collected in two posthumous volumes, *Questions d'art et de littérature* (1878) and *Questions politiques et sociales* (1879). Her twenty-volume autobiography, *Histoire de ma vie* (1854-1855; *History of My Life*, 1901), is considered by some to be her masterpiece. Georges Lubin produced an excellent annotated edition of this work and other autobiographical writings for Gallimard in 1970. Other important nonfictional works include *Lettres d'un voyageur* (1837; *Letters of a Traveller*, 1847), *Lettres à Marcie* (1837), and *Un Hiver à Majorque* (1841; *Winter in Majorca*, 1956). Sand's plays were published in five volumes in 1877. She wrote more than nineteen thousand letters and was called by André Maurois "the best French epistolary writer." From 1964 onward, Lubin devoted himself to a new multivolume edition of Sand's letters, many of which were previously unpublished or had been published only in truncated form. The twenty-sixth and final volume of that series was published in 1995.

ACHIEVEMENTS

To her contemporaries, George Sand was a great novelist and a fallen woman. The controversy surrounding her life has continued into the twenty-first century. Until the late 1980's, scholars neglected her enormous production of literary works to concentrate on biographical quarrels. She was recognized as a major novelist by Honoré de Balzac, Ivan Turgenev, Victor Hugo, and Henry James. She was widely read in the United States and Great Britain, where she influenced writers such as the Brontë sisters (Anne, Charlotte, and Emily) and George Eliot. In Russia, where political treatises were banned, her novels passed on progressive ideas and inspired political thinkers such as Mikhail Bakunin as well as novelists such as Fyodor Dostoevski. Gustave Flaubert called Sand "My Dear Master," and Marcel Proust's most poignant childhood memories involved his mother reading Sand's rustic novels to him.

This picture of Sand's pastoral or rustic novels persists in France today, where the average reader considers her a writer of sentimental stories for children. Because of this image, she has been attacked by political liberals who accuse her of supporting the status quo with her tales of happy peasants. Scholars, on the other hand, regard her rustic novels as the perfection of a literary genre. To the nineteenth century public, Sand's novels calling for the emancipation of women (and men) from arranged marriages, equality between the sexes, and education for women seemed outrageously feminist. Her novel *Lélia* shocked readers with its explicit analysis of female sexuality. Modern-day feminists, however, point to the limits of Sand's feminism, especially to her opposition to the participation of women in political affairs, for she felt that women should be educated before they were given the right to vote.

Because of the volume of Sand's work and the speed at which she was forced to write to support her family, her artistic circle, and her charitable contributions, the quality of her fiction is uneven, yet literary critics admire her fluid style and her techniques of psychological analysis. All agree in considering *Mauprat, Consuelo*, and the rustic novels as powerful masterpieces.

BIOGRAPHY

George Sand was born Amandine-Aurore-Lucile Dupin in Paris on July 1, 1804, to parents who had been married scarcely a month. Her father, Maurice Dupin, was a descendant through bastard lines of the king of Poland, Augustus the Strong, and her mother, Sophie Delaborde, was a camp follower and the daughter of a Paris bird seller. Thus, from the beginning, Sand was exposed to the class struggle. When she was four years old, her father was killed in a fall from a horse; three years later, her mother gave up custody of her to her aristocratic maternal grandmother, who brought her up as a lady

at her country estate of Nohant in the Berry region. Sand nevertheless reached out to her mother in Paris and the working class she represented.

In 1817, Sand returned to Paris, where she entered the Couvent des Anglaises for her education. In 1820, she returned to the country while her grandmother attempted to arrange a suitable marriage for her; Sand preferred to read books and ride horses. After the death of her grandmother in 1821, Sand returned to Paris to live with her mother. This arrangement proved unsatisfactory because of her mother's violent temper, and the girl sought refuge at the country estate of her father's friends, the Roëttiers. Through the Roëttiers, she met Casimir François Dudevant, the illegitimate but recognized son of a baron; she married Dudevant in 1822.

At first, the couple seemed happy enough, but after the birth of their son Maurice in 1823, their incompatibility became evident. A second child, Solange, was born in 1828. After a fight with her husband, Sand arranged to spend half of each year in Paris, where Dude-

George Sand. (Library of Congress)

vant would send her an allowance from the revenues of her land. In 1831, she left for Paris to live with Jules Sandeau, a law student who aspired to become a writer. To supplement her meager pension, Sand obtained a job writing for *Le Figaro*, a newspaper run by Hyacinthe de Latouche, an acquaintance from Berry. In collaboration with Sandeau, Sand wrote several short stories and at least one novel, which was signed "J. Sand." When Sand wrote *Indiana* alone at Nohant and returned to Paris to publish it, de Latouche suggested that she keep the name "Sand" and choose another Christian name. She chose "Georges" (soon anglicized to George) because it seemed to her to be typical of the Berry region. *Indiana*, the first novel signed "George Sand," was published in 1832. More than seventy others were to follow.

In 1833, Sand fell in love with the poet Alfred de Musset and left with him for Venice, the city that all the Romantic writers dreamed of visiting. There they both fell ill. Following several violent incidents resulting from Musset's overindulgence in wine and women, they agreed to separate. When Musset's illness recurred, Sand nursed him faithfully but fell in love with his Italian doctor, Pietro Pagello. Barely restored to health, Musset returned to Paris while Sand and Pagello stayed in Italy. Sand addressed much of her correspondence in *Letters of a Traveller* to Musset in Paris. In 1834, she returned to Paris with Pagello but neglected him, feeling herself drawn again to Musset. Musset wrote some of his most famous poems about this relationship and analyzed it in his *La Confession d'un enfant du siècle* (1836; *The Confession of a Child of the Century*, 1892). After Musset's death in 1857, Sand reevaluated their adventure in *She and He*.

After many painful scenes, Sand finally broke with Musset in 1835. Later that year, she met and fell in love with the Republican lawyer Michel de Bourges. When she returned to Nohant, she had a definitive fight with her husband and sued for a legal separation, since divorce did not exist in France at that time. De Bourges acted as her lawyer.

In 1838, Sand began a relationship with Frédéric Chopin, whom she met through a mutual friend, Franz Liszt. For nine years, Sand was Chopin's mother, mistress, and nurse, protecting him and enabling him to write some of his best music. The most famous event in their years together was the ill-fated trip they took with Sand's children to Majorca in the winter of 1838-1839, which she describes in *Winter in Majorca*. Most literary critics agree that Sand was satirizing her relationship with Chopin in her novel *Lucrezia Floriani*. Sand and Chopin separated in 1847, disagreeing over the marriage of her daughter Solange to the sculptor Jean-Baptiste Auguste Clésinger.

In 1848, Sand returned to Paris as soon as she received word that the monarchy had been overthrown. She wrote most of the official bulletins for the new Republican government, which included many of her old friends. When the Republicans were arrested in May, Sand took refuge at Nohant. Although she continued to intercede with the Emperor Napoleon III for her friends, Sand has been accused of turning her back on the Revolution to write bourgeois pastoral novels.

After 1848, Sand spent more time at Nohant than in Paris, but she returned to Paris often, frequently for the openings of her plays. From 1850 to 1865, Alexandre Manceau, an engraver and a friend of her son Maurice (who was an artist, a pupil of Eugène Delacroix), was Sand's private secretary and lover. In 1864, Manceau bought a small house near Paris, where they lived in order to leave Nohant to Maurice and his new wife, Lina, the daughter of the engraver Luigi Calamatta, an old friend of Sand. After Manceau's death from tuberculosis in 1865, Sand traveled, lived in Paris, visited Flaubert at Croisset, and went to the Ardennes region to document a novel, but she considered Nohant her home again. There, she received Flaubert and Turgenev as well as other friends. She died at Nohant of a painful intestinal blockage on June 8, 1876.

ANALYSIS

Faced with the enormous number of George Sand's novels, literary critics quickly moved to divide them into categories. The traditional categories include feminist novels, socialistic novels, and rustic novels. While this oversimplification is inaccurate, it does help the reader to identify the major themes that recur in most of her novels.

VALENTINE

Valentine is a good example of the critics' dilemma. The novel recounts a love story of a married noblewoman and an educated peasant that ends tragically with the death of the lovers. The plot is a Romantic one, both in the sense of "a love story" and in the literary-historical sense of the term, for it contains several of the essential themes of French Romanticism: the passing of time, the passing of love with time, and a search for the meaning of the universe beyond the limits of human life. In *Valentine*, Sand's Bénédict is a melancholy, meditative person who resembles François-René de Chateaubriand's René. He is killed accidentally by a jealous husband, but Valentine, the heroine, dies from sorrow soon after his death. At first reading, the novel seems to be primarily Romantic, yet Valentine's fruitless attempts to find personal happiness and satisfaction, despite her financially arranged marriage and her indifferent and absent husband, suggest classification among the feminist novels. The beautiful descriptions of the Berry countryside and details of the daily life of the peasants are characteristic of her rustic novels. The love affair between two people of different social classes suggests classification as a socialistic novel. The conclusion is obvious: Most of Sand's novels contain Romantic elements, Romanesque elements, feminist elements, rustic elements, and socialist elements.

The novels that contain the highest percentage of feminist elements are the early ones. Clearly, Sand's unhappy personal experiences were reflected in novels such as *Indiana*, in which the heroine leaves her despotic husband, is betrayed by her lover, and ultimately finds happiness with her cousin, who serves as a father figure for her and becomes her lover on a lush tropical island in a primitive paradise that owes something to Jean-Jacques Rousseau and Jacques-Henri Bernardin de Saint-Pierre. Sand's feminist novel par excellence is *Lélia*, which reinterprets the metaphysical dilemma of the Romantic hero in feminine terms.

Sand's socialistic novels are generally less successful artistically than her work in other genres, perhaps because her theoretical digressions are not well integrated into the plots. One exception, *The Companion of the Tour of France*, was reedited by the University Press of Grenoble in the late 1980's and then began to receive long-overdue critical attention. In addition to its story of the love between the lady of a manor and a carpenter-artist, the novel contains a study of secret trade guilds

and a portrait of the daily life of workers—a class that was neglected by Balzac in *La Comédie humaine* (1829-1848; *The Comedy of Human Life*, 1885-1893, 1896; also known as *The Human Comedy*, 1895-1896, 1911). *The Miller of Angibault* is also a successful socialistic novel, but it contains many elements of the rustic novels as well. *The Sin of Monsieur Antoine* and *La Ville noire* expose the problems of factory workers, making Sand the only French novelist before Émile Zola to analyze seriously the effects of the Industrial Revolution.

JEANNE

Sand's experiments with the rustic novel began with *Jeanne*, whose peasant heroine is compared to Joan of Arc and Napoleon. In the rustic novels, Sand saw herself as an intermediary between Paris and Nohant, between bourgeois and peasant. She hoped to bring about a reconciliation between the two by portraying the best qualities of the country folk to make them acceptable to urban readers. She did not, however, neglect the very real problems of rural life. Her peasants are often hungry and overworked, but they have a noble character that enables them to conquer all obstacles and a resourcefulness that comes from living in harmony with nature.

Sand never claimed to be a realist, even though she documented her novels carefully. There are realistic elements in her psychological analyses, in her landscapes, and in her portrayal of the everyday life of workers and peasants. Nevertheless, what counted for Sand, as she states in the introduction to *The Devil's Pool*, was "ideal truth" rather than "a slice of life." She wanted to inspire readers to live up to their potential, in contrast to the productions of the realist and naturalist schools, which, she felt, depressed people by showing the ugly side of life. In her autobiography, she quotes Balzac as saying to her, "You search for man as he should be, while I take him as he is. Believe me, we are both right."

LÉLIA

Lélia is a flawed masterpiece. Its lyric tone and mystical examination of God, love, the universe, and the nature of truth make it both a profound philosophical work and a difficult novel for most readers. The characters tend toward allegory: Lélia represents doubt, according to a document published in *Sketches and Hints* (1926); Trenmor, expiation and stoicism; Sténio, poetry and credulity; Magnus, superstition and repressed desire; and Pulchérie, the senses (as opposed to the mind or soul). They also represent different aspects of Sand's own personality. She wrote in *Journal intime* (1926; *The Intimate Journal*, 1929), which was published with *Sketches and Hints*, "Magnus is my childhood; Sténio, my youth; Lélia is my maturity; Trenmor will perhaps be my old age. All these types have been in me."

When Sand published *Lélia* in 1832, it had a *succès de scandale*. A novel by a woman treating explicitly the problem of female frigidity, briefly touching on lesbian sexuality, and creating a superior heroine to rival melancholy Romantic heroes (Chateaubriand's René, Étienne de Senancour's Obermann, Johann Wolfgang von Goethe's Werther, and Benjamin Constant's Adolphe) was more than even Paris was prepared to accept. Sand's passionate cry of suffering was so revealing, however, that Musset and many of her contemporaries called her "Lélia."

Sand, who ordinarily did not rewrite novels, rewrote *Lélia*, cutting out the sexually explicit passages and transforming its profoundly skeptical and pessimistic tone into a more positive and progressive one. The second version, published in 1839, was chosen by the author to be included in an edition of her complete works. After that, the 1832 edition disappeared from view until André Maurois titled his 1952 biography *Lélia: Ou, La Vie de George Sand* (*Lélia: The Life of George Sand*, 1953). Maurois asserted that the first *Lélia* was, with *Indiana* and *Consuelo*, one of Sand's finest novels and artistically superior to the 1839 version. In 1960, Pierre Reboul published the text of the 1832 *Lélia*, and scholars now generally agree with Maurois. Östen Södergård published a comparison of the two editions in 1962 and showed how and why Sand changed her novel.

In the first *Lélia*, the heroine is presented to the reader as seen from afar by the young poet Sténio, who worships and fears her. The question the first part of the novel asks is whether Lélia will be able to love Sténio. Trenmor, a rehabilitated gambler resigned to a calm philosophical life, says no. Lélia is older and wiser than Sténio and so frustrated by unsatisfying love affairs that she is no longer capable of physical love. She proposes a more spiritual love, but the poet insists that ideal love unites the senses with the spirit. After many vain power struggles, Lélia leaves Sténio with her courtesan-sister Pulchérie, with whom he makes love, believing her to be Lélia. In this way, Lélia hopes to teach him that sensual love is unreliable. Instead, Sténio, disillusioned by the experience, decides that pleasure alone is real and throws himself into debauchery. Finally, he drowns himself in a lake; while Lélia weeps over his body, she is strangled by Magnus, a priest who has become an atheist and has been driven insane by his desire for Lélia. At the end, Lélia and Sténio, the lovers who could not agree on earth, are united as stars in Heaven; and the philosopher Trenmor continues his pilgrimage alone.

The love story at the center of *Lélia* is less important than Lélia's desperate search for God, herself, and truth—what Maria Espinosa, the translator of the original version of *Lélia* into English, calls the "spiritual odyssey" of Lélia and, of course, of Sand herself. Lélia searches for a man who is perfect, like God; not finding one, she makes a god of the man she loves. When she realizes her mistake, it is too late for her ever to obtain the fresh, pure love of which she dreams. She has lived too much without enjoyment, and her fantasies surpass any possible realization. This makes her doubt God and hate herself while she is filled with a burning and insatiable physical desire. Seeking relief in a year's voluntary claustration, Lélia waits in vain to achieve the stoic resignation of Trenmor, who is emotionally dead. Since, for her, physical love represents a submission of the woman to the man, she finds it distasteful and tries to solve her dilemma by taking the dominant male role in love scenes. For this reason, she treats Sténio like her son and loves him most when he is passive—sleeping or dead. Unable to find a solution to her problems, Lélia is finally content to be killed by Magnus.

In the 1839 version, Lélia becomes a nun who teaches girls how to resist men and reforms the Church. Trenmor becomes a reformed murderer and acquires a secret identity as Valmarina, a benefactor of the poor and needy as well as the head of a mystico-political secret society somewhat like the Italina Carbonaros. Even though Lélia dies in disgrace at the end of the second version, the reader feels that she will be vindicated. Both Trenmor and Lélia thus find meaningful things to do with their lives as Sand passes from Romantic pessimism to preach active reform of society.

MAUPRAT

The reader who finds the lyric and philosophical passages of *Lélia* long and painful will be enchanted by *Mauprat*. The latter, a more traditional novel, combines the beautiful exterior scenes of Sand's rustic novels with a historical adventure story of the type written by Sir Walter Scott or Alexandre Dumas, *père*. Political and philosophical reflections are carefully woven into the fabric of the work so as not to impede the swift movement of the plot toward its suspense-filled conclusion, for *Mauprat* also contains a detective story. These disparate elements are skillfully united to form a bildungsroman. The central focus of the novel is the education of Bernard de Mauprat, that is, the transformation of a wild barbarian interested only in sensual gratification into a sensitive, loving, and cultured man. This transformation is the work of Bernard's cousin Edmée, who uses his love for her to force him to change.

From the outside, Edmée seems to resemble Lélia. She is cold and proud; she dominates Bernard and treats him like her son. Edmée is not frigid, however; she merely appears that way because she suppresses her own desire for Bernard and patiently waits for him to become her equal, emotionally and morally, before she agrees to marry him. Meanwhile, like Sand herself, Edmée carries a knife with which to commit suicide if necessary to protect her virtue.

Bernard, who was taken at age seven by his grandfather Tristan de Mauprat to a disintegrating castle, grew up in an atmosphere of violence and crime as his marauding uncles filled the countryside with terror, recreating in the eighteenth century their family's feudal domination of the peasants. Bernard's slow progress from this life of darkness to the light of civilization begins when Edmée de Mauprat, the sole heir of the respectable younger branch of the family, loses her way in the forest and is captured by the evil uncles. She convinces Bernard, who only wants to make love to her, to rescue her and flee from the castle with her. In order to do this, she promises Bernard that she will belong to no other man before him.

This solemn promise shapes the future of both the young people. Bernard, who is seeking only instant physical gratification, slowly and painfully discovers that Edmée will withhold this from him for many years, while

he, like the medieval knight, is forced to overcome obstacles to merit her love. Chivalrous motifs are reinforced by a young man named Arthur, who serves as Bernard's friend and guide in the American Revolution, explaining to him what he must do to earn the favors of the fair maiden. The medieval knight had to conquer dragons (exterior enemies) while Bernard must conquer his own savage nature. For Edmée, on the other hand, this promise to make love is tantamount to a promise of marriage.

Sand states in her preface to *Mauprat* that the trauma of the legal separation from her husband made her begin to reflect upon the dream of an ideal marriage and an eternal love; thus, Bernard de Mauprat, who narrates his story at the age of eighty, tells his listeners that he loved only one woman in his entire life, before his marriage, during his marriage, and after her death. This is certainly a strong response to Sand's contemporaries, who criticized her for attacking the institution of marriage.

As the love story gives unity to the plot, the theme of the perfectibility of humankind forms the center of the philosophical framework of the novel. Here, Sand is undoubtedly following one of her first mentors, Rousseau. In a sense, Edmée is like Julie in Rousseau's *Julie: Ou, La Nouvelle Héloïse* (1761; *Eloise: Or, A Series of Original Letters*, 1761; also known as *Julie: Or, The New Eloise*, 1968; better known as *The New Héloïse*), who moves from a passionate lover, Saint-Preux, to a reasonable husband, Wolmar, creating a utopia out of her farm. The major difference is that Sand unites Saint-Preux and Wolmar to form one character, Bernard. Edmée does create a utopia with the aid of Patience, an old hermit who gives up his solitary lifestyle to help Edmée build a life of dignity and honor for the peasants. Bernard and Edmée are happy to give up their wealth with the arrival of the French Revolution, which they see as a step toward a more equitable society.

In *Mauprat*, Sand uses the medieval trappings, the plot of an adventure story, and the psychological developments of a love story to interest her reader in the essential message—that the human race can improve with education. This progressive theme signals Sand's own movement toward a more optimistic view of the world.

CONSUELO

Consuelo and its sequel, *The Countess of Rudolstadt*, form, like *Mauprat*, a bildungsroman. This time, however, the person who learns and grows by overcoming obstacles is a woman. *Consuelo*, considered by many to be Sand's masterpiece, has been called France's answer to Goethe's saga of Wilhelm Meister. The novel is set in the eighteenth century, in Venice, Bohemia, Vienna, and Berlin—for Consuelo is a talented singer, born in Spain of a Gypsy mother, who travels in Europe perfecting her voice and developing her career. The character is roughly based on Pauline Garcia Viardot, a close friend of Sand; as a prototype of the Romantic artist, Consuelo also shares many traits with Sand herself. Consuelo has the misfortune of being ugly until she is transformed by her music. As Béatrice Didier has pointed out, her ugliness may not be a disadvantage after all, because it saves her from easy success and venal protectors, enabling her to keep her independence and grow in her art.

The bildungsroman operates on three levels, as Consuelo follows an artistic itinerary that leads to her becoming a composer, a political itinerary that makes her aware of the evils of despotism and dedicated to helping the poor and suffering, and a spiritual itinerary that culminates in her initiation into the secret society of the Invisibles, who work to correct social injustice. Consuelo's artistic voyage begins when the famous maestro Porpora agrees to give the poor girl free music lessons in Venice. After Porpora teaches her the fundamentals of her art, Consuelo becomes an opera star. At this point, Porpora feels he must warn her to beware of men—both would-be protectors such as Count Justiani and would-be lovers such as Anzoletto, her childhood friend. Porpora persuades Consuelo to devote her life to art and sends her off to the Castle of the Giants in Bohemia to give music lessons to the young Baroness Amélie.

In this castle, which has all the subterranean passageways and mysteries of the gothic novel, Consuelo meets Albert de Rudolstadt, Amélie's cousin, who is subject to temporary mental disorders during which he imagines that he is the reincarnation of the Prince Podiebrand or the Hussite hero Jean Ziska. He plays violin music that has a magical influence on Consuelo. Albert and his deranged peasant friend Zdenko teach her the history of Bohemia and its suffering under political and religious oppression. They introduce her to folk music and begin her initiation into the occult. After saving Albert's life by carrying him through secret underground passages, tun-

nels, and wells, Consuelo becomes ill and is nursed back to health by Albert, who falls in love with her. She refuses to marry him and leaves the castle for Vienna to pursue her study of music.

On the trip to Vienna, Consuelo dresses up like a man to protect herself. This loss of female identity gives her a freedom that helps her develop as an artist. She accidentally meets young Joseph Haydn, who accompanies her on the long trip on foot. As a result of this journey, she learns about war, despotism, and the oppression of the peasants. In Vienna, she finds Porpora again and learns about tyranny from Maria Theresa.

As she is leaving Vienna for Berlin, Consuelo receives a message that Albert is dying. She rushes to the Rudolstadt castle and agrees to marry him *in extremis*. After his death, she renounces his wealth and title and continues on to Berlin, where she is imprisoned by Frederick the Great for conspiracy. In prison, she discovers the joys of musical composition and memorizes her creations, moving even closer to traditional folk music. She is freed from prison by the Invisibles, who take her to a palace where she studies their mysteries and decides to become a member of their secret society. She falls in love with her mysterious rescuer Liverani, only to discover that Albert is still alive and an Invisible. Forced to choose between love and duty, Consuelo follows her higher instincts and chooses Albert, who reveals that he is Liverani. After her initiation into the Invisibles, which takes place in another castle, with the symbolic name of Castle of the Grail, the marriage of Consuelo and Albert is renewed.

In the epilogue, the reader learns that the Invisibles have been forced underground and that Consuelo has lost her voice and Albert his reason. She has become a composer writing music for Albert's poems. They wander with their children through the countryside, bringing hope to the poor and needy. Consuelo is thus as poor at the end of the novel as she was at the beginning, but she has become the "Good Goddess of Poverty." She has fulfilled her artistic destiny by becoming a creator—a complete Romantic artist. She has fulfilled her political and spiritual destiny by helping the needy. Finally, she has fulfilled her destiny as a woman by uniting physical and spiritual love in her relationship with Albert. She is the whole woman Lélia wanted to be. She lives up to her name "Consuelo" by bringing "consolation" to those around her.

The religious and political philosophy of Albert and the Invisibles, which Consuelo adopts at the end of the novel, was inspired by Pierre Leroux, a Socialist thinker whom Sand admired. In *Consuelo*, the Invisibles base their doctrine on a belief in absolute equality between sexes and classes. They also proclaim the right of the people to participate as fully as the priests in religious sacraments. Their motto, The Cup to the People, refers to the communion chalice. This desire to reform the Catholic Church was a constant preoccupation of Sand, best expressed in *Spiridion*, which develops a religious philosophy of history. Parallel to her desire to reform the Church is her desire to reform society, which finds in *Consuelo* its most complete expression.

This novel, which is epic in scope, has been called a novel of initiation as well as a bildungsroman. Because of its length, it is a challenge to most modern readers. Its beautiful landscapes, fascinating characters, and exciting plot, however, reward readers for their perseverance.

THE DEVIL'S POOL

If *Consuelo* can be likened to an epic poem, *The Devil's Pool* is more like a folk song. Considered the perfect example of Sand's rustic novels, it is short, simple, and tightly structured. The novel has only two major characters, Germain, a thirty-year-old widower with three children, and Marie, a poverty-stricken sixteen-year-old girl. The title of the novel leads one to think that the occult might play as large a role in this novel as in *Consuelo*. Actually, the Devil's Pool, which forms the center of the narrative structure, is magic only because it makes people lose their way in the forest at night. Marie and Germain, accompanied by Germain's oldest child, Pierre, lose their way near this pool and there discover the truth about themselves—that they love each other. The major theme of the novel is thus quasi-biblical: "Those who think they are lost are found," or "One finds one's way by losing it."

The conflict in the plot arises from the fact that Germain must remarry to ensure the economic viability of the family unit, although at first he has no desire to do so. Marie is considered an unfit wife for him because of her youth and poverty. In the forest, however, she shows her true character—she is provident, attuned to nature,

and clever at caring for children. After Germain recognizes her special gifts, he still has to persuade the elders of his family that she is an appropriate bride for him. Until the end of the story, he is uncertain whether Marie returns his love.

The ideological basis of this novel springs from Rousseau's theories about the purity of country life and the corruption of the cities. Germain and Marie, the innocent country people, find their opposites in the vain, materialistic Cathérine Guérin, a widow whom Germain was supposed to marry, and the Farmer of Ormeaux, the licentious master who attempts to seduce Marie. It is important to note that they are both members of the middle class as well as inhabitants of a village. Sand's vision of the country, however, is more than simply an ideological construct. She grew up in the country, and her portraits of the peasants of Berry have done much to preserve the language and folklore that were beginning to disappear.

There is an innate conflict in the rustic novels between Sand's desire to conserve and preserve a disappearing way of life and her avowed purpose of reforming society by promoting understanding between the bourgeois and the peasant. Her rustic novels have been read for more than a century as tributes to the status quo and have been used by the French educational system to keep people in their place. This is clearly not what Sand intended when she wrote in the introduction to *The Devil's Pool*, "It is necessary for Lazarus to leave his dungheap so that the poor will no longer rejoice in the death of the rich. It is necessary that all be happy so that the happiness of the few may not be criminal and cursed by God." In this introduction, Sand explains that the novel was inspired by an engraving by Hans Holbein the Younger showing death as the only recompense for a life of hard labor in the fields. Sand believed that nineteenth century laborers should have life rather than death as a reward and that inequities should be rectified on earth rather than in Heaven. In this way, *The Devil's Pool* joins the technical perfection of a new genre of novel with an expansion of Sand's constant concern for the suffering of humanity.

Lucy M. Schwartz

OTHER MAJOR WORKS

SHORT FICTION: *Contes d'une grand'mère*, 1873, 1876 (*Tales of a Grandmother*, 1930).

PLAY: *Théâtre complet de George Sand*, 1877 (5 volumes).

NONFICTION: *Lettres à Marcie*, 1837; *Lettres d'un voyageur*, 1837 (*Letters of a Traveller*, 1847); *Un Hiver à Majorque*, 1841 (*Winter in Majorca*, 1956); *Histoire de ma vie*, 1854-1855 (20 volumes; *History of My Life*, 1901); *Questions d'art et de littérature*, 1878; *Questions politiques et sociales*, 1879; *Letters*, 1896 (9 volumes); *Journal intime*, 1926 (*The Intimate Journal*, 1929); *Sketches and Hints*, 1926; *Correspondance*, 1964-1995 (26 volumes); *Œuvres autobiographiques*, 1970-1971 (2 volumes).

MISCELLANEOUS: *Works*, 1887 (38 volumes).

BIBLIOGRAPHY

Atwood, William G. *The Lioness and the Little One: The Liaison of George Sand and Frédéric Chopin*. New York: Columbia University Press, 1980. Offers a careful and scholarly account of a part of Sand's life and career that has often been distorted and sensationalized.

Barry, Joseph. *Infamous Woman: The Life of George Sand*. Garden City, N.Y.: Doubleday, 1977. Presents an illuminating overview of Sand's life and writing. Chronicles her development as an artist, her tumultuous love affairs, her relationships with her children and her mother, her role in French politics, and her stand against traditional female roles.

Cate, Curtis. *George Sand*. Boston: Little, Brown, 1975. Sound, comprehensive biography includes a preface that provides an insightful discussion of Maurois's classic biography (cited below) and the fluctuations of Sand's literary reputation.

Crecelius, Kathryn J. *Family Romances: George Sand's Early Novels*. Bloomington: Indiana University Press, 1987. Informative study discusses topics such as Sand's handling of heroic romance and bourgeois realism and her role as a woman artist. Separate chapters cover her novels *Lélia*, *Mauprat*, and *Valentine*.

Eisler, Benita. *Naked in the Marketplace: The Lives of George Sand*. New York: Basic Books, 2006. Biography draws on Sand's substantial body of correspondence to explore the complicated personality of the radical nineteenth century feminist. Focuses especially on Sand's impressively active and lengthy love life and its impact on her literary output.

Goodwin-Jones, Robert. *Romantic Vision: The Novels of George Sand*. Birmingham, Ala.: Summa, 1995. Presents a thematic analysis of about forty of Sand's novels, including *Valentine*, *Indiana*, *Mauprat*, and *The Companion of the Tour of France*. Includes an introductory discussion of Sand as a novelist.

Harkness, Nigel. *Men of Their Words: The Poetics of Masculinity in George Sand's Fiction*. London: Legenda, 2007. Examines questions of masculinity in Sand's fiction within the context of the nineteenth century French novel, describing how Sand's novels repeatedly depict the connections among masculinity, power, and language.

Jack, Belinda Elizabeth. *George Sand: A Woman's Life Writ Large*. New York: Vintage Books, 1999. Biography pays especial attention to Sand's childhood and its influence on her later life and career. Includes illustrations and index.

Massardier-Kenney, Françoise. *Gender in the Fiction of George Sand*. Atlanta: Rodopi, 2000. Argues that Sand's novels express a complex and extremely modern conception of gender in which she questions prevalent patriarchal modes of discourse and redefines masculinity and femininity.

Maurois, André. *Lélia: The Life of George Sand*. New York: Harper and Brothers, 1953. Classic biography by one of the genre's most renowned practitioners. Less scholarly than Cate's biography (cited above), but written with verve and a sure grasp of both the subject and her period.

Powell, David A. *George Sand*. Boston: Twayne, 1990. Provides an excellent introduction to Sand's life and works. Approaches Sand as a major Romantic and feminist writer and places her work within the context of French social history.

JOSÉ SARAMAGO

Born: Azinhaga, Ribatejo, Portugal; November 16, 1922

Also known as: José de Sousa Saramago

PRINCIPAL LONG FICTION

Terra do pecado, 1947

Manual de pintura e caligrafia, 1976 (*Manual of Painting and Calligraphy*, 1994)

Levantado do chão, 1980

Memorial do convento, 1982 (*Baltasar and Blimunda*, 1987)

O ano da morte de Ricardo Reis, 1984 (*The Year of the Death of Ricardo Reis*, 1991)

A jangada de pedra, 1986 (*The Stone Raft*, 1994)

História do cerco de Lisboa, 1989 (*The History of the Siege of Lisbon*, 1996)

O Evangelho segundo Jesus Cristo, 1991 (*The Gospel According to Jesus Christ*, 1993)

Ensaio sobre a cegueira, 1995 (*Blindness*, 1997)

Conto da ilha desconhecida, 1997 (*The Tale of the Unknown Island*, 1999)

Todos os nomes: Romance, 1997 (*All the Names*, 1999)

A caverna, 2000 (*The Cave*, 2002)

O homem duplicado, 2002 (*The Double*, 2004)

Ensaio sobre a lucidez, 2004 (*Seeing*, 2006)

OTHER LITERARY FORMS

In addition to his novels, José Saramago (sah-rah-MAH-goh) has written various other literary works, including several collections of poetry, short stories, plays, and an extensive personal diary. He has translated many European authors' works, including those of Colette, Georg Wilhelm Friedrich Hegel, Leo Tolstoy, Charles Baudelaire, Nicos Poulantzas, Guy de Maupassant, Étienne Balibar, Jean Cassou, Henri Focillon, Jacques Roumain, André Bonnard, and Raymond Bayer. Saramago has also worked as an editor for the newspaper *Diário de Noticias* and later published several newspaper articles.

ACHIEVEMENTS

José Saramago received the Prémio Cidade de Lisboa in 1980, an award that is critical to achieving recognition in Portugal. International acclaim came to Saramago with the publication of *Baltasar and Blimunda* in 1982. For this novel, he received Portugal's most prestigious literary honor, the PEN Club Award (1983 and 1984). This award was followed by the Prémio da Crítica da Associação Portuguesa 1986, an important journalism prize. *The Gospel According to Jesus Christ* was nominated for the European Literary Prize (1992), awarded by the European Writers' Congress, but Saramago's name was removed from the list of nominees by the Portuguese government. Later, he earned the Prémio Vida Literária (1993) and the Prémio Camões (1995). Most significant, his novel *The Stone Raft* received the 1998 Nobel Prize in Literature. Saramago is the only native writer in Portuguese to have received this highly coveted award, which includes one million U.S. dollars. *The Stone Raft* and his earlier novels were soon translated into many languages.

BIOGRAPHY

José Saramago was born into a poor family in the village of Azinhaga, Portugal, about sixty miles outside Lisbon on November 16, 1922. His name would actually have been a traditional Portuguese last name (de Sousa), but he accidentally received his father's nickname Saramago (Portuguese for "wild radish"). In 1924, the family moved to Lisbon.

Saramago has said that he was a good student. His family could not afford to provide him with a general education that emphasized grammar and writing. At the age of twelve, he was forced to enter a technical school, where he studied for five years to become a mechanic. Nonetheless, he was able to take courses in French. During this period, he borrowed money to buy Portuguese grammar books. After completion of his training, he became a mechanic for two years. At night, he would frequent the public library, where his interest and skill in reading poetry and prose literature inspired him to advance his writing skills without being mentored.

José Saramago. (AFP/Getty Images)

In 1944, Saramago married Lida Reis; in 1947, Violante, their only child, was born. It was also in 1947 that Saramago published his first novel, *Terra do Pecado*, and his only published work for the next twenty years. Saramago himself said that he did not publish during this period because he had nothing worthwhile to say. In 1951, he started work at a publishing firm (Estúdios Cor), where he would meet Portuguese authors. He then began working as a translator of literary works. From 1955 until 1981, these translations provided him a stable income so that he could also begin to seriously write poetry. In 1966, he published his first collection of poetry, *Possible Poems*. Later, he became a journalist for *Diário de Notiças*. In the late 1970's and early 1980's, he published essays that focused on Portuguese politics.

Saramago had joined the Communist Party in 1969

(an affiliation he has maintained), and he also became an atheist, which was directly counter to the traditionally conservative government of Portugal and the tenets of the Catholic Church. In 1991, Saramago left Portugal to live on the Spanish island of Lanzarote in the Islas Canarias (Canary Islands), off the western coast of North Africa. His self-exile came after the Portuguese government removed his name from a list of nominees for the European Literary Prize. The government believed that his nominated work *The Gospel According to Jesus Christ* was divisive and was offensive to the majority of Portuguese citizens.

Undeterred by the opposition and criticism, Saramago continued to publicly express his views. In 2002, in response to what he believed were immoral Israeli actions in Palestine and Lebanon, he wrote in *El País* (a Spanish newspaper) that the radical Judaism of Israel created an attitude that allowed the brutal suppression of the Palestinians. In addition, during the 2006 Lebanon War, he signed a statement declaring the actions of Israel to be a war of genocide against the Palestinian Nation. In response, the Anti-Defamation League, a Jewish civil-rights group based in the United States, said his remarks were anti-Semitic.

Saramago's play *In Nomine Dei* was published at the beginning of 1993, and in the same year, he started writing a series of diaries. Five volumes have been published as *Cadernos de Lanzarote: Diário* (1994-1998).

ANALYSIS

José Saramago's works are often fantastic and surreal. His readers, and his characters, are forced to confront the basis for the existence of humanity; that is, what it is to be human in ever-changing modern civilizations. His characters struggle to find meaning at precisely the moment of greatest change in their respective social settings. His protagonists must not only justify their interpersonal relationships but also renew and redevelop their individuality, often outside previously understood religious, economic, and political structures. Saramago's use of fantasy settings and situations form, many have argued, a new style of writing that combines the regional Magical Realism (the use of fantastic deeds and settings as commonplace) of Latin America with the global outlook of Europe.

Saramago's style, especially in the novels published after 1986, forms a uniquely individual experiment in writing. His novels often display lengthy sentences—lengthy even for Hispanic literature, which is known for its verbosity. His baroque descriptions of the most minor settings and events often continue for pages and pages. He does not use colons, semicolons, hyphens, or quotation marks in his writing, a style that can confuse the reader as he or she attempts to determine who is speaking (including the narrator). Quotations are difficult to distinguish from the narrative; in marking a quotation, Saramago uses a limited number of commas and capitalizes the first word of a new speaker. Although this style can be frustrating, it forces the reader to pay close attention to who is speaking at any given moment. Oftentimes, Saramago eliminates the use of proper nouns and instead refers to characters with vague descriptive terms, such as "the doctor's wife." This inexactness of terminology reflects one of the author's major themes: the recurring mystery of human impermanence.

THE STONE RAFT

The Stone Raft addresses Portugal's national identity and its political, cultural, and social destiny. In an almost magical turn of events, a postcolonial Iberian society must confront its open-ended future. *The Stone Raft* is an ethnographic tale that explores modern strategies for survival within a previously isolated population. It is not by coincidence that the work was published the same year that Portugal joined the European Union. Portugal had been Europe's last surviving colonial empire, a nation that had only recently begun its voyage of self-acceptance as one of Europe's most enterprising and progressive member-nations.

Like all of Saramago's fictional works, the novel evolves like a present-day fable. The story begins with an event that marks the end of a fundamental concept of accepted reality. In this case, the entire Iberian Peninsula breaks from the European continent and starts drifting in the Atlantic, first toward the Azores and then toward some unknown destination (and destiny) between Europe and the United States. The story follows five characters who represent the entire population of the strange "stone raft."

Unlike many of his later works, Saramago chooses to use specific names for his characters in *The Stone Raft.*

Perhaps representative of the evolution of the populace, one of the characters, a dog, has a name that changes throughout the Atlantic adventure. The dog starts as Pilot, later becomes Faithful, and ultimately is named Constant. The newly formed group of pilgrims, united by their search for answers, roam seemingly without purpose from Lisbon to Galicia. As with other Saramago novels, the focus of *The Stone Raft* is on how humans survive in unknown circumstances.

The pilgrims are ordinary people in extraordinary circumstances. Saramago does not conduct a useless search for cause and blame; instead, he focuses on what occurs with human renewal and adaptation: love and companionship, the ability to find love in the strangest of times, and the timeless determination of humans in situations that seem impossible. Saramago shows his readers that everyone must eventually learn to start anew. This collective renewal is symbolized in the novel by the pregnancies of almost all of the women on the floating landmass.

Drifting west at eighteen kilometers per day, the populace slowly begins to accept that the impossible has occurred and that they must prepare for a future that none could have imagined. The society abruptly faces new geopolitical realities, as it soon becomes obvious that the floating landmass will probably hit the Azores. The populations of Lisbon, Coimbra, Oporto, and other coastal cities are abandoned for inland areas. The collision with the Azores is avoided, however, and the floating landmass, the entire Iberian Peninsula, comes to rest somewhere in the South Atlantic between the United States and South America. Furthermore, it soon becomes clear that the United States and Canada are more interested in the economic and political effects of the newly located Iberian Peninsula than in what the consequences will be for the new nation and its people.

Saramago's approach to narration in this work is somewhat complicated, but effective. The reader is presented with single speaking characters *and* with dual narrators. One narrator speaks in an omnipresent voice, as if to explain the meanderings of the protagonists and the drifting landmass. Another, perhaps the writer himself, speaks directly to the reader, as if to justify the style of the work itself. The characters question themselves and the strange series of events, while the narrators question the values of the changes and of the work itself. In spite of the doubt, the "semimagical" tale proceeds forward into an unknown future. As the end of the work states, the journey continues.

The Gospel According to Jesus Christ

In this controversial novel, Saramago brings the reader into a time and space that is located within the Christian world, but not a part of a commonly recognized Christianity. The novel explores themes found in the New Testament, such as pain, suffering, guilt, and the struggle for justice and forgiveness, but does so in a manner that goes far beyond the dogma associated with the Gospels of Jesus Christ. The tone of the work is light, even humorous at times. As with other Saramago novels, Magical Realism is employed throughout the work. The sparse descriptions of the events and characters from the Bible are replaced with detailed and fantastical portrayals. For example, in place of the standard concept of an angel as an enlightened and magical entity, the reader finds humanlike figures acting out the miraculous deeds assigned to them. Mary, the mother of Jesus, is informed of her pregnancy in a magical manner, but the angel appears in the form of a common beggar.

The novel describes the life of Jesus, Mary, and Joseph. In an interesting reinterpretation of biblical accounts, Saramago describes a relationship between Joseph and Jesus that is much closer than that between Mary and Joseph. After the birth of his son, Joseph finds out about the plan by King Herod to kill every child over the age of two years in Bethlehem. Joseph hides his son Jesus in a remote part of a cave, thereby preventing his death. However, Joseph later repents, and his life is filled with guilt. Eventually, in an effort to justify his guilt, Joseph gives his own life to save another. His son Jesus would later meet the same fate. Before his death, however, Jesus confronts his other father, God, and engages in a heated debate about the right of God to demand so much of humanity to gain recognition. He decides to rebel against God's plan for him, but in the end, he is deceived and is crucified.

Several predominant themes, or fundamental doubts and questions, arise from the text. The first is the presence of guilt in Joseph's life. Why did he not warn the other families of the impending slaughter of the young children in Bethlehem? Joseph's inaction displays the theme of limited skepticism, and the consequence of his inaction is used to raise questions about the very nature of a god that justifies his cruelty, hunger for power, and anger to get his way. Other controversial themes in the novel include the mutually beneficial relationship between God and the devil, and the plan by God to use humans as slaves to achieve his goal of a single global religion.

Blindness

The setting for the novel *Blindness* is an unnamed city, where people suddenly start to go blind. The illness is contagious, and as it advances, the city's social fabric degenerates and unravels rapidly. Initially, the blind are rounded up, put in a sanatorium, and left to exist there by whatever means possible. The government then attempts to control the sanatorium and its population by using increasingly repressive and unsuccessful measures. Gangs form within the sanatorium and, eventually, all order collapses. At this time, a doctor and his wife start a group that slowly entices the population to construct a new society, with a new form of existence. Once human-centered harmony is restored, people regain their eyesight.

Saramago's long sentences and limited separation of quotes is present in this work as well. Indeed, here it is most effective, as it requires the reader to navigate speech without the usual visual cues. Paragraphs are extensive and punctuation is sparse. Names are not given. Irony is employed throughout the work. For example, the sanatorium doctor is an eye doctor. The doctor's wife is the only one who can see, but she must hide this fact in order to be persuasive to the others.

The theme of blindness in this novel is used as a means to explore the fragility of human societies. Blindness here mimics how one limited problem in a civilization can lead to a complete breakdown of social systems. The reader becomes a spectator to the negative consequences of "blind" ambitions for power. In the end, however, one of Saramago's literary traits comes into play: The new situation brings about a search for new ways of implementing the dignity of the human race. When forced to rely only upon each other, humans can and do reach out.

Paul Siegrist

OTHER MAJOR WORKS

SHORT FICTION: *Objecto quase*, 1977.

PLAYS: *A noite*, pb. 1979; *Que farei com este livro?*, pb. 1980; *A segunda vida de Francisco de Assis*, pb. 1987; *In nomine Dei*, pb. 1993.

POETRY: *Os poemas possíveis*, 1966; *Provàvelmente alegria*, 1970; *O ano de 1993*, 1975.

NONFICTION: *Deste mundo e do outro*, 1971; *A bagagem do viajante*, 1973; *As opiniões que o DL teve*, 1974; *Os apontamentos*, 1976; *Viagem a Portugal*, 1981 (*Journey to Portugal*, 2000); *Cadernos de Lanzarote: Diário*, 1994-1998 (diaries; 5 volumes); *Discursos de Estocolmo*, 1999; *Folhas politicas, 1976-1998*, 1999; *Candida Höfer: In Portugal*, 2007 (art exhibition catalog; with Shelley Rice).

BIBLIOGRAPHY

Askin, Denise Theresa, and Teresa Méndez-Faith, eds. *On the Eve of a New Millennium: Belief and Unbelief as Expressed in Literature, Philosophy, Theology, and the Visual Arts.* Manchester, N.H.: Saint Anselm College Press, 1999. Selected papers of a regional meeting of the Conference on Christianity and Literature. An interesting viewpoint that incorporates ideas about Saramago's controversial view of God and religion. Includes a short, but well-written chapter on *The Gospel According to Jesus Christ.* Also includes a bibliography.

Bloom, Harold. *José Saramago.* Philadelphia: Chelsea House, 2005. An extensive critical work on Saramago. Bloom finds Saramago to be one of the best living authors. Well written and informative. Includes a bibliography.

Frier, David Gibson. *The Novels of José Saramago: Echoes from the Past, Pathways into the Future.* Cardiff: University of Wales Press, 2007. Good critical analysis of Saramago's novels. Uses a European-based perspective of place and time. Includes a bibliography.

Hart, Stephen M., and Wen-chin Ouyang, eds. *A Companion to Magical Realism.* Rochester, N.Y.: Tamesis, 2005. A good source for an international perspective on Magical Realism, with a chapter devoted to the unique style employed by Saramago. Includes an extensive bibliography.

WILLIAM SAROYAN

Born: Fresno, California; August 31, 1908
Died: Fresno, California; May 18, 1981
Also known as: William Stonehill Saroyan

PRINCIPAL LONG FICTION

My Name Is Aram, 1940
The Human Comedy, 1943
The Adventures of Wesley Jackson, 1946
Rock Wagram, 1951
Tracy's Tiger, 1951
The Laughing Matter, 1953 (reprinted as *The Secret Story*, 1954)
Mama I Love You, 1956
Papa You're Crazy, 1957
Boys and Girls Together, 1963
One Day in the Afternoon of the World, 1964

OTHER LITERARY FORMS

Despite his many novels, William Saroyan (suh-ROY-ehn) is more famous for his work in the short story, the drama, and autobiography. Each of these areas received emphasis at different stages in his career. In the 1930's, he made a spectacular literary debut with an avalanche of brilliant, exuberant, and unorthodox short stories. Major early collections were *The Daring Young Man on the Flying Trapeze, and Other Stories* (1934), *Inhale and Exhale* (1936), *Three Times Three* (1936), and *Love, Here Is My Hat, and Other Short Romances* (1938). *My Name Is Aram*, a group of stories detailing the experiences of Aram Garoghlanian growing up in a small California town, marks the culmination of his short-story artistry.

Most of Saroyan's plays and his productions on Broadway were concentrated in the years between 1939 and 1942. *My Heart's in the Highlands* was produced by the Group Theatre in April, 1939. His second major production, *The Time of Your Life* (pr., pb. 1939), was awarded both the Pulitzer Prize and the New York Drama Critics' Circle Award and is still considered Saroyan's best play. *Hello Out There* (pr. 1941), a one-act play, is also regarded as a fine drama.

In 1951, Saroyan and Ross Bagdasarian published a popular song, "Come On-a My House." Saroyan also wrote several television plays, including an adaptation of *The Time of Your Life*. Starting with *The Bicycle Rider in Beverly Hills* (1952), Saroyan composed extensive memoirs, including *Here Comes, There Goes, You Know Who* (1961), *Not Dying* (1963), *Days of Life and Death and Escape to the Moon* (1970), *Places Where I've Done Time* (1972), *Sons Come and Go, Mothers Hang in Forever* (1976), *Chance Meetings* (1978), and *Obituaries* (1979).

ACHIEVEMENTS

By the age of twenty, William Saroyan had already decided his role in life was to be that of a professional writer, and throughout his remaining fifty years he dedicated himself to that vocation, publishing voluminously in all literary forms, with the exception of poetry. The sheer bulk of his work and his admission that much of it was done merely to earn money have worked against him. Further, his frequent arguments with his critics and his increasingly difficult personality left him with few strong critical advocates.

Saroyan's lasting literary achievement is in the area of the short story, where he expanded the genre by linking narrative form to the essay and infusing his work with a highly individual vision of poetic intensity. Many of his stories feature a character modeled on Saroyan, a writer-persona who, though often obsessed with his own ideas and feelings, is vitally alive to the world of his immediate experience. Several of the most successful stories concern childhood experiences in an ethnic, small-town environment modeled on Saroyan's Fresno. Saroyan impressed his early readers with his rediscovery of the wondrous in the texture of ordinary American life. *The Saroyan Special: Selected Stories* (1948) is a collection of his best stories. *My Name Is Aram* delineates with

some beautiful character portraits Saroyan's sense of the poetic interplay of values in the ethnic community.

Saroyan's plays oppose the vitality of personality and individual dreams to the force of social institutions and the threats of war. In their sense of improvised movement, his plays were a deliberate challenge to the strictly plotted productions of the commercial theater.

Starting in the mid-1940's, Saroyan turned his attention to longer fiction, writing over the next two decades a series of novels concerned with marriage and divorce. Apparently inspired by his own experiences, the books become increasingly skeptical about romantic love and reflect Saroyan's growing cynicism about the man-woman relationship while retaining his fondness for the charm of childhood.

Saroyan's longer fiction grows gradually out of those short stories concerned with growing up in a small town. *My Name Is Aram*, a story collection moving toward novelistic unity, leads directly to *The Human Comedy*, where Saroyan finally succeeds in making a novel out of his childhood material. While *The Adventures of Wesley Jackson* must be regarded as a failed attempt to write in the picaresque mode, *Rock Wagram* is a surprisingly mature handling of the thematic scope provided by the novel form. Whereas *The Adventures of Wesley Jackson* presents marriage as an idyllic goal for the solitary man, *Rock Wagram* focuses on the crushing effect of the title character's failed marriage. Several shorter book-length works—Tracy's Tiger, Mama I Love You, and *Papa You're Crazy*—seem more tied to Saroyan's earlier material in their confinement to the perspectives of childhood and youth and, for the most part, are limited in theme and story situations.

Saroyan's other novels—*The Laughing Matter, Boys and Girls Together*, and *One Day in the Afternoon of the World*—are deliberate forays into social areas where relationships are often intense and events are somber in their finality. Like *Rock Wagram*, each of these books centers on a male's struggle with marriage, death, and divorce. The last novel, *One Day in the Afternoon of the World*, features a character who at last seems to have acquired the wisdom to deal with such personal crises. Though his longer fictions are professionally wrought, Saroyan's achievements in the novel form are limited.

The mood of the later novels is picked up and carried

to greater extremes in Saroyan's memoirs, a series whose loose formats encourage the author to reveal, often in free associations, his deep anxiety about his relationship to his society. Saroyan's memoirs, generally his weakest works, become increasingly preoccupied with death, the significance of his literary achievements, and with his struggle to ward off a bitterness that he occasionally admits but wants to deny.

BIOGRAPHY

So much of the work of William Stonehill Saroyan—especially his fiction—is drawn from the circumstances of his life that it has a biographical dimension. He was born in 1908, in Fresno, California, the city where he died on May 18, 1981. The child of Armenian immigrants, he faced his first hardship when, at his father's death in 1911, he was placed for four years in the Fred Finch orphanage in Oakland. During these years, his mother worked in San Francisco as a maid, finally gathering the money to move back to a house in Fresno with her four children. Here Saroyan lived from age seven to seventeen, learning Armenian, acquiring an irreverence for the town's chief social institutions—the church and the school—and working as a newspaper boy and as a telegraph messenger to help support the family.

At age fifteen, Saroyan left school permanently to work at his Uncle Aram's vineyards. In 1926, he left Fresno, first to go to Los Angeles, then, after a brief time in the National Guard, to move to San Francisco, where he tried a number of jobs, eventually becoming at age nineteen the manager of a Postal Telegraph branch office. In 1928, determined to make his fortune as a writer, he made his first trip to New York. He returned to San Francisco the following year, somewhat discouraged by his lack of success. In the early 1930's, however, he began to write story after story, culminating with his decision in January, 1934, to write one story a day for the whole month. That year, *Story* published "The Daring Young Man on the Flying Trapeze," and suddenly Saroyan stories were appearing in many of the top periodicals. His first book of stories was published that year, and the following year he had enough money to make an ethnic return, a trip to Soviet Armenia.

Except for a few months in 1936 spent working on motion pictures at the Paramount lot, Saroyan spent the majority of the 1930's in San Francisco. By 1939, he had shifted his activities to drama, writing and producing plays on Broadway. After *The Time of Your Life* won both the New York Drama Critics' Circle Award for the best play of 1939 to 1940 and the Pulitzer Prize, Saroyan made headlines by rejecting the Pulitzer on the grounds that he was opposed to prizes in the arts and to patronage. More controversy followed when he wrote *The Human Comedy* as a screenplay for Metro-Goldwyn-Mayer, then argued about directing the film and tried to buy his work back for twenty thousand dollars, more than he was paid for it. At that time he also was, in a letter to *The New York Times*, publicly denouncing the Broadway theater.

Even though he had pacificist sympathies, Saroyan was inducted into the U.S. Army in October, 1942, and

William Saroyan. (D.C. Public Library)

served until 1945. His most traumatic experience in the 1940's, however, was his marriage to Carol Marcus, which lasted from 1943 to 1949 and which was resumed briefly from 1951 to 1953, before a final divorce. The couple had two children, Aram and Lucy.

In the 1950's, Saroyan began to write more long fiction, much of it dealing with marital difficulties. In addition, in 1951, he was the coauthor of a hit song, "Come On-a My House," and in the late 1950's, he began writing television plays. From 1952 to 1959, he lived in a Malibu beach house, an environment that encouraged him to work very steadily. During this time, he lived a less public existence and, feeling monetary pressure because of his gambling and his huge income tax debt, he increasingly developed a reputation as a difficult personality.

In 1960, after some travel about the world, he settled in a modest apartment at 74 Rue Taitbout, Paris. The following year he was briefly a writer-in-residence at Purdue University in Indiana. By 1962, he had arranged to buy two adjacent houses in Fresno and thereafter alternated living between Fresno and Paris. He spent most of the last fifteen years of his life working on various volumes of memoirs. Five days before his death he called the Associated Press to give this statement: "Everybody has got to die, but I have always believed an exception would be made in my case. Now what?" After much success (much money earned by writing, much money lost by gambling), international travel, controversy, fame, and obscurity, Saroyan died of cancer in his hometown in 1981.

ANALYSIS

William Saroyan's work habits were a major determinant (for better or worse) of his unique literary effects. He regarded writing as work, something that required disciplined effort, but also as an activity whose chief characteristic was the free play of the mind. As he explained his practice, Saroyan would often give himself assignments, a story or a chapter a day (or so many hours of writing), but would seldom work from a detailed organizational plan. Uncomfortable with mulling over possible styles, attitudes, narrative directions, he would often prefer to plunge into writing, fueled by coffee and cigarettes, hoping that whatever got down on paper would in-

spire the story to "take off on its own." Whatever relationships would be worked out would be those of deep structure, drawn from his inner being rather than from rhetoric.

At times Saroyan would begin with a "theory" or abstract idea. (For example, the theory stated at the end of "War" is that hatred and ugliness exist in the heart of everyone.) The act of writing itself was to clarify and refine the idea for the writer. In "Myself upon the Earth," the writer's own situation, his dead father, and his attitudes toward the world begin to weave into the free connections that substitute for a conventional plot. Thematically, the apparently undisciplined becomes the true discipline as the dedication expressed in an attitude toward life—toward humanity—is transformed through the narration into a dedication to art.

There are obvious difficulties with this method of composition. "The Man with His Heart in the Highlands" begins in the course of its improvisation to split in two; when Saroyan puts it into the form of a full-length play, the theme of the importance of acceptance in forming the new American community is finally seen as a basic articulation in the material. Saroyan also acknowledged revision as an important stage in the writing process, but much of his work suffers from a lack of objectivity, the ability to see his own work clearly and revise it accordingly.

While the act of writing was for Saroyan both a kind of thinking and a performance, the materials of his art were usually the materials of his life. Much in the manner of Thomas Wolfe (an early influence), Saroyan's fiction was often drawn directly from his experience. A letter to Calouste Gulbenkian (in *Letters from 74 Rue Taitbout*, 1969) shows how Saroyan drew in detail on his external experience and his frame of mind for most of the content of "The Assyrian." Writing, he came to believe, was connected with "noticing" life and with the sense that life itself was theatrical. Although Saroyan acknowledged that the process of writing had to discover form in its materials and that the writer had to be transformed into a character framed by his art, the sense of witnessed scene and character in his best work lends a necessary solidity to his creative exuberance.

The favorite writer-personas in Saroyan's early fiction were poet-philosophers in the manner of Walt Whitman, American wise guys (the young grown suddenly smarter about the ways of the world than their elders), or combinations of the two. His later long fiction featured the writer as a veteran of life, sometimes bitter but with his own philosophical resignation, a mode of stoic humility about what he might be able to accomplish. Saroyan's typical themes—the advocacy of love and a condemnation of war and violence—are less important than the way in which he plays the narrator (usually a writer) against the narrator's circumstances. In the most deep-seated manifestation of this paradigm—the ethnic boy responding to his American environment—Saroyan associates the ethnic self in the ethnic community with naturalness, lack of self-consciousness, true being, and dignity of person. The American environment, while it promises opportunity with its training and its competitive games, also has institutions that seem to specialize in modes of restriction, punishment, and prejudice.

The ethnic boy responds to his environment with a complex involvement and detachment. On one hand, he is willing, even eager, to be assimilated; on the other hand, however, he is always aware of a kind of existence that has no adequately defined relationship to the American world of conventional social fact. The ethnic's psychological relationship to the world recalls Whitman's democratic paradox of people being intensely individual and at the same time like everyone else. In Saroyan's fiction, there is at times an emphasis on the individual's alienation—as when the protagonist in "The Daring Young Man on the Flying Trapeze" feels "somehow he had ventured upon the wrong earth" and the central character in "1,2,3,4,5,6,7,8" feels the room he is living in is not a part of him and wants a home, "a place in which to return to himself." Invariably, however, the ethnic family and its small-town environment expand quite naturally for Saroyan into a version of the democratic family of people.

This sense of communal home, however, is not easily preserved—as Saroyan's novels with their marital catastrophes and lonely protagonists repeatedly demonstrate. From the beginning, the fate of Saroyan's ethnicity was complicated by the fact that his deepest allegiance was to a national community that no longer existed. In an early story, "Seventy Thousand Assyrians," the Assyrian states, "I was born in the old country, but I want to get

over it . . . everything is washed up over there." Though Saroyan could be sympathetic to such practicality, he tried to achieve, often with a deliberate naïveté, a poetic point of view that would embrace both existence in the old community of family values (which was a basic part of his being) and existence in the practical new world (which offered the only opportunity for becoming).

From the perspective of Saroyan's writer-persona, the world outside is continually new, funny, sometimes strange, often wonderful, a place of innocent relationships and suspended judgments. A recurring situation in his work has someone who is apprehended for theft trying to explain that he is not guilty because his value system is different from that of his accusers. On one hand, Saroyan believes in an attitude of joyful acceptance: Here he sees man "on the threshold of an order of himself which must find human reality a very simple unavoidable majesty and joy, with all its complications and failures." On the other hand, he imagines, like Whitman, a more somber mystic vision based on "the joyous sameness of life and death." In this mysterious crucible, life is fate, perhaps only glimpsed fully when "drawing to the edge of full death every person is restored to innocence—to have lived was not his fault." Saroyan's basic impulse is to preserve, recapture, and restore the innocence that the world has lost that state of being that sees experience only as a fantastic fate that serves ultimately to redeem the primal self.

MY NAME IS ARAM

Like Sherwood Anderson's *Winesburg, Ohio* (1919) and William Faulkner's *The Unvanquished* (1938), *My Name Is Aram* is a book that falls midway between short-story collection and novel. The stories are separate and distinct, but they all concern the small-town experiences of the same boy, Aram, with his Armenian relatives. There is little sense of sequence but rather an accumulated manifestation of the potential wisdom in this world. Saroyan emphasizes the preservation of innocence, the warding off of the absolute element in the values of the adult culture. Aram and his friends turn social rituals into human games, and in the course of their experiences demonstrate that the many social failures in these stories have really two constituents, the innocent immediacy of the experience (its essential value) and the cultural "truths" and judgments applied to it. Through vital participation in their world, Aram and his friends begin to negotiate its preconceived ideas.

THE HUMAN COMEDY

The setting, the characters, and the young man's perspective that predominate in *The Human Comedy* all have their sources in Saroyan short stories. The background is World War II, and the California small town has accordingly become "the home front." In the book's basic drama, the innocence in this environment—its vulnerable children, young people, and women and its emotional closeness—must come to terms with death and its finalities.

Within the context of the small-town milieu, the novel focuses primarily on the Macauley family and most often on Homer Macauley, a fourteen-year-old telegraph messenger boy. As Homer delivers telegrams announcing the deaths of soldiers, he finds himself getting caught up psychologically in the shock of the family reactions. On his first such delivery, to Rosa Sandoval, the woman responds with an eerie, calm hysteria in which she confuses Homer with her dead son and begins to think of both as little boys. Feeling at first both compassion and an urge to flee, Homer gradually arrives at an awareness of the meaning of death. With the help of his mother (whose husband has recently died), he fights through feelings of loneliness and isolation toward the idea that death and change afford perspectives for redeeming the values of innocence, love, and life itself.

The ideal of the community dominates the book. The novel implies in its moments of crisis and healing—Homer becoming briefly transformed into the son of another woman; Tobey taking the place of the dead Marcus in the Macauley family—that humankind is a single family. Though the fact of death and the awareness of death are constant threats to the individual, the book, as the allusions to Homer's *Odyssey* (c. 725 B.C.E.; English translation, 1614) imply, is about to return home, the coming back from the ugly realities of the outside world to the love and security that humankind can provide.

The book seems intent on assuring its readers that despite economic tribulations, the discontent of restless desire, the anxiety connected with competition, and the confining tendency of its institutions, the community is an active, positive force. A working out in the rhythms of experience of the differences between people—age, sex, degrees of formality—invariably shows positive contrasts. The many relationships Homer has with older people are all thematically active ingredients for dramatizing the closeness of the community. *The Human Comedy* insists—perhaps too facilely at times—on the capacity of the American community to regulate the experience of life and the encounter with death.

THE ADVENTURES OF WESLEY JACKSON

The Adventures of Wesley Jackson may be Saroyan's worst novel. It is marred by two closely related problems, an uncertain grasp of form and a confusion about its issues. Saroyan's indiscriminate use of his own military experience takes the novel hopelessly out of control. Evidently attempting to give himself ample latitude with the novel form, Saroyan chose to employ the picaresque form, referring in his comments on the novel to Mark Twain's *Adventures of Huckleberry Finn* (1884). Unfortunately, Wesley is much too introverted to be an effective picaro of any kind. He is intended to be a nonconformist, but, except for a few anti-Army establishment opinions, his personal idealism and prosaic earnestness only serve to make him seem as remote from the realities of Army life as from the realities of war. Lacking a feeling for the actual operations of the Army, the book meanders haphazardly from the bureaucratic to the personal, from one location to another, from family concerns to writing ambitions, succeeding finally in giving the impression of an Army journal rather than a picaresque novel.

At times the book develops an antiwar theme; at times the theme seems to be the pettiness of the Army bureaucracy. No one theme, however, is developed consistently. Wesley's self-absorbed narration does provide some shaping by turning the officers into bad fathers (cruel figures of authority), the women into sympathetic (though vague) images, and his fellow soldiers into boys, sometimes naughty but basically innocent. In sporadic, almost desultory, fashion the first part of the book features Wesley's search for his father, the essentially good man who has been displaced and ignored by organized society. The last part of the book becomes concerned with Wesley's search for a son (actually a search for a woman to bear him a son). Were Wesley's narration less limited, less egotistical, these thematic threads might have made firmer connections.

ROCK WAGRAM

The split structure of *Rock Wagram*—approximately half the novel taking place in September, 1942, and half in February, 1950—emphasizes the drive of Rock Wagram (pronounced vah-GRAM) to be married to Ann Ford and his resultant puzzled desperation when that marriage fails. The chronological gap, by omitting the marriage and Rock's military experience, accents the negative quality of this part of his life. Yet by leaving out the specific difficulties that are so much a part of his later depression, the novel makes Rock's psychology a problematic frame for understanding events instead of using the events of the past to put his psychology in an understandable perspective. At times, the failure of the marriage seems explained by Ann's frivolous, lying character. At other times, the failure seems to grow out of Rock's ethnic assumption that people must become involved in a family existence.

Rock Wagram explores the tensions between people as individuals and people as social animals. In his motion-picture career, Rock has become successful as an individual star, but his acquaintance with Ann Ford kindles his memories of certain values from his Armenian background, particularly the notion that a man is not complete until he had founded his own family, been husband to his wife, father to his children. Unhappily for him, Ann turns out to be like so many other characters whose departures from their true natures disturb him; her lies signify to him that she is refusing to be herself, hoping for something better. Earlier Rock has met a series of males rebelling against their heritage: Paul Key, the Hollywood producer who hates being a Jew; Sam Schwartz, Paul's nephew, who devotes himself to becoming the image of success; and Craig Adams, the completely assimilated Armenian. Although these men are denying both their heritage and their own individuality, they are better adapted to the world of casual social relationships than he, and the book raises doubts about the possibilities of a deeply authentic existence.

Rock chooses to see his life—and the life of humans—as involving continual adjustment to a Shavian life force, a power that, once he begins to perceive it through his Armenian ethnic environment, becomes his ultimate guide to true being. To get in tune with this force, he tries to be uninhibited in his social relationships, to go with the flow of events, to pay attention to his circumstances and to the people he is with, and to be, as he puts it, "a good witness" to his own experience and to his world.

Part of Rock's effort to live in terms of true being is a half-conscious cultivation of strategies toward death. His reaction to the death of his brother Haig is rage; at the death of his friend Paul Key, he affects a Hemingway-esque stoicism; and to his mother's death, he responds by plunging deeply and intensely into his subjective nature. In spite of all attempts to come to terms with the reality of death, he seems at last depressed, left with a sense of being part not only of a dying culture but also of a dying world. As he goes back to acting at the end of the narrative, his feeling for his art is one of obligation rather than enthusiasm for an individualized expression of himself. Yet, as the humor in his last statement indicates, he is finally not without hope in probing his lonely situation for its satisfactions.

THE LAUGHING MATTER

The laughter of *The Laughing Matter* is that of black comedy. From the time Swan Nazarenus announces to her husband that she is pregnant with another man's child, *The Laughing Matter* moves powerfully but erratically toward what seems an almost self-indulgently gruesome ending. The story line is captive to the emotional tensions and explosions of Evan Nazarenus as he attempts to sort out a future direction for himself, Swan, and their two children, Red and Eva. As he resorts successively to drink, violence, a return to family harmony, an abortion, and more violence, the problem-pregnancy tends to be obscured by his confusing attempts at solution. Since his personality is never clarified in the characterization, and since he often gives the impression of running aimlessly about the countryside, Evan becomes progressively less sympathetic in his shifting relationship to people and events.

The accompaniment to the mad rhapsody of his behavior is more carefully controlled. The children are innocent victims, becoming increasingly aware that something is wrong and even acting out some of the tensions themselves. The Walzes, a neighbor couple, have their own fights, and Evan's brother, Dade, who has, after years of domestic turbulence, lost his family entirely, conveniently defines one possible outcome.

Complicating the question of what to do is the issue of who is to blame. In one scene between Evan and Dade, the two brothers—who often speak in an old-country tongue—review their ethnic fate as heads of families, Evan wondering what they as males have done wrong. Evan debates whether he ought to be more feminine, more kindly, or strive to retain his masculine pride in the face of what may be an essential challenge to his person. His solution, the abortion, is less an act of harsh morality (as he later views it) than the result of a desire to begin again, to regain a kind of innocence by reversing events.

The ironies and the deaths pile up so rapidly at the conclusion that they achieve only a blurred effect. The fact that so much violence results from simple ignorance begins to make the characters comic rather than tragic, and this may have been the prompting behind Saroyan's title. When Evan accuses the wrong man as the adulterer (pushing the poor lonely man toward suicide), and when he shoots and kills his brother Dade under the mistaken notion that they have been responsible for Swan's death from abortion, Evan seems more the incompetent than the grief-stricken victim. His own death in an auto accident may have been meant to suggest that the whole chain of events was merely a series of accidents, but this must be weighed against the remarks of the doctor who explains to Dade that Swan committed suicide and that she had evidently had a strong death wish for several years. For all its masculine madness, this book begins and ends by pointing an accusing finger at the woman.

BOYS AND GIRLS TOGETHER

Boys and Girls Together is a realistic study of a husband-wife relationship that moves with an understated satire toward black humor. The husband, Dick, is a writer who finds that his current domestic relationship has made it impossible for him to work, thus heaping financial strain upon his already turbulent marriage to Daisy. In the course of their sporadic fighting, the couple discovers greater and greater depths of incompatibility. Dick comes to the conclusion that she is ignorant, trivial, and selfish; Daisy accuses him of being egotistical and immature. Were it not for the two children (Johnny, age five, and Rosey, age two and a half), the writer, who is a family man, would undoubtedly leave.

As this account of a few days in their lives demonstrates, what keeps the marriage together is their social-

izing with other couples. The slight story line follows the meeting of Dick and Daisy with two other couples for a few days of fun in San Francisco. Though only casual friends, all the couples have common characteristics: In each instance, the husband has achieved prominence in the arts; in each case, the husband is many years older than the wife; and in each instance, the difference in age seems part of the strain on the marriage. Before all six can get together, the oldest husband, Leander, dies of a heart attack, an episode witnessed by Oscar Bard (the actor) and his wife, and by Leander's wife Lucretia. Dick and Daisy arrive soon after the attack and seem generally ineffective in preventing the scene from sliding from seriousness to farce. Dick eventually begins to act as satiric observer, commenting on Oscar's egotistical discomfort and on Lucretia's performance as grieving widow.

The scene has its climax in Oscar's long speech on the difficulties of their kind of marriage. While he begins by pointing out realistically that the women they have married are not for them, he finally comes to the conclusion that it is sexual attraction that gives the necessary life to all partners in such marriages and that makes them continue to put up with each other. Dick does not disagree. Soon the survivors are planning a trip to Reno as another distraction from the harsh realities around them. Earlier, Dick had resented it when his wife teased him about being a fool for sex. In the last part of the novel, his understated satiric vision outlines them all as characters in a sexual farce.

If all of Saroyan's writing can be regarded as his attempt to understand and define his position in the world, his long fiction must be seen as his deliberate recognition of the crueler circumstances in that world—death, the failure of love, divorce, the recalcitrant details of life itself. His own marital troubles undoubtedly inspired the novels of the 1950's and 1960's with their fragmented families, and while the intently masculine perspective in these books reveals a serious but virtually unexamined reverence for love and marriage, it also demonstrates the author's own very personal irritation with wives.

In nearly all of Saroyan's novels, the formal problem tends to be the male protagonist's varied reactions to his situation. In *Rock Wagram* and *The Laughing Matter*, Saroyan is successful in focusing these reactions by means of intense emotional pressures, but his confusion about final blame for the marital breakdown makes a fictional closure difficult. With *Papa You're Crazy* and *Mama I Love You*, he moves to the detachment of the child's point of view but is still uncertain about the extent to which the world's facts ought to—and must—impinge on the individual family member. (To what degree, for example, does the particular existence of the parent doom or mold the life of the child?) In *Boys and Girls Together* and *One Day in the Afternoon of the World*, Saroyan gets mixed results from mining the attitudes of his male protagonists for a perspective that would be both a consistent and legitimate interpretation of their marital situations. In Saroyan's long fiction, as well as in his other writing, both his strengths and his weaknesses derive from his insistent emotional presence.

Walter Shear

OTHER MAJOR WORKS

SHORT FICTION: *The Daring Young Man on the Flying Trapeze, and Other Stories*, 1934; *Inhale and Exhale*, 1936; *Three Times Three*, 1936; *The Gay and Melancholy Flux: Short Stories*, 1937; *Little Children*, 1937; *Love, Here Is My Hat, and Other Short Romances*, 1938; *The Trouble with Tigers*, 1938; *Peace, It's Wonderful*, 1939; *Three Fragments and a Story*, 1939; *The Insurance Salesman, and Other Stories*, 1941; *Saroyan's Fables*, 1941; *Forty-eight Saroyan Stories*, 1942; *Dear Baby*, 1944; *Some Day I'll Be a Millionaire: Thirty-four More Great Stories*, 1944; *The Saroyan Special: Selected Stories*, 1948; *The Fiscal Hoboes*, 1949; *The Assyrian, and Other Stories*, 1950; *The Whole Voyald, and Other Stories*, 1956; *William Saroyan Reader*, 1958; *Love*, 1959; *After Thirty Years: The Daring Young Man on the Flying Trapeze*, 1964; *Best Stories of William Saroyan*, 1964; *The Tooth and My Father*, 1974; *The Man with the Heart in the Highlands, and Other Early Stories*, 1989.

PLAYS: *The Hungerers: A Short Play*, pb. 1939; *My Heart's in the Highlands*, pr., pb. 1939; *The Time of Your Life*, pr., pb. 1939; *The Beautiful People*, pr. 1940; *The Great American Goof*, pr. 1940; *Love's Old Sweet Song*, pr., pb. 1940; *The Ping-Pong Game*, pb. 1940 (one act); *Subway Circus*, pb. 1940; *Three Plays: My Heart's in the Highlands, The Time of Your Life, Love's Old Sweet Song*, 1940; *Across the Board on Tomorrow Morning*, pr., pb. 1941; *Hello Out There*, pr. 1941 (one act); *Jim Dandy*, pr., pb. 1941; *Three Plays: The Beautiful People, Sweeney in the Trees, Across the Board on Tomorrow Morning*, 1941; *Razzle Dazzle*, 1942 (collection); *Talking to You*, pr., pb. 1942; *Get Away Old Man*, pr. 1943; *Sam Ego's House*, pr. 1947; *A Decent Birth, a Happy Funeral*, pb. 1949; *Don't Go Away Mad*, pr., pb. 1949; *The Slaughter of the Innocents*, pb. 1952; *The Cave Dwellers*, pr. 1957; *Once Around the Block*, pb. 1959; *Sam the Highest Jumper of Them All: Or, The London Comedy*, pr. 1960; *Settled Out of Court*, pr. 1960; *The Dogs: Or, The Paris Comedy, and Two Other Plays*, 1969; *An Armenian Trilogy*, 1986 (includes *Armenians, Bitlis*, and *Haratch*); *Warsaw Visitor and Tales from the Vienna Streets: The Last Two Plays of William Saroyan*, 1991.

SCREENPLAY: *The Human Comedy*, 1943.

NONFICTION: *Harlem as Seen by Hirschfield*, 1941; *Hilltop Russians in San Francisco*, 1941; *Why Abstract?*, 1945 (with Henry Miller and Hilaire Hiler); *The Twin Adventures: The Adventures of William Saroyan*, 1950; *The Bicycle Rider in Beverly Hills*, 1952; *Here Comes, There Goes, You Know Who*, 1961; *A Note on Hilaire Hiler*, 1962; *Not Dying*, 1963; *Short Drive, Sweet Chariot*, 1966; *Look at Us*, 1967; *I Used to Believe I Had Forever: Now I'm Not So Sure*, 1968; *Letters from 74 Rue Taitbout*, 1969; *Days of Life and Death and Escape to the Moon*, 1970; *Places Where I've Done Time*, 1972; *Sons Come and Go, Mothers Hang in Forever*, 1976; *Chance Meetings*, 1978; *Obituaries*, 1979; *Births*, 1983.

CHILDREN'S LITERATURE: *Me*, 1963; *The Circus*, 1986; *Horsey Gorsey and the Frog*, 1968.

MISCELLANEOUS: *My Name Is Saroyan*, 1983 (stories, verse, play fragments, and memoirs); *The New Saroyan Reader*, 1984 (Brian Darwent, editor).

BIBLIOGRAPHY

Balakian, Nona. *The World of William Saroyan*. Lewisburg, Pa.: Bucknell University Press, 1998. Balakian, formerly a staff writer for *The New York Times Book Review*, knew Saroyan personally in his last years, and her observations of him color her assessment of his later works. She viewed it as her mission to resurrect his reputation and restore him to his place among the finest of twentieth century American writers. Her book traces Saroyan's evolution from ethnic writer to master of the short story, to playwright, and finally to existentialist.

Floan, Howard R. *William Saroyan*. New York: Twayne, 1966. Floan's study remains one of the best extensive critical monographs on Saroyan's work. It focuses on Saroyan's early literature, glossing over the post-World War II period as less productive and durable. Contains a valuable annotated bibliography through 1964.

Foster, Edward Halsey. *William Saroyan*. Boise, Idaho: Boise State University Press, 1984. A condensed but helpful survey stressing Saroyan's unique voice. This work draws parallels between his work and that of the Beat generation. Includes bibliography.

Haslam, Gerald W. "William Saroyan." In *A Literary History of the American West*, edited by Thomas J. Lyon et al. Fort Worth: Texas Christian University Press, 1987. A good introduction to Saroyan's life and work. Haslam focuses on the writer's post-World War II decline in popularity and its cause. Includes a select bibliography.

_____. "William Saroyan and San Francisco: Emergence of a Genius (Self-Proclaimed)." In *San Fran-cisco in Fiction: Essays in a Regional Literature*, edited by David Fine and Paul Skenazy. Albuquerque: University of New Mexico Press, 1995. Haslam's discussion of the influence of San Francisco on Saroyan's work is included in this collection of essays that examine the relationship between the "real" city and its fictional depiction.

Keyishian, Harry, ed. *Critical Essays on William Saroyan*. New York: G. K. Hall, 1995. A collection of essays on Saroyan, from early reviews to critical articles. Some of the essays discuss Saroyan in California, the writer and his critics, and Saroyan's study of ethnicity.

Lee, Lawrence, and Barry Gifford. *Saroyan: A Biography*. New York: Harper & Row, 1984. Lee and Gifford's study is rich with anecdotes and segments of interviews with Saroyan's family, friends, and associates. Supplemented by a chronology and a bibliography.

Leggett, John. *A Daring Young Man*: *A Biography of William Saroyan*. New York: Alfred A. Knopf, 2002. Leggett relies heavily on Saroyan's journals to produce a sustained look at the author that is neither admiring nor forgiving. Includes a bibliography and an index.

NATHALIE SARRAUTE

Born: Ivanovo Voznesensk (now Ivanovo), Russia; July 18, 1900
Died: Paris, France; October 19, 1999
Also known as: Nathalie Ilyanova Tcherniak

PRINCIPAL LONG FICTION

Portrait d'un inconnu, 1948 (*Portrait of a Man Unknown*, 1958)
Martereau, 1953 (English translation, 1959)
Le Planétarium, 1959 (*The Planetarium*, 1960)
Les Fruits d'or, 1963 (*The Golden Fruits*, 1964)
Entre la vie et la mort, 1968 (*Between Life and Death*, 1969)
Vous les entendez?, 1972 (*Do You Hear Them?*, 1973)
"Disent les imbéciles," 1976 (*"Fools Say,"* 1977)
Tu ne t'aimes pas, 1989 (*You Don't Love Yourself*, 1990)
Ici, 1995 (*Here*, 1997)

OTHER LITERARY FORMS

In 1932, Nathalie Sarraute (sah-ROHT) began to write the short texts that make up *Tropismes* (1939, 1957; *Tropisms*, 1963). These short fictions cannot be called short stories because they have neither the plots nor the characters traditionally associated with the genre. The texts provide, rather, glimpses into the inner psychological workings of anonymous beings designated only by pronouns. This book is the basis of all of Sarraute's later creations; it is interesting to note that she returned to this form (a collection of short fictions) in *L'Usage de la parole* (1980; *The Use of Speech*, 1980). While she was developing her novelistic techniques, Sarraute began to write critical essays on the evolution of the novel form. These essays were published in a collection titled *L'Ère du soupçon* (1956; *The Age of Suspicion*, 1963). Sarraute turned to dramatic literature in 1963 when she was commissioned by a German network to write radio plays. Her first two plays, *Le Silence* (1964; *Silence*, 1981) and *Le Mensonge* (1966; *The Lie*, 1981), were originally presented on the radio; they were subsequently staged by Jean-Louis Barrault. Sarraute regularly wrote a play after each novel she published; for her, writing plays seemed to be a form of "relaxation." She published a collection of five plays in 1978.

ACHIEVEMENTS

The publication of Sarraute's *Tropisms* in 1939 went unnoticed by the general public, with only a single critical review, yet the movement that Sarraute was unaware of starting became the "New Novel" movement of the late 1950's. When *Tropisms* was republished by Minuit in 1957, it was read in the light of the critical theories expressed in *The Age of Suspicion*, which was actually written after *Tropisms*. By this time, Sarraute had already published two novels, and her third, *The Planetarium*, received a friendly critical reception and became a best seller. In 1964, *The Golden Fruits* won the Prix International de Littérature, and Sarraute became secure in her reputation as an established writer. Along with Alain Robbe-Grillet, with whom she sometimes disagreed, she was considered a leader and an important theorist of the New Novel movement. Although Sarraute liked to point out her differences with the New Novelists, there are many things on which they agreed. They all saw the traditional concepts of plot and character in a novel as outmoded and in need of renewal. It is certain that without the notoriety of this movement, the genius of Sarraute would have gone undiscovered for many more years.

BIOGRAPHY

Nathalie Sarraute was born Nathalie Ilyanova Tcherniak on July 18, 1900, in Ivanovo Voznesensk, Russia. Her parents were Russian Jews who met in Geneva, where they had gone to acquire university educations because Czar Nicholas II prevented Jews from attending universities in Russia. When she was two years old, her parents divorced. Sarraute claimed that French was her first language because she moved to Paris with her mother at age two and later attended nursery school there. Until the age of eight, when she settled in Paris with her father, who had remarried, she was shuttled back and forth between France, Switzerland, and Russia. At the age of seven she wrote a novel, which she timidly presented to a Russian writer, a friend of her mother. His only comment, "Learn to spell before you write novels," discouraged her for almost thirty years. By the age of twelve she was fluent in French, Russian, English, and German.

After studying at the Lycée Fénelon in Paris, Sarraute received the *baccalauréat* degree and then a *licence* in English from the Sorbonne in 1920. In the academic year 1920-1921, she studied toward a bachelor's degree in history at Oxford University. During the winter of 1921-1922, she studied sociology under Werner Sombart in Berlin. In 1922, she enrolled in the University of Paris Law School, where she met Raymond Sarraute in 1923. They were married in 1925 and were both admitted to the Paris bar. For twelve years, she worked as a lawyer, and during this time she gave birth to three daughters, Claude in 1927, Anne in 1930, and Dominique in 1933. In 1932, Sarraute's literary career began, and her biography merged with the story of the long, painful process of getting her works recognized and published. During World War II, Sarraute took refuge in the town of Parmain (Seine-et-Oise). There, under the name of Nicole Sauvage, she masqueraded as the governess of her own daughters in order to hide from the Germans.

Biographical details about Sarraute are scarce—first, because she saw her life as banal, and second, because she believed that a writer's private life has nothing to do with the individual's public persona. She also maintained that the idea of a public persona (which she ridicules in several of her novels) has little relation to the consciousness of the writer who creates literary works.

Nathalie Sarraute. (AP/Wide World Photos)

ANALYSIS

In her preface to *The Age of Suspicion*, Nathalie Sarraute attempts to explain the concept of "tropisms"— the subterranean movements she tries to capture in her fiction. She calls them "the secret source of our existence" and claims that they are "at the origin of our gestures, of our words and of the emotions that we believe we feel." Although few people recognize or pay attention to these rapid changes at the limit of consciousness, Sarraute insists, they occur in every human being. Because they are deeper than the "subconscious" mind and exist before thoughts are put into words, these emotional movements are extremely difficult to record. The method that Sarraute adopts is to translate these tropisms into images—provoking in the reader emotional reactions similar to those she is seeking to portray. Because these movements are very rapid, she attempts to slow them down and take them apart so that the reader can follow the interaction of tropisms, usually between two or

more people. Often, she devotes three or four pages to "events" that take place in a matter of seconds. Sarraute compares this technique to a slow-motion film.

In addition to showing the interaction of tropisms between different persons, Sarraute also studies the interplay of two levels of discourse. The first level, which she calls "conversation," realistically and sometimes ironically imitates the banal clichés that people exchange in everyday life or in the dialogue of traditional novels. The second level, called "subconversation," contains the images that convey the tropisms and all the other unvoiced feelings and approximations of feelings that go on behind (Sarraute would say "below") ordinary conversation. Her later novels wander freely between these two levels with few signposts to orient the reader. The extra work required from the reader, his or her "collaboration" in making the novel, is one of the characteristics of the New Novel.

Because Sarraute was fascinated by tropisms and sought to portray them in her novels, she discarded the traditional notions of plot and character, which she believed created an awkward distance between the reader and the tropisms she was trying to isolate. She numbered among her predecessors Fyodor Dostoevski, who also showed contradictory characters with illogical motivations; James Joyce, who pioneered in techniques of the interior monologue; and Franz Kafka, whose characters were caught in an irrational world where no human contact was possible. Sarraute was especially fascinated by Marcel Proust, who, she believed, was studying the same movements that interested her; he saw them only in the past, however, frozen by memory.

In her novels, Sarraute captures her tropisms while they are still moving and makes the reader participate in this rapid movement. Otherwise, Sarraute saw her characters as dead, frozen, all of one piece, wax statues of the Musée Grévin—her most negative words of condemnation. In *Between Life and Death*, her writer-protagonist's alter ego explains that there are only two judgments possible for a work of art: It is alive, or it is dead.

PORTRAIT OF A MAN UNKNOWN

Her first two novels, *Portrait of a Man Unknown* and *Martereau*, are constructed around the tension between the first-person narrator, a sensitive person who is aware of tropisms and seeks to discover them in others, and other characters, who appear at first to be solid, reliable, easily defined, all of one piece. In *Portrait of a Man Unknown*, the narrator attempts to discover the secret relationship between a miser and his old-maid daughter. Sarraute pointed out that this novel could have been Honoré de Balzac's *Eugénie Grandet* (1833; English translation, 1859) if she had concentrated on the exterior of the characters. The narrator imagines scenes of crisis between the father and the daughter and even goes to a "specialist" to be cured of his mania. After the specialist (probably a psychologist or a psychiatrist) recommends that he forget the world of tropisms by traveling, the narrator sees in an art museum in Holland the painting that gives the book its title. It is an unfinished portrait by an anonymous artist, but its eyes have a strange power. The narrator prefers the ambiguity of this unfinished work of art to the finality and limits of finished masterpieces. This experience convinces him that he is right to continue to look for tropisms, but his search and the novel are ended by the appearance of a character from a traditional novel who has a full name and physical appearance. Louis Dumontet marries the daughter and puts an end to the tropisms.

MARTEREAU

Martereau seems to begin where *Portrait of a Man Unknown* leaves off. The first-person narrator of this novel lives with his aunt, uncle, and cousin in a world filled with tropisms. He wistfully admires a man named Martereau (the only character with a name), who seems to live in a more clearly defined universe. Martereau is simply a good, upstanding, cordial man, all of one piece—or is he? When the uncle asks Martereau to do him a favor and purchase a house for him so that he can avoid paying taxes on the money, the narrator begins to suspect that Martereau is not so honest as he appears. First, he refuses to give a receipt for the money; then, he moves into the house to "supervise the repairs." The most interesting scene in the novel is imagined by the narrator, who hypothesizes four different but plausible exchanges between Martereau and his wife that explain his motives. Finally, Martereau gives the house to the uncle, and the tropisms disappear, but the narrator retains his doubts.

THE PLANETARIUM

After her first two novels, Sarraute abandoned first-person narration for a third-person technique that allowed

her to move rapidly from the inside of one character to another. These first two novels share a preoccupation with the notion of character. The third novel, *The Planetarium*, continues this exploration but also introduces a preoccupation with aesthetic values that becomes more important in *The Golden Fruits*, *Between Life and Death*, *Do You Hear Them?*, and the play *C'est beau* (pb. 1973; *It's Beautiful*, 1981). The notion of character has almost entirely disappeared from *The Golden Fruits*, where a novel of that name is the "protagonist." Sarraute's novel describes the tropisms surrounding the rise and fall of *The Golden Fruits* and incidentally provides an amusing satire of Parisian literary circles. *Between Life and Death* recounts the same process from the point of view of the artist. *Do You Hear Them?* and *It's Beautiful* center on intergenerational feuds over the definition of beauty in art. Two of Sarraute's subsequent works indicate a slightly new direction. *"Fools Say"* and *The Uses of Speech* return to the subject of her first plays, *Silence* and *The Lie*, the paradox of the simultaneous necessity and impossibility of real human communication with words.

The Planetarium is both more complex and more traditional than Sarraute's first two novels. After the reader has mastered the technique of deciphering what critic Vivian Mercier has called Sarraute's "third-person stream of consciousness," a traditional plot appears. This plot revolves around several questions concerning Alain Guimier, a young man supposedly working on a thesis in art history, who emerges as the central consciousness of the novel. He has inherited the sensitivity of the first-person narrators of *Portrait of a Man Unknown* and *Martereau*. The questions are as follows: Will Alain succeed in convincing his family to buy him an antique armchair rather than leather club chairs? Will Alain talk his Aunt Berthe out of her spacious apartment in a prestigious section of Paris? Will Alain be admitted into the circle of admirers of the famous writer Germaine Lemaire? In addition to this skeletal plot, *The Planetarium* has another vestige of the traditional novel—characters, who also have names if one is willing to search for them. Alain's wife is named Gisèle; his father, Pierre; his mother-in-law, Madeleine.

Despite these elements of the traditional novel, which tempt the reader to construct characters and adventure, the essence of the novel is elsewhere. In an interview with François Bondy published in *Der Monat*, Sarraute explained the symbolism of the novel's title. A planetarium is a false sky, and the characters are like false stars rotating in elliptical orbits. This artificial reality—art objects, material success, social status—is the surface under which the real dramas, the tropisms, lie. These dramas concern interpersonal relations in two worlds—the family and the social circle of the artist. Critics have variously suggested that Alain, Germaine Lemaire, or Aunt Berthe is the star at the center of this solar system, but the universe of *The Planetarium* seems to have no star, or at least no center of gravitational pull. The characters collide with one another at random. They are all seeking love, acceptance, possession (of other human beings), domination—in a word, human contact. Critics have said that Sarraute's novels contain no love or other warm human emotions, yet both Alain's father, with his desire for Spartan discipline, and his Aunt Berthe, with her need to lavish gifts on him, love Alain in their own ways. Gisèle is torn between her love for her mother and her love for Alain. She seeks security and protection in his love. Even Alain has tender thoughts about his aunt on occasion and takes refuge in the security of his wife's presence after his battles on the social front.

Beyond these psychological insights, Sarraute leads the reader to question his or her own cherished values. The epigraph of the novel could be the reaction of Germaine Lemaire to a critical article that makes her see that her books are dead: "Alone on a burnt out star. Life is elsewhere." Lemaire quickly forgets this criticism, however, to bask in the praise of her admirers. Just as she refuses to search for authentic art, the other characters refuse to live authentic lives, taking refuge in shallow satisfactions.

Nothing is any more final in this novel than in everyday life, however. The reader is never sure that Alain is a spoiled brat, that Berthe is a possessive maniac. Their lives are filled with contradictory feelings and desires that resist all attempts to simplify them. In the last scene of the novel, Alain begins to have doubts about the good taste of his idol, Germaine Lemaire. Perhaps he is capable of finding the authentic existence she glimpsed briefly and brushed aside.

BETWEEN LIFE AND DEATH

In a review of *Tropisms*, Yvon Belaval claimed that Sarraute's subject was "creation in the process of being born." This description seems to fit *Between Life and Death* perfectly. A writer who is only a minor character in *The Planetarium* becomes here the main focus of Sarraute's microscopic analysis. The writer is hanging between life and death, looking for his own identity and meaning in life. For him, this identity can be found only in the act of writing; the work of art itself also hangs between life and death while the implacable critic, the alter ego of the artist, pronounces his verdict: "It's alive" or "It's dead."

Critics who have studied this text have attempted to create a hero, "The Writer," out of the portions of the novel narrated in the first person, yet Sarraute warns against this interpretation on the cover of the book. Her novel contains many experiences of many writers, and the pieces of the puzzle do not fit together to form a unified character. At the beginning of the novel, the reader hears a famous writer talking to an admiring audience about how he creates a work of art. He makes it sound mechanical: "I tear out the page. I crumple it up. I throw it away. I begin again." This famous writer, or perhaps another one, appears in the last scene of the novel repeating the same gestures to another audience, but this writer seems older, more disillusioned with life and art. Between these two scenes, many writers, or many faces of the writer, struggle in their relationships with other people and with the process of creating a work of art.

Since the Romantic period in French literature, the writer has been considered an outcast, a genius misunderstood by the masses. The dynamics of Sarraute's novel are constantly shifting, but Sarraute usually places "the one" alone facing "the many." The writer, even as a child, is different from the others. Despite his attempts to be "just like everybody else," he stands out like a sore thumb. He plays with words. He is sensitive to accents and word usages. The crowd is quick to place labels, names, masks on him: He is "predestined," "precocious," "a misfit." He does not fare any better among artists. They tell him they are "just like him," but he protests. He wants to retain his individuality, his "special relationship" with art. They protest; they, too, have "special relationships." Wherever he turns, he is alone and misunderstood. His father is sure his son could not get a book published without paying for it himself. His mother has been convinced from his birth that he is an artist and can see no faults in his work. When his book is published, a famous critic praises a passage in it that does not exist, and his "friends" insist they know the "sources" of different parts of the book. Finally, he is surprised to find himself developing into a public personality whom he does not recognize. His humble teakettle becomes a samovar with which he performs daily rituals.

Juxtaposed to texts that show the writer confronting society are texts in which the writer confronts the work of art. Here he is alone. In his solitude, he searches for life, for the gleam, the movement of authentic life. He tries to follow it, to capture it in words. When he is finished, he calls in the judge, his double, who decides whether the page will be tossed or saved. At the end of the novel, the writer has become old and famous, and the judge no longer functions well. He knows that he is dead, that his standard speech, "I tear out the page . . . ," is taking place in a funeral home. This is the moment of truth that Germaine Lemaire faces in *The Planetarium*, only to push truth aside to hide behind her fame. The protagonist of *Between Life and Death* does not push aside this truth. Over the heads of his admirers, he sees the *petite chose*, the unnameable thing that signifies life to him, and he leaves the crowd to follow her wherever she may lead. He struggles again to create a work of art that is truly alive. With his alter ego, he examines it closely and there, perhaps, he sees the fine mist made by breath on a mirror that indicates life.

"FOOLS SAY"

Sarraute's novel *"Fools Say"* weaves together several themes that interested Sarraute for many years, carrying them to their logical conclusion. In *Portrait of a Man Unknown*, *Martereau*, and *The Planetarium*, she was especially concerned by the masks people place on others. In *The Golden Fruits*, *Between Life and Death*, and *Do You Hear Them?*, a major theme is the relativity and subjectivity of aesthetic ideas. In *"Fools Say,"* Sarraute analyzes the processes by which people place masks, labels, or names on other people in order to denigrate their ideas. The ultimate insult to an idea, according to Sarraute, is to claim that it is said by a fool. By attacking the personality of the creator of the idea, one elimi-

nates the necessity, or even the possibility, of a rational discussion of the merits of the idea itself.

The novel has no characters in the traditional sense—only voices that sometimes seem to coalesce to form a central consciousness. In certain sections, there are also relationships implied between people: grandmother-grandchild, master-admirers, two lovers, newlyweds, and so on. The central consciousness, which may belong to one person or to many, usually speaks in the first person and is almost always alone in protesting the use of "fools say" to silence opponents. He sees himself as infinite. He, like everyone, conceives of himself as a subject and cannot "see himself as others see him," as an object. For this reason, he does not recognize photographs of himself. The little boy who refuses to see his grandmother as "cute" is probably the same one who is shocked to be told he has Uncle Frank's undercut jaw. When he overhears others saying that he is not really intelligent, he accepts their judgment at face value, until an adult points out to him that he must defend himself by calling the people imbeciles who say he is stupid. Later, he realizes that anyone who calls someone else an imbecile is one himself. (Sarraute cannot resist an ironic comment here: What does that make a person who writes a book on the subject?) When this boy, or another one, becomes more mature, he attempts to avoid this labeling by really examining a repugnant idea. This proves so distasteful that he is finally forced to use name-calling to escape from the situation.

The consciousness (or consciousnesses) who calls himself "I" fluctuates between a declaration that there are no limits between people ("There is no longer any I, any he, any separations, any fusion") and a recognition that individuals do exist ("Each in his place. Each is what he is"). This dilemma of identity makes the name-calling even more ludicrous. Finally, after starting a riot by declaring that he is "empty . . . a hole of air," he seems to be subdued by the "forces of order" and admits that ideas do come from people. He then becomes important; he is "someone." At the ironic ending of the novel, "he" is accused of conceiving and almost saying the words "That is what fools say."

In *"Fools Say,"* Sarraute points out how language can become a tool of repression and tyranny. By exploring the ambiguity of personal identity, which always fascinated her, she shows how futile it is to characterize a person by a word or a gesture. In this way, she protests against the use of language to attack individuals and to silence ideas.

Lucy M. Schwartz

OTHER MAJOR WORKS

SHORT FICTION: *Tropismes*, 1939 (revised 1957; *Tropisms*, 1963); *L'Usage de la parole*, 1980 (*The Use of Speech*, 1980); *Ouvrez*, 1997.

PLAYS: *C'est beau*, pb. 1973 (*It's Beautiful*, 1981); *Théâtre*, 1978 (*Collected Plays*, 1980); *Pour un oui ou pour un non*, pb. 1982.

RADIO PLAYS: *Le Silence*, 1964 (*Silence*, 1969); *Le Mensonge*, 1966 (*The Lie*, 1969).

NONFICTION: *L'Ère du soupçon*, 1956 (essays; *The Age of Suspicion*, 1963); *Enfance*, 1983 (autobiography; *Childhood*, 1984); *Entretiens avec Nathalie Sarraute*, 1999 (interviews).

MISCELLANEOUS: *Œuvres complètes*, 1996.

BIBLIOGRAPHY

Angelini, Eileen M. *Strategies of "Writing the Self" in the French Modern Novel: C'est moi, je croi*. Lewiston, N.Y.: Edwin Mellen Press, 2002. Examination of the nature of autobiographical fiction discusses Sarraute's work along with that of Marguerite Duras and Alain Robbe-Grillet.

Barbour, Sarah. *Nathalie Sarraute and the Feminist Reader: Identities in Process*. Lewisburg, Pa.: Bucknell University Press, 1993. Feminist analysis of Sarraute's early works demonstrates how Sarraute places her fiction within the tradition of psychological realism while simultaneously bringing new innovations to this tradition.

Besser, Gretchen R. *Nathalie Sarraute*. Boston: Twayne, 1979. Presents an analysis of Sarraute's early work, placing the writer within the context of the French New Novel.

Cothran, Ann. "Nathalie Sarraute." In *French Women Writers: A Bio-bibliographical Source Book*, compiled by Eva Sartori and Dorothy Wynne Zimmerman. Westport, Conn.: Greenwood Press, 1991. Useful resource includes a brief biography of Sarraute, discussion of her works, and bibliographies of primary and secondary sources.

Jefferson, Ann. *Nathalie Sarraute, Fiction and Theory: Questions of Difference*. New York: Cambridge University Press, 2000. Reassesses Sarraute's fiction and other writing, exploring her fundamental ambivalence to differences of various kinds, including questions of gender and genre. Includes bibliography and index.

O'Beirne, Emer. *Reading Nathalie Sarraute: Dialogue and Distance*. New York: Oxford University Press, 1999. Discusses Sarraute's growing disillusion with the reader over the course of her literary career and how this disappointment is reflected in the changing style of her prose.

Peebles, Catherine M. *The Psyche of Feminism: Sand, Colette, Sarraute*. West Lafayette, Ind.: Purdue University Press, 2004. Uses psychoanalytic and feminist approaches to examine Sarraute's novel *You Don't Love Yourself* as well as works by George Sand and Colette. Includes bibliography and index.

Phillips, John. *Nathalie Sarraute: Metaphor, Fairy-Tale, and the Feminine of the Text*. New York: Peter Lang, 1994. Analyzes Sarraute's novels and plays from psychoanalytic and feminist perspectives, focusing on issues of genre and gender in her work. Includes bibliography.

Ramsay, Raylene. *The French New Autobiographies: Sarraute, Duras, and Robbe-Grillet*. Gainesville: University of Florida Press, 1996. Comparative study of autobiographical writings by Sarraute, Marguerite Duras, and Alain Robbe-Grillet focuses on Sarraute's autobiography *Childhood* and her novel *You Don't Love Yourself*.

Willging, Jennifer. *Telling Anxiety: Anxious Narration in the Work of Marguerite Duras, Annie Ernaux, Nathalie Sarraute, and Anne Hébert*. Toronto, Ont.: University of Toronto Press, 2007. Examines the depictions of anxiety in works by Sarraute and three other women writers and argues that these works reflect skepticism about the ability of language to describe the death and destruction of World War II.

MAY SARTON

Born: Wondelgem, Belgium; May 3, 1912
Died: York, Maine; July 16, 1995
Also known as: Eléanore Marie Sarton

PRINCIPAL LONG FICTION

The Single Hound, 1938
The Bridge of Years, 1946
Shadow of a Man, 1950
A Shower of Summer Days, 1952
Faithful Are the Wounds, 1955
The Birth of a Grandfather, 1957
The Fur Person: The Story of a Cat, 1957
The Small Room, 1961
Joanna and Ulysses, 1963
Mrs. Stevens Hears the Mermaids Singing,
    1965
Miss Pickthorn and Mr. Hare: A Fable, 1966
The Poet and the Donkey, 1969
Kinds of Love, 1970
As We Are Now, 1973
Crucial Conversations, 1975
A Reckoning, 1978
Anger, 1982
The Magnificent Spinster, 1985
The Education of Harriet Hatfield, 1989

OTHER LITERARY FORMS

A poet as well as a novelist, May Sarton published a considerable number of volumes of verse. Her *Collected Poems, 1930-1973*, appeared in 1974 and *Collected Poems, 1930-1993*, appeared in 1993. She also wrote a fable, *Miss Pickthorn and Mr. Hare*; an animal fantasy story, *The Fur Person: The Story of a Cat*; several volumes of autobiography, including *I Knew a Phoenix: Sketches for an Autobiography* (1959), *Plant Dreaming Deep* (1968), and *A World of Light: Portraits and Celebrations* (1976); and several journals of her life in Nelson, New Hampshire, and York, Maine.

ACHIEVEMENTS

It was after World War II, with the novel *The Bridge of Years* and the poems collected in *The Lion and the*

Rose (1948), that May Sarton's reputation began to grow. Her novels met with a mixed response from critics and reviewers, sometimes condemned for awkward or imprecise style, an odd charge against a practicing poet. Even Carolyn Heilbrun, Sarton's defender, admitted that confusing shifts of viewpoint occur in her fiction. On the other hand, Sarton's honesty in presenting human problems, seeing them from varied perspectives, has generally been acknowledged. In some ways, novels such as *Mrs. Stevens Hears the Mermaids Singing* and *Crucial Conversations* are dramatized debates about art, feminine culture, interpersonal relationships, tradition, and memory.

Sarton also was accused of sentimentality and preciousness, and she tried to shift her style to a more direct, less self-conscious one after the early 1970's, perhaps answering critics of *Mrs. Stevens Hears the Mermaids Singing*, who saw it as too arch, too knowing. She tended to take current issues or fashions such as the Vietnam War, death-and-dying, feminine consciousness, and Jungian psychology as material for her novels. Autobiographical material frequently enters into her fiction, particular characters being reinvoked in various works and especially types such as authoritarian women, supportive women, and rebellious young people.

Sarton complained of the lack of serious critical scrutiny of her work and expressed disappointment as well at her failure to achieve a large popular success. She has been stereotyped as a woman's writer, presumably creating slick plot situations, overdramatic dialogue, and conventional characters in romantic duos or trios. Some of these charges are true; she herself, noting the difficulty of supporting herself by her work even as late as the 1970's, although she was a prolific and well-established writer, spoke of the difficulties of being a single woman writer not sustained by a family or a religious community. Nevertheless, she affirmed the possibility of self-renewal, commenting, "I believe that eventually my work will be seen as a whole, all the poems and all the novels, as the expression of a vision of life which, though unfashionable all the way, has validity." The surge of interest in her work at the end of the twentieth century, particularly among feminist scholars, would seem to confirm Sarton's hopes.

BIOGRAPHY

May Sarton was born Eléanore Marie Sarton in Wondelgem, Belgium, on May 3, 1912. Her mother, Mabel Elwes Sarton, a designer who worked at Maison Dangette, Brussels, was a determined craftsperson and an uncompromising seeker of high standards. Her father, George Sarton, pampered by his Belgian upper-middle-class family after losing his mother early, was an active socialist who did mathematical studies at the University of Brussels before settling into his life's work as a major historian of science; he founded the leading journal in the field, *Isis*, in 1912. He was a methodical scholar who even after his day's scholarly labors would make notes in the evening concerning recent research by other scholars. May's mother compromised her talents for her husband's career, but her gift of "refashioning things magically" inspired her daughter's own verbal artistry.

One close friend of Sarton's mother was Céline Dangotte Limbosch, or Mamie, whose home near Brussels Sarton has recalled as the one place in the world that would not change and whose traits appear in the heroine of *The Bridge of Years*. Mamie's husband, Raumond Limbosch, a poet who never published his poems, also figures in that novel as a philosopher.

Sarton's earliest years were spent in Belgium, but with the coming of World War I, the family fled to England. In 1915, the Sartons went to the United States, staying briefly in New York before settling in Washington, D.C., where the Carnegie Institute gave support to George Sarton's projected history of science. Mabel Sarton founded Belgart, specializing in handmade fashion apparel. Sarton's father's somewhat informal appointment at Harvard University led the family to Cambridge, Massachusetts, in 1918. There, young Sarton attended Shady Hill School, a Spartan institution run by an educational innovator, Mrs. Hocking, wife of a well-known philosopher, who combined the study of philosophy with poetry. Miss Edgett, an imaginative math teacher, inspired Sarton to be a poet, but Sarton also received encouragement from a family friend in Cambridge, Edith Forbes Kennedy. Kennedy was the inspiration for a character, Willa MacPherson, in *Mrs. Stevens*

Hears the Mermaids Singing, whose friendship and encouragement push young Hilary Stevens along on her poetic career. School plays also awakened Sarton's interest in drama.

In 1919, the family briefly returned to settle their affairs in Belgium. For a short time, Sarton attended the Institute Belge de Culture Française, which she later attended for a year at age twelve. The institute was presided over by Marie Closset, who published poetry as Jean Dominique, and two other women. Literature was taught from great works, and memorization was required. Sarton spent that year with the Limbosches while her parents were in Beirut, Lebanon, so that her father could learn Arabic for his research. The literary atmosphere and general culture that she encountered there influenced Sarton greatly.

A 1926 graduate of Cambridge Latin High School, Sarton recalled attending Boston Repertory Theater, reading poems with friends, and feeling revolutionary about Henrik Ibsen during these years. Her parents had settled into Channing Place, Cambridge, which was the center of Sarton's life until her parents' deaths. Sarton spent two years wanting to be an actor, doing summer stock in Gloucester before joining Eva LeGallienne's Civic Repertory Theater in 1929. She spent three years with the theater company; from 1931 to 1932, Sarton was in Paris working as director of the company's apprentices. While in Paris, she became friends with Aurélian-Marie Lugné-Poë, a founder of Théâtre de L'Œuvre, a theater that brought many new plays to France. Lugné-Poë appears as a director in *The Bridge of Years*. Although he thought Sarton had more talent as a writer, he was willing to help her improve her acting skills. Their unsuccessful romantic relationship parallels that which occurs in *A Shower of Summer Days*, whose heroine goes to a country home in Ireland to overcome a love affair.

When LeGallienne ran out of money, Sarton, together with Eleanor Flexner and Kappo Phelan, kept the Apprentices Theater going, settling in Dublin, New Hampshire, and appearing elsewhere on tour. That venture failed after two years, a considerable shock for Sarton that turned her in the direction of writing fiction. In the following year, she wrote several short stories, none of which sold. In June, 1936, she went to Cornwall,

England, first staying with Charles Singer, the historian of science, and then moving to London. She met Elizabeth Bowen, who was to become a friend over the next several decades and was the subject of passionate feelings; Juliette and Julian Huxley, at whose apartment over the London Zoo she spent a month; and Virginia Woolf. She also met James Stephens, the Irish poet, and became a particular friend of S. S. Koteliansky, editor and mentor of various writers, including Katharine Mansfield.

From 1936 to 1940, Sarton visited Belgium each spring, and for decades she could not decide whether she was European or American. She began writing poetry at the age of twenty-six. Needing funds and having no settled career, she returned to the United States in 1939 to read her poetry at various colleges. Despite feeling "the inward disturbance of exile," she felt the love and friendship of many different people.

During the years of World War II, Sarton worked for the U.S. Office of War Information in the film department. In 1943, she set up poetry readings at the New York Public Library to provide cultural experience for wartime workers. She returned to England in 1944 to visit her friend Bowen, who also visited Sarton whenever she was in the United States. With *The Bridge of Years*, Sarton's novel writing began again in earnest. Novels and other fiction and volumes of poetry have appeared at close intervals since. Her early poetry won her the Gold Rose for Poetry and the Edward Bland Memorial Prize (1945).

Sarton supported herself by teaching, serving as Briggs-Copeland instructor in composition at Harvard from 1950 to 1952, poet-in-residence at Bryn Mawr from 1953 to 1954, and lecturing on poetry at Harvard, the University of Iowa, the University of Chicago, Colorado College for Women, and Wellesley and Beloit colleges. In 1953, she met Louise Bogan, whose calm and order she valued considerably, though Bogan, poetry editor of *The New Yorker*, did little to advance Sarton's career. Other novels appearing in the early 1950's earned Sarton a Guggenheim Fellowship from 1954 to 1955.

Her reputation had grown with *A Shower of Summer Days*, though the critical reception, as with later novels, was mixed.

The Birth of a Grandfather came at a turning point in Sarton's life: Her mother had died in 1950 after a long illness and her father died quite suddenly in 1956. The family home in Cambridge was sold, and Sarton moved in October, 1958, to an old house equipped with a barn and thirty-six acres in Nelson, New Hampshire, a small village. Sarton then settled briefly in Ogunquit, Maine, and then in York, Maine, in an old house on the coast, writing further volumes of poetry, autobiographical sketches, and journals. Her love for animals is reflected in *The Fur Person*, a story about a gentleman cat's adventures.

Sarton's career reflected her conviction that "art must become the primary motivation, for love is never going to fulfill in the usual sense." Increasingly, she took her stand as a feminist: "We [women] have to be ourselves." Her understanding of her own sexual orientation seems

May Sarton. (Gabriel Amadeus Cooney)

to have grown partly out of her isolation as a woman and as a writer and her sense that marriage and family would detract from her creativity. She died in Maine in 1995.

ANALYSIS

The Small Room, a novel dealing with women training women as intellectual disciples in the atmosphere of a small women's college, was written while Sarton lived in Nelson. The novel also introduced a lesbian love affair between Carryl Cope, a brilliant but flinty scholar, and Olive Hunt, a benefactor of the college. *Mrs. Stevens Hears the Mermaids Singing*, which Sarton wrote at a time of gloom because of worries over her financial situation, was at first refused publication because it depicted a lesbian relationship, and the publishers required excisions before the book was accepted. *Kinds of Love*, *As We Are Now*, *Crucial Conversations*, and *A Reckoning* explore various marital or amatory dilemmas along with the problem of being a woman and an artist. *The Bridge of Years* is, perhaps, Sarton's most complex work. This is partly because the prototypes of the main characters were close to Sarton's own experience and the themes were motivated by intellectual friendships established in Europe prior to World War II.

THE BRIDGE OF YEARS

Based on Sarton's student years in Belgium and memories of her own family, *The Bridge of Years* centers on a Belgian family, Paul and Melanie Duchesne, and their three daughters, during four segments of their lives. These periods, besides accounting for personal growth in the major characters, also demarcate the stages of political change after World War I: optimism in the immediate postwar period; the decline of public morale and search for political solutions to the Depression of the 1930's; the fear of renewed European conflict attendant upon the rise of Adolf Hitler; and the outbreak of that conflict as liberal, humanitarian values come under attack with World War II.

Melaine Duchesne, a designer of furniture, a stickler for fine craftsmanship, a courageous and optimistic woman whose country home is a model of stability, is based on Sarton's mother and her longtime friend Céline Limbosch. Paul, the temperamental philosopher who cannot express his thoughts, is partly based on Raymond Limbosch and partly on George Sarton, May's father,

especially in his need for an ordered existence and exact routine. Paul's breakthrough into true philosophical statement under the pressure of the war is, as much as anything, Sarton's own search for authentic expression. Her father's leftist socialism and critical intelligence are reflected in Pierre Poiret, the university student son of close friends of the Duchesne family. The immemorial Bo Bo, the stiff but protective Teutonic nursemaid, is a portrait of Sarton's childhood governess.

Of the daughters, Colette, the youngest, is the poet, a romanticist living in a fairy world, Sarton's view of herself as a child. Solange, who becomes a veterinarian, has the patient skill with animals that Sarton herself possessed. The eldest daughter, Françoise, with her long affection for Jacques Croll, a fatigued soldier from World War I, believes that art is everything, turning herself inward when Jacques, maneuvered by Melanie, marries a local girl. Françoise feels compromised when Jacques tips her a wink as he walks down the church aisle with his bride. Her resulting emotional breakdown, and the awareness that art cannot be everything when "life [is] lived near the point of conflict," reflect Sarton's own emotional turmoil in the 1930's as she sought to become an artist.

Paul Duchesne's skepticism about the perfectibility of the human spirit is tempered by his German friend, the intellectual Gerhard Schmidt, who sees the need for individual effort to resist tyranny. After escaping from his homeland during Hitler's purge of intellectuals, he goes to fight with the Loyalists in Spain while his son, Hans, hypnotized by the Nazis, becomes a storm trooper. This opposition of father and son is repeated in the case of Emile Poiret, a pious Catholic floral illustrator with a sense of cosmic presence in things, and his antireligious son, Pierre. The novel presents facets of the European response to the breakdown of democratic civilization in the 1920's and 1930's and, at a more personal level, reflects the idea that some persons must extend themselves in love if civilization is to continue.

THE BIRTH OF A GRANDFATHER

The question of who one is, especially in the context of generations and of change, was a continuing concern of Sarton. It is presented through the dramatic, carefully staged scenes of *The Birth of a Grandfather*, in which the omniscient author moves among the characters, heightening the effect by the questions they ask themselves. The interior speculation is in the style of Henry James, though the consciousness attributed to a given character does not always seem consistent with his personality or inner life. This novel begins at the Maine island retreat of the wealthy and established Wyeth family. Tom Dorgan, a Boston Irish Catholic, is romantically involved with Betsy Wyeth, Frances and Sprig Wyeth's daughter. In contrast to these young lovers, Lucy, Frances's sister, is undergoing a divorce. It is Frances, the major character, and her husband, Sprig, from the middle-aged generation, whose painful readjustment to marriage and to age form the basis of the plot.

The older generation includes Uncle Joe, an urbane retired diplomat, Aunt Jane, a wise old woman capable of immersing herself in others, and Gran-Quan, Sprig's father, a man consumed by dramatic self-pity over the death of his wife and constantly supported by his sister, Jane. The Wyeths' son, Caleb, is reluctantly in the heart of family matters, biding his time until he gains independence from them. Appropriately enough, a major scene is the family's Fourth of July celebration on a nearby island. The fireworks are, for Frances, like moments of purity amid darkness, but they also herald the sudden death of Aunt Jane and the breaking up of Gran-Quan's private world and descent into insanity. Betsy and Caleb see their parents in new ways: Frances represents human frailty, and Sprig is seen as one sheltered from the pains of life.

The second part of the novel, "Ice Age," set in Cambridge, Massachusetts, shows the threat that tension and obligation bring to family unity. Tom and Betsy have married, and a child is on the way. This potentially joyful event threatens Sprig, who cannot accept the loss of direction in his life, which has settled into traditional philanthropy and conservation of the family wealth. By contrast, his friend Bill Waterford, who treats life with saving grace, calmly announces his impending death from cancer. Bill's life has had a sense of purpose. Two dinner scenes set forth two perspectives: In one, Hester, Sprig's sister, sees Sprig and Frances trying vainly to avert the emotional threat of Caleb's demand to be allowed to go alone to Greece for a year. In another, Tom Dorgan, innocently holding forth on the coming prospect of family life, exacerbates the conflict of generations, but he also sees that the Wyeths can admit to being wrong and remain loyal to each other. Caleb puts aside his immediate demand for independence, recognizing his father's own imprisonment in his reticence and sense of responsibility.

Coming to terms with Caleb leaves Sprig uncertain about his love for his wife, and a visit to Bill provokes the question of what real life is. Bill's wife, Nora, warns him that one may fail to exercise one's talents out of fear of freedom and power, a question that Sarton explored in various ways in probing the nature of the artist. Caleb's destination, Greece, awakens other echoes in Sprig, reminding him of the Greek scholarship for which he had once wished; Sprig then realizes his potential for continued growth.

In the third part, the grandfather is reborn, both in the sheer physical sense of the new grandchild and in meeting the meaning of his own life. Sprig must surrender his friendship with Bill, and he must test his own talent, no longer relying on Bill's support. Frances wonders whether she has not turned self-detachment into a prison; the answer comes with the realization that birth and death, the march of ongoing generations, has significance. This insight strikes her when, while visiting Bill, she encounters his nearly exhausted wife, Nora; a seemingly unsuitable marriage has worked because Bill was able to give of himself. Upon the departure of Caleb, to whom Sprig has given financial independence so that Caleb may try what he has wanted, Sprig himself turns to translating Greek plays as a self-imposed test. He acknowledges also that he has loved himself rather than Caleb in their relationship. With new honesty and willingness to assume self-defined responsibility, Sprig reconnects to the exuberance of his youth. He and Frances reaffirm their faithfulness, and love wins out as absolute value.

Sarton uses imagistic motifs, such as the current in the Charles River and the isles of Greece, to suggest important ideas in the novel. The shifting omniscient viewpoint highlights dramatic intensities, but it is used at times without strong motivation or without a careful build-up of character. It also can turn into undisguised narrative commentary. Moral implications do come through in catchwords such as "escape" and "freedom," which reverberate through the novel. Occasionally, moral judgments become banal. The novel has shown

Sprig's life as empty of personal demands on himself and his resistance to his children as a fearful reaction to his own aging, but the moral tends to blunt the focus.

MRS. STEVENS HEARS THE MERMAIDS SINGING

Coming roughly at the middle of Sarton's career, *Mrs. Stevens Hears the Mermaids Singing* is the author's most intense study of the female artist. Here, too, the style received mixed reviews, one critic praising the music of the prose, another objecting to the fussiness and humorlessness of the writing. What one critic found to be a well-done presentation of the mystery of the creative impulse a second found to be "an embarrassing probing of art" and "acute self-consciousness," and a third found the novel's characters "musechasers who believe themselves to be delicate vessels of talent." Scholar Heilbrun, in noting that the novel deals with the poet Hilary Stevens's escape from the passivity of a feminine destiny, sees Sarton as aware that "the real artist is not the fantasy creature imagined by women trapped in domesticity." Art comes, as Hilary insists, at the expense of every human being, the self and the self's ties with other people.

The plot interweaves Hilary's initiation of Mar Hemmer, a potential poet recovering from an intense relationship with a man, with her reveries as she is being interviewed about her own poetic development. Mar, despite his lack of emotional proportion, helps her to see her own life in perspective. Married to an unstable war veteran in England, Hilary began to write poetry after his sudden death. An intellectual friend, Willa MacPherson, encourages her to continue writing poetry and provides one night of passionate sexual exploration. Another friend, however, creates self-doubt, which Hilary identifies with the masculine force in herself. She knows that she can preserve her artistry only by caring about life, which does not necessarily mean sparing others from pain. As Hilary later points out to Mar, poetry and feeling are connected only if the poet understands that "true feeling justifies whatever it may cost." One cannot be anesthetized against the pain of life.

Philippa Munn, Hilary's proper girlhood governess with whom she is infatuated, plays the role that Sarton's own teachers did in her youth. Poetry diffuses sensuality, Hilary learns; it creates a moment of revelation, not sim-

ply of indulgence. As Hilary's wise physician tells her as she lies in the hospital recovering from a breakdown over her husband's death, she must write poems about objects and about a person to whom she can fasten herself deeply, but she should not confuse love for someone with poetry. Poetry can become "passionate decorum" in which love is presented as a mystique; what gives strength to poems is form.

Mrs. Stevens Hears the Mermaids Singing mixes the Platonic tradition of poet as maker whose creations surpass his or her own conscious understanding with an Aristotelian stress on the formal artifact that has its own laws of being and is autonomous. The notion of the poet as rapt by emotional experience lies also within the Platonic tradition of poetry as ecstasy. The events making up the life of Hilary Stevens have parallels with Sarton's own life, and the novel is a justification of that life. The presentation of the poet as a solitary individual misunderstood by the world also reflects Sarton's romanticism.

A RECKONING

As the heroine of *A Reckoning*, Laura Spelman, resident of an upper-middle-class Boston suburb, faces terminal cancer, she interprets her growing "death-wish" as a return to the Jungian "house of gathering." It is a world of timeless personages; Sarton had been reading Jung before writing the book. She had also become more concerned with feminism and more open about lesbian sexuality. As Laura is alienated from her own body, she works to resolve her unexamined passions by assessing her life. She comes, according to one critic, to an "understanding of life as an amalgam of human relationships, culture, and the natural world."

The novel also shows Harriet Moors, a budding novelist and lesbian, trying to put her life into art, an issue complicated by the opposition of her lover to any fiction that might hint at the truth of their liaison. It seems that not only marriage but also a binding lesbian attachment is fatal to art: Harriet Moors will have to suffer the loss of her lover as the price of continuing with her art.

Laura has to sort out her feelings for her mother, Sybille, a woman of dazzling power whose beauty and charm have oppressed her daughters. Jo, Laura's sister, after her mother had interrupted Jo's passion for a woman, had fled into the sterile intellectuality of academic life. Daphne, Laura's other sister, has become insecure and emotionally dependent. Laura has found escape in marriage. The destructive Sybille is a less flattering version of Céline Limbosch, of whom Sarton has said that she forced friends into decisions they did not wish to make and attacked their authentic being. Even in her senility in a nursing home, Sybille is someone about whom her daughter treads warily. Earlier in her life, Laura had had an intense friendship with Ella; the reader may strain, in fact, to realize it was a lesbian relationship. Harriet Moors's visits for advice on her novel rekindles in Laura her memories of Ella. She comes to realize that if love is painful, then art is mutilating. Yet in dying, Laura finds positive answers in music and in poetry.

The final reckoning is instigated by Laura's warm and helpful Aunt Minna, whose reading aloud to Laura forces her to consider that "journey into being a woman" and what women are meant to be. Women are locked away from one another in a man's world, she decides. Marriage may be normal destiny, but for those living intensely, a mystical friendship is the hope—of women for women, of men for men. Sybille, according to Ella, feared "the tenderness of communion."

Laura's loss of lonely autonomy is convincingly presented, but the master image, that of weaving a pattern, is imposed rather than dramatized. Ella's appearance at the end does not really complete the final weaving of the pattern by mystical friendship; the scene reminds the reader of sentimental fiction often found in women's magazines. Clearly, too many issues have come within the compass of the heroine's last months. Death may force its victims to focus their lives and aspirations, but the last days of Laura Spelman are not deeply and plausibly linked to her life as a married woman and parent or even to her efforts to approach art. As in *Mrs. Stevens Hears the Mermaids Singing*, reminiscence plays a key role. Whole scenes are recalled in dramatic form, but the very selectivity of memory and its often self-serving quality may raise questions about the honesty and sheer structural relationship between what Laura recalls and what she really was—a Boston upper-middle-class housewife with delusions of creativity, the kind of thing against which Sarton herself warned. *A Reckoning* lacks the strengths of Sarton's best work: thematic depth, balanced characters, organic use of imagery, adequate plot development, and motivated action.

Roger E. Wiehe

OTHER MAJOR WORKS

PLAY: *The Underground River*, pb. 1947.

POETRY: *Encounter in April*, 1937; *Inner Landscape*, 1939; *The Lion and the Rose*, 1948; *The Land of Silence, and Other Poems*, 1953; *In Time Like Air*, 1958; *Cloud, Stone, Sun, Vine: Poems, Selected and New*, 1961; *A Private Mythology*, 1966; *As Does New Hampshire, and Other Poems*, 1967; *A Grain of Mustard Seed: New Poems*, 1971; *A Durable Fire: New Poems*, 1972; *Collected Poems, 1930-1973*, 1974; *Selected Poems of May Sarton*, 1978 (Serena Sue Hilsinger and Lois Byrnes, editors); *Halfway to Silence*, 1980; *Letters from Maine*, 1984; *The Silence Now: New and Uncollected Earlier Poems*, 1988; *Collected Poems, 1930-1993*, 1993; *Coming into Eighty*, 1994.

NONFICTION: *I Knew a Phoenix: Sketches for an Autobiography*, 1959; *Plant Dreaming Deep*, 1968; *Journal of a Solitude*, 1973; *A World of Light: Portraits and Celebrations*, 1976; *The House by the Sea*, 1977; *Recovering: A Journal*, 1980; *Writings on Writing*, 1980; *May Sarton: A Self-Portrait*, 1982; *At Seventy: A Journal*, 1984; *After the Stroke: A Journal*, 1988; *Honey in the Hive: Judith Matlack, 1898-1982*, 1988; *Endgame: A Journal of the Seventy-ninth Year*, 1992; *Encore: A Journal of the Eightieth Year*, 1993; *At Eighty-two*, 1996; *May Sarton: Selected Letters, 1916-1954*, 1997 (Susan Sherman, editor); *Dear Juliette: Letters of May Sarton to Juliette Huxley*, 1999; *May Sarton: Selected Letters, 1955-1995*, 2002 (Sherman, editor).

CHILDREN'S/YOUNG ADULT LITERATURE: *Punch's Secret*, 1974; *A Walk Through the Woods*, 1976.

MISCELLANEOUS: *Sarton Selected: An Anthology of the Journals, Novels, and Poems of May Sarton*, 1991 (Bradford Dudley Daziel, editor); *May Sarton: Among the Usual Days*, 1993 (Sherman, editor); *From May Sarton's Well: Writings of May Sarton*, 1994 (Edith Royce Schade, editor).

BIBLIOGRAPHY

Evans, Elizabeth. *May Sarton, Revisited*. Boston: Twayne, 1989. Updates the 1973 Twayne series volume on Sarton by Agnes Sibley. A revaluation of Sarton's lifetime achievements, offering careful analysis of her work in four genres. Includes a helpful chronology of Sarton's life and accomplishments.

Fulk, Mark K. *Understanding May Sarton*. Columbia: University of South Carolina Press, 2001. Consciously avoids assuming that Sarton is of interest only to students of feminist or lesbian writers, attempting to come "closer to the spirit of Sarton's work as she saw it."

Hunting, Constance, ed. *May Sarton: Woman and Poet*. Orono, Maine: National Poetry Foundation, 1982. Twenty-four essays on Sarton's novels, journals, and poetry, including analyses of her journals and memoirs and the French influences on her writing style. Includes a bibliography and an index.

Peters, Margot. *May Sarton: A Biography*. New York: Alfred A. Knopf, 1997. In this first full-length biography, Peters examines why Sarton inspired such a devoted following among readers and discusses her uncertainty about the literary value of much of her work.

Sarton, May. *May Sarton: Selected Letters, 1916-1954*. Edited by Susan Sherman. New York: W. W. Norton, 1997.

_____. *May Sarton: Selected Letters, 1955-1995*. Edited by Susan Sherman. New York: W. W. Norton, 2002. A collection of correspondence that offers invaluable insight into Sarton's life and work. Includes indexes.

Sibley, Agnes. *May Sarton*. New York: Twayne, 1972. An early book-length treatment of Sarton's novels, and her poetry, through the 1960's. Groups the novels under two themes: "detachment" for the early novels and "communion" for the later ones.

Swartzlander, Susan, and Marilyn R. Mumford, eds. *That Great Sanity: Critical Essays on May Sarton*. Ann Arbor: University of Michigan Press, 1992. Thoughtful essays on Sarton's works, including discussions of Sarton and contemporary feminist fiction and of art and lesbian sexuality in her novel *Mrs. Stevens Hears the Mermaids Singing*.

Whitelaw, Lis. "The Education of May Sarton: Love Between Women in Four Novels by May Sarton." In *Beyond Sex and Romance? The Politics of Contemporary Lesbian Fiction*, edited by Elaine Hutton. London: Women's Press, 1998. This analysis of Sarton's novels from the perspective of queer theory is included in a collection of essays in which lesbian feminist critics examine works by lesbian authors.

JEAN-PAUL SARTRE

Born: Paris, France; June 21, 1905
Died: Paris, France; April 15, 1980
Also known as: Jean-Paul Charles Aymard Sartre

PRINCIPAL LONG FICTION

La Nausée, 1938 (*Nausea*, 1949)
L'Âge de raison, 1945 (*The Age of Reason*, 1947)
Le Sursis, 1945 (*The Reprieve*, 1947)
La Mort dans l'âme, 1949 (*Troubled Sleep*, 1950; also known as *Iron in the Soul*; previous three novels collectively known as *Les Chemins de la liberté*, in English as *The Roads to Freedom*)

OTHER LITERARY FORMS

Around the time that he published *Nausea*, Jean-Paul Sartre (SAHR-truh) drew considerable attention as a promising writer of short fiction with the stories collected in *Le Mur* (1939; *The Wall, and Other Stories*, 1948). Trained as a philosopher, Sartre went on to define and develop his concept of existentialism in *L'Être et le néant* (1943; *Being and Nothingness*, 1956), turning also to the theater with such famous plays as *Les Mouches* (pr., pb. 1943; *The Flies*, 1946), *Huis clos* (pr. 1944; *In Camera*, 1946; better known as *No Exit*, 1947), and *Les Mains sales* (pr., pb. 1948; *Dirty Hands*, 1949), in which the basic tenets of his thought are brilliantly executed and easily grasped. He is known also for essays and reviews collected in several volumes of the journal *Situations* as well as for psychological criticism of such authors as Charles Baudelaire, Gustave Flaubert, and Jean Genet. In 1964, he published a partial autobiography, *Les Mots* (*The Words*, 1964).

ACHIEVEMENTS

For students and readers of long fiction, Jean-Paul Sartre is perhaps most notable as the author of *Nausea*, an unsettling and groundbreaking work that exercised considerable influence over developments in the novel during the postwar era. His later efforts in the genre—the unfinished tetralogy *Roads to Freedom*—are viewed less charitably by most of his commentators, who would contend that Sartre had by that time turned his finest efforts toward the drama. Some scholars, however, have argued that Sartre's later novels have simply been obscured by the sensational publicity afforded his plays and other writings. In any event, Sartre himself appears to have lost interest in the writing of fiction, preferring such alternative forms as his essays on Baudelaire and Flaubert. Nevertheless, Sartre's influence on fiction, both long and short, has been considerable. In 1964, Sartre was awarded the Nobel Prize in Literature, which he declined to accept.

BIOGRAPHY

Born in Paris in 1905, Jean-Paul Sartre grew up in a book-filled, if fatherless, household. Sartre was a brilliant student, and his secondary schooling at the time-honored Lycée Henri IV was followed by competitive admission to the École Normale Supérieure. Although he failed his first attempt at the likewise competitive *agrégation*, or teaching credential, before successfully retaking it in 1929, Sartre had opted early for a life of the mind and had written at least one novel (later destroyed for want of a publisher) while still in his teens. He had also made the acquaintance of Simone de Beauvoir, a fellow philosophy student who would remain his companion for life, even as both rejected as "inauthentic" the "bourgeois" institution of marriage. During the 1930's, Sartre taught philosophy in *lycées* at Le Havre and elsewhere, traveling during vacations with the help of a small inheritance, before settling into the life of the professional writer and thinker as author of *The Wall, and Other Stories* and *Nausea*.

Briefly incarcerated by the Germans as a prisoner of war in 1940 and 1941, Sartre was nevertheless able to pursue his literary and philosophical work during the Occupation with a minimum of interference. As founding editor of the liberal periodical *Les Temps modernes* (ironically named for the 1936 Charles Chaplin film *Modern Times*, which both he and Beauvoir admired), Sartre became perhaps the most frequently quoted spokesman of the intellectual French Left, even as he "kept his options open" and refrained from the ultimate commitment of membership in the Communist Party. As the leading proponent of existentialism, Sartre also attracted the attention of the print and broadcast media, achieving during the postwar years celebrity status as existentialism was widely discussed and misinterpreted, seen by many commentators as the immediate ancestor of such phenomena as the Beat generation. His plays, meanwhile, shone brightly as the strongest and most durable of his creative efforts, performed worldwide before increasingly appreciative audiences.

During his later years, Sartre traveled widely and, when in Paris, spent most of his time and energy on his psychobiographical study of Flaubert, *L'Idiot de la famille: Gustave Flaubert, 1821-1857* (1971-1972; partial translation *The Family Idiot: Gustave Flaubert, 1821-1857*, 1981, 1987), a massive work conceived in much the same spirit as his earlier studies of Baudelaire and Jean Genet. Sartre died in Paris on April 15, 1980.

ANALYSIS

Hailed in the immediate prewar years as a rising master of prose fiction, Jean-Paul Sartre soon deserted the form and would leave unfinished the fourth and final volume of *The Roads to Freedom*, originally announced as a tetralogy. As it turned out, his creative talents were perhaps indeed better suited to the theater; encouraged by the eminent director Charles Dullin, Sartre, between 1943 and 1959, turned out eight original plays, fully half of which survived him and are still included in the world's repertory. Unlike his onetime friend and colleague Albert Camus (1913-1960), who repeatedly tried and failed to apply his gifts to the stage, Sartre possessed a particularly dramatic imagination that proved especially well suited to the exposition even of the most difficult philosophical concepts originally expounded in

Jean-Paul Sartre. (Library of Congress)

his essays. To be sure, a number of his concepts found their earliest, albeit undeveloped, expression in *Nausea* and in the stories to be collected in *The Wall, and Other Stories*; nevertheless, Sartre found fiction a comparatively inefficient vehicle for the communication of his ideas.

NAUSEA

Completed as early as 1936 under the working title of "Melancholia" (inspired by Albrecht Dürer's engraving *Melancholia I*, 1514), *Nausea* proved to be as unconventional in content as it was apparently conventional in form. Cast in the more or less familiar format of a diary discovered after the death (or disappearance) of its author, a convention in turn derived from the time-honored epistolary form, Sartre's first novel bodied forth a disoriented, disorienting vision of the world as perceived through the eyes of its rapidly changing protagonist and narrator: Antoine Roquentin, a thirty-year-old historian and former teacher, finds himself suddenly overcome by the sensation of his own existence, a sensation that soon evokes in him the nausea of the book's eventual, pub-

lisher-selected title. Overwhelmed by the evident contingency of his own being, Roquentin soon senses the same contingency in others, and in inanimate objects as well: In one memorable scene, Roquentin watches and describes his own hand as if it were a monstrous creature quite divorced from his existence, a beached crab with hair; in another scene, a glass of beer appears to be spying on him. His eventual and perhaps inevitable conclusion is that he is superfluous (*de trop*), a quality shared by most of the things and people around him.

Had Sartre limited *Nausea* to Roquentin's record of the changes taking place in his own mind, the book might well have been dismissed as an inventive simulacrum of a psychological case history. What assures the viability and power of *Nausea* is the nature and aptness of Roquentin's powers of observation, powers that alternately feed on and are fed by the operations of his mind. Even without the record of Roquentin's depression, *Nausea* might well have earned a respectable place in French literary history as a rare work of biting yet perceptive social satire in which few conditions of life are spared. To his credit, Sartre in *Nausea* repeatedly manages portraits that closely approach caricature yet stop short of straining the reader's credulity.

Trained as a historian, Roquentin is perhaps well chosen as an observer, yet not even he is presented wholly without satire. Dissatisfied with teaching, able to survive (if barely) on a small but regular unearned income, Roquentin probably is superfluous, at least by certain people's standards; in 1932, when he begins his journal, he has been working for some three years on the study of one Marquis de Rollebon, a minor survivor of the French Revolution whose descendants have willed the Marquis's papers to the city of Bouville (Mudville, equated by most of Sartre's commentators with the port city of Le Havre). Roquentin's daily work at the public library of Bouville has exposed him to a small but highly memorable cast of characters, including the Corsican librarian and especially the Self-taught Man (*l'auto-didacte*), a drab civil servant and World War I veteran who spends all of his free time in the library, attempting to educate himself by reading all of the books in alphabetical order, as filed under the author's name: "He has passed brutally from the study of coeleopterae to the quantum theory," observes Roquentin, "from a work on

Tamerlaine to a Catholic pamphlet against Darwinism, he has never been disconcerted for an instant." Later in the novel, the Self-taught Man will emerge as a deeply committed if somewhat fuzzy-minded Socialist not unlike those satirized around the same time by George Orwell in Britain; Roquentin, decreasingly proud (or even certain) of his own humanity, will turn a deaf ear to his acquaintance's declarations of predigested humanism. In a brief scene near the end of the book, the Self-taught Man stands cruelly revealed and judged as a barely repressed pederast, permanently expelled by the Corsican from the library that has come to represent his entire life. The greater part of Sartre's satire and Roquentin's scorn is reserved for the bourgeois "city fathers," however, whose portraits hang proudly on the walls of the civic museum—"*les salauds*," Roquentin calls them, using a term perhaps best rendered into English as "the bastards." For Sartre, as for Roquentin, the *salauds* are perhaps the most superfluous of all, born into a system that was set in place by their ancestors and that they themselves accept without question even as they perpetuate it; such individuals were to serve as models for Sartre's diatribes against inauthentic or "received" behavior. Roquentin, perversely fascinated by one portrait of particularly fearsome aspect, makes no secret of his pleasure upon learning that the man portrayed stood barely five feet tall.

Inevitably, Roquentin abandons his work on the life and career of Monsieur de Rollebon, having long since begun to suspect its futility. A brief visit to Paris and his former girlfriend, Anny, yields little more of consequence; Anny, a second-rate actor apparently addicted to striking poses, freely announces that she has become another man's "kept woman" and that, moreover, she is about to leave the country. Roquentin notes with some satisfaction that Anny has grown quite fat and wonders, between the lines of his journal, why he ever lent his collusion to her endless poses and "game-playing." With love thus discredited, Roquentin then moves on to the oddly Proustian conclusion that art alone offers a possible clue to life's meaning, if any, and a potential cure for his "nausea." Perhaps, he thinks, he might have found more meaning in life if he had written a novel. In any case, it is now too late, and the journal trails off into nothingness.

Throughout the diary, to be sure, Roquentin's only solace against his disquieting revelations has come through art, *authentic* art as opposed to the commissioned excrescences on display in the Bouville museum. A particular favorite is a jazz tune that he first heard on the lips of American soldiers during 1917, now preserved on a record on the jukebox in the Railwaymen's Café. As he continues his journal, the record grows in importance until, toward the end, Roquentin conjures up a vision of a Jewish musician and a black woman vocalist, who in less than five minutes of recorded playing time have achieved their immortality. The song, initially associated in Roquentin's mind with Anny, has long since acquired an authentic life of its own; by then, however, Roquentin has tacitly rejected the option of creative salvation for himself. Instead, he simply disappears, leaving the diary behind.

From the 1940's onward, it was customary to read *Nausea* in the reflected light of Sartre's subsequent efforts, finding Roquentin's memoirs complete illustration of such Sartrean categories as "essence," "existence," "anguish," and "bad faith." As James Arnold and other scholars have shown, however, the novel originally conceived as "Melancholia" represents a somewhat earlier stage in the evolution of Sartre's thinking, and such examples as there are (such as the implicit "bad faith" of the *salauds*) must be seen as prototypical rather than exemplary; those in search of specific illustrations might be better advised to consider such plays as *The Flies, No Exit*, or *Dirty Hands*. To be sure, Sartre's particular concept of "existence" receives its first exposition in *Nausea*, as Roquentin discovers and explores the "unjustified" fact of his being in all of its contingency; the "nausea" that overwhelms him as a result might likewise be interpreted as an early manifestation of the state later described as *angoisse* (anguish). Still *Nausea* demands to be read and appreciated as an independent work of art rather than as an existentialist manifesto. As Arnold has pointed out, moreover, the novel is also rich in autobiographical elements, however skillfully reworked and transposed; the character of Anny, for example, was drawn quite closely from life, in the person of an artist-actor with whom a very young Sartre once believed himself to be in love and whose perennial posing provided him with an invaluable object lesson in the "art" of inauthentic behavior. Like "The Wall" and its companion stories, *Nausea* must thus be seen, regardless of its thought-provoking "content," above all as a work of literary art.

It was not until well after *Nausea*, during the wartime and postwar years, that Sartre would truly emerge as an original and provocative thinker. His ideas, afforded scholarly and rather ponderous exposition in *Being and Nothingness*, soon gained widespread exposure through his plays, particularly *The Flies* and *No Exit*, as well as in essays and columns initially published in *Les Temps modernes*. Soon a coherent existentialist attitude began to emerge, roughly delineated as follows: Of all beings, Sartre maintains, only the "human animal" is capable of *creating* itself through continual, fully conscious acts of *choice*; at birth, people share *essence* with rocks, plants, and other animals, but they must then proceed toward a uniquely human *existence* of their own choosing. Those who refuse to choose, or to accept responsibility for choices already made, are guilty of "bad faith" (*mauvaise foi*) in renouncing their potential "existence" (*poursoi*) for a subhuman fixed "essence" (*en-soi*) that is tantamount to death. Indeed, as the godless prefigured hell of *No Exit* makes abundantly clear, those who reject the "anguish" of perpetual free choice for the illusory comfort of self-applied "labels" are in fact already dead to the world. Only after real, physical death should it be possible to draw the bottom line, to add up the total of a human life; until that time, any effort to complete the phrase "I am . . ." with a predicate, adjective, or noun identifies the speaker as a person "in love with death," one who has forsaken the unique human privilege and potential of existence. Sartre applies this theory with particular clarity in his *Réflexions sur la question juive* (1946; *Anti-Semite and Jew*, 1948), in which bigotry is portrayed not as an "opinion" or "reaction" but rather as a "passion," a predisposition that antedates its object. Bigots, Sartre maintains, are at bottom terrified of their own freedom, of their own capacity for change; they have therefore opted, in conscious or unconscious bad faith, for the fixed essence of a position that they perceive as self-protective: Refusing to consider the possibility that the world is simply ill-made, they choose to blame all of its ills on a particular minority—Jews, blacks, or Arabs, for example. "If the Jew did not exist," concludes Sartre with the persuasion of simple logic, "the anti-Semite would have to invent him."

As Hazel E. Barnes has pointed out, much of Sartre's argument against anti-Semitism, and against bigotry in general, is outlined in his prewar novella *L'Enfance d'un chef* (*Childhood of a Boss*), the longest of the tales collected in *The Wall, and Other Stories*. Frequently too broad in its satire of bourgeois mentality and morality to be thoroughly credible, *Childhood of a Boss* nevertheless announces, even more clearly than *Nausea*, the provocative blend of philosophy, psychology, and politics that would become characteristic of Sartre's mature output: The life of Lucien Fleurier is a life lived almost totally in bad faith, including a constant search for comforting, self-applied labels and dilettantish flirtation with the artistic "fads" of the time, most notably Surrealism. Insecure from his earliest childhood onward, Lucien constantly seeks to hide behind something larger and stronger than himself, ultimately finding refuge in Fascist anti-Semitism. Haunted also by suspicions of his homosexuality, he relates to women only insofar as he can "objectify" them, to be objectified by them in his turn. In the end, Lucien is so strengthened by his reactionary politics as to have crystallized into the archetypal, unbending capitalist "boss" of the title, not unlike the *salauds* of Bouville.

THE ROADS TO FREEDOM

In the projected tetralogy *The Roads to Freedom*, begun around the same time as *Being and Nothingness* and the early plays, Sartre endeavors to illustrate his developing philosophy through the lives of several continuing characters, most of whom are fortunately drawn less close to caricature than the hapless Lucien Fleurier. Although narration throughout is in the objective, "affectless" third person, the apparent central character in the three published novels is one Mathieu Delarue, a disaffected intellectual in his thirties who resembles Sartre even more than does Antoine Roquentin. The first volume, ironically titled *The Age of Reason*, deals mainly with Mathieu's efforts to secure an abortion for his unloved and unlovely live-in mistress, Marcelle; only at the end, having met with odd opposition from unexpected quarters, will Mathieu ruefully conclude that he has at last reached "the age of reason." Among the more intriguing characters of *The Age of Reason* and its sequels is Mathieu's friend Daniel, a gay man who nevertheless cherishes his clandestine friendship with Marcelle and refuses Mathieu a loan for the abortion, claiming that he does not have the money when in fact he does. A protracted earlier scene has shown Daniel contemplating suicide, planning first to drown his three beloved cats in order to be free of his last responsibilities; unable to kill the cats, he will likewise lack the nerve to carry out his projected self-annihilation. At the end of *The Age of Reason*, he will astound the reader and his fellow characters alike by choosing to marry Marcelle, ostensibly to assure her unborn child a home and father but also, and perhaps more likely, to lock himself into a situation in which he will be condemned to feel false, deserving of contempt as well.

For Barnes, Daniel is perhaps the archetypal character in existentialist fiction, defined not by heredity or environment, as in the traditional novel, but rather, simply by choice. As Barnes points out, nothing is revealed of Daniel's parentage, childhood, or early sexual encounters; Daniel is shown only *in situa*, defining himself (however negatively) through continuous and conscious acts of choice. It is Daniel's *choice* to be reviled and hateful, for whatever unknown reasons. Like Lucien Fleurier—although with far greater lucidity, reflecting the subsequent evolution of Sartre's thought—Daniel is so terrified of his potential freedom that he repeatedly uses that freedom to turn himself into a detestable object, a walking testimonial to the negative effects of bad faith. Mathieu, in turn, "has discovered his freedom but does not know what to do with it." Less interesting as a character than is Daniel, although perhaps equally complex, Mathieu functions throughout the existing trilogy less as protagonist than as catalyst, a common acquaintance shared by the variety of characters portrayed. Toward the end of the third novel of the series, *Troubled Sleep*, which portrays the end of the "phony war" and the start of the Vichy regime, Mathieu falls in battle and is apparently left for dead, his "central" position being assumed by the committed Communist Brunet; from Sartre's descriptions of the projected fourth volume, however, as well as from excerpts from it published in *Les Temps modernes* during 1949, it was clear that Mathieu would survive his wounds and that Daniel, perhaps too predictably, would collaborate with Occupation forces.

As in *Nausea*, Sartre in *The Roads to Freedom* proves to be a keen observer of human nature as well as a social satirist of no mean talent; among his more skillful portraits are those of Mathieu's brother Jacques, a successful lawyer (who in turn will refuse to lend Mathieu the abortion money) and Jacques's wife, Odette, an intelligent but bored (and boring) bourgeoise. By the early 1940's, however, social satire had lost ground in relative importance to the development of Sartre's philosophical and political attitudes; diverting though the social portraiture may be, it is clear throughout *The Roads to Freedom* that what really matters are the choices facing, and made by, each of the characters, whether consciously or unconsciously. As early as 1939, Sartre had addressed himself as a critic to the delineation of character in fiction, calling for a clear-cut distinction between exposition and "advocacy" on the part of a supposedly omniscient narrator, berating François Mauriac, in particular, for assuming a "godlike" attitude in denying his characters their "freedom." "God is no novelist," Sartre opined in a now-famous statement, "and neither is François Mauriac."

In *The Roads to Freedom*, Sartre appears to have been quite determined to allow his characters their freedom, even at the cost of plausibility; taking care to preserve their integrity by denying his personages the customary justifications of heredity and/or environment, Sartre frequently strains readers' credulity by asking them to accept the validity of voluntary, seemingly unmotivated actions, a practice perhaps derived from André Gide's earlier concept of the *acte gratuit*, or unmotivated gesture, exemplified in the murder of Fleurissoire in *Les Caves du Vatican* (1914; *The Vatican Swindle*, 1925; better known as *Lafcadio's Adventures*, 1927). Perhaps not surprisingly, Sartre's ideas received considerably more credible and effective presentation in his plays, in which actors could accomplish the necessary mediation between text and audience; one is reminded, in particular, of Electra's sudden but thoroughly plausible recourse to bad faith in *The Flies*.

In all of Sartre's published fiction, perhaps the best illustration of his developing theories is to be found in his story "The Wall," narrated throughout by an unprivileged first-person narrator from inside a situation that threatens him with imminent extinction; that Pablo survives to tell the tale at all is surely among the greater, and more skillfully managed, ironies in all modern fiction. In the longer form, however, Sartre proved somewhat less skillful at bridging the gap between theory and practice; indeed, few of his commentators expressed any real surprise when his tetralogy was left unfinished.

With or without the support of Sartre's unfolding existentialism, *The Roads to Freedom* appears not to have stood the test of time. However carefully observed, the disaffected, often marginal characters of the trilogy seem unlikely to capture or maintain the reader's interest, perhaps least of all in what might have become of them in the projected fourth volume. Of the existing volumes, *The Reprieve* has perhaps deservedly received the greatest critical attention, owing mainly to Sartre's skillful experiments with time and simultaneity, a technique admittedly borrowed from the cinema by way of John Dos Passos. On balance, however, Sartre was doubtless well advised to turn his talents elsewhere.

David B. Parsell

OTHER MAJOR WORKS

SHORT FICTION: *Le Mur*, 1939 (*The Wall, and Other Stories*, 1948).

PLAYS: *Les Mouches*, pr., pb. 1943 (*The Flies*, 1946); *Huis clos*, pr. 1944 (*In Camera*, 1946; better known as *No Exit*, 1947); *Morts sans sépulture*, pr., pb. 1946 (*The Victors*, 1948); *La Putain respectueuse*, pr., pb. 1946 (*The Respectful Prostitute*, 1947); *Les Jeux sont faits*, pr., pb. 1947 (*The Chips Are Down*, 1948); *Les Mains sales*, pr., pb. 1948 (*Dirty Hands*, 1949); *Le Diable et le Bon Dieu*, pr. 1951 (*The Devil and the Good Lord*, 1953); *Kean: Ou, Désordre et génie*, pb. 1952 (adaptation of Alexandre Dumas, *père*'s play; *Kean: Or, Disorder and Genius*, 1954); *Nekrassov*, pr. 1955 (English translation, 1956); *Les Séquestrés d'Altona*, pr. 1959 (*The Condemned of Altona*, 1960); *Les Troyennes*, pr., pb. 1965 (adaptation of Euripides' play; *The Trojan Women*, 1967).

NONFICTION: *L'Imagination*, 1936 (*Imagination: A Psychological Critique*, 1962); *Esquisse d'une théorie des émotions*, 1939 (*The Emotions: Outline of a Theory*, 1948); *L'Imaginaire: Psychologie phénoménologique de l'imagination*, 1940 (*The Psychology of Imagination*, 1948); *L'Être et le néant*, 1943 (*Being and Nothingness*,

1956); *L'Existentialisme est un humanisme*, 1946 (*Existentialism*, 1947; also known as *Existentialism and Humanism*, 1948); *Réflexions sur la question juive*, 1946 (*Anti-Semite and Jew*, 1948); *Baudelaire*, 1947 (English translation, 1950); *Qu'est-ce que la littérature?*, 1947 (*What Is Literature?*, 1949); *Situations I-X*, 1947-1975 (10 volumes; partial translation, 1965-1977); *Saint-Genet: Comédien et martyr*, 1952 (*Saint Genet: Actor and Martyr*, 1963); *Critique de la raison dialectique, précédé de question de méthode*, 1960 (*Search for a Method*, 1963); *Critique de la raison dialectique, I: Théorie des ensembles pratiques*, 1960 (*Critique of Dialectical Reason, I: Theory of Practical Ensembles*, 1976); *Les Mots*, 1964 (*The Words*, 1964); *L'Idiot de la famille: Gustave Flaubert, 1821-1857*, 1971-1972 (3 volumes; partial translation *The Family Idiot: Gustave Flaubert, 1821-1857*, 1981, 1987); *Un Théâtre de situations*, 1973 (*Sartre on Theater*, 1976); *Les Carnets de la drôle de guerre*, 1983 (*The War Diaries of Jean-Paul Sartre: November, 1939-March, 1940*, 1984); *Lettres au Castor et à quelques autres*, 1983 (2 volumes; volume 1, *Witness to My Life: The Letters of Jean-Paul Sartre to Simone de Beauvoir, 1926-1939*, 1992; volume 2, *Quiet Moments in War: The Letters of Jean-Paul Sartre to Simone de Beauvoir, 1940-1963*, 1993); *Le Scénario Freud*, 1984 (*The Freud Scenario*, 1985).

BIBLIOGRAPHY

Aronson, Ronald, and Adrian van den Hoven. *Sartre Alive*. Detroit, Mich.: Wayne State University Press, 1991. Provides a judicious and well-informed introduction to Sartre's work followed by sections on Sartre's continuing political relevance, on his political and philosophical thought, on his fiction and biography, on his relationships with Simone de Beauvoir and other writers, and on concluding assessments of his career.

Bloom, Harold, ed. *Jean-Paul Sartre*. Philadelphia: Chelsea House, 2001. Collection of critical essays on Sartre is supplemented by an editor's introduction, a brief biography, and a chronology of events in Sartre's life. Includes bibliography and index.

Fournay, Jean-François, and Charles D. Minahen, eds. *Situating Sartre in Twentieth-Century Thought and Culture*. New York: St. Martin's Press, 1997. Sartre scholars offer varied interpretations on the significance of Sartre's philosophical and literary works.

Hayman, Ronald. *Sartre: A Life*. New York: Simon & Schuster, 1987. Well-written biography shows the historical contexts within Sartre wrote various works, suggesting how and why Sartre explored different literary genres in search of the most accessible vehicle for his ideas.

Hill, Charles G. *Jean-Paul Sartre: Freedom and Commitment*. New York: Peter Lang, 1992. Discusses Sartre's qu est for freedom and authentic actions as well as his recognition of the ambiguities of commitment. Chapter 2 discusses the novel *Nausea*. Includes chronology, notes, and bibliography.

Howells, Christina, ed. *Sartre*. New York: Longman, 1995. Collection of essays presents critical analyses of Sartre's dramatic works and literary fiction, including all his novels. Includes bibliography and index.

McBride, William L., ed. *Existentialist Literature and Aesthetics*. Vol. 7 in *Sartre and Existentialism*. New York: Garland, 1997. This volume, part of a multivolume series on Sartre and his philosophy, examines his literary works and how existentialism is expressed in them. Includes bibliography.

Rowley, Hazel. *Tête-à-Tête: Simone de Beauvoir and Jean-Paul Sartre*. New York: HarperCollins, 2005. Chronicles the relationship between the two French writers, discussing their writings, their politics, their philosophical legacy, and their commitment to each other. Includes bibliography and index.

Silvester, Rosalind. *Seeking Sartre's Style: Stylistic Inroads into "Les Chemins de la liberté."* Lewiston, N.Y.: Edwin Mellen Press, 2003. Offers a detailed philosophical and linguistic analysis of *The Roads to Freedom*, analyzing Sartre's use of language in the novel trilogy. Includes bibliography and index.

Van den Hoven, Adrian, and Andrew Leak, eds. *Sartre Today: A Centenary Celebration*. New York: Berghahn Books, 2005. Collection of essays includes discussion of Sartre's existential philosophy and his thoughts on psychology and politics.

Wardman, Harold W. *Jean-Paul Sartre: The Evolution of His Thought and Art*. Lewiston, N.Y.: Edwin Mellen Press, 1992. Critical examination of Sartre's literary works traces the author's philosophical development through his writings, charting his changing ideas about religion, art, human relationships, and politics. Includes bibliography and index.

DOROTHY L. SAYERS

Born: Oxford, England; June 13, 1893
Died: Witham, Essex, England; December 17, 1957
Also known as: Dorothy Leigh Sayers

PRINCIPAL LONG FICTION

Whose Body?, 1923
Clouds of Witness, 1926
Unnatural Death, 1927 (also known as *The Dawson Pedigree*)
Lord Peter Views the Body, 1928
The Unpleasantness at the Bellona Club, 1928
The Documents in the Case, 1930 (with Robert Eustace)
Strong Poison, 1930

The Five Red Herrings, 1931 (also known as *Suspicious Characters*)
The Floating Admiral, 1931 (with others)
Have His Carcase, 1932
Ask a Policeman, 1933 (with others)
Murder Must Advertise, 1933
The Nine Tailors, 1934
Gaudy Night, 1935
Six Against the Yard, 1936 (with others; also known as *Six Against Scotland Yard*)
Busman's Honeymoon, 1937
Double Death: A Murder Story, 1939 (with others)
Striding Folly, 1972

"The Scoop" and "Behind the Scenes," 1983 (with others)
"Crime on the Coast" and "No Flowers by Request," 1984 (with others)

OTHER LITERARY FORMS

In addition to the twelve detective novels that brought her fame, Dorothy L. Sayers (SAY-uhrz) wrote short stories, poetry, essays, and plays, and distinguished herself as a translator and scholar of medieval French and Italian literature. Although she began her career as a poet, with the Basil Blackwell publishing house bringing out collections of her verse in 1916 and 1918, Sayers primarily wrote fiction from 1920 until the late 1930's, after which she focused on radio and stage plays and a verse translation of Dante. She also edited a landmark anthology of detective fiction, *Great Short Stories of Detection, Mystery, and Horror* (1928-1934; also known as *The Omnibus of Crime*).

Apart from her fiction, the essence of Sayers's mind and art can be found in *The Mind of the Maker* (1941), a treatise on aesthetics that is one of the most illuminating inquiries into the creative process ever written; in her essays on Dante; and in two religious dramas, *The Zeal of Thy House* (pr., pb. 1937), a verse play written for the Canterbury Festival that dramatizes Sayers's attitude toward work, and *The Man Born to Be King: A Play-Cycle on the Life of Our Lord and Saviour Jesus Christ*, a monumental series of radio plays first broadcast amid controversy in 1941-1942. The latter work addressed what Sayers regarded as the most exciting of mysteries: the drama of Christ's life and death, the drama in which God is both victim and hero. Of her many essays, the 1946 collection *Unpopular Opinions* and the 1947 *Creed or Chaos?, and Other Essays in Popular Theology* provide a good sampling of the acumen, wit, and originality with which Sayers attacked a variety of subjects, including religion, feminism, and learning.

In 1972, James Sandoe edited *Lord Peter*, a collection of all the Wimsey stories. Two other collections, both published during Sayers's lifetime (*Hangman's Holiday*, 1933, and *In the Teeth of the Evidence, and Other Stories*, 1939), include non-Wimsey stories. At her death, Sayers left unfinished her translation of Dante's *Cantica III: Paradise*, which was completed by her friend and colleague Barbara Reynolds and published posthumously in 1962 as the final volume in the Penguin Classics edition of Dante that Sayers had begun in 1944. An unpublished fragment of an additional novel, to be called "Thrones, Dominations" and apparently abandoned by Sayers in the 1940's, was also left unfinished, as was her projected critical/biographical study of Wilkie Collins. This last fragment was published in 1977. From 1973 to 1977, the British Broadcasting Corporation (BBC) produced excellent adaptations of five of the Wimsey novels for television, thus creating a new audience for Sayers's work.

ACHIEVEMENTS

One of the chief pleasures for readers of Dorothy L. Sayers is the companionship of one of fiction's great creations, Lord Peter Wimsey, that extraordinarily English gentleman, cosmopolite, detective-scholar. Although the Wimsey novels were created primarily to make money, his characterization demonstrates that his creator was a serious, skillful writer. As the novels follow Wimsey elegantly through murder, mayhem, and madness, he grows from an enchanting caricature into a fully realized human being. The solver of mysteries thus becomes increasingly enigmatic himself. Wimsey's growth parallels Sayers's artistic development, which is appropriate, since she announced that her books were to be more like mainstream novels than the cardboard world of ordinary detective fiction.

Lord Peter is something of a descendant of P. G. Wodehouse's Bertie Wooster, and at times he emulates Arthur Conan Doyle's Sherlock Holmes, but in Wimsey, Sayers essentially created an original. Sayers's novels integrate elements of earlier detective fiction—especially the grasp of psychological torment typified by Joseph Sheridan Le Fanu and the fine delineation of manners exemplified in Wilkie Collins—with subjects one would expect from a medieval scholar: virtue, corruption, justice, punishment, suffering, redemption, time, and death. The hallmarks of her art—erudition, wit, precision, and moral passion—provoke admiration in some readers and dislike in others.

Sayers's novels are filled with wordplay that irritates those who cannot decipher it and delights those who can. Her names are wonderful puns (Wimsey, Vane, Freke, de Vine, Snoot, Venables), her dialogue is embedded with literary allusions and double entendres in English, French, and Latin, and her plots are spun from biblical texts and English poetry. Reading a Sayers novel, then, is both a formidable challenge and an endless reward. Hers are among the few detective novels that not only bear rereading, but actually demand it, and Sayers enjoys a readership spanning several generations. To know Sayers's novels is to know her time and place as well as this brilliant, eccentric, and ebullient artist could make them known. Because of her exquisite language, her skill at delineating character, and her fundamentally serious mind, Sayers's detective fiction also largely transcends the limits of its time and genre. Certainly this is true of novels such as *Strong Poison*, *The Nine Tailors*, *Gaudy Night*, and *Busman's Honeymoon*, books that did much toward making the detective novel part of serious English fiction.

BIOGRAPHY

Dorothy Leigh Sayers was born on June 13, 1893, in the Choir House of Christ Church College, Oxford, where her father, the Reverend Henry Sayers, was headmaster. Mr. Sayers's family came from county Tipperary, Ireland; his wife, the former Helen Mary Leigh, was a member of the old landed English family that also produced Percival Leigh, a noted contributor to the humor magazine *Punch*. Sayers's biographer James Brabazon postulates that her preference for the Leigh side of the family caused her to insist on including her middle initial in her name; whatever the reason, the writer wished to be known as Dorothy L. Sayers.

When Sayers was four, her father left Oxford to accept the living of Bluntisham-cum-Earith in Huntingdonshire, on the southern edge of the Fens, those bleak expanses of drained marshland in eastern England. The contrast between Oxford and the rectory at Bluntisham was great, especially as the new home isolated the family and its only child. Sayers's fine education in Latin, English, French, history, and mathematics was conducted at the rectory until she was almost sixteen, when she was sent to study at the Godolphin School, Salisbury, where she seems to have been quite unhappy. Several of her happiest years followed this experience, however, when she won the Gilchrist Scholarship in Modern Languages

and went up to Somerville College, Oxford, in 1912. At Somerville, Sayers enjoyed the congenial company of other extraordinary women and men and made some lasting friends, including Muriel St. Clare Byrne. Although women were not granted Oxford degrees during Sayers's time at Somerville, the university's statutes were changed in 1920, and Sayers was among the first group of women to receive Oxford degrees in that year (she had taken first honors in her examination in 1915).

Following her undergraduate days, Sayers did various kinds of work for several years: first as poetry editor for Blackwell's in Oxford from 1916 to 1918, then as a schoolmistress in France in 1919, and finally in London, where she worked as a freelance editor and as an advertising copywriter for Benson's, England's largest advertising agency. At Benson's, Sayers helped create "The Mustard Club," a phenomenally successful campaign for Colman's mustard. Around 1920, when Sayers's mind was focused not only on finding suitable employment but also on surviving economically, the character of Lord Peter Wimsey was miraculously born, and Sayers's first novel, *Whose Body?*, introduced him to the world in 1923.

Her early years in London were scarred by two bitterly disappointing love affairs, one of which left Sayers with a child, born in 1924. The novelist married Oswald Atherton Fleming, a Scottish journalist, in 1926, and shortly thereafter assumed financial responsibility for him as he became ill and ceased working several years after they wed. Perhaps these pressures encouraged Sayers to keep turning out the increasingly successful Wimsey novels.

By the end of the 1930's, however, Sayers was in a position to "finish Lord Peter off" by marrying him to Harriet Vane, the detective novelist who first appeared in *Strong Poison* and who, like Wimsey, reflected part of Sayers's personality. After the Wimsey novels, Sayers was free to do the kind of writing she had always wanted to do: manifestly serious work such as religious dramas and a translation of Dante that would occupy most of her time from 1944 to 1957. While working on these demanding projects and writing incisive essays on a wide range of issues, Sayers also became something of a public figure, playing the role of social critic and Christian apologist with great brilliance and panache.

Dorothy L. Sayers. (Library of Congress)

On December 17, 1957, Sayers died of an apparent stroke while alone in the house that she had shared with Fleming from 1928 until his death in 1950. Although she left an unpublished autobiographical fragment, "My Edwardian Childhood," much of Sayers's life is reflected in her novels, which depict the Oxford of her college days (*Gaudy Night*), the Fen wastes of her girlhood (*The Nine Tailors*), and the excitement and confusion of the London she knew as a young writer (*Murder Must Advertise*). Excellent though much of her other work is, Sayers will probably be remembered primarily for her novels.

ANALYSIS

If one should wish to know England as it was between the two world wars—how it was in its customs, among its different classes, and in its different regions, how it regarded itself and the world, what weaknesses festered, what strengths endured—there is no better place to learn its soul or to revel in its singular delights and peccadilloes than in the novels of Dorothy L. Sayers.

When Harriet Vane marries Peter Wimsey in *Busman's Honeymoon*, she happily realizes that she has "married England," revealing that Sayers herself recognized the symbolic import of her hero. As a survivor of World War I, a war that decimated a generation of young Englishmen and left their society reeling, Wimsey represents England's fragile link with a glorious past and its tenuous hold on the difficult present. His bouts of "nerves" and persistent nightmares dramatize the lasting effects of this "War to End All Wars," while his noble attempts at making a meaningful life represent the difficult task of re-creating life from the rubble.

Sayers's England encompasses tiny villages unchanged for centuries (*Busman's Honeymoon*), the golden-spired colleges of Oxford (*Gaudy Night*), the "gloom and gleam" of London (*Murder Must Advertise*), the deceptive calm of the southern seacoast (*Have His Carcase*), the brooding Fens (*The Nine Tailors*), and the primitive north counties (*Clouds of Witness*). The novelist ranges throughout this varied landscape with some constants: Accompanied by his indefatigable "man," Bunter (who is Jeeves transformed), Lord Peter reasons his way through all but one mystery (he is absent from *The Documents in the Case*). Through Wimsey's well-wrought consciousness, Sayers maintains a certain *Weltanschauung* that seems a peculiar blend of mathematical rigor and lush, witty, insightful language.

Carolyn Heilbrun's praise for Sayers's special blend of "murder and manners" points out to an understanding of both the novelist's appeal and her place in English fiction: Sayers is an inheritor not only of the more literary branch of detective fiction but also of the older tradition of the comedy of manners. She can reveal a character, time, or place in a bit of dialogue or one remark. From a brief sentence, for example, the reader knows the Duchess of Denver: "She was a long-necked, long-backed woman, who disciplined herself and her children." A short speech summarizes all *The Unpleasantness at the Bellona Club*, revealing not only a character but also the values and condition of his world:

> Look at all the disturbance there has been lately. Police and reporters—and then Penberthy blowing his brains out in the library. And the coal's all slate. . . . These things never happened before the War—and great

heavens! William! Look at this wine! . . . Corked? Yes, I should think it *was* corked! My God! I don't know what's come to this club!

The character on whom Sayers lavishes most of her considerable talent is Lord Peter. Although it is possible, as some of her critics have said, that Sayers created Wimsey, the perfect mate for an intellectual woman, because actual men had disappointed her, the psychobiographical approach can explain only part of her novels' motivation or meaning. In Wimsey, Sayers dramatizes some significant human problems, including the predicament of the "lost generation," the necessity of every person's having a "proper job," and the imperative synthesis of forces that are often perceived as opposites but are really complementary: intellect and emotion, good and evil, male and female. When viewed in these terms, Sayers's fictional world fits naturally into the entire cosmos of her creation, because it deals with some of the very subjects she addressed in other, more patently serious forms.

It is appropriate to speak of all Sayers's work as one, for, as she concludes in *The Mind of the Maker*, "the sum of all the work is related to the mind [of the artist] itself, which made it, controls it, and relates it to its own creative personality." From beginning to end, Sayers's work investigates the possibility of creative action; for her the creative act consists of establishing equilibrium among competing powers, of drawing together disparate, even warring elements. Of course, given that she writes detective novels, Sayers focuses on the opposite of creative action in the crimes of her villains, crimes that destroy life, property, sanity, peace. Wimsey, who solves the mysteries and thereby makes a life from destruction, is the creative actor.

The Mind of the Maker argues that there is a discoverable moral law, higher than any other, that governs the universe. In a way, Sayers's novels attempt to discover or reveal this universal moral law, which in its most superficial form is reflected in civil codes. This process of moral discovery, however, becomes increasingly complex and ambiguous; if Sayers's subjects are constant, her understanding of them deepens as her art matures. Since Sayers's artistic maturation parallels her hero's development, a comparison of how Wimsey func-

tions in the early and late novels will elucidate both the consistency and the change that mark Sayers's fiction.

WHOSE BODY?

The most striking quality of *Whose Body?* as a first novel is the deftness with which it presents Sayers's hero and his world. In its opening pages, the reader gets to know Lord Peter Wimsey, the dashing man-about-town and collector of rare books (which, amazingly, he seems to read). Keen of mind and quick of tongue, like an exotic bird chirping in a formal English garden that, perhaps, conceals a jolly corpse or two, he is a remarkable personage at birth. Wimsey is also quite marvelously a wealthy man who knows how to spend both his time and his money; his elegant apartment's only acknowledged lack is a harpsichord for his accomplished renditions of Domenico Scarlatti. The product of an older England marked by civility, restraint, and order, Wimsey is accompanied in his first tale by two challengers to his wits and position: his valet, Bunter, and the middle-class Inspector Parker of Scotland Yard, who will make sure that Wimsey never nods during fourteen years of fictional sleuthing. Even his mother, the delightfully balmy Duchess of Denver, is introduced here, and the reader quickly guesses from their relationship that Sayers is interested in how men and women coexist in this world. The Dowager Duchess and her son are as different in appearance as they are similar in character, the narrator remarks, thus signaling that the superficial differences between men and women often conceal more important similarities. Wimsey and his entourage enter the world nearly complete, and their creator has a firm grasp of character, dialogue, and the mystery plot from the beginning of her career.

The theme of *Whose Body?* plants the seeds of one of Sayers's ever-flourishing ideas. Her first and perhaps most horrid villain, Sir Julian Freke, suffers from one of the great problems facing modern people: the disassociation from mind and heart that often renders "civilized" people incapable of moral behavior. The great surgeon Freke, who is aptly named because he is a freakish half-human, denies the importance of intangibles such as the conscience, which he considers akin to the vermiform appendix. With this perfectly criminal attitude, Freke coolly kills and dissects an old competitor, ironically from one of the oldest, least rational of motives, jealousy and revenge. Freke therefore demonstrates Sayers's point: that people, as creatures of both intellect and passion, must struggle to understand and balance both if moral action is to be possible. Freke, the dissector of life, destroys; the destruction he causes awaits the truly healing powers of a creative mind.

The somewhat surprising link between moral action and detective work is suggested by Wimsey, who observes that anyone can get away with murder by keeping people from "associatin' their ideas," adding that people usually do not connect the parts of their experience. The good detective, however, must study the fragments of human life and synthesize the relevant data. This synthesis, the product of imagination and feeling as well as reason, reveals not only "who did it," but how, and why. Thus, according to Sayers's own definitions, her detective pursues moral action in his very sleuthing, not only in its final effects of punishment for the criminal and retribution for society. Wimsey's detective method typifies this creative synthesis by incorporating different aspects of a rich experience: poetry, science, history, psychology, haberdashery, weather reports. When Wimsey finally realizes that Freke is the murderer, he remembers "not one thing, nor another thing, nor a logical succession of things, but everything—the whole thing, perfect and complete . . . as if he stood outside the world and saw it suspended in infinitely dimensional space." In this moment, Wimsey is not merely a successful detective, he is a creator, his mind flashing with godlike insight into human life. The story has moved, therefore, from destruction to creation because disparate aspects of life have been drawn together.

Freke's failure as a human being is exemplified in his failure as a physician, just as Wimsey's successful life is instanced in the skillful performance of his "job," his compulsive "hobby of sleuthing." More than a hobby, detection is actually Wimsey's "proper job." In a crucial discussion with Inspector Parker, Wimsey admits to feeling guilty about doing detective work for fun, but the perceptive Parker warns him that, as a basically responsible person for whom life is really more than a game, he will eventually have to come to terms with the seriousness of his actions. What is clear to the reader at this point is that Wimsey, an English aristocrat displaced by social change and scarred by World War I, is at least

carving out a life that is socially useful while it is personally gratifying. He is not simply feeding the Duke of Denver's peacocks.

If Wimsey seems almost too perfect in the early novels, Sayers redeems him from that state by slowly revealing the finite, flawed, and very human man within the sparkling exterior. To make this revelation, she has to create a woman capable of challenging him, which she does in the character of Harriet Vane. By the time he appears in *The Nine Tailors*, Wimsey is less of a god and more of a human being. After all, the great lover has been humiliatingly unsuccessful in wooing Harriet Vane, whom he saved from the hangman four years earlier in *Strong Poison*. The beginning of *The Nine Tailors* finds Wimsey, the super-sleuth, wandering about the Fens, that bleak terrain of Sayers's childhood, muttering about the misery of having one's car break down on a wintery evening and dreaming of hot muffins. When offered shelter at the rectory of Fenchurch St. Paul, the great connoisseur of haute cuisine is delighted with tea and oxtail stew. The greatest change in Wimsey's character and in Sayers's fiction, however, is evidenced in the novel's richer, more subtle structure, and in its newly complex view of crime and punishment, of good and evil.

THE NINE TAILORS

Indicative of Sayers's increasing subtlety, *The Nine Tailors* is as much a metaphysical meditation on time and change as it is a murder mystery; there is not even a corpse until Part 2. In place of Lord Peter's jolly but rather macabre singing of "We insist upon a [dead] body in a bath" (in *Whose Body?*), *The Nine Tailors* resonates with the sound of church bells and an explication of campanology (bell or change-ringing). The bells at Fenchurch St. Paul, which are rung for both weddings and funerals, seem ambiguously to stand for both life and death, good and evil. The whole question of good versus evil is quite complicated here, for unlike the wholly innocent victim of the cold-blooded murder in *Whose Body?*, the man killed here is probably the worst person in the book, and he is accidentally killed by the ringing of holy bells. Locked in the church's bell chamber as a precaution by someone who knows of his criminal past, Geoffrey Deacon is killed by the intense sound of the bells, and ultimately by the hands of every man who unwittingly pulls a bell rope that New Year's Eve. This group includes Wimsey, who just happens to be there because of several coincidences.

Although Deacon perhaps deserves to die, not only for his jewel robbery but also because of a generally dishonorable life, his death forces Wimsey to reexamine himself and his motives. In ringing the changes, Wimsey thought he was simply following a set of mathematical permutations to a neat conclusion; in reality, he was taking a man's life. This greatly sobers the old puzzle-solver, who has always had some qualms about attacking life as a game. Indeed, Wimsey's role in Deacon's death is but an exaggerated version of the detective's role in any mystery: He causes the villain or criminal to come to justice, which usually means death. Wimsey cannot ignore the consequences of his actions in *The Nine Tailors*, because they are direct, obvious, and significant in human terms. He voices his concern about the morality of all his "meddling" to the rector, who assures him that everyone must "follow the truth," on the assumption that this path will lead invariably if somewhat indirectly to God, who has "all the facts" in the great case of life. Thus, it is impossible to be too curious, to probe too far, to ask too many questions, even though some answers or consequences may be painful.

In this great novel, Wimsey actually experiences the central Christian paradox, that of good coming from evil or of the two being inextricably linked. The mystery is over when he realizes, in a grisly pun, that Deacon's killers are already hanged, since they are the very bells in the church's tower. As one of the inscriptions on this ancient church says, the nine tailors, or the nine peals, "make a man," suggesting that the bells not only signify a man when they toll his passing but also stand as timeless, disinterested judges of human behavior. The dead man, Deacon, mocked honorable work in his thievery, and thus began the cycle of destruction that ends in his own death, a death that ironically leads to Wimsey's discovery or creative act. From evil thus confronted and comprehended, good may grow. Mr. Venables, the rector, wittily pricks Wimsey with the irony that "there's always something that lies behind a mystery . . . a solution of some kind." For Wimsey, as for Sayers, even the solution to a mystery leads to further mysteries; the answer to the mystery of Deacon's death leads to a more subtle inquiry into one of the essential mysteries of life: how to

determine responsibility or meaning for human action. In this paradoxical world, victims may be villains and right action is often based in error, chance, or even transgression.

Wimsey leaves this complex novel with greater insight into himself and the ambiguous nature of life; he is, therefore, finally ready to come to terms with the greatest mystery of his life, Harriet Vane, who is also about ready to accept his inquiry. In *Gaudy Night*, Wimsey reaches his fulfillment, a fulfillment that is expressed in terms of resolving the conflict between man and woman, between intellect and emotion, and between good and evil. In fact, Wimsey's fulfillment represents the culmination of Sayers's search for a resolution of these forces. The novel's subject is also one of Sayers's oldest: the moral imperative for every person to do good work that is well done, and the terrible consequences of not doing so. All of these ideas come into play in this subtle novel, which is on one level the mystery of the "Shrewsbury Poison Pen" and on another, more important one, an unusual and profound love story. Reflecting the subtlety and delicacy with which Sayers spins her tale, there is not even a death in this book; the psychological violence caused by the Poison Pen is alarming, but here evil is banal, and all the more powerful for being so.

GAUDY NIGHT

Gaudy Night takes place at Oxford, which held happy memories for Sayers as the place of her birth and formal education, and the entire novel is a paean to that golden-spired city. Harriet Vane goes to Oxford to attend the Shrewsbury Gaudy, an annual spring homecoming celebration, where she has the opportunity to judge her old classmates and teachers in terms of how well they, as women, have been able to live meaningful lives. Shrewsbury is obviously a fictional version of Somerville, Sayers's college, and just as clearly Vane, a famous detective novelist who is wrestling with the question of "woman's work" and with the problem of rendering reality in fiction, is to some extent Sayers, the self-conscious artist. Having been pursued by Wimsey for five frustrating years, Vane finally accepts him at the end of *Gaudy Night*. She accepts him because the experiences in this book teach her three interrelated things: that Wimsey, as an extraordinary man, will not prevent her from doing her "proper job," a consequence she feared from any relationship with a man; that men and women can live together and not destroy each other, but create a good life; and therefore, that there can be an alliance between the "intellect and the flesh." Vane's discoveries in this novel thus signal the solution of problems that had preoccupied Sayers throughout her career.

Vane learns all of these things through Wimsey's unraveling of the mystery of the Poison Pen, who is a woman frightfully flawed because she has never been able to strike a balance between the intellect and the flesh, and therefore has never done her proper job. Annie Wilson, the Poison Pen who creates so much confusion and instills so much fear in the intellectual women of Shrewsbury, is the victim of sentimentality and a radically disassociated sensibility; she hates all learning because her dead husband was punished long ago for academic dishonesty. Ironically, Harriet Vane suffers from the same problem, but in its other manifestation; she begins the novel capable of trusting only the intellect, and fears any bonds of the flesh or heart. When she finally sees that neither the sentimentality of Annie nor the hyperintellectualism of Shrewsbury can solve the "problem of life," Harriet realizes that it is only through balancing intellect and passion that creative or truly human action is possible.

Wimsey, who solves the mystery because he is able to bring these forces into equilibrium and to acknowledge the potency of both, is rendered acceptable to Vane because of this ability. Her new willingness to admit her feelings reveals to her what Sayers's readers had known for a long time: She loves Wimsey. The man she loves has changed, too. He is no longer an unattainable paragon who sees good and evil as discrete and life as a game, but a middle-aged man who fears rejection and death, who is idiotically vain about his hands, and who, to Harriet's surprise, looks as vulnerable as anyone else when he falls asleep: the man behind the monocle. All of this does not argue that Wimsey is less extraordinary than he was; in fact, perhaps what is most extraordinary about him now is that he seems a real person—flawed, finite, vulnerable—who is yet capable of that rare thing, creative action. Indeed, his very life seems a work of art.

Busman's Honeymoon

Wimsey and Vane finally embark upon marriage, that most mundane and mysterious of journeys, in *Bus-*

man's Honeymoon, the final novel that Sayers aptly called a "love story with detective interruptions": The detective novelist had moved that far from the formula. In the closing scene of this last novel, Wimsey admits that his new wife is "his corner," the place where he can hide from a hostile, confusing world and shed tears for the murderer whose execution he caused. This is not the Wimsey who blithely dashed about in the early novels, treating criminals as fair game in an intellectual hunting expedition, but it is the man he could have become after fourteen years of living, suffering, and reflecting. Indeed, it was a masterful stroke for Sayers to create Harriet Vane, a woman who could match Wimsey's wits and passions, because through her and through his loving her, the reader can learn the most intimate facts of this once-distant hero. If a man is to cry in front of anyone, that witness should most likely be his wife, especially if she is an extraordinary person who understands his tears. The early Wimsey may have been the kind of man that an intellectual woman would imagine for a mate, but the mature Wimsey is one with whom she could actually live. The unpublished fragment of a later novel to be called "Thrones, Dominations" indicates that the Wimsey-Vane marriage was just this workable.

Finally, the marriage of Wimsey and Vane symbolizes the paradoxical and joyful truth of good coming out of evil, for if Harriet had not been falsely accused of murder, they would never have met. She quiets Wimsey in one of his familiar periods of painful self-scrutiny about his "meddling" by reminding him that if he had never meddled, she would probably be dead. The point seems clear: Human actions have consequences, many of which are unforeseen and some painful, but all of which are necessary for life. It is not difficult to imagine a novelist with this vision moving on shortly to the drama of Christ's crucifixion and resurrection, or even the next step, her study and translation of that great narrative of good and evil, desire and fulfillment, mortality and eternity, Dante's *La divina commedia* (c. 1320; *The Divine Comedy*, 1802). Indeed, all of Sayers's work is of a piece, creating that massive unity in diversity by which she defined true art.

Catherine Kenney

OTHER MAJOR WORKS

SHORT FICTION: *Hangman's Holiday*, 1933; *In the Teeth of the Evidence, and Other Stories*, 1939; *Lord Peter*, 1972 (James Sandoe, editor).

PLAYS: *Busman's Honeymoon*, pr. 1937 (with Muriel St. Clare Byrne); *The Zeal of Thy House*, pr., pb. 1937; *The Devil to Pay, Being the Famous Play of John Faustus*, pr., pb. 1939; *Love All*, pr. 1940; *The Just Vengeance*, pr., pb. 1946; *The Emperor Constantine*, pr. 1951 (revised as *Christ's Emperor*, 1952).

POETRY: *Op 1*, 1916; *Catholic Tales and Christian Songs*, 1918; *Lord, I Thank Thee—*, 1943; *The Story of Adam and Christ*, 1955.

RADIO PLAY: *The Man Born to Be King: A Play-Cycle on the Life of Our Lord and Saviour Jesus Christ*, 1941-1942.

NONFICTION: *The Greatest Drama Ever Staged*, 1938; *Strong Meat*, 1939; *Begin Here: A War-Time Essay*, 1940; *Creed or Chaos?*, 1940; *The Mind of the Maker*, 1941; *The Mysterious English*, 1941; *Why Work?*, 1942; *The Other Six Deadly Sins*, 1943; *Making Sense of the Universe*, 1946; *Unpopular Opinions*, 1946; *Creed or Chaos?, and Other Essays in Popular Theology*, 1947; *The Lost Tools of Learning*, 1948; *The Days of Christ's Coming*, 1953 (revised 1960); *The Story of Easter*, 1955; *The Story of Noah's Ark*, 1955; *Further Papers on Dante*, 1957; *Introductory Papers on Dante*, 1957; *The Poetry of Search and the Poetry of Statement, and Other Posthumous Essays on Literature, Religion, and Language*, 1963; *Christian Letters to a Post-Christian World*, 1969; *Are Women Human?*, 1971; *A Matter of Eternity*, 1973; *Wilkie Collins: A Critical and Biographical Study*, 1977 (E. R. Gregory, editor); *The Letters of Dorothy L. Sayers, 1937-1943*, 1998.

TRANSLATIONS: *Tristan in Brittany*, 1929 (of Thomas the Troubadour's romance); *The Heart of Stone, Being the Four Canzoni of the "Pietra" Group*, 1946 (of Dante's poems); *The Comedy of Dante Alighieri the Florentine*, 1949-1962 (*Cantica III* with Barbara Reynolds); *The Song of Roland*, 1957.

CHILDREN'S LITERATURE: *Even the Parrot: Exemplary Conversations for Enlightened Children*, 1944.

EDITED TEXTS: *Oxford Poetry 1917*, 1918 (with Wilfred R. Childe and Thomas W. Earp); *Oxford Poetry 1918*, 1918 (with Earp and E. F. A. Geach); *Oxford Poetry 1919*, 1919 (with Earp and Siegfried Sassoon); *Great Short Stories of Detection, Mystery, and Horror*, 1928-1934 (also known as *The Omnibus of Crime*); *Tales of Detection*, 1936.

BIBLIOGRAPHY

Brabazon, James. *Dorothy L. Sayers: A Biography*. New York: Charles Scribner's Sons, 1981. Authorized biography draws on Sayers's private papers and contains an introduction by her only son, Anthony Fleming. Demonstrates that Sayers's real desire was to be remembered as an author of poetry and religious dramas and as a translator of Dante.

Brown, Janice. *The Seven Deadly Sins in the Work of Dorothy L. Sayers*. Kent, Ohio: Kent State University Press, 1998. Links Sayers's literary and religious works by analyzing the author's representations of the seven deadly sins in her mystery fiction and religious plays. Includes bibliography and index.

Coomes, David. *Dorothy L. Sayers: A Careless Rage for Life*. New York: Lion, 1992. Concentrates on reconciling the author of religious tracts with the detective novelist in order to provide a portrayal of a more "complex Sayers." Draws heavily on Sayers's papers at Wheaton College.

Dale, Alzina Stone. *Maker and Craftsman: The Story of Dorothy L. Sayers*. Rev. ed. Wheaton, Ill.: H. Shaw, 1992. Revised edition of a work originally published in 1978 recounts the events of Sayers's life and describes her many and varied writings.

_____, ed. *Dorothy L. Sayers: The Centenary Celebration*. New York: Walker, 1993. Collection of memoirs and essays situates Sayers within the history of detective fiction. Includes an essay by mystery writer Anne Perry about Sayers and Dante, a brief biography, and an annotated bibliography.

Downing, Crystal. *Writing Performances: The Stages of Dorothy L. Sayers*. New York: Palgrave Macmillan, 2004. Presents an analysis of Sayers's writing from the perspective of performance theory. Argues that Sayers was a modernist whose work anticipated postmodernist irony.

Gaillard, Dawson. *Dorothy L. Sayers*. New York: Frederick Ungar, 1981. Brief volume seeks to establish a link between Sayers's detective fiction and her other literary works. Devotes four chapters to her mystery novels, one to her short stories, and a sixth to a summary of Sayers's literary virtues.

Hall, Trevor H. *Dorothy L. Sayers: Nine Literary Studies*. Hamden, Conn.: Archon Books, 1980. Nine critical essays discuss topics such as the connection between Sayers's creation, Lord Peter Wimsey, and Arthur Conan Doyle's creation, Sherlock Holmes. Also speculates in some detail on the influence of Sayers's husband, Atherton Fleming, on her writing.

McGregor, Robert Kuhn, and Ethan Lewis. *Conundrums for the Long Week-End: England, Dorothy L. Sayers, and Lord Peter Wimsey*. Kent, Ohio: Kent State University Press, 2000. Focuses on how Sayers used the character of Wimsey to comment on British society in the period between the two world wars.

Reynolds, Barbara. *Dorothy L. Sayers: Her Life and Soul*. New York: St. Martin's Press, 1993. Recounts Sayers's life story through the author's letters and conversations and through passages from her writings, depicting a woman of great intellect and generosity.

LEONARDO SCIASCIA

Born: Racalmuto, Sicily, Italy; January 8, 1921
Died: Palermo, Sicily, Italy; November 20, 1989

PRINCIPAL LONG FICTION

Il giorno della civetta, 1961 (*Mafia Vendetta*, 1963)

Il consiglio d'Egitto, 1963 (*The Council of Egypt*, 1966)

Morte dell'inquisitore, 1964 (*Death of the Inquisitor*, 1969)

A ciascuno il suo, 1966 (*A Man's Blessing*, 1968; also known as *To Each His Own*)

Il contesto: Una parodia, 1971 (*Equal Danger*, 1973)

Todo modo, 1974 (*One Way or Another*, 1977)

Candido: Ovvero, Un sogno fatto in Sicilia, 1977 (*Candido: Or, A Dream Dreamed in Sicily*, 1979)

Cronachette, 1985 (novella; *Little Chronicles*, 1990)

1912 + 1, 1986 (novella; English translation, 1989)

Porte aperte, 1987 (novella; *Open Doors*, 1991)

Il cavaliere e la morte, 1988 (novella; *The Knight and Death*, 1991)

Una storia semplice, 1989 (novella; *A Straightforward Tale*, 1991)

The Knight and Death, and Other Stories, 1991

Open Doors, and Three Novellas, 1992

OTHER LITERARY FORMS

Leonardo Sciascia (SHAH-shah) was a prolific writer whose works in a wide variety of literary forms are unified by a passion for justice, an Enlightenment devotion to reason, and an obsession with Sicily and its violent history. Sciascia published poetry (*La Sicilia, il suo cuore*, 1952), drama (*L'onorevole*, pb. 1965), and short stories (*Gli zii di Sicilia*, 1958 [*Sicilian Uncles*, 1986]; *Il mare colore del vino*, 1973, including work by others [*The Wine-Dark Sea*, 1985]) in addition to his novels, but he was particularly productive as a writer of nonfiction. The concerns of his novels, most of which adopt the form of the mystery or detective novel and are based on real incidents, are reflected in his accounts of true crime, *La scomparsa di Majorana* (1975; *The Mystery of Majorana*, 1987), *I pugnalatori* (1976), and *L'affaire Moro* (1978; *The Moro Affair*, 1987).

Among Sciascia's many other books are several works dealing with Sicilian history, two studies of his fellow Sicilian Luigi Pirandello, and several collections of essays and miscellaneous prose, including *Le parrocchie di Regalpetra* (1956; *Salt in the Wound*, 1969), *La corda pazza* (1970), and *Cruciverba* (1983).

ACHIEVEMENTS

Leonardo Sciascia is widely acknowledged as one of the major voices of postwar Italian literature, a gifted novelist, essayist, playwright, and social critic and the preeminent contemporary chronicler of his native Sicily. His novels combine a sophisticated awareness of literary form—like many postmodern novelists, he appropriates and often parodies the conventions of the mystery genre—with an aroused social conscience. His novels, neither affectedly literary and self-referential nor clumsily didactic, resemble the most accomplished fictions of Voltaire and Denis Diderot, with their blend of philosophical inquiry, social indignation, and playful wit.

Among the many literary honors awarded to Sciascia are the Premio Crotone, the Premio Libera Stampa Lugano, and the Premio Prato.

BIOGRAPHY

Leonardo Sciascia was born on January 8, 1921, in Racalmuto, Sicily, the son of a sulfur miner. Completing his schooling at the Istituto Magistrale in Caltanissetta, he began teaching at an elementary school there in 1949; his first book, *Favole della dittatura*, a collection of fables satirizing the Fascists, appeared in 1950. During this period, he also began a career as a journalist and editor, pursued for some time concurrently with his teaching. By the mid-1950's, Sciascia had published several more books, establishing the pattern for his prolific output. All of his works are informed by his lifelong attachment to Sicily and things Sicilian.

ANALYSIS

Leonardo Sciascia's novels usually develop from a single dramatic incident, through which his characters emerge slowly. The subtle analysis of poverty and deluded hope characteristic of his early essays is developed in his fiction to include the corruption of an entire social and political system. He goes beyond appearances to the core of each situation and brings out abuses and contradictions, finding in history the root causes for evils mistakenly held to be incurable. According to the writer's definition, the present struggle for liberty and justice against political and social power is deeply rooted in the past.

The epigraphs of Sciascia's novels indicate his emphasis on historical parallels and relationships. In *Mafia Vendetta*, his first novel, Sciascia uses a line from William Shakespeare's *Henry VI, Part 3* (1591) to suggest that power and corruption existed then as they exist now. *Mafia Vendetta*, *A Man's Blessing*, *Equal Danger*, and *One Way or Another* all deal with the social evils found in Sicily and elsewhere. Each of the four novels is based on actual facts. The story then unfolds like a puzzle: Everything falls into place, piece by piece, as its hidden pattern comes to light. Persuaded by the rigorous logic of the protagonists, the reader understands the workings of society and is awakened to the dishonesty of the system.

MAFIA VENDETTA

Mafia Vendetta opens at a bus stop on a small town square where some fifty people are already seated on board the bus. A man in a dark suit—indicative of his social status—jumps on the running board as the bus is about to leave and suddenly falls to the ground, shot through the back. He was a small building contractor who had ignored the Mafia system of protection. By the time the police arrive, many of the witnesses to the crime have vanished; those who remain claim that they saw nothing. Later, a police informant and a young man who has seen the assassin are also gunned down. The informer had become so nervous after tipping off the police that he unwittingly betrayed himself. On the day he was shot, he had scribbled two names on an airmail letter, adding the words "I am dead. Regards" and his signature. Captain Bellodi, the officer in charge of the investigation, to whom the letter was addressed, feels deep compassion for the agonizing despair that prompted the helpless victim in his fatal decision to speak out.

The Captain is from Parma, and his way of thinking and acting underlines the cultural differences between the North and the South of Italy. Believing firmly that the Mafia must not go unpunished, he spares no effort to solve the case, but he is alone and helpless as he struggles against the law of *omertà*, the Mafia's code of silence, and against complicity on the national as well as the local level.

The conspiracy of silence, a recurrent theme in all of Sciascia's novels, originated in Sicily as a protective measure for the defense of the people against tyranny and injustice. In time, however, it degenerated into an oppressive social system and became one of the basic tools of the Mafia as it is known today: a secret society oriented toward the protection of vested interests.

Courageous and fearless, Captain Bellodi has Don Mariano Arena, the aging *capo mafia* whose name was one of the two on the informer's last letter, brought to the barracks for the twenty-four hours of preliminary arrest, like any other common criminal. Sciascia's account of the interrogation is a masterpiece of realism and dramatic urgency; particularly compelling is the characterization of the Mafia chieftain. Don Mariano divides humanity into five categories. The Captain falls into the first: "Men! and they are few." He recognizes the Captain's integrity, but, like all Sicilians, Don Mariano is deeply devoted to his family. Moreover, he has always been protected by the *omertà* of both the honest and the dishonest. Through his network of connections with influential politicians, he succeeds easily in sabotaging Bellodi's investigation. In fact, when it becomes apparent that Captain Bellodi is too close to the truth, he is reassigned to his home city, Parma, in Northern Italy, where he sadly ponders Sicily's crushing heritage of injustice and death. After Bellodi's departure, everything he has accomplished is undone "like a house of cards blown down by the winds of incontrovertible alibis."

A MAN'S BLESSING

Similar concerns inform Sciascia's third novel, *A Man's Blessing*. The Italian title, *A ciascuno il suo* (to each his due), derives from the Latin expression *unicuique suum*, a term referring to a principle of Roman law that means simply that the punishment should fit the crime. Here the concept is applied ironically.

The story develops from a dramatic incident, a double murder, out of which the characters' and the Sicilians' world gradually takes form. One afternoon, an anonymous letter is delivered to a pharmacist, Manno, informing him that he has been sentenced to death for something he has done. The honest man and his friends dismiss it as a joke. On August 23, 1964, the opening day of the hunting season, both the pharmacist and his constant hunting companion, Dr. Roscio, are mysteriously shot. The wheels of a ponderous bureaucracy begin to turn slowly and ineffectually.

The main character, Professor Laurana, begins his own investigation, out of intellectual curiosity, starting from the first detail that the police had dismissed as in-

significant. When the letter containing the death threat was held open by an officer of the *carabinieri*, with the light of the lamp falling slantingly on it, Professor Laurana happened to notice the word *unicuique* on the reverse side of the threat, which had been made up with words cut out and pasted on the paper. After the murder, Laurana realizes that the word represents the first clue to the mystery, because it had been cut from the masthead of *L'osservatore romano*, a Vatican newspaper. Despite this deduction and several similar intuitions worthy of the great detectives, Laurana is essentially a parody of the brilliant, eccentric amateur. Indeed, he is frequently shown to be quite obtuse, and his solution of the mystery is largely fortuitous. The corruption he discovers is social as well as personal: In this case, the Mafia is represented by the "respectable" lawyer Rosello, a cousin of Dr. Roscio's lovely widow, to whom Laurana is attracted. Dr. Roscio had known of his wife's affair with her cousin and had been planning to blackmail the lawyer Rosello. The pharmacist, then, was an innocent victim whose murder was intended to distract attention from the murder of the real target: Dr. Roscio.

Sciascia's vivid rendition of small-town gossip, of ambiguous remarks dropped at the men's club and in cafés, and of family ties and old prejudices, all of which are brought out during the investigation, reveal a society not only Sicilian but universal. Among the novel's stimulating characters are the bold, frank parish priest and old Benito di Montalmo, both reminiscent of many of Pirandello's characters. In a real sense, the whole town becomes the protagonist in this novel, even though the story centers on Laurana, who naïvely discloses all of his clues to the two cousins, Rosello and Mrs. Roscio. At the end, the beautiful widow invites Laurana to a café in a nearby town but fails to appear. A disappointed Laurana, on his way to the railroad station, accepts a ride from a casual acquaintance and thus seals his fate. Laurana's intellectual value, in an irrational world, is summed up cynically in the brief and merciless comment of his three male friends at the end of the book: "He was a fool!" In other words, he failed to observe the traditional code of silence and accordingly was killed.

EQUAL DANGER

In *Equal Danger*, Sciascia analyzes the legal system through an incident that takes place in an imaginary city where court, police, politicians, protestors, and journalists are equally involved. Complications arise when Cres, who has served five years in prison for a crime that he did not commit, takes the law into his own hands upon his release, murdering the first two judges who sentenced him.

During the subsequent inquiry, Inspector Rogas, assigned to the investigation, discovers a wide net of corruption that includes the two murdered judges. At this point, he is ordered to suspend the inquiry. He rebels and begins to consider Cres no longer as a criminal but as a dispenser of justice. Later, he decides to join Amar, a revolutionary leader, in his plot to overthrow the state to bring about a new real order. Both are mysteriously killed in a museum where they were to meet. Once again, Sciascia confirms that the road to truth is fraught with danger and that misuse of reason results in disaster.

ONE WAY OR ANOTHER

In a completely different setting, *One Way or Another* elaborates upon the issue of the entangled logic of justice. On September 1, 1971, Sciascia made a note of his impressions of a religious retreat; the note appears in his book *Nero su nero* (1979), a Stendhalian journal spanning a period of ten years. This single entry became the genesis of the novel. Hidden in an isolated and unspecified milieu, Don Gaetano, a learned but ambiguously diabolic priest, manages the monastery hotel of Zafer. He organizes spiritual retreats for prominent men, including government ministers, members of Parliament, industrialists, and academics. What is supposed to be a spiritual gathering for the good of the soul turns into a vacation and, between one rosary and another, provides the opportunity to work out profitable negotiations and to plot intrigues. A clever man of the cloth, Don Gaetano fosters corruption.

The story is told by an anonymous painter who by chance stops at the monastery and who cannot refrain from investigating on his own the reasons behind the mysterious murders that occur during the retreat. Once again, however, the truth is not entirely unraveled. The progression that began with the honorable society's racket in *Mafia Vendetta* and became a crime of passion in *A Man's Blessing* and a personal vendetta against the judges in *Equal Danger* culminates in *One Way or Another* in all-pervasive political corruption. Particularly in these two later novels, Sciascia dwells on the hypocrisies and compromises that lie beneath the surface of respectability.

CANDIDO

In *Candido*, a novel inspired by Voltaire's eighteenth century masterpiece, innocence and reason once again clash with the realities of an absurd system. Born one night between July 9 and 10, 1943, after a bombardment, Candido's life is in continuous conflict with the lives of other people, including those of the members of his close family. His insatiable curiosity and desire for truth often get him into trouble. It is not his intention to reveal the hypocrisy of those around him, but he does so by a fortuitous series of incidents: He uncovers his father's illicit activities and causes his suicide; he reveals his grandfather's Fascist past; and he is punished for his honesty and generosity. When Candido inherits his family estate, he is not allowed to cultivate the land, and when he tries to bequeath his property first to the hospital and then to the Italian Communists, some incongruous laws and regulations keep him from doing so. Candido's independence of spirit and love of truth estrange him from all society. After traveling outside Sicily, in Northern Italy and abroad, Candido and his second mistress move to Paris, away from false ideology. This justifies the ambiguous subtitle of Candido's vanished "dream dreamed in Sicily."

Sciascia's prose is vivid, incisive, and richly allusive. Enlivened by a subtle, oblique irony, it underlines the ills derived from a system based on compromise and subterfuge. At times, his language is complex, rich with metaphors, inversions, quotations, and indirect literary allusions. Sciascia uses Sicilian colloquialisms most frequently in his early works, adding a touch of spontaneity and color.

Like the writers of the Enlightenment, however, Sciascia is above all committed to clarity, to freedom from cant. The bitter defeat of Captain Bellodi and the deaths of Professor Laurana, Inspector Rogas, and others are redeemed by these characters' defiance, their refusal to surrender to injustice and compromise; all remain true to themselves, like Sciascia the man and the writer.

Iole F. Magri

OTHER MAJOR WORKS

SHORT FICTION: *Favole della dittatura*, 1950; *Gli zii di Sicilia*, 1958 (*Sicilian Uncles*, 1986); *Il mare colore del vino*, 1973 (with others; *The Wine-Dark Sea*, 1985); *Death of an Inquisitor, and Other Stories*, 1990.

PLAYS: *L'onorevole*, pb. 1965; *Recitazione della controversia liparitana dedicata ad A.D.*, pb. 1969.

POETRY: *La Sicilia, il suo cuore*, 1952.

NONFICTION: *Pirandello e il Pirandellismo*, 1953; *Cronache scolastiche: Nuovi argomenti*, 1955; *Le parrocchie di Regalpetra*, 1956 (essays; *Salt in the Wound*, 1969); *Pirandello e la Sicilia*, 1961; *Feste religiose in Sicilia*, 1965; *La corda pazza*, 1970; *Atti relativi alla morte di Raymond Rousel*, 1971; *La scomparsa di Majorana*, 1975 (*The Mystery of Majorana*, 1987); *I pugnalatori*, 1976; *I Siciliani*, 1977 (with Dominique Fernandez); *L'affaire Moro*, 1978 (*The Moro Affair*, 1987); *Dalle parti degli infedeli*, 1979; *Nero su nero*, 1979; *La Sicilia come metafora*, 1979 (*Sicily as Metaphor*, 1994); *Conversazione in una stanza Chiusa Leonardo Sciascia/Davide Lajolo*, 1981; *Teatro della memoria*, 1981; *Kermesse*, 1982; *La sentenza emeorabile*, 1982; *Cruciverba*, 1983; *Alfabeto pirandelliano*, 1989; *Fatti diversi di storia letteraria e civile*, 1989.

MISCELLANEOUS: *L'onorevole; Recitazione della controversia liparitana; I mafiosi*, 1976; *Opere*, 1987-1996 (3 volumes).

BIBLIOGRAPHY

Cannon, JoAnn. *The Novel as Investigation: Leonardo Sciascia, Dacia Maraini, and Antonio Tabucchi*. Toronto, Ont.: University of Toronto Press, 2006. Cannon examines detective novels by Sciascia and two other writers whose works denounce social ills in late twentieth century Italy. Cannon focuses her discussion on Sciascia's *Open Doors* and *The Knight and Death*, examining how these works condemn the death penalty and abuses of power.

_____. *Postmodern Italian Fiction: The Crisis of Reason in Calvino, Eco, Sciasca, Malerba*. Rutherford, N.J.: Fairleigh Dickinson University Press, 1989. Cannon devotes one of the four essays in her book to an analysis of Sciascia's postmodern novels, placing these works within the social and intellectual context of post-World War II Italy.

Farrell, Joseph. *Leonardo Sciascia*. Edinburgh, Scotland: Edinburgh University Press, 1995. The first critical study of Sciascia. Farrell examines the man, the writer, and the politician, treating both his detective fiction and his historical novels.

Glynn, Ruth. "*Il Consiglio d'Egitto*, Leonardo Sciascia." In *Contesting the Monument: The Anti-Illusionist Italian Historical Novel*. Leeds, England: Northern Universities Press, 2005. Glynn analyzes *The Council of Egypt* and novels by other writers in her examination of the historical novel, which was popular in Italy from the mid-1960's through the early 1990's.

Jackson, Giovanna. *Leonardo Sciascia, 1956-1976: A Thematic and Structural Study*. Ravenna, Italy: Longo Editore, 1981. Jackson provides a comprehensive study of Sciascia's work completed between 1956 and 1976.

"Leonardo Sciascia." In *Dictionary of Italian Literature*, edited by Peter Bondanella and Julia Conaway Bondanella. Rev. ed. Westport, Conn.: Greenwood Press, 1996. The entry on Sciascia in this collection on Italian literature examines his life and works.

Wren-Owens, Elizabeth. *Postmodern Ethics: The Re-Appropriation of Committed Writing in the Works of Antonio Tabucchi and Leonardo Sciascia, 1975-2005*. Newcastle, England: Cambridge Scholars, 2007. Owens examines current debates about the role of the intellectual in Italian society by studying the works of the two authors. She argues that Sciascia uses his writings as a form of dialogue with society and a means of commenting on terrorism, justice, and other social issues.

SIR WALTER SCOTT

Born: Edinburgh, Scotland; August 15, 1771
Died: Abbotsford, Scotland; September 21, 1832
Also known as: First Baronet Scott

PRINCIPAL LONG FICTION

Waverley: Or, 'Tis Sixty Years Since, 1814
Guy Mannering, 1815
The Antiquary, 1816
The Black Dwarf, 1816
Old Mortality, 1816
Rob Roy, 1817
The Heart of Midlothian, 1818
The Bride of Lammermoor, 1819
Ivanhoe, 1819
A Legend of Montrose, 1819
The Abbot, 1820
The Monastery, 1820
Kenilworth, 1821
The Pirate, 1821
The Fortunes of Nigel, 1822
Peveril of the Peak, 1823
Quentin Durward, 1823
St. Ronan's Well, 1823
Redgauntlet, 1824
The Betrothed, 1825
The Talisman, 1825
Woodstock, 1826
The Fair Maid of Perth, 1828
Anne of Geierstein, 1829
Castle Dangerous, 1831
Count Robert of Paris, 1831
The Siege of Malta, 1976

OTHER LITERARY FORMS

Sir Walter Scott's first published work was a translation of two ballads by Gottfried August Bürger, which appeared anonymously in 1796. In 1799, he published a translation of Johann Wolfgang von Goethe's 1773 drama *Götz von Berlichingen mit der eisernen Hand* (*Goetz of Berlichingen, with the Iron Hand*). In 1802, the first two volumes of *Minstrelsy of the Scottish Border* appeared, followed by the third volume in 1803. This

was a collection of popular ballads, annotated and often emended and "improved" with a freedom no modern editor would indulge in. A fascination with his country's past, formed in his early years and lasting all his life, led him to preserve these ballads, the products of a folk culture that was disappearing. In 1805 came *The Lay of the Last Minstrel*, the first of the series of long narrative poems that made Scott the most widely read poet of the day. It was followed by *Marmion: A Tale of Flodden Field* (1808). *The Lady of the Lake* (1810) brought him to the height of his popularity as a poet.

The later poems were less successful, and Scott was gradually eclipsed by Lord Byron. In 1813, he completed the manuscript of a novel he had laid aside in 1805. This was *Waverley*, which appeared anonymously in 1814. (Scott did not publicly admit authorship of his novels until 1827.) It created a sensation and launched him on the series that remained his chief occupation until the end of his life. Other important works were his editions of John Dryden (1808) and of Jonathan Swift (1814); a series of lives of the English novelists, published in 1825; and *The Life of Napoleon Buonaparte: Emperor of the French, with a Preliminary View of the French Revolution*, begun in 1825 and published in nine volumes in 1827. *Chronicles of the Canongate* (1827) comprises three short stories: "The Highland Widow," "The Two Drovers," and "The Surgeon's Daughter."

ACHIEVEMENTS

The central achievement of Sir Walter Scott's busy career is the series of novels that is conventionally designated by the title of the first of them. The sheer bulk of the Waverley novels is in itself impressive, as is the range of the settings the novels present. For example, *Ivanhoe* is set in twelfth century England, *The Talisman* in the Holy Land of the Third Crusade, *Quentin Durward* in fifteenth century France, *The Abbot* in the Scotland of Queen Mary, *Kenilworth* in the reign of Elizabeth I, and *The Fortunes of Nigel* in that of James I. In spite of his wide reading, tenacious memory, and active imagination, Scott was not able to deal convincingly with so many different periods. Moreover, he worked rapidly and sometimes carelessly, under the pressures of financial necessity and, in later years, failing health. Some of the novels are tedious and wooden, mechanical in their plots and stilted in their dialogue. Scott himself was aware of their flaws, and he sometimes spoke and wrote slightly of them.

Most readers, however, find that even the weaker novels have good things in them, and the best of them have a narrative sweep and a dramatic vividness that render their flaws unimportant. The best of them, by common consent, are those set in Scotland as far back as the latter part of the reign of Charles II. When Scott attempted to go further back, he was less successful, but in such novels as the four discussed below—*Waverley*, *Old Mortality*, *Rob Roy*, and *The Heart of Midlothian*—Scott's sense of history is strong. They are among the most impressive treatments of his great theme, the conflict between the old and the new, between Jacobite and Hanoverian, between the heroic, traditional, feudal values of the Tory Highlands and the progressive commercial interests of the Whig Lowlands, between stability and change. Though some of the other novels offer historical conflict of a comparable kind (*Ivanhoe* and *Quentin Durward*, for example), the Scottish novels present the conflict with particular insight and force and convey a strong sense of the good on both sides of it. Scott values the dying heroic tradition even as he recognizes the benefits that change brings. Earlier writers had mined the past to satisfy a market for the exotic, the strange, or the merely quaint. Scott saw the past in significant relation to the present and created characters clearly shaped by the social, economic, religious, and political forces of their time, thus providing his readers with the first fictions that can properly be called historical novels.

BIOGRAPHY

An important factor in the vividness of the Scottish novels was the strong oral tradition to which Sir Walter Scott had access from his early childhood. After a bout with polio in his second year, he was sent away from Edinburgh to his paternal grandfather's house at Sandyknowe in the Border country, in the hope that the climate would improve his health. It did, and though he remained lame for the rest of his life, his boyhood was an active one. In this region from which his ancestors had

sprung, he heard stories of Border raids, Jacobite risings, and religious struggles from people for whom the past survived in a living tradition. Throughout his life he added to his fund of anecdotes, and his notes to the novels show how very often incidents in them are founded on actual events about which he had learned from the participants themselves or from their more immediate descendants.

Scott's father was a lawyer, and in 1786, having attended Edinburgh High School and Edinburgh University, Scott became an apprentice in his father's office. In 1792, he was admitted to the bar, and all his life he combined legal and literary activities. After losing his first love, Williamina Belsches, to a banker, he married Charlotte Carpenter in 1798. In 1805, he entered into a secret partnership with the printer James Ballantyne, and four years later they formed a publishing firm. This firm ran into financial difficulties, and in 1813, Scott escaped ruin only through the intervention of another publisher, Archibald Constable. Scott continued to overextend himself. In 1811, he had bought a farm on the Tweed at a place he named Abbotsford, and in the years that followed he wrote furiously to provide funds for building a splendid house and buying additional land. His ambition was to live the life of a laird. In 1826, the financial collapse of Constable and Ballantyne ruined Scott. In his last years, he worked tirelessly to pay his creditors. The effort told on his health, and he died in 1832, at the age of sixty-one. The debts were finally cleared after his death by the sale of his copyrights.

ANALYSIS

Waverley displays, at the start of Sir Walter Scott's career as a novelist, many of the features that were to prove typical of his best work. In the Jacobite rebellion of 1745, he saw an instance of the conflict between the older feudal and chivalric order, strongly colored with heroic and "romantic" elements, and the newer order of more practical and realistic concerns that had already begun to supplant it. His focus is not on the great public figures whose fates are at stake, and this too is typical. The Pretender, Prince Charles Edward, is not introduced until the novel is more than half over, and most of the major events of this phase of his career are only alluded to, not presented directly. He is shown almost exclusively in his dealings with the fictional character for whom the novel is named, and largely through his eyes.

WAVERLEY

Edward Waverley, like so many of Scott's heroes, is a predominantly passive character who finds himself caught between opposing forces and "wavering" between his loyalty to the House of Hanover and the attractions of the Stuart cause. Though his father occupies a post in the Whig ministry, he has been reared by his uncle Sir Everard, a Tory who had supported the earlier Jacobite rebellion of 1715, though not so actively as to incur reprisals when it was put down. His father's connections procure Edward a commission in King George's army, and he is posted to Scotland. Shortly after arriving there, he makes an extended visit to his uncle's Jacobite friend, the Baron of Bradwardine, and his daughter Rose. When a Highland raider, Donald Bean Lean, steals several of the baron's cows, Waverley goes into the Highlands in the company of a follower of Fergus MacIvor, a chieftain who has the influence to secure the return of the cows. Waverley is impressed by Fergus and infatuated with his sister Flora. They are both confirmed Jacobites preparing to declare for the Pretender upon his arrival in Scotland.

As a result of Waverley's protracted absence and of a mutiny among the small band of men from his family estate who had followed him into the army, Waverley is declared absent without leave and superseded in his office. By coincidence, his father also loses his government position. Waverley's resentment at this twofold insult to his family by the Hanoverian government is heightened when, on a journey to Edinburgh to clear himself, he is arrested. Rescued by Donald Bean Lean, he is later brought to Edinburgh (now in the hands of the Jacobites), meets the Pretender, and is won over to his cause. He takes part in the Jacobite victory at Preston, but is separated from Fergus's troop in a skirmish at Clifton, in which Fergus is captured. After a period in hiding, Waverley is pardoned, through the good offices of Colonel Talbot, whom he had saved from death and taken prisoner at Preston. Fergus is executed for treason.

Objections to *Waverley* usually center on the character of the hero, whom Scott himself called "a sneaking piece of imbecility." Certainly it is possible to be impatient with his lack of self-awareness, and the frequency with which he is acted upon rather than acting puts him often in a less than heroic light. Waverley, however, is not intended to be a Romantic hero, and his susceptibility to external influence is necessary to enable Scott to show within a single character the conflict between the two forces that compose the novel's theme. For most of the book, Scott's view of the hero is ironic, emphasizing his failings. There is, for example, his vanity. One of the things that reconciles his Jacobite Aunt Rachel to his serving in the Hanoverian army is the fact that he is becoming infatuated with a local girl. Scott mocks Waverley's feelings, first by giving their object the inelegant name of Cecilia Stubbs, and then by telling the reader that on Waverley's last Sunday at the parish church he is too preoccupied with his own dashing appearance in his new uniform to notice the care with which Miss Stubbs has arrayed herself. The complement of this detail occurs later in the novel when Waverley, having joined the Jacobites, puts on Highland dress for the first time, and one of Fergus's followers remarks that he is "majoring yonder afore the muckle pier-glass." More seriously, the memory of "the inferior figure which he had made

Sir Walter Scott. (Library of Congress)

among the officers of his regiment," resulting from his inability to keep his mind on detail and routine, contributes to his decision to change sides.

In addition to exposing his vanity, Scott often undercuts Waverley's Romantic view of experience. On finding himself for the first time in the Highlands, he muses over "the full romance of his situation." It occurs to him that "the only circumstance which assorted ill with the rest, was the cause of his journey—the Baron's milk cows! this degrading incident he kept in the background." If, instead of deploring Waverley's inadequacy as a Romantic hero, one attends to the irony with which Scott undercuts his fascination with romance and heroism, one will be better prepared for the author's reluctant dismissal of heroic virtues at the end of the novel. Waverley's character is perfectly appropriate to one who will survive into the new age, an age in which the dashing but destructive energies of Fergus have no place.

The real problem with the character is not his passivity or his ordinariness, but Scott's occasional failure to dramatize certain features of his personality, as opposed to merely making assertions about them. On two occasions he is credited with remarkable conversational powers, but no sample of them is given. During Waverley's period in hiding, Scott declares, "he acquired a more complete mastery of a spirit tamed by adversity, than his former experience had given him," but there is no demonstration of this "mastery." These flaws, however, hardly justify dismissing the characterization as a failure. The eagerness of Waverley's response to the new scenes and experiences he encounters, the growth of his resentment against the established government and his conversion to Jacobitism, his delayed recognition of his love for Rose, the cooling of his regard for Fergus as he comes to see the chieftain's selfishness and then the reawakening of that regard when Fergus is in danger— all these phases of his development are convincingly presented. Moreover, in a few scenes he shows real firmness (for example, his confrontation with Fergus when he has been shot at by one of Fergus's men), and in several he displays active generosity.

This said, one may concede that Waverley remains a rather slender figure to carry the weight of a novel of such length. He does not have to, however, for Scott surrounds him with a number of vivid characters from a wide range of classes and backgrounds. It is chiefly through their speech that he makes his characters live. The dialogue is not consistently successful: The bright small talk between Fergus and Flora can be downright dreadful, and some of the language of the other upper-class characters is stiff. The speech of most of the secondary characters, however, is convincing, and the dialect writing is particularly effective. Scott's most important contribution here is the achievement of a wide variety of tones in dialect speech. Before Scott, dialect was almost exclusively a comic device, but he was able to write dialect in different keys all the way up to the tragic. The best evidence of this is the scene in which Fergus and his follower Evan Dhu Maccombich are condemned to death. When Evan Dhu offers his life and the lives of five others in exchange for his chieftain's freedom, volunteering to go and fetch the five others himself, laughter breaks out in the courtroom. In a speech that loses nothing in dignity by being couched in dialect, Evan Dhu rebukes the audience and then proudly rejects the judge's invitation to plead for grace, preferring to share his chieftain's fate.

Fergus is perhaps the most interesting of the major characters. He possesses throughout the capacity to surprise the reader. Scott prepares the reader carefully for his first appearance. Waverley first hears of him in chapter 15 as an extorter of blackmail or protection money and is surprised to learn that he is nevertheless considered a gentleman. When he is introduced several chapters later, the reader discovers that this feudal leader of a troop of half-savage Highlandmen is a polished and literate individual with a very good French education. He is clearly fond of his sister and yet quite prepared to exploit her as bait to draw Waverley into the Jacobite ranks. In the early part of the novel, the emphasis is on his courage, his hospitality, and his ability to inspire loyalty, and he is for the most part an attractive figure.

Gradually, however, both Waverley and the reader come to view him more critically. It grows increasingly clear that his commitment to the Jacobite cause is founded on self-interest. On learning that Prince Charles Edward is encouraging Bradwardine to leave his estate to Rose instead of to a distant male relative, he attempts to make the prince promote his marriage to Rose. When the prince refuses, he is furious, later saying that he could at that moment have sold himself to the devil or King George, "whichever offered the dearest revenge." As the Jacobite fortunes ebb, however, his generosity returns, and for the first time he attempts to use his influence over Waverley for the latter's good, telling him there is no dishonor in his extricating himself from the now certain wreck of their cause and urging him to marry Rose: "She loves you, and I believe you love her, though, perhaps, you have not found it out, for you are not celebrated for knowing your own mind very pointedly." He refuses to allow Waverley to witness his execution, and, by a generous deception regarding the hour at which it is to take place, he spares his sister the pain of a final interview. As he strides out of his cell, it is he who is supporting Waverley.

Throughout the novel, the portrait of Fergus is sharpened by a number of contrasts, explicit and implicit, between him and other characters. The contrast with Waverley is obviously central. There is also a contrast between him and his sister. While Fergus's Jacobitism is tinged with self-interest and he sometimes resorts to duplicity to advance the cause, Flora's devotion to the Stuarts is absolutely pure. She cannot reconcile herself to her brother's dealing with a thief of Donald Bean Lean's stripe even in the interest of the cause, and she resists his wish that she encourage Waverley's infatuation with her in order to win him to their side. Fergus's preoccupation with the more practical aspects of the campaign is set against Bradwardine's comically pedantic concern with form and ceremony in the question of whether and how to exercise his hereditary privilege of drawing off the king's boots. Bradwardine's old-fashioned loyalty lacks all taint of self-interest, however, and, although he has been largely a comic figure, he behaves after the failure of the rebellion with a gallant fortitude comparable to that of Fergus. In the latter part of the novel, a new character enters to serve as Fergus's complete antithesis. Colonel Talbot, who supplants him in guiding Waverley's fate, differs from Fergus on practically every count—political affiliation, disinterested generosity, attitude toward women, and even age.

Several other characters are paired in contrast. Flora's strength of character, heroic bent, intellectual accomplishments, and striking beauty are repeatedly contrasted with the less remarkable gifts of the placid and domestic Rose. Sir Everard Waverley and his brother Richard are opposite numbers in all respects. When Waverley is arrested on his way to Edinburgh, Melville and Morton, the magistrate and the clergyman who hear his defense, take differing views of his case. One of Fergus's henchmen, Callum Beg, commits a crime for his master when he attempts to shoot Waverley, while Humphry Houghton, one of Waverley's followers, involves himself in a conspiracy and mutiny. Both are carrying out what they mistakenly believe to be their masters' wishes, and they receive differing treatment for their actions.

This network of contrasts contributes much to the unity of a novel that is sometimes criticized as loosely structured. Scott's general preface to the 1829 edition of the whole series lends credence to this charge: "The tale of Waverley was put together with so little care, that I cannot boast of having sketched any distinct plan of the work. The whole adventures of Waverley, in his movements up and down the country with the Highland cateran Bean Lean, are managed without much skill." Whatever Scott meant by this, it cannot really be said that the book is loosely plotted. A glance at the retrospective explanations contained in chapters 31 and 65 will remind any reader of the great number of details that at first looked unimportant but that turn out to be essential to the mechanics of the plot. Such after-the-fact explanations may be technically awkward, and they may lay Scott open to the charge of unnecessary mystification in the episodes leading up to them, but they certainly evidence some careful planning.

It is rather for excessive reliance on coincidence that the plot can be criticized. The retrospective explanations just mentioned make some of these appear less unreasonable and incredible, but there are still a great many of them, and this is true of all Scott's novels. Also, the pace of the narrative is at times uncertain. Although the opening chapters describing Waverley's education are important to an understanding of the character, they make an undeniably slow beginning, and some of the set pieces retard the narrative flow.

In spite of its flaws, however, the novel is sustained by its central theme of the process of historical change and by Scott's ability to do justice to both sides in the conflict. Part of him responded strongly to the gallant romance of the Jacobite and to the love of tradition behind it. At the same time, he realized that the world had passed all that by. As Waverley himself points out, there have been four monarchs since James II was deposed, and the divine right absolutism for which the Stuarts stood would have sorted ill with the political and economic realities of the mid-eighteenth century. So Fergus is executed, his head is stuck up over the Scotch gate, and the Edinburgh youth whom Waverley has engaged as a valet comments, "It's a great pity of Evan Dhu, who was a very weel-meaning, good-natured man, to be a Hielandman; and indeed so was [Fergus MacIvor] too, for that matter, when he wasna in ane o' his tirrivies [tantrums]." In a snatch of dialogue, the heroic perspective is replaced by one more down-to-earth and commonplace. The threat to the prevailing order that the rebellion represented is already diminishing in importance in the popular view. To the common man secure in the established order, the energies that burned in Fergus amount to no more than "tirrivies."

OLD MORTALITY

Old Mortality deals with an earlier rebellion, one in which the issue is religious. Charles II had won the support of the Scottish Presbyterians by subscribing to the Solemn League and Covenant, which provided for the establishment of Presbyterianism as the state religion in Scotland and in England and Ireland as well. After the Restoration, however, Charles sought to impose episcopacy on Scotland, and the Covenanters were persecuted for their resistance to the bishops. In 1679, the assassination of the Archbishop of St. Andrews by a small party of Covenanters led by John Balfour of Burley sparked a gathering of insurgents who managed at Drumclog to defeat the Cavalier forces, under John Graham of Claverhouse, that were sent against them. A few weeks later, however, the Covenanters, divided by moderate and extremist factions, were routed at Bothwell Bridge by an army commanded by the duke of Monmouth. The novel's title is the nickname of an old man who travels through Scotland refurbishing the markers on the graves of the martyred Covenanters.

Out of these events, Scott built one of his starkest and swiftest plots. Once again he portrays a hero caught between conflicting forces. Just after the Archbishop's murder, Henry Morton gives shelter to Burley because

Burley and his father had been comrades-in-arms and Burley had saved the elder Morton's life. Henry Morton's moderate principles lead him to condemn the murder, but he also deplores the oppression that provoked it, and Burley hopes that he will eventually take up arms with the Covenanters. Morton is, however, drawn to the Cavalier side by his love for Edith Bellenden (one of Scott's more pallid heroines) and by his friendship for her granduncle.

Morton receives some firsthand experience of the oppressive measures of the Cavaliers when he is arrested for harboring the fugitive Burley and is brought before Claverhouse. This figure is Burley's opposite number, rather as Talbot is Fergus MacIvor's in *Waverley*, except that Talbot is wholly admirable while Claverhouse is a more complex character. Like Burley, Claverhouse sees in Morton qualities of courage and leadership that could be valuable to the rebels. He is about to have him executed when one of his subordinates, Lord Evandale, intervenes. Evandale is a suitor of Edith, and at her request he generously asks Claverhouse to spare his rival's life. Morton is carried along as a prisoner with Claverhouse's troops, and when they are defeated by the Covenanters at Drumclog, he is set free. Under Burley's auspices, he is given a high post in the rebel army.

In this phase of the novel, Morton shows himself a much more active hero than Waverley. He quickly repays his debt to Evandale by saving his life in the rout of the loyalist forces, and he does so again in a later chapter, when Evandale has become Burley's prisoner. He plays a prominent part in the Covenanters' attempts to take Glasgow. He draws up a statement of the rebels' grievances and presents it to Monmouth just before the battle of Bothwell Bridge, and even though the Covenanters obstinately refuse the terms he secures, he does not defect, but instead fights heroically in the battle that ensues.

In spite of the vigor with which Morton fulfills his commitment to the Presbyterians, they distrust him, and Scott sharply dramatizes their ignorance, factiousness, bigotry, and cruelty. He also exposes the unscrupulous streak in Burley's enthusiasm. This zealot is convinced that the most barbaric cruelties and the rankest deceptions are justified by his cause. He is surrounded by a gallery of fanatics, of whom the most horrifying is the insane preacher Habbakuk Mucklewrath. In flight after the defeat at Bothwell Bridge, Morton and his servant Cuddie stumble upon a group of Covenanting leaders in an isolated farmhouse at Drumshinnel. They have been praying for guidance, and the arrival of Morton, whom they irrationally regard as the cause of their defeat, convinces them that God has sent him to them as a sacrifice. They conduct a kind of trial, though the verdict of death is never in doubt. It is the Sabbath, however, and they are unwilling to execute him before midnight. Eventually, Mucklewrath jumps up to put the clock ahead, crying, "As the sun went back on the dial ten degrees for intimating the recovery of holy Hezekiah, so shall it now go forward, that the wicked may be taken away from among the people, and the Covenant established in its purity."

This display of the Covenanters' fanaticism is the complement of the earlier trial before Claverhouse, in which Morton was threatened with the arbitrary cruelty of the Cavalier side. Ironically, it is Claverhouse who now arrives to save Morton. (He has been led to the farmhouse by Cuddie, who had been allowed to escape.) Most of the Covenanters are slaughtered. Riding back to Edinburgh in the custody of his rescuers, Morton is divided between horror at Claverhouse's habitual cold indifference to bloodshed and admiration for his urbanity and his valor. Claverhouse admits that he is as much a fanatic as Burley but adds, "There is a difference, I trust, between the blood of learned and reverend prelates and scholars, of gallant soldiers and noble gentlemen, and the red puddle that stagnates in the veins of psalm-singing mechanics, crack-brained demagogues, and sullen boors." Scott counters this assessment in the very next chapter by showing the fortitude of one of the Covenanting leaders, Ephraim MacBriar, as he is brutally tortured and then condemned to death. The reader may also recall that it was prolonged imprisonment by the Cavaliers that drove Mucklewrath insane. As in *Waverley*, Scott sees both sides objectively.

Morton is sentenced to exile, and there is a gap of ten years in the narrative. In 1689, when the Glorious Revolution has put William and Mary on the throne, Morton is free to return to Scotland. Edith is on the point, finally, of accepting marriage to Evandale. Claverhouse, loyal to the Stuarts, is now ironically a rebel in his turn. He is killed in the battle of Killecrankie, but his army is victo-

rious. He had once said to Morton, "When I think of death . . . as a thing worth thinking of, it is in the hope of pressing one day some well-fought and hard-won field of battle, and dying with the shout of victory in my ear—*that* would be worth dying for, and more, it would be worth having lived for!" The rather too crowded closing pages describe the deaths of Burley and Lord Evandale.

The novel displays Scott's dramatic gifts at their best. Though the language of Morton, Edith, and Evandale is sometimes stiff, the dialogue of the rest of the characters is vigorous and precisely adjusted to their various stations and backgrounds, and the language of the Covenanters, loaded with scriptural allusions, idioms, and rhythms, constitutes a particularly remarkable achievement. In addition to the characters already discussed, three others stand out. One is Sergeant Bothwell, who is descended from an illegitimate son of James VI and resents his failure to attain preferment. He is one of the novel's chief embodiments of the bullying oppression and extortion to which the Covenanters are subjected, but he is also capable of the courtesy and bravery that he regards as incumbent on one of his blood. Another is Mause Headrigg, whose compulsive declarations of her extreme Presbyterian principles are always ill timed, to the chagrin of her pragmatic son Cuddie, who has no ambition to become a martyred Covenanter. The third is Jenny Dennison, Edith's maid. Like her mistress, Jenny has a suitor on each side of the conflict, and Scott thus creates a comic parallel to the Morton-Edith-Evandale triangle. She chooses Morton's servant Cuddie over her other suitor, a soldier in the Cavalier army, and this match foreshadows the eventual union of Edith and Morton. Jenny, however, has more vitality, resourcefulness, and charm than her mistress. She has been criticized for trying to promote Edith's marriage to the wealthy Evandale with a view to securing the future of herself, her husband, and their children. One can admit this fault and go on to point out that it is related to the success of the characterization. The most convincing characters in *Old Mortality* are those in whom Scott reveals a mixture of motivations or a blending of admirable with deplorable traits.

ROB ROY

Rob Roy is probably the least successful of the four novels considered here. It resembles *Waverley* in that it takes a young Englishman into the Highlands during a Jacobite rising, this time that of 1715. Like Edward Waverley, Frank Osbaldistone has a Romantic and poetical turn and responds eagerly to the unfamiliar world of the Highlands. Like Waverley, he has a touch of vanity and of obstinacy in his temper. Like Waverley, he is slow to understand his feelings for the heroine. That he is not as slow as Waverley was to realize that he loved Rose may be attributed to two factors: There is only one possible object for Frank's affections, not two; and that object, Diana Vernon, bears a much closer similarity to Flora, who captivated Waverley immediately, than to Rose.

Frank Osbaldistone, however, is a less interesting hero than Waverley, largely because he does not experience any serious internal conflict. In spite of his love for Diana, a committed Jacobite, he never considers supporting the Pretender. His conflicts are all external. Having angered his father by refusing to follow him into trade, Frank is sent to stay with his uncle's family in Northumberland, to be replaced in the firm by one of his cousins. Though it is understandable that his father should turn to a nephew when his son has disappointed him, it is not clear what point he has in sending Frank to Osbaldistone Hall. Frank's uncle and five of his cousins are boors with no interests beyond hunting and drinking. The sixth son, Rashleigh, is clever, villainous, ugly, and lame. He is the one chosen to take Frank's place in the firm. He had been tutor to Diana, who is his cousin on his mother's side, but had attempted to seduce her, and she has since kept him at a distance. Nevertheless, their common Jacobite sympathies remain a bond between them. Rashleigh, resenting Diana's obvious liking for Frank and smarting under an insult from him, forms a plan that will ruin the Osbaldistone firm and at the same time hasten the rising of the clans in support of the Pretender. The financial details of this scheme are not clear, and it therefore lacks credibility. This flaw in the plot is fairly serious because in *Rob Roy* commercial activity has considerable thematic importance.

Once in London, Rashleigh wins his uncle's confidence and then absconds with certain crucial documents. Frank's task is to follow him to Glasgow and then into the Highlands to recover them. It is in fact not Frank but Diana Vernon's father (whose identity is a mystery to Frank and the reader until the end of the book) who gets the documents back, and this in spite of the fact that he is also a Jacobite and might thus be expected to further rather than thwart Rashleigh's plot. Punishment comes to Rashleigh not from Frank but from the Highland chieftain Rob Roy. Rashleigh turns traitor to the Jacobites, and, after the failure of the rebellion, he arranges the arrest of Diana and her father. In the process of rescuing them, Rob Roy kills Rashleigh.

Thus, though Frank is a party to his fair share of adventures, he is too often merely a party rather than the chief actor, even though he is clearly meant to be the hero. Although Rob Roy appears at practically every crisis of the story, those appearances are intermittent, and the crises mark stages in the experience of Frank. Everything, down to the use of Frank as first-person narrator, points to him as the central character. (Everything, that is, except the title, but a writer with Scott's sense of what sells would hardly call a book *Osbaldistone*.) At too many crucial points, however, Rob Roy displaces Frank as the focus of the reader's interest. Though their relationship may appear to resemble that of Waverley and Fergus or of Morton and Burley, Morton and even Waverley are more active characters than Frank and thus are never eclipsed by Burley and Fergus to the extent that Frank is by Rob Roy. This seems to be largely a result of the bonds that unite Fergus with Waverley and Morton with Burley in a common enterprise for much of their respective stories. The cause shared by each pair of characters makes it possible for each pair to share the spotlight, so to speak, against a common background without compromising the novel's unity. Rob Roy and Frank, by contrast, do not act together in a public cause, since Frank is not a Jacobite. Furthermore, the distance between them is emphasized in the early part of the novel by the fact that, though he takes action several times in Frank's behalf, Rob Roy's identity is unknown to Frank until the novel is half over. In short, the plot keeps these characters separate as Waverley is not kept separate from Fergus or Morton from Burley, and as a result the novel seems marred by a divided focus.

There is also a failure to unify the public and the private themes as convincingly as in the other two novels. The vagueness of the link between the ruin of the Osbaldistone firm and the rising of the clans has already been noted. A related problem is the absence of specificity about Diana Vernon's Jacobite activities. A wary reader will recognize Scott's irony in having Frank respond to an early warning about Diana with the words, "Pshaw, a Jacobite?—is that all?" There is, however, a lack of concrete detail about her role in the conspiracy. This is perhaps inevitable, given the first-person point of view and the fact that Diana keeps Frank out of the secret of the conspiracy, but it weakens the characterization of the heroine. In contrast, Flora MacIvor's political obsession is fully convincing. Diana is perhaps not meant to seem as much a fanatic as Flora, yet she too has sacrificed all personal inclination to the cause—or to her father's will. At the end of the novel, the reader learns that her father has been a central figure in the conspiracy and has often stayed at Osbaldistone Hall in the disguise of a priest, and that Rashleigh's hold over Diana resulted from his having penetrated her father's disguise. This is a fairly dramatic situation, but the reader is, so to speak, asked to do the dramatizing in retrospect. The specifics about Diana's part in the conspiracy are too little, too late.

Since Sir Frederick Vernon has no identity for the reader until the closing pages, he can never be more than a minor figure, yet Scott assigns to him the account of the actual rebellion. In the penultimate chapter, the rebellion and its collapse are perfunctorily described by Sir Frederick in less than two pages. This is a signal failure to unify the personal and historical dimensions. Instead of the climax that it should have been, the 1715 rising seems almost an afterthought.

There is, however, a good deal of effective characterization in the novel. Diana Vernon is probably the most attractive and interesting of Scott's heroines. She is well educated, strong-minded, outspoken, aggressive, and witty. She may not quite hold her own in the company to which critical opinion sometimes promotes her, the company of William Shakespeare's Beatrice and Jane Austen's Elizabeth Bennett, but the dialogue Scott gives her does indeed amply express intelligence and vitality. If there is one false note, it is Scott's finally allowing her to marry Frank, but one's reservations may be qualified by the consideration that Frank seems politically almost neutral. If he does not support the Stuarts, he is not in the debt of Hanover either. It is not quite as if Flora MacIvor had married Edward Waverley.

Diana first appears before Frank on horseback wearing "what was then somewhat unusual, a coat, vest, and hat, resembling those of a man, which fashion has since called a riding-habit." Scott several times underlines her firm and forthright behavior by comparing it to a man's. There is a much stronger masculine streak in the only other important female character in this book, which has just four speaking roles for women. Rob Roy's wife, Helen, is a virago capable of ambushing a British troop with only a small band and of cold-bloodedly ordering the drowning of a hostage. She should have been a powerful figure, but the language she speaks is impossibly bookish and rhetorical, an objection that is not sufficiently answered by Scott's later remarking that her "wild, elevated, and poetical" style is caused by the fact that she is translating from Gaelic into English, "which she had acquired as we do learned tongues."

The characterization of Rob Roy himself is on the whole successful, despite a certain lack of impact in his first few appearances, during which a reader who has skipped Scott's unusually cumbersome prefatory material may not even realize that this is the titular character. He gains added weight by being the chief embodiment of one side of the novel's main thematic conflict. The focus of the novel is not on the Jacobite-Hanoverian struggle but on the related but distinguishable conflict between the half-barbaric feudal life of the Highland clans and the modern commercial world of trade. Rob Roy is an outlaw relying on blackmail to support himself and his followers, who acknowledge no leader but him. Their way of life breeds narrow loyalties (a point emphasized also by the judge in the trial of Fergus MacIvor). Helen MacGregor cannot "bide the sight o' a kindly Scot, if he come frae the Lowlands, far less of an Inglisher." The clansmen are a threat to peace and order because rebellion and disorder are conditions far more likely to improve their lot. As Rob Roy says of the expected uprising, "Let it come . . . and if the world is turned upside down, why, honest men have the better chance to cut bread out of it."

Rob Roy is contrasted with the Glasgow weaver and magistrate Bailie Nichol Jarvie. A business associate of the Osbaldistone firm, he accompanies Frank in his pursuit of Rashleigh. Scott makes Rob Roy and Jarvie kinsmen in order to point out the contrasts between them more sharply. These contrasts are most clearly drawn in two fine scenes, one in the Glasgow jail midway through the novel and the other near the end. In the latter scene, when Bailie Nichol Jarvie deplores the ignorance of Rob Roy's sons, the Highlander boasts, "Hamish can bring down a black-cock when he's on the wing wi' a single bullet, and Rob can drive a dirk through a twa-inch board." Jarvie retorts, "Sae muckle the waur for them baith! . . . An they ken naething better than that, they had better no ken that neither." Rob Roy scorns his kinsman's offer to take his sons as apprentices: "My sons weavers! . . . I wad see every loom in Glasgow, beam, traddles, and shuttles, burnt in hell-fire sooner!" Shortly afterward, however, he admits to Frank that he is troubled at the thought of his sons "living their father's life." That kind of life in fact remained possible for only about three more decades, for after the rising of 1745, the rule of law was extended into the Highlands and the power of the clans was permanently broken.

That defeat in effect completed the Union of England and Scotland that had been established in 1707. In chapter 27, when Andrew Fairservice, Frank's servant, speaks disparagingly of the Union, Jarvie sternly rebukes him:

> Whisht, sir—whisht! it's ill-scraped tongues like yours, that make mischief atween neighbourhoods and nations. . . . I say, Let Glasgow flourish! . . . judiciously and elegantly putten round the town's arms, by way of by-word—Now, since St. Mungo catched herrings in the Clyde, what was ever like to gar [make] us flourish like the sugar and tobacco trade? Will ony body tell me that, and grumble at the treaty that opened us a road westawa' yonder?

Jarvie expresses Scott's own sense of the benefits that the growing commercial activity of the eighteenth century had brought to Scotland. Emotionally, he admired the Romantic and adventurous character of Rob Roy's way of life, but his reason put him finally on the Bailie's side. Jarvie states the theme in terms of honor versus credit: "I maun hear naething about honour—we ken naething here but about credit. Honour is a homicide and a bloodspiller, that gangs about making frays in the street; but Credit is a decent honest man, that sits at hame and makes the pat play [pot boil]."

THE HEART OF MIDLOTHIAN

The Heart of Midlothian is regarded by many as Scott's best work. In addition to the familiar virtues of a fully realized specific historical milieu and a large cast of characters from a variety of social levels who create themselves through the dialogue, the novel has for its heroine one of the common people, with whom Scott's powers of characterization were at their surest, and it has a truly serious ethical theme in the heroine's refusal to lie to save the life of her younger sister. Jeanie Dean's dilemma enables Scott to examine the relation of the law to justice and to mercy.

The novel opens with an extended presentation of an actual historical event, the Porteous riots in Edinburgh in 1736. Immediately after the execution of a smuggler named Wilson, John Porteous, captain of the City Guard, reacts to a minor disturbance among the spectators by needlessly ordering his troop to fire on the crowd. Several people are killed, and Porteous is sentenced to be hanged. On the very day set for his execution, he is reprieved by Queen Caroline. That night a mob storms the prison, the Tolbooth (to which the novel's title is a reference). Porteous is dragged out and hanged.

In Scott's version, the mob is led by George Robertson, an accomplice of Wilson, who would have died along with him had Wilson not generously made possible his escape. Robertson has another reason besides revenge on Porteous for breaking into the Tolbooth. In the prison is Effie Deans, who has been seduced by him and has borne his child. She is to stand trial under a statute that stipulates that if a woman conceals a pregnancy and then can neither produce the infant nor prove that it died a natural death, she shall be presumed to have murdered the child and shall suffer the death penalty. Once inside the prison, Robertson seeks her out and urges her to make her escape in the confusion, but she refuses. (One wonders why he does not remove her forcibly, but evidently he has his hands full directing Porteous's fate.) The next night, Robertson summons Effie's sister Jeanie to a remote spot and tells her that the case can be removed from under the statute if Effie is found to have communicated her condition to anyone. Jeanie refuses to lie about her sister's having done this, and she repeats her refusal in an affecting interview with Effie just before the trial. When Effie is condemned to death, Jeanie travels on foot all the way from Edinburgh to London, wins the support of the duke of Argyle, and persuades Queen Caroline to pardon her sister. A few days after Effie is released, she elopes with Robertson.

At this point the novel is in effect finished, or nearly so, but Scott added a fourth volume to stretch the book to the length for which he had contracted. In it, the duke of Argyle arranges for Jeanie, her new husband Reuben Butler (a clergyman), and her father to remove to a remote part of Scotland under his protection. This pastoral coda contrasts too strongly with the tone of the rest of the novel, and there is an unfortunate emphasis on the material blessings showered on Jeanie that rather qualifies one's sense of the disinterested heroism of her achievement. The closing chapters are, to be sure, tied to the main plot by the reappearance of Effie and her husband and by the discovery of their son, now a member of a small gang of bandits. Robertson is killed in an encounter with this gang, probably by his own son. There is an interesting variation on the novel's central situation, for the son, probably actually guilty of unnatural murder as his mother Effie was not, escapes when Jeanie goes to the room where he is confined and in her compassion loosens his painfully tight bonds. If this repetition of the novel's central event, Jeanie's saving a prisoner from execution, is aesthetically interesting, it is nevertheless ethically problematic, for the youth is a lawless individual who shows no compunction at what he has done and who does not hesitate, once Jeanie has loosened his bonds, to endanger her life by setting a fire in order to effect his escape. Jeanie's mercy seems in this case ill-judged.

It is the first three volumes that contain the most effective probing of the relation of the law to justice and to mercy. Scott contrasts a number of characters, each of whom stands in a different relation to the law. Wilson is a criminal justly condemned for smuggling, but his last offense is the generous one of saving a life by enabling his young accomplice to escape, and it wins him the sympathy of the populace and sets him in sharp contrast to the enforcer of the law, the captain of the City Guard. Porteous's excessive zeal in the performance of his office leads to the loss of life and earns him the hatred of the populace when he gives the order to fire on the crowd. His callousness is also shown by his earlier refusal to loosen Wilson's painfully tight handcuffs on the way to the execution, pointing out that all his pain will soon be at an end.

Among the mob that punishes Porteous, Robertson is concerned to preserve order because he wishes to stress the justice of their action, yet in his own person he has much to fear from justice. He is, moreover, clearly moved more by a desire for revenge than by a true concern for justice, and also, as has already been noted, he has in Effie Deans an ulterior motive for storming the Tolbooth.

Of all the prisoners the novel describes, Effie is in the worst plight, since she is entirely innocent of the crime she is charged with and since the statute does not even require that a crime be proved to have occurred. Moreover, she is in a sense to suffer for the guilt of others, for the government wishes to make an example of her because of the increasing frequency of child murder. Also, the queen's anger at the response to the pardon of Porteous makes a royal pardon for Effie unlikely. Her situation is rendered more hopeless by these two factors that in strict justice have no bearing on her case.

Effie is linked with Wilson in that he and she have both sacrificed themselves for Robertson. Effie staunchly refuses to reveal her seducer's identity, even when she is "offered a commutation and alleviation of her punishment, and even a free pardon, if she would confess what she knew of her lover." In her desire to protect Robertson, she goes so far as to withhold all information concerning Meg Murdockson, the woman to whom Robertson had sent her when her child was due.

Robertson clearly does not deserve her generosity (or Wilson's, for that matter). He is completely selfish. Effie is not the first girl he has abused. Meg Murdockson had long been a servant in his family, and he had seduced her daughter Madge. When her mother put Madge's infant out of the way so it would not pose an obstacle to Madge's finding a husband, Madge lost her wits. She is one of a number of pathetic simpletons who wander through Scott's novels, a company that includes David Gellatley in *Waverley* and Goose Gibbie in *Old Mortality*. Robertson's guilt in Madge's case has far-reaching consequences, for it is anger at the prospect of Effie's taking her daughter's place that moves Meg Murdockson to spirit away Effie's infant and later to attempt to waylay Jeanie on her journey to London.

Robertson's real name is Staunton. He has been among other things an actor, and this is appropriate, for, besides being selfish, he is the rankest hypocrite. In the scene where he confronts Jeanie to explain how she can save her sister, he heaps blame on himself liberally, but it is all empty gesture and rhetoric. He expects someone else to solve the problem. Jeanie is to save Effie by telling a lie when he could do it by surrendering himself and telling the truth. When Effie has finally been sentenced, then indeed he leaps on his horse with the intention of securing her reprieve by giving himself up as the leader of the Porteous mob, but his horse loses its footing and Staunton is thrown and severely injured. Jeanie learns of this on her journey to London when, by a remarkable coincidence, she meets him in his father's house, where he is recuperating. He authorizes her to trade his life for that of her sister, but only if her own unsupported plea is refused.

When Effie is reprieved and Staunton marries her, he becomes an actor in good earnest, and so does she. Sir George and Lady Staunton live for years in fear that their past will be discovered, and his unhappiness is much aggravated by the fact that they are childless. A series of coincidences reveals that their son is not dead, but is part of a small gang of bandits in the very vicinity where Jeanie and her family now live. When Staunton arrives in search of him and is killed, Jeanie prepares the body for burial. She discovers "from the crucifix, the beads, and the shirt of hair which he wore next his person, that his sense of guilt had induced him to receive the dogmata of a religion, which pretends, by the maceration of the body, to expiate the crimes of the soul." The verb "pretends" conveys Scott's view of the appropriateness of Staunton's conversion to Roman Catholicism.

Jeanie Deans, in contrast, is firmly anchored in her father's rigid Presbyterianism and has a horror of every kind of pretense or falsehood. Her principles prevent her from lying to save Effie, but her generosity enables her to accomplish what all of Staunton's empty heroics are powerless to achieve. It is interesting to consider a misunderstanding that arises between Jeanie and her father, David Deans, regarding her testifying at Effie's trial. Deans is a Cameronian, the strictest kind of Scottish Presbyterian, and his memory goes back to the battle of Bothwell Bridge and the persecutions that followed it. He is doubtful of the propriety of even appearing in court, as doing so might seem to constitute an acknowledgment of a government that has abandoned the Solemn League and Covenant and that exercises what he regards as undue influence over the Kirk. Though Deans has never before hesitated to tell anyone what to do, in the present case he says to himself, "My daughter Jean may have a light in this subject that is hid frae my auld een—it is laid on her conscience, and not on mine—If she hath freedom to gang before this judicatory, and hold up her hand for this poor cast-away, surely I will not say she steppeth over her bounds." The inconsistency is too touching and too clearly rooted in his love for Effie to be called hypocrisy. It is another instance of the conflict between principles of conduct and emotional claims, and it enriches the character and underlines his relation to the central theme.

When he attempts to convey to Jeanie his resolution of his scruples, she, who has no thought of refusing to appear in court, takes it that he is encouraging her to give false testimony. The misunderstanding increases her sense of isolation and lack of support and thus makes her behavior all the more heroic.

The heroic impact of the journey itself is marred somewhat by the melodramatic events with which Scott seeks to enliven it. The lurid coloring is overdone in the scene of Jeanie's captivity at the hands of Meg, Madge, and two underworld cronies of theirs (to whom the old woman is known as Mother Blood). Scott is more successful when he modulates into comedy in the scene in which the demented Madge, in the absence of Meg and the others, leads Jeanie to a nearby village and then into church, where Madge's fantastic behavior causes her captive considerable embarrassment. The tension between the comic elements here and the very real danger of Jeanie's situation makes a strong effect. Shortly afterward, however, the tone shifts back to melodrama with the coincidental meeting with the convalescent Staunton, and the dramatic temperature drops during one of those retrospective narratives that Scott's complex plotting often forced on him.

The climactic confrontation with the queen is very well done. Oddly enough, although Scott often had trouble finding a convincingly natural mode of utterance for his invented characters of the upper class, for actual historical figures he often succeeded in writing dialogue that is elevated without being stilted, polished without being wooden. Such is the language of Prince Charles Edward in *Waverley*, of Claverhouse in *Old Mortality*, and of Queen Caroline here.

The psychology of the queen and her language are noteworthy. Jeanie's simple plea is effective, but it is not, or not only, emotional considerations that cause the queen to grant the pardon. Even her response to Jeanie's main speech—"This is eloquence"—suggests objective evaluation of the speech more than emotional assent, and Scott keeps the scene well clear of sentimentality by a persistent emphasis on the political factors in the queen's decision. She is divided between resentment of the Scots for their response to her pardoning of Porteous and her inclination to remain on good terms with Jeanie's sponsor, the duke of Argyle. Even though he is at present out of favor, her policy is based on the principle that political allies may become opponents and opponents may again become allies. Another element in the scene is her complex attitude toward Lady Suffolk, also present at the interview. The queen has so arranged matters that Suffolk is both her chief confidant and the king's mistress. After inadvertently making a remark that the queen construes as a reflection on herself, Jeanie rights herself with a chance reference to "the stool of repentance," the punishment in Scotland "for light life and conversation, and for breaking the seventh command." The queen is amused at the obvious embarrassment of "her good Suffolk."

The novel as a whole indicates that although the law is an absolute necessity, it can never do more than approximate justice because it is made and administered by human beings. It is ironically the generous instincts of Effie (in protecting Staunton) and the uncompromising honesty of Jeanie that make Effie the victim of a law that, it is repeatedly suggested, is a bad law because it exacts punishment in cases where there may have been no crime. It seems unjust too that the strict enforcement in the present instance is caused by factors external to Effie's case, the rise in child murder and the royal anger over the Porteous affair. Moreover, the author tends to place the human agents who enforce the law in an unflattering light. Porteous abuses the authority vested in him. The Doomster, or executioner, is a kind of untouchable who inspires horror in everyone when he makes his ritual appearance at Effie's sentencing. Ratcliffe, a thief four

times condemned to the gallows, is the only prisoner besides Effie who rejects the opportunity to escape when the mob breaks into the Tolbooth. His reason is that he wants the post of underturnkey. The authorities actually grant this audacious request after considering how valuable his knowledge of the underworld is likely to prove. Scott provides a striking emblem of the amount of practical compromise involved in the enforcing of the law when he shows Ratcliffe and Sharpitlaw, the superintendent of police, at the start of the interview in which they bargain over Ratcliffe's request: "They sate for five minutes silent, on opposite sides of a small table, and looked fixedly at each other, with a sharp, knowing, and alert cast of countenance, not unmingled with an inclination to laugh."

The scene with the queen indicates that the prerogative of mercy that is intended to mitigate the sternness of the law or correct miscarriages of justice is likewise governed by considerations of policy and expediency. The outcome of that scene, however, shows that the gap between ideal justice on one hand and policy or expediency on the other can be bridged by the selfless exertions of someone motivated simply by love.

Although the four novels discussed here are likely to appear on anyone's list of the best of Scott, they are by no means the only ones worthy of a modern reader's attention. *The Antiquary*, *The Bride of Lammermoor*, *A Legend of Montrose*, and *Woodstock* have all found advocates among modern critics. There is also a very successful third panel in what might be called the Jacobite triptych that includes *Waverley* and *Rob Roy: Redgauntlet*, set in the 1760's, describes the last throes of the Jacobite movement. In addition to a plot full of intrigue, it is noteworthy for its combination of letters and journals with third-person narration and for autobiographical elements in the main characters of Alan Fairford and Darsie Latimer. Obviously Scott will never again have the huge audience he enjoyed throughout the nineteenth century, but he is more than merely a chapter in literary history. In addition to establishing the genre of the historical novel and influencing nineteenth century historiography, he wrote several novels that can be judged major achievements by any but the most narrow and rigid criteria.

John Michael Walsh

OTHER MAJOR WORKS

SHORT FICTION: "Wandering Willie's Tale," 1824; *Chronicles of the Canongate*, 1827 (2 volumes); "Death of the Laird's Jock," 1828; "My Aunt Margaret's Mirror," 1828; "The Tapestried Chamber," 1828.

PLAYS: *Halidon Hill*, pb. 1822; *Macduff's Cross*, pb. 1823; *The House of Aspen*, pb. 1829; *Auchindrane: Or, The Ayrshire Tragedy*, pr., pb. 1830; *The Doom of Devorgoil*, pb. 1830.

POETRY: *The Eve of Saint John: A Border Ballad*, 1800; *The Lay of the Last Minstrel*, 1805; *Ballads and Lyrical Pieces*, 1806; *Marmion: A Tale of Flodden Field*, 1808; *The Lady of the Lake*, 1810; *The Vision of Don Roderick*, 1811; *The Bridal of Triermain: Or, The Vale of St. John, in Three Cantos*, 1813; *Rokeby*, 1813; *The Ettrick Garland: Being Two Excellent New Songs*, 1815 (with James Hogg); *The Field of Waterloo*, 1815; *The Lord of the Isles*, 1815; *Harold the Dauntless*, 1817.

NONFICTION: *The Life and Works of John Dryden*, 1808; *The Life of Jonathan Swift*, 1814; *Lives of the Novelists*, 1825; *The Life of Napoleon Buonaparte: Emperor of the French, with a Preliminary View of the French Revolution*, 1827; *Religious Discourses by a Layman*, 1828; *Tales of a Grandfather*, 1828-1830 (12 volumes); *The History of Scotland*, 1829-1830; *Letters on Demonology and Witchcraft*, 1830.

TRANSLATIONS: *"The Chase," and "William and Helen": Two Ballads from the German of Gottfried Augustus Bürger*, 1796; *Goetz of Berlichingen, with the Iron Hand*, 1799 (of Johann Wolfgang von Goethe's play).

EDITED TEXTS: *Minstrelsy of the Scottish Border*, 1802-1803 (3 volumes); *A Collection of Scarce and Valuable Tracts*, 1809-1815 (13 volumes); *Chronological Notes of Scottish Affairs from the Diary of Lord Fountainhall*, 1822.

BIBLIOGRAPHY

Crawford, Thomas. *Scott*. Rev. ed. Edinburgh: Scottish Academic Press, 1982. Revision and elaboration of Crawford's widely acclaimed study of Scott, originally published in 1965. Examines Scott's work as a novelist, poet, and balladist.

Cusac, Marian H. *Narrative Structure in the Novels of Sir Walter Scott*. The Hague: Mouton, 1969. Study of Scott's narrative structure separates his fiction into three classifications: romances, chronicles, and the mediocre hero history. Supplemented with informative appendixes, including classifications of Scott's novels and significant recurring elements. Includes a bibliography.

DeGategno, Paul J. *"Ivanhoe": The Mask of Chivalry*. New York: Twayne, 1994. Provides a good general introduction to one of Scott's most compelling and long-lived works. Places the novel within its literary and historical context and then focuses on an analysis of the book; emphasizes the novel's pertinence to its own time and its importance as a reflection of Scott's society.

Dekker, George. *The Fictions of Romantic Tourism: Radcliffe, Scott, and Mary Shelley*. Stanford, Calif.: Stanford University Press, 2005. Argues that Scott, Ann Radcliffe, and Mary Shelley were not only Romantic novelists but also "contributors to the discourse of Romantic tourism." Analyzes the relationship between this discourse and novels of the late eighteenth and early nineteenth centuries, demonstrating how these writers "brought the tour into fiction and fiction into the tour."

Gamer, Michael. *Romanticism and the Gothic: Genre, Reception, and Canon Formation*. New York: Cambridge University Press, 2000. Examines works by Scott and other Romantic writers to demonstrate how these authors were influenced by many of the conventions of earlier gothic literature.

Humphrey, Richard. *Waverley*. New York: Cambridge University Press, 1993. Brief volume provides a useful introduction to a seminal Scott novel, with the analysis divided into four parts: "Scott's changing world and the making of *Waverley*," "*Waverley* as story," "*Waverley* as history," and "*Waverley* as initiator"—by which Humphrey means that the novel provided a model not only for subsequent Scott works but also for novels written by many other writers. An interesting appendix contains contemporary accounts of the Battle of Prestonpans.

Lauber, John. *Sir Walter Scott*. Boston: Twayne, 1989. Provides a good starting point for a study of Scott. The first three chapters present an overview of Scott's career; the rest discuss the novels, with the final chapter devoted to the topic of the Waverley novels and their literary reputation. Includes a chronology and a select bibliography.

Lincoln, Andrew. *Walter Scott and Modernity.* Edinburgh: Edinburgh University Press, 2007. Examines Scott's novels and poems and argues that these were not works of nostalgia; rather, Scott used the past as a means of exploring modernist moral, political, and social issues.

Mitchell, Jerome. *Scott, Chaucer, and Medieval Romance: A Study in Sir Walter Scott's Indebtedness to the Literature of the Middle Ages.* Lexington: University Press of Kentucky, 1987. Describes the influences of Geoffrey Chaucer and medieval romances at work in Scott's narrative poetry, early novels, middle novels written during his financial collapse, and novels of his declining years. Analyzes the style and structure of the novels.

Sutherland, John. *The Life of Walter Scott.* Malden, Mass.: Blackwell, 1995. Narrative account is particularly valuable for its presentation of the darker areas of Scott's life and for the clarity with which it relates Scott's work to his life and times.

W. G. SEBALD

Born: Wertach im Allgäu, Germany; May 18, 1944
Died: Norwich, Norfolk, England; December 14, 2001
Also known as: Winfried Georg Maximilian Sebald

PRINCIPAL LONG FICTION

Schwindel: Gefühle, 1990 (*Vertigo*, 1999)
Die Ausgewanderten, 1992 (*The Emigrants*, 1996)
Die Ringe des Saturn, 1995 (*The Rings of Saturn*, 1998)
Austerlitz, 2001 (English translation, 2001)

OTHER LITERARY FORMS

In the United States, W. G. Sebald (ZAY-bahlt) gained recognition primarily as a writer of novels. In Germany, his literary output included poetry and critical essays, only a portion of which have been translated into English. His writing as a critic first appeared in his work on German Expressionist playwright Carl Sternheim, *Carl Sternheim: Kritiker und Opfer der Wilhelminischen Ära* (1969; Carl Sternheim: critic and victim of the Wilhelminian era) and in his dissertation on the novelist Alfred Döblin, titled "Der Mythus der Zerstörung im Werk Alfred Döblins" (1973; the myth of destruction in the work of Alfred Döblin).

Sebald's history of Austrian literature, *Die Beschreibung des Unglücks: Zur österreichischen Literatur von Stifter bis Handke* (the description of melancholy in Austrian literature from Stifter to Handke), appeared in 1985, and his edited collection of critical essays on modern German theater, *A Radical Stage: Theatre in Germany in the 1970's and 1980's*, in 1988. In 1999, Sebald's extended meditation on post-World War II German literature's reluctance to examine the consequences of the bombings of Germany in World War II, *Luftkrieg und Literatur* (*On the Natural History of Destruction*, 2003), was published. A collection of his critical essays, *Campo Santo*, appeared in 2005. Sebald's important 1998 collection of critical essays on Robert Walser, Gottfried Keller, and others, *Logis in einem Landhaus* (lodgings in a country house), remains untranslated into English. After his death, two volumes of Sebald's poetry—*For Years Now* (2001) and the English translation of his 1988 collection *Nach der Natur: Ein Elementargedicht*, titled *After Nature* (2002)—were published.

ACHIEVEMENTS

From the very beginning of his career, critics recognized W. G. Sebald's artistic genius, and he received numerous awards and literary prizes for his work. In 2007, the secretary of the Swedish Academy observed that

Sebald would have been a worthy recipient of the Nobel Prize in Literature if he had lived. In 1990, he received the Feder-Machow Prize for Lyric Poetry for *After Nature*. Sebald's second novel, *The Emigrants*, won several awards, including the Berlin Literature Prize and the Johannes Bobrowski Medal in 1994 and, in 1997, the Heinrich Böll Prize and the Mörike Prize. His third novel, *The Rings of Saturn*, won the Los Angeles Times Book Prize for fiction in 1999. Sebald received the Heinrich Heine Prize and the Josef Breitbach Prize in 2000, and he was posthumously awarded the 2002 National Book Critics Circle Award for fiction for *Austerlitz* as well as the Literary Prize of the City of Bremen.

BIOGRAPHY

Winfried Georg Maximilian Sebald was one of four children born to Georg and Rosa Genovefa Sebald in the quiet southern Bavarian village of Wertach im Allgäu. Because Sebald knew little of his father, who was mostly absent from the family, working in larger towns and engaging in military service under Adolf Hitler, Sebald's maternal grandfather, Josef Engelhofer, played a significant role in raising the young boy.

Almost all of Sebald's writings deal in some way with the Holocaust and with Germany's inability to understand the political and social scope and gravity of the event. After attending elementary school in Wertach and Sonthofen, Sebald learned about the Holocaust in his secondary school in Oberstdorf, where his teachers showed their students pictures of the camps and the consequences of the activities in the camps. None of his teachers was able, however, to explain adequately to the students the significance of the Holocaust or the meaning of the pictures. Frustrated with this overwhelming silence, Sebald left Germany to study German literature in Switzerland, where he received a *licence des lettres* from the University of Fribourg in 1966, and where he also began his lifelong love of French literature. He also married a fellow student, Ute, in 1967.

His work in Fribourg began his move away from Germany, and he moved among teaching positions in England, Switzerland, and Germany over the next decade. He began his academic career at the University of Manchester in 1968. After completing his dissertation on the work of novelist Alfred Döblin in 1973 at the University of East Anglia in Norwich, Sebald returned to Germany in 1975 to work at the Goethe Institute. After only one year, however, he went back to the University of East Anglia to teach German literature. He became professor of modern German literature in 1988 and the director of the British Centre for Literary Translation in 1989, and he spent the remainder of his academic and writing career at East Anglia.

From 1989 until his death in 2001, Sebald increasingly gained recognition for his novels. When his first novel, *Vertigo*, was published in 1990, critics hailed him as an original voice and praised his mysterious and sublime prose. Over the course of the next decade, his three other novels—*The Emigrants*, *The Rings of Saturn*, and *Austerlitz*—won numerous prizes and awards. Sebald's lyrical prose and his haunting and evocative scenes of melancholy exiles sifting for meaning through the detritus of the past won him the admiration of critics and readers, who saw him as being part of the long tradition of philosophical novelists from Franz Kafka and Robert Walser to Rainer Maria Rilke. His untimely death in an automobile accident at age fifty-seven in December, 2001, prompted critics to compare Sebald to Albert Camus, another European writer whose promising career as a novelist was cut short by a car crash. Like Camus, Sebald often dealt with themes of exile, alienation, and evil in his novels, and his focus on the Holocaust resembles Camus's own concerns with the consequences of Hitler's rise to power and the marginalization of Jews in Nazi Germany.

ANALYSIS

Anyone picking up one of W. G. Sebald's novels for the first time might be initially perplexed. Are these really novels, or are they documentaries? Multiple shifts of point of view, the use of photographs that depict everything from family reunions to historical events, the lack of specific plot, the use of real people as characters (Stendhal, Michael Hamburger), and the mixture of fact and fiction create a surrealistic world where expectations and events change from moment to moment. Like Kafka, Walser, and Thomas Mann before him, Sebald records the lives of individuals who wander though their lives searching the past for some clues about their identities. These characters often drift through broken landscapes littered with the debris of shattered families, madness, and the shards of history as they try to remember how they came to their particular historical moment and discern ways to live within that moment. More than any other contemporary German novelist, Sebald explores the ways that individuals manage to carry—or cannot manage to bear—the unbearable weight of history in their lives. Much like the spiritual wanderers of Hermann Hesse's novels and the pilgrim in Dante's *La divina commedia* (c. 1320; *The Divine Comedy*, 1802), Sebald's characters find themselves ever restless, always on a quest—either through their consciousness or through journeys through cities such as Dresden—to reach that ever-receding horizon that promises revelation and knowledge.

All four of Sebald's novels are extended meditations on the function of memory. In his first novel, *Vertigo*, for example, the narrator engages in a long process of reconstructing his identity through writing down—literally, since the novel itself functions as the preservation of his writing, and figuratively, as he writes a journal or a novel as the central part of the novel's action—the events of his life, the political affairs through which he has lived, and the women he has loved. As the narrator of this particular novel discovers, memory can be both unreliable and accurate. By the end of the novel, has he learned any more about himself than he knew at the beginning? Has the reader learned any more about him? All of Sebald's other novels involve similar exercises in which the narrators set out to recall, in whatever fashion they have at hand, the events that have led them to their present state, as well as to use those events to reveal to themselves something of the character of their lives. As Sebald's characters discover, memory often unsettles them, forcing them to uncomfortable recognitions about themselves and others, or it lulls them momentarily into thinking that indeed they have found the keys to their identities.

Exile and homelessness are also two major themes of Sebald's novels. Every one of his novels features a narrator who is wandering throughout Germany, England, or Europe, trying to find some semblance of the home he has left behind. The German title of his second novel, *Die Ausgewanderten* (which comes from a word whose root is "to wander"), literally expresses these themes.

W. G. Sebald. (© Jerry Bauer/Courtesy, New Directions Publishing)

The novel features stories of four such wanderers who must endure the loneliness and pathos of their attempts to construct for themselves a new home in a foreign land. Given that Sebald himself was an emigrant—a German writer living in England—and that many of his narrators are thinly veiled doubles for himself, it is perhaps not surprising that homelessness, exile, and wandering dominate his novels.

VERTIGO

Although *Vertigo* was Sebald's first novel, it did not appear in English translation until after two of his other novels—*The Emigrants* and *The Rings of Saturn*—had been published. By the time it was published, critical acclaim for Sebald had been building. *The Emigrants* and *The Rings of Saturn* had established Sebald as a brilliantly original thinker whom critics called a rare and elusive species and the epitome of literary greatness. *Vertigo* merely confirmed critical opinion of Sebald and reinforced opinions regarding his genius.

Much as its title indicates, *Vertigo* is a dizzying journey through European history and through the minds of several different narrators trying to find their identities within those Wordsworthian "spots of time" in which they find themselves ensconced. The book consists of four sections, each narrated by a different narrator (although the narrators of the second and fourth parts of the book may be the same individual). The point of view shifts from the third person in the first and third sections to the first person in the second and fourth sections. All of the narrators are wanderers, traveling through various settings in Europe and involved in particular events in those settings. The settings here range from Italy and France, Austria and Italy, to England and Germany.

Each section of the novel also takes place roughly during a certain period of time. The first section occurs in 1813, the year in which Napoleon I is finally defeated. The third section takes place in 1913, the year prior to World War I and its history-altering consequences. The second section takes place in Italy and Austria around 1980, and the fourth section occurs in Italy around 1987. As in other Sebald novels, the narrators of the sections move from historical individuals (Stendhal in the first section and Kafka in the third) to fictional characters (a writer in the second and fourth sections—although the narrator in each of these sections resembles Sebald himself).

With its line drawings and its observations about the nature of the writing life and the nature of love, the first section of *Vertigo* resembles Stendhal's own "autobiography," *Vie de Henry Brulard* (1890; *The Life of Henry Brulard*, 1925). In the aftermath of his reluctantly undertaken military service, Marie Henri Beyle (Stendhal) resolves to become the greatest writer of all time. In addition, he falls in love with a married woman, pursues her surreptitiously, loses her through his incautious manner, and mourns this loss (she never loved him in the first place, but his love for her is eternal) in his little book *On Love*. The second section is also a story of wandering abroad (the title of the section), and it resembles Dante's *Divine Comedy* in its search for a road out of the chaos in which the narrator (who resembles Sebald and may be him) finds himself. Here, the road may be through writing, as the narrator jots down a long account—his memoir?—of his travels and his personal history.

In the third section, "Dr. K. Takes the Waters at Riva," the third-person narrator weaves passages from Kafka's diaries and letters into an account that identifies Kafka with his own story, "Der Jäger Gracchus" (1931; "The Hunter Gracchus," 1946). In this section of *Vertigo*, much as in that story, the identity of the main character remains mysterious, his secrets confined to a shrouded past. Finally, in the fourth section, the narrator of the second section returns to Germany ("Il ritorno in patria," or "return to the Fatherland," is the section's title) in an attempt to find out whether he belongs in a country that still proclaims its superiority through its nationalistic spirit. As he wanders through the mountains, he feels his foreignness and realizes that he has never gazed into such chasms before. Sebald's *Vertigo* explores the uncanny ways in which memory shapes identity and provides human beings with some kind of hope for the future.

THE EMIGRANTS

As in *Vertigo*, Sebald's *The Emigrants* follows the lives of individuals who are "wandering out" (*Ausgewanderten*) in search of their identities. *The Emigrants* contains Sebald's characteristic blend of fact and fiction, documentary and photography, and the narrator of at least two of these stories may be Sebald himself. The characters in the four sketches that constitute the novel have voluntarily migrated from their homelands to various places in Europe and must confront the loneliness and isolation that such emigration brings with it. Although each of the characters hopes in some way to begin his life anew in a new place, the longing for home is unbearable. Unable to bear the weight of such longing, each of these individuals commits suicide, so that all the tales become cautious reflections on the burden of memory and the hope of emigration.

In the first story, the narrator meets Henry Selwyn, a Lithuanian Jew who had emigrated to London quite by accident. Through a series of conversations with various other characters, Selwyn reveals that he has kept his Jewish identity a secret (his real name is Hersch Serewyn) even from his wife, and he realizes that he must come to terms with the guilt of his past. When he realizes he can never be free from these memories, he ends his life, and the narrator uses this death as the starting point for his own reflections on the nature of memory and the weight of the past.

The second story focuses on schoolteacher Paul Bereyter, who adores his students but also reviles them for their disrespectful attitudes toward art, music, and literature. While Paul considers his students the hope for a more open future—without the prejudices that characterize the nationalistic pride of Germany—he is also disheartened by his students' failures to recognize or understand beauty. Sebald likely modeled this character on one of his own teachers.

The third story is a family tale of Great Uncle Ambros Adelwarth (perhaps Sebald's own uncle), who emigrates to New York, works for a wealthy family, becomes the lover of the family's younger son, loses his lover to death, and goes through a deep depression leading to his own death. In the end, Adelworth is exiled not only from his community but also from himself.

Sebald modeled the main character of the final story, Max Ferber, on the English Jewish painter Frank Auerbach. The narrator of this story—who may be Sebald—meets Ferber in Manchester, England, where Ferber has been living for twenty-two years. As the two begin to talk about the present and the past, they offer each other the community of exiles in a strange place. Only after Ferber's death does the narrator understand the gravity of the secrets Ferber has kept hidden and the horrors from which neither his exile nor his memory would allow him to escape.

THE RINGS OF SATURN

Much like Sebald's previous novels, *The Rings of Saturn* is a diary of a wanderer. Unlike his previous novels, however, this work focuses on one narrator—who again at times appears to be Sebald himself—and his journey through eastern England. As in much of Sebald's other work, in this novel the borders between illusion and reality, fact and fiction, and dreams and life are porous and permeable. In a stream-of-consciousness description of his reveries and dreams, the narrator reflects on the dust and ash that surround him from the destruction of the war. Like the rings of Saturn, which are particles of ash and dust remaining after the destruction of one of the planet's former moons, the ashes to which Sir Thomas Browne refers in his *Hydriotaphia: Or, Urn Burial* (1658) signify for the narrator the waning of human civilization. Saturn also plays another role in the novel, for both the narrator and Browne were born under the sign of Saturn.

Like Homer's *Odyssey* (c. 725 B.C.E.; English translation, 1614), Dante's *Divine Comedy*, and James Joyce's *Ulysses* (1922), among others, Sebald's *The Rings of Saturn* depicts a journey or a quest to find one's way back home or to move out of a mysterious stage of life into a place where new directions for life are revealed. Memory plays a major role here, as it does in *Vertigo*, especially as the narrator looks to the distant past for models of individuals looking for the transformative power of Nature.

As he ambles through the countryside, like Samuel Taylor Coleridge's Ancient Mariner, the narrator feels a joyous sense of freedom in Nature but also a sense of revulsion when he encounters destruction in Nature, primarily from the bombings of World War II. He recollects his own search for the skull of Sir Thomas Browne, with whom the narrator feels a close kinship. Like Browne, he is captivated by the idea that nothing of the human remains after death. For the narrator, life is simply the metamorphosis from one form into another. Browne's poem about burial urns reflects humans' attempts to somehow mark this transformation from the living to the dead. As he continues on his journey, the narrator, like the Ancient Mariner, recognizes the organic unity of all life and starts to understand the ways in which transformation can be destructive and destruction can be transformative. As he learns, however, the journey toward transformation and revelation is never-ending.

AUSTERLITZ

Unlike *Vertigo*, *The Emigrants*, and *The Rings of Saturn*, *Austerlitz* contains a relatively straightforward plot that most readers can follow without much difficulty. The characters often speak interchangeably, and without quotation marks to distinguish speakers, but Jacques Austerlitz does not meander too far off his path when he tells his story. More than any of Sebald's other novels, however, *Austerlitz* offers a powerful meditation on memory and self-identity. Ironically, the English translation of *Austerlitz* was published only two months before Sebald's untimely death in December, 2001.

Raised as Dafyyd Elias in Wales, Jacques Austerlitz is now living in Britain, which he believes to be his native country. The narrator meets up with Austerlitz in

Belgium, where they strike up a friendship based on their mutual love of history and architecture. Ten years later, the two meet again in London, where Austerlitz begins to tell the story of his origins, unfolding for himself and the narrator his own identity and history. As he begins to talk to the narrator, Austerlitz learns more about himself than he is prepared to face. When he learns that his mother shipped him off to England in the *Kindertransport* (in which Jewish children were transported out of Nazi Germany and German-occupied territories to safety in the United Kingdom in the months preceding World War II), he realizes that his past is lost to him and that he can recover it only through a painful process of recollection. He no longer knows whether his own family is alive, and they do not know his fate. His attempts to return to the past often paralyze him, for he does not have a language to describe himself or his past.

Just as the memory of the past is an unbearable burden for the characters in all of Sebald's novels, so Austerlitz must learn how to bear this burden without losing himself in the pathos of fear and guilt. As the narrator helps Austerlitz slowly to recover his past by looking at photographs in various archives, these moments both horrify and transport him. Eventually, Austerlitz comes to an understanding of himself, though he knows that he must continually open the doors of his memory as he seeks to know himself. He also relearns his native language, a skill that allows him symbolically to return to his homeland and to open doors to himself and a world he thought he had lost. *Austerlitz* provides a snapshot of Sebald's major themes: the burden of the past, the quest for self-identity, the alienation and loneliness that come from exile, and the transformative power of memory.

Henry L. Carrigan, Jr.

OTHER MAJOR WORKS

POETRY: *Nach der Natur: Ein Elementargedicht*, 1988 (*After Nature*, 2002); *For Years Now*, 2001; *Unerzählt: 33 Texte und 33 Radierungen*, 2003 (*Unrecounted: 33 Poems*, 2004; includes lithographs by Jan Peter Tripp, essays by Sebald and Andrea Köhler, and two additional poems by Hans Magnus Enzensberger).

NONFICTION: *Carl Sternheim: Kritiker und Opfer der Wilhelminischen Ära*, 1969; *Die Beschreibung des Unglücks: Zur österreichischen Literatur von Stifter bis Handke*, 1985; *Unheimliche Heimat: Essays zur österreichischen Literatur*, 1990; *Logis in einem Landhaus*, 1998; *Luftkrieg und Literatur*, 1999 (*On the Natural History of Destruction*, 2003); *Campo Santo*, 2005 (essays); *The Emergence of Memory: Conversations with W. G. Sebald*, 2007 (Lynne Sharon Schwartz, editor).

EDITED TEXT: *A Radical Stage: Theatre in Germany in the 1970's and 1980's*, 1988.

BIBLIOGRAPHY

Blackler, Deane. *Reading W. G. Sebald: Adventure and Disobedience*. Rochester, N.Y.: Camden House, 2007. Argues that Sebald's novels encourage readers to step outside the boundaries of their own lives in their attempts to overcome loneliness and isolation.

Doctorow, E. L. "W. G. Sebald." In *Creationists: Essays, 1993-2006*. New York: Random House, 2006. Focuses on Sebald's novel *The Emigrants*, praising Sebald for his ability to weave various leitmotifs into the novel to capture the themes of displacement and movement.

Long, J. J. *W. G. Sebald: Image, Archive, Modernity*. New York: Columbia University Press, 2008. Argues that Sebald's novels are not merely responses to the Holocaust and the trauma following it; rather, they examine the problem of modernity.

Long, J. J., and Anne Whitehead, eds. *W. G. Sebald: A Critical Companion*. Seattle: University of Washington Press, 2004. Collection of essays explores Sebald's life, his influences, and the themes of his writings.

McCulloh, Mark R. *Understanding W. G. Sebald*. Columbia: University of South Carolina Press, 2003. Highly accessible work provides an excellent student guide to Sebald's life and work as well as discussion of the critical reception of his works.

Patt, Lise, with Christel Dillbohner. *Searching for Sebald: Photography After W. G. Sebald*. Los Angeles: Institute of Cultural Inquiry and ICI Press, 2007. Monumental collection of essays takes Sebald's use of images in his novels as the starting points for discussions of art history, cultural theory, and photographic studies.

Santner, Eric L. *On Creaturely Life: Rilke, Benjamin, Sebald*. Chicago: University of Chicago Press, 2006. Offers a fine portrait of the ways in which Rainer Maria Rilke and Walter Benjamin influenced Sebald's creative process.

Schwartz, Lynne Sharon, ed. *The Emergence of Memory: Conversations with W. G. Sebald*. New York: Seven Stories Press, 2007. Collection of interviews with Sebald provides insights into his life and his creative work.

ANNA SEGHERS

Born: Mainz, Germany; November 19, 1900
Died: East Berlin, East Germany (now Berlin, Germany); June 1, 1983
Also known as: Netty Reiling; Antje Seghers; Netty Radványi

PRINCIPAL LONG FICTION

Aufstand der Fischer von St. Barbara, 1928 (*The Revolt of the Fishermen*, 1929)
Auf dem Wege zur amerikanischen Botschaft, und andere Erzählungen, 1930
Die Gefährten, 1932
Der Kopflohn, 1933 (*A Price on His Head*, 1960)
Der Weg durch den Februar, 1935
Die Rettung, 1937
Das siebte Kreuz, 1942 (*The Seventh Cross*, 1942, partial translation)
Transit, 1944 (English translation, 1944)
Der Ausflug der toten Mädchen, und andere Erzählungen, 1946
Die Toten bleiben jung, 1949 (*The Dead Stay Young*, 1950)
Die Entscheidung, 1959
Der Bienenstock: Gesammelte Erzählungen in drei Bänden, 1963
Das Vertrauen, 1968
Sonderbare Begegnungen, 1973
Werke in zehn Bänden, 1977

OTHER LITERARY FORMS

Although Anna Seghers (SAY-gehrs) was primarily a writer of fiction, known for her tightly structured novellas and novels that express the theme of revolutionary solidarity, there is extant a considerable body of her essays, speeches, and letters, notably the three-volume collection *Über Kunstwerk und Wirklichkeit* (1970-1971; on the work of art and reality). As a writer committed to communism, Seghers endeavored to define the concept of realism in the so-called debate on expressionism that took place among leftist exiled writers in the late 1930's. After her return from exile, Seghers participated in the various discussions concerning the function of literature in the German Democratic Republic (GDR). Her short stories "Die Hochzeit auf Haiti" (the wedding on Haiti) and "Die Wiedereinführung der Sklaverei auf Guadeloupe" (the reestablishment of slavery on Guadeloupe) depict liberation movements—albeit unsuccessful ones—in the Caribbean during the French Revolution and the Napoleonic period. Although these stories are not completely devoid of relevance to their time of publication, they do not deal directly with their author's contemporary reality.

Also noteworthy is Seghers's radio play *Der Prozess der Jeanne d'Arc zu Rouen 1431* (pr. 1937; the trial of Joan of Arc at Rouen in 1431), which was adapted and staged by Bertolt Brecht. A collection of Seghers's essays, *Glauben an Irdisches: Essays aus vier Jahrzehnten*, edited by novelist Christa Wolf, was published in 1974.

ACHIEVEMENTS

Because of her openly professed sympathies for the communist cause, there is no unanimity among critics as to Anna Seghers's literary stature. Celebrated to the point of uncritical adulation in the GDR, her works have been far more cautiously received in the West. Whereas Western critics tend to emphasize those novels and prose narratives that were written and published before her return from exile in 1947, East German critics regard Seghers as the chief representative of the new Socialist literature that portrays life in the GDR according to the doctrines of Socialist Realism. Seghers achieved fame and critical recognition as early as 1928, when *The Revolt of the Fishermen*, a narrative about an abortive strike and uprising, was praised as a masterpiece in the style of the New Objectivity and awarded the prestigious Kleist Prize.

The novel *The Seventh Cross*, a vivid portrait of life in Adolf Hitler's Germany, was published in German in Mexico and in English in the United States. The degree of its popular success may be gauged by the fact that it appeared on several best-seller lists in the United States; Hollywood also produced a film that was based on the novel. Robert Pick wrote in the September 26, 1942, issue of *Saturday Review of Literature* that the novel "is not only the most important contribution to world literature made, so far, by any exiled German author, but also one of the most remarkable books to come out of these times of chaos and moral danger."

American critics tended to rank the novel *Transit*, first published in English translation, not as highly as its predecessor; still, this Kafkaesque tale that pits refugees whose lives are threatened by the advancing Nazi armies against the intransigent bureaucracy in Marseilles during World War II is a gripping account of a world in turmoil.

Der Ausflug der toten Mädchen, und andere Erzählungen (the excursion of the dead girls, and other stories), a narrative in which Seghers skillfully blends autobiographical events from past and present, is generally praised by Western critics; conversely, East German critics tend to consider the novel *The Dead Stay Young* and its two sequels as a literary justification of the brand of socialism practiced in the GDR. Seghers was awarded many prizes by the GDR; although the Federal Republic was far more reluctant to honor her, both the university and the city of Mainz made the Mainz native an honorary citizen in 1977 and 1981, respectively.

BIOGRAPHY

Although notoriously reticent about her personal history, Anna Seghers freely admitted that her hometown of Mainz and its environs, notably the Rhine River, have left distinct traces in her work. Born Netty Reiling on November 19, 1900, the daughter of a respectable, well-to-do Jewish family (her father was an art dealer), Seghers grew up in middle-class comfort and received a solid education that enabled her in 1919 to enroll at the University of Heidelberg, where she studied art history, history, and philology. In 1924, she received her doctorate after completing her dissertation "Jude und Judentum im Werke Rembrandts" (Jew and Jewishness in the work of Rembrandt), which was published in 1981. Questions of Jewish identity or problems related to race are, however, only rarely to be encountered in her later literary work; only the story "Post ins gelobte Land" (mail to the Promised Land) deals specifically with Jewish experiences.

Seghers's upbringing had not prepared her for a career as a socially committed writer. In Heidelberg, she met her future husband, Hungarian sociologist László Radványi, whom she married in 1925. In retrospect, Seghers attributed her developing political consciousness to the influence of Radványi and other refugees from Central and Eastern Europe. As a result of this association with political activists, Seghers became attuned to social injustices. Her first, recently rediscovered story, "Die Toten auf der Insel Djal" (the dead on the isle of Djal), is a "legend from the Dutch" in the manner of pirate and ghost stories rather than a text propounding a social message. It was for this story that she first used the pen name Antje (later, Anna) Seghers—derived from Jan Seghers, the hero of her story, rather than, as has often been claimed, from the Dutch painter and graphic artist of the Baroque period, Hercules Seghers. Seghers's literary work achieved major recognition in 1928 when she was awarded the Kleist Prize; in the same year, she joined the Communist Party and, in 1929, the Bund Proletarisch-revolutionärer Schriftsteller, a Communist writers' organization.

When the Nazis came to power in 1933, Seghers was arrested but released shortly afterward; she managed to escape to France via Switzerland. In Paris, Seghers became one of the prominent figures of the German exile community; both in her literary work and in public speeches and appeals, she continued her fight against Nazi Germany. Her most famous novel, *The Seventh Cross*, which depicts resistance inside the Third Reich, originated in France. When German troops invaded France in 1940, Seghers fled from Paris to Marseilles; in the following year, she and her family were able to leave France on a cargo ship that eventually took them to Mexico. The novel *Transit* was, in part, based on the harrowing experiences Seghers underwent before she could obtain passage.

Unlike other exiled writers, Seghers continued her literary productivity even under adverse conditions; in Mexico City, she participated fully in the cultural and political affairs of the exiles. In 1947, she returned to Germany and took up residence in the Soviet sector of Berlin. In the same year, she received the Büchner Prize, named after the nineteenth century writer Georg Büchner, one of Seghers's literary models. Until 1977, this was the only official recognition from West Germany for the returned writer, who, in the meantime, had become one of the chief cultural representatives of the GDR. Seghers died in East Berlin on June 1, 1983.

ANALYSIS

Although the publication of Anna Seghers's first major work, *The Revolt of the Fishermen*, coincided with her decision to join the Communist Party, her fiction exhibits an ambivalence that does not fit the mold of revolutionary and proletarian literature. As the critic Fritz J. Raddatz has noted, the level of political consciousness attained by the figures in Seghers's fictional universe often remains below that of the author, who has been unswerving in her support of communism. In particular, Seghers's male protagonists rarely conform to the stereotype of the class-conscious, proletarian hero whose dedication to the cause and moral integrity are beyond question.

The author is less interested in the socioeconomic determinants of character than in the depiction of a shadowy world that is derived from both Franz Kafka and Fyodor Dostoevski.

THE REVOLT OF THE FISHERMEN

The Revolt of the Fishermen begins with a statement about an abortive uprising:

> But long after the soldiers had been withdrawn and the fishermen were at sea again, the revolt remained sitting on the empty, white, summery and bare market place and thought quietly of his own, those whom he had born, bred, taken care of, and sheltered for that which was best for them.

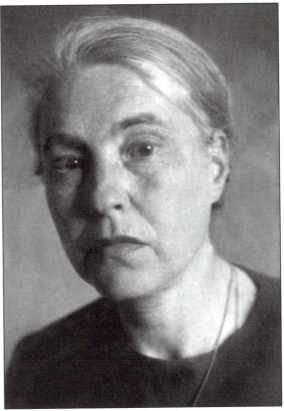

Anna Seghers. (DPA/Landov)

Whereas Marxist critics interpret both this anthropomorphic passage and the text as a whole in terms of future successful uprisings, the lack of any concrete historical and geographical details and the narrator's dispassionate stance tend to create a mood of ambivalence and resignation. The same fishing vessel that had been severely damaged by the fisherman Andreas, who single-handedly attempted to prevent strikebreakers from gaining the upper hand, is the first one to be taken out fishing again after the strike has been definitely crushed; this is indicative of futility rather than hope.

Like Andreas, the strike leader, Hull, is a vitalistic rebel who joins the fishermen only when the uprising is imminent. Hull is not a class-conscious revolutionary in the strict sense; in his vitalistic orientation, Hull resembles George Heisler, the hero of *The Seventh Cross*.

THE SEVENTH CROSS

Among the seven men who have escaped the concentration camp, Heisler is by no means the one who is most dedicated to the proletarian cause. Rather than the steadfast and determined union representative, Wallau, Heisler is the only fugitive who is not recaptured and who manages to flee Germany. Thus the last of the seven crosses that have been erected in the concentration camp for the purpose of crucifying the caught fugitives remains empty and becomes a symbol of hope and resistance.

Not Heisler, but his former friend, Franz Marnet, whose girlfriend Heisler had taken away from him only to abandon her later, formulates the maxim that can serve as a justification for the fight against the Nazis. His "desire for justice," Marnet claims, changed his life and caused him to join the revolutionary movement. Although Heisler possesses the will for survival, his ultimately successful escape is only in part the result of his own resourcefulness; he is dependent on both chance and the solidarity of those who, in disregard of the danger to themselves, help him along the way. The novel, then, is concerned not only with Heisler and his fellow inmates' suspenseful flight but also with the depiction of life within Germany under Nazism.

The characters in the large cast demonstrate varying attitudes toward the new rulers—from active support to indifference and outright resistance. In this way, the author avoided an undifferentiated portrayal that equated the Nazis with the German people as a whole. Actually, Heisler's escape serves as the catalyst for the revival of human decency in the face of brute force. The worker Paul Röder, for example, although he benefits in a modest way from the Nazis' social measures, does not hesitate to hide Heisler. Seghers's ambivalent socialism is evident from the fact that, like Röder, many of her figures act out of a sense of basic humanism rather than an ideological motivation.

Unlike *The Revolt of the Fishermen*, *The Seventh Cross* does not end in complete defeat. When the empty seventh cross was taken down, the unidentified narrator reports in the prologue, the concentration camp inmates reacted with "a weak, strange smile . . . of hope and scorn, of powerlessness and boldness." In the epilogue, the narrator evokes that "unassailable" and "inviolate" inner sphere of man that gives him the strength to resist powerful forces—an indication that for the author the category of hope could not be grasped exclusively in

terms of the contemporary political situation. One of the initial passages of the novel, in fact, establishes a historical framework that transcends the time of action. Seghers applies the historical perspective to intimate that the Third Reich is only a passing, if particularly brutal, episode in the lives of the successive generations populating her native region, situated between Mainz on the Rhine and Frankfurt on the Main. At the same time, the historical perspective is not intended to instill futile hope; the aforementioned Marnet explicitly conceives of the struggle for a better future of humankind not in abstract terms but in those of the concrete here and now.

TRANSIT

Like Heisler, Seidler, the first-person narrator of *Transit*, is an unexceptional hero, yet he ultimately decides not to flee France after the Nazi invasion. Instead, he joins the Resistance movement—an act that enables him to find his true identity by breaking out of the vicious circle of hopelessness and despair in which the endangered fugitives from Hitler's Germany are caught while they are waiting for their overseas passage in the port city of Marseilles. Whereas *The Seventh Cross* depicts deeds of defiance within Nazi Germany, *Transit* compellingly evokes the fate of those exiles who live in constant fear of being captured by the advancing German armies or the secret police. Their often futile efforts to obtain the necessary visas, transit permits, and other documents that would enable them to leave France bring them into contact with a complex and intransigent bureaucracy; indeed, this bureaucracy exerts a powerful influence on the refugees' lives that is reminiscent of Kafka's fictional universe. As one critic observed about Seidler, "He moves in a sort of miasma; [he is] enveloped in the mistrals of Marseilles spiritually as well as physically." Consequently, "his strength of purpose is neutral; it lacks fire and drive."

As a corollary to her unexceptional yet adventuresome male characters, Seghers introduces women figures who are usually content with traditional role models and who do not exhibit any emancipatory urge. Raddatz has noted that Seghers's women are characterized by their lack of conspicuous female physical attributes; for all practical purposes, they have become desexed. Moreover, they tend to appear in subservient roles that do not permit them to participate actively in the affairs of men. Thus, Marie in *The Revolt of the Fishermen* suffers from casual sexual exploitation by a number of men; in *The Seventh Cross*, the narrator condescendingly mentions speeches by the Socialists August Bebel and Karl Lieb-knecht "that could even be read to women, while they were mending the truly devilish holes in all the socks." In her dedicated but futile search for her husband—who had committed suicide in Paris—Marie Weidel in *Transit* represents yet another type of devoted woman in Seghers's work.

DER AUSFLUG DER TOTEN MÄDCHEN

In *Der Ausflug der toten Mädchen*, generally considered an exception in Seghers's fiction in that the first-person narrator is largely identical with the author herself, a number of subtly differentiated female figures occupy center stage. In her Mexican exile, the narrator relives in memory an excursion with her girls' school classmates that took place before World War I. The narrator is present in the story as both narrating subject and narrated object—a narrative stance that is designed to contrast the happy state of adolescence with the eventual fate of the girls. With the exception of the narrator, all the girls have died as a consequence of the Nazi terror and World War II. The initially harmonious relationship among the girls, exemplified by the intimacy between beautiful Marianne and her friend Leni, deteriorates with the advent of Nazism. Marianne, married to an officer of the SS, refuses to help Leni, whose husband opposes Hitler. Leni ultimately perishes in a concentration camp; Marianne, however, also dies prematurely, in a bombing raid on Mainz. Victims and oppressors, then, suffer the same fate—but neither victims nor oppressors are entirely defined in ideological or political terms. Rather, the girls' future development is largely determined by their degree of humanity and understanding. It is Marianne's indifference and lack of conscience that enable her to remain noncommittal and hostile in the face of a former friend's real suffering.

In both its pattern of an antagonistic grouping of figures and its symbolic indication of hope by means of a surviving child from the ranks of the oppressed, *Der Ausflug der toten Mädchen* anticipates Seghers's far more ambitious project, the novel *The Dead Stay Young*.

THE DEAD STAY YOUNG

In this chronicle of Germany from the end of World War I to the end of World War II, Seghers provides a broad panorama of society, from workers and farmers on one hand to industrialists and aristocratic officers on the other. Several major figures dominate separate but parallel and occasionally intersecting plot lines. The author endeavored to impose a somewhat superficial thematic unity on the novel through the parallelism alluded to in the title. In the beginning, Erwin, the former soldier turned revolutionary, is murdered by counterrevolutionary officers; the same officer who has participated in Erwin's murder orders the shooting of Erwin's son, Hans, a soldier and anti-Nazi activist. Because of Hans's likeness to his dead father, Hans appears to the officer as the dead person who had remained miraculously young. Thus, the title is indicative of the unbroken continuity of the revolutionary movement—a movement that, as the presumable survival of Hans's unborn child demonstrates, cannot be annihilated by the representatives of the old order.

The novel is concerned with the depiction of the class struggle during the Weimar Republic and the Third Reich, and the characters are clearly divided between murderers and victims. It is surprising, then, that Seghers provides four fictional biographies of figures from the ranks of the former group as compared to only one account devoted to a figure from the latter. The biographies of the representatives of the aristocratic officer caste, the landed gentry, and the wealthy industrialists are supplemented by that of the small farmer Nadler, who serves as a willing and eager tool of his reactionary military superiors. These figures will eventually perish, but Marie, the mother of the murdered Erwin's son, Hans, provides the biological link in the chain of revolutionaries. The main quality she imparts to her son is a basic humanity rather than any well-defined ideology. As a consequence, some East German critics objected to the absence in the novel of an upright, class-conscious, proletarian hero. This lack was particularly noticeable, they claimed, in view of the more than adequate representation of the reactionary camp. At the same time, the novel was poorly received by Western critics; Marcel Reich-Ranicki charged that, in *The Dead Stay Young*, Seghers had confined herself "to the transformation into fiction of the view concerning the epoch between the two world wars as it was to be found in Communist publications."

There is no question that the novel offers a one-sided explanation of the disastrous developments in recent German history; Seghers's intention was to instill in her readers a sense of hope, a faith in Socialist democracy as an alternative societal model that, at the time of her writing, seemed a viable possibility. Seghers's works are, in fact, most convincing when they express the hope for a better, Socialist future that is to replace the old order of injustice and oppression. Perhaps it is an indication of the deficiencies of both GDR socialism and its cultural policies that the two sequels to *The Dead Stay Young*, *Die Entscheidung* (the decision) and *Das Vertrauen* (trust), both of which treat conditions in the GDR, may qualify as literary adaptations of officially sanctioned views, but hardly as great literary works.

Siegfried Mews

OTHER MAJOR WORKS

SHORT FICTION: *Benito's Blue, and Nine Other Stories*, 1973.

PLAY: *Der Prozess der Jeanne d'Arc zu Rouen 1431*, pr. 1937 (radio play).

NONFICTION: *Frieden der Welt: Ansprachen und Aufsätze 1947-1953*, 1952; *Über Tolstoj, Über Dostojevskij*, 1963; *Briefe an Leser*, 1970; *Über Kunstwerk und Wirklichkeit*, 1970-1971; *Glauben an Irdisches: Essays aus vier Jahrzehnten*, 1974 (Christa Wolf, editor).

BIBLIOGRAPHY

Cernyak, Susan E. "Anna Seghers: Between Judaism and Communism." In *Exile, the Writer's Experience*, edited by John M. Spalek and Robert F. Bell. Chapel Hill: University of North Carolina Press, 1982. Seghers is one of the writers discussed in this collection of essays about German authors in exile from Nazi Germany.

Fehervary, Helen. *Anna Seghers: The Mythic Dimension*. Ann Arbor: University of Michigan Press, 2001. A reexamination of Seghers's life and work that focuses on her use of fairy tales, biblical legends, and mythology. Fehervary places Seghers within the wider context of Central European intellectual history.

Gutzmann, Gertruad. "Literary Antifascism: Anna Seghers's Exile Writings, 1936 to 1949." In *Facing Fascism and Confronting the Past: German Women Writers from Weimar to the Present*, edited by Elke P. Frederiksen and Martha Kaarsberg Wallach. Albany: State University of New York Press, 2000. Gutzmann's analysis of Seghers's exile writings is included in this study of writers who were silenced by the Nazi regime. The essays discuss, among other topics, the authors' representations of gender, patriarchy, and feminism.

Huebener, Theodore. *The Literature of East Germany*. New York: Frederick Ungar, 1970. Seghers is one of the authors discussed in this examination of literature from the former German Democratic Republic. Includes a bibliography.

LaBahn, Kathleen J. *Anna Seghers' Exile Literature: The Mexican Years, 1941-1947*. New York: Peter Lang, 1986. Analyzes the literature Seghers created while in exile from Germany, focusing on the historical and political factors that influenced these works. LaBahn also discusses Seghers's involvement in antifascist activities during her years in Mexico.

Maier-Katkin, Birgit. *Silence and Acts of Memory: A Postwar Discourse on Literature, History, Anna Seghers, and Women in the Third Reich*. Lewisburg, Pa.: Bucknell University Press, 2007. Maier-Katkin examines Seghers's novel *The Seventh Cross* and her other exile literature, focusing on its depiction of women, in order to form an "acceptable memory" of private life in the Third Reich.

Plapp, Laurel. "Le Parfum des Antilles: The Caribbean Revolutions in the Works of Anna Seghers and André Schwarz-Bart." In *Zionism and Revolution in European-Jewish Literature*. Hoboken, N.J.: Taylor & Francis, 2007. This study of twentieth century Jewish writers whose work challenges imperialism includes a look at Seghers's and Schwarz-Bart's depiction of Caribbean rebellions by a coalition of Jews and African slaves.

Wallace, Ian, ed. *Anna Seghers in Perspective*. Amsterdam: Rodopi, 1998. Discusses Seghers's early works, the Kafkaesque imagery in her novel *Transit*, and her "politics of affirmation." Includes a bibliography and an index.